OF Blood AND Battles:

Oswego's 147th Regiment

NATALIE JOY WOODALL

outskirts
press

To the men of the 147th Regiment who fought to preserve the Union and to the women who bade them go this book is gratefully dedicated.

Give me for a friend in these trying times the one that took my hand when I left home to join the army, and bid me go do my duty like a man . . . Tears and deep drawn sighs are very good for outward show, but, after all, they are not as satisfactory (to me at least) as the firm, unshaken lip and steady speech of him who bid me, "Go." Charles Freeman Biddlecom

Erected by the Grand Army of the Republic this monument stands in the Mexico Village Cemetery and honors all the men from the town who served in the Civil War.

Author's Collection

Preface

THIS BOOK WAS conceived as a companion to *Men of the 110th Regiment: Oswego's Own* but it soon took on a life of its own. While the 110th was a fairly cohesive unit, such was not the case for its sister regiment. All too quickly I realized my "Oswego regiment" was eventually filled with men who had served in the 30th and the 76th Regiments, as well as a few others. I decided the easiest way to handle the biographies of the more than 2,000 men who served in the 147th was to separate them into three categories which I labeled "The Originals," "'63 and Beyond," and "76ers." In the course of my research I found a few men who were associated with the 147th but who for one reason or another never actually served in that organization. Rather than ignore them I placed them in a section I humorously titled "Et Cetera Nomina." In this section I also added short biographies of two women whose names are legend in Oswego County, Elmina Spencer and Dr. Mary Walker. Both justly deserve to be associated with the 147th. I even found room for some of the deserters in a chapter which I call "The Draft, Dodgers, and Deserters." A dear friend teases me at times for my regard for the soldiers whose stories I attempt to tell within the pages of this book. While some have eluded me I admit I have become quite intimately acquainted with many. Seeing their pictures, reading their letters, and visiting their graves has forcefully driven home the fact that they were real people, that they lived, sacrificed, and, in not a few cases, died for a cause larger than themselves. They deserve to be remembered.

Much has already been written about the fourth Oswego County regiment and it was imperative that I present my findings in a way not yet fully exploited. A combination of genealogy and regimental history, with emphasis on the former, seemed to be the logical solution to the problem. I do not pretend to be an expert of any kind when it comes to the Civil War. My plan throughout was to allow the soldiers, reporters, and editors to tell the story as it unfolded. In that I hope I have succeeded.

Material for the biographies of the soldiers and their families has been gleaned from *The Adjutant-General's Reports*, Ancestry.com, Familysearch.com, Findagrave. com, military and pension records, newspapers articles, obituaries, gravestones, secondary sources such as local histories, and the kind and generous assistance of researchers all over the United States. I have endeavored to be as accurate and complete as possible, always keeping in mind that further revelations will add detail to the stories. As always, my mistakes are my own and no one else's.

Natalie Joy Woodall
Oswego, NY
December 31, 2018

Acknowledgments

NO ONE WRITES a book such as this without the assistance of many people and I gratefully acknowledge the help and advice I have received over the past two years. The National Archives, cemetery records in the Oswego Public Library, Tom Tryniski's Fultonhistory.com, NYS Historic Newspapers.com, and the 76th New York Volunteer Homepage have all made my research fuller and more accurate. I also acknowledge the following: Chad Miller, for information on Asa and Rosetta Sparrowk Forbes and for permission to use the photo of Asa's gravestone; Julie Litts Robst, researcher extraordinaire; Charlene Cole, Town of Sandy Creek historian; Justin White, Oswego County historian; Roger Zarn of the Nobles County, MN Historical Society for information on Ira and Sally Turner; Dawn Krul, Wolcott town clerk, for information about Mary J. Upcraft Neal; Lowell Newvine, Hannibal town historian for assistance with several local families; Treva Neiman, Crawford County, KS Genealogy Society for information on Henry and Sarepta Rice James; Christine Filippelli of the Troy Public Library, for information on Lawrence Dorsey; Sharon Fellows, Cattaraugus County historian, for information on Alexander Mudgett; Darrell Klute, Deputy Cattaraugus County Clerk, for copies of divorce proceedings of Annette "Nettie" Mudgett vs. Alexander Mudgett; Nettie NM, for material on the DeCory family; Polly H. Held, Madison County Historical Society, for information on Stephen Emblen; Kathy Clair, Reddick Public Library, Ottawa, IL, for information on Thomas J. Gabler; Arlington National Cemetery, for information on William and Charles Hyde; Kevin Farrell, for extensive information on the LeRoy family; great grandson Robert L. Farrell, for permission to use a photograph of Oliver LeRoy; Margaret and Ruth Lewis, for information on Lemuel Kirby; Michelle Davis, for material on Henry J. and Eliza Lewis; Dayton Public Library for the obituary of William Kirk; Corey Wright, for information about Velsor Montross and for permission to publish a photo of Victor Hallock; Alexander P. Merrill, Kalamazoo Public Library, for searching for the grave of Robert Watson Webb; Rev. Marshall Hudson-Knapp, for material pertaining to Alexander and Emeline Chapman King and for permission to use Alexander's photo; Larry E. Crosby, for information on Charles Fay Wheeler and for permission to use

Wheeler's photo; Sutter County, CA Library for obituary for Robert Jenkins Tubbs; Sherry Sponseller, Genealogical Society of Isabella County, MI, for information about Cyprian and Magdalena Depore; Karen Osburn, Geneva City historian, for locating the grave of and for information on Areana Woodyard Denison; Jeffrey Kowalis, for permission to use the photograph of Charles Hamilton; Robert Lutey, curatorial assistant, Monroe County, MI Museum, for obituary of Horace C. Graves; Peter Lowell, for permission to use a picture of Levi Powell; Robert Byrnes, for permission to use Findagrave.com picture of William Hungerford's gravestone; Sebastian Nelson, for permission to use picture of Thaddeus Bradley posted on 76th Regiment Homepage; Wes Anderson of the Barnes County, ND Historical Society, for information concerning Charles Richardson and for permission to use a photograph of Mr. Richardson; Theresa Richardson of the Riverside Cemetery, Waterbury, CT, for information on and permission to use photo of John and Ida Stephen's gravestone; Paul Friday, reference librarian, New Hampshire Historical Society for material relating to the death of Gideon Silver; Gary Woodward, for information about and permission to use a photo of George Watrous; "fabusys," for information on Thomas and Lydia Sharp Wilbur; Harold Stoddard, for information on Arvilla Thornton Willey, AKA Lazell; William Van Valkenburg for material relating to Emeline Van Valkenburg; Debra Waggoner of the Prairie Pioneer Genealogy Society, Grand Island, NE, for information on the later life of Olive Yarton Vest; Kim Wals, for picture of C. D. Bouton, from the Ken Eaton Collection, Homeville Museum, Homeville, NY; Richard Roth for permission to use a photo of Charles R. Hoag; Sharon Talmadge, Amsterdam, NY Public Library, for locating the obituary for John Greenwald; Eric Parsons, superintendent of Evergreen Cemetery, Orwell, for assistance in locating graves and for permission to use a photo of James Draper's gravestone; David Sigler for information on and permission to use a photograph of John Mistler; Nancy J. Van Blaricum and the Dexter Area (Michigan) Historical Society for information on Hiram Pierce; St. John Lodge No. 82 RA & AM for permission to use a photograph of John Shay's gravestone; Shawn Doyle, president of Half-Shire Historical Society, Richland, NY, for permission to use a photograph of Darius Ballou and for information on and permission to use a photograph of William McCaw; great grandson Willard Loomis and Williamstown Historical Society, for permission to publish a photo of Alexander McAuley; Pulaski Lodge #415 F & AM for permission to publish a photograph of Lafayette Barber; Gary Heinmiller, for extensive information on soldiers in the 147th Regiment who were Masons; Marie Sweet, New Haven town historian, for help in locating persons buried in New Haven Rural Cemetery; James Gandy, New York State Military Museum, for permission to use photos of George Harney, Delos Gary, John McKinlock, Francis Miller, James Volney Pierce, Henry H. Lyman, and George Hugunin. The following persons are gratefully acknowledged for permission to use photographs: Christine Kenzie, Sarah Fish Brownell; Michelle Hompe-Barr, John Hompe; Michael Sayre, Oliver LeGault; Aleta Klahn McLain, Daniel Louth; Shawn Herron, Andrew Warner; Paul Kamalsky, Charles F. Biddlecom's gravestone; John Hart, Henry Grawbarger's gravestone; Sue Sullivan, Ambrose Marcely's gravestone; Mary Lou Thomas, John McFee Keller; Dorothy Morgan Monahan, Joseph Morgan.; S. J. Sheret, Dudley Farling's gravestone; Kathy Scott, Solomon and Mary Ann Rima's gravestones; Erin Cassidy, Charles T. Hilbert; Diane Gravlee, Dr. Newton A. Lindley's gravestone; Karen Halstead, William and Jennie Calvert Myers' gravestone; Ron Baublitz, Henry and Ellen Eastham's gravestones; Steve and Linda Malkson, John W. Northrop's gravestone; William Yates, George Harney's gravestone; Wayne Ashley, George Whitefield Cranston's gravestone; Special Collections and College Archives, Gettysburg College, photo of Lewis Tway; US Naval Historical Center, photo of USS General Lyon. I acknowledge the Library of Congress for the pictures of the executed deserter, Fort Lawton, GA, the siege works at Petersburg, and for the painting of the Battle of the Wilderness.

I also acknowledge three persons who trekked through cemeteries with me during the past two years to help me find the graves of veterans and their families: Elaine DeLong, Sally Woolson, and Aubrey Woolson. I especially thank my friend Darlene Woolson for accompanying me on many forays to visit cemeteries all over Oswego County and for permission to use her photos of David Dexter and of the 147th Regiment's monument at Gettysburg. I also gratefully acknowledge another good friend, Joanne Paino, for her technical skills when dealing with recalcitrant computers and technologically challenged operators. To friends unlucky enough to have had to listen to stories about "my men" I tender sincere thanks for their patience and forbearance.

If I have omitted anyone, please know it has not been intentional. I appreciate every bit of information and every photo I have obtained while compiling this book.

Table of Contents

The Summer of '62

We are coming, Father Abraham!

SUMMER IS ALWAYS welcomed in Oswego County. The dreary days and nights of a cold, harsh winter give way to warm, sunny days and cool, comfortable nights. Farmers hope for bumper crops, children rejoice at having a holiday from school, local businesses look forward to the many travelers and tourists who visit the region for fishing and sightseeing. Churches, charities, and fraternal organizations host parties and fundraising efforts to benefit the less fortunate.

The summer of 1862 was no different. On July 17th, *The Mexico Independent* reported that farmers were worried about the effect of a drought upon the hay crop. The courts were handing down decisions. Benefit strawberry festivals and church picnics were the order of the day. New manufacturing was coming to Mexico and Pulaski. Missionaries were holding lectures to instruct the citizenry about the work they had done abroad.

Among all that mundane reporting, however, was an undertone of grief, stress, and loss. Soldiers in the 24th and the 81st Regiments, both raised in Oswego County, were in the front lines of the effort to put down the rebellion which had raged since 1861. Funerals were announced for the latest casualties, wounded and sick soldiers were mentioned, names of men taken captive and facing an unknown fate were reported. Most significant of all, a county-wide War Committee had been formed, its purpose being to induce volunteers to enlist in order to save Oswego from the dreaded draft which had been announced by President Lincoln on July 1st.

The so-called War of the Rebellion, predicted to last no longer than 90 days, was now in its second year and both sides realized that the thought of an early end was a pipedream which had metamorphosed into a political and cultural nightmare. Members of the War Committee were well aware of the hesitation of families to offer up more husbands, fathers, brothers, and sons to a cause which appeared, at the time, on the brink of being lost. Nevertheless, they persevered. Rallies were held throughout the county to garner support for a new regiment, ultimately dubbed the 110th. The deal was sweetened by the institution of bounties available only to volunteers. So persuasive was the combination of the rallies and the liberal bounties that the 110th Regiment ultimately had a roster of 1,025 men.

Capitalizing on the enthusiasm shown by Oswego residents, the War Committee announced in August that it planned to form yet another regiment: "We learn that the

War Committee have determined to raise another regiment of volunteers in order to make up the quota of Oswego county, without drafting. They will start with a capital of nearly or quite three hundred men already enlisted. A call is in circulation for another meeting of the Board of Supervisors to raise the bounty to the same figure as that provided for Col. Littlejohn's regiment."[1]

Four days later that same newspaper announced that Andrew S. Warner of Sandy Creek had been selected as colonel of the as yet unnamed organization. Unlike DeWitt Clinton Littlejohn, the colonel of the 110th, Warner had military experience, enrolling in 1844 in the 168th Regiment, New York Militia, and rising to the rank of major.[2] He was a Republican and had served in both the New York State Assembly and Senate. He was described as a man of "abundant strength and vitality . . . possessed of a powerful will" and "well fitted to be a leader of men."[3] Dudley Farling, editor of *The Daily Palladium*, was chosen to be adjutant. This man, described as

Andrew S. Warner was the organizer and first colonel of the 147th Regiment.
Shawn Herron

having "much good feeling and genuine goodness of heart," would be both a contro-versial figure and a brave soldier in the months and years to come.[4]

Recruiting was brisk all over the county. War meetings were held in New Haven, Constantia, and Parish.[5] Delos Gary and John McKinlock, among others, organized companies in Oswego City. Reuben Slayton raised a company of neighbors and friends in Parish. Chauncey Gridley was hard at work in New Haven and Alexander Hulett in Fulton. The success of the effort was reported in this gleeful article: "The prospects for the completion of Col. Warner's regiment are excellent, if our War Committee and citizens generally take hold of the work in earnest. The country is ripe for the work, and if a perfect avalanche of meetings are held within the next few days the regiment will be a success. Let us be prepared for the work, and let all unite in it, without raising distracting side issues or attempting to carry on any other object than that of filling up our quota of volunteers. This is the task before us. Shall we not unite in it?"[6] The official excitement displayed by the *Times* was evidenced by the fact that as of August 27th eleven printers had volunteered.[7]

As September 15th, the rescheduled date of the threatened draft, loomed closer, even greater emphasis was put on the advantages of volunteering for the new regi-ment, particularly the bounties which might mean a son would be able to provide for aging parents or a husband for his wife and children if he should decide to do his patriotic duty: "Gov. Morgan announces by proclamation that the State bounty of fifty dollars will be continued to those who volunteer in the new regiments until Saturday, the 6th day of September, and that after that day it will be paid only to those who enlist for three years to fill up the old regiments. – All, therefore, who desire to secure the State, County, and City Bounty, amounting to one hundred and thirty dollars, besides the one hundred dollars Government bounty at the end of the war, *should enlist in our new regiment immediately*. Let the word go forth; let it be rung in every neighborhood, on every street corner, at every household shrine: *the fourth Oswego County Regiment must be completed this week!* . . . Unless our quota is raised *drafting will take place in this county*. Let no man say after he is drafted, that he did not have fair warning. Volunteering must be hurried forward with more briskness and enthusiasm now than ever. Every man to the work. Let it be the great business of the week. Hurry up the enlistments. The wounded and dying soldiers on the field cry for help. A bleeding country demands instant and tremendous efforts and sacri-fices for its salvation. To the work, then; to the work! Work with your money, work with your brains, -- work up our new volunteer force to a full regiment and running over, before Monday morning next."[8] The enthusiasm shown by the newspaper was reflected in an incident occurring at a rally in Oswego City on September 4th: ". . . Wm. I. Preston, Esq., closed the meeting with an address full of the fire of patriotism, concluding his remarks by saying he was prepared to give $10 extra bounty to any qualified person who would enlist on the spot. The offer was immediately accepted, and again repeated and accepted. Loud cheers greeted the new recruits. The scene continued till six able-bodied muscular men had enrolled their names . . . ."[9]

The companies gathered in Oswego City, as reported on September 15th: "We yesterday afternoon made a brief visit to the encampment, which, during the past week, has had several new streets added to it. There are now ten companies in camp, numbering in the aggregate nearly 1000 men. The men appear in fine spirits, and all will heartily welcome the reception of marching orders. Two or three of the companies are short of their maximum number, occasioned by the rejection of some by the mustering officer. An effort should be made immediately to fill up these companies. When the regiment will receive orders to leave for the seat of war is unknown, but probably the present or next week at the farthest, will witness the departure of the Fourth Oswego County Regiment . . . ."[10]

On September 15th the regiment still had not received its designation, a question which undoubtedly was of interest to all concerned and was finally answered: "Col. Warner's regiment has been officially designated as the 147th regiment New York Volunteers . . . ."[11] Two days later it was announced that Col. Warner had "received his marching orders, and that the 147th regiment will depart for the seat of war on Monday, the 22nd inst. The regiment lacks but a few men of being up to the maximum standard. Let all our citizens united in indevoring [sic] to fill it up during the present week."[12] Despite the news of the anticipated departure date, the regiment was still in camp on September 22nd, when formal mustering began. Not until September 27th did the regiment actually depart. Eight hundred thirty-seven souls boarded railroad cars and set out, ignorant of the horrors awaiting them: blood and battles, deprivation, loss of life, limb, and in some cases, mind.[13]

NOTES

1. "A New Regiment," *Oswego Commercial Times* (Thurs. Eve.) August 14, 1862, n. p. Where the newspaper obtained the figure of 300 surplus men is unknown. *The Adjutant-General's Report for the 147th Regiment* notes that 46 men who originally planned to enlist in the 110th were instead sent to the 147th.
2. "Col. Andrew S. Warner," *Sandy Creek News* (Thurs.) October 4, 1934, 3.
3. "Hon. Andrew S. Warner," *Sandy Creek News* (Thurs.) December 29, 1887, 1.
4. "Adjutant of the New Regiment," *Oswego Commercial Times* (Tues. Eve.) August 26, 1862, n. p.
5. "War Meeting at New Haven," *Oswego Commercial Times* (Mon. Eve.) September 1, 1862, n. p. See also "War Meeting in Parish" and "War Meeting in Constantia," same edition and page.

OF BLOOD AND BATTLES: OSWEGO'S 147TH REGIMENT

6. "The New Regiment," *Oswego Commercial Times* (Wed. Eve.) August 27, 1862, n. p.

7. "Two More Printers Gone," *Oswego Commercial Times* (Wed. Eve.) August 27, 1862, n. p.

8. "Enlist Now and Save Your Bounty," *Oswego Commercial Times* (Tues. Eve.) September 2, 1862, n. p.

9. "War Meeting Last Evening," *Oswego Commercial Times* (Fri. Eve.) September 5, 1862, n. p.

10. "The Camp," *Oswego Commercial Times* (Mon. Eve.) September 15, 1862, n. p. Among the rejects were Eli Cornwell and Michael O'Brien. Cornwell lied about his age, alleging he was 18 when he was only 17. O'Brien was probably too old. He said he was 44 but it is likely the enlisting officer did not believe him.

11. "Local Affairs," *Mexico Independent* (Thurs.) September 18, 1862, n. p.

12. "Marching Orders," *Oswego Commercial Times* (Thurs. Eve.) September 18, 1862, n. p.

13. "The Gallant 147th," *Oswego Palladium (Wed.)* July 3, 1886, n. p.

Trials and Tribulations

The fourth Regiment from Oswego county will shortly now be in the field, and we doubt not will render a good account of itself.

SEPTEMBER 1862 WAS a busy time in Oswego County. Crops were being harvested, schools were opening, and men were preparing, once again, to go off to war. After the departure of the 110th Regiment on August 27th attention was turned to filling the ranks of the fourth Oswego regiment, the 147th. Newspapers were full of dire warnings about the looming threat of a draft and offered strenuous advice about the benefits of enlisting: "... *All those, therefore, who desire to enlist in the new Fourth Oswego Regiment before the full bounties cease must do so THIS WEEK*. We know there are those who desire to enlist, and expect to do so sooner or later. To all such we say *now* is the time . . . ."[14] Appeals were made to the different ethnic groups in the area: "A German boy, from the 1st ward, who has seen service under Gen. Sigel in 1849, and who when only 17 years old was engaged in eleven battles under him, enlisted yesterday in Capt. Gary's company. Fall in! – Fall in, Germans; and follow the example of your compatriot of 1849."[15] Other optimistic reporting appeared: "The prospects for the completion of Col. Warner's regiment are excellent, if our War Committee and citizens generally take hold of the work in earnest. The country is ripe for the work, and if a perfect avalanche of meetings are held within the next few days, the regiment will be a success. Let us be prepared for the work, and let all unite in it, without raising distracting side issues or attempting to carry on any other object than that of filling up our quota of volunteers. This is the task before us. Shall we not unite in it?"[16] By mid-September, at the time designated for the dreaded draft, the regiment was in camp in Oswego City and the newly minted soldiers were anticipating their departure: "We yesterday afternoon made a brief visit to the encampment, which, during the past week, has had several new streets added to it. There are now ten companies in camp, numbering in the aggregate nearly 1000 men. The men appear in fine spirits, and all will heartily welcome the reception of marching orders. Two or three of the companies are short of their maximum number, occasioned by the rejection of some by the mustering officer. An effort should be made immediately to fill up these companies. When the regiment will receive orders to leave for the seat of war is unknown but probably the present or next week at the farthest, will witness the departure of the Fourth Oswego regiment . . . ."[17] Presentations to various officers took place shortly before the regiment left Oswego.[18]

Although it had been predicted that the regiment would depart Oswego on September 20th, logistical problems made that date impossible. Mustering occurred on September 22-23. Not until September 27th did the soldiers board the railroad cars late in the day to begin their journey. Amid the crowds of friends and relatives, the soldiers marched through the city to the late arriving transportation: ". . . A little after six o'clock the battalion formed in line and took up its march for the depot, headed by the Mechanic's Sax Horn Band. Leaving the encampment ground it proceeded down Schuyler street as far as Seventh street; along Seventh to Seneca; down Seneca to first, and up First street to the depot. By this time the shades of evening were falling, and the display was rather dimly witnessed. Arriving at the depot, it was found that the cars were not yet ready for their reception. The men were kept in line as well as possible . . . About nine o'clock, however, 'all aboard' was called, and the cars moved from the depot amid the cheers of an immense assemblage. The Fourth Regiment from Oswego county will shortly now be in the field, and we doubt not will render a good account of itself. The present destination of the 147th we have not ascertained. It will doubtless however be Baltimore or Washington, where some time must necessarily be occupied in perfecting the men in the drill before they are brought before the enemy."[19]

The regiment's itinerary was detailed in a letter Captain Cyrus Hartshorn sent to his local newspaper: ". . . We left Oswego city on Saturday evening, and arrived at Geneva, which is at the foot of Seneca lake, at 2 o'clock Sunday morning – There were three steamers in readiness to convey us up the lake. Thus far our journey was in the night, and but little can be said of it. Sunday morning found us moving rapidly along the beautiful sheet of water. Hemmed in as it is by a rich farming section of country, all enjoyed the scenery on either side very much. We arrived at Jefferson, a village at the head of the lake, at 10 ½ A. M., and marched from the boat to the cars . . . The whistle sounds, the cars start, and on we go up the narrow valley of the Chemung, securely guarded and hemmed in on either side by high and rugged hills, and at 2 P. M. we arrived at Elmira, safe and sound. Here we drew our rations for one day, which consisted of cooked ham and beef, bread and cheese. Here too we received our arms – the Enfield rifle, which is considered the best in the service. – the boys were all well pleased with them and thought that if used by brave men, would teach the rebels a lesson not soon to be forgotten. At 4 ½ P. M. we took seats in a long train of freight cars, fitted up with temporary seats with that real Yankee spirit which always accommodates itself to the circumstances in which he is placed. Some of the boys stretched themselves on the floor, some on the benches, and others under them, thus making themselves as comfortable as they could while being whirled, with the power and fierceness of steam, through the deep, narrow ravines that wound themselves amid the rugged, mountainous region of Pennsylvania. At 12 M. it was announced that we had crossed into the State of Maryland. Here, for the first time, we saw evidences that treason existed in our once happy land. Most of the inhabitants cheered us heartily, others remained sullen, and apparently displeased with the present state of things. – Every bridge was well guarded, and numerous encampments were stationed along the railroad to Baltimore, at which place we arrived at 3 P. M. Leaving the cars, we marched through the streets to the depot of the Baltimore and Washington railroad, expecting to immediately take the cars for Washington. In this we were disappointed, as there were two regiments ahead of us awaiting transportation, and it became evident that we would not leave until the next day. Our regiment was invited to a bountiful repast, gratuitously furnished by the citizens, which was disposed of by our boys with a right good will. Baltimore has its rebels; it also has many true friends of the Union, who are nobly feeding the thousands of soldiers who are daily passing through that noted city. – Night came on and found us with arms stacked, awaiting orders. Soon the good news came that we must march to Camp Patterson and encamp for the night. This order was most cheerfully obeyed, as it gave us an opportunity of visiting our friends of the 110th. We were received and entertained like brothers . . . The camp is two and a half miles from the depot and pleasantly situated on an eminence, giving a good view of the city, a small portion of the Chesapeake, Fort McHenry, and the surrounding country. After a treat of good coffee and bread and a lively chat of an hour or two, all was quiet, and all were soon asleep. Tuesday morning, Sept. 30th. – Morning came and with it a pleasant sunrise, and the prospect of a fine day . . . [W]e marched back to the city and took breakfast at the same place where we were entertained the night before. Thus far the weather has been fine and our journey prosperous . . . ."[20]

A soldier identified only as P. H. F. continued the story: ". . . .We left Patterson Barracks at 8 o'clock next morning, and at 12 we left Baltimore, but were delayed at Annapolis Junction, so that we did not arrive at Washington until evening. We retired for the night at Washington Barracks. Next morning we had orders to march to Camp Chase, Va., five miles from Washington. It was a severe march, for it was uncommonly warm here, and some of the boys in other companies fell by the way; but every man in Capt. Hartshorn's company, I believe came through sound. I remember hearing some of his most slender men say, 'I'll get through as soon as the captain.' That's the grit for a soldier. One remark of the captain was: 'I'll go with my boys if I go on a bob-sled.' Then the old cattle cars rang with cheers for Capt. Hartshorn. There was a reserve car for officers, but such as the captain of company F are not afraid to fare with their boys. Our camp is quite pleasant. It is very warm and very dry here. At present there is a great stir among the troops . . . ."[21]

On October 3rd the regiment went to Camp Morris at Tennallytown, DC and despite early enthusiasm and good well, circumstances quickly evoked less happy reports.

Captain Hartshorn reported that the 147th was put to work building a seven mile long road from Fort McClellan to Fort Pennsylvania. He also noted that illness had appeared among the troops but letters from home were helping alleviate homesickness.[22] Letters from the soldiers demonstrated how disaffected they were quickly becoming with their superiors and the army in general, witness a letter composed by William Henry Skinner, dated November 2, 1862: ". . . Our camp today is wrapt in gloom, caused by the first death in the regiment. Corporal A. D. Fuller, from Fulton, a member of company D, died at 11 o'clock this morning, after a short but severe illness. He was apparently as well and hearty yesterday morning, and in ten hours from the time he was taken sick he was a corpse. His remains are to be embalmed and sent home . . . It is almost impossible to keep clean here; but upon this point the understrappers in rank and file do not agree with the shoulder strappers in command. If any of our friends in Mexico are anxious to do anything for the comfort of us soldiers who are (not) fighting for our country, they can do it by sending us a little box with a jug of cider in one end, a paper of tobacco in the other, and a baked goose in the middle . . . ."[23]

That same issue of the *Mexico Independent* also carried a less subtle description of conditions in camp. Identified only as "A Volunteer," the writer delivered a scathing assessment of his surroundings: "Having a few moments to spare, I thought I would write a few lines to you, knowing they would be read with interest by many friends in Oswego county. We are all in as good health as can be expected under the present circumstances. We have a number of sick on hand and it's only through the mercies of God that they are cared for. They will not take them in the hospital, or give them any stove or bedding. We are trying to have a little better place to put the sick in; we are putting up a new tent for them. We have to drive down crooked stakes and lay poles on them; in this way make the beds. It keeps the sick off the ground. They have lain on the ground heretofore, and if they have care, it comes from one of their kin or friends in the same company; and that is all they have to rely on, and if the friend's money is gone, the sick soldier must suffer for the want of care. Now, if Oswego county has sent her sons in the field to fight the enemy, will she, or will she not, when they are in pain and standing on the edge of the grave, stretch forth her hand and with gentleness assist them either to descend in respect or help them out? We enlisted out of patriotism to save the country from destruction, but we can see our mistake now. Speculation is the theme, and we enlisted to maintain it; for some of the time we do not get half of our rations, and never all that the law allows us to have. But what can we do? Will you, the inhabitants of Oswego county, allow this treatment to your sons? If so, we must bear it patiently till Christ relief doth send by death; for that relieves the wounded soul of the trouble of this world. While I am writing I hear the groans of the sick. May their groans go to God, and may he relieve them of their pain and trouble. If we don't get some help, we shall have to bury some of our boys like dogs. ** We are told that the government gives plenty to the soldier, but who gets it? – We do not. When we left home the boys were full of patriotism, but it has all fled, and it will not return unless we get better treatment . . . ."[24] Even the officers recognized that the 147th was being used for a purpose for which the members had not signed on, as a comment by Captain Reuben Slayton revealed: ". . . We as a regiment are at work on a fort about a half mile from camp. We have not drilled much except with pick and shovel."[25]

Discontent over poor food and health issues are apparent in William Skinner's letter dated October 18, 1862: ". . . Our regiment is at present acting in the capacity of sappers and miners, and all the drilling we have had as yet has been with the pick axe and shovel. The health of our regiment is improving some, but there are many sick ones. Most of the sickness is occasioned by the scant supply of *inferior food*. When we left our friends and homes we expected to encounter many hardships and endure many privations, but we did not expect to forfeit our claims to the title of human beings. A man to be a good soldier must forget that he ever had a home, or has ever enjoyed the common comforts of life, and the society of 'dear ones far away.' We know as yet but little of a soldier's life, but few of you at home can duly appreciate the horrors of civil war, and the hardships and privations incident to a soldier's life. The history of this unfortunate war purchased by the lives and blood of thousands of men must be found in the hospitals . . . There have been several desertions from our camp . . . ."[26]

By December the editors of *The Mexico Independent* were alarmed enough to publish an article condemning the alleged ill treatment of volunteer soldiers: "Can it be possible that the men of the 147th regiment, who are encamped close to Washington, where there is an abundance of provisions, have not enough to eat? It seems incredible. Yet we are continually receiving letters from the boys (as also are their parents), complaining most bitterly of the scantiness and inferiority of their rations. They write that they never get their full rations, and sometimes not one half of them; and what they do obtain are often times of the most inferior quality and scarcely fit for a dog to eat. Some of the men write begging their friends to send them provisions, so that they can eat and be satisfied. If they could have all the rations that are allowed them by Government they say that they would have ample to eat, and would feel contented. We know the writers of some of these letters, and believe them to be men whose word can be relied on. We have received more letters of complaint from the 147th regiment, respecting their fare and the conduct of some of their officers, than from all the other Oswego regiments put together. At first we refused to publish some of the letters, and omitted sentences and paragraphs in others, thinking the statements contained therein were greatly exaggerated, and that giving them publicity would do much more harm than good. But as letters now come to us (two of which appear in this week's paper, written by reliable men), thicker and faster, and as fathers who have sons in the regiment bring in letter after letter to read, all telling the same sad tale – not enough to eat, and what they do have is very poor – we cannot help thinking there is something wrong somewhere. If the men in the 147th regiment are not the greatest eaters in the army they must be the greatest grumblers, or those officers whose business it is to see that the men have the whole of their rations, and they are wholesome, are very remiss in their duty, and ought to be severely reprimanded or dismissed from the service."[27]

The officer most criticized for not looking after his company's gastronomical needs was Captain Hartshorn. He attempted to refute the charge in a letter to Rev. A. P. Burgess, in response to one received by him on December 3, 1862. Hartshorn explained the procedure required for requisitioning food and then added: ". . . Our fare is not what it used to be at home. We are enduring many privations as soldiers, and I hope that whether we live to return from the war or not, our friends will remember with grateful respect every soldier, however humble his station. Be assured, it has been my first thought and most earnest wish that my men should fare well as to food, clothing and labor. If they had been wronged by speculators, whether officers or not, far be it from me to utter one word in opposition to complaints which you refer to; and if there has been dishonesty in relation to the men's rations I am not only ignorant of the fact, but fail to see any appearance of it. O, I wish that deficiency of food had been our only trial! Not so. Disease and death have entered our ranks in a way to teach us the uncertainty of life. And while our friends at home have been anxious as to our food, my constant labor by day and anxious, watchful hours by night, in view of the fact that our men were dying and our sick list increasing, have made it the severest trial of my life . . . ."[28] William W. Hathaway was among those who supported Hartshorn's denial of the charges: ". . . There are men in the Company that would like to ruin his character, if they could. Some of them have written letters to the Mexico Independent that were, in many respects, false. My opinion is that Capt. Hartshorn has done the best for his men that he could. It is possible that they have treated him so bad since I left the regiment that he has resorted to some severe punishment, but I doubt it. Tell Mrs. Hartshorn for me, not to give herself any trouble about it, for she may feel assured that these reports will all prove false."[29] Three days after this letter appeared, however, Hartshorn resigned and returned to Oswego County and civilian life.

In the midst of the controversy over rations and treatment of the sick, the soldiers had an experience few probably forgot. While arranged for the presentation of a flag to the regiment, the soldiers saw a carriage approach. Adjutant Dudley Farling explained what happened next: "At this juncture, as the colors were again stationed to front and centre, and the battalion was being reformed in line of battle, the President of the United States, accompanied by Secretary Seward, drove on to our parade ground and stopped, calling to Col. Warner to approach. It being a little darkish, we did not recognize our distinguished visitors at first, but Warner came on, reached the carriage, and signaled me to follow. After shaking hands and a brief chat about the progressing battle, of which neither the President or ourselves had any definite information except from the sense of hearing, about the condition and health of the 147th regiment, &c., the regiment was informed that the President and Secretary of State were present. They were saluted by 'Present Arms' and the waving of our colors. The President then wheeled his carriage, came up on the right and drove close along the whole line, his head bared, and was greeted, of course, by the vociferous cheers of the regiment. The President then waved us an adieu, and proceeded on to Washington. The honor of this unexpected visit was peculiarly gratifying to the regiment, and inspired the men with new enthusiasm and zeal."[30]

The 147th was ordered to Acquia Creek on November 30th, as described by George Hugunin: "I write you but a few words merely to let you keep track of us. We left our camp at or near Georgetown, Sunday night the last day of November. – We marched five days through Maryland, and finally, came to *water* at Liverpool, landing on the Potomac above Aquia Creek about sundown Thursday afternoon . . . ."[31] A letter written by Wallace Barnes on December 5th further described the move: "As I believe that our numerous friends will be anxious to hear from us and learn our destination, I embrace the earliest opportunity since we left Washington to send a few lines. This morning finds us at Acquia Creek. We arrived here this morning at 4 o'clock, and are now resting and waiting for supplies. Where we are going is more than we can tell, and our officers seem to be as ignorant of our destination as the men. It is believed, however, that Fredericksburg is the place, to reinforce Burnside, as a battle is expected to take place before many days. If we go there we are to be held back as a reserve. It is reported that the rebels there are an immense force. I am sorry we have not been better drilled, but we are going to 'pitch in' if called upon, and do our best. We are brigaded with some other regiments, making about 8,000 strong. We left Washington on Sunday at 6 P.M., and have been on the road ever since, marching most of the time night and day. The 24th are encamped within four miles of us. I stand the march first-rate, although my load was rather heavy along towards night. I had to throw from my knapsack such things as I could get along without. Anson Drake and Alonzo Lewis, of our company, deserted as soon as they found we had marching orders. I must bring this to a close, as I write in great haste. I have just learned that Fredericksburg is our destination, which is only 14 miles distant. The 81st are there to join with us. I want a chance to pop the Secesh . . . ."[32] Adjutant Farling wrote a long letter on December 8th, thanking the Oswego folk for the Thanksgiving box containing cooked fowl and mince pies, then describing the regiment's departure: ". . . An unexpected and sudden order set the regiment in motion before the first report was digested. That order was for us to 'march,' *immediately*, to a point near Fredericksburgh, the present scene of great military operations in Virginia, where two immense armies lie confronting each other and where a stupendous battle may be fought before this reaches its destination. The turkeys and pies then came as a God-send, for the men were compelled to take two days' rations in their haversacks, and five days' rations were to be sent after them in wagons. Company K 'filled up' with choice cuts of turkey, and the writer put his in requisition for the same service which gave him good supply for two days, with his Sergeant and Clerk. Under these peculiar circumstances Company K is anxious that their hearty and cordial thanks should be appropriately returned to the generous citizens who so beneficently remembered them on this occasion. Having thus expressed the thanks of company K, in accordance with their request, it may not be uninteresting to say something of the late movements of the 147th regiment. We are now in camp about one mile from Aquia Creek, Va., and ten miles from Falmouth, opposite Fredericksburgh, surrounded by the camps of many thousand of other troops, several brigades of which followed directly in our track from the vicinity of Washington and arrived the next day after ourselves . . . The 147th did not expect so sudden an order to march, after an order only a few days before to 'go into winter quarters at Camp Morris,' and also because not one day's opportunity had been given for military drill since the regiment was organized. For ten weeks the men labored daily with the shovel on the 'Northern Defences of Washington,' and they worked faithfully, hoping that soon they would be permitted to learn something of drill and prepare for the field. But it was ordered otherwise, and the Regiment received the order to march with cheerfulness and prompt obedience, being the first on the march of the six regiments of the brigade that moved with us. The order came at 3 ½ P. M., and at 5 P. M. we were on the road – our backs upon our old camp and our faces set towards Fort Carroll, Md., across the east branch of the Potomac, eight miles distant, where we arrived at two o'clock on Monday morning, and bivouacked in the open field till ten o'clock. Some of the other regiments then came up with us, and we moved on, in the midst of quite a brisk shower. For some reason our line of march was an indirect one, and we were on the road from 5 P. M. Sunday, continuing most of the night, till Saturday morning, being on the march five days and two nights, averaging some fifteen miles per day. The first day's march was very trying to the men, their heavy knapsacks and accoutrements, with 100 rounds of cartridge, weighed them down, and many of them were compelled to fall out by the roadside and afterwards work their way up at night, but a considerable number did not overtake us till the end of the journey. After the first day, however, the men seemed to have gained new vigor, and scarcely a man fell out . . . After Monday the weather was delightful and the roads good . . . Precisely what is the destination of the regiment I cannot tell at present. We are sending out heavy details of pickets and guards daily. It is rumored that we are to return to Aquia Creek and go into winter camp there. But of this we shall know more in a day or two. It is not probable we shall remain in this spot long. Perhaps we shall be in the expected contest at Fredericksburgh, which all seem to think is close at hand, judging by the long train of ambulances that are daily moving toward the front . . . Our regiment is unfortunate in one respect. Its field officers are all absent, sick, but the Major. Col. Warner is lying ill at Washington, and Lieut. Col. Butler is ill in New York. Quartermaster Lewis was also too ill to come on with us from Camp Morris. Major Miller and the Adjutant are therefore laboring under extraordinary duties. We hope to see all our field officers and staff present in health in a few days . . . ."[33]

While the soldiers in the 147th were grumbling about the lack of training and complaining about their rations, events were unfolding in Washington which were to have a bearing on the course of the war and their participation in it. On November 5th, finally completely disenchanted with General George McClellan's handling of the war effort, President Lincoln relieved him of command of the Army of the Potomac and installed a most unwilling Ambrose Burnside in his place. Although Burnside considered himself not competent enough to assume command, nevertheless, as a good soldier, he obeyed the president's order. The problem with McClellan had been his indecisiveness. Lincoln needed a victory. Not only was he dealing with the Confederates he also had unhappy Northerners and a less than thrilled Congress to deal with, to say nothing of his own Cabinet. He hoped Burnside could give him a victory before the end of 1862. Burnside tried. He thought that if the Union Army could take Richmond the war would come to a speedy conclusion. To accomplish this goal he determined the best way was to go through Fredericksburg. In theory it was an admirable plan. Lee's army was divided at this time and Burnside called for pontoon bridges to be built across the Rappahannock River to facilitate crossing the thousands of soldiers and equipment. All would have been well except that through various snafus in communication the pontoons were not forthcoming. By the time they did arrive, together with the 50th New York Engineers to construct them, Lee had discovered Burnside's plan and was taking steps to thwart it. Late in the night of December 10th the engineers began their task. At daybreak they came under fire from Confederate sharpshooters. In response, Burnside ordered his artillery to shell the city. Burnside was finally able to send three regiments across the river and street fighting, as well as wholesale pillaging, took place as the residents scurried away to safety. Burnside spent the entire day of December 12th ferrying the remainder of his troops across the Rappahannock. This delay gave Lee ample time to arrange his now combined forces to resist the predicted onslaught. When December 13th dawned, the area was engulfed in fog. Burnside did not know that Lee and a portion of his army were arranged on a ridge outside of town known as Marys Heights. Other parts were stationed at various places on both sides of him. Partway up the heights was a stone wall over which Burnside's soldiers attempted to climb at least fourteen times that day. More men were lost in a field later dubbed the Slaughter Pen. When dusk finally called a halt to the carnage, approximately 12,500 of the 106,000 Union soldiers were either killed, wounded, or missing, compared to Confederate losses of only 5,300 of 72,500 men. On December 14th Burnside retreated to Washington, having accomplished nothing but sacrificing thousands of men in a botched up operation.[34]

The battle for Fredericksburg had special meaning for Oswego County since both the 24th and the 81st Regiments saw action. While the battle was raging, the 147th, although not actually fighting, was put to good use, as Adjutant Farling explained in a letter dated December 13th while the battle was in progress: ". . . Our regiment is kept constantly on the alert. One half of the men are out daily on picket duty and guard duty, at Falmouth, opposite Fredericksburgh; also to guard the railroad from this point to Fredericksburgh, and to guard bridges between Aquia Creek and Falmouth. The other half is kept constantly lying on their arms ready to spring to action any moment. We sent five companies out this afternoon, under Capt. Harney, to guard the Potomac Creek bridge, some seven miles off, where a raid is expected from the rebels. We are informed that a considerable body of rebel cavalry are between us and our main army on the Rappahannock, having an eye upon the large depot of military supplies at this point, which the 147th and *four* or *five* other regiments are left to protect; also to picket the roads, bridges, and shore of the Potomac hereabouts . . . ."[35]

Although kept in reserve the 147th was beginning to see the action the troops avowed they had desired when they enlisted. In the coming months their situation would change dramatically and they would exchange their pick axes and shovels for bullets and bayonets.

NOTES

14. "The Last Chance," *Mexico Independent* (Thurs.) September 4, 1862, n. p.
15. "Good for Capt. Gary," *Oswego Commercial Times* (Thurs. Eve.) August 26, 1862, n. p.
16. "The New Regiment," *Oswego Commercial Times* (Wed. Eve.) August 27, 1862, n. p.
17. "The Camp," *Oswego Commercial Times* (Mon. Eve.) September 15, 1862, n. p.
18. See "Presentation to Lieut. Pierce," "Legal Tender," and "Presentation to Lieut. Hugunin," all in *Oswego Commercial Times* (Fri. Eve.) September 20, 1862, which reported that a horse and equipment were to be presented to Adjutant Dudley that afternoon.
19. "Departure of the One Hundred and Forty-seventh Regiment," *Oswego Commercial Times* (Mon. Eve.) September 29, 1862, n. p. See also "The 147th Regiment," *Mexico Independent* (Thurs.) October 2, 1862, n. p.

20. "Letter from Capt. Hartshorn," *Mexico Independent* (Thurs.) October 9, 1862, n. p.

21. "Letter from the 147th Regiment," *Mexico Independent* (Thurs.) October 16, 1862, n. p. See also "From Virginia," *Oswego Commercial Times* (Thurs. Eve.) October 9, 1862, n. p.

22. "Letter from Capt. Hartshorn," *Mexico Independent* (Thurs.) October 16, 1862, n. p. See also "Letter from the 147th Regiment," *Mexico Independent* (Thurs.) November 6, 1862, n. p. The letter was dated October 26, 1862 and its anonymous writer lamented the necessity to be away from home and business to fight a war so far away only "that the chains of slavery, that have bound for nearly a century more than four millions of human beings, may be riveted still tighter. And is this all? An echo answers, All . . . ."

23. "Letters from the 147th Regiment," *Mexico Independent* (Thurs.) November 13, 1862, 1.

24. "Letters from the 147th Regiment," *Mexico Independent* (Thurs.) November 13, 1862, 1.

25. "Letter from Capt. Slayton," *Mexico Independent* (Thurs.) November 27, 1862, 1.

26. "Letter from the 147th Regiment," *Mexico Independent* (Thurs.) October 30, 1862, 1. See also "Letter from the 147th Regiment," *Mexico Independent* (Thurs.) December 4, 1862, n. p. Dated November 24, 1862 and signed by "A Volunteer" this letter too alludes to the inferior quality of the regiment's food and its scarcity.

27. "Can It Be Possible?" *Mexico Independent* (Thurs.) December 4, 1862, n. p. See also "Letter from the 147th Regiment" written by "A Volunteer" on the same page. The letter, dated November 24th, repeats the lament that the men were not being fed well.

28. "Letter from Capt. Hartshorn," *Mexico Independent* (Thurs.) January 1, 1863, n. p. See also "Letter from Capt. Hartshorn," *Mexico Independent* (Thurs.) November 20, 1862, 1 where he first attempted to detail how food was acquired.

29. "Capt. Hartshorn," *Mexico Independent* (Thurs.) January 22, 1863, 1. Hathaway's assessment was appended to a letter from "Colosse" which also defended the captain. Even Col. Warner felt compelled to interject his opinion of the situation, saying, ". . . The food is good, as good as can be had anywhere. If at any time there should by chance be anything drawn that was not of the best quality, the company officers are directed to return it at once, and get such as is good . . . ." See "Letter from Col. Warner," *Oswego Commercial Times* (Sat. Eve.) December 27, 1862, n. p.

30. "'Old Abe's Visit to the Oswego Boys," *Oswego Commercial Times* (Fri. Eve.) November 7, 1862, n. p.

31. "From the One Hundred and Forty-Seventh Regiment," *Oswego Commercial Times* (Thurs. Eve.) December 18, 1862, n. p. Hugunin's letter was dated December 12th.

32. "Letter from the 147th Regiment," *Mexico Independent* (Thurs.) December 11, 1862, n. p. See also "Military," *Oswego Commercial Times* (Fri. Eve.) December 12, 1862, n. p., which reported that the regiment was put to work unloading provisions and forage from transports.

33. "From the 147th Regiment," *Oswego Commercial Times* (Sat. Eve.) December 13, 1862, n. p.

34. Many works are available which deal with the Fredericksburg Campaign. I have used Francis Augustin O'Reilly, *The Fredericksburg Campaign: Winter War on the Rappahannock* (2006); Hubbard Cobb, *American Battlefields* (1995); Bruce Catton, *Reflections on the Civil War* (1994); Kelly Knaer, ed., *The Civil War: An Illustrated History* (2011). See also "Saturday's Fight at Fredericksburg," *Rochester Evening Express* (Mon.) December 15, 1862, n. p.; "The Week's Topics," *Oneida Weekly Herald and Gazette and Courier* (Tues. Morn.) December 16, 1862, 1, which contains a day by day account of the battle; "Letter from Capt. Frank's Battery," *Mexico Independent* (Thurs.) January 29, 1863, written by Jerome Loucks (1843-1894), which describes the carnage and aftermath of the battle; "Malignant Opposition," *Oswego Commercial Times* (Sat. Eve.) December 20, 1862, n. p. which reviews negative opinions of Democratic newspapers after the disaster at Fredericksburg, among them *Albany Argus, Rochester Union,* and *New York World. See also* "The Deadly Stone Wall," *Oswego Daily Times* (Sat. Eve.) November 15, 1902, 6. For a report from the opposing side, see "Report of the Rebel Gen. Lee on the Battle of Fredericksburgh," *St. Lawrence Republican* (Tues.) December 20, 1862, 1. Although Burnside took the blame for the defeat at Fredericksburg, there was plenty to go around, starting with the War Department. Members of Congress agitated to have certain of Lincoln's Cabinet members removed, but the president refused their resignations. See, for example, "Resignation of Secretary Seward," *Troy Daily Whig* (Mon. Morn.) December 22, 1862, n. p. and "First Edition," *Syracuse Daily Standard* (Tues.) December 23, 1862, n. p. which reported that the Congressional Committee on the Conduct of the War had met on the previous day to hear testimony on "matters connected with the battle of Fredericksburgh."

35. "Another Letter from the One Hundred and Forty-Seventh," *Oswego Commercial Times* (Thurs. Eve.) December 18, 1862, n. p. See also "Sketches," *Sandy Creek News* (Thurs.) August 6, 1931, 7, which reprints a letter from Sgt. J. A. Robinson, dated December 14, 1862 and published in *Sandy Creek Times* (Sat.) December 27, 1862.

On to Glory

"The 147th regiment got it rather tight.
Only 86 men remain to tell the tale."
Homer Ames, Battery G, 1st NY LA

". . . On the first day of January, in the year of our Lord one thousand eight hundred and sixty-three, all persons held within any State or designated part of a state, the people whereof shall then be in rebellion against the United States, shall be then, thenceforward, and forever free . . . ." With these words, President Abraham Lincoln transformed the focus and scope of the War of the Rebellion from preserving the Union to abolishing slavery.[36] Reaction to his decision was both positive and negative in all regions of the divided country. In Oswego County, home of many who advocated abolition and were committed to the Underground Railroad, residents generally considered the decision correct: "The expected proclamation of President Lincoln was duly issued, according to announcement, and was laid before your readers yesterday afternoon. We think most of our readers will concur with us in the opinion that it is a model document . . . Whatever effect it may immediately produce, none can doubt that it is the entering wedge destined to split asunder the institution of Human Bondage, sooner or later. It is the beginning of a movement that must end in divorcing the Government of the United States from all responsibility for the continuance of Slavery. It is an advance forward which decrees the final death of the monster that has long threatened to destroy our beloved country . . . Since the Declaration of Independence no document has been issued as the Emancipation Proclamation . . . At last the government of the Union is on the side of Justice, Humanity and Religion. At last we dare to proclaim Liberty as our watchword, and to fight under her banner and in her dear name."[37]

In Virginia, however, the issuance of the proclamation seems to have evoked little response from the 147th Regiment.[38] Concerned as they were over food, ill health, and mounting deaths among the ranks, the president's decision was probably perceived as distant to the regiment's situation. An unsigned letter dated January 13, 1863 and sent from Belle Plain, VA underscored current concerns: "Our regiment made another grand march yesterday to Belle Plain, about nine miles from where we have been encamped. We are now on the extreme left of Franklin's division, where, should we be called upon, we should have to fight; but that probably will not be this winter. We are located on the bank of the Potomac. There is considerable business done by steamers, but not as much as at Falmouth. Joseph Munger died last Sunday night and was buried the following morning just before our regiment started on its march. A board was placed at the head of his grave with his name, the letter of his company and the number of his regiment, so his friends can find his grave without any trouble. There is a great amount of sickness and many deaths. Last week there were three deaths in one hospital in one day. It seems to be a small matter for a man to die in camp. Our officers are becoming awake to the fact, as well as Dr. Coe, who has been acting brigade surgeon for some time past, and has in consequence been away from the regiment. He has now returned to see to the sick himself. Ellery Gillett has been in the hospital for some time past. I learn he is slowly gaining. It was expected that when we marched the sick would all be sent to Washington, but the Medical Director told Col. Warner that he must keep them with the regiment, so they were all brought to this place in ambulances. Mr. Goss has been discharged and has returned home. Col. Warner and Quartermaster Lewis are both here. They look rather feeble for duty . . . I learn that one of the men in our regiment has been sent to headquarters, and is sentenced to carry a ball and chain for two years, without pay, for the crime of sleeping on his post while on picket duty near the enemy. The Mexico boys are well."[39]

The anonymous writer's prediction that the soldiers would be quartered at Belle Plain until spring was rendered false on January 20th when General Burnside initiated what was later nicknamed the Mud March.[40] Just five weeks after the disastrous defeat at Fredericksburg, Burnside decided once again to attempt to reach Richmond and end the war. And once again, pontoons to cross the Rappahannock were a part of the plan. This time, however, Mother Nature was the deciding factor in Burnside's failure. Adjutant Dudley Farling's account of the maneuver left little to the imagination: "The vast Army of the Potomac on Monday commenced moving. Our brigade and regiment started at noon, on Tuesday last. The weather was fine and the roads in fair condition at that time. After proceeding some ten miles, however, and night closed upon us, the rain began to fall fast and steady and continued all night. About 10 P. M. we halted in the rain in the woods, we pitched our little shelter tents and spent a very wet uncomfortable night, the horses having nothing to eat, and standing out in the driving rain. In the morning we moved on, but the roads had broken up. The artillery and supply trains got stuck in the mud. We marched on till 4 P. M. through a perfect mortar bed and in the rain, when our brigade and in fact the whole army, was compelled to halt. We filed into a dense pine forest and encamped for the night. – There we lay on the ground till Friday morning, when the order came for the great army to retrace its steps, as it was impracticable to proceed any further, as the wagons and the artillery could not proceed, and it is impossible for any army to move without supplies of food for soldiers, and ammunition and big guns. We started back and marched fifteen miles through indescribable mud, through fields and forests, leaving hundreds of dead horses and mules behind which expired from mere exhaustion. We camped some two miles short of this spot Friday night, and came up on Saturday afternoon, and took our old camp which was most disgustingly muddy and dirty, as an Ohio regiment had occupied it during our absence. We are now again getting settled, and feel more comfortable, as a day's sun has dried the mud partially. The object of our movement, was, to surprise the rebel army, cross the Rappahannock above Fredericksburgh and come down and attack them in the rear. The whole thing was a failure, however, and it is probable that the rebels would not have been surprised, had the roads continued good; for they were at the ford we intended to cross, before we got there, and swept the woods on this side with their cannon during the night. Had we crossed the river, or attempted to cross, it would have been a desperate and bloody conflict. Whether any other movement will be attempted during the winter, of course I am unable to tell. All we know is what orders reveal when they come. Would that I had time to describe to you the picture of the movement of the great army. But I cannot. It would require many pages. Imagine a vast column of soldiers, some fifteen miles in length, every man with gun and knapsack, containing his blanket, clothing, &c., his haversack with three days' rations in it, his cartridge box with forty rounds of ball cartridge in it – all moving forward together. Then imagine some hundreds of cannon and the caissons (which carry the ammunition for the guns) each gun and caisson, drawn by six to twelve and fourteen horses, driving forward, the drivers yelling and the whole crashing and pounding onward. – Then imagine, besides this, other hundreds of four, six, eight, and ten horse wagons loaded with rations for the men, forage for the horses of the vast army, and a full supply of ammunition for cannon and muskets for any emergency. Then imagine the incessant yells and shouts of all this vast body of men, as they press on – and when you have worked all this up in your imagination, you will have but a faint conception of the scenes – especially if you attempt to conceive of the horrible mud and the dying and dead animals that line the road, and the scenes presented by the vast army lying tired and exhausted in the woods after the halt, with the ten thousands of fires at which the soldiers cook their coffee and such pork as they might have. The Twenty-fourth regiment was with us in the march, and we camped near together, and they and we have both again returned to our old camps. Of course there is a strong sympathy between the two regiments."[41]

In later years H. H. Lyman had occasion to comment on the infamous march: "They [the members of the 147th Regiment] had not got fairly settled in their new quarters when, on January 20th, the Burnside mud march was begun. Whatever the object may have been which General Burnside hoped to accomplish by this dead-of-winter movement, the result was disaster and demoralization to the Army of the Potomac, and a waste of men and material never fully realized by the country. The One-hundred and forty-seventh received its full share of damage and demoralization from this unfortunate movement. Scores of its men were exhausted and broken down by the four days' exposure to chilling rains and the strain of poaching through the endless slough of deep, sticky mud, and on returning to camp were prostrated with typhoid fever, pneumonia, dysentery and other complaints, from which many never recovered. As a direct result of this terrible four days' march, forty-four men died in camp at Belle Plain within the next two months. Demoralization was evinced by the resignation of the colonel, four captains, and three lieutenants, between January 25th and February 4th. Had the privilege extended to enlisted men, the list would have been larger . . . ."[42]

Lincoln sacked Burnside on January 26th, installing General Joseph Hooker in his place.

While military strategists grappled with the latest disaster, the 147th was experiencing its own misery. Sergeant Lewis D. Rulison of the 24th Regiment wrote on January 12th near Belle Plain: ". . . The 147th regiment has just passed here. – They have been assigned to Gen. Paul's brigade (late Patrick's) of our division. They are very much afflicted with sickness in that regiment. Capt. Slayton told me that he buried two of his boys the day before, that his first lieutenant had gone home, that his second lieutenant was sick and that he had not a sergeant for duty in his company. . . ."[43] In February Colonel Warner, Rev. Chapin, Quartermaster Lewis, Captains Hartshorn, Woodbury, Howlett, Seeley, well as Lieutenant Gridley and Lieutenant Gregware, all resigned, most of them for ill health. Rev. Chapin died of tuberculosis a year later.[44] Warner's departure led to the promotion of John G. Butler to the rank of full colonel.

Despite the dismal beginning of 1863 things were slowly improving. Hooker announced on February 7th that soft bread, fresh potatoes, and onions would be issued several times each week. He sacked quartermasters who either could not or would not do their job properly. Furthermore, he demanded that army camps be cleaned properly, offering furloughs to those regiments passing inspection. These improvements greatly raised morale among the ranks. An excerpt from Lansing Bristol's letters lends credence to the efficacy of Hooker's orders: ". . . As to your coming here I think that there is no doubt but that you will find us here if you come when you spoke of, & we will try & entertain you comfortably. You need not bring any hard tack. I have 300 lbs of it in my shanty also ½ doz loaves of bread, 20 lbs coffee, 3 lbs tea, 40 lbs Rice, 25 lbs sugar, & 100 lbs pork, & ½ barrel of flour, one bush beans & a few onions . . . ."[45]

Changes in command throughout the Army of the Potomac meant that the 147th finally received the formal battlefield training the men had so desperately hoped for.

As early as the first week in January, General Gabriel R. Paul, in charge of the Third Brigade, First Division, First Army Corps, took it upon himself to "perfect the organization and discipline of his brigade, attending to the details of drill and sanitary policing, and the personal and soldierly bearing of officers and men."[46] In March 1863 the regiment found itself transferred from the Third Brigade to the Second Brigade of the same division. As spring approached the Union Army once again was stirring itself with plans to begin a new offensive against Lee and the Confederates.

Hooker, brimming with confidence, was advised and encouraged by President Lincoln to forget about Richmond and instead to concentrate on destroying the Confederate Army. The Chancellorsville campaign, which lasted from April 27th through May 4th, ultimately led to another Confederate victory but not without great personal cost to Lee since he lost his ever faithful Lt. General Thomas J. "Stonewall" Jackson to friendly fire.[47] Hooker's plan called for splitting his 134,000 troops into two parts. His group would cross the Rappahannock to the north and take a place called Chancellorsville. To the south General Sedgwick was to cross and once again attack Fredericksburg. The unpredictable weather notwithstanding, the plan was put into operation. The 147th was with Hooker and Lieutenant Joseph Dempsey described their experiences in a letter dated May 14th: "I take this opportunity of writing you a brief sketch of the doings of the 147th regiment, during the last two weeks. On the 28th of April, our regiment marched from camp near Belle Plain for the Rappahannock. About dark we halted in a piece of woods two miles from the river. We started from there about two A.M., and arrived at the river before daylight, four miles below Fredericksburg. The morning was foggy, and as soon as the fog began to rise the enemy's pickets began to fire on our pontooners and drove us back. Then our skirmishers began to fire in return. The rebel pickets were protected by rifle-pits, and behind buildings, but our artillery opened on them over our heads, which made great fun for our boys to see the rebels run. The firing was kept up for two hours, when some of the 6th Wisconsin boys went over in a boat, and then the pontoons were run over the river. General Wadsworth then crossed over, and first after him was the 147th. We marched up the bank filed to the right, and halted in front of a large brick house which our General division then formed in line of battle and advanced our pickets. We remained in this condition all that day, and laid on our arms that night. The next day nothing was to be seen in our front but the enemy's made his headquarters. We took about twenty prisoners. I counted seven dead rebels on the ground. Our division then formed in line of battle and advanced our pickets. We remained in this condition all that day, and laid on our arms that night. The next day nothing was to be seen in our front but the enemy's pickets. About three P. M. Major-General Reynolds and staff rode along our lines. We immediately formed in line of battle, and supposed we were going to advance on the enemy. By this time we could see the rebels forming for battle. In a few moments a couple of teams drove along in our rear with shovels and picks, and we were ordered to stack arms, and each man armed himself with a pick or shovel and went to work throwing up breast-works. That was more than the rebels could stand, and they opened on us again with artillery. Our batteries replied to them from the opposite side of the river. The firing was kept up till after dark. This was a trying time for the regiment. The shells fell all around us thick and fast. Here two men in Co. C were wounded, one of whom has since died, but our men kept at work until the breastworks were finished, and we slept in them that night. Nothing more of moment transpired until Saturday morning at eight o'clock, when the rebels opened on us again, but were soon silenced by our guns. In the meantime we were ordered to lie down in our rifle-pits, which we did, creeping out into a ravine to the river bank, where we crossed over to the north bank, which place we reached about eleven o'clock A. M. We then marched to Chancellorsville, reaching that place the next morning about six A. M. We formed the second line of battle – the regulars the first – we being the reserve to them. The regiment in our immediate front was the 14th, commanded by Major Giddings, well-known in Oswego. Our boys were very anxious to have the rebels give us battle here, as we had very strong breast-works. Our general orders were not to permit any live rebel to cross the road which was in our front, and running east and west. The rebel line was on the south side of this road. Our breast-works ran along this road for about six miles. Our regiment was stationed about a quarter of a mile from the Chancellorsville House, where the hardest battle of the war was fought. The rebels charged seven times on Sunday, and were repulsed every time by our centre, which was our weakest point. On Sunday evening I went up there to see how things looked. It reminded me of a large pasture of sheep lying down, to see the dead rebels covering the ground for acres in their gray uniforms. Every time they would charge you could hear them scream for miles. That is the way they frightened the Eleventh Corps. The only way to stop them was to try lungs in the same way. The rebels tried us down the river in the same way, but we silenced them at that game. There was about thirty pieces of cannon at that point raking in all directions. It is nearly all woods here for miles, and mostly oak, about a foot in diameter. On Sunday night all was quiet. On Monday the rebels made a charge about ten A. M. and another at three. During the forenoon our General sent for me and told me to take fifty men out of the brigade and lay out a road parallel with the line of battle for artillery, and to intersect with the roads to the pontoons, and east of the Chancellorsville House, which I did in a short time, and just in season for the three o'clock charge, which I had a splendid chance to see from where I was near the Chancellorsville house. The rebel skirmishers would advance first and fire on our skirmishers, ours falling back as they advanced, then came the main army in close column, their line of battle extending a half mile in length, cheering like fiends – our men in the mean time lying behind breast-works, would pour their whole charge along the lines, and cross fire, which would stop them for a few seconds. Then about the time they would gather, our artillery would mow them down with grape and canister. By that time, the infantry would be loaded to give them another shot. But our artillery was enough. It seemed as though every shot would fairly raise them from the ground. Then they would look around and run back, and some who were nearest our lines, would lay down their arms and run to us as prisoners. About this time our regiment was ordered to the right to support men there, for our scouts reported that the enemy was going to force our lines at that point. We waited there until after dark for them, but they did not come. Then we went back and resumed our old place near the centre. We remained there until the next day, when we were ordered to the extreme right, to protect two batteries of twelve guns. We expected a rebel charge on our right flank. At about four P. M. it began to rain in torrents; at eight o'clock in the evening we received orders to retreat in five minutes without noise. We marched out on the road for that purpose, when the order was countermanded. We were then ordered to go to bed and take a good sleep. – About three o'clock the next morning we received orders to fall in quietly, which we did and marched out on the road. The artillery and men were all gone from the breast-works. We then marched for the pontoons, where we arrived at ten A. M.; we halted, made some coffee, and after two hours' rest, crossed the pontoons, and marched that day through the mud to within four miles of Falmouth. The 147th was the last regiment to cross the river, not a rebel being in sight. When we left the other side of the river, we supposed we were going to help the Sixth Corps re-take Fredericksburg, but we were disappointed when we came here into camp. We were not beaten, for there was two thirds of the army that did not fire a gun. Our army is in the best of spirits. We are getting some large siege guns at Falmouth. Life is sweet, but I would give a leg or an arm to see something done. When our General told us not to let a live rebel cross that road I got a rifle, and bayonet, and my pocket full of cartridges, and thought I would sell my life as dear as I could. We have great confidence in Gen. Hooker, and I tell you that Gen. Wadsworth is a brave man. Our misfortune was with the Eleventh and Sixth Corps undertaking to do too much. If our Corps had remained with the Sixth we would now be in Fredericksburg. We lost Capt. Sisson, of Co. D, of Fulton, by fever on the 12th. He was a good officer. Mr. Osborne, formerly of the *Oswego Times*, but now reporter for the New York *Herald*, was in our camp today. – Capt. McKinlock arrived here today. Col. Butler has gone to Washington on a sick leave. There are more officers here sick than men. James Kingsley's papers have been sent on for commission as Lieutenant. May 15th. – Last night we were called up at two A. M. to march. We picked up everything, and got under arms, but the order was countermanded, and here we are waiting for orders to move. Gen. Hooker has promised to move soon, in general orders. The army have great confidence that they can do something when they are led across the river again . . . The rebel pickets are very quiet on the other side of the river. For the last ten days there has been no New York papers allowed to circulate in the army. We only get Washington papers at present. My health was never better than at the present writing; I stand the marches well. We have eight days' rations in our haversacks, ready to march."[48]

The discipline and willingness to fight of the 147th did not escape the notice of their commanders. On May 10, 1863 General Cutler reported: ". . . The several regiments of this brigade behaved with great coolness during the time they were under fire from the enemy's batteries, on April 29 and 30 and May 1 and 2, and were at all times ready and eager to be led into action. The One hundred and forty-seventh New York Volunteers were under fire for the first time, and behaved with the coolness of veterans . . . ."[49]

As the Army of the Potomac licked its wounds, the war continued on other fronts. General Ambrose Burnside, now in charge of the Department of Ohio, arrested former Congressman Clement Vallandigham for violating his General Order 38, accusing him of treason because of his vitriolic public speeches encouraging open opposition to the war effort. General Ulysses S. Grant began the siege of Vicksburg. In Louisiana General Nathaniel Banks and the Nineteenth Corps, to which the 110th Regiment belonged, in conjunction with Admiral David Farragut, were endeavoring to take Port Hudson on the Mississippi in a plan to divide the Confederacy and prevent delivery of materiel to the interior. Black men all over the country were flocking to recruiters to enlist in the newly created United States Colored Regiments. In Washington, President Lincoln was increasingly frustrated with Gen. Hooker's inaction.

In the meantime, Robert E. Lee had his own problems. He needed a way to remove the Union Army from Virginia, one which would also relieve the strain on the state's resources and would simultaneously provide his own forces with fresh supplies of food, equipment, and horses. After reorganizing his army into three parts, he set out for Pennsylvania.[50] He hoped to elude Hooker for as long as possible to give his soldiers the opportunity to avoid conflict as they made their way through the Shenandoah Valley and Maryland into Pennsylvania. Hooker, sensing something was afoot, sent General Alfred Pleasanton and his cavalry to reconnoiter across the Rappahannock. Pleasanton surprised Lee's cavalry on June 9th at a place called Brandy Station. Although the Confederates ultimately prevailed, Hooker now knew where Lee was and what he was planning.

If only Hooker had followed Lee, American history might have been quite different. His decision to attempt another assault on the now less well defended Richmond instead of pursuing the Confederate Army was not only poorly thought out but contrary to Lincoln's order to disregard that city and concentrate on destroying Lee: "Lee's army and not Richmond is your sure objective point."[51] After several arguments with General Henry Halleck over strategy and requests for more troops, Hooker asked to be relieved of command and Lincoln obliged him.[52] On June 28th he promoted General George Meade to be head of the Army of the Potomac. Meade was at first worried that Baltimore or Washington was Lee's objective but as soon as he deduced that the Confederate leader had other plans he set out after him and met him at Gettysburg. The battle was joined by accident on July 1st when Henry Heth's soldiers met advancing Union forces near the village.

Much has been written about the battle of Gettysburg, quite a bit of it about the role of the 147th Regiment.[53] We are fortunate that the soldiers themselves have left letters and reminiscences of their experiences. Grove Dutton, for example, described the long, arduous march: "The march through Maryland was very severe. The roads generally were fair but at times very dusty, though when we passed through Frederick City they were the reverse. Maryland, or at least the portion we passed through, is a beautiful farming country. The growing wheat was nearly fit for cutting. Everything indicated thrift, so much different from the devastated fields of Virginia. The ravages of the Army soon became apparent. Fences were burned for fuel and ofttimes the grain trampled down. One night near Frederick City we camped in a field of several acres enclosed by a crooked rail fence . . . The next day we marched thirty-three miles. My feet were blistered as they have never been since. June 29 we mustered for pay, 380 men answering to their names. This included mule drivers and all detailed men. This was at Marsh Creek, Pa. . . . And now we were about to engage in a battle, which has become historic, where I witnessed sights that will never be effaced from my memory . . . ."[54] Francis Pease continued the story: ". . . July 1st we were routed out at daybreak and ordered to march. We started at seven o'clock. When we got within a couple of miles of Gettysburg, off to the South of the town, we saw two or three shells burst in the air. It was the rebel batteries shelling our cavalry, which was on ahead. There was hard fighting to be done and we were ordered to load, which we did without delay. Then came the order, double quick, and the men started towards the front on a run. The road became so crowded, however, that we were compelled to slacken the pace and could only get over the ground on a run at rare intervals. The horses of the artillery were coming up at a mad gallop. Soon the rebel cannon balls began to whistle over our heads, some of them pretty close and probably the greatest battle of the rebellion was raging. Our batteries soon began to return the fire and as we came up in a little hollow we were ordered to lay down. The rebel batteries were firing away, but the balls flew over our heads and we could see them strike in the distance and plow up the turf and scatter the dust. We were soon ordered to march by the right flank and were soon within thirty or forty rods of the rebels, whose colors were flying. We were then ordered to get down upon one knee and then the order came to fire and volley after volley was sent into the ranks of the Johnnies. The rebel bullets whistled about our heads like hail. The men were falling thick and fast around us, some dead others wounded. Corporal Franklin Halsey, of Mexico, stood right by my side to the left. He was hit by a ball in the head and killed instantly. For fifteen or twenty minutes we fought hard, when the rebels flanked us on the right and began advancing upon us in large numbers. The firing from both sides was very rapid. Finally we got the order to retreat and we lost no time in obeying, leaving an awful sight of dead and wounded upon the field. As we retreated we got into a railroad cut or ravine. We were moving as fast as we could, which was not very fast, because the ravine was crowded and there were a good many wounded men that had to be helped along. After we got into the cut the rebel bullets whistled over our heads. Soon the Johnnies were upon both sides of us, standing upon the banks in large numbers, and we were compelled to throw down our arms and surrender . . . ."[55] Lieutenant Volney Pierce provided more details: ". . . We had been firing but a short time when I saw the right of our regiment suddenly swing back, then formed to the rail fence on our right and fired very rapidly . . . At the same moment I noticed Hall's battery limber up, and dash down the Chambersburg Pike all but 2 guns – and they very soon went – for I saw a squad of rebs rush up to a rail fence and fire at them and I directed some of my men to give them a few shots . . . We were now nearly surrounded and the fight very hot – We stubbornly held that line. No order to fall back had been received. Col. Miller was wounded, early in the action and left the field. Maj. Harney was close up on the line with us. I saw an officer whom [sic] I think was H. [Lt. Homer] Chisman of Gen. Cutler's staff ride down towards us and wave his sword as a signal for us to fall back. In the meantime a brigade of Rebs crossed the fence on our right and rear, and we then broke for the rear ourselves. The left of the regiment myself included went off into the R. R. cut – when it was about two feet deep. I was no sooner in the cut than I found it was a death trap; for the Rebs had fortified the lower end (north) of the cut and the moment we got off in there to avoid the charge on our right they opened on us with a score of rifles. How we climbed out we can hardly realize, but I know I climbed up the steep sides and got out and Sergeant Wyburn with me, as he carried the regimental colors. At this moment we were all liable to capture by the Confederate brigade on our right rear and but for the prompt action of Col. [Rufus] Dawes of the 6th Wisconsin we should the whole forty of us gone to the rear as prisoners of War . . . Our regiment reformed on the Chambersburg Pike south of Seminary ridge and immediately returned, and went in to the woods on the right of the R. R. cut and joined our brigade for the rest of the fight . . . ."[56] Lansing Bristol reported that the remnant of the 147th was repulsed about 4 p.m. and regrouped "on the hill back of the Village." On July 2nd he and others were sent to assist the 12th Brigade at dusk. The fighting, he noted, lasted until late into the night when the soldiers were relieved. The 147th was stationed in the rifle pits on July 3rd.[57]

By July 4th all was quiet. Lee began his retreat into Virginia and never attempted to invade the north again. Sidney Cooke wrote to his father from the battlefield on July 5th: "We have had a hard battle. I think the hardest of the war, at Gettysburg. We went in the morning of the first and opened the battle. Out of 31 we took into the battle of this company, 13 are killed and wounded, a large number are missing. Among the killed are Lieut. Taylor, Simson, and Albert Potter. Ed and Elam Goodrich and Asa are among the wounded. Mr. Turner is not hurt, he is with us now. I am all right. I got a crack on my thumb, but it did not injure the bone. So I was able to go on every time. We slaughtered the rebbels (sic) awfully, they charged right up to our works. I think the rebbels (sic) are in full retreat."[58]

On July 6th B. E. Parkhurst, now a patient in US General Hospital, West Philadelphia, wrote to his father: "I presume you will be looking for a letter from me rather anxiously, so I take this my first opportunity since the battle to write to you. I came here yesterday. I left the battlefield on Wednesday. We had a hard fight I can tell you. I have not heard from our company since I left the battle field. Our brigade led the advance on that day. We were within a very short distance of the rebels, and such fighting as our corps did was never before known. Our corps did not number over 8,000 men, and with that force we held the whole rebel army for two hours. At first we drove them back for half a mile, then they were reinforced, and we had to fall back nearly two miles. Then our corps rallied and held their ground till the 11th corps came up and relieved us. Then our corps fell back to the town of Gettysburg, and were held as a reserve for the 11th corps; but they did not stay there long before the 11th corps broke and run like a set of cowards. Our corps then had to come in again and handle the rebels till the 12th corps came up. We then knew that we had men that would stand by us. So we held the ground till next morning, when, most of the army coming up, our corps was relieved for a short time. – They had got pretty well cut up by this time, so that there were not a great many men in the corps. It was the first time our regiment was exposed to infantry fire, but they fought more like tigers than anything else. They had to be told twice to retreat before they would move. I think that more than half of them were killed or wounded. I know that there were a great many wounded in our company . . . There were four men killed and seventeen wounded in our company when I left the field. How many there are now I do not know. I think that was pretty hard for our company, for we only had about 35 men when we first went into the battle; and taking 21 out of that were killed and wounded, I think it must leave the company pretty small . . . ."[59] The official record states that 380 men from the 147th entered the fray on July 1st and by the end of the three-day battle, 76 had been killed or mortally wounded, 146 more were wounded, and 79 were missing. Among the missing was Francis Pease who was paroled and sent to Carlisle parole camp until exchanged later in the summer. Grove Dutton, who had been wounded severely, was taken to a hospital in Philadelphia to recover.[60]

Residents of Oswego County were aware of Lee's attempt to invade the north, as evidenced by an article published on July 1st: ". . . We shall be surprised if the rebels are not badly defeated before they escape from the trap. It seems to us that nothing but culpable negligence or cowardice on the part of our forces can save the invading army from annihilation. We eagerly await the result, possessing considerable confidence that it will redound to the glory of the national arms."[61] Over the next few days news of casualties trickled in and finally confirmation of the great victory was announced: "The good news holds out. Every dispatch as it reaches us over the wires adds something to the glorious record of valor which the Army of the Potomac has made. The defiant foe, under its favorite commander who affected to despise our army, after fighting with a fury almost superhuman, an energy that amounted to madness, has been disastrously and fearfully beaten. His shattered columns are flying in every direction, pursued by our victorious forces, smiting them at every step. After three days of obstinate fighting which never had an equal in the annals of the world, the morning of the glorious Fourth of July dawned on a ghastly and stricken field – sad and sickening – but yet glorious for the Republic. How doubly glorious is this victory when we consider the circumstances under which our brave soldiers fought. Brave but unfortunate, the Army of the Potomac seemed to have been wedded to disaster. Time after time hurled against the enemy, it went into conflict only to be beaten, or if it were victorious, to see the fruits of valor wrested from it by incompetency and mismanagement . . . Gen. Lee evidently planned and inaugurated his late campaign in perfect contempt of the force against which he had so often contended. He must have known the facility with which Hooker, or whoever commanded our army, could bring it upon his rear, to sever his communications, and force him to give battle. But he calculated that, having got into a convenient position for advance or retreat, he would turn about, engage and destroy this army, and thus be free to make his other movements, with no fear that the North could concentrate fresh levies upon him so rapidly as to destroy him. How awfully he has been disappointed the daily telegrams reveal. He will be fortunate, indeed, if he gets across the Potomac with even the remnant of an army, and at the most, he can take back to Richmond a force little better than a mob, stripped of arms, cannon, munitions of war, and wagon trains. Lee has lost his Waterloo. Rebellion has received its mortal stab and is already stricken with the agonies of impending dissolution. Honor to our noble army! Honor to its commanding General, who has so nobly, so heroically, so modestly performed his duty! In the midst of our rejoicing our hearts are filled with sadness at the fearful sacrifice of life, and we drop the tear of sympathy for afflicted friends who have lost those near and dear to them. Let us not forget our duty to the survivors; and let us, if possible, assuage their grief by pointing to the fact that this blood has not been shed in vain – that those who fell heroically battling the enemies of our Republic met their death in the most noble cause which ever enlisted the courage and patriotism of man."[62]

Survivors who returned home shortly after the battle confirmed the news: "By the return of Captains Slattery, Wright, Parker and Gary last evening from the battle-file of Gettysburgh, we have corroboration from participants of the bloody nature of the contest. Capt. Wright describes the conflict as far more terrible than any which he has witnessed. The storm of iron and lead was terrific, and entire regiments were nearly annihilated. – The 147th suffered terribly, but of course, it is impossible to yet ascertain definitely the number of killed and wounded. There was only a portion of the regiment engaged, the remainder being in hospital or on detached duty. At the last call of the roll before the above officers left the scene of action, but sixty-nine answered to their names. – It must not be surmised, however, that the balance of the number engaged have fallen. In the excitement of a general engagement men become detached from their regiments and days frequently elapse before they again rejoin them."[63]

Meade chased Lee to Hagerstown, MD but then refused to pursue his advantage, a step which reportedly reduced Lincoln to tears. A series of messages between General Halleck and General Meade in the wake of the battle illustrates the frustration felt on both sides. Lincoln, through Halleck, was insisting that Meade pursue Lee before he crossed the Potomac. Meade, however, contending not only with scattered artillery, barefoot soldiers, lack of food and equipment but also the weather, thought it singularly foolish to attempt such a move. The two sparred with each other until July 14th when Halleck wrote: "I hardly say to you that the escape of Lee's army without another battle has created great dissatisfaction in the mind of the President, and it will require an active and energetic pursuit on your part to remove the impression that it has not been sufficiently active heretofore." The same day Meade tendered his resignation to which Halleck responded: "My telegram stating the disappointment of the President at the escape of Lee's army was not intended as a censure, but as a stimulus to an active pursuit. It is not deemed a sufficient cause for your application to be relieved." Meade may have been restrained when writing to his superiors but he vented his true feelings to his wife, Margaretta: ". . . They have refused to relieve me, but insist on my continuing to try to do which I know in advance it is impossible to do. My army (men and animals) is exhausted; it wants rest and reorganization; it has been greatly reduced and weakened by recent operations, and no reinforcements of any practical value have been sent. Yet, in the face of all these facts, well known to them, I am urged, pushed and *spurred* to attempt to pursue and destroy an army nearly equal to my own . . . ."[64]

In fact, Meade did pursue Lee, as evidenced by entries in Lansing Bristol's diary. He mentioned on July 7th that the soldiers started for Middletown, MD, arriving there on July 8th. Two days later they set out for Hagerstown, arriving in that place on July 12th. After several more days of marching and crossing the Potomac, the regiment, together with other elements of the army, reached Warrenton Junction, VA on July 25th.[65]

Bristol noted that several men from the 147th were headed to Elmira to bring back recruits and conscripts. Throughout the summer the draft was in full force in Oswego County and new men were constantly being added to the ranks.[66] Among them were Ned "Dennis Degan" Lee, Captain John Hurley, Alexander Penfield, and John B. Audlin, all enrolling in Oswego City. Many more were recruited from every part of the state, Charles Biddlecom from Macedon, Wayne County among them, thus rendering the outfit no longer an "Oswego regiment." A good number was drafted; still others enrolled as substitutes; some actually enlisted.

While the 147th rested and regrouped, a controversy arose pitting Major George Harney and Captain Dudley Farling against other regimental officers. Lt. Colonel Francis Miller was badly injured in the head on the first day of the battle of Gettysburg. His horse bolted, taking him off the field. Harney assumed command and it was he who gave the order to retreat. In Miller's absence Harney became the *de facto* second in command after Colonel J. G. Butler, who was frequently absent on account of illness. It has been suggested that Harney and Farling, both Democrats, used the fact that New York now had a Democratic governor, Horatio Seymour, to advance their military ca-

George Harney was a controversial yet brave soldier in the 147th Regiment.
New York State Military Museum

reers. Harney wanted to be colonel and, when Lt. Col. Miller was absent recovering from his wound, began to agitate for the position, hinting that Miller's hasty retreat from the field on July 1st looked suspiciously like cowardice. At the time the 147th had been organized Edwin Morgan, a Republican, was governor and consequently most of the officers were of the same party. Employing General Orders No. 100 which permitted any regimental officer to request the discharge of company officers absent more than 60 days and obtaining the consent of General James Rice, Harney used Farling, as adjutant, to discharge 10 officers for "disability" to date November 5, 1863. These included Delos Gary, Patrick Slattery, Nathaniel Wright, and George Hugunin. Most of them had returned from their sick leave before hearing the news. Only Hugunin and Slattery protested officially and won back their commissions. Harney's ploy, however, only went so far. Col. Butler resigned to date November

5, 1863 but it was Miller who obtained the colonelcy.[67] One local newspaper exulted: "We are glad to chronicle the fact that Lieutenant Colonel Frank Miller, of this city, has been promoted to the rank of colonel of the 147th regiment. This is as it should be. Col. Miller is not only a brave soldier who has nobly done his duty in the field, but he is also a genial man and a gentleman in all his social relations. Much opposition was made to his appointment, by a few ambitious men, and we rejoice that justice has been done in giving him the promotion that he has justly won . . . ."[68]

As summer wound into autumn Lee again decided to attempt a campaign against the Union forces. Both he and Meade had been forced to send troops to Tennessee but Lee was undaunted. He wanted either to force Meade to retreat to Washington, DC or put him into such a position that he, Lee, would be able to destroy part of the Union army. Meade, although he still commanded a greater force than his Confederate rival, knew that Lincoln and Halleck looked upon him disapprovingly

COL. JOHN G. BUTLER.

Colonel John Germond Butler was forced to resign his commission on account of continued ill health.
Syracuse Journal

and wanted to do what was right by his soldiers. In mid-October Lee, supported by his various cavalry divisions, implemented his latest plan. For the next several weeks he and Meade waged what was called the Bristoe Campaign. Although both sides won minor skirmishes by November neither commander could say with certainty that he had won any clear victory. The effort resulted in many casualties. In addition, thousands of prisoners were captured on both sides. The 147th was engaged in this campaign and on October 19th at a place called Haymarket, while doing picket duty, several members were taken prisoner. Willard S. Smith, a soldier in Co. B, wrote to his father: "I wrote you on the 18th but had no chance to send it until this morning, and when I will send this I don't know. Perhaps today and perhaps not for several days to come. The mail came again this morning, but there was nothing for me. You see by the heading of my letter that we have moved since my last. Yesterday morning we left Centreville (raining hard) and are now about eleven miles to the front of it, near Manassas Gap, and on the Manassas railroad. We had to ford four creeks nearly knee deep. We halted about 4 P. M., and a picket was thrown out immediately. We pitched tents, and, had got our supper fairly eaten, when firing was heard on our picket line. We packed up and started out, loaded, and formed line of battle. The first Division, as usual, being in front. The 14th N. Y. Militia (Brooklyn) were sent forward as skirmishers. We heard the rebel pickets halt them but they can't have fallen back, for we heard firing afterwards in advance of them. There was some artillery firing. At nearly 9 o'clock we withdrew. Oct. 21st. – I quit writing last night because we had marching orders. I was speaking about the pickets. About two-thirds of those from our regiment were gobbled by the rebs. From our Company were corporal Skippen, private Gifford, Ed. Carroll and Walter VanAlstyne. You can tell Walter's folks that he is unhurt but is a prisoner. We marched five miles last night in as many hours, and such a road! The rebs. fell back from the Gap and we came through. I have received the *Palladium* you sent. That's the paper. There was more news in it than I have seen or heard before in a month. We are now in a splendid place on a high hill and mountains all round us. Good water and lots of rail fences all around. We will probably leave in the morning, if we do not move before."[69]

General Meade, still at odds with the president, Halleck, and others in the administration, made one more effort against Lee to prove he was a capable and competent commander. The ill-fated campaign, known as Mine Run, began on November 26th and ended on December 2nd. Hampered by bad weather, rugged geography, and bad communications, neither side fared well and the two armies went into winter quarters to await the coming of spring and a renewal of hostilities.[70]

The 147th Regiment participated in this campaign and a soldier identified only as H. described his adventures in a letter dated December 17, 1863: "Our camp is situated on the south side of the Rappahannock and close to Kelley's Ford. You must almost know the place, you have heard so much about it in the newspapers. It is a desolate looking place now. Kelleysville is almost torn down; the few houses that are left standing are well marked with shot and shell which passed through them. The hills in the vicinity of the Ford are also well marked with field works, rifle pits, &c. The country around is dotted with the graves of the brave men of both armies, who died gallantly fighting for the cause each loved best. Our Division Camp is situated in a large belt of timber. The men have their huts all finished; some of them are very nice and comfortable, but the location is unpleasant and unhealthy; the camp now looks like a vast bed of black mortar. The surface is covered with a thick coat of decayed vegetation – men and horses traveling through the camp will sink, the horses up to their knees in some places, and the men above their shoes. There are quite a number getting sick already; indeed it would almost make a man sick to look at the camp this morning. I have just returned from a two days' tour of picket duty and am under the care of Dr. Coe. I am not very sick, only a little worn and tired; the duty was very hard and I had not fully recovered from the fatigue of the last expedition. I may as well say a few words here in relation to the trip across the Rapidan. The cause of our failure is given fully in the newspapers; it would be unnecessary to speak of that here; I will give a short sketch of the part the regiment took in that expedition. We broke camp at day break Nov. 26th, crossed the Rappahannock, marched all day through the woods, (the artillery using the road,) and went into camp about 10 p.m. near the Rapidan. We lay there a few hours, was called up and was on the road again at 3 A. M. on the 27th. We then crossed the Rapidan and marched all day through a region known as 'the wilderness,' and halted about 10 P. M. During that day (the 27th) an incident occurred which I will relate, as it helps to illustrate the character of the guerrillas of Virginia. A part of the train in front of our Division while traveling through a very heavy timber was stopped by a few men dressed in our uniform, and the teamsters informed that they were on the wrong road, and told that if they would turn to the left they would soon gain the right road. The teamsters not suspecting anything wrong did as advised; a large portion of the train followed, until at last one of the teamsters suspecting something wrong, refused to go any farther, -- a fight ensued, in which the teamster was killed; the guerrillas came out of their hiding places – some formed in line to protect others who employed themselves in robbing the wagons and turning the mules and horse lose [sic]. They did not have much time to do their work, for three regiments of the First Brigade of our Division immediately deployed, and with a yell charged on the rebels and sent them flying in all directions. Our boys ran them out of sight in less than five minutes. November 28th we moved out at 2 A. M. and went into position in front of the enemy at Robinson's tavern. Our regiment was detached, and I was directed to relieve a regiment of the Second Corps, which I did and had my skirmish line established before daylight. The enemy did not advance as was expected. Our Brigade was formed in two lines of battle (our regiment in the front line) and advanced through a thick growth of timber, driving the enemy before us. We then came to an open plain close to Mine Run and under the enemy's guns; we then halted, the rain began falling heavily; companies I and G skirmished with the enemy until dark, we remaining in position to support them. At dark firing ceased; we had only one man wounded, Private Dirkee, Co. I. The ball passed through his cheek bone and settled in his neck. Capt. McKinley commanded his company (I) although suffering from fever. The Captain could not be induced to remain in hospital while there was any fighting going on; the exposure of that day nearly killed him. He was sent to Washington a few days ago for medical treatment; I hope he will soon recover, for he is as good a soldier as ever drew a sword in the service of the United States. An army of such men could not be beat. Nov. 29th and 30th the regiment remained under arms. December 1st the regiment was detailed on picket duty. I was directed to cross Mine Run, hold and protect two bridges which had been thrown across the creek during the day. I crossed and posted the men close to the rebels, and ready for a fight next morning, but it was decided not to make an attack on the rebel works, so I was ordered to fall back and destroy the bridges, which I did at 8 o'clock the next morning, taking up the bridges and setting fire to the timbers, without losing a man. The night was piercing cold; I got chilled through, and have not got over it yet. We found it would not do to attack the rebels -- the reasons of this you have learned through the papers some time ago. The regiment did very well during this expedition, only a few of the conscripts were badly frightened; one fellow shot himself through the hand and another through the foot, in order to be sent to the rear. But if this regiment is properly handled this Winter it will be a good one in the Spring."[71] Little did the writer know what 1864 would present to the Army of the Potomac.

NOTES

36. See Doris Kearns Goodwin, *Team of Rivals* (New York: Simon and Schuster, 2005), 497-502 for reaction in Washington, DC and elsewhere to his decision.

37. "The Proclamation," *Oswego Commercial Times* (Sat. Eve.) January 3, 1863, n. p.; see also "The Proclamation and the Supreme Court," *Oswego Commercial Times* (Tues. Eve.) January 10, 1863, n. p., and "The Proclamation," *Oswego Commercial Times* (Wed. Eve.) January 14, 1863, n. p.

38. That is not to say that the troops had no opinions about the war. See for example, Joyce Hawthorne Cook, Ed., *The Civil War Diary and Letters of Lieutenant Lansing Bristol, 147th New York Volunteers* (Oswego, NY: Mitchell Printing, 2004), 14. In a letter dated January 19, 1863, Bristol wrote to his father: ". . . You enquired what the feelings of the Soldiers were as regards the war Negroes &c. It is a universal feeling among the old Soldiers that they have had enough & many of them say that they will never go into another fight, & the new Recruits are not spoiling for a fight by any means. & as regards the Nigger a majority of them would say damn the Nigger. It is a queer state of things. It looks like an absurdity, fighting as we are & the fighters feeling as they do . . . ."

39. "Letter from the 147th Regiment," *Mexico Independent* (Thurs.) January 22, 1863, n. p.

40. Burnside's optimistic General Order, dated January 20, 1863, makes for interesting reading: ". . . they are about to meet the enemy once more. The late brilliant actions in North Carolina, Tennessee, and Arkansas have divided and weakened the enemy on the Rappahannock, and the auspicious moment seems to have arrived to strike a great and mortal blow to the Rebellion and to gain that decisive victory which is due to the country. Let the gallant soldiers of so many brilliant battlefields accomplish this achievement, and

a fame the most glorious awaits them. The Commanding General calls for a firm and united action of officers and men, and under the Providence of God the Army of the Potomac will have taken the great step toward restoring peace to the country, and the Government to its rightful authority." See "War News of the Week," *Sabbath Recorder* (Thurs.) January 29, 1863, 15.

41. "Letter from Adjutant Farling," *Oswego Commercial Times* February 3, 1863, n. p. Captain Reuben Slayton reported on this fiasco as well. See "Letter from Capt. Slayton," *Mexico Independent* (Thurs.) February 12, 1863, n. p. See also "The 'Mud March' Nor'easter, January 20-23, 1863," http://www.weatherbook.com/Mudmarch.htm.

42. H. H. Lyman, "Historical Sketch," Major- General Daniel J. Sickles and others, eds., *Final Report of the Battlefield of Gettysburg* (Albany: J. B. Lyon Company, 1902), vol. 3, 998-999.

43. "Letter from the 24th Regiment," *Mexico Independent* (Thurs.) January 29, 1863, 1.

44. "Resignations in the 147th Regiment," *Mexico Independent* (Thurs.) February 26, 1863, n. p.

45. Cook, 16. The letter was dated February 22, 1863 and sent from Belle Plain, VA.

46. Crisfield Johnson, *History of Oswego County, 1789-1877* (Philadelphia: L. H. Everts & Co., 1877), 84.

47. Jackson suffered a bullet wound which shattered the bone just below the left shoulder. The arm was amputated and although it appeared he would survive he died of pneumonia on May 10th.

48. "The One Hundred and Forty-Seventh Regiment – The Battle at Chancellorsville," *Oswego Commercial Times* (Fri. Eve.) May 22, 1863, n. p. See also Cook, 25-27. Burns Elwood Parkhurst wrote of his terrifying experience at Chancellorsville in a letter to the editor published in *The Mexico Independent* (Thurs.) May 7, 1902, n. p. It is quoted in Parkhurst's biography in "The Originals." A summary of his exploit may be found in "Tribute to B. E. Parkhurst," *Oswego Semi-Weekly Palladium* (Fri.) January 29, 1915, 4. See also Dorothy Kincheloe Hendrix, *A Leaf from Army Life: Background and Experiences of a Civil War Soldier* (Independently published, 1995), 118-119, and Cook, 25-26.

49. *Report of Brig. Gen. Lysander Cutler, U. S. Army, Commanding Second Brigade, April 27-May 6, 1863 – The Chancellorsville Campaign,"* http://www.civilwarhome.com/cutlerchancellorsville.htm.

50. Richard S. Shue, *Morning at Willoughby Run: The Opening Battle at Gettysburg, July 1, 1863* (Gettysburg: Thomas Publications, 1998), 2-5.

51. Carol Reardon and Tom Vossler, *The Gettysburg Campaign, June-July 1863*

(Washington, DC, Center of Military History, United States Army, 2013), 12. See also Harry W. Pfanz, *Gettysburg – The First Day* (Chapel Hill: University of North Carolina Press, 2001), 5-9 for a discussion of Hooker's efforts to determine Lee's plans and to protect against them. An ostensible obituary for Henry Heth, "Led to Gettysburg," *Oswego Daily Times* (Sat. Eve.) November 1899, 7, contains an excellent review of events leading up to the battle on July 1st.

52. Goodwin, 531.

53. See, for example, Bret. Brig. Gen. John W. Hofmann, "General Hofmann on the Action of the 147th New York At the Opening of the Battle," *National Tribune* (June 5, 1884); Henry H. Lyman, "Battle of Gettysburg: Opened by Cutler's Brigade, And Not By Any Single Regiment," *National Tribune* (August 25, 1887); James Coey, "Cutler's Brigade: The 147th N. Y.'s Magnificent Fight on the First Day of Gettysburg," *National Tribune* (June 15, 1910). See also Sickles , vol. 1, 11-13. In vol. 3, see Capt. J. V. Pierce, "Dedication of Monument, 147th Regiment Infantry," 988-997.

54. Hendrix, 119.

55. "He Fought at Gettysburg," *Oswego Daily Palladium* (Mon. Eve.) April 11, 1898, 6. Pease's letter, which was written to his parents, passed to his widow, Katherine Lord Pease Dutcher, who gave permission for it to be published.

56. "Letter of Lt. J. Volney Pierce," *The Bachelder Papers*, ed. David L. Ladd and Audrey J. Ladd (Dayton, OH, 1994), vol. 2, 910-913.

57. Cook, 33. See also "The Battle at Gettysburg," *Oneida Weekly Herald* (Tues.) July 7, 1863, 8 which provides an excellent eyewitness account of events occurring on July 2nd. See also "From the 123rd," *Syracuse Daily Standard* (Tues. Morn.) July 14, 1863, n. p. detailing that regiment's participation in the battle on July 3rd. For the Confederate perspective, see "The Rebel Telegrams," *Oswego Commercial Times* (Mon. Eve.) July 13, 1863, n. p. which quotes the Richmond *Examiner* alleging that Lee had won at Gettysburg!

58. "Recalls Part of Fultonian in War Between States," *Oswego Palladium-Times* (Mon.) June 27, 1938. The letter was in the possession of Sidney Cooke's son, Thornton.

59. [No Headline], *Mexico Independent* (Thurs.) July 23, 1863, n. p. D. H. Crosier, writing in the *Albany Atlas and Argus* (Tues. Morn.) October 6, 1863, n. p., opined that the First Corps, to which the 147th belonged, did not receive sufficient credit for its participation in the battle of Gettysburg: ". . . The First Corps is entitled to the credit of withstanding the full brunt of the first day's fight, with the exception of some aid afforded by the Eleventh Corps – a large portion of whose men broke and ran away, on the first assault of the enemy on our right. But for three hours, the 1st corps alone held the overwhelming force of the

enemy to check, and took over 2000 prisoners. In the afternoon, when in danger of being flanked by the Rebel left wing, which drove back the 11th Corps, the gallant 1st slowly retired, and took positions on the heights in the rear, and held them, while the other Corps came up, and took position preparatory to the renewal of the struggle on the second day. It is no more than just that the 1st Corps should have the credit due. Its mere skeletons of regiments that came out of that awful first day's fight, very emphatically told the story of their terrible and bloody struggle against a greatly superior force; and among those who breasted the hottest of that deluge of iron and lead, was the 147th N. Y., the 4th regiment went to the field from Oswego county . . . ."

60. Dutton disagreed with the official record: "This [figure] out of 380 would leave but 79, but there could not have been that number (380) that went into the fight for as I have mentioned before that number included mule drivers, company cooks and all detailed men . . . ." See Cook, 122. See also "The Battle at Gettysburg," *Oswego Times and Express* (Wed. Eve.) July 2, 1884: "Twenty one years ago yesterday the one hundred and forty seventh Oswego regiment opened the fight at the battle of Gettysburg. The regiment went into the battle 450 strong and mustered at roll call after the fight only 91 . . . ." General Abner Doubleday's official report on the battle contained the following: ". . . During the half hour which elapsed before he [Harney] could be relieved his loss was 207 killed and wounded out of 380 . . . ." See Hendrix, 67.

61. "The Rebel Invasion," *Oswego Commercial Times* (Wed. Eve.) July 1, 1863, n. p. That same issue contained an editorial about the feud between Halleck and Hooker.

62. "Victory Is Ours!" *Oswego Commercial Times* (Tues. Eve.) July 7, 1863, n. p.

63. "The One Hundred and Forty Seventh Regiment," *Oswego Commercial Times* (Tues. Eve.) July 7, 1863, n. p. Over the next few days and weeks both the *Oswego Commercial Times* and the *Mexico Independent* published list after list of men confirmed dead or found in various hospitals. See for example, "From the 147th Regiment," *Oswego Commercial Times* (Thurs. Eve.) July 16, 1863 which is a letter dated July 13th and sent from Baltimore by O. J. Harmon and Philo Bundy who had traveled south especially to locate survivors: ". . . The wounded were scattered around for miles, but they are being rapidly transferred to hospitals – mostly to Philadelphia . . . The whole country seems to be rushing there [Gettysburg] to look after their wounded friends. Everything indicates that the carnage of that battle was terrible . . . ."

64. "George Meade's Failure to Pursue Robert E. Lee," https://www.gettysburg. edu/dotAsset/4a2eaf8-8a64-4d64-9f1e-12a6a2be2631.pdf .

65. Cook, 35-36.

66. See, for example, the numbers listed in "Record of the 147th," *Sandy Creek News* (Thurs.) January 24, 1895, n. p.

67. As may be imagined, the news of the officers' dismissal caused a great stir in Oswego. The newspapers ran several articles pertaining to the situation. See "A Presentation," *Albany Atlas and Argus* (Tues. Morn.) October 6, 1863, n. p., which describes the sword presentation to Major Harney and contains the veiled accusation against Miller. See also "From the One Hundred and Forty-seventh Regiment," *Oswego Commercial Times* (Tues. Morn.) October 6, 1863, n. p., an abbreviated version of the first article, but contains the name of the writer, D. H. Crosier, clerk of Company A; "Dismissed the Service," *Oswego Commercial Times* (Tues. Eve.) November 17, 1863, n. p.; "Adjutant Farling's Letter," *Oswego Commercial Times* (Tues. Eve.) December 1, 1863, n. p.; "Letter from Adjutant Farling," *Oswego Commercial Times* (Tues. Eve.) December 1, 1863, n. p.; "Adjt. Farling and the *Times*," *Oswego Daily Palladium* (Wed. Eve.) December 2, 1863, n. p.; "Adjutant Farling," *Oswego Commercial Times* (Sat. Eve.) December 26, 1863, n. p.; "Adjutant Farling Again," *Oswego Commercial Times* (Mon. Eve.) December 28, 1863, n. p. It is interesting that although Harney appears to have been the instigator of this plot it was Farling who responded to the resultant criticism. It is ironic that Maj.-General John Adams Dix issued General Orders No. 15 on October 31, 1863, extending the furloughs of all New York State soldiers until November 15th at which time they were required to report either to a hospital or to their regiments. See "Furloughs Extended," *Oswego Commercial Times* (Mon. Eve.) November 2, 1863, n. p. The controversy continued into 1864 when the *Mexico Independent* (Thurs.) February 11, 1864 complained that Lt. Cheney Barney, Co. H, had been passed over for promotion because he was an "outsider."

68. "Col. Miller Promoted," *Oswego Commercial Times* (Fri. Eve.) November 27, 1863, n. p. Charles Biddlecom, who was a draftee, had definite opinions about who was the "real leader" of the 147th. In a letter to his wife, Esther, dated January 24, 1864 he wrote: "Our Colonel has come back to the regiment again after being gone ever since the Battle of Gettysburg (he got hit on the side of the head, just enough to draw blood and show off his limbering to the rear without losing his commission). He managed to get on detached service (to look after conscripts) at Elmira and while there, got his Eagles. Whereas, the man entitled to wear the Eagles, Harney, the officer that led the regiment in the fight at Gettysburg, was severely wounded in the hand and stayed with his command all summer and fall until we were in winter quarters gets but the Silver Oak Leaves for his reward . . . ." See Katherine M. Aldridge, ed., *No Freedom Shrieker: The Civil War Letters of Charles Freeman*

Biddlecom (Ithaca: Paramount Market Publishing, Inc., 2012), 93-94. See also "One Hundred and Forty-Seventh," *Oswego Commercial Times* (Wed. Eve.) January 6, 1864, n. p., which contains the following: "We understand that Major Harney has been appointed Lieut. Colonel and Adjutant Farling, major of this regiment. We rejoice to record these promotions. When we first knew Lieut. Col. Harney he was a Sergeant in the 7th U. S. Infantry stationed at Fort Ontario, and his term of service having expired in that regiment, he recruited a company for the 147th. From the position of Captain, he has, through meritorious and soldierly conduct, been promoted to his present position. He is a popular and worthy officer." How sincere these good wishes were is open to debate.

69. "From the 147th," *Oswego Daily Palladium* (Wed.) October 28, 1863, n. p. The letter was written at Haymarket and dated October 20th.

70. An excellent review of the Mine Run Campaign appeared in "The Army of the Potomac," *New York Times* (Sat.) December 12, 1863, 1.

71. "From the 147th Regiment," *Oswego Commercial Times* (Mon. Eve.) December 28, 1863, n. p. The private named Dirkee in the letter was Charles Andrew Durkee of Company I, a draftee who had enrolled in the 147th at Barton, Tioga, NY on July 14th.

Of Blood and Battles

The new year has come and with it has come
another year of war. I fear for this toil worn army . . . .
Charles Biddlecom, Co. A, 147th Regiment

JANUARY 1864: AS the new year began in Oswego, the newspapers were full of local news. The snow was deep enough for good sleighing but too deep to permit the fire department to put out a bad fire at Mitchell's cooper shop. Residents and business-men were admonished to keep the snow shoveled off their sidewalks. Coal was being sold from $7.25 to $8.10 per ton. St. Paul's Catholic Church held a multi-day bazaar to raise funds for a new school. A request for 5,000 pairs of mittens had recently been made and the members of the Soldiers' Relief Association were busy knitting them. Plans were being made to welcome home the 81st Regiment. Lake Ontario Commandery was scheduled to meet. Capt. A. A. Fellows of the 110th Regiment wrote to say the soldiers were in good health. John Doyle, brother of Capt. James Doyle, 110th Regiment, had recently died in Buffalo, NY and his remains were being sent to Oswego. Delos Gary, late of the 147th Regiment, was once again practicing law. Henry Adriance, local bookseller, had the latest issues of *Harper's, Eclectic,* and *Atlantic Monthly*. John Garahan was arrested by the local provost-marshal for at-tempting to induce a recruit at Fort Ontario to desert. Lastly, the bachelors of Oswego County were warned that 1864 was a leap year and the ladies were free to make the first move!

On the national scene, Native Americans were warring with homesteaders in Minnesota. A group from Wisconsin was hoping to convince the US House of Representatives to impeach an unnamed Supreme Court justice for corruption and bribery when he was a circuit judge from 1861-1863. President Lincoln's amnesty proclamation was going to be presented to the approximately 40,000 rebels in Union prisons and it was predicted that about 30% would take the oath of allegiance. On January 12th Senator John Henderson from Missouri submitted a joint resolution to abolish slavery which would eventually become the 13th Amendment to the US Constitution.

All was quiet in the camp of the 147th Regiment in Culpeper, VA. Lansing Bristol recorded in his diary that January 1st was windy and cold but he and his tent mates were keeping a good fire. In a letter to his sister Persis, dated January 13th, he said the weather was warmer and the troops were now dealing with mud. Camp inspections and drilling of soldiers were taking place.[72] Grove Dutton provided a humorous anecdote about the exercises. Maria Louisa, wife of Colonel Miller, had come to stay with her husband for a while, causing the following: "At Culpepper we went into winter quarters in a beautiful camp on a side-hill near the timber. Here we went into the usual routine of camp life, company and battalion drills. Our Colonel, Frank Miller, was an excellent drill master. His wife came and kept him company most of the winter. One day we were drilling battalion drill on the parade ground in front of his quarters and in our manoeuvres the order was given to double quick. Mrs. Miller was watching us and as the battalion came around in front of their tent again she said, 'Double quick them again, Frankie. I want to see the boys fly.' The men of course took it up and for a long time after that when we were ordered to run, the Colonel would be embarrassed by someone calling, 'Double quick them again, Frankie'."[73]

A correspondent known only as "Spraker" visited the 147th Regiment in February, sending home periodic reports to the newspapers. He ostensibly traveled to Virginia to check on his son but his observations provide an excellent glimpse of the state of the regiment. A letter dated February 1st, for example, contained the following: ". . . The 147th is a splendid regiment. They have not a single man in their hospital today sick. The officers are all veterans and gentlemen. They have nice quarters, all having built themselves nice little log huts, and the Colonel has had a nice little school house erected which would compare with the houses of our youthful days. This school house is to be used for religious purposes, and as a school for the regiment . . . ."[74] A few days later he reported on the movement which came to be known as the Advance on Morton Ford: "I have seen what but few civilians see during the course of their lives – the breaking up of camps and the marching of three whole corps of our army to meet an enemy that has gained a reputation for fighting unsurpassed by any army in the annals of history. I mean the Rebel army of Virginia, commanded by Gen. Lee. The 1st, 2d and 3d corps of the Army of the Potomac presented a magnificent spectacle as they left their cantonments to encounter the rebel host. On Saturday morning last, the 6th inst. about 5 o'clock, the Adjutant of the 147th regiment kicked at the door of the little log hut with a tent cover, in which your correspondent was fast asleep, together with his son, Capt. P_____. 'Well,' says the Captain, 'what's up now?' 'Fall in your company at six o'clock, with three days' rations, one hour's notice to leave winter quarters,' was the astounding reply. The Captain got up and gave the orders to his men. Then there was hurrying to and fro in camp – to the Quartermasters for rations, to the officers for orders, and all the bustle and confusion incident to the breaking up of camps. At six o'clock the order came loud and stern from the lips of Col. Miller, 'Fall in! Right face! Forward march!' and the 147th regiment took up the line of march for Brigade headquarters, which was near Col. Hoffman, who was in command of the Second Brigade. The Colonel informed me he was ordered to take his Brigade to

Raccoon Ford, on the Rapidan . . . ." Spraker was advised to remain in camp: ". . . Well, it rained all day, and as the camps were all deserted I passed a dreary time. It was then, within sound of those cannon, that I for the first time realized the solemnity of war, in its awful grandeur. Nor was this feeling unmixed with uneasiness, for I had friends near and dear, in the direction from which came the ominous boomings, in quick succession. Yes, more than friends, I had a son there, and I involuntarily walked back over the hills to the camp, listening to the boding sounds. I met an aid [sic], his horse foaming, going at the top of his speed towards Culpepper. 'What's the news?' said I. 'Fighting,' said he, and galloped on. Arrived at camp, I found Lieut. Wybourn who was left to look after it and those who were not able to march, and it was there I heard a terrible crashing sound which the Lieutenant said was the Enfields at work, and which he professed a liking to hear. I informed him I could not see the point. -- . . . ." The following morning Spraker rode out and encountered many ambulances carrying the wounded. He asked about the First Corps and was relieved to learn it had not been engaged in the fight: ". . . On my arrival at the encampment of the 2d brigade, I found the 147th lying in a swamp about one and a half miles from Raccoon Ford. I borrowed a camp glass and rode to the front with Col. Miller, got under range of the rebel picket fire, and viewed the south bank of the Rapidan. For six or seven miles I found the bank to rise, say fifty rods from above, abruptly from diminutive hills to mountains, on which was built Forts, ranging from two miles above Raccoon Ford to below Morton's Ford, embracing a distance in all of about seven miles[;] I counted eight forts on those hills and mountains, besides rows of rifle pits between there and the river, and near these fords two and three rows, and there seemed to be plenty of camps but most of them were situated in the woods, and you could see by the white tents and smoke that across above the trees that they were densely oc-cupied with rebel troops . . . ." Although some Union troops managed to cross the river, the attack was eventually called off due to the strength of the opposing forces. Spraker continued: ". . . On returning to the camp I found everything in commotion. Orders were read to return, and such splashing through the mud as the troops made, and the pontoon train, artillery and ambulances, together with officers galloping about and wallowing through the mud, interspersed with a number of adjectives, not proper for ears polite, from the unfortunate privates stuck in the mud, formed a scene not easily forgotten. We finally reached camp about 11 o'clock on Sunday night, several of the boys in the 147th Regt. barefooted through losing their shoes in the mud . . . I observed by the Philadelphia *Inquirer* and the Washington *Chronicle*, that the expedition was a 'success!' – our forces having taken about thirty of the rebel pickets prisoners when we first crossed the Rapidan!"[75]

Lansing Bristol's perception of this foray was less effusive: ". . . Saturday morn we were aroused early with orders to march at 6 ½ Oclock so of course we had livly times as we had had not notice . . . we started for some unknown place, camped in the Afternoon on a very wet pice of woods. It was then reported that the 2nd Corps was over the river & that we were near Raccoon ford. We could hear firing in front. We lay there until last night at 6 Oclock when we started back for camp. about 8 miles to be traveled after dark in the mud & it over ditches &c. Lots of boys would fall headlong in the mud or going through choppings where there were lots of brush, get trip[ped] up. on such times where there are 10,000 or over coming the same way we see but little road. I did not fall, but going through one ditch, I went into the mud over my boot legs. We got back to camp between 10 & 11 Oclock . . .[T]his forenoon I have been busy getting things to rights . . . [H]ad a thorough wash, took 2 great chunks of mud & worked at them until I have succeeded to find a pair of boots . . . ."[76]

While the 147th was dealing with short rations, mud, and boredom, matters of importance to them were occurring in Washington, DC. In late February Congress passed a bill reinstituting the rank of lieutenant general and it was widely suspected that Ulysses S. Grant, who until recently had been with the army in Tennessee, would be named to the post. In so doing, Grant would replace General Halleck and become George Meade's superior officer. Meade, whose relationship with the press was, to put it mildly, unpleasant, found himself under increasing attacks in the newspapers. About the same time that Grant arrived in Washington to assume his new command, Meade unexpectedly found himself summoned to testify before the Committee on the Conduct of the War. Previously, and unknown to him, Generals Sickles and Doubleday had also testified, alleging that Meade should not have been given credit for the victory at Gettysburg and had in actuality wished to retreat. Without any warning Meade found himself answering questions put to him by Senator Benjamin Wade of Ohio. Even before he had been ordered to appear, Wade and others had approached Lincoln, petitioning him to relieve Meade and appoint another general. Hooker's name was mentioned but the Congressmen stated they would be happy with anyone Lincoln might like to select. Lincoln was not duped and insisted that Meade be heard before he made any decisions. In February Halleck had told Meade some of his officers were not loyal to him, leading to Meade's plan to reorganize the Army of the Potomac. The five corps of the Army of the Potomac were reduced to three in March and the 147th Regiment found itself transferred to the Second Brigade, Fourth Division, Fifth Corps. Thanks to letters Meade sent to his wife, Margaretta, we know that he and Grant met soon after Grant received his promotion. Meade had already told her Grant might relieve him in favor of another of his own choosing. Grant, however, avowed he had no such plan. Henceforth, Meade would be in nominal command of the Army of the Potomac but Grant, who determined to travel with them, was recognized as the person in control. As Meade wrote to Margaretta: ". . . you may look now for the Army of the Potomac putting laurels on the brows of another rather than your husband."[77]

Grant, by all accounts, was the general Lincoln had sought so unsuccessfully for three years. He immediately made plans for an aggressive move against Lee and he told Meade to be wherever Lee was. The rest of the war was bloody and costly in terms of lives, equipment, and property but Grant pushed on, as Lincoln had hoped, increasing the expectation that the North would at last prevail and the war would end. Grant's own words reflect the seriousness with which the effort to crush the rebellion once and for all was undertaken: "Soon after midnight, May 3d-4th, the Army of the Potomac moved out from its position north of the Rapidan, to start upon that memorable campaign, destined to result in the capture of the Confederate capital and the army defending it. This was not to be accomplished, however, without as desperate fighting as the world has ever witnessed; not to be consummated in a day, a week, a month, or a single season. The losses inflicted, and endured, were destined to be severe; but the armies now confronting each other had already been in deadly conflict for a period of three years, with immense losses in killed, by death from sickness, captured and wounded; and neither had made any real progress towards accomplishing the final end . . . The campaign now begun was destined to result in heavier losses, to both armies, in a given time, than any previously suffered; but the carnage was to be limited to a single year, and to accomplish all that had been anticipated or desired at the beginning in that time. We had to have hard fighting to achieve this . . . ."[78]

Between May 5th and June 12th the 147th Regiment was involved in no less than eight significant battles. The first occurred on May 5-6 and became known as the battle of the Wilderness. Perhaps the best eye-witness account was written by Thomas Kearney in a letter he sent to his brother John in New York City. Dated May 17, 1864 and sent from the field near Spotsylvania, Kearney's letter graphically described the events of those fateful two days: ". . . We started on the march from Culpepper, Va., on the 2d inst., at 12 ½ o'clock at night, marching all night, until 10 o'clock A. M., when we crossed the Rapidan at Germania Ford, and continued marching until we came to Gold Mine, where we encamped for the night. On Thursday, May 5th, we marched up the road to the right about two miles, where we formed in line of battle and marched to the west towards Mine Run. We had not gone far before we met the rebels in the woods in two lines of battle marching to meet us. Here our battle opened; our line and the rebels fired at about the same time. After each fire of the first line of the rebels, they lay down and let the second line fire; thereby keeping a continuous fire upon us all the time, which proved very destructive to our regiment. Our Colonel (Miller) fell here mortally wounded, while rallying his men on the left of his regiment. This place was called 'the Wilderness,' and true enough it was a wilderness. Col. Miller acquitted himself on this occasion very creditably. No officer in the army of the Potomac could display more courage and bravery than he did that day. The losing of such a brave and gallant officer threw gloom over the whole regiment. Meanwhile, the right of the regiment was manoeuvred by Lieut. Colonel Harney with great coolness and bravery – Company K (our company) was the second in line, forming the 1st division. The casualties in our company were very heavy. – Our 1st Lieutenant, Hamlin, was wounded in both arms – one broken below the elbow, and the other having a flesh wound. Our killed, wounded and missing, the first day, were twenty-one men; the company went in with 57 guns, and came out with 28. After being under such a destructive fire for some time, we received orders to fall back, but not until the rebels were close upon us. Much credit is due to Captain Dempsey, for a braver and cooler officer or better soldier there can not be found in our army. As the rebels were within hailing distance of us, one of our corporals called out to him that he was wounded; and Capt. D. immediately went to his rescue, regardless of his own life; and while in the act of assisting the poor wounded man, one of his sergeants fell mortally wounded in the head. Meanwhile the rebels had been advancing. They were but a few yards from the Captain when we called out to him from behind, for God's sake to come on or he would be taken prisoner. He turned, saw the rebels and how he was situated, and what few men he had, ordered to fire; but at that time the rebels let fly a volley from the left, which compelled him to fall back. The Captain then fired a gun, the rebels perceiving where the smoke issued from, poured in a deadly volley. I thought our Captain Joe was no more; but thanks to kind Providence, who saved him that time, and he immediately fell back and rallied his men on the clearing in line of battle. It is my opinion that our division had to stand before a whole division of rebels; and what was more, there was not even the slightest reserve to fall back on. About 5 P. M., the whole division again formed in line of battle, and marched in the woods to the east, the line running north and south. We charged the rebels in the woods for the purpose of getting possession of the road leading to Spottsylvania [sic] C. H. We drove them steadily before us until dark . . . ."

The battle was rejoined on May 6th: ". . . At the break of day, we were ordered to move forward, which we did, and drove them three quarters of a mile out of the woods. When we came to the edge of the woods we saw Gen. Wadsworth (our Division General) riding up and down the line (between our's and the rebel's fire), hat in hand, cheering on his men. Our boys gave him three hearty cheers and moved forward on the double-quick across a clearing about fifteen yards wide, which brought us on to a pine thicket. We fired a volley through the thicket, and in return received a terrible charge of grape and canister which mowed down men and trees like so many scythes. It seems the rebels had a masked battery about four rods off, which they opened on us when they got us near enough to them. At this charge Gen. Wadsworth was killed. We were then ordered to fall back slowly. Part of our brigade went south east through the woods, and getting possession of the Spottsylvania road commenced throwing up breastworks; and soon after the Second Corps came up and did likewise. In the afternoon about 4 P. M. the rebels charged our breastworks in front of the 2d Corps, and planting their colors on their works, captured two stands of colors. Gen. Rice, commanding our brigade, ordered his men to charge the rebels, which they did, and recaptured the colors, and jumping over the breastworks after the rebels, killed and wounded many. One of the rebel prisoners we captured said that the charge in which Gen. Wadsworth was killed was led by Lee in person. Our line of battle now extended from the Rapidan, on our right, to about four miles on the plank road leading to Spottsylvania Court House. On this day we were reinforced by the arrival of the Ninth Corps, which immediately went into action and commenced throwing up breastworks. This day our company lost two men by being wounded; and a chum of mine from Oswego, Dennis Deegan, is missing yet . . . ."[79]

The second day of the Battle of the Wilderness was as fierce and bloody as the first.
Library of Congress

Dutton's description of his experiences in the Wilderness graphically illustrates the near impossibility of seeing the enemy: ". . . The bushes were so thick we could not see a rod ahead, but the rebels were lying down and could see us better . . . After the first scare, however, a line was formed somewhat in the rear of our first position and there was fighting back and forth, though on account of the thick forest we could not see them or they us. They opened on us from the left flank as well as from the front. Every soldier knows how demoralizing this is and soon we were on the retreat, forming and firing at intervals. Most of us bore to the left in our retreat but some kept straight to our rear and ran right into the enemy and were made prisoners. I never was so turned around in my life, and I think most of us were confused as regards points of compass. This was the beginning of the Battle of the Wilderness . . . After we formed in the open it was a sight to see the wounded coming back --- it seemed as though there was no end to them. The woods, meanwhile, had caught fire and the smoke was dense . . . ."[80]

The battle raged until May 7th. Although the brigade was ordered to assist the Sixth and Ninth Corps, nothing of import occurred and they were relieved at 5 p.m. They marched first back to Gold Mine and then to Spotsylvania, a distance of 15 miles, traveling all night.[81]

Between May 8th and the 12th the Army of the Potomac engaged the Army of Northern Virginia at Spotsylvania, Piney Branch Church, Laurel Hill, and the Salient. Kearney's letter described heavy firing, cannonading, loss of men, capture of guns and prisoners. He reported the death of General Rice and the wounding of both Harney and Dempsey. Biddlecom wrote to Esther on May 13th: "This is the eighth day of Battle and I am as yet unharmed. I pray to God that it may continue so to the end. More than ¾ of our company are either killed, wounded, or missing. In great haste I write this . . . ."[82]

The telegraph kept government officials and newspapers informed about the progress of the campaign. For example, on May 13th the *Syracuse Daily Courier* reported: ". . . The woods between the contending armies were all on fire, and the wind blowing strong to the [?], gave the enemy a decided advantage over our troops, who were stifled and blinded by the heat and smoke. Numbers on both sides must have been consumed by the heat and smoke . . . The accounts of our losses vary from 18,000 to 25,000, but owing to the nature of the contest, which is mostly in the woods, thousands may be lying dead or wounded, of which no records can be made . . . ." Grant's dispatch to Secretary of War Stanton, dated May 12 was quoted: "The eighth day of the battle closes, leaving between 3,000 and 4,000 prisoners in our hands, for the day's work, including two general officers, and over thirty pieces of artillery. The enemy are obstinate, and seem to have found the 'last ditch.' We have lost no organization – not even a company – whilst we have destroyed and capture [*sic*] one division (Johnson's), one brigade (Dobb's), and one regiment, entire, of the enemy's." An exultant Chief Quartermaster of the Army of the Potomac General Rufus Ingalls wrote to Senator Nesmith: ". . . Grant is a giant and hero in war; but all our generals are gallant, and as to our men, the world never had better."[83]

A letter from an unnamed soldier in the 147th written at Spotsylvania Court House and dated May 16th not only apprised the folks back home of the carnage the boys from Oswego had recently endured but also reflected the optimism now felt by all: ". . . We began fighting on the 5th (our Division opening the ball and by the way we got terribly cut up) and have kept it up since. Col. Miller was killed by almost the first fire and Farling was taken sick. So Col. Harney has had some work to do. He had a narrow escape on the 10th while making an attack on the enemy's works. – A shell cut a long scar on the left side of his face and produced a severe contusion, his head, face and neck swelling, and disabling his teeth so that he could not grind hard tack. He rode to the Hospital, however, had his wound dressed and returned to duty. Major Farling, Capts. McKinlock, Pierce and Gillet are in hospital sick. Lieut. James Brown had a leg taken off by a shell on the 12th inst. I am afraid he will not recover; he was an excellent officer. – Capt. McKinley is well, but he had a close call. The shell which took off Lieut. Brown's leg tore a large hole in McKinley's pants just below the knee. Things look bright so far. We have the inside track, and Grant seems determined to keep it. The army of the Potomac never worked so hard before. You will soon hear of us from Richmond. Lee is pushed closer than ever he was before. Every move he has made has been closely watched and whenever he changes his troops daylight the next morning shows our forces drawn up in front ready to fight him if he feels disposed to advance. An unusual quantity of rain has fallen lately. The roads are in a horrible state. I hope it will clear up for I am confident if we have good roads we can beat Lee on a march to Richmond, whenever he starts in that direction. If we can get to Richmond before Lee does and form a junction with Butler we will whip him all to pieces in less than three days after he attempts to attack us. Our regiment and brigade have been in seven fights already and are pretty well cut up, but our courage is good. We gave the rebels worse than they gave us; we took some prisoners who fought in front of our brigade line in the last engagement. They say we shot so close they thought we were a lot of sharpshooters. Our regiment has lost, as near as I can get at it, one officer and twenty-nine men killed; six wounded; one officer and seventy-seven men missing."[84]

If the men of the 147th expected a bit of respite from the fighting they were sorely mistaken as Grant pushed on. Grove Dutton related that the army moved from Spotsylvania to North Anna River where they "almost immediately were engaged with the enemy, this time they being the aggressors . . . That night we built rifle pits as usual but soon left them and moved again to the left of Bethsaida Church near Cold Harbor . . . [W]e moved toward the Tottopottany [sic] and occupied breastworks there. This fight I have described was part of the battle of Cold Harbor, but we were not in it with as great a loss as our comrades of the Second and Eighteenth Corps. I was detailed for picket. It was very dangerous relieving the picket on account of the rebels shooting at us. We accomplished this by running from one tree to another until we arrived at the desired position, the rebels meanwhile putting in the balls thick and fast . . . Soon after we were marched to the left near the Chichahominy [sic] River . . . And now about the middle of June after some of the most terrible fighting on record of which I have been able to convey but a slight idea, the army was about to make a change of base and attack them at Petersburg . . . ."[85]

Let us allow Crisfield Johnson the final word on the events begun at the Wilderness and ending with the crossing of the James River on June 16th: ". . . The regiment by this time had become much enfeebled by constant vigils and long, weary marches in the heat of a Virginia summer. Since May 5 it had been almost constantly in the presence of the enemy, and more than half of the time under fire. It often slept in the trenches when the enemy's shells were bursting thick and fast around them as a lullaby. The losses of the armies in their fierce struggles from the Wilderness to the James river were never officially published; probably because they were so enormous that the authorities deemed it unwise to appall the country by making known their magnitude. The whole scene of contest from the Rapidan to the Chickahominy was one Golgotha. In many places in the dense thickets the dead were left without sepulture, and their bleaching skeletons were seen upon the return of some of their comrades after the surrender at Appomattox Court-House (1865), who passed through there to revisit the scenes of their former struggles . . . ."[86]

Grant withdrew the Army of the Potomac from Cold Harbor on June 12th and headed to Petersburg, undertaking a campaign which lasted from June 15, 1864-April 2, 1865. Only 24 miles from Richmond, Petersburg was the junction of five railroads. Grant theorized that if he could wrest control of this area from the Confederacy he could deny Lee an ability to resupply the rebel army and thereby force him to surrender. A letter written to his father by Lt. James Ells illustrates his perception of Grant's design: "We are having some terrible fighting here. Almost half of the Army of the Potomac is down here besieging Petersburg. The other half is strongly entrenched on Malvern Hill ready to dash into Richmond whenever the opportunity offers. Richmond is doomed. I think Grant's design is to take Petersburg first, and thus cut off their retreat in that direction, and then Richmond next. Petersburg is the key to the whole Confederacy. One half of the workshops and ammunition factories of the South are there; besides it is an immense depot for supplies. Petersburg in a military point of view is a hundred times more important than Richmond ever was. We are within about one-half mile of Petersburg. Our main force is out of sight. We keep enough in sight to scare them pretty well. It is evidently Grant's intention to let Lee reinforce Petersburgh [sic] as much as he will, then move out two corps, which he has massed in good positions, cut off their retreat to Richmond, and gobble the whole. I tell you that Grant is a brick and the army has perfect confidence in him, and that is one-half of the battle. You will hear great news in a short time. Grant seems to have ignored all the principles of military strategy and adopted a tactic of his own.

The rebels acknowledge this, and say they do not understand his movements at all."[87]

An attempt to take Petersburg on June 15th had failed even though the Union forces greatly exceeded those defending the place. On June 18th Grant tried again with the Fifth Corps, as related by Grove Dutton: "June 18th we crossed the James River, and an order was received that we could go in bathing. In a few minutes there were thousands of men in the water. We soon fell in and marched toward Petersburg. The road was dry and dusty and the weather hot. There was heavy firing in our front. It was understood by us that the Ninth Corps had made a charge and had been repulsed. We passed by some forts captured by our men inside of which a number of the rebel dead were still unburied. Soon we came in sight of their works about a quarter of a mile in our front and our hearts sank within us at the thought of charging these formidable defenses. They were full of men and cannon and had evidently recently been strengthened. They were about a quarter of a mile in our front. About twenty rods in front of these breastworks was a line of abates and a few rods in front of this was another. These were made of trees about seven or eight inches in diameter, merely the ends of the limbs being cut off and the butts of the trees buried in the ground, placing the trees side by side, the limbs toward us and all wired together making it an extremely difficult obstacle to get through, especially considering that while we would be making the effort they would be pouring shot and shell into us. We lay down in the hot sun expecting every minute the order to attack. About noon I noticed an Aide coming along our line and when about where my company lay, inquired for General Cutler, our Brigade Commander. He was only a few paces in our rear and I heard him

The assailing Union soldiers were faced with formidable siege works along the Rebels' defensive line at Petersburg.
Library of Congress

say after saluting, 'General, you will advance your command immediately within the enemy's works.' So it must be. We were to go forward to what seemed to be almost certain death. What chance have we over that open field? I had hardly time for these thoughts when the order came 'Rise up!' and 'Uncap pieces!' 'Fix bayonets!' 'forward, double quick.' As we rose up the shells came bursting over our heads terribly close and bullets to whiz around us, striking the earth or finding its home in the body of some of my comrades. Our brigade was in the front line, the First Brigade in our rear. As I glanced to the right and left I noticed how short our line was seemingly, but few except my regiment arose to go on the charge. With a yell we started down the incline through the corn, the shells and missiles raining toward us, making the most unpleasant music I ever heard. It seemed to me now the most foolish, reckless thing in the world to expect us to take those works at that time. Perhaps it was intended that the whole Corps should charge at once but the rest certainly did not at that time. This was June 18th, 1864. The ground from where we started was downward about two thirds of the way and then upward gradually toward their works. When we got down the ravine, looking back the ground we had gone over was well spotted with our dead and wounded. But a very few were left. Some had undoubtedly run back; others had not started all. Dick Esmond of my company, than whom a braver man we did not have, has told me since there were only thirty five men when we got to the foot of the hill. Of course it would have been madness to attempt to go further with our force and we dare not run back. The right of the ravine extended to their works and here they had a cannon posted and every few moments they would plank a shell into us. It did not seem possible to escape. Here Miner was killed and Stratton wounded. Esmond raised up and discovered that the rebels had sent a force from our front (they were on higher ground and we could not see them when lying down) to capture us. Our men in the rear dare not fire for fear of hitting us. 'Rise up! and give them a volley,' our Lieutenant Colonel called out, which was obeyed and they ran back. Meanwhile we were burrowing in the ground for all we were worth using our tin cups and plates to dig with and getting down as low as possible. After a short time a shell from one of our batteries dismounted the gun that had troubled us the most, but their musketry from our right kept peppering into us without cessation. Darkness came at last and never more welcome, so it gave us an opportunity to retire without being seen, which was done as soon as we could get away. I had no sooner got back to the main line when our First Sergeant who had 'slinked' out of the fight detailed me for picket. In the charge (it must be remembered that our ranks had been much reduced since starting the campaign and the regiment numbered at that time less than one hundred) we lost fifteen killed and over forty wounded, among whom was Will Ellis by a piece of shell. Toppings was wounded in the leg, necessitating amputation. He was sent to Philadelphia and died of small pox. The picket line was a hot place.

That night we formed a line and threw up skirmish pits . . . The next day we did not dare raise our heads for the bullets were directed toward our little pits, making them a vey unsafe place unless we hugged the earth which we were willing to do. At night we were relieved and returned to the regiment . . . ."[88]

According to Dutton the remnant of the 147th was pulled off the line and sent to the rear to do "fatigue duty, building roads, forts, etc."[89] Although ordered to prepare to attack once again after the Confederate fortifications were bombed on July 31st, the resultant failure of the plot meant the soldiers stayed where they were.

Very soon the 147th was to be engaged in the battle known as Weldon Railroad or Globe Tavern. In June 1864 Grant had unsuccessfully attempted to take control of this vital railroad which connected Richmond to Wilmington, NC. In August he determined to try again since, as he wrote: ". . . This road was very important to the enemy. The limits from which his supplies had been drawn were already very much contracted, and I knew he must fight desperately to protect it . . . ."[90] The Fifth Corps moved toward the railroad early in the morning on August 18th and, although facing tough opposition from the Confederates over the next three days, finally destroyed a good part of it and established permanent control of the area. Henceforth Lee would need to obtain supplies by circuitous routes, thus weakening his forces considerably.

Although the telegraph and the local newspapers kept people informed of current events, it was the letters sent home which revealed the awful truth about this engagement. Robert Spencer's letter dated August 21st provided a list of casualties, including three deaths, those of Sgt. McGrath, Co. K, Private Edward Dahm, Co. G, and Private John Smith O'Riley, Co. K. He continued: ". . . These are all the casualties I know. There are others. Owing to the late heavy rains the roads are quite bad, and it is difficult transporting the wounded from the front. The wounded in the above list were brought to the General Field Hospital at this point, night before last, and will probably be sent north in a day or two. Capt. Hugunin is too dangerously wounded to be moved and will remain here. I shall probably get more definite information and further news today, and will write again tomorrow. The 147th has again stood manfully in the breach, while other regiments of the same brigade gave way. Again have the Oswego boys won the approbation and 'especial notice' of their division commander; and when you get the particulars of the fight, and learn how the enemy were routed, and by whom, who were the thirty volunteers called for by the Colonel commanding the brigade from the 147th, and by whom and how they were led to the fray, then you will know how justly you may pride yourselves on the 147th N. Y. V. . . . ."[91]

A letter written by Colonel Harney and sent to Major Farling, who was home on furlough due to sickness, bore witness to the carnage wrought at the battle: ". . . We are getting rather lonesome now. Our numbers are decreasing rapidly. We have but a few officers present. Sickness as well as the bullets of the enemy, is telling upon us. Capts. McKinlock and Hubbard, Lieuts. Lawlor, Wyborn, and Kingsley, are sick in hospital. Capts. Pierce and Hugunin were wounded in a skirmish on the 18th inst. So you see I have met quite a loss in officers within a short time. I suppose you have learned through the papers, ere this, of the movements of the 5th corps, its occupation of the Weldon Railroad, &c., &c.; but a few words from me, relating to the regiment and brigade, may not be uninteresting. The 5th corps marched around the left flank of the army on the 18th inst., and met the enemy's pickets early in the forenoon, capturing some and driving the remainder before them as far as the Weldon Railroad; thence along the Railroad in the direction of Petersburg. When arriving within three miles of the city the enemy was found in force, and dispositions for a battle were made at once. The 4th division was ordered forward in the order of battle. The 2d brigade (embracing the 147th) as usual was assigned the post of honor, and advanced in good style under a sharp artillery fire. Upon arriving on the outskirts of a piece of heavy timber it was halted. The 147th, deployed as skirmishers, advanced and engaged the skirmishers of the enemy. The 6th Wisconsin moved forward in the support of the 147th. The enemy was driven back; then our men rallied and drove the rebels back. This was kept up until late in the afternoon, when the rebels seemed to give it up for a bad job, and made no further effort to regain lost ground. It was then determined that we should make a charge on the rebel skirmishers, which we did; but coming suddenly upon a rebel line of battle, which delivered a well directed fire, our skirmishers were forced to fall back. Here Capts. Pierce and Hugunin were wounded. Night coming on we were relieved by pickets from the 3d division of our corps and we rejoined the brigade. The loss of the regiment in this affair was two men killed; two officers and four men wounded. Next day (the 19th) we went into position on the south side of the railroad and threw up breastworks. On the afternoon of this day the enemy made a fierce attack on our whole line. All on our right gave way and the enemy captured a number of men. Our brigade held their works and repulsed the enemy, capturing one stand of colors and some prisoners. The works taken by the enemy were subsequently recaptured and quiet restored. The 147th in this affair, lost a few men by shelling from our own batteries. The 20th passed off quietly. At night our division was moved to the left, and worked almost all night on new breastworks. Next morning our skirmishers came running in, followed by a long line of battle (Rebs.) with colors flying and seeming determined to drive everything before it. Gen. Mahon's brigade (Rebel) came against ours, under a heavy fire. The poor fellows fought bravely but they could not get over our works. The slaughter was fearful. After fighting for a time they surrendered. The 2d brigade (ours) captured four stand of colors and a large number of prisoners. I do not know the exact number, but think it was nearly *as many as we had in our brigade,* present. The prisoners all say they never were broken before, and one rebel Captain, upon coming within our line, sat down and cried like a child; said he did not care what became of him; he was completely discouraged. The 147th, and all our brigade, was very lucky in the affair, owing to the fact that the rebels did not fire much. Their intention was to run over us and capture everybody. They certainly made a good attempt, for they came close upon us before surrendering. They were brave fellows, and although rebels, are entitled to great credit for the fearless manner in which they charged our works. The 147th had but one man killed in the affair. We are now making our works almost impregnable, and the Weldon railroad is lost to the enemy. I think the 5th corps is entitled to a great deal of credit for gaining possession of, and holding this road. You remember the 2d corps and the 6th corps, with a large number of cavalry, sought for the possession of this work sometime ago, and after suffering a fearful loss were forced to retire. It is evident the enemy feels very sore over the loss of this road, for they did all they could to regain its possession, and rebel officers captured say that Lee will have the road again if it takes him a whole army to do so. But let him come on. The corps feel now like men who cannot be conquered . . . ."[92]

Another letter contained more graphic details: ". . . Our boys stood the shock as become veterans, and hurled them back to the cover of the trees with awful slaughter. After the second charge upon the 4th division, 5th corps, to which the 147th belong, the rebels finding they could not move them, and after a fearful loss of life and limb, they attempted to flank the 4th division by massing their forces, and with demoniac yells charging upon the 2d division, 5th corps, which lay to the left and a little in the rear of the 4th division. When the rebels had passed and were in close engagement with the 2d division, old *Iron Gray*, our division commander, (Gen. Cutler,) who led the brigade at Gettysburg, gave the word to the 4th division to jump their works and advance, which they did with a will; and by swinging around towards the left, the 4th attacked the rebels in the rear, while they were fighting the 2d division in front. Now came the tug of war upon open field – hand to hand, and muzzle to muzzle. Nothing could stand before our veterans, who had been praying all summer for the 'Johnnies' to come out from behind their cover and give them an open field and a fair fight. Our brigade took three stand of colors. The Johnnies soon found they had caught a Tartar – fought desperately for a while, but soon yielded, and with fixed bayonets the 4th division drove an entire brigade of rebels to the rear, prisoners of war. I cannot tell how many prisoners we have taken, or how many we have lost, but since the 18th we have had hard fighting. Our losses are not heavy . . . ."[93]

Harney's letter to Farling mentioned losses by friendly fire which was elaborated on in an obituary for William Boyce: ". . . At the battle of Weldon railroad, in front of Petersburg, Boyce did an act that saved the brigade to which he was attached from annihilation and won for him the everlasting gratitude of the officers and men. The brigade with which the 147th was fighting was stationed on both sides of a railroad, the 147th just to the left of the track. It was on the 18th day of August. The entire brigade which had been fighting gloriously was cut off and ordered to fall back. The aid [sic] who carried the order from the commanding officer had to pass over a long space swept by the rebel bullets. He reached the regiment on the right side of the railroad track, and gave the order, and told the officer to pass it down the line to the regiments on the other side, and then returned. The order was not promulgated, and only that portion of the brigade on the right of the railroad fell back. The others held their ground. Gen. Warren, supposing that all the regiments on the line had fallen back and seeing from a distance the three regiments on the left supposed them to be rebels and ordered a battery to open upon them. At this time the three regiments had been successful in repelling the enemy, when their own battery in the rear sent a shower of shells into their midst. Thus were they receiving a fire from friend and foe and for a while were obliged to dodge from one side of the breastworks to the other for protection. A number of the Oswego regiment had been killed by their friends, when Major Harney, who was in command, called for a volunteer to go up to the battery and inform the men of their mistake. Such an undertaking meant almost certain death. Without a moment's hesitation, Mr. William Boyce volunteered and started toward the battery. He walked boldly toward the front of the battery, while the huge guns were belching forth their shot and shells. His comrades, those who could see him, actually forgot the rebels for the time, and watched Boyce in admiration. He reached the battery in safety, and it was at once silenced. The brigade then with the 147th in the front and left drove the 'rebs' . . . ."[94]

The siege continued. The 147th was transferred twice in the summer of 1864. In August the men, until then assigned to the Second Brigade, Fourth Division, Fifth Corps, were sent to the Third Brigade, Second Division. In September they were moved to the Third Brigade, Second Division. From September 29-October 2 the 147th was involved in a minor engagement known as the battle of Peeble's Farm in which Meade and his Union forces achieved a small success. Worse was to come in late October at Hatcher's Run or Boydton's Plank Road, for it was here that Col. Harney disappeared without a trace. Dr. A. S. Coe informed Dudley Farling, now in Oswego because he had been discharged, in a letter dated October 29, 1864: "I have the melancholy tidings to give you of the loss of Col. Harney. He was either killed or taken prisoner on the 27th inst. Early in the morning of that day, the 9th, 5th and 2d corps set out to capture the South Side Railroad. The 9th corps occupied the right, immediately in front and advance of their entrenched camp. The 5th the centre, and the 2nd the left of the line. The country in which the 2nd and 5th corps operated was almost an unbroken pine thicket, and the surface very uneven, and cut up by ravines, worse if anything, than the wilderness. Here was a large gap in the line of battle between the 2d and 5th corps, as it was advanced into the dense thicket. Col. Hoffman, (commanding the Brigade) ordered Col. Harney to march the regiment by the left flank, in order to protect the Brigade from surprise on the left, the Brigade advancing in line of battle. By that means our regiment got separated from the brigade. The wood was so dense that the Col. could not keep the brigade in sight, and consequently lost the direction it took – or rather, the brigade changed its direction more to the right, which would make them diverge more widely as they advanced. Colonel Harney at length found himself entirely separated from the line. He then halted and waited some time. Finally one of Hoffman's aids came up and ordered the Col. to strike across and join the regiment on to the left of the 5th corps picket line. He advanced cautiously and halted the regiment several times – riding in advance alone to find the picket line – about dark he found the extreme right of the 2d corps, and it was there he was last seen. He started from there to the right to find our line. Immediately a heavy roll of musketry was heard in the direction he took, and soon after the enemy came in heavy force into the gap upon the right flank of the 2d corps. The attack, while it lasted, was fierce and terrible, and was made simultaneously in front and on both flanks. The corps made but a short stand, then broke and fled in all directions utterly disorganized. I hardly think Col. Harney is killed or wounded. We will hear from him probably in a few days. His loss has cast a gloom upon the whole regiment. He seems to have had the confidence of officers and men alike, and the regiment feel his loss very sensibly. The *fiasco* of the 2d corps lost us the day, and of course we had nothing to do but retrace our steps, and get back into our entrenched camps as soon as possible, where we arrived last night."[95]

The 147th Regiment was to take part in one more expedition before winter arrived. Grant, fearing that Lee was somehow still obtaining supplies, sent General Warren and the Fifth Corps south along the Petersburg and Weldon Railroad with orders to destroy as much of the track as possible. Between December 7-12, while simultaneously fending off Confederate attacks, the soldiers were able to so completely destroy between 16-17 miles of track that Lee's supply line was again lessened considerably. This engagement came to be known as the Stony Creek Raid or Warren's Raid on Weldon Railroad.

Good news arrived in late December when Col. Frank Miller, whose death had been mistakenly reported in May, was released from Confederate custody. He returned to Oswego for some time before returning to the regiment and reassuming command of the 147th.[96]

Charles Biddlecom gets the final word for the year 1864. Writing to Esther he mused: ". . . 'Tis a bad thing to be too reliable. Our regiment has a reputation for standing fire that is anything but enviable, especially when we want to have a rest. I sometimes think that we will be rushed in as long as there is but a man of us left. 'Tis nothing but the 147th and 76th New York, the rest of the brigade without those two regiments is not worth the rations the men eat. The three Pennsylvania regiments are assumed to run and leave us to fight it out alone, and they have done it some half dozen times this last summer. The 147th is the last to turn their backs to the foe and the first to rally for another trial, is the talk in the brigade, in the division, in the corps, and, in fact, in the Army of the Potomac. Wherever known our reputation is notorious. Johnny Rebs know our tar bucket hats and had as soon meet the Devil as the 147th. Well, 'tis all very fine to talk about, but to make the name cost us many a good man and no doubt it will cost us dear to keep it . . . .[97]

Biddlecom's pessimistic opinion seems, from the vantage of over 150 years, prophetic. The 147th Regiment and the Army of the Potomac were indeed to pay dearly with more blood and battles as the final year of the war opened.

NOTES

72. Cook, 52-53.
73. Hendrix, 125.
74. "From the 147th," *Oswego Daily Palladium* (Mon. Eve.) February 4, 1864, n. p.
75. "From the 147th N. Y. V. – Advance at Morton's Ford," *Oswego Daily Palladium* (Thurs. Eve.) February 18, 1864, n. p. While Spraker does not identify his son, it is possible that he was referring to Captain J. Volney Pierce or to Captain Edward David Parker.
76. Letter to his father, dated February 8, 1864 in Cook, 54. See also Aldridge, 104-106.
77. George Gordon Meade, ed., *The Life and Letters of George Gordon Meade* (New York: Charles Scribner's Sons, 1913), vol. II, 161-183.
78. Ulysses S. Grant, *Personal Memoirs* (New York: The Modern library, 1999), 401. The *Memoirs* were originally published posthumously in 1885.
79. "The 147th in Action," *Oswego Daily Palladium* (Tues. Eve.) June 14, 1864, 1-2. Thomas W. Kearney's life is shrouded in mystery. See "The Draft, Dodgers, and Deserters" for details.
80. Hendrix, 125-126. See also Cook, 64-67. Bristol's diary entries attest to the confusion of the battle.
81. "The 147th in Action," 1-2.
82. Aldridge, 144.
83. "By Telegraph; The Afternoon Report," *Syracuse Daily Courier* (Fri.) May 13, 1864, n. p.
84. "From the One Hundred and Forty-Seventh Regiment," *Oswego Commercial Times* (Mon. Eve.) May 23, 1864, n. p. Lt. James Brown died of his wounds on July 5th. The news that Colonel Miller had been killed was erroneous. He had been seriously wounded and was taken prisoner.

85. Hendrix, 130-131. See also Cook, 67-72 and Aldridge, 144-151. Although the 147th Regiment took no real part in the battle of Cold Harbor, nevertheless many of its soldiers were either wounded or killed between June1-3. See "Further Casualties in the 147th," *Oswego Daily Palladium* (Fri. Eve.) June 10, 1864, n. p.

86. Johnson, 98.

87. "An Encouraging Letter," *Oswego Commercial Advertiser* (Mon. Eve.) June 27, 1864, n. p. James Smith Ells, Jr. (May 28, 1843-August 24, 1890) was the son of James (1807-1873) and Roxa Penfield Ells (1811-1884). He was mustered into Co. A, 12th NY Cavalry at Oswego on November 19, 1862 as a private and discharged in March 1864 to accept a commission in the 2nd USC Cavalry.

88. Hendrix, 131-133. See also Aldridge, 160-164 and Cook, 73-77. A list of the wounded from the 147th appeared in the *Mexico Independent* (Thurs.) July 7, 1864, n. p.

89. Hendrix, 133.

90. Grant, 487.

91. "More Casualties in the 147th Regiment," *Oswego Daily Palladium* (Wed. Eve.) August 24, 1864, n. p. A part of this letter was reprinted in the *Mexico Independent* (Thurs.) September 1, 1864, n. p.

92. "From the 147th," *Oswego Daily Palladium* (Tues. Eve.) August 30, 1864, 1. The letter was dated August 23rd.

93. "The 147th in the Weldon Railroad Fight," *Oswego Daily Palladium* (Tues. Eve.) August 30, 1864, n. p. See also Hendrix, 133-134.

94. "William Boyce," *Oswego Palladium* (Fri.) June 27, 1884, n. p.

95. "Death or Capture of Col. Harney of the 147th Regiment," *Oswego Daily Palladium* (Thurs. Eve.) November 3, 1864, n. p. See also "From the 147th: Col. Harney Missing," *Oswego Commercial Times (Thurs. Eve.)* November 3, 1864, n. p., a letter by Charles Vauvilliez to his parents dated October 29th announcing Harney's disappearance. Harney was not released until February 1865 but was able to muster out with the regiment on June 7, 1865.

96. See "From Col. F. C. Miller," *Oswego Commercial Advertiser* (Thurs. Eve.) July 31, 1864, n. p.; "Letter from Col. Miller," *Oswego Commercial Advertiser* (Tues. Eve.) October 18, 1864, n. p..; "Letter from Col. Miller," *Oswego Commercial Times* (Tues. Eve.) October 25, 1864, n. p.; "At Home," *Oswego Commercial Times* (Mon. Eve.) December 19, 1864, n. p.; "Return of Colonel Frank Miller, An Account of his Sojourn in Dixie," *Oswego Commercial Times* (Tues. Eve.) December 20, 1864, n. p.; "Sword presentation to Col. Miller," *Oswego Commercial Times* (Sat. Eve.) January 22, 1865, n. p.

97. Aldridge, 252. The letter was dated December 6th and was therefore composed just before the regiment set out on the Stony Creek raid.

The Final Act

The longest day must have its close –
The gloomiest night will wear on to a morning.
An eternal, inexorable lapse of moments is ever
hurrying the day of the evil to an eternal night,
And the night of the just to an eternal day.
--Harriet Beecher Stowe

THE 147TH REGIMENT to which Col. Frank Miller returned in January 1865 was much different from that which he had left in May 1864. Lt. Col. George Harney and Adjutant Henry H. Lyman were prisoners of war; Major Dudley Farling had been discharged in November for "disability." Many of the soldiers whom he had known from the early days of the war were either dead or discharged for various types of disability. Conscripts from all parts of the state filled their places. For a man who had survived a serious wound to the side and seven months in various southern prisoner of war camps this reality must have provided an unwelcome, gloomy shock. Nevertheless, duty awaited and he re-assumed command and set about doing his part to bring the conflict to a speedy conclusion.

Even before he left Oswego to rejoin the regiment, which was at this time camped southeast of Petersburg, VA in winter quarters, Miller received word that the 76th Regiment was being disbanded and that all soldiers who had not fulfilled their term of service were being transferred to the 147th.[98] By this action the strength of the 147th was estimated to be about 900 men. As soon as Miller returned to active duty, he had the responsibility of coalescing

Francis Miller served as the 147th Regiment's third and last colonel. *New York State Military Museum*

a well-established regiment into the ranks of another, with whom its members had served for several years. According to muster roll cards, the official transfer of men occurred on January 28th. A few whose date of transfer was given as January 31st were for the most part prisoners of war or prisoners whose deaths had not yet been reported.

The relative quiet of winter quarters was ended in early February as General Grant determined once again to extend his line of fortifications around Petersburg, thereby forcing General Lee to devote more of his already thin ranks to defending those new extensions. Between February 5-7 the 147th, under the command of General Warren, participated in the second battle of Hatcher's Run. Grove Dutton provided a detailed account of the effort: ". . . The 6th of February, 1865, Grant determined to extend his line around the right flank of the enemy, which led to the battle of Hatcher's Run. Here I saw a fine exhibition of courage by my comrade, Lieutenant Dick Esmond, then on Brigade Staff, while we were advancing in line of battle in the woods, the enemy from their works firing into us. Dick grasped the brigade colors and rushed forward, waving them toward the enemy heedless of the balls that were flying thick and fast, but we were after him in a few moments and were soon engaged in firing with the rebels but a short distance from us. Glancing to my left I saw my friend, Lieutenant Lansing Bristol, fall. I rushed to him but could not catch the words that were passing his lips and in a moment he had breathed his last, a brave soldier and a good officer . . . Major James Corey was shot in the face and a number of other officers were seriously wounded. Asa Raddick of my company was killed. After this we went into camp . . . ."[99] Although the outcome of this battle was indecisive, Grant's objective was reached.

Near the end of February the Confederates began exchanging soldiers and the local newspapers were full of names of the living and the dead: "We are happy to announce that Lieut. Col. George Harney, of the 147th regiment, has been exchanged. He will probably visit this city on leave of absence before going into active service. His many friends here will greet him with heart-felt pleasure . . . ."[100] Lyman was released soon thereafter: "Among the recently released prisoners arrived at Annapolis, we notice the name of Adjutant H. H. Lyman, of the 147th N. Y. S. V."[101] Later that month Colonel Miller sent a list of soldiers from the 147th who survivors said had died in rebel prisons. Among the names were Sanford Alsaver, Lorenzo Horton, and John Wetherby.[102]

In the meantime plans were being made which would end the war. Grant, noting in his *Memoirs* that the nation "had already become restless and discouraged at the prolongation of the war," determined to oust Lee from Petersburg and to capture Richmond.[103] The final push, known as the Appomattox Campaign, got under way on March 28th and from that date until April 9th the Army of the Potomac, including the 147th Regiment, relentlessly pursued Lee. The battle of White Oaks was fought from March 29-31 and Five Forks, April 1st. Grove Dutton reported: "On April 1st, after some hard marching we brought up at Five Forks where there was quite a force of the enemy. In these moves Grant's idea was to encircle them, cut off their supplies and force them out of their position at Petersburg or make them surrender there. His line now was over twenty five miles long. Of course the rebs were inside this circle and the lines shorter, but they had less men and in places their lines were thinly manned . . . ."[104] As the noose tightened Lee had little choice but to evacuate Petersburg on April 2nd. Richmond fell on April 3rd. On April 9th Lee, after an exchange of letters with Grant, formally surrendered the Army of North Virginia.[105]

Although fighting continued for a time in the western part of the country, the war was, for all intents and purposes, over. Captain James McKinley of the 147th wrote: "I have just returned to camp from witnessing the formal surrender of Lee's Army of Northern Virginia. It was a humiliating affair to them. The 147th Regiment have gone through this campaign very successfully, losing only about twenty men. We were engaged on the 1st of April in the memorable charge on the South Side Railroad. We claim that the fighting on that road caused the evacuation of Petersburg and Richmond."[106]

It was time to think about going home.

Amid the joy surrounding the end of the war was the national grief attending the assassination of President Abraham Lincoln. In later years veterans of the 147th Regiment would recount their own stories in relation to this catastrophe.

The people of Oswego County welcomed home their veterans of all the Oswego units. Life went on. Farms were tilled, lawsuits contested, and children educated. The following years were good for some veterans but not for others. At least two were tried for murder. Several committed suicide. Others succumbed to their wounds or were so incapacitated by their wartime experiences that they were able to do little work. Many whose health had not been impaired moved west, settling in Michigan, Minnesota, Nebraska, and parts beyond, hoping perhaps to obliterate wartime memories with new surroundings.

On July 1, 1888, veterans of the 147th met on the battlefield at Gettysburg to dedicate a monument commemorating the regiment's participation in that historic battle. It was an opportunity to greet old comrades, to reflect on three days of bloody combat, and to remember the ones who did not return when the war ended. As J. Volney Pierce said so simply, yet so eloquently, "We turn towards the South Land and view the finger marks of war in the graves of comrades dead, and raise the old tin cup of black coffee, and drink to the memory of those who never came home."[107] Although he spoke of those who died at Gettysburg, in a larger sense he was eulogizing all those who had fought and died to preserve the Union.

The monument commissioned by the veterans of the 147th Regiment stands near the site where the regiment joined the battle.
Darlene Woolson

NOTES

98. "From the 147th," *Oswego Commercial Times* (Mon. Eve.) January 23, 1865, n. p. The order from the War Department was dated December 31, 1864.

99. Hendrix, 135-136. James' surname was Coey and Asa's was Reddick. See also "The 147th Regiment," *Mexico Independent* (Thurs.) February 16, 1865, n. p. It was for his bravery at Hatcher's Run that Coey was awarded the Medal of Honor.

100. "Exchanged," *Oswego Commercial Times* (Thurs. Eve.) March 2, 1865, n. p.

101. "Adjutant H. H. Lyman," *Oswego Commercial Times* (Fri. Eve.) March 10, 1865, n. p.

102. "Death of Members of the 147th Regiment," *Mexico Independent* (Thurs.) March 23, 1865, n. p. The list, dated March 14th and sent from Annapolis, MD, had originally been published in the *Oswego Commercial Times* (Tues. Eve.) March 21, 1865, n. p.

103. Grant, 548.

104. Hendrix, 136. Dutton was wounded at Five Forks and heard the news that the war had ended while lying in a hospital bed.

105. Grant, 575-583.

106. "From the 147th Regiment," *Oswego Daily Palladium* (Fri. Eve.) April 21, 1865, n. p.

107. "Address by Capt. J. V. Pierce," in *Monuments Commission for the Battlefields of Gettysburg and Chattanooga*, 988-997.

The Originals

Time engraves our faces with all the tears we have not shed.
– Natalie Clifford Barney

James S. Abbott – Co. C

b. 1825 England
d. *post* 1865 ?
m. Dianna Irons Whitmore (October 1820-May 27, 1907) *ca.* 1860

NOTE: Abbott was a cabinet maker by trade. He was captured at Gettysburg on July 1, 1863 and paroled the same day. He deserted from Parole Camp on October 20, 1863 and was sentenced by General Court Martial to make up the absence of five months and fifteen days. Nevertheless, he was discharged on June 9, 1865. Dianna had previously been married to William Delos Whitmore/Wetmore (1818-1853), who allegedly drowned in Lake Superior, as evidenced by the 1860 census which listed three of her six Whitmore children in the Abbott household. Although Abbott's death cannot be fixed exactly, Dianna was living in Detroit, Mi by 1876 where she styled herself "widow of James." In 1896 she unsuccessfully applied for a widow's pension in Michigan, which implies he had abandoned her and she was unaware that he might still be living. She died in Los Angeles, CA at the home of her daughter, Mary Davis.

George B. Acker – Co. D

b. August 9, 1839 Cato, Cayuga, NY
d. June 13, 1886 National Soldiers' Home, Hampton, VA
m. Hattie G. _____ (1849-*post* 1865) *ca.* 1865

NOTE: Acker, the son of Henry and Hannah Acker, received a gunshot wound to the leg on July 1, 1863. He was discharged from the service at David's Island on January 29, 1864 and applied for a pension on February 23, 1864. Because his pension card does not list a widow, I infer that Hattie predeceased him. His application to the National Home in 1885 lists his brother James H., living in Tornah, WI, as his closest relative. George is buried in the Hampton National Cemetery. His brother William served in the 110th Regiment NYSV and died on February 8, 1863 in New Orleans, LA.

John Quincy Adams – Co. D

b. 1836 Monroe County, NY
d. March 27, 1908 Jamestown, Greene, OH

m. Laura B. Spahr (March 4, 1842-April 9, 1922) October 25, 1866

NOTE: John was the son of Zina B. (1801-1844) and Eliza Ann Sharp Adams (1811-1885). He was discharged from the147th on February 24, 1864 to accept a commission in Co. B, 30th Regiment USCT. He was seriously wounded in the left leg at the battle of the Crater on July 30, 1864 and furloughed to recover. He returned to "light duty" as part of JAG and assisted with courts-martial in and around Washington, DC until July 1865 when he returned to his regiment, now a captain, and served until mustered out on December 10, 1865. He and Laura had no children. They are buried in Old Silvercreek Cemetery, Jamestown, Greene, OH.

Chester Adner – Co. H

b. 1840 Lewis County, NY

d. April 15, 1888 Natural Bridge, Jefferson, NY

m1. Elizabeth _____ (1842-*post* 1882) *ca.* 1870

m2. Albina C. Armstrong (February 1851-November 17, 1925) *ca.* 1883

NOTE: Chester's surname on his muster roll card is Edner. Although his gravestone gives a DOB of 1838, he said he was 22 when he enlisted and most records favor 1840 as his birth date. He was captured on May 5, 1864 and held until December 5th. His pension card states he served in Co. H, 91st Regiment and Co. H, 14th NY HA but his name does not appear in either form in *The Adjutant-General's Reports*. He applied for a pension in 1881 but it was not granted. His muster roll card notes that he "never joined Regt since capture" and perhaps there was a question of possible desertion despite the fact that he was discharged on July 17, 1865 at Albany, NY. Chester and Elizabeth were the parents of at least three children, Millie (1871-?), Lillian (1875-?), and Edward "Eddie" (1878-?). On March 15, 1882 *The Lewis County Democrat* reported the following: "Not long ago Mrs. Chester Adner, of the town of Diana, eloped with her four [*sic*] children with David Baucus, it is supposed, to parts unknown. She and her husband have had considerable trouble the past year, supposed to have been caused by Baucus." After the elopement, the couple and the children disappeared from history. It is unknown whether Chester got a divorce from Elizabeth. His obituary appeared in *The Watertown Herald* April 28, 1888, 1: "The funeral of Chester A. Adner was held at the Universalist church on Tuesday of last week, Rev. F. P. Stoddard officiating. He was buried by E. B. Steele post, G.A.R., of Carthage, of which he was a member. He enlisted in August, 1862, in the 147th N.Y. Volunteers, and served until July 17th, 1865. He was confined for 9 months in Andersonville and 9 months in Libby prisons. He leaves a wife and brothers who deeply mourn his loss. His age was 50 years, and he was sick for some time with typhoid pneumonia." There is no evidence he spent time in Libby Prison. When he died Albina applied for and received a widow's pension. In 1890 she said that Chester had been injured in the hip and back from being kicked by a horse but she did not specify the date of the injury. Chester and Albina are buried in Black Creek Cemetery, Wilna, Jefferson County, NY. Chester and brother Charles (1843-1917), who served in Co. D, 10th NY HA, were the children of George W. (1814-1868) and Laura Ingraham Adner (1805-1846).

Ebenezer Adsit – Co. E
b. August 1846 Rome, Oneida, NY
d. April 8, 1888 Redfield, NY
m. Charlotte Haines (October 1847-February 14, 1910) April 9, 1865

NOTE: Ebenezer's parents were Sylvanus (1793-February 16, 1881) and Hannah Bronson Reed Adsit (1820-*post* 1875). He was wounded at Gettysburg and again at Dabneys Mills, VA. He was discharged from Felton General Hospital, Wilmington, DE on May 22, 1865. He is buried in Redfield Village Cemetery. Charlotte married James E. Secor (July 1840-March 8, 1906) on July 16, 1891 as his second wife. He had served in the 146th Regiment and, according to the 1890 Veterans' Census, had a "leg shot off by shell." Secor is buried in Maple Hill Cemetery, Taberg, Oneida, NY. Charlotte is buried in Forest Park Cemetery, Camden, Oneida, NY.

William Aiken – Co. I
b. 1840 Ireland
d. ?
m. ?

NOTE: Aiken was captured at Gettysburg and paroled at an unknown date. He was captured again at the battle of the Wilderness on May 5, 1864. According to *The Registers of Officers and Enlisted Men* he was "a prisoner 10 months." Since he was discharged on May 30, 1865 from Summit Hospital, Philadelphia, PA he probably was held until February when prisoner exchanges began in earnest. His post-war life is sketchy. In 1869 he was the secretary for the Oswego Co-Operative Painting Company.

David W. Alger – Cos. B, A
b. November 10, 1843 Oswego, NY
d. October 20, 1924 Chicago, Cook, IL
m. Annie _____ (1847-May 9, 1889) *ca.* 1874

NOTE: Alger's parents were George H. (1807-*post* 1860) and Phinanda Parker Alger (1813-*post* 1870). He was a chair maker. Annie was born in Norway. She and David were the parents of two children, Edward (1875-?) and Frances (1878-1957). David is buried in Forest Home Cemetery, Chicago, Cook, IL. Since Annie also died in Chicago, it is possible she is buried there too. David's brother, George P. (1837-1928), served in Co. B, 24th from May 1861-May 1863 and in Co. B, 184th from August 1864-June 1865.

George H. All – Cos. A, B
b. 1838 Herkimer County, NY
d. ?
m. ?

NOTE: All previously served in Co. D, 24th Regiment. His muster card for the 147th shows his POB as Irion Brier, Canada, but other documents prove he was born in Herkimer County. His brother, Lorenzo Hamilton (1841-1920), served in the 21st Battery NY LA from 1863-1865. Their parents were Sylvester (1813-*post* 1880) and Sarah "Sally" All (1823-*post* 1880). No information about George, a harness maker, can be found after 1865.

Alexander Allen – Co. D
b. !821 Granby, NY
d. April 25, 1883 Green Bay, Brown, WI
m. Lucinda Wright Proud (May 5, 1819-November 27, 1898) *ca.* 1855

NOTE: Lucinda's first husband was Henry Proud (1811-May 13, 1853). In 1850 Alexander was living with them in Granby. Alexander is buried in Fort Howard Memorial Cemetery, Green Bay, WI. Lucinda died in Michigan and is buried in Stephenson Township Cemetery, Stephenson, Menominee, MI. Her COD was the result of a fractured femur. "Old age" was listed as a contributing factor on her death certificate.

Morgan Laben Allen, Sr. – Co. C
b. 1807 Williamstown, NY
d. July 21, 1863 Seminary Hospital, Gettysburg, PA
m. Nancy Patchin (1813-April 27, 1890) *ca.* 1834

NOTE: Allen, Sr. was wounded on July 1st. According to *Deaths of Volunteers*, his COD was a fracture of the left thigh. Records dispute whether he died July 12th or July 21st. He is buried in Gettysburg National Cemetery. His son, John Frank Allen (1835-1908), served in the 3rd Wisconsin Cavalry. For another son, see below. In 1880 Nancy was living in Russia, Herkimer, NY with her son Julian (1853-?).

Morgan Allen, Jr. – Co. C
b. 1844 Williamstown, NY
d. 1864 Andersonville, GA
m. ------

NOTE: The 1865 New York census says young Allen died on July 1, 1863 at Gettysburg: "Supposed to be dead[;] have not heard from him since battle [?]." His entry in *Registers of Officers and Enlisted Men* also says he died at Gettysburg. According to *The Town Clerks' Registers*, however, he "died in prison in the South." The National Park Service's "Prisoner Details" says: "Reported to have died at Andersonville, date unknown."

Amos Allport – Co. G
b. February 15, 1840 Scriba, NY
d. February 22, 1919 Oswego City, NY
m. Melinda E. Baker (1840-April 23, 1918) 1866

NOTE: Amos was the son of Zachariah (1802-1874) and Phebe Edwards Allport (1805-1875). His life is best summarized in an obituary appearing in *The Syracuse Post-Standard* February 23, 1919, 1: "The funeral of Amos Allport, 79, Civil War veteran and former sheriff of Oswego county, who died today at his home, No. 77 West Second street, will be held Monday afternoon . . . He had been in poor health for the past four years, having suffered a stroke of paralysis. Mr. Allport was born in the town of Scriba and resided there most of his life. A few months ago the family moved to the city for the winter. After that time his wife was taken ill and expired. Mr. Allport's parents, the late Mr. and Mrs. Zachariah Allport, were among the earliest settlers of Scriba. During the Civil War, Mr. Allport served in Company B [*sic*], 147th New York Volunteer Regiment. At the close of the war he returned to the Allport farm, situated in the Broadway road, near Lansing. In politics he was a Republican and took an active interest in county affairs. In 1883 Mr. Allport was elected supervisor of Scriba and represented that town on the board for a continuous period of four years. In the fall of 1890 he was elected sheriff of the county and served one term of three years. Prior to that time he served in the local customs house as inspector for two years. He was a member of the M. E. Church at Lansing and is survived by one son, Roscoe B. Allport of this city." Allport, who belonged to Lewis Porter Post No. 573 GAR, was wounded in the right arm at Petersburg in 1864. Melinda reportedly died "following a lingering illness." She was the sister of Joel A. Baker (see below). Amos and Melinda are buried in Riverside Cemetery, Scriba.

Sanford Alsaver – Co. H
b. 1837 Parish, NY
d. September 3, 1864 Andersonville, Sumter, GA
m. Lucetta Smith (February 18, 1839-July 22, 1911) December 20, 1860

NOTE: Sanford was the son of Frederick (1801-1890) and Betsy Capels Alsaver (1803-1853). He was captured at Gettysburg and later paroled. He was captured again on

May 5, 1864 at the battle of the Wilderness and was sent to Andersonville. His DOD varies from September to November 1864. Aaron Burr's list of soldiers who died at Andersonville, found in *The Pulaski Democrat* August 29, 1923, 6, concurs with *Deaths of Volunteers* that he died on September 3rd. Sanford's COD was scurvy, but since his muster roll card reports death was caused by "chronic diarrhea," one could have exacerbated the other. He is buried in Andersonville National Cemetery. Lucetta married John L. King (April 27, 1843-February 21, 1904) on June 10, 1869. He had served in the 5th US Cavalry and was pensioned for "disease of eyes, chronic diarrhea, piles, disease of heart, rheumatism." In 1863 near Falmouth, VA he contracted smallpox and lost the sight in one eye. He and Lucetta are buried in Mount Pleasant Cemetery, Wales Township, St. Clair, MI. Her COD was cancer of the liver and uterus. Sanford's brother Nelson (September 26, 1846-April 2, 1920) served in Co. I, 184th Regiment.

Walter Ames – Co. C
b. February 1835 Sandy Creek, NY
d. June 25, 1911 Watertown, Jefferson, NY
m. Rebecca McClary Spicer (April 1861-October 23, 1944) 1890

NOTE: Ames, son of David (1804-1877) and Betsy Ames (1807-*post* 1880), saw duty in the newly organized Ambulance Corps in 1863. Rebecca had previously been married to James A. Spicer (May 31, 1849-June 8, 1885) as his second wife. Spicer and his first wife Mary J. Washburn are buried in Sulphur Springs Cemetery, near Watertown, NY. An obituary, published in *The Watertown Re-Union*, reveals why he died in Watertown: "While enjoying a visit at the home of friends here, Walter Ames, 76 years old, of Richland, a retired farmer and a veteran of the Civil war, suffered a stroke at 8 o'clock Sunday morning, which resulted in death a half hour later. Mr. Ames, accompanied by his wife, came here Saturday on the Club train, and they were spending a couple of days as guests of the Obleman family at No. 881 West Main street, before proceeding to Carthage, where they had planned to visit Mrs. William Sanders, a stepdaughter. Mr. Ames had been in poor health since March, although able to be about. Before leaving Richland Saturday he suffered from short breathing and consulted his physician. He felt better in the afternoon and decided not to postpone the trip here and to Carthage. He was walking towards the bathroom when suddenly stricken . . . ." Rebecca's death was announced in *The Pulaski Democrat* October 26, 1944: "Mrs. Rebecca Spicer Ames, 83, widow of Walter Ames, died at the home of her son, Clarence Spicer, at Richland, Monday morning. She was born in 1861, on Wolf Island, daughter of Louis and Lucretia Bowman McClary, and was a member of the Church of Christ, Richland. Besides her son, Clarence, she is survived by another son, Earl Ames, of Syracuse . . . ." Walter and Rebecca are buried in Richland Cemetery, Oswego County.

Louis Amgen – Co. E

b. 1833 Bavaria

d. July 1, 1863 Gettysburg, Adams, PA

m. ?

NOTE: Amgen's first name was also spelled Lewis. Nothing else is known about this man, including his burial site.

David Anson – Co. K

b. 1814 Vermont

d. *post* 1870 ?

m1. ?

m2. Elizabeth Wooldridge _____ (1840-*post* 1870) *ca.* 1865

NOTE: Anson, a stone mason, originally enlisted in the 110th Regiment. He was wounded on July 1, 1863 and eventually transferred to the VRC and discharged on July 3, 1864. On the 1865 New York census for Granby, NY both he and Elizabeth said they had been married twice. A son, John, 10, probably was the unknown first wife's child since Elizabeth would only have been fifteen at the time of his birth. Furthermore, the 1865 census indicates she had had no children. In 1870 the family, including three more sons, Wilson, 4, Edwin, 2, and Egbert, 4/12, was living in Poughkeepsie, Dutchess, NY. No further documents have been located but Elizabeth may have predeceased David because his pension card does not list a widow. John was married in Michigan in 1879 and died in Oregon in 1921. It is possible the entire family migrated there with him.

Sylvester Auringer – Co. F

b. September 2, 1831 Palermo, NY

d. May 1864 Virginia

m. Catherine Jane Blankman (1837-1918) March 16, 1854

NOTE: Sylvester was the son of John (1804-1834) and Sally Foster Auringer (1805-1905). A note in *The Town Clerks' Registers* remarks cryptically: "The last seen or known of him was May 8, 1864 being taken sick on the march toward Battle of the Wilderness – supposed to be dead." His wife applied for a pension for herself and her children and in the file is a deposition by Sgt. Edward Sabins, dated July 30, 1869, who recalled: ". . . for some time prior to May 8th 1864 said Auringer had been sick and was in the regimental hospital and was at times out of his head & when on the march would sometimes fall down . . . at such times his nerves would be unstrung & he would tremble all over & deponent thought at sometimes that he had fits. That some thought he was playing off; that deponent had known said Auringer for years before he enlisted in said service and was & is fully satisfied that he was suffering from some nervous disease the result probably of exposure & hardship as he had been in the service with said Regiment since Sept. 1862. That said 8th day of May 1864 Lieut. James Brown now deceased having died from wound rec'd in action, was in command of said Co. F & deponent was orderly sergeant over all who were in the Regimental Hospital [and all] who were able to march were directed to march. Deponent being wounded at the time & in the regimental hospital marched with the others in the hospital and saw said Auringer on the march in company with others from the regimental hospital and conversed with him and saw that he was unable to go any further with the rest and last saw him sitting by a log or the fence where deponent advised him to wait till the Dr. should come along with an ambulance as deponent could do no more for him. That deponent never saw said Auringer or heard of him after that day . . . deponent believes said Auringer must have died on or about said 8th day of May 1864 probably when deponent left him in the field away from any house or assistance . . . ." It would appear, then, that Auringer died after, not before, the battle of the Wilderness. Sylvester and Catherine were the parents of five. After his death, they were "farmed out" to other families because their mother could not afford to care for them. The youngest, Jane, born April 1, 1863, was adopted formally by Madison Keller of Palermo, NY on February 1, 1865. Jane never remarried. She is buried in Oakwood Cemetery, Syracuse, Onondaga, NY. Her gravestone also memorializes Sylvester.

Alpheus Austin – C. A

b. 1839 Volney, NY
d. June 1864 Andersonville, Sumter, GA
m. ------

NOTE: Alpheus, a sailor by occupation, was the son of Milo Stratton (1817-1893) and Harriet Eliza Hagadorn Austin (1824-1898). He was captured at Haymarket, VA on October 19, 1863 and sent to Andersonville where he died in June 1864. The exact DOD is disputed: Aaron Nash Burr recalled he died on June 5th while a note in *Registers of Officers and Enlisted Men* puts the date at June 6th. *Deaths of Volunteers* and "Andersonville POWs" both claim he died on June 8th. COD was "chronic diarrhea." He is buried in the Andersonville National Cemetery.

Christopher Jenkins Avery – Co. F

b. March 10, 1821 Schoharie County, NY
d. May 2, 1874 Scriba, NY
m. Minerva Polly Fairchild (July 10, 1818-May 14, 1898) *ca.* 1847

NOTE: Avery, son of Whitfield (1788-?) and Amanda Avery (?-?), originally enlisted in the 110th Regiment. He mustered out with the regiment near Washington, DC on June 7, 1865. His remains were buried in Mexico Village Cemetery. Although Polly, as she was known, moved to Iowa after her husband's death *The Mexico Independent* May 25, 1898 published a lengthy obituary based on an earlier article published in *The Grundy* [Iowa] *Courier* May 20, 1898: "Mrs. P. M. Avery, mother of our townsman, H. W. Avery, died at her home in Iowa Falls, Saturday, May 14, 1898, and her remains were brought to Reinbeck for burial Monday. Mrs. Avery was quite well known here, having resided here about three years fifteen years ago. Funeral services were held at the M. E. church, conducted by Rev. Trimble, who read the following sketch of her life: 'The venerable lady whose obsequies we attend today lacked only a few risings and settings of the sun to have reached the eightieth milestone of her life. She was born in New Bedford, Conn., July 10, 1818. At the age of 25 she was married to Christopher Avery of Oswego County, N.Y. In 1861, at the beginning of the civil war, they moved to the little village of Prattville in the town of Mexico, N.Y., where she remained with her seven children while the husband and father served his country in the war. On his return from the field of strife they moved to Scriba, where they lived until the death of Mr. Avery which occurred in 1874. She then came west and lived with her eldest son in Waterloo, Iowa. Since then she has spent most of the time with her children. Mrs. Avery is survived by six children . . . At her death, which occurred on last Saturday night, at 11:30, all of her living children were present. Four days before, she was stricken down and had suffered much, but at the last all pain seemed to subside and she was given a peaceful hour to close her long and eventful life. In her early married life she united with the Baptist church at Colosse, N.Y. For many years she has not been able to attend church regularly. Most of her children are Methodists and it was her custom to go with them when she could. That her life was Christian, none who knew her ever doubted. The secret of this beautiful life is to be found in that ever-consoling passage, Matt.11.28, that says, "Come unto me all ye that labor and are heavy laden and I will give you rest." This was quoted thousands of times. In this she rested in life; by it she was supported in death; through it she entered into the everlasting rest'." She was buried in Reinbeck, IA, perhaps in Reinbeck Cemetery, since her son, Harmon Whitfield, is there.

Edwin Griffen Aylsworth – Co. G

b. 1841 Oswego County, NY
d. July 3, 1863 Seminary Hospital, Gettysburg, PA
m. ------

NOTE: Aylsworth, whose parents were Welcome Y. (1812-1896) and Marian Adkins Aylsworth (1818-1862), previously served in the 81st Regiment. During the retreat of the 147th at Gettysburg on July 1st, Lt. Volney Pierce and Sgt. Peter Shutts came across Aylsworth who had been severely injured in the right leg. He begged them for help but the press of the enemy was so great that they were forced to leave him to save their own lives. Aylsworth was eventually rescued and taken to hospital. On July 3rd his leg was amputated and he may have died that day although his DOD is disputed. While his entry in *Deaths of Volunteers* provides a date of July 1st, the Interment Control Form gives a date of July 8th. Some researchers claim he died July 10th. He was buried in Associate Reformed Graveyard, Gettysburg but is now interred in Gettysburg National Cemetery. In 1890 Welcome successfully applied for a pension.

Charles H. Backus – Co. D
b. 1838 Oswego County, NY

d. September 1863 Annapolis, Anne Arundel, MD

m. ------

NOTE: Charles was the son of Matthew (1805-*post* 1865) and Nancy Backus (1807-*post* 1865). His DOD is disputed. The muster roll card says he died September 29th but his entry in *Deaths of Volunteers* states he succumbed on September 23rd. COD was "secondary syphilis."

William Backus – Co. A
b. 1840 Phoenix, NY

d. May 5, 1864 Wilderness, VA

m. ------

NOTE: William, whose parents are unknown, was a boatman by occupation. Although he died at the battle of the Wilderness and was buried in Fredericksburg National Cemetery a note in *The Town Clerks' Registers* reported he "died at Gettysburg & [was] buried there."

Frank P. Baehr – Co. G
b. 1837 Bavaria

d. October 24, 1908 Oswego City, NY

m. Amelia Bishop (1840-April 23, 1916) 1859

NOTE: Baehr, a sailor, immigrated to the United States in 1842 and became a naturalized citizen. His parents are reputed to be Dionisius "David" Baehr and Walburga Hodapp. His obituary in *The Oswego Daily Times* October 26, 1908, 4, revealed how he was viewed in the community: "Frank P. Baehr, a well known Civil War veteran, died Saturday night, at his home, No. 157 East Eighth Street, after a lingering illness. Mr. Baehr was 72 years of age and during the Civil War he served as First

Lieutenant of G Company, 147th New York Volunteers. For many years he has lived a retired life. Mr. Baehr was well liked by all who knew him and in their bereavement his family have the sympathy of many friends. He is survived by his wife, three sons and two daughters . . . Mr. Baehr was a devout member of St. Peter's Church from which his funeral will be held tomorrow morning. It is expected that members of the G. A. R. will attend the funeral." Baehr was a charter member of Post O'Brien 65 GAR. He and Amelia are buried in St. Peter's Cemetery, Oswego City.

Harvey Murphy Baird – Co. H
b. June 30, 1837 Springfield, Otsego, NY
d. November 24, 1913 National Soldiers' Home, Bath, Steuben, NY
m. ------

NOTE: On his muster roll card Harvey said he was a "horse doctor." He was the son of Barnes (1792-1871) and Eliza Barker Baird (1800-1888). After the war he lived for a time in New York City. He was admitted to the home on November 2, 1907 and died there six years later. Although COD was not recorded he was suffering from heart disease when he entered the home. He is buried in Bath National Cemetery.

Benjamin O. Baker – Co. F
b. July 1845 Flint, Oneida, NY
d. May 12, 1919 Mexico, NY
m. Sarah C. _____ (July 1845-January 2, 1909) 1864

NOTE: Baker's parents are unknown. He was discharged from the 147th on September 24, 1863 for "disability" and a deposition he gave for Henry Mayo's widow on December 17, 1864 describes what that disability was: ". . . he the deponent was wounded in his left arm and left upon the Battle field & subsequently taken prisoner at the Battle of Gettysburg in the State of Pennsylvania on the first day of July AD 1863 and subsequently paroled and returned within the lines of the Army of the United States on the 3rd day of July AD 1864 [sic] . . . ." The gunshot wound resulted in total disability of his left hand. He and Sarah are buried in Mexico Village Cemetery. The cemetery record erroneously gives his DOD as 1913.

Joel A. Baker – Co. G
b. June 4, 1842 Scriba, NY
d. July 1, 1885 Oswego City, NY
m. Florence Morse (March 1850-September 18, 1934) December 14, 1871

NOTE: On July 1, 1885 The Oswego Palladium published the following encomium for a much esteemed member of the community: "As we write Joel A. Baker, chief of police, lies dying at his home in this city. All hope has fled and only a few hours at most of life remain to him. He is surrounded by his heart stricken wife and family. The sympathy of the whole community goes out to them. Mr. Baker has been confined to his house for about ten days with erysipelas. Something like two weeks ago Chief Baker accompanied a fishing party to Pleasant Point where they engaged in a game of base ball. While standing behind C. W. Ott who was knocking the ball he was accidentally struck in the ear, the skin being broken. The wound did not heal as speedily as could be desired and in a few days erysipelas set in. At first the chief did not pay much attention to the matter, but soon the wound became very annoying and he was confined to the house. Medical aid was summoned, but the disease spread to the base of the brain and brain fever set in. Late last week his friends became alarmed and the leading physicians of the city were summoned. Everything which medical skill could suggest was done for him, but he continued to sink. This morning the physicians were forced to admit that the case was a hopeless one and that the patient's lease of life did not exceed a few hours. Joel A. Baker was born in that part of the town of Scriba known as 'The Kingdom,' and spent his early life on his father's farm. He was educated at the district school, but so great was his desire for knowledge that he devoted himself faithfully to his books and when a young man was able to take charge of a school himself. When the war of the rebellion broke out Chief Baker was ready to serve his country and in August 1862 he enlisted in Company G, 147th regiment, Capt. Geary, and served with honor until mustered out. So excellent a soldier was he that he was successively promoted to the position of orderly sergeant, sergeant and major, second and first lieutenant and ultimately became captain. A portion of the time he also served on Gen. Coulter's staff. On the battle field, the march and in the camp he was always at his post and merited the esteem of his superiors and the good will of his subordinates. He served in every battle in which the glorious 147th was engaged, and was with them at all times. After being mustered out he went back to home in Scriba and became a school teacher. In 1868 while teaching school at Lansing in the town of Scriba he was nominated by the democrats for the office of supervisor and though the republicans placed in nomination a well known and respected citizen of the town, Squire Simpson, Mr. Baker was elected. He served his constituents creditable [sic] and in 1869 was re-elected, again defeating Squire Simpson, by an increased majority. Some months after his election and before meeting the board, he was appointed under-sheriff by the late James Doyle and resigned the office of supervisor, Dr. Snyder being appointed to fill the vacancy. He faithfully discharged the duties of this office till June 7, 1871, when he was chosen chief of the Oswego police force, a position which he has since held. As chief of police, Mr. Baker has distinguished himself in many ways, proving himself a thoroughly competent officer . . . Chief Baker was in every respect a worthy man. Modest and retiring in demeanor, he was nevertheless cool, firm and level-headed, always ready for emergency and always steady in the management of the most difficult cases. Perfect self command in trying circumstances was his distinguishing trait, and it made him a most excellent officer. During the entire existence of the present police system in this city, Mr. Baker was in command of it and in all of that time there never was an occasion that he did not come fully up to the standard of requirement. He was warm-hearted and generous, true to his friends and just to all. It is true to say that aside from some wrongdoers, whom, in the discharge of his duty, he brought to justice, he had not an enemy. As husband and father, he was true to every obligation; as a friend and Christian he stood blameless. The announcement of his death is to us a sad duty and it will be received with general and unfeigned sorrow by the whole community." Baker's funeral was impressive, attended by members of the 147th Regiment and Post O'Brien No. 65 GAR, of which he was a charter member. He had been a member of Oswego Lodge No. 127 F & A M, Lake Ontario Chapter No. 165 RAM, and Lake Ontario Commandery, Knights Templar No. 32 and all those bodies sent representatives. Graveside services were conducted by the Masons. Florence married Frank A. Moss (1853-July 20, 1925) on October 30, 1912 as his third wife. The couple lived in Sterling, Cayuga, NY. Florence died in Oswego "after having been ill for the past six months." She and Joel are buried in Riverside Cemetery, Scriba.

Joseph Baker – Co. K
b. 1818 Canada
d. July 2, 1900 Scriba, NY
m. Melissa Pelo (1822-April 30, 1913) ca. 1846

NOTE: In 1890 Baker claimed his disability was a "wound" and he apparently was wounded and listed MIA until August after the battle of Gettysburg. He said he had been "formerly" in the army on the 1865 New York census. Melissa, also born in Canada, said she was the mother of ten children on the same census. Both said they had been married only once. Joseph's death was reported in *The Fulton Patriot* July 4, 1900, 1: "Joseph Baker, aged 83 years, who lived at Seneca Hill and the husband of the fortune teller ought to have known better than to leave the world in the manner he did Saturday. He was seen alive about nine o'clock and it is supposed that he went to the barn, placed the ladder against the inside, tied the rope around his neck, went to the top, attached it to the ladder and dropped between the rungs. The attempt was a success. He was found about two o'clock in the afternoon and the coroner was notified." He was buried in Riverside Cemetery, Scriba. Melissa died at her home in Oswego City. Her funeral was held at St. Louis' Church but her grave has not been located.

Miles M. Baker – Co. D

b. 1840 Manchester, Bennington, VT

d. November 30, 1907 Granby, NY

m. Jane _____ (1834-October 11, 1911) 1858

NOTE: Baker's parents have not been identified. He was wounded July 1, 1863 at Gettysburg and subsequently transferred to the VRC. In 1890 he told the enumerator that his disability was "chronic diarrhea and catarrh." His DOB varies from document to document. According to his muster roll card, he was born in 1840. On the 1900 federal census he said he was born in December 1829. His gravestone contains the birth date of 1838. He and Jane are buried in Lewis Cemetery, Granby, NY.

Robert W. Baker – Co. G

b. 1834 Chautauqua County, NY

d. November 20, 1863 US General Hospital, Washington, DC

m. Henrietta B. Mickle (December 30, 1839-April 10, 1925) December 10, 1859

NOTE: Robert, whose parents may have been Simeon (1799-1874) and Patience Baker (1802-1876), was a carpenter by occupation. He succumbed to typhoid fever and was buried in the Soldiers' and Airmen's Cemetery, Washington, DC. Henrietta married Seth P. Handy (1820-March 8, 1871) on December 14, 1870. He died in Easton, Washington, NY and was buried in Greenwich Cemetery, Greenwich, WA. Her third husband was Elisha Hoag Gifford (May 9, 1824-February 1, 1911) whom she married November 11, 1882. Henrietta, who died in Oakland, CA, is buried with Elisha and his first wife, Anna Hoag (1829-1881), in Easton Cemetery, Easton, Washington, NY.

Orrin H. Balch – Co. G

b. March 31, 1835 Orwell, NY

d. August 28, 1920 Mannsville, Jefferson, NY

m1. Catherine Elizabeth Curry (October 22, 1834-October 14, 1876) September 4, 1856

m2. Clara Vernon Brown (September 1847-May 7, 1920) 1877

NOTE: Orrin was the son of John (1792-1882) and Eunice Stowell Balch (1808-1873). He was captured at the battle of Gettysburg and spent time in Libby Prison, Richmond. He detailed his experiences as a POW in an article entitled "Gettysburg Prisoners. Brutality and Inhumanity of the Rebels and Robbers Who Were Their Guards on the March and In Prison," *National Tribune* August 11, 1904. Paroled sometime prior to October 16, 1863 he was officially discharged on November 30, 1863. Later he was accused of desertion but the charge was dismissed. In 1910 Orrin and Clara were residing in Horseheads, Chemung, NY but by 1911 they had moved to Mannsville. Orrin belonged to Calvin Burch Post No. 345 GAR in Ellisburg, Jefferson, NY. He was also a member of Lake City Lodge No. 127, F & A M, Oswego City. Clara was the widow of DeAlton Brown (1846-?). She, Orrin, and Catherine are all buried in Maplewood Cemetery, Mannsville.

Ransom G. Ball – Co. D

b. April 7, 1845 Volney, NY
d. March 1, 1899 Washington, DC
m1. Lydia A. Davis (1847-August 4, 1877) *ca.* 1866
m2. Anna M. _____ (1841-January 15, 1902) *ante* 1880
m3. Anan E. Williams Potts (1856-February 28, 1924) May 10, 1889

NOTE: Ransom was the son of Ashley King (1822-*ca.* 1878) and Laura A. Barnes Ball (1821-1856). He was injured at the Battle of Gravelly Run, March 31, 1865. Lydia, daughter of Dean Elijah (1822-1893) and Phebe Remington Davis (1823-1905), of Palermo, NY, was a schoolteacher before her marriage. She was killed in a boating accident. According to *The Oswego Daily Times* August 8, 1877 the Balls had joined two other couples for a trip on the Hattie E, a steam-driven pleasure yacht: ". . . Just before entering the lock . . . Mrs. Ball sat upon a camp stool immediately in front of the partition which divided the engine and boiler from the forward part of the boat and less than one foot from the boiler . . . The water had been lowered in the lock until it had nearly reached the lower level when without any warning a terrific explosion occurred. The boiler of the yacht had exploded. In an instant the entire party with the exception of Mr. Taylor were thrown into the water, Mrs. Ball, Wolf and the engineer being first lifted several feet into air by the force of the explosion . . . Mrs. Ball immediately sank to the bottom of the lock. Mr. Ball sank twice but rose again to the surface, when some one in the crowd, which was gathered by the explosion reached him a pole to which he clung, until the water was let into the lock to raise it to the upper level . . . In a few minutes the water was raised to the upper level and all but Mrs. Ball were taken out. The search for her which of course began immediately after she sank was continued and in a moment or two she was found on the bottom near the lower gate and was brought up with a pike pole which was hooked into her dress. Under the supposition that she was drowned, every effort was made to resuscitate her, but the blood which flowed from her mouth showed that she was internally injured. It soon became evident that life was extinct. There were no external injuries of a serious character. It is a question whether Mrs. Ball was drowned or killed by the shock of the explosion . . . ." Lydia and her parents are buried in Sayles Corners Cemetery, Mexico. Little is known about Ransom's second wife, Anna. According to the marriage license for his third marriage, he and Anna were divorced, but because of the fact that Anna contested Anan's claim to a widow's pension, she may have assumed they were still married. Add that to the fact that Ransom and Anan Potts were married in Pennsylvania. Anan's first husband, whom she married *ca.* 1875, was Charles Potts (1847-1884). Ransom's death was reported in a lengthy, informative obituary appearing in *The Oswego Daily Times* March 6, 1899, which is here excerpted: "On Wednesday, March 1, 1899, at his home in Washington, D.C., occurred the death of Ransom G. Ball, from liver trouble, resulting in blood poisoning, after an illness of a little more than two weeks, aged fifty-four years . . . He was born in the town of Palermo, April 7, 1845, and received the usual education imparted at country schools, but being unusually bright and active, very early in life manifested an interest in all public affairs. He came into the years of his early manhood amid the stirring and stormy scenes of the darkest days of the Rebellion, and under the call that brought the 147th New York Volunteers Infantry into existence, enlisted in Company D, of that Regiment . . . Although less than eighteen years of age Mr. Ball was made 1st Sergeant of his company, and served with distinction until his final discharge after the close of the war. In fact the history of the 147th is his war record, for he was with his regiment from date of enlistment until discharge except for a period of three months, when he was home on furlough, from a wound in his right side, received at Spottsylvania in 1864 . . . After the expiration of his furlough he returned to his regiment in time to participate in the closing scene around Petersburg and was in the various engagements in which the 147th participated until the battle of Five Forks, when he was again wounded, this time in the left leg, and was so severely that he was obliged to suffer amputation of the limb. His work however was done, and the dawn of peace was already illuminating the horizon. A few days more and Richmond had fallen, and Lee had surrendered. After lingering several weeks in the hospital he was discharged August 2, 1865, and returned to his home in Palermo. The romance of Mr. Ball's life began in his teens, and before his heart was stirred by the call of his country the little love god had already transfixed it with an arrow, which, with all the excitements and changes of his eventful life was never withdrawn. Before he went to war he had met and loved a sweet young girl, the daughter of a neighbor, Lydia Davis, and when her youthful hero and lover came home, although so sadly maimed, they were married. Their married life was an especially happy and congenial one, but it lasted only about eleven years, and its end was the most tragic of any of the scenes through which the young husband had ever passed. Many of your readers will recall the accident which occurred on Oneida Lake on August 4, 1877, by the explosion of the boiler of the steam launch . . . By this explosion Mrs. Ball was instantly killed. From the shock of this terrible loss the loving husband never recovered, although he manfully took up the burden of life, and in later years, when time had seared his heart wounds, and dimmed the past, he found another wife. Few men in Oswego County were more widely known in the county than Mr. Ball. He was eminently a politician, and he made it his business to know and be able to call by name any one he might meet. He was an ardent Republican and as such with his peculiar gifts and wide experience he was very useful to the leaders of his party, both in council and at the polls. He held many places of trust and responsibility, and at different times was in the Custom House, County Clerk's office, Canal Collector's office and other positions of minor importance. About ten years ago Mr. Ball left Oswego County and engaged in business in Syracuse, where he met and married Mrs. Anan Potts, who still survives him. Shortly after this marriage under a Civil Service examination he was called into the Departmental Service at Washington, D. C., and was assigned to the Pension Bureau. Here his genial manner made him hosts of friends and his attention to his duties made him a valued clerk. At the beginning of the present administration he was promoted to a chief of section in the Certificate Division, which he held at the time of his death. He was an active and honored member of the Grand Army and the Union Veteran Legion, and both of these organizations escorted his remains to their final resting place. In accordance with his oft-repeated request he was wrapped in the flag he had so faithfully assisted in defending and for which he had sacrificed so much . . . ." Anan applied for a widow's pension on April 6, 1899. On December 19, 1900 Anna M. Ball applied as a "contesting widow." Anan ultimately received the pension, giving credence to the assertion that the couple had indeed divorced. Anan and Ransom are buried in Arlington National Cemetery. Anna is buried in Riverside Cemetery, Scriba.

Thomas W. Banister – Co. K
b. 1816 St. Lawrence County, NY
d. July 1, 1863 Gettysburg, Adams, PA
m. Hannah Bullis (1818-March 10, 1907) February 8, 1836

NOTE: Thomas, whose parents are unidentified, and Hannah were married in Cape Vincent, Jefferson, NY. He is buried in an unknown grave in Gettysburg National Cemetery. Hannah, born in England, was illiterate and signed all her pension papers with "X." She never remarried. Upon her death, *The Oswego Daily Palladium* March 11, 1907, 8, published a lengthy, somewhat fanciful, obituary: "Mrs. Hannah Banister, one of Oswego's oldest residents, died at the home of her daughter, Mrs. L. W. Brunot, at the corner of East Fifth and Lawrence streets, yesterday. She was Miss Hannah Bullis before her marriage and was born in Sheepshead, England, January 2d, 1818. She came to Oswego with her family in 1842 and has lived here ever since. Her husband was the late John [sic] Banister who was killed at Gettysburg in the Civil War, and in the family plot at Riverside is not only his body, but on one side that of his father, John Banister, who was a veteran of the War of 1812, and on the other his son, John Banister, who went out to the Civil War with his father. Mrs. Banister joined the First Baptist church in 1844, sixty-three years ago, and at the time of her death was probably the oldest member of that body. She was an aunt of Superintendent of Schools George E. Bullis . . . ." The Banister son who went to war was Thomas (1847-1881) who served in Co. F, 184th Regiment from August 1864-June 1865. John, mentioned in the obituary, was born in 1851 and died in 1927. Hannah was buried in the family plot in Riverside Cemetery, Scriba, together with several of her children. The handsome family gravestone in Riverside is also a cenotaph for Thomas, Sr.

Gothelp Barap – Co. C
b. 1808 Denmark
d. *post* 1865 probably in Richland, NY
m. ?

NOTE: Research for this man is hampered by the variety of spellings for his name. He originally enlisted in the 110th Regiment but was sent to the 147th. Because of his age it is difficult to comprehend why he was accepted for service. His muster roll card shows he spent time at Convalescent Camp in Alexandria, VA. He was discharged for "disability" on August 3, 1863. After his discharge, the only document located for him is the 1865 New York census. He was living with Andrew and Ann Mathewson and claimed to be a widower. His occupation was "artist."

Elijah Barbarick – Cos. K, D
b. July 1845 Oswego County, NY
d. May 18, 1916 Biteley, Newaygo, MI
m1. Margaret Pluff Van Waren (1840-May 31, 1896) September 24, 1865
m2. Laura Atkins (September 1859-September 2, 1921) February 12, 1898

NOTE: Elijah, son of William (1794-1863) and Nancy Elmer Barbarick (1795-1850), was also known as Ephraim. He originally enlisted in the 110th but was transferred to the 147th. He was discharged from service on August 4, 1863 at Convalescent Camp, Alexandria, VA. His COD was "influenza" with "acute cystitis" listed as a contributing factor. He is buried in Volney Cemetery, Volney, Newaygo, MI. Laura allegedly first married Andrew Cook in Monroe, MI, in 1875. He reportedly died July 15, 1877 in Fulton, NY. In 1920 Laura was living in the Newaygo County Almshouse. Her COD was "senile dementia." She was buried in an unmarked grave at the Newaygo County Poor Farm. According to the records, her parents were "unknown." Margaret died in Leavitt, Oceana, MI of "pneumonia of the lungs." Her grave has not been located.

John H. Barbarick – Co. D

b. 1836 Oswego County, NY
d. May 24, 1908 Berlin Heights, Erie, OH
m. Roseanne Brown (May 11, 1847-July 11, 1924) 1861

NOTE: John, brother of Elijah, originally enlisted in the 110th Regiment. He was wounded at Gettysburg on July 1, 1863, subsequently transferred to the VRC, and finally discharged from the service on September 15, 1863. Later he was accused of desertion but the charge was removed in 1894. Roseanne married Ely Baker Tillman (October 30, 1838-December 1, 1921) on September 10, 1913. He had served in Co. A, 40th and Co. I, 51st OH. He is buried in Willow Cemetery, Oregon, Lucas, OH. The name of his first wife, Seretta A. Lloyd (1839-1912), is on the gravestone but she is buried in Preston Cemetery, Alger, Hardin, OH. Roseanne is buried in Association Cemetery, Sylvania, Lucas, OH. John's grave has not been found.

Theophilus R. Barbarick – Co. K

b. 1839 Granby, NY
d. July 1, 1863 Gettysburg, Adams, PA
m. ------

NOTE: Like his brothers Elijah and John, Theophilus originally enlisted in the 110th Regiment. He was killed in action and is buried in an unknown grave in Gettysburg National Cemetery.

Lafayette D. Barber – Co. C

b. December 3, 1841 Albion, NY
d. November 11, 1933 Pineville, NY
m. Calsadana "Callie" Wade (1846-December 12, 1928) December 1865

NOTE: Lafayette was the son of John (1815-1899) and Julia Ann Thomas Barber (1814-1882). The following informative obituary was published in *The Oswego Palladium-Times* November 11, 1933, 9: "Lafayette D. Barber, one of the oldest and best known residents of [Pulaski], died Saturday noon at his home in Pineville after a long illness. He had been in fair health the past few years. He had always lived in Pineville and was a member of J. B. Butler Post G.A.R., having served with the 147th Regiment, New York Volunteers, during the Civil War. Mr. Barber was born Dec. 3, 1841, son of the late Julia Thomas and John Barber. He had always been a sawyer and was employed in several mills of this section until his health failed. He was one of the oldest members of Pulaski Lodge 415, F. & A. M. No near relatives survive . . . ." Callie's death was marked by an obituary in *The Oswego*

Palladium-Times December 14, 1928: "Mrs. Callie S. Barber, wife of Lafayette D. Barber, 82 years old, died suddenly Wednesday afternoon about 2 o'clock at her home in Pineville. Mrs. Barber was born in the town of Amboy and was a daughter of the late Ransom and Elizabeth Brown Wade. Mrs. Barber who had spent her entire life in the vicinity of Pineville was exceedingly alert and active. Mrs. and Mrs. Barber were married Dec. 1865 by Squire Wright who was justice of the peace at that time. In the early days of their married life, Mr. Barber operated a sawmill but at the beginning of the Civil War, Mr. Barber enlisted and Mrs. Barber, in her later life, enjoyed discussing the various experiences of her husband during that period. For many years she was an active member of the Methodist Episcopal church in Pineville . . . ." Lafayette and Callie were the parents of one child, Cora E. (1866-1874). She is buried with her parents in Pineville Cemetery.

Lafayette Barber was one of the last five surviving members of J. B. Butler Post No. 111 GAR and a Freemason for 44 years at the time of his death.
Pulaski Lodge #415 F & AM

Samuel Simon Barbo – Co. B

b. 1841 Oswego, NY
d. May 12, 1864 Laurel Hill, Augusta, VA
m. ------

NOTE: Samuel was the son of Peter (1820-1888) and Martha Anderson Barbeau (1821-1900), as shown by early census records. He was killed in action. According to *Deaths of Volunteers* he died at Spotsylvania Court House, VA. His mother successfully applied for a pension on May 12, 1877. A brother, Augustus Barbeau (1847-February 23, 1865), was a member of the 24th NY Cavalry and died of acute dysentery.

William W. Bargy – Co. E

b. February 9, 1842 Utica, Oneida, NY
d. June 16, 1913 Boylston, NY
m. Amelia A. Harrington (March 18, 1833-February 16, 1907)

NOTE: William's parents were Jacob (1809-1894) and Sally Van Auken Bargy (1809-1853). In 1890 he stated that he had lost toes on his left foot "in Andersonville Prison" but it is unknown when he was captured. His death was noted in *The Sandy Creek*

News June 19, 1913, 8: ". . . Wm. Bargy, a lifelong resident of [Boylston], passed away Monday night, June 16, at the home of Mrs. Sarah Porter, where he has made his home for the past few years. Mr. Bargy has been in poor health since March last but has been able to be around until a few days previous to his death [when] he suffered a slight shock from which he never recovered." When Amelia died, *The Sandy Creek News* February 28, 1907, published the following: "Mrs. Amelia Huntington [*sic*] Bargy died at the family home in Boylston Saturday, February 16 of typhoid pneumonia, aged 76 years. In the death of Mrs. Bargy the neighbors and community lose a kind friend and the husband a faithful companion. She leaves to mourn her loss a husband and one sister. She was born in Pulaski and spent the early years of her life there. She was a relative of the late Judge Huntington of Pulaski. Burial at North Boylston." Both William and Amelia were buried in North Boylston Cemetery. The gravestone does not provide his DOD.

Charles Hiram Barker – Co. K
b. May 29, 1835 Oswego City, NY
d. July 31, 1911 Oswego Town, NY
m. Martha J. King (1834-January 2, 1909) October 8, 1855

NOTE: Charles was the son of Hiram D. (1808-1894) and Sophia Morrow Barker (1814-1904). He mustered out with the regiment on June 7, 1865 near Washington, DC. *The Oswego Daily Palladium* July 31, 1911, 5, published the following obituary for him: "Charles H. Barker, an old and respected resident of Oswego Town, died at his home in Southwest Oswego at an early hour this morning as the result of a stroke of apoplexy received about three weeks ago. He was born in this city seventy six years ago. Mr. Barker was a volunteer soldier, being a member of the old 147th Regiment and prominent member of Post Stevenson, G.A.R. He was also a member of the Southwest Oswego Lodge No. 206, I.O.O.F. Mr. Barker is survived by three sons and one daughter . . . The funeral will be held on Wednesday morning at eleven o'clock from his late home under the auspices of the G.A.R." Charles and Martha are buried in Rural Cemetery, Oswego Town. *The Oswego Daily Palladium* January 4, 1909 reported that she died on January 2nd "after an illness of about a year" while *The Oswego Daily Times* January 4, 1909 stated she died "somewhat unexpectedly" that morning. The New York Death Index confirms the January 2nd date.

James Rhodes Barker – Co. C
b. 1839 Camden, Oneida, NY
d. August 25, 1868 on the road between Syracuse and Central Square, NY
m. Margaret _____ (1842-*post* 1885) *ante* 1860

NOTE: Barker was wounded at Gettysburg and transferred to the VRC, mustering out on June 28, 1865 at Washington, DC. His parents were James (1817-?) and Hannah Maria Stearns Barker (1822-?). His death in a freak accident was reported in *The Mexico Independent* September 9, 1868: "On the 25th ult., James Barker, of Dugway, when between Syracuse and Central Square, on his way home, fell from his wagon, the wheels (so we are informed) passing over his body. We are unable to give particulars but learn that he lived only a short time after the accident." He was buried in Dugway Cemetery. Margaret applied for a widow's pension in November 1885 but her activities between James' death and that date are unknown. What happened after 1885 is unknown. Since she did not obtain the pension, it is possible she died before the process could be completed.

Wallace W. Barnes – Co. F
b. January 20, 1840 Mexico, NY
d. February 2, 1912 Salem, Rensselaer, NY
m. Alice Levina Broughton (October 5, 1843-May 8, 1925) 1870

NOTE: Wallace's parents were Sardius B. (1809-July 2, 1898) and Hannah Hutchens Barnes (1812-1877). When S. B., as he was known, learned his son was in hospital, he went to Virginia to try to win him a discharge, as reported in *The Mexico Independent* March 5, 1863: "Our friend, S. B. Barnes has returned from a visit to the 147th regiment, in Virginia. The object of the visit was to get the discharge of his son Wallace but he was entirely unsuccessful, as the authorities would neither permit his discharge, nor consent to a leave of absence on furlough, nor permit his removal to a hospital at Washington. He has been sick about ten weeks, first with fever; now his lungs are very much affected, accompanied with diarrhea. The surgeons advised his discharge, but the medical director would not consent. It looks like a hard case." On April 10th, however, he was discharged from Douglas Hospital, Washington, DC, for "disability." When Barnes enlisted, he was a schoolteacher. In later life he was a painter. His death elicited the following notice in *The Troy Times* February 5, 1912, 10: ". . . Wallace Barnes, who dropped dead at his residence Friday evening, had not been in good health for several months, having suffered a stroke of paralysis during the summer, but had been about his duties as usual. About ten years ago Mr. Barnes moved to Salem from Hoosick Falls. He was about seventy years of age, a veteran of the Civil War and a parishioner of St. Paul's Episcopal Church . . . ." Alice's obituary appeared in *The Salem Press* May 14, 1925, 4: "After a short illness, Mrs. Alice Levina Barnes, aged eighty-one years, died at the home of her daughter, Mrs. Albert Hanna, on Friday afternoon, May 8, at about 3:00 o'clock. Mrs. Barnes was born at Hampton, N.Y. on October 5, 1842 . . . In her younger days Mrs. Barnes was an active worker in the organization of St. Paul's Episcopal church here, and she acted as organist for several years when the church was first started. All her life she had been a great worker, both in her home and in the church and she was loved by all who knew her. After her marriage to Wallace Barnes they resided in Hoosick Falls for several years, later moving to Salem, where Mr. Barnes died February 2, 1912. Mrs. Barnes spent the remainder of her life here. The funeral was held at St. Paul's church Monday afternoon at 2:00 o'clock, after which the body was taken to Hoosick Falls for burial. After a life well spent she has crossed the Silent River to join the great white throng who have washed their Robes, and stand continually before the Throne of God and serve him day and night, and 'God shall wipe away all tears from their eyes'." Wallace and Alice are buried in Maple Grove Old Cemetery, Hoosick Falls, Rensselaer, NY.

Cheney Deloss Barney – Co. H
b. 1833 Hartwick, Otsego County, NY
d. April 16, 1895 Parish, NY
m. Frances R. Law (1843-August 21, 1929) *ca.* 1870

NOTE: Cheney, whose parents were Daniel P. (1787-1872) and Martha Barney (1789-1858), appears to have used his Christian names interchangeably. He was a dentist by occupation. When he was discharged for "disability" on April 12, 1864, he held the rank of first lieutenant. In 1890 he said his disability was "rheumatism and varicocele." He was a member of Melzar Richards Post No. 367 GAR in Mexico. He and Frances are buried in Pleasant Lawn Cemetery, Parish, NY.

John Bartlett – Co. C
b. 1830 Herkimer County, NY
d. May 21, 1910 Williamstown, NY
m. Mary A. Harger (1836-October 3, 1883) *ca.* 1856

NOTE: Bartlett, whose parents are unknown, was a sawyer by trade. He was wounded at Gettysburg and transferred to the VRC on March 21, 1864 although in 1890 he claimed no disability. His DOB and DOD are disputed. His gravestone lists 1825 but his muster roll card records a birth date of 1830. In 1900 he said he was born in April 1832. Although his gravestone says he died in 1905, this too must be erroneous because he reapplied for his pension on March 4, 1907. His pension payment card confirms he died in 1910. He and Mary, the mother of at least seven children, are buried in Fairview Cemetery, Williamstown, NY.

Albert E. Bartley – Co. D
b. 1844 Fulton, NY
d. July 1, 1863 Gettysburg, Adams, PA
m. ------

NOTE: Albert's parents were Gilbert (1816-May 28, 1898) and Clarissa Mooney Bartley (1821-December 30, 1891). Albert is buried in Gettysburg National Cemetery. On August 7, 1889 his mother applied for his pension. After her death Gilbert also successfully sought a pension based on Albert's service.

Alfred Nathaniel Beadle – Co. E
b. April 13, 1837 Orwell, NY
d. October 13, 1912 Pulaski, NY
m. Mary Frances Bently (October 30, 1838-October 19, 1895) September 6, 1865

NOTE: Beadle, son of Nathaniel (1802-1837) and Anne Wellman Beadle (1813-1852), was a schoolteacher when he enlisted. During his military career he was promoted several times. Alfred received a lengthy obituary, published in *The Sandy Creek News* October 17, 1912, 2: "Alfred N. Beadle, aged seventy-seven, for many years a resident of Oswego, was found dead in his chair Sunday evening at the home of Timothy Lawler on Lake street, Pulaski, where he had been boarding for several weeks. He had not complained of feeling unwell and had been about as usual during the day. During the afternoon he took a short walk about the village returning about six o'clock. When Mrs. Lawler entered the reception room to summon him to supper she received no reply and going to his chair she found him dead. Coroner Hollis was notified. Mr. Beadle was a native of the town of Orwell and for many years was engaged in a hardware business at Pulaski as a member of the firm of Beadle, Hollis & Lyman. In 1881 Mr. Beadle was appointed deputy sheriff by Sheriff Edward L. Huntington and had charge of the Pulaski court house. In 1885 he was elected sheriff of Oswego county and made his home in Oswego. Mr. Beadle was a veteran of the Civil war, serving in company E, 147th Reg., N.Y. Vol. He was a member of Pulaski Lodge, F. and A. M. since 1865 . . . ." Mary's death in 1895 occasioned the following obituary in *The Pulaski Democrat* October 23, 1895: "The community was very much shocked Saturday to hear of the death of Mrs. Alfred N. Beadle, in Oswego. She was well known in this community and much loved and respected by a large circle of friends. She suffered something like a shock a few days before her death so that to the family the dread hour was expected. The funeral took place at the home in Oswego and regular services at the Congregational church in this village at one o'clock. Rev. Dr. Bacon, of Oswego and Rev. A. S. Emmons of this place conducted the services at the church which were impressive. Dr. Bacon gave a biographical sketch in which he dwelt upon the loveable traits and the excellent character of the deceased. A large congregation of her old neighbors and friends were present. Burial took place at Orwell. Mary Frances Bently was born in the town of Sandy Creek, October 30, 1838. She was a daughter of Elias and Sarah Bently. In 1860 she removed to this village with her mother, her father having died that year. She was inclined to literary occupation and besides teaching in other schools she was at one time preceptress of Waterford, N. Y. Academy. Sept. 6, 1865, she was married to Alfred N. Beadle. To them six children were born, three sons and three daughters[;] only the daughters are now living. She united with the Congregational church in this village some years ago and always remained in connection with her first church society. In 1885, with her family, she removed to Oswego, where she resided until her death . . . The deepest sympathy of this entire community goes out to the sorrowing husband and daughters." Alfred and Mary are buried in Evergreen Cemetery, Orwell.

John N. Beadle – Co. K
b. June 7, 1841 Orwell, NY
d. February 12, 1881 Buffalo, Erie, NY
m1. Mary Clark (1847-*ca.* 1875) *ca.* 1865
m2. Amelia "Millie" A. Gibson (1843-September 28, 1928) March 2, 1876

NOTE: The son of Henry (1810-1888) and Calista Reynolds Beadle (1807-1885), John said he was an engineer when he enlisted. He mustered out with the regiment on June 7, 1865. A note in *The Town Clerks' Registers* says that he was present at the surrender of General Robert E. Lee. Mary, 18, was living with John's parents in 1865. Her exact DOD and gravesite are unknown. On the 1875 New York census John was enumerated as a married man living with his parents. Mary was not a member of the household. John is buried in Evergreen Cemetery, Orwell. A large stone records his death as 1880 while a smaller one gives the correct date of 1881. Amelia, who also died in Buffalo, is buried in Elmlawn Cemetery, Kenmore, Erie, NY.

Orange Beardsley – Co. C
b. April 11, 1825 Hounsfield, Jefferson, NY
d. May 23, 1864 5th Army Corps Hospital, VA
m. Sarah "Sally" M. Westcott (April 21, 1828-November 7, 1911) February 27, 1847

NOTE: Orange, son of Chauncey (1796-1875) and Nancy Smedley Beardsley (1802-1882), had previously served in the 10th NY ART. He was fatally wounded at North Anna River, VA, on May 22, 1864, his "cranial bone" having been fractured. An interesting death notice was published in *The Mexico Independent* September 15, 1864: "Died – At Field Hospital, Va., May 24, from wounds received in the battle of North Anna, on the 23d of May, Orange Beardsley, aged 39 years,1 month and 13 days. He was a private in Co. C., 147th regiment. Dearest husband, thou hast left us,/Here thy loss we deeply feel;/ But 'tis God that has bereft us,/He can all our sorrows heal." Sally, the mother of ten children, died after suffering a stroke in Burnes, Shiawassee, MI. She is buried in Montrose, Genesee, MI. Orange's brother, Isaac Hungerford Beardsley (1838-1912), also served in the 10th NY ART.

George C. Beckwith – Co. C

b. September 11, 1839 Oneida County, NY

d. *post* 1865 ?

m. ?

NOTE: The 1865 New York census shows George C. Beckwith, currently in the Army, residing in Williamstown, NY with his adopted father, Joseph F. Beckwith, aged 68, and a widower whose wife, according to the 1850 census, had been Diana _____ (1810-?). She was probably George's mother. No other document can be found for either George or Joseph after the 1865 enumeration.

Ezra Marshall Bedell – Co. H

b. October 22, 1842 Constantia, NY

d. May 4, 1891 Soldiers' and Sailors' Home, Grand Island, Hall, NE

m. Florinda J. Bingham (April 6, 1847-December 28, 1936) November 7, 1867

NOTE: Bedell's parents were Richard (1815-1867) and Elizabeth Dickinson Bedell (1816-1891). He was captured at Gettysburg and paroled at an unknown date, mustering out with the regiment on June 7, 1865 near Washington, DC. Ezra and Florinda were married in McLean, IL and were the parents of at least six children, the youngest, Roger, born in 1886. Ezra was buried in Grand Island Cemetery. Florinda married Andrew Jackson Britton (February 1850-January 2, 1924) in 1892. When he died she applied for a pension as a "remarried widow." Florinda was 90 years old when she died. According to an obituary published in *The Miami Daily News-Record* December 29, 1936, 1, she had lived in Miami for "the greater part of her life" and was considered a pioneer in the area. She was a member of Holiness Church. She and Andrew are buried in the GAR Cemetery, Miami, Ottawa, OK. A brother, Adelbert Bedell (1847-1919), served in Co. F, 189th Regiment.

Charles Wheaton Beers – Co. D

b. July 14, 1831 Cayuga County, NY

d. February 20, 1908 Bellevue, Eaton, MI

m. Sarah Ann Ida Peckham (May 2, 1830-December 9, 1919) April 7, 1852

NOTE: Charles, son of John Wesley (1806-1884) and Eliza Ann Leverich Beers (1811-1894), was a butcher when he enlisted. He was a subject in *The Past and Present of Eaton County,* 187-191, which is excerpted here: "Charles W. Beers . . . was reared on the old homestead farm, in New York state, and there received a common-school education. In 1851 he came to Eaton county, working on a farm in Bellevue township one summer and then returning to New York where he was shortly afterward married. He then engaged in farming in Oswego county . . . also doing a butchering business, operating a meat wagon in the farming community . . . and being successful in his efforts. In May, 1862, responding to President Lincoln's second call for volunteers, he enlisted in Company D, One Hundred and Forty-seventh New York Infantry, and he served three years . . . He was assigned to detail service and never took part in any battles. He passed two weeks in the hospital at Belle Plaines, Va., where he witnessed the death of several hundred soldiers. At the battle of Gettysburg and in the engagement at Seminary Hill he was on duty as driver of a forage wagon. He was with his command within twelve miles of Appomattox at the time of Lee's surrender . . . Mr. Beers left his wife and four small children to go forth in his country's service, and he made a record of which he may be proud, having done the duty assigned him and having seen his full share of the horrors and hardships of war, even though he was not a participant in the great battles waged about him. After the war he returned to his home in New York, having duly received his honorable discharge. His parents had removed to Eaton county, Michigan, in 1853 . . . and they expressed an earnest desire that he should also bring his family here. He accordingly sold his property in New York and removed to Eaton county, arriving in August, 1865. He purchased forty acres of his father's old homestead and a tract of one hundred and twenty acres on the opposite side of the road. He erected a good frame house and barns, set out a large orchard and otherwise improved his land, continuing to reside there until 1877, when he moved to the village of Bellevue, where he opened a meat market, continuing to be identified with this line of enterprise until 1901, when he virtually retired, buying a small piece of land south of the village, and here having an attractive home. He raised some crops each year, preferring not to be idle, and he is held in high esteem in the community, having made the record of a reliable business man and upright citizen. He has been identified with the Republican party from the time of its organization, is affiliated with the Grand Army of the Republic and the Independent order of Odd Fellows, and both he and his wife are zealous members of the Methodist Episcopal church, with which they have been identified from their youthful days. April 7, 1852, Mr. Beers was united in marriage to Miss Sarah A. Peckham, who was born in Hannibal, Oswego county, New York, May 2, 1830, being a daughter of David and Polly (Potter) Peckham . . . ." Charles was appointed postmaster in Moorland, Eaton, MI on February 14, 1888. His death certificate reveals he died of influenza with heart disease and Bright's disease as contributing factors. Sarah was the mother of five, all of whom were living in 1900. Her COD was "old age." She and Charles are buried in Bellevue Cemetery, Bellevue, MI. Charles' brother, Josiah Luther (1835-June 6, 1864), was a member of Co. E, 6th MI Infantry. He died at Andersonville. Sarah's brother, Isaac Hiram Peckham (1828-1894), was a captain in Co. F, 110th Regiment.

Chester Sanford Belknap – Co. H

b. December 4, 1831 Frankfort, Herkimer, NY

d. November 2, 1920 Valley City, Barnes, ND

m. Mariah "Marie" Eckert (1835-December 22, 1919) 1851

NOTE: Charles was the son of Oran (1802-1866) and Nancy Kelch Belknap (1810-*ante* 1850). He was discharged for "disability" on September 12, 1863 after spending three months in Fairfax Seminary Hospital, VA. He and Mariah were the parents of nine children. Mariah died in Austin, Mower, MN. When Chester died, his body was shipped to Minnesota and he was buried with his wife in Greenwood Cemetery, Glenville, Freeborn, MN.

Dexter D. Belknap – Co. K

b. March 4, 1825 Brattleboro, Windham, VT

d. September 21, 1894 Boston, Middlesex, MA

m1. Mary Coleman (July 6, 1840-October 12, 1862) June 10, 1858

m2. Sarah J. "Jennie" Girdler (1839-May 28, 1915) January 23, 1868

NOTE: Dexter was the son of Cyrus (1799-1859) and Sally Lawton Belknap (1800-1890). He deserted the regiment on January 12, 1863 near Falmouth, VA but returned September 7, 1864. A general court martial sentenced him to forfeit all pay and make up the lost time. As a result, he was transferred to Co. I, 91st Regiment on June 5, 1865 and mustered out on July 3rd near Washington, DC. In later life he was a cement manufacturer. He and Sarah lived in Louisville, KY and, according to *The Louisville Courier-Journal* September 22, 1894, 1, he was on a business trip to Boston when he died. COD was "paralysis of the brain." Sarah married Americus Whedon (July 30, 1840-October 18, 1921) on August 24, 1907 as his third wife. When she died *The Madison Courier* May 27, 1915 reprinted an obituary originally appearing in *The Louisville Times*: "News of the death of his sister, Mrs. Jennie Belknap Whedon, in Washington this morning was received by Louis Girdler, of 113 East Front street, Jeffersonville. The telegram said that the body will reach Louisville Friday morning on the C. & O. train at 11 o'clock for interment in Cave Hill cemetery by the side of her first husband, Dexter Belknap, who died twenty-five years ago. Mrs. Whedon had no children, but is survived by Mrs. W. O. Bonnie, a step-daughter. Mrs. Whedon was the wife of Americus Whedon. She was seventy-six years old and was born in Marblehead, Mass. She resided in Louisville until eight years ago, when she moved to Washington to take up her residence there. She was well known in Louisville, and her death is mourned by many friends." Americus is also buried in Cave Hill Cemetery.

John Milton Belknap – Co. H

b. 1842 West Monroe, NY

d. April 30, 1915 Brewerton, Onondaga, NY

m. Amanda Landers (August 1848- February 19, 1914) 1868

NOTE: John, son of Oran and Rhoda Phillips Belknap (1809-*ante* 1855), was Dexter's half-brother. He spent three months in Finley Hospital suffering from typhoid fever and was finally discharged on September 26, 1864 for a disability of "lung disease." He was a member of William Pullen Post No. 595 GAR, Brewerton. John died of pneumonia and eight days later his son, Albert, died of the same disease. John and Amanda, who died "after an illness of less than a week," are buried in Hillside Memorial Park and Cemetery, Central Square, NY.

Isaac L. Bentley – Co. C

b. October 24, 1837 Trenton Falls, Oneida, NY

d. August 28, 1913 Albion, NY

m. Dora A. Thompson (February 7, 1856-August 17, 1924) April 7, 1874

NOTE: Isaac, son of William (1810-1883) and Roxy Warren Bentley (1806-1885), originally enlisted in the 110th Regiment. According to *The Town Clerks' Registers*, his wound was a "ball through the left thigh." In 1910 Isaac claimed to be a widower although Dora was still living. His obituary appeared in *The Pulaski Democrat* September 3, 1913, 4: "Isaac Llewellen [*sic*] Bentley was born in Oneida County seventy-six years ago. He came to the town of Albion when a young man with his parents on the Pineville road about four miles east of this village. When the war broke out he enlisted in the 147th regiment, Co. C and served his country in the heat of the great struggle. He came back to Pineville and has resided there since. Though his health was not the best for some time past he was about up to a week before his death which occurred Thursday night. He was a member of Post E. L. Bentley of Altmar, named for his brother, who died in the army. The funeral was held at the Pineville church, Sunday afternoon, Rev. T. J. Wheeler, of Fernwood, officiating . . . ." Dora's obituary appeared in *The Pulaski Democrat* on August 20, 1924, 4: "Mrs. Dora Thompson Bentley, 68, widow of Isaac Bentley, died Sunday at her home following an illness of about three weeks. She had been passing some time at Lowville with her son, Samuel J. Bentley, and was taken ill while there and returned to her home here. Mrs. Bentley was a native of Oswego county. She was born February 7, 1856, in the town of Albion but had passed nearly all her life in this vicinity . . . ." Isaac and Dora are buried in Pineville Cemetery, Richland, NY. A brother, Elisha L Bentley (1844-1864), for whom GAR Post #265 in Altmar, NY was named, was killed at Cold Harbor, VA on June 3, 1864. He was a member of Co. K, 14th NY HA.

Throop Hazeltine Bentley – Co. B
b. 1833 Washington County, NY
d. May 5, 1864 Wilderness, VA
m. ------

NOTE: Little is known about this soldier. His father was James Bentley (1775-1841). His mother, Lydia N. Dunham (1794-1890), outlived three husbands: John Tibbets (1790-1830); Bentley; and William Cain (1794-1881). In 1850 and 1855 Throop was living in Oswego City with his half-brother John Tibbets (1821-December 1910). He was KIA and his body was apparently buried on the battlefield. When Lydia died *The Oswego Daily Times* November 19, 1890 published the following: "The death of Mrs. Lydia N. Cain took place at the residence of her daughter, Mrs. L. W. Drury at Martville, Cayuga Co., on Saturday last. Mrs. Cain has reached the ripe age of 94. Her surviving children are John H. Tibbits [*sic*] of this city, Mrs. Drury of Martville and Mrs. A. Reed of Greene Lodge, Michigan. Mrs. Cain was a highly estimable lady and had many friends in Oswego."

Josiah F. Benton – Co. H
b. December 1836 Palermo, NY
d. January 1, 1911 Hastings, NY
m1. Hannah Gregory (1842-July 11, 1892) *ca.* 1866
m2. Catherine _____ Bristol (April 1847-*ante* 1910) 1893
m3. Harriet Holcomb Gard (1843-January 30, 1929) October 12, 1910

NOTE: Josiah, son of John W. (1819-?) and Welthey Widger Benton (?-post 1836), was wounded at the battle of Gettysburg on July 1, 1863 and in 1890 said he had had "one arm shot off." In 1900 he and Catherine had been married seven years. Living with them was her son DeForest Bristol (December 1883-September 14, 1962) by William J. Bristol (1816-1892). Catherine had been his second wife. Harriet was the daughter of Edward and Polly Church Holcomb. Her first husband was John Gard (1832-?). On February 10, 1914 she married James K. Bates (1841-December 30, 1928) from Graling, MI as his third wife. Born in England, he was 73 years of age. He and Harriet died in Syracuse, NY. Josiah and Hannah are buried in Hillside Memorial Cemetery and Park, Central Square, NY. Graves for Catherine and Harriet have not been located.

John Bergin – Co. I
b. 1829 Ireland
d. ?
m. ?

NOTE: Bergin said he was a laborer on his muster roll card. He was discharged on May 4, 1863 for "disability" and appears to have returned to Oswego since he is listed in the 1864 *Oswego City Directory.* Nothing can be documented after that year. Research is hampered by the many men with his name.

Horatio N. Berry – Co. H
b. April 1841 Black River, Lorain, OH
d. October 13, 1914 Great Valley, Cattaraugus, NY
m. Catherine M. _____ (September 1844-June 3, 1930) 1884

NOTE: Berry was the son of Philemon (1816-1888) and Christiana Dickinson Berry (1815-*post* 1900). He was a musician. For part of 1863 he was on detached duty with the Ambulance Corps. On February 27, 1865 he was transferred to the 3rd Brigade Band. He and Catherine are buried in Holy Cross Cemetery, Ellicottville, Cattaraugus, NY.

James N. Berry – Co. C
b. November 1834 Erie County, OH
d. December 18, 1923 Crestline, Crawford, OH
m. Margaret C. Stevens (1842-October 25, 1919) 1866

NOTE: James N. Berry was an alias for William W. DeGaugh, son of Joseph (1806-1904) and Maria Headley Burdue DeGaugh (1813-1860). He enlisted in the 147th Regiment in Albion, NY and transferred to Battery L, 1st ART on December 28, 1863. His COD was apoplexy. He and Margaret are buried in Edwards Grove Cemetery, Greenwich, Huron, OH. His DOD, which is not given on the gravestone, was found on his pension card. Joseph DeGaugh was a member of Co. D, 17th PA Cavalry. He is buried in Leavenworth National Cemetery.

William Wakeland Berry – Co. H
b. June 1836 Cattaraugus County, NY
d. July 4, 1866 Sugartown, Cattaraugus, NY
m. ------

NOTE: William and Horatio were brothers. Like Horatio he was a musician and transferred to the 3rd Brigade Band on March 1, 1863 but returned to the regiment in June. He was sent to hospital on July 17, 1863 and did not return to the 147th until March 1864. On August 12, 1864 he was admitted to City Point Hospital, VA and then to Whitehall Hospital in Philadelphia, PA where he was discharged on May 18, 1865. Although his disability is not stated it apparently was severe enough that he lived only a little over a year after returning home. William is buried in Sugartown Cemetery with his parents. In 1872 his mother Christiana applied for and received a pension.

John Bettinger – Co. F
b. December 10, 1840 Mexico, NY
d. January 28, 1890 East Syracuse, Onondaga, NY
m. Permilia C. Bohannon Mosher (November 24, 1836-May 30, 1915) December 25, 1865

NOTE: John, son of John (1811-*post* 1865) and Harriet Bettinger (1812-*ante* 1865), was erroneously listed as "killed in action" on July 1, 1863 at Gettysburg, though it would have been no surprise had he succumbed. According to a deposition given by Permilia on May 13, 1890, John "was wounded six times at the battle of Gettysburg July 1, 1863, through the body, through the head (losing one eye) through the left shoulder, three times in the left arm . . . ." His COD was "la grippe" which he had contracted three weeks previous to his demise. Permilia had formerly been married to Warren W. Mosher of Co. K 21st Wisconsin Infantry who was killed at Perryville, KY on October 8, 1862, having been mustered in on September 5, 1862. She had two sons, George (1858-?), and Adelbert (1860-?) by him. By Bettinger she had two children, William (1876-*post* 1915), and Grace (1885-*ante* 1915). When Will was four years old he caught his foot in the railroad ties and when the other children attempted to pull him out of the way of an approaching train his foot was fractured so badly that much of it had to be amputated. John, who ran a hotel in Syracuse, had received a pension since 1864 but when he died he left Permilia practically penniless. The estate appraiser wrote that the only things of value were a few pieces of furniture, worth no more than $50. Permilia applied for pensions for both herself and Will who was crippled as a result of the accident. For five years she fought the government on Will's behalf and was finally told that since he was not "insane, idiotic, or otherwise permanently helpless" he did not qualify for a pension. She struggled another five years for herself but was rebuffed each time on the grounds that John's death was not "war-related." In 1901 she tried another tactic. As a remarried widow she now was eligible to claim her first husband's pension and this application was successful. Until she died she received $12.00 a month. She wrote several heart-rending letters to various government officials, including President Wilson, begging for an increase but all her pleas fell on deaf ears. John is buried in Oakwood Cemetery, Syracuse. He had been a member of Philip Eckel Post No. 596 GAR and a member of Central City Commandery, KT. Permilia is buried in Pulaski Village Cemetery.

Samuel J. Beyet – Co. H
b. June 1835 Montreal, Canada
d. April 9, 1910 Chicago, Cook, Il
m. Edmere Maria Philips (November 1848-September 30, 1901) 1863

NOTE: Beyet, whose parents were Joseph (1803-1894) and Marie Anne Dion Beyet (1809-1846), was discharged from the army for "disability" in Washington, DC at an unknown date. His disability must have been severe since he applied for a pension on September 29, 1863. Samuel and Edmere are buried in Calvary Cemetery, Evanston, Cook, IL.

Isaac Smith Bickley – Co. K
b. February 14, 1832 Victory, Cayuga, NY
d. January 9, 1915 Kansas City, Jackson, MO
m1. Octavia Guyant (1837-July 25, 1909) *ca.* 1853
m2. Anna Telfer (1848-January 31, 1917) 1876

NOTE: Isaac, son of John (1825-1907) and Sallie Newell Bickley (1825-*post* 1880), has been difficult to trace, to say the least, because of conflicting information. His DOB varies. I use the one on his death certificate. It appears he was taken prisoner at Gettysburg and sent to Libby Prison. According to his muster roll card he was discharged from the army on January 16, 1864 at Central Park Hospital, New York City. He is listed twice on *The Town Clerks' Registers*, one entry containing no information, the other saying he was exchanged on February 16, 1864 and discharged in Syracuse, NY on August 28, 1865. On February 9, 1865 he enrolled in Co. D, 193rd Regiment but deserted on May 5th. He did not apply for a pension until December 22, 1877. Two women claimed to be his wives and perhaps there was a third. On the 1855 New York State census he was married to Freelove, aged 23, and was the father of a daughter, Julia, aged nine months. By 1860 he was married to Octavia, 22, and the father of Augustus, 3, and Lydia J., seven months old. The couple was listed on the 1870 census for Oswego City but by 1874 Isaac had left for Missouri. Only Octavia and Augustus appeared in the city directory and on the 1875 New York census. If correct, he married Anna Telfer in 1876 without bothering to obtain a divorce from Octavia. By 1880 Octavia was calling herself a widow. Strangely enough, in 1892 she applied for Isaac's pension. Perhaps she thought he was dead. She did not receive it because she was told he was still very much alive. Octavia lived with Augustus, who worked on the railroad, and his family in Buffalo. She is buried in Forest Lawn Cemetery, Buffalo. In 1910 Anna claimed to have been married three times but I have not found any previous husbands. After Isaac's death in 1915 she applied for a widow's pension which she apparently did not receive. Perhaps she could not prove she and Isaac were married. It is also possible she died before the process was completed. Anna's COD was chronic nephritis and cirrhosis of the liver. She and Isaac, who died of chronic bronchitis, are buried in Elmwood Cemetery, Kansas City.

Celestin Bircklee – Co. G

b. 1819 Germany

d. July 1, 1863 Gettysburg, Adams, PA

m. ?

NOTE: According to his muster roll card, Celestin was a cooper who enlisted in the 147th in Oswego City. He was killed in action. There are no other available documents and even his burial site seems to be unknown.

John Henry Blowers – Co. H

b. July 1845 Marshall, Oneida, NY

d. May 9, 1881 Towanda, Bradford, PA

m. Mary Alice Bowman (February 1849-1936) *ca.* 1877

NOTE: John, whose parents were Barton (1814-1886) and Elisabeth Santos Blowers (1814-1879), was the brother of Barton (1843-1864) and Alfred (1839-1863), both of whom served in the 110th Regiment and died in service. He was a member of Kellogg Post No. 554 GAR, Monroeton, PA. He and Mary Alice were the parents of Ralph (1879-?) and Susan (1880-?). The couple is buried in Cole Cemetery, Monroeton, Bradford, PA.

James Boady – Co. I

b. 1840 Canada West

d. December 23, 1862 Hospital at Aquia Creek, VA

m. ------

NOTE: James, a painter by occupation, was the son of William and Elizabeth Spark Boady. According to *Deaths of Volunteers* his COD was "inflammation of the lungs." His entry in *The Town Clerks' Registers* says he died from disease and "his remains [were] buried there."

Patrick Bond – Co. D

b. March 17, 1832 Ireland

d. May 20, 1922 Soldiers' and Sailors' Home, Grand Rapid, Kent, MI

m. Angelina Buske (August 1, 1841-March 1, 1913) 1855

NOTE: Bond's DOB varies. I use that contained in his death certificate. He mustered out with the regiment on June 7, 1865. Patrick's COD was "general arterio-sclerosis." According to his death certificate, he was 90 years, one month, and 3 days old when he died. Angelina's death certificate says she was a chronic alcoholic who froze to death while intoxicated. He and Angelina are buried in the Grand Rapids Veterans' Home Cemetery.

Narcisse Bondeau – Co. A

b. 1818 France

d. September 29, 1898 Fife Lake, Grand Traverse, MI

m. Euphrosine Gauthier (June 9, 1816-February 20, 1898) ?

NOTE: Narcisse and Euphrosine were both tailors. He was transferred from active duty to the VRC at some unknown date and mustered out on July 10, 1865. He belonged to Lt. Frank Fowler Post No. 286 GAR at Fife Lake. Euphrosine, born in Canada, was the mother of five children. Her COD was influenza. Both are buried in Saint Aloysius Catholic Cemetery, Fife Lake, MI.

Chauncey H. Booth – Co. D

b. 1835 Oswego County, NY

d. June 16, 1912 Pulaski, NY

m1. Adelia Huntington (1835-1889) *ca.* 1866

m2. Leora Enos (1855-August 16, 1936) 1898

NOTE: Chauncey, a miller, was captured at Gettysburg on July 1, 1863 and paroled at an unknown date. He was subsequently transferred to the VRC and discharged from service at Rochester, NY on July 24, 1865. He was a member of J. B. Butler Post No. 111 GAR and upon his death the post published the following memorial in *The Pulaski Democrat* July 3, 1912, 5: "The officers and members of J. B. Butler Post, No. 111, G.A.R., are called upon to mourn the death of another comrade, Chauncey H. Booth, who died June 16, 1912. He enlisted in 1862 in the 147th N.Y. Vols., and served till the close of the war. He was a respected member of this Post and we will miss him at our meetings . . . ." Leora's death was announced in *The Oswego Palladium-Times* August 17, 1936, 7: "Mrs. Leora E. Booth, 81, former resident of Adams, N.Y., died early Sunday morning at the home of her step-son, Clarence Booth . . . where she had resided for three years. Mrs. Booth suffered a stroke a week ago and her condition had since been critical. She was a member of the Baptist church at Adams . . . ." Chauncey, Adelia, and Leora are all buried in Maple View Cemetery, Mexico, NY.

Henry Bougie – Co. A

b. 1839 Canada East

d. December 1, 1879 Oswego City, NY

m. Eliza Hickey (1848-October 21, 1893) *ca.* 1867

NOTE: Henry's surname was variously spelled. I use that on his gravestone in Rural Cemetery, Oswego Town, NY. Eliza married Abraham Ladue (December 1839-*post* 1900) *ca.* 1880 since her first child by him, George, was born in 1881. Eliza's grave has not been located.

Peter Bowman – Co. H

b. March 15, 1833 Herkimer County, NY

d. November 9, 1908 North Syracuse, Onondaga, NY

m. Demeris Kezia Rhody West (April 2, 1835-January 29, 1907) January 24, 1857

NOTE: Bowman was transferred to the VRC on September 26, 1863. In 1890 he said his disability was "spinal 25 years." Peter's death was announced in *The Oswego Palladium* November 14, 1908, 1. He and Kezia are buried in West Monroe Cemetery. Peter's parents were Adam (1801-1876) and Lana Piper Bowman (1805-*post* 1875).

George W. Box – Co. C

b. 1844 Pulaski, NY

d. September 22, 1863 1st Division AC Hospital, Culpepper, VA

m. ------

NOTE: Box initially enlisted in the 110th Regiment. His DOD varies, depending on the source. One FAG entry claims he died on September 20, 1863. His muster roll card states he died September 22, 1863 "at camp in the field." *The Town Clerks' Registers* entry shows a date of September 23, 1863. *The Registers of Officers and Enlisted Men* and *Deaths of Volunteers* both provide a date of September 27, 1863. This is probably correct since his entry in the Burial Registers says he was buried in Alexandria National Cemetery on September 30, 1863. The entry also says that the body was removed on December 28, 1863. If accurate, he is buried in Pulaski Village Cemetery with his father John (1807-1866) and his mother Frances (1810-1846). Another FAG entry says he died on January 4, 1864 but it is more likely this was the date he was buried in Pulaski.

John F. Box – Co. A

b. January 25, 1838 Pulaski, NY

d. May 21, 1899 Pulaski, NY

m. Helen "Nellie" Munger (1838-October 11, 1922) *ca.* 1865

NOTE: John and George Box were brothers. John was wounded on July 3, 1863 and lost an arm. His obituary, published in *The Sandy Creek News* May 25, 1899, offers an interesting synopsis of his life: "John F. Box, one of the leading citizens of Pulaski died at his home in that village last Sunday afternoon. Mr. Box was born in that village sixty-two years ago. At the age of twenty-five he responded to the call of his country for volunteers to help put down the rebellion and went out with the 147th N.Y. Infantry. He was a good soldier and earned promotion until he reached the rank of first lieutenant. During the third day at the battle of Gettysburg he was shot in the left arm and the member was removed close to the shoulder[;] thus in his young manhood he sustained an injury which was indeed hard to bear, yet with the courage of his nature he came home and established himself in the drug business and has built up a trade which is one of the most important commercial enterprises in this part of the county. He married Miss Helen Munger, who with the three sons, Dr. Frank A., George M. and John F. Jr., survive [sic] him . . . ." An obituary appearing in *The Oswego Daily Palladium* May 22, 1899, 6 revealed he had suffered from diabetes for nearly ten years and had died from complications of that disease. Box was a member of J. B. Butler Post No. 111 GAR. When Helen died, *The Pulaski Democrat* October 18, 1922, 4 printed the following: "Mrs. Helen M. Box, who has been ill for some time died Wednesday noon, October 11. Mrs. Box was born in this village eighty-one years ago and has spent her life here. She was widow of John F. Box who died several years ago. Mrs. Box was a member of St. James Episcopal church and she was the first president of J. B. Butler W. R. C. She is survived by two sons, Mr. George M. Box, of Pulaski and Dr. John F. Box, of Rome . . . ." John and Helen are buried in Pulaski Village Cemetery.

William Boyce – Co. K

b. 1835 Roscommon County, Ireland
d. June 26, 1884 Oswego City, NY
m. Mary Elizabeth Riley (1836-July 10, 1903) *ca.* 1856

NOTE: Boyce, the son of Michael (?-?) and Bridget O'Connor Boyce (?-?), immigrated to the United States in 1856. When he died all former members of the 147th Regiment were encouraged to attend his funeral. William is buried in St. Paul's Cemetery, Oswego City. He and Mary were the parents of James (1859-October 16, 1939) and Mary Catherine (May 18, 1857-April 30, 1927). When James applied for a passport in 1921 he was living in Albuquerque, Bernalillo, NM. He stated he had left Oswego in 1886. In fact, he, Mary, and Catherine, who had married Edward McGuire (1857-1938), all moved west. With the exception of Edward, who is buried in St. Paul's Cemetery, Oswego, they are buried in Santa Barbara Section of Mount Calvary Cemetery, Albuquerque.

Giles S. Bradley – Co. D

b. June 10, 1834 Volney, NY
d. February 5, 1909 Indianapolis, Marion, IN
m1. Cornelia Oliver (1835-*post* 1875) *ca.* 1859
m2. Zeruah C. Bailey (1849-July 8, 1895) 1884

NOTE: Giles, son of Eli (1796-*post* 1855) and Sally Bradley (1801-*post* 1855), was discharged from the 147th on November 28, 1862 for "disability." He subsequently enlisted in Co. A, 24th NY Cavalry on December 18, 1863 and was mustered out on May 27, 1865. Bradley was married when he joined the 147th but alleged in later years that he divorced Cornelia on May 18, 1868 in DeKalb County, IN. He and Zeruah had no children but they adopted a daughter, Lulu Pearl (1873-1936). After Zeruah died of a brain tumor, Lulu cared for her father until his death. In 1908, a man named Walter Bradley visited Giles and alleged he was his son. The old man rejected him, asserting that he and Cornelia had no children when he left New York State. The records prove otherwise. On the 1870 census Cornelia Bradley was living with her father, Caleb Oliver, in Volney. One of the members of the household was Walter Bradley, aged 10. Giles was so worried that Walter would attempt to claim part of his substantial estate, valued at $40,000-50,000, that he specified in a codicil that Lulu was his sole heir. According to an article in *The Indianapolis News* February 9, 1909, 4, "The codicil further said that the adopted daughter had cared for him for thirteen years, twelve of which he had been an invalid, and that her untiring attention had been given him, although the task 'was, no doubt, arduous, repulsive and, at times, discouraging.' For this, in small return for her many acts of kindness, he desired to leave what little happiness fortune could bring. Miss Bradley became Mrs. Drummond several years ago and her husband is now dead. At the time of her marriage she received a large part of the estate, the remainder of which is now willed to her." Lulu had married Robert Drummond (1871-August 20, 1900) on July 16, 1900. They were on their honeymoon when he unexpectedly died a month later. Bradley's obituary in *The Indianapolis Star* February 6, 1909, 10 details his career in real estate: "Giles S. Bradley, 74 years old, died at 5 o'clock yesterday afternoon of a complication of diseases at his residence, 2238 College avenue. He had been in feeble health for fifteen years and had been unable to leave his home for four years. For more than twenty-five years Bradley was active in the real estate business. He was a member of the firm of Bradley & Denny, which now bears the name Denny & Denny. He laid out various additions and at one time owned Norwood. He purchased ground on the outskirts of the city and did not deal in down-town property. He retired fifteen years ago, when his health began to fail. Relatives say his illness had its beginning in the civil war and his health gradually failed as a result of hardships experienced in service . . . ." His official COD was chronic cystitis, with "years of chronic asthma" listed as a contributing factor. Giles, Zeruah, Lulu, and Robert Drummond are all buried in Crown Hill Cemetery, Indianapolis. Cornelia disappears after the 1875 New York census and may have remarried. Walter died in St. Petersburg, Pinellas, FL on July 22, 1943 after a long and successful career in contracting. A lengthy obituary appeared in *The Oswego Palladium-Times* July 28, 1943, 8. He and his two wives are buried in Mt. Adnah Cemetery, Fulton.

Louis Brassard, Jr. – Co. A

b. January 1843 Canada East

d. January 1910 Champlain, Clinton, NY

m1. Elizabeth LaFontaine (1849-August 20, 1879) *ca.* 1868

m2. Laura Petrie (October 28, 1862-April 26, 1951) 1884

NOTE: Louis' surname was variously spelled. I use that found on Elizabeth's gravestone. He originally enlisted in the 110th but was sent to the 147th. He was a shoemaker by trade. He was a member of Angell Post No. 411 GAR, located at Mooers, NY and a member of Champlain Lodge #237 F & A M. Elizabeth was buried in Old St. Mary's Cemetery, Champlain. Louis was eulogized in *The Plattsburgh Sentinel* January 28, 1928: ". . . At a special meeting, Tuesday evening, the village board unanimously adopted the following resolution: 'Whereas, the late Louis Brassard, who was elected a village trustee in the spring of the year 1894 and has since faithfully served on this board, constantly working for the greatest benefit of the people and gratuitously devoting a large part of his time for the advancement of public works, be it Resolved, that the members of the village board deeply feel the loss of this useful servant of the people and are sharing in the general sorrow at the death of this most respected and beloved citizen. That a vote of sympathy be given to the family of the deceased and a copy of this resolution be sent them and also to the Plattsburgh Sentinel for publication.' Mr. Brassard was one of the twenty-five citizens, many of whom are now dead, who signed the application for incorporating the village of Champlain, August 14, 1873. He enlisted at the age of nineteen, in Oswego where he was working at his trade of a shoemaker, in 1861 [*sic*] and remained in the army three years, taking part in many battles of the Civil War, finally being made prisoner. He was sent to the Andersonville camp, Georgia, where he contracted the disease which caused him so much suffering and brought his relatively early death. Among the thirty friends who marched in procession at the funeral Thursday of last week and accompanied the remains to the cemetery, were several veterans of the Civil War and representatives of the Angell Post, of Mooers . . . ." I have found no evidence that Louis spent time in Andersonville or any other POW camp. Laura's COD was pneumonia. She and Louis are buried in Prospect Hill Cemetery, Champlain.

James S. Brayton – Co. H

b. 1844 Herkimer County, NY

d. April 7, 1888 Union County, OR

m. Barbara Smith (1857-October 20, 1930) *ca.* 1878

NOTE: James was the adopted son of Moses (1802-January 16, 1877) and Margaret Mary Steele Crimm (1805-1872). He mustered out with the regiment on June 7,

1865. On the 1880 census for Indian Valley, Union, OR, Brayton and Barbara had a one year old daughter, Estella. In 1881 they became the parents of Albert (January 22, 1881-February 26, 1957). James served as postmaster of Elk Flat, Union, OR in the 1880s. Barbara married Jacob Groth (1846-?) on April 13, 1890. They were the parents of a daughter, Jessie (October 22, 1891-April 17, 1965). By 1910 Barbara, Jessie, and Albert were living in Joseph, Wallowa, OR. Barbara said she was divorced. The family lived in Gooding, ID in 1920 and in Kern County, CA in 1930. James Brayton is buried in Highland Cemetery, Union County, OR. Barbara's gravesite has not been located.

George Wales Briggs – Co. G

b. December 1840 Oswego, NY
d. November 4, 1913 Lee Memorial Hospital, Fulton, NY
m. Eunice E. Morse (1848-1924) February 12, 1867

NOTE: George, son of Gardner (1809-1890) and Harriet A. Wales Briggs (1819-1890), deserted the regiment on January 5, 1863 and did not return until June 13, 1864. An interesting article appeared in *The Oswego Daily Palladium* June 20, 1864: "The Rochester *Union* of Saturday says that Geo. Wales Briggs, a man who was brought to that city in a buggy, from Oswego, to go to Canada, has been arrested as a deserter. His father and mother are also under arrest for having aided him to desert." He was court-martialed and sentenced to a loss of all allowances. He forfeited $10 of his pay for eighteen months and was required to make up the time he was missing. On January 1, 1865 he was promoted to quarter-master sergeant. Although he was transferred to Co. D, 91st Regiment, he does not appear on *The Adjutant-General's Report* for that regiment. His pension index card shows no evidence that he ever served in the 91st. He died after being struck by a train, as was reported by *The Oswego Daily Palladium* November 4, 1913, 5: "G. Wales Briggs, who was thrown from his rig that was struck by the New York Central train which left Oswego at 10:45 o'clock yesterday, on the Battle Island crossing, died at four o'clock this morning in the Fulton hospital. The remains were taken in charge by undertaker John F. Dain, of this city, and removed to his home north of Fulton. Interment will be in Riverside cemetery. Mr. Briggs never fully recovered consciousness after the accident. His skull was fractured and his body was badly bruised. From the time he was taken to the hospital his physician, Dr. L. Fowler Joy, of Fulton, despaired of his recovery. Born in Volney seventy-three years ago, the son of the late Mr. and Mrs. Gardner Briggs, he was one of the best known residents of that town. He was a student at a commercial college in this city when the Civil War broke out and he enlisted as quartermaster sergeant of Company G, 149th [sic] New York State Volunteers, remaining three years in the service. Returning from the war he engaged in various public works and managed a line of boats on the Oswego canal until 1888, when he bought the Summit House at Seneca Hill. In that capacity he made many warm friends in Oswego who will learn with regret of his death. Several years ago Mr. Briggs sold the Summit House and retired to a farm near Battle Island, where he had since resided. He was a member of Fulton Grange and the Fulton Lodge of Odd Fellows . . . The accident that cost Mr. Briggs his life has aroused the people living in the vicinity of the Battle Island crossing to take steps to have it protected. The crossing is a blind one and the automobile clubs of this city and Fulton are to co-operate with the residents about there to see if protection can not be secured. A few years ago Jasper Brown was killed at the same crossing." Eunice, who was left with practically nothing when her husband died, sued the railroad for $10,000, charging negligence. She also secured a widow's pension. When she died she had a will and left an estate of $6,000 so it is possible she won her suit. She and George are buried in Riverside Cemetery, Scriba, as are George's parents.

Ira Blake Briggs – Co. E

b. February 26, 1824 Schodack, Rensselaer, NY
d. January 31, 1903 Boylston, NY
m. Catherine E. Goodrich (July 1833-March 8, 1902) October 1853

NOTE: Ira was the son of James Blake (1787-1854) and Bersheba Barrus Briggs (1808-1830). His POB is a matter of dispute. His obituary says he was born in Vermont and the 1855 New York census claims he was born in Herkimer County. His muster roll card, *Registers of Officers and Enlisted Men*, and the 1865 New York census all say he was born in Rensselaer County. His DOD is also disputed. His gravestone provides a date of January 29th but his obituary offers a date of January 31st, as does the New York State Death Index. His obituary was published in *The Sandy Creek News* February 12, 1903, 1: "Ira B. Briggs was born February 26, 1824 at Brattleboro, Vermont. His early life was spent in Danube, Herkimer County, N.Y. He was married in October 1853 to Catherine Goodrich of Lacona, who died March 8, 1902. He enlisted August, 1862 in the 147th N.Y. volunteers, was wounded in the battle of Gettysburg, but served his country faithfully until the close of the war. On Tuesday evening, January 27, after eating his supper as usual, he suddenly became unconscious and fell from his chair to the floor. Although he was conscious part of the time, he was unable to speak or take any nourishment but passed quietly away January 31 at 8 o'clock. The funeral was held at his late home February 3d, Rev. F. L. Knapp officiating. He leaves one sister, and five children to mourn the loss of a loving father and brother." Ira and Catherine are buried in Woodlawn Cemetery, Sandy Creek.

Jacob L. Briggs – Co. G
b. 1846 Volney, NY
d. March 22, 1893 Chicago, Cook, IL
m. Hattie Gale (1852-*post* 1910) *ca.* 1875

NOTE: Jacob, son of William (1820-1896) and Mary "Sally" Worden Briggs (1825-1891), lied about his age when he enlisted. He was discharged on April 10, 1863 but joined Co. L, 20th NY Cavalry on August 26, 1863 serving until July 3, 1865 when he was discharged at Manchester, VA. In 1880 he and Hattie were living in Middletown, Orange, NY with his parents. He was a member of Robson Post No. 5, Albert Lea, Freeborn, MN. His obituary was published in *The Middletown Times-Press* March 25, 1893, 3: "J. L. Briggs, a former well known conductor on the O. & W., died at Chicago, Wednesday, of this week. Mr. Briggs was in charge of trains 1 and 2, the mail trains on the middle division, for a long time. At the time of his death he was in the employ of the Chicago, Rock Island and Pacific railroad. Mr. Briggs was about 45 years of age. He was a son of William Briggs, the flagman at Wickham avenue. Mr. Briggs went to Chicago about 13 years ago. He leaves a wife and four children. The remains will arrive here tonight and the funeral will be held at his father's residence, No. 18 Beattie avenue, tomorrow. He was a member of the Masonic order and of the order of RR Conductors. All railroad men are invited to meet at the K. of H. hall at 1 o'clock tomorrow, to attend the funeral." Briggs is buried in Hillside Cemetery, Middletown. Hattie last appears on the 1910 census but her exact DOD has not been determined. She may have remarried.

Lansing Bristol – Cos. D, K
b. 1838 Granby, NY
d. February 6, 1865 Hatcher's Run, VA
m. ------

NOTE: The son of Elera Enoch (1810-1874) and Adah Brewer Bristol (1812-1887), Lansing survived all the battles fought by the 147th only to have his luck run out a mere two months before the war ended. He kept a still extant diary which contains interesting information on the day-to-day activities of a soldier. He was eulogized in an editorial in *The Oswego Commercial Advertiser* February 13, 1865: ". . . Among the fallen we are more than usually pained to find the name of Lieutenant Lansing Bristol, of Granby. We speak of Lieutenant Bristol because we have for years enjoyed his personal friendship. And his real worth, true patriotism, and unswerving devotion to the cause of his country, are personally known to us. Young Bristol was a teacher by profession, entered the service as a private, and was awarded a commission for his merit and bravery. He has served faithfully and with distinction through the career of the 147th, never flinching from duty, and had richly earned the reputation of a brave soldier and an accomplished officer. He was an estimable young man in all the relations of life, and his early loss will be alike sincerely mourned by the members of the regiment in which he served, and the large circle of acquaintances and friends in this county, by whom he was respected and beloved." His friends succeeded in having the body embalmed and sent home, as reported in *The Oswego Commercial Times* March 1, 1865: "The remains of Lieut. Bristol, of Company K, 147th Regiment, were brought to Fulton on Saturday last . . . He was a brave officer, and his death is greatly regretted by the officers and men of the regiment, as well as his numerous friends in this vicinity." He was buried in Granby Center Cemetery.

Darius Clark Broughton – Co. C

b. August 12, 1830 Hamden, Delaware, NY

d. February 4, 1913 Oswego City, NY

m. Bedee Ophelia Richardson (1833-October 22, 1915) 1852

NOTE: Darius was the son of John Urial (1792-1870) and Orial Barber Broughton (1796-1869). His life and career were summarized in an obituary appearing in *The Oswego Palladium* February 5, 1913: "Darius C. Broughton, one of the best known residents of the city, died at the home of his daughter, Mrs. S. H. Potter, 86 East Oneida street, yesterday. The end came peacefully while members of his family were at his bedside. Born in Delaware county, this State, August 12th, 1830, Mr. Broughton was a veteran of the Civil War, enlisting in Company C, 147th New York Volunteers, August, 1862, and being discharged for disability in a Philadelphia hospital January 3d, 1863. For over forty years Mr. Broughton has resided in this city and for fifty-two years he was in the railroad service. Mr. Broughton was for a number of years employed by the old Rome, Watertown & Ogdensburg Railroad Company at Richland and then he came to this city, where he had charge of the freight yards, going from the former to the O. & W. Company. He had a large acquaintance among railroad men. For three years he had been an invalid . . . ."

Darius Broughton worked for the railroad over 50 years. Although he and Bedee died in Oswego City they were buried in Evergreen Cemetery, Orwell.
Author's Collection

Bedee's death was announced in *The Sandy Creek News* October 28, 1915, 7: "Mrs. Bedee Richardson, widow of the late Darius C. Broughton, passed away Friday, October 22 at the home of her daughter, Mrs. S. H. Potter in Oswego, aged 82 years. She was a native of Richland and was the last surviving child of Azel W. Richardson, who for many years was a resident of the towns of Sandy Creek and Richland . . . She had resided in the city of Oswego for the past forty-three years and is survived by four children . . . ." Bedee had fallen on October 9th and dislocated her hip, an accident which contributed to her death. She and Darius are buried in Evergreen Cemetery, Orwell, NY.

Asa S. Brown – Co. C
b. December 30, 1830 Fairfield, Herkimer, NY
d. November 10, 1904 Sandy Creek, NY
m. Sylvina "Vina" Adelaide Johnson (February 9, 1841-July 28, 1916) December 2, 1856

NOTE: Asa was the son of Joseph (1794-1876) and Mary Green Brown (1796-1874). He was discharged from the service on December 29, 1863 for "disability" although in 1890 he claimed none. His obituary appeared in *The Mexico Independent* November 16, 1904: ". . . Asa S. Brown died at Sandy Creek, N.Y., Nov. 10, 1904, aged 74 years. The funeral was held Monday at the home of his daughter, Mrs. Woodrick, at Sandy Creek, Rev. M. D. Sill, pastor of the Methodist church here, officiating. The service at the grave was conducted by the [J. B. Butler] G.A.R. Post, of Pulaski, and the bearers were members of Melzar Richards Post, G.A.R., of this village . . . Mr. Brown had been in feeble health for many years; was a veteran of the Civil War and was highly respected and esteemed. The many friends of the family deeply sympathize with them in their bereavement." Sylvina's death was reported in *The Sandy Creek News* August 3, 1916: "Once more the angel of Death has entered our home and taken our dear mother. Last Friday morning at 4:50 a.m., the Death Angel came so suddenly and took her from us. She had been failing for some time but none thought her time could be so near. How are we to measure the great influence for good which has been wrought by her noble life, on the lives and characters of all those who came under her influence in their childhood and since gone forth into the world and become men and women. Sylvina A. Johnson was born in Cherry Valley, near Cooperstown, N.Y., February 9, 1841, and died at the summer home of her daughter, Mrs. J.A. Cole, in Sandy Creek, N.Y., July 28, 1916. She was the eldest of a large family of whom two survive. December 2, 1856 she was united in marriage to Asa S. Brown of Lowville, N.Y., and for many years they were residents of Sandy Creek, owning the Wilbur Jamerson farm west of the Ridge road school house. To them were born seven children, four of whom survive . . . The funeral services were held at the home of her daughter, Mrs. Widric [sic], Sunday, July 30, Rev. Spencer Bacon officiating . . . ." Asa and Sylvina are buried in Pulaski Village Cemetery.

Charles A. Brown – Co. C

b. 1836 Canada

d. November 22, 1864 South Richland, NY

m. ------

NOTE: Charles was the son of Abner (1805-1877) and Lucy French Brown (1805-1882). A death notice in *The Mexico Independent* December 8, 1864 suggests he died while on furlough: "In South Richland, on the 22d of November, of chronic diarrhea, Charles A. Brown, of Co. C., 147th regiment, N.Y.V., aged 28 years and 7 months." He is buried in Maple View Cemetery, Mexico with his parents.

Cyrus Eugene Brown – Co. D

b. February 2, 1840 Oswego Town, NY

d. September 14, 1932 Volney, NY

m. Savalla Louisa Druse (1847-November 24, 1922) August 1, 1880

NOTE: Cyrus, son of Reuben (1809) and Almira Everts Brown (1822-1892), was wounded at Gettysburg and again at Wilderness. In 1890 he reported he was "shot through thighs and L[eft] shoulder." His obituary, published in *The Palladium-Times* September 15, 1932, 11, provided more of the story: "Funeral services for Cyrus E. Brown, 92-year-old Civil war veteran, will be held at his home in North Volney at 2:30 p.m. Saturday with the Rev. William Lord of Mount Pleasant church officiating and burial in North Volney cemetery. Mr. Brown was wounded seriously during the war, left for dead on the battlefield. A stretcher bearer picked him up several days later and, despite the predictions of doctors, he rallied slowly. He never fully regained his strength. Last winter he was seriously ill, but recovered enough to be fairly active during the summer. A native of Oswego Town, he was a son of Mr. and Mrs. Reuben Brown. He had lived most of his life in Volney and had always been a farmer. In 1862 he volunteered for service in Company D, 147th New York volunteers. In the battles of the Wilderness and Gettysburg, he was wounded seriously. He was a member of the old Schenck Post, G.A.R., of which four members are left . . . ." Savalla is also buried in North Volney Cemetery.

Henry Brown – Co. I

b. 1835 Sweden

d. ?

m. ?

NOTE: Very little can be found for this man. His muster roll card says he was a "mariner" and he probably was a lake sailor. He was discharged for an unspecified disability on March 14, 1863 and after that date nothing has been located. He should not be confused with Henry G. Brown, 18, who deserted from the regiment.

James Brown – Co. B
b. 1836 Troy, Rensselaer, NY
d. July 5, 1864 Douglas Hospital, Washington, DC
m. ?

NOTE: Little is known about Brown's life before he came to Oswego. He does not appear on the 1860 census but according to the city directory he was a saloon keeper in Oswego City in 1862. He enlisted as a private but after Guilford Mace was killed at the battle of Gettysburg, he was promoted to first lieutenant. During the battle at Spotsylvania on May 10, 1864 he had a leg shot off. His condition was reported in *The Oswego Daily Palladium* June 15, 1864: "Lt. Brown of the 147th regiment, who lost his leg at the Wilderness, was seen a few days ago by L. H. Conklin, Esq., our County Treasurer, who took the necessary trouble to find him at the Douglas hospital in Washington. Mr. Conklin says Lieut. Brown was in good spirits, not disheartened and determined to get well." He succumbed to pyaemia brought about by the amputation and was buried in the Soldiers' and Airmen's Home Cemetery, Washington, DC. His burial record states he was unmarried. An entry in *The Town Clerks' Registers* confuses him with another James Brown who served in the 24th Regiment.

John Duncan Brown – Co. I
b. March 1823 Herkimer County, NY
d. April 22, 1904 Worcester, Washington, VT
m1. Amanda M. _____ (1824-*ante* 1865) *ca.* 1853
m2. Lotisa "Lottie" Debora Cox (June 1843-September 14, 1914) *ca.* 1867

NOTE: John, who had been transferred to the VRC, was discharged from service on April 28, 1863 for "disability." He was the son of Jesse (1790-?) and Persis Duncan Brown (1790-?). His COD was heart failure and toxemia resulting from a gangrenous condition of his leg. Although he died in Worcester, his remains were taken to Plainfield, VT for burial. Amanda's grave has not been located. Lottie died in Redgate, St. Mary's, MD but her grave has not been located. She had lived with her son, Dr. Clayton Brown, for many years.

Orrin Brown – Co. A
b. 1815 Preble, Cortland, NY
d. July 14, 1863 Seminary General Hospital, Gettysburg, Adams, PA
m. Eliza Ann Thatcher (September 1830-April 13, 1893) *ca.* 1845

NOTE: Orrin, whose parents are unidentified, was a tailor. Although he said he was born in 1819 when he enlisted he actually was born in 1815 and was, therefore, technically ineligible to serve. He had originally joined the 110th Regiment but was sent to the 147th. A comment in *The Town Clerks' Registers* reports that he died on July 1st but his entry in *Deaths of Volunteers* shows he died two weeks later in hospital. COD was "right leg fractured." Eliza died in Albion, Orleans, NY and is buried in Mt. Albion Cemetery.

Patrick Joseph Brown – Co. I

b. February 1840 Trenton, Ontario, Canada
d. November 25, 1909 Oswego City, NY
m. Margaret A. Barrett (December 1844-July 11, 1921) 1870

NOTE: Captain Brown was the son of Richard (1807-1885) and Ellen Conroy Brown (1806-1876). An article published in *The Oswego Daily Palladium* January 7, 1864 contained the following: "Patrick Brown, of this city, lately orderly sergeant of Co. I, of the 147th Regiment, has been promoted to the office of 2d Lieutenant. He fought gallantly at the battle of Gettysburgh, where he lost an arm. He has always proved himself a good soldier, and we rejoice at this recognition of his services." His obituary, which appeared in *The Post-Standard* November 29, 1909, 11, offers details of his injury and provides an excellent summary of his life: "Shortly before midnight at his home, No. 215 East Sixth street, [Oswego] occurred the death of Captain P. J. Brown at the age of nearly 71 years. Captain Brown was a well-known citizen and an active member of Post O'Brien G.A.R. He was born at Trenton, Ont., and at the age of 5 came to this city with his parents. There were six sons and when the War of the Rebellion was declared four of them, including the deceased, enlisted. Patrick was assigned to Company I of the 147th regiment, of which the late Captain James McKinley was in command. He was mustered in as first sergeant and on July 1, 1863, was wounded and captured at Gettysburg, being hit in the right shoulder with a rifle ball. General Robert E. Lee, who was near, ordered that the wounded man be placed in charge of a Confederate surgeon, who removed the arm from its socket. For a number of years Captain Brown was a prominent business man here and took an active part in politics. He was also a foreman in charge of construction work when the Capitol at Albany was being erected . . . ." I have only located five sons for the Brown family: Matthew Charles (1834-1912); Patrick; Thomas (1842-1925); David E. (1844-1921); Dominic D. (1847-*post* 1877). Matthew served in the 23rd Iowa Volunteers. Thomas served in the 147th (see below). I have not located military service for David. Dominic was too young to join the military. Margaret's death elicited the following obituary in *The Oswego Daily Times* July 11, 1921, 5: "Word was received here this forenoon of the death of Mrs. Margaret Brown, widow of Capt. Patrick Brown, at the home of her son, Dr. J. C. Brown in New York. She had been ill but a week. Mrs. Brown was a lifelong resident of Oswego and removed to New York in December last. She was a member of St. Paul's church and the Rosary Society of that parish . . . The remains will be brought to Oswego for interment.

Time of arrival and of services at St Paul's church will be announced later. Capt. Brown who was a well known Civil War veteran died nearly twelve years ago." Patrick, a "man of great courage," and Margaret are buried in St. Peter's Cemetery, Oswego.

Samuel James Brown – Co. E

b. June 5, 1831 Fryeburg, Oxford, ME
d. July 15, 1898 Orwell, NY
m. Melissa J. Clements (1834-May 28, 1921) April 14, 1855

NOTE: Samuel, son of Robert (?-?) and Esta Jennes Brown (?-?), was discharged from the 147th at Finley Hospital, Washington, DC on December 12, 1862. He also served in Co. B 7th NY Cavalry (October 1861-March 1862) and in Co. E 189th NYSV (August 1864-May 1865), for which he received a bounty of $900. His obituary appeared in *The Sandy Creek News* July 21, 1898, 1: ". . . Samuel Brown, a veteran of the War of the Rebellion and an old resident of this place [Pine Meadows], died at his home here on Thursday. Mr. Brown was sixty-seven years of age and had been an invalid for several years. He was a member of the W. M. Church here . . . The family have the sympathy of all in their affliction . . . ." Melissa married William E. Tanner (January 1829-June 1913) in 1904 as his second wife. She was residing with a daughter in Verona, Oneida, NY when she died. She and her two husbands are buried in Riverside Cemetery, Altmar, NY.

Thomas F. Brown – Co. I

b. 1842 Canada
d. December 31, 1925 Oswego City, NY
m. ------

NOTE: Thomas, brother of Patrick Joseph, was wounded at the battle of Gettysburg and discharged for "disability from wounds" on September 22, 1864. For many years he was a guide at the State Capitol Building in Albany, NY. He was a member of William A. Jackson Post No. 644 GAR, Albany. His grave has not been located.

Wyatt Lyman Brown – Co. D

b. April 17, 1842 Jefferson County, NY
d. March 26, 1915 Lansing, Ingham, MI
m. Emily Cross (October 30, 1842-February 17, 1924) 1863

NOTE: Wyatt, son of Lyman (1801-1870) and Saloma Hungerford Brown (1809-1897), sometimes was known by his middle name. He transferred to Battery L, 1st NY ART on December 8, 1863 and was mustered out at Elmira, Chemung, NY on June 17, 1865. His COD was "general decay." Emily's COD was "senility." Both are buried in Mount Hope Cemetery, Lansing.

Charles S. Brownell – Co. F

b. November 14, 1843 Sullivan, Madison, NY

d. May 5, 1864 Wilderness, VA

m. ------

NOTE: Charles, a son of Benjamin (1801-January 1864) and Sarah "Sally" Fish Brownell (1803-1877), was one of at least 11 children. Sally did not apply for a mother's pension until 1869 because she did not know she was eligible. Her husband had been totally disabled for ten years when he died of a "lingering disease quite like consumption." Charles had supported his parents for several years before he enlisted and testimony provided by George Robbins and Joseph Baker on June 30, 1869 demonstrates how bad her situation was after his death: ". . . no property whatever & no means of support – that she is old and feeble and has done a little knitting to support herself for the last few years." Sally was assisted by charity and by Elijah Brownell, Charles' uncle, prior to applying for a pension. She lived with her son, Amos, in Palermo, until her death in 1877. A cenotaph for Charles Brownell stands in Sayles Corners Cemetery, Vermillion, NY.

This stone is a cenotaph for Charles Brownell who died at the battle of the Wilderness.

Author's Collection

Elijah Brownell – Co. F

b. December 1832 Sullivan, Madison, NY

d. February 21, 1904 Oswego, NY

m1. Harriet Lord (1834-1872) 1860

m2. Emma Hagaman Valentine (1844-*ante* 1900) October 21, 1874

NOTE: Elijah was Charles' brother. His DOB varies. I use that on the 1900 census. He mustered out with the regiment on June 7, 1865. He entered the Bath National Home in 1903 and said his disabilities were epithelioma "since the war," disease of the scrotum, and a gunshot wound of the right hand suffered in the war. His obituary appeared in *The Oswego Daily Times* February 22, 1904, 4: "Elijah Brownell, a veteran of Company F, 147th Regiment, N. Y. I., died in Oswego Hospital last evening of Bright's disease. He was about 70 years old and was for some time an inmate at the Soldiers' Home at Bath. Several weeks ago he left that institution claiming the discipline was too severe and he stopped with friends at Mexico. About a week ago he was brought to the Hospital. His only survivor is a brother who lives in the Eastern end of the county. His funeral will be held from Dain's undertaking parlors tomorrow at 2 o'clock." Several sisters also survived him: Nancy Baker (1831-1907), Mexico; Mrs. Fox, Michigan; Mrs. Ouderkirk, Granby. Emma was previously married to Henry Valentine (1833-1864), by whom she had a daughter, Ida (1862-?) and a son, William (1863-?). Graves for her, Harriet, and Elijah have not been located.

Sarah Fish Brownell, the mother of many children, was able to obtain a pension based on the military service of son Charles. Her grave has not been located.
Christine Kenzie

John Buel, Jr. – Co. D
b. 1838 Oswego County, NY
d. August 1864 ?
m. Elizabeth O'Grady (1842-September 14, 1884) *ca.* 1860

NOTE: John was the son of John, Sr.(1791-1863) and Luna Whelan Buel (1814-1898). His exact DOD and POD are mysteries. Allegedly he was sick at City Point, VA, put aboard a transport although he was dying, and was buried at sea. Crisfield Johnson, *History of Oswego County, 1789-1877*, 409, states: "Supposed to have died on a transport, and to have been buried at sea in Aug. 1864." He is also reported to have died as a result of the battle of Weldon Railroad sometime between August 18-24. After his death, Elizabeth applied for a pension for herself and for her three children, Harriet, John H., and Anna C. John is memorialized with a cenotaph in Lewis Cemetery, Granby, and another in St. Mary's Cemetery, Fulton, which also serves as a gravestone for Elizabeth.

John J. Bunn – Co. D
b. 1844 Schoharie County, NY
d. November 30, 1917 Burkett, Hall, NE
m1. Mary Jane Philips Chase (1846-*ante* 1900) June 16, 1870
m2. Anna Maria Irvins Chapman (1839-April 20, 1918) September 5, 1913

NOTE: John, son of Jacob (1810-1846) and Elizabeth McLyman Bunn Guild (1817-?), was captured at the battle of Gettysburg and later paroled. He mustered out with the regiment on June 7, 1865. In 1890 John was living in Douglas, NE and he said his disability was "wounded." He spent a brief period in the Soldiers' Home in Hot Springs, SD in 1909, listing his disabilities as chronic arthritis, rheumatism, and myalgia. Mary Jane may have died in Nebraska but her gravesite has not been identified. Since John said he was single on his land claim dated May 1900 Mary Jane must have died beforehand. Her first husband is unidentified. Anna was previously married to Charles Henry Chapman (1839-1899). She and John are buried in Burkett Cemetery, Burkett, Hall, NE. This cemetery is also known as the Soldiers' and Sailors' Cemetery.

Warren Alonzo Burgess – Co. H

b. May 22, 1840 Bennington County, VT

d. August 9, 1903 Mt. Holly, Rutland, VT

m. Lydia Nutting (April 12, 1850-April 21, 1912) *ca.* 1865

NOTE: Warren was the son of Warren (1914-1896) and Sarah A. Stanley Burgess (1816-1886). Captain Reuben Slayton reported that Warren had suffered a severe injury on November 16, 1862: ". . . Quite a serious accident happened to one of my men yesterday while cutting down a tree to procure some brush. Warren A. Burgess had his two fore fingers cut off near the first joint. They were dressed immediately by the surgeon, and he is as comfortable as can be expected . . . ." Burgess was discharged from the service on February 6, 1863. His COD was a pulmonary hemorrhage with "aortic regurgitation" listed as a contributing factor. When Lydia died *The Syracuse Journal* April 22, 1912, 7 printed the following: "Funeral services for Mrs. Lydia Nutting Burgess, 62, who died Sunday at her home in N. Syracuse, will be held at the family home at 2:30 p.m. Tuesday. Burial will be at North Syracuse. Mrs. Burgess had been an invalid for 30 years. She was a daughter of the late Rev. William Nutting and a sister of the late Congressman Newton W. Nutting, who was at one time a judge in Oswego county. She was also a sister of the late State Senator Harmon Nutting of Virginia . . . ." Lydia was a member of Free Will Baptist Church. Warren is also buried in North Syracuse Cemetery.

Edward Orvis Burnett – Co. H

b. April 22, 1847 West Monroe, NY

d. November 1, 1908 Minneapolis, Hennepin, MN

m. Louisa Catherine "Kate" Carson (1854-May 18, 1916) May 2, 1874

NOTE: Edward, son of Joseph Isaac (1823-1863) and Charlotte Sedgwick Burnett (1830-1854), lied about his age when he enlisted, alleging he was eighteen. He was discharged on January 12, 1864 for "disability." On March 14, 1864 he enlisted in

Co. D, 149th Regiment at Otisco, Onondaga, NY and was wounded on June 20, 1864. According to *The Adjutant-General's Report* he was transferred to Co. I, 102nd NYSV "absent, wounded. No further record." His pension cards show only service for the 147th and the 149th. Kate's DOB varies from document to document. She was the mother of five, four of whom were living in 1900. She and Edward are buried in Mound Cemetery, LeSueur, LeSueur, MN but their graves have no stones.

Thomas F. Burns – Co. I
b. 1843 Ireland
d. 1899 ?
m. ?

NOTE: Burns, a blacksmith, was the son of Anthony (1815-*post* 1865) and Bridget Dowd Burns (1810-*post* 1865). He was wounded at Gettysburg on July 1, 1863. According to his muster roll card he was discharged for "disability" on January 7, 1864. His entry in *The Town Clerks' Registers* says he was wounded and captured at Gettysburg, paroled on the field, sent to hospital, and discharged. He applied for a pension on February 10, 1864. Further documentation of his life has been difficult. His DOD is found on his pension card although a POD is not included. His marital status is unknown. On August 26, 1899 a man named Thomas "Tom" Burns, 57, a widower born in Ireland, committed suicide by slashing his throat in the Mancelona Jail, Antrim, MI. His death certificate shows an unsuccessful attempt was made to save his life. His body was sent to Ann Arbor for burial. Whether or not this is the correct person is open to question.

Aaron Nash Burr – Co. C
b. December 22, 1837 Ellisburg, Jefferson, NY
d. February 1, 1927 Pulaski, NY
m. ------

NOTE: Aaron was the son of Elisha (1794-1879) and Charlotte Willis Burr (1799-1890). His long, active life was summarized in *The Pulaski Democrat* February 9, 1927, 1: "With his work all done and well done, Aaron N. Burr answers the call of the Great Commander to join the mighty host who had gone over to swell the ranks of the triumphant host, where peace and rest await the veteran, from which he will never more be separated. He had not been well for a little time before his passing which occurred Feb. 1st in the home he had so long occupied. Aaron N. Burr will be missed on Salina st., where he was seen every day, when in health. He was interesting to meet and in his reserve and modest manner he carried the marks of a gentleman. He was clean in habits, sound in speech and positive in his convictions.

The many years he was employed by the N. Y. C. as baggage man at the depot gave him opportunity to prove his methodical and faithful qualities in public service. As each duty came to him he met it with scrupulous care. Aaron N. Burr was born in the town of Ellisburg, Jefferson county, December 22, 1837. He came from stock that had no fear of the terrors of war and was conspicuous in the ranks of the war heroes of this section. His grandfather, I. Burr fought in the Revolution and his father, Elisha L. Burr, was in the war of 1812 having part in the activities about Sackets Harbor. Coming down to Civil War days Mr. Burr and three brothers enlisted. Joseph R. Burr, one of the brothers, was killed while in service. Three brothers came home and all settled at Pulaski where they had made their home since 1857 when they removed here from Ellisburg. One brother, Adelbert H. died some five or more

Aaron Burr and many members of his family are buried in Willis Cemetery, Fernwood, NY.
Online photograph, Union Drummer Boy Civil War Artifacts

years ago and Elisha L, the other brother, died last October. While in the service, Mr. Burr saw some real service but escaped untouched by shot or shell except being hit in a finger by a bullet which severed the member. He enlisted in 1862 in Co. C, 147th N. Y. Vols. and served to the close of the war being honorably discharged May 12, 1865. Mr. Burr was a charter member of J. B. Butler Post No. 111, G. A. R. and served as commander for a term or more and for more than a quarter of a century he served as adjutant, [and] also was careful custodian of the Post rooms and also the valuable relics and souvenirs. He was a member of Oswego Co. Veteran's Association. Last rites for Mr. Burr were held at the home, Thursday afternoon . . . The burial service of the Sons of Veterans was conducted by Past Commander, O. Bert Trowbridge with Edward S. Parker, as chaplain . . . Burial was made in Willis cemetery . . . Mr. Burr never married." Adelbert H. Burr (1844-May 11, 1926) served in Co. I, 184th NYSV.

Elisha L. Burr, Jr. – Co. C
b. January 15, 1841 Ellisburg, Jefferson, NY
d. October 13, 1926 Pulaski, NY
m. Caroline Jones (March 14, 1843-May 9, 1917) 1872

NOTE: Elisha mustered out with the regiment on June 7, 1865 near Washington, DC. *The Pulaski Democrat* October 20, 1926, 1 published an informative obituary: "In the death of Elisha L. Burr, which occurred last Wednesday evening following a period of illness and a fall which left him in a critical condition, the ranks of Civil War veterans has [sic] been further reduced. All through his illness he had been cared for by his daughter, Mrs. David P. Rogers, husband and daughter, Constance. Mr. Burr was born in Ellisburg, January 15, 1841. He was son of Mr. and Mrs. Elisha Burr who were pioneer settlers of the country and figured prominently in the early civil and military life of the land where they settled. When Elisha was fourteen years of age his parents moved to this town and in 1861 [sic] he, with three other brothers, enlisted in the service of the Federal army of the United States, he going with Co. C, 147th regiment N. Y. Vols. At the close of the war three of the four brothers came home, namely Adelbert H., Aaron and Elisha L. Joseph W., the other brother was killed in the battle of Gettysburg, July 1, 1863. The grandfather was a soldier in the Revolutionary War and the father was a soldier in the war of 1812[;] as we understand it, he was among those who assisted at the Battle of Big Sandy. There were nine children in the family, only one of whom remains, Aaron, now past 86 years of age, but active. In 1872 Mr. Burr was united in marriage with Miss Caroline Jones, who died in 1917. They built their home on the spot where they spent all their married life and where Mr. Burr spent his last days and where the only child, Mrs Rogers now resides. Mr. Burr was a member of J. B. Butler Post, G.A.R., No. 111, and when he was able was very regular in attendance. Of his comrades, except his brother, but four were able to attend his funeral; they were Hartwell Douglass, Sylvanus Wolcott, Adelbert Hillaker and George Bushnell. The services were held at the home, Saturday afternoon, at 2 o'clock, conducted by Byron G. Seamans, commander of Andrew S. Warner Camp, who spoke on the theme, 'When the Storms of Life Are Passed.' There was a large gathering of relatives and friends at the service and the floral tributes were beautiful and abundant. Burial was made in Willis cemetery." Caroline is also buried there.

Joseph Warren Burr – Co. C
b. August 1836 Ellisburg, Jefferson, NY
d. July 1, 1863 Gettysburg, Adams, PA
m. Catherine M. Casler (1840-April 7, 1885) July 4, 1856

NOTE: Joseph is buried in Gettysburg National Cemetery but a cenotaph for him is located in Willis Cemetery, Fernwood. He and Catherine were the parents of two sons, William H. (April 10, 1860-?), and Daniel E. (December 25, 1862-1923). Catherine married Royal "Riley" L. Nutting (October 1816-March 24, 1905) on November 18, 1868 as his second wife. Her obituary appeared in *The Pulaski Democrat* April 23, 1885: "Mrs. Riley Nutting died at her residence, April 7, 1885, aged 35 years. Mrs. Nutting had been a resident here for many years, and was known as the Widow Burr before she became Mrs. Nutting. She has been greatly afflicted in health for the past 5 years but her sweet trust in Christ has helped her to bear it all cheerfully. The great kindness of her many friends and neighbors shows how much she was loved and respected by all. She leaves a husband and two sons to mourn her loss. A friend." Catherine is buried in Willis Cemetery, Fernwood, as is Royal.

Charles C. Burroughs – Co. F
b. 1829 Rome, Oneida, NY
d. April 8, 1882 Hastings, NY
m. Mary A. _____ (1831-July 9, 1918) *ca.* 1860

NOTE: Charles was the son of Herrick (1798-1851) and Asenath Burroughs (1796-*post* 1865). He was discharged from the army on January 6, 1864 at Emory Hospital, Washington, DC for "disability." His obituary appeared in *The Mexico Independent* on April 19, 1882: "Charles C. Burroughs died April 8, 1882 at his home in Hastings, aged 53 years, 6 months and 11 days. Deceased was born in Rome, Oneida county, and in 1841 removed with his parents to this county. He enlisted in 1862 but before his term of service expired, he was discharged on account of poor health. Since that time he has been the victim of a complication of ailments, suffering intensely the past few years from asthma and cancer; but through all afflictions possessed a spirit of patience and resignation. He leaves a wife and one daughter. On Monday his funeral was attended by a large circle of relatives and friends, Rev. A. P. Phinney officiating. The remains were taken to New Haven for interment . . . ." He and Mary are buried in New Haven Rural Cemetery.

Alvin P. Burtch – Co. F
b. December 21, 1834 St. Lawrence County, NY
d. July 3, 1864 Liverpool, Onondaga, NY
m. Jerusha Adams (July 1842-February 18, 1920) September 10, 1860

NOTE: Burtch originally enlisted in the 110th Regiment. He suffered a compound fracture of his right thigh at Gettysburg. He died while on furlough, as Newton Stowell's deposition of May 25, 1867 shows: ". . . at the request of Mrs. Burtch he [Stowell] started for Baltimore after the said Burtch who was then sick in the USA Gen'l Hospital; that he left his home the 20th day of June 1864 & went to Baltimore – That on the 22nd day of June he left Baltimore with the said Burtch in charge on his way to Elmira – that he arrived at Elmira said 22nd day of June & reported to Surgeon Way in charge of Hospital –On examining the papers & furlough of the said Burtch Surgeon Way concluded to forward the furlough & other papers to Gen'l Dix at New York. That the transfer was made & permission given by Surgeon Way for said Burtch to go to his home in Mexico[,] Oswego County NY & that he would be required to report to U.S.A. General Hospital at Elmira NY – that we left Elmira for the home of said Burtch on the 1ˢᵗ day of July & arrived at Liverpool[,] Onondaga the same day when Burtch was not able to proceed further on his way home – That the said Burtch died at Liverpool on the 3d day of July 1864 & on the 4ᵗʰ day his body was carried to Mexico NY the residence of his family where his body was buried & that this deponent saw the said Burtch buried . . . ." Burtch's COD was acute dysentery, according to *Deaths of Volunteers*. He is buried in Mexico Village Cemetery. Jerusha married Alexander Fleming (November 15, 1847-December 25, 1937) on July 22, 1875 as his second wife. They are buried in New Haven Rural Cemetery.

Asahel D. Butler – Co. H

b. 1844 Amboy, NY

d. March 28, 1868 Amboy, NY

m. ------

NOTE: Asahel, whose parents were John Taylor (1809-1881) and Catherine Wright Butler (1820-1867), was wounded at the battle of Gettysburg on July 1, 1863 and was subsequently transferred to the VRC. A notation in his Findagrave.com entry lists COD as pneumonia. He and his parents are buried in Butler Cemetery, Amboy.

John Germond Butler – regimental colonel

b. March 16, 1834 Utica, Oneida, NY

d. October 4, 1917 Syracuse, Onondaga, NY

m1. Annie Huntington Rosekrans (1838-November 1, 1907) August 8, 1861

m2. Mabel Helen Mason Gilmore (March 16, 1866-December 25, 1911) June 2, 1890

NOTE: John's parents were Ammi Todd (1806-1888) and Susan Jennette Mott Butler (1814-1889). He joined the regiment on September 13, 1862 in New York City and became regimental colonel when A. S. Warner resigned on February 5, 1863, serving until November 5, 1863 when he was discharged for "disability." His lengthy obituary, published in *The Syracuse Journal* October 5, 1917, 4 chronicles his extensive career and community service: "A veteran of two wars, Col. John G. Butler, 83 Syracuse's 'Grand Old Man of the Army,' died at 5:15 o'clock Thursday afternoon at the Hospital of the Good Shepherd, following a long illness. Colonel Butler had been a patient at the hospital since Sept. 11, and had undergone two operations, death closely following the second. A sudden turn for the worse shattered the hopes for his recovery that had been entertained by the physicians. Colonel Butler had served under the city administration for 25 years in the capacity of cashier of the Water Bureau and during this time made more acquaintances in Syracuse than perhaps any other man. Colonel Butler was the soldier who in the early part of the Civil War was called 'Fighting Jack Butler.' He also served in the Spanish-American war and he was deeply interested in the present conflict for democracy. He was born in Utica March 16, 1834, and came to Syracuse at the age of four where he lived ever since. His grandfather was an officer during the Revolutionary War and his father was Ammi Todd Butler, one of Syracuse's former dry goods merchants. The colonel, after graduating from Hoyt's private school, became a clerk in the Syracuse City Bank, of which his father was a director. Later he was teller of the Crouse Bank and then worked for a bank at Rome. From there he went to New York City and returned to accept a position as teller for the Merchants Bank here. At the declaration of the Civil War he formed a company of 40 men from this city and, being chosen their captain, they were named Butler's Zouaves. They offered their services to Lincoln and took part in the first real battle of the war, at Big Bethel. At the outbreak of the Spanish-American War Colonel Butler was 64 years old, and led the Forty-first Company, of which he was captain, away from Syracuse when they were called. He was commander of Root Post No. 151, Grand Army of the Republic in 1896 and 1897, and was recently made a life member by Col. John Butler Camp No. 26, United Spanish War Veterans, named in his honor. He was also a member of Central City Lodge No. 305, F. & A. M., the Onondaga Historical Society and the Citizens Club . . . ." What happened to the marriage of J. G. and Annie, his first wife, is unknown. When she died *The Utica Tribune* published the following obituary on November 3, 1907: "Mrs. Annie H. Butler died unexpectedly at the home of her daughter, Mrs. Lloyd Taylor, in New York, Friday. Mrs. Butler left here the latter part of September for a visit with her daughter, and while there was taken ill. Mrs. Butler was the daughter of Judge Rosecrans, for many years a Justice of the Supreme Court of the State of New York. Her mother was a sister of William A. Beach who was distinguished in the practice of his profession and who was one of the counsel engaged in the celebrated Beecher-Tilton case more than a quarter of a century ago. She was born in Glens Falls . . . There was a tinge of romance about the marriage of this young girl to Col. John G. Butler. Report came to her that he had been killed in the battle of Big Bethel in the Civil War, and while she was grieving for the death of her lover, he returned to her and they were married soon thereafter . . . ." Annie was buried in Glens Falls Cemetery, Warren Co., NY. Helen's obituary appeared in *The Syracuse Herald* December 26, 1911, 3: "Mrs. Ella [sic] Mabel Butler, wife of Col. John G. Butler, 48 years old, died last night at her home, No. 424 James street after a short illness. Mrs. Butler was born in Baltimore, Md., and was married to Colonel Butler 25 years ago. She was a member of the Eastern Star and the Root Post Relief Corps of the G.A.R. Besides her husband, she is survived by a son, Jack, two sisters . . . and two brothers of Baltimore." Col. Butler and Helen are buried in St. Agnes Cemetery, Syracuse.

John Steele Butler – Co. D

b. March 15, 1841 Oswego County, NY

d. July 1, 1863 Gettysburg, Adams, PA

m. ------

NOTE: John's parents were Joseph Wetmore (1801-1882) and Nancy C. Steele Butler (1806-1858). He was a brother of Joseph Bradley Butler (1834-1863), a member of the 110th Regiment who was killed at Port Hudson, LA on June 21, 1863 and for whom J. B. Butler Post No. 111 GAR was named. Although John lies in Gettysburg, a cenotaph for him can be seen in Mt. Adnah Cemetery, Fulton, NY.

George Button – Co. F

b. March 29, 1836 Volney, NY

d. December 31, 1862 College Hospital, Georgetown, DC

m. Mary R. Smith (May 6, 1843-June 8, 1921) February 17, 1859

NOTE: George's COD was a combination of typhoid fever and tuberculosis. According to a deposition given by Mary, she had gone to Georgetown to be with her husband and when she left on December 31st, he appeared to be "much better and nearly or quite out of danger." On January 1, 1863, however, Hettie Painter, a ward nurse, sent her tragic news: "I am under the painfull necessity of informing you of the death of your husband[.] He appeared as you left him until about 4 ½ O.C. of the day you left (Dec. 31st)[.] He then sent for me to come to him. I went but I saw he was dying. Dr. Smith was in the ward. I called him but nothing could be done, he was past speaking. The Dr. was aware he had organic disease of the heart, but had thought he could be raised again. It is impossible to know how long life can be prolonged where the heart is diseased. Then too you know he had consumption. He died without a struggle . . . be assured you have my warmest sympathy & kindest regards; here we miss you & little Eddie. Kiss him for me & don't allow him to forget to repeat my name; he done it so prettily, bless his little heart. With wishing you the blessing of home & friends on this bright & beautifull New Years, I bid you adieu. Please write me. Your friend Hettie H. Painter." Button was buried in the National Asylum Cemetery, Washington, DC. In my book, *Men of the 110th Regiment: Oswego's Own*, 233-4, I erroneously wrote that Mary R. Smith was the wife of George Washington Button (1836-1895), an error I should like to correct now. Mary Smith Button, widow of George Button who died December 31, 1862, married Richard DeWitt Fort on March 28, 1867. He had previously been married to Amanda Fellows (1842-1866) and was the father of two sons, Leander (1861-?) and Willis (1864-1917). In 1870 he, Mary, Willis, Leander, Jennie, born 1869, and Addison Button, Mary's son by her first husband, were living in Palermo. In 1872 Nettie was born. According to documents filed when Mary attempted to regain her pension as a remarried widow, Fort deserted her that year. For many years Mary alleged she had no idea where he was but her application for a pension brought out the ugly truth. After Fort left her, he married again, evidently without bothering to obtain a divorce. The Michigan Marriage Records show that DeWitt Fort, aged 38, born in Oswego, NY, married Sarah J. Thayer, 24, born in Hamburg, Erie, NY, on July 12, 1875. The Michigan Death Records show that Sarah J. Fort, 29, died on December 18, 1879. Her COD was "congestive brain." Fort's

Mary Smith Button Fort lies in an easily missed grave near the front of Upson's Corners Cemetery, Palermo.
Author's Collection

admission form to the Ionia County Home, MI, gave as his next of kin a daughter, Mrs. Mary (Floyd A.) Totten. When Mary and Totten were wed in November 1898 she was nineteen, meaning she was born in 1879, probably shortly before her mother died. She said her father was DeWitt Fort and her mother was "unknown." Fort never left the County Home, dying there on January 9, 1918. He was buried in Keene Township Cemetery, Ionia, MI. Mary was old and feeble in 1920 when she applied for the renewal of her widow's pension and she died of apoplexy and Bright's disease before the process could be completed. She is buried in Upson's Corners Cemetery, Palermo.

Louis Byron – Co. A

b. 1815 France
d. August 3, 1884 Mexico, NY
m. Sarah M. Fairchilds (1815-September 28, 1904) *ante* 1875

NOTE: Louis, whose name was also spelled Lewis, first appeared on the 1855 New York census. He was a boarder in Hastings, NY, a shoemaker who had been there for two years. Since he was not married or widowed, one must infer he was unmarried. He was wounded at Gettysburg and transferred to the VRC in October 1863. Sarah was the daughter of Harmon and Ruth Fairchilds. She probably was born in Connecticut although on the 1900 census she said she had been born in New York State. In that same year she said she was the mother of five children, two of whom were living. I have not found any of them and have been unable to determine the couple's marriage date. In 1886 Sarah unsuccessfully applied for a widow's pension. She and Louis are buried in Maple View Cemetery, Mexico.

Martin Cahill – Co. G
b. 1847 Belleville, Ontario, Canada
d. January 11, 1909 Oswego City, NY
m1. Mary A. _____ (1843-1892) *ca.* 1870
m2. Mary F. Mahar (December 1853-*post* 1931) July 31, 1895

NOTE: Martin, son of Thomas (?-*ante* 1865) and Mary Fray Cahill (1810-*post* 1865), enlisted as a musician in Oswego City. At this point, young boys were being allowed to enlist provided their parents agreed. He mustered out with the regiment on June 7, 1865. In 1890 he claimed the following disabilities: sunstroke, diabetes, smallpox, and typhoid fever. His obituary, which appeared in *The Oswego Daily Times* January 12, 1909, 4, documented his long career: "Martin Cahill, one of Oswego's well known citizens and a prominent locomotive engineer, died shortly before six o'clock yesterday afternoon at his home, No. 236 West Fourth street. Death resulted from cancer of the jawbone and with that ailment Mr. Cahill had suffered for a little more than a year. Mr. Cahill was born at Belleville, Ont., in 1847 and was in his sixty-second year. When a child he came to Oswego with his parents. When he was a boy of fifteen he enlisted in the One Hundred Forty-seventh New York Volunteers as a drummer boy and served with distinction throughout the Civil War. After the war he entered the employ of the New York Central, then the R. W. & O., and for twenty seven years he served as an engineer. For years Mr. Cahill had the run between Oswego and Suspension Bridge and he had a large acquaintance along the entire division. Mr. Cahill was a member of Division No. 152 Brotherhood of Locomotive Engineers and took a leading part in promoting and extending the influence of the brotherhood. A few years ago he was one of a party of engineers to make a tour of the United States. The party went from Buffalo to New Orleans, then to Arizona and California back over the Rocky Mountains to Denver and then to New York. Stops were made in all the principal cities and the traveling engineers were received and entertained by the members of the brotherhood in the cities visited. Mr. Cahill acted as spokesman for the party and his remarks made a fine impression everywhere. He enjoyed remarkable fine health until about a year ago when a cancer developed in his mouth and he failed rapidly until the end came. Specialists in New York and other cities were consulted but the relief given was only temporary. Mr. Cahill was well informed on the affairs of the world. He was particularly interested in municipal affairs and was a strong advocate of municipal ownership of the water plant. He was extremely active in the original water controversy and was one of the organizers of the Municipal League. He was devoted to his home and because of his pleasant manner enjoyed a large acquaintance. In addition to his membership in the brotherhood Mr. Cahill was a member of the Columbian club . . . ." He and his first wife are buried in St. Paul's Cemetery. His second wife's DOD has not been located. She appeared in the Oswego city directory for the last time in 1931. Someone named

Mary Cahill died in Ogdensburg, St. Lawrence, NY on March 16, 1933 but it is unknown if this is the correct person.

John Callahan – Co. G

b. 1803 Ireland
d. March 13, 1890 Waupaca, Waupaca, WI
m. Ann _____ (1811-1894) *ca.* 1835

NOTE: Callahan lied about his age when he enlisted, saying he was 44 and thus still eligible for service. He was transferred to the VRC on September 26, 1863 and discharged on June 29, 1865 at Washington, DC. He and Ann, who was also born in Ireland, are buried in the Wisconsin Veterans' Memorial Cemetery, King, Waupaca, WI.

William Campbell – Co. I

b. September 15, 1846 Oswego, NY
d. July 23, 1885 New York City, NY
m. Isabella "Bell" _____ (1846-1876) ?

NOTE: William, son of James (1817-1885) and Eleanor Margaret Bradt Campbell (1820-1858), was sixteen when he enlisted as a musician in the 147th. His brother James Campbell served in the 110th Regiment. James was taken sick at Port Hudson, LA and died on October 20, 1863. A death notice in *The Oswego Times and Express* July 25, 1885, 5 announced William's death: "In New York, July 23, Wm. H., son of James Campbell, formerly of this city. Funeral services will be held at the East Baptist church tomorrow afternoon at four o'clock. Friends are invited." He was buried in Riverside Cemetery, Scriba. The gravestone also acts as a cenotaph for James. Isabella probably died in New York City but she was buried in Riverside on December 2, 1876.

Loren Caples - Co. H

b. 1839 Herkimer County, NY
d. August 10, 1876 Mallory, NY
m. Diantha Ostrander (1844-January 5, 1919) July 14, 1862

NOTE: Loren was the son of William (1805-1861) and Lucy Jane Lower Caples (1818-*post* 1892). His father abandoned the family in 1861 and died in the Onondaga County Almshouse on July 10, 1861. Loren was wounded at Gettysburg on July 1, 1863 and discharged on October 1st. He had been shot in his shin bone and was forced to use crutches. After he returned from the war he evidently decided he did not want to be married. In a deposition given in 1887 Diantha testified that Caples refused to support her so she left him, saying she would support herself. She "married" Alfred Ingerson (1844-1938) on December 31, 1866 in Brewerton. By 1880 they were the parents of four children. In the meantime Caples had begun living with Catherine Fidler (1850-*post* 1875). He and Catherine are listed as married on the 1875 New York census. Loren died of tuberculosis and was buried in Pine Grove Cemetery, Mallory, NY. In June 1880 Lucy, his mother, applied for his pension. An investigation ensued and it was discovered that Loren and Diantha were never divorced. Diantha told examiners Lucy had threatened her with prosecution for bigamy if she attempted to hinder her application. John Fidler, Catherine's father, testified on January 31, 1887: "Loren Caples lived for a time with my daughter Catherine as man and wife after his return from the army but I don't think they were ever married." Lucy married William Carpenter (1813-1887) on February 11, 1882. In the end no one got the pension! Diantha and Alfred are buried in West Monroe Cemetery. Loren's brother, Lorenzo (1837-1916), served in the 148th Regiment.

Elisha H. T. Carman – Co. D
b. January 1824 Onondaga County, NY
d. November 5, 1912 National Soldiers' and Sailors' Home, Milwaukee, Milwaukee, WI
m. ------

NOTE: Elisha's father is unknown but he was living in Granby, NY in 1860 with his mother, Cornelia (1786-?). He originally enlisted in the 110th Regiment but was transferred to the 147th. He mustered out on June 7, 1865. In 1890 he was living in Mishicot, Manitowac, WI and claimed chronic diarrhea as his disability. The enumerator noted that he was "old and feeble; completely used up." Elisha entered the home in Milwaukee on July 29, 1903 and remained there until his death. Chronic diarrhea, rheumatism, prostate problems, and senility were listed among his disabilities. It is relatively certain that he never married although in 1900 he said he had been married for eight years. At the time he was 76 and his senility may have generated this information. His COD was "general paresis and arteriosclerosis." He was buried in Wood National Cemetery, Milwaukee.

Samuel Carpenter – Co. E
b. March 17, 1841 Sandy Creek, NY
d. July 10, 1863 Seminary Hospital, Gettysburg, Adams, NY
m. ------

NOTE: Samuel was wounded on July 1st but lingered until July 10th. A gravestone proclaiming him the son of George (1798-1888) and Nancy Dean Carpenter (1805-1888) can be seen in Woodlawn Cemetery, Sandy Creek. Because of a poem on the reverse of the stone, I infer that he was brought home and buried: "From that fatal field returning/We have lain him down to rest/But the patriot's fire is burning/Brightly in each loyal breast./And we think while tears are falling/Thickly o'er that hallowed sod/We have yielded up our brother/To our country and our God."

James Loren Carroll – Co. H
b. June 1844 Vienna, Oneida, NY
d. September 15, 1910 Buffalo, Erie County, NY
m. ------

NOTE: James, a butcher, deserted from the regiment on June 25, 1864 and did not return until December 5. For this offense he lost all pay and allowances and was required to forfeit $10.00 each month. He was also ordered to make up the time and thus was transferred to Co. F, 91st Regiment on June 6, 1865. He mustered out with that regiment on July 3rd near Washington, DC. He returned to his parents' home and last appears on the 1875 New York census. James' parents, James (1806-1882) and Almira Davis Carroll (1808-1876), are both buried in Cleveland Village Cemetery but his whereabouts are a mystery until 1910. His death was announced in *The Buffalo Enquirer* September 16, 1910, 2: "The funeral of the late James L. Carroll, a well-known Civil War veteran, who died yesterday morning after a brief illness, will be held from Moest's undertaking room . . . under the auspices of Chapin Post No. 2, G. A. R. Mr. Carroll was born in Cleveland, Oswego County, sixty-six years ago, and was first sergeant of Co. H, 147th New York Infantry, recruited at Oswego. He is survived by two brothers, Charles Carroll of Chittenango and Milan Carroll of Buffalo." James is buried in Forest Lawn Cemetery, Buffalo.

Samuel Carpenter's service and death at Gettysburg are memorialized by the monument erected by family members.
Author's Collection

Justus Cary – Co. D
b. 1836 Ira, Cayuga, NY
d. April 25, 1863 Granby, NY
m. Artemiscia "Mary" Miller (April 2, 1838-February 16, 1924) May 13, 1860

NOTE: Justus, son of John (1795-1875) and Mary Kelly Cary (1795-1875), was sent home on furlough "on account of illness" and died there. There had been a question as to what disease he had: was it rubella or typhoid fever? Dr. Samuel Andrews, the family physician, corroborated Artemiscia's opinion that her husband was suffering from typhoid fever when he died. Artemiscia applied for pensions for her and for her son Justus Ellsworth (1862-*post* 1924). On January 19, 1868 she married John Knapp (1815-October 2, 1887) at Lysander, Onondaga County. Several years later when the Pension Law was amended to permit a remarried widow to reapply for her original pension, she took advantage of the change. The deposition she gave on October 22, 1902 graphically details her life with Knapp: "I am the widow of John Knapp who died Oct. 2, 1882 in the Oswego Co. Almshouse. He was never a soldier. I married him on Jan. 19, 1868 and was never divorced from him. I was the widow of Justus Cary who died in the service April 23, 1863 and I drew a pension as his widow until I remarried Knapp. I lived with Knapp to about May 23, 1868 from the time of our marriage. He had been a Methodist minister before in his younger days and was highly recommended but he became a spiritualist and drunkard. He would come home drunk and abuse me shamefull [sic]. He went down terribly and brought a man and woman to the house and wanted me to consent to exchange husbands and said the other man would support me. He pounded me once and broke ten ribs and I was obliged to go on crutches and in a chair for five years. It caused abscesses in my bowels and I was completely used up and broken hearted. I could not live with him. He continued to live in Oswego [illegible]. My health is poor and I have not a cent ahead. I have no source of income except what I can earn sewing and own no property except this little house worth $500. It is assessed at $300. I shall be obliged to mortgage it soon if I cannot get my pension restored. I have earned only 80 cts. in the past three weeks. Anyone who knows me can testify I have not been divorced or remarried and own no property except this home . . . ." She was granted the pension and drew it until her death "after a short illness." She and Justus are buried in Mt. Adnah Cemetery, Fulton.

Edward Caryl – Co. B
b. August 12, 1841 England
d. January 14, 1910 Norwich, New London, CT
m. Mary Ann Newton (September 1842-May 6, 1923) 1867

NOTE: Edward, son of John (1816-1841) and Matilda Williamson Caryl (1816-1876), mustered out with the regiment on June 7, 1865. He was a painter by trade. He and Mary Ann are both buried in Yantic Cemetery, Norwich, CT.

John Caryl – Co. B
b. August 12, 1841 England
d. August 12, 1908 Norwich, New London, CT
m. Martha J. Newton (January 1847-1932) March 25, 1884

NOTE: John mustered out with the regiment on June 7, 1865. He and his twin, Edward, married sisters. Like his brother, John was a painter. Their father John died in Portugal in 1841 and sometimes the boys said they were born in that country. John, who died on his birthday, and Martha are buried in Yantic Cemetery, Norwich, CT.

Nathan B. Case – Co. C
b. 1843 Williamstown, NY
d. June 1, 1863 Divisional Hospital, Aquia Creek, Stafford, VA
m. ------

NOTE: Nathan was the son of Jonathan (1789-1880) and Amy Lott Worthington Case (1797-1889). His COD reportedly was typhoid fever but chronic diarrhea may also have been a contributing factor. Amy applied for a mother's pension on January 17, 1870, alleging that Nathan had been her primary support for many years because her husband had been disabled "by reason of old age & imbecility or insanity" for ten years. Nathan had used his wages, bounty money, and army pay to support his parents. Jonathan and Amy are buried in Fairview Cemetery, Williamstown.

Patrick Cashman, Jr. – Co. I
b. 1841 Ireland
d. *post* 1870 ?
m. ?

NOTE: This soldier's parents were Patrick (1817-*post* 1870) and Margaret Foley Cashman (1820-*ante* 1870). He was captured on July 1, 1863 at Gettysburg and paroled, mustering out with the regiment on June 7, 1865. In 1870 he was living with his father in Oswego City. I have found no documents after the 1870 census.

James A. Castle – Co. H
b. 1833 Oneida County, NY
d. November 18, 1863 Libby Prison, Richmond, VA
m. Jane E. Piney (1841-?) December 30, 1860

NOTE: James, whose parents are unknown, was taken prisoner on July 1, 1863 and sent to Libby Prison. Although it was reported in *The Town Clerks' Registers* that he died on June 10, 1864, a letter sent to Jane from Benjamin Rainalls, dated January 10, 1864, disproves that assertion: "Dear friend: I was requested to rite a few lines to you stating the deth of youre husband[.] he died between two and three months ago[.] he had the Diarrhea and got all run down[.] before he died he told me tow send youre likeness to you and I did so his last thoughts was ov you and home[.] pleas anser this Direct to Bengamond Rainnal vergena celie 18 Rigmint prisoner of war[,] Richmond." A subsequent letter, dated December 13, 1864, specified that James died November 18, 1863. Jane married Alfred S. Hall (1834-?) in Watertown, Jefferson, NY on June 19, 1865. After that she disappears.

William Castor – Co. E
b. 1844 Redfield, NY
d. May 8, 1864 Virginia
m. ------

NOTE: William's parents were John (1810-1886) and Esther Washburn Castor (1814-*post* 1880). According to *The Town Clerks' Registers* he "was mortally wounded in the lungs [in] a charge of the enemy in action of Wilderness May 5, 1864 – died 8th May 1864. Remains buried."

Lawrence Cavanaugh – Co. B
b. 1834 Ireland
d. *ca.* 1886 Geddes, Onondaga, NY
m. Ellen Bambry (1835-January 22, 1918) *ca.* 1870

NOTE: Lawrence, son of Bernard (1818-1879) and Ann McMahon Cavanaugh (1830-1881), was wounded at Gettysburg and transferred to the VRC on March 1, 1864. He was discharged on June 29, 1865 and applied for a pension on July 21, 1865. He and Ellen were the parents of at least four children, the youngest, James (1881-1917). Lawrence's exact DOD is unknown but Ellen applied for a pension on March 17, 1886. By 1900 she was living in Syracuse with James. She, James, and a daughter, Katherine (1876-1960), are buried in St Agnes' Cemetery, Syracuse.

John Chambers – Co. E
b. 1823 New York State
d. August 23, 1864 Andersonville, Sumter, GA
m. ?

NOTE: Chambers enlisted first in the 30th Regiment but was unassigned and sent to the 147th which he joined on September 26, 1862 in Watervliet, Albany, NY. His capture date is unknown. He was sent to Andersonville where he died of diarrhea. He is buried in the Andersonville National Cemetery. Nothing else has been learned about this man.

Dr. Harvey Ezra Chapin – chaplain
b. August 12, 1811 Paris, Oneida, NY
d. January 29, 1864 Sandy Creek, NY
m. Deborah Fenton (November 10, 1811-December 15, 1891) January 12, 1833

NOTE: Rev. Chapin was the son of Rev. Harvey (1785-1861) and Dolly Campbell Chapin (1785-1863). He was discharged from the service on February 4, 1863 and died less than a year later of "consumption." When Deborah died *The Sandy Creek*

News December 17, 1891 published the following: "Mrs. Deborah Fenton Chapin relict of the late Rev. Harvey E. Chapin was born in Fulton county N. Y. Nov. 10, 1811, and died in Sandy Creek NY. Dec. 15th, 1891, aged 80 years 1 month and 5 days. Her father was brother to ex-Governor Fenton. In her father's family there were eight children, only three of whom are now living, viz., the Rev. Isaac C. Fenton of Washington county, N. Y., Mrs. Lucinda Watson and Mrs. Isaac Howe. The subject of this sketch was married with the Rev. H. E. Chapin, January 12, 1833. Four children were born to them, two sons and two daughters. The sons died early but the daughters both lived to womanhood; one became the wife of Mr. William Hooker but departed this life twenty-one years since; the other became the wife of Mr. S. H. Barlow and with him mourns the loss of a dear mother, whose memory will ever be precious and her name as ointment poured forth. In the death of Mrs. Chapin the family has sustained a great domestic loss, the community a true neighbor and friend, and the Methodist church one of its most valued members. On account of her superior intelligence and good judgment, she was a safe counselor on all questions pertaining to church interests, and therefore will be greatly missed in her relation to the church as well as to the family and community. Her life was filled with deeds of benevolence and kindness in all directions for the good of others . . . ." The two daughters were Deborah (1843-1918), who married Smith Barlow, and Caroline (1849-1870), who married William Hooker. Harvey, Deborah, and Caroline are buried in Woodlawn Cemetery, Sandy Creek.

Daniel Chapman – Co. D
b. 1843 Oswego County, NY
d. July 24, 1914 Saginaw, Saginaw, MI
m. Margaret Sweet (October 10, 1845-March 20, 1912) 1867

NOTE: Daniel's parents were John (1817-?) and Jane (1817-?) Miller Chapman. He mustered out with the regiment on June 7, 1865. According to the 1865 New York census for Granby, NY, John and two sons, Daniel and Duane (1846-?), were all in the army. John joined the 184th Regiment in August 1864 and Duane enlisted in the 147th in February 1864 (see his entry). Margaret's COD was chronic bronchitis. Daniel's COD was senility and fibrosis of the lungs. Both are buried in Forest Lawn Cemetery, Saginaw.

John Chawgo – Co. E
b. June 10, 1842 Onondaga County, NY
d. January 1, 1900 Lacona, NY
m1. Frances Ann Fitch (1841-April 26, 1868) *ca.* 1860
m2. Mary _____ (1845-August 6, 1891) *ca.* 1869
m3. Elizabeth Ann Bunn Dwight (March 6, 1850-April 25, 1902) *ca.* 1892

NOTE: John was the son of Henry, Jr. (1810-May 11, 1873) and Sarah "Sally" Chrisman Chawgo (1803-September 23, 1887). He mustered out with the regiment on June 7, 1865. It appears that his third marriage was stormy because in May 1893 he "advertised" Elizabeth (called Ann in the notice). In 1897 he moved to Port Ontario but whether Elizabeth went with him is unknown. *The Pulaski Democrat* March 15, 1899 reported the following: "Mrs. John Chawgo who has been insane for the last five weeks was taken to Ogdensburg Monday." She had previously been married to Theodore E. Dwight (1840-1886) by whom she had a daughter, Nettie. When the 1900 census was taken, she was living with Nettie and her husband, C. Eugene Plummer. Elizabeth Ann applied for a widow's pension on March 20, 1902 but died before the process could be completed. She is buried in Daysville Cemetery, Richland, with her first husband. Frances Fitch Chawgo is buried in Scripture Cemetery, Sandy Creek. John and Mary Chawgo are buried in Woodlawn Cemetery, Sandy Creek.

William H. Chawgo – Co. E
b. 1836 Madison County, NY
d. April 18, 1902 Sandy Creek, NY
m. Angelette "Nettie" Robbins (1848-March 30, 1914) 1867

NOTE: William's parents were George H. (1805-1890) and Mary "Polly" Chawgo (1812-1895). In 1890 he said his disabilities were rheumatism and diarrhea. Angelette was sometimes called Jennette or Gennette. She and William were the parents of one child, Mary C. (October 1884-1914). As reported in *The Sandy Creek News* April 2, 1914, Nettie died at the home of her daughter, Mrs. John (Mary) Dingman in Pulaski, NY. Two weeks later *The Syracuse Post-Standard* April 15, 1914, 20, reported the following: "Mrs. Mary C. Dingman, 30, widow of John Dingman, died this morning at her home in Mill street [Pulaski] after an illness of about a week with pneumonia. Surviving are three small children. Mrs. Dingman was born at Sandy Creek. Her mother, Mrs. Gennette Chawgo, who lived with Mrs. Dingman, died two weeks ago after an illness of five days with pneumonia. John Dingman died about a year ago . . . ." John Dingman (1874-February 1, 1913) died of appendicitis. They are all buried in Woodlawn Cemetery, Sandy Creek.

Horace Dyer Cheever – Co. F
b. 1838 New Haven, NY
d. November 8, 1863 Parole Camp, Westchester, PA
m. ------

NOTE: Horace was wounded in the foot and captured at Gettysburg. After being paroled, he was sent to Parole Camp, Westchester, PA where he developed chronic diarrhea. His father, William Cheever, wrote the following letter to Hannah Paxton on

October 28, 1863: "I have just received your letter of the 21st, you can see how it was delayed. If my son is yet alive, which I hope is the case, give him all the care possible. If he is not alive, enclosed please find $20 which you say will pay all the expenses except transportation. If he is dead and buried, I do not think it advisable to have him removed. If such be the case, please return the $20, and what few things he left, direct to me by express. Yours with respect, William A. Cheever. P.S. If you ship the body, telegraph to Mr. L. L. Kinyon, Express Agent, Oswego, New York." *The Mexico Independent* November 19, 1863 finished the story: "Died at Westchester, Pa., on the 8th inst., Corporal Horace D. Cheever, of Co. F, 147th regiment, aged 26 years. The remains of the deceased were brought home and buried at New Haven on Friday last. The friends of the deceased tender their heartfelt thanks to the surgeon and the ladies who so kindly and unremittingly administered to his wants during his sickness." Horace was buried in New Haven Rural Cemetery.

Horace Cheever's remains were brought home from Pennsylvania and buried in New Haven Rural Cemetery.

Author's Collection

Jonathan B. Church – Co. F

b. 1822 Onondaga County, NY

d. July 27, 1863 Court House Hospital, Gettysburg, Adams, NY

m1. Melinda _____ (1818-*ante* 1858) *ca.* 1845

m2. Caroline L. Bernasky (1834-June 14, 1887) October 10, 1858

NOTE: Jonathan, whose parents are unknown, had seen previous service as a musician in Co. C, 101st Regiment from October 1, 1861-April 11, 1862 when he was discharged for "disability." According to testimony provided by Lt. Charles B. Skinner, Co. F, 147th Regiment, Church "was shot in the hip and his hip bone [was] broken from the effects of such wound or shot and that he died from the effects of such wound July 27, 1863 . . . ." Caroline must have been shocked when she received the news of his death because O. J. Harmon had written her an optimistic letter dated July 24, 1863 which was later published in *The Mexico Independent* August 20, 1863: "Mrs. Caroline L. Church will be pleased to know that we saw her husband, Mr. J. B. Church, of Co. F, 147th regiment, during our recent visit to the battle field at Gettysburgh. He is in the hospital there, severely wounded in the right thigh. It is quite possible that amputation of the limb may become necessary. He desired me to write to you. It was a great comfort to me and will be to you to know the happy condition of mind your husband was in. He had learned to put his trust in his Saviour, whose promises of help in time of need have never failed his people. He expresses perfect resignation to the divine will, whatever it might be; though he desired much to see his wife and family. But if it was the will of his Heavenly Father that he should be denied this comfort, he hoped to meet them in Heaven. Your husband has every care possible. Every want is supplied by strange but kind and sympathizing hands. You have made a noble offering to your country and you cannot lose your reward." Caroline is buried in Upson's Corners Cemetery, Palermo. A cenotaph for Jonathan is also located there.

John A. Clagg – Co. B
b. 1824 England
d. July 6, 1893 Fonda, Montgomery, NY
m. Jemima _____ (1833-December 17, 1911) *ca.* 1850

NOTE: John, a blacksmith by trade, mustered out with the regiment on June 7, 1865. In 1890 he said he had been shot in the leg, had a sprain in his side, was deaf, and suffered from rheumatism. His sad end was reported in *The Rome Semi-Weekly Citizen* July 8, 1893, 2: "An unknown man aged about 60 was found dead on the New York Central railroad. From papers and a ticket found on his person it is supposed his name is John Clagg, an old soldier of Oswego Falls [Fulton], N.Y." He and Jemima are buried in Mt. Adnah Cemetery, Fulton.

John Clagg was killed in a railroad accident, perhaps because of his profound deafness.
Author's Collection

Abiather L. Clark – Co. A
b. October 1843 Volney, NY
d. April 19, 1913 Volney, NY
m. Margaret _____ (1852-December 27, 1899) *ca.* 1870

NOTE: Abiather, son of Loren (1822-1869) and Rosana Beals Clark (1827-1909), was captured at Gettysburg and later paroled. On February 6, 1865 he was wounded at Hatcher's Run. He reported in 1890 that he had been shot in the left foot. Other disabilities were rheumatism and heart disease. He was a member of Lewis B. Porter

Post No. 573 GAR, Scriba. When he died he left an estate of over $9,000 to be divided between his son, Willis, and daughter, Lucy Clark Fairbanks. He and Margaret are buried in Mount Pleasant Cemetery, Volney.

Ambrose Eugene Clark – Co. C

b. 1843 Oswego, NY

d. March 10, 1881 Montcalm County, MI

m. Irena Ann Omans (July 12, 1844-October 22, 1900) September 26, 1862

NOTE: Ambrose, the son of Luman (1798-1874) and Lucy Clark (1802-?), originally enlisted in the 110th Regiment but was sent to the 147th. He was wounded on July 1, 1863 at Gettysburg and discharged for "disability" on December 31, 1863. Diana Grace Felix Bastion, writing in *The Mayflower Quarterly* 69, 1 (March 2003), 134, reported that his left "leg ended up 3 inches shorter than the right." He and Irena were the parents of three. Irena married Warner Lott (1833-1911) on December 5, 1881. By him she was the mother of two sons. Irena's COD was Bright's disease. She and Ambrose are buried in Ferris Center Cemetery, Vestaburg, Montcalm, MI. Lott, who was married at least five times, had served in the 6th MI HA. He is buried in Oak Hill Cemetery, Battle Creek, Calhoun, MI.

Loren R. Clark – Co. A

b. January 18, 1822 MA

d. June 18, 1879 Volney, NY

m. Rosana M. Beals (1827-May 26, 1909) *ca.* 1842

NOTE: Loren, a clergyman, and Rosana were the parents of Abiather Clark. He was discharged on September 20, 1863 for "disability." They are buried in Mount Pleasant Cemetery, Volney.

Franklin "Frank" Benjamin Clary – Co. C

b. 1827 Richfield, Otsego, NY

d. July 1, 1863 Gettysburg, Adams, PA

m. Arminda Wright (1835-1860) *ca.* 1856

NOTE: According to *The Town Clerks' Registers* he was "killed instantly by ball through head at Battle [of] Gettysburg 7/3/1863." His DOD in *Deaths of Volunteers* is July 1st. He is buried in Gettysburg National Cemetery. Arminda is buried in Albion Center Cemetery. A cenotaph is located there for Frank.

Albert Clemens – Co. E
b. 1841 Greenboro, NY
d. February 4, 1863 US General Hospital, Windmill Point, VA
m. ------

NOTE: Albert's surname was variously spelled. His parents were Samuel (1813-1880) and Julia Castor Clemens (1812-February 5, 1905). His COD was described as "disease" and his body was sent home and buried in Greenboro Cemetery, Redfield, NY.

Charles H. Cobb – Co. E
b. July 1838 Jefferson County, NY
d. July 24, 1910 Boylston, NY
m. Mary Elizabeth Hollis (September 1843-February 22, 1922) 1866

NOTE: Charles, whose parents were Stevenson H. (1800-1880) and Zoa Penniman Cobb (1806-1884), was wounded on April 1, 1865 at the battle of Five Forks, VA. He and Mary are buried in Woodlawn Cemetery, Sandy Creek.

John D. Cody – Co. K
b. 1820 Ireland
d. October 9, 1906 Syracuse, Onondaga, NY
m. Mary Kelly (1819-August 17, 1885) *ca.* 1840

NOTE: John, son of William (?-?)) and Mary Morrissey Cody (?-?), was transferred to the VRC on April 29, 1864 and subsequently discharged on June 29, 1865 at Albany, NY. On the 1865 New York census Mary said she was the mother of twelve children. Both are buried in St Paul's Cemetery, Oswego.

Dr. Algernon Sidney Coe – surgeon
b. September 18, 1828 Norway, Herkimer, NY
d. October 17, 1893 Oswego City, NY
m1. Mary Bates Goit (1832-July 19, 1862) *ca.* 1852
m2. Cathlina Bogart Fort (July 19, 1830-July 19, 1914) 1869

NOTE: Dr. Coe was the son of Ira (1790-1861) and Elizabeth Norton Coe (1795-1877). His standing in the community was demonstrated by the lengthy obituary appearing in *The Oswego Daily Palladium* October 18, 1893, 5: "The people of Oswego were greatly shocked this morning to learn of the death of Dr. A. S. Coe, which occurred at his home last evening after a very brief illness. He had been ill but a day and no apprehension was felt by his family or friends. The summons came when least expected, bringing uncommon affliction to those who knew him well and a shade of grief to the entire community. Dr. Algernon Coe came from New England stock. He was born at Norway, Herkimer county, September 18, 1828. He remained on his father's farm, received the benefits of the common schools of that time and was finally graduated at Fairfield Academy. Later he was graduated in medicine and surgery at the New York College of Physicians. He became a pupil of his brother, Dr. A. B. Coe, whom many citizens still remember, and in 1853 began the practice of his profession for himself. When the war with the South broke out Dr. Coe was mustered into the service of the United States as Surgeon of the 147th New York Volunteers, August 29th, 1862, and served with his regiment in the Army of the Potomac until its discharge . . . In January, 1863, at Belle Plain, he was detailed as Brigade Surgeon, and from that time till the close of the war was almost continuously in charge of the medical department of the Brigade or division. His ability as a surgeon, together with his faithful attention to duty and thorough discipline of assistants and subordinates, made him a favorite with the commanding officers of the old First and Fifth Corps in which he served. He was known as a line-of-battle surgeon and was with his command on every march and in every battle. No surgeon in the whole army did more or better work than he. During his whole term of service he was never absent a single day. He was deservedly popular with the brave and faithful officers and men under his immediate charge and in the whole corps, but never much of a favorite with malingers [sic] and beats, with whom he had no sympathy. Since the war he has always taken great interest in matters pertaining thereto and has left some valuable contributions to the history of the One Hundred and Forty-seventh New York and to the brigade and corps in which it served. The article in 'Oswego County History' under head of 'Oswego in the Rebellion,' was written by him and is a faithful tribute to the gallantry and patriotism of Oswego's boys in blue. Soon after returning home he was the head of the Board of Pension Examiners in which responsible capacity his justice and skill deserved and obtained the highest esteem as well with the authorities at Washington as with the soldiers themselves. We can pen no more faithful eulogy on the character and virtues of the deceased than the following written this morning by one of his professional brethren: 'To catalogue his virtues would be to go over the whole circle of human merits. To an integrity and honor so exalted that he was absolutely incapable of guile or indirection, or even of concealment, he added uncommon generosity of character, a fellow-feeling that suffered with all who suffered, and a devotion that left no obligation of duty unfulfilled. With these was joined that righteous wrath for bad men and bad actions which is a necessary part even of divine justice. Thus whatever praise may be inscribed on the stone that covers his mortal frame will not surpass his merits . . . .'" When Cathlina died, the managers of the Oswego Orphan Asylum eulogized her in *The Oswego Daily Times* July 22, 1914, 8: ". . . In the death of Mrs. Coe another beloved associate and fellow worker has been taken from our number, called from her loving service here, to the higher service above. For over thirty years she had filled the position of directress and first vice-president with a faithfulness and unswerving loyalty most marked. The welfare of our home and the little ones within it was ever near her heart, and she gave most practical proof of that interest and devotion. For many years her hospitable home was open for our monthly meetings during the winters when inclement weather prevented our going to the asylum. Tenderness, loving sympathy and charity were marked features of her character, which, with her gracious, kindly personality, presented in most attractive combination the graces of a Christian woman. With choice native gifts, developed by a refining and practical culture, she fitly filled every place in which she was called to act, true to all the proprieties of life. Earth is the poorer, heaven the richer, by her translation, and she has left a shining track in which we [fain] would follow. Our hearts are full of the deepest, tenderest sympathy for her beloved ones, whom we tenderly commend to the Divine Consoler . . . ." Dr. Coe, Mary, and Cathlina are buried in Riverside Cemetery, Scriba.

John Ellsworth Coe – Co. G

b. January 24, 1837 Scriba, NY
d. October 23, 1889 Oswego City, NY
m. Frances J. "Frank" _____ (November 1841-June 27, 1922) *ca.* 1857

NOTE: Coe, son of Simon (1808-1897) and Sarah Prosser Coe (1813-1891), was wounded on July 1, 1863 at Gettysburg and transferred to the VRC on February 11, 1864. He was a member of Lewis B. Porter Post No. 573 GAR and of Lycoming Lodge IOOF. His unexpected death was reported by *The Oswego Daily Palladium* October 23, 1889, 3: "Coroner [Christopher] Vowinkel was notified this morning that a man had been killed at the Sparks Hill crossing in East Seneca street by the Phoenix train for Syracuse, which left this city at 11o'clock. The police patrol wagon conveyed the Coroner and a Palladium reporter to the scene of the accident. The victim of the accident, who proved to be John E. Coe, of Lycoming [North Scriba] was not dead, but was found unconscious in the house of Mrs. Meyers suffering from a bruise on the back of the head and from other injuries which will probably cause his death. Mrs. Meyers, who witnessed the accident, told the reporter that she saw Coe driving down the hill toward the crossing, and from this it is impossible to see the approach of a train from either direction. He apparently did not hear the train and his wagon was just on the track when struck by the train. The horses were thrown upon one side of the track, and the wagon and man upon the other. The train was stopped as soon as possible, and the train hands carried the injured man to the house of Mrs. Meyers. The point where he was picked up is fully 100 feet from the crossing. After the arrival of the patrol wagon Doctors Langdon and Richards came upon the scene. They dressed the injuries and were working over the injured man when the reporter left.

They gave it as their opinion that the injury on the head was caused by coming in contact with a stone where the man struck the ground. Mr. Coe, who kept a store at Lycoming, was on his way home from the city with a load of groceries when the accident occurred. The wagon was broken into kindling wood and the contents strewn for 50 feet along the track. One horse was badly injured. Mr. Coe is 53 years old and has a wife and son, the latter a physician in Lycoming. He has been telegraphed for. The injured man is widely known throughout the county. He has been quite a prominent politician and has represented his town on the Board of Supervisors and has also been Postmaster . . . Coe died at two o'clock this afternoon. Coroner Vowinkel impaneled a jury, and viewed the remains. The body was then removed to his home at Lycoming." John, Frances, and their son, Dr. Charles Coe, are all buried in North Scriba Union Cemetery.

James Coey – Co. E MEDAL OF HONOR RECIPIENT
b. February 12, 1841 New York City, NY
d. July 14, 1918 Berkley, Alameda, CA
m. Maria L. Reynolds (March 1844-April 24, 1925) *ca.* 1870

NOTE: James was the child of William John (?-*ante* 1865) and Elizabeth Jane Carlisle Coey (?-*post* 1870). When he died *The Oswego Daily Palladium* July 25, 1918, 3 published the following: "General James Coey, former Postmaster of San Francisco, died in Berkley, Cal., July 14th. He enlisted from Redfield in 1862 with the 147th N.Y. and was soon promoted to Colonel. He was advanced in the ranks until he became a general. He won honors for gallantry in the battles of the Wilderness and Laurel Hill. He was given [the] Congressional Medal of Honor for distinguished bravery in the battle of Hatcher's Run when he was dangerously wounded. In 1868 he organized the G.A.R. department of California, Oregon, Nevada and Arizona, serving as first department commander for several terms. General Coey is survived by his widow and two daughters . . . ." The brief notice concerning Hatcher's Run does not do justice to the man's courage. The citation for his MOH gives more detail: "The President of the United States of America, in the name of Congress, takes pleasure in presenting the Medal of Honor to Major James Coey, United States Army, for extraordinary heroism on 6 February 1865, while serving with 147th New York Infantry, in action

GENERAL JAMES COEY

For his bravery at Hatcher's Run Coey was awarded the Medal of Honor.
History of the Grand Army of the Republic

at Hatcher's Run, Virginia. Major Coey seized the regimental colors at a critical moment and by a prompt advance on the enemy caused the entire brigade to follow him; and, after being himself severely wounded, he caused himself to be lifted into the saddle and a second time rallied the line in an attempt to check the enemy." Coey was wounded in his first attempt to encourage the men forward in the face of the advancing Confederates. A bullet hit him in the head just below the left eye and exited behind his right ear. He became unconscious and was being carried off the battlefield when he awoke. Instead of leaving, he insisted on mounting a horse, returning to the line, and continuing his exhortation of the troops. Hatcher's Run, however, was not the first battle in which he was wounded. He had received a leg wound at Laurel Hill, VA on May 10, 1864. His brother, David Norwood Coey (1837-1905), served in the 69th Regiment. Another brother, Stark Andrew Coey (1844-1903), served in the 189th Regiment. James and Maria are buried in San Francisco National Cemetery.

Charles Henry Cole – Co. A
b. 1842 Oswego, NY
d. July 1, 1863 Gettysburg, Adams, PA
m. ------

NOTE: Charles, son of Claudius (*ca.* 1815-?) and Martha (1822-?), was a lake sailor. He was probably buried on the field at Gettysburg.

Harrison H. Cole – Co. E
b. October 4, 1840 Adams, Jefferson, NY
d. August 4, 1916 Sandy Creek, NY
m. Arabella Wilds (August 1842-December 5, 1916) 1868

NOTE: Harrison, son of Joseph (1798-1873) and Fanna A. Reynolds Cole (1800-1843), was a musician in the 147th Regiment. His obituary, appearing in *The Sandy Creek News* August 10, 1916, outlined a long and active life: "One of the prominent residents of the Ridge, Harrison H. Cole, died suddenly last Friday at eventide. Mr. Cole had been about the house and, while not in the best of health, his death was not anticipated. Dr. Cook was hastily summoned and reached his side a few moments before he passed away. The deceased was born October 4, 1840 in Adams, his parents being Joseph and Fanny Nobles [*sic*] Cole, natives of Hebron Washington Co., N.Y., who settled in Adams in 1818 and who came to Sandy Creek in 1846. Mr. Cole's life was largely spent in this town. He went to the front during the Civil war, enlisting in September, 1862, in the 147th N.Y. Vol. as a musician, and remained till the close of the conflict. He was leader of the 3d Brigade band, 3rd Div. 6th Corps. Several members of this band were killed at Gettysburg and Comrade Cole barely escaped capture by the Confederates.

He was also at Fredericksburg and all through the Wilderness. His brother, L. J. Cole, now deceased, was captain of Co. G, N.Y. Cav. Mr. Cole was a musician of more than ordinary ability, and for years was leader of the Sandy Creek Cornet band. So popular was he with his townsmen that for sixteen years he was a collector of taxes. He purchased the farm of 90 acres where he resided in 1869. In addition to general farming and dairying, he kept a large apiary. In 1868 he married Arabella daughter of James and Mariah Wilds, of Sandy Creek, who survives him. In the early days of ballooning Mr. Cole took an interest in aeronautics, and made a balloon ascension at the Sandy Creek fair grounds. He was Ridge road correspondent of the Sandy Creek News since its establishment. For many years he served as trustee of the Congregational church of which both Mr. and Mrs. Cole were regular attendants . . . Mr. Cole was a member of Post Barney . . . ." Harrison and Arabella are buried in Woodlawn Cemetery, Sandy Creek.

Barney Colgan – Co. H
b. 1825 Ireland
d. September 28, 1880 Celina, Mercer, OH
m. Julia Horrey (1827-June 4, 1889) ca. 1852

NOTE: Barney, whose parents are unknown, lived in Constantia, NY. In 1855 he and Julia had resided there fore three years. He claimed to be a laborer. Colgan, whose name was variously spelled, was captured at Gettysburg on July 1, 1863 and paroled at an unknown date. He and Julia moved to Ohio at some time after the 1875 New York census. In 1865 Mary said that she was the mother of seven. She and Barney are buried in St. Mary's Catholic Cemetery, Celina.

Patrick Connell – Co. I
b. 1839 Ireland
d. ?
m. ?

NOTE: Patrick, who joined the 147th in Oswego City, was a sailor, probably on the Great Lakes. He transferred to Batt. L, 1st NY ART on December 31, 1863. I have located nothing else about him.

Dennis Conley – Co. D
b. 1830 Ireland
d. December 19, 1882 Flint, Genesee, MI
m. Mary "May" Bush (1840-December 27, 1909) ca. 1857

NOTE: Research on this man has been difficult due to variations of his surname. His parents are unidentified but he claimed to be a sailor when he enlisted. He was captured on July 1, 1863 and paroled, date unknown. He mustered out with the regiment on June 7, 1865. Dennis applied for a pension under the name Connoly on August 25, 1879. According to his FAG entry he had suffered a gunshot wound to the head resulting in vertigo, for which he was awarded $4.00 per month. In 1890 Mary was enumerated as a war widow. She said Dennis had been "shot in the head & killed." What she meant by that is uncertain. Both are buried in Avondale Cemetery, Flint.

Abraham Conterman – Co. H

b. September 5, 1824 Minden, Montgomery, NY

d. March 16, 1906 Central Square, NY

m. Phebe Hoyt (December 16, 1823-July 6, 1896) *ante* 1855

NOTE: Abraham was the son of John Adam (1791-1868) and Margaret Wohlgemuth Conterman (1789-1847). His DOB varies. I use that on his gravestone. When he enlisted in the 147th he was a blacksmith. In 1875 he was a section boss on the railroad. He was discharged from the army on January 8, 1863 for "disability," specifically, chronic diarrhea and rheumatism. His DOD is not given on his gravestone but was deduced from an obituary appearing in *The Oswego Daily Palladium* March 22, 1906, 8: "Abraham Conterman, aged eighty years, a respected citizen of [Central Square], died on Friday afternoon after a short illness. He was a member of Central Square, No. 622 F. and A.M., Central Square lodge No. 798, I.O.O.F., Isaac Waterbury Post No. 418, G.A.R., and of the Eastern Star and the Rebekah degrees. The funeral was held [March 19] at the Baptist church. Burial at West Monroe. Mr. Conterman is survived by one brother, William Conterman, West Monroe. The funeral was conducted by the Masonic fraternity . . . ." Abraham and Phebe had no children, making a more exact marriage date impossible to determine. They are buried in West Monroe Cemetery.

William Cotton Cook – Co. B

b. July 17, 1824 Wallingford Town, New Haven, CT

d. October 25, 1896 Oswego City, NY

m. Mary Angeline Dodge (June 2, 1825-November 7, 1915) *ca.* 1850

NOTE: William, son of Caleb (1786-1852) and Amelia Lewis Cook (1788-1840), transferred to the US Navy in 1864, enlisting on May 4th for a year and a half. He and Mary lived in Oswego City where he was a grocer. Her death was marked by an informative obituary in *The Oswego Daily Palladium* November 9, 1915: "The death of Mrs. Mary A. Cook occurred early last Sunday morning, following an illness of but a few days. Born in Richland, N.Y., June 2d, 1825, she had reached the advanced age of ninety years. Nearly sixty years ago she came with her husband, the late William C. Cook, to Oswego, which had since been her home and where she and her husband will be remembered by the older residents of the city. In her death the old First Presbyterian Church loses another loved member, a member of no uncertain creed, and while strength permitted ever active in the upbuilding of her church. She will be remembered as a woman of rare culture and personal charm . . . ." Mary and William, the parents of two children, are buried in Pulaski Village Cemetery.

William H. Cook – Co. D

b. May 11, 1817 Madison County, NY

d. September 1, 1911 Fulton, NY

m. Nancy M. Sears (April 5, 1825-February 26, 1905) 1840

NOTE: William, son of William H. (1792-1876) and Nancy Rector Cook (1796-1886), was a farmer. He transferred to Batt. L, 1st NY ART on December 8, 1863. He and Nancy were the parents of five children, only two of whom were alive in 1900. William is buried in Mt. Adnah Cemetery, Fulton. Nancy is buried in Mt. Pleasant Cemetery, Volney.

Sidney Granger Cooke – Co. E

b. June 18, 1846 Fulton, NY

d. August 15, 1926 Leavenworth, Leavenworth, KS

m. Helen Maria Thornton (April 24, 1847-May 22, 1941

NOTE: Sidney was the son of Horace Nelson (1811-1888) and Jane Ann Forman Cooke (1809-1883). An article published in *The Oswego Palladium-Times* March 13, 1941, 4 tells the story of a Bible Cooke bought from a Confederate soldier and how his son, Thornton, returned it to its rightful owners. This article is valuable for the material it contains about Cooke's experiences as a POW and later a soldier awaiting exchange. The muster roll entry for him does not specify where he was taken prisoner, but this story does: ". . . Then came the Battle of the Wilderness. My father, sent out in charge of a small detachment to find the enemy, came upon them very suddenly, turned to give a command, and was struck by a bullet just below the base of the brain. His men examined him and left him for dead within the Confederate lines . . . Sidney Cooke was taken to Andersonville for six months, then to Millen, then to Savannah, where, seven months after he was shot (in the back of his neck), he sneezed the bullet out of his nose. From Savannah, he was shipped to Annapolis, where he took charge of the men in the parole camp. After his exchange he was commissioned second lieutenant and was in command of his company when barely nineteen . . . ." Over the next few years Cooke received a degree from the University of Rochester, became a school superin- tendent, and eventually a lawyer, among others. In 1904 he was appointed governor of the National Home in Leavenworth, KS, a post he held for several years. Thornton spoke of his father's humanity towards Confederate veterans: ". . . Then the no-firing agreement of the Confederate pickets on the Rappahannock, the decency of the soldiers who didn't take his boots, the service of the Southern surgeon, the chivalry of the Confederate major who got his letter through two armies to his mother, paid dividends. Every now and then some old Confederate soldier would straggle into camp and be referred to Governor Cooke. Against the regulations and proud of it, he would order the man taken up 'Temporarily at Post.' So the old Confederate would get good square meals and a rest, and medical attention, too, if he needed it, until it became impossible to keep up longer the pretense that his eligibility was under investigation . . . ." Sidney was elected to the commandery of the Kansas Division of the Loyal Legion in 1901. He was elected honorary president of the 147th Reunion Committee in 1915. Sidney and Helen are both buried in Leavenworth National Cemetery.

Andrew Coon – Co. K
b. March 13, 1844 Oswego, NY
d. November 17, 1912 Central Lake, Antrim, MI
m1. Maria _____ (1837-*post* 1873) *ca.* 1869
m2. Margaret J. "Jennie" Davis Walker (May 1859-1930) December 1, 1882

NOTE: Andrew Coon was an alias for Charles Andrew Mason, son of William (?-?) and Mary E. Hutchins Mason (1826-?). When he enlisted he said he was a boatman. Coon mustered out with the regiment on June 7, 1865. His COD was heart disease with "dropsy" as a contributing factor. He and Margaret are buried in Southern Cemetery, Central Lake, MI.

George W. Coon – Co. G
b. 1841 Scriba, NY
d. April 13, 1863 Regimental Hospital, Belle Plain, VA
m. ------

NOTE: George was a son of Alvin Joseph (1802-1893) and Ruth Sweet Coon (1821-1903). His COD was "chronic diarrhea." A note in *The Town Clerks' Registers* reports he died on April 12th. His mother applied for a pension in 1890 and obtained a certificate.

John Henry Coon – Co. G
b. 1846 Scriba, NY
d. April 3, 1863 Regimental Hospital, Belle Plain, VA
m. ------

NOTE: John, son of Jacob W. (1815-1872) and Mary Sweet Coon (1818-1892), lied about his age in order to enlist, proved by a cenotaph in Worden-Sweet Cemetery, Scriba, which says he was "Aged 16 years 7 mo. & 22 Days." His muster roll card says he died in March 1863 but according to *Deaths of Volunteers*, he died of "chronic diarrhea" on April 3, 1863. *The Town Clerks' Registers* and his cenotaph both say he died April 2ⁿᵈ. He is buried in Fredericksburg National Cemetery. In 1889 his mother applied for and obtained a pension.

John N. Coon – Co. G

b. December 9, 1842 Oswego County, NY

d. August 14, 1864 probably Scriba, NY

m. ------

NOTE: John was a son of Calvin (1804-1878) and Sarah Amsbron Coon (1812-*ante* 1875). According to his muster roll card, he was discharged from the service on May 18, 1864, returned home and died on August 14ᵗʰ. His DOD was August 1ˢᵗ, according to *Registers of Officers and Enlisted Men*. His grave has not been located.

Oscar Mervale Coon – Co. G

b. May 3, 1846 Scriba, NY

d. July18, 1898 Scriba, NY

m. Rebecca E. Touse (April 1853-June 10, 1928) *ca.* 1875

NOTE: Oscar, a son of Joseph (1813-1895) and Ruth Smith Coon (1815-1888), lied about his age when he enlisted. According to *The Town Clerks' Registers*, he was captured at the battle of the Wilderness on May 5, 1864 and sent to Andersonville Prison. In 1890 he said his disability was "dyspepsia" and the enumerator noted he had been a "Prisoner at Andersonville." His parole date is unknown but he mustered out with the regiment on June 7, 1865. He was a member of Lewis B. Porter Post No. 573 GAR which published the following in *The Oswego Daily Times* July 23, 1898, 7: "Whereas the last great enemy has again attacked our Post and our roll call reveals the fact that Comrade Oscar M. Coon has been lost to us by transfer from our Grand Army of volunteers to the Grander Army of the immortal, and, Whereas in each of these warnings we realize another link is broken in the circle that from henceforth must ever grow less, therefore be it Resolved, That in the death of Comrade Coon this post regrets the loss of one more of our little company and with the desire to fittingly express our kind remembrance of the deceased and sacred regard for our fallen comrade be it Resolved, That we send to the bereaved family of this dead soldier our sincere sympathy and regret at their loss . . . ." Oscar and Rebecca are buried in North Scriba Union Cemetery.

James F. Cooper – Co. D

b. August 23, 1838 Saratoga County, NY

d. October 19, 1898 Fulton, NY

m. Nancy Wakeley (1833-December 29, 1903) *ante* 1860

NOTE: James was the son of Jarvis (1810-1886) and Doanda Moody Cooper (1811-1897). He was discharged from Finley Hospital, Washington, DC on June 15, 1863 for "disability." In 1890 he reported typhoid fever had affected his lungs. His obituary in *The Oswego Daily Palladium* October 20, 1898 recounted his long and active life: "In the death of James F. Cooper, which occurred at his home at the corner of Oneida and Fourth streets, yesterday, Fulton lost one of her old and most respected citizens. Mr. Cooper was born in Saratoga August 23, 1838, and was the son of Jervis and Doanda Cooper, whose families were Quakers and farmers. He removed to Hannibal, where he lived until 1843, when he came to this village, living here ever since. He was married to Nancy Wakeley, who survives him. During the War of the Rebellion he enlisted in Company D, 147the N.Y.V., in which he served one year. He was a carpenter and millwright by trade, but for a number of years was prominently connected with the schools, being principal of the school in district No. 1 for twenty-eight consecutive terms, before it was consolidated. At the time of his death he was principal of the Oswego Falls school. He was a prominent member of Hiram Lodge, F. and A.M., and Zion Episcopal church. Funeral services will be held Saturday at 10:30 A.M., the Rev. George F. Potter officiating." James and Nancy are buried with their parents in Union Cemetery, Ira, Cayuga, NY.

Thomas Cooper – Co. K
b. 1818 England
d. *post* 1863 ?
m. ?

NOTE: Cooper, who enlisted in Oswego City, was wounded at Gettysburg on July 1, 1863 and was discharged from the army at Convalescent Camp, Alexandria, VA on September 18, 1863. His application for a pension, filed on December 7, 1863, was successful. His parents were James (?-?) and Mary Cooper (?-?), according to *The Town Clerks' Registers*, which also stated he resided in Weedsport, Cayuga, NY. No information can be located after 1863. His pension card does not list a widow, so he either was not married or his wife predeceased him.

John Corcoran – Co. B
b. 1824 Ireland
d. July 12, 1895 Oswego City, NY
m1. Mary _____ (1835-*ante* 1875) *ca.* 1852
m2. Bridget _____ (July 1831-April 20, 1918) 1888

NOTE: John was taken captive at Gettysburg and paroled at an unspecified time. He was discharged for "disability" on January 11, 1864. John, a member of May Stacy Post No. 586 GAR, Oswego, is buried in St Paul's Cemetery. In 1900 Bridget said she and John had been married seven years which I interpret to mean seven years before his death, that is, 1888. Bridget's death was announced in *The Oswego Daily Palladium* April 20, 1918, 4: "Mrs. Bridget Corcoran, wife of the late John Corcoran, died at 4:30 o'clock this morning at the home of her niece, Mrs. Fred Dowie, 144 Liberty street. She was born in Ireland eighty-seven years ago, but had long been a resident of this city, having many friends who will be pained to learn of her death. She was a member of St. Mary's Church, from where the services will be held, probably on Monday morning. Several nephews and nieces survive." Graves for Mary and Bridget have not been located.

Eli Cornwell – Co. H
b. 1820 Oswego, NY
d. ?
m. ?

NOTE: Eli was captured on May 5, 1864 and was probably sent to Andersonville, GA. He was paroled in Savannah, GA on November 30, 1864 and transferred *in absentia* to Co. A, 91st Regiment under the name of Elijah Cromwell with the notation "absent-at Parole Camp. See 147 for final record." He does not appear in *The Adjutant-General's Report* for that regiment. Since there are no further documents I theorize he died while at parole camp.

Louis N. Cottet – Co. H
b. November 1, 1841 Mexico, NY
d. August 24, 1920 Crookston, Polk, MN
m. Minerva Elizabeth Dunn (February 8, 1849-October 25, 1921) September 21, 1869

NOTE: Louis' parents may have been James (1800-?) and Madeline Cottet (1797-?), both born in France. He mustered out with the regiment on June 7, 1865. He and Minerva were married in Jackson County, IA. His death was announced in *The Warren Sheaf* September 1, 1920, 12: ". . . Louis Cottet, who was next to the last member of Col. Cobham post of the G.A.R. of Crookston, died Aug. 24, at his home in said city. Deceased was born in Oswego, N.Y., in 1844 [*sic*] and was 77 years of age at his death. He came to Euclid 41 years ago from Bellevue, Iowa, but he has resided in Crookston the past 20 years. Death was due to a stroke of paralysis." Cottet gave his age as 21 when he enlisted in 1862 and all census records show he was born in 1841 even though his gravestone shows a DOB of 1844. He and Minerva are buried in Oakdale Cemetery, Crookston.

Arthur T. Coulson – Co. B
b. August 25, 1847 Oswego County, NY
d. November 11, 1930 Marshalltown, Marshall, IA
m. ------

NOTE: Arthur was the son of William (1821-ca. 1853) and Helen Gridley Coulson (1821-*post* 1905). In 1855 he, with his widowed mother and two siblings, lived in New Haven. He joined the 147th as a drummer and mustered out with the regiment on June 7, 1865. He was living in Iowa when he applied for a pension in 1890. Arthur, a Quaker, was buried in Earlham Cemetery, Earlham, Madison, IA. The All-American Legion Post 158, Earlham, ordered his gravestone.

William Wallace Court – Co. K
b. August 23, 1842 Ogdensburg, St. Lawrence, NY
d. June 2, 1925 State Hospital, Pontiac, Oakland, MI
m. Esther Mary Corcoran (February 1846-1919) May 6, 1868

NOTE: William's DOB varies from document to document. His death certificate says he was born May 13, 1841 but *The Town Clerks' Registers* provide a date of August 23, 1842. In 1900 he said he was born in May 1842. He was a son of James (1810-1880) and Martha Jenette Bocquet Court (1825-1892). According to *The Town Clerks' Registers* he was wounded at the second battle of Bull Run, which is impossible since that battle was fought August 28-30, 1862, about the time the 147th was being organized. It is probable, however, that he was wounded at some point since he was not discharged from the service until July 15, 1865. He and Esther, who was born in Ohio, were married in Middlesex, Ontario, Canada. In 1900 she said she was the mother of eight, six of whom were living. William's COD was arterio-sclerosis and senility. Their graves have not been located.

Martin Hathaway Cox – Co. D
b. 1822 Onondaga County, NY
d. March 26, 1886 Hannibal, NY
m. Sally Ann _____ (1823-September 20, 1886) January 1, 1844

NOTE: Martin was the son of Rev. Gabriel (1798-1858) and Lydia Farnum Cox (1807-1861). He mustered out with the regiment on June 7, 1865. His death was announced in *The Oswego Times-Express* March 27, 1886, 1: "Another one of Hannibal's prominent and respected citizens has been called away by the relentless hand of death. Friday afternoon Martin H. Cox died at his home at North Hannibal, aged 63 years. For weeks and months disease wasted away his body but his intellect seemed to brighten as the time of his end approached and he passed away peacefully and happy and left behind him many words of cheer and blessings to his afflicted family which consists of a wife and five children . . . Mr. Cox was a veteran of the late war, and served his country nobly and well. By his neighbors he was held in the highest esteem for his noble traits of character, as he was a man of large generosity, honesty and truthfulness. For about fifteen years he was postmaster at North Hannibal and carried on the mercantile business for eighteen years. He was identified with the republican party, and advocated strongly the cause of temperance and kindred reforms. His family and friends feel deeply his loss, but his influence for good is left indelibly on their hearts and the grandeur of his character is left as a monument to guide those who knew him . . . ." He and Sally Ann are buried in Fairdale Cemetery, Hannibal.

Moulton Gabriel Cox – Co. A
b. May 14, 1838 Oswego County, NY
d. October 18, 1896 Binghamton, Broome, NY
m. Lucretia E. Wadleigh (1840-January 29, 1914) May 1872

NOTE: Moulton was a brother of Martin H. Cox. He originally enlisted in the 110th Regiment but was sent to the 147th. He was discharged for "disability" on March 27, 1865 and in 1890 he said his disability was a "gunshot wound in back." He and Lucretia are buried in Floral Park Cemetery, Johnson City, Broome, NY. Two other Cox brothers also served in the Civil War. George M. Cox (1833-1914) served in Battery E, 1st Michigan LA. Charles H. Cox (1835-1892) was a member of the 75th Regiment NYSV. He was captured at Sabine Pass, TX on September 8, 1863 and paroled at an unknown date.

Norman Crafts – Co. G
b. April 3, 1829 Prattsburg, Steuben, NY
d. February 3, 1899 Scriba, NY
m. Jeanette E. Waggoner (1839-April 28, 1923) November 23, 1858

NOTE: Norman, son of Elijah (1786-1874) and Dilla "Dolly" Trescott Crafts (1788-1833), was wounded July 1, 1863 at Gettysburg and transferred to the VRC on February 6, 1864. He belonged to Lewis B. Porter Post No. 573 GAR, Scriba. Norman, a farmer, and Lucretia are buried in New Haven Rural Cemetery.

John C. Cratsenberg – Co. C
b. August 23, 1842 Champion, Jefferson, NY
d. May 5, 1875 Adams Center, Jefferson, NY
m. Jane "Jennie" E. Bailey (December 1848-July 29, 1917) ca. 1869

NOTE: John, son of Adam (1819-1901) and Esther Averill Cratsenberg (1818-1889), was wounded at the battle of Gettysburg on July 1, 1863 and discharged, according to *The Town Clerks' Registers*, on May 9, 1864 "by reason of wounds received in service." In 1870 he said his occupation was "horse dealer." The 1875 New York census shows he and Jane were the parents of three children, Zoe, 5, Marshall, 3, and Bessie, 0. John was buried in Union Cemetery, Adams Center, NY. His gravestone erroneously says he served in the 146th Regiment. Although John did not receive an obituary *The Jefferson County Journal* July 21, 1875, 4 noted the following: "Cratsenberg-at Clayton, N.Y., July 3d, Bessie infant daughter of the late John C. Cratsenberg of Adams Center, N.Y., aged three months." Jane and Zoe lived together for the rest of their lives. In 1900 Jane was a nurse and Zoe (November 1869-1959) was a dressmaker. Jane's death was reported in *The* [Potsdam] *Commercial Advertiser* July 31, 1917: "At her home on Court street after an illness of several years, Mrs. Jane E. Cratsenberg passed away Sunday night, July 29 at about midnight. Mrs. Cratsenberg's condition had been such that death was momentarily expected . . . The death of Mrs. Cratsenberg removes one of the very fine elderly women of [Canton]. Mrs. Cratsenberg was born sixty-nine years ago and lived for a great many years in the house on Court street where death came. She was a sister of the late Sylvester S. Bailey who died here a few years ago. She was a member of the M. E. Church and when in health a constant attendant and worker in the church. She leaves surviving her a daughter, Miss Zoe Cratsenberg, who cared for her mother with devotion during the long months of her late illness. A son there is also, Marshall Cratsenberg, who resides at Los Angeles." Jane and Zoe are buried in Fairview Cemetery, Canton, St. Lawrence, NY. Marshall (1872-June 16, 1936) died in Los Angeles, CA. John's father, Adam I. Cratsenberg, served in the 14th NY HA, was wounded and captured at Cold Harbor, VA on June 2, 1864. He lost an arm as a result of his injury. He was sent to Andersonville Prison but was paroled on August 13, 1864. He was discharged because of his wound on January 20, 1865. He and Esther are buried in Riverside Cemetery, Cape Vincent, Jefferson, NY. His DOD does not appear on his gravestone. It was located on a pension index card.

John Crinnon – Co. H
b. August 1818 Ireland
d. *post* 1865 ?
m. ------

NOTE: According to *The Town Clerks' Registers*, John was born August 1813, son of William (?-?) and Nina Whalan Crinnon (?-?). All existing records indicate he never married. He was wounded in the foot at the siege of Petersburg and discharged on March 22, 1865. He appears on the 1865 New York census, aged 52, single, a laborer, "formerly in Army." After that the trail goes cold.

Albert B. Crocker – Co. C

b. November 1840 Richland, NY

d. July 8, 1916 National Soldiers' Home, Bath, Steuben, NY

m. ------

NOTE: Albert was the son of Abraham (1787-1859) and Maria Cook Crocker (1805-1872). His was a checkered military career. He was "absent – sick" in the summer of 1863. His muster roll card records he went AWOL in March 1864 and was sentenced to forfeit $10 of that month's pay "for leaving His Co. while in front of the enemy." The clerk also noted, "Is now absent without leave having sneaked away and been left behind." Despite his transgressions he was honorably discharged on July 12, 1865, successfully applying for a pension in 1880. Albert entered the home in 1906. He is buried in Bath National Cemetery.

Daniel Cronk – Co. C

b. 1843 Constable, Franklin, NY

d. June 16, 1869 Richland, NY

m. ------

NOTE: Daniel's parents were Elijah (1800-1880) and Marsha M. Cronk (1803-?). He was discharged from the army for "disability" on April 10, 1865. His COD, "lung consumption," is found on the 1870 Mortality Schedules and was probably the reason he was discharged. Daniel is buried in Willis Cemetery, Fernwood.

Freeman H. Cross – Co. C

b. July 14, 1848 Richland, NY

d. April 13, 1911 Pulaski, NY

m. Delia Gates (June 1848-May 28, 1927) November 25, 1869

NOTE: Freeman, a musician, was the son of Henry (1807-1884) and Eliza A. Winters Cross (1808-1895). He mustered out with the regiment on June 7, 1865. His death was reported in *The Pulaski Democrat* April 19, 1911, 1 in an obituary with an over line of "A Patriotic Youth – A Loyal Citizen": "It was no little surprise to this community, when Friday morning,

Daniel Cronk succumbed to tuberculosis probably acquired in the service. He was only one of thousands of veterans who died shortly after the war ended.

Author's Collection

announcement was made that Freeman H. Cross had passed away about midnight. Mr. Cross had been ailing for some time but not confined to the house until Tuesday. Monday he came to the Democrat office with the telegram he had just received announcing the death of Mrs. Burch, of Grand Rapids, and he sat and visited in the sanctum for half an hour or more and little did we think it would be the last of the always welcome calls he would make. He was about town that day and made calls which were his farewells, but he did not expect they were such. He began to decline that night and went down rapidly. Mr. Cross was born in this village, July 14, 1848. He was a mere lad, only fourteen years of age, when he was accepted as a drummer boy in the 147th Regiment, N.Y.V. and served three years. After the war he returned to Pulaski and learned the trade of machinist and later took up the profession of correcting deformation by use of appliances which has made the lame to walk in hundreds of cases. He was so skilled that no deformity of limb seemed too severe for him to help the patient. His work was not confined to this locality alone but was called for in the remotest parts of the country. He was one of the charter members of J. B. Butler Post, No. 111, G.A.R. and served in various offices up to the Commander's station which he has held with credit for the past 4 years and was the incumbent of that office at the time of his death. He was the youngest member of the Post and on him the older members relied for much of the work which keeps the organization moving. Mr. Cross married Delia Gates, Nov. 25, 1869 who, with one son, Willard G., of Rochester, survive [sic] him . . . His funeral was held from the home, Monday, at two o'clock, Rev. Frederick Maunder officiating. The bearers were sons of veterans from A. S. Warner Camp and the burial ceremony of the Grand Army was conducted by the Post. The floral tributes were most abundant and exceedingly impressive in design and beauty. The passing of Mr. Cross takes from our community a man who will be greatly missed. He was a good citizen, a good husband and father, a willing supporter of all that pertains to the welfare of the community, the church and the school." Freeman and Delia, who died in Rochester, NY, are buried in Pulaski Village Cemetery.

William Cullen – Co. B

b. 1830 Ireland
d. May 5, 1864 Wilderness, Virginia
m. Bridget _____ (1825-1907) *ca.* 1848

NOTE: William was killed in the battle of the Wilderness. Bridget never remarried and raised her family alone. Although illiterate she applied for and received a widow's pension. She is buried in St. Paul's Cemetery, Oswego.

James Cummins – Co. H

b. February 1843 Constantia, NY

d. October 26, 1920 Lee Memorial Hospital, Fulton, NY

m. Margaret Ellen Mowers (1852-July 1906) *ca.* 1869

NOTE: James was the son of Alvah (1800-1885) and Lana Cummins (1810-?). Frequently their surname was spelled Cummings. He was absent, sick, when the regiment mustered out. An entry on his pension card noted he had received gunshot wounds to his right leg and left thigh. He and Margaret, generally called Ellen, were the parents of three daughters. She died in Port Leyden, Lewis, NY where the family had resided for many years. James was living with a nephew, Milo, when he died "after an illness of several months." Their graves have not been located. His brother Alvah (1838-?) served in the 1st NY LA.

James Henry Cummins – Co. G

b. 1844 Oswego, NY

d. March 26, 1924 Oswego City, NY

m. Mary Boddy (1846-June 24, 1906) November 30, 1864

NOTE: James Henry was the son of Samuel (1820-1898) and Eliza Barlow Cummins (1821-1898). His surname was subject to frequent variations. His DOB also varies. I use 1844 because he said he was eighteen when he enlisted. His obituary, which appeared in *The Oswego Daily Palladium* March 26, 1924, contained a little known story: "An eye-witness to preparations which John Wilkes Booth, assassin of president Abraham Lincon made preliminary to the crime that shook the nation, and of the escape which the actor made after shooting the President, James H. Commins, veteran of the Civil War, died this morning at the home of his son-in-law, Thomas Dietz . . . after a lingering illness. Mr. Commins was in his 82d year and for many years following his discharge from the Army of the Potomac was employed by T. Kingsford & Son. In recent years he had lived quietly and was retired from all business activity. Mr. Commins was not a member of the G.A.R. or any veteran organization, and hence except to members of his family, the story of his intimate acquaintance with circumstances surrounding the assassination of President Lincoln did not become publicly known until after his death. Mr. Commins enlisted in Company D [*sic*], 147th Regiment, N.Y. Volunteer Infantry, and served throughout the campaigns in which that unit was engaged. After Appomattox he was detailed to duty in Washington, and on the night that the President was shot at Ford's Theatre in Washington, he had driven a high ranking army officer to the theatre. A few minutes after a man whom he afterwards knew to be John Wilkes Booth came along the street, and looked into the carriage which Mr. Commins had driven. Then Booth went into the stage entrance of the theatre. Mr. Commins noticed that a colored boy was holding a spirited saddled and bridled horse a few feet away down the street, but thought nothing of it. He was curious as to what Booth was doing, and followed him into the theatre, and as he was in uniform readily gained admission to the back of the theatre. He spoke to Booth and asked him what he was doing. Booth made reply that he was an actor, which was true, and as he was known to the stage hands and attaches, Mr. Commins thought no more of it, and after looking at the President seated in a stage box, Mr. Commins left the theatre and took his place again on the seat of the carriage to wait until the performance was over. Perhaps twenty minutes later, although he kept no account of time, Booth limped at a rapid pace out from the stage entrance and swept aside the boy holding the horse, mounted the latter and escaped. A few seconds later Mr. Commins learned that the President had been shot, although the sound of the galloping horse had scarcely died away. Mr. Commins was a member of the First M. E. church, but did not belong to any other organization, preferring his home and the associations with his family to clubs and social work . . . ." James and Mary are buried in Riverside Cemetery, Scriba.

Lewis Cummins – Co. E

b. August 17, 1834 Oneida County, NY
d. February 20, 1914 Sandy Creek, NY
m. Mary McDougall (April 10, 1832-September 16, 1905) 1857

NOTE: Lewis' parents were Alvinas (1810-1884) and Cynthia Maria Clark Cummins (1816-1905). Upon his death *The Sandy Creek News* March 5, 1914, 1 published the following: "Lewis Cummins passed away at his home in the southern part of the town of Sandy Creek on Friday, February 20, 1914, at six o'clock, after an illness of two weeks, aged 79 years 6 months 3 days. Mr. Cummins was born in Vermont [sic] in 1834 and came to this state when three years of age. He was married to Miss Mary McDougall in 1857. To them were born nine children, all of whom survive except one daughter. He enlisted in the Civil war as a private in Co. E on September 21, 1862, and was discharged September 4, 1863 . . . The funeral services were held from his late home on the North road February 23, Rev. Shares, pastor of the Wesleyan church, officiating. Burial in the Wesleyan cemetery beside his wife and daughter . . . ." The cemetery mentioned is the Sandy Creek-Boylston Wesleyan. All existing documents have led me to conclude Lewis was born in Oneida County, not Vermont.

Alverson B. Curtiss – Co. B

b. 1835 Lewis County, NY
d. September 21, 1900 Oswego City, NY
m. Mary Jane Meeker (1838-July 22, 1902) May 21, 1856

NOTE: Alverson, whose name was also spelled Alvinson, was the son of William (1797-1870) and Betsy Galpin Curtiss (1800-1887). His obituary, published in *The Oswego Daily Palladium* September 22, 1900, chronicled his life and career: "Alvinson B. Curtiss died suddenly at his home, 188 East Oneida street, last night at 10:30 o'clock of paralysis of the heart. Early in the evening he left home to attend a meeting of Post J. D. O'Brian, G.A.R., and was apparently in good health. After the meeting he chatted with friends on the street, among them being Superintendent of Works F. J. O'Brien. He reached home rather early and retired, making no complaint of being ill. He was in bed but a few minutes when he complained of pains about his heart. Mrs. Curtiss aroused her grandchildren and sent one of them for Doctor Richards, while she, with the assistance of the others endeavored to relieve the stricken man. Mr. Curtiss was beyond all aid, however, and died before the physician could reach him. When he arrived, Doctor Richards pronounced paralysis of the heart as the cause of death. The announcement of Mr. Curtiss's death caused general regret throughout the city today. His prominence in certain branches of public affairs during his lifetime made for him many friends. He was sixty-five years old and lived here practically all of his life. For many years he was a prominent contractor and many of the largest buildings along the water front were built by him. Among the structures which he built were the Northwestern, Corn Exchange, Columbia and Washington elevators. The three latter were destroyed in the great elevator fire several years ago. Mr. Curtiss also built other leading structures throughout the city. He was Superintendent of Streets for three years and had charge of the removal of the dead from the Fifth and Fourth ward cemeteries, when the city decided to convert the burying-places into public parks. Mr. Curtiss was a competent, efficient official and performed his duties to the satisfaction of all. For the past few years he has been employed as a lock-tender on the Oswego canal. Mr. Curtiss was a veteran of the Civil War. He enlisted in the 147th Regiment and took part in all the bloody engagements of that gallant command. At the battle of Gettysburg he was shot through the jaw, and although the injury was a dangerous one, he ultimately recovered. Mr. Curtiss was happily married early in life . . . Mr. Curtiss was prominent in Masonic circles and was an active member of [Frontier Lodge No. 422]." Alverson had been discharged from the service because of his wounds on December 9, 1863 at a hospital in Albany, NY. He and Mary Jane are buried in Riverside Cemetery, Scriba.

George Dahm – Co. G
b. 1838 Germany
d. ?
m. ?

NOTE: Very little is known about this soldier. He said he was a sailor when he enlisted and was probably a lake sailor. He was discharged for "disability" at an unspecified date. Someone named George Dahm, 25, enlisted in Co. F, 52nd Regiment NYSV in New York City on December 12, 1863 as a substitute but it is unknown if this was the same man. No other documents have been located.

Michael Daley – Co. K
b. 1839 Ireland
d. June 3, 1868 Oswego City, NY
m. ------

NOTE: Michael was a son of John (1800-1877) and Mary Daley (1824-1894). Although a note in *The Town Clerks' Registers* says he was discharged in 1865, his pension application, dated September 9, 1864, proves otherwise. His disability was "a neurosis of the elbow joint." He did not receive a pension, probably because he died before the process could be completed. He is buried in St. Paul's Cemetery, Oswego City. Two brothers also served in the military, John (1844-1864) in the 147th (see "'63 and Beyond"), and Daniel (1842-?) in Co. K, 160th Regiment.

Edward Damm – Co. G
b. 1824 Baden, Germany
d. August 18, 1864 Weldon Railroad, VA
m. Catharine Weber (1821-1887) April 26, 1854

NOTE: Edward was killed in a skirmish line at the battle of Weldon Railroad. When Catharine applied for a widow's pension she related she had come to the United States in 1851 and could not speak English. She and Edward were married in New York City but she had lost her marriage certificate and could not remember the name of the minister. Furthermore all the witnesses to the marriage were strangers to her. She and Edward were the parents of Edward Felix (1857-1912) and Catharine (1859-1938), both of whom were baptized in St. Mary's Church, Oswego. All are buried in Rural Cemetery, Oswego Town. A cenotaph is there for Edward.

Patrick J. Danaher – Co. I
b. 1839 Ireland
d. April 22, 1894 National Soldiers' Home, Dayton, Montgomery, OH
m. Mary Bergen (1828-October 1883) *ca.* 1866

NOTE: Patrick was discharged from the service on May 29, 1865 at Washington, DC. He had contracted typhoid fever. He was originally admitted to the Bath National Home on July 23, 1884 at which time he said his nearest relative was his son, John. Patrick and Mary are buried in St. Paul's Cemetery, Oswego City.

Ephraim Darling – Co. H

b. 1841 Constantia, NY

d. January 10, 1863 Regimental Hospital, Falmouth, Stafford, VA

m. ------

NOTE: According to *Deaths of Volunteers*, Ephraim died of typhoid fever. His parents may be William (1811-*post* 1890) and Roxa Darling (1808-1871). His father successfully applied for a pension in 1890. Although Ephraim is buried in Fredericksburg National Cemetery a cenotaph for him can be seen in Constantia Center Cemetery.

James Alan Darrow – Co. G

b. October 16, 1833 Scriba, NY

d. June 16, 1897 Scriba, NY

m. Emeline Bracy (April 1841-April 20, 1919) September 13, 1855

NOTE: James was the son of Rial (1804-1882) and Catherine Hodges Darrow (1803-1885). He was wounded at Gettysburg on July 1, 1863 and again at Petersburg, VA on June 17, 1864. In 1890 he said he had been wounded in the left wrist. He and Emeline are buried in North Scriba Union Cemetery. Her COD was heart disease.

Charles Dashner – Co. A

b. February 8, 1833 Lachine, Montreal, Canada

d. May 27, 1907 Oswego City, NY

m. Amelia Brisebois [Woods] (March 21, 1842-February 18, 1924) June 21, 1857

NOTE: Charles was the son of Vincent Voshon (1803-1850) and Margaret Latour Dagenais (1797-188). He anglicized his surname after immigrating to the United States. He was captured at Buckland's Mills, VA on October 19, 1863. After a short stay at Libby Prison he was sent to Andersonville and was finally paroled at Aiken's Landing, VA on February 24, 1865. After spending several months in a Rochester, NY hospital he was discharged on June 27, 1865. Amelia also anglicized her surname to Woods, as evidenced by the 1865 New York census. In 1900 the couple said they were married in 1860 although a date of June 21, 1857 has also been suggested. Charles and Amelia, who died after a brief illness, are buried in St. Peter's Cemetery, Oswego.

Richard Day – Co. D

b. 1824 England

d. June 11, 1901 Granby Center, NY

m. Susan L. Huggins (May 30, 1832-January 3, 1915) 1851

NOTE: Richard, whose parents were Gabriel (1801-*post* 1850) and Maria Day (1806-*post* 1850), was captured at Gettysburg on July 1, 1863. His parole date is unknown but he mustered out with the regiment on June 7, 1865. An obituary appearing in *The Fulton Patriot* June 1901 stated: "Richard Day who died in Granby Center last week Tuesday, was one of the typical patriots of America. He came to this country from England in 1831. At the commencement of the Civil War he became a member of the 147th Regiment from Granby, participated in the battle of Gettysburg, was captured and taken to Libby prison and at the close of the war returned to farm life at Granby Center. Mr. Day was the father of Richard Edwin Day, for many years the editorial writer on the Syracuse Standard and now an editor at the Regents office at Albany. He was also related through marriage with Senator N. N. Stranahan." Susan's death was reported in *The Fulton Patriot* January 11, 1915: "Mrs. Susan L. Day, who died Jan. 3, at the home of her daughter, Mrs. William Grant on S. 6th st., was in the 83rd year of her age. Mrs. Day was born at Lysander, Onondaga county and was the daughter of the late Alfred Higgins [*sic*] and Mary Ann Kellsey. Her early life was spent at West Granby; the family was a prominent one of that section. For her educational training, Mrs. Day came to Fulton and entered Falley Seminary, from which institution she graduated later and in 1851 she became the bride of Richard Day.. They made their home at Granby center but in 1901 the husband died. After this the widow made her home with her youngest daughter, Mrs. William Grant of Fulton. Mrs. Day was a member of Zion Episcopal church. She was a person of strong character and vigorous mind, and keenly sensitive to all manifestations of beauty in nature. Surviving are four children . . . ." Richard and Susan are buried in Granby Center Cemetery.

Archibald DeCory – Co. G
b. April 1825 Cape Vincent, Jefferson, NY
d. December 22, 1905 Syracuse, Onondaga, NY
m1. Polly Dawson (1836-*ante* 1880) *ca.* 1856
m2. Nancy _____ Crawford (1846-May 3, 1899) *post* 1870

NOTE: Archibald was the son of Joseph (1796-1865) and Lydia DeCory (1808-1865). He transferred to Batt. L, 1st NY ART on November 16, 1863 and was discharged June 17, 1865 at Elmira, NY. Polly and Archibald were the parents of five children. Nancy was previously married to Darwin M. Crawford (1849-*post* 1870) and was the mother of two children, William Crawford (1868-?) and Elizabeth Crawford (1869-?). She and Archibald were married before 1880. In 1890 he said his disability was "disease of the lungs." They are buried in Hannibal Center Cemetery. Polly's grave has not been located.

James DeCory – Co. C
b. 1843 Ellisburg, Jefferson, NY
d. November 3, 1913 Oswego Hospital, Oswego, NY
m1. Emiline Mott (1846-*post* 1880) April 25, 1876
m. Adelia Cole Bloodworth (May 1830-May 5, 1908) November 26, 1895

NOTE: James was Archibald's brother. His DOB varies from document to document. I use that given on his muster roll card. His gravestone says he was born in 1842 and the 1900 census provides a DOB of February 1842. Transferred to the 16th VRC on February 1, 1865, he was discharged from the service on July 6, 1865. Little is known about Emiline. She and James were married in Seneca Falls, Seneca, NY. In 1880 she, James, and her mother, Abigail Mott, were living in Phelps, Ontario, NY. Adelia was first married to Edward Bloodworth (1830-1892) who died of consumption in New Haven, NY. He left all his property to "Delia my beloved wife." She and James were married in Scriba, NY. Adelia is buried with Bloodworth in New Haven Cemetery. James, who was a farmer all his life, met a sad end, as reported by *The Oswego Daily Times* November 4, 1913, 5: "James Decory, a Civil War veteran, 71 years old, died at the Oswego Hospital last night as the result of injuries sustained Friday night by falling downstairs at the house of Gilbert Barrows, town of Scriba, where he boarded. It was at first believed that the body would not be claimed and would have to be buried at public expense. But the comrades of Mr. Decory in Post Porter, the army post at Scriba, would not permit their former associate to fill a nameless grave and they arranged to take charge of the funeral and burial. The details of the interment have not yet been decided upon but the services will probably be held tomorrow afternoon. The accident to Mr. Decory occurred last Friday but the seriousness of his condition was not known until yesterday morning. Mr. Decory had said that he only wrenched his foot. Dr. A. C. Baxter was called yesterday and found the man's right hip fractured, and that he was suffering from internal injuries. His condition was serious and Dr. Baxter ordered that he be taken to the Oswego Hospital. The ambulance was called and the injured man was brought to the hospital. He had been there but a short time when he passed away. Coroner Vowinkel was notified of Mr. Decory's death and ordered the body taken to Dain's undertaking rooms. The coroner learned that a niece survived Mr. Decory but she could not be located. When officers of Porter Post heard that the body had not been claimed arrangements were at once made for the funeral. Mr. Decory spent most of his life in the town of New Haven, residing in the village of that name for many years. He served in the Seventy-fourth New York volunteers in the Civil War and was a member of the Grand Army." Decory did not serve in the 74th Regiment. His service was spent entirely in the 147th and the 16th VRC. The GAR men fulfilled their promise to the old man. He was buried in Riverside Cemetery, Scriba.

William H. Delamater – Co. B
b. September 16, 1839 Lockport, Niagara, NY
d. January 15, 1863 Regimental Hospital, Belle Plain, VA
m. ------

NOTE: William was the son of Frederick (1811-1862) and Maria Beebe Delamater (1812-?). Like his father, he was a miller. His COD, as recorded in *Deaths of Volunteers*, was "P*neuma Typhoides*." The same document gives a DOD of January 16th. His gravesite is unknown. William's father is buried in Prospect Hill Cemetery, Guilderland, Albany, NY.

Samuel C. Delano – Co. D
b. 1831 Jefferson County, NY
d. December 2, 1863 General Hospital #21, Richmond, Henrico, VA
m. Phebe Jane _____ (1840-*post* 1891) *ca.* 1857

NOTE: Samuel was captured by the enemy on July 1, 1863 and sent to Libby Prison. His entry in *Deaths of Volunteers* says his COD was "chronic diarrhea." He was buried among the "unknowns" in Richmond National Cemetery. Samuel and Phebe, who used her two Christian names interchangeably, were the parents of Harrison (1858-?). On June 11, 1881 Phebe married Thomas Connor (1843-?) in Sumpter, Wayne, MI. It is supposed he died by 1891 because Phebe applied for a widow's pension under her original married name on November 30, 1891 in Michigan. The record shows she obtained the pension but nothing more has been found.

John DeLong – Co. C
b. 1825 Onondaga County, NY
d. December 7, 1889 Richland, NY
m. Jane E. Pitcher (1833-August 9, 1913) 1852

NOTE: John's parents are unidentified. He was a cooper by trade. He transferred to the VRC on January 21, 1864 and was discharged from that unit on July 14, 1865 at Elmira, NY. John, who is buried in Daysville Cemetery, did not receive an obituary but when Jane died *The Oswego Daily Palladium* August 14, 1913, 6 published the following: "Mrs. Jane Delong died at the home of her son Jasper on Saturday morning, August 9th after an illness of less than a week. She was born in Palermo in 1833, daughter of Gottlieb and Eunice Pitcher. In 1852 she was married to John Delong, who died in 1889. Of the union eight children were born, three of whom have died. Those remaining are Dwight, Fernwood; Jasper, of this place; Mrs. Henry Schrieffer, Chicago, Ill., Mrs. Runah Keller, Fulton, and Mrs. Dwight Hall, New Haven. When a girl she united with the Baptist Church at Palermo, afterward, upon taking up her residence [in the Manwarren District], uniting with the Daysville M. E. Church. She leaves besides the children named several grandchildren, a nephew, Charles Fleming, of this place, and numerous other relatives and friends who will mourn her loss. But we feel that what is our loss will be her gain, for she had been heard to say many times that she was prepared to meet her Maker at any time. Funeral services were conducted by the Rev. R. F. Thomas, Fernwood, on Tuesday. Burial took place in the family plot in Daysville cemetery. Her children were all present at the funeral, with other relatives from Utica, Fulton and other places."

Lewis DeLong – Co. H
b. 1827 Canada
d. July 13, 1898 Oswego City, NY
m. Margaret _____ (1829-February 10, 1897) ca. 1849

NOTE: Lewis' name was generally spelled Louis. His DOB varies. I use that found on his muster roll card but according to his obituary and his gravestone he was born in 1821. He was transferred to the VRC on March 26, 1864 and discharged for "disability" on February 17, 1865. In 1890 he said his disability was an "injury to scrotum and testicle." He was a member of Post O'Brien No. 65 GAR whose members attended his funeral in a body. Lewis and Margaret were the parents of at least six children, one of whom, Lewis, Jr., committed suicide by shooting himself on March 23, 1893. They and their son are buried in St. Paul's Cemetery, Oswego.

Joseph Dempsey – Co. K
b. August 1828 Ireland
d. April 14, 1902 Oswego City, NY
m. Mary Manning (1826-September 22, 1865) ca. 1850

NOTE: Joseph was the son of Edward (1808-?) and Mary Tyge Dempsey (1808-?). Despite what his obituary says, he was born in Ireland and came to the United States in 1829. He organized Co. K, 147th Regiment and was made a second lieutenant. He had only been home a few months when his wife died. He never remarried. Upon his death, *The Oswego Daily Palladium* April 14, 1902, 4 published a lengthy, informative obituary: "Captain Joseph Dempsey, aged seventy-five years, died at his home, 119 East Eighth street, at 3:30 o'clock this morning after a sickness of two weeks, up to which time he was in excellent health. Mr. Dempsey suffered an attack of acute indigestion about two weeks ago, which aggravated an old heart trouble and resulted in his death. The deceased was born in this city in 1827 [sic] and married Miss Mary Manning, who died thirty-six years ago. He is survived by four children . . . Captain "Joe" Dempsey, as he was familiarly called, was considered one of the most gallant and brave soldiers from Oswego county, which sent out so many gallant boys in blue during the days of the Civil War. In 1862 he was commissioned a Second Lieutenant in K Company, 147th Regiment. His first promotion came when he was advanced to take the place of his First Lieutenant, who was killed in action. When Captain N. A.

Wright was wounded and discharged from the service Lieutenant Dempsey was promoted to the command of the company, which position he held during the rest of the war. He was in all the battles in which the 147th took part, including Fredericksburg, Gettysburg, Spotsylvania and Hatcher's run. At the latter place he was wounded three times and in 1868, when President Andrew Johnson issued the brevet to the officers who had taken part in the Civil War Captain "Joe" Dempsey received two – that of Major for gallant and meritorious service at [Hatcher's] Run and that of Lieutenant-Colonel for gallant and meritorious service during the war. Major Wright, in speaking of his old comrade this morning, said: 'All that I can say of "Joe" is that he was one of the few men in the Army who did not fear a bullet. He was as gallant and brave a soldier as ever wore the blue and instead of being wounded but three times it was a wonder he was not wounded a hundred times, for he was utterly fearless and faced death during the war a thousand times.' On his return from the war Mr. Dempsey held several impor-

Joseph Dempsey served bravely during the war and had an influential civic career later.
Author's Collecion

tant political appointments, being Under-Sheriff under the late Colonel H. H. Lyman. He was also in the Custom-House under Collectors Clark, Root, Fort and Lamoree. Mr. Dempsey was a highly respected citizen and his many friends will learn of his death with regret." The Dempseys are buried in Riverside Cemetery, Scriba.

Francis Granger Devendorf – Co. B
b. August 25, 1832 Hastings, NY
d. July 13, 1864 Andersonville, Sumter, GA
m. ?

NOTE: Francis, a carpenter by trade, was wounded and captured at the battle of the Wilderness. His DOD is disputed, with some records saying he died July 12th. His COD is also disputed. Although his muster card says he died of his injuries, *Prisoner of War Records* lists acute diarrhea as COD. Francis is buried in Andersonville National Cemetery. His parents were Joseph ((1805-1862) and Elizabeth Douglas Devendorf (1808-1865). One brother, Daniel Douglas (1829-1894), served in the 110th Regiment and another brother, Edwin Crosswell (1826-1900), served in the 184th Regiment. Francis' marital status remains a mystery. Someone named A. Richardson, guardian, applied for a minor's pension on September 22, 1866, suggesting a remarried widow although Francis was listed as a single man in *The Town Clerks' Registers*. There is no indication the pension was granted and it is possible the entry was put on the wrong card.

Darius Tallman Dexter – Co. D

b. 1834 Oswego County, NY

d. March 10, 1863 Islington Hospital, Philadelphia, PA

m. Marilla N. Powell (December 6, 1836-October 8, 1920) July 31, 1859

NOTE: Darius was a son of Rodman (1796-1874) and Elizabeth Tallman Dexter (1797-1877) who settled in the area of Oswego County known as Dexterville. His COD was smallpox and he was buried in Philadelphia National Cemetery. He and Marilla had no children. On February 9, 1868 she married Jacob S. Haws (1823-September 11, 1900) as his second wife. He died of *cholera morbus* and heart disease and was buried in Conquest Village Cemetery, Cayuga, NY.

Marilla applied for a remarried widow's pension on June 14, 1901. She revealed that she was working as a domestic for $1.25 a week plus board. She drew the pension until her death in Utica State Hospital. A brief obituary published in *The Utica Herald-Dispatch* October 10, 1920, 8 revealed she had died from "a complication of diseases." She was buried in Conquest Village Cemetery.

David Harry T. Dexter – Co. D

b. 1836 Granby, NY

d. July 11, 1904 Granby, NY

m. Alamanza Cross (July 1843- February 22, 1910) *ca.* 1860

NOTE: David, a carpenter, was a brother of Darius T. Dexter. He was mustered out of the service on June 7, 1865. In 1860 he and Alamanza, aged 16, had been "married within the year." On the 1900 census they alleged they had been married in 1865 but since their first child, Albert, was born in 1862 that assertion must be

David and Darius Dexter were sons of Rodman and Elizabeth Tallman Dexter, settlers of Dexterville, NY.

Darlene Woolson

incorrect. He and Alamanza were the parents of four, all living in 1900. The couple is buried in Fairdale Cemetery, Hannibal, NY.

Nelson Diamond – Co. A
b. 1835 Quebec, Canada
d. June 14, 1897 Morrisonville, Clinton, NY
m. Olive Charlotte Dashner (1845-October 1902) *ca.* 1858

NOTE: Nelson, whose surname was also spelled Dimond, was wounded and captured at Gettysburg. In 1887 he was accused of desertion from Parole Camp, Westchester, PA, a charge later dropped. He was officially discharged from the army on December 3, 1863. In 1890 he claimed his disability was "a gunshot wound in head." Although he said he was a boatman when he enlisted in later life he was a barber. He was a member of W. H. Benedict Post No. 366 GAR which offered the following in *The Plattsburgh Daily Press* July 24, 1897: "*Whereas* Death has again visited our membership and removed therefrom our comrade, Nelson Diamond, late Private Co. A 147 N. Y. Inf., therefore *Resolved*, that, as God in his infinite wisdom has removed from among us our much beloved comrade and brother, Nelson Diamond, to his eternal rest and reward, that we most humbly submit to his overruling power. *Resolved*, that the sympathy and condolence of the members of this Post with a copy of these resolutions be transmitted to the bereaved family and friends . . . ." Olive's death was announced in *The Plattsburgh Sentinel* November 14, 1902: "--- Mrs. Olive Dimond, widow of Nelson Dimond, died after a brief illness from liver trouble last week at the age of 51 years. Her last illness was induced by injuries sustained from a fall several years ago from which she never fully recovered. She was buried on Sunday, Nov. 2, from St. Alexander's church, in the R. C. cemetery, Rev. Father Grenathier officiating." She and Nelson are buried in Saint Alexander's Old Catholic Cemetery, Morrisonville.

Asahel Dibble – Co. I
b. April 19, 1814 Wilmington, Windham, Vermont
d. December 21, 1864 Post Hospital, Fort Magruder, VA
m. Cynthia L. Barry (1817-*post* 1885) October 11, 1835

NOTE: Asahel, son of Ira (1791-*post* 1865) and Elizabeth Bessy Dibble (1790-*post* 1865), had a long military career. He first served in the 4th US HA from 1848-1849. He was discharged at Key West, FL for "disability." He next served in the 147th, saying he had been born in 1819 in Deerfield, Franklin, MA. His time with the 147th was brief since he was discharged for "disability" on February 13, 1863. Subsequent service was in Co. L, 16th NY ART which he joined on January 5, 1864 at Ira, Cayuga, NY. His COD was "chronic dysentery." In 1885 Cynthia was living with her daughter and son-in-law in Middletown, Jackson, MN. I have located no further records. Asahel's brother, Ira, Jr. (1818-1875), served in Co. K, 9th NY HA.

Adoniram Judson Dickinson – Co. B

b. July 1839 Oswego County, NY
d. July 25, 1928 New York City, NY
m. Sarah Louise Bosworth (February 10, 1842-March 27, 1910) 1860

NOTE: Adoniram's surname was also spelled Dickison. He was a son of William (1798-1856) and Lydia Marsh Dickison (1803-1869). He served as a lieutenant in the 147th and was assigned to several different companies. In a letter to his parents dated October 29, 1864 and published in *The Oswego Commercial Times* November 3rd Charles Vauvilliez spoke about Dickinson's capture on the same day Harney disappeared: ". . . The writer states that Jud. Dickson [*sic*], who is attached to the ambulance corps, was taken prisoner the same evening, but managed to effect his escape. His capture was made in this manner. He observed three of his ambulances driving off and riding up to them, found they were in possession of the rebels, who immediately made him a prisoner. Just after dark, cavalry approached the rebel detachment which held him a prisoner, and Dickson made his escape in the confusion which ensued and safely returned to camp . . . ." Dickinson mustered out on June 7, 1865. Before the war he was a ship-carpenter but in 1901 he gave his occupation as insurance salesman. Sarah is buried in Homewood Cemetery, Pittsburgh, Allegheny, PA with the surname "Dickison." After she died Adoniram moved to New York City to live with his daughter Clara Ross. He too is buried in Homewood Cemetery but under the surname "Dickinson."

Julius Dietz – Co. G

b. August 1830 Baden, Germany
d. November 1, 1903 Oswego City, NY
m. Maria Sophia Rapp (1841-October 14, 1922) 1866

NOTE: Dietz, a baker by occupation when he enlisted, transferred to the VRC on August 19, 1863. His FAG entry says he was seriously wounded when impaled by a branch during the campaign at Chancellorsville. In 1890 his disability was a "hernia ventral." His death elicited the following obituary in *The Oswego Daily Times* November 2, 1903, 8: "Julius Dietz, one of the oldest and best known residents of the First Ward, died at the family residence in West Eighth street yesterday morning after a lingering illness. Mr. Dietz died from a complication of diseases. He was born in Germany but came to this country when a young man. For thirty-seven years he resided in the First Ward and he was held in the highest esteem by his neighbors and friends. He was a faithful employee of the Standard Oil Company for nineteen years. Mr. Dietz was a kind husband and faithful, and the stricken family has the sympathy of numerous friends. Mr. Dietz had reached the advanced age of seventy-three years. He was always a loyal Republican . . . ." Dietz was a Freemason. He and Maria are buried in Rural Cemetery, Oswego Town.

Julius was one of thousands of immigrants who served in the Union Army.
He is buried next to his wife, Maria.
Author's Collection

William H. Dillenbeck – Co. C

b. 1834 Jefferson County, NY
d. March 13, 1892 Pulaski, NY
m. Harriet A. Stillwell (1835-May 17, 1910) *ca.* 1860

NOTE: William, a carpenter, was transferred to the VRC on February 18, 1864. His stint must have been brief because he applied for a pension on April 23, 1864. He listed no disability in 1890. William was the son of Henry (1795-1868) and Elizabeth Ronnes Dillenbeck (1796-1874). He and his parents are buried in Pulaski Village Cemetery. Harriet lived with her only child, Emma Peck (1861-?), in Gloversville and apparently died there. I have not located her grave.

Joseph W. Distin – Co. D

b. April 9, 1837 Volney, NY
d. July 1, 1863 Gettysburg, Adams, PA
m. Mary Diana Babcock (1842-October 16, 1890) December 19, 1860

NOTE: Joseph, son of Eli Delos (1808-1850) and Sarah Ann Gregg Distin (1812-1892), was killed in action and buried "site unknown." He and Mary were the parents of a son, Adna Warren (1861-1931). She obtained a widow's pension but her life cannot have been easy. According to documents in the pension file she suffered with cancer for seven years and had been bedridden for months before her death. Her brother, George, applied to the government for $84.00 for reimbursement for her funeral expenses. The estate appraiser, Norman Adams, reported that "said Mary D. Distin left no property except a small amount of clothing & a carpet, all her means having been exhausted in her support before her death – that the value of the property left by her did not exceed $20." *The Oswego Daily Times* October 25, 1890 printed a touching obituary: "The funeral services of Mrs. Mary D. Distin were held in the church at Bundy's Crossing Sunday, Oct. 19th. The house was filled with friends and neighbors, come to pay the last tribute of respect to one who was loved and esteemed by all. Mrs. Distin was a member of the M. P. church and an earnest Christian. Her life has been full of toils and afflictions but they seemed to bring out the virtues of a beautiful character. Of a loving, cheerful disposition, her influence for good cannot be estimated. The months of intense suffering have been bravely and patiently lived. She died trusting in the Savior she loved and served. A large circle of relatives and friends mourn her loss." Mary was buried in Fairview Cemetery, Bundyville, NY with her father Oliver (1811-1887) and mother Amanda Bacon Babcock (1810-1872).

Monroe Almond Doane – Co. C
b. April 27, 1843 Richland, NY
d. December 3, 1925 S. Marysburgh, PEI, Ontario, Canada
m1. Hannah M. _____ (1849-*post* 1891) 1869
m2. Georgiana Ackerman (1859-March 25, 1902) November 25, 1896
m3. Nancy Ostrander (September 2, 1855-December 24, 1925) October 15, 1902

NOTE: The son of Isaac (1810-?) and Sophie Bennett Doane (1810-?), Monroe used his Christian names interchangeably. He was transferred to Batt. L 1st NY ART on December 28, 1863. Monroe stated he was a sailor when he enlisted and he continued in that occupation after he moved to Canada, as evidenced by the 1881 Canada census. His death certificate says he succumbed to "uranium poisoning." Nancy, who died only weeks later, suffered a cerebral hemorrhage. Monroe and Nancy are buried in South Bay Cemetery, S. Marysburgh, and it appears Hannah and Georgiana are buried there too. Monroe's brother, Samuel (1841-1909), served in the 110th Regiment.

Francis Lemuel Dodd – Co. H
b. April 1844 Cleveland, NY
d. July 3, 1863 Fairfax Seminary Hospital, VA
m. ------

NOTE: Francis was the son of John (1797-1871) and Jane Smith Dodd (1802-1867). His COD was typhoid fever. His gravesite has not been located.

James Edward Dodd – Co. H
b. January 1842 Cleveland, NY
d. June 7, 1863 Divisional Hospital, Aquia Creek, VA
m. ------

NOTE: James was a brother of Francis. His COD was also typhoid fever. Within the space of a month their parents lost two sons. No grave has been located for him.

Judson Dolbear – Co. F
b. May 30, 1837 Palermo, NY
d. July 1, 1863 Gettysburg, Adams, PA
m. ------

NOTE: Judson's parents were Humphrey (1769-1845) and Mary Trim Dolbear (1798-1870). He was killed in action and buried in Gettysburg National Cemetery, exact location unknown.

Theodore Dolloway – Co. B
b. 1844 Oswego County, NY
d. January 18, 1863 Regimental Hospital, Belle Plain, VA
m. ------

NOTE: The son of William H. (1783-1860) and Huldah Johnson Dolloway (1805-1865), Theodore succumbed to typhoid pneumonia. He was originally buried in Wallace's Farm, VA but now rests in Fredericksburg National Cemetery. His parents are buried in Rural Cemetery, Oswego Town and a cenotaph honors his memory.

John Donner – Co. B
b. 1822 Germany
d. ? ?
m. ?

NOTE: Very little has been learned about this soldier. His parents, as revealed in *The Town Clerks' Registers*, were John (?-?) and Mary Donner (?-?). He was married but his wife is unidentified. According to his muster roll card, he was a confectioner. He mustered out with the regiment on June 7, 1865 and disappeared.

John Dooley – Co. I
b. 1838 Port Byron, Cayuga, NY
d. July 27, 1863 St. John's Hospital, Annapolis, MD
m. Julia Elizabeth Sterling (1845-?) September 26, 1862

NOTE: John's DOB varies from document to document but since he said he was 24 when he enlisted I use the date of 1838. Furthermore, his death certificate assigns him an age of 24. He apparently was taken prisoner at Gettysburg. His entry in *The Registers of Officers and Enlisted Men* contains this memorandum: "Had been a prisoner[;] exchanged died." COD was chronic diarrhea. He had already enlisted in the 147th when he and Julia were married in Oswego City. She obtained a pension but disappeared by 1865 and may have remarried. John's mother Rosana (1805-*post* 1890) applied for a pension on September 19, 1890. She did not receive a certificate probably because she died before the process could be completed. John's father was Edward Dooley (1803-?), born in Ireland. He appears only on the 1855 New York census living with his family in Port Byron.

Robert Dore – Co. K
b. 1819 Ireland
d. September 2, 1882 Oswego City, NY
m. Mary _____ (1827-May 30, 1886) *ante* 1854

NOTE: According to the 1862 Oswego City Directory, Robert was a sailor. His DOB is variously given and he apparently lied in order to enlist. The dates range from 1814 to 1829. I use that given on his gravestone. He mustered out with the regiment on June 7, 1865. In later years he was the sexton of St. Paul's Cemetery which is located a short distance down Mitchell Street from where the family resided. *The Oswego Palladium* May 31, 1886 noted Mary's death: "Mrs. Robert Dore died quite suddenly at her home at an early hour Sunday morning. She had been ailing for some time but was able to be about. Saturday night about four o'clock she went downstairs and soon after complained of serious illness. The deceased was a highly respected woman and her death is greatly regretted by all that knew her." Robert and Mary are buried in St. Paul's Cemetery, Oswego City.

William Walter Dority – Co. H
b. March 1845 Amboy, NY
d. May 21, 1909 State Hospital, Ogendsburg, St. Lawrence, NY
m. Maria Taber (April 1849-April 1, 1931) 1865

NOTE: William was wounded in the leg at Gettysburg and in January 1864 he was transferred to the VRC, finally being discharged July 3, 1865. His parents were William (?-*post* 1845) and Ruth Daniels Dority (1818-?). Although he said he was a blacksmith when he enlisted, in later years he was a grocer in Brewerton, Onondaga, NY. Upon his death *The Syracuse Herald* May 22, 1909, 3 published the following death notice: ". . . W. W. Dority of Brewerton died yesterday at the St. Lawrence State hospital at Ogdensburg. Armory Lodge No. 895 I.O.O.F, of which he was a member, will meet tonight at the office of A. C. Schumacher in West Onondaga to take action on the death." He was also a member of William Pullen Post No. 595 GAR, Brewerton. From 1886-1889 he served as Brewerton's postmaster. *The DeRuyter Gleaner* April 6, 1931, 5 noted Maria's death: ". . . -----Mrs. Maria E. Dority, 80, died Saturday at her home in Brewerton. Funeral services were held Tuesday afternoon at her late home with burial in Cicero. She leaves a daughter, Mrs. N. M. Pierce of Brewerton, a sister, Mrs. Milo Warner of Fulton and three grandchildren. Deceased was the daughter of Benjamin and Susan Taber and resided in Mariposa as a young girl. Her father, a Civil war soldier, died in Andersonville prison . . . ." Benjamin Taber served in Co. K, 111th Regiment. He was captured on October 30, 1864 near Petersburg, VA. According to pension records he died on or about November 18, 1864 at Salisbury, NC of intermittent fever. He had enlisted on September 1, 1864 as a substitute. William and Maria are buried in Cicero Cemetery.

Martin W. Dowd – Co. I
b. 1837 Ireland
d. July 1, 1863 Gettysburg, Adams, PA
m. ------

NOTE: This man appears first on the 1855 New York census. He had come to Oswego City five years earlier, was still an alien, and worked as a painter. *The Town Clerks' Registers* provide two entries. One lists a Charles W. Dowd, Co. I, single, painter. His parents were Martin Dowd (?-?) and Anna Corcoran (?-?). No one by that name served in the 147th. The other entry lists him as Martin Dowd, Co. G, painter, but gives no other information. I theorize that Charles and Martin W. Dowd were the same person. He is buried in Gettysburg National Cemetery.

John H. Doxtater – Co. A
b. 1830 Amboy, NY
d. March 3, 1886 Embarrass, Waupaca, WI
m1. Laura A. Deinhart (1835-*ante* 1860) 1850
m2. Elizabeth Austin (1838-?) *ante* 1860
m3. Zilpha _____ (1841-*ante* 1880) *post* 1860
m4. Olive Jane Fox Prichard (September 18, 1860-September 7, 1932) June 25, 1880

NOTE: John was the son of Christian (1800-1874) and Elizabeth Hanna Boyer Doxtater (1803-1869). He mustered out with the regiment on June 7, 1865. The information given on his wives may be considered conjectural at best except for Olive Jane. In 1850 John and Laura were married and living with his parents. She was 15. She gave birth to Martin L. in 1851 and she appears to have died *ante* 1855 because only John (who said he was married) and Martin were living with Christian and Elizabeth that year. In 1860 John was married to Elizabeth and living in Amboy. They did not say they had been married within the year. Martin, however, was still living with his grandparents. By 1865 Elizabeth was replaced by Zilpha. She, John, Martin, and John, Jr., aged 4, were living in Scriba. I think John, Jr. was Elizabeth's child but have no proof. The next record located is the 1880 census for Packwaukee, Marquette, WI. Martin was married to Alice Fox and the father of a baby, Ralph. His father, John, was living with them and was widowed. Olive Jane had married Leslie Prichard September 5, 1879 and had given birth to Arthur on September 24, 1879. She was a sister of Alice Fox Doxtater and was living in the same household as the others in 1880. She said she was married but we know she and John were married on June 25, 1880 because the marriage record is available online. Leslie married Lizzie Jamieson in Columbia County, WI on June 16, 1883. John, Sr. is buried in Clintonville Cemetery, Waupaca, WI. Olive died in Lone Rock, Richland, WI and is buried in Lone Rock Cemetery.

Michael Doyle – Co. B
b. 1836 Ireland
d. July 1, 1863 Gettysburg, Adams, PA
m. ------

NOTE: Michael was a malster by occupation which assisted in differentiating him from other Michael Doyles living in Oswego. He is buried in an unknown grave in Gettysburg National Cemetery.

Chester D. Drake – Co. F
b. December 11, 1838 New Haven, NY
d. April 24, 1875 New Haven, NY
m. Matilda _____ Larabee (April 1845-August 22, 1917) *ante* 1875

NOTE: Chester, whose parents have not been positively identified, transferred to Co. G, 18th Regiment VRC on March 10, 1865, and was discharged at Point Lookout, MD on June 29th. It is possible that he was first married to Mary Dean (1841-1860). The 1875 New York census shows that Matilda was the mother of Delia Larabee, 15. *The Syracuse Daily Journal* April 29, 1875 published the following, somewhat cryptic, notice: "Mr. Chester Drake, a resident of the north part of the town of New Haven was taken suddenly ill last Friday morning and died Saturday night." He was buried in Daysville Cemetery. Matilda was living in Mexico, NY when she died. Her grave has not been located.

Henry Melzer Drake – Co. B
b. August 1843 Palermo, NY
d. January 29, 1924 North Bay, Oneida, NY
m. Adelia "Adell" Castler (1852-*post* 1879) *ca.* 1871

NOTE: Henry, child of Cornelius (1780-*post* 1850) and Phoebe Phillips Drake (1820-*post* 1850), was discharged from the service at Fairfax Seminary Hospital, VA on July 11, 1863 for "disability." He enlisted in Co. D, 24th NY Cavalry on April 14, 1864 and was transferred to Co. D, 1st NY Provisional Cavalry when the two units were consolidated. Little is known about Adell. Perhaps she was Adelia Castler whom he met while they were working at a boarding house in Sandy Creek in 1870. In 1875 they and their son, Herbert, 3, lived in Sandy Creek. After that the couple apparently parted company. Adell Drake, 28, born Jefferson County, entered the Oswego County Poorhouse in June 1878 and stayed until March 11, 1879. She was described as "destitute" with "bad" habits. In 1880 Henry and Herbert were living with Henry's sister Cynthia and her husband Otis Allen in Volney. Adell disappeared after leaving the Poorhouse although Henry stated in 1880 he was married. In 1900 he claimed to be single. In 1910 he said he was a widower. His death occasioned several obituaries. The most informative appeared in *The Fulton Patriot* February 6, 1924: "At his home in North Bay, N.Y., on January 29th, Henry Melzer Drake passed away in the 83rd year of his age. He was a native of Oswego county and had resided in North Volney, South Hannibal and Fulton up to eight years ago when he purchased a small farm in the town of Vienna, Oneida county. He was a veteran of the Civil war, having been a member of Co. D, 147th Regiment, N.Y.S. volunteers. He was a member of Post Sherman, G.A.R. of Vermilion. Surviving are one son, Herbert Drake of Fulton and two sisters, Mrs. Annie Allen of R.D. 3, Fulton, and Mrs. L. J. Morgan of . . . Cleveland, Ohio. The funeral was held on Friday, Feb. 1st, from the Sanborn undertaking rooms at North Bay. The body was placed in the Camden vault to await burial in the spring in the soldiers' plot in the Camden cemetery."

James W. Draper – Co. E
b. 1843 Orwell, NY
d. December 29, 1863 Orwell, NY
m. ------

NOTE: James, son of Stephen (1815-1861) and Sophronia Barnum Draper (1815-November 7, 1907), was discharged from the service at West Philadelphia Hospital, PA for disability "resulting from fever" on October 12, 1863. He had previously served in Co. B, 7th NY Cavalry from October 12, 1861-March 31, 1862 when the unit was mustered out at Troy, NY. He is buried in Evergreen Cemetery, Orwell. By

1865 his mother had married Joshua Ostrum (1817-1881) and later the couple spent time in Wisconsin before returning to Oswego County. Sophronia successfully applied for a mother's pension in 1882. She and Stephen are buried in Evergreen Cemetery, Orwell. A brother, Nathan Draper (1836-1897), served in the 20th NY Cavalry.

James Draper was discharged from the service in October 1863 and died from an unknown disability in December.
Eric Parsons

Bernard James Driscoll – Co. C
b. 1841 Western, Oneida, NY
d. October 6, 1899 Syracuse, Onondaga, NY
m. Julia Elizabeth Bishop (June 14, 1849-May 14, 1936) July 6, 1875

NOTE: Driscoll, the son of John (1800-*post* 1860) and Mary (1804-*post* 1860), enlisted under the name James. He was discharged for "disability" which in 1890 was "chronic diarrhea." In later years he was accused of desertion, a charge which was dropped. He was officially discharged to date from March 24, 1864. He and Julia are buried in Oakwood Cemetery, Syracuse.

Dennis Driscoll – Co. I
b. July 1843 Ireland
d. February 4, 1912 Oswego City, NY
m. Eleanor "Ellen" Farden (November 1854-June 14, 1941) 1876

NOTE: Driscoll was discharged from the service on May 16, 1865 and applied for a pension on May 30th. When he enlisted he said he was a mariner but in later years he worked in the R. W. & O. railroad shops. He was a member of St. John's Catholic Church. Eleanor's death elicited the following obituary in *The Oswego Palladium Times* June 14, 1941: "Mrs. Ellen Driscoll, widow of Dennis Driscoll, died shortly after 10 o'clock [this] morning at the family home . . . She had been in impaired health for several months and during the past week her condition became critical. Mrs. Driscoll was born in Baldwinsville, the daughter of the late James and Mary Breen Farden, for many years prominent residents of Sterling. She was a communicant of St. John's Church and a member of its Rosary Society and other societies of the church. Her chief interests were in her home and church. Of a quiet and unassuming manner,

Mrs. Driscoll was charitable and helpful to others and among her friends she was esteemed the most highly for her many admirable traits of character . . . ." Dennis and Eleanor are buried in St. Peter's Cemetery, Oswego City.

Oliver Dubo – Co. K
b. 1830 Canada
d. December 6, 1910 ?
m. Angeline _____ (1831-February 25, 1895) *ca.* 1852

NOTE: Oliver, son of Louis (?-?) and Harriet Gunier Dubo (?-?), was a cooper. The various spellings of his surname have hampered research. The names of his parents appear in *The Town Clerks' Registers* and may also be incorrectly spelled. According to the 1855 New York census Oliver had been in Oswego City for six years and was an alien. Angeline had been in Oswego for three years. At that time they were the parents of Margaret, 2. Later they would become the parents of Edward (1862-1911). Oliver was wounded in the left eyelid and right wrist at the battle of Gettysburg on July 1, 1863 and was discharged for "disability" at Washington, DC on February 8, 1864. He apparently abandoned the family sometime before 1880. When Angeline died, no mention was made of her husband in her brief obituary. Oliver's DOD is taken from his pension card but where he died is unknown. Perhaps he returned to Canada. Edward "Eddie" spent time in Auburn State Prison for assault. He died after falling from a stool in a restaurant in Oswego and breaking a hip. The coroner ruled that alcoholism was the primary cause of death. Margaret died in Oswego on August 30, 1934. Graves for these people have not been located although reportedly they are buried in St. Paul's Cemetery, Oswego.

Benjamin Jacob "Jake" Dunn – Co. H
b. June 20, 1832 Canajoharie, Montgomery, NY
d. September 17, 1899 Constantia, NY
m. Harriet Redfield Lewis (1835-October 25, 1911) January 30, 1855

NOTE: Benjamin's parents were John Henry (1801-1875) and Eliza Merchant Dunn (1805-1894). He mustered out with the regiment on June 7, 1865. In 1890 he said he had had "rheumatism 26 years – contracted in military service." Upon his death *The Oswego Daily Palladium* September 27, 1899, 6 published a lengthy obituary: "Benjamin J. Dunn died at his home in North Constantia on Sunday, September 17th, 1899, in the sixty-eighth year of his age. He was born in Canajoharie, N.Y., and came to this town about forty-seven years ago. He was a veteran of the Civil War. He enlisted as a private in Company H, 147th Regiment New York Infantry, August 25th, 1862 and served until the close of the war and was honorably discharged near

Washington in June, 1865. He was very highly respected, of refined feelings, sensitive and affectionate, always remembering with deep gratitude favors shown. On the other hand, a frown at once enshrouded him in gloom. His love for his family was unbounded and his greatest desire in life was to make them happy, which was duly appreciated and reciprocated by them. They left nothing undone to relieve him of suffering or contribute to his happiness. About thirty years ago he embraced the Saviour and became connected with the Methodist church and has led a devoted and Christian life since. He was honored by all people of his acquaintance for his mild and genial disposition and the innocent, artless simplicity of his nature, who often gave him words of cheer notwithstanding his poor health. Cheerful scenes and objects buoyed up his spirits and he seemed to enjoy the comforts of life. But all is over, and he rests in peace . . . ." Dunn was a member of Daniel B. Lewis Post No. 419 GAR which organized his funeral. Harriet's obituary appeared in *The Oswego Daily Palladium* October 31, 1911, 8: "On Wednesday, October 25th, at her home in [Constantia] occurred the death of Mrs. H. R. Dunn, aged seventy-six years, seven days. For the past year she had been a sufferer from cancer, had undergone two operations and help failing she suffered excruciating torture until a few days before she died, when the pain quieted and the death angel carried her very peacefully 'into that city from whence no traveler returns.' She was born in the town of Amboy when the country was new and spent her entire life in that town and this one, where her death occurred. Shortly before the Civil War she married Benjamin J. Dunn, Constantia, whose demise occurred some years ago . . . A kind neighbor, an earnest church worker, a loving mother, she leaves to mourn her a host of friends and relatives, while in her home she [leaves] a vacant place which can never be filled . . . ." Harriet had cancer removed from her tongue in February 1911 but it returned and finally killed her. She and Benjamin were buried in Amboy Center Cemetery.

Orrin Watson Dunn – Co. G

b. August 1843 Ontario, Canada
d. December 25, 1922 Stanford University Hospital, Palo Alto, Santa Clara, CA
m1. Melissa "Sunbeam" Woolley (July 11, 1850-December 28, 1930) September 27, 1870
m2. Harriet Lavinia Holcomb (April 7, 1859-April 18, 1946) December 24, 1885

NOTE: Born in Canada, Orrin arrived in Cape Vincent, Jefferson, NY in March 1862. He was a carpenter by trade and served with the 147th until mustering out on June 7, 1865. Orrin abandoned Melissa and married Harriet in Grand Rapids, Kent, MI. As late as 1920 Melissa said she was married. Orrin, a salesman for the Bissell Company for many years, was described as a "pioneer resident of the Stanford campus," and his obituary in *The San Francisco Chronicle* December 27, 1922, 3 details his connection with the university: "Orrin W. Dunn, 76 [*sic*], for thirty years a resident of Stanford, known to students of Stanford University as the 'dad of the self-supporting student,' died last night in the Palo Alto Hospital. Dunn, during the many years he lived near the institution, befriended the students in numberless ways and found employment for scores of those who would otherwise have been unable to attend the university. Born in Canada, Dunn came to the United States early in his life, served in the Northern Army during the Civil War and at the time of his death was commander of McKinley Post of the Civil war veterans in Palo Alto." Harriet established a scholarship in his name at Stanford. Orrin's grave has not been located but Harriet is buried in Cypress Lawn Cemetery, Colma, San Mateo, CA. Melissa died in Buffalo, Erie, NY and her obituary is revealing for the numbers of friends she possessed: "Funeral services for Mrs. Melissa Dunn, a woman whose sweetness of disposition, despite serious physical handicaps, won hundreds of friends for her throughout the country, will be held at 3 p.m. today in the Johnson & Wilkins funeral parlors, 448 Delaware avenue. Mrs. Dunn, better known as Sunbeam, a nickname given her because of her consistent cheerfulness, was a patient in the El Nathan Home for Old Ladies, 26 Richmond avenue, for the last 22 years. She died Sunday after a brief illness. She was 80 years old. A broken hip and arthritis confined her in bed during the entire residence at El Nathan. But in those years hundreds of visitors to the home, including Buffalo persons and those from many other cities and nations, became acquainted with Sunbeam. Some called regularly to see her. Others came less frequently. For all she had had the same smile and the same cheery spontaneous conversation. Sunbeam could entertain a dozen persons at her bedside, and often did, according to Mrs. Abigail Luffe, who manages the home. Visitors later would write letters almost daily from widely separated sections, Mrs. Luffe said. Sunbeam was a patient at the Erie County hospital when Mrs. Luffe found her, and took her to the home which she founded. El Nathan is a home for elderly women unable to support themselves. It is a faith home, where no contributions for its support are sought, but only volunteer offerings accepted. Sunbeam's nearest relatives are two nephews and a great nephew in Buffalo who will be pallbearers at the funeral. They are Theodore Wooley, Charles Wooley and William Wooley. Other bearers will be Werner Piehl, George Diehl and Chauncey Henderson. Burial will be in Elmlawn cemetery."

Thomas Dunn – Co. I
b. 1841 Ireland
d. May 30, 1863 Aquia Creek, VA
m. ------

NOTE: Thomas' parents were Cornelius (1814-ca. 1900) and Elizabeth Kelly Dunn (1820-1855). According to the 1855 New York census Cornelius, a grocer, had lived in Oswego for thirteen years. Thomas, 13, had lived there for twelve years. All his younger siblings were born in Oswego. *The Town Clerks' Registers* say, erroneously, that Thomas was "taken sick after the battle of Bull Run and sent to Division Hospital at Acquia Creek; died May 29th 1863. Remains buried in Oswego." It is more likely that he became ill after the battle of Chancellorsville since Bull Run had been contested in August 1862 while the 147th was being organized. DOD is also disputed. Most records say he died May 30th. His headstone card, however, gives a date of March 29, 1863. *The Oswego Commercial Times* June 12, 1863 published a letter from Adjutant Farling, dated May 31, 1863, which announced Dunn's death and offered a different date: ". . . Sergeant Dunn, son of Cornelius Dunn, Of Oswego, was removed from our regimental hospital to the Division Hospital at Acquia Creek, on the 28th, where he could have better treatment and attention. He died the next day. We did not suppose he was in any serious danger when he was removed. He was a faithful and good soldier, always doing his duty promptly; he was quick, steady, intelligent and generally respected by officers and men. His body will be embalmed and sent home. We cannot get permission for any one to go home with the remains. Military restraint here is too rigorous." *The Oswego Commercial Times* June 16, 1863 described the preparations for his funeral: "Brother Firemen, -- We are called upon to mourn the loss of another brave and gallant Fireman, who has given up his life in defence of our country's flag; and it is fitting for us, and also due to the brave and noble youth, that we should unite in performing the last sad rites of burial to our deceased brother, Sergeant Thomas Dunn, of Company I, 147th Regt., N.Y.V., and a late member of Union Fire Company No. 2, therefore we cordially invite you to unite with us in performing such ceremony. Funeral services at 2 ½ P.M., June 17th. The line of march will form in front of the Market Hall, at 2 P.M., and thence proceed to the residence, corner of West Fifth and Fitz streets. Yours respectfully, P. Hourigan, Foreman. P. Griffin, Secretary." Thomas was originally buried in Oswego's Fifth Ward Cemetery but today lies in St Peter's.

Daniel T. Dunsmoor – Co. G

b. November 9, 1843 Oswego Town, NY
d. October 1, 1864 Albany, Albany, NY
m. ------

NOTE: A son of Clinton (1811-1893) and Paulina Dunsmoor (1817-1880), Daniel was wounded on May 5, 1864 at the battle of the Wilderness. An article published in *The Oswego Daily Palladium* October 4, 1864 tells the rest of the story: "Sergeant Dunsmoor joined the 147th regiment on its organization two years ago, as a private, but his good conduct at the battle of Gettysburg won for him the position which he occupied at the time of his death . . . Daniel passed unharmed through all the engagements and campaigns in which the 147th regiment had taken part, until [on] the 5th day of May in the battle of the 'Wilderness,' Va., he was wounded and left on the field in the hands of the enemy. Before proper assistance could be afforded him his wounds compelled the amputation of his right limb above knee. His sufferings, which were intense, brought no words of complaint from his lips during the five months he was confined to his bed. Thus another soldier has laid down his life and passed from sight, to be known no more, only in memory. His home circle is again broken, and grief is around the hearthstone. Comrades around the camp fire will tell of the noble qualities which distinguished him in camp and field, and of his courage and soldierly conduct in the time of battle. He is now done with marches and battle. He has finished his work, but the memory of his many noble traits will remain in the hearts of all who knew him. – COM." Daniel is buried with many members of his family in Rural Cemetery, Oswego Town. His brother Delos (1835-1862), a member of the 81st Regiment, died of "disease" at Fortress Monroe, VA on July 1, 1862 and was buried there. Another brother, David (1846-1931), joined the 2nd NY HA in 1864, was wounded at Cold Harbor, VA and finally discharged for "disability" on March 12, 1865.

James Durant – Co. K
b. *ca.* 1820 England
d. May 16, 1888 Oswego City, NY
m. Catherine Haley Supple (1824-*ante* 1875) *ca.* 1853

NOTE: James' DOB is a matter of conjecture. When he enlisted he said he was 42, but his listing in *Registers of Officers and Enlisted Men* claimed he was 47. He was wounded in action on July 1, 1863 at Gettysburg and discharged for "disability" on June 3, 1864. In 1865 Catherine indicated she had been married twice and was the mother of nine children, one of whom was Mary Supple, 19, born in Ireland. Graves for these people have not been located.

Grove Henry Dutton – Co. D
b. July 5, 1846 Granby, NY
d. March 15, 1910 Granby, NY
m. Bettie Maria Austin (1852-December 5, 1919) March 27, 1878

NOTE: Dorothy Kincheloe Hendrix' *A Leaf from Army Life: Background and Experiences of a Civil War Soldier* contains extensive biographical information on this young boy who twice attempted to join the army before being accepted by the 147th.

At 16 he was too young to enlist without parental approval which he eventually obtained. A son of Orson Homer (1808-1884) and Sophia Church Dutton (1810-1910), he took part in many of the engagements of the 147th Regiment. An article appearing in *The Oswego Daily Times* August 1, 1904, 4 reported on a new position and reviewed his military career: "Ex-Supervisor Grove H. Dutton of Granby has been assigned to duty as Deputy Collector and Inspector by Collector Cooper in place of William Griffin who has retired from the service. Mr. Dutton receives his assignment to duty under a change in the Civil Service rules which provides for the reinstatement without examination of a veteran who has already been in the service. Mr. Dutton held a position in the local Custom House under the late Henry H. Lyman. Mr. Dutton has one of the finest military records of any soldier that ever left Oswego County. He enlisted in Company D, 147th Regiment N. Y. on September 5, 1862 at the age of sixteen. He participated with his command in many battles and on all occasions displayed remarkable bravery. The battles included Chancellorsville, Gettysburg, Mine Run, Wilderness, Laurel Hill, Spottsylvania, north Ann [sic], Bethesda Church, Totopotomey, Petersburg, Weldon Road, Hatcher's Run, Chapin's farm, Boyden plank road, White Oak road and Five Forks. At Gettysburg on July 1, 1863 Mr. Dutton was wounded in the wrist which resulted in the loss of one of his arms after the war. He was sent to the general hospital at Chestnut Hill, Philadelphia. At the battle of Five Forks on April 1, 1865 he was again wounded but recovered in time to march with his regiment in the grand review in Washington after the war. Mr. Dutton was discharged with his company on June 23, 1865 [*sic*] with the rank of Sergeant. Mr. Dutton served as a member of the Board of Supervisors and he proved to be a faithful public servant. He will make an excellent official. He has assumed his new duties." Dutton actually mustered out with the regiment on June 7, 1865 and returned to the family farm in Granby where he spent the rest of his life. He and Bettie were the parents of five sons and three daughters. In 1907 he wrote a series of articles about his wartime experiences which were published in *The* [Fulton] *Observer*. In addition to belonging to Post Schenck No. 271 GAR he was also a member of Lower Falls Grange No. 719. His daughter Bessie wrote that her father's old war wound caused blood poisoning and necessitated the amputation of most of his hand. When that failed to stem the septicemia, the doctors removed the rest of the hand. The entire arm below the elbow was amputated in 1888. At his death an obituary appeared in *The Oswego Daily Palladium* March 16, 1910, 8: "Many Oswego friends will learn with sorrow of the death of Grove Dutton, of the town of Granby, for the past six years a Deputy Collector and Inspector of Customs here. Mr. Dutton had been in poor health for some time and shortly after the close of the season of navigation last Fall he went to Rome for an operation for internal trouble. He has since been at the home in Granby, where his health has been gradually failing, though very few of his friends here were prepared for the news which came today. Mr. Dutton was born in Granby in 1846 and has always made his home there. He was a farmer by occupation, but when the Civil War broke out he enlisted and went out as a member of Company D, 147th New York Volunteers, and served throughout the war. At Gettysburg he was hit in the arm and though the wound healed at the time, it ultimately resulted in the loss of his arm. Mr. Dutton had been prominent as a member of the G.A.R., belonging to Schenck Post, Fulton. He was an ardent Republican and had served his town as Supervisor and other positions of trust. In August, 1904, he was appointed to a position in the Customhouse and during the Summers since has spent most of his time in this city, where he made many warm friends . . . ." The esteem with which he was held was evident at his funeral where eight former members of the 147th Regiment served as honorary pallbearers. *The Fulton Patriot* December 10, 1919, 4 announced Bettie's passing: "Died at her home in Ilion, Dec. 5th, Mrs. Betty [*sic*] M. Dutton, aged 68 years . . . The remains were brought to this city Saturday and taken to the home of her sister-in-law, Mrs. C. M. Strickland . . . where funeral services were held Monday . . . Mrs. Dutton was the widow of Grove H. Dutton, formerly of Granby. She was born in Volney and for over 40 years had resided in Granby. She was an active member of Columbia Circle, Ladies of the G.A.R., and was prominent in the Presbyterian church and only last year visited this city and attended the services in that church, when a service flag in honor of the members in the military service was unfurled. At that time she had the distinction of pinning three stars on the flag for her sons in war." Grove and Bettie are buried in Mt. Adnah Cemetery, Fulton.

Timothy Dwyer – Co. B
b. 1841 Ireland
d. October 22, 1881 National Soldiers' Home, Dayton, Montgomery, OH
m. ------

NOTE: According to *The Town Clerks' Registers,* Timothy was wounded at Laurel Hill on June 18, 1864, but more probably was injured at Petersburg, VA since the battle of Laurel Hill occurred on May 10th. It also stated he mustered out at the end of the war. His muster roll card, however, states he was discharged on January 5, 1865 for gunshot wound through the jaw. His pension card shows he applied for a pension on February 8, 1864! A son of Timothy (?-?) and Margaret Murphy Dwyer (?-?), he never married. He was an inmate at several soldiers' homes and apparently was not an easy man to deal with. A notation in the records of the Milwaukee Home says: "Expelled Oct.29.72 [for] insubordination, absence without leave, drunkenness." A doctor authorized his re-admission in July 1873 but he was transferred in June 1875 to the Southern Branch. Eventually he was transferred to Dayton where he died of *homophysis*, a disease incipient to consumption. Dwyer was buried in

Dayton National Cemetery. At the time of his death at age 40, his net worth was $24.83.

Byron C. Earl – Co. F
b. August 17, 1838 Ellisburg, Jefferson, NY
d. November 27, 1907 New Haven, NY
m. ------

NOTE: Byron, a farmer, was the son of James (1798-1875) and Phebe Taylor Earl (1803-1888). He transferred to Co. B, 19th Regiment VRC on January 22, 1863 and was discharged from the service on July 13, 1865 at Elmira, NY. In 1890 he claimed no disability. He became a member of Melzar Richards Post No. 367 GAR in Mexico and later transferred his membership to James Doyle Post No. 591 in New Haven. He and his parents are buried in New Haven Rural Cemetery.

Albert Eaton – Co. C
b. 1839 Oneida County, NY
d. May 5, 1864 Wilderness, VA
m. Sarah Hortensia Sloper (September 16, 1840-November 27, 1932) December 3, 1858

NOTE: Albert's parents were Simeon (1809-?) and Tamar Eaton (1814-?). Albert and Sarah were the parents of Julia Adelia (1860-1945) and Albert Warren (1862-1952). On July 19, 1865 Sarah married Nathan Hamblin (October 10, 1844-January 13, 1907). By him she had four more children. When Hamblin died Sarah applied for and obtained a remarried widow's pension. Her death was announced in *The Sandy Creek News* December 1, 1932, 2: "Sarah Hortensa [*sic*] Hamblin, aged 92 years – died at Altmar, November 27, 1932. Sarah Hortensa Sloper was born at Pitcairn, St. Lawrence county, September 16, 1840, the daughter of William and Phila Murdock Sloper. When a young girl, her family moved to a farm in this vicinity where she has since made her home. She was united in marriage to Albert Eaton and to them were born two children . . . Mr. Eaton enlisted when the call came for northern volunteers and gave his life for his country in the Battle of the Wilderness, leaving his young wife with her two small children. Later, she married Nathan Hamblin who died twenty-six years ago . . . Mrs. Hamblin was a faithful member of the Altmar M. E. church, and a charter member of the Aid Society in both of which organizations she was deeply interested and faithfully attended as long as health permitted. Three weeks ago she sustained a fall, and while she was about the house until a few days before her death, she has gradually failed until the end came Sunday night . . . Funeral services were conducted from the Methodist Episcopal church Wednesday afternoon at two o'clock." Hamblin served in Co. F, 153rd Regiment. He was an excise commissioner and member of Elisha L. Bentley Post No. 265 GAR at Altmar. He and Sarah are buried in Riverside Cemetery, Altmar.

James Eaton – Co. C
b. August 7, 1842 Utica, Oneida, NY
d. February 16, 1915 Pulaski, NY
m. Sarah Ann Bohannon (June 19, 1844-August 7, 1935) 1862

NOTE: James was Albert's brother. He mustered out with the regiment on June 7, 1865. He was a box maker by occupation and a member of J. B. Butler Post No. 111 GAR. His unexpected death, caused by a heart attack, was reported in *The Pulaski Democrat* February 17, 1915: "The community was greatly shocked yesterday morning, when it was known that Mr. James Eaton had died on the porch of his home on Bridge street. Mr. Eaton arose about five o'clock and went out to shovel some snow away from the walk and when Mrs. Eaton went to call him to breakfast she was shocked to find him on the steps unconscious. She summoned help and Mr. Eaton was taken into the house but life was extinct. James Eaton was born in Oneida County seventy-two years ago the 7th of last August. He married Sarah Bohanan [*sic*], of this town fifty two years ago last October. He enlisted in the 147th regiment and served in the civil war nearly three years. He has lived all his married life in this village except two years he lived in Oswego . . . The funeral will be held at the home Friday at two o'clock." Sarah received a lengthy obituary in *The Pulaski Democrat* August 14, 1935, 1: "With the death of Mrs. Sarah Bohannon Eaton, 91, at her home on Bridge street, last Wednesday night, one of Pulaski's most highly respected and best beloved citizens passes. For some three weeks Mrs. Eaton had been in failing health, but able to be about her home and receive her friends and neighbors who called. She fell Sunday, August 4 suffering a dislocated shoulder and a fractured elbow and greatly from shock. This hastened her death. Two years ago she also fell at her home sustaining a badly strained wrist, but she recovered remarkably from this and was soon able to write and take care of her usual home duties. Mrs. Eaton was born June 19, 1844 at Port Ontario, a daughter of Alpheus and Mary Anne Corbin Bohannon, pioneer residents of this section. Many of Mrs. Eaton's very early recollections were associated with activities in those far off days, when as a young girl living at the Port and Selkirk she recalled many of the stirring events in our early history. She came to Pulaski when a girl of 18, and early became a member of the Baptist church of this village. Most of her life was active in home duties and church work wherein her nature and attitude toward life fitted so admirably. Mrs. Eaton was a woman of splendid Christian character, with a quiet, serene nature; always thinking of and doing the things which made life pleasanter for others. For many, many years this community has been blessed by her presence in it, and there are many who mourn her passing.

She was one of those saintly souls whose womanly grace and virtues were as natural with her as breathing. Her home was a place where friends were always made welcome and greeted with a kindly, gracious courtesy that inspired their admiration and love . . . ." James and Sarah are buried in Pulaski Village Cemetery.

William Franklin Eaton – Co. B

b. February 22, 1841 Oswego County, NY

d. December 27, 1900 Washington, DC

m. Emma Sophia Creaser (1849-April 7, 1928) 1871

NOTE: William, the son of William (1815-*post* 1865) and Sarah Andrews Eaton (1822-*post* 1865), was wounded in action on July 1, 1863 and transferred to the VRC on February 8, 1864. His muster roll card says he was a clerk and in 1880 he was a clerk in the Pension Office in Washington, DC. He and Emma, who died in Pinellas County, FL, are buried in Rock Creek Cemetery, Washington.

William Eccles – Co. I

b. March 1828 England

d. May 15, 1904 Oswego City, NY

m1. Adelia _____ (1837-July 9, 1863) *ca.* 1856

m2. Mary Crimmins (1845-July 10, 1919) *ca.* 1865

NOTE: William, a sailor, and Adela do not appear on the 1860 census and probably arrived in the United States within the year. He lied about his age when he enlisted. He was captured by the Confederates on July 1, 1863 and paroled at an unknown date. He and Adelia were the parents of a daughter, Matilda (1857-*post* 1885). Adelia's sudden death was reported in *The Oswego Commercial Times* July 9, 1863: "About four o'clock this morning a woman named Adela [sic] Eccles died very suddenly at the Empire Saloon, of heart disease. The deceased was a boarder there, and for some time past has not been in the enjoyment of good health. She was a married woman, and her husband, whose name is Wm. Eccles, is a member of the 147th regiment." Her age, 26, was given in a death notice the same day in that newspaper. It has been suggested that Adelia heard of his capture and the news hastened her death. Her gravesite is unknown. Eccles and Mary Crimmins were the parents of six children. What happened to Matilda is unknown except for a report under "Police Court," *The Oswego Daily Palladium* March 18, 1885: "Matilda Eccles, charged with violating a city ordinance in using profane and obscene language. The case was put over until Friday morning at 10 o'clock in order to procure witnesses." Her father's obituary appeared in *The Oswego Daily Times* May 16, 1904: "William Eccles, a well known resident of the East Side, died about 8 o'clock last evening at his home in East Fifth Street after a lingering illness. Mr. Eccles had lived in Oswego a great many years and he had a large number of friends who will regret to learn of his death . . . ." He and Mary are buried in Rural Cemetery, Oswego Town.

Charles Henry Edick – Co. H
b. July 1838 Parish, NY
d. January 6, 1905 Bismarck, Burleigh, ND
m. Orlinda Wilcox (September 1842-September 8, 1922) January 1, 1860

NOTE: Charles mustered out with the regiment on June 7, 1865. He was appointed postmaster of Parish, NY in 1861 and again in 1871. When he enlisted he gave blacksmith as his occupation but in 1900 he was a coal mine operator. Charles' brother Cornelius (1844-1911) was for many years the superintendent of schools in Bismarck. The men were the sons of Daniel (1813-1902) and Minerva Richards Edick (1819-1894). His obituary appeared in *The Bismarck Tribune* January 10, 1905, 3: "The funeral of C. H. Edick was held from the First Methodist church Sunday after-noon at two o'clock, Rev. Magin conducting the services. In his remarks the Rev. Magin paid marked tribute to the departed giving a sketch of his life and the services he had rendered to his country in the strife of '61. The many friends of the deceased were present to pay a last tribute and the local Post, G.A.R., of which Mr. Edick was a charter member attended in a body." The post referred to was James P. McPherson No. 2. He was buried in St. Mary's Cemetery, Bismarck. Subsequent to her husband's death, Orlinda returned to Oswego County. Her COD was a stroke. She, together with several family members, is buried in Pleasant Lawn Cemetery, Parish.

George Edmonds – Co. C
b. 1840 Richland, NY
d. February 1,1863 Windmill Hospital, Aquia Creek, VA
m. ------

NOTE: George's parents were John (1798-1860) and Margaret Edmonds (1812-*post* 1870). After he succumbed to chronic diarrhea, Margaret applied for a pension on April 29, 1864, claiming that George had been her primary means of support after the death of her husband. In 1865 Margaret said she was the mother of twelve children.

William Edmonds – Co. F
b. 1836 Livingston County, MI
d. September 17, 1863 General Hospital, Turners Lane, Philadelphia, PA
m. ------

NOTE: According to *The Town Clerks' Registers*, William was wounded in the shoul-der on July 1, 1863. The injury was his COD. He is buried in Philadelphia National

Cemetery. His mother, Ann Edmonds (?-*post* 1886), successfully applied for a pension in August 1886 in Michigan.

James H. Edwards – Co. B
b. 1817 Ireland
d. February 17, 1893 National Soldiers' Home, Bath, Steuben, NY
m. Margaret J. Gokey (1827- January 8, 1891) May 11, 1845

NOTE: According to *The Town Clerks' Registers*, James' parents were Patrick and Mary Edwards. Although he claimed to have been born in 1822 when he enlisted, almost every document, including his death announcement, puts the lie to that statement. A short article published in *The Oswego Commercial Times* October 16, 1863 reported that James H. Edwards, of the 147th Regiment, had been injured by a train on October 7th in New York City. His injuries were slight and he was released from hospital on October 8th. Edwards was discharged from the service on December 27, 1864 from the hospital on David's Island, New York City Harbor but no reason was given. It is unknown whether or not the train accident contributed to his discharge. In 1890 he said his disabilities were "right shoulder, left knee hurt" and the 1880 census noted a "lame arm." Margaret signed her will on January 1, 1891 and died a week later. Her executors began probate proceedings on February 5, 1891. Her obituary appeared in *The Oswego Daily Palladium* January 9, 1891, 5: "Mrs. Margaret Edwards, wife of James H. Edwards, died at the family residence in Moore street yesterday morning after a lingering illness in the 64th year of her age. Mrs. Edwards was before marriage Mrs. [*sic*] Margaret Gokey. She was born in Canada, but when yet a child removed to this city with her parents and has made her home here ever since . . . The funeral occurs tomorrow from the family residence at 1:30 o'clock and from St. Mary's at 2 o'clock." On the 1855 New York census Margaret said she had been born in St. Lawrence County, NY. James and Margaret are buried in Rural Cemetery, Oswego Town.

John E. Eggleston – Co. B
b. April 1842 West Monroe, NY
d. July 2, 1929 National Soldiers' Home Hospital, Bath, Steuben, NY
m1. Lucy Smith (1844-*ante* 1870) *ca.* 1864
m2. Hannah Catharine Rubennault (November 8, 1850-May 31, 1931) *ca.* 1870

NOTE: John's parents have not been identified. He previously served in Co. B, 1st NY LA from September 20, 1861 to March 4, 1862 when he was discharged for "disability." He was discharged from the 147th on December 30, 1863. When he entered Bath Soldiers' Home in 1925 his disability was "senile dementia." He was re-admitted on May 1, 1929 and died of gangrene in his feet and myocardia. He is buried in Bath

National Cemetery. Lucy's grave has not been located but Hannah is buried in West Lawn Cemetery, Canton, Stark, OH.

Frank Ehart – Co. D

b. 1844 Germany
d. June 6, 1924 Beaver Falls, Lewis, NY
m. Augusta Kohl (August 1840-March 25, 1926) 1865

NOTE: Frank, whose surname was given as Ehrhardt on his muster roll card, was wounded in action on July 1, 1863. In later years when he applied for a pension he was accused of desertion from the hospital on October 20, 1863. Records show, however, that he enlisted in Co. D, 15th NY Cavalry on August 19, 1863 in Syracuse, NY, mustering in on August 26th. He was transferred on June 17, 1865 to Co. D, 2nd NY Provisional Cavalry and mustered out on August 9, 1865 at Louisville, KY. The charge of desertion was removed on June 21, 1886 and he was officially discharged from the 147th as of August 10, 1863. His obituary appeared in *The Lowville Journal and Republican* June 12, 1924, 1: "Frank Ehart died Friday evening, June 6, soon after retiring for the night. He had been in his apparently good health and had worked in his garden the greater part of the day. He was born in Saxony, Germany, and came to this country when a boy. Fifty years ago he settled in this village. Mr. Ehart was a veteran of the Civil war and served in the 15th New York Cavalry, and was a member of the Evangelical church for many years. Funeral services were held Monday at 2:30 o'clock from the home. Rev. Herman Rex officiated. He leaves his wife, Augusta Cole Ehart, and six children . . . ." *The Lowville Journal and Republican* April 1, 1926, 1 noted Augusta's passing: "Mrs. Frank Ehart died at her home Thursday, March 25, aged 86 years. Mrs. Ehart was born in Saxony, Germany, and came to America with her parents, Mr. and Mrs. Cole, when seven years of age, and has been a resident of this place for 56 years. Her husband died about two years ago. Mrs. Ehart was a member of the Evangelical church . . . ." Frank and Augusta's family consisted of six children, 21 grandchildren, and 14 great grandchildren. The couple is buried in Beaver Falls Old Cemetery.

Newton G. Ehle – Co. E

b. February 9, 1838 Sandy Creek, NY
d. May 30, 1863 ?
m. ------

NOTE: Newton was a son of David (1807-1874) and Sarah Richards Knollin Ehle (1816-1848). His DOD is disputed. His cenotaph in Woodlawn Cemetery, Sandy Creek, says he died May 30th, but *The Town Clerks' Registers* provide a date of April 15, 1863 while his entry in *Deaths of Volunteers* records the date as May 31st. His muster roll card says he died in June 1863. I use that on the cenotaph. Even his POD is conjectural. His muster roll card says he died at Aquia Creek, VA but a note in *The Town Clerks' Registers* says he succumbed at Windmill Point Hospital, Fredericksburg, VA. Since he is buried in Fredericksburg National Cemetery, the latter is probably the correct location. COD was typhoid fever. *The Sandy Creek News* July 4, 1863, 1 published a poem by D.R.K. written in memory of this young man. While not the best piece of literature ever penned, its sentiment was nevertheless heartfelt.

Johan Frederick Ehrisman – Co. G
b. 1806 Wuertemberg, Hohenklingen, Germany
d. July 8, 1863 White Church Hospital, Gettysburg, Adams, PA
m. Jantien Kamping (1810-*post* 1875) May 3, 1854

NOTE: Frederick, who lied about his age in order to enlist, was wounded on July 1, 1863 at Gettysburg and died from that wound. His parents are unknown. He and Jantien "Johanna" were married in Amsterdam, Holland. The couple lived in Oswego City where Frederick was a baker. After his death she obtained a widow's pension of $8.00 per month. In 1863 when she made application she was 53 years old. Jantien was last listed in the Oswego City Directory in 1875. Her grave has not been located.

Joseph B. Eldred – Co. D
b. October 8, 1841 Cayuga County, NY
d. August 10, 1916 Saginaw, Saginaw, MI
m. Amelia Ann Madison (April 2, 1841-February 25, 1916) February 25, 1857

NOTE: Joseph, whose parents were Thomas Chauncey (1800-1886) and Orilla Woolridge Eldred (1802-1890), originally enlisted in the 110th Regiment but was sent to the 147th. He was captured July 1, 1863 and paroled at an unknown date. Amelia's death was announced in *The Saginaw Daily News* February 25, 1916, 12: "Amelia A. Eldred died [this] morning at the family residence on the Shattuck road, Carrollton, of Bright's disease after an illness of four weeks. Amelia A. Madison was born in Oswego county, New York, April 2, 1841, and was married to Joseph Eldred in 1857, coming to Saginaw to reside 30 years ago, where she had a large acquaintance of friends . . . The funeral will take place from the residence, Sunday afternoon at 2 o'clock . . . ." Her COD was Bright's disease. When Joseph died a few months later, *The Saginaw Daily News* August 11, 1916, 2 published the following: "The funeral of Joseph B. Eldred took place [this] afternoon at 2:30 o'clock from his home, 900 Johnson street. Rev. Mr. Volz officiated . . . Mr. Eldred was a member of Camp Sherman No. 1. He was born in New York in 1838 [*sic*]. He joined Co. D, New York Volunteers No. 147, August 5, 1862. He served about three years with the army, more than a year of which was in Libby Prison, and was mustered out at Oswego, N.Y. [*sic*], June 7, 1865. Immediately after he came to Michigan which had since been his home. He leaves two sons and two daughters, 11 grandchildren and four great grandchildren, practically all residing in Saginaw . . . ." His COD was "chronic cystitis." He and Amelia are buried in Forest Lawn Cemetery, Saginaw.

Charles Eldridge – Co. B
b. 1835 Essex County, NY
d. February 24, 1864 Richmond, VA
m. Catherine Harper Razey (1835-April 16, 1906) January 17, 1859

NOTE: Charles' parents are unidentified. He was taken prisoner at Gettysburg on July 1, 1863 and died in Libby Prison of chronic diarrhea. He is buried in Richmond National Cemetery. Catherine had previously been married to Joseph Razey (1828-1911) and they were the parents of Andrew (1850-?) and Walter (1852-*post* 1910). Apparently Joseph abandoned her *ca.* 1855 and settled in Iowa where he married Mary Ann Mix in 1865 and reared a second family. After Charles and Catherine married the two boys took his surname. In 1900 Walter was living in Lamar, Powers, CO with his second wife and second family. Catherine was living in Syracuse, caring for the children from his first marriage. She does not appear on the 1905 New York census, evidently having moved to Colorado some time after the 1900 census. She is buried in Riverside Cemetery, Lamar.

John W. Elliott – Co. K
b. 1817 Ireland
d. November 20, 1863 Syracuse, Onondaga, NY
m. ?

NOTE: John's parents are unknown. He lied about his age in order to enlist. Both *Registers of Officers and Enlisted Men* and the 1865 New York census confirm he was born in 1817. He previously served in Co. E, 24th NYSV from May 4, 1861-April 5, 1862 when he was discharged at Upton's Hill, VA for "disability." He next enlisted in the 110th but was sent to the 147th. He was captured at Gettysburg and paroled at an unknown date. *The Oswego Daily Palladium* November 21, 1863 reported the following: "John Elliott, of Co. K, 147th Regiment, was arrested at Syracuse on Tuesday last as a deserter, having, as he claimed, lost his furlough, and was confined in the jail of that city. He had been drinking very hard for several days before he was arrested, and yesterday died quite suddenly in a fit of delirium tremens. After lying down for some time he got up and sat on a stool and immediately fell off dead." According to an article published in *The Oswego Commercial Times* November 27, 1863 the funeral was held in Fulton on Sunday, November 22nd. John is buried in Mt. Adnah Cemetery, Fulton. Elliott's widow may have been Julia _____ (1827-?). In 1850 John Elliott, 35, and Julia, his wife, 22, had been married within the year. They were living in Granby, NY with Bridget Whalen, who may have been Julia's mother. In the section on the 1865 New York census which enumerated deceased soldiers, John reportedly left two minor children, a fact confirmed by *Registers of Officers and Enlisted Men*. The unnamed woman who applied for a pension in July 1864 did not obtain it and it is relatively certain she had died. As for the two children, the 1865 New York census enumerated John Elliott, 12, and Thomas Elliott, 7 in the household of John and Nancy Sheridan. These may or may not be John's children.

Alonzo Ellis – Co. F
b. 1820 Waterville, Oneida, NY
d. February 12, 1863 Regimental Hospital, Belle Plain, VA
m. Caroline Morgan (May 1820-September 16, 1900) April 20, 1840

NOTE: Alonzo was the son of John (1786-?) and Rhoda Ellis (1789-?). He and Caroline were the parents of Fidelia (1840-1914), William (1842-1929), and Amelia (1843-*post* 1881). At some point Caroline went insane and by 1850 Alonzo was living with Melissa Hinds (1831-June 8, 1909). According to a deposition made by John Forsyth, justice of the peace, Alonzo "married" Melissa on July 17, 1847 in Fulton, NY. After Alonzo died of "pneumonia after measles," Caroline's legally appointed guardian, John Parsons, superintendent of the Oswego County Poor House and Insane Asylum where she lived from time to time, took charge of applying for a pension for her. Melissa also filed as a "contesting widow." By 1863 she was the mother of Huldah (1851-1918), Julius (1855-1925), Ezra (1857-1920), and Ida (1861-1931). An investigation ensued at the conclusion of which Melissa's children were excluded because they were "illegitimate being the fruit of adulterous cohabitation of soldier and their mother while his legal wife was still living and insane." Caroline was living with Fidelia in Fulton, NY when she died. Her grave has not been located. Melissa married Merritt Hodges (1815-June 11, 1885) in 1866. After his death she married Hiram Guile (1814-June 11, 1899) on June 22, 1892.

Russell Ellis – Co. B
b. 1826 Oneida County, NY
d. May 5, 1864 Orange Court House, VA
m. ?

NOTE: Russell, parents unknown, had previously served in Co. A, 81st Regiment from October 1861-February 1862 when discharged for "disability." He was wounded at the battle of the Wilderness and, according to the statement of Captain George Hugunin, died the same day. Very little has been learned about this man. Someone by that name was a soldier in the Regular Army stationed at Fort Ontario in 1846. No one filed a claim for a widow's pension so he probably was not married.

Samuel Ellis – Co. I
b. 1844 England
d. September 7, 1910 National Soldiers' Home, Johnson City, Washington, TN
m. Sophia Glen Whidden (April 1,1834-April 2, 1907) December 25, 1888

NOTE: Samuel's parents are unidentified. He was discharged from the army on April 22, 1864 at Culpeper, VA in order to enlist in the US Navy, serving in that organization from May 4, 1864-June 11, 1865. After the war he moved to Sanibel Island, Lee, FL where he married Sophia who, according to Betty Anholt's *Sanibel's Story*, 29, was part Native American. She had already been married three times: James Henry Thompson (1834-1864) December 24, 1858; John E. Savage (1840-*post* 1876) March 26, 1871; John Underhill (1823-?) April 20, 1876. (She divorced Savage on April 20, 1876 and apparently married Underhill the same day. Underhill died at a "cow camp" between 1885-1888 and "was buried where he died on the range.") When Samuel entered the home in 1908 he claimed a lengthy list of disabilities, among which were a urethral fistula extruding from his scrotum, hemorrhoids, cardiac hypertrophy, and kidney disease. He is buried in the Mountain Home National Cemetery, Johnson City, TN. Sophia, whose COD was bronchial pneumonia, complicated with Bright's disease and senile gangrene of the right leg below the knee, died on Sanibel Island and, according to her death certificate, was buried there.

William Ellis – Co. D
b. January 6, 1842 Palermo, NY
d. February 19, 1929 Fulton, NY
m. Jennie M. Hart (January 1852-December 17, 1915) 1870

NOTE: William was the son of Alonzo and Caroline Morgan Ellis. He mustered out of the regiment on June 7, 1865. In 1890 he said he had been "bruised in left hip and wounded in left knee" during the war. He was a member of Daniel F. Schenck Post No. 271 GAR. His obituary, appearing in *The Fulton Patriot* February 27, 1929, is excerpted here: ". . . Although well advanced in years, Mr. Ellis took an important part in the patriotic gatherings in this city and vicinity . . . He was seen about our streets nearly every day until a short time [ago], when he fell and fractured his hip, which hastened his death." William and Jennie, the mother of four, are buried in Mt. Adnah Cemetery, Fulton.

Charles Elmer – Co. D

b. 1843 Granby, NY

d. March 2, 1901 National Soldiers' Home, Marion, Grant, IN

m. Harriet "Hattie" Corey (1860-July 23, 1896) October 18, 1881

NOTE: Charles, whose mother may have been Hannah (1813-*post* 1865), was discharged from the service for "disability" on February 12, 1863. He enlisted in Co. A, 184th Regiment on August 22, 1864 and served until June 29, 1865 when he was mustered out at City Point, VA. *The Indianapolis News* March 2, 1901, 11 reported his death: "Charles D. Elmer, a member of the Soldiers' Home, committed suicide last night, in barrack No. 11, by taking morphine and was found dead in bed this morning. He belonged to Company D [*sic*], One hundred-and-eighty-fourth New York and resided for thirty years in Michigan. He has a daughter in the Soldiers' Orphan Home, at Knightstown, and a son." I have found no evidence of a son but his daughter was Daisy (1887-?) who married William Fleming on June 3, 1905 in Delaware County, IN. Charles is buried in Marion National Cemetery. Harriet's gravesite is unknown.

Jasper William Emblen – Co. C

b. March 1841 Rome, Oneida, NY

d. March 14, 1934 Elmira, Chemung, NY

m. Amanda V. Parsons (October 6, 1842-May 2, 1926) August 2, 1863

NOTE: Jasper was a son of James (?-?) and Chloe Loomis Emblen (?-?), both of whom died young. His name was erroneously spelled Emblem on his muster roll card. He had previously served in 1st NY ART from October 1861-February 1862. He was discharged from the 147th on February 11, 1865 when that regiment was consolidated with the 76th. His obituary, appearing in *The Elmira Star-Gazette* March 12, 1934, 2, detailed a long and active life: "Jasper W. Emblen, veteran of the Civil War and master carpenter, died Sunday evening after a brief illness. He observed his 93rd birthday anniversary Thursday. Mr. Emblen was in charge of the construction of the Northside Baptist Church and St. Luke's Congregational Church. He also superintended the erection of several other of Elmira's larger buildings before his retirement several years ago. As a member of the 147th New York Volunteers, he took part in some of the most important Civil War battles. His regiment fired the first volley in Battle of Gettysburg. Other engagements in which he took part were Chancellorsville, Piney Branch Church, Laurel Hill, Spotsylvania and Petersburg. He was mustered out at the close of the war with the rank of first sergeant. Mr. Emblen was a past master of Chemung Valley Lodge, F. & A. M., was noble grand and chief patriarch Newtown Lodge IOOF. He was four times commander of Walter C. Hull Post, GAR, of Waverly. At the time of his death he was a member of Baldwin Post, GAR, of Elmira." His graveside service was conducted by members of Chemung Valley Masonic Lodge. Amanda, like her husband, led a full and busy life, as revealed in her obituary published in *The Elmira Star-Gazette* May 4, 1926, 11: "Mrs. Amanda V. Emblen, a former resident of Elmira, died unexpectedly Monday night at 11:30 o'clock of a heart seizure at the family home in Chemung. Mrs. Emblen was born Amanda V. Parsons, October 6, 1842 and was married with Jasper W. Emblen August 2, 1863. They celebrated their sixty-fifth anniversary of their wedding last August at their home in a quiet manner. For many years Mr. and Mrs. Emblen resided in the northeastern section of the city and Mr. Emblen was engaged as a contractor and builder. They were prominent members of the Free Will Baptist Church, which later became the Northside Baptist Church. The family removed to Florida in 1882 and returned to Elmira in 1884. Several years ago Mr. and Mrs. Emblen established their home at Chemung where they have lived very happily and comfortably. Mrs. Emblen was a woman of true motherly character, who gave her life's work for the benefit of her family and those persons in need of her care and assistance. Quiet in manner and unselfish in her work she had the love and respect of many friends during her long life. Mr. and Mrs. Emblen were members of the Methodist Episcopal Church at Chemung which building adjoined their home . . . ." Jasper and Amanda are buried in Woodlawn Cemetery, Elmira.

Stephen Washington Emblen – Co. C

b. September 25, 1842 Albion, NY
d. July 11, 1898 Elmira, Chemung, NY
m. ------

NOTE: Stephen was Jasper's brother. On January 1, 1864 he transferred to Co. F. A year later, on February 27, 1865 he was transferred to the Brigade Band. According to *The Town Clerks' Registers* he lived in Floyd, Oneida, NY after the war. In 1890 his address was Bennett's Corners, Oneida, NY. By 1892 he was living in Lenox, Madison, NY. When he died he was living with his brother Jasper in Elmira. The county paid for his burial in Woodlawn Cemetery.

Richard Emmons – Co. B

b. 1838 Rome, Oneida, NY
d. August 14, 1898 Ithaca, Tompkins, NY
m. Emma E. Short Wright (1845-September 3, 1906) *ca.* 1873

NOTE: The son of Richard (1811-?) and Susan Hartman Emmons (1811-*post* 1875), Richard was a carpenter and joiner when he enlisted in the 147th Regiment. He was discharged from the service on March 21, 1864 at Washington, D. C. for "disability." When Richard died, Emma and a "contesting widow," Annie C. Emmons, claimed his pension. Richard's relationship with Annie is mysterious. In 1860 he was living with his parents, but both *The Town Clerks' Registers* and *Registers of Officers and Enlisted Men* show him as a married man. In 1870 he was living with Ann, 29, and an adopted daughter, Mary Jane Lewis, 11. By 1875 he was married to Emma, who had two children from her first marriage, George (1868-?) and Mary (1871-?) Wright. He and Emma were the parents of Fanny, two months. The actual marital status of Richard and Ann is unknown but Emma obtained the pension. Perhaps Annie could not prove she and Richard had been legally married. *The Ithaca Daily News* August 15, 1898 reported the following: "On Sunday morning at 12:45 occurred the death of Richard Emmons, age 56 years. Mr. Emmons has been ill for the past two years, but has been confined to bed only one week. He was a great sufferer, and a man who was well thought of by the community at large. He was a veteran of the civil war, and served in Co. D [*sic*], 147th New York Volunteers . . . The funeral will be held from his late residence, No. 140 North Tioga street, on Tuesday afternoon at three o'clock. Sydney Post No. 41, G.A.R., and the Sons of Veterans will attend the funeral in a body . . . ." Emma's death elicited the following obituary in *The Ithaca Daily News* September 5, 1906, 5: "The funeral of Mrs. Emma Emmons, who died at the Robinson hospital Monday night, was held from the home of her daughter, Mrs. William C. Cummings, at No. 612 North Tioga street, this afternoon at 3 o'clock, the Rev. Herbert W. Hutchinson officiating . . . The pall bearers were taken from among the veterans of Mix and Sidney posts, Mrs. Emmons having been a member of the Ladies' auxiliary to the Sons of Veterans. Each of these organizations, together with the other fraternal orders to which she belongs, was largely represented at the funeral. The floral tributes offered by the several societies were very beautiful. The Ladies' auxiliary to the National Protective Legion gave a large floral star, with the emblem of the society thereon. A design representing a sheath [*sic*] of wheat and a sickle was given by the Sons of Veterans, and a pillow on which were the words, 'Our Neighbor,' by the Modern Woodmen . . . ." Richard and Emma are buried in Ithaca City Cemetery.

Ernest Richard Esmond – Co. D

b. April 1845 Oswego County, NY
d. November 7, 1910 Manhattan, NY
m1. Rose Lasher (?-?) *ca.* 1873
m2. Julia Augusta Wilson (July 4, 1850-December 22, 1942) 1887

NOTE: Richard, son of Joseph (1819-1898) and Rhoda Titus Esmond (1820-*post* 1892), attended Falley Seminary, Fulton, as a boy. He was a lieutenant in the 147th and at the battle of Hatcher's Run (Dabney's Mills) distinguished himself, as reported by Brig.-General Henry A. Morrow, commanding Third Brigade: ". . . First Lieut. Richard Esmond, One hundred and forty-seventh New York Volunteers, acted as an aide on my staff, and deserves a brevet for his gallant conduct. He was present throughout the engagement, and in the execution of his duties displayed remarkable courage and coolness. In the charge of Mahone, already referred to, this young officer mingled freely among the troops, and by words and example rendered most valuable service. In the severest part of the conflict he offered to take the brigade colors in advance of the line, hoping thereby to induce the troops to charge the enemy. This he was not allowed to do, as I deemed it a deed of too hardy a character to be attempted by any one. I earnestly recommend him to the favorable consideration of the Government." Esmond mustered out with the regiment on June 7, 1865. When he enlisted, Esmond, who used his Christian names interchangeably, said he was a clerk. In later life he was an electrical engineer and he served as a captain in Co. L, 1st US Volunteer Engineers during the Spanish-American War. He and Rose Lasher were the parents of Mabel Esmond (1879-January 13, 1843). When Mabel, a trained nurse, applied for Social Security benefits, her mother's maiden name was required on the form. She died in San Diego, CA and was cremated. With the possible exception of the 1875 New York census, Weedsport, Cayuga, NY, I have located no other records for Rose. Richard and Julia became the parents of a son, Henry "Harry" Lambden, on September 27, 1889 in New York City. He died very suddenly in Herkimer, NY January 17, 1917. After Julia and Richard separated some time before the 1892 New York census, he lived in New York City until his death. He was by all accounts a successful businessman and held several patents for heavy machinery. His death was announced in *The New York Times* November 9, 1910, but a fuller obituary was published in *The Ilion Citizen* November 17, 1910, 2: "Major E. [Richard] Esmond died suddenly in New York city, Nov. 7, 1910. He enlisted with the 147th Regiment of Volunteers of New York in the Civil War and was brevetted major for special service at the end of the war. He also enlisted as Captain of the 1st Regiment of Engineers in the Spanish American War. The interment was made in Herkimer, Friday, Nov. 11." Albert S. Roe wrote a remembrance of Esmond which appeared in *The Fulton Times* December 7, 1910, 12 and is here excerpted:". . . I know not how recent years have dealt with him, but of this I am sure, had death overtaken 'Dick' in those gala days of Old Falley Seminary he would have taken out of life one of the merriest youngsters who ever called John P. Griffin 'Professor.' It was just pure, continuous, unqualified fun that bubbled perennially from an apparently exhaustless source. Everybody liked 'Dick' . . . He had dignity enough when necessary, to make himself a veritable 'Little Corporal,' for such was Napoleon when he impressed himself on the minds of his fellow soldiers of France. Our small lad of the seminary started in the 147th . . . It was no picnic party into which Corporal Esmond's regiment was led for, from Gettysburg to Five Forks, the Oswego County boys had their share of all there was in sight . . . The 147th was one of the Fighting Regiments forever immortalized by Colonel Fox in his famous volume, and I love to think that the rollicking, mischievous friend of my boyhood was one of the bravest and best of the entire army. I have understood that his coolness in danger, his ceaseless activity soon won him positions where such qualities were appreciated and that he found his proper position as a staff officer. At any rate he attained his First Lieutenancy, January 13, 1864, and the government later recognized his valiant worth by giving him the brevet rank of Captain and Major. What an alert, inspiring sight he was when he came home with his honors still fresh upon him. How all of us regretted that he was not inclined to accept the cadetship offered him at Annapolis, asking that the honor be conferred upon his brother, Titus . . . What more can I write? I had not seen him since the earliest days after the bloody struggle. Perhaps he had grown a bit more sedate, manlike, but he could laugh just as heartily then as in the earlier Sixties. He won his fame in the 'Sixties' of the Century and he died in the Sixties of his age. For the sake of Auld Lang Syne, for all he was and did, may God bless him and ever keep his memory green. Is there one who knew him and loved him, to whom these words may come who will not breathe a fervent 'Amen'." Julia lived in Herkimer, NY until her death with her unmarried sisters Eliza (1852-1925) and Josephine Wilson (1848-1929). Another sister, Harriet (1848-1927), was married to Richard's brother, Zadok Titus Esmond (1848-1918). At one time Julia was the landlady of a boarding house. She took an active interest in community affairs and her name was repeatedly mentioned in the newspapers as a donor to Chautauqua programs held in the area. Her obituary appeared in *The Utica Daily Press* December 23, 1942, 14: "Mrs. Julia Esmond, 93, one of Herkimer's oldest residents, died Dec. 22, 1942, in a Utica nursing home where she had been confined for several months. Mrs. Esmond was born in Canastota, daughter of John Alexander and Emmaliesa [*sic*] Penfield Wilson. She attended the Canastota schools and the Oswego Normal. Her husband, Major Richard Esmond, veteran of the Civil and Spanish-American wars, died several years ago. She lived for many years in 420 Margaret St., and was very active until her health failed over a year ago. Mrs. Esmond was a member of the reformed church . . . ." Graves for Richard, Rose, and Julia have not been located.

Hudson Henry Evens – Co. B
b. February 23, 1843 Brooklyn, NY
d. November 25, 1874 Syracuse, Onondaga, NY
m. Eliza Jones (October 19, 1848-February 13, 1929) *ca.* 1866

NOTE: Hudson's parents were George (1804-*ante* 1855) and Hannah Howard Evens [Clark] (1817-*post* 1881). Although the surname was often spelled Evans, I use the version located on the gravestone. He mustered out with the regiment on June 7, 1865. In 1870 the family, consisting of Hudson, Elisa [*sic*], Margarett, 3, and Mary, 1, was living in Syracuse. Hudson's COD was "consumption." He and Eliza are buried in Oakwood Cemetery, Syracuse.

Joseph H. Everts – Co. G
b. January 18, 1840 Orleans County, NY
d. December 1, 1914 Otter Lake, Lapeer, MI
m. Ida Frances Randall (June 2, 1858-June 29, 1928) October 22, 1874

NOTE: Joseph's parents were James Everts (?-*ante* 1865) and Jemima _____ Everts Townsend (1802-*post* 1865). Although his muster roll card indicates he was born in Orange County, NY, his death certificate says his POB was Orleans County, NY. As a young man he was a boatman but in later years he was a mail carrier in Otter Creek. Joseph's COD was heart disease complicated by asthma. Ida married Joseph O. Jones (1851-August 8, 1929) in Clio, Genesee, MI on September 26, 1917 as his second wife. She died of liver cancer and is buried with Everts in Otter Lake Cemetery.

Peter Fannon – Co. K
b. 1841 Oswego County, NY
d. May 21, 1899 Oswego City, NY
m. Ann Delaney(1844-April 22, 1899) *ca.* 1866

NOTE: Peter was a son of Malachi (1805-*post* 1865) and Ellen Keegan Fannon (1815-*post* 1865). Peter's unexpected death was reported in *The Oswego Daily Palladium* May 22, 1899, 8: "Peter Fannon, aged fifty-six, of Rochester, died suddenly of heart disease at the home of his sister, Mrs. Willis Rogers, in East First street, over Ryan's restaurant, yesterday afternoon at one o'clock. Mr. Fannon has been visiting Mrs. Rogers for the past three weeks. Yesterday morning he arose and ate his breakfast. He made no complaint of feeling ill during the morning, but at noon told Mrs. Rogers that he did not wish any dinner. Between twelve and one o'clock Mr. Fannon said that he was sick and asked that a physician be sent for. A doctor was summoned but before his arrival Fannon toppled over, dead. Mr. Fannon was a resident of Rochester and lived there a number of years. He served in the Civil War and was honorably discharged. About a month ago his wife died and it is believed that her death caused his health to be undermined. He leaves a family of nine grown-up children in Rochester. Before the war Mr. Fannon was a resident of Oswego and went to the front from this city as a member of company K, 147th New York Volunteers, Captain N. A. Wright, commanding. He was a good soldier, and the announcement of his death will be received with sorrow by many of his old comrades in arms. In the Winter of '62 Mr. Fannon was stricken with brain fever; recovering he rejoined his regiment and remained until the close of the war. August 18th, 1864 he was wounded in the hip and on February 5, 1865 he was shot in the arm at Hatcher [*sic*] Run." Peter is buried in St. Paul's Cemetery, Oswego City. Ann is buried in Holy Sepulchre Cemetery, Rochester. Peter's brother, Thomas (1843-1870), served in the 21st New York Cavalry.

Another brother, Malachi (1837-November 28, 1864), served in the 5th NY HA and died of typhoid fever at Harper's Ferry, VA.

Leonard S. Fargo – Co. D
b. 1817 Rutland Co., VT
d. April 7, 1881 Fulton, NY
m. Nancy _____ Graves (1820-June 5, 1905) *ca.* 1852

NOTE: Leonard, whose parents are unknown, was a farmer. In August 1863 he was reported "absent, sick" and at an unknown date he transferred to the 50th Company, Second Battalion VRC. His discharge date is also unknown. He and Nancy were the parents of six children but she apparently was married previously since she had a son, Orville T. Graves, with whom she was living in Fulton when she died. Leonard's tragic ending was reported in *The Oswego Daily Palladium* April 7, 1881: "Leonard Fargo, about sixty years old went to the river this morning for a pail of water, fell in and was drowned. The body was recovered after being in the water two hours . . . ." The community's perception of him was revealed in an article appearing in *The Syracuse Daily Standard* April 13, 1881: "Three girls named Mary Martin, Mary Gillard and Mary Sullivan are under arrest at Oswego Falls, charged with having disturbed the funeral of one Leonard Fargo, an eccentric individual, who was drowned last week. The prisoners are accused of indecent conduct, loud and boisterous language and laughter. They were arrested under the law prohibiting interference with religious services." Leonard and Nancy are buried in Mt. Adnah Cemetery, Fulton.

Dudley Farling – adjutant
b. April 1818 Tompkins County, NY
d. December 3, 1882 Newfield, Tompkins, NY
m. Rebecca Van Nortwick (June 1819-January 25, 1876) *ca.* 1842

NOTE: Farling's parents are unidentified. His occupation was newspaper printing and publishing. He was the foreman of *The Albany Argus* in 1853 when he bought *The Oswego Palladium*. In 1861 he ran for the New York State Assembly from Oswego County. After the war, he served as secretary-treasurer for the Palladium Printing Company for a number of years. Although his gravestone says he died in 1883, his obituary, published in *The Ithaca Daily Journal* December 7, 1882, disproves that assertion: ". . . Mr. Dudley Farling who died so suddenly Sunday morning of heart disease, had been with his daughter Mary, residing at Mrs. C. H. Seabring's, in Seabring Settlement, since last spring. He was a member of the 147th N.Y. Volunteers, entering the service as adjutant of the regiment, and was subsequently promoted to major, November 5, 1863." Further evidence of a DOD of 1882 may be found in his son

Samuel's application to the Surrogate Court in December 1882 to send his father's estate to probate. He and Rebecca were the parents of five children. She died of pneumonia and is buried in Ithaca City Cemetery with her husband.

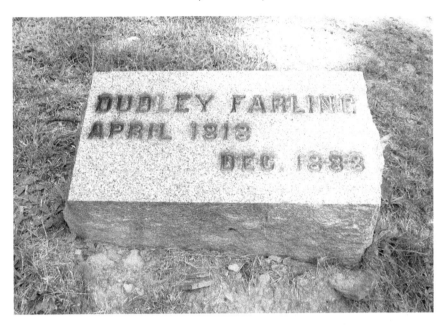

A newspaper man by profession, Dudley Farling served the Union well, despite his controversial actions with regard to other officers.
S. J. Sheret, FAG

George Madison Farnham – Co. A

b. 1841 Hannibal, NY

d. November 18, 1922 Syracuse, Onondaga, NY

m. Margaret Tilford (April 1849-September 10, 1922) 1872

NOTE: George, son of Truman (1805-?) and Sybil Moon Farnham (1808-?), was discharged from the 147th on November 14, 1862 in order to enlist in the US Regular Army. In 1900 the family lived in Washington, TN. He and Margaret, the mother of four all living in 1900, are buried in North Syracuse Cemetery.

Mason David Farnham – Co. A

b. June 27, 1837 Oswego County, NY

d. January 29, 1870 Pittsfield, Berkshire, MA

m. Augusta M. Warren (November 1849-April 9, 1904) ca. 1866

NOTE: Mason was the son of David (1814-1909) and Julyette Mason Farnham (1816-1865). Although he originally enlisted in the 110th Regiment, he was sent to the 147th. He was discharged from the service on January 24, 1863 for "disability" which might have been the tuberculosis which ultimately killed him. He is buried in Hannibal Village Cemetery. He and Augusta were the parents of William (1867-1867) and Lora E. (1868-1869). Augusta married Emory Upton Parshall (July 16, 1864-April 9, 1914) on December 7, 1890 at Pierstown, Otsego, NY. Her death was announced in *The Otsego Farmer* April 15, 1904, 4: "It was with sorrow that the friends learned of the death of Mrs. Emory U. Parshall which occurred last Saturday forenoon the 9th, after a brief illness with pneumonia. A little over a week ago she was in Cooperstown attending to business interests and arranging to leave for the West to join her husband who travels in the interest of Hastings Industrial Co. of Chicago. Mrs. Parshall was intending to leave for Chicago the 6th to visit for a few days after which she intended to meet Mr. Parshall at Monticello, Minn. She had cousins in Minneapolis where she was to spend some time. After this she was to make her home with Mrs. Joseph Warren and Mrs. Seymour of Monticello where Mr. Parshall would have joined her on Sundays. He had planned to have her with him in traveling. At the time of her sickness, Mr. Parshall was in western Minneapolis. His friends had written every day but all letters had failed to reach him. A telegram found him in Windom. Mr. Parshall came as quickly as the fastest trains could bring him arriving here Sunday noon, he not knowing of her death until his arrival in Binghamton where the sad news was broken to him by a friend . . . Mrs. Parshall was a loving daughter of Wm. Kendrick Warren who died the 7th of last June, and was a member of the First Baptist church of Cooperstown. A true and pure Christian wife and daughter . . . ." Emory also died on April 9th after a bout with pneumonia lasting two weeks. They are buried in Lakewood Cemetery, Cooperstown, Otsego, NY.

Thomas E. Farr – Co. F

b. May 26, 1828 Warwickshire, England

d. October 9, 1899 Texas, NY

m. Mary C. Clapsaddle (1845-September 21, 1906) *ca.* 1866

NOTE: Farr, son of Charles (1802-1885) and Catherine Shuttleworth Farr (1800-*post* 1875), was wounded at Gettysburg during Picket's Charge on July 3, 1863. Nevertheless, he mustered out with the regiment on June 7, 1865. In 1890 he claimed paralysis as his disability. He was a member of Melzar Richards Post No 367 GAR. For some years he managed the Lake Grove House at Mexico Point, NY "on strictly temperance principles." His life and death were chronicled in *The Oswego Daily Palladium* October 18, 1899, 3: "Texas, Oct. 12. – Our community was again shocked on Tuesday morning to hear that Thomas E. Farr had been found dead in bed. Mr. Farr, whose health had been feeble for years past, had only been confined to the house for ten days and was then able to be around. On Monday he appeared more cheerful than for some days past. He ate a hearty supper, read the *Daily Palladium* and went upstairs to bed at half-past eight o'clock. At a quarter past ten Mrs. Farr went upstairs and found him dead. He had passed away easily without struggle or outcry. Coroner Box was summoned and declared that death resulted from gangrene and paralysis, caused by a gunshot wound he received at Gettysburg while facing the rebel General Pickett's charge, which settled the destiny of the Confederate States. Mr. Farr was born in Warwickshire, England, May 26th, 1828. He came to this country when a young man and for many years traveled extensively, crossing the ocean several times. In 1862 he enlisted in the 147th Regiment, N. Y. V. He was promoted to be Orderly Sergeant of Company F and served till the close of the Rebellion, never missing an engagement in which his regiment participated. Politically he was an ardent Republican until 1884, when he supported Grover Cleveland for President. He continued to act with that party till 1896, when he supported William McKinley. The funeral was held at the Wesleyan Methodist church yesterday. The services were conducted by the Rev. E. E. Curtis who delivered an eloquent address to the many old veterans present who were waiting to tenderly bear their old comrade to his last resting place." Mary was living in Black River, Jefferson, NY with her son John (1867-*post* 1920) when she died. Her remains were returned to Oswego County. She and Thomas are buried in Daysville Cemetery, Pulaski.

James Farrell – Co. B

b. 1832 Ireland

d. May 15, 1877 Oswego City, NY

m. Julia Parkhurst (September 25, 1835-April 26, 1861) *ante* 1860

NOTE: James Farrell, parents unknown, was a painter when he enlisted in 1862 at Oswego City. He transferred to the US Navy on April 22, 1864. He has two entries in *The Town Clerks' Registers*. One provides no information at all. The other says he was a sailor born in Pennsylvania. In 1860 he and Julia were living in Scriba with her parents Isaac R. (1809-1882) and Eliza Sheldon Parkshurst (1810-1898). His POB was Canada. Julia was a sister of Byron Dwight Parkhurst, for whom see below. James' death was announced in the *Oswego Daily Times* May 15, 1877: "Mr. Farrell, brother of Edward Farrell was found dead in bed this morning. Mr. Farrell had been ill for sometime [*sic*], and it is supposed he died of heart disease." James is buried in St. Paul's Cemetery,

James Farrell, a native of Ireland, served in both the 147th Regiment and in the US Navy.
Author's Collection

Oswego City. Julia's grave has not been located although her parents are buried in Worden-Sweet Cemetery, Scriba, and she may also be there.

Patrick Farrell – Co. B
b. 1833 ?
d. ?
m. ?

NOTE: Very little has been learned about this man, but he and James may have been brothers. He enlisted at Oswego City. He was wounded at Gettysburg but was able to muster out with the regiment on June 7, 1865. *The Town Clerks' Registers* provide no information and his muster roll card contains no biographical material.

John B. Featherstonhaugh – Co. K
b. 1840 Oswego County, NY
d. May 6, 1893 Chicago, Cook, Il
m. Eliza J. Connolly (January 1850-November 11, 1917) *ca.* 1867

NOTE: John's surname was pronounced "Fanshaw." A son of Henry (1818-?) and Mary Ann Lee Featherstonhaugh (1818-?), he was a sailor when he enlisted. He was wounded in the leg on July 1, 1863 at Gettysburg and later transferred to the US Navy, serving aboard the frigate Niagara until his term of service expired. Although he was born in Oswego County, his POB varied from census to census. He and Eliza were the parents of a large family, two of whom, Mary Capers (1870-?) and Clara Niles (1871-?), were still alive in the 1940s. John is buried in Calvary Cemetery, Chicago. In 1910 Eliza was living in Chicago with William, John's brother. See below. Another brother, Henry F., was a lake captain. In November 1893 the schooner Emma Flora broke its moorings in Oswego Harbor during a gale. Henry, the captain of the tug Eliza Redford, set out to rescue the crew. The schooner beached itself and the tug smashed into it. Most of the tug's crew escaped but Henry was trapped in the pilot house which was ripped off in the storm. His body was recovered the next day. He had been scalded by the exploding steam engine and had drowned.

William W. Featherstonhaugh – Co. K
b. 1844 Oswego County, NY
d. May 26, 1916 Chicago, Cook, IL
m. ------

NOTE: William had previously served in Co. H, 24th Regiment. While a member of the 147th he was captured prior to August 1863. His parole date is unknown but he mustered out with the regiment on June 7, 1865. In 1873 he was sent to Auburn State Prison (NY) for four years for grand larceny. In October 1903 William and Eliza, John's widow, took out a marriage license but evidently never got married. William applied for a pension on June 17, 1886 and renewed it on January 16, 1911. Eliza had obtained a widow's pension after John died and perhaps she and William decided that two pensions were better than one. He is buried in Elmwood Cemetery, Chicago. Eliza, whose DOB varies from document to document, is buried with John in Calvary Cemetery, Chicago.

Justin W. Ferrington – Co. G

b. April 1842 Clinton County, NY
d. January 22, 1901 Greenleaf, Brown, WI
m. Elva Viola Ellis (March 1850-January 13, 1932) 1868

NOTE: Justin, the son of David (1770-*post* 1850) and Nancy Ferrington (1802-*post* 1850), served one day in Co. K, 16th Regiment, May 15, 1861-May 16, 1861, before he was discharged for "disability." He enrolled in the 147th at Oswego City and mustered out with the regiment on June 7, 1865. He and Elva were the parents of seven children, all born in Wisconsin. In 1900 he was a blacksmith. Elva never remarried and when she died *The Green Bay Press-Gazette* published the following: "Mrs. Elva V. Ferrington, 81, a pioneer resident of Greenleaf, died this morning at her home there after an illness of about three weeks. Complications caused her death. The funeral of Mrs. Ferrington will be held Friday afternoon with services at two o'clock at the home. Interment will be in Fairview cemetery. Mrs. Ferrington was born in the state of Vermont, came to Greenleaf about 60 years ago, and had lived there since that time. She was the widow of Justin Ferrington, who preceded her in death in 1901. She is survived by four sons, Benjamin, Greenleaf; William, Green Bay; Carl, Harlowton, Mont., and Elmer, Chicago." Justin is also buried in Fairview Cemetery, Greenleaf.

Bazael Fiel – Co. F

b. February 16, 1827 France
d. December 19, 1902 Syracuse, Onondaga, NY
m. Mary _____ (March 1828-March 1903) 1849

NOTE: This man's name was variously spelled, from "Fiel" to "File" to "Phile." His Christian name suffered the same fate: "Bazell," "Bazel," and "Brazil." His government gravestone says "Bazel File" but the cemetery record reads "Brazal." He and Mary, also born in France, came to the United States in 1843 and he became a naturalized citizen. He was transferred from the 147th to the VRC on August 17, 1863. In 1880 the family was living in Minnesota but by 1900 they were in Syracuse. He is buried in Oakwood Cemetery, Syracuse. It is possible that Mary returned to

Minnesota. One source says she died in Monticello, Wright, MN where her son, Sylvester (1855-1942), was living. Her grave has not been located.

John C. Fitzgibbons – Co. F
b. 1844 Oriskany, Oneida, NY
d. April 22, 1915 Goldhill, Jackson, OR
m. ?

NOTE: John, son of Patrick (1806-1866) and Catharine Fitzgibbons (1816-1892), mustered out with the regiment on June 7, 1865. In 1910 he was living in Foots Creek, Jackson, OR. He was a gold miner and said he had been married once for 32 years. I have, however, found no wife and when he died no widow claimed his pension. His parents are buried in Mexico Village Cemetery and a man named John Fitzgibbons, died in 1915, is also there.

John Fitzsimmons – Co. H
b. 1824 Meath County, Ireland
d. ? ?
m. Catharine _____ (1825-1887) ca. 1847

NOTE: John's parents are unknown. His muster roll card says he was wounded in the head at Gettysburg. He was also wounded in the leg at battle of the Wilderness, May 5, 1864, and taken prisoner. According to the *Registers of Officers and Enlisted Men* he spent seven months in prison. Other documents indicate he was sent to Andersonville. His parole date is unknown but he mustered out with the regiment on June 7, 1865. He entered the National Soldiers' Home at Bath, Steuben, NY on November 4, 1885, claiming to have suffered a gunshot wound at the battle of the Wilderness, a claim he confirmed in 1900. He left that place "summarily" on September 15, 1886. He was admitted to the Dayton Home on July 16, 1887 and was discharged February 25, 1896. By 1887 he was widowed and he gave his son Edward as his next of kin. Someone named John Fitzsimmons died in Oswego City on March 22, 1897 and could be this man. Graves for him and Catharine have not been located.

Michael Fitzsimmons – Co. B
b. 1825 Ireland
d. May 3, 1887 Muskegon, Muskegon, MI
m. Anna _____ (1832-August 6, 1902) ca. 1853

NOTE: Michael, a sailor, was the son of Michael and Elizabeth Kelly Fitzsimmons. He said he was 37 in 1862, suggesting he was born in 1825. His gravestone, however, says he died at age 58, implying a DOB of 1829. He was discharged from the army on August 29, 1864 for "disability" and applied for a pension on September 28, 1864. According to Michigan Death Records, his COD was a "diseased limb." He and Anna are buried in Oakwood Cemetery, Muskegon. His stone erroneously places him in the 174th Regiment. No such person served in that organization.

William Flack – Co. G

b. August 7, 1838 Drumgoon, Cavan, Ireland
d. October 15, 1928 Oswego, NY
m1. Mary Louise Martin (1841-February 18, 1901) 1865
m2. Sarah Josephine Crites Woodcock (August 1850-May 12, 1926) October 29, 1904

NOTE: William's parents were Samuel (1807-1867) and Margaret Jane Hall Flack (1807-1872). The family immigrated to the United States in 1845. William was wounded July 1, 1863 at Gettysburg and in 1890 said he had been wounded in the left leg. He was transferred to the VRC on January 22, 1864 and discharged at Elmira, NY on July 13, 1865. He alleged he was 22 in 1862 but his gravestone provides a DOB of 1838. He was 90 years old when he died. He and Mary Louise were the parents of at least six children. Sarah was previously married to Herbert L. Woodcock (1851-1903) in 1878. William and Mary Louise are buried in Rural Cemetery, Oswego Town. Sarah is buried in Lewis Corners Cemetery, Granby, and Herbert, in Mt. Adnah, Fulton.

Peter Flavin – Co. I

b. 1818 Ireland
d. ? ?
m. ?

NOTE: Peter, a mariner, was wounded near Chancellorsville, VA on May 3, 1863 and discharged from service on October 7, 1863 for "disability." On October 19, 1863 he successfully applied for a pension. No one claimed a widow's pension. No other information has been discovered.

Harvey O. Flint – Co. F

b. 1830 Schoharie County, NY
d. November 23, 1862 Camp near Tennallytown, DC
m. Minerva Marshall (1832-March 23, 1915) July 4, 1853

NOTE: Harvey, son of Alexander (1806-1890) and Asenath Joyce Flint (1811-*post* 1880), was a 2nd lieutenant. His DOB varies but since his gravestone says he was 32 when he died, I use a DOB of 1830. When he became sick with typhoid fever, Minerva, as she deposed in November 1908, nursed him: "I went down three weeks before he died and took care of him and brought him home to Palermo, Oswego Co., N.Y. and buried him." Harvey is buried in New Haven Rural Cemetery. He and Minerva had adopted a foundling left on the steps of "Lawyer Haskins" in Oswego City. She claimed in her 1908 deposition that the boy, whom they named John Wood Flint, was nine days old when they adopted him on May 9, 1860. As an officer's widow, she was entitled to a pension of $15 per month: ". . . After I had drawn my pension . . . for a little over three years, the neighbors made a fuss about my drawing a pension because I had this little boy, and they also wrote to Washington, to the Pension Bureau, and they stopped my pension, and I got so indignant over it and never paid any more attention to it . . . The little boy, John Wood Flint, above mentioned, that we adopted, as stated, died when he was six years and six months old . . . ." She never claimed a pension for little John. Minerva later married another officer from the 147th, Chauncey Gridley, and her story will continue below.

Lieutenant Harvey Flint's body was returned to New Haven for burial. The worn inscription says, "I miss you, Husband."
Author's Collection

James Hershal Foil – Co. H

b. 1837 Amboy, NY
d. September 29, 1899 Amboy, NY
m. Catharine E. Harris (1842-February 7, 1885) *ca.* 1860

NOTE: James' surname was variously spelled. I use that on his gravestone. The son of James (1798-1857) and Margaret Chambers Foil (1808-1875), he was a farmer. He mustered out with the regiment on June 7, 1865 near Washington, DC. In 1890 he claimed "rheumatism" as his disability. He and Catharine are buried in West Amboy Cemetery. They were the parents of 10 children.

Erwin Roselle Fonda – Co. D

b. October 18, 1844 Deerfield, Oneida, NY
d. August 23, 1919 Salisbury, Rowan, NC
m. Marion R. Berry (December 30, 1849-March 30, 1934) May 8, 1873

NOTE: Erwin was the son of James Robert (1816-1891) and Alzina Bacon Fonda (1813-1852). His story is detailed in an obituary appearing in *The Salisbury Evening Post* August 23, 1919, 1: "Capt. E. R. Fonda died shortly before noon today at his home at the Federal cemetery, of which he was superintendent. The funeral services will be held at the residence Sunday at 5:30 and conducted by Dr. Abernathy, and Dr. Lambert, of High Point, and the remains will be shipped to Pawpaw, Ill., for burial, this being in carrying out the wish expressed by the deceased some time ago. Capt. Fonda would have been 74 years old the 18th day of October. He was born in Deer Field, N.Y., and was a veteran of the civil war, fighting with the Union forces. Later he moved to the West and was for 28 years an engineer on the Union Pacific railroad, and was for a long time secretary to the committee on adjustment of grievances for this railroad. He continued his membership in the Brotherhood of Locomotive Engineers throughout his retired life and was a member of the order at his death. He was also an honorary member of the Eastern Star, a 23rd [*sic*] degree Mason and a Modern Woodman . . . Capt. Fonda had been in declining health for several years and three weeks ago suffered an attack which confined him to his bed. He was not thought to be in a critical state and had been dead some minutes when he daughter went up to his room just before noon to see how he was resting. He was a great reader and clasped in his hands was a newspaper which he had been reading. Capt. Fonda was a prince of [a] good fellow, exceeding pleasant and courteous and was always cheerful. He made a host of friends since coming to Salisbury as super-intendent of the Federal cemetery eight years ago. He was a regular attendant upon the services of the First Methodist church and an officer in the Baraca class. He took deep interest in political affairs and matters of state and was well posted on all public matters and discussed them intelligently and interestingly. He was at one time one of city officials of Council Bluff, Iowa, and at one time a candidate for mayor of that city. While a Union soldier he always participated in events in which the Confederate soldiers held in this city and delighted to meet and converse with his former foes. He was a friend of these men and of all who were in distress or want. In his death Salisbury loses a valuable citizen and his acquaintances a true friend. His death will cause genuine sorrow in this city." His funeral resulted in the following article in *The Salisbury Evening Post* August 25, 1919, 2: ". . . [The funeral] was a sad occasion and was attended by a large number of people. Dr. Lambeth made a beautiful talk and read the Scriptures which Capt. Fonda carried with him through the civil war and which is still stained with his own blood from a wound received in battle. On a visit of Dr. Lambeth during a previous illness, Captain Fonda had him read from this Bible. There were many floral offerings and some of these came from Confederate soldiers, one being sent by Col. A. H. Boyden. Quite a number of Confederate sol-diers, men who loved Captain Fonda and whom he loved, were present to pay tribute to a former foe but later a warm friend. The funeral was an impressive one, held on a spot the deceased loved and overlooking the hillside on which more than 12,000 of his comrades in blue are buried. A number of negro people attended the services and many called at the residence to view the remains of a man they claimed as a friend. The remains were shipped this morning on Western No. 11 to Pawpaw, Ill., to be laid beside the graves of his parents . . . Captain Fonda was the possessor of several articles which he valued highly although their monetary value was not great. One was his war Bible, another a gold headed cane presented to him by his G.A.R. Camp at Council Bluff, Ia., and another his Baraca pin, a gift from the class of the First Methodist church of this city. He always wore these two pins and frequently carried his cane. The simple insignia on the casket were his Masonic apron and a piece from the Eastern Star of which he was an honorary member. Another thing prized by this former Union soldier was a picture, taken at a Confederate reunion here when he and the late Capt. John A. Ramsay, of Confederate artillery fame, stood with clasped hands. Today, August 25, is the anniversary, both as to date and day of week of the enlistment of Captain Fonda in the Union army, having entered this service almost at the outbreak of the war, in 1861." Erwin was one of numerous siblings since his father married twice and had large families by both wives. He was a 32nd degree Scottish Rite Mason. His COD was heart disease and nephritis. He is buried in East Paw Paw Cemetery. His full brother, Fitch Fenton Fonda (1840-1864), enlisted in the 59th Regiment at Brookfield, NY on January 1, 1864 under the name "Fundy." He was captured near Petersburg, VA on June 22, 1864 and died of starvation and diarrhea at Andersonville, GA on October 4, 1864. He is buried in Andersonville National Cemetery.

Asa "Acey" Philip Forbes – Co. H
b. June 1846 Granby, NY
d. January 26, 1927 State Hospital, Ogdensburg, St. Lawrence, NY
m. Rosetta "Nettie May" Sparrowk (1861-February 25, 1908) April 16, 1875

NOTE: Asa, sometimes called Acey, was the son of Simeon (1807-?) and Nancy Mariah Muckey Forbes (1817-1889). He enlisted with two of his stepbrothers, Volney and Decatur Russell, the same day. See below their stories below. Asa was captured at Gettysburg on July 1, 1863. He entered Libby Prison, Richmond, VA on July 21, 1863 and was paroled at City Point, VA on September 29, 1863. He mustered out with the regiment on June 7, 1865. He and Rosetta were the parents of two sons, Herbert (1876-1939) and Homer (1877-1914). Homer drowned in Oswego Harbor on August 29, 1914 and was buried in St. Paul's Cemetery. According to an article published in *The Oswego Daily Times* August 31, 1914, 10, his family in Watertown informed authorities that they could not afford to have the body shipped home and asked that it be buried in

Oswego. Asa was a heavy drinker and frequently in trouble with the law. Mental problems ran in the family. A brother, William Forbes (1848-*post* 1910), was an inmate in the State Hospital in Ogdensburg. A sister, Mary, who married Volney Russell, hanged herself in 1884. Asa had his own mental problems. In January 1872 he reportedly bit off the nose of an elderly man named Solomon Baker. He was finally declared insane in November 1896 and taken to Ogdensburg where he died in 1927. He was buried in North Watertown Cemetery. In 2013 Chad Miller, his 3x great grandson, succeeded in having a handsome government stone placed on his ancestor's grave. Rosetta was the daughter of Reuben (1829-1892) and Jane Stevenson Sparrowk (1842-1923) who are buried in Pleasant Lawn Cemetery, Parish. In 1892 Rosetta, called Ann, was living with Asa and her sons in Williamstown. Next door was a man named George Russell (1867-1934), a cabinet maker. In 1900 Homer and his family were living in Syracuse and next door was George Russell and his wife, Nettie May. They claimed they had been married since 1889 and Nettie May said she had had no children. When Nettie May died her obituary appeared in *The Syracuse Daily Journal* February 26, 1908 which proved beyond a doubt that she was identical with Rosetta Sparrowk Forbes since many of her siblings were named as survivors. It is doubtful that she and Russell were actually married but they are buried together in Pleasant Lawn Cemetery, Parish.

Chad Miller, descendant of Asa Forbes, obtained this government gravestone for his 3x great grandfather.
Chad Miller, FAG

James J. Forbes – Co. K

b. 1813 England
d. March 23, 1863 Regimental Hospital, Washington, DC
m. Elizabeth _____ (1819-*post* 1855) *ca.* 1850

NOTE: James' parents are unidentified. Although he claimed he was born in 1818 when he enlisted, the 1855 New York census proves he lied in order to qualify. His COD was "diarrhea and pleurisy." Originally buried at Wallace's Farm, VA, today he lies in Fredericksburg National Cemetery. Little is known about Elizabeth and their son, William (1852-?). No evidence exists that she applied for a widow's pension which may mean she remarried or died. She was also born in England but William's POB was Oswego County. I located a William Forbes, 13, living in a "house of refuge" in Rochester, Monroe, NY in 1865. His POB was England but it is altogether possible that the person being interviewed did not actually know his birthplace but guessed based on information about his parents.

George French – Co. A
b. 1842 Boston, Suffolk, MA
d. ? ?
m. ?

NOTE: George said he was a sailor when he enlisted. His entry in *The Town Clerks' Registers* says merely that he transferred to the navy in 1864 and, indeed, he joined the US Navy at Brooklyn, NY on May 4, 1864 for a term of 18 months. His parents are unknown. No further information has been located.

George B. French – Co. C
b. 1837 Leyden, Lewis, NY
d. December 11, 1889 near Pulaski, NY
m. -------

NOTE: George, whose parents are unidentified, transferred to Batt. L, 1st NY ART on December 28, 1863 and mustered out at Elmira, NY on June 17, 1865. His death was reported in *The Mexico Independent* December 18, 1889: "Last Friday [December 12th] the body of George B. French was found in Wright's woods, near Pulaski. A bottle of laudanum was found near him, and the coroner's jury gave a verdict that it was a case of suicide. Several years ago the deceased was employed in the foundry here. He served his country faithfully during the late war in the 147th regt. and in battery L, New York Artillery . . . ." It is ironic that he had applied for a pension on December 3, 1889. He is buried in Mexico Village Cemetery.

George R. French – Co. D
b. August 1830 Granby, NY
d. April 22, 1912 Fulton, NY
m. Jane Philpott (January 1840-November 15, 1914) 1860

NOTE: George, son of Lyman (1804-?) and Eliza French (1807-?), mustered out with the regiment on June 7, 1865. In 1890 he claimed no disability. Although he said he had been born in 1832 when he enlisted, other documents give a DOB of 1830, including his obituary, published in *The Oswego Daily Palladium* April 24, 1912, 3, which said he was 82 when he died. He and Jane were the parents of three children. The Frenches are buried in Mt. Adnah Cemetery, Fulton.

William Isaac Frost – Co. C

b. November 6, 1839 Albion, NY
d. February 19, 1924 Saginaw, Saginaw, MI
m. Harriet Sophia Doane (May 27, 1842-June 17, 1927) 1860

NOTE: William was a son of Isaac (1805-1863) and Olive Scofield Frost (1810-1890). He was discharged from the service on July 15, 1863 at Finley Hospital, DC for "disability." He enrolled in Co. B, 184th Regiment on August 26, 1864 and served until mustered out at City Point, VA on June 29, 1865. He and Harriet were the parents of twelve children. The couple is buried in Forest Lawn Cemetery, Saginaw. William's COD was a cerebral hemorrhage and old age. Harriet's official COD was senility.

Amos D. Fuller – Co. D

b. 1825 Syracuse, Onondaga, NY
d. November 2, 1862 Camp Morris, Tennallytown, DC
m. Frances Elizabeth Bennett (1830-May 5, 1863) March 30, 1850

NOTE: Amos, son of Judah Lyman (1788-1832) and Azuba Russell Fuller (1797-1885), died, according to Captain Alexander Hulett, of an "inward rupture caused by overexertion." Other sources cay he died of "bilious colic." Frances and her children were living in Chili, Monroe, NY when she died. She left a will naming William Beach, Fleming, Cayuga, NY the guardian of her sons, Truman Seeley (1857-?), and William H. (1859-?). Frances is buried in Mt. Hope Cemetery, Rochester.

Thomas Jefferson Gabler – Co. H

b. January 25, 1818 Geneva, Seneca, NY
d. January 26, 1892 Ottawa, LaSalle, IL
m1. Rachael _____ (1828-ante 1853) ca. 1846
m2. Clarissa _____ (February 1835-October 13, 1881) ca. 1853
m3. Mary Anne Murphy Dowling (ca. 1837-ante 1892) December 31, 1886

NOTE: Gabler's parents were Gottlieb Godfrey (1782-1856) and Susanna Madeira Gabler (1784-1858). His mother's maiden name has several variants. An alternate DOB of 1816 for Thomas is found in *Registers of Officers and Enlisted Men*. His three wives present their own mysteries. Rachael apparently died in Sand Lake, Rensselaer, NY before 1853 since Thomas was married to Clarissa and had a 6 month old son, Thomas, in 1855. Clarissa's name might actually have been Theresa or Amelia Theresa. All three are found on census records. Mary Anne's first husband, whom she married on April 4, 1858, was Patrick Dowling (1834-December 11, 1886). He died of Bright's disease in Chicago, Cook, IL shortly before Mary Anne and Thomas were married. The Cook County Death Records say he was single but that entry may have been erroneous. I theorize that it was his death which precipitated the marriage between Thomas and Mary Anne. *The Ottawa Republican-Times* January 28, 1892, 1 published an interesting obituary: "From this field of life's short battle into the celestial realms of eternal peace, from the midst of earthly turmoil into the rest of his heavenly home, goes the true heart and soul into his last blessed reward. Thos. Jefferson Gabler was born at Geneva, N.Y., January 25, 1818; died Tuesday A.M. at his home on north LaSalle street after a long protracted illness of pneumonia. In the late war he served in the Union army and most nobly and bravely defended his country's flag. In 1871 he came to Ottawa, and for 21 years had been one of her most faithful and honored citizens and soldiers. He leaves to mourn his loss three sons and two daughters. Funeral services will be held at the house, 12131 LaSalle street, at 10 this (Thursday) A.M. conducted by Seth C. Earl Post. The members of the Post are requested to assemble at the hall at 9 A.M. sharp." Thomas is buried in Ottawa Avenue Cemetery, Ottawa.

Dennis Galvin, Jr. – Co. I
b. May 7, 1847 Ireland
d. December 16, 1919 Chicago, Cook, IL
m. Anna "Annie" _____ (April 1851-February 3, 1904) 1886

NOTE: Dennis was the son of Dennis (1816-December 19, 1872) and Margaret Connelly Galvin (?-*ante* 1855). Dennis, Jr. was a musician in the 147th Regiment and, according to his muster roll card, was discharged February 14, 1865 "in the field." His father made his will December 15, 1872, four days before his death, and excluded Dennis, suggesting perhaps a rift in the family. The 1900 census shows Dennis and Anna living in Chicago. He was a liquor merchant. His original pension application was dated March 24, 1892. Dennis is buried in Calvary Cemetery, Evanston, Cook, IL and presumably Anna is there too.

John Galvin – Co. I
b. August 1843 Ireland
d. December 26, 1912 Oswego City, NY
m. Jane "Jennie" E. _____ (November 1851-August 25, 1916) 1869

NOTE: John immigrated to the United States in 1847 with his parents, Michael (1805-1887) and Catherine "Bridget" Higgins Galvin (1815-1880). He mustered out with the regiment on June 7, 1865. In 1890 he claimed chronic diarrhea as a disability. An obituary, published in *The Oswego Daily Times* December 26, 1912, detailed his post-war activities: "Mr. John Galvin, one of the oldest and most respected residents of the Fifth ward, died today at his home, West Sixth and Albany streets. Mr. Galvin had been in ill health for several months and his recovery was not expected. The deceased was about 70 years old and was born in Ireland. He came to this country in his early manhood and had made his home in Oswego ever since, except the time spent at the front during the Civil war as a member of the 147th regiment. Returning to this city Mr. Galvin engaged in the iron business and conducted a shop in West First near Schuyler street for many years. The deceased was a brother of the late William, Michael and Patrick Galvin, all of whom were prominent in the affairs of the Fifth and Seventh wards. He was a man of high character and was justly respected by all who knew him. Mr. Galvin was a devout member of St. John's church . . . ." Jane's death was announced in *The Oswego Daily Times* August 25, 1916, 8: "Jane E. Galvin, wife of the late John Galvin, died very suddenly at her home, No. 210 West Sixth street, early this morning. She was born in Ireland but has been a resident of this city practically all of her life. She was 65 years of age, a devout member of St. John's church and of the Rosary society connected with that church. One daughter, M. Frances Galvin, survives . . . ." John and Jane are buried in St. Peter's Cemetery, Oswego City.

James Gard, Jr. – Co. A
b. 1846 Oswego County, NY
d. November 3, 1863 David's Island, New York Harbor
m. ------

NOTE: James was the son of James (1828-?) and Jane Gard (1829-*post* 1871), both of whom were born in Vermont. In 1855 the family was living in Hastings, NY and had lived there for nine years. James, Jr. was nine years old. In 1861 he attempted to enlist in the 81st Regiment, actually spending thirteen days in uniform before he was discharged for being underage. In the summer of 1862 he enlisted in the 110th but was sent to the 147th. It is unknown if he had parental approval. Nevertheless he was accepted and went out with the unit. His death was the result of an accidental shooting. He is buried in Cypress National Cemetery, Brooklyn. His mother applied for a pension on February 4, 1871 but apparently did not obtain it.

John Garner – Co. B
b. 1841 England
d. July 22, 1864 Andersonville, Sumter, GA
m. ------

NOTE: His entry in *The Town Clerks' Registers* says he was captured at Gettysburg but more likely it happened at the battle of the Wilderness on May 5, 1864. The same entry gives a COD of "starved to death." His muster roll card and *Andersonville*

Prisoners both say he died of diarrhea. Death probably resulted from a combination of factors. He is buried in Andersonville National Cemetery.

Delos Gary – Co. G

b. September 10, 1831 Oneida County, NY
d. July 27, 1870 Binghamton, Broome, NY
m. Catherine Martin (1840-October 14, 1864) 1859

NOTE: Captain Gary was the son of the Rev. Dr. George (1793-1855) and Elizabeth Armitage Gary (1798-1838). He was wounded severely at Gettysburg and discharged from the service for "disability" on November 5, 1863. In his short life he held many positions, as his lengthy obituary, published in *The Oswego Daily Press* July 28, 1870, attests: "This event [Gary's death], which has been expected for some little time, and almost hourly for the past three or four days, has at length occurred and it is now announced that Recorder Gary is no more. He died at Binghamton about half past eleven yesterday forenoon, though the dispatch announcing the sad event was not received here till after our hour of going to press . . . Delos Gary was the son of Rev. George Gary, a Methodist preacher of considerable eminence, and was born in Oneida county, in September, 1831. He was educated at the Wesleyan University, Middletown, Conn., and after graduating at that institution came to Mexico, Oswego county, as principal of the Mexico Academy. How long he retained that position we are unable to say. From Mexico he came to Oswego and on the organization of the Oswego High School in 1853, was appointed its first Principal, which position he retained for one year. During his connection with the High School, he had been paying some attention to the study of the law, for which he had a taste, and on leaving the school he entered the office of Albertus Perry, Esq., and there studied the law till the time he was admitted to the bar. He had a predilection for politics and entered the lists with considerable success. In April, 1856, he was appointed Under Sheriff by Rufus Hawkins, Esq., which he retained during Mr. Hawkins's term and on the election of Chas. Perkins, Esq., as Sheriff in 1858, he entered the office with him in the same capacity. This position he did not long continue to occupy. In September, 1862, Mr. Gary raised Co. G of the 147th N. Y. Vols., and went to the front with them as their Captain. At the battle of Gettysburg, while in command of his Company, gallantly facing the enemy's fire, he was wounded in the head by a gun shot, which disabled him for the time. Returning to Oswego, he resumed the practice of law with C. T. Richardson, Esq., under the firm title of Richardson & Gary. He continued his practice till 1867, in the fall of which year he was elected Recorder, which position he held at the time of his death. In 1850 Mr. Gary married a daughter of R. W. Martin, Esq., of this city, who died in 1865 [*sic*], without issue. Mr. Gary did not remarry. For the past year or two Recorder Gary's health had been unsound, and on one occasion he was confined for some weeks by an attack of pleurisy. Subsequently he met with an accident which interfered with the bodily exercise, which for a man of his habits was absolutely necessary to preserve health. From these and other causes his constitution appeared subjected to a test too heavy to be borne unimpaired. For the past year, particularly, his health had weakened rapidly, and those who noted his failing steps felt certain that his days on earth were nearly numbered. At various times during the year he was obliged to relinquish the Recorder's chair for short terms of recreation. On the 27th of last April he again vacated the chair, as he supposed temporarily, but he was destined never again to occupy it. About six weeks ago he went to Binghamton, where he had a sister living, and there sought to regain the priceless boon of health. His letters home, we believe, almost uniformly breathed a spirit of hopefulness and he seemed to feel considerable confidence that he would recover, but that was not to be. We have little need to speak of Recorder Gary in the community where he was so well known. As a lawyer he was one of the most careful and successful members of the Oswego County bar. His talents were conspicuous among his legal brethren, and by force of them he was rising rapidly. As a Judge, he was ready to decide and conscientious in his ideas of exact and equal justice, which was the basis of his action in all cases. No man ever brought better legal abilities to the Recorder's bench, and none ever more intelligently and faithfully executed the functions of his office for the protection of the public interests and still for the reformation of criminals and the purification of society. As a companion and friend he was genial and open-hearted as well as open-handed, and in this connection there are hundreds who will mourn his death and over his lifeless dust will breathe with fervency the prayer, 'May he rest in peace.' The remains will arrive here on the 4:10 train this afternoon. The funeral services will occur at 10 a.m. tomorrow and the body will be interred at Riverside." The profound effect of his death upon the community was reflected in resolutions passed by both the Grand Jury and by the Common Council, both of which appeared in *The Oswego Daily Press* July 28, 1870. I quote an excerpt from the latter: ". . . Resolved, That by the death of Judge Gary, the City has lost an able and upright magistrate, the State, an intelligent and patriotic citizen, and society, a genial gentleman and an honest man. And while we regret the public loss sustained by his decease, in the prime of life and in the midst of his usefulness, we would extend our sympathies to his relatives and numerous friends who have been

Captain Delos Gary had an extensive career as an educator, soldier, attorney, and judge.
New York State Military Museum

bereaved of a kind and affectionate brother, and generous and faithful friend . . . ." Delos is buried in Riverside Cemetery, Scriba, with his wife and her family. Catherine Gary's death was reported above as occurring in 1865, but it actually happened in 1864, as a short article published in *The Oswego Commercial Advertiser* October 14, 1864 noted: "Mrs. Catherine Gary, wife of Delos Gary, died suddenly, in convulsions at 11 o'clock this morning. Mr. G. was absent from the city, and returned at 2 o'clock, to find his wife whom he had left in ordinarily good health, a corpse."

Sidney C. Gaylord – Co. E
b. April 9, 1844 Florence, Oneida, NY
d. June 18, 1864 Petersburg, VA
m. ------

NOTE: Sidney's parents were Charles (1807-1896) and Catherine Mills Gaylord (1815-1873). According to *The Town Clerks' Registers*, Lt. Gaylord was "killed in action [in] front of Petersburg VA June 18, 1864 while galently [sic] at the head of his men, charging the Enemy's works. Remains buried in cemetery Redfield, Oswego Co., NY." He and his parents are buried in Redfield Village Cemetery. In 1878 his father applied for and obtained a pension based on his son's military service.

Frank Gier – Co. A
b. 1837 Canada East
d. *post* 1866 ?
m. ?

NOTE: This man's parents are unknown and his surname variously spelled. He originally enlisted in the 110th but was sent to the 147th. He was wounded on July 1, 1863 at Gettysburg and subsequently transferred to the VRC. He successfully applied for an invalid's pension on December 13, 1866. No widow is listed on the pension card and no other documents have been located.

Alanson "Lanson" Gifford – Co. B
b. March 1823 Hannibal, NY
d. May 26, 1909 Hannibal, NY
m. Hannah A. Van Patten (March 1824-August 7, 1910) 1843

NOTE: Alanson, son of Elihu Wing (1782-1848) and Mary "Polly" Carley Gifford (1782-1868), was discharged for "disability" at a hospital in Annapolis Junction, MD. In 1890 he said his disability was "disease of the lungs." He also stated he had been a captive in Belle Isle Prison for five months. Alanson and his parents are buried in Hannibal Center Cemetery. His gravestone erroneously assigns him to the 24th

Regiment and the FAG entry erroneously says he died on August 7, 1910. That is Hannah's DOD, although her obituary, published in *The Oswego Daily Times* August 8, 1910, said she died that day. She was to be buried "in Hannibal cemetery" but to date her grave has not been located. Hannah told the enumerator in 1900 that she was the mother of 15 children, 12 of whom were still living.

Charles Gilbert – Co. G
b. August 1836 Sodus, Wayne, NY
d. December 8, 1911 Oswego Town, NY
m. Elizabeth Ann Rowe (1839-February 13, 1896) *ca.* 1872

NOTE: Charles, son of John (1811-*post* 1865) and Betsey Penfield Gilbert (1819-1860), mustered out with the regiment on June 7, 1865. *The Oswego Daily Palladium* December 11, 8 published his obituary: "Charles Gilbert died at his home in Oswego Town on Friday. Mr. Gilbert has lived on his farm for the past forty-five years. He is survived by two children, Charles H. Gilbert, of this city, and one daughter, Miss Nellie E. Gilbert, who kept house for him since the death of his wife fifteen years ago. He was a veteran of the Civil War, having enlisted in the 147th Regiment, Company G, and served three years." Charles and Elizabeth are buried in Rural Cemetery, Oswego Town. His gravestone erroneously places him in Company C.

Herbert Curtis Gilbert – Co. C
b. 1844 Orwell, NY
d. June 19, 1864 4th Division Hospital, Petersburg, VA
m. ------

NOTE: Herbert was the son of Edward (1795-1882) and Mary "Polly" Balch Damon Gilbert (1803-1893). He was wounded at Gettysburg and, according to *Deaths of Volunteers*, suffered a "penetrating wound of abdomen" on June 18th in front of Petersburg. He died of that wound the following day. Edward Gilbert was a veteran of the War of 1812 and his first wife was Anna Balch (1798-1840), Polly's sister. Polly married him on March 19, 1843. He abandoned the family in 1860 and Herbert became his mother's sole support, providing clothing, groceries, etc. When he enlisted he gave her his bounty money and sent pay home to her. Polly had first been married to Daniel Damon (1801-1835) and by him was the mother of Mary Damon (1832-March 5, 1893), first wife of Albert Potter (1833-1918), a member of the 110th regiment. According to *North American Histories*, 220, Damon "was killed June 2, 1835; he was a constable, and went into the woods in the town of Boylston, N.Y., to serve some paper, and was there killed." Polly was illiterate and when she applied for Herbert's pension Albert and Mary were her witnesses and Albert was ever ready to assist her in her legal issues. In fact she died at his home, as revealed in *The Sandy Creek News* September 21, 1893, 1: ". . . Mrs. Polly Gilbert, an old lady aged nearly ninety, died Monday morning at the home of her son-in-law, Mr. A. J. Potter. Her funeral was held Wednesday and conducted by Rev. W. H. Jago . . . ." All these people are buried in Evergreen Cemetery, Orwell, except for Herbert who is memorialized by a cenotaph.

John Gill – Co. I

b. 1841 Portage, Livingston, NY
d. September 15, 1913 Oswego City, NY
m. Sarah _____ (1853-December 14, 1921) 1866

NOTE: John, a son of Anthony (1819-1887) and Winifred Gill (1820-1880), mustered out with the regiment on June 7, 1865. His obituary, published in *The Oswego Daily Palladium* September 16, 1913, 5, detailed his life and career in Oswego: "John Gill, for thirty-five years a member of the Oswego police force, died about six o'clock last evening at the

Herbert died from injuries sustained June 18, 1864 at Petersburg, VA.
Author's Collection

family home, 31 West Ninth street, after an illness of only a few days. Born in this city seventy years ago Mr. Gill in early life went into the shipyards and with his father and brother learned the shipbuilding trade. When the Civil War broke out he enlisted in Company B [*sic*], 147th New York Volunteers, and served through the war. He returned to his trade after the close of the war and for years afterward was in the employ of the late George Goble. From there he went to the Lackawanna railroad shops, and being an expert [illegible] was employed on coach finishing work. In 1876 he was appointed to a position in the police department and held it until two years ago, when he retired, having since lived quietly at his home, respected and esteemed by all who knew him. Besides being a veteran of the Civil War Mr. Gill was an old volunteer fireman, a former member of Engine Company No. 2 . . . ." Gill had been forced to retire because he injured his foot when attempting to make an arrest. He and Sarah, who died in Brooklyn, NY, are buried in

St. Paul's Cemetery, Oswego City. One of his siblings, Michael (1838-1890), served in Co. A, 12th NY Cavalry.

Ellery Cory Gillett – Co. F
b. 1829 Cherry Valley, Otsego, NY
d. February 9,1865 Elmira, Chemung, NY
m. Mary Elizabeth Huntington (September 12, 1830-May 3, 1886) November 19, 1848

NOTE: Ellery, son of Joel (1806-1846) and Charity Finch Gillett (1805-1875), originally enlisted in the 110th but was sent to the 147th. He was discharged on February 12, 1863. He enlisted in Co. G, 1st NY ART on January 4, 1864 and served until discharged for "disability" on February 6, 1865. Three days later he was dead. Mary married Edwin R. Carpenter (1826-1910), a veteran of the 184th Regiment, in 1872 as his second wife. Residing with them was Mary's daughter, Adelaide Gillett (1851-February 20, 1931). After her mother died, Adelaide "Addie" married Carpenter *ca.* 1888 and had two children by him. Ellery, Mary Elizabeth, and Edwin are all buried in Wellwood Cemetery, Mexico. One mystery remains: Ellery's pension card says he applied for a pension on February 14, 1865 but all available evidence shows he was dead by that time. The only plausible explanation is that the clerk put the date on the wrong line. Instead of putting it on the soldier's line he should have put it on the widow's line.

William Johnson Gillette – Co. B
b. June 9, 1840 Oswego, NY
d. October 21, 1903 Buffalo, Erie, NY
m. Sarah J. McCarthy (1843-October 30, 1895) 1862

NOTE: William was the son of Elisha (1806-1854) and Esther Phelps Gillette (1806-1874). His surname was also spelled Gillett. He mustered out with the regiment on June 7, 1865. He was a carpenter and his occupation directly contributed to his death, as reported in *The Syracuse Evening Herald* October 21, 1903: "William J. Gillette, the Syracuse contractor, was instantly killed by the falling of a portion of the old Grand Turk freight station here [Buffalo] at 1:10 o'clock this afternoon. Mr. Gillette took the contract for erecting a new freight station for the New York Central railroad here a few weeks ago. Part of the contract called for the tearing down of the Grand Trunk freight house, which had been purchased by the New York Central. Mr. Gillette was personally supervising the work of demolition when the accident occurred. The men had only resumed their work after the noon hour when, without warning, part of the roof gave way and tumbled to the ground. Mr. Gillette and a laborer were standing directly beneath and were caught and buried beneath the debris. Two heavy timbers struck the Syracuse man, crushing his life out instantly . . . ." An obituary appearing in *The Daily Palladium* October 22, 1903, 1 added details: "William Johnson Gillett [sic], born in Oswego June 9th, 1840, educated in the public schools of this city, died at his home in Syracuse yesterday. For many years he was a well known contractor, having learned the mason and carpenter trades. For a period in his younger days he was gold mining in Central America and later was engaged in the asphalt industry in Venezuela. He was one of the first promoters of asphalt paving in Syracuse. Mr. Gillett was a veteran of the Civil War, having organized Company B, 147th Regiment in this city. He was a prominent member of the G. A. R., a thirty-second degree Mason and a member of the Citizens' Club, Syracuse. His wife died several years ago. He had no children . . . ." William and Sarah are buried in Oakwood Cemetery, Syracuse.

James Glinn – Co. H

b. April 1844 Lockport, Niagara, NY
d. August 14, 1921 National Soldiers' Home, Dayton, Montgomery, OH
m. Caroline "Carrie" S. Perry (January 1850-November 27, 1928) 1869

NOTE: James Glinn was an alias for Charles C. Glenn, a son of Alexander (1811-?) and Sarah Glenn (1822-?). He was wounded at Gettysburg on July 1, 1863, transferred to the VRC on March 16, 1864 and finally discharged on May 2, 1865 at Johnson's Island, OH. He succumbed to pneumonia and was buried at Dayton National Cemetery. Caroline, the mother of seven, died at the OES Home in Cincinnati, Hamilton, OH. She is buried in Spring Grove Cemetery, Cincinnati.

Thomas Glynn – Co. K

b. 1841 Ireland
d. June 9, 1896 Philadelphia, Philadelphia, PA
m. ?

NOTE: Thomas, a cooper, was the son of John (1809-July 11, 1863) and Margaret Roach Glynn (1813-October 31, 1899). His marital status is a mystery. The 1865 New York census shows he was married once, but does not indicate his current condition. His entry in *The Town Clerks' Registers* lists him as single, which may simply mean he was not married at the time, but his death certificate says he was widowed. He was wounded on July 1, 1863, transferred to the VRC on March 16, 1864 and finally discharged for "disability" at USA General Hospital, Philadelphia, PA on April 12, 1865. In 1896 his mother applied for his pension but apparently did not obtain it. Thomas' parents are buried in St. Paul's Cemetery, Oswego City. He is buried in

Fernwood Cemetery, Yeadon, Delaware, PA. His brother Patrick (1844-?) served in the 24th NY Cavalry.

James Monroe Goodell – Co. G
b. July 13, 1819 West Boylston, Worcester, MA
d. May 2, 1901 Union Springs, Cayuga, NY
m. Emily H. Kingsbury (1824-January 26, 1904) 1848

NOTE: James, son of Ezra (1789-1861) and Marsena Perry Goodell (1787-1876), lost his right arm at the battle of Cold Harbor, VA on June 2, 1864. He was discharged from the service for "disability" on October 24, 1864. His obituary appeared in *The Auburn Bulletin* May 4, 1901, 4: "James M. Goodell died at his home in Homer street, Union Springs, Thursday evening of organic disease of the heart. Mr. Goodell was 82 years of age and was an old soldier. He has a son in this city. Funeral services will be held at the family residence tomorrow afternoon at 2 o'clock. The remains will be taken to Hannibal, Oswego county, Monday for burial." James and Emily are buried in Hannibal Village Cemetery.

Asa W. Goodrich – Co. E
b. August 9, 1838 Ellisburg, Jefferson, NY
d. April 22, 1905 Sandy Creek, NY
m. Marietta Cummins (September 1847-February 15, 1903) 1867

NOTE: Asa was discharged from the VRC on July 14, 1865. In 1890 he said his disability was a dislocated left shoulder joint. His obituary in *The Sandy Creek News* May 4, 1905 provides an excellent review of his life: "Asa W. Goodrich, one of the most highly respected residents of the eastern part of the town of Sandy Creek, where he has made his home for many years, died at the residence of his son at the Outlet House in the western part of this town April 22. Mr. Goodrich was born in Ellisburg on August 9, 1838, and at the age of nine years moved with his parents, William and Cyrena (Stillwell) Goodrich, to the town of Sandy Creek. In early manhood he was married to Miss Mary Cummins of Boylston, about 1867, and together they trod life's pathway for over forty years. Two children were born to them, who still survive, Francis Goodrich and Mrs. Josa James, both of this town. Mr. Goodrich was united with the Methodist Protestant church thirty years ago. In the early days of the war he gave himself to his country's cause, and in 1861 enlisted in Co. B, 7th N.Y.V. Black Horse Cavalry, where he served six months and was honorably discharged in the fall of 1862; he then enlisted in Co. E of the noted 147th Infantry, serving three years and was honorably discharged. Mr. Goodrich was taken prisoner at the battle of Gettysburg after being wounded in the battle and was taken to Richmond, thence to Bell Isle where he remained nearly three months. With the exception of the four years spent on the southern battlefields, his entire manhood was passed on the old homestead until January last. He was an excellent citizen, a kind husband and father, and few were more devoted and self-sacrificing. As a Christian none doubted his sincerity or questioned his profession . . . ." Marietta, who predeceased Asa, was eulogized in an obituary appearing in *The Sandy Creek News* February 26, 1903: "Mrs. Mary Goodrich, wife of Asa Goodrich, passed away quietly and peacefully to her final rest February 15, 1903, after a year's sickness, most of the time confined to her bed, a patient sufferer. She had many friends and kind neighbors, ready to do all in their power for her comfort. One of her neighbors, whom she had known from her childhood, could be found at her bedside daily, cheerfully studying everything for her welfare. Mrs. Goodrich was converted at the age of eleven years and at the age of thirteen years joined the M.P. church at Hemlock and was a member of North Boylston M. P. church when she died. In the fall of '67 she married Mr. Goodrich. She was a model wife, an affectionate mother, a kind friend and a good neighbor. She retained her senses to the last, waved her farewell to her loved ones and passed over the river . . . ." Asa and Marietta are buried in the Boylston-Sandy Creek Wesleyan Cemetery, Lacona.

Edwin W. Goodrich – Co. E

b. November 4, 1839 Sandy Creek, NY
d. January 13, 1909 National Soldiers' Home, Bath, Steuben, NY
m. Flora Woodruff (1842-December 31, 1878) 1862

NOTE: Edwin's parents were Samuel (1795-1880) and Esther Luce Goodrich (1806-1891). He was discharged from the military in 1864 for "disability" at US General Hospital, West Philadelphia, PA but the exact date varies from document to document. His COD was "edema of the lungs." He and Flora are buried in Woodlawn Cemetery, Sandy Creek.

Elum Goodrich – Co. E

b. 1826 Sandy Creek, NY
d. April 10, 1919 Dexter, Jefferson, NY
m1. Nancy Ann Dye (April 29, 1829-February 5, 1871) *ca.* 1850
m2. Malvina "Vine" Schell Skinner (April 10, 1842-February 1, 1909) January 1, 1872

NOTE: Elum, whose name was also spelled Elam, was Edwin's brother. He also served in the 7th NYV Black Horse Cavalry in 1861-2. He was wounded at Gettysburg and discharged on March 12, 1864 at US General Hospital, Philadelphia, PA on account of the wound. His first wife, Nancy Ann Dye, is buried in Fairview Cemetery, Rodman, Jefferson, NY. His second wife, Malvina, also predeceased him. An informative obituary was published in *The Sandy Creek News* February 4, 1909: "A life long resident of this vicinity passed away on Monday in the person of Mrs. Elum Goodrich. Mrs. Goodrich suffered a paralytic shock two weeks ago and rapidly failed two or three days previous to her death. She was born in the town of Ellisburg, April 10, 1842 and was the second of four children born to Daniel and Nancy Schell . . . She was married at the age of nineteen to Andrew Skinner of Elliburg . . . [He] passed away in 1869 and on January 1, 1872 Mrs. Skinner was married to Elum Goodrich who survives. Mr. Goodrich is in advanced years and was largely dependent on his wife in many ways so that the blow is a severe one that falls upon his shoulders, already bowed with age. For the past twenty-seven years Mr. and Mrs. Goodrich have resided in the town of Sandy Creek and for the greater part of that time in their home on Powers avenue in the village of Lacona . . . ." Elum's death was announced in *The Sandy Creek News* April 17, 1919: "At the home of his son, Oren Goodrich, on Thursday evening last, April 10, occurred the death of Elam Goodrich, one of the oldest sons of the town of Sandy Creek, having been born near its eastern border on the Boylston Center road 93 years ago. He was married to Ann Rye [*sic*] of Rodman, and of this marriage, one son, Oren Goodrich of Dexter survives. Later after the death of his wife he was married to Mrs. Vine Shell [*sic*] Skinner, who passed away a few years ago; since then he has made his home mostly with his son in Dexter. At one time he ran a restaurant and grocery in Lacona. He built the home where Captain Peters resides . . . ." Elum and Malvina are buried in Woodlawn Cemetery, Sandy Creek.

Francis E. Goodrich – Co. E
b. 1841 Jefferson County, NY
d. April 3, 1868 Sandy Creek, NY
m. ------

NOTE: Francis was Asa's brother. He was discharged from the service on June 13, 1865 at Washington, DC. He is buried in Woodlawn Cemetery, Sandy Creek. Another brother, William (1845-1924), served in the 24th Regiment. He is buried in Boylston-Sandy Creek Wesleyan Cemetery. Their mother, Cyrena (1805-1886), successfully applied for a pension in 1873, based on Francis' service.

Reuben Franklin Goodrich – Co. H
b. December 1828 Oneida County, NY
d. September 15, 1906 Constantia, NY
m1. Julia A. _____ (1834-*ante* 1868) *ca* 1855
m2. Elizabeth _____ Miller (1839-*ante* 1898) *ca.* 1868
m3. Esther R. Fairbanks Beebe (September 1837-April 13, 1918) 1898

NOTE: Reuben's DOB and POB vary from document to document but since his parents, Elisha (1806-*post* 1880) and Elizabeth Friest Goodrich (1806-*ante* 1880) lived much of their lives in Oneida County, he was probably born there. I use the birth date given on the 1900 census. Reuben deserted from the 147th on November 3, 1862 and was not apprehended until May 2, 1864. As part of his sentence he had to make up the time lost. Therefore, on June 5, 1865 he was transferred to Co. F, 91st Regiment although a note in *The Town Clerks' Registers* says he was sent to the 91st HA. He was discharged when the 91st was disbanded in July. He successfully applied for a pension in 1887. In 1890 he said his disability was a ruptured vein in his left leg. Little has been learned about his wives. In 1880 Esther Fairbanks, 41, single, was the housekeeper for Nathan Beebe (1835-1893) whom she subsequently married. Reuben is buried in Cleveland Village Cemetery but I have not located his wives' graves.

Ichabod F. Goss – Co. F
b. 1820 Oneida County, NY
d. March 22, 1891 Lenox, Madison, NY
m1. Lucy Wilcox (1827-*ante* 1870) *ca.* 1850
m2. Barbara J. _____ (1847-*post* 1892) *ante* 1870

NOTE: Ichabod, whose parents are unknown, was discharged from the service for "disability" on June 7, 1863. In August 1864 he enlisted in Co. A, 184th Regiment and served until mustered out at City Point, VA on June 30, 1865. In 1890 he said his disability was an injury to his back. Since he and his wives produced no children, it is difficult to estimate marriage dates. He and Barbara must have spent some time in Indiana because he applied for his pension in that state. Barbara settled his estate in 1891 and was enumerated in Lenox, Madison, NY in 1892. She then disappeared and may have remarried. Ichabod is buried in Pleasant Lawn Cemetery, Parish. Lucy's grave has not been located.

John Granger – Co. H
b. 1836 Martinsburg, Lewis, NY
d. August 15, 1864 Andersonville, Sumter, GA
m. Almira Jane Smith (1841-*post* 1885) October 15, 1859

NOTE: John was the son of Samuel (1802-1867) and Ruhannah Kenyon Granger (1810-*post* 1870). When he enlisted he and Almira were the parents of Luther E. (1860-1925) and Harriet Elizabeth (1862-1945). He was captured at the battle of the Wilderness on May 5, 1864. The exact date of his death from chronic diarrhea or dysentery is disputed. Most records claim he died August 15, 1864, including *Deaths of Volunteers* and Andersonville Prisoners of War. Almira alleged he had died on July 20, 1864 and her pension started on that date. The births of the children are important for this story because in 1870 Almira was living in Weeping Water, Cass, NE with three children, Luther, Harriet, and Roxana, aged 5. Obviously John was not Roxana's father and since Almira petitioned to have her pension sent to Nebraska, it was perhaps because she was the subject of adverse community scrutiny. In 1865 she was living in Constantia with her mother and father and several siblings. Maybe her family disowned her after the birth of an illegitimate child. In 1870 John's mother Ruhannah petitioned to obtain John's pension, based on her assertion that the couple never was married. In fact, however, A. N. Hough, the justice of the peace who married John and Almira, offered not only a sworn statement but an exact copy of the record. Furthermore, according to the 1860 census, John and Almira were living with Ruhannah and her invalid husband Samuel. His death in 1867, Ruhannah's subsequent dependence on the local authorities for support, plus the inferred "bad behavior" of Almira, may have driven her to seek a mother's pension. She did not obtain it although the pension file clearly shows she caused Almira considerable stress. In 1870 Almira and her children were living next door to Henry Forbes (ca. 1842-?) and his father Elias. She and Henry were married on January 20, 1876. The last known reference to Almira appears on the 1885 Nebraska census when she and the children were living in Jefferson County, NE. Henry was not enumerated with them. Luther died at Fort Smith, Sebastian, AR and was buried in Oak Cemetery. Harriet died in Weeping Water, Cass, NE and was buried with her husband Albert Leaper in Prairie Home Cemetery, Diller, Jefferson, NE. Roxana married Frank W. Lloyd in Jefferson County, NE on March 24, 1886. Nothing has been learned about her subsequent life. John is buried in Andersonville National Cemetery.

Patrick Gray – Co. H
b. *ca.* 1825 Ireland
d. *post* 1875 Oneida County, NY
m. Margaret _____ (1825-February 27, 1901) *ca.* 1849

NOTE: Patrick, whose parents are unidentified, and Margaret immigrated to the United States *ca.* 1851. On August 27, 1862 he enrolled in the 147th Regiment at Amboy. Although his entry in *The Town Clerks' Registers* states he deserted, that probably is incorrect. His muster roll card for August 1863 shows he had been on detached service with Battery L, 1st NY LA since February 9th. It would appear that he never returned to the 147th since he was classified as "absent, sick" at muster out. Even though he does not formally appear on the roster for the 1st LA a notation in "Civil War Soldiers" shows he was a member of that organization. It is interesting to note as well that no children were born to Patrick and Margaret during the years 1863-1865. In 1870 the family was still living in Amboy but by 1875 had moved to Utica, Oneida County. Patrick last appears on the 1875 NY census for Utica. Margaret never remarried. On September 26, 1890 she applied for a widow's pension which was denied. On October 31, 1891 the New York Adjutant-General asked the War Department for Patrick's records and on November 2nd was told that when the regiment mustered out on June 7, 1865 he was "absent, sick." A comment was added: "Investigation fails to elicit any further information." Poor recordkeeping seems to be the reason Margaret was denied a pension. She died in Utica but to date graves for her and Patrick have not been located.

Henry C. Green – Co. F
b. September 26, 1846 Scriba, NY
d. January 29, 1912 Buffalo, Erie, NY
m. Emma Louise Hallenbeck (1858-March 25, 1926) January 30, 1877

NOTE: Henry's muster roll card reveals he lied to enlist. He was only 16, not 30 as he claimed. He mustered out with the regiment on June 7, 1865. Tracing his family has been difficult. Researchers identify his parents as John Stanton (1815-1885) and Mary Elizabeth Congdon Green (1816-?) but he lived with his grandfather, Henry, in 1850. His father was living in Wayne County with Mary Anne and two daughters. I theorize that Mary Elizabeth died shortly after Henry's birth and that Mary Anne was a second wife. Henry and Emma were the parents of one child, Floyd (1893-1970). In 1890 the couple was living in North East, Erie, PA. Henry said his disability was "chronic diarrhea and rheumatism." He was a member of Chapin Post No. 2 GAR and when he died in 1912 he was the third member of the post to die in 48 hours. *The Buffalo Commercial* January 29, 1912, 11 reported his death: ". . . Henry C. Green was 65 years old and lived at 871 Broadway. He served during a large part of the war as a member of Company F, 147th New York infantry. He participated in many of the important battles of the war. Mr. Green's death was due to apoplexy. He is survived by his wife and one son . . . ." Henry and Emma are buried in Buffalo Cemetery, Cheektowaga, Erie, NY.

Henry P. Green – Co. H
b. 1835 West Monroe, NY
d. April 24, 1863 Finley Hospital, Washington, DC
m. Mary _____ (1838-*post* 1875) *ca.* 1855

NOTE: Henry's father is unknown. In 1850 he was living with his mother, Sally (1795-?) and two siblings in West Monroe. His COD was "chronic diarrhea." He is buried in Soldiers' and Airmen's Home National Cemetery, Washington, DC. He and Mary were the parents of Warren R. (1859-?). Mary next married Charles Devendorf

(1843-February 19, 1895) *ca.* 1865. They were the parents of Mary (1866-?). He apparently abandoned her because in 1868 he married Ella Caroline Dodge (1847-1936). Mary then married Jacob Kitts (1836-*post* 1892) *ca.* 1869. By him she was the mother of Arthur (1870-*post* 1892). Apparently the couple separated because in 1875 she and the children were living in West Monroe and Mary was calling herself a widow. That she was not a widow is evidenced by the 1892 New York census. Jacob, 58, and Arthur, 22, were living in Syracuse, NY. Nothing else has been learned about these people.

John Putnam Green – Co. H

b. October 6, 1837 Washington County, NY
d. July 1, 1863 Gettysburg, Adams, PA
m. Emily Ann Blanchard (1842-*post* 1864) August 8, 1858

NOTE: When he enlisted, John, son of Ephraim (1800-1852) and Phebe Bixby Green (1809-1866), stated he had been born in Constantia. The 1855 New York census, however, shows he was born in Washington County, but had lived 17 of 18 years in Constantia. He was listed as MIA on July 1, 1863 and subsequently declared dead. He is buried in Gettysburg National Cemetery but a cenotaph for him is located in Lakeside Rural Cemetery, Bernhards Bay, NY. Emily applied for a widow's pension on July 11, 1864 and obtained it. She subsequently disappeared and probably remarried.

Jonathan Green, Jr. – Co. D

b. 1843 St. Lawrence County, NY
d. January 10, 1863 in camp near Falmouth, VA
m. ------

NOTE: Jonathan, whose parents were Jonathan (1803-*post* 1866) and Christianna Green (1805-?), originally enlisted in the 110th Regiment but was enrolled in the 147th in Fulton, NY. COD was termed "disease." Originally buried at Phillips Farm, VA today he rests in Fredericksburg National Cemetery. His father unsuccessfully applied for a pension on November 19, 1866. Perhaps he died before the process could be completed.

Philip Schuyler Green – Co. F

b. March 18, 1821 New Hartford, Oneida, NY
d. September 23, 1911 Long Beach, Los Angeles, CA
m. Lovisa Rider Wilcox (January 25, 1826-December 11, 1905) March 22, 1852

NOTE: Philip, son of Jonathan (1788-1877) and Sally Green (1787-1847), mustered out with the regiment on June 7, 1865. By 1880 the family was living in Madison,

Poweshiek, IA. He was a member of J. T. Drake Post No. 321 GAR in Brooklyn, IA. Lovisa died in Brooklyn after a lengthy illness and was buried in Kent Cemetery, Brooklyn. In 1910 Philip was living with his widowed daughter, Alta Scott, in Long Beach, CA. He is buried in Sunnyside Cemetery, Long Beach.

William Green – Co. G
b. October 8, 1821 England
d. July 10, 1899 Madison County, NY
m. Sophia Isam (1821-June 7, 1885) August 24, 1846

NOTE: William, a gardener by trade, and Sophia were married in Blakesley, England. His parents are unknown. He lied about his age to enlist, saying he had been born in 1824. His muster roll card shows he was working as a hospital attendant in August 1863. He mustered out with the regiment on June 7, 1865. In 1890 he claimed "disease of the brain" as a disability. He and Sophia are buried in Vermillion Cemetery, Mexico, NY.

Edward Gregware – Co. A
b. June 7, 1838 Canada
d. January 24, 1916 State Hospital, Kalamazoo, Kalamazoo, MI
m. Margaret Monroe (May 1837-August 17, 1907) 1856

NOTE: Edward, a shoemaker, was a son of Joseph (1800-?) and Mary Ophmaster Gregware (1800-?). His father was born in France and the surname originally was Gregoire. Edward first served as a lieutenant in the 81st Regiment. He also served as a lieutenant in the 147th, resigning his commission on January 9, 1863. He succumbed to arteriosclerosis and was buried in Forest Lawn Cemetery, Saginaw, Saginaw, MI. Margaret died in Seattle, King, WA but her grave has not been located. Two brothers also served in the Civil War. Joseph Gregoire (1826-June 3, 1864), a member of Co. B, 81st Regiment, was killed at the battle of Cold Harbor, VA. His remains were buried on the field. Jedediah Grigwar/Grigware (1840-1914) served first in Co. F, 24th Regiment and later in Co. B, 81st. He died in the National Solders' Home in Milwaukee, WI and was buried in Wood National Cemetery.

Chauncey Gridley – Co. F
b. September 7, 1818 Oneida County, NY
d. July 28, 1881 Scriba, NY
m1. Sarah Cummings (1821-June 22, 1863) *ca.* 1845
m2. Minerva Marshall Flint (1830-March 23, 1915) October 8, 1867

NOTE: Chauncey's parents are unidentified. By his own admission he had accepted a commission as first lieutenant to encourage others to enlist and this statement came back to haunt him towards the end of his life. He became ill after the famous "mud march" in early 1863 and tendered his resignation. Fellow officers, doctors, and other soldiers testified that he had developed liver and kidney troubles. All spoke of his jaundiced appearance both before and after his discharge. Over the years his health continued to decline, so much so that frequently he could perform no labor and was confined to his bed. Dr. G. D. McManus attended him and testified his condition was "that of great suffering & pain with emaciation, jaundice, dyspepsia, and with coma & fainting – and that he died of same July 28, 1881." In 1878 Chauncey had finally applied for a pension but when the examiners looked at his resignation letter they rejected his claim on the basis that he had said nothing about his health being a cause for leaving the military. Chauncey and Harvey Flint knew each other well since both lived in New Haven. After Sarah, Chauncey's wife, died, he asked Minerva Flint to keep house for him and his three young children, Lewis (1847-1916), Alice (1849-1898), and Sarah (1855-1924). Minerva alleged years later that she and Chauncey did not live together "as husband and wife" until their marriage but the 1865 census tells a slightly different story. She and her little boy, John, were enumerated in the Gridley household. Minerva also alleged many years later that she had been the object of adverse scrutiny because of the boy and had lost her pension on account of neighbors' letters to the Pension Board. While the extant letters do mention the child, the main focus is her cohabiting, however innocently, with Chauncey. She actually was paid her pension until shortly before her marriage to him in 1867. As the examiner said, she cared more for Chauncey than for the pension. The problem was that since Chauncey did not qualify for a pension neither did Minerva as his widow and her application was rejected. For the next few years she lived alone and supported herself by nursing. In 1886 Peter Moot, a widower twice over, came from Owego, Tioga, NY to visit his brother Gabriel in New Haven. He and Minerva apparently got along well and decided to get married. The ceremony took place on September 15, 1886 and the very next day Minerva said good-bye to New Haven and moved to Owego where she lived with Moot until he died on October 30, 1896. The enactment of the Remarried Widows' Act of March 3, 1901 gave Minerva another chance to obtain a pension and she applied on August 18, 1908. All the old rumors and gossip were dredged up, Minerva's half-truths re-examined, and various laws, especially the Act of August 7, 1882 which excluded widows "living in open and notorious adulterous cohabitation" from receiving a pension, considered. The examiner who questioned Minerva ruled out that law as grounds for rejection, pointing out that even if she had lived with Chauncey "adulterously" the law could not be construed to be retroactive. The pension was granted by letter dated March 16, 1909. By now Minerva was elderly, living on a farm in Owego with her niece, Emma, and her husband

William Mahar. Minerva had purchased the farm where she and Moot lived and she deeded it to Emma and William in return for supporting her and paying her funeral expenses. All admitted it was a purely verbal agreement. When she died of "epidemic influenza and debility incident to old age," Emma applied to the Pension Bureau for reimbursement for nursing and burial costs. The "last straw" was the government's rejection of the claim because of that verbal agreement between Minerva and the Mahars. Harvey Flint, Chauncey Gridley, Sarah Gridley, and Minerva Moot are all buried in New Haven Rural Cemetery.

Anthony Griffin – Co. I

b. October 1841 Ireland

d. June 9, 1901 Syracuse, Onondaga, NY

m. Catherine Hawks (April 1847-July 23, 1926) 1870

Chauncey Gridley is buried with his first wife, Sarah. Nearby are the graves of Harvey Flint and Minerva Marshall Flint Gridley.
Author's Collection

NOTE: Anthony's parents were Anthony (1810-*ante* 1860) and Bridget Murphy Griffin (1810-*post* 1860). In 1855 the family was living in Oswego, having moved there nine months earlier. An informative obituary published in *The Oswego Daily Times* June 10, 1901, 4 detailed Griffin's career as a soldier and a civilian: "Anthony Griffin, a former well known Oswegonian, passed away at his home in Syracuse yesterday morning after an illness of about two years. Mr. Griffin was a veteran printer and was born in Ireland in 1841. After coming to this country he settled in Oswego and entered the office of the *Palladium* where he learned the printing trade. He next went to Utica and was engaged as a printer on the Utica *Herald* for seven years. He worked for the Syracuse *Courier* and was employed on the Syracuse *Herald* for seventeen years. Two years ago he was compelled to retire from active work owing to ill health. He fought in the Civil War and was a member of Company I, One Hundred and Forty-seventh Regiment, New York Infantry. Later he was color bearer of the 147th and was wounded in an engagement in front of Petersburg. He enlisted at Oswego, August 20, 1862, and received an honorable discharge on June 6, 1865. He was a member of the Root Post, G.A.R., and also a member of Typographical Union No. 55 . . . ." The engagement mentioned in the article was the battle of Weldon Railroad, VA in August 1864. Anthony and Catherine, the mother of three, are buried in St. Agnes' Cemetery, Syracuse.

Richard Thomas Griffith – Co. I
b. 1836 Ireland
d. January 21, 1909 Parishville, St. Lawrence, NY
m. ------

NOTE: Richard's parents are unknown. His surname is erroneously spelled Griffin on his muster roll card. He was wounded on May 2, 1863 at Franklin's Crossing, VA and transferred to the VRC on September 26, 1863. As the result of a general court-martial he was dishonorably discharged from the service on March 25, 1865 for being absent without leave and was sentenced to serve a year in Clinton State Prison. Prison records show he was received at the facility on May 8, 1865. Little can be found about him until 1900 when he appeared on the Parishville, NY census. He said he was born in 1836, immigrated to the United States in 1855, and was naturalized. Under "occupation," he said he was an Army pensioner and, indeed, his application for a pension in 1877 was granted. He is buried in Hillcrest Cemetery, Parishville. The stone gives a DOB of 1826.

Amos Groesbeck – Co. D
b. 1838 Cicero, Onondaga, NY
d. January 1, 1863 Armory Square Hospital, Washington, DC
m. Charlotte G. Clapper (1844-May 14, 1929) February 17, 1859

NOTE: Amos, whose parents were Benjamin (1810-*post* 1860) and Olive Groesbeck (1812-*post* 1860), succumbed to typhoid fever and was buried in Soldiers' and Airmen's Home Cemetery, Washington, DC. He and Charlotte had one child, Alonzo (January 10, 1861-1939). Charlotte was granted guardianship of her son and by the time his pension was granted in 1867 he and his mother were living in Norton, Muskegon, MI. Charlotte married Ambrose J. Abbey (1831-*post* 1880) on September 27, 1867 in Detroit, Wayne, MI as his second wife. The couple moved to Iowa in 1876. Abbey last appears on the 1880 census. Charlotte next married Calvin Edward Fletcher (1856-1935) in 1882. On August 17, 1890 she was baptized as a member of the Reorganized Church of Jesus Christ of Latter Day Saints and she attended the Shenandoah, Page, IA branch. Charlotte and Calvin are buried in Rose Hill Cemetery, Shenandoah, Page, IA. Abbey's DOD and grave have not been located.

James William Gulliver – Co. F

b. 1826 England

d. December 16, 1862 New Haven, NY

m. Emily Sarah Dagwell (1818-June 10, 1895) September 17, 1851

NOTE: James was the son of Lemuel (1804-1879) and Abigail Jarvis Gulliver (1802-1884). He was a harnessmaker by occupation. Gulliver was discharged from the service on November 28, 1862, suffering from chronic diarrhea and *phthisis pulmonalis* (tuberculosis). Dr. Amos Austin deposed that Gulliver only lived two weeks after arriving home and was in the last stages of the disease. John Woodall and Samuel Merriam both testified they had known Gulliver for 15 years and had not seen any signs of the disease before he enlisted in the 147th. Emily's application for a pension for herself and for her four children under the age of 16 was allowed. She and James are buried in New Haven Rural Cemetery.

Charles Guernsey – Co. C

b. 1817 Jackson, Washington, NY

d. June 20, 1864 City Point Hospital, VA

m. Elizabeth "Betsey" Taylor (1830-*post* 1875) July 26, 1846

NOTE: Charles was the son of Lewis (1777-1862) and Sarah Guernsey (1788-1862). He was wounded in the neck and shoulder near Petersburg, VA on June 18, 1864 and sent to City Point Hospital where he succumbed. In 1864 the couple, who were married in Fulton, NY, had four children under the age of 16: Mary Jane (1850-?); George (1856-?); Almina (1859-?); and Emma Eugenie (1861-?). The family last appears on the 1875 New York census living in Oswego City.

Alexander Guyatt – Co. G

b. August 16, 1832 Watertown, Jefferson, NY

d. January 8, 1900 Scriba, NY

m. Amelie "Millie" Walker (1836-May 11, 1918) *ca.* 1853

NOTE: Alexander's surname was variously spelled. He was the son of Alexander Clement (1803-1873) and Mary O'Clare Guyatt (1814-?). He was discharged in Philadelphia, PA for "disability" and in 1890 said his disability was "paralysis of the lower limbs." Alexander was a member of Lewis Porter Post No. 573 GAR in Scriba. *The Oswego Daily Palladium* January 26, 1900, 6 published a memorial resolution enacted by the members on January 17, 1900: "Whereas the Great Commander of us all has removed by death from among us, our respected comrade and friend, Alexander Guyatt, late of Company G, 147th N.Y.V.I., therefore be it resolved, that while we tearfully submit to the inexorable order, and make this expression of our sorrow, and sympathy for the family, we desire to express our own grief, for the loss to our order of an earnest and faithful member, and one whose cheerful disposition and benevolent and forgiving nature we may all do well to emulate . . . ." Alexander and Millie were the parents of seven children. On September 3, 1903 Millie, a native of Canada, married Edward D. Kelly (1858-September 21, 1924) in Oswego City. The couple was living in Granby when she died. She and Alexander are buried in North Scriba Cemetery. The gravestone does not contain her DOD. It was found in the New York State Death Index.

David Hadin – Co. B
b. 1840 Trenton, Ontario, Canada
d. July 1, 1863 Gettysburg, Adams, PA
m. ------

NOTE: David's surname was more commonly spelled Hayden or Heyden and the latter is the name on his gravestone in Gettysburg National Cemetery. Very little is known about this soldier who said he was a sailor on his muster roll card. His entry in *The Town Clerks' Registers* contains no mention of parents and says nothing about his death.

Horace B. Hale – Co. C
b. 1839 Williamstown, NY
d. July 1, 1863 Gettysburg, Adams, PA
m. ------

NOTE: Horace, killed in action, is buried in Gettysburg National Cemetery. His parents were Samuel (1800-*post* 1868) and Deborah Beckley Hale (?-February 5, 1845). Samuel applied for his son's pension, alleging that he was "entirely helpless because of a shock of paralysis in 1860" and that Horace had supported him for eight years before he enlisted and afterwards. As proof, Samuel said that Horace had given him $100 of his bounty money and had sent home $65 of his Army pay. Described as a "town pauper," Samuel was supported by the town of Williamstown. He received the pension, $8 per month. In 1868 he applied for and obtained an increase in his pension but I have located nothing about him after that date.

Anthony Haley – Co. I
b. 1837 Ireland
d. September 27, 1891 Trinidad, Las Animas, CO
m. ------

NOTE: Anthony, parents unknown, whose occupation was mariner on his muster roll card, was wounded on July 2, 1863 at Gettysburg. He mustered out with the regiment on June 7, 1865. He is buried in the Masonic Cemetery, Trinidad.

William N. Haight – Co. H

b. 1833 Otsego County, NY

d. February 17, 1863 Regimental Hospital, Belle Plain, VA

m. Martha A. Miller (1839-1866) *ca.* 1858

NOTE: William, son of Benjamin (1795-1851) and Sally Haight (1800-1854), died from typhoid fever and pneumonia. He and Martha were the parents of Charles W. (1859-1924). In 1865 Martha and Charles were living with her parents, Adam (1815-1889) and Roxana Miller (1824-*post* 1880). Martha's father petitioned the Surrogate Court in Oswego for letters of administration on April 21, 1866.

Adelbert P. Hall – Co. B

b. October 5, 1844 Volney, NY

d. July 1, 1863 Gettysburg, Adams, PA

m. ------

NOTE: According to *The Town Clerks' Registers*, Adelbert was "killed instantly at the battle of Gettysburg July 1st, 1863 and is supposed to have been buried there." His parents were Amasa (1819-1906) and Clarissa Claud Hall (1818-*post* 1880). His muster roll card says he was a boatman.

Amasa Hall – Co. B

b. April 18, 1819 Scriba, NY

d. August 17, 1906 Oswego City, NY

m1. Clarissa Claud (1818-*post* 1870) 1843

m2. Nancy A. _____ (1828-February 11, 1908) ?

NOTE: Amasa, son of Merritt (1783-1842) and Rhoda Jackson Hall (1791-1878), was wounded in the head at Gettysburg and was discharged in early 1865 with the consolidation of the 76th Regiment. He was Adelbert's father. Clarissa's exact DOD and gravesite have not been discovered, nor has a marriage date for Amasa and Nancy. In 1900 they claimed they had been married 57 years which was not the truth. Amasa died at the home of his daughter, Jane "Jennie" Nichols, in Oswego. The local newspaper erroneously reported he served in the 181st Regiment although his brother Horace (1820-?) served in Co. D, 184th Regiment from August 1864-June 1865. Amasa was a member of Post O'Brian No. 65 GAR. He and Nancy are buried in Riverside Cemetery. Jennie died of pneumonia on January 17, 1908 in Auburn, Cayuga, NY at the Hub Hotel. She too is buried in Riverside.

Colin Hall – Co. I
b. 1848 Oswego County, NY
d. *post* 1870 ?
m. ?

NOTE: This soldier's Christian name was Colon, although he apparently used Frederick at times such as for the 1870 census. He was a son of Daniel (1818-1895) and Roxana Murray Hall (1818-April 1, 1908). It appears he lied to enlist since in 1865 he was only 17 years old. He mustered out with the regiment on June 7, 1865. He last appeared in the 1870 census living with his mother and father in Mexico, NY. I have found no records for him beyond that date. I theorize he died sometime before the 1875 census when his parents and sister Sarah, aged 14, were living in New Haven, NY. He probably was not married.

Jason Hall – Co. B
b. 1844 Oswego County, NY
d. November 17, 1891 Scriba, NY
m. Bridget _____ (1845-October 20, 1898) *ca.* 1870

NOTE: Jason was the son of Horace (1818-July 17, 1875) and Mary Clancey Hall (1817-*post* 1880). According to *The Town Clerks' Registers*, he was wounded in action at Gettysburg and transferred to the VRC from which he was discharged on July 31, 1865 at Wilmington, DE. He applied for a pension on August 11, 1865 and in 1890 he said he was crippled because he had been shot in the elbow. He was a member of Post O'Brian No. 65 GAR and later of Lewis B. Porter Post No. 573 GAR. Jason and Bridget are buried in Riverside Cemetery, Scriba. Two brothers also served in the Union Army. George (1846-1865) was a member of the 2nd NY HA and was taken prisoner at Reams Station, VA. He was sent first to Libby Prison, then to Salisbury. He was paroled and died on March 25, 1865, two days after arriving home on furlough. Lorenzo (1848-1913) served in Co. D, 184th Regiment from 1864-1865. He mustered out with the regiment at City Point, VA on June 29, 1865. Their father, Horace, also served in Co. D, 184th Regiment. He was killed in a shipyard accident in Oswego City.

Llewellyn J. Hall – Co. I
b. July 1845 Oswego County, NY
d. October 16, 1928 Liverpool, Onondaga, NY
m. Sarah A. Borden (August 1857-December 28, 1951) 1873

NOTE: Llewellyn was Colon's older brother. He was discharged for "disability" on March 18, 1865 and in 1890 said his disability was the "loss of left foot." His entry in *The Town Clerks' Registers* spells his name "Luellen" and says he fought in both battles of Bull Run "and many more" and died in Richmond Hospital. It also says his remains were buried there. In reality, he was buried in Liverpool Cemetery. *The Watertown Daily Times* October 17, 1928, 2 published his obituary: "Services for Llewellyn J. Hall, 83, a Civil War veteran who died Tuesday morning will take place tomorrow afternoon at his home on the Liverpool road. Burial will be in Liverpool. One of the last survivors of Company I, One Hundred and Forty-Seventh regiment, Mr. Hall served for more than two years and took part in many famous battles. He was a native of Oswego and resided nearly all his life on the Liverpool farm. He was a member of Butler Post G.A.R. Pulaski . . . ." Sarah died in Leyden, Lewis, NY. According to an obituary published in *The Lowville Leader* January 4, 1952, 6, her body was put in the vault for interment in Liverpool in the spring.

Silas Halleck – Co. G
b. 1834 Scriba, NY
d. July 1, 1863 Fairfax Seminary Hospital, VA
m. ------

NOTE: Silas was the son of Richard (1800-1873) and Electa Crippen Halleck (1802-1876). According to *Deaths of Volunteers* his COD was "chronic diarrhea."

Victor B. Hallock – Co. H
b. November 1829 Coxsackie, Greene, NY
d. February 24, 1914 Oneida, Madison, NY
m. Julia L. Montross (September 8, 1836-January 13, 1917) 1853

NOTE: Victor was the son of Epenetus (1791-1877) and Patience Halstead Hallock (1794-1875). He was wounded at Gettysburg on July 1, 1863 and discharged on April 8, 1865. Victor wrote a letter to President Lincoln which is still extant. I transcribe it as he wrote it: "Mr. Presedent I wood like to heare from you if you stope so low as to rite to a poor soldier witch I now you think a goodeal of soldiers I cast a vote for you four years ago and I exspect to if I have the privilege to put in a vote this fall for you I don't do this to git my discharge but I am in ernest about it I remain your obedient servent Victor B. Hallock, Co. H 147th reg N.Y.S. Vol." In 1890 Victor said he had been wounded in the right thigh. The enumerator noted that he was "quite deaf." His death elicited the following obituary in *The Oswego Daily Palladium* February 27, 1914: "Victor Hallock died Tuesday night at the home of his son, Herbert Hallock, at Oneida where he has made his home since last Fall. Funeral services will be held in Temperance Hall here [in Bernhards Bay] at eleven o'clock tomorrow morning, the Rev. A. F. Pennock, of Madison, a former pastor, having charge. Mr. Hallock was eighty-four years last November, and had been married for sixty years. The greater part of his life was spent here. He was a soldier of the Civil War. Surviving are his widow, one son, five grandchildren and several great-grandchildren." Julia's death was announced in *The Oswego Daily Palladium* January 18, 1917, 2: "Mrs. Julia Hallock, aged eighty years, passed away on Saturday afternoon at the home of her son Herbert Hallock, in Oneida. The body was brought here [Bernhards Bay] on Tuesday morning and funeral held from the church, the Rev. G. W. Wood, of Cleveland, officiating. Mrs. Hallock had spent nearly all her life here until four years ago, when she and her husband went to Oneida to live with their son. Mr. Hallock died three years ago . . . ." The Hallocks are buried in Lakeside Cemetery, Bernhards Bay. Julia was a sister of Velsor Montross. (See below.) Her DOD is not on the gravestone.

Private Victor Hallock
147th New York

Victor Hallock showed his support for President Lincoln's reelection by sending him a personal letter in 1864.
Cory Wright

Franklin "Frank" N. Halsey – Co. F

b. October 21, 1842 Mexico, NY
d. July 1, 1863 Gettysburg, Adams, PA
m. Sarah "Nellie" E. McCumber (1844-*post* 1864)
August 25, 1862

NOTE: Frank, son of William (1807-1861) and Elizabeth Miller Halsey (1814-1843), married Sarah shortly before leaving for the front. *The Mexico Independent* July 16, 1863 published the letter announcing to her that her husband had been killed: "I am very sorry to announce to you the death of your husband. He was shot on the first day's fight – the 1st of July. No one knows where he is buried . . . Dear Madam, you must look to Heaven to comfort you, and there also you will again meet your beloved husband. He fell while nobly fighting for his country, and the country's honor will be his reward. Daniel L. Anerty, 147th Reg't N.Y.S.V." Anerty is unidentified and the name may be a corruption based on poor penmanship. Below this letter was another short one, written by Benjamin O. Baker to his father to tell him he had been captured and paroled. At the end he wrote: "Frank Halsey was shot in the forehead. All he said when wounded was, 'Please tell Nellie'." A notation in Halsey's pension file to "marriage Feb'y 10 '64" may refer to Sarah's remarriage. She does not appear on the 1865 New York census. Frank is buried in Gettysburg National Cemetery.

Franklin "Frank" Norton Hamlin – Co. K

b. November 18, 1831 Annsville, Oneida, NY
d. June 25, 1864 Seminary Hospital, Georgetown, DC
m. ------

NOTE: Franklin, son of John (1787-1870) and Cynthia Deming Hamlin (1792-1866), was mustered into the 147th as a first lieutenant. He was remembered in a lengthy obituary published in *The Oswego Commercial Times* July 14, 1864: "Among the many officers who have fallen in the recent advance towards Richmond, no one was more intimately connected by the ties of friendship and association with the citizens of this vicinity than Lieut. Frank Hamlin, -- Inspired by that spirit of patriotism which has swelled the ranks of our armies with the flower of the young men of the country, he left the comforts and luxuries of a model home and entered the ranks as a private in Company K, 147th Regiment N.Y.V. He occupied this position but a short time, when he received a commission as First Lieutenant in the same company, which position he held at the time of his death. On the 5th day of May, 1864, at the battle of the wilderness, Lieut. Hamlin was wounded in both arms, the bones of the left arm being badly shattered. He was removed to Washington and placed in Seminary Hospital, at Georgetown, D.C. The prostration caused by

Hamlin's death occurred as the result of wounds suffered at the battle of the Wilderness. If his obituary is to be believed his body was sent home for burial. *Author's Collection*

loss of blood and the fatigue of the journey to Washington, proved too much for a constitution already undermined by disease contracted in the service. He lingered in suffering, with varying prospects, until the 25th day of June, when death released him from his sufferings and extinguished the hopes of his friends. Lieut. Hamlin was a resident of the town of Scriba. Few men of his age have acquired the respect and esteem with which he was regarded in the community where he resided. – No man was more ready than he to assist the needy and relieve the distressed. By his cheerful disposition, his warm heart, and his never varying, never ceasing kindness to the miserable and the unfortunate, he has left a memory in the hearts of his friends at home, and his comrades in the army, more precious than marble shaft or monument of brass could bestow. His aged parents are deeply stricken – the staff of their declining years is broken. They have the sympathy of the large circle of friends who, with them, mourn their loss; but God alone, who 'tempers the wind,' can heal their bleeding hearts. He fell in the prime of life – in the 33rd year of his age, a victim of the rebellion, and in the country church-yard, near the home of his childhood, among the friends of his youth, 'he sleeps well'." He is buried in North Scriba Union Cemetery.

Degrass Hanness – Co. C
b. 1843 Schoharie County, NY
d. July 1, 1863 Gettysburg, Adams, PA
m. ------

NOTE: Degrass, son of Elias and Ann Eliza Hummel, was killed in action. Although some researchers claim he was born in Parish, NY the 1855 New York census confirms his POB was Schoharie County. He is buried in Gettysburg National Cemetery.

Elias Hanness – Co. C
b. 1819 Schoharie County, NY
d. July 15, 1863 Spangler's Warehouse Hospital, Gettysburg, Adams, PA
m. Ann Eliza Hummel (1822-post 1880) May 9, 1842

NOTE: Elias, son of Abraham (1788-1870) and Catherine Hanness (1789-post 1870), was wounded on July 1, 1863 and died from his injuries. He is buried in Gettysburg National Cemetery. Ann Eliza married Elijah Fairchild (1812-April 10, 1898) on January 28, 1867 as his second wife. By Fairchild she was the mother of Frederick (1868-1937). Fairchild is buried with his first wife, Harriet West (1816-1866), in Colosse Cemetery, Mexico. Ann's DOD and POD have not been located.

George Harney – Co. B
b. May 5, 1832 Tipperary, Ireland
d. November 23, 1881 Georgetown, Clear Creek, CO
m. ------

NOTE: Lt. Col. George Harney's early life is sketchy. Even his DOB varies from document to document. I use that found on his Naturalization Record. It appears he arrived in the United States in June 1848. He may have worked as a shoemaker until he entered military service. He enlisted in Co. A, 7th US Infantry in Boston, MA on October 9, 1852 and re-enlisted in the 7th US Army on August 9, 1857 at Fort

Belknap, TX for another five-year term. He was stationed at Fort Ontario before enlisting in the 147th. Over the course of his service, he rose to the rank of lieutenant-colonel. On October 27, 1864 near Dabney's Mills he was captured by the Confederates and spent time in Danville Prison, VA. He was granted a furlough as a paroled prisoner on February 26, 1865 so he must have been freed in the general exchange of prisoners occurring at that time. He mustered out with the regiment on June 7, 1865. In September 1865 he was in Massachusetts completing the formalities to become a naturalized citizen. He noted on the record that he had been a member of the 147th Regiment. By 1870 he was living in Clear Creek County, Colorado Territory. The census record says he was "mining." What happened to him between 1870 and 1880 is unknown. The only

After the war George Harney moved west where he became a miner.
William Yates (FAG)

name approximating his was Geo. W. Harne, living in Nevada and working as a bartender in 1880. I suspect he was unavailable for the 1880 census even though he was living in Colorado. His DOD is also disputed, variously given as November 20, 22, and 23. He is buried in Alvarado Cemetery, Eagle, Clear Creek, CO. A government gravestone without any dates marks his grave.

Thomas J. Harrigan – Co. A

b. 1834 Hannibal, NY
d. April 10, 1863 Armory Square General Hospital, Washington, DC
m. Arvilla Lum (1831-1883) July 14, 1858

NOTE: Thomas' parents may have been Michael (1796-*post* 1865) and Ellen Olnine Harrigan (1815-*post* 1865). His COD was typhoid fever. His DOD is disputed but most documents, including *Deaths of Volunteers*, placed it on April 10th. He is buried in the Soldiers' and Sailors' Home Cemetery in Washington, DC. Thomas and Arvilla were the parents of one child, Samuel T. J. Harrigan, born April 13, 1863, three days after his father's death. Arvilla, who lived with her parents, David and Catherine Lum, in Granby, does not appear on the 1880 census and I can find no confirmable record for Samuel after 1870. Her apparent DOD is 1883 because her estate was sent to probate on June 25, 1883. She died intestate and Marshall Foster was appointed executor.

George Calvin Harris – Co. K
b. 1834 New Brunswick, Canada
d. March 3, 1873 Painesville, Lake, OH
m. Teresa Caroline Bowhall (1846-*post* 1896) March 21, 1870

NOTE: George was the son of Hezekiah Harris (1803-?) and an unidentified mother. He collected a bounty of $300 upon enlisting in the 147th Regiment. He transferred to the US Navy, date unknown, and according to a Navy Rendezvous Card he was discharged on June 7, 1865. A brief death notice appeared in *The Northern Ohio Journal* March 8, 1873, 3: "HARRIS – At his residence, over the river, on Monday March 3rd, of consumption, George C. Harris, in the 39th year of his age. The deceased served two years in the United States army and two in the navy during the late rebellion, where it is thought he contracted the disease from which he died. He leaves a wife and one small child." To date his grave has not been located. The child mentioned in the text was Mabel Amelia (1871-1933). Teresa married Archibald Chisholm (1839-*post* 1910), a native of Scotland, on February 28, 1877. In March 1896 she attempted to obtain a widow's pension under George's name, implying her marriage to Chisholm had ended. She was unsuccessful. No more records for her have been found. In 1910 Chisholm was working as a hired hand in Perry, Lake, OH. He claimed to be a widower.

Gilbert Harris – Co. E
b. July 12, 1837 Jefferson County, NY
d. December 5, 1908 Valparaiso, Porter, IN
m. Emeline A. Ehle (1839-July 21, 1904) February 27, 1866

NOTE: Although Gilbert said he was born in Sandy Creek, NY when he enlisted, the 1855 and 1865 New York census records show he was born in Jefferson County, as does his entry in *Registers of Officers* and *Enlisted Men*. His parents were Ariel (1805-?) and Emily Harris (1807-*ante* 1865). He was wounded June 18, 1864 at Petersburg, VA, transferred to the VRC on August 29, 1864, and discharged June 28, 1865 at Washington, DC. He and Emeline were married in DuPage, IL. His death resulted from a fall which injured his spine. Emeline's COD was breast cancer. Both are buried in Maplewood Cemetery, Valparaiso.

Alexander Harrison – Co. K
1821 Ireland
d. ??
m. ?

NOTE: Very little has been located about this man. His parents are unidentified. On his muster roll card he said he was a "soldier" and it well may be he had been a soldier in the Regular Army stationed at Fort Ontario, Oswego City, where he enlisted. He mustered out with the regiment on June 7, 1865 and disappeared.

Robert Harrison – Co. K
b. 1819 Ireland
d. November 21, 1898 National Soldiers' Home, Milwaukee, Milwaukee, WI
m. ------

NOTE: Harrison, a sailor, was wounded on July 1, 1863 at Gettysburg. In 1890 he stated he had been shot in the right arm and had also lost an eye. He was transferred to the VRC and finally discharged on July 29, 1865 at Harrisburg, PA. His COD was tuberculosis and he was buried in Wood National Cemetery.

Haynes Lord Hart – Co. B
b. 1844 Oswego, NY
d. February 21, 1900 Auburn, Cayuga, NY
m. Rosantha L. Jones (1845-July 16, 1924) *ca.* 1868

NOTE: Haynes, a son of Edwin (1801-1892) and Aurel Ann Anderson Hart (1802-1870), was discharged for "disability" on February 12, 1863 at Washington, DC. His later life was detailed in an obituary published in *The Oswego Daily Palladium* February 22, 1900, 5: "Word has been received here of the death of Haynes L. Hart, which occurred at his home, 6 Ross Place, Auburn, yesterday of pneumonia, after a brief illness. The deceased formerly lived in Oswego and was well known here. He was born here about fifty-eight years ago, was educated in the public schools and, after graduation, entered the retail shoe business. When a young man he was proprietor of a store in East Bridge street, now occupied by Burden & Marsden. Later he bought the building, finally selling it several years ago to E. D. Stacy. A few years ago Mr. Hart went to Kansas City, where he engaged in the real estate business and also manufactured a brand of printer's ink. From Kansas City Mr. Hart removed to Williamsport, Pa., where he manufactured metal valves. Two years ago he went to Auburn, where he has lived ever since. Mr. Hart was prominent in Masonic circles. He was a thirty-third degree Mason, a Past Master of Oswego Lodge, 127, and also a Past Commander of Lake Ontario Commandery, No. 22, K.T. For many years Mr. Hart was secretary of Lake Ontario Chapter, No. 165, R.A.M., and was the first Commander-in-Chief of Lake Ontario Consistory, No. 12 S.P.R.S. [Sublime Princes of the Royal Secret], organized about fifteen years ago. Mr. Hart married while living here, Miss Rosie Jones, who lived East of the city and who now survives, as do three children . . . The funeral will be held from the family home in Auburn at eleven o'clock tomorrow morning and the body will be brought to Oswego for burial in Riverside cemetery.

The members of the Masonic Order will go to the train at three o'clock tomorrow afternoon and escort the body to the cemetery, where Masonic services will be held." Rosantha's death was announced in *The Oswego Daily Palladium* July 18, 1924, 7: "Mrs. Rosantha J. Hart, 79, wife of the late Haynes L. Hart and a former resident of Oswego, died Wednesday at Phoenix. Mrs. Hart is survived by two daughters, Mrs. Paul D. Sexton, of Syracuse, and Miss R. Belle Hart, Phoenix. Private funeral services were held yesterday at the family home in Phoenix and the body was brought here for burial in the family plot in Riverside. Haynes L. Hart, late husband of the decedent, was a former merchant here for many years. He conducted a shoe store in East Bridge street where the Burden & Marsden store is now located. The family home at that time was at 81 East Fourth street, between Bridge and Oneida streets. Mr. Hart moved from Oswego to Auburn, where he continued in the shoe business for a number of years." Haynes and Rosantha are buried in Riverside Cemetery, Scriba.

John Hart – Co. C

b. ? Sligo County, Ireland
d. July 2, 1863 5th Army Corps Hospital, Gettysburg, Adams, PA
m. Mary Carroll (May 1820-June 2, 1900) *ca.* 1860

NOTE: John claimed to be 37 when he enlisted which meant he was born in 1825. On the 1860 census, however, he said he was 40, implying a DOB of 1820. An entry in *Registers of Officers and Enlisted Men* shows an age of 30 when he was killed. Mary's dates are also confusing. In 1900 she said she had been born in May 1820 and was 80 years old and her gravestone gives an age of 80 at her death, confirming the date. The 1860 census, however, put her age at 30, or a DOB of 1830. John's DOD is also a matter of conjecture. His entry in *Deaths of Volunteers* says he was KIA on July 1, 1863 but his muster card says he died on July 2nd of wounds sustained the previous day. His gravestone shows a DOD of July 2nd. John and Mary were the parents of one child, Michael (March 1862-October 13, 1901). He was fatally injured by a train in Buffalo, NY. For two weeks his body lay unidentified until his wife, Frances, whom he had deserted several months earlier, heard that it might be his and went to Buffalo to identify it. Mary is buried in Holy Cross Cemetery, Williamstown. Her gravestone also commemorates her husband John.

Jeremiah Hartigan – Co. I

b. 1843 Oswego, NY
d. October 29, 1925 National Soldiers' Home, Danville, Vermilion, IL
m. ------

NOTE: Jeremiah, son of Daniel J. (1815-*post* 1865) and Margaret Hannon Hartigan (1823-*post* 1865), was wounded at Gettysburg on July 1, 1863 and discharged from the service on September 8, 1864. He applied for a pension on September 26, 1864 and on his home admission forms he said he had suffered gunshot wounds to the right knee and left foot at Gettysburg. His COD was chronic myocarditis and myocardial infarction. He is buried in Danville National Cemetery.

Cyrus Veber Hartshorn – Co. F

b. May 11, 1823 Exeter, Otsego, NY
d. November 1, 1895 Oswego City, NY
m. Louisa Elizabeth Palmer (October 2, 1824-February 18, 1898) June 13, 1844

NOTE: Cyrus was the son of John (1797-1857) and Lucy Veber Hartshorn (1794-1877). A farmer and merchant of farming implements, Hartshorn was also very active in his church, serving as superintendent of the Sunday School for seven years before he resigned to enter the military. He was also a dedicated member of South Richland Grange No. 156. In 1862 he raised a company of volunteers for the 147th Regiment from the Mexico area. Having been involved in a dispute over food distribution, he resigned his commission in late January 1863 and returned home. He and Louisa were the parents of four children, two of whom were living in 1895. His death was announced in *The Mexico Independent* November 6, 1895, 2, reprinted from *The Oswego Daily Palladium*: "Mr. Cyrus V. Hartson [*sic*], who suffered a stroke of paralysis on the 20th ult., peacefully fell asleep this morning [November 1st] at the home of his son, Mr. J. F. Hartson, 38 West Third street. Mr. Hartson was afflicted with paralysis about seven years ago and had not been strong since that time. He was born in the town of Exeter, Otsego county, May 11th, 1823, removing in 1855 to Union Square, this county, which has been his home since that time. Mr. and Mrs. Hartson spent the greater part of last year with their younger son in Dallas, Texas, returning to make their home with Mr. John F. Hartson in this city. In early life Mr. Hartson united with the Baptist church, of which he was a member up to the time of his death. He was an earnest, active Christian and filled well several church offices, including that of Sunday School Superintendent. He was kind, benevolent, consistent and was loved and respected by all who knew him. His wife to whom he was united in marriage in 1844, survives him with two sons . . . ." *The Oswego Daily Palladium* November 5, 1895 reported on his funeral: ". . . The services at Mr. Hartson's old home in Union Square were attended by a large concourse of mourning friends and were solemn and impressive. The Rev. Dr. Lewis Halsey, of the West Baptist church, in this city, gave a discourse from Second Corinthians 1, 3, paying an earnest tribute to the memory of the departed. The services at the grave were conducted by the South Richland Grange, of which Mr. Hartson had been for years an honored member, in accordance with their beautiful ritual. A touching tribute to the memory of the departed and one which the friends will never forget, was the flag of the neighboring school-house which was flying at half-mast during the day." Louisa, too, received a lengthy obituary, published in *The Mexico Independent* March 3, 1898: "The death last Friday of Mrs. Louisa P. Hartson, mother of Mr. John F. Hartson of this city, removes from the West Baptist church one of its most faithful and earnest members. Mrs. Hartson has been a member of this church about four years, and her constant, loving, and loyal service proved how deeply sincere was her religion, and how sweet was her character and disposition. It is a fact worthy of special mention that Mrs. Hartson's Christian service of more than sixty years' duration had been divided among only four churches. It can readily be seen from this how thoroughly and deeply rooted her life must have grown into the life of the churches with which she was connected. Everywhere the same record had been made, of unswerving devotion to the church and its interests, and, home and social life, of the most beautiful unselfishness, sympathy and kindliness in her relations with those around her. It is interesting to note that Mrs. Hartson inherited from a long line of ancestors a strong and sturdy character, coming of a family of long-lived, God-fearing people. Her mother, grandmother, and great-grandmother, living to ages ranging from ninety-three to one hundred and six years, died after devoting almost their entire lives to the service of God and the church. The influence of such lives and of the one just ended, cannot be estimated. Mrs. Hartson's sweet face, kind words, and beautiful life will be long and lovingly remembered by the West Baptist church and by friends in other churches in which she has worked." Cyrus, Louisa, John, and Lucy are all buried in Maple View Cemetery, Mexico.

William W. Hathaway – Co. F
b. 1823 Wareham, Plymouth, MA
d. May 16, 1891 Mexico, NY
m. Matilda _____ (1820-December 29, 1891) *ca.* 1845

NOTE: Hathaway's parents are unknown. He transferred to the VRC on December 18, 1863 and was discharged at Philadelphia, PA on September 21, 1865. In 1890 he said his disability was "piles – 25 [years]". A carpenter by occupation, Hathaway was a member of Melzar Richards Post No. 367 GAR. He is buried in Pleasant Lawn Cemetery, Parish. Matilda's grave has not been located. She died in Cicero, Onondaga, NY.

George M. Havens – Co. C
b. 1843 Jefferson County, NY
d. March 7, 1863 Regimental Hospital, Belle Plain, VA
m. ------

NOTE: George's POB on his muster card is Sandy Creek, NY but the 1855 census showed that the family was living in Ellisburg, NY and that all children had been born in Jefferson County. His official COD was typhoid fever. A Surgeon-General's certificate dated August 3, 1868 contains the notation: "Remarks – It appears written in pencil-mark opposite his name, 'This man was subject to fits previous to enlisting'." Whether or not this statement is true, George was the main financial support of his family. His father, William (1803-July 12, 1873) was, according to Dr. Frank Low, "completely broken down." He had been disabled for ten years prior to applying for George's pension in 1866, suffering from "neuralgia & rheumatic swellings." William applied for a pension on July 30, 1866 and his wife Betsey Burt Havens (1806-May 23, 1884) applied on October 31st, receiving a payment of $8 per month. The pension records show that George had supported the family for several years before enlisting and had bought a house and lot for the family. He had $10 set aside from his army paycheck each month to be sent to them. There were eight children in the family and it appears that George and Judith were twins. In one deposition dated April 6, 1868 William revealed the family had not heard from their son, Riley (1836-?) in nine years and thought he was dead. In actuality he was very much alive. The last known dated reference to him was 1882 when he was living in Sutter, CA. William and Betsey are buried in Richland Cemetery.

Luther Merwin Hayes – Co. H
b. April 22, 1827 Parish, NY
d. April 8, 1912 Detroit, Wayne, MI
m1. Laura J. Carpenter (*ca.* 1840-1872) *ca.* 1855
m2. Catharine Ann "Kate" Barnes Drummond (1830-July 26, 1895) 1874
m3. Fanny Lavington (May 17, 1868-November 9, 1949) 1890

NOTE: Luther was the son of Joel Post (1800-1881) and Clarissa Redington Hayes (1804-1877). He served as a second lieutenant in the 147th and was discharged on April 1, 1863. He and Laura, who is buried in Pleasant Lawn Cemetery, Parish, NY, had no children. Catharine was first married to Captain Thomas Drummond (1832-April 2, 1865), a member of the 5th US Cavalry who was killed at the battle of Five Forks, VA. They were the parents of Fitz Henry Warren (1861-1927) and Thomas Fletcher (1864-1943). In 1875 these boys were living with Luther and Kate. Also living with them was an unnamed baby, later named George Luddington Hayes (1875-1952). It appears that Luther and Kate parted company because she died in Nebraska and is buried in Wyuka Cemetery, Lancaster County. Her gravestone says she was the "wife of Thomas Drummond." Luther and Fanny had a daughter, Marion (1892-1961). Luther's death certificate says he was buried in Elmwood Cemetery, Detroit but he also has a stone in Pleasant Lawn, Parish. His obituary in *The Detroit Free*

Press April 9, 1912, 4 solves the apparent mystery: "Luther Merwin Hayes, a distant relative of President Rutherford B. Hayes, died at his home, 692 Second avenue, yesterday morning. Mr. Hayes was over 85 years old. About a year ago, he sustained a fall which caused a general breakdown. Mr. Hayes was a native of New York state and for many years conducted a hotel at Mexico, Oswego county, of that state. He moved to Detroit about 13 years ago, and retired from active business . . . Funeral services will be held this afternoon from the family residence at 2 o'clock. The body will be placed in the vault at Elmwood cemetery and later taken to Mexico, N.Y. for burial." Fanny died at Marion's home in Hollywood, CA. Her body was shipped to Parish and buried in Pleasant Lawn Cemetery. Luther's sister, Emily Hayes (1829-1913), was married to Dr. Tobias John Green (1818-1916), a physician attached to the 110th Regiment.

William Alonzo Hayes – Co. F
b. January 6,1825 Camden, Oneida, NY
d. January 28, 1906 Detroit, Wayne, MI
m1. Abigail Spencer (1825-1849) *ca.* 1848
m2. Fanny Miranda Smith (February 28, 1821-January 30, 1887) October 7, 1851

NOTE: William was Luther's brother. He was discharged from the army for "disability" on April 6, 1863 at Douglas Hospital, Washington, DC. *The Detroit Free Press* January 29, 1906, 5 published an interesting obituary: "A familiar figure to Detroiters, and especially to visitors at the Wayne hotel, passes away in the death of William A. Hayes, father of James R. Hayes, proprietor of the Wayne; Frank H. and Addison J. Hayes, all of Detroit. Mr. Hayes, who had been failing for some time, died yesterday afternoon of heart disease at his rooms in the hotel, aged 81 years 22 days. Mr. Hayes was born in Durham, Oswego county, N.Y., January 8, 1825, and passed the first part of his life in central New York where he was married and his three sons were born. He engaged in barrel manufacturing at Chittenango, and later in the lumber business at Red Mills. At the outbreak of the war he enlisted in the 147th New York Volunteer Infantry, and was assigned to the charge of the commissary department. He sustained a severe injury by being thrown from his horse. For this, he was granted a pension. After the war Mr. Hayes moved to Grand Rapids, where he conducted a cooperage establishment for many years. Ten years ago he came to Detroit to spend his last days with his children. He soon became a warm friend of the boarders and regular guests at the hotel. Between him and former Gov. John T. Rich there was established a firm friendship, and the governor is one of the sincerest mourners at his death. Mr. Hayes was a third cousin of former President Rutherford B. Hayes. He was a member of Custer Post, G.A.R., of Grand Rapids, and was highly esteemed in both cities. His death occurred exactly nineteen years after that of his wife . . . ." William was buried in Elmwood Cemetery, Detroit. Fanny, whose COD was consumption, is buried in Greenwood Cemetery, Grand Rapids. Many members of the Hayes family are buried in Pleasant Lawn Cemetery, Parish, NY and it is possible Abigail is there.

Charles D. Hayward – Co. K
b. March 1841 Canada
d. February 23, 1915 Seattle, King, Washington
m. Mary E. Fales (1850-March 11, 1928) July 4, 1874

NOTE: Charles was the son of Orin (?-?) and Jerusha Winters Hayward (?-?). According to the 1900 census he immigrated to the United States in 1862 and became a naturalized citizen. He enlisted as a musician and on October 7, 1864 was transferred to the Brigade Band. He married Mary E. Fales in Grand Rapids, Kent, MI and they became the parents of four children: Alfred "Fred" (1877-1921); Mary Adelaide "Addie" (ca. 1877-1952); Maud A. (1879-1901); Earl (1881-1903). By the early 1890s Charles and Mary had separated and he was living in Washington State, working as a mason. Mary and the children resided in Grand Rapids, MI. Mary's life after her husband left cannot have been happy. Maud, a telephone operator, died of typhoid fever July 26, 1901. Earl was a lineman for the Michigan Telephone Company and on July 15, 1903 was electrocuted by a live wire while working on a line. Alfred probably had tuberculosis. A death announcement said he died of "congestion and hemorrhage of the lungs." Addie married Harry Felton (1881-?) in 1906 and became the mother of Earl Felton, a Hollywood writer. She is buried in Hollywood Cemetery, CA. Mary, Maud, Fred, and Earl are all buried in Oak Hill Cemetery, Grand Rapids. I have not located Charles' gravesite.

Harvey H. Heburn – Co. E
b. June 29, 1840 Western, Oneida, NY
d. June 8, 1905 McConnellsville, Oneida, NY
m. Helen E. Crandall (1845-September 7, 1928) April 3, 1866

NOTE: Harvey's story is one of the most confusing, and yet most entertaining, of all the men of the 147th Regiment. Despite the fact that his muster roll card says he died on July 1, 1863 he lived a good long life! Instead of being killed, he was taken captive that fateful day, paroled, and sent to Harrisburg, PA. While there he and a friend, Menzo W. Griffin, made a rash decision. On March 5, 1903 Griffin offered the following testimony which I transcribe as written: ". . . We wer both captured by the Confederates at the Battle of Gettisburgh, Pa on July 1st 1863 and both Harvey Heburn and myself Menzo W. Griffin of Co K 147 Regt NYS Vol Inft. wer Paroled on the field of Battle at the Battle of Gettysburgh. After being released by the

Confederates and again entering our lines we wer transported to a Parole Camp at Westchester Pa. from information we received while in Parole camp their had ben and was a Genral order that no Soldier should accept a Parolle on the Field of Battle, and that the Government were intending to send us to our Regiments without being exchanged. We did not know of the order forbidding the Parole on the Field of Battle. So as we did not feel disposed to return our Regt under our own names before we wer exchanged we left Parole Camp and went into the State of New Jersey and enlisted in the 2 NJ Vol. Cav. at Mansfield, Burlington Co New Jersey Sept 8 1863. I inlisted under the alias of Henry Brayman [and] Harvey Heburn inlisted under the alias of Harvey McDonald . . . and serv'd in said Regt. untile the close of the War and wer Honorable discharged . . . ." Menzo does not mention it, but he and Harvey both accepted local bounties, too. While serving in the New Jersey Cavalry Harvey was wounded twice. In June 1864 he lost his right index finger to a Rebel bullet at Guntown, MS. In September he was wounded again in the right hand near Memphis, TN. In 1866 using the alias of Harvey McDonald he applied for and obtained a pension based on those wounds. Eventually someone turned him in and he was arrested and put on trial for obtaining a pension fraudulently. He was acquitted but told he would have to apply to have his pension restored. Despite his best efforts to explain away his actions, the restoration was denied. He was considered a deserter from the 147th; he had joined a second outfit while still under obligation to the first; he had collected a hefty bounty from local authorities in New Jersey. Harvey's COD was liver cancer and chronic rheumatism. *The Utica Herald-Dispatch* June 9, 1905, 5 published an interesting, if somewhat fanciful, obituary: "Harvey Heburn died at his home in [McConnellsville] at 4:30 o'clock yesterday afternoon after a lingering illness from a complication of diseases. Mr. Heburn was born in the city of Rome [*sic*] June 29, 1840. At the outbreak of the Civil War he was one of the first to answer the call for volunteers and enlisted in Company E, One Hundred and Seventh [sic] regiment, New York Volunteers, where he served three years. At the end of this term of service he re-enlisted in the New Jersey Cavalry, where he served until the close of the war. Mr. Heburn married Miss Helen Crandall of Lowell in 1866. Seven children were born to them . . . At the time of his death Mr. Heburn was surrounded by his children. Deceased was a member of the Grand Army post of Camden. Mr. Heburn had followed the calling of a farmer nearly all his life, and had lived at the farm where he died nearly thirty years. He was of a genial disposition and made friends easily, retaining them to the end . . . ." After Harvey died, Helen, who had had no part in his desertion and subsequent re-enlistment, nor the years of deception, attempted to collect a widow's pension. She was flatly denied on the grounds that Harvey was never honorably discharged from the 147th and that his subsequent service was of no legal consequence. She married Abraham Goring (1848-1934) on September 5,

1920 as his second wife. Although they lived in Frankfort, Herkimer, NY, she was buried in Grandview Cemetery, Whitesboro, Oneida, NY with Harvey.

Adam Heller – Co. G

b. 1813 Herkimer County, NY
d. September 22, 1875 Oswego City, NY
m. Rebecca G. _____ (ca. 1820-July 21, 1896) ca. 1845

NOTE: Although Adam, whose parents are unidentified, alleged he was born in 1818, census records prove he lied in order to enlist. He was discharged from the service June 22, 1863. Rebecca applied for a pension on July 6, 1882. The investigation into Adam's service revealed a charge of desertion. Not until 1886 was the charge removed from his record. Instead he was considered AWOL and Rebecca was granted her pension. The Hellers were the parents of at least six children. Myron, one of the youngest, moved to Michigan in 1879 to work on the railroad. On March 17, 1879 while at work he caught his foot in the track and before he could extract it, a train backed over him, killing him instantly. His body was returned to Oswego. Rebecca died in Ogdensburg and her body too was brought home for burial. She, Adam, and Myron are all buried in Butterfly Cemetery, Mexico.

Calvin Arnold Herrington – Co. E

b. September 1844 Ellisburg, Jefferson, NY
d. May 13, 1928 Whittier, Los Angeles, CA
m. ?

NOTE: Calvin was the son of Harvey (1811-?) and Betsey Herrington (1814-?) but was adopted by John and Cynthia Bentley. He was wounded in the forearm at Gettysburg on July 1, 1863. According to *The Town Clerks' Registers* he was captured but I have found no evidence of it. He was transferred to the VRC on February 6, 1864. After the war he traveled west and spent many years in Osage, KS where he was a member of Canby Post No. 11 GAR. In 1919 he was senior vice commander. It is unknown if he was married. Some census records identify him as a widower while others as a single person. He is buried in Rose Hills Memorial Park, Whittier.

John Hibbard – Co. B

b. 1842 Montreal, Quebec, Canada
d. ?
m. ?

NOTE: John's surname was also spelled Hibbert, as evidenced by his pension application dated June 26, 1865. He was wounded in the right arm at Gettysburg on

July 1, 1863 and transferred to the VRC on March 10, 1864. He was re-transferred to the 147th on October 10, 1864 and mustered out with the regiment on June 7, 1865. He and his widowed mother, Julia (1800-?), appear on the 1865 New York census. She said she was the mother of 11 children. His pension application is the last document located for him. He and Julia may have returned to Canada.

David Hickey – Co. G
b. 1827 Ireland
d. ?
m. ?

NOTE: David, whose parents were James (?-?) and Mary Miner Hickey (?-?), was a ship carpenter when he enlisted. His entry in *The Town Clerks' Registers* says he was wounded at Gettysburg on July 2, 1863, again at Petersburg on June 18, 1864, and finally discharged with the regiment. That probably is not entirely true. His muster card shows that he was discharged from the 147th in April 1864 in order to enter the US Navy. It is very possible that the David Hickey, age 40, ship carpenter, born Ireland, who enlisted in the Navy on May 4, 1864 at Brooklyn Naval Yard is the same man. He was among a group of transferred soldiers and signed on for a term of 18 months. Nothing more can be confirmed.

Michael Hickey – Co. I
b. 1843 Oswego, NY
d. *ante* 1905 ?
m. ?

NOTE: Michael, son of Edmond (1808-1876) and Catherine King Hickey (1816-April 10, 1905), was a mariner. His muster card listed him as MIA after the battle of Gettysburg and *The Adjutant- General's Report* says he was captured on July 1st, 1863 and paroled at an unknown date. He apparently rejoined the regiment and mustered out on June 7, 1865. There the trail ends. When his mother Catherine died in 1905 she received a lengthy obituary which included names of surviving children. His name was not among them. Edmond and Catherine are buried in St. Peter's Cemetery, Oswego.

Morgan Hill – Co. K
b. 1819 Pawlet, Rutland, VT
d. *ante* 1875 Scriba, NY
m. Freelove Ann Rathbun (November 15, 1823-December 25, 1897) *ca.* 1843

NOTE: Hill's parents are unidentified. He originally enlisted in the 110th Regiment, but was sent to the 147th where he served until August 26, 1863 when he was discharged for "disability" at Convalescent Camp, VA. On October 4, 1864 he enlisted in Company D, 16th US Infantry at Buffalo, serving until February 21, 1867 when he was discharged at Atlanta, GA, again for "disability." He and Ann are buried in Rural Cemetery, Oswego Town. His government stone contains no dates. He did not appear on the 1875 New York census.

Henry Adelbert Hilliker – Co. E

b. March 7, 1845 Sandy Creek, NY
d. July 13, 1936 Pulaski, NY
m. Roxie Hough Fillmore (May 7, 1859-August 15, 1943) 1887

NOTE: Henry was the son of Job (1801-1888) and Sally Fitch Hilliker (1808-1907) and commonly known by his middle name. His DOB varies from document to document. He mustered out with the regiment on June 7, 1865. *The Pulaski Democrat* July 15, 1936, 1 published an informative obituary: "Henry Adelbert Hilliker, one of the two remaining members of J. B. Butler Post, G.A.R., and commander of the post since the death of Hartwell Douglass last winter, died at his home on North street, Monday night at 10:30. Mr. Hilliker was stricken with the intense heat while on an auto ride Sunday, pneumonia set in and, at his advanced age, proved fatal. Mr. Hilliker was born in the Town of Sandy Creek, March 7, 1845 a son of Job and Sally Hilliker. He enlisted in Company E, 147th N. Y. Vol. in 1861 [*sic*], and served throughout the civil war. Forty years ago he came to Pulaski and has made his home here since. He was an attendant at the Methodist church, and an honorable and upright citizen. He had been a member of J. B. Butler Post for years and had filled several offices in the organization, being elected commander at a recent meeting. With his passing his old comrade, Frank Fancher, is left the sole survivor of that once large and noble band of men who kept alive for so many years the true spirit of American patriotism in this community . . . The funeral will be held at the home at 2 o'clock Thursday afternoon with the Rev. Henry Bridge officiating. Burial with military honors in charge of Robert Edwards Post, American Legion, in Pulaski cemetery." Roxie's obituary appeared in *The Pulaski Democrat* August 19, 1943, 1: "Mrs. Roxie Hough Hilliker, 85, died Sunday morning at her home in North street following a long illness. She was born May 7, 1859 on the Syracuse road and had lived her entire life in the vicinity of Pulaski. Mrs. Hilliker was twice married. Her first husband was the late Silas Fillmore. Her second husband, Adelbert Hilliker, was one of the last surviving veterans of the Civil war in Pulaski. He died several years ago. She was a life member of the Methodist church and of the Maunder class of that church. She was also one of the oldest members of the J. B. Butler Post, Women's Relief Corps . . . Funeral services were conducted Tuesday afternoon at the home with Rev. W. A. Gardner, officiating. Burial was in Pulaski cemetery."

Frederick "Fred" M. Hills – Co. F
b. 1842 Chaumont, Jefferson, NY
d. June 3, 1925 Oswego City, NY
m. Ruth A. Head (1849-March 22, 1919) 1872

NOTE: Fred, son of Eugene (1820-1876) and Abigail Savage Hills (1823-1895), originally enlisted in the 110th but was sent to the 147th. He was wounded in the hand and
foot at Gettysburg on July 1, 1863 but was able to muster out with the regiment on
June 7, 1865. Fred's obituary appeared in *The Oswego Palladium-Times* June 4, 1925,
4: "Fred M. Hills, 84, a veteran of the Civil War, died last evening at 10 o'clock at the
home of his son, William H. Hills . . . after an illness of several weeks. Deceased was
born in Chemung [*sic*], Jefferson County. He was a member of the 147th Regiment,
Co. F, New York Volunteers. He was a farmer by occupation and for a number of years
conducted a large dairy farm on the East State road. He retired several years ago and
made his home with his son, who is his only survivor . . . ." Ruth's death was announced in *The Oswego Daily Palladium* March 24, 1919, 3: "Mrs. Ruth Hills, aged
seventy-one years, died yesterday afternoon [*sic*] at the home of her son, William
Hills . . . after a lingering illness. Mrs. Hills was born in New Haven, the daughter
of the late Cyrus and Ruth Head. She has lived in this city for the past twenty-two
years and was a member of the First Baptist church. Besides her husband, two sons,
William and Frank, of this city survive. Funeral will be held on Thursday afternoon at
two o'clock." Fred and Ruth are buried in Riverside Cemetery, Scriba.

John Larmer Himes – Co. B
b. June 27, 1834 Scriba, NY
d. February 18, 1925 Pulaski, NY
m. Mary E. Neal (1845-July 22, 1915) 1866

NOTE: John was a son of James Larmer (1792-1862) and Sarah "Sally" Pullman Himes
(1795-1872). He was wounded in the right foot at the battle of the Wilderness, May
5, 1864 and in the left hand at Hatcher's Run, February 6, 1865. He was discharged
from the service at Syracuse on August 7, 1865. In 1890 he claimed his disabilities
were rheumatism, heart disease, and a wound in his right heel. *The Pulaski Democrat*
February 25, 1925, 1 published an informative obituary: "One by one, and their
deaths grow fewer, the Veterans of the Civil War are being mustered out of the earthly
ranks to take their places in the Greater Grand Army under the Grand Commander
of the triumphant host. Wednesday afternoon of last week, the long life of Veteran
John L. Himes came to a close and he was at rest at the end of a journey reaching
ninety years and more than half of his ninety-first year. He had been a resident of
this village for several years coming here from Orwell and his home was with his

daughter, Miss Katherine Himes, of Jefferson St. John L. Himes was born in Scriba, Oswego Co., June 27th, 1834. In 1873 he settled in the wilds of Orwell, and engaged in farming, having previously been engaged in carpenter work. The section known as New Scriba was where he settled and the name was adopted to that region because a number of people came from Scriba to settle there. James Himes, father of John L. Himes, who fought in the war of 1812, served in Captain Reed's company and which formed a part of General Brown's army of 12,000 men. The wife of James Himes was Sally Pullman, a close relative of the late W. M. Pullman, Chicago, well known as founder of the Pullman Car company. In August, 1863 [sic], Mr. Himes enlisted at Oswego in Company B, 147th Regiment, New York Volunteers, remaining in service about three years. He was wounded at the battle of the Wilderness, being confined for six months in a hospital. Two brothers, Marshall Himes and Lucius Himes, also served in the Civil war. Mr. Himes was a member of J. B. Butler Post No. 111, Grand Army of the Republic, of which he had served as senior vice-commander and also filled other offices . . . ." The graveside services, held at Evergreen Cemetery, Orwell, where John and Mary were buried, were conducted by the officers of J. B. Butler Post GAR. Marshall Himes (1822-1899) was a physician attached to the 96th Regiment. Lucius (1839-1864), a member of the 9th NY HA, was killed at the battle of Cedar Creek on October 19, 1864. Mary's COD is unknown but a brief mention in *The Oswego Daily Palladium* July 28, 1915, 3 gives some idea of the attendant pain: ". . . Mrs. Mary Himes, wife of veteran J. L. Himes, was buried last Sunday. She was a great sufferer for a long time and death was a welcome release from her sufferings. A good many friends miss her . . . ."

William Henry Harrison Himes – Co. K

b. May 27, 1840 Oswego, NY
d. July 1, 1916 Muskegon, Muskegon, MI
m. Caroline "Carrie" Louise Dickinson (1848-November 5, 1918) 1885

NOTE: William, son of Whitford (1798-1858) and Philena Van Buren Himes (1807-1890), mustered out with the regiment on June 7, 1865. In 1890 he claimed he had been "wounded in head and heel." He and Caroline had no children but adopted Mary Louise Lake (1872-?). He died after suffering a stroke. *The Muskegon Chronicle* July 1, 1916, 14 published his obituary: "William Henry Harrison Himes, aged 76, died at his home, 126 Monroe avenue, this morning, after a brief illness. Mr. Himes was a past master of Lovell Moore Lodge, No. 182 F. & A. M., and a veteran of the Civil war. Mr. Himes was born in Otsego [sic], New York state, and when the war broke out, joined the New York Volunteers, 147, Company K. He came to Muskegon in 1880. He was a sawyer by trade and worked for several years in the mill owned here by the late John Torrent . . . ." The Masons attended his funeral in a body and members of the

Past Masters' Society were pallbearers. Carrie's death was reported by *The Muskegon Chronicle* November 12, 1918, 7: "Mrs. Carrie L. Himes, formerly of Muskegon, died November 5, at Los Angeles, Calif., where she had made her home for the past two years with her niece, Mrs. Herman Lankheet. Mrs. Himes was a member of Mizpah Chapter, No. 88, Order of the Eastern Star; Bethesda Shrine, No. 21, of the White Shrine of Jerusalem; Scandinavian Hive No. 7, of the [Ladies Of The Maccabees]; and Phil Kearney Post, No. 105, of the W. R. C. Her body was cremated and her ashes will be sent to Muskegon for interment . . . ." William and Carrie are buried in Oakwood Cemetery, Muskegon. Mrs. Lankheet was Mary Louise, their adopted daughter.

John Hinchcliff – Co. K

b. 1826 England
d. July 1, 1863 Gettysburg, Adams, PA
m. ?

NOTE: John's surname was variously spelled. For example, his entry in *The Town Clerks' Registers* spelled it Hickliff. The same reference says that his parents were John (?-?) and Hannah (?-?) and that he was single. He was the color sergeant in Co. K. His bravery has been immortalized in numerous articles about the role of the 147th on the first day of fighting at Gettysburg. Called "the big Swede" by men in his company, he reportedly stood over six feet tall. As the regiment was retreating he was shot in the chest and instantly killed. According to a chapter in Johnson's *History of Oswego County,* allegedly written by H. H. Lyman, "Sergeant Hinchcliff, the colorbearer conspicuous for his bravery and fine soldierly bearing was shot through the heart, and had fallen upon the colors. Major Harney was about to return in person to bring them off, when Sergeant Wybourn, Company I, volunteered to rescue them. He returned, rolled Sergeant Hinchcliff off the colors, and bore them off triumphantly amidst a storm of bullets . . . ." Dr. Algernon S. Coe, in his speech at the dedication of the 147th monument at Gettysburg, subsequently published in *The Oswego Daily Times* July 2, 1888, referred to Hinchcliff as "the stalwart color bearer" who was "shot through the heart . . . ." Hinchcliff is buried in Gettysburg National Cemetery. Other biographical material is non-existent. Hinchcliff died intestate and Edward Sykes, perhaps a brother-in-law, was appointed the administrator of his estate in 1864.

George Washington Hindes – Co. A

b. August 16, 1834 Vermont
d. June 19, 1897 Lincoln County, OK
m1. Lydia Jemima Green (1845-*ca.* 1869) January 22, 1865
m2. Sophia Day (1848-*ca.*1876) July 16, 1870
m3. Ellen M. Van Alstine (July 22, 1847-April 13, 1912) *ca.* 1877

NOTE: George was the son of Silas (1787-1877) and Anna Maria Crane Hindes (1802-1880). His surname is variously spelled. I use that found on the pension card. Dates are a stumbling block to researching this man. According to *The Town Clerks' Registers* he was "in the Battle of Gettysburgh and was wounded in the privates and lost the right thumb – discharged March 1863." If this statement is true, he could not have been at Gettysburg. His muster roll card says he was discharged for "disability" on January 24, 1863 yet he did not apply for a pension until October 4, 1864. In 1890 he said his disability was "sore eyes." George and Lydia appear to have had no children, but the 1875 New York census shows he and Sophia were the parents of Lydia, 4. I tentatively date his marriage to Ellen as 1877 because their son, Charles Henry, was born on January 1, 1878. George's gravesite has not been located. In 1900 Ellen was living with Charles (1878-1965) in Cimarron Township, Payne, OK. She married Thomas Lewis Black (1831-1906) sometime after that date as his second wife. They are buried in Black Cemetery, Stroud, Lincoln, OK. Lydia only appears on the 1875 New York census and may have died around the same time as her mother.

Calvin Hinman – Co. A

b. 1838 Oswego County, NY
d. January 28, 1885 Detroit, Wayne, MI
m. ------

NOTE: Calvin, son of Peleg (1787-1850) and Mary Jones Hinman (1808-1891), originally enlisted in the 110th Regiment. He was wounded and captured on May 5, 1864 at the battle of the Wilderness. His remarkable escape was chronicled in *The Oswego Daily Palladium* July 29, 1864: "Sergeant Calvin Hinman, of Company A, 147th Regiment, Capt. McKinlock, called upon us yesterday, and we gathered some interesting facts connected with his escape from the hands of the enemy. Sergeant Hinman was severely wounded in the left breast, and taken prisoner at the first day's fight at the Wilderness. There were five others of the 147th sent to the rear on that day. They occupied hospital tents from that date (May 5th) till the night of June 1st, when Sergeant Hinman and eleven others started under cover of darkness, to make their way to the Federal lines. They took the Chancellorsville turnpike towards Mine Run, and passed over the bloody field of the Wilderness, on which they had been taken prisoners. The scene was one of the most horrible character. The dead had not been buried, and the bloated and putrified bodies of men and horses almost entirely covered the ground. The deadly stench sickened some of the party so that it was with difficulty that they were gotten along. The night was windy, and heavy clouds were driven along the sky. As the moon occasionally cast its pale light on this horrid field, covered with its seething load of corruption, the strongest shuddered, and of the twelve who started, four gave out, and went back. The remaining eight crossed the field, constantly stepping on, and stumbling over the dead. At daylight they went into the woods to avoid pursuers, guerrillas and bushwhackers. The provisions were here divided, and they found that they had two hard crackers each. These with some very bad water, furnished a breakfast. – They staid in the woods all that day, and at night cut across the old Chancellorsville battle ground, and reached a point about five miles above where the Rapidan emptied into the Rappahannock; crossed the Rapidan and made for the Rappahannock in the direction of Ellis' Ford; saw rebel scouts but escaped their notice by dodging into the woods. They spent the next day in the woods in sight of the Rappahannock, but durst not move from their cover on account of the scouts, which were very plenty at this point. When darkness came, they made for the river and followed it up to Ellis' Ford. At this place the whole party came near to being retaken by a troupe of cavalry. Luckily they were able to conceal themselves until the horsemen passed down when the party plunged into the river, and after a good deal of difficulty succeeded in reaching the opposite shore. At this point, one of the party who had been badly wounded in the leg, seemed about to give out. He couldn't swim, so was put on to a plank and towed across. The wet and weary party then pushed on down the river towards Fredericksburg, and made about eight miles before daylight. They went into the woods and slept about two hours. Hunger began to tell on the poor fellows, but they kept up courage and pushed on by daylight, in the hope of coming within our lines at Aquia Creek. – They reached the latter place at dark and found it deserted. Not a living thing could be found. They set to work and by three o'clock A.M. had made a raft. There was a dense fog on the river which did not clear off till about eight o'clock, when the party embarked on their raft, and after a sail of about two hours towards the Maryland shore were picked up by a Federal transport and restored to that liberty which they had encountered so much to obtain. Besides Hinman, Corporal [David] Welsh, of Company K, was the only member of the 147th who escaped on this occasion. We are glad to find that Sergeant Hinman is recovering from his wound and will soon be himself again." Hinman was discharged for "disability" on December 31, 1864. His COD was consumption. His grave has not been located.

Erastus R. Holdredge – Co. C
b. February 24, 1820 Frankfort, Herkimer, NY
d. May 2, 1908 Albion, NY
m1. Jane E. _____ (1824-December 29, 1847) 1843
m2. Maria E. Erskine (1815-February 17, 1896) *ca.* 1848
m3. Melona J. _____ (July 1817-March 24, 1907) *ca.* 1896

NOTE: Erastus was the son of Deacon Charles Eldridge (1795-1871) and Isabel Rathbone Holdredge (1795-1828). He was discharged from the service on August

26, 1863. In 1890 he said his disabilities were "rheumatism, diarrhea, catarrh." *The Pulaski Democrat* May 6, 1908 published an interesting obituary: ". . . Another old resident of this place, E. R. Holdredge, passed away at the home of his daughter, Mrs. X. A. House, Saturday morning, May 2, at 8 o'clock, of heart disease from which he had suffered for a long time. Mr. Holdredge was born in Frankfort, Herkimer Co., Feb. 24, 1820, where he lived until 1848, when he removed to Holmesville (now Fernwood), Oswego Co., and three years later he came to Albion and purchased the place which has since been his home. Although not a member of a church Mr. Holdredge was a regular attendant at church as long as he was able to go and only a few days before his death expressed the belief that all was well and he was ready for the summons at any time. He was not able to get far away from home, yet he enjoyed meeting and visiting with old friends and always had a pleasant greeting for all who came his way, and his mind remained clear to the last . . . Funeral services were held at the home, Tuesday afternoon, at two o'clock, Rev. W. H. Hall, of Dugway, officiating . . . ." Erastus, Jane, and Maria are buried in Willis Cemetery, Fernwood. In 1905 Erastus claimed to be a widower. In 1906 Melona, living in Racine, WI, said she was Erastus' widow. Apparently the couple had separated. Her grave has not been located.

Rodolphus Hollenbeck – Co. K
b. February 8, 1835 Albany County, NY
d. September 5, 1908 Binghamton, Broome, NY
m. ?

NOTE: Rodolphus, a tailor by trade, was a son of Peter (1801-?) and Sarah Hollenbeck (1799-?). He was discharged from service on March 14, 1863 at an unnamed hospital. He was listed as married in Draft Registrations of 1863 and in *Registers of Officers and Enlisted Men* but I have found no evidence of a wife. Little verifiable information is available. He appears to have lived in Binghamton, Elmira, and Manhattan. In 1873 he lived in Binghamton and was a tailor but by 1880 he was a street sprinkler. In 1900 he was living in Manhattan with a brother, Walter (1826-1903). On January 3, 1903 he was baptized at the Chapel of the Messiah, New York Protestant Episcopal City Mission Society. In 1907 he was a witness to Milo Kinyon's application for a pension increase. A short article in *The Binghamton Press* September 5, 1908 noted his passing: ". . . Rodolphus Hollenbeck, aged 74 years, died this morning at 9 o'clock at his home, 60 Clinton street. The funeral will be held at Watrous undertaking rooms tomorrow afternoon at 3 o'clock. Burial will be in Floral Park Cemetery." He is buried in the GAR section of the cemetery.

John B. Hompe – Co. D

b. February 4, 1846 Amsterdam, Holland
d. December 15, 1937 Soldiers' Home Hospital, Minneapolis, Hennepin, MN
m. Ella Nottingham (May 30, 1857-October 19, 1917) April 1, 1879

NOTE: John Hompe's death was reported in a short obituary in *The St. Cloud Times* December 16, 1937, 11: "John B. Hompe, civil war veteran, Minnesota legislator for 40 years, school teacher, farmer and merchant, died last night in the hospital of the old soldiers' home after a long illness. He would have been 92 years old next February. Funeral services have not been completed but he will be buried in Deer Creek, Minn., where he lived all the time he was in the legislature. He is survived by four sons, Harold, of Monticello, Minn., and Howard, Bernard and Edward of Deer Creek." The article does scant justice to the man's accomplishments. John's parents, Anthony Peter (1823-1909) and Henrietta Weiman Hompe (1821-1887), brought their family to America in 1849, eventually settling on a farm in Hannibal, NY. John was only 16 when he enlisted in the 147th Regiment, mustering out on June 7, 1865. It was said he never missed a roll call. After the war John went to Ionia, MI to teach school. Later he migrated to Minnesota where he hired out as a teamster and sawyer. Following an eighteen-year stint as a homesteader he moved to Deer Creek and opened a store. In 1889 he was elected to the state legislature, serving two terms as a senator. After a hiatus of 20 years he was elected to the House in the Minnesota legislature. He was re-elected nine times and in 1931, at the age of 85, he had the honor of being the oldest legislator in the country. At the time he was also the only Civil War veteran serving in a legislative body. In addition to his professional occupations, John found time for personal interests. He was a Mason, a member of the Modern Woodmen of America, and a Knight of the Maccabees. He and Ella were the parents of five sons, two of whom, Bernard (1883-1967) and Edward (1897-1968), also held office in the Minnesota legislature. John and Ella are buried in Oak Hill Cemetery, Deer Creek. To finish the story: John's father, Anthony, 44, enlisted in the 184th Regiment in August 1864 and served until mustered out at City Point, VA on June 29, 1865. He and Henrietta are buried in Fairdale Cemetery, Hannibal.

John B. Hompe had a long legislative career after the Civil War and in 1931 was the oldest legislator in the United States.
Michelle Hompe-Barr

James Homes – Co. H

b. December 1837 Madison County, NY

d. September 20, 1917, Font du Lac, Font du Lac, WI

m. Mary Ann Van Wormer (August 1844-1912) 1866

NOTE: In 1850 James and two siblings were living with their mother, Hannah Homes (1818-?) and maternal grandparents, James and Mary Lord, in West Monroe, NY. Despite the fact that West Monroe is noted as his POB on his muster roll card, other documents confirm that he was born in Madison County. His unknown father was born in Pennsylvania, according to the 1900 census. James was captured at Gettysburg and paroled at an unknown date, mustering out with the regiment on June 7, 1865. A cooper by trade, James said he was a bridge builder on the 1905 Wisconsin census. Census records frequently spell his surname Holmes. He and Mary Ann are buried in Rienzi Cemetery, Font du Lac. Mary's DOB is erroneously given as 1854 on the gravestone.

Lorenzo Warren Horton – Co. C

b. 1828 Richland, NY

d. October 26, 1864 Andersonville, Sumter, GA

m. Mary Potter Mandigo (1824-May 18, 1902) February 19, 1856

NOTE: Lorenzo, whose parents are unknown, was captured at the battle of the Wilderness and sent to Andersonville. *The Mexico Independent* March 23, 1865 published a list sent by Colonel Miller, dated March 14, 1865, of men from the 147th who had died in what he termed "Southern Hells." Among them was Lorenzo Horton. The exact DOD can be fixed thanks to the testimony of William Bargey: ". . . That I was a Private in Co. 'E' in the 147th Regiment of New York State Volunteers. That I was well acquainted with Lorenzo W. Horton who was a Private in Co. 'C' in the said Regt. from the time he entered the service of the United States until the day of his death. That on the 6th day of May A.D. 1864 at the battle of the Wilderness Va. said Lorenzo W. Horton & myself were both captured and taken Prisoner by the enemy. That we were both prisoners in the hands of the enemy and confined in the Rebel Prison at Andersonville, Georgia. That to my own personal Knowledge said Lorenzo W. Horton died at Andersonville aforesaid while he was a prisoner in the hands of the enemy on the 26th day of October, A.D. 1864 by reason of Chronic Diarrhoea. That I was with said Horton when he died & saw him die . . . ." Mary was previously married to Joseph Mandigo (1823-*ca*. 1850). She died in the Town of Ellisburg, Jefferson, NY and was buried in Woodlawn Cemetery, Sandy Creek.

Stephen R. S. Horton – Co. D
b. January 1820 Oneida County, NY
d. March 27, 1905 Pasadena, Los Angeles, CA
m. Olive Dexter (1826-October 6, 1899) March 24, 1847

NOTE: Stephen, whose parents are unknown but were allegedly born in Rhode Island, was promoted to commissary sergeant on March 1, 1863 and discharged December 31, 1864 when the 76th Regiment was consolidated with the 147th. He and Olive were the parents of at least six children, most of whom died young. By 1880 the family was living in Cordona, Rock Island, IL. Olive, a sister of Darius and David Dexter, died in Grant Township, Cass, IA. The bodies of both Olive and Stephen were shipped to Fulton and buried in Mt. Adnah Cemetery together with several children.

William Henry Horton – Co. G
b. 1840 Scriba, NY
d. August 16, 1883 San Bernardino, San Bernardino, CA
m. Linnie A. Connolly (1858-May 12, 1925) June 1, 1881

NOTE: William, frequently known by his middle name, was the son of Laurens (1807-1881) and Almira Coe Horton (1810-1842). After his mother died, he and his mentally handicapped sister, Emily (1855-*post* 1871), lived with their maternal grandmother, Phebe Smith Coe (1788-1871), even though their father married Laura Bennett Dutcher (1821-1867), widow of Peter C. Dutcher and the mother of Gilbert (1844-1898) and Himan Dutcher (1846-1928), both of whom served in the 184th Regiment. On December 1, 1862 Horton was admitted to Finley General Hospital, Washington, DC for diarrhea and was transferred to West Philadelphia Hospital on December 12th. On January 20, 1863 he left the hospital without permission and went home, which action led to a charge of desertion. *The Oswego Commercial Times* May 19, 1863 gives details about the outcome of this adventure: "Sunday night Deputy U. S. Marshal Reid and Police officer Chauncey arrested two deserters near Richland Station, named respectively Henry Horton and Wm. Churchill. The former is a member of the 147th regiment, and the latter of the 81st regiment. The first named had his baggage marked 'Henry Coe,' and the other's has [sic] the name of 'Wm. Turner.' At the time of the arrest they were only about half a mile from the station, whither they were being taken in a wagon driven by a man named Merrick DuBois, of the town of Scriba. The latter was also arrested for assisting the deserters off. The party were brought to the city and lodged in Fort Ontario." The records show Horton was returned to duty on June 23rd. On July 1st he was wounded in the shoulder and did not return to duty until November 28, 1863. He mustered out with the regiment on June 7, 1865 and subsequently returned to Oswego where he resided for a few years before heading west. An article in *The* [Yuma] *Arizona Sentinel* December 7, 1878 reveals what he was doing for a living: "The heaviest single shipment ever made into Arizona of wines and liquors, came in here this week for Mr. Henry Horton; there were over 40,000 pounds of it. These goods are all of the best kind and well-assorted. They are now being forwarded to Tucson, where Horton is about to open a wholesale liquor house. During the eighteen months that he has lived here he has conducted his business in first class style and has made many friends." Despite his successful business venture, William was plagued by ill health, especially chronic diarrhea. His pension file is replete with testimony from doctors who attempted to alleviate his pain and suffering with little success. The bright spot in his life was his wife, Linnie, whom he married in San Bernardino. Their marriage was to be of short duration, as *The Los Angeles Herald* August 18, 1883, announced: "From the annexed, which we clip from the San Bernardino *Index* of the 16th instant, it will be seen that Henry Horton, of Tucson, Arizona, died suddenly at that place on Thursday morning. Deceased was a nephew, we believe, of Mr. A. E. Horton, of San Diego, and was well known in this city. He had been engaged in business at Tucson, for several years, having been a partner in that city of Mr. Solon W. Craigue & Co., formerly of Lips, Craigue, & Co., of this city. Mr. Horton moved to Los Angeles with his family some weeks ago, in the hope that our genial climate would benefit his health, and only returned to San Bernardino a few days ago. The *Index* gives the following account of his death: Henry Horton was discovered dead in his room, No. 20 of the Southern Hotel, this morning. For several months Mr. Horton has been ill, and his physicians said he was beyond all remedies. But he lingered on, and was out on the street yesterday. In the evening he was seized with a spasm, and passed the night in great pain. About 3 o'clock in the morning an adjoining lodger heard him calling for help, and on entering his room Horton said he was poisoned – that he had taken too much medicine. A physician was sent for, but failed to arrive. A man considerably under the influence of liquor was in the same room with him all night, but was oblivious to the circumstances of his death. He probably died between 4 and 5 o'clock, but it was not known until a couple of hours later. Mr. Horton was until recently engaged in business at Tucson, Arizona, when he sold out and came to San Bernardino for his health. He leaves a wife, who was in Los Angeles at the time of his death. The deceased was about 40 years of age." Linnie applied for a widow's pension, securing testimony about her husband's health from such Oswego notables as Joel Baker and Amos Allport. Initially her claim was denied because of that charge of desertion against Henry. In 1887 the charge was removed since the law had been changed to allow soldiers who illegally checked themselves out of hospitals to be considered AWOL. The pension was granted and Linnie collected it until she died in Los Angeles in 1925. Their graves have not been located.

John Albert Hough – Co. C

b. 1841 Parish, NY

d. February 19, 1863 Camp Hospital, Belle Plain, VA

m. ------

NOTE: John was a son of James E. (1818-1857) and Laura Hatch Hough (1818-September 16, 1891). His COD is listed as "fever" or "typhoid fever" or "diarrhea" but was probably a combination of maladies. He was buried at Wind Mill Point, VA. His widowed mother applied for a pension on July 2, 1863, alleging that John had been the family's sole support since the death of her husband, who also died of typhoid fever. The family consisted of two younger brothers, Henry E. (1848-1927) and James T. (1850-1861), whom Laura endeavored to keep in school, as well as two daughters, Sarah (*ca.* 1839-?), and Mary Loretta (1843-1864), who supported themselves after their father's death but could not support their mother. Laura, described as "in indigent circumstances," obtained her pension. She and James are buried in Fairview Cemetery, Williamstown. Her stone does not contain any dates. Her DOD was found in the New York State Death Index. A cenotaph for John is also there.

Luman Hough – Co. K

b. 1818 Genesee County, NY

d. September 24, 1870 Williamstown, NY

m1. Louisa L. Phillips (1830-*ante* 1860) 1847

m2. Sarah "Sally" A. Lyon (1825-January 19, 1884) *ca.* 1860

NOTE: Luman, whose name was also spelled Lyman, was the son of Russell (1796-1826) and Mary Knapp Hough (?-*post* 1855). His uncle, also named Luman (1794-1878), was a medical doctor. The younger Luman was discharged from the 147th at an unknown date. Sally applied for a pension on June 28, 1880 but did not obtain it. Perhaps she died before the process could be completed. Graves for these people have not been located.

Lucius Howard, Jr. – Co. H

b. July 1823 Vernon, Oneida, NY

d. January 10, 1899 Cleveland, NY

m. Katherine G. Fisher (September 18, 1822-May 18, 1869) *ca.* 1848

NOTE: This man's muster roll card erroneously named him Louis. He was the son of Lucius (1795-*post* 1855) and Matilda Ward/Wood Howard (1804-February 1, 1832). He mustered out of the service on June 7, 1865. In 1890 he was living in Kenwood, Madison, NY. He said his disability was rheumatism. A woman named Elizabeth Howard, residing in Cleveland, NY and calling herself Lucius' widow, is also listed on the Veterans' Schedules. Both entries say he was a member of Co. H, 147th Regiment. His gave the correct muster out date of June 7, 1865. Hers said he did not leave the service until May 29, 1866. No disability was noted but the enumerator wrote, "This discharge is as near as can find." The entry is suspicious, as if provided by a person not familiar with the details of the soldier's service. If Elizabeth was Lucius' second wife, few viable candidates present themselves. The woman had to predecease him since his pension card does not show a widow applying for benefits. In 1880 a woman named Elizabeth Howard, 53, born in Canada, married, was living with three children in Constantia, all using the Howard name but definitely not Lucius' because of their ages. She shows up again in 1892, 67, born in Canada, again living in Constantia. This is the last known reference to her. I suspect this person was indeed a second wife who died before 1899. When Lucius died in 1899 he was living in Madison County and that was where his estate was probated. His daughter, Catherine Hammond (1859-1929), was named administrator. Lucius and Katherine are buried in Cleveland Village Cemetery.

William Monco Howard – Co. E

b. January 21, 1842 Oswego County, NY
d. April 26, 1887 Ellisburg, Jefferson, NY
m. Sophronia Kast (1838-March 19, 1926) *ca.* 1866

NOTE: William was the son of Daniel (1796-1866) and Phebe Winters Howard (1819-1899). He had the dubious distinction of being wounded in the hip at Gettysburg on July 1, 1863, the left knee at the battle of the Wilderness on May 5, 1864, and again in the left knee at Petersburg on June 18, 1864. The last incident resulted in amputation of the leg. He was discharged from the service for "disability from wounds" on June 22, 1865. Sophronia's death was announced in *The Jefferson County Journal* March 24, 1926, 6: "Mrs. Sophronia A. Howard, 87, an aged resident of this vicinity passed away at the home of her son, Fred Howard, about five miles west of Mannsville. Death was due to old age. Mrs. Howard lived alone for 39 years following the death of her husband until two months ago when she went to live with her son. Mrs. Howard was born in the Mohawk Valley, a daughter of the late Henry and Catherine Christman Kast and came with her parents to this region when young. She later became the bride of William Howard and lived here the remainder of her life. Always a great lover of flowers her home was much admired for the interior and exterior flower gardens. At her funeral the room was profusely banked with the flowers she loved so well, the gift of neighbors. Just 25 years ago yesterday an elder sister passed away in the same room about the same time and four weeks ago another sister, Mrs. Sophia Kendall died . . . The funeral was held Sunday afternoon at 1 o'clock . . . Burial was made in the Ellisburg [Rural] cemetery beside the body of her husband."

Henry Harrison Hubbard – Co. D

b. July 17, 1839 Volney, NY
d. June 23, 1868 Volney, NY
m. Harriet E. Distin (July 12, 1840-September 29, 1929) January 10, 1867

NOTE: The son of Rev. Thomas Markham (1811-1896) and Huldah Ann Beardsley Hubbard (1815-1885), Henry rose to the rank of captain and mustered out with the regiment on June 7, 1865. He and Harriet had one daughter, Jessie (October 17, 1868-March 20, 1874), who died in New Jersey. Henry's COD was *phthisis pulmonalis* (tuberculosis). He is buried in Mt. Pleasant Western Cemetery, Volney. Harriet married James H. Pittinger (1831-1912) on September 18, 1877 at Volney as his second wife. He died September 11, 1912 in Branchville, Sussex, NJ. He and Harriet are buried in Green-Wood Cemetery, Brooklyn.

George Hugunin – Co. A

b. December 11, 1829 Oswego Town, NY
d. June 6, 1892 Syracuse, Onondaga, NY
m. Huldah McChesney (June 23, 1833-March 15, 1902) December 12, 1854

NOTE: George was the son of Abraham (1787-1860) and Fanny Boynton Hugunin (1792-1870). His father was taken prisoner in May 1814 when the British attacked Oswego and forced Fort Ontario to surrender. He was compelled to do pilot duty for the British and was detained a long time. George, discharged for "disability" in 1863, fought to regain his commission although he left the military on December 21, 1864. His lengthy obituary, published in *The Oswego Daily Palladium* June 7, 1892, 8, provides a detailed description of the man's career: "The news of the death of Colonel George Hugunin in Syracuse yesterday will be received with a feeling of sadness in Oswego, where he was born and where most of his life was spent. Colonel Hugunin was born on December 11, 1829, and was a son of the late Abraham D. Hugunin. Before the war he was a member of the Old Oswego Guards, and always took a deep interest in military matters. He was, in fact, a born military man and took great pride in everything connected with the local military. He entered the service as Lieutenant of Company A, 147th New York Volunteers, in August, 1862, and was with that regiment in many of its fierce engagements. In January, 1864, he was promoted to Captain. He was severely wounded at the battle of Weldon Railroad, the ball entering his side and lodging in one of his lungs, where it remained some years, gradually dropping down to the right hip, where it formed an abscess which was opened by Dr. C. C. P. Clark about two years ago and the ball extracted. He was brevetted Major of New York Volunteers and also Major of the United States Volunteers March 31st, 1865. He was also Colonel of the Forty-eighth Regiment N.G.S.N.Y., and resigned in 1878. Colonel Hugunin was a brave soldier, a strict disciplinarian, and one of the best drill masters that Oswego county sent into the service. After the war he returned to Oswego where he held the office of Tax Collector for some time, and afterwards was appointed Postmaster by President U.S. Grant. Like his military service, his official duties were performed to the entire satisfaction of the people whom he served. He was a most courteous and affable gentleman, of strict integrity and was held in high esteem by all who knew him. For several years he has lived in Syracuse, where he was in the employ of his brother-in-law, George H. McChesney, but for more than a year he has been unable to attend to his duties owing to his enfeebled health. It was Colonel Hugunin's last wish that his body be taken to the

George Hugunin had extensive military experience before and after the war.
New York State Military Museum

State Armory, this city, his casket opened, and his old comrades given an opportunity to look upon his face. In respect to this wish the body will arrive here at 12:30 o'clock tomorrow and will be received at the station by a detail of the 48th Separate company and the Grand Army and escorted to the Armory, where it will lie in state for two hours, under guard. Burial will be from the Armory later. The funeral will take place from the Armory at 3 P.M. The Forty-eighth Separate Company and band, with veterans of Posts O'Brian and Stacey will escort the body to the city line. All G.A.R. men are requested to meet at the Armory at 2:30 P.M., sharp. All members of the 147th N.Y. Volunteers are requested to meet at the Armory, Oswego, N.Y., at 2:30 P.M. tomorrow to attend the funeral of Colonel George Hugunin. The officers of the old 48th regiment are also asked to join the escort." Colonel Hugunin authored a family history for his son which is still extant. Huldah's death elicited the following obituary in *The Oswego Daily Palladium* March 17, 1902, 5: "Mrs. Huldah McChesney Hugunin, widow of Colonel George W. Hugunin, died Saturday at the home of her son, Weldon Hugunin, No. 62 Belden avenue. She was sixty-eight years old, and had been an invalid for about a year. She was born at Pulaski, Oswego county, and for a number of years lived in Oswego . . . The funeral was held from her late home today, the Rev. Phillip H. Cole, officiating . . . ." The colonel and his lady are buried, together with his parents, in Riverside Cemetery, Scriba. Her DOD is erroneously given as 1904 on the gravestone.

Alexander Hulett – Co. D

b. 1823 Washington County, NY
d. November 27, 1892 Brooklyn, Kings, NY
m. Rebecca A. Brackett (1830-April 19, 1899) 1849

NOTE: Alexander, son of Hopkins (1794-1869) and Phoebe Hulett (1796-1875), served as a captain in the 147th. His COD was "cerebral apoplexy." *The Oswego Daily Times* November 29, 1892, 8 published his obituary: "The remains of Alexander Hulett of New York city are expected here Wednesday morning by the D. L. & W. road . . . Mr. Hulett resided here many years and was in business here several years . . . He was a genial, and kind hearted man honored by all who knew him. He was captain of a company in the 147th regiment, N.Y.S.V. He removed from here twenty-five years ago. He was aged sixty-nine years. His burial will be on a lot in Mt. Adna [*sic*]. He leaves a wife and daughter." Alexander was a member of Erastus T. Tefft Post No. 355 GAR in New York City. Rebecca also died in Brooklyn of "neuralgia of the heart." She, Alexander, and their only child, Ella Julia (1851-1902), are buried in Mt. Adnah, Fulton.

Charles M. Huested – Co. D

b. 1829 Cayuga County, NY
d. November 1898 Sherburne, Chenango, NY
m1. Harriet Duley (January 31, 1847-January 31, 1878) *ca.* 1864
m2. Nancy _____ (1832-April 28, 1903) *ca.* 1880

NOTE: Gaps and questions abound in this soldier's story. His muster roll card says he was born in Cayuga County but the only other available document which records POB is the 1875 New York census which lists Onondaga County as his birth place. He first served in Co. H, 24th Regiment, enlisting in Fulton on May 9, 1861. He was discharged for "disability" on April 12, 1862 at Upton's Hill, VA. The 1880 census says his right arm was amputated in 1863 after he was wounded at Chancellorsville (April 29, 1863-May 2, 1863). He applied for a pension on July 10, 1863 but was not discharged until September 12, 1863. In the meantime he was on detached service with Batt. L, 1st NY ART in August! He and Harriet are buried in Sherburne Quarter Cemetery under the surname "Husted." Nancy is buried in Sherburne West Hill Cemetery under the surname "Huested."

Willard Hunt – Co. H

b. 1820 Otsego County, NY
d. February 10, 1864 Camden, Oneida, NY
m. Samantha Cotton (1835-*post* 1905) *ca.* 1850

NOTE: Willard's parents are unknown. According to the testimony of Clark Norton, he contracted chronic diarrhea while marching on August 10, 1863. He was sent to

Division Hospital and eventually allowed to go home. His death was reported in *The Rome Daily Sentinel* February 22, 1864: "Warren [*sic*] Hunt, a member of the 147th Regiment, who has been home since November last, sick and confined to his house, died on Tuesday last and was buried on Thursday. He enlisted, we are told, from the town of Amboy. He had experienced a great deal of suffering, and his death leaves a family without support." Hunt was buried in "Camden Village Cemetery" which may be Forest Lawn. Samantha and the children moved west. In 1885 she was running a boarding house in Eagle, CO. George was a rancher and Charles was working on the railroad. In 1905 Samantha and George resided in Wakeeney, Trego, KS. George (1850-1926) is buried in Wakeeney City Cemetery and perhaps his mother is there too.

James Hutson – Co. K
b. 1822 England
d. July 1, 1863 Gettysburg, Adams, PA
m. Lucretia Duvall (1828-*post* 1870) *ca.* 1844

NOTE: This soldier's surname was also spelled Hudson. His parents are unidentified. Some documents claim James was killed July 2nd but Captain Joseph Dempsey testified to the earlier date. Dates are generally a problem when tracing this family. Marriage dates of October 13, 1848 and October 14, 1849 were provided in the pension records. Nevertheless, James and Lucretia were the parents of Elizabeth, born in 1845. Either Elizabeth was not Lucretia's child or the marriage date was inaccurately reported. Lucretia's DOB is likewise variously offered, as early as 1828 and as late as 1838. If Elizabeth was born in 1845, Lucretia could not have been born in 1838. The 1860 census assigned her an age of 29 and for that reason I think she was born in 1828. Lucretia received a widow's pension until she married William White in Hannibal, NY on July 17, 1865. No other information about him has been located. Her five minor children were assigned a guardian, Emery S. Pardee, and they received pensions. In 1869 Lucretia was living in Canastota, NY with Ella and Mary. The source for this information, A. C. Livingston the local post master, did not say where White was but he did refer to her as Lucretia White. In 1870 Lucretia, Ella, and Mary were in Flint, Genesee, MI. She called herself "Mrs. Hudson." The last payment for the youngest child, Mary Angeline (1861-1923), was sent to her guardian, Henry Lovell, in Detroit, MI but that does not necessarily mean Lucretia was still living.

Charles E. Hyde, Jr. – Co. A
b. 1847 Oswego, NY
d. ? ?
m. ?

NOTE: Charles, son of Charles E. (1820-?) and Lavina Barnes Hyde (1819-*ca.* 1857), was discharged from the 147th on December 5, 1862 for "disability." He was under-age. In 1863 he enlisted in the US Navy, re-enlisting in February 1864. On February 17, 1865 he joined the 16th US Army, in which organization his brother William (1849-December 2, 1919) had been a member since 1862. William was only thir-teen when he enlisted as a drummer at Fort Ontario, Oswego, and served throughout the war. Charles' history comes to an abrupt end with his last enlistment. William moved from Oswego in 1913 to enter the Soldiers' Home in Washington, DC. He is buried in the Soldiers' and Airmen's Home National Cemetery.

Joseph Hyde – Co. A
b. 1844 Oswego, NY
d. February 25, 1865 Oswego, NY
m. ------

NOTE: Joseph was the brother of Charles and William. He was discharged from the service on December 8, 1862 for "disability." He lied about his age when he enlisted, for his muster roll card gives an age of 20. His COD is unknown but it was probably the reason he was discharged. He is buried in Rural Cemetery, Oswego Town.

Jenkins Hyland – Co. A
b. 1832 Ireland
d. October 21, 1866 Oswego City, NY
m. ------

NOTE: Jenkins and his widowed mother, Jane Thompson Hyland (1791-*post* 1869), arrived in America from Liverpool, England on April 29, 1861 aboard the Resolute. From that time until he enlisted he was her sole support, as evidenced by testimony of neighbors, co-workers, and friends. George Hugunin described how Jenkins be-came so ill he was unfit for duty for months: ". . . said Jenkins Hyland was a healthy man until the 25th day of February 1863. On the 20th of February 1863 the said Jenkins Hyland started with his said command from Belle Plain Va. on a march to the Rappahannock River & on reaching the Rappahannock the said Command returned to Belle Plain & and said Jenkins Hyland returned with it. That during said March the said Jenkins Hyland was much exposed to the wet and cold and thereby contracted a cold & suffered from a cough and other indications of a severe cold. After that time said Hyland never performed duty as a soldier. He continued with the regiment about two months when he was sent to the Hospital. From the time of his return to Belle Plain as above stated he continued to grow more feeble every day until he was sent to the Hospital . . . ." Hyland was finally discharged on a surgeon's certificate for "disease of the heart." He was deemed too ill to serve in the VRC. Attorney Robert Martin testified that Jane wanted her son to apply for a pension but because Jenkins was too weak to attend to the matter the papers were never filed. Jenkins' COD was said to be dropsy and disease of the lungs. In 1867 Jane applied for a mother's pension. The file reveals that while Jenkins was absent she had had to resort to the city Poor Master for assistance, despite the fact that he had continued to send her funds. After his death she was assisted by the Commissioners of Charity. Jane had no property and an appraiser said her net worth was about $10, consisting mainly of furniture. Her house was described as a "shanty." Jane obtained a pension of $8.00 per month. Graves for her and Jenkins have not been located.

Elisha Ingraham – Co. H
b. 1807 Litchfield, Herkimer, NY
d. October 29, 1903 Syracuse, Onondaga, NY
m. Cecilia _____ (1819-1881) ca. 1850

NOTE: Elisha's surname was spelled Ingram on his muster roll card. His parents are unknown. Although he claimed to be 42 when he enlisted in 1862, he was much older. *Registers of Officers and Enlisted Men* assigned him an age of 55 and in 1900 he said he was born in July 1809. When he celebrated his birthday in 1903 he claimed to be 95, suggesting a birth date of 1808. He was discharged on September 11, 1863 and in 1890 he said that "chronic diarrhea" had been the reason for leaving the service. He worked for the railroad after leaving the military and in 1892 was involved in an incident which could have caused a disaster. The initial report published in *The Syracuse Evening Herald* June 8, 1892 was answered by an indignant letter from Ingraham and a further explanation by the *Herald*: "Under the heading 'False Representation' the *Evening News* last Saturday printed the following letter: *The Evening Herald* said much last Thursday concerning a gate-tender who works on the Rome, Watertown & Ogdensburgh crossing on West Genesee street. The article contained only two words of the truth. It seems that *The Herald* is very much in need of news when it cannot get news – without printing falsehoods against a poor man who attends to his work as faithfully as the highest official on any of the railroads. The person who wrote the article criminating [sic] the gate-tender is better adapted for a ticketeer on the Erie canal than for a writer. *The Herald* pretends to be a friend of all who toil hard for a living while it has ever shown its hostility to honorable labor in a low way. [signed] Elisha Ingraham, Syracuse, N.Y. . . . *The Herald* has procured an official investigation of its statement that the gate-tender at the West Genesee street crossing was absent from his post, that the gates were up when an express train came along, and that the train was stopped barely in time to avert disaster to persons and teams crossing the track. Ingraham admitted to the investigating officer that he had left his post, was told that there was no excuse for it, was reprimanded, and was informed that if such a thing occurred again he would be discharged. Ingraham told the investigating officer that he left the gate in charge of the tender at the next crossing north. That is not true, for when the train had stopped that tender came running down the track from his own gate." Using 1807 as his DOB, Ingraham was 85 years old when this incident occurred. *The Evening Herald* March 5, 1903 may have redeemed itself by publishing an extensive article celebrating Ingraham's 95th birthday: "Few people live to see their 95th birthday. Elisha Ingraham of this city not only saw it but enjoyed it immensely. For the past sixteen years Mr. Ingraham had made his home with Mrs. DeWitt C. Spencer, who keeps a boarding house at No. 600 South State street and last night she planned a little celebration among the boarders in his honor. Mr. Ingraham in spite of his advanced age enjoyed the evening as much as any of those present and entertained them with stories of his early experiences. Mr. Ingraham was born in Litchfield, Herkimer county. He helped build the Rome, Watertown & Ogdensburg railroad, working on that road as a section boss. He was connected with this road from the time it was built until three years ago, when he left the employ the company on account of his advanced years. During the last eight years of his service on the Northern road he was flagman at the West Genesee street crossing and will be remembered by a number of people who live in that vicinity. Mr. Ingraham delights in telling a story of how he walked from Sandy Creek to Parish, a distance of eighteen miles, twice a day for a week while the road was being constructed between those two places. When the Civil war broke out, Mr. Ingraham enlisted in the One Hundred and Forty-seventh regiment, serving throughout the war . . . Twice every week Mr. Ingraham walks to the barber shop in that vicinity and gets shaved and up to this winter he has gone down town almost every day. He smokes and drinks moderately and enjoys the best of health, in fact, Mrs. Spencer says that he eats more than most of her boarders do. If his present health continues, there is no reason why Mr. Ingraham should not live to be 100 years old." That, however, was not to be. He was one of three elderly men to die of pneumonia within 48 hours at Mrs. Spencer's establishment. Elisha and Cecilia are buried in Pleasant Lawn Cemetery, Parish.

George W. Jackson – Co. C

b. 1818 Richfield, Otsego, NY
d. ? ?
m. ------

NOTE: This soldier seems to have no history except for the small amount of information gleaned from his muster roll card and *Registers of Officers and Enlisted Men* which says he was born in 1820. He mustered out with the regiment on June 7, 1865 and disappeared.

John Wesley James – Co. G

b. August 7, 1844 Camden, Oneida, NY

d. March 12, 1923 Mayville, Tuscola, MI

m. Maria Jane Moutray (December 28, 1850-July 1, 1930) July 1, 1874

NOTE: John, son of William (1808-*post* 1855) and Ann Taylor James (1811-*post* 1855), was a carpenter. He served in Co. B, 93rd Regiment from December 1861 until January 1862 when he was discharged for "disability." He mustered out of the 147th on June 7, 1865. He and Maria, the parents of seven children, were married in Canada. The couple is buried in Fremont Township Cemetery, Mayville. Although John's gravestone gives a DOB of 1845 I use that borne on his death certificate.

Sardius D. Jenkins – Co. F

b. February 27, 1842 Mexico, NY

d. January 10, 1918 Lincoln County, OR

m1. Hannah _____ (1842-February 8, 1913) *ca.* 1863

m2. Celestia Jane Moore Reed (December 1849-February 19, 1937) October 5, 1898

NOTE: Sardius was the son of Charles C. (1815-1850) and Dorcas Olds/Oles Jenkins (1812-*ante* 1900). He originally enlisted in the 110th Regiment but was sent to the 147th. He was discharged from the military on February 12, 1863 for "disability" and in 1890, while living in Columbia, Clark, WA, he stated he had been "poisoned." He also claimed "general debility." The Jenkins family moved several times over the years. In 1870 they lived in Denver, Newaygo, MI and in 1880 were at home in Bloomfield, Davis, IA. In 1889 Hannah and Sardius were in Klickitat County, WA. At some time while living in Washington they parted company. In 1900 Sardius and his second wife, Celestia, were living in Bandon, Coos, Oregon, where he was a homesteader. By 1910 it appears that Celestia and Sardius had also separated. He was living in Kern, Lincoln, OR and was "widowed." She was living in Bandon, Coos, OR and also was "widowed." Hannah lived in Ohop, Pierce, WA in 1910 with three of her sons. She said she had been married once and was still married. Her DOD is taken from Sardius' obituary which does not mention another wife. Celestia had previously been married to Isaac Walter Reed (1843-1887) who had served in Co. B, 37th Illinois Regiment. He died on April 28, 1887 from the effects of overdosing on laudanum. Celestia is buried in Averill Pioneer Cemetery, Bandon, OR. Graves for Sardius, who died "after a lingering illness of several months," and Hannah have not been located.

John Johnson – Co. I

b. June 13, 1820 Ireland

d. June 4, 1898 Hospital, National Soldiers' Home, Bath, Steuben, NY

m. ?

NOTE: John was the son of Philip (?-?) and Mary Johnson (?-?). Although his muster roll card spells his surname Johnston, all evidence points to Johnson as the correct version. He mustered out of the service on June 10, 1865 at Albany, NY. His entry in *The Town Clerks' Registers* reported that he took part in every battle in which the 147th participated and gave a current address of Oswego City. He was living there in 1890 and said his disability was "kidney affected." According to the *Registers* he was married but no widow claimed a pension, indicating he either was unmarried or the wife had predeceased him. The DOD on his pension card is incorrect. John is buried in Bath National Cemetery.

David Henry Johnston – Co. H
b. 1834 West Monroe, NY
d. December 29, 1864 General Hospital, Annapolis, Anne Arundel, MD
m. Margaret Vickery (1835-March 17, 1902) July 19, 1854

NOTE: David, son of David Henry (1797-1874) and Betsey Patty Richmond Johnson (1803-1859), was wounded on July 1, 1863 and apparently was granted a furlough since his daughter, Ann, was born August 18, 1864. When Margaret applied for a pension she said that David had been captured at the battle of the Wilderness, a statement which has caused confusion for later researchers. Lieutenant Luther Hayes, Co. H, testified on April 15, 1867 that he was well acquainted with Johnston and "that said Johnston was a good and robust man up to within a few days of his death which happened on or about the 29 day of Dec. 1864. That deponent verily believes said Johnston died of sickness received in the service. That said Johnston died at or near Annapolis in the state of Md." This statement makes clear that Johnston had not been taken by the Confederates but had been with his company until he was taken ill and sent to the hospital. His official COD was "chronic diarrhea." He is buried in Annapolis National Cemetery but a cenotaph may be seen in McAlister Cemetery, West Monroe. Margaret never remarried. She died in Cicero Center, Onondaga, NY but her grave has not been located.

James Johnston – Co. H
b. 1843 West Monroe, NY
d. January 10, 1863 Regimental Hospital, Falmouth, Stafford, VA
m. ------

NOTE: James was David Henry's brother. His COD was typhoid fever. In 1870 his father, David, successfully applied for a pension. A cenotaph for James is located in McAlister Cemetery, West Monroe.

Jonathan Carmont Johnston, Jr. – Co. F

b. June 15, 1819 Stockbridge, Madison, NY

d. November 4, 1909 Syracuse, Onondaga, NY

m1. Sophronia Wilson (July 2, 1828-April 22, 1897) *ca.* 1845

m2. Lucy _____ Keech (December 1825-1906) *ca.* 1900

NOTE: Jonathan, son of Jonathan C., Sr. (1793-1867) and Nancy Johnston (1799-1878), was discharged from the service at Armory Square Hospital, Washington, DC on May 23, 1863. He enlisted in Co. I, 184th Regiment at Mexico, NY on August 23, 1864, mustering out at City Point, VA on June 29, 1865. *The Oswego Daily Times* November 9, 1909, 6 published an obituary: "The subject of this sketch, Jonathan Carmont Johnston, was born in the town of Stockbridge, Madison County, N.Y., June 15, 1819, and departed this life Nov. 3 [*sic*], making him 90 years, 4 months and 20 days old. Jonathan was married, date unknown, to Miss Sophronia Wilson . . . The deceased was a veteran, a member of the 184 N.Y.S.V., and a professed Christian. The funeral services were held at the Upson's M. P. church on Saturday, Nov. 6th, at 11 a.m., conducted by Rev. H. F. Snow, assisted by Rev. W. H. Spaulding, after which he was laid to rest in the cemetery near by beside the chosen one of his youth, his beloved companion. His children have the sympathy of all." Another obituary, published in *The Syracuse Post-Standard* November 5, 1909, 7, revealed he had died at son Oscar's home after an illness lasting a year. Jonathan and Sophronia are buried in Upson's Corners Cemetery, Palermo. Little is known about Lucy. Her maiden name is unknown but in 1900 her daughter Delilah Keech, 57, and single, was living with Lucy and her husband Jonathan, in Eaton, Madison, NY. Her first husband was Ephraim Keech (1810-1893).

Amos D. W. Jones – Co. C

b. April 1841 Brownville, Jefferson, NY

d. December 21, 1912 Detroit, Wayne, MI

m. Louisa Phoebe Cratsenberg (February 6, 1842-November 21, 1907) *ca.* 1862

NOTE: According to *The Town Clerks' Registers*, Amos was wounded in the groin at Spotsylvania but an entry in *Registers of Officers and Enlisted Men* says he was wounded in the hip at the battle of the Wilderness. These battles occurred only several days apart and the information may have been inaccurately reported. He mustered out with the regiment on June 7, 1865. A son of Silas (1808-?) and Sarah Ann Witt Jones (1810-?), he grew up in Jefferson County and was enumerated there in 1865. By 1880 he and Louisa were living in Michigan. On both the 1880 and the 1900 censuses Amos said he was a bartender. He and Louisa had one child, Adam Earl (1883-1933). Louisa's COD was breast cancer. Amos succumbed to myocarditis. They are buried in Oak Hill Cemetery, Owosso, Shiawasee, MI.

Benjamin Gendron Jones – Co. A
b. 1838 Canada East
d. June 15, 1897 Auburn, Cayuga, NY
m. Henrietta "Hattie" Mary LeRoy (1847-August 15, 1901) December 25, 1865

NOTE: Jones, whose parents are unidentified, was a boatman by trade. He mustered out with the regiment on June 7, 1865. *The Auburn Bulletin* June 15, 1897, 6 published an interesting obituary: "There were two sudden deaths in the western part of the city this morning. One of them was Benjamin Jones, of 33 West street, about 61 years of age, who died from the effects of an apoplectic stroke. Mr. Jones seemed to be in his usual health Sunday. He had his dinner and afterwards went out for a walk. He returned to his home in the afternoon and feeling sleepy laid [*sic*] down on a sofa in the parlor. He was soon asleep and breathing regularly. He slept on into the evening and when the members of his family thought it was time to arouse Mr. Jones they attempted to do so but their efforts were of no avail. Notwithstanding every effort was made to arouse the sleeping man he remained unconscious. The family then became alarmed and word was sent for Dr. Frank Putnam. On arrival the doctor saw that Jones had suffered a stroke of apoplexy. Jones lived until this morning at 6 o'clock when death came. During that time he had not regained consciousness once. He would move his arms and legs slightly and at times seemed to comprehend in a slight degree what was being said, but it was only for very brief intervals . . . ." Henrietta was a sister of Oliver LeRoy of the 147th (see below). She and Benjamin are buried in St. Joseph's Cemetery, Auburn.

George Gray Jones – Co. A
b. January 22, 1842 Oneida County, NY
d. May 30, 1924 Long Beach, Los Angeles, CA
m. Martha J. Scovill (*ca.* 1845-*post* 1920) 1867

NOTE: George, son of Orlando H. (1814-1864) and Hannah Jones (1824-?), transferred to 3rd Brigade, 3rd Division, 5th Army Corps Band at an unspecified date. He was a member of Long Beach Post No. 181 GAR. He is buried in Angelus Rosedale Cemetery, Los Angeles. His obituary, published in *The Long Beach Press* May 31, 1924, mentions his daughter Daisy but not Martha so it is possible she predeceased him.

Gilbert R. Jones – Co. G
b. 1842 Scriba, NY
d. February 5, 1863 1st Army Corps General Hospital, Wind Mill Point, VA
m. ------

NOTE: Gilbert, son of Erastus (1821-*ca.* 1901) and Esther Mary Jones (1823-1876), died of "chronic rheumatism." According to *Deaths of Volunteers* he died on February 5, 1863 but *Registers of Officers and Enlisted Men* and *The Town Clerks' Registers* both say the DOD was February 8th. A pension card gives a DOD as October 5, 1863. I use that found in *Deaths of Volunteers*. Erastus successfully applied for a pension in 1887.

Horace Jones – Co. A

b. 1844 Oneida County, NY
d. May 23, 1884 Fulton, NY
m. Selina "Lina" Niles (September 1852-January 19, 1928) *ca.* 1875

NOTE: Horace, brother of George Gray Jones, originally enlisted in the 110th Regiment. He mustered out with the regiment on June 7, 1865. He and Selina were the parents of one child, Luella (1879-?). He is buried in Lewis Cemetery, Granby. Selina married DeWitt C. Whipple (1858-July 15, 1926) in 1886 as his second wife but the marriage did not last. By 1900 he was living with Lucinda Inman (1868-1949) who claimed to be his wife. Selina and Luella were living in Fulton in 1900. Whipple and Lucinda are buried in Morrisville Rural Cemetery. Selina successfully applied for a remarried widow's pension shortly after DeWitt died in 1926. She died in Utica, NY but her grave has not been located.

Isaac Jones – Co. C

b. 1844 Brownville, Jefferson, NY
d. ?
m. ?

NOTE: Isaac was the brother of Amos D. W. Jones. He mustered out with the regiment on June 7, 1865. No further information has been located. His entry in *The Town Clerks' Registers* contains only the names of his parents. He apparently never applied for a pension. It is possible he died shortly after returning home.

Michael Jordan – Co. I

b. 1836 Ireland
d. July 1, 1863 Gettysburg, Adams, PA
m. ?

NOTE: Little has been learned about this man. His brief entry in *The Town Clerks' Registers* says he was born in Ireland in 1840. Crisfield Johnson dated his death to July 3rd but information contained in *The Oswego Commercial Times* July 20, 1863 confirms he was KIA on July 1st. No one applied for a pension.

Albert Juno – Co. G

b. 1844 Phoenix, NY

d. May 5, 1864 Wilderness, VA

m. ------

NOTE: Albert was the son of Augustus (?-April 25, 1862) and Marie Esther Allard Juno (1800-*post* 1870). His entry in *The Town Clerks' Registers* says he was killed at Spotsylvania on May 10, 1864. Esther applied for a mother's pension on June 3, 1864 suggesting a real financial hardship. She alleged in a deposition dated May 27th that her husband had died of consumption and that Albert had supported the family for some time, working in a saw mill for $26.00 a month. She named her other children and detailed why none of them was able to assist her. Albert not only supported her but also a widowed sister, Kate Brady, and her son, John, for several years. Albert gave Esther his bounty money and sent part of his pay to her whenever he was paid. Esther also said she had received charity from the Town of Granby and the Oswego County Superintendent of the Poor. She obtained the pension. Albert's brother George (1835-1917) served in the 81st Regiment.

Augustus Juno – Co. G

b. 1823 Montreal, Canada

d. November 21, 1905 Manlius, Onondaga, NY

m. Almira _____ (June 1835-February 13, 1909) 1854

NOTE: Augustus, the brother of Albert, immigrated to the United States in 1827 as a small child. He was discharged from the service on June 3, 1865 and applied for a pension on June 17th. When his mother, Esther, applied for a pension, she described Augustus as "a poor man and has a wife and three small children and who is now a private in Co. G of the 147th Regiment . . . ." Although Augustus and Almira died in Onondaga County, their bodies were returned to Oswego for burial. They were members of St. Louis' Church and were buried in St. Peter's Cemetery. Augustus' pallbearers were members of the GAR.

Thomas Kane – Co. F

b. 1837 Ireland

d. November 25, 1862 College Park Hospital, Georgetown, DC

m. ?

NOTE: Thomas Kane, whose parents are unknown, originally enlisted in the 110th Regiment but was sent to the 147th. He died of peritonitis, according to *Deaths of Volunteers* which erroneously assigned him to the 147th Pennsylvania Infantry. He is buried in the Soldiers' and Airmen's National Cemetery, Washington, DC.

Michael Kelly – Co. B

b. September 1845 Ireland

d. September 27, 1926 Syracuse, Onondaga, NY

m. Rose Martin (April 1851-April 15, 1913) 1868

NOTE: Michael was the son of Daniel (1816-1893) and Margaret McDonald Kelly (1814-1891). The family immigrated to the United States in 1847. Kelly's experiences in the military rival those of Harvey Heburn. His muster roll card reports he was captured at Spotsylvania, VA on May 21, 1864 and sent first to Richmond on May 25th and then to Andersonville, GA on May 31st. While confined there he became "galvanized," that is, he enrolled in Co. D, 10th Tennessee (CSA) Infantry. He was re-captured at Egypt Station, MS on December 28, 1864 and sent to Alton, IL where he entered the Military Prison on January 23, 1865. On April 14th he enlisted in Co. C, 5th US Volunteers and served until discharged on October 11, 1866 at Fort Kearney, NE. Despite his temporary allegiance to the Confederacy his application for a pension in 1891 was successful. He and Rose, the mother of nine, both died in Syracuse. Their bodies were returned to Oswego and buried in Rural Cemetery, Oswego Town.

George Warren Kennedy – Co. D

b. 1820 Lysander, Onondaga, NY

d. August 8, 1874 Lysander, Onondaga, NY

m. Martha _____ (1825-*post* 1894) *ca.* 1842

NOTE: George, a miller by trade, sometimes was known by his middle name. His father, Dr. Dennis Kennedy (1789-1863), was the first physician in Lysander. In addition to keeping a tavern, he owned a mill which is probably where his son worked. George was discharged from the service for "disability" on May 28, 1863. He applied for a pension on July 20, 1863 but seems not to have obtained it. His gravestone, located in Lysander Union Cemetery, does not contain DOD. That information was taken from the order card for his government stone. His father and his mother, Ann (1794-1834), are also buried there. Martha, the mother of four in 1865, was living with her daughter Ida in Syracuse in 1894, the last year her name appeared in the Syracuse city directory. Her DOD and grave have not been located.

Isaac Eugene Kennedy – Co. B

b. 1841 Allegany County, NY

d. March 31, 1879 Oswego City, NY

m. Julia A. Sherman (1851-May 23, 1900) May 1870

NOTE: Isaac may have been the son of Sidney R. (1808-?) and Julia Ann Kennedy (1808-?). He was discharged from the army on February 12, 1863 at Washington, DC for "disability." On January 3, 1865 he enlisted in the 34th US Infantry in Oswego City and served until he was discharged in Grenada, MS at the end of his term on February 3, 1868. Upon his death the following was published in *The Oswego Morning Herald* April 3, 1879: "At a meeting of former members of DeWolf Hose No. 7, held at the house of Engine Co. No. 1, Mr. Wm. Hancock presiding, the following preamble and resolutions were unanimously adopted: Whereas the Great Chief has summoned our late friend and brother fireman from active duty, and in view of the loss we have sustained by the decease of our former associate, Isaac E. Kennedy, and by the still greater loss sustained by those who were nearest and dearest to him, therefore be it Resolved, that we are grateful to a divine Providence for protection in the hour of danger, when in discharge of our duty as firemen, and that we have all been spared since the organization of DeWolf Hose Co., save the one who has this day been dropped from our roll. Resolved, that we sincerely condole with the Family of the deceased and commend them for consolation to Him, who orders all things for the best, and whose chastisements are merciful. Resolved, That we attend the funeral of our late comrade, and that this heartfelt testimonial of our sympathy and sorrow be forwarded to the family of our departed friend. J. H. Mattoon, Secretary. April 1st." Julia, the mother of at least three children by Kennedy, married John Williamson (1823-December 24, 1900) as his second wife at an unknown date. She gave birth to William Williamson on May 10, 1888. Julia is buried with Isaac and John is buried with his first wife Sarah (1826-1881) in Riverside Cemetery, Scriba.

Engelbert Kerfene – Co. G
b. July 7, 1832 Prussia
d. April 3, 1891 Oswego City, NY
m. Ellen _____ (1832-March 31, 1916) *ca.* 1859

NOTE: This soldier's surname was variously spelled. According to *The Town Clerks' Registers*, it was spelled Korfin, and he was the son of John (?-?) and Catherine Prince Korfin (?-?). His muster roll card spells it Korfen. The spelling on the family gravestone is what I use. Engelbert was wounded on July 1, 1863 at Gettysburg, taken prisoner, and paroled on July 4th. In 1890 he said he had suffered a gunshot wound to his hip. He and Ellen are buried in St. Peter's Cemetery, Oswego.

Elmer S. Kilborn – Co. B
b. 1839 New Haven, NY
d. *post* 1866 ?
m. ?

NOTE: Elmer's story is shrouded in mystery. His father is unknown. His mother Paulina (1819-1858) married for her second husband Horatio Jones (1810-?) who had previously been married to Almira _____ (1817-1852). In 1855 Paulina and Horatio with members of both families were living in New Haven. The couple had a baby, John W. D., two months old. After Paulina died Horatio married Dulcina _____ (1827-1884). In 1860 they were the parents of a baby, Stephen Hollister, five months old. None of the Kilborn children lived at home in 1860. Elmer lived in Oswego City with the Perry family which explains how he happened to enlist in that place. He mustered out with the regiment on June 7, 1865 and successfully applied for a pension on September 14, 1866. After that date, he disappeared. Many of the members of his family are buried in New Haven Rural Cemetery, including his mother and brother Lewis (1845-1878).

Lemuel Weeks Kilby – Co. F

b. September 29, 1829 Camillus, Onondaga, NY
d. May 9, 1907 Ottumwa, Wapello, IA
m. Emma Florilla Kendall (January 1834-July 2, 1903) September 18, 1851

NOTE: Lemuel was the son of John Belden (1789-1883) and Violetta Barnard Kilby (1793-1857). On January 15, 1863 he was discharged from the military for "disability" and later documents reveal that he suffered from rheumatism, bronchitis, and chronic diarrhea for years after leaving the army. Emma's COD was apoplexy. *The Ottumwa Review* May 10, 1907 published the following upon Lemuel's death: "After more than forty years [of] residence in Ottumwa, Lemuel Weeks Kilby, one of the most prominent and progressive of the early settlers of Wapello county, passed to rest at 8:30 o'clock last night at the age of seventy-seven years, eight months, and ten days . . . L. W. Kilby was born in Onondaga county, New York September 29, 1829. He was the son of Mr. and Mrs. John B. Kilby. On September 18, 1851 he was united in marriage to Miss Emma F. Kendall, also of Onondaga county, New York. Mr. and Mrs. Kilby moved to Iowa in 1865 immediately after the close of the civil war, of which Mr. Kilby was a veteran. Mr. Kilby settled in Wapello county about three miles south of Ottumwa. Here he resided for several years, working most of the time in Ottumwa as a contractor. In 1868 he moved into the city and has since resided there. He was one of the best known early contractors in this part of Iowa. Mrs. Kilby passed away July 2, 1903. For the past twenty years Mr. Kilby has been living a retired life in Ottumwa. During his active life he took an interest in the affairs of the city and his death is mourned by a large number of friends." His official COD was "paralysis of the heart." He and Emma are buried in Ottumwa Cemetery.

Alexander King – Co. D

b. September 18, 1825 Cambridge, Washington County, NY

d. October 26, 1900 Volney, NY

m1. Mary J. Smith (1825-1849) *ca*.1845

m2. Emeline Tabitha Chapman Pierce (May 28, 1827-September 13, 1903) 1852

NOTE: The son of Ira (1800-1859) and Eliza King (1800-1835), Alexander had several occupations. According to his daughter, May King Loomis (1866-1936), he taught school, mined for gold in California, and raised flax. Her family history reveals that after he was wounded at Gettysburg in the right arm by a piece of exploding shell, a "little girl fanned him all the afternoon when he was taken to the rear of the lines . . . When he went to a reunion at Gettysburg, thirty years

Alexander King had several careers in his lifetime, including teacher, miner, and flax grower.
Rev. Marshall Hudson-Knapp

afterward, he located the woman who was that child." Loomis continues: "Father was with Grant all through the Wilderness Campaign, was present at the surrender at Appomattox, saw Lee hand his sword to Grant, and saw the Northern Army begin to divide their food with the starved southern troops. He was in the great parade at Washington at the close of the war and shook hands with Lincoln." His discharge dated to June 7, 1865. King was a member of Post Schenck No. 251 GAR in Fulton. Emeline's parents were Deacon John Chapman (1800-1853) and Annis Wood (1801-1862). Annis was first cousin to Almon Wood (1840-May 26, 1863), a member of the 110th Regiment who was killed in an ambush near Franklin, LA. Emeline was first married, according to her daughter, to Almond Pierce (*ca.* 1820-1845) when she was only 16. He reportedly died two years later. She and Alexander, the parents of three children, are buried in Mt. Adnah Cemetery, Fulton.

James Wakefield Kingsley – Co. K

b. March 7, 1842 Pittsfield, Berkshire, MA

d. January 9, 1908 National Soldiers' Home Hospital, Leavenworth, Leavenworth, KS

m. ------

NOTE. James was a son of Oliver (1813-1868) and Laura Borden Kingsley (1813-1862). Known to friends as "Slim Jim," he was a bricklayer by trade. He rose to the rank of first lieutenant and mustered out with the regiment on June 7, 1865. He first entered the Home on March 26, 1886 and said his disability was a gunshot wound to the right shoulder. In 1890, while was staying at the St. Charles Hotel in Lincoln, Lancaster, NE, he elaborated on his disabilities, claiming he had been "wounded in head and left foot by sabre[;] gunshot wound [in] left temple & left thigh." Kingsley's COD was "mitral insufficiency." An obituary appeared in *The Oswego Daily Palladium* on January 13, 1908: "News has been received here of the death on Thursday at the Soldiers' Home, Leavenworth, Kansas, of James Kingsley, a former resident of this city. He was about sixty-eight years old. Mr. Kingsley was a mason by trade and spent his summers in Denver where he worked. He went out to the war with the 147th N. Y. V. and rose to the rank of Second Lieutenant of Company I. He was also a member of Fire Company No. 4 before the war . . . ." He was buried in Leavenworth National Cemetery. His brother, Gale Brewster Kingsley (1837-1900), served in the 24th Regiment NYSV. Their mother was mistakenly identified as Louisa in *The Town Clerks' Registers*.

William Kinney – Co. K

b. 1841 Oswego, NY
d. November 6, 1875 Oswego, NY
m. ------

NOTE: William, a cooper by occupation, was the son of Thomas (1815-*ante* 1875) and Johanna "Annie" Hallihan Kinney (1816-*post* 1875). He was wounded on July 1, 1863 at Gettysburg. He mustered out on June 7, 1865 holding the rank of second lieutenant. He is buried in St. Paul's Cemetery, Oswego City. COD is unknown. An alternate DOD of November 4, 1878, based on the order card for a government headstone, has been proposed.

Llewellyn Laird – Co. F

b. 1839 Onondaga County, NY
d. June 23, 1864 City Point, Virginia
m. ------

NOTE: Llewellyn, son of Chauncey Boyd (1804-1873) and Sally E. Adams Laird (1806-1844), was wounded at Gettysburg on July 1, 1863. He spent time in McDougal Hospital, Fort Schuyler, New York City but succumbed to his wounds in Virginia. He is buried in City Point National Cemetery, Hopewell, VA.

David Lally – Co. I

b. 1841 Ireland
d. April 13, 1902 National Soldiers' Home, Wauwatosa, Milwaukee, WI
m. Sarah Aiken (1844-October 24, 1899) *ca.* 1865

NOTE: David was the son of David (?-?) and Mary Mills Lally (1795-?). He was a painter by occupation. He was transferred to the VRC on September 26, 1863 and discharged at Cincinnati, OH on July 6, 1865. He and Sarah resided in Chicago, IL where she died. David entered the National Soldiers' Home on July 7, 1891, listing varicose veins and rheumatism as his disabilities. His COD was "pulmonary tuberculosis." His body was shipped to Chicago and buried with Sarah in Rosehill Cemetery.

Thomas Lanigan – Co. I
b. 1839 Oswego, NY
d. October 28, 1884 National Soldiers' Home, Roseburg Branch, Hampton, VA
m. ------

NOTE: Thomas, a seaman, was the son of Thomas (1800-?) and Ann Lanigan (1808-?). He was wounded in the wrist and thigh at Gettysburg on July 1, 1863 but mustered out with the regiment on June 7, 1865. He entered the Bath Home on November 24, 1880 but was "summarily" discharged on March 18, 1881. He was admitted to the Roseburg Home on October 10, 1884, dying 18 days later. He is buried in Hampton National Cemetery.

John Lapage – Co. I
b. 1832 Canada
d. ? ?
m. ?

NOTE: John said he was a laborer when he enlisted in Oswego City. He was wounded at Gettysburg on July 1, 1863 and discharged for "disability" on March 4, 1864. No further information is available.

Gideon LaPlante – Co. H
b. 1842 Canada
d. May 30, 1927 St. Hilaire de Rouville, Quebec, Canada
m. Marie Julie Zephinine Cordelia Authier Delisle (April 20, 1859-June 9, 1942) March 25, 1871

NOTE: Gideon, whose name in French was Gedeon Plante and is so spelled on Canadian census records, was a blacksmith when he entered the military, enlisting in Parish, NY. He mustered out with the regiment on June 7, 1865. His entry in *The Town Clerks' Registers*, under Gideon Lapland, contains an interesting remark: "Is still living. Served with the Regt. until it was discharged. Was a good & faithful soldier. Officers say [he] never tried to shirk from duty. Left the states for Canada soon after he was discharged where his parents live." His parents are unidentified. Gideon and Cordelia, the parents of at least six children, are buried in the parish cemetery.

Edward Lawlor – Co. E

b. 1838 New York City, NY

d. ? ?

m. ?

NOTE: Many men had this name but the closest was Edward Lawlor, born 1840 in Ireland. In 1860 he was living with his apparently widowed mother Ann in New York City. It is possible that he was the person who came to the United States in 1859 aboard the Kangaroo and was married to Ann Murphy. This is conjecture. What follows is taken from his muster roll card and *The Town Clerks' Registers*. His entry says he was born in New York City, as does his muster roll card, but in 1840. Why he enlisted in Redfield, NY remains a mystery. He was promoted first to sergeant in September 1862 and then to first lieutenant in 1863. He was wounded at Gettysburg on July 2, 1863 and again at the Wilderness on May 6, 1864. He was finally discharged for "disability" at Annapolis, MD on November 3, 1864. According to *The Town Clerks' Registers*, he returned to New York City. There the trail ends.

Augustin Jesse Laduke, Jr. – Co. A

b. 1844 Canada East

d. ? ?

m. ?

NOTE: Research into this man's life has been hampered by the variety of names he and his parents used. His muster roll card identifies him as Gesler LaDuke, Jr. but other names, such as Gesler LeDuck, Justin LaDuke, and Jessy or Jesse LaDuke, have been found. His father was variously called Jesse and Justin. His mother had several maiden names, ranging from Cassidy/Cassady to Purty to Jolith to Putley and even "unknown." What follows can be taken as fact. This soldier's parents were Augustin Jesse Laduke, Sr. (1818-*post* 1887) and Mary Angeline _____ Laduke (1823-February 8, 1880). Angeline died of asthma in Saginaw, Saginaw, MI and is buried in Oakwood Cemetery. Their son has two entries in *The Town Clerks' Registers*. One merely gives his name as Gesler LaDuke. The other, under the name of Jessy LaDuke, says he lived in Oswego but was born in Canada. His parents were identified as Jesse LaDuke and Angeline Cassady. The entry also says he was wounded at Gettysburg, died from his wounds, and was buried on the field. While the identification of his parents is almost correct, the rest of the entry is definitely false. Laduke's muster roll card states that he was wounded August 27, 1864 at Yellow House, VA. Yellow House or Globe Tavern was part of the Weldon Railroad Campaign fought August 18-21, 1864 and since Robert Spencer sent a letter listing casualties to *The Oswego Daily Palladium* dated August 21, 1864 which was reprinted in *The Mexico Independent* September

1, 1864 and mentioned Justin LaDuke, he must have been wounded prior to the date of the letter. Spencer's letter not only named casualties but also their wounds: ". . . Private Justin LaDuke, Co. A, slightly in side." The 1865 New York census shows the Laduke family was living in Oswego City. Jesse/Justin was among the members of the household, aged 20, born Canada, "in the Army now." It is interesting that in the notes for men in the military located in that census Jesse/Justin was not included! The only other reference to this soldier is contained in *Records and Profiles of Civil War Soldiers* which claimed he survived the war. That may be so but I do not think he survived it by much. On August 18, 1871 his mother, under the name of Angeline Ladd, applied for a pension which she obtained. The state from which the application was filed was not given. At an unknown date the entire family moved to Michigan. Many members, including Justin/Jestin LaDuke, aged 64, widowed, born Canada, were enumerated on the 1880 census. He was living with one of his married daughters. On October 28, 1887 he applied for a pension in Michigan and obtained it. His DOD has not been located. Nowhere is there any mention of the son who went off to war, died at Gettysburg and later was wounded "slightly" in Virginia!

John W. Lavigne – Co. A

b. November 5, 1845 Montreal, Quebec, Canada
d. August 9, 1919 Carrollton, Saginaw, MI
m. Alice Bager (November 15, 1848-April 6, 1921) November 5, 1865

NOTE: The spelling of this soldier's surname on his muster roll card is LeVene. He was wounded at Gettysburg on July 1, 1863. On June 7, 1865 he mustered out with the regiment. He and Alice celebrated their fiftieth wedding anniversary and his 70th birthday in 1915, an event reported in *The Saginaw Daily News* November 6, 1915, 6. His death four years later elicited a lengthy obituary in *The Saginaw News Courier* August 11, 1919, 3: "John W. Lavigne, for more than half a century a resident of Carrollton, died at his home there Saturday midnight of stomach trouble after an illness of six months. He was in his seventy-fourth year. Mr. Lavigne was a veteran of the civil war and during his 52 years' residence in Carrollton held every office within the gift of the people of that township, as well as the position of postmaster of the village for 17 years. He and Mrs. Lavigne, who survives him, celebrated the fiftieth anniversary of their marriage November 5, 1915, simultaneously with his seventieth birthday anniversary. Mr. Lavigne was born in Oswego, N.Y. [*sic*] and lived there until 1863 [*sic*], when he enlisted in the union army and saw active service throughout the remainder of the war. He fought in the battle of Gettysburg. He received his honorable discharge from the service at Oswego at the close of the war, then holding rank as a sergeant in Company A, 147th New York infantry, and the same year was married to Miss Alice Bager. In 1867 Mr. and Mrs. Lavigne came to Carrollton which since has been their home. He was the first police officer of the village and held some village or township office during practically all of his residence there. At various times he was highway commissioner, township clerk, township treasurer, justice of the peace, supervisor and village postmaster. He was a lifelong Republican . . . ." According to his death certificate, COD was carcinoma of the prostate. Alice's death was reported in *The Saginaw News Courier* April 6, 1921, 2: ". . . Mrs. Alice Lavigne, 72 years old, widow of John W. Lavigne, former postmaster and supervisor of Carrollton township, died Wednesday morning at her home on Maple street, Carrollton, of pneumonia. She was born in Covington, N.Y., November 15, 1848, was united in marriage to Mr. Lavigne at Oswego, N.Y. November 5, 1865 and in 1866 came to Carrollton . . . The funeral will take place Friday morning at 9 o'clock from St. John Baptist church, Carrollton . . . ." John and Alice are buried in Mt. Olivet Cemetery, Saginaw.

Horace Gaylord Lee – Co. D

b. November 4, 1837 Fulton, NY

d. March 24, 1904 Wichita, Sedgwick, KS

m1. Sarah E. _____ (January 2, 1851-March 14, 1900) *ca.* 1885

m2. Dora Caroline Nicholas Hadler (February 4, 1855-November 11, 1940) September 30, 1902

NOTE: Horace, a merchant and real estate agent, was the son of Dr. Moses Lindley (1805-1876) and Elizabeth "Betsey" Ann Case Lee (1804-1883) and brother of Brigadier-General Albert Lindley Lee (1834-1907), for whom A. L. Lee Memorial Hospital in Fulton, NY was named. Horace and Sarah were the parents of Howard (1886-1901). Sarah and Howard are buried in Highland Cemetery, Wichita, KS. On June 7, 1902 Horace made a will but at the time he was unmarried so he left everything to his brother, Albert. He never bothered to update the will and after he died Dora found she had been left nothing. She was appointed administratrix of the estate on April 12, 1904. In the end Albert was declared the heir but, to his credit, he turned everything over to Dora. Horace's body was shipped to Fulton and buried in the family plot in Mt. Adnah. Dora, born in Germany, moved to California where in 1917 she applied for a widow's pension. She had previously been married to Conrad H. Hadler (1848-1897) and was the mother of several children. She is buried in Forest Lawn Cemetery, Glendale. Her gravestone erroneously gives a DOB of 1865.

Oliver LeGault – Co. A

b. 1844 Canada

d. July 1, 1863 Gettysburg, Adams, PA

m. ------

NOTE: Very little has been learned about this soldier. His entry in *The Town Clerks' Registers* says he died August 1, 1863. His remains, originally buried on the field, today lie in Gettysburg National Cemetery.

Joseph Lemaine – Co. A

b. 1843 Canada East

d. July 1, 1863 Gettysburg, Adams, PA

m. ------

NOTE: Joseph's surname was also spelled Lemay. He originally enlisted in the 110th Regiment but was sent to the 147th. He was listed under the name Lemay as "killed in action" in *Deaths of Volunteers*. No other information is known but presumably he is buried in Gettysburg National Cemetery.

Very little is known about LeGault, a Canadian who fought and died at Gettysburg.

Michael Sayre

Levi George Lennox – Co. K

b. 1827 Canada West

d. *ca.* 1867 Oswego City, NY

m. Lucinda "Lucy" _____ (1830-January 16, 1905) *ca.* 1852

NOTE: Levi, a sailor, sometimes was known by his middle name. He mustered out with the regiment on June 7, 1865. He was erroneously listed as a member of the 12th NY Cavalry in *The Town Clerks' Registers*. An exact DOD has not been determined but since Lucinda applied for a pension on May 8, 1867 he probably died a few weeks beforehand. His government stone in St. Paul's Cemetery, Oswego City contains no dates. In 1880 Lucinda married Joseph Gordon Lennox (1835-1915) who may or may not have been Levi's brother. Joseph, also a sailor, served first in the 24th Regiment NYSV from May 1861-January 1863. He enlisted in the 24th NY Cavalry on January 19, 1864, serving until May 2, 1864 at which time he transferred to the US Navy. Joseph died at the Bath National Home and is buried in Bath National Cemetery. Lucinda is buried with Levi in St. Paul's Cemetery, Oswego.

Alexander LeRoy – Co. A

b. ? Montreal, Quebec, Canada

d. July 1, 1863 Gettysburg, Adams, PA

m. Adele "Delia" DeRosier (1837-*post* 1880) July 13, 1853

NOTE: When Alexander enlisted he said he was 44 years old but the 1860 census assigned him an age of 35. Until he married Adele, his surname was Rousson. After their marriage he began to use the surname of LeRoy. Originally reported wounded at Gettysburg he died the same day. He and Adele were the parents of Margaret (1854-1930), Medora "Delia" (1857-?), and Helen Sophia (1861-?). A son, Alexander, seems to have died young. Adele married Jackson S. Miller on March 3, 1864 and immediately departed from Oswego, leaving the children in dire straits. Margaret and Delia were living in St. Francis' Orphanage in 1865, completely dependent on family and charity for their support. In 1865 their maternal grandmother, Delia DeRosier, went to court to have herself named the girls' guardian. She alleged that her daughter never returned to claim her children and therefore she had abandoned them. The goal, to obtain pensions for the girls as a soldier's orphans, was successful. Interestingly enough, Adele DeRosier LeRoy Miller, living in North Bay, Oneida, NY applied for a pension in 1880 as Alexander's widow, declaring she had remained unmarried since his death! The outcome of this application is unknown. Adelia disappeared after 1880 and may have remarried.

Oliver LeRoy – Co. A

b. Boharneau, Quebec, Canada

d. May 7, 1913 Oswego City, NY

m. Celestia Serow (1848-August 8, 1925) April 19, 1866

NOTE: Oliver was the son of Joseph (1812-1886) and Margaret Gilly LeRoy (1810-1897). He immigrated to the United States with his family when he was four years old. During his lifetime he worked as a miller and as a boatman. He was wounded in the left knee on July 1, 1863 and spent many months recuperating, not rejoining the regiment until October 4, 1864. He mustered out on June 7, 1865. His obituary was published in *The Oswego Daily Palladium* May 8, 1913, 8: "Oliver Leroy, one of the old and respected residents of the Eighth ward, died at his home, No. 234 East Sixth street, at ten o'clock last night. Deceased has not enjoyed the best of health for the past four years and his death was not unexpected. Born in Canada 70 years ago, Mr. Leroy came to this country when a boy and when the Civil War broke out enlisted in the 147th New York Volunteers and served throughout the entire war, participating in many of the leading battles, including Gettysburg. Mr. Leroy was a charter member of St. Louis's church. Besides his wife, he is survived by five children . . . ." Celestia's death was announced in *The Oswego Palladium-Times* August 10, 1925: "Mrs. Celestia LeRoy, widow of Oliver LeRoy, 78, a well known and highly esteemed resident for many years of the Eighth ward, died at her home . . . late Saturday afternoon after a brief illness. Mrs. LeRoy was born in Prescott, Ontario, and came to this city in 1863, where she lived continuously. She was a member of St. Louis's church and was keenly interested in its welfare. She was a member of St. Ann's Society . . . Funeral will be held on Wednesday morning from the family home at 9 o'clock and at St. Louis's church at 9:30 o'clock." Oliver and Celestia are buried in St. Peter's Cemetery, Oswego City.

Oliver's family came to the United States from Canada when he was a small boy. His descendants have mementoes of the many reunions he attended later in life.
Robert Farrell, great grandson

Samuel LeSage – Co. A
b. 1833 Montreal, Quebec, Canada
d. 1863 Gettysburg, Adams, PA
m. ?

NOTE: This man's parents are unknown. He originally enlisted in the 110th Regiment. His DOD is a matter of some dispute. His muster roll card contradicts itself by saying, "wounded 7/1" as well as "killed 7/1." Other documents such as quarter-master burial cards record his DOD as July 3, 1863. No contemporary newspaper accounts list him among the dead on the first day of fighting. Part of the problem seems to be spelling. *The Utica Morning Herald* July 18, 1863, for example, states: "Samuel Lafarge, A, wounded in left leg badly, broken above knee, doing well." Travis and John Busey, *Union Casualties at Gettysburg: A Comprehensive Record*, say that he died on September 8, 1863 at Letterman Hospital, Gettysburg and was first buried in the hospital's graveyard. Today he lies in Gettysburg National Cemetery.

Levi Palmer Lester – Co. E
b. December 1847 Oswego County, NY
d. December 30, 1910 Fort Madison, Lee, IA
m. Mary Emeline Hurd (1852-1928) 1876

NOTE: Levi, son of Samuel (1810-1881) and Mary Jane Lester (1826-1865), lied in order to enlist, alleging he was 18. He was discharged from the service on February

19, 1865 at Armory Square Hospital, Washington, DC. A GAR roster says discharge occurred because of "wounds" but for an enrollment record for the assessor's office in Kansas he said he left the military because of disease. He and Mary Ann Stevens (1853-1928) produced a son, Jay Durwood (1873-1969), but never married. Later she married Cyrus Stowell (1829-1914), a veteran of the 110th Regiment, as his second wife. According to his FAG entry, Levi was working in a farm implement factory when he died. An obituary appeared in *The* [Lawrence, KS] *Gazette* January 3, 1911, 3: "The body of the late Levi P. Lester, who died of pneumonia last week Friday at his home in Fort Madison, Iowa, arrived here last night, accompanied by his daughter Mrs. Fred W. Fein and Mr. Fein. The body was taken to the Lescher & Power undertaking rooms, from which place the funeral will be held tomorrow. The G.A.R. will have charge of the body at the grave . . . ." Levi was a member of Buford Post No. 189 GAR in Halstead, Harvey, KS. He and Mary are buried in Oak Hill Cemetery, Lawrence.

Benjamin Franklin Lewis – quartermaster
b. October 8, 1817 Redfield, NY
d. April 24, 1883 Orwell, NY
m1. Lura W. Reynolds (January 25, 1821-July 5, 1875) June 15, 1841
m2. Catherine "Kate" Doyle Brayton (December 31, 1842-April 30, 1920) May 5, 1880

NOTE: Benjamin was the son of Friend (1765-1840) and Sarah Bennett Lewis (1787-1862). A Democrat, he was elected to the New York State Assembly for 1850. In 1859 he was appointed postmaster of Orwell. He was commissioned a first lieutenant and quartermaster in August 1862 but only served until January 24, 1863. The reason for his discharge is unknown but contemporary letters from soldiers in the 147th referred frequently to his absences due to illness. He and Lura, the mother of one child, Franklin, are buried in Evergreen Cemetery, Orwell. Catherine was first married to Stephen Brayton (1838-May 13, 1869). In March 1870 the local newspaper reported that Kate had paid $10.00 for his grave. Kate's death elicited the following obituary in *The Pulaski Democrat* May 5, 1920: "Mrs. Kate C. Lewis, who resides in the home [where] she has passed nearly all her life, at Meadow Brook Farm, two miles north of Pulaski, was called from this life Friday morning, between the hours of two and five, when no one was near to see her breathe her last. Mrs. Lewis had been in poor health for some time but her faithful sister, Mrs. Annie Williams, who lived with her, went to her at two o'clock Friday morning and found her comfortable and when she went to her bed at five she spoke to her but received no reply, --she then went closer and found that death had taken her peacefully away. Mrs. Lewis was born in Deerfield, Oneida Co., December 31st, 1842. When a young woman she was united in marriage with Mr. Stephen Brayton. They came to reside on the Brayton farm, two miles north of this village, and after Mr. Brayton's death his widow remained there for a time. Later she united in marriage with Benjamin Lewis and went to Orwell where she resided for a time, then came back to Meadow Brook where she has spent many years. Mrs. Lewis was a person who had worlds of friends. She was of a most sunny nature and lovable disposition . . . Funeral services were held at the home Sunday at two o'clock[;] Rev. Charles N. Olney was present and offered a prayer and then spoke most fitting and timely words over the casket of the loved one. Mrs. Nettie D. Holmes and Mrs. Charles Brooks sang 'Beautiful Isle of Somewhere.' A great number of friends were present, some coming from Deerfield, Oswego, Sandy Creek, Altmar and Orwell." Kate is buried in Pulaski Village Cemetery.

Daniel Bartlett Lewis – Co. H
b. March 4, 1845 Fabius, Onondaga, NY
d. July 17, 1883 Amboy, NY
m. Amanda Betsey Lewis (1845-May 23, 1926) *ca.* 1867

NOTE: Daniel was the son of Christopher (1800-1866) and Emily Phoebe Wood Lewis (1810-?). Following the death of John Hinchcliff and the wounding of William Wybourn during the first day's fighting at Gettysburg, Daniel became the regimental color bearer and was promoted to sergeant. He carried the colors until April 1864. On June 1, 1864 he was seriously wounded at Cold Harbor. He described the wound thus: "[It was a] severe flesh wound through left thigh by minie ball which entirely disabled me from field service." He was subsequently transferred to the VRC and discharged on July 1, 1865. In 1894 during a reunion of the 147th Regiment, H. H. Lyman offered the following resolution which was published in *The Oswego Daily Times* August 30, 1894, 4: "Resolved, That the extra 'Gettysburg Medal of Honor', now in the hands of the secretary [Lyman], be presented with the compliments of this association to Daniel B. Lewis of Amboy, N.Y., son of Daniel B. Lewis, deceased, a brave and honorable soldier, who was for a long time color bearer of our regiment, who after the death of color sergeant Hinchcliff and subsequent wounding of Sergeant Wybourn, gallantly carried our colors through the three days' fighting at Gettysburg, as well as many other severe engagements, and whose conspicuous bravery and devotion to duty did credit to his regiment and great honor to himself and his posterity . . . ." Daniel and Amanda, daughter of Thomas Jefferson (1808-1892) and Betsey Stone Luke Lewis (1813-1904), are buried in Amboy Center Cemetery. When her will was admitted to probate, it was revealed that she made an interesting request: she wanted her family to visit her grave at least once a year and ensure that it be "suitably cared for." Daniel Lewis was the brother of John Wood Lewis (1833-1864), a member of the 110th Regiment who died at Key West, FL of yellow fever.

Henry James Lewis – Co. G

b. 1848 Mexico, NY

d. October 31, 1881 County Poor House, Sennett, Cayuga, NY

m. Eliza A. Foster (1842-June 21, 1907) November 6, 1866

NOTE: Henry was the son of James (1822-1892) and Betsy Stoutenger Lewis (1826-June 6, 1858). He lied about his age in order to enlist in the 147th. His military career was cut short when he developed rheumatism and spent considerable time in the hospital. He never recovered from the disease. On November 13, 1863 he transferred to the VRC and was discharged from the service on June 23, 1865 at Camp Cleveland, OH after another soldier's gun fell to the floor and accidentally discharged, hitting Henry in the hip. In 1879 he applied for and received a pension, having been bedridden and unable to work in months. His disability was serious enough that it was noted on the 1880 census. Dr. D. B. Horton examined him in January 1881 and declared him completely disabled since all his joints were enlarged, tender or stiffened. His right hand was "worse than useless" and he needed constant care since he could not even feed himself or attend to personal hygiene. According to Dr. Horton, ". . . he was worse than anyone I ever saw. He was a most pitiable object to behold. He was almost in a dying condition at the time." Henry and Eliza were the parents of six children, though in 1880 three of them were living with neighbors because the family was so poor. On October 25, 1881 Henry was admitted to the Cayuga County Poor House. He died there six days later and was buried in the poor house cemetery with a number on his gravestone. Eliza, who had been born in England and immigrated to the United States in 1848 with her parents, applied for and received a widow's pension. In 1900 she lived with son George (1877-?) in Butler, Wayne, NY. By 1905 she was living in Wolcott, Wayne, NY with her son Richard (1875-?). I have not located her grave.

Franklin Lince – Co. H

b. February 1841 Rome, Oneida, NY

d. December 11, 1862 Finley Hospital, Washington, DC

m. ------

NOTE: Lince, the son of John (?-?) and Alvira Moores Lince (?-?), was a boatman. He died of typhoid fever or bronchitis, depending on the source of information. A letter sent by Captain Reuben Slayton, dated December 23, 1862 and published in *The Mexico Independent* January 1, 1863, offers insight into his untimely end: "Again I am compelled to ask you [the editors] to record the death of another volunteer of my company. Franklin Lynch [sic], of Constantia, died at Finley Hospital, Washington, D.C., December 11. His disease was bronchitis. His funeral took place at 3 o'clock, Dec. 12. He was about 20 years of age, and when well he was always ready and prompt to do his duty as a soldier . . . ." He is buried in the Soldiers' and Airmen's Home National Cemetery, Washington, under the name Lynce. A cenotaph for him stands in Constantia Center Cemetery.

Briggs Lindsey – Co. E

b. 1841 Sandy Creek, NY

d. June 23, 1914 Homer, Calhoun, MI

m. Mary Azubah Pendleton (September 15, 1847-January 12, 1914) October 5, 1870

NOTE: This man's parents were Robert (1797-1856) and Harriet Briggs Lindsey (1804-1881). On February 1, 1864 he was discharged for "disability" which must have been severe since he applied for a pension on July 19th. He and Mary were married in Quincy, Branch, MI. In 1910 she said she was the mother of three, all living. Mary died in Litchfield, Hillsdale, MI of arthritis and chronic bronchitis. Six months later Briggs died of apoplexy and heart disease. His death was announced in *The Sandy Creek News* July 2, 1914, 4: "Gilford Lindsey has received the sad news that his uncle, Briggs Lindsey, died June 23, 1914, at Litchfield, Mich. He was about 71 years old, and was a brother of Asa Lindsey, who resides in the western part of the town and was well known in Sandy Creek in years gone by. He was a soldier in the Civil war and was a member of the 147th regiment, New York Infantry." Briggs and Mary are buried in Mount Hope Cemetery, Litchfield.

Daniel Linihin – Co. I

b. 1841 ?

d. *post* 1863 ?

m. ?

NOTE: Daniel's surname may have been Lenahan. Such a person was listed in the Oswego city directory in 1862, working at the Kingsford starch factory. His POB was noted as Oswego, NY on his muster roll card but it is more likely he was born in Ireland since he seems to have no history until 1862. He was discharged for "disability" on June 12, 1863 and promptly disappeared. He did not apply for a pension and it is possible he died soon after leaving the military.

James White Lish – Co. K

b. March 26, 1834 New Jersey

d. February 23, 1917 Wilmington, Grundy, IL

m. Lucinda Barker (January 1, 1842-January 9, 1898) January 28, 1858

NOTE: James, whose parents were Byrum (1807-1885) and Jane White Lish (1815-1835), was a painter. He was wounded at Gettysburg on July 1, 1863 and spent time in the hospital at Fort Schuyler, New York City. He was discharged on June 20, 1865 at Washington, DC. He and Lucinda, the mother of at least three children, were married in Kankakee, IL. They lived in Scriba, NY in 1860 but their son, Charles H., 2, was born in Illinois. James and Lucinda are buried in Essex North Cemetery, IL.

John H. Lloyd – Co. I
b. November 11, 1837 Sterling, Cayuga, NY
d. March 28, 1884 West Spring Creek, Warren, PA
m. Clarissa Sanderson (June 4, 1839-June 23, 1913) *ca.* 1858

NOTE: John's parents were John (?-*ante* 1865) and Susan Furber Lloyd (1798-*post* 1870). He was a farmer by occupation. According to *The Town Clerks' Registers*, on June 2, 1864 at Cold Harbor, VA John was "wounded in left thigh [and] ball remains." He was transferred to Co. H, 14th VRC on November 7, 1864 and discharged at Washington, DC on July 1, 1865. Although he and Clarissa spent most of their married life in Sterling, by 1880 they were living in Pennsylvania. His COD is unknown but that ball may have had something to do with it. In 1890 Clarissa said that her husband had been "shot through left leg & hip." Interestingly enough, Clarissa's parents were William (?-?) and Dorothy Furber Sanderson (?-?). John and Clarissa, who died in Concord, Erie, PA, are buried in West Spring Creek Cemetery. Her COD was arteriosclerosis.

Daniel C. Louth – Co. B
b. November 1833 Hess Darmstadt, Germany
d. February 19, 1915 Oswego City, NY
m. Caroline Eick (1851-September 23,1926) 1870

NOTE: Daniel's parents were Johann Friedrich (1811-1846) and Johanna Margaretta Magdalena Bauer Louth (1810-?). He immigrated to the United States in 1851 and became a naturalized citizen. He was wounded at Cold Harbor in June 1864 but was able to muster out in June 1865. He and Caroline were the parents of at least six children but by 1900 the couple was no longer living together. His obituary appeared in *The Oswego Daily Times* February 19, 1915, 6: "Daniel Louth, one of the oldest members of St. Paul's Lutheran church of this city, and a well-known veteran of the Civil War, died this morning at 8:30 o'clock at

Daniel Louth was active in the GAR after the end of the war.
Aleta Klahn McLain

the home of his daughter, Mrs. J. W. Muldoon, 37 John street, after a long illness. He was born in Germany eighty-two years ago, but came to this country 67 years ago and in 1862 went to the front in the Civil War as a member of Company B, 147th N.Y. Volunteers, and served until the close of the war, when the regiment was mustered out of service. He was a member of Post O'Brian, G.A.R., and had many friends in this city who will learn of his death with regret. He lived for a time in Oswego Center, but of late years had made his home in this city . . . ." He is buried in Rural Cemetery, Oswego Town. After his death Caroline applied for and obtained a widow's pension. She died in Ogdensburg, NY and is buried in Lewis Cemetery, Granby.

John Love – Co. A

b. 1841 Ireland

d. January 30, 1870 Oswego City, NY

m. Margaret M. Hanes (January 1846-February 7, 1934) *ca.* 1862

NOTE: John's DOB varies from 1841 to 1844. I use that on his muster roll card. He was wounded on July 1, 1863 at Gettysburg and subsequently transferred to the VRC. He was discharged from that organization on June 27, 1865 at Washington, DC. The 1870 Mortality Schedules indicate John died of consumption. Margaret, whose parents were Henry (1796-?) and Sarah Hanes (1815-?), never remarried. In 1900 she said she was the mother of three children, of whom one survived. She and John are buried in Riverside Cemetery, Scriba. He had originally been buried in Hall Road Cemetery, Scriba, but his body was moved on July 30, 1901. His father, Andrew Love (?-August 30, 1862) enlisted in Co. E, 14th USA on November 9, 1861 at Elmira, NY. He claimed to be 30 but unless he was only 11 years old when John was born, that number cannot be accurate. It is more likely he was 40. Andrew was KIA at the battle of Bull Run, VA on August 30, 1862. His gravestone in Riverside Cemetery is in all likelihood a cenotaph. I have not identified John's mother.

Francis Lovine – Co. D

b. 1823 Canada

d. July 7, 1895 National Soldiers' Home, Bath, Steuben, NY

m1. Mary _____ (1813-September 23, 1879) *ca.* 1838

m2. Agnes _____ Goodroe (1821-December 17, 1899) March 1880

NOTE: This soldier's parents are unknown. The family surname was variously spelled. I use that appearing on his gravestone. He was discharged from the service for "disability" on May 19, 1865 at Campbell Hospital, Washington, DC. He experienced several medical problems while in the service, a hernia at Aquia Creek; typhoid fever; sunstroke at Laurel Hill. In 1890 he claimed "general debility" and "breach." When he entered the Bath National Home on May 18, 1895 his disabilities included sunstroke, hernia, rheumatism, paraplegia, and "senile condition generally." His COD two months later was paraplegia. His remains were shipped to Fulton in care of his son-in-law, Charles Vogelsang. Francis and Mary are buried in Mt. Adnah Cemetery. Agnes Goodroe and her first husband John (1809-April 1, 1869) were neighbors of Mary and Francis. They are buried in Granby Center Cemetery.

Louis Joseph Alfred Lukin – Co. A
b. 1842 Canada East
d. November 21, 1862 Regimental Hospital, Camp Morris, Tennallytown, DC
m. ------

NOTE: A letter from "A Volunteer" to the editors of *The Mexico Independent* December 4, 1862 and dated November 24, 1862 announced Alfred's death: ". . . Two deaths have occurred recently. One was a young man named Lukin, of company A. He died on Thursday morning last, after a brief illness. His friends started a subscription among the boys of his company, and in 24 hours raised $100 for the purpose of embalming the body and sending it home. His people live, I believe, in Canada . . . ." Alfred died from typhoid fever. His mother, Hermengilde Matte Lukin, whose address was Napierville, Quebec, Canada, applied for a pension in 1869, claiming that her husband Jean-Baptiste Lukin had died on September 18, 1852. Alfred was her sole means of support for four years prior to entering the service. He had also sent her $80 which constituted part of his bounty money. She was granted the pension and at her death on June 2, 1887 she was receiving $12.00 per month. Graves for this family have not been located.

Alphonse Lukin – Co. B
b. 1841 Canada East
d. *post* 1872 probably California
m. Mary Adele Senecal (1843-February 19, 1871) October 18, 1866

NOTE: Alphonse was Alfred's brother, although published family trees do not include him. He was discharged for "disability" on February 13, 1863. He may have enlisted in Co. K, 59th PA militia which saw service from June 15-September 9, 1863. On January 25, 1864 he enlisted in Co. I, 153rd NYSV at Washington, DC. He was wounded in action on September 19, 1864 and spent time in hospital in Philadelphia. According to the records he had "not been heard from since wounded at Opequan, VA – no discharge furnished or muster out of organization." Since Alphonse did not apply for a pension it probably means he deserted. He married Mary Adele Senecal, born in Canada, in Lowell, MA. The couple, together with their daughter, Mary Elias

[Eloise?], 2, were living in Rocklin, Placer, CA in 1870. Alphonse was a clerk in a store. Mary Adele died in San Francisco and was originally buried there. Today she lies in Holy Cross Catholic Cemetery, Colma, San Mateo, CA, one of "nearly 40,000 deceased who [were] reinterred from a San Francisco cemetery to the Holy Cross section called Calvary." What happened to the child is unknown although a woman named Mary Lukins, DOB unknown, died on August 18, 1918 and was buried in Rose Hills Memorial Park, Whittier, Los Angeles, CA. Alphonse's ultimate fate is unknown but an article published in Stockton's *Daily Evening Herald* December 13, 1871, 3 sheds some light on his activities after his wife's death: "Three men were examined by Drs. Stockton and Thorndike, at the County Jail, last evening, and were found to be insane. They were committed to the Asylum by order of Judge Greene. Their names are James Welch, Alfonzo [*sic*] Lukins and _____ Laclaa. Welch has been in the Asylum before; Lukins is the man who was injured by falling into a cellar on main street last Saturday night, and Laclaa is a stranger, in relation to whom no information can be obtained." The asylum to which the article referred was the Stockton State Hospital and its record for Alphonse is still extant. His age was given as 28 and he had been in California for eight years and was "probably" married: "The evidence of insanity is general appearance and inability to converse connectedly; is neither homicidal, suicidal nor incendiary; this attack appeared last summer, disease increasing; no rational intervals; no hallucinations; is dangerous to himself for want of care; is not disposed to injure others; is not filthy or distinctive; has probably used wine to excess; has been injured on the head; class of insanity, probably dementia. Condition of patient when received about the same as represented above. Had the appearance of cuts on the head." Alphonse was released on January 5, 1872. There is no record of his movements after that date. It is interesting to note that in 1863, Alphonse, claiming to be 47, attempted to get his mother a pension as her "attorney in fact" in Philadelphia. The effort was unsuccessful. Yet another Lukin brother, Peter Hector (1838-1921), served in Co. E, 98th NYSV. He died in Montana and is buried in St. Michael's Catholic Cemetery, Browning. His wife was Mary Last Calf (1844-1919), a Native American.

John Lumprey – Co. K
b. May 5, 1844 Oswego, NY
d. ? ?
m. ?

NOTE: This man began life as John Morgan. On the 1850 federal and the 1855 New York censuses he was living with Louis/Lewis (?-February 10, 1878) and Frances Meyers Lumprey (1806-*ante* 1870) in Oswego City. The 1855 census specifically states he was an orphan. By 1862, however, he had assumed their surname. The

1865 New York census again showed the family in Oswego. John, 20, was single and in the army. He was wounded at Gettysburg on July 1, 1863 but mustered out with the regiment on June 7, 1865. In 1870 John was living in Oswego City with Joseph Lumprey, 85. This man is probably Lewis/Louis. When Lewis died the local newspapers published lengthy articles, focusing on his age – some estimates had him as old as 95 -- and the stories he liked to tell about working in the fur trade and avoiding the draft in Canada during the War of 1812. He had lived in the poor house for over a year before his death. In 1850 he was 55 years old, making him 83 when he died, provided he told the truth. Between 1850 and 1855 he only aged a year! None of the articles mentioned any family members but the 1875 Oswego city directory shows a John Lumprey living there even though he did not appear on the 1875 census. It is altogether possible that John left Oswego *ca.* 1875 for parts unknown. The mystery deepens: on May 1, 1900 John Morgan, veteran of Co. K, 147th Regiment, applied for a pension but did not secure it. The card does not show where the claim was filed. Is this John Lumprey using his birth name? Did he die before completing the process? No other men in any company of the 147th had this surname. Even among the deserters there was no one named John Morgan.

Henry Harrison Lyman – Co. C
b. April 15, 1841 Lorraine, Jefferson, NY
d. May 4, 1901 Oswego City, NY
m1. Flora T. Clark (1841-February 21, 1866) September 16, 1862
m2. Emily Vorce Bennett (March 29, 1842-July 12, 1938) May 2, 1867

NOTE: H. H. Lyman, as he was frequently called, was the son of Silas (1794-1883) and Cynthia Waugh Lyman (1799-1883). He was one of the most prominent members of the 147th Regiment. His death was widely reported, for, example, *The New York Press, Utica Sunday Journal, Buffalo Courier, Rochester Democrat and Chronicle*, to name only a few. *The Oswego Daily Times* May 6, 1901, 4 provided a lengthy, informative obituary which is excerpted here: "Henry Harrison Lyman, for many years one of the city's oldest and distinguished citizens passed quietly away at the family residence Saturday night at 8:45 o'clock . . . Mr. Lyman had been low for several days and his death had been momentarily expected. He grew gradually weaker until six o'clock Saturday evening when he lost consciousness and continued in that state until peacefully passed out of this life. The news of his sad death spread rapidly about the city and expressions of sincere sorrow were heard on every side. Few men were better known than Mr. Lyman and the ending of so brilliant a career cast a deep gloom over the entire community. His death was due to heart and nervous troubles. His former robust constitution was severely tested the first year as State Excise Commissioner and after organizing the department he was obliged to return to this city for a rest. In February last he contracted the grip in Albany and was confined to his bed in that city several weeks. This was the beginning of his physical breakdown. His heart, which had been affected, began to give him trouble and several weeks ago he returned to this city and took to his bed . . . his condition was not considered serious until about three weeks ago. His illness then took a more serious turn and Dr. H. Eisner, a Syracuse specialist, was called into consultation. He made a careful examination and stated that Mr. Lyman was beyond earthly aid and his death was only a question of a short time. He displayed wonderful vitality throughout his illness and was able to converse with his faithful [?] and children up to within a few hours of his death. Mr. Lyman was a self-made man in every sense of the word. As a soldier he showed the same bravery and ability as he did when administering the affairs of several public positions which he so ably held. He was a kind and loving husband and father and loved his home above all other earthly things. Whether on the streets of Oswego or in his busy office at Albany he was the same democratic fellow and the pity is that he could not be spared longer. Mr. Lyman was born at Lorraine, Jefferson County, in 1841 . . . When a boy he worked upon his father's farm attending the district school when in session, until 1856, from which time to 1859 he attended the Pulaski Academy, teaching school in winters. Having made a special study of surveying and engineering he was employed in that business from 1859 to 1862. In the summer of 1862 he enlisted as a private in the One Hundred and Forty-Seventh New York Volunteers and served with that regiment until his discharge in 1865 having been promoted through various grades to that of Adjutant and Brevet Major. At the Battle of the Wilderness Mr. Lyman, then the Adjutant of the regiment, was captured by the Southern forces and for some time was held a prisoner at Macon, Savannah, Charleston, and Columbia prisons. He was a brave and competent officer and was very popular with the men under him. He took an active part in all of the engagements in which the regiment participated and for great bravery he was brevetted a Lieutenant Colonel. He was an active member of Post O'Brien, G.A.R., and was a conspicuous figure at all of the annual reunions of the 147th Regiment and in 1898 he prepared and had published an interesting history of the Regiment. In 1866 he was appointed Lieutenant Colonel by Governor Fenton to organize a second regiment of National Guard in Oswego County but early in 1868, it having been decided to reduce rather than increase the Guard, his regiment was disbanded and he left the service. At the close of the war Mr. Lyman engaged in the hardware business in the village of Pulaski, N.Y. It was in 1871 that he made his first appearance in county politics and he quietly became one of the principal leaders and advisers. His first public position was that of Supervisor and he represented the town of Richland in 1871 and again in 1872. His ability as a public officer was readily recognized and in 1873 he was unanimously nominated for Sheriff of the county. His election by a handsome majority followed and he then moved from Pulaski to this city. His administration of affairs was pleasing to the taxpayers of the county and he served until 1876 when he was appointed Deputy County Clerk, which position he held until John J. Lamoree was made collector of the port and he selected him as his deputy. For several years he was superintendent of the Oswego Water Works Company, during which time the same was largely improved. He resigned this position to become collector of the port under President Harrison, serving from 1889 to 1898. Upon the consolidation of the Fish and Game with the Forest Board and the organizing of the Fisheries, Game and Forest Commission he was made a member of the commission by Governor Levi P. Morton. It was his first State position and although he only served for a year he made a record which will long be remembered. He succeeded in bringing about any number of reforms in the way of reducing expenses and improving the management of affairs. He went at his work in a fearless manner and his great efficiency attracted the attention of all of the public officers with whom he came in contact, including Governor Morton. When the State liquor tax law was passed in 1896 it was feared that the enforcement of the new law would hurt the Republican administration. It gave unlimited power to the State Excise Commissioner and it was felt that the office required an honest and capable man, one with great ability as an organizer. Governor Morton who had been watching the work of Mr. Lyman while on the Fish and Game Commission was quick to appreciate his value and selected him as State Excise Commissioner. The responsibility of the success of the Raines law rested almost entirely upon him and the wisdom of the Governor's choice has been demonstrated over and over again. It would have been difficult to find another man who would have administered the affairs of the department in such a thorough business way. For the first two years he worked early and late and all of the details of the office received his personal attention. He finally succeeded in organizing one of the strongest and most business-like departments in the State. Not a word of criticism was ever heard and his grand, good work was recognized a short time ago when he was reappointed by Governor Odell and on the same evening the Senate unanimously confirmed his nomination . . . Mr. Lyman attended the Church of the Evangelists and gave liberally to charity. He was Vice President and Director of the First National Bank, a Director and Secretary of the Oswego Water Works Company, Trustee of the Oswego City Savings Bank. He was also a member of the Fortnightly and City Clubs of this city, the Loyal Legion and the Fort Orange Club of Albany. He was the author of several books including the genealogy of the Lyman family which was issued in December last and copies of which have been distributed among his relatives and friends. 'A Cruise Among the Bermudas' was the title of another book the material for which was gathered by Mr. Lyman over a year ago when he visited the islands with his wife on a pleasure trip." This brief biographical sketch cannot possibly do justice to the esteem with which the Oswego community held H. H. Lyman. His widow received telegrams of condolences from men of all walks of life beginning with the governor himself. She even got a telegram from Lt. Johnson, CSA, the man who had captured Lyman and relieved him of his sword. Many years later the two men met again and Johnson returned the sword to its rightful owner. Among the mourners was George Washington, a black man who had accompanied Lyman to New York State and had become a clerk in his hardware store. Emily, Lyman's wife, never remarried. When she died *The Oswego Palladium-Times* July 12, 1938, 7 published the following: "Mrs. Emily V. Lyman, 96, wife of the late Col. Henry H. Lyman . . . died at 9 o'clock Tuesday morning in the family home . . . where she has lived continuously for 63 years. Mrs. Lyman had been in declining health since January. Prior to that

Henry Harrison Lyman was one of Oswego's best known and influential residents who spent much of his adult life in the service of his country and his fellow citizens.

New York State Military Museum

time she had been quite well. Native of Pulaski, this county, Mrs. Lyman was born March 29, 1842, the daughter of David and Margaret Frasier Bennett, pioneer residents of that village. Her mother was a native of Scotland. She was educated in the Pulaski schools. Her marriage to Henry Lyman, also of Pulaski, took place May 2, 1867 and was a happy union . . . Mrs. Lyman was his trusted helpmate and counselor during his years of success and eminence, but her preference was for activities of the home and family. Her charm of personality, coupled with sincerity of purpose and friendly interest, attracted many friends. She [?] those happy relations and treasured the confidence and love of all who came to know her. Mrs. Lyman never lost touch with life, and enjoyed the contacts with visitors to her home. She was a devout member of the Church of the Evangelists, attending services regularly as long as her health permitted. Too, she was a member of the societies of that parish and of the Episcopal diocese of Central New York . . . Funeral services will be privately held from her late home . . . Thursday afternoon at 2 o'clock . . . ." Henry, also a member of Pulaski Lodge No. 415 F & AM, and Emily are buried in Riverside Cemetery, Scriba. Flora is buried with her parents in Pulaski Village Cemetery.

William Lyon – Co. F

b. 1830 Sandy Creek, NY

d. February 25, 1863 Regimental Hospital, Belle Plain, VA

m. ------

NOTE: The POB on his muster roll card is Sandy Creek and, if that is correct, he may have been born after his father died. According to his mother Fanny's pension file, her husband Abram Lyon, died in Penfield, Monroe, NY on April 23, 1830. She applied for William's pension at the age of 63 and her recollection of dates may have been somewhat blurry. Her testimony, however, is the best available information and forms the basis for this sketch. She married Jeremiah Cummings (1776-August 22, 1859), veteran of the War of 1812, on June 17, 1837 as his second wife and bore him several children. When several of his sons migrated to Dunn County, Wisconsin Jeremiah went with them, the plan being that after things were settled Fanny and her daughters would follow. That, however, was not to be. His stepfather died in Wisconsin and William, whose surname is also spelled Lyons, became his mother's sole support. Depositions given by neighbors and friends attested to the fact that he used much of his pay to buy food, wood, and clothing for his mother. He originally enlisted in the 110th Regiment but was sent to the 147th. He gave her part of his bounty money and sent money to her from his Army paychecks. His untimely death of pneumonia left her practically destitute. William, as revealed in a deposition by Capt. Cyrus Hartshorn, became ill on the "Mud March" and only with difficulty was able to return to camp: ". . . William Lyons complained of being unwell and that he had taken cold and felt very bad but with assistance succeeded in returning with his company to camp and that he was immediately taken to the Regt. hospital and was taken with a fever and soon deranged and continued to grow worse for about two weeks . . . ." Hartshorn left the military about this time and another witness, Benjamin O. Baker, finished the tale: ". . . and deponent states that he saw said Lyons each day while he was sick until he died of Chronic Diarrhea and deponent states that he helped make his coffin and helped dig his grave and bury him . . . ." Although Baker claimed his friend died of chronic diarrhea, all official records say he died of pneumonia or "inflammation of the lungs." Meanwhile Fanny was dependent on charity and the kindness of neighbors to sustain herself. She testified that she was trying to earn money through her own labor but her age made that difficult. She owned no property of any kind except a few clothes which William had purchased for her. The unnamed persons with whom she was living contacted the overseer of the poor in the town of Volney to assist her. A collection was taken by her son-in-law, Jeremiah "Jerry" Dawley (1840-1906) which helped temporarily. The entire process of applying for the pension occupied the better part of five years but finally on August 20, 1868 Fanny obtained her son's pension retroactive to February 25, 1863.

On both the 1870 and the 1880 censuses Fanny was enumerated in the Dawley household. Her daughter, Mary Cummings, was Dawley's wife. Mary's obituary in *The Mexico Independent* June 20, 1935, 1 stated she had been born in Sandy Creek on February 14, 1837 which probably means Fanny and Jeremiah Cummings were married in 1836, not 1837, as Fanny remembered when applying for her pension. The last known reference to Fanny occurred in 1883 when she was named on the Oswego County Pension List. Jerry and Mary are buried in Mexico Village Cemetery. "Mother Cummings" is also there but no dates are given on her stone.

John A. MacDonald – Co. K
b. 1843 Canada
d. July 17, 1908 Chicago, Cook, IL
m. Louisa Peters (April 4, 1848-October 29, 1925) *ca.* 1871

NOTE: John, whose parents are unidentified, was a sailor by occupation. After enlisting in the 147th he rose through the ranks, eventually becoming a second lieutenant. He was wounded on July 1, 1863 at Gettysburg, mustering out with the regiment on June 7, 1865. He also served in Co. H, 1st US Cavalry. In 1880 he was living in Chicago with Louisa and two sons, Fred (1871-?) and Charles (1879-?). He gave "peddler" as his occupation. In 1900 John was working in a bookstore. Next door to him and Louisa were her parents, Carl (1819-?) and Dorothea Peters (1819-?). They had been born in Germany, as was Louisa. Although he died in Illinois an obituary for John appeared in *The Oswego Daily Times* July 22, 1908: "David Welsh of 200 East Bridge Street has received word of the death of John A. McDonald [*sic*], a former Oswegonian which occurred in Chicago July 17. Mr. McDonald lived in Oswego before the Civil War and was employed as a bartender in the saloon which stood at the corner of East First and Bridge Streets where the Metropolitan restaurant is now located. Mr. McDonald served through the war as Second Lieutenant of Company K, 147th Regiment, and shortly after left for Chicago where he has since made his home. Many friends and former comrades of Mr. McDonald will regret to learn of his death." John and Louisa are buried in Montrose Cemetery, Chicago. The square and compass design on his gravestone attests to his membership in the Masonic fraternity.

Guilford Dudley Mace – Co. F
b. 1832 Oswego County, NY
d. July 1, 1863 Gettysburg, Adams, PA
m. Catherine E. Farrell (April 1837-December 30, 1910) April 14, 1856

NOTE: Guilford was the son of Amos (1800-1884) and Hannah/Anna Ferris Mace (1800-1882). A mechanic by profession, he married Catherine in New York City.

His two older children, Catherine (1858-?) and Amos (1861-?), were born there. He and Catherine were living in Palermo, NY when he enlisted. The youngest child, Guilford, was born May 23, 1863 while his father was away fighting. Guilford began his military career as a private but by January 1863 he had been promoted to 1st sergeant. A letter he sent to an uncle from Belle Plain, VA and dated January 28, 1863 bears witness to his disgust with officers in general and Captain Cyrus Hartshorn in particular. It is excerpted here: ". . . For the last two months we have been guarding the sacred port of Virginia and trying to keep ol' Johnny Rebel from routing Uncle Abraham from his very comfortable quarters at Washington. No man has the least idea of soldiering in the field until he takes a hand at it himself. Some of our milk and water officers of a [?] turn of mind have concluded that they were not made for the business and have resigned. Among the rest – our Wooden Capt. – who made such great promises while raising his company and who has fulfilled them in such a cowardly and contemptible manner. He started for home this morning [and] the men rejoice that he has gone. If your Country is ever called upon to raise more men never put a man in for an office who is not willing to enlist as a private . . . They come here for the pay alone and care nothing for these men or the country. Our company has been nearly ruined by the Capt. Some of them have deserted [and] others have become discouraged under his mismanagement and sickened and died. We now report 51 men present 24 absent in the various hospitals of Philadelphia and Washington. Some of those will probably be returned to duty but the majority will be discharged for disability. Our 1st lieut. McGridley [Chauncey Gridley] has sent in his resignation which will probably be accepted. He is a man we all love and respect and shall be sorry to part with him. Our second Lieut. [Horace] Lee will try for the captaincy of the Co. I expect to get a commission either 1st or 2nd Lieut. The Capt's position belongs to me by right but a man cannot get his rights when there are rich men's sons to be provided for[;] at least that has been my experience. I like the business well enough if it has got to be done. I am in good health and can sleep in the water several inches deep without great inconvenience. We had a march in the mud for the last week and got stuck and have had to return to our old quarters at this place. Such a bedlam as an army on the march makes you cannot conceive especially if it storms and the soil is clay of the stickiest kind[;] however our lads stood it well. Will Ure, Jud Dolbear and others with whom you are acquainted went through it like old veterans. It rained all last night and to cap the climax, it is snowing today . . . ." Mace was promoted to 1st lieutenant when Gridley resigned. His death was graphically reported in *The Mexico Independent* July 16, 1863: "The details of the late battle near Gettysburg are very meager, and slow in coming in, but we learn by a few letters from the men that Co. F, 147th regiment, was almost annihilated, nearly all of them being killed, wounded or prisoners. In addition to the loss of our men, we are pained to learn of the death of Lieut. G. D. Mace, who was in command of the company. He fell on Wednesday, the first day of the battle, at the head of his company while gallantly leading them against the rebels. He was wounded slightly, but would not leave the field, and when he saw the regiment falling back, he stood in front cheering his men, and said, 'Do not fall back, boys, but give the rebels what they deserve;' when he was struck by a ball and mortally wounded, and almost at the same time he was literally torn in pieces by the explosion of a shell. Thus fell one of the noblest men that have been sent forth from Oswego county to do battle for their country. Through his efficiency, Co. F was pronounced by their Colonel to be one of the best in the regiment. Mr. Mace has stood by his company through evil as well as good report, and it is thought he has never been absent from his post of duty a single day since he left Oswego . . . ." A friend, identified only as H. N. G., eulogized Mace in an article appearing in *The Fulton Patriot and Gazette* August 1863 and is excerpted here: "Among the names of the many noble heroes who fell at the battle of Gettysburg, none, perhaps, are more deserving of a word of praise than that of Lieut. Guilford D. Mace. I knew him well. Fifteen years ago he was a class-mate at Falley Seminary, and although then but a youth of fifteen summers, his quick perception and his wonderful capacity for learning made him older than his class. He became a splendid scholar. This, together with his kind and genial nature, won for him many warm friends. In after years he visited Brooklyn, entered the profession of ship building, and soon rose to the position of master mechanic. One year ago he visited his native town of Volney. It was about the time the Government was so loudly calling for volunteers . . . He fell on Wednesday, July 1st, in the first engagement, at the terrible battle at Gettysburg, while gallantly leading his men. He was first wounded slightly . . . Col. Miller writes to his brother that he was first shot in the neck, then he was hit in the back, which broke it; and while lying on the field, among his wounded men, conscious that he must die, sent word to me, to write to his wife, and tell her he was killed. He had not more than told it, before a shell exploded, blowing him all to pieces, and killing several more men lying near him. 'Tis terrible! Guilford was idolized by his men, and loved by all who knew him. Poor boy! he seemed like a brother to me, and I think I could not feel worse, if he really had been. But he has gone. He, by his example, inspired his men with that confidence and courage, that made many a Rebel bite the dust. We have lost a brave and noble officer . . . ." After Guilford died Catherine obtained a widow's pension. She never remarried. She is buried in Mt. Adnah Cemetery, Fulton. The lot also contains a cenotaph for her long-dead husband who lies in Gettysburg National Cemetery. Their youngest child, Guilford, was killed in a hit and run accident in Fulton on January 7, 1935.

Charles Mahler – Co. H

b. 1826 Germany
d. April 4, 1908 Pulaski, NY
m. Caroline E. Sheridan (1826-December 23, 1889) *ca.* 1852

NOTE: Mahler, whose parents are unidentified, was wounded at Gettysburg on July 1, 1863 and discharged on May 1, 1864. In 1890 he said his disability was "gun shot and saber cut." His obituary appeared in *The* [Syracuse] *Post-Standard* May 7, 1908: ". . . The remains of Charles Mahler, who died Saturday at the residence of his son-in-law, Mortimer D. Compton, will be taken to Dugway tomorrow afternoon, where the funeral will be held. The deceased was a member of Parish Post, G.A.R., and members of Post Butler of Pulaski will act as bearers and a delegation accompany the remains to Dugway . . . ." Charles was buried in Dugway Cemetery, Albion Center, NY. Caroline, mother of at least three children, died in Dugway and presumably is also buried there.

Cane O. Mahoney – Co. I

b. December 1819 Ireland
d. May 1879 Oswego Town, NY
m. Catherine _____ (1824-April 6, 1890) ?

NOTE: According to *The Town Clerks' Registers*, Cane was the son of John (?-?) and Catherine Mahoney (?-?), but an examination of his gravestone suggests their surname was O'Mahoney. He was discharged from the service for "disability" on March 10, 1863 and applied for a pension on May 5th. He and Catherine were the parents of at least three children, all born in England: Elizabeth (1852-1921), Cornelius (1853-1928), and Mary (1858-1898). Cane and Catherine, together with their children, are buried in Old Irish Cemetery, Oswego Town.

James Mahoney – Co. B

b. 1823 Ireland
d. July 11, 1863 Gettysburg, Adams, PA
m. Johanna Keating (1833-?) November 8, 1852

NOTE: James' parents are unknown. His entry in *The Town Clerks' Registers* reveals he was "wounded at battle of Gettysburg – lay three days on the field – sent to hospital and died." He and Johanna were married in St. Paul's Catholic Church, Oswego City and their daughters, Mary Ann (1855-?) and Margaret Elizabeth (1857-?), were baptized in that church. Johanna married Martin Melvin in the same church on April 14, 1866. She was named the girls' guardian and they obtained pensions. In 1870 Margaret, aged 13, was a servant in a private home in Oswego. The family cannot be traced farther.

Thomas Maillieth – Co. H

b. 1822 Switzerland

d. *post* 1864

m. ?

NOTE: Little is known about this soldier who was also known as Thomas Meyers or Myers. He was wounded at Gettysburg on July 1, 1863 and discharged from the army on November 3rd at Philadelphia, PA under the name "Myers." He applied for a pension on February 11, 1864, again using the name Myers. In 1870 Thomas Myers, 54, born in Switzerland, without an occupation, was living with Adam Jennis in Palermo, NY. This may or may not be the correct man. Nothing further has been located.

Charles Maiz – Co. G

b. 1833 Prussia

d. *post* 1870 probably Iowa

m. Augusta _____ (1845-?) *ca.* 1868

NOTE: Very little has been learned about this soldier. He transferred to the US Navy in April 1864 but I have located no relevant records. In 1870 a man named Charles Maiz, 37, born in Prussia, was living with his wife Augusta, 25, also born in Prussia, and daughter, Augusta, 1, in Council Bluffs, Pottawattamie, IA. The child had been born in Iowa. Whether or not this is the correct person is conjectural.

Peter Market – Co. A

b. 1843 ?

d. ? ?

m. ?

NOTE: This man, claiming to be a sailor, enlisted in the 147th Regiment at Oswego City on September 2, 1862, mustering into Co. A. His biographical material is missing from the muster roll card. According to *The Town Clerks' Registers* he was captured at Gettysburg and deserted from parole camp on July 12th at Westchester, PA. At an unknown date he returned and transferred to the US Navy. It is possible that this man is actually Peter Marcotte/Marcot/Marcott, who was born in Canada to Peter and Melissa Marshall Marcot. In 1850 the family was living in Salina, Onondaga, NY. If this is the correct man he married Theresa Trombley (1841-February 15, 1915) in Detroit, Wayne, MI on October 6, 1871. He gave his occupation as sailor. For some strange reason he claimed he had been born in Oswego County. His death certificate, which lists Peter Marcott (1806-*post* 1850) and Melissa Marshall (1823-*post* 1850) as his parents, is identical to the family listed on the 1850 census except that in 1850 the enumerator spelled the surname Market. I have located no pension record for Peter which may be on account of his desertion in 1863 even though he allegedly returned and served in the Navy. Peter Marcott died on November 30, 1928 of arteriosclerosis and a cerebral hemorrhage. Theresa succumbed to peritonitis. She and Peter are buried in Mt. Olivet Cemetery, Detroit.

Daniel Marks, Jr. – Co. H
b. 1839 Oneida County, NY
d. September 3, 1915 Syracuse, Onondaga, NY
m1. Lucy _____ (1835-*post* 1880) *ca.* 1862
m2. Catharine Kelley (November 1856-August 12, 1935) 1887

NOTE: Daniel, a shoemaker, was the son of Daniel, Sr. (1816-1878) and Frances Mary Crowe Marks (1820-1890). He was discharged from the service at Chestnut Hill Hospital, Philadelphia, PA on April 3, 1863 where he had been since November 30, 1862. On August 27, 1864 he enlisted in Co. C, 184th Regiment and served until mustered out on June 28, 1865 at City Point, VA. He was a member of Melzar Richards Post No. 367 GAR in Mexico, NY. His first wife, Lucy, had been married before and was the mother of Anna M. (1853-?) and Sarah Ann (1856-?). By his second wife Daniel was the father of Frances Percival (1888-1946) and Catherine Loretta (1894-1925). *The Syracuse Herald* September 4, 1915, 6 published the following upon Daniel's death: "Funeral services for Mr. Marks, 72, a veteran of the Civil war, who died last night, will be held privately at his home . . . at 9 o'clock Monday morning and a half hour later at St. Patrick's church. Burial will be in Assumption cemetery. During the war he served in the 147th and Eighty-fourth [*sic*] New York regiments. He is survived by his widow and two daughters." Loretta is buried in Assumption and probably her mother is there too.

Ira Marks – Co. B
b. 1839 Mexico, NY
d. July 30, 1920 Mexico, NY
m. Lucinda _____ (1844-January 6, 1914) 1861

NOTE: Ira, son of James (?-*ante* 1850) and Ann _____ Marks (Hesson) (1808-1861), lived most of his life in Mexico. He transferred to the VRC on January 24, 1864 and was discharged in June 1864. In 1890 he said his disability was "injury to hip and spine." His obituary appeared in *The Oswego Daily Palladium* August 2, 1920, 3: "Mexico, Aug. 2. – Ira Marks, 81, an old war veteran, died Saturday at his home in Lincoln avenue after an illness of several weeks. Mr. Marks was born in the town of Mexico and had lived here all his life. He was a soldier belonging to the 147th Regiment, Company A. He was a member of Melzar Richard [sic] Post . . . His funeral was held this afternoon at two o'clock from his late home3 in Lincoln avenue. The Rev. Hamilton H. D. MacNeal, rector of the Episcopal church, officiated . . . ." He and Lucinda were the parents of Allen DeForest (1870-March 8, 1933) and Mary (1872-January 2, 1951). Allen hanged himself after a fire destroyed an apartment building he owned in Baldwinsville. All are buried in Mexico Village Cemetery.

William Marsden, Jr. – Co. A
b. October 26, 1816 Oswego County, NY
d. ? ?
m1. ?
m2. Huldah Hindes (1836-April 15, 1905) *ca.* 1853

NOTE: William was the son of William (1778-1865) and Sarah H. Waring Marsden (1785-1865). The 1855 New York census shows him, his wife Huldah, 20, daughter Frances E., 1, and son Minot J., 14. Unless Huldah's age was incorrectly entered, she could not be Minot's mother. The 1860 census showed her age as 24, thus confirming that she was born in 1836. William's military career is fraught with problems. He was reported sick on October 29, 1862 and again at muster out. Another document says he did indeed muster out on June 7, 1865. Yet another says he applied for a pension on January 30, 1863 although he did not obtain it. In 1870 Huldah, 30, Fanny, 16, Sarah, 14, Charley, 9, and Grant, 3, were living in Elk Rapids, Antrim, MI. Therefore, William could have died no sooner than 1866. Huldah's marital status was not recorded in 1870 but it appears she was widowed because in 1871 she married Alexander McKay (1840-1917) by whom she had a daughter, Jennie V. (1877-?). It is interesting that Huldah began using the name Anna after she had married McKay. Her COD was enteritis. The attending physician noted that a contributing factor was injuries received in a fall in August 1900. She and Alexander are buried in Pine Hill Cemetery, Sheboygan, Sheboygan, MI. Minot deserves a mention. He served in the 1st Independent Wisconsin LA and was killed at Parker's Crossroads, TN on February 1, 1863.

George H. Marshall – Co. B
b. 1836 New Haven, NY
d. October 19, 1893 Oswego City, NY
m1. Henrietta _____ (1841-*ante* 1879) *ca.* 1865
m2. Anna Rose Dennee (1839-September 11, 1933) *ca.* 1879

NOTE: George's parents were Jacob Livingston (1796-1871) and Margaret Herkimer Marshall (1796-1870). He was a chair maker. George was discharged for "disability" on January 4, 1865 and applied for a pension eight days later. His death was briefly announced in *The Oswego Daily Times* October 20, 1893 but a fuller account appeared in *The Oswego Daily Palladium* October 21, 1893: "The funeral of the late George Marshall took place from the residence, East Schuyler street, this morning and was attended by many of his old comrades and friends of the family. A fine floral piece from Charles Bechstedt's, representing the corps badge of his regiment and the words 'Our Comrade, 147th N. Y.,' and the old flag, in defense of which he received a wound in the Wilderness May 6th 1864, together with floral offerings from neighbors, covered the casket. The remains were taken to New Haven for burial. The bearers were Comrades VanAlstyne, Watson, Colson and Neville, all of his company B, 147th Regiment. The Rev. Mr. Coit of Trinity M. E. church performed the service." Anna's death forty years later elicited the following in *The Oswego Palladium-Times* September 12, 1933: "Mrs. Anna Rose Marshall died Monday evening at the family home, 214 Duer street, after an illness of two weeks. Mrs. Marshall was born at Amberet Island, Canada, and had resided in Oswego [?] years. She was a member of Trinity Methodist church. Among her neighbors and friends she was highly respected, having possessed a kindly and charitable nature . . . Funeral Wednesday at 2 o'clock at the family home . . . ." George and Anna Rose are buried in New Haven Cemetery. Henrietta's grave has not been located.

Joseph A. Marshall – Co. B

b. 1835 New Haven, NY
d. January 17, 1896 Kidders, Seneca, NY
m. Elizabeth J. _____ (1843-November 18, 1925) *ca.* 1857

NOTE: Joseph was George's brother. He went AWOL on December 17, 1862 at Washington, DC and did not return until April 14, 1864. He was sentenced "to make good all time lost" and because of that was transferred to Co. G, 91st Regiment on June 5, 1865, mustering out on July 3, 1865. Upon his death, *The Farmer Review* January 25, 1896, 1 published the following: ". . . Joseph A. Marshall died at his home near Kidders last Friday afternoon at 5 o'clock, aged 62 years, and was buried at Sheldrake Tuesday, Rev. E. B. Van Arsdale conducting the services. Mr. Marshall was born in Oswego County in 1835. In August 1862, he enlisted in Co. B, 147th regiment, N.Y.V., serving two years, 11 months and 23 days, or until mustered out at the close of the war." Joseph did not apply for a pension but Elizabeth did on April 15, 1897 and was successful in her application. The general index card makes for interesting reading: it erroneously states that Joseph also served in Co. B, 81st Regiment. A man named Joseph Marshall did indeed serve in that outfit but he and this soldier are different men. Elizabeth, born in England, died in Demster, NY. She and Joseph are buried in Lake View Cemetery, Interlakin, Seneca, NY.

Frederick G. Martin – Co. F
b. December 1843 Pulaski, NY
d. April 24, 1922 Oswego City, NY
m. Malissa Smith (1853-May 15,1919) 1877

NOTE: Frederick, son of Augustin/Austin (1814-1892) and Jane Perreault Martin (1823-1853), tried to enlist in the 110th Regiment but was rejected. He was more successful with the 147th. On June 7, 1865 he mustered out with the regiment. His obituary in *The Oswego Daily Palladium* April 25, 1922 contained an interesting piece of information: "Frederick G. Martin, 78, well known resident of Scriba, who had the distinction of having had president Lincoln as a guardian in view of the fact that he went to the Civil War under age and had the President act for him so that he could get into service, died at the Oswego Hospital last night after a long illness. Mr. Martin was born in Pulaski but had lived in Scriba in recent years. The body was taken to Coe's undertaking rooms at North Scriba and the funeral will be held from the Mexico M. E. church Thursday at 2 p.m. Burial will be in Daysville cemetery. Mr. Martin was a veteran of Company F, 147th New York Volunteers, and a member of Butler Post G.A.R., of Pulaski . . . ." Although the obituary stated he would be buried in Daysville, he and Melissa, the mother of eight, were actually buried in Willis Cemetery, Fernwood. President Lincoln may indeed have assisted Frederick in enlisting but it could not have been because he was under age. All records show he was born in 1843.

Samuel Martin – Co. I
b. 1841 Ireland
d. April 21, 1924 National Soldiers' Home, Bath, Steuben, NY
m. ------

NOTE: Samuel's parents were John (?-?) and Mary Smith Martin (?-?). He claimed to have become a naturalized citizen in 1862 although his immigration year is unknown. He mustered out with the regiment in June 1865. He was admitted to the Bath National Home on three occasions, the last being on August 5, 1914. He never left. He is buried in Bath National Cemetery although a cenotaph is located in Rural Cemetery, Oswego Town.

William Martin – Co. B
b. 1833 Scriba, NY
d. July 1, 1863 Gettysburg, Adams, PA
m. ------

NOTE: William, a carpenter, was the son of John (?-?) and Nancy Herman Martin (?-?). He was killed in action and lies with the "unknowns" in Gettysburg National Cemetery.

DeWitt Clinton Mathews – Co. H

b. 1840 Rome, Oneida, NY

d. November 24, 1909 Ypsilanti, Washtenaw, MI

m. Catherine E. Brasington LaValley (1840-February 23, 1916) April 19, 1870

NOTE: DeWitt, a sailor, was the son of Abram (1815-?) and Ruhannah Russell Mathews (1820-?). In later life he was a schoolteacher. His time in the military was brief since he was discharged on February 24, 1863. Catherine was first married to Peter LaValley (1836-1863). He served in Co. A, 5th Michigan Cavalry and was killed at Gettysburg on July 2, 1863. DeWitt's COD was chronic nephritis. Catherine died from "cancer of the appendix." Both are buried in Highland Cemetery, Ypsilanti. DeWitt's brother, Charles C. (1844-1913), served in Co. H, 184th Regiment.

Charles Matthews – Co. B

b. 1837 Norwalk, Huron, OH

d. ?

m. ?

NOTE: This man's muster roll card says he was absent at muster out but a notation in *Soldier Records and Profiles* says he not only was promoted to first sergeant but also mustered out with the regiment on June 7, 1865. No other information is available except that he was a sailor when he enlisted.

Henry B. Mayo – Co. F

b. 1832 Madison County, NY

d. July 1, 1863 Gettysburg, Adams, PA

m. Lucy J. Miller (1836-January 16, 1879) September 10, 1852

NOTE: Henry was the son of Elisha (1805-1869) and Gertrude Fisher Mayo (1805-1884), both of whom died in Palermo, NY and are buried in Upson's Corners Cemetery. Benjamin O. Baker offered testimony on December 17, 1864 as to what he saw occurring near him on the battlefield on July 1st, 1863. He had been wounded and left behind but before he was captured by the Confederates he observed Mayo lying near him: ". . . And that while deponent was upon the said Battle field wounded, and after the remainder of said Company & Regiment had been driven back by the enemy, deponent saw the said Henry B. Mayo lying upon the Battle field seriously wounded, and upon being interrogated by deponent as to the nature and extent of his wound replied that he had been shot through the body and that the said Mayo appeared to be entirely helpless and in a dying condition when deponent was taken prisoner and removed to the rear of the Rebel Army since which time deponent has heard nothing from the said Henry B. Mayo and that from the appearance of the said

Henry B. Mayo when deponent last saw him he (deponent) is satisfied and verily believes that the said Henry B. Mayo is dead and that he survived but a very brief period after deponent last saw him . . . ." Henry and Lucy were the parents of four minor children and she applied for pensions for herself and for them. In 1878 Lucy became ill with tuberculosis and according to the testimony of Julia A. Smith, who cared for her, she was sick for 22 weeks and during the "last 4 weeks [was] not able to turn herself in bed." She died in Palermo. The total value of her estate was $10 and consisted of a few pieces of furniture. To date her grave has not been found.

Alexander McAmbly – Co. G
b. 1806 Ireland
d. July 1, 1863 Gettysburg, Adams, PA
m1. ?
m2. Anne Groves (1804-October 4, 1875) December 2, 1838

NOTE: Although Alexander, son of Alexander (?-?) and Betsey Fetter McAmbley (?-?), claimed to have been born in 1818, 1806 is a more likely date since his cenotaph in Riverside Cemetery, Scriba says he was 57 years old. When he married Anne he had an 11-year-old son, Jesse, who testified that he had attended the wedding. The name of Jesse's mother is unknown. Anne's gravesite has not been located. Jesse (1827-July 24, 1894), who was married three times, served in Co. B, 81st Regiment. He is buried in Riverside. Alexander's brother, Major John McAmbly, also a member of Co. B, 81st Regiment, was killed at Fair Oaks, VA on May 31, 1862 and his body buried on the field. A cenotaph for him is located in Riverside Cemetery.

Daniel McAssey – Co. I
b. 1838 Oswego, NY
d. July 1, 1863 Gettysburg, Adams, PA
m. ------

NOTE: Daniel's parents were George W. (?-*post* 1875) and Mary Knowlin McAssey (?-?). His brothers, James and Thomas, were appointed administrators of his estate since Daniel died intestate. His father applied for a pension in 1875 but did not obtain it. According to *The Town Clerks' Registers*, McAssey, a second lieutenant, was "probably buried on [the] field."

Alexander McAuley – Co. C
b. 1832 Oswego County, NY
d. October 10, 1911 Williamstown, NY
m. Mary Mellen (July 11, 1837-September 12, 1917) September 15, 1862

NOTE: Alexander, son of John (1787-1881) and (possibly) Martha McLean McKindley McAuley (1789-1857), was principal musician in his company. His entry in *The Town Clerks' Registers* lists only his father who, according to the 1865 New York census, had been married twice and was at that time a widower. Alexander mustered out with the regiment on June 7, 1865. In 1890 he claimed rheumatism as a disability. When he enlisted he said he was a sailor; in later census records he consistently said he was a wagon or carriage maker. He and Mary, who had been born in Troy, NY, were the parents of six. The couple is buried in Fairview Cemetery, Williamstown, NY.

McAuley was a musician in his company. Later in life he was a wagon and carriage maker.
Willard Loomis, great grandson, and Williamstown Historical Society

Charles H. H. McCarty – Co. C

b. 1836 Richland, NY

d. May 6, 1863 Fitzhugh House Hospital, Falmouth, VA

m. Maria Sears (July 10, 1842-September 1, 1886) April 23, 1861

NOTE: Charles, son of Daniel (1811-1878) and Elizabeth Harding McCarty (1812-*post* 1878), was fatally wounded in the chest by a shell while constructing rifle pits near Fredericksburg, VA. A letter written by Capt. E. D. Parker and published in *The Mexico Independent* June 4, 1863 announced the sad news to Maria: "It becomes my painful duty to inform you that Charles is no more. He was wounded with a shell on the 3d, and sent to the rear to a hospital, where, I understand, he lived till the sixth. He had all done for him that could be, and every comfort he could have had at home. He was past all help from human hands. A piece of shell struck him in the breast and went clear through him. He could talk, and fully realized his situation. He wished someone to write to you, and I think some of his friends did. He did not seem to repine any at the thought of death. He called for me soon after he was hurt. I went to him. He said, 'Captain, I can help you no more; I can never get well.' He seemed to think he had lost his life while doing his duty for his country. He has always been a good, faithful soldier doing his duty to the best of his ability. I am truly sorry you should be called upon to make such a sacrifice for your country in the losing of your beloved husband but you have the consolation that you have sacrificed upon your country's altar the greatest sacrifice that human nature can be called upon to make; and I hope our country will show that it is not ungrateful for the sacrifices that have been made to save it; and may the sacrifices we are all making be sufficient to save and speedily restore our country to peace and unity. Then will our trials not be in vain. But we speak with pride and satisfaction of the sacrifices we have made to preserve our country, and amongst all the patriots none have made the sacrifices for their country that she has made who has sacrificed a beloved husband. Hoping that you may find comfort in the belief that your husband has yielded up his life for the good of his country and in the cause of humanity . . . ." Charles and Maria were the parents of one child, George F. (1862-1930). He is buried in Daysville Cemetery, Richland. Maria married Leonard H. King (1842-July 1913) on February 21, 1866. Her death was announced in *The Pulaski Democrat* September 8, 1886: ". . . In South Richland, Sept.1, 1886, of paralysis, Maria, wife of Leonard King, aged 44 years. Mrs. King, in former years, became a member of the Protestant Methodist church and until her health became impaired was an active member in church matters. She was a kind hearted, sincere Christian lady, a devoted wife and fond mother, and from her home circle and many kind friends will sadly missed. The funeral took place from the Methodist church on Thursday afternoon. The services were conducted by Rev. Mr. Barnes, of Mexico, in accordance with an arrangement made by Mrs. King. 'In the Christian's Home in Glory,' and 'Sweet By and By' were the hymns she had selected." Maria and Leonard were buried in Willis Cemetery, Fernwood.

William McCaw – Co. E
b. 1829 Ireland
d. September 21, 1915 Utica, Oneida, NY
m1. Leticia Kelly (1842-1881) September 6, 1864
m2. Clara Hulser Darling (1838-January 22, 1899) March 24, 1886

NOTE: William was the son of William (1800-1850) and Mary Lawson McCaw (1800-1850). He claimed in 1900 to have immigrated to the United States in 1849. His DOB varies from document to document: I use that on his gravestone. On his muster roll card someone wrote he had been born in Co. Antwerp, Ireland. There is no such place. He most likely was born in Co. Antrim. He was seriously wounded in the right leg on July 1, 1863 and was discharged in May 1864. He limped for the rest of his life. His life ended suddenly on Busy Corner, Utica, NY, as reported by *The Utica Herald-Dispatch* September 22, 1915, 4 which originally used an incorrect surname: "William McCall [sic], aged 86, of 1546 Miller street, was struck by an automobile owned and driven by George L. Randall of 814 Genesee street, New Hartford, at 5 o'clock yesterday afternoon just north of the Busy Corner, and taken to the General Hospital, where he died about 11 o'clock last night. Dr. A. A. Mahady, the Coroner, has begun an investigation. The accident happened at an hour when

Genesee and adjacent streets were crowded, the theater crowds pouring into the streets and the fashion week throngs adding to the crowds. Traffic Officer Peter Dressel, who was directing the traffic at the Busy Corner, did not see the accident, but he was one of the first to reach the prostrate man, who had been struck by the machine and hurled several feet. A crowd quickly gathered. The officer ordered the police ambulance summoned and Barney's ambulance was also called upon, but neither the police or Barney's ambulance was available at the time, both being engaged on calls elsewhere. The injured man was taken into the Antlers Hotel, conducted by Henry Bauer, in front of which place the accident occurred, and soon after an automobile was pressed into service and Mr. McCall was hurried to the General Hospital, where the physicians gave him immediate attention. He was unconscious. It was found he had suffered a fracture of the pelvis, had sustained several bad bruises and was badly shocked. Later he

William McCaw's life came to a tragic end when he was fatally injured in an automobile/pedestrian accident in Utica, NY.
Shawn Doyle

regained consciousness, but he was not able to withstand the shock and injuries. Traffic Officer Dressel took Randall, who is past middle age himself, to police headquarters where he was questioned concerning the accident. He told police he was going south in Genesee street and moving slowly at the time. This statement did not coincide with statements by witnesses gathered by the police that the automobile was travelling at a good rate of speed. Mr. Randall said he blew his horn, but that McCall evidently did not hear it, as he continued on across the street. After the automobile hit the aged man it continued on for a little distance and struck the rear end of an automobile owned by W. T. Farley of New York City, damaging the Farley car somewhat. A few years ago Mr. Randall's car struck a boy. William McCall was born in Ireland and came to this country at the age of 10, having resided in the United States 66 years. His first residence was in New York City and later he went to Redfield, this State, where he made his home until two years ago, when he came to Utica to spend the evening of his life with his daughter, Mrs. Charles E. Marks of 1546 Miller street, to whom the fatality was a great shock. Mr. McCall was married to Letichia [sic] Kelly of Albany while the Civil War was raging and a few months after his marriage he enlisted in Company E, One Hundred and Forty-seventh New York, serving with bravery until he was wounded in battle at Gettysburg. The wounds proved of a nature to make an invalid of Mr. McCall for several years but he was of a vigorous nature and years in the open as a farmer restored his health. He was a man of kindly nature and held the respect and esteem of all who knew him. Mr. McCall's first wife died about 38 years ago and in 1889 he was united in marriage to Clara Redfield of Deerfield . . . Mr. McCall was a member of Post Gaylord G.A.R., of Redfield and of the Odd Fellows. He was a member of the Episcopal Church . . . ." An inquest was held but no charges were made. Apparently unsatisfied, James McCaw and Isabelle Humphrey, two of McCaw's children, sued Randall for $5,000. The case was heard in October 1916 and the jury returned a verdict of "no cause for action." McCaw and his wives are buried in Redfield Village Cemetery. Clara, whose surname was erroneously given as Redfield in her husband's obituary, had previously been married to a man named Darling but nothing has been learned about him.

Andrus McChesney – Co. A
b. 1844 Pulaski, NY
d. February 26, 1863 Belle Plain, VA
m. ------

NOTE: This soldier's real name was Merritt Andrew McChesney, although he was also known as Anthony. He died of "typhoid pneumonia" and, according to *The Town Clerks' Registers*, his body was sent home and buried in Pulaski Village Cemetery. George Hugunin testified that McChesney had become ill on the infamous "mud march" and had died as a result. His parents were William (1798-1863) and Huldah Lord McChesney (1805-1893). William died of *phthisis pulmonalis* on August 7, 1863 and Huldah subsequently applied for her son's pension. She claimed that Andrus had contributed towards the family finances before he enlisted, had given his parents $200 of his bounty money, and had sent home part of his army pay. She was granted a pension of $8.00 per month. A lengthy obituary for her appeared in *The Oswego Daily Times* May 16, 1893, 4 which is excerpted here: "Huldah Lord, widow of William McChesney, died peacefully Sunday morning at the home of her youngest son, George H. McChesney, No. 607 James street [Syracuse]. She was born in New Hartford, N.Y., July 21, 1805, and she had therefore nearly completed her eighty-eighth year. In 1821 she was married to William McChesney and the young couple moved to the town of Richland, Oswego county, where the husband engaged actively in business and died in 1862 [*sic*]. Fourteen children were born to them, twelve of whom grew up to adult age, and six of these survive their mother. Shortly after the death of her husband Mrs. McChesney made her home with her son George in Oswego, and when he came to [Syracuse] in 1868 to engage in business, she came also and continued to be a cherished inmate of his home until her death. During her long residence in Oswego county, Mrs. McChesney was a member of the Methodist church of Pulaski. Shortly after her removal to this city she united with the Reformed Dutch church, during the pastorate of Rev. Dr. Martin L. Berger. She was the oldest member of that church, much revered on that account and much beloved for her sincere and simple piety. Those who knew this aged lady knew well that hers was no ordinary character. Along with her bodily faculties and her memory she retained to the last her strong common sense, cheerfulness, humor and serenity. She was kind to all and companionable with all, young and old. Her last years were ideal ones for old age, spent in a beautiful home which she adorned with her 'meek and quiet spirit,' and which she fully appreciated, while she looked forward with trust and joy to the home above. The end of life, for which she calmly waited, came as she wished it to come, and she was called home suddenly and painlessly, surrounded by the kindred who had cherished her, leaving a precious memory to her children's children . . . Funeral services will be held at No. 607 James street on Wednesday at 11 o'clock, and the burial will be at Pulaski the same day." Huldah and William are buried with their lost son, Andrus, and many other members of the family. .

John Smith McCoy – Co. G
b. March 16, 1845 Oswego Town, NY
d. June 30, 1929 National Soldiers' Home, Fort Leavenworth, KS
m. Lovina Emma Barstow (1845-1932) 1868

NOTE: John, also known by his middle name, was the son of John S. (1799-1861) and Rachel Cowan McCoy (1799-1876). His DOB is variously given. I use that on his gravestone. According to *The Town Clerks' Registers*, he participated in every battle in which the regiment was engaged. He mustered out with the regiment on June 7, 1865. In 1900 he was a conductor on the railroad. The membership list for Capt. Ames Post No. 318 GAR, Merriam, KS, dated December 30, 1916 showed he held the office of adjutant. The burial records for the national home note that his body was shipped home. He and Lovina were buried in Shawnee Cemetery, Johnson, KS.

Nicholas McCoy – Co. K
b. March 1815 Atlantic County, NJ
d, January 8, 1864 General Hospital, Alexandria, VA
m. Jane Richmond (July 31, 1811-January 5, 1903) December 22, 1835

NOTE: Nicholas, the son of Robert (1785-?) and Sarah Newton McCoy (1790-?), and Jane were married in New Jersey and all their children were born there. In 1855 they had resided in Verona, Oneida, NY for a year. Nicholas was a glassblower. He evidently lied about his age when he enlisted for he gave an age of 44. He contracted smallpox and was absent from duty from November 1863 until he died. He is buried in Arlington National Cemetery. A charge of desertion was later dropped. In 1900 Jane was living with her son Benjamin in Kane, McKean, PA. He is buried in Forest Lawn Cemetery but she apparently is not there. Her DOD is taken from the pension file.

Ira McDaniels – Co. H
b. January 5, 1827 Camillus, Onondaga, NY
d. May 26, 1898 Camden, Oneida, NY
m1. Catherine Innes (1829-September 14, 1886) *ca.* 1850
m2. Eliza Banks (1847-February 23, 1885) *ca.* 1879
m3. Bridget McNamara Swan (1849-August 18, 1919) May 26, 1886

NOTE: Ira, son of Samuel (1792-1862) and Mehitable Tubbs McDaniels (1799-1880), was discharged at an unknown date. In 1890 he said he left the military on a "surgeon's certificate of disability." He and Catherine divorced some time after the 1875 New York census was taken when they were enumerated with four children. In 1880 he was living in Glenmore, Oneida, with Eliza and three children, Rosa, 6, Lizzie, 3, and Homer, 2 months. The little girls provide testimony as to the reason for the divorce. It is possible that Eliza died in Glenmore but her grave has not been located. In 1885 Ira and two children were homesteaders in Polk County, MN. His exact address in 1890 was Crookston. The records suggest he and Bridget also parted company since he died in Camden, NY and she applied for his pension in Washington State. Bridget died in the Mission Hospital, Desmet, Benewah, ID. Her COD was chronic nephritis. The informant for her death certificate was the Sister Superior of the hospital. She was to be buried in Spokane, WA but her grave has not been located. Although Ira and Catherine divorced they are buried together in North Bay Cemetery, Vienna, Oneida, NY.

Deglin McGrath – Co. I
b. 1832 Ireland
d. July 1, 1863 Gettysburg, Adams, PA
m. Catherine _____ (1829-January 15, 1905) *ca.* 1853

NOTE: Deglin's parents are unknown. His names were variously spelled. Subsequent records show the surname was actually McGraw. His entry in *The Town Clerks' Registers* says his remains were buried on the battlefield. Catherine never remarried. *The Oswego Daily Times* January 16, 1905, 4 published her obituary: "Mrs. Catherine McGraw died suddenly at the home of her son-in-law, Timothy Mahaney, No. 280 West Fifth Street, yesterday afternoon. Coroner Vowinkel decided that death was due to paralysis. Mrs. McGraw was in her sixty-fifth year. Two daughters, Mrs.

Mahaney of this city and Mrs. R. A. Hemingway of Chicago, survive." Catherine is buried in the Mahaney plot in St Paul's Cemetery, Oswego City.

Dennis McGrath – Co. I
b. 1842 Newfoundland, Canada
d. July 1, 1863 Gettysburg, Adams, PA
m. ------

NOTE: This man's surname was also spelled McGraw, evidenced by his entry in *Deaths of Volunteers* and a list of casualties published in *The Oswego Commercial Times* July 20, 1863. He was a mariner by occupation. His parents are unidentified.

Patrick McGrath – Co. K
b. 1819 Ireland
d. November 8, 1878 Oswego City, NY
m. Margaret _____ (1822-ca. 1876) ca.1850

NOTE: Patrick, son of Thomas (?-*ante* 1843) and Mary Egan McGrath (?-1879), was born into a family of 12 children. He listed as sick on the muster roll for August 1863. He eventually transferred to the VRC. Although *The Town Clerks' Registers* had him dying at the battle of Weldon Railroad, he was confused with his brother, Richard (see below), and survived the war. Patrick met a tragic end, as reported in *The Oswego Daily Times* November 9, 1878: "At 2:30 o'clock this morning a small house owned and occupied by Patrick McGrath, corner of East Ninth and Cook streets, was discovered to be on fire and it was subsequently burned to the ground. McGrath, who was a man 60 or 65 years of age, lived alone in the house, his wife having died about a year ago. Henry Miller, who lives across the street from McGrath, was awakened by the light and heard a scream in the direction of McGrath's house. He ran across the street and kicked open the door of the house when the flames burst out in his face and drove him back. McGrath slept in the front room, a room 12 by 14 feet, his bed being in the southeast corner of the room. After the house had burned down, it became known that McGrath was missing and had not escaped from the burning building. His charred remains were found near the place where the bed stood, the head being towards a window, indicating that he attempted to reach the window and was probably suffocated by the smoke. The flesh was completely burned off the bones and nothing was left but the charred and blackened skeleton. The neighbors say that McGrath was in the habit of frequently keeping a lamp burning all night. No one appears to know whether he had put up a stove and kept a fire in the house. It is said no stove was found in the ruins of the house. The deceased was a cartman. He also drew a pension, having been wounded at the battle of Chancellorsville, while a member of Capt. Dempsey's company, 147ᵗʰ Regiment. He leaves two daughters . . . ." A coroner's inquest was held and the verdict was that McGrath had accidentally been burned to death. Patrick is buried in St. Paul's Cemetery, Oswego City. Margaret's grave has not been located. A brother, William, served in Co. D, 184ᵗʰ Regiment and was seriously injured at the Battle of Cedar Creek. He drowned in the Oswego River on January 30, 1886 after he suffered a seizure and fell through the ice.

Richard McGraugh – Co. K
b. 1822 Ireland
d. August 19, 1864 Weldon Railroad, VA
m. Mary Hyde (1820-May 14, 1895) 1843

NOTE: Richard was Patrick McGrath's brother. He and Mary were married in Montreal, Canada and became the parents of five children, two of whom, Jane and Richard, were minors when their father was killed. In January 1865 it was announced that his body was being returned home. A funeral notice was published in *The Oswego Commercial Times* March 18, 1865. "The remains of Sergeant Richard McGrath of the 147ᵗʰ regiment were interred in the Roman Catholic Cemetery in this city yesterday, with military honors. The funeral cortege was headed by the band of the 16ᵗʰ U.S. Infantry. Two companies of the National Guard formed the military escort. The large attendance at the funeral testified the respect in which the deceased was held by his former fellow citizens." Mary obtained pensions for herself and for the children. Another child, Thomas (1846-1884), served in Co. F, 24ᵗʰ NY Cavalry. Mary and Richard, together with Thomas and other members of the family, are buried in St. Paul's Cemetery, Oswego City.

Patrick McGuire – Co. I
b. 1842 Ireland
d. *post* 1865 ?
m. ?

NOTE: This soldier was wounded at Gettysburg on July 1, 1863 and discharged at Baltimore, MD on July 6, 1865. He said he was a miller when he enlisted at Oswego City. No other verifiable information, including names of parents, has been located.

Richard McKee – Co. B
b. 1840 Newfoundland, Canada
d. December 7, 1916 Providence Retreat, Buffalo, Erie, NY
m. Mary Ann McIntosh (1840-January 25, 1927) *ca.* 1868

NOTE: Richard, a blacksmith, was also known as Richard McGee, the name on his muster roll card. His father is unknown but in 1855 he and several brothers were living in Oswego City with their widowed mother, Catherine (1818-?) His DOB is variously given. I use that on his muster roll card. He mustered out with the regiment on June 7, 1865. He and Mary Ann were the parents of James (May 20, 1869-July 11, 1938), who is buried in Mt. Carmel Cemetery, Cook County, IL. According to the 1880 census, Richard was living with his brother Thomas, also a blacksmith, in Fleming, Cayuga, NY. Under the Defective, Delinquent notes obtained that year it was revealed that Richard had his first attack of "dementia" at age 25, or shortly after the war ended. He had spent three years in Ovid Asylum and had been released in 1879. Richard's name was included in a lengthy list of Civil War pensioners residing in Oswego County published in *The Oswego Times and Express* October 17, 1883. His disability was insanity and he was collecting a pension of $50 per month. Richard was living with an uncle, John Malone, 72, in Oswego City in 1900 but by 1905 he was residing in Providence Retreat, a hospital established by the Sisters of Charity specifically for mental patients. He resided there until his death. Mary Ann applied for and obtained a widow's pension. She died in Chicago and was buried in Calvary Cemetery. Richard's gravesite has not been located.

James A. McKinley – Co. I
b. 1836 Kingston, Ontario, Canada
d. October 25, 1905 Oswego City, NY
m. Jane Reid (September 1838-March 19, 1917) 1862

NOTE: James' parents were John (?-?) and Sarah McCaffrey McKinley (?-?). His obituary, published in *The Oswego Daily Palladium* October 26, 1905, 1, detailed a long and eventful life: "Captain James A. McKinley, one of Oswego's best known residents, died last night at his home . . . after a long illness of stomach trouble. Captain McKinley was born in Kingston, Ont., and came to this city when a very young man with his brother, the late William P. McKinley, who was one of the first superintendents of the old Midland railroad. Captain McKinley was apprenticed to George A. Crotius and learned the blacksmithing trade. He was popular with his associates and was by them elected foreman of Champion Engine Company, No. 3, in the days of the Old Volunteer Fire Department. With the expiration of his term of office he was elected foreman of Lightfoot Hose Company No. 2, and held that position when the War of the Rebellion broke out. In 1862, when the 147th N.Y. Volunteers was organized, Captain Patrick Regan was elected Captain of Company I and Captain McKinley was First Lieutenant. Shortly after entering the service Captain Regan resigned and Lieutenant McKinley was named as Captain. Nearly the entire hose company of which he had been foreman joined his company and fought till the end of the war. Captain McKinley was beloved by his men and participated in every engagement in which the Army of the Potomac fought from 1862 until the close of the war in 1865 . . . With the close of the war Captain McKinley returned to Oswego and became interested in canalboats. For several years he conducted these boats successfully and retired to take a position, superintending the construction of bridges and culverts on the old Midland railroad at Norwich, where for several years he made his home. Returning to this city he entered the employ of the R. W. & O. road and was in the company's blacksmith shop, where he remained until a few years ago, when he resigned, owing to failing health and has since lived quietly at home. Captain McKinley was a good citizen, an indulgent husband and parent and a devout member of St. Mary's church. He had the respect and esteem of all who knew him . . . ." A writer who signed his name "Veteran," penned the following which appeared the same day: "By the death of Captain James A. McKinley Oswego loses one of her most distinguished veterans. Probably no soldier of our country had a more creditable record. As a member of the famous 147th New York Volunteers, he did his full share in making its fighting record. He was a typical volunteer soldier, brave, kind hearted, cool when coolness was required, fiery as Sheridan when dash and daring were called for, quick to take offense, but quicker still to apologize if he was in the wrong. A lovable man and a good citizen. It is pleasant to know that his intense patriotism has been transmitted to his children as an essay written and read by one of them before the Normal school will show. Hail and farewell to you, Captain James." James and Jane were the parents of eight children. When Jane died, the following obituary appeared in *The Oswego Daily Palladium* March 19, 1917, 8: "Jane McKinley, widow of Captain James A. McKinley, died late last night at her home . . . after an illness of about three months. Mrs. McKinley was born near the city of Limerick, Ireland, coming to Oswego with her parents seventy years ago, and having made her home here practically all of that time. She was a member of St. Mary's Church and the League of Prayer. While the announcement of her death has been expected at almost any time for the past week or two, it nevertheless came as a shock to many friends . . . ." James and Jane are buried in St. Peter's Cemetery, Oswego City.

John McKinlock – Co. A

b. 1833 New York City, NY
d. October 28, 1912 Chicago, Cook, IL
m1. Margaret McCormick (1835-1894) *ca.* 1855
m2. Bertha Bart (January 27, 1869-July 1966) 1901

NOTE: John, who gave his occupation as sailor in 1855, was the son of Henry McKinlock (?-?). His mother's name is unknown. After moving to Oswego City in 1852 he became involved in the local militia and was a member of the Old Oswego Guards. A brief death notice in *The Brooklyn Daily Eagle* October 29, 1912, 5 contained a tantalizing comment relating to his military career: "Chicago, October 29

– Captain John McKinlock, who mustered three companies for the Civil War, going out as the head of the last one, the One Hundred and Forty-seventh of New York, died at his home here yesterday. He was born in New York City seventy-nine years ago." When the 81st Regiment was being formed in late 1861 and early 1862, McKinlock raised a company and expected to go to the war as its lieutenant. Instead, Lieut. Col. Jacob DeForest installed a brother as leader of the company. Despite a rumor reported in *The Oswego Commercial Times* January 23, 1862 that DeForest had been dismissed and that McKinlock was to be reinstated, such did not occur. Apparently undaunted by this political ploy, McKinlock placed advertisements in *The Oswego Commercial Times* that he and Captain Austin had consulted with Col. Johnson Butler Brown of the newly formed 101st Regiment (Syracuse) and were recruiting riflemen for that organization. Later in the year McKinlock was foiled from raising a company for the 110th because so many had already been raised. He had better luck with the 147th, as reported by *The Oswego Commercial Times* August 15, 1862: "Capt. McKinlock has recruited over fifty as stout, able bodied men as ever carried a musket, and is still at work to fill up his company. He will go into the new regiment. Let our citizens all help him. Capt. McKinlock's company should now be filled up before another infantry company is started in our city. It is due to him as a gentleman and as a soldier, that he should have a good position in some Oswego regiment. He was most shabbily treated in the organization of the Eighty-first, and he is left out of Col. Littlejohn's regiment on account of there being so many other companies started. We go for McKinlock. He is one of the best drilled officers in the city, and a most deserving young man. If our citizens organize themselves into a Committee for the work, his company can be filled up next week. Shall it be done?" The newspaper offered further encouragement in its August 19th edition: "Capt. McKinlock is still recruiting slowly, but surely. We wish his company might be filled up at once. How many of our wealthy men have interested themselves in his case? How many have asked him whether he needed any money in his enterprise? The services of an officer so thoroughly drilled as he is will be found valuable in any regiment – more valuable than politicians or others, who never had any experience in military affairs. We talk plainly, for that is our fashion. Capt. McKinlock expended all the money he had in the world to raise a company for the 81st, and then got kicked out to make room for a man from Albany. Is he to be treated in the same way again?" Finally McKinlock recruited 83 men, the minimum for the company which was designated with the letter A. It was customary to present a new officer with a gift from friends and fellow soldiers, generally in the form of a sword or a horse. McKinlock's friends gave him the gift of financial security, as reported in *The Oswego Commercial Times* September 23, 1862: ". . . The men having been drawn up in order, O. H. Hastings, Esq., in behalf of the citizens of the First Ward made a presentation to Capt.

McKinlock of a policy of insurance on his life for $5,000 in the Connecticut Mutual Life Insurance Company. This most appropriate gift will enable the Captain to leave his family with an assurance that they will be provided for should accident befall him . . . Mr. Hastings happily alluded to the difficulties which Capt. McKinlock had encountered – to the ill-treatment he had uncomplainingly suffered in the organization of the 81st regiment, and also to the obstacles he had encountered in raising his present company . . . As Captain McKinlock declared himself more of a fighting man than a talking man, at his request Ira D. Brown spoke in his behalf, returning his heartfelt thanks to the citizens of the First Ward for the appropriate gift, and thanking them for their interest in his behalf which

John McKinlock served faithfully in the 147th Regiment and enjoyed a fulfilling career in the post war era. *New York State Military Museum*

had sustained, cheered and encouraged him in the work. Captain McKinlock promised to repay this generous kindness in the only way he could – by striking a good blow for his county when opportunity offered . . . ." McKinlock temporarily assumed command of the regiment in late October 1864 when Lieut. Col. George Harney disappeared while on patrol. He mustered out with the regiment on June 7, 1865 and returned to Oswego. In 1870 John, Margaret, and their four children were living in Buffalo, but the family subsequently moved to Detroit, MI and then to Chicago where John engaged in the electrical supply business. He is buried in Oak Woods Cemetery. His wives' graves have not been located. A brief mention of his children is in order: George (1857-1936) organized and led the Central Electric Company in Chicago; William (1859-1918) was also involved in the electrical field in Connecticut; John (1861-1944) became a medical doctor specializing in surgery and gynecology in Chicago; Letitia (1866-1940) married Charles E. Sharp (1865-1938) on April 18, 1889 in Detroit, MI. Sharp was an exporter of electrical supplies. Letitia and Charles lived in St. Louis, MO and were active in society affairs.

Edward McKittrick – Co. I
b. 1829 Oswego, NY
d. ? ?
m. Mary Ann _____ (1834-?) *ca.* 1850

NOTE: Edward and Mary Ann, together with Michael, 4, and Clarissa, 2, appear on the 1855 New York census. They had resided in Oswego City for 11 years. Edward said he had been born in Oswego County but it is possible he was born in Canada, as was Mary Ann. His parents are unknown. Both children were born in Oswego. Edward, a sailor, transferred to Batt. L, 1st NY ART on December 21, 1863 and then to the US Navy. The weekly rendezvous sheet showed him enlisting at Brooklyn, NY on May 5, 1864. The entire family subsequently disappeared.

Thomas McManus – Co. K
b. 1844 Ireland
d. *post* 1873 ?
m. ------

NOTE: Thomas, whose parents are unidentified, transferred to the 16th Regiment VRC in August 1864 and was finally discharged in August 1866. He spent considerable time in various soldiers' homes. One record reveals he was extensively burned on the right side and arm and lost the sight in his right eye when a cannon exploded on July 4, 1865. He applied for a pension on October 19, 1866. Despite his many residencies in national homes, no record of his death has been located.

Silas McNett – Co. K
b. March 30, 1844 Oswego County, NY
d. February 18, 1917 Rochester, Monroe, NY
m. Margaret Homer (1840-April 21, 1913) 1866

NOTE: Silas, a musician, was the son of Silas (1818-*post* 1865) and Caroline Clark McNett (1828-*post* 1865). He was discharged from the service on February 13, 1865 when the 147th and the 76th Regiments were being consolidated. He and Margaret were the parents of seven children, only three of whom were alive in 1900. Silas is buried in the GAR section of Holy Sepulchre Cemetery, Rochester. Margaret is also buried there in Section M.

Bernard McOwen – Co. E
b. 1812 Ireland
d. April 12, 1863 David's Island, New York Harbor, NY
m. Mary Doyle (1815-February 24, 1899) January 8, 1845

NOTE: Bernard claimed to have been born in 1818 but his cenotaph gives a more accurate DOB of 1812. His surname is variously spelled. Although he listed Redfield, NY as his POB on his muster roll card, other evidence points to Ireland as his birthplace. His COD was Bright's disease. Mary applied for and obtained a pension for herself and also for her four minor children. Upon her death *The Oswego Daily Palladium* March 7, 1899, 6 published a lengthy obituary: "The death of Mrs. Bernard McOwen, which occurred on the evening of February 24th, is deserving of more than passing mention, marking as it does, the passing away of another of the oldest and most respected citizens of the town of Redfield. Mrs. McOwen's maiden name was Mary Doyle. She was married in Albany, in 1844 [*sic*], to Bernard McOwen. Mr. and Mrs. McOwen were both born in county Westmeath, Ireland. The early years of their married life were spent in Saugerties, Ulster county, N.Y., until 1860, when they removed to Redfield. September 21st, 1862, Mr. McOwen, espousing the cause of his adopted country, enlisted in Company E, of the 147th Regiment, and gave his life in the service of his country, dying at a hospital on Ford's Island from disease contracted in the service. All honor to those brave men, though of alien birth, who fought to give us a united country; debtors all are we to them . . . On Tuesday, the 28th, funeral services conducted by the Rev. Father Brennan were held at St. Mary's church, Florence, of which Mrs. McOwen was a most exemplary and devoted member. The very large concourse of people was an elegant tribute to the high esteem in which Mrs. McOwen was held by Catholic and Protestant alike . . . ." Bernard and Mary's son Hugh served in Batt. L, 1st NY ART. His mother's obituary erroneously stated he served in the 147th. Bernard is buried in Cypress Hills National Cemetery, Brooklyn. Mary is buried in St. Mary's Church Cemetery, Florence, Oneida, NY.

Oscar McQueen – Co. F

b. June 14, 1841 Palermo, NY
d. October 14, 1929 Mexico, NY
m1. Harriet Story (December 24, 1835-November 19, 1907) November 27, 1871
m2. Josephine Grant (October 1852-March 10, 1933) October 23, 1912

NOTE: According to *The Town Clerks' Registers*, Oscar became ill on November 13, 1862 and was discharged on February 7, 1863 from the Convalescent Camp, Alexandria, VA. In 1890 he claimed lung disease and catarrh as his disabilities. His obituary appeared in *The Mexico Independent* October 17, 1929, 1: "Oscar McQueen, 88, died suddenly Monday morning at his home in this village. Mr. McQueen has been in failing health for the past year, but was able to be about and to go downtown occasionally. He had complained of not feeling well on Sunday, but arose as usual Monday morning, and was at the breakfast table with Mrs. McQueen when the end came before medical aid could be summoned. He was born in the town of Palermo June 14, 1841, the son of Ephraim and Catherine Pierce McQueen, and is the last survivor of his family. The greater part of his life was spent in the town of Palermo . . . where he was a prosperous farmer and highly respected citizen. In 1917 he moved here where he has since resided . . . He was a civil war veteran, having enlisted in the 147th regiment, Company F and was a member of Sherman Post, Vermillion, until it disbanded. Mr. McQueen retained his mentality and enjoyed life in general, possessing a social nature, and those who knew him best can testify to his helpfulness. He will be greatly missed, not alone in his home, but in the neighborhood where he was so favorably known . . . ." When Harriet died, *The Mexico Independent* November 27, 1907 published the following: ". . . The subject of this writing, Miss Harriet Story, was born in the town of Hastings, Oswego county, New York, Dec. 24, 1835, and departed this life Tuesday, Nov. 19, 1907. The deceased was married to Oscar McQueen, Nov. 27, 1871 . . . The services were held at their late home in Palermo, where the two had lived all their married life. The funeral was conducted by Rev. H. F. Snow. Text may be found in 1 Cor.13:12. 'For I now know in part, but then we shall know as we are known' . . . The deceased was indeed a very estimable woman, possessing veracity and honesty, loved in her home, admired by her neighbors. Her prayer in home was that God will bless her husband and children. She will be missed by many, but most of all by her companion and children, but she is gone and it is hopeful to a better world. Let us all pray that the blessings of the Almighty God may rest on the afflicted family and comfort them." Harriet and Oscar are buried in Sayles Corners Cemetery, Mexico. Josephine died at the Ogdensburg State Hospital. She buried with her parents, Nathan (1810-1899) and Cornelia Blankman Grant (1821-1901), in Hastings Cemetery. Her stone does not contain a DOD.

Henry F. Mellen – Co. C
b. 1843 Albion, NY
d. March 5, 1863 Kalorama Hospital, Washington, DC
m. ------

NOTE: Henry, son of Felix (1806-1888) and Ann Dugan Mellen (1812-1887), died of typhoid fever and was buried in Arlington National Cemetery. H. F. Mellen Post No. 497 GAR, Williamstown, was named in his honor. Ann, who obtained a mother's pension, and Felix, both born in Ireland, are buried in Holy Cross Cemetery, Williamstown.

Henry Hezekiah Mellen – Co. C
b. 1820 Richland, NY
d. December 13, 1892 Minneapolis, Hennepin, MN
m. Charlotte Maria Ferguson (May 4, 1831-May 30, 1905) 1853

NOTE: Henry, also known by his middle name, was the son of Henry (1793-1861) and Alice Harris Mellen (1789-1888) and the eldest of at least six children. He was quartermaster sergeant and later first lieutenant. He was discharged for "physical disability" on October 12, 1864 and in 1890 said he was bothered by "piles and heart trouble." Henry was appointed postmaster of Richland in 1861 and again in 1868. Two of his brothers, Daniel (1829-1862) and Chester (1822-1864), went west. Daniel died in Olivia, NM. Chester was murdered by Native Americans in Yavapai, AZ. In

1865 Henry was appointed administrator of Chester's estate. Although Henry died in Minneapolis, his body was returned to Richland. Charlotte died in Clermont, IA at the home of a brother. Her body too was returned to Richland and was buried with her husband in Richland Cemetery.

Hugh D. Mellen – Co. C
b. July 1841 Albion, NY
d. September 11, 1928 Rome, Oneida, NY
m. Elinor "Ellen" Smith (October 16, 1850-February 28, 1928) 1872

NOTE: Hugh was a brother of Henry F. Mellen. He lost his right arm on July 1, 1863 at Gettysburg and was discharged from the service on January 18, 1864. His death was announced in *The Rome Daily Sentinel* September 11, 1928, 2: "Hugh D. Mellen, who had spent the greater part of his life in Fairport, N.Y., but for the past few months, since the death of his wife, had made his home with his son, Dr. Dan Mellen, 305 N. Washington street, died there at 1:40 o'clock this morning. He was in his 88th year and death was due to complications attendant upon advanced age. Mr. Mellen was born in Oswego. He had been an active member of the Masonic order for 65 years and was a veteran of the Union forces in the Civil War. Mr. Mellen was an entertaining story teller and his recounting, particularly his reminiscences of the inter-states conflict, were sources of keen enjoyment to hearers on many occasions. For several years Mr. Mellen was justice of the peace in Fairport. The late Mr. Mellen was a keen observer of the political situation and up to the last retained a lively interest in local, state and national issues. He was an amiable and friendly man and during his short stay in Rome had made a large circle of friends who will hear with regret of his passing. He attended the Methodist Church. Besides Dr. Mellen he is survived by three daughters and three other sons." Hugh, a Democrat, was active in local political affairs. He was a member of H. F. Mellen Post No. 497 GAR. In 1885 he was appointed postmaster at Kasoag, NY. His wife died only a few months before his demise. *The Rome Daily Sentinel* February 29, 1928, 11 carried her obituary: "Mrs. H. D. Mellen, 77, died at her home in Fairport on Tuesday afternoon, at 4:30 o'clock, after several months of poor health . . . Mrs. Mellen was born in Auburn on October 16, 1850, daughter of the late Mr. and Mrs. John Smith. Her maiden name was Ellen Smith. After spending part of her early life in Auburn and other cities, she was married 53 years ago in Oswego to Mr. Mellen, who survives . . . ." Hugh and Ellen are buried in Greenvale Rural Cemetery, Fairport.

Joseph Mellen – Co. C

b. June 8, 1839 Williamstown, NY

d. July 6, 1900 Bouckville, Madison, NY

m. Electa J. Mowers (July 20, 1844-June 5, 1903) 1867

NOTE: Joseph was a brother of Henry F. and Hugh. He was discharged for "disability" on February 14, 1863 but on August 23, 1864 he enlisted in the 184th Regiment and served until mustered out at City Point, VA on June 29, 1865. In 1898 he and his family moved to Bouckville. Although he died there, his body was taken to Williamstown and buried in Holy Cross Cemetery with other members of the family. Another brother, Oliver (1833-1904), was a member of the 184th Regiment. He too is buried in Holy Cross Cemetery. Electa's COD was blood poisoning and traumatic erisypelas. She is buried in Madison Village Cemetery.

Harris James Merrill – Co. B

b. ? ?

d. March 23, 1907 Gibson, Bay, MI

m. Mary Tobin (1847-April 1, 1897) *ca.* 1864

NOTE: The DOB and POB of Harris, son of John Jeremiah (1808-1887) and Almira Whelpley Merrill (1806-1881), apparently depended upon the moment. His muster roll card says he was born in 1836 in Delaware County, NY. In 1850 and 1880 he claimed to have been born in 1837 in NYS. In 1870 he said he had been born in 1840 in NYS, but in 1900 the date and place became 1837 in PA. Several researchers report he was born on January 3, 1837. His death certificate says he was born September 20, 1842 in PA although the DOB on his gravestone is 1837. Other mysteries exist: His muster roll card says he was "absent, sick" at muster out but his entry in *Records and Profiles* states specifically that he mustered out on June 7, 1865. No pension card has been located nor does his name appear on the 1890 Veterans' Schedules. The family was living in Gibson in the 1880s. Harris worked in a saw mill. He and Mary are buried in St. Patrick Cemetery, Bay City. Their graves are marked with stones which merely say "Father" and "Mother."

Chauncey G. Miller – Co. D

b. October 28, 1843 Granby, NY

d. May 21, 1871 Fulton, NY

m. ------

NOTE: Chauncey's parents were Tobias (1794-*ante* 1860) and Abigail Montague Miller (1802-July 31, 1893). He was wounded at Gettysburg on July 1, 1863 but mustered out on June 7, 1865. Chauncey is buried in Mt. Adnah Cemetery, Fulton.

His father was a veteran of the War of 1812. His mother applied for a pension on November 21, 1889 but apparently died before the process could be completed.

Francis "Frank" Charles Miller – regimental colonel
b. 1831 Mohawk, Herkimer, NY
d. August 17, 1878 Oneida, Madison, NY
m. Maria Louisa _____ (1833-January 22, 1897) ca. 1853

NOTE: A carpenter by trade, Francis or "Frank" as he was familiarly known, was the son of John D. (1805-1869) and Catherine Getman Miller (1811-1882), both of whom are buried in Rural Cemetery, Oswego Town. A lengthy obituary appearing in *The Oswego Daily Times* August 17, 1878 chronicled his military career and post-war experiences: "Col. Francis C. Miller died at his residence in Oneida last night at 12 o'clock. Some days since he was taken with what seemed to be cramping while bathing in Oneida lake, at the head of which he had a summer cottage. He was rescued from drowning with difficulty, and was attacked immediately with brain fever, and was delirious the most of the time until his death. Thus has departed another of the brave men who periled their lives that the Union might live. Col. Miller was the oldest son of the late John D. Miller, for many years a well known citizen of Oswego. He was born in Mohawk, Herkimer County, and came with his father to reside in this city when six years old. When the rebellion broke Col. Miller was a young man in this city. He had been an officer in the Oswego Guards a well-known military company of this city, and had acquired a knowledge of military tactics. When the call for volunteers came he raised Company C of the Twenty-fourth Regiment of New York Volunteers and took it into the field. He was with his company through the entire career of the regiment, until on the march to Antietam he received word of his promotion to the position of Major of the 147th, with orders to report at once for duty, to his regiment. He filled the position of Major until the resignation of Col. Warner when he was promoted to the Lieutenant Colonelcy, and upon the resignation of Col. Butler, he was made Colonel and continued in command of the regiment which he had had for some time in the absence of his predecessor. In the Battle of the Wilderness while at the head of his regiment, Col. Miller was shot directly through the body, the bullet passing out near the spine. The ball struck the case of his watch, as it entered his body and was slightly diverted from its course, and otherwise would have shattered the spinal column. He was thrown from his horse in a state of insensibility, and was captured by the enemy, his regiment supposing he was killed. He was reported killed and his regiment and friends at home so supposed for several weeks. When the enemy found that he was still alive and might possibly recover they sent him to Lynchburg, Virginia, and when he was well enough to travel they sent him to Charleston, and in company with about two hundred other Union officers he was placed under fire to deter Gen. Gilmore from shelling the city. He was subsequently exchanged and resumed command of his regiment, and was with it at the surrender of Lee at Appomattox. After the close of the war Col. Miller returned to this city for a short time but soon after went into the lumber trade in the village of Oneida, where he acquired the respect and confidence of the whole community. He was at one time President of the village, and was universally regarded as an enterprising, public spirited and popular man. As a soldier and officer, Col. Miller was brave, intrepid and popular with his officers and men. As a citizen he was patriotic, honorable, highminded, and genial. The people of Oswego, as well as of Oneida will deeply regret his death." Miller's rumored death at the battle of the Wilderness elicited numerous articles and letters about him as a soldier and a man. The news that he had survived came as a pleasant surprise to all. Two men, Adjt. O. V. Tracy, 122nd Regiment, and Andrew Sheav, 6th US Cavalry, had met him in prison and after they escaped both sent letters to Maria Louisa, assuring her that her husband was indeed alive and recuperating from his wounds. Although the obituary states he was taken directly from Lynchburg to Charleston, such was not the case. A short article in *The Oswego Commercial Times* October 4, 1864 reported that he, Lieut. H. H. Lyman, and many other officers had been moved from Savannah, GA to Charleston, SC. A letter written to his wife and published in *The Oswego Commercial Advertiser* October 18, 1864 confirmed the report. At some unspecified date in early December 1864 Col. Miller was exchanged. He wrote to his wife from Annapolis, MD that he would soon be home and he arrived in Oswego on December 19, 1864, much to the delight of his many friends. On January 23, 1865 a large crowd witnessed the presentation of a sword and sash to him from a grateful citizenry. Making the presentation was the Hon. D. G. Fort, whose remarks were reported in *The Oswego Daily Palladium* January 23, 1865: ". . . Colonel Frank Miller, you say that when you lay wounded and bleeding upon the bloody field at the battle of the Wilderness, you have an indistinct impression that rebels stole your sword. We have met here this afternoon to leave upon your mind a very distinct impression that what rebels stole patriots have restored . . . ." Miller returned to the 147th and remained in command until the end of the war, mustering out on June 7, 1865. His obituary said his COD was brain fever but the 1880 Mortality Schedules claimed he died of diarrhea. He is buried in Glenwood Cemetery, Oneida. He and Maria Louisa were the parents of one son, Frederick Charles (1855-June 7, 1903). He was a physician in Tacoma, Pierce, WA when he died of diphtheria. Maria's death was reported in *The Syracuse Daily Journal* January 25, 1897, 5: ". . . The funeral of Mrs. Maria L. Miller was held from St. John's Episcopal church at 2:30 this afternoon, Rev. John Arthur officiating. There was a large attendance. The body was placed in the vault at Glenwood, where it will remain until spring . . . ."

Henry Miller – Co. B

b. 1846 Eaton, Madison, NY

d. July 9, 1863 Gettysburg, Adams, PA

m. ------

NOTE: The son of William (1789-*post* 1850) and Ruth Howard Miller Maxwell (1807-*post* 1868), Henry lied about his age in order to enlist. He was wounded at Gettysburg and, according to *The Utica Morning Herald* July 18, 1863, 1, his leg was amputated. *The Oswego Commercial Times* July 20, 1863 reported him among the wounded. His FAG entry says he died July 3rd. His muster roll card says he died on July 9th while a note in *Registers of Officers and Enlisted Men* states he died as late as August 3rd. He is buried in Gettysburg National Cemetery. In 1868 his mother filed for and obtained a pension.

Henry Miller – Co. B

b. 1820 Stafford, Tolland, CT

d. October 7, 1887 Oswego City, NY

m. Alice _____ (December 26, 1835-March 1, 1911) *ca.* 1855

NOTE: Henry, son of David (?-?) and Hester Walbridge Miller (?-?), lied about his age to enlist since subsequent census records point to a DOB of 1820, not 1830. His muster roll card says he was wounded in action "in both legs" but does not provide an exact date. He was transferred to the VRC in August 1863 and eventually discharged for "disability." He and Alice were the parents of at least seven children. In 1865 Martin was 5 months old. *The Oswego Daily Palladium* October 8, 1887, 8 chronicled his untimely demise: ". . . last night the body of Henry Miller, a moulder, who lived at 144 West Erie street, was found on the West bank of the Varick canal, about one hundred feet north of the bridge leading to the Gordon malt house. A number of persons who were in the vicinity saw the deceased go down the bank, and when he did not return they became alarmed. Andrew Curran, who lives on Garrett street, passed by the place and seeing the crowd asked what the trouble was, and was informed that they thought a man had been drowned. Mr. Fred Sayer went search of a lantern and Curran went down the bank and found deceased lying on his face with his head in the water. He picked the body up and placed it on the bank and found that life was extinct. An alarm was given and police and Coroner Mattison were notified and the body was taken to Dain's undertaking room. A jury was summoned and an adjournment taken until this morning. At the inquest today Dr. W. J. Bulger testified to having made an examination of the body and found no marks of violence with the exception of a slight abrasion of the skin on the left cheek. There was no water in the lungs or any other sign that death resulted from drowning except that the head and shoulders were wet. In his opinion he said death resulted from apoplexy or some disease of the heart. Andrew Curran testified that when he found the body the head was lying in the water face down and the feet extending up the steep embankment. Mrs. Miller, wife of the deceased, testified that he worked all day yesterday and was at home in the evening as usual. After supper he went to visit a sick neighbor and then went downtown. That was the last time she saw him alive. Mrs. Miller said that her husband had been suffering from inflammatory rheumatism ever since he left the army and had done but little work since. About three weeks ago he went to work at his trade in the moulding shop of the Kingsford foundry, and his wife says he was feeling unusually well. The deceased was an old soldier and served throughout the war and received a pension. He was about 60 years of age. He was the father of Police Officer George Miller who was killed in Chicago at the time of the Anarchist riots. The jury found that death resulted from heart disease." Henry was originally buried in the Fifth Ward Cemetery but his body was moved to the City Plot, Riverside, Scriba, on November 7, 1889. Alice, who obtained a widow's pension, is buried in St. Paul's Cemetery, Oswego City. Their son, George F. (1857-May 6, 1886), had been a police officer a little more than 18 months when he died. According to *Officer Down Memorials,* he "was one of many officers detailed to disperse protesters near Haymarket Square on May 4, 1886. Suddenly, a bomb exploded and a gun battle ensued. Officer Miller suffered severe wounds. Eight other officers died in this incident. Eight men were arrested and charged with the officers' murders. Seven were convicted of murder and sentenced to death. The other one was sentenced to 15 years . . . ." Officer Miller's body, which had suffered six gunshot wounds, was shipped to Oswego and buried in St. Paul's Cemetery.

James Knox Polk Miller – Co. H
b. 1843 Oneida County, NY
d. April 1, 1863 Regimental Hospital, Belle Plain, VA
m. ------

NOTE: The son of James H. (1809-*post* 1879) and Mary Miller (1810-January 17, 1856), James enlisted in the 24th Regiment on May 4, 1861 and served until August 26, 1861 when he was discharged for "disability." The family was living in West Monroe when he enlisted in the 147th. His COD was typhoid fever. In 1879 his father applied for and obtained a pension. Mary Miller is buried in West Monroe Cemetery. Graves for her husband and son have not been located.

John Miller – Co. G
b. April 15, 1810 Germany
d. May 6, 1864 Wilderness, VA
m. Catharine Pfannemuller (August 20, 1805-March 16, 1893) December 17, 1833

NOTE: John claimed to be 43 when he enlisted but he was much older. He and Catharine immigrated to the United States in 1847 and settled in Oswego. All five of their children were born in Germany. His muster roll card says he died while a prisoner of war, but Lt. Frank Baehr testified that he had erroneously been listed as MIA by Captain Gillette. Baehr alleged that he had brought the mistake to Gillette's attention and was told it would be corrected. He stated emphatically that Miller died on the battlefield on May 6th. Catharine died in Oswego City but her grave has not been located.

William F. Miller – Co. I
b. 1817 ?
d. *post* 1880 ?
m. Harriet _____ (1831-*post* 1880) *ca.* 1848

NOTE: Very little has been learned about this soldier. He stated on his muster roll card that he was born in Salem, Essex, Massachusetts but existing census records show he was born in NYS. His parents are unknown. He and Harriet were the parents of Ezra (1850-?), Wallace (1852-?), Cora (1855-?), and Josephine (1856-?). The family's last appearance on a census roll was in 1880, although Josephine was missing. They were living in Granby. I have located no pension card. After 1880 the family disappeared.

Harlow Mills – Co. C
b. 1836 Redfield, NY
d. July 1, 1863 Gettysburg, Adams, PA
m. Mary L. West (December 13, 1834-November 30, 1914) January 24, 1861

NOTE: Harlow, a sawyer by occupation, was the son of Francis (?-August 31, 1865) and Catherine Braddock Mills (1804-*post* 1865). After he was killed, H. H. Lyman sent condolences, dated August 4th, to Mary which were published in *The Mexico Independent* August 20, 1863: "Dear madam: Your communications concerning your husband were received last night, and as neither Lieut. Potts nor Capt. Parker have been present since the Gettysburgh fight (both being wounded then), your questions concerning Harlow I will answer as well as I am able. His effects I can say nothing about, for I knew not what money he had with him. But all was lost, as we did not get possession of the field where he fell until all the dead were buried. *** In the loss of your late husband you have the sympathy of the whole company and all who knew him here. Although my knowledge of him was short, and only in the capacity of a soldier, yet I had learned to place implicit confidence in him as a true and honest man, always cheerful in the discharge of ever so disagreeable duties. Mr. Mills was one of the first who fell in my company. He was shot, I think, in the head. Could hardly have time to tell in the confusion of the fight. I regret very much that I could not get back on the field to secure and bury our dead. But it was impossible, and, hard as it seems, it could be no different. Anything which I can do in aiding you in your deep affliction I will cheerfully perform. I need not repeat his virtues, so well known to you. He is gone, we trust, where there are no more wars to come between loved ones; where all is peace, joy and love. Let us bear the chastening of the Divine Hand patiently, believing that He doeth all things well . . . ." His death also occasioned an interesting obituary written by "A Bereaved One" which appeared in *The Mexico Independent* August 6, 1863: "Harlow Mills was killed in the late battle at Gettysburg by a minie ball entering the left eye and passing out the back part of his head. He enlisted August 28, 1862, in the 147th reg't, Co. C. His tent mate in speaking of him said, 'When we went to the fight we were all in good spirits, your husband with us. Feeling the importance of the attack, and the justice of our cause, gave inspiration to all of us.' His heart was full of Patriotism, and it was only by the entreaties of his companion that he was prevented from enlisting in the 81st reg't, that left your place one year before. He was beloved by all who knew him. He won the esteem and confidence of his officers and tent mates. But he is gone, he leaves fond parents, a sister and a brother (now in the service) to mourn a kind and affectionate brother and son, a wife is bereft of her loving husband in her youthful days, who is now left to walk the path of life alone, yet her trust is in Him who doeth all things well. May they be all gathered in an unbroken family, where there will be no more war, but all Heavenly love and unison. 'He's fought his last battle/ And conquered his last foe'." The brother mentioned above was Samuel (1839-August 1, 1921), who served in the 81st Regiment. Mary applied for and obtained a widow's pension which was supposed to stop if she remarried which she did, marrying Lyman Matteson (March 16, 1837-September 6, 1865) on December 13, 1864. He died nine months later. She next married George Potter (November 13, 1819-February 11, 1899) on March 18, 1873. Under the Act of March 3, 1901 remarried widows were given the opportunity to apply for a pension and Mary did so on August 27, 1901. She either could not or would not provide the correct date for her marriage to Lyman Matteson, claiming it was either 1866 or 1868. A special examiner was appointed in 1906. He discovered that "someone" had received pension checks until March 64, 1866 and accused Mary of attempting to defraud the government. He even took her to the cemetery to see Matteson's gravestone after which she admitted they had married in 1864. She emphatically denied receiving the pension checks, however, saying, "I knew better than to draw it [the pension] after my remarriage." In fairness to Mary she was 72 years of age when she was deposed in 1906. Mr. Hotaling, the examiner, mentioned in his report that she had a good reputation, worked hard to support herself, and was a "good Christian woman." He recommended that the Chief of the Board of Review examine his findings and render a decision. When all was said and done, she collected a pension from August 29, 1901, minus the payments erroneously paid her after her remarriage. Mary's death occasioned the following obituary published in *The Sandy Creek News* December 10, 1914: "Mrs. Mary L. Potter died in Mexico, N.Y., November 30, 1914. She was born in the town of Western, Oneida county, December 13, 1834. She was a daughter of the late Willison and Hannah Hicks West and spent the greater part of her life in Oswego County. She was married to Harlow Mills, of Albion, in 1860 [*sic*]. He was killed at the battle of Gettysburg. Her second [*sic*] marriage was with George Potter of Orwell, who died in 1899. Mrs. Potter had been a member of the Methodist church for many years but had been unable for some time to attend church owing to failing eyesight. She was wonderfully comforted in her last days by the faith she had in the Father above. Those who cared

Lyman Matteson's gravestone assisted a Pension Bureau investigator and Mary West Mills in determining his DOD.
Author's Collection

for her in her last sickness speak of her repose in the hope she enjoyed. Most of her past few years were spent in the home of her nephew, William. H. West of Mexico, where she found kind and tender care at the hands of Mr. and Mrs. West. Aside from the nephew her only near relative surviving is a sister, Mrs. Johnson of Rome. The funeral was held in the Methodist church, Thursday, December 3, at two o'clock, Rev. Mr. Townsend, assisted by Mr. B. G. Seamans, officiating. Mr. Seamans a friend of Mrs. Potter for many years, spoke at request, in which he mentioned the estimable traits of the departed. Burial was made in Mexico cemetery. 'I will bring the blind by the way that they know not, I will lead them in paths that they have not known; I will make darkness light before them and crooked things straight.' Isaiah 42:16. – Democrat." Harlow Mills is buried in Gettysburg National Cemetery. Lyman Matteson is buried in Arthur Cemetery, Mexico, with Willie (1866-1866), his son by Mary. George Potter is buried with his first wife, Lucinda (1828-*post* 1870), in Evergreen Cemetery, Orwell, NY. Mary is buried in Mexico Primitive Cemetery.

Andrew Mires – Co. K

b. 1827 Germany

d. June 30, 1909 National Soldiers' Home, Bath, Steuben, NY

m. Catherine _____ (1832-August 2, 1917) *ca.* 1861

NOTE: Andrew, whose surname was variously spelled, including "Meyers" and "Myers," originally enlisted in the 110th Regiment. He was wounded at Gettysburg on July 1, 1863. He mustered out with the regiment on June 7, 1865. In 1890 he claimed "chronic diarrhea and piles" as his disabilities. He last appeared in the Oswego city directory in 1888. By 1890 he was living in Bath. He is buried in Bath National Cemetery under the name "Mier" or "Meir." Catherine, born in Ireland, died in Syracuse, NY and was buried in St. Mary's Cemetery, Fulton.

John Nicholas Mistler – Co. D

b. October 13, 1837 France

d. January 13, 1878 Hillsdale, Hillsdale, MI

m. Frances E. Young (1842-November 5, 1918) *ca.* 1862

NOTE: John, whose parents are unidenti-fied, attained the rank of second lieuten-ant and mustered out with the regiment on June 7, 1865. He was a marble cutter and in Hillsdale was a partner in Mistler and Jennings, a firm specializing in grave stones. Mistler was a member of Hillsdale Lodge #176 F & AM and his own grave-stone, situated in Oak Grove Cemetery, Hillsdale, is decorated with the square and compass. John's COD was consump-tion. He is buried with an infant son, Willie (1875-1877). On June 3, 1878 Frances married William F. Keith (1849-December 26, 1919) but apparently the marriage did not last. In 1900 she was living in Stockton, San Joaquin, CA with a daughter, Grace Armbrust, and a son, Frank. Her grave has not been located.

John Mistler was a stone mason after the war, specializing in grave markers.

Daniel Sigler

Velsor Montross – Co. H

b. September 20, 1840 Rensselaerville, Albany, NY

d. October 27, 1909 Vienna, Oneida, NY

m. Adella Reed (1649-July 6, 1917) 1868

NOTE: Velsor was the son of Jacob (1813-1900) and Ann Eliza Denio Montross (1816-1884). His sister Julia was the wife of Victor Hallock, also a member of the 147th Regiment. Velsor was captured at Gettysburg and paroled at an unknown date. He returned to the regiment and was wounded in the left hand at Five Forks, VA on April 1, 1865. He was discharged from Whitehall Hospital, Philadelphia, PA on June 15, 1865. His obituary, published in *The Rome Daily Sentinel* October 28, 1909, 8, chronicled a full, active life: "Velsor Montross died about 10 a.m. on Wednesday while sitting in a chair at his home. He had been ill with Bright's disease for a long time. He was born in Rensselaerville, Albany county, and celebrated his 69th birthday September 20. For a time he lived at Bernhard's Bay, then West Vienna, and 30 years ago he moved to North Bay, where he had lived since. He was a horseshoer and blacksmith by occupation, and conducted a shop on Main street during all of his residence here until poor health compelled him to give up work. It has since been conducted by his son, who became his father's partner some years ago. He served three years in the army during the Civil War, and was a member of Company H, 147th Regiment, New York Volunteers, and for some time was confined in one of the southern prisons. In politics he was a Democrat, and has held the offices of town clerk and commissioner of highways. He was also a Mason, a member of Vienna Masonic Lodge, and the funeral will be partly in charge of the Masons. He was married 41 years ago to Miss Della Reed, a daughter of the late Luther Reed of this place, who survives with three sons . . . Mr. Montross was well known and one who enjoyed the acquaintance of a large circle of friends, who will learn with much regret of his death, and deeply sympathize with the bereaved ones . . . ." Adella died at the home of her son, Bert, in Auburn, Cayuga, NY. She and Velsor are buried in North Bay Lawn Cemetery, Vienna.

Ebenezer Moore – Co. I

b. 1838 Canada

d. November 11, 1880 Fernwood, NY

m. Mary Angeline Wood (1840-January 1910) *ca.* 1857

NOTE: Ebenezer was the son of Giles (1805-1850) and Sally Draper Moore (1815-?). He transferred to the VRC on March 20, 1865. His application for a pension was filed on October 19, 1865. On the 1880 census he was listed among the Paupers and Indigents as receiving town assistance on account of consumption. He was termed "habitually intemperate." He is buried in Daysville Cemetery, Richland. Mary Angeline applied for a pension on March 19, 1881 but did not receive it, most likely because she married Royal Nutting (1816-March 24, 1905) *ca.* 1881 as his third wife. She is buried in Daysville Cemetery, Richland. Royal Nutting is buried in Willis Cemetery, Fernwood.

George Moore – Co. E
b. 1830 Sandy Creek, NY
d. August 9, 1865 Sandy Creek, NY
m. Matilda Baldwin (June 25, 1833-August 14, 1910) December 14, 1848

NOTE: George, son of John (*ca.* 1785-September 1869) and Hannah Ferguson Moore (1796-April 25, 1882, and Matilda were married in Lorraine, Jefferson, NY and at the time of his death were the parents of six minor children. He was discharged from the 147th on February 5, 1863 and re-enlisted in Go. G, 184th Regiment on August 31, 1864. When he was discharged on June 29, 1865 at City Point, VA he was suffering from chronic diarrhea which, according to Major William Ferguson of the 184th, he had contracted on or about February 25, 1865 at Harrison's Landing, VA. The disease had rendered him unfit for duty. Moore headed home but got no farther than his mother's house in Sandy Creek on July 14, 1865, a few miles from his own home and that is where he died. He is buried in the Moore Family Plot, Boylston, although the dates do not coincide. A stone confirms he was a member of the 147th Regiment but lists his DOD as August 20, 1864. Matilda, who was illiterate, applied for and obtained pensions for herself and the children. On June 29, 1873 she married Charles Rowbotham (1834-December 18, 1908) in Lorraine, Jefferson, NY. Rowbotham had already been married twice. His first wife, Jane Fair (1838-August 25, 1882), left him in 1867 and made her way to Chicago where she reportedly married a man named _____ Murphy by whom she had three more children in addition to the four she and Charles produced. Apparently Jane attempted to start divorce proceedings against Charles but the matter was quashed, perhaps because she left him for another man. After Jane departed, Rowbotham moved to Ohio where on May 14, 1870 he married Esther Rowe (1847-June 24, 1872). Upon her death he returned to New York State where he married Matilda. He did not enjoy a very good reputation as a worker and provider and there were allegations that he attempted to force Matilda to hand over a good share of her children's pension money. She steadfastly maintained, however, that her reason for leaving him was that she did not know about Jane until she heard one of her stepsons tell his aunt his mother was coming for a visit. After confronting her husband who corroborated the boy's story, she immediately separated from him. Matilda and her children moved to Michigan where on December 21, 1881 she married Loran D. Hancock (1813-November 30, 1898). They lived together until his death of cancer. Hancock is buried with his first wife, Susan (1816-1880), in Rich Township

Cemetery, Lapeer County, MI. In 1902 Matilda applied for restoration of her pension under the Remarried Widows' Act of March 3, 1901. She also asked for arrears from the time she "married" Rowbotham until 1881 when she married Hancock, claiming that she was entitled because her marriage to Rowbotham was null and void. Many years passed before the claim was settled but in 1908 she was granted the arrears and she was also awarded a pension under the provisions of the Act of March 3, 1901. By that time she was a very old woman. She died of "dropsy" and was buried in Riverside Cemetery, Vassar, Tuscola, MI.

John Moore – Co. A
b. 1842 ?
d. June 9, 1887 Tucson, Pima, AZ
m. Carmen Suastegui (March 4, 1859-January 23, 1937) 1877

NOTE: John Moore's parents and POB are unknown. According to his muster roll card, he was born in Oswego County. His entry in *The Town Clerks' Registers* noted he was born in Buffalo, Erie, NY. On the 1880 census he said both he and his parents had been born in Pennsylvania. John enlisted at Oswego City on August 14, 1862. He was wounded at Gettysburg on July 1, 1863 and again at Cold Harbor, VA on June 3, 1864. His discharge was dated to March 13, 1865. After the war he migrated west. His occupation on the 1880 census was police officer in Tucson. His COD is unknown but he is buried in Evergreen Memorial Park, Tucson. A note attached to his FAG entry states his exact grave location is unknown but the marker was placed in the approximate spot. Carmen was the daughter of Rafael Suastegui and Emilia Pompa. She came to the United States in 1875 and became a naturalized citizen. She had at least four sisters, Beatrice, Emilia, Mariana, and Clara, with whom she lived for many years after John died, and a brother, Francisco. Carmen's death elicited the following obituary in *The Arizona Daily Star* January 24, 1937, 6: "Mrs. Carmen S. Moore, 77-year-old resident of Tucson, died yesterday afternoon after a long illness at her home, 630 South Fourth avenue. Mrs. Moore was born in 1859 in Hermosillo, Sonora, Mexico, and came to Tucson in 1875. Here she married John Moore in 1877. She had lived in Tuscson since that time . . . ." Carmen is buried in Holy Hope Cemetery, Tucson.

Lawrence Moore – Co. B
b. 1827 Ireland
d. November 8, 1887 Oswego City, NY
m. Mary _____ (1834-October 7, 1906) *ca.* 1857

NOTE: Moore's parents are unknown. He was a laborer by occupation. He was transferred to the VRC on February 15, 1864. According to a casualty list published in *The Oswego Commercial Times* July 20, 1863, Moore was among the wounded at Gettysburg. In1890, Mary reported her husband had been shot in the arm and disabled so he could not work. She told the enumerator he died from the effects of the wound. Moore's application for a pension dated September 13, 1865 was successful. Mary's death was noted in *The Oswego Daily Times* October 8, 1906, 1: "Mrs. Mary Moore for a great many years a highly respected resident of the First Ward died last evening at her home 201 West Seneca. She had been ill for a long time the result of having broken her hip by a fall. Mrs. Moore was the wife of the late Lawrence Moore and she is survived by one daughter, Miss Mary Moore of this city." Lawrence and Mary are buried in St. Paul's Cemetery, Oswego City.

Joseph W. Morgan – Co. I

b. May 1841 Oswego, NY
d. February 1, 1914 Chicago, Cook, IL
m. Catharine Murphy (March 1850-February 13, 1915) 1869

NOTE: Joseph, son of John (1800-1858) and Sarah Marshall Morgan (1800-*post* 1880), was a painter by occupation. He was captured at Gettysburg on July 1, 1863. According to *The Town Clerks' Registers*, he escaped and rejoined the regiment. He was wounded at the battle of the Wilderness, May 5, 1864, transferred to the VRC on October 5, 1864 and finally discharged on June 27, 1865 at Washington, DC. Although his FAG entry shows he was born in 1846, all early census records indicate he was born in 1841. He and Catharine, the parents of five children, are both buried in Mt. Olivet Cemetery, Chicago. A brother, Hugh (1837-September 18, 1900), served first in Co. A, 6th NY Cavalry and later in Co. A, 2nd NY Provisional Cavalry. He never married and spent many years

Joseph and Catherine Murphy Morgan were the parents of five children. The couple is buried in Mt. Olivet Cemetery, Chicago.
Dorothy Morgan Monahan

entering and leaving soldiers' homes and poorhouses. He died in Cleveland, Cuyahoga, OH and is buried in Woodland Cemetery.

George Morrall – Co. F
b. 1819 England
d. August 13, 1889 Vermillion, NY
m. Jane _____ (1829-December 6, 1911) *ca.* 1845

NOTE: George's surname was variously spelled. I use that on his gravestone. He was transferred to the VRC on March 1, 1864 and discharged at Washington, DC on June 29, 1865. He and Jane, who had been born in Columbia County, NY, lived in New Haven, where he was a blacksmith. Jane's death elicited a short obituary in *The Oswego Daily Times* December 13, 1911, 6: "On Wednesday, Dec. 6, in the very early morning occurred the death of Mrs. Jane Morrall, widow of the late George Morrall, aged 85 years. Mrs. Morrall was much esteemed for her Christian virtues. She is survived by her son, John Morrall, of Binghamton, who was present when the end came. The funeral was held from the Vermillion Methodist Episcopal church Friday, Dec. 8, at 2 p.m., Rev. D. C. Haven officiating . . . ." George and Jane are buried in Vermillion Cemetery. John (1846-1913) was the couple's only child. When only 15 he enlisted in the 59th Regiment NYSV and served for three years. He was severely wounded at Antietam on September 17, 1862. John is buried in Floral Park Cemetery, Binghamton.

Henry F. Morton – Co. F
b. 1838 Mexico, NY
d. July 26, 1863 Gettysburg, Adams, PA
m. Kate Himple (1842-April 18, 1921) *ca.* 1860

NOTE: Henry, son of Gad Waite (1800-1883) and Betsy Wing Morton (1808-1880), was a cooper. He originally enlisted in the 110th Regiment. He was wounded on July 1, 1863 and died of his wounds. He is buried in Gettysburg National Cemetery. He and Kate, who was born in Germany, were the parents of Frederick Henry (1861-May 25, 1956). In 1864 Kate married Daniel Morton (1844-October 26, 1918), Henry's brother. He was a member of Co. A, 81st Regiment. According to an article in *The Mexico Independent* December 17, 1863 while in Washington, DC he "was accidentally shot through the right arm, which was so injured that amputation became necessary." Later in life he was a constable in Mexico. He and Kate were the parents of Medora "Dora" (1865-1942). Daniel, Kate, and Dora are all buried in Mexico Village Cemetery.

Abram Mowers – Co. C
b. January 16, 1834 Parish, NY
d. December 3, 1917 Parish, NY
m1. ? (?-?) ?

m2. Julia Ann Smith Duel (February 4, 1830-April 7, 1900) *ca.* 1868

m3. Sarah Hannah Campbell Cole (1837-May 8, 1916) April 14, 1913

m4. Mary Weed DeWolf (May 4, 1846-May 13, 1928) October 24, 1917

NOTE: Abram, also known as Abraham, was the son of John (?-*ante* 1850) and Adelia Woodbeck Mowers (1801-*post* 1850). He was wounded and captured at Gettysburg on July 1st, but according to *The Town Clerks' Registers*, was returned the next day. He transferred to the VRC on November 15, 1863 and was discharged from the service on July 1, 1865. He applied for a pension on January 25, 1879 and the enumerator for the 1880 census wrote he "has fits" and was an invalid. When he and Mary applied for a marriage license Abram alleged he was marrying for the fourth time. I have not located any information about his first wife. He was enumerated in his brother's house in 1865 and described as single. Julia was previously married to Seth Duel (1810-*ante* 1868). Abram and Julia are buried in Bidwell Cemetery, Parish. The gravestone does not show his DOD. Sarah had previously been the wife of Alvin Cole (1830-*post* 1910). When she and Abram went to Fulton to obtain a marriage license, *The Syracuse Herald* April 13, 1913 reported they were the oldest couple ever to obtain a marriage license in that city. Sarah is buried in Mt. Adnah Cemetery, Fulton. Mary Weed had previously been married to William DeWolf (1820-October 19, 1901) as his third wife. *The Sandy Creek News* September 20, 1894, 4 carried a delightful story about William's wooing and winning of his last bride. Mary applied for a pension on June 1, 1921 but did not obtain it. An obituary appeared in *The Mexico Independent* May 17, 1928: "Mrs. Mary Mowers, 82, died in the City of Ogdensburg, Sunday evening, May 13, 1928. Mrs. Mowers had been a life long resident of the northern part of the town of Mexico until about one year ago. She was a member of the Methodist Episcopal church of Parish, N.Y. The only surviving relative is one sister, Mrs. Floretta Sainsbury with whom she had lived up to [the] time of leaving Mexico for Ogdensburg. The remains arrived at Mexico and were taken in charge by undertaker Edw. J. Fish and removed to the home of her sister where funeral services were held Wednesday afternoon at two o'clock, Rev. B. L. Waters, pastor of the First Methodist Episcopal church of Mexico officiating. Interment was in Willis cemetery . . . ." Although the obituary does not say so, Mary died in the State Hospital.

Joseph Sidney Munger – Co. F
b. February 5, 1841 Palermo, NY
d. January 11, 1863 Falmouth, VA
m. ------

NOTE: Joseph was the son of Hiram (1805-1862) and Caroline Moss Munger (1808-1881). His muster roll card says he died of "disease" and a notation in *The Town Clerks' Registers* states that his COD was "quiet consumption." A letter written to the editors of *The Mexico Independent* by an unidentified soldier at Belle Plain, VA on January 13, 1863 and published on January 22nd announced Joseph's passing: ". . . Joseph Munger died last Sunday night, and was buried the following morning just before our regiment started on its march. A board was placed at the head of his grave with his name, the letter of his company and the number of his regiment, so his friends can find his grave without any trouble. There is a great amount of sickness, and many deaths. Last week there were three deaths in one hospital in one day. It seems to be a small matter for a man to die in camp . . . ."

Thomas Murphy – Co. D

b. 1824 Ireland
d. May 8, 1864 Laurel Hill, VA
m. Honora "Nora" Dwyer (1829-November 26, 1906) *ca.* 1853

NOTE: Thomas, whose parents are unknown, was a shoemaker. According to *Deaths of Volunteers*, he died in Spotsylvania General Hospital of a gunshot wound to the abdomen. Honora applied for a widow's pension and in 1867 applied for pensions for her minor children, using the name Honora Irons. Richard Irons (1817-*ca.* 1869), also a shoemaker, was born in England. In 1860 he, wife Rhoda, and three children were living in Cape Vincent, Jefferson, NY. By 1865 the family was living in Oswego City. At some time between 1865 and 1870 he and Honora were married. By 1870 Honora was again a widow. In that same year she and her children by Murphy were living in Dennis Scanlon's (1830-?) home. They must have been married before the census was taken because she listed herself as Honora Irons in the 1870 Oswego city directory. By 1880 Scanlon had disappeared and Honora's household consisted of two of her children and three Scanlon stepsons. Dennis Murphy (1857-October 1, 1902), a son, fell into the Oswego River and drowned. His obituary mentioned Scanlon, saying he "died several years ago." Dennis Murphy and Honora are buried in St. Paul's Cemetery, Oswego City. No other graves have been located.

Peter Murray – Co. E

b. September 3, 1818 Burlington, Chittenden, VT
d. September 18, 1888 Ellisburg, Jefferson, NY
m. Mary Ann Kilborn (1820-September 13, 1914) February 19, 1838

NOTE: Peter went AWOL on November 30, 1862 and did not return to the regiment until March 7, 1865. He was required to forfeit all his pay and allowances and to make up the time lost. He was transferred to Co. K, 91st Regiment on June 5, 1865 and discharged July 3rd. He is buried in Woodlawn Cemetery, Sandy Creek. His gravestone cites his membership in the 91st Regiment. Mary Ann, the mother of four, died in Oswego City. A short obituary appeared in *The Oswego Daily Palladium* September 14, 1914, 8: "The death of Mrs. Mary Murray occurred at the home of her daughter, Mrs. D. F. Smith, 68 Mitchell street, yesterday afternoon, after a lingering illness. She was born in Rutland, Vt., ninety-four years ago, but has been a resident of this city for many years. She was a member of Trinity M. E. Church. Besides her daughter she leaves one son, William L., of this city." Mary is buried in Riverside Cemetery, Scriba.

John Mushizer – Co. G
b. 1840 Rome, Oneida, NY
d. July 3, 1863 Gettysburg, Adams, PA
m. ------

NOTE: John, son of Francis (1815-1895) and Mary Mushizer (1810-1885), was a miller. He was wounded on July 1, 1863 and succumbed to those injuries. The following appeared in *The Oswego Commercial Times* October 8, 1863: "The body of J. Mushoeser, of the 147th regiment, who was killed at Gettysburgh, has been brought to this city. The funeral will take place on Sunday at 2 o'clock P. M. on the corner of East Seneca and Fifth streets. – The German Guards will attend the funeral." He was buried in St. Paul's Cemetery, Oswego and his name appears on the family monument. The name of a brother, Peter (1843-November 20, 1864), also appears on the stone. To date I have located nothing about this man although one researcher claims Peter died in Chicago in 1874. The inscription on the base of the monument reads: "May their souls rest in peace." Mary Mushizer applied for and obtained a pension. Her husband Francis successfully applied for a pension after her death.

John Mushizer – Co. G
b. 1843 Oswego County, NY
d. March 13, 1863 ?
m. ------

NOTE: This man appears nowhere except on his muster roll card which states he was a cooper. The card specifically states he died March 13, 1863 but does not give the POD.

Isaac H. Neville – Co. B
b. 1824 Jefferson County, NY
d. October 17, 1905 Oswego City, NY
m. Eliza J. Core (1836-March 25, 1919) *ca.* 1854

NOTE: Isaac's parents are unknown. He was a teamster by occupation. He was discharged from the army for "disability" at an unknown date. In 1900 Eliza said she was the mother of 18 children, six of whom survived. Isaac is buried in Rural Cemetery, Oswego Town, with several of his children. Eliza moved to Syracuse, NY in 1918 and died there. Her death elicited the following obituary in *The Oswego Daily Times* March 26, 1919, 7: "Mrs. Eliza Neville, widow of the late Isaac Neville and for many years a well-known resident of this city, died at her home, 1225 West Pleasant avenue, Syracuse, yesterday. The body will be brought here tonight and funeral will be held tomorrow at 11 o'clock from Dain's funeral parlors. The funeral services will be conducted by the Rev. A. G. Judd, pastor of the First M. E. church. A son and two daughters survive, Eugene Neville of this city, and Miss Harriett Neville and Mrs. John Chauncey of Syracuse." Eliza's grave has not been located.

Andrew Jackson Newton – Co. E
b. April 18, 1835 Sandy Creek, NY
d. April 19, 1908 Oswego Center, NY
m1. Mary Jane Kent (1842-August 14, 1864) December 29, 1858
m2. Alice Nancy Carpenter May 9, 1844-September 20, 1927) January 1, 1866

NOTE: Andrew was the son of Jotham (1796-1889) and Sarah Ann Titus Newton (1800-1881). He mustered out with the regiment on June 7, 1865. His obituary, published in *The Sandy Creek News* April 23, 1908, detailed his long life: "In the death of Andrew Jackson Newton, which occurred at the home of his son, Ora, at Oswego Centre, Easter Sunday, April 19, this town lost one of its highly respected and greatly esteemed citizens. He was born on the Ridge road April 18, 1835, being the son of Jotham and Sarah (Titus) Newton. His parents were among the town's pioneers, and possessed the sturdiness and integrity of their New England ancestors. To this couple twelve children were born, of whom only two survive, Mrs. Admatha Hadley and Miss Viola Newton of Sandy Creek. The departed was first married to Mary Kent, who after a brief married life passed away. In 1867 [sic] he was again united in marriage to Alice Carpenter, who with three children, survive him, Hosea, living in Pulaski, Ora at Oswego Centre, and Miss Lucia at home with her mother. Their oldest son, Jotham, and their youngest son, Perry, a student at Brown's university, a young man full of promise, died several years ago. Mr. Newton at the opening of the war responded to his country's call for defenders and experienced the privations of a soldier's life, until the confederacy became a lost cause. After being honorably discharged he returned to his former home, where he was engaged in farming. He was a member of the G.A.R. post and took great interest in all that appertained to its welfare. The immediate cause of his death was pleurisy, aggravated by disease contracted in the army. His obsequies were held at his late home April 23, Rev. T. T. Davies officiating. Interment in the family lot in Woodlawn cemetery. The departed was a man of sterling worth, upright in character and clean in his private life. He was loved and trusted by a large circle of friends. He is now at rest and has fallen asleep, in Jesus."

Andrew most likely belonged to Andrew J. Barney Post No. 217 GAR. When Alice died, *The Sandy Creek News* September 22, 1927, 4 published a lengthy obituary: "Mrs. Alice N. Newton, widow of the late Jackson Newton of Sandy Creek, departed this life at her home on South Main street, Tuesday morning September 20, 1927, after being satisfied with a long and beneficent life. The immediate cause of her death was an infection of the throat, affecting the glands of the neck. She was born on the Ridge road, on the farm now owned by Thomas Soule, May 9, 1844, being the daughter of George and Nancy Dean Carpenter. Her father was one of the early settlers of this town, moving hither from Vermont in an ox-team, which at that time was as great an undertaking as a journey from here to California would mean today. The land upon which he located was covered with great pine trees which in the process of time he cleared, and converted the forest land into a place of human habitation. What a wonderful race of people the pioneers of this town, and other towns, must have been. There were giants on the earth in those days. Little we realize in these days of ease and utility the amount of labor required to subdue the forest and erect suitable buildings for the shelter of man and beast. Jan. 1, 1866 she was married to Jackson Newton, who departed this life several years ago. Five children blessed their union, of whom three survive, Lucia Newton and Hosea Newton, Syracuse, and Ora Newton, Sandy Creek. Mrs. Newton has been a life long resident of this town. Her education was obtained at Pulaski and Belleville Academy. Her early life was devoted to teaching, having, in 1865, sixty pupils attending her district school on the Ridge Road among whom twelve of her former pupils still are living. She was a charter member of the W.C.T.U. and rendered efficient service to the union in the years that are gone. She rendered valuable assistance to the W.R.C. as long as the organization functioned. In her church affiliation she belonged to the Disciple Church at Richland. During many years she conducted an extensive correspondence with friends far and near. She wrote many letters, and numerous were the friends that kept in touch with her. Her funeral will be held at the Congregational Church Friday, Sept. 23, at 2:30 p.m. Rev. T. T. Davies is in charge. Interment will be in the family lot at Woodlawn cemetery." Alice was a sister of Samuel Carpenter, a member of the 147th Regiment who died at Gettysburg and is buried in Woodlawn.

Charles Nichols – Co. D
b. 1824 Arlington, Bennington, VT
d. January 2, 1904 Fulton, NY
m1. ?
m2. Rosella Guyette Carvey (1826-January 23, 1919) *ca.* 1865

NOTE: Charles said he was a laborer when he enlisted but by 1870 he was working on the railroad. In 1890 his disability was a gunshot wound to the left breast. He mustered out with the regiment on June 7, 1865. Charles was married twice but his first wife's name is unknown. He had a son, Stephen (1859-May 19, 1927), and a daughter, Orilla (1851-*post* 1919). On the 1860 census both children were living with other families. Rosella was first married to James Carvey, Jr. (1827-1864), a member of Co. A, 12th NY Cavalry. He was captured at Plymouth, NC April 20, 1864 and died in the Florence, SC stockade on October 10, 1864. Their marriage on August 8, 1852 produced five children. Charles and Rosella are buried in Mt. Adnah Cemetery, Fulton.

James R. Nichols – Co. D
b. October 1844 Litchfield, Herkimer, NY
d. May 12, 1925 Syracuse, Onondaga, NY
m. Theresa Mary Ballard (April 1851-October 11, 1920) 1869

NOTE: James' middle initial is R. only on his muster roll card. All other documents say it was K. He was the son of Daniel (1822-1897) and Louisa Maria Langworthy Nichols (1817-1864). He was wounded on July 1, 1863 at Gettysburg, transferred to the VRC on June 18, 1864, and ultimately discharged on June 29, 1865 at Washington, DC. He is buried in Mt. Adnah Cemetery, Fulton, NY. Theresa's COD was Bright's disease. She is buried in St. Mary's Cemetery, Fulton.

John L. Nichols – Co. E
b. July 16, 1818 Sandy Creek, NY
d. May 16, 1896 Sandy Creek, NY
m1. Martha Ann Richardson (December 2, 1825-April 4, 1884) February 22, 1849
m2. Alza Martin Stannard (1837-December 24, 1909) 1889

NOTE: John was discharged on March 26, 1863 for "disability" and in 1890 he said he was disabled by rheumatism. His death occasioned the following obituary in *The Sandy Creek News* May 21, 1896: "Mr. John L. Nichols, one of the older residents of the town, entered into rest at his home in this village after an illness of a few hours on Saturday morning last. Mr. Nichols was subject to neuralgia of the heart and suffered from two attacks on the street on Friday, the second being specially severe. He however ate a hearty supper and was about as usual though retiring somewhat early. Shortly before one o'clock Saturday morning he suffered another attack from which his physician, Dr. Cook, found no relief though he applied the most powerful medicines. He retained his consciousness to within a few moments of his death which took place at 7:30 when he entered peacefully into rest. Mr. Nichols was born in the town of Sandy Creek, July 16, 1818, being the second of three children born to Thomas B. and Susannah Nichols. He had survived all the members of his father's family . . . He was married February 22, 1849, to Miss Martha A. Richardson, daughter of Axel Richardson of Richland . . . Mrs. Nichols died in the spring of 1884, and in the fall of 1889 he married Mrs. Alza Stannard of Parish, who survives her husband. Mr. Nichols spent most of his life in this county. He responded to his country's call in 1862 and enlisted in Company E, 147th regiment, New York Volunteers. Through exposure he contracted disease in the following year and was sent home to his cot never to regain the vigor of his former manhood . . . ." Martha's COD was termed "congestion." She and John are buried in Woodlawn Cemetery, Sandy Creek. Alza's first husband, Henry Stannard (1839-November 3, 1888), died in Sandy Creek and is buried in Oakwood Cemetery, Chittenango, NY. She is buried in Eaton Village Cemetery, Madison County, NY.

John Nicholson – Co. C
b. June 1842 South Richland, NY
d. July 25, 1897 Richland, NY
m. Matilda McClelland (1847-February 13, 1933) *ca.* 1867

NOTE: John, son of Joseph (1792-1865) and Dimmis Loomis Nicholson (1795-1887), was discharged for "disability" on October 14, 1863. He was a member of J. B. Butler Post No. 111 GAR. Upon his death the post published the following resolutions in *The Pulaski Democrat* August 18, 1897: ". . . Whereas, Comrade John Nicholson, late Co. C, 147th Regt. N.Y. Inf., has in the providence of Almighty God been summoned by death from time to eternity, therefore, Resolved, That we honor his name who went forth in response to his country's call and served with her brave defenders. We tender to his bereaved widow and family our heartfelt sympathy in this time of their bereavement and sorrow. Resolved, That the rooms of Post J. B. Butler, No. 111, G.A.R., of which he was a member, be draped in mourning for thirty days and a copy of these resolutions be presented to the family of our deceased comrade and be spread upon the records of the Post . . . ." Matilda married J. Wilbur Bushnell (1833-1915) *ca.* 1898 as his second wife. He died in Washington, DC and his body was shipped home. He and his first wife, Harriet Carter (1835-1897), are buried in Willis Cemetery, Fernwood. John and Matilda, who died in Syracuse, NY, are also buried there. John's brother, George (1828-1864) served in Co A, 2nd NY HA, enlisting on January 4, 1864. He was wounded in the foot on June 9, 1864, place not stated but perhaps Petersburg, VA, and died at Stanton General Hospital, Washington, DC of typhoid fever contracted after being wounded.

Peter Bunker Nickerson – Co. H
b. October 24, 1818 Broome, Schoharie, NY
d. November 6, 1876 Martinsville, Harrison, MO
m. Mary Ann Knowles (June 7, 1821-February 24, 1907) October 27, 1839

NOTE: Peter's parents were Andrew (1787-1844) and Theodosia Burch Nickerson (1788-1883). He was discharged from the service on May 30, 1863 at David's Island,

New York City. He and Mary Ann were the parents of ten children. After the war the family moved to Missouri. Mary Ann married Jacob McLey (1824-1903) in 1880 as his third wife. Mary Ann and Peter are buried in Kidwell Cemetery, Martinsville. Jacob may be buried in Cat Creek Cemetery, Harrison County, MO.

Reynolds Knowles Nickerson – Co. H
b. September 1, 1843 Schoharie County, NY
d. January 31, 1912 Bethany, Harrison, MO
m1. Margaret Rowe (March 2, 1845-February 6, 1904) April 11, 1867
m2. Nancy "Nannie" Jane Empshwiller Walker (April 12, 1850-February 21, 1921) 1905

NOTE: Reynolds was the son of Peter and Mary Ann Nickerson. He was transferred to the VRC on September 26, 1863 and discharged at Washington, DC on June 26, 1865. When his father died, he was appointed guardian of his minor siblings. He was the superintendent of the almshouse in Bethany, MO in 1910. Reynolds' COD was heart and kidney disease. Although Nannie officially died of a cerebral hemorrhage, an article in *The Albany Capital* February 10, 1921, 3, offers insights into her demise: "Mrs. Nannie Nickerson, relict of the late R. K. Nickerson, returned from Kansas City Sunday, where she had been visiting her son, John Walker, and proceeded to her home in the south part of town, to settle down to her ordinary life. She started her baseburner and retired that night in usual health. When she did not appear the next morning neighbors investigated and could hear her breathing but could get no response. Dr. Harned was passing at the time and was called to their aid, and immediately broke a window and entered the house. He found her in an unconscious condition and the house full of hard coal gas. She was given every aid possible, but remained unconscious all day Monday and Tuesday, and at the time this is written (Tuesday night) no hopes are entertained for her recovery." Reynolds, Margaret, and Nannie are buried in Miriam Cemetery, Bethany, MO.

James Nolan – Co. D
b. 1836 Ireland
d. August 20, 1864 David's Island, New York City, NY
m. Harriet Lum (1844-May 3, 1930) *ca.* 1862

NOTE: James, parents unidentified, was wounded in action but the place was not specified, although it was probably Petersburg. He was buried in Cypress Hills Cemetery, Brooklyn. He and Harriet were the parents of Mary Ann Nolan [Wilson] (1862-1963). Harriet married Thomas L. Green (1840-November 29, 1919) *ca.* 1865. He had served in Co. D, 50th NY Engineers from 1861-June 13, 1865. He, Harriet, Mary Ann, and their daughter Nora are all buried in Lewis Cemetery, Granby.

George A. Northrop – Co. G
b. January 8, 1841 Oswego Town, NY
d. May 29, 1868 Granby, NY
m. ------

NOTE: George's parents were David (1801-November 10, 1855) and Polly Barker Northrop (1807-December 23, 1895). He transferred to Batt. L, 1st NY ART on November 16, 1863. His mother 's application for a pension on October 3, 1870 was successful. George is buried in Lewis Cemetery, Granby. His mother died in Oswego City. Graves for her and David have not been located.

Birdsey Norton – Co. H
b. November 1840 Parish, NY
d. February 14, 1929 Syracuse, Onondaga, NY
m. Jane "Jenny" A. Nicholson (1848-November 28, 1925) 1869

NOTE: Birdsey, whose name was variously spelled, was the son of Birdsey (1806-*ante* 1850) and Lemira Norton (1805-*post* 1860). He was a carpenter by trade. He and Jane were the parents of four children. Upon his death, *The Syracuse Journal* February 15, 1929, 2 published the following: "Birdsey Norton, 88, Civil War veteran, answered his last roll call last night. He passed away at the home of his son, William Norton . . . after a brief illness. He was a member of Lilly Post, 66, G.A.R. During the Civil War he was a member of the 147th Regiment and was later transferred to Company L, First Regiment, New York Light Artillery. Mr. Norton participated in 12 important battles in the Civil War and was honorably discharged in Elmira, June 17, 1865. After returning home he married Miss Jane Nicholson, of New York City and resided in the First Ward until his death . . . Funeral services will take place from the home of his son tomorrow . . . ." He and Jane are buried in Woodlawn Cemetery, Syracuse.

Clark H. Norton – Co. H
b. May 30, 1841 Parish, NY
d. October 10, 1926 Syracuse, Onondaga, NY
m. Nellie M. Brown (August 17,1846-March 30, 1919) 1867

NOTE: Clark, a cooper by occupation, was the son of Stephen (1819-?) and Mary Richards Norton (1821-?). He attained the rank of second lieutenant in February 1865 and mustered out with the regiment on June 7, 1865. After the war he moved to Michigan with his brother Pliny and lived in Saginaw where he worked as a raftsman and was elected deputy sheriff. Upon returning to Syracuse in 1873 he became active in local affairs. In 1888 he was chosen to command the delegation representing the 147th Regiment for the dedication of the regimental monument at Gettysburg. He was a member of Syracuse Lodge No. 501 F & A M. He was also very active in Post Root No. 151 GAR, Syracuse. In June 1902 while serving as post commander he was nominated and elected to the office of senior vice commander for the New York Department. *The Abstract of General Orders and Proceedings of The Annual Encampment, Department of New York, G.A. R.,* 333-4 contains Captain Alexander Penfield's speech to second his nomination: ". . . I speak from the position of an associate with him in the Army. I was Captain of the company of which he was a sergeant and afterwards promoted to Second Lieutenant. He served faithfully as has been told you here . . . doing every duty cheerfully, meeting every responsibility that was imposed upon him without a murmur. You know that when a soldier does that he is a pretty good one. I have slept with him. To know a man through and through you have to sleep with him, eat hard tack with him, drink out of the same canteen and share each other's toils and perils. Therefore I

Clark H. Norton was very active in the Grand Army of the Republic and in local political affairs.
Syracuse Post-Standard

speak of it honestly and with a knowledge that would satisfy any comrade who knows." In 1898 Norton was elected to the Syracuse City Board of Assessors and served as president twice. He and Nellie, the mother of three, are buried in Morningside Mausoleum, Oakwood Cemetery, Syracuse. Clark's brother, Pliny (1844-1900), served in Co. E, 24th NY Cavalry. He died at the Soldiers' Home, Grand Rapids, MI and was buried in the Soldiers' Home Cemetery.

Martin J. O'Brien – Co. I
b. 1824 Ireland
d. May 31, 1887 Oswego City, NY
m. Winifred _____ (1827-*ante* 1880) *ca.* 1854

NOTE: Martin's parents are unknown. He served in Co. I, 24th NYSV from May 17, 1861-June 17, 1861. He was discharged for "disability." His time with the 147th ended on June 9, 1863 when he was again discharged for "disability." He and Winifred, also born in Ireland, were the parents of Charles (1854-?) and Catherine (1858-?). In

1880 Martin, enumerated as a widower, was living in Oswego with Catherine and her husband Theophilus Cavellier (1852-ca. 1943). Graves for Martin and Winifred have not been located.

Michael John O'Connor – Co. B
b. 1827 Ireland
d. June 7, 1895 Phoenix, NY
m. Mary Norton (1835-November 9, 1900) *ante* 1860

NOTE: Michael, who styled himself a retired grocer in 1870, was the son of Michael (1805-*ante* 1905) and Bridget Byrne O'Connor (1805-March 12, 1904). He enlisted in the 147th on August 28, 1862 and was mustered in on September 22, 1862. He was discharged for "disability" on November 22, 1862. He applied for a pension on January 23, 1864 but apparently was refused, probably because he had not served the required 90 days. Mary also unsuccessfully attempted to obtain a pension. Michael died at the home of his daughter, Mrs. Mary Hornbeck, in Phoenix, NY and his body was shipped by rail to Oswego where the funeral was held in St. Paul's Church. Mary, the mother of six children, was living Mary Hornbeck in 1900. Their graves have not been located.

Owen W. O'Connor – Co. H
b. 1840 Ireland
d. October 6, 1918 Buffalo, Erie, NY
m. Mary Anne Crowe (?-*post* 1879) *ca.*1872

NOTE: Owen, son of Nicholas (1800-?) and Ann Gordon O'Connor (1810-1865), saw prior duty in Co. A, 20th NY Mil. Inf. from May 1, 1861-August 1, 1861. He was captured at Gettysburg and paroled at an unspecified date, mustering out with the regiment on June 7, 1865. Information about his home life has been difficult to obtain. I obtained his wife's name because his son Nicholas Edward (1879-March 24, 1944) got married. Owen's obituary revealed he had another son, Eugene Joseph (1873-*post* 1933). His marriage license confirmed the mother's name. Owen's pension card does not indicate a widow. Therefore either Owen and Mary Ann divorced, which is unlikely, or she died some time after the birth of Nicholas. *The Buffalo Evening News* October 8, 1918, 14 published the following: "The funeral of Owen W. O'Connor, Civil war veteran and old resident of Buffalo, was held this morning at 92 Niagara street and later in Saint Joseph's old cathedral. Mr. O'Connor served throughout the Civil war and was with Grant's army when Lee surrendered at Appomattox. He was taken prisoner at Gettysburg but escaped. He had been ill less than a week of pneumonia. He is survived by two sons, Eugene J. and Nicholas O'Connor and two sisters, Mrs. John Delahunt of Cleveland, N.Y. and Mrs. Mary Kelly of Syracuse." Mrs.

Delahunt's name was Doretta (1844-1926). Mary (1842-1920) was the wife of Patrick Kelly. Graves for Owen and Mary have not been located.

Patrick O'Connor – Co. B
b. 1829 Ireland

d. June 14, 1864 Virginia

m. ------

NOTE: Patrick's parents were Thomas (?-?) and Margaret Glahaven O'Connor (?-?). According to a casualty list published in *The Oswego Daily Palladium* June 14, 1864, he was wounded in a "skirmish with the enemy" on May 25th. It is ironic that the list was printed the day he died. He was buried in Arlington National Cemetery. His FAG entry says he was seriously wounded in the leg at North Anna River, VA. The leg was amputated and death resulted. His gravestone erroneously assigns him to the 47th Regiment.

George W. Oliver – Co. D
b. 1835 St. Lawrence County, NY

d. January 6, 1879 probably Fulton, NY

m. Electa _____ (?-*post* 1881) ?

NOTE: George was the son of Caleb (1804-*post* 1855) and Eliza Oliver (1809-*ante* 1860). In 1855, the only census record I have located which names him, the family, consisting of mother, father, and seven children, all born St. Lawrence County except the youngest, Eliza, 3, who was born in Oswego County, was living in Fulton where George later enlisted in the 147th. He transferred to 22nd Regiment, VRC on January 14, 1864 and was mustered out in Trenton, NJ on July 14, 1865. He does not appear in *The Town Clerks' Registers*. Electa's name appears only on George's general pension index card. George's DOD was located on the order form for a government gravestone. According to that card, he was buried in Mt. Adnah. It is altogether possible that Electa remarried but she should have appeared on the 1880 census since her eligibility for a pension depended upon her remaining a widow. It is also possible that the widow's name was entered incorrectly on the index card.

George W. Omans – Co. C
b. March 10, 1841 Clay, Onondaga, NY

d. January 19, 1922 Joplin, Jasper, MO

m. Melissa Susan Nelson (April 18, 1847-May 30, 1930) July 5, 1861

NOTE: George, son of James (1819-1885) and Anna McLoring Omans (1825-1908), originally enlisted in the 110th Regiment. His time in the 147th was brief. On November 11, 1862 he transferred to the US Regular Army. On January 4, 1864 he enlisted in the 11th NY Cavalry. He mustered out in Memphis, TN on September 30, 1865. On July 11, 1886 he was baptized and ordained as a deacon in the Reorganized Church of Jesus Christ of Latter Day Saints at Luce, Otter Tail, MN. George and Melissa were married in Texas, NY. By 1900, when the family was living in North Campbell Township, Greene, MO, Melissa had borne 10 children, seven of whom survived. George was a grocer. His COD was ruled either apoplexy or a cerebral hemorrhage. *The Joplin Globe* January 20, 1922, 3 published his obituary: "George W. Omans, 80 years old, died at 11 o'clock yesterday morning at his home, No. 2802 Moffet avenue. Mr. Omans, who was a veteran of the civil war, had resided in Joplin fifteen years. In 1862 he enlisted in Company C of the 147th New York volunteers, later being transferred to the regular army in which he fought until the war ended. He was a member of O. P. Morton post, G.A.R., and was affiliated with the Latter Day Saints church . . . ." Melissa was also baptized into the Mormon Church on July 11, 1886. She died in Brooking Township, Jackson, MO of bronchial pneumonia. She and George are buried in Forest Park Cemetery, Joplin.

John O'Neil – Co. K

b. 1815 Ireland
d. *post* 1880 probably Oswego City, NY
m. Maria/Mary _____ (1818-*post* 1880) *ca.* 1843

NOTE: John's parents were Edward (?-?) and Sophia Campbell O'Neil (?-?). Many men were named John O'Neil but the best candidate is John O'Neil/O'Neal who arrived in Oswego City in 1850. Although he said he was born in 1818 when he enlisted, available census records demonstrate that 1815 was the actual DOB. He transferred to the VRC on April 25, 1865 and was discharged at Washington, DC on June 28, 1865. He and Maria were the parents of 10 children. Their graves have not been located.

John O'Rafferty – Co. I

b. 1841 Ireland
d. May 4, 1907 Oswego City, NY
m. Catherine O'Leary (1858-May 23, 1901) *ca.* 1876

NOTE: John, a miller, came to the United States in 1848 and was naturalized. He was wounded on February 6, 1865 at Hatcher's Run, VA. He apparently was in hospital when the regiment mustered out but he applied for a pension on July 19, 1865. He and Catherine, who immigrated in 1874, were the parents of six children, one of whom, Willie, 13, was killed on the railroad tracks on June 29, 1891 in a bizarre, gruesome accident. John was active in city politics. He stood as the Democratic candidate for constable in 1866. In 1895 he was elected second vice-president of Branch 140, Catholic Mutual Benevolent Association (CMBA). He was elected president of the 147th Regiment Reunion in 1898 and presided at the 1899 event. He was also a member of Post O'Brian No. 165 GAR. John was an avid fisherman and on several occasions the local newspaper announced he had caught the first mullet of the season. His funeral was described in an article appearing in *The Oswego Daily Times* May 6, 1907, 8: "There was a large attendance including several members of the G.A.R. at the funeral of John O'Rafferty which was held this morning from his home, No. 164 West Sixth Street. The Rev. Father Hopkins conducted the services at St. Mary's Church and burial was in St. Peter's Cemetery. A firing squad from Post O'Brien fired the usual volleys at the grave. The bearers were Captain P. J. Brown, John Galvin and John Gill, veterans of the One Hundred Forty-seventh Regiment; W. D. Mackin, William Murtha and James McCaffrey of Branch 140 C.M.B.A." Catherine's death was announced in *The Oswego Daily Palladium* May 24, 1901, 4: "Mrs. Catherine O'Rafferty, wife of John O'Rafferty, died yesterday at the family home . . . after a lingering illness. Mrs. O'Rafferty was forty-four years of age. Last winter she was taken down with an attack of the grip and then she had a relapse. Other complications arose and for some days past it has been known to her family and friends that she could not recover. She was a member of St. Mary's church and a woman who had the love and esteem of all who knew her. Besides her husband she is survived by a daughter and son, and a brother and sister, all of this city." Catherine is also buried in St. Peter's Cemetery, Oswego City.

John Smith O'Riley – Co. K
b. 1822 Ireland
d. August 18, 1864 Weldon Railroad, VA
m. ?

NOTE: Little has been learned about this soldier who enlisted at Oswego City and said he was a laborer. An entry in *Deaths of Volunteers* says he was killed in action. His name appeared in a list of casualties appearing in *The Oswego Daily Palladium* August 24, 1864 which had been compiled by Robert H. Spencer.

Thomas O'Rourke – Co. K
b. 1818 Ireland
d. ? ?
m. ?

NOTE: O'Rourke, who said he was a bricklayer, may or may not have been born in 1818. He does not appear in any Oswego directories. He is not listed in *The Town Clerks' Registers* and no pension card has been located. He transferred to the VRC on

July 16, 1863, was discharged at Washington, DC on August 21, 1865 and promptly disappeared. No biographical information has been obtained.

Henry John Orton – Co. C

b. December 29, 1832 Williamstown, NY
d. March 31, 1911 Richland, NY
m. Maria L. Woods (July 22, 1833-March 25, 1914) 1854

NOTE: Henry, son of Joseph (1812-1908) and Hannah Stewart Orton (1804-1880), was a farmer. He was wounded on July 1, 1863 but was able to muster out with the regiment on June 7, 1865. Upon his death *The Pulaski Democrat* April 5, 1911, 5 published a lengthy, informative obituary: "Henry J. Orton, 78 years old died at 12:30 o'clock March 29 [*sic*] at his home [one] mile and a half north of Pulaski. Mr. Orton has been failing in health for nearly five years[;] eight weeks ago he was confined to his bed with severe illness which caused his death. He bore intense suffering without a murmur putting his whole trust in his blessed Saviour. Mr. Orton was born in Williamstown, N.Y. When at the age of 14 years old he moved with his father and mother on a farm near Richland. Shortly after the outbreak of the Civil War, Mr. Orton enlisted in Co. C one hundred and forty-seventh New York Volunteer Infantry. He served until the close of the war [and] he was present in nearly all of the large battles fought. In one battle his life was saved by a small testament which he carried in his breast pocket which deadened the speed of a bullet by which it was struck[;] the bullet lodged in the testament severing every leaf [but] his only injury from it was a slight flesh wound. After the war Mr. Orton bought a farm near Pulaski where he has since resided. He was greatly interested in church work [and was] also a member of G.A.R. Besides his widow Mrs. Maria Wood Orton, he is survived by five children . . . ." Henry's children appended a five-stanza poem to the obituary, one of which is: "When life's bright prospects did unfold,/Then thou was't called to die./But now doth dwell in heaven's fold,/In realms beyond the sky." Maria followed her husband three years later, as reported in *The Oswego Daily Palladium* March 26, 1914, 3: "Maria, widow of Henry Orton, died suddenly yesterday while making a call at the home of Eber James, a neighbor, on the Jefferson road, about a mile north of this village [Pulaski]. Mrs. Orton was eighty-one [years] old, and had just arrived at the James house when she was stricken with paralysis, and died before a physician arrived. She was a lifelong resident of the town of Richland. She made her home here with a daughter, Mrs. A. Burdette Frary . . . ." Henry and Maria are buried in Pulaski Village Cemetery.

Jerome Barnum Ostrom – Co. E
b. September 1844 Orwell, NY
d. October 2, 1921 Arapahoe, Furnas, NE
m. Emma Martindale (October 1852-May 14, 1926) September 10, 1871

NOTE: Jerome was the son of Barnum (1829-1914) and Ursula Eleanor Fuller Ostrom (1822-1890). His was an interesting military career. Originally assigned to Co. E, he spent some time on detached duty with Batt. L, 1st NY ART. He went AWOL on March 16, 1864, returning on May 14, 1864. His pension card states he was "unassigned" in the 24th NY Cavalry but this cannot be accurate unless he attempted to join that outfit while absent from the 147th. Upon his return he was required to make up time and was transferred to Co. K, 91st Regiment on June 5, 1865, ultimately being discharged on June 20, 1865. Despite his lapses, his application for a pension, made in 1877, was accepted. Like many others, Jerome headed west after the war. He and Emma were married in Eaton Township, Clark, WI. By 1900 the family was living in Edison, Furnas, NE. Emma was a school teacher and the mother of three. Jerome was a plasterer. The 1910 census found them in Eckley, Yuma, CO. Ten years later they were back in Furnas County. A brief death announcement in *The Omaha World-Herald* October 5, 1921, 5 reported that Jerome had died after being ill for two years. He and Emma are buried in Edison Cemetery, Arapahoe.

Romine Ostrom – Co. E
b. 1821 Rush, Herkimer, NY
d. February 12, 1903 Rural Hill, Jefferson, NY
m1. Hannah Louise _____ (1825-*ante* 1877) *ca.* 1850
m2. Sarah Margaret Huffstater Edgett (1838-June 18, 1923) *ca.* 1877

NOTE: Romine was Jerome's uncle. His parents were David (1779-1872) and Mary "Polly" Van de Water Ostrom (1781-1860). His DOB varied. I use that in his obituary. Romine was discharged from the 147th for "disability" on January 7, 1863. In 1890 he claimed he suffered from rheumatism. Romine and Hannah were the parents of Mary J. (1855-*post* 1880). Hannah's exact DOD and grave have not been located. Sarah, also known as Margaret, was first married to Henry Wellington Edgett (1829-November 15, 1871). He was killed by Alexander Murray, whose cow had injured one of the Edgett boys. The two men got into an argument over the incident and Murray fatally struck Edgett with a club. He was convicted of manslaughter on May 28, 1874. Sarah and Romine had two children, Don (1878-1952), and Martha (1879-1863). Don married Minnie Alexander (1885-1965), granddaughter of Eli Alexander (1815-1863), a member of the 110th Regiment. Romine, Sarah, and Henry Edgett are buried in Evergreen Cemetery, Orwell, though her stone has no dates.

Elijah Oyer – Co. H

b. July 24, 1838 Herkimer County, NY

d. January 19, 1863 Stewart's Mansion Hospital, Baltimore, MD

m. ?

NOTE: Elijah, son of Jacob (1799-1854) and Elizabeth Harvey Oyer (1803-1882), lived in West Monroe when he enlisted. According to *Deaths of Volunteers*, his COD was typhoid fever. His entry in *The Town Clerks' Registers* states, "widow draws pension," but I have located no such person. Elijah is buried in Loudon Park National Cemetery, Baltimore. His surname is spelled Oyier on the marker.

Adelbert Paddock – Co. E

b. 1841 Boylston, NY

d. August 27, 1914 East Florence, Oneida, NY

m1. Paulina "Lina" Baird (April 1840-January 27, 1908) 1864

m2. Rhoda Riker Murphy Meacham (1843-May 25, 1920) October 31, 1909

NOTE: Adelbert's parents were Rev. Solomon (1800-1878) and Samantha "Mattie" Arnold Paddock (1822-1876). He was discharged from the army for "disability" at Douglass Hospital, Washington, DC on April 11, 1863. In 1890 he was living in Florence, Oneida, NY. Paulina is buried in Forest Park Cemetery, Camden, Oneida, NY. Adelbert's death was reported in *The Sandy Creek News* September 3, 1914: "The death of Adelbert A. Paddock, an old and respected resident of East Florence, occurred at his home between 5 and 6 o'clock Thursday morning, Aug. 27, after an illness of about ten months of a complication of diseases. Mr. Paddock was a son of Rev. Solomon and Samantha Arnold Paddock and was born in Orwell and was 72 years old. He was a veteran of the Civil War, having been a member of Co. A [*sic*], 147th Regiment, New York Volunteers. He had been a resident of East Florence for the last 45 years. He has been twice married[;] his first wife was Miss Lina Baird of Orwell who died six years ago on July 27. By this marriage there were three sons, Fred, Charles, and Chester, who are all living in Syracuse. His second wife was Mrs. Rhoda Meacham of Altmar, who survives him . . . ." It is possible that Adelbert is buried with Paulina. Rhoda was married three times. Her first husband was Samuel White Murphy (1834-1910) whom she married on November 10, 1862. That marriage did not last since he married Mary Eugenia Harrington (1848-1937) on November 18, 1869. Rhoda next married William Meacham (1835-1900) in 1882. In 1919 she applied for Murphy's pension and obtained it, thereby proving the couple had never been divorced. He had been a member of Co. H, 184th Regiment. After Adelbert's death, Rhoda lived with her daughter Ellen Murphy March (1864-1931) in Altmar, NY and died there. She is buried in Riverside Cemetery, Altmar.

Charles Richardson Paddock – Co. G

b. April 18, 1841 Liverpool, Onondaga, NY

d. February 7, 1894 Brooklyn, NY

m. Ann Minerva Sykes (September 25, 1840-July 1, 1919) November 20, 1866

NOTE: Charles was the son of Henry (1806-1885) and Henrietta Molther Paddock (1810-1893). He was a hospital steward during his time with the 147th. When the 147th and the 76th Regiments were consolidated at the end of January 1865, he was discharged. In later life he was a druggist in Brooklyn. He died intestate and Ann Minerva petitioned the court to be administrator of the estate, valued at $6,000. Not until 1908, however, did she apply for a pension. Charles and Ann Minerva were the parents of three children, one of whom, Raymond (1874-?), disappeared on December 31, 1904, abandoning his wife Anna and his mother. He was never heard from again and it was presumed he committed suicide. Charles and Ann Minerva, who also died in Brooklyn, are buried in Hannibal Village Cemetery, as are her parents Bernice R. (1808-1895) and Elvira Augusta Wilson Sykes (1806-1893).

Hiram Palmer – Co. B

b. December 7, 1834 Oswego, NY

d. October 28, 1917 Chicago, Cook, IL

m. Martha L. Anderson (1839-June 17, 1921) 1860

NOTE: Hiram, the son of William (1784-1854) and Sarah Palmer (1795-*post* 1855), was a millwright and carpenter by trade. He mustered out on June 5, 1865 at Washington, DC. He and Martha, the mother of three children, are buried in Oakwoods Cemetery, Chicago.

Austin Pangburn – Co. F

b. October 2, 1835 Herkimer County, NY

d. February 16, 1900 Palermo, NY

m. Sabrina _____ (1841-November 25, 1912) *ca.* 1858

NOTE: Austin was the son of Jedediah "Dyer" (1807-1871) and Philinda "Lydia" Rounds Pangburn (1810-1851). He was captured on July 1, 1863 and, according to the 1890 Veterans' Schedules, he suffered from kidney disease and "rupture" acquired while a prisoner in Libby Prison. He was paroled at an unspecified date and discharged for "disability" at Armory Square Hospital, Washington, DC on December 14, 1863. His death was announced in *The Oswego Daily Palladium* February 22, 1900, 6: "Austin Pangburn died at his home on Friday, February 16th, aged sixty-four years. Funeral services were held at the Methodist Protestant church at Upson's Corners on Monday, February 19th. He leaves a widow and four children. The Rev.

J. R. Guthrie, of Wayne county, officiated, after which the G.A.R. Post, of Central Square, of which he was a member, took charge of the remains. The afflicted family wish to thank the neighbors and friends for the kindness shown to them; also the Central Square Post and other comrades." Austin belonged to Isaac Waterbury Post No. 418 GAR. He and Sabrina are buried in Upson's Corners Cemetery, Palermo. A word must be said about "Dyer" Pangburn. He apparently considered himself a Mormon and had children by several women. In 1858 he was convicted of bigamy and sentenced to two years in Auburn State Prison. On August 15, 1871 he beat his wife, Nancy Roland Sprague Pangburn (1831-August 15, 1871), to death, then retreated to a nearby barn where he hanged himself.

Clark Stewart Parke – Co. H
b. 1845 Constantia, NY
d. November 12, 1862 Presbyterian Hospital, Georgetown, DC
m. ------

NOTE: Clark, usually known by his middle name, was only 17 when he enlisted as a musician. His father, Smith Parke (1816-1862), had enlisted in Co. D, 24th Infantry in April 1861 but was discharged near the end of 1861 because he was ill with consumption, a disease he had had for several years prior to enlisting. He arrived at home in Amboy Center on January 4th and died on February 17th. He left his widow Harriet J. Stewart Parke with five minor children, the youngest only three years old. There were two other children: Mary Almira (1841-*post* 1905) and Joel Sage (*ca.*1842-died young). Harriet herself died on July 12, 1862 at the age of 42, probably of consumption. Neighbors testified that Stewart had almost solely supported the family since 1858 and he thought it his duty to support his siblings by enlisting even though he was underage. His death was reported by Captain Reuben Slayton in *The Mexico Independent* November 27, 1862: ". . . Stewart Park, aged 18 years, died at Georgetown hospital with typhoid fever, on Wednesday, Nov. 12th. He was among the first who enrolled themselves in my company, and when well was a good, prompt soldier; and, for the benefit of his friends, I will state that during his illness he was well cared for. This young man's father served as a soldier in the 24th regiment, under Capt. Richards, for about eight months, when he was allowed to return home on account of poor health, having taken a severe cold, which settled on his lungs, and terminated in consumption. He lived but a short time after reaching his family. Thus father and son have both laid down their lives for the benefit of their country . . . ." Clark was buried in the Soldiers' and Airmen's Home National Cemetery, Washington, DC. John W. Howard was appointed the guardian of Harriet (1849-1878), Martha (1853-*post* 1880), DeWitt (1855-1921), and Fannie (1859-1879). The children were destitute, and it was revealed that the poor master of Town of Amboy had sold what little property there was in order to pay for the parents' funerals. The children obtained pensions at the rate of $8.00 per month. Harriet married Asahel Wallace; Martha became a school teacher in Putnam, Windham, CT; DeWitt was a deputy sheriff for many years in Putnam and at the time of his death he was in charge of the Windham County Temporary Home for Children; Fannie died in Putnam, CT and was buried in DeWitt's plot in Grove Street Cemetery, Putnam. Smith and Harriet are buried in Amboy Center Cemetery.

Edward David Parker – Co. C
b. December 6, 1828 Billerica, Middlesex, MA
d. May 10, 1889 Auburn, Cayuga, NY
m1. Mary E. Fields (1836-1868) 1854
m2. Sarah "Satie" C. Evans (1839-September 23, 1893) November 10, 1887

NOTE: Edward, son of David (1786-1874) and Achsah Crosby Parker (1786-1857), was a tanner by trade. He was a captain in the 147th. His obituary, published in *The Auburn Bulletin* May 11, 1889, 1, attests to an extensive military and civilian career: "Edward David Parker died at his residence, 190 German street, at midnight. He had been ill since Sunday afternoon with peritonitis and grew gradually worse from the first moment until death. Mr. Parker was born in Billerick, Mass., in 1828 and was next to the youngest in the family of ten children. He was educated in the common schools and left home at 22. In 1850 he located in Oswego county and engaged in the tanning business with a brother, C. E. Parker. After a few years he removed to Moravia and was engaged in different enterprises until the beginning of the war. At the first call for troops he enlisted in the Nineteenth regiment as ensign, served three months and came home. A few days after his return, he re-enlisted in the One hundred and forty-seventh regiment and remained in the service until after the Battle of Gettysburg in which he was wounded in the thigh and disabled. He returned home again and remained until fall when he was assigned to the Veteran Reserve corps and was appointed adjutant of the camp at Concord, N. H., where he remained until after the close of the war. In 1867 he removed to Auburn and engaged with Ira Gaston in the tanning business in Wall street. He retired from the firm in 1871 to engage in the wholesale liquor business at 7 State street with Col. W. N. Thomas. The firm built to a good trade and did a prosperous business from the beginning. Mr. Thomas retired from the firm a number of years ago and shortly afterward David W. Tocht (?) bought an interest in the firm, which has since been conducted under the firm name of E. D. Parker & Co. Mr. Parker was married in Moravia in 1854, to Mary Elizabeth Field. Three children were born to them . . . Mrs. Parker died in 1868. On November 10, 1887 Mr. Parker married Satie C. Evans of Utica for his second wife, who also survives." Another obituary, published in *The Oswego Daily Times* May 13, 1889,

1, paid tribute to his bravery: ". . . He was loved and respected as a good man and brave officer by every man of his regiment. At Gettysburg he had the credit of doing much toward making the record of the 147th N.Y., the grand one of the first day's fight, by his personal bravery and efforts encouraging and holding the left companies at the railroad cut next to Hall's Battery to their work after they were outflanked and almost completely enveloped by the enemy; and to him as much as any one man is due the credit of saving the battery and making possible the brilliant success of Wadsworth's division at the opening of that great battle. Since the war Major Parker has always taken a lively interest in the welfare of the union soldier and has held many honorable positions in the Grand Army. His death will be sincerely lamented by his old comrades and citizens generally of this locality. His funeral takes place at Auburn tomorrow, Tuesday, the 14th, at 4 p.m. A delegation of his regiment from this city will attend to do honor to the memory of their brave comrade . . . ." David is buried in Fort Hill Cemetery, Auburn. Mary's grave has not been located. Sarah, who obtained a widow's pension, died in Auburn. Her death was announced in *The Auburn Argus* September 29, 1893, 1: ". . . Mrs. Sarah Evans Parker, relict of the late Major E. D. Parker, died at the home of her step-daughter Mrs. George B. Wright in Elizabeth street on Saturday of diphtheria. She was visiting at the house at which she died, having returned from Chicago, on her way to her home in Utica." Her grave has not been located.

Orlando J. Parker – Co. A

b. March 4, 1835 Oswego County, NY

d. March 5, 1910 Grand Haven, Ottawa, MI

m. Zilpha Ann Farnham (November 27, 1835-February 7, 1926) December 1, 1854

NOTE: Orlando was the son of Solomon (1805-1848) and Elizabeth Maria Schofield Parker (1806-1882). He transferred from the 147th to Batt. L, 1st NY ART on February 4, 1863. He then transferred to the US Navy on April 22, 1864, serving aboard the USS North Carolina, Merrimac, and Vermont. He and Zilpha were in Michigan as early as 1866 where he was selected for petit jury duty at Hillsdale. Orlando had several occupations. When he enlisted he claimed to be a teamster. In 1880 he said he was a cooper. In 1900 he was a pilot on a steamboat and was still in that position when he died, one day after his birthday. His COD was heart disease, with asthma as a contributing factor. He was buried in Lake Forest Cemetery, Grand Haven. Zilpha, the mother of four, moved to California to live with a daughter. Upon her death *The Los Angeles Times* February 7, 1926 printed the following: "Mrs. Zilpha A. Parker, for forty years a member of the Order of the Eastern Star and for twenty-six years a member of the Women's Relief Corps, passed away today at the home of her daughter, Mrs. B. O. Holbrook, 426 West Harvard street, Glendale, aged 91 years. Funeral services will be conducted Monday afternoon at 2 o'clock at Grand View Cemetery, Rev. Clifford E. Cole, pastor of the Central Christian Church officiating. Mrs. Parker who was born at Oswego New York, in 1835 . . . had been a resident of Glendale for the past six years."

Burns Elwood Parkhurst – Co. F
b. July 23, 1843 Colosse, NY
d. January 25, 1915 Pulaski, NY
m. Janette "Nettie" Edick (1848-January 31, 1909) December 12, 1866

NOTE: B. E., as he was generally known, was the son of Leander (1806-1886) and R. Josephine Brown Parkhurst (1816-1851). He was severely wounded at Gettysburg. Upon his death *The Sandy Creek News* January 28, 1915, published a lengthy obituary attesting to his long, active life: "Burns E. Parkhurst was born at Colosse, in the town of Mexico, July 26, 1843. Died at his home on Salina street, Pulaski, January 25. Mr. Parkhurst enlisted in the 147th regiment of New York Volunteer Infantry, August 21, 1862, and served three years, until the close of the war. Was with the regiment during the Chancellorsville campaign and received honorable mention by his colonel for gallant and meritorious conduct. He was seriously wounded during the three days' fight at the battle of Gettysburg. After the close of the war Mr. Parkhurst returned to Oswego County. On December 12, 1866 he was united in marriage with Nettie M. Edick, with whom he lived until her death, January 31, 1909. For the past thirty-five years Mr. Parkhurst has lived in Pulaski, engaged in the practice of law. For more than twenty years was Justice of Peace of the town of Richland. He has been an invalid for the past three years. Mr. Parkhurst was an active member of the Methodist church, a member and past commander of J. B. Butler Post G.A.R. No. 111; member of Pulaski Lodge, I.O.O.F., No. 348; Salmon River Encampment, I. O. O. F., No. 131; Pulaski Lodge, F. and A. M., and Pulaski Chapter, R.A.M. . . . The funeral was held at the Methodist church, Wednesday at 2 o'clock." *The Adjutant-General's Report* of 1904 states that Parkhurst was awarded the Medal of Honor for bravery, but that is incorrect. He was, as his obituary states, officially cited for his actions at Chancellorsville. Burns wrote about his experiences there in a letter published in *The Mexico Independent* May 7, 1902: ". . . In the Chancellorsville campaign our regiment was attached to the Second Brigade, First Division, First Corps. It was desired to cross the Rappahannock river, below Fredericksburg, at a place called Fitzhugh Crossing or Pollock's Mill Creek. Ours was the first regiment to cross the pontoon bridge to the south bank of the river. In the afternoon of April 30, 1863, we were ordered to throw up breastworks, and as soon as we commenced to do so the enemy began to fire at us from a battery in front with 12 pound shells. Three guns of this battery were nearly in front of our regiment and one of them directly in front. Our batteries in rear of us replied to the enemy's firing over our heads. One of those guns of the enemy fired to the left of our regiment and one fired to the right at our batteries that were firing at them. The other gun was in the centre of these, firing directly at us. Soon two of our men were hit by pieces of bursting shell, and died a few days after from the effects. The regiment was commanded by Col. Jno. Butler; Co. F, to which the writer belonged, was commanded by Capt. H. G. Lee. Right after these men were struck the writer was given an order by Capt. Lee to occupy a special position in front of this gun of the enemy and to watch, and when it was fired to give the order 'down,' when the men, by falling flat upon the ground were enabled to protect themselves until the shell had passed over. I occupied this position, exposed to the enemy's fire from this gun for over an hour, until the breastworks were high enough to protect the men, and it was no longer necessary for me to remain, when by an order I resumed my place in the company. From my position and knoll, which I was directed to occupy, I could look into the mouth of this gun, and when it was fired I could see the red flame down in the throat of the gun, lighting up the inside and in the center of the flame I could see a dark spot that I knew to be the shell starting on its mission of destruction. As the firing (?) came from the gun it almost seemed as if I could feel it scorching my face, for I was a boy then, and not man enough to wear a beard, and my cheeks were as smooth as a girl's. My anxiety of mind and strain upon my nervous system were great, not only on account of my personal danger, but that I might not warn the men in time for them to protect themselves by dropping upon the ground when the gun was fired. But none were injured . . . When the gun was fired I would give the word, 'down!' then would drop on hands and knees . . . One experience of that kind will do me for a lifetime. I am not in a hurry for another. I was very glad when I received the order from Capt. Lee that I might return to my place. I received a report of this service from Col. Butler in the fall of 1897 over 34 years after the battle of Pollock's Mill Creek, Va., but it is now on record in the War Department at Washington, D.C." Nettie died of heart disease. She too was active in the Methodist Church. She was a member and past president of the Women's Relief Corps. B. E. and Nettie are buried in Pulaski Village Cemetery.

Byron Dwight Parkhurst – Co. G
b. November 25, 1840 Scriba, NY
d. February 20, 1879 St. John's, Clinton, MI
m. ------

NOTE: Byron was the son of Isaac (1809-1882) and Eliza Sheldon Parkhurst (1810-1898). He was wounded in the left leg at Petersburg, VA on June 18, 1864 but mustered out with the regiment on June 7, 1865. In later life he was a saloon keeper in Michigan. Upon his death *The Oswego Morning Herald* February 22, 1879, 1 published the following: ". . . Captain Byron D. Parkhurst, who won honor and distinction in the 147th N.Y.V., died at his home in St. John's, Mich., Thursday. He was born in Scriba and had a large circle of warm friends in this city. He was here on a visit last summer and was then in the bloom of health." His COD was consumption. Although he is buried in Mountain Rest Cemetery, St. John's, a cenotaph for him is located in the Worden-Sweet Cemetery, Scriba.

Silas E. Parsons – Co. B
b. 1843 St. Lawrence County, NY
d. May 5, 1864 Wilderness, VA
m. ------

NOTE: Silas, whose parents were William B. (1816-1887) and Sophronia Chesbro Parsons (1820-1898), was transferred to Co. K on December 1, 1862. After her husband died, Sophronia applied for and received a mother's pension. When she died *The Oswego Daily Palladium* March 21, 1898, 8 published an obituary detailing the family history: "Sophronia E. Chesbro,

Byron D. Parkhurst moved to Michigan after the war and managed a saloon.
Author's Collection

relict of the late William B. Parsons, of this city, died at her late residence in East Sixth street last evening, aged seventy-eight years. Mrs. Parsons was born in Otsego county, this state, and was the daughter of Nicholas Chesbro, for many years a prominent resident of the North part of the town of New Haven, and who moved to that town when the subject of this sketch was five years old. In 1840 she married William B. Parsons, of Gouverneur, and a year or two after moved to Oswego, where they continued to reside until 1867, when they moved to the old Chesbro homestead, where Mr. Parsons died about eleven years ago. In 1895 Mrs. Parsons again returned to Oswego. She leaves four children . . . One son, Silas Parsons, was wounded at the Battle of the Wilderness and subsequently reported missing and from whom no further tidings were ever obtained. About three years ago Mrs. Parsons suffered a severe attack of pneumonia and from which she never recovered. The funeral service will be held at the residence in East Sixth street Wednesday morning at nine o'clock and from the Congregational church at New Haven at 11:30. The interment will be made at the cemetery at that place. Mrs. Parsons was a good woman, kind, charitable and a mother whose life and energy was largely given to her husband and children." Sophronia was a descendant of William Chesbro, the founder of Stonington, CT. Both she and her husband William are buried in New Haven Cemetery. Silas was undoubtedly buried on the field.

Francis "Frank" M. Pease – Co. F

b. February 28, 1844 Oswego County, NY

d. March 11, 1886 Scriba, NY

m. Catherine "Katie" Lord (June 23, 1851-January 22, 1904) February 13, 1877

NOTE: Francis was the son of Albert (1816-1891) and Christiana G. Worden Pease (1812-1886). He was captured at the battle of Gettysburg and sent to West Chester, PA where he wrote a letter to his family back home detailing his participation in the battle. Many years later Katie permitted *The Oswego Daily Palladium* April 11, 1898, 6 to publish it. It is extremely long and can only be excerpted here: ". . . July 1st we were routed out at daylight and ordered to march. We started at seven o'clock. When we got within a couple of miles of Gettysburg, off to the South of the town, we saw two or three shells burst in the air. It was the rebel batteries shelling our cavalry, which was on ahead. There was hard fighting to be done and we were ordered to load, which we did without delay. Then came the order, double quick, and the men started toward the front on a run. The road became so crowded, however, that we were compelled to slacken the pace and could only get over the ground on a run at rare intervals. The horses of the artillery were coming up at a mad gallop. Soon the rebel cannon balls began to whistle over our heads, some of them pretty close and probably the greatest battle of the rebellion was raging. Our batteries soon began to return the fire and as we came up in a little hollow we were ordered to lay down. The rebel batteries were firing away, but the balls flew over our heads and we could see them strike in the distance and plow up the turf and scatter the dust. We were soon ordered to march by the right flank and were soon within thirty or forty rods of the rebels, whose colors were flying. We were then ordered to get down upon one knee and then the order came to fire and volley after volley was sent into the ranks of the Johnnies. The rebel bullets whistled about our heads like hail. The men were falling thick and fast around us, some dead others wounded . . . . For fifteen or twenty minutes we fought hard, when the rebels flanked us on the right and began advancing upon us in large numbers. The firing from both sides was very rapid. Finally we got the order to retreat and we lost no time in obeying, leaving an awful sight of dead and wounded upon the field. As we retreated we got into a railroad cut or ravine. We were moving as fast as we could, which was not very fast, because the ravine was crowded and there were a good many wounded men that had to be helped along. After we got into the cut the rebel bullets whistled over our heads. Soon the Johnnies were upon both sides of us, standing upon the banks in large numbers, and we were compelled to throw down our arms and surrender . . . ." Pease was eventually paroled and returned to the 147th. He was captured a second time on May 5, 1864 at the battle of the Wilderness and spent the next ten months in Andersonville and Florence Prisons. He was ultimately exchanged at North East Ferry, NC on February 27, 1865, mustering out with the regiment on June 7th. Life for Pease after the war was difficult since prison conditions and horrible food had left him weak and sickly. He considered writing a book about his wartime experiences but it never materialized. He also took some courses at the local business school. He joined Beacon Light Lodge, IOOF. Very often, however, he was too sick to work. His pension file is replete with testimony describing his poor health. Towards

Francis M. Pease suffered for years from the effect of spending 10 months in Confederate POW camps.
Author's Collection

the end of his life he developed a tumor below his right ear. Despite attempts to remove it, the tumor returned and was described by Dr. Algernon Coe as being "as large as a two-quart pail." When Francis died the official COD was "innutrition caused by diseased stomach together with extensive necrosis of the tumor." Katie, now a widow with a young daughter, Mabel (1881-1965), became the third wife of Hiram Dutcher (1846-1928) in March 1891. Her official COD was arteriosclerosis. She had been an invalid for three years. She and Francis are buried in North Scriba Union Cemetery.

John Edwin Peere – Co. A
b. 1835 New York County, NY
d. May 8, 1864 Spotsylvania, VA
m. Electa Diana Jones (April 9, 1837-January 21, 1917) October 13, 1853

NOTE: John's surname was also spelled Peer. His POD and DOD vary and his parents are unidentified. His muster card states that he died at Spotsylvania on May 8, 1864, but according to *Deaths of Volunteers*, he died on May 5, 1864 at the battle of Wilderness. In 1890 Electa, too, said he was killed at the Wilderness. His entry in *The Town Clerks' Registers* says he was killed at Laurel Hill, VA on May 9, 1864. His pension card puts his death at May 26, 1864, place not stated. Electa married attorney Melvin Fayette Stephens (1826-March 17, 1911) in 1878. He had served in Co. B, 12th NY Cavalry. Electa's death occasioned the following which was published in *The Fulton Patriot* January 31, 1917, 2: "Mrs. Electa Diana Jones Stephens, widow of the late Melvin F. Stephens who died at her home . . . at 9 o'clock Sunday evening, January 21, 1917, was a daughter of Ira and Diana Jones, who were among the early settlers in Oneida county, formed by the partition of Tryon county as it existed at the time of the Revolutionary war. The original settlers of the Jones family were of Welsh origin. Her family was a large one, consisting of 13 sons and daughters. At the time of her birth, her parents lived at New Hartford, near Utica, but in her early childhood moved to a farm a few miles east of Oswego, where they lived for many years. Shortly before the outbreak of the civil war, she was married to John Peer [sic], whom she had met a year or two before during a visit to her oldest sister in New York. Their marriage was a short one for at the call for volunteers, Mr. and Peer and four other members of Mrs. Stephens' immediate family enlisted in the 147th regiment of New York volunteer infantry. Mr. Peer and his two nephews, George and Horace Jones, the sons of Orlando Jones, were in Company A of this organization and participated in the battle of the Wilderness. On the second day of the battle, May 5 [sic] 1864, Mr. Peer was instantly killed by a bullet wound through the head. He was seen to fall by his friends, but his body was never recovered. Soon after this, Mrs. Peer moved to Fulton and there conducted a dressmaking establishment for many years. On the 31st of July, 1878, she was married to Melvin Fayette Stephens . . . During the 70 years that Mrs. Stephens has lived in Oswego county her life has been a good one. She was a devoted member of the Universalist church of this city, was active in various ? and organizations, and in recent years has been much interested in the cause of woman suffrage . . . ." Electa and Melvin are buried in Mt. Adnah Cemetery, Fulton.

Joseph Pelow – Co. B
b. 1832 Canada
d. February 25, 1863 Armory Square Hospital, Washington, DC
m. Margaret Perkins (April 5, 1838-May 27, 1921) January 8, 1853

NOTE: Joseph was the son of Albert (?-?) and Catherine Pelow (?-?). His COD was typhoid fever. Margaret married John Gouler (*ca.* 1833-August 23, 1919) on September 22, 1864. He died after being struck by a car and suffering a fractured skull and was buried in Mt. Olivet Cemetery, Detroit. Margaret, the mother of 13 children, died of "apoplexy" and arteriosclerosis. She is buried in Calvary Cemetery, Flint. Joseph's brothers, Nelson (1838-1916) and Godfrey (1840-1911), served in the 110th Regiment.

Peter Perry – Co. D

b. 1828 St. Lawrence County, NY
d. 1891 Grand Rapids, Kent, MI
m1. Sophia Rocque (1835-*post* 1880) *ca.* 1849
m2. Honora O'Connor _____ (*ca.* 1835-*post* 1895) March 11, 1891

NOTE: Peter's parents were Francis (?-?) and Mary Gonyeaux Perry (?-?). He originally enlisted in the 110th Regiment but was sent to the 147th. He was captured on July 1, 1863 and paroled at an unspecified date, mustering out with the regiment on June 7, 1865. By 1880 he and Sophia were living in James, Saginaw, MI. Her DOD and grave site have not been located. In 1890 Peter, residing in the Soldiers' Home in Grand Rapids, MI, said his disability was "general debility – war." The following year he married Honora. Their marriage license shows both were marrying for the second time but she was using her maiden name. Peter's exact DOD is unknown but he is buried in St. Andrew's Catholic Cemetery, Grand Rapids. Honora's application for a widow's pension on June 24, 1892 was unsuccessful. She was last listed in the Grand Rapids City Directory in 1895. Nothing else has been learned about her.

William Perry – Co. G

b. July 11, 1843 Granby, NY
d. *post* 1865 ?
m. ?

NOTE: William was the son of Jeremiah (1805-1891) and Huldah Perry (1819-*ante* 1880). Little has been learned about him. He was accused of desertion from General Hospital, Frederick, MD on August 13, 1863. On December 16, 1864 he was transferred to the VRC. According to his muster roll card he was discharged at Philadelphia, PA on September 1, 1865. On the 1865 New York census he was listed as married and serving in the army. I have not located a wife. No other confirmable information is available.

Asa Pettingill – Co. F

b. 1842 Parish, NY
d. July 1863 Gettysburg, Adams, PA
m. ------

NOTE: Asa was the son of Charles (1783-1866) and Phylena Seamans Jackson Pettingill (1792-1874). He was wounded in action at Gettysburg on July 1, 1863. His muster card says he died on July 1st, but it also notes that in August 1863 he was in hospital sick with wounds received on July 1st. The Quartermaster's Interment Form and Veterans' Gravesites both say he died July 1st. His listing in *Civil War Soldier*

Records and Profiles gives a date of July 5th. Asa is buried in Gettysburg National Cemetery, but was originally buried in Presbyterian Graveyard, Gettysburg.

Irving Sedgewick Pettis – Co. D

b. October 23, 1831 Oneida County, NY
d. August 8, 1903 National Soldiers' Home, Quincy, Adams, IL
m. Martha Ophelia Treat (1834-October 20, 1880) *ca.* 1855

NOTE: Irving, a schoolteacher, was the son of Micajah (1806-1881) and Tryphena Sedgewick Pettis (1803-1842). He was discharged from the army for "disability" on April 26, 1863. He and Martha are buried in Oakwood Cemetery, Geneseo, Henry, IL.

James Phair – Co. I

b. 1834 Ireland
d. *ca.* 1898 ?
m. ?

NOTE: No biographical information about this soldier is available except he was a sailor when he enlisted in Oswego City. His name was variously spelled. His entry in *The Town Clerks' Registers* states, "Was in all the Battles Reg't was in – mustered out with the Reg't." A charge of desertion was removed from this soldier's record on December 8, 1897 and a discharge date of May 19, 1865 was determined. Someone named Margaret Smith, minor, applied for a pension on April 25, 1898 from New York State. Who this person was has not been established but she did not obtain a certificate. Nevertheless, these dates suggest, but do not absolutely prove, that Phair died either in late 1897 or early 1898.

George Washington Philbrick – Co. C

b. 1845 Richland, NY
d. October 12, 1909 Pulaski, NY
m1. Martha Adelia Price (December 25, 1852-September 26, 1904) 1872
m2. Melissa "Mittie" House Walts (January 1854-October 6, 1920) *ca.* 1905

NOTE: George was the son of Albert (1811-1869) and Eunice Nye Philbrick (1811-1884). His DOB varies, but early census records demonstrate he was born in 1845 although his gravestone shows March 14, 1847. He served in Co. B, 7th NY "Northern Black Horse" Cavalry from October 2, 1861-March 31, 1862 and his record assigned him an age of 16 when he enlisted. In 1890 he did not claim any disability but said he had been a prisoner for five months in Libby and Bell Island Prisons. No mention of capture is noted on his muster roll card. George's death occasioned the following, published in *The Sandy Creek News* October 21, 1909, 5: "George W. Philbrick, aged about 65 years, a Civil war veteran, died at the home of his sister, Mrs. Ralph Price, at 4 Tuesday afternoon, of last week after an illness of but a few hours' duration. The deceased had for some time past made his home at the residence of Mr. and Mrs. Ralph Price, who live at the lower end of Lake avenue, Pulaski. Relatives are visiting the family and an outing at Selkirk Beach, a nearby summer resort, was planned for Tuesday. Mr. and Mrs. Price, accompanied by their relatives, including Mr. Philbrick and others, started to drive to the lake and had gone but a short distance when Mr. Philbrick was suddenly stricken with a severe shock of paralysis, becoming unconscious. The party at once returned to the Price residence and Dr. James L. More of Pulaski was called on the telephone. Mr. Philbrick remained in an unconscious condition up to the hour of his death. During the Civil war he served in the 147th regiment, New York volunteers. He was a member of Post Butler, G.A.R., of Pulaski. Besides the widow, who lives in Fulton, he is survived by two brothers, Newton Philbrick and Willis Philbrick, both of Pulaski, and also by two sisters, Mrs. Price and Mrs. Mary A. Wheeler of Sandy Creek." Martha's obituary appeared in *The Mexico Independent* October 5, 1904: "Many old friends will regret to learn of the death of Martha Philbrick, which occurred at her home in Arthur, Sept. 26th, 1904. Martha A. Price was born in the town of Richland in 1852 in which town she spent her girlhood days. At the age of twenty-two she was united in marriage to George Philbrick. In 1898 she removed to Arthur and resided in that place up to the time of her death. She was a kind neighbor and a loving wife and mother. She leaves to mourn her loss a husband and two sons and one daughter, Harrie and Homer Philbrick of Arthur and Mrs. Blanche Watson of Palermo. The funeral services were held at North Mexico church, conducted by Rev. M. D. Sill. Interment at Mexico." George and Martha are buried in Mexico Village Cemetery. The gravestone does not include his DOD. Melissa's obituary appeared in *The Fulton Patriot* October 13, 1920, 1: "The death of Mrs. Mittie Walts Philbrick, aged 62 years, occurred at the home of her daughter, Mrs. Chas. Dumont, on the Rowlee road, in Volney, Oct. 6th. Mrs. Philbrick was the widow of George Philbrick and resided on South First street. About ten days ago she went to visit her daughter, where she was taken ill and passed away. Funeral services were held from Mrs. Dumont's home Friday afternoon; interment at Chase Cemetery . . . ." Mittie had previously been married to Thomas Walts (1849-1901) and was the mother of at least four children. She and Thomas are buried in Chase Cemetery, Lysander, Onondaga, NY.

Hiram Pierce – Co. H
b. January 28, 1838 Otsego County, NY
d. August 10, 1916 Lansing, Ingham, MI
m. Florence Augusta Ferris (June 7, 1850-April 7, 1905) May 6, 1868

NOTE: Hiram's parents were Jonathan (1806-*post* 1860) and Cordelia Pierce (1814-*post* 1860). He was a cooper by trade. Hiram was discharged from the army on April 18, 1863 in Washington, DC. He and Florence were married in Washtenaw County, MI. In 1900 Florence said she was the mother of three children. She died of "edema of the lungs" and an "uncompensated heart lesion" and was buried in Forest Lawn Cemetery, Dexter, Washtenaw, MI. Hiram's COD was "acute supporative prostatitis" and "chronic cystitis." His death was reported in *The Lansing State Journal* August 11, 1916, 5: "Hiram Pierce, 79 years old, a resident of this city for the past two months, and formerly mayor of Dexter, died at the home of his daughter, Mrs. Lois Hunter, 334 South Grand ave., at 8:45 o'clock Thursday evening. He had been ill since Sunday . . . Short funeral services will be conducted at the home where he died Saturday morning at 11 o'clock. The body will be taken to his former home in Dexter for services and burial Saturday." A more extensive article appeared in *The Dexter Leader* August 17, 1916: "Hiram Pearce [*sic*] was born in Springfield, Otsego Co., N. Y., January 28, 1838, and died in Lansing, Mich., August 10, 1916. When he was seven years of age his father moved onto a farm in Otsego, N. Y. On August 30, 1862, he enlisted in Company H Regiment 147, and served his country two years. At the close of the war in 1865 he came to Michigan. He carried on a prosperous coopering business at Dover six miles north of Dexter for a number of years. Later he moved on a farm in Ionia Co. near Portland, where he lived eighteen years. He moved to Dexter village two years ago. In 1868 he was united in marriage with Miss Florence Ferris. They lived together thirty eight years. Mrs. Pearce passed away April 7, 1905. Mr. Pearce was a member of the F. & A. M. He was a member of the M. E. church at Dexter and was faithful and true to the end. He loved the prayer meeting and always took an active part and gave evidence of being in close fellowship with God. He was a loving and thoughtful husband and father and did all he could to make his family happy and comfortable while he lived, and no needy person ever came to his door without receiving relief and consolation. He has been in failing health for a number of years. About four months ago his daughter, Mrs. James Hunter, came and took him to her home in Lansing, where he gradually declined till his death. His remains were brought to Dexter by his daughter. The funeral services were conducted by Rev. D. H. Campbell in the M. E. Church, August 13, and he was laid to rest beside his life partner in Forest Lawn Cemetery . . . ." The farm to which the family moved when Hiram was seven years old was in Parish, Oswego County, NY.

Jonathan Pierce – Co. D
b. 1820 Granby, NY
d. February 7, 1898 Coleman, Midland, MI
m. Celista Burnham (December 9, 1824-January 5, 1920) *ca.* 1849

NOTE: Jonathan was the son of Benjamin B. (1785-1875) and Polly French Pierce (1791-1869). He was transferred to the VRC on July 27, 1863 but his discharge date is unknown. His COD was poliomyelitis combined with "exhaustion." Celista's COD was "inflammation of spinal vertebrae and membranes with neuritis of spinal nerve," together with a cerebral hemorrhage. They are buried in Warren Township Cemetery, Coleman.

James Volney Pierce – Co. G

b. July 19, 1835 Rutland, Jefferson County, NY
d. December 12, 1904 Los Angeles, Los Angeles, CA
m. Susan Augusta Maxwell (1847-October 16, 1910) September 30, 1868

NOTE: J. V., or Volney, as he was usually known, was the son of James, Jr. (1797-1870) and Cynthia Ann Weatherbee Pierce (1807-1897). He mustered out as captain of Co. D. After the war he headed west, marrying Susan in Chicago, IL. He was involved in the banking industry, and managed a bank in Walnut, KS which failed, causing considerable financial woes for the residents. He later established and ran a more successful bank at Osage Mission, KS. He advocated exploring and developing the gas reserves in Neosho County, KS. He was a member of the Ancient Order of United Workmen (AOUW), a fraternal and benevolent organization. On July 1, 1888, Pierce delivered a speech at the dedication of the 147th Regiment's monument at Gettysburg, a portion of which is here excerpted: ". . . Comrades, I have brushed aside some of the cobwebs that have obscured your history since the battle day of July 1, 1863. As it stands corrected it is a grand history; it is full of glorious and heroic deeds . . . We point with pride to the record, and claim the still higher credit that by holding the right of the line like a forlorn hope, we saved the entire line from destruction and made the battle of Gettysburg possible. Had our regiment flinched for one moment, or allowed the three Confederate

James Volney Pierce had the honor of delivering the dedicatory speech when the 147th Regiment's monument was unveiled at Gettysburg.
New York State Military Museum

regiments to have marched over the field unopposed, Hall's battery and the left of the line would have been taken in flank and rear, with results no man can appreciate.

God only knows the possible result. To the memory of our honored dead who laid life's tribute on the sacred altar of home and country we leave this monument of respect and honor from the hands of the people of the Empire State . . . ." Volney and Susan moved to California because of health issues. When he died members of Bartlett-Logan Post No. 6 GAR assisted with his funeral. Graves for him and Susan have not been located.

Peter James Piguet – Co. H
b. May 1837 Hastings, NY
d. January 9, 1920 St. Joseph's Hospital, Syracuse, Onondaga, NY
m. Frances "Fannie" Lawton West (October 1843-February 1910) 1860

NOTE: Peter's parents were Francis Victor (1800-1853) and Mary Tackley Piguet (1810-1897), both of whom were born in France. The family surname was spelled variously. On Peter's gravestone it appears as Piggah. His muster roll card spelled it Piggy. He was wounded at Gettysburg on July 1st and sent to Baltimore where he was in hospital in August. He transferred to the VRC on August 10, 1864 and was discharged on June 17, 1865 at Philadelphia, PA. In 1890 he was listed on the Veterans' Schedules as Abijah Teeter. He stated he had been afflicted with rheumatism for 20 years. He and Fannie were the parents of seven children. Her DOD is recorded as 1910 on the gravestone in St. Francis' (Little France) Cemetery, Central Square, NY but some researchers claim she died in 1909. On the same stone Peter's death is given as 1919 but his obituary, published in *The Oswego Daily Palladium* January 13, 1920, proves the date on the stone is incorrect: "Peter J. Piguet, eighty-two years old, died at St. Joseph's Hospital, Syracuse, on Friday. For years Mr. Piguet was a resident of the town of West Monroe. Several months ago he went to Syracuse to live with his son, James Piguet. A week ago he was taken to the hospital for an operation . . . The funeral was held at St. Francis's church, Little France, at ten a.m. today. Burial was made in Little France cemetery."

Henry Pitsley – Co. C
b. 1842 Parish, NY
d. December 5, 1863 David's Island, New York Harbor
m. ------

NOTE: Henry was the son of Elijah (?-*post* 1880) and his second wife, Rhoda Quimby Pitsley (*ca.* 1817-May 4, 1877). In 1855 they were the parents of seven children. Henry's COD was *phthisis pulmonalis* and chronic diarrhea. He was buried in Cypress Hills National Cemetery, Brooklyn, NY. In 1866, Elijah and Rhoda moved to Toledo, OH. They were paupers and were helped to make the move by the poor master of the town of Richland and charitable contributions. In 1867 Rhoda applied for and obtained a pension based on Henry's service. For several years before enlisting he had been the primary means of support for his mother and his father who was described as "a man of mental imbecility" who was "physically & mentally disqualified almost totally from doing any business or labor to support himself." The couple returned to Oswego County and were living in Albion in 1875. Elijah was living with Frederick and Charlotte Lewis in Albion when the 1880 census was taken. His DOD has not been located nor have the graves for him and Rhoda.

John Place – Co. C
b. October 12, 1828 Richfield, Otsego, NY
d. January 9, 1863 Falmouth Station, VA
m. Mary E. Hubbard (1836-April 17, 1938) *ca.* 1858

NOTE: John, son of William (1800-?) and Phoebe Robinson Place (1802-?), died of typhoid fever. According to *The Town Clerks' Registers*, his body was shipped home and buried in Pineville Cemetery, Richland. Mary and her daughter Coraette (1859-1945) moved to Minnesota where on January 14, 1873 she married Theodore "Dory" Owen (1823-*ante* 1895). By him she had another daughter, Hattie (1877-?). Mary died at the age of 102 at Hattie's home, as reported by *The Bellingham Herald* April 18, 1938, 8: "Mrs. Mary Owen, 102, of Everett, died yesterday at the Seattle home of a daughter, Mrs. Frank Mechener. She celebrated her birthday anniversary last January. Until a week ago she lived with another daughter, Mrs. Cora Wildey, in Everett." Graves for Theodore and Mary have not been located.

Simeon Gardner Place, MD – assistant surgeon
b. June 30, 1809 Rhode Island
d. August 29, 1871 Oswego, NY
m1. Mary Mornton (1816-March 22, 1840) September 14, 1836
m2. Mary Gilchrist (1820-June 9, 1850) *ca.* 1841
m3. Mary "Polly" Albina Colby (1827-January 16, 1899) January 8, 1851

NOTE: Simeon or Simon was the son of Peleg (1778-1849) and Hannah Lewis Place (1781-1862). He was discharged from the 147th on November 5, 1863. On March 22, 1865 he joined the 8th NY HA and was transferred to the 4th NY HA in June, ultimately being discharged June 12, 1865. In 1865 he said he had been married three times. All his wives are buried with him in Rural Cemetery, Oswego Town. Henry Peleg (1838-1903), Simeon's son by Mary Mornton, served in Co. B, 75th NYSV. His entry in *The Town Clerks' Registers* is interesting. Besides assigning him the incorrect mother, it rather euphemistically states he was taken prisoner, escaped "but somehow failed to return to his regiment." *The Adjutant-General's* Report of 1901 explained it somewhat differently:

"Deserted February 21, 1863 at Brasher City, La." George A. Place (1843-1907), whose mother was Mary Gilchrist, also served in Co. B, 75th NYSV. His notation in *The Town Clerks' Registers* also makes for interesting reading: "Accompanied Banks' expedition up Red River. At Sabin Pass Com. B, to which he belonged was totally lost. He being at the time an ordinance sergeant was on the flag-ship [and] consequently saved." George died in New Orleans, LA.

Stephen Plantee – Co. B
b. 1841 Ogdensburg, St. Lawrence, NY
d. July 1, 1863 Gettysburg, Adams, PA
m. ------

NOTE: Stephen's parents were Antoine (1815-1908) and Esther Plantee (1828-1869). Although probably buried at Gettysburg, he was memorialized on the family monument in Rural Cemetery, Oswego Town.

Simeon Alavandus Plumb – Co. H
b. December 1844 Oswego County, NY
d. June 22, 1864 near Petersburg, VA
m. ------

Simeon Place, MD, is buried with his three wives in Rural Cemetery, Oswego Town.
Author's Collection

NOTE: Alavandus' parents were Simeon (1803-1884) and Rhoda Hall Plumb (1805-1853). He was called Simeon Alexander in *The Town Clerks' Registers*. A note in *Registers of Officers and Enlisted Men* claims he died at Gettysburg on June 22, 1864! In 1865 he was listed on the New York census with the notation "formerly in Army." His family erected a cenotaph for him in Lakeside Rural Cemetery, Bernhards Bay, NY.

Seth Porter, Jr. – Co. E
b. 1841 Sandy Creek, NY
d. July 1, 1863 Gettysburg, Adams, PA
m. ------

NOTE: Seth's parents were Seth (1793-1885) and Rhoda Porter (1798-1884). He was killed at Gettysburg and buried in Evergreen Cemetery, Gettysburg. His mother applied for a pension in 1878 but seems not to have qualified. *The Sandy Creek News* January 31, 1884 announced her death: ". . . Mrs. Rhoda Porter, wife of Seth Porter, died at the residence of her son Uri last Friday, Jan. 25th, at the advanced aged of 86 years. Mrs. Porter has been a resident of this place over 60 years and leaves a husband aged 92 years. She was only sick a week, with congestion of the lungs. Her funeral was held Sunday, with sermon by Rev. Cowles, and her remains interred in the East road cemetery. The deceased was the mother of fourteen children." Seth was a veteran of the War of 1812. Upon his death *The Sandy Creek News* April 23, 1885 noted: ". . . We are again called upon to announce the death of another of our aged neighbors, Mr. Seth Porter, better known in this section as uncle Seth. Mr. Porter has been in poor health for some time and his disability began to increase of late, and on the 17th he died at the ripe age of 92 years . . . ." The East Road Cemetery, mentioned in Rhoda's obituary, has not been identified.

Stephen Plantee's short life is memorialized on two family gravestones located in Rural Cemetery.
Author's Collection

Albert D. Potter – Co. E

b. April 22, 1845 Boonville, Oneida, NY
d. July 1, 1863 Gettysburg, Adams, PA
m. ------

NOTE: Albert was the son of Ephraim (1807-1869) and Abigail Clark Potter (1810-1851). According to *The Town Clerks' Registers*, his "remains [were] buried on field of battle." His parents are buried in Redfield Village Cemetery.

John E. Potter – Co. E

b. December 6, 1840 Boonville, Oneida, NY
d. April 9, 1916 Redfield, NY
m. Clarissa N. Brockway (1851-April 24, 1914) 1869

NOTE: John was a brother of Albert D. He transferred to Batt. L, 1st NY ART on November 16, 1863 and was mustered out at Elmira, NY on June 17, 1865. John's death was reported in *The Sandy Creek News* April 13, 1916: ". . . John Potter, Sr., who has been ill with pneumonia, died at the home of his daughter, Mrs. Henry Lake, in Orwell, Sunday morning, April 9. Mr. Potter was a life long resident of the town of Redfield. He enlisted as a soldier during the Civil War and served in the Artillery division. He was wounded in the arm for which he drew a pension. This pension was increased a few days before his death as he had passed the 75th mile stone of his life. Since the death of his wife he has lived among his children, three of which survive him . . . Mr. Potter was a kind and generous man and a good neighbor. He was one who always spoke only good of every one he knew. He will be sadly missed by his many friends." Although it is evident that John survived the war, his entry in *The Town Clerks' Registers* contains a strange comment: "Suffered. Transferred to Gettysburg National Cemetery." John and Clarissa, who also died of pneumonia, are buried in Evergreen Cemetery, Orwell.

Lathum Denison Potter – Co. K

b. March 27, 1839 Orwell, NY
d. May 22, 1903 Pulaski, NY
m. Martha A. Doane (October 1834-October 7, 1906) October 17, 1866

NOTE: The DOB for Lathum, whose name was variously spelled, differs from document to document. I use that contained in his obituary. His parents were John (1801-1880) and Jane Davis Potter (1802-1885). One of his brothers was Albert Jackson Potter (1833-1918), who served in the 110th Regiment. Lathum mustered out with the 147th on June 7, 1865. According to *The Town Clerks' Registers* he "was at the surrender of Gen. Lee." His obituary, published in *The Pulaski Democrat* May 27, 1903, details a long and useful life: "A shadow was cast over our community, Friday evening, when the news reported that Lathum D. Potter had expired after less than an hour of unconsciousness which came over him while milking his cow. Mr. Potter had been failing this spring, but no one realized that he was declining so fast as his sudden death proves he must have been. He returned from the funeral of T. D. Spencer at Port Ontario, which he attended with his brother masons and had gone to the barn to milk his cow when the boy who drives the cow to pasture found him in an unconscious condition in the stable, where he had fallen from the stool. Dr. Caldwell was called and help soon carried Mr. Potter to the house where every means possible was used to revive him but of no avail. Lathum D. Potter, son of John Potter and Jane Davis, was born in the town of Orwell, March 27, 1839. He attended the district school and helped about the farm in boyhood, and afterwards attended and graduated from a business college. At the opening of the rebellion he enlisted in the 147th N.Y. Inf. He was promoted to the office of Mail Messenger and was discharged in 1865. In 1866, October 17th, he married Martha Doane, of this village, and they resided in Richland four years, when they moved to this village where they have since resided. In 1872 Mr. Potter entered the U.S. mail service and ran (?) between Richland and Syracuse. He continued in that service until about 1886. He served as assistant P.M. under J. T. McCarthy and D. C. Bishop. He was serving his third term as Justice of the Peace of this town. He was a charter member of Post Butler, 111, G.A.R.; a charter member of Pulaski Lodge A.O.U., which order he served as financier for several years; was a member of Pulaski Lodge, 415, F. & A. M. He served the village as collector and is numbered among the Past Commanders of J. B. Butler Post. He was a member of St. James Episcopal church, holding the office of Senior Warden and Treasurer. The funeral was held from his late home, in North street, yesterday, at ten o'clock, with masonic honors, the bearers being members of the G.A.R. Post. Rev. W. N. Hawkins, rector of St. James church, officiated . . . We cannot close this memorial sketch without expressing a deep sorrow over the death of our esteemed friend and brother. He has been so well known in this community, and in so many ways manifested his willingness to help and encourage where he was able to extend a helping hand, he will be missed. Mr. Potter has met with reverses and discouragements which caused no one to suffer more than himself and deep was his regret that so busy a life, one so full of work and so rounded with service could not be within reach of resources by which he could do more for those he wished to help. He was never indifferent to calls for service in the church or any organization to which he belonged. He felt a responsibility in the welfare and lively exuberance of the various societies with which he held membership, thus his demise will be felt with keen regret." When Martha died, *The Pulaski Democrat* October 10, 1906 published the following: "Martha A. Potter was born in Pulaski, Oct. 9, 1832 [sic], and was the daughter of Captain Ira Doane. All her life was spent in this village. She was married to Latham D. Potter about thirty-five years ago, and to them were born two sons, who both died in infancy. Mr. Potter died very suddenly three years ago last spring. A week ago last Sunday Mrs. Potter was called to the home of Mr. Burton, whose death occurred that day, and on her return home she was stricken with paralysis and lapsed into unconsciousness from which she never rallied, her death occurring last Sunday, after just a week's illness. Mrs. Potter was a most loyal member of St. James' Episcopal church. Her life has been one of patient devotion to all members of her household and her mild and lovable disposition endeared her to all with whom she became associated. She was of a quiet retiring nature, yet the rare fragrance of her sweet, self-sacrificing life was felt by the large circle of friends and relatives who mourn her departure . . . The funeral will be held at the late home on North street, today at 2 p.m., being conducted by Rev. J. O. Ward . . . ." Lathum and Martha are buried in Pulaski Village Cemetery.

Luke Potter – Co. C

b. 1829 Ellisburg, Jefferson, NY

d. February 12, 1863 Mount Pleasant Hospital, Washington, DC

m. Caroline Reynolds (1832-November 3, 1884) October 20, 1852

NOTE: Luke was the son of John R. (1803-*post* 1860) and Caroline Gillett Potter (1808-1880). He and Caroline were married in Pierrepont Manor, Jefferson, NY and became the parents of Rosetta (1854-1912) and Willis (1859-1926). According to *Deaths of Volunteers*, Luke died of pneumonia. He was buried in the Soldiers' and Airmen's National Home Cemetery, Washington, DC. On September 27, 1865 Caroline married an Englishman, Robert Brown (1830-March 20, 1916). The family moved to Fairfield, Ontario, Canada where Caroline became the mother of two more children, Charles Newton Brown (1868-1930) and John Robert Brown (1870-1932). Caroline died of "inflammation of the lungs," after being sick one week. Robert died of uraemia. His obituary said he was to be buried in Athens, Leeds, Ontario, Canada but graves for him and Caroline have not been located.

Simeon F. Potter – Co. E

b. August 18, 1842 Boonville, Oneida, NY

d. July 1, 1863 Gettysburg, Adams, PA

m. ------

NOTE: Simeon was the brother of Albert D. and John E. Potter. According to *The Town Clerks' Registers*, his "remains [were] buried on field of battle." In 1868 his father Ephraim applied for and obtained a pension based on Simeon's service.

William R. Potts – Co. C

b. 1827 Oneida County, NY

d. April 8, 1890 Williamstown, NY

m. Sarah A. Kelsey (1831-March 2, 1906) *ca.* 1857

NOTE: William, whose parents were John (1795-?) and Margaret Shonts Potts (1803-1865), was a carpenter by trade. He was wounded at Gettysburg on July 1, 1863 and discharged for "disability from wounds" on November 5, 1863. His death was reported in *The Pulaski Democrat* April 17, 1890: "W. R. Potts died on Tuesday, April 8, aged sixty-three years. Mr. Potts was a member of the church and an elder, and will be greatly missed in society. He was a first lieutenant in the late war and received a bullet wound. His funeral was held from the Presbyterian church on Friday, April 11, Rev. Vincent officiating. George Potts, of St. Louis, Mo., came home last Wednesday to attend the funeral of his father." Sarah's COD was heart disease. She and William are buried in Fairview Cemetery, Williamstown. The stone does not contain her DOD.

Virgil M. Powers – Co. E
b. 1844 Sandy Creek, NY
d. October 13, 1865 Sandy Creek, NY
m. ------

NOTE: Virgil, whose birth name was Crosby, was the adopted son of Parley H. (1826-1879) and Nancy Cole Powers (1824-1882). He transferred to the 3rd Brigade Band on January 23, 1865. His COD is unknown but he is buried in Woodlawn Cemetery, Sandy Creek.

William Davis Pratt – Co. K
b. *ca.* 1821 Bristol, England
d. June 1879 Oswego City, NY
m1. Helen "Ellen" Eliza Howe (*ca.* 1818-1856) *ca.* 1839
m2. Mary D. Sweeney (*ca.* 1820-April 4, 1885) November 28, 1856

NOTE: William, a sailor, was the son of Thomas (?-?) and Elizabeth Davis Pratt (?-?). His DOB has been difficult to determine because he changed it often. In 1855 his age was 40; in 1860 he was 39; in 1865 he was 44. When he died his age on the Mortality Schedules was 65. A biography of Armieger Howe Pratt, appearing in *History of Whatcom County*, vol. 2, 142-43, provides information on his father: "Armieger Howe Pratt, who has for a number of years been successfully engaged in the real estate business at Bellingham, WA, has resided within the borders of Whatcom county for a period of forty-three years and has therefore been a witness of its remarkable development and progress. His birth occurred in Boston, MA on 5 Sep 1852, his parents being William David Pratt and Helen Howe, natives of Bristol, England, who immigrated to America in the '40s of the past century and settled in Boston. The father, who was a sea captain, at one time had a line of ships of his own out of Bristol. It was about 1858 that he abandoned a sea faring life and removed to Oswego, New York, after which he was a sailor on the Great Lakes until the time of his enlistment in the Union army in the latter part of 1861 [*sic*]. Two years later he became sick and was discharged. Recovering from this illness, he reenlisted and served until the cessation of hostilities . . . When the war was over, William Davis Pratt, broken in health, returned to Oswego, New York, where he spent the remainder of his life in retirement passing away in 1876. He gave his political support to the republican party and attended the services of the Episcopal church. William D. and Helen (Howe) Pratt were the parents of three sons and two daughters, namely, Thomas, Elizabeth, William H., Ella and Armieger H. The wife and mother departed this life in 1856 and the following year William D. Pratt was again married, his second union being with Mary Sweeney, a native of Nova Scotia. To them were born three children: Thomas and Mary, who died in infancy; and Sarah Jane, who is the wife of John Cole and now resides at Oswego, New

York . . . ." While Armieger's recollections were interesting, they were slightly erroneous. William enlisted in the 147th on August 22, 1862. His tenure was short since he was discharged for "disability" from General Hospital, location not specified, on March 18, 1863. On February 25, 1865 he enlisted in Co. D, 193rd Regiment at Lenox, Madison, NY, serving until mustered out on August 11, 1865 at the Post Hospital, Harper's Ferry, VA, again for "disability." Although Armieger (September 5, 1852-Nobvember 29, 1926) professed that his father died in 1876, in truth he died in June 1879 of "paralysis," as is confirmed by the 1880 Mortality Schedules. Mary, whose marriage date is confirmed by a record filed in Boston, MA, was the mother of one child not in the biography. Sophia (1865-1866) and her half-brother, Thomas (1840-1862), are buried in St. Paul's Cemetery, Oswego City. Mary last appeared in the 1882 Oswego City Directory living with Sarah Jane, a dressmaker and milliner. Graves for her and William have not been located. William H. Pratt (1846-November 19, 1897) served in Co. E, 140th Regiment. He was captured at the battle of the Wilderness on May 5, 1864 and spent ten months in Andersonville Prison. He lived in Boston, MA at the time of his death. His body was returned to Oswego and buried in Riverside Cemetery.

Leonard A. Preeman – Co. F
b. 1841 Canada
d. October 24, 1864 Andersonville, Sumter, GA
m. ------

NOTE: Leonard, son of John (1815-1892) and Mary Herbert Preeman (1818-1854), originally enlisted in the 110th Regiment. He was captured at Haymarket, VA on October 19, 1863 and sent to Andersonville. He was reported dead by exchanged prisoners. His COD was diarrhea. His father, who was widowed twice over by 1860, applied for a pension on July 19, 1869. Leonard's brother, John, Jr. (1835-1914), served in Co. A, 14th US Infantry from 1861-1864.

Lewis Preeman – Co. F
b. 1843 Knowlesville, Orleans, NY
d. July 1, 1863 Gettysburg, Adams, PA
m. ------

NOTE: Information about this soldier is scant. His POB on the 1855 New York census was Canada. At the time he was living in Palermo, NY as a servant. His muster roll card, however, shows he was born in New York State. It is possible he was Leonard's brother but this theory is unconfirmed. He too tried to enlist in the 110th but was sent to the 147th. If Leonard is a brother, then too is John, Jr., who gave a POB of Genesee County, NY when he applied for GAR membership. Although Lewis died at

Gettysburg, I have located no record about his gravesite. He may have been buried on the battlefield.

Alonzo Bailey Prior – Co. F
b. January 18, 1846 Lenox, Madison, NY
d. August 9, 1926 St. Charles, Saginaw, MI
m1. Florine Allen (May 1851-August 28, 1932) *ca.* 1867
m2. Christena G. Cook (1859-April 5, 1939) June 17, 1882

NOTE: Alonzo, son of Asahel (1813-1880) and Rachel A. Taber Prior (1830-1865), lied about his age when he enlisted. He attempted to join the 110th but was sent to the 147th. He transferred to the VRC on November 28, 1863 and was discharged at Rochester, Monroe, NY on July 24, 1865. His marriage to Florine did not last and he moved to Michigan where he married Christena in East Saginaw. In 1890 he said his disabilities were Bright's disease and rheumatism, but his COD was "heart trouble." He and Christena are buried in Riverside Cemetery, St. Charles. Florine married John S. Seamans (June 1835-1925), a member of the 147th Regiment, in 1880. (See his entry below.)

Matthew Purdy – Co. H
b. 1838 Ireland
d. July 25, 1869 Philadelphia, Philadelphia, PA
m. Mary Jane _____ (1841-September 1871) *ca.* 1865

NOTE: This man's muster roll card spells his name Mathew Purey but all other documents show Matthew Purdy. The key to finding him lies in his pension card. Although his muster roll card states he was absent at muster out, *Soldier Records and Profiles* shows clearly he mustered out on June 7, 1865. His application for a pension on June 30, 1865 was successful. His widow Mary Jane applied for a pension on November 2, 1869. On March 12, 1872 N. B. Browne, guardian, applied for a minor's pension. The only Matthew and Mary Jane Purdy fitting these criteria are those identified here. Even so, there are problems. In 1862 Matthew said he was born in Ireland. All death records show Canada as POB. The 1870 Mortality Schedules provide an occupation of glassblower and a COD of consumption. The records for the Odd Fellows Cemetery in Philadelphia, where he and Mary Jane were originally buried, list stone cutter as his trade and a COD of tetanus. Mary Jane died of typhoid fever. Where they are buried now is unknown. The bodies in this Odd Fellows Cemetery were removed when the land was sold for a housing development and were reinterred either in Lawn View Cemetery, Rockledge, Montgomery, PA or Mount Peace Cemetery, Philadelphia. N. B. Browne's identity is unknown but a man by that name was a trustee at the University of Pennsylvania in 1872. He may have been appointed guardian of Eliza (1865-?) and Charles (1868-?) who appear with their mother on the 1870 census for Philadelphia. They were living with Michael and Elizabeth Murphy, who may have been Mary Jane's parents.

Sylvester Earl Quick, Jr. – Co. K
b. 1841 Onondaga County, NY
d. July 3, 1863 Gettysburg, Adams, PA
m. Ellen "Nell" Loveland (1845-*post* 1880) *ca.* 1861

NOTE: Sylvester's parents were Sylvester (1800-1840) and Louisa Stevens Quick (1810-1874). It would appear that the son was a posthumous child. He gave "clerk" as his occupation when he enlisted. His DOD is contested. An entry in *Deaths of Volunteers*, signed by Dr. A. S. Coe, says he died on July 1st. *The Adjutant-General's Report* states he died on July 3, 1863 and his FAG entry says he was mortally wounded on Culp's Hill on July 3rd, a statement confirmed by his muster roll card. He is buried in Gettysburg National Cemetery. He and Ellen were the parents of Henrietta (1862-1929). Ellen married Daniel Christmas (1815-1903) as his second wife. By him she was the mother of Angeline (1864-?) and John (1872-1953). In 1880 the family was living in Hannibal, NY. In 1900 Daniel, widower, was living in Sunderland, Bennington, VT with John. Graves for him and Ellen have not been located.

Daniel Quigley – Co. K
b. March 1828 Ireland
d. September 2, 1907 Fulton, NY
m. Margaret S. Boland (1822-*post* 1906) 1858

NOTE: Daniel's mother was Bridget Quigley (1797-*post* 1875). In 1855 they lived in Oswego City and alleged they had resided there eight years. Bridget was a widow. Birthdates for Daniel and Margaret vary considerably but it is relatively certain that she was the elder of the two. I use the dates listed on the 1900 census. Daniel was discharged from a hospital at Washington, DC on June 26, 1863. When he was admitted to the Bath National Home on June 15, 1906 he gave Margaret as his next of kin but his pension card does not list a widow's application, an indication that she had predeceased him. He is buried in St. Mary's Cemetery, Fulton. No further information has been located about her except that in 1900 she claimed to be the mother of eight, none of whom was alive. If this statement is true, all must have died very young because no children appear on any census records.

William Quinlan – Co. K
b. 1833 Ireland
d. September 3, 1895 Oswego City, NY
m. Ellen H. _____ (1835-May 14, 1909) *ca.* 1852

NOTE: The many spellings of this man's surname have made researching him a challenge but the discovery of a pension card with the spelling given above has solved the mystery. According to his muster roll card William, whose parents are unknown, was on detached service with Batt. L, 1st NY ART on February 1, 1863. On May 18, 1863 William applied for (but did not obtain) an invalid pension, indicating he had been discharged. An article appearing in *The Oswego Commercial Times* October 17, 1863, which uses one variation of his surname, hints that he had been back in Oswego for some time: ". . . William Quinlivan was charged with creating a disturbance yesterday on the Flats. Mrs. McMahon, the complainant, witnessed that he came about her place very drunk and noisy, and upon her requesting him to go home quietly, he used abusive language towards her, and finally pushed open the door of her room, wielding a billet of wood in a most vicious manner, threatening to strike her. Defendant [*sic*] alleged that he said, 'If you were a man I would strike you.' Whatever he may have said, his conduct was proved to have been very unruly, as it has been on previous occasions. He is a returned soldier, from the 147th Regiment. Sentence suspended." On December 12, 1890 William made a will, naming Ellen as his executrix. The will was not recorded until May 25, 1896, months after William's death. Graves for these people have not been located although William's funeral was held at St. John's Catholic Church, Oswego.

Frank Rattle – Co. H
b. 1830 Germany
d. March 1, 1895 Rome, Oneida, NY
m. Jane Robotham (November 13, 1831-December 4, 1898) *ca.* 1868

NOTE: Frank's surname was also spelled Ratle and Rathle. His parents are unidentified. He was wounded at Gettysburg on July 1, 1863 and sent to hospital where he was discharged for "disability" on September 3, 1863. Ironically, in 1890 he did not claim any disability. His COD is unknown. A lengthy obituary for Jane appeared in *The Rome Daily Sentinel* December 6, 1898, 2: "Mrs. Jane Rattle, widow of Frank Rattle, died of cancer of the stomach at her home, 218 Expense street, at noon on Sunday, aged 68 years. She had been confined to the bed since the first of September. She suffered intensely, but bore her pain with remarkable fortitude. Mrs. Rattle was born in Yorkshire, England. When she was 8 years [old] she came with her father, Thomas Robotham, to this country and Mr. R. located near Floyd Hill. Afterward the family moved to Ridge Mills and about thirty years ago the deceased was married in

Constantia to Frank Rattle and for a time they made their home in Clinton, moving about eight years ago to this city, where Mr. Rattle died in March, 1895. Mrs. Rattle was a member of the Wesleyan M. E. Church of this city and was a devout Christian woman. She leaves one sister and one brother, the only surviving members of her family. They are George Robotham and Mrs. Emma Pense, both of Rome." Frank and Jane are buried in Wright Settlement Cemetery, Rome.

John David Rau – Co. G

b. 1830 Prussia
d. July 1, 1863 Gettysburg, Adams, PA
m. Elenore Modrag (November 2, 1834-January 15, 1917) May 7, 1857

NOTE: John's parents were Christian (?-?) and Elizabeth Rau (?-?). He and Elenore were married in Poland. In December 1864 Captain Delos Gary testified as to what he knew about Rau's fate. After describing the order to retreat on July 1st, he stated: "[The regiment] had already suffered severely in killed and wounded and it was compelled to retreat under a sharp fire by which it lost many more men in killed and wounded. The enemy immediately occupied the ground and continued to occupy it until the morning of July 4th – Many of the dead had been buried before any member of the Regiment had an opportunity to revisit the ground. In the precipitate retreat made by the Regiment under a sharp fire it was impossible to tell who was killed and who was not until the Company was again assembled. David Rau was then found to be missing. There were more men left on the ground the Company had occupied, apparently dead than the members of the Company could give names of those whom they knew positively to be killed. No one as far as deponent could learn could say that Rau was certainly killed, but I have no doubt that his body was one of the number left dead upon the field and whose names could not at that time be positively given. All the men taken prisoner have been heard from. Every one of them has been exchanged. As far as I have heard there is no difference in opinion among the officers and men of the Company as to the fate of David Rau. All are satisfied that he was killed in action at Gettysburg on the 1st day of July, 1863 . . . ." Elenore, left with three minor children, married George Walter (1837-December 29, 1902) on April 16, 1865. He too had been born in Germany. He died of "neuralgia of the heart" in Oswego City. *The Oswego Daily Palladium* January 16, 1917 announced Elenore's death: "Mrs. Eleanor Walters of 72 Stone Street, Oneida was found dead in her bed yesterday by Chief of Police Wilcox. When the neighbors failed to see her out and about, the police were called, with the above results. Coroner W. T. Tanner was called and ordered the remains taken in the undertaking rooms of Munro and Dunbar. The cause of death was a ruptured heart. Mrs. Walters was about eighty-three years of age . . . The body arrived in this city at 12:30 o'clock today and was removed to the home of Gustav Rowe. The deceased was born in Berlin, Germany and came to this country when twenty years old . . . ." George and Elenore are buried in Rural Cemetery, Oswego Town.

Patrick Regan – Co. I
b. 1821 Ireland
d. December 6, 1891 Auburn, Cayuga, NY
m. Susan Newman (1831-February 20, 1904) *ca.* 1847

NOTE: Regan's parents are unidentified. He was discharged from the service on September 27, 1863 and enjoyed a long and active career, as demonstrated by his obituary, published in *The Auburn Bulletin* December 7, 1891, 1: "Captain Patrick Regan died at his home, 110 Fulton street, yesterday from an attack of pneumonia with which he was stricken a little over a week ago. Mr. Regan was born in Ireland 69 years ago, and came to this country when a child. He lived in Utica, where he received his early education and learned the trade of shoemaking. When a young man he located in Oswego and commenced business for himself. At the outbreak of the war he enlisted for service in the 147th regiment, New York State volunteers, which regiment he helped organize. He was made a captain and served through the war with distinction. He afterwards resumed business in Oswego and continued until he removed to this city to take charge of the shoemaking department in the prison, in which John Dunn was interested. He remained there for a number of years, afterwards establishing himself in the shoe business on State street. Mr. Regan was a kind, courteous gentleman and made a large circle of friends who will be pained to hear of his death. He was a trustee of St. Mary's church and accountant of the Equitable Aid Union . . . ." Susan was the mother of five, four of whom were living in 1900. Her death was announced in *The Auburn Citizen* February 21, 1914: "Mrs. Susan Newman Regan, widow of Capt. D. [*sic*] Regan passed peacefully away at her residence, 105 Fulton Street, yesterday. Mrs. Regan was the oldest resident of Fulton Street, having resided in that street for 40 years. By her kind and lovable disposition she made hosts of friends, who will sympathize with her family . . . ." Patrick and Susan are buried in St. Joseph's Cemetery, Auburn.

George Washington Remore – Co. F
b. February 1838 Camden, Oneida, NY
d. August 4, 1911 LeRoy, Mower, MN
m1. ?
m2. Sarah A. Hutchins (March 1850-April 27, 1907) 1871

NOTE: Remore's surname was also spelled Reymore. His parents were David (1796-?) and Catherine Lentz Remore (1803-?). He mustered out with the regiment on June 7, 1865. In 1890 he said his "left leg [was] hurt by a mule falling on it." He was a member of James George Post No. 23 GAR, located in LeRoy. His obituary, published in *The Austin Daily Herald* August 8, 1911, 2, contained some intriguing material: "George Remore whose sudden death occurred last Friday at his home in LeRoy was one of the pioneer settlers in that section of the state. He took up a farm near the old town, which for many years was the Poor Farm of the county until it was removed to Austin vicinity. It was when serving as manager of this farm, that his young wife contracted typhoid fever in the care of one of the inmates and died after she had been married to Mr. Remore but two years. He was later married again and the second wife died about four years ago, after having been married to Mr. Remore about thirty-seven years. They leave one daughter, Edna, wife of Will Armstrong, who since their mother's illness, have made their home at the old homestead farm. For seven years Mr. and Mrs. Remore had charge of the Poor Farm near Austin. During their residence there they made many friends who always valued their friendship. Mr. Remore was seventy-three years of age in February. While in his usual health he had suffered from a weak heart and his daughter had kept close watch of him. Friday his daughter thought he was working with her husband in the field. When the husband returned at noon Mr. Remore was not with him, but he had seen him lining a fence. They went at once to where he had been seen and found him dead with his hammer in his hand and his back against a tree. The funeral was held Sunday from his old home and was largely attended. Mr. Remore was an old soldier and a man of unimpeachable character. He was noted for loyalty to friends, integrity in business dealings, and kindliness in his home life. He was just such a man as the world has need of and is to be missed when his work is over." Sarah's death was reported in *The Austin Daily Herald* April 27, 1907, 2: "The many Austin friends of Mrs. George Remore will be exceedingly sorry to learn of her death which occurred at her home in LeRoy this morning at 1:15 o'clock after several months' illness of cancer. The funeral will be held Monday at 2:30 p.m. from the house . . . A year ago last fall Mrs. Remore began to feel that she was stricken with cancer and a year ago last March submitted to an operation. But the dread disease was not stayed and after suffering for many weeks, death came. The sorrowing husband and daughter who are left to mourn the loss of so good a wife and mother, have the sympathy of many of our people in their sorrow." Graves for George and Sarah have not been located.

Herman Reynolds – Co. C
b. 1841 Sandy Creek, NY
d. 1906 probably Michigan
m. ?

NOTE: Herman's name was variously spelled. I use that found on his pension card. He was the son of Timothy (1811-1870) and Almira Murdock Reynolds (?-ca. 1850). In 1850 Herman/Heman was living with his widowed father and three siblings in Richland. He was captured at Gettysburg on July 2, 1863 and paroled on September 21st. He was discharged on June 9, 1865 at Washington, DC. On April 24, 1867 he applied for a pension. No widow is listed on the card and I can find no evidence of a wife. In 1870 he was living with his brother Edson (1837-1911) in Dryden, Lapeer, MI. In 1890 he was living in Allegan County, MI and he said he had been wounded in the head and hip during the war. His DOD is found on his pension card but no location is provided. Some researchers say he died as late as 1933 but I have found no evidence for this.

David S. Rice – Co. F
b. 1815 Smithfield, Madison, NY
d. June 18, 1864 Petersburg, VA
m1. Lucy _____ (1825-*ante* 1857) *ca.* 1849
m2. Evaline Doty Rafferty (May 1837-*post* 1915) September 27, 1857

NOTE: David's parents are unidentified. He and his first wife Lucy (1825-*post* 1850) were the parents of Amanda (1845-*post* 1870), Charles W. (1846-*post* 1870), and George D. (1848-?). On the 1850 census he said he had been born in Connecticut. Evaline, whose name was variously spelled, may have been the daughter of Cyrus Berry Doty, Sr. (1807-1886) and Jane Elizabeth Brower (1811-1859). Her first husband was James Rafferty (?-*ante* 1857) by whom she was the mother of Thomas (1852-?) and James (1854-?). She and David were the parents of Mary Jane (1858-?), Cora (1860-?) and Clara (1862-?). Rice was KIA. Alvin Richardson, guardian for the children, testified that he was mortally wounded by a "rifle ball shot through the lungs by the rebels while on picket duty from which he died in 5 minutes." On December 31, 1864 Evaline married Egbert Wingate (1836-*post* 1915). Their first child, Frank (1865-?), was born in NYS. Clarence (1872-1940) and Walter (1874-1949) were born in Outagamie County, WI. In 1900 Evaline said she was the mother of 13 children, of whom eight survived. In 1910 she said she had been married three times, confirming earlier documents. In 1915, Egbert and Evaline were in Seymour, Outagamie, WI. No further information is available for them. Clarence lived in the Outagamie County Home for at least 20 years and is buried in Outagamie County Cemetery. His obituary named Walter as his only surviving relative. Walter is buried in Elm Lawn Cemetery, Maple Grove Township, Shawano, WI.

Henry O. Rice – Co. D
b. 1834 Washington County, NY
d. May 21, 1879 Manchester, Ontario, NY
m. Elizabeth Howland (1833-January 23, 1895) *post* 1860

NOTE: Henry was the son of James (1811-?) and an unidentified mother. He was discharged from the service for "disability" on April 28, 1863. He and Elizabeth had no children, making determining a marriage date impossible. In 1860, however, she was still single. They were married by 1870. It is probable they were married soon after he returned from the war. His brief death notice does not reveal the cause. When Elizabeth died, however, *The Rochester Democrat and Chronicle* January 26, 1895, 4 printed the following: ". . . Mrs. Elizabeth Rice, of Farmington, died of apoplexy Wednesday evening at the residence of Christopher Tilden, three miles south of Palmyra, at the age of 62 years. She was on a visit and was taken ill suddenly Saturday, never rallying. The funeral services will be held at the residence of her nephew, Winifred [*sic*] Mink, of Manchester, at 12 o'clock today, the Rev. Leonard Woods Richardson, rector of Zion Episcopal Church, of Palmyra, officiating . . . ." Henry and Elizabeth are buried in South Farmington Cemetery. The "nephew" mentioned in the obituary was Wilfred Mink, husband of Elizabeth's niece, Mary Howland Mink.

John Wesley Rice – Co. C
b. October 1844 Hounsfield, Jefferson, NY
d. September 15, 1918 Fulton, NY
m. Helen G. Connell (October 1851-May 15, 1937) 1869

NOTE: John, who frequently used his middle name, was the son of Francis (1790-?) and Lovina Sadler Rice (1818-1906). He was discharged from the service for "disability" on October 31, 1863 after his leg was amputated. In 1890 he said his disabilities were kidney and heart disease. The enumerator remarked, "Very bad." Rice was a member of Post Schenck No. 271 GAR. He and Helen, who died after a long illness, were the parents of five children. They are buried in Mt. Adnah Cemetery, Fulton.

Guy Richards – Co. K
b. 1844 Adams, Jefferson, NY
d. 1888 Iosco County, MI
m. ?

NOTE: This soldier's parents are unknown. He was a sailor and originally attempted to enlist in the 110th Regiment. On March 17, 1864 he was transferred to Co. K, 12th Regiment VRC and finally discharged on June 28, 1865 at Washington, DC. His entry in *The Town Clerks' Registers* contains almost no information. He applied for a pension in Michigan on November 2, 1883 but was unsuccessful. A definite DOD has not been located. He is buried in Greenwood Cemetery, East Tawas, Iosco, MI and his government gravestone contains no dates at all. No evidence of a wife has been found.

John Richardson – Co. C

b. December 12, 1828 Ireland
d. January 27, 1916 Altmar, NY
m. Amanda V. Briggs (1850-July 9, 1928) 1871

NOTE: John, whose parents are unknown, was discharged from the service for "disability" on May 30, 1864. A detailed obituary appeared in *The Pulaski Democrat* February 2, 1916: "John Richardson was born in Ireland, Dec. 12, 1828 and died in Altmar January 27th, 1916. He came to this country with his parents when a small child and lived for many years in the town of Richland. He was a blacksmith by trade and worked in the Ingersoll shop in Pulaski for 18 years. He was a veteran of the civil war, having enlisted twice, once in the 147th and once in [the] 110th Regiments, going from the town of Richland. Mr. Richardson had been a resident of Altmar for 33 years and for the past twenty-five years had been an invalid. During his long illness he was devotedly cared for by his faithful wife who survives him . . . The funeral services were held from the home Saturday morning, Rev. W. E. Baker, pastor of the Methodist church officiating . . . ." Amanda's death occasioned the following which was published in *The Sandy Creek News* July 12, 1928: "Funeral services for Mrs. Amanda Richardson, an aged resident of Altmar who died Monday, were held at the M. E. Church Wednesday at 2 o'clock with the Rev. G. M. Sleeman officiating. Mrs. Richardson was the widow of the late John Richardson a veteran of the Civil War. Since her husband's death she had made her home with Mr. and Mrs. Arthur Dawley. She is survived by one sister, Mrs. Green of Phoenix . . . ." Although John's obituary stated he was a member of the 110th, such was not the case. On September 24, 1861 he attempted to enlist in the Band of the 35th Regiment but was unassigned. In 1900 Amanda said she was the mother of two children, neither living. She and John are buried in Riverside Cemetery, Altmar. Her DOD is not given on the stone and John's is erroneously given as 1915.

Martin Van Buren Richardson – Co. F

b. October 19, 1829 Hastings, NY
d. March 20, 1897 Kansas City, Jackson, MO
m. Armina D. Munger (May 21, 1830-September 25, 1915) *ca.* 1850

NOTE: Martin was the son of Freeman (1801-1878) and Phebe Cornwall Richardson (1802-1865). He was wounded at Gettysburg on July 1, 1863. His entry in *The Town Clerks' Registers* states: "Wounded through both shoulders July 1st at the battle of Gettysburg – Discharged Oct. 21, 1863. Still living but disabled." In 1890 Martin was living in Rolla, Phelps, MO. The enumerator wrote: "Wounded in left shoulder & discharged for that reason." He and Armina are buried in Elmwood Cemetery, Kansas City.

William Harrison Richardson – Co. F

b. January 30, 1825 Manlius, Onondaga, NY

d. October 18, 1891 Hastings, NY

m. Polly Ann _____ (1827-May 6, 1906) *ca.* 1850

NOTE: William, also known by his middle name, was a brother of Martin V. B. He was wounded at Gettysburg on July 1, 1863 and subsequently transferred to the VRC. According to *The Town Clerks' Registers* he was discharged for "physical disability" in August 1864. He is buried in Coit Cemetery, Hastings, as are several members of his family. Polly died in Syracuse, Onondaga, NY. Her death notice said she was going to be buried in Hastings.

Ezra Alonzo Rider – Co. D

b. 1844 Oswego County, NY

d. July 1, 1863 Gettysburg, Adams, PA

m. ------

NOTE: Ezra, frequently called by his middle name, was the son of Ezra (1785-*post* 1865) and Sarah J. Rider (1823-*post* 1865). His muster roll card listed him MIA on July 1, 1863 with the notation: "Has not been heard from since." A casualty list published in *The Mexico Independent* July 23, 1863 also numbered him among the missing under the name Alonzo Rider. He was probably buried on the field.

Alpheus H. Ridgeway – Co. E

b. 1837 Wayne County, NY

d. February 14, 1884 Watertown, Jefferson, NY

m. Sarah C. Goodrich (1840-Jully 29, 1896) 1857

NOTE: Alpheus, the son of Allen (1804-1882) and Sophronia Hastings Ridgeway (1822-*ante* 1850), was a brother of James Henry (1832-1911) and Benjamin A. Ridgeway (1845-1912), both of whom served in the 110th Regiment. He was discharged from the army on January 1, 1865 for "disability." He and Sarah were living in Watertown when the 1880 census was taken. A lengthy, detailed obituary for Sarah appeared in *The Sandy Creek News* August 27, 1896: "Mrs. Sarah Ridgeway was a daughter of William and Cyrena Goodrich and was born in Ellisburg, Jefferson county, in 1840. She was united in marriage to Mr. Alpheus Ridgeway in 1857, to whom four children were born, Jennie, Emma, Rena and Earl, all of whom survive to mourn the loss of a loving mother. Mr. Alpheus Ridgeway, the father, was the son of Rev. Allen Ridgeway and starting out for himself in early youth his life was one of constant and ceaseless activity until twelve years ago when his health began failing. He was confined to his bed only a short time when he crossed the river and went to his reward. The son Earl was then less than three years old, and after the death of her husband Mrs. Ridgeway seemed to be ever over anxious for the welfare of her son. We believe Earl will always retain the advice his mother gave him along the line of temperance, education and Christianity. Jennie and Emma, who reside in Missouri, were unable to attend the funeral, though they sent a beautiful wreath of flowers. Mrs. Ridgeway's health appeared as good as usual, having just returned from visiting her sister, Mrs. Baxter, in Boylston. Her general health had, however, been slowly failing for the past two years. In early life she gave her heart to God, and her anchor held as firmly in the storm as sunshine. On the evening of July 29 she fell asleep to awake in the home above. Three brothers and five sisters survive to mourn her death . . . ." Sarah's COD, so euphemistically mentioned here, was reported more fully in *The Watertown Re-Union* August 1, 1896: "Mrs. Sarah Ridgeway was found dead at her home in [Sandy Creek] early this morning. When found she was fully dressed and was lying on the floor, by the side of a chair, from which she had evidently fallen. She was about her home as usual yesterday. Dr. Crockett, who was Mrs. Ridgeway's attending physician, says that she probably died last evening, and that heart trouble was undoubtedly the cause of her death." Alpheus and Sarah are buried with other members of the family in the Boylston-Sandy Creek Wesleyan Cemetery, Lacona, NY.

Frederick "Fred" Rife – Co. G
b. 1832 Germany
d. July 1, 1863 Gettysburg, Adams, PA
m. ?

NOTE: In 1860 Rife, whose parents are unidentified, was a porter at the Revenue House in Oswego. He either was not married or his wife was living elsewhere. When he enlisted in 1862 he said he was a gardener. He held the rank of corporal on July 1, 1863. On July 1, 1888, at the dedication of the 147th Regiment's monument at Gettysburg, Captain J. Volney Pierce's address memorialized Rife's actions that day: ". . . While we were advancing in the wheat field the battle opened on our right, and the bullets from the Confederate line commenced their harvest of death. Men dropped dead, and the wounded men went to the rear before they had emptied their muskets; Corp. Fred Rife and his file closer, Hiram Stowell, dropped dead, one upon the other . . . ." His grave has not been located.

Owen Riley – Co. I
b. May 5, 1844 Ireland
d. May 8, 1878 Mexico, NY
m. Elizabeth "Lizzie" Meade (1844-December 5, 1920) *ca.* 1869

NOTE: Owen's parents were Michael (?-*ante* 1855) and Mary McGowan Riley (1825-*post* 1880). Although wounded at Gettysburg on July 1, 1863, he mustered out on June 8, 1865 at Washington, DC. Owen was a baker by trade. *The Oswego Daily Palladium* November 29, 1873 published the following: "Drs. Read and DeWitt, appointed a commission of lunacy in the case of Owen Riley, have made an examination, pronounced him a lunatic, and Judge Whitney having granted an order for his conveyance to Utica, he was taken thither today by officer Walrod. Riley, who, as a baker, has worked for Mr. Worts a long time, has always been a hard-working man, being master of his trade. His insanity resulted from overwork. The case is peculiarly a sad one." His obituary was published in *The Oswego Daily Palladium* May 9, 1878: "Owen Riley, a young man well known in this city, died in the insane asylum at Mexico last night. He had been in Mr. Mannister Wort's employ for several years and was greatly esteemed by all his friends." Elizabeth never remarried, rearing three sons alone. She and Owen are buried in St. Paul's Cemetery, Oswego City.

Solomon F. Rima – Co. H
b. December 9, 1825 Herkimer County, NY
d. July 7, 1882 Lincoln County, NE
m1. Mary Ann Aldrich (October 11, 1824-December 2, 1874) *ca.* 1847
m2. Jennie _____ Elliott (1841-?) July 12, 1876

NOTE: Solomon, son of George (1805-1889) and Mary Rima (1800-1876), was transferred to the VRC on October 13, 1864. His discharge date is unknown but it was definitely before the 1865 New York census was taken. On that census, under "Men formerly in the military," a note says he was "wounded by team and ankle broke." Mary, born in Massachusetts, was the mother of seven children. The family migrated to Nebraska where Mary died. Little is known about Jennie Elliott. She was born in Michigan and apparently had been married since her marriage license listed her as Mrs. Elliott. It is possible the marriage did not last since in 1880 Solomon F. Rima, widower, was working as head cook in a boarding house in Plattsmouth, Cass, NE. He and Mary Ann are buried in North Platte Cemetery, Lincoln, NE. Their son, George Henry (1848-1864), served in Co. I, 24th NY Cavalry. He died in Lincoln US Hospital, Washington, DC on July 3, 1864 of "congestion of the lungs." Another son, Alonzo Randolph (1852-1901), died in the Ingleside Insane Asylum, Adams County, NE.

Solomon and Mary, the parents of 11 children,
are buried in North Platte Cemetery, Lincoln, NE.
Kathy Scott

Jesse Robbins – Co. F

b. 1840 Jefferson County, NY

d. March 23, 1926 Ogdensburg, St. Lawrence, NY

m1. Marguerite Vance (?-?) *ca.* 1867

m2. Emerette Merrill Case (1865-September 27, 1923) April 15, 1890

NOTE: Jesse, son of James (1802-1877) and Eliza Jane Mesock/Mesick Robbins (1810-1889), has been mistakenly identified as "Pepe" on the 1855 New York census because of the enumerator's penmanship. He originally enlisted in the 110th Regiment. He was wounded on July 1, 1863 at Gettysburg and sent to a hospital in Philadelphia. He transferred to the VRC at an unspecified date. A pension payment card said his disability was "disease of brain and spinal cord [the] result of sun stroke." Very little is known about Marguerite. I date their wedding in relation to the DOB of their elder son, William J. Robbins, MD (1868-1935). He was born in Canada, as was his mother. The younger son, Lewis H. (1871-1942), was also born in Canada. In 1880 the boys were living with their grandmother, Eliza, in Richland. Because both sons died in Michigan it is evident they and Jesse migrated there during the 1880s. Emerette was married three times, first to Colin W. Case, date unknown, whose name she used when she and Jesse married; second, to Robbins; third, to Michael E. Gregg (1858-1948) on March 29, 1893. Her marriage to Robbins was, therefore, short-lived. Jesse's obituary, which contained several errors, appeared in *The Pulaski Democrat* March 31, 1926: "Jesse Robbins, aged 87, who was about this village about a year ago and whose mental condition was so bad he was taken to Ogdensburg state hospital, died there last Wednesday and his body was brought to Mexico. Burial will be made at Daysville in the spring. Mr. Robbins was born in New Haven. He was a veteran of the Civil War. He leaves two sons, William and Lewis, of Dugway, Mich.; one daughter, in Michigan; two sisters, Mrs. Elizabeth Hager, Mrs. Edwin Sypher, of Central Square and a brother, Lewis, of Hermon, N.Y." I have been unable to locate any information on the unnamed daughter. Jesse was buried in New Haven Cemetery. His COD was pneumonia. William was buried in Plainwell Cemetery, Plainwell, Allegan, MI. Lewis was buried in Forest Lawn Cemetery, Tower, Cheboygan, MI.

William H. Robbins – Co. C

b. 1845 Canada West

d. May 14, 1863 Fitzhugh House Hospital, First Army Corps, Falmouth, VA

m. ------

NOTE: William was a brother of Jesse Robbins. *The Adjutant-General's Report* of 1904 noted he died at an unspecified date from wounds received on May 1, 1863, but *Deaths of Volunteers* provides the exact date, together with COD as recorded by Dr. Algernon S. Coe, regimental surgeon: "shell wound in Rt. hip – spine back." If the date is correct, he was wounded during action at Pollock's Mill Creek, VA. William's mother Eliza applied for a pension on October 6, 1866 and received it. Two other brothers, John A. (1833-1864) and James R. (1844-1923), enlisted in the 147th Regiment. According to *The Adjutant-General's Report*, John deserted on November 27, 1862 at Tenallytown, DC under the name Robins. On January 4, 1864 he joined the 11th New York Cavalry and died on March 20, 1864 of measles in Campbell Hospital at Washington, DC. James deserted on December 22, 1862 from an unnamed hospital. His obituary in *The Sandy Creek News* August 9, 1923 says nothing about military service, but his gravestone, which does not give DOD, in Willis Cemetery, Fernwood, clearly shows he served in Co. C, 147th.

William Rider Robbins – Co. H

b. January 20, 1829 Vienna, Oneida, NY

d. March 26, 1899 Fayetteville, Onondaga, NY

m1. Elmina Ferris (1838-February 12, 1917) *ca.* 1854

m2. Nancy Maria Snedecker (1842-July 15, 1913) 1872

NOTE: William was the son of Jeremiah (1805-1860) and Anna Maria Rider Robbins (1805-1888). Although his muster roll card says he was born in Oneida County, state census records consistently show he was born in Oswego County. He was wounded and captured at Gettysburg on July 1, 1863 and paroled at an unknown date. On March 16, 1864 he transferred to the VRC and was discharged at Cincinnati, OH on July 5, 1865. He and Elmina were the parents of four sons. After he married Nancy he became the father of Worth Meade Robbins (1880-June 1913). Nancy applied for a widow's pension but did not receive it, possibly because William was never officially divorced from Elmina. On February 3, 1875 Elmina married Harrison King Reed (1845-1885) and by him was the mother of two more sons. Reed had served in Co. I, 142nd Regiment. Robbins' lengthy obituary appeared in *The Fayetteville Recorder* March 30, 1889, 1: "William Robbins died on Sunday afternoon, March 26th, at his home on South Mill Street, of Bright's disease, aged 70 years. He was born on the 20th of January 1829, at Vienna, Oswego Co. [*sic*]. In 1862 he enlisted in the 147th regiment and was at the battle of Gettysburg, where he was shot in the leg. After he had fallen as the result of the wound he was run over by the wheel of a gun carriage, and sustained injuries thereby, which brought on the troubles resulting in his death. In 1864 he was transferred to the reserve corps and later, his term of enlistment being over, returned to civil life. His occupation was that of a boat builder and he continued that until failing health compelled him to abandon it. In 1872 he married Miss Nancy M. Snedecker, of Manlius Center, who with one son, Worth M., survives him. In 1882 he engaged in the bakery business and this was continued until increasing infirmities compelled him to relinquish the business. A year ago last November as the effect of his physical ailments Mr. Robbins became subject to attacks of insanity and these increased in frequency and violence until the end came. Funeral services were held at the Presbyterian church, of which deceased was a member, on Tuesday afternoon, Rev. Quincy J. Collins officiating. At the cemetery the ceremonies were conducted according to the ritual of the G.A.R. Post, R. H. Hayes, No. 657, of which Mr. Robbins was a member . . . ." Nancy's death occasioned the following, published in *The Fayetteville Bulletin* July 18, 1913, 1: ". . . Mrs. Nancy M. Robbins died Tuesday morning at her home in Mill street. Her son, Worth M. Robbins, died only three weeks ago and at one time during his illness she cared only to live as long as he did. She leaves a sister, Mrs. Aurilla Post, and a brother Perrin Snedecker. The funeral was held Thursday afternoon from her home . . . ." Worth died in June 1913 of complications from diabetes. William, Nancy, and Worth are all buried in Fayetteville Cemetery. Elmina died in Hannewa Falls, St. Lawrence County. Her death was announced in *The* [Potsdam] *Courier and Freeman* February 21, 1917: "The death of Mrs. Elmina Reed occurred Monday, Feb. 12, after a long illness of heart trouble. Her funeral was held Thursday in the Methodist church, the pastor Rev. Strong officiating. Interment was in Colton cemetery. Mrs. Reed was 78 years old and had lived in this place a good many years with her son Dan Reed. She was a loving mother and was ever ready to help in all ways to lighten the burden of others. She lived a Christian life in her home from day to day. The beautiful flowers given by neighbors and friends bore testimony of sympathy and love to the family. She leaves four sons, one in Syracuse, one in Michigan and Charles Reed of Baldwinsville, and Dan Reed of this place." The son living in Syracuse was Gilbert Robbins (1855-*post* 1917) and the son living in Michigan was Jeremiah "Jerry" Robbins (1857-1920). Elmina and Daniel (1878-1929) were buried in Pleasant Mound Cemetery, Colton, St. Lawrence County. Harrison Reed was buried in Pierrepont Hill Cemetery, Pierrepont, St. Lawrence County. Charles Reed, born in 1875, died in 1954.

Charles Franklin Robe – Co. G
b. November 23, 1841 Canastota, Madison, NY
d. July 2, 1910 San Diego, San Diego, CA
m1. Kate Eloise Stevens (1842-December 29, 1903) February 13, 1867
m2. Mary Elizabeth Richmond Kendall (October 2, 1843-October 12, 1918) October 3, 1905

NOTE: Charles was the son of Harvey "Harry" Wayne (1807-*post* 1855) and Parlyncia Maria Stevens Robe (1815-*post* 1850). He was a first lieutenant upon entering the 147th but was promoted to captain when Delos Gary left the service. On March 11, 1864 he was transferred to the VRC with the rank of captain. An obituary published in *The Los Angeles Times* July 3, 1910, 11 summarized his lengthy military career: "Gen. Charles F. Robe, U.S.A., retired, died suddenly early this morning. He was in good health when he retired, following a visit with friends. He died at the home of his daughter, Mrs. George Rogers. He had lived in San Diego seven years, coming here soon after his retirement. Gen. Robe was born in New York in 1841. He served in the Civil War as first lieutenant and captain in the Hundred and Forty-seventh New York Volunteers. He was appointed as first lieutenant in the Twenty-ninth United States Infantry in 1866. At the time of his retirement, with the rank of brigadier-general, in 1903, he was colonel of the Ninth United States Infantry, in charge of Madison Barracks. He belonged to numerous military organizations, including the Loyal Legion, United States Cavalry Association, Military Service Institution, Sons of the American Revolution, and was honorary president of the Reunion Association of the One Hundredth and Forty-seventh New York Volunteer Infantry . . . ." His funeral was described in *The San Diego Union* July 4, 1910, 7: ". . . As the remains were carried from the chapel to the hearse the two companies of regulars, standing in line on Seventh street, presented arms at the command of Major G. H. McManus, commanding officer of Fort Rosecrans. The command remained at present arms until the hearse started on the way to Mt. Hope cemetery . . . At Mount Hope cemetery, where the body of General Robe was interred beside that of his wife, a musician from the fort sounded taps as the remains were lowered into the grave . . . ." Mary was first married to Charles Freeman Kendall (1844-1894) a well to do businessman in Kansas. Their three children all died in infancy. Mary and Charles were married in Chicago, Cook, IL but the marriage was rocky. In November 1906 she sued for divorce in California, as reported in *The Salina* [Kansas] *Evening Journal* November 30, 1906, 1: "Brigadier General Charles F. Robe, retired, now living in San Diego, is defendant in a divorce suit in which Mrs. Mary R. Robe charges extreme cruelty because her husband was cold and unsympathetic, and extended her less consideration than did her former spouse, one Charles Kendall. They were married in Chicago last year. In Grand Rapids, she alleges Robe bought theater tickets for them and her [*sic*] daughter, but omitted her sister, who was hurt by his inattention. Once when she fainted on the street, Robe, she says, offered no assistance, allowing her sister to support her. In registering at a hotel, she declares, Robe omitted her name. Even when she had an ulcerated tooth no sympathy was offered." It is not known when or if the divorce was granted but on the 1910 census Robe called himself a widower. When Mary died in Los Angeles of heart disease 1918 she was using the surname Kendall. She left an estate of $100,000. Her body was shipped to Topeka where she was buried in Topeka Cemetery next to her first husband.

Joseph A. Robinson – Co. E
b. 1844 Sandy Creek, NY
d. *post* 1865 probably Sandy Creek, NY
m. ?

NOTE: Joseph was the son of Hiram (1799-*ante* 1860) and Almira Morgan Robinson (1803-1880). He previously served in Co. G, 24th Regiment from April 30, 1861-March 10, 1862 and was discharged for "disability" at Upton's Hill, VA. He mustered out with the 147th on June 7, 1865. He appears on the 1865 New York census but nothing after that date has been located. His brother, Lafayette (1839-1916), served briefly in Co. G, 24th Regiment and subsequently in Co. B, 7th New York Cavalry. Lafayette was ordained as a Methodist minister in 1867. He is buried in Forest Park Cemetery, Camden.

Daniel Rogers – Co. D
b. May 1832 Lenox, Madison, NY
d. November 4, 1909 County Poorhouse, Mexico, NY
m. ------

NOTE: This soldier's parents are unknown and his early life has been difficult to track. He originally enlisted in the 110th Regiment but was sent to the 147th. At some unspecified date he was transferred to the VRC and discharged for "disability" on March 24, 1864. He applied for a pension in 1890 and again in 1907. In 1890 he was living in Mt. Pleasant, near Fulton. He claimed no disability in 1890. He apparently went from one farming job to another. He was admitted to the Oswego County Poorhouse on November 1, 1909. His admission form carried the following information: "No record could be procured of this man. Too sick to answer questions. No one able to give any further information." He died four days later. Members of Post Daniel F. Schenck No. 271 GAR hastily put together a funeral and took charge of burying him in Mt. Adnah Cemetery, Fulton. His gravestone erroneously puts him in the 110th Regiment.

Elbridge Thomas Rogers – Co. B
b. February 27, 1838 Guilford, Windham, VT
d. ? ?
m. Olive Elizabeth Hodgerney (April 5, 1843-1918) June 26, 1859

NOTE: Elbridge's parents were Samuel (1793-?) and Mary Cannon Rogers (?-?). In 1862 he was a shoemaker in Oswego City. He mustered out with the regiment on June 7, 1865 at Washington, DC. He and Olive were the parents of seven children, the youngest, Leonard, born in 1878. Olive and the children were living in Grafton, Worcester, MA in 1880 but Elbridge was not in the household. He does not appear on any census record or Massachusetts vital record and it is possible he "went west" and assumed a new identity. Olive married Charles W. Duntley (1832-1915) as his second wife on August 30, 1894. Lovina Watson, his first wife, died in 1892. It is probably safe to say Elbridge died *ante* 1894. Charles and Lovina are buried in Pine Grove Cemetery, Farmington, Stafford, NH. Olive, whose exact DOD has not been located, is buried with several of her children in Riverside Cemetery, Grafton.

Edward M. Rowbotham – Co. E
b. 1837 Richland, NY
d. November 25, 1862 Armory Square Hospital, Washington, DC
m. ------

NOTE: Edward's father is unknown but he allegedly was born in England and was dead by 1850. His mother Frances "Fannie" Rowbotham (1811-February 1887) also had at least two daughters, Lucy Jane (1835-1899), and Mary (1847-1927). Edward's COD was typhoid fever. He was buried in Soldiers' and Airmen's Home Cemetery in Washington, DC under the name Edwin Rowbotham. His stone provides only the initials "E. M." Fannie and Lucy, who married Daniel White (1822-1882) in 1851, are buried in Woodlawn Cemetery, Sandy Creek. Mary is buried with her second husband, William Plantz (1852-1942), in North Boylston Cemetery.

Nathan Rowlee – Co. D
b. 1839 Oswego County, NY
d. December 22, 1862 Georgetown, DC
m. ------

NOTE: Nathan's parents were George Washington (1813-1884) and Jane DeMott Rowlee (1812-1892). His COD was typhoid fever. A letter written by Dr. Mary Walker appearing in *The Oswego Commercial Times* December 27, 1862 and dated December 24, 1862 contained the following: "The 147ᵗʰ were not engaged in the terrible fight at Fredericksburgh but some of them have taken up their final residence in the 'Silent City' in Washington. They were left in the hospitals in Georgetown, when the regiment moved from here . . . Nathan Rowlee, Co. D, died Dec. 22d – typhoid fever . . . ." His burial site is problematic. Markers for him are located in both Riverview Cemetery, Baldwinsville, and Mt. Pleasant West Cemetery, Volney but whether or not he is buried in either is unknown.

Anson M. Runyon – Co. F
b. 1827 Canada
d. January 23, 1916 Mexico, NY
m. Jane Burdick (1826-April 3, 1916) *ca.* 1854

NOTE: As a young man, Anson, whose parents are unknown, was a sailor. He was a sergeant when discharged from the service on December 31, 1864 as a result of the consolidation of the 147ᵗʰ and the 76ᵗʰ Regiments. Anson was a member of Melzar Richards Post No. 367 GAR in Mexico. On the 1910 census Jane was listed as having been married twice. Since she was 18 in 1855 and was at the time married to Anson, this notation must be erroneous. In 1865 she stated she had been married once. In 1900 Jane said she was the mother of no children but the 1865 New York census belies that statement since a daughter, Martha, 11, was living with them. Anson's death notices assigned him an age of 39. He and Jane are buried in New Haven Rural Cemetery.

Decatur Russell – Co. H
b. 1840 Vienna, Oneida, NY
d. November 28, 1863 Fort Schuyler Hospital, Bronx, NY
m. Mary Jane Muckey (1843-June 26, 1917) January 21, 1861

NOTE: Decatur was the son of Elias (1806-1892) and Clarissa Beebe Russell (1804-1853). He was wounded in the right knee at Gettysburg on July 1ˢᵗ and died from blood poisoning. He and Mary Jane were the parents of Minerva, born on April 6, 1863. Mary Jane married Alonzo Alger (1837-1892) on April 29, 1866. By him she was the mother of four more children. In 1902 Mary Jane applied for a remarried widow's pension. She owned a small farm, five cows, one horse, and a few farming tools. She claimed to be dependent on her own labor for support and alleged no one was financially responsible for her. Her son, Burton (1874-1949), bought the farm in 1903 and supported her until 1913 when she went to live with daughter Clara (1881-1967). Mary Jane died of "carcinoma of the gall bladder." Her obituary appeared in *The Oswego Daily Palladium* June 28, 1917: "The funeral of Mrs. Mary Alger, seventy-eight, was held at two o'clock today from the West Amboy M. E. Church, the Rev. P. O. Wilcox officiating . . . Mrs. Alger died at the Homeopathic Hospital in Rochester, where she underwent a surgical operation a few days ago. She was born in Hastings, her grandfather being Colonel Muckey, a soldier of the Revolution . . . ." A cenotaph for Decatur stands in the Old Dutch Hill Cemetery, Parish. Mary Jane and Alonzo, who died of pneumonia, are buried in West Amboy Cemetery.

Volney Russell – Co. H

b. 1845 West Monroe, NY
d. January 8, 1925 Constantia, NY
m1. Mary P. Forbes (1844-December 27, 1884) 1865
m2. Mabel B. Gillis Spring (1858-July 28, 1936) February 21, 1906

NOTE: Volney was Decatur's brother. His DOB varies. I use that found on his gravestone. He was captured at Gettysburg on July 1, 1863 and paroled at an unspecified date, mustering out with the regiment on June 7, 1865. In 1890 he said he had had "chronic diarrhea 26 years." Mary Forbes was a sister of Asa Forbes. *The [Baldwinsville, NY] Gazette & Farmers' Journal* January 1, 1885 carried the following sad news: "Mary, wife of Volney Russell, of Gayville, Oswego county, hung herself Friday afternoon, during the absence of the rest of the family. She was subject to fits and despondency." The marriage between Volney and Mabel was announced in *The Syracuse Journal* February 22, 1906: "While about everybody was out at luncheon yesterday afternoon Volney Russell and Mabel Spring were married by [Oneida City] Mayor Scheifele. The wedding took place in his office with Joseph H. Bussett acting as best man. In the absence of a maid-of-honor, a Western Union messenger, Charles Creedon, was impressed for the other subscribing witness. The groom hails from Constantia and the bride came over from Canastota." Volney left an estate of $13,500 upon his death for which Mabel and her son John Spring were named executors. Volney and Mary are buried in Union Settlement Cemetery. Mabel was first married to Michael Spring (1848-1897), who had served in the 20th NY Cavalry. He and Mabel are also buried there. Another brother, Abram Russell (1844-1891), served in the 110th Regiment and died in Wisconsin.

Thomas Ryan – Co. K
b. 1827 Ireland
d. December 16, 1876 Oswego City, NY
m. Bridget Dwyer (July 1836-September 20, 1902) August 28, 1853

NOTE: Thomas' parents are unknown. He was wounded at Gettysburg on July 1, 1863 and discharged for "disability" in a hospital in Baltimore, MD. He and Bridget were married in St. Paul's Church, Oswego. Bridget's death occasioned the following obituary in *The Oswego Daily Palladium* September 22, 1902: "Mrs. Bridget Ryan, for over fifty years a resident of this city, died Saturday afternoon at the family home, 114 East Oneida street. Mrs. Ryan was the widow of Thomas Ryan, who was a member of Company K, 147th New York Infantry, and died in 1876. Mrs. Ryan was born in the County Tipperary, Ireland, sixty-eight years ago, and came to this city with her parents when a very young girl. To within a short time her general health had been good. Her last hours were peacefully spent, surrounded by members of her family . . . The funeral occurs tomorrow morning from St. Paul's Church." Thomas and Bridget, the parents of at least seven children, are buried in St. Paul's Cemetery, Oswego City. One of Bridget's siblings was Honora Dwyer Murphy Irons Scanlon (1829-1906) who was married to Thomas Murphy.

Timothy Ryan – Co. K
b. 1827 Ireland
d. March 30, 1863 Regimental Hospital, Belle Plain, VA
m. Mary Catherine Shanahan (1828-*post* 1875) April 10, 1849

NOTE: Timothy and Mary were married Easter Sunday, 1849 and the next day sailed for America where they settled in Oswego City. They were the parents of three daughters, Catherine "Katie" (1851-?), Julia (1854-*ca.* 1862), and Mary (1858-?). Timothy died of typhoid fever. On September 20, 1865 Mary married John Carroll (1805-*post* 1875) as his second wife. She was named guardian of her surviving children and obtained pensions for them. In 1875 Mary Ryan, 17, was living with John and Mary Carl (Carroll) in Oswego City. Further information has not been obtained.

Edward Franklin Sabins – Co. F
b. October 1836 Hastings, NY
d. April 25, 1910 Syracuse, Onondaga, NY
m. Angela "Angie" M. Calley (1843-January 1, 1917) 1870

NOTE: Edward Franklin Sabins was an alias for Edward F. Coville. His parents were Horatio Nelson (1804-1858) and Annis Sabins Covell (1809-1869). He was captured at Gettysburg on July 1, 1863 and paroled at an unspecified date. He was wounded on May 5, 1864 at the battle of the Wilderness but was able to muster out with the regiment on June 7, 1865. He and Angie had no children but adopted a daughter, Ruth E. Headson (1890-1957). Edward was a druggist in Cicero for many years. He died after suffering a stroke. He and Angie are buried in North Syracuse Cemetery.

Charles Salem – Co. G
b. 1822 Prussia
d. February 6, 1908 Chittenango, Madison, NY
m. Dora Auer Sullivan Newsbaum (August 1830-July 5, 1904) *ca.* 1866

NOTE: Charles' POB is taken from his muster roll card. His parents are unknown. He was transferred to the VRC on September 10, 1863 and discharged at Washington, DC on June 28, 1865. In later years he was a member of Joseph Bonney Post No. 64, GAR. His death was announced in *The Madison County Times* February 7, 1908: "Charles Salem died at his home in the northern part of the village Thursday morning, February 6th, at about 8 o'clock, after a short illness of pneumonia. Mr. Salem was 85 years old and was born in Belgium, coming to this country when a boy and had always made this village his home. He was a veteran of the Civil War, having served three years in the 147th New York Volunteers. The deceased was a carpenter by trade but for the last few years had retired from active work on account of poor health. Charles Salem was a well known and respected citizen, a loyal friend and a kind hearted and accommodating neighbor . . . Funeral services will be held at the home, Sunday afternoon at 2 o'clock, Rev. Charles O. Wright, a former pastor of the Baptist church here, officiating . . . ." Dora's death occasioned the following in *The Madison County Times* July 8, 1904: "Dora Auer, wife of Charles Salem, died at her home here Tuesday morning at 5 o'clock. She had been sick a long time, and was a great sufferer. The deceased was born in Grosreiden, Germany, in 1830, and came to this country in 1848, locating in Little Falls where she lived a year, then came to Chittenango which has since been her home. She was married three times and is survived by her last husband, Charles Salem, and six children . . . Mrs. Salem was a devout Christian woman, a kind neighbor, and will be greatly missed . . . . Charles and Dora are buried in Oakwood Cemetery, Chittenango.

Mark Sampson – Co. F
b. 1844 Meadville, Crawford, PA
d. ? ?
m. Delia L. Doolittle (September 15, 1852-July 14, 1940) March 1870

NOTE: Mark Sampson was an alias for Hugh Lyle Allen whose parents were Ethan (1804-1881) and Lillias Newton Allen (1812-?). He enlisted in the 110th Regiment but was sent to the 147th and mustered out with the regiment on June 7, 1865. I have been unable to ascertain Hugh's DOD or POD. He and Delia were the parents of four, the youngest of whom, Guy, was born in 1883. In 1890 Hugh, living in Wattsburg, Erie, PA, claimed no disability. In 1900 Delia was living with her parents, Davis and Alvira Burlingame Doolittle, in Venango, Erie, PA, using her maiden name and calling herself a widow. It is possible that a man named Hugh Allen, who died on July 20, 1898 and was buried in the Old Almshouse Cemetery, Fairview, Erie, PA was her husband. He does not appear on the 1900 census. Hugh had applied for a pension in 1887 but was rejected although Delia's application in 1906 was successful. Delia, who died in Union City, Erie, PA of gastroenteritis and old age, is buried in Lowville Cemetery, Wattsburg. There is a government marker for Lyle but since neither it nor the burial card indicates DOD it is possible the stone is a cenotaph.

William M. Sanderson – Co. G

b. May 2, 1819 Canada
d. September 9, 1897 Johnstown, Fulton, NY
m. Mary Teat (1825-*ante* 1880) September 11, 1852

NOTE: William's parents were William (1790-?) and Dorothy "Dolly" Sanderson (1793-1886). He and Mary were married in Wayne County, MI. In 1870 the couple was living in Oswego but by 1880 William, a widower, was living with his widowed sister, Mary Wert (1821-1898), and his widowed mother in Johnstown. William transferred to the VRC on November 24, 1863 and in 1890 he said his disabilities were chronic diarrhea and a scalp wound. His death was announced in *The Johnstown Daily Republican* September 19, 1897, 3: "William M. Sanderson, a veteran of the late rebellion, was mustered out, by death, at the residence of his sister, Mrs. John Wert, 412 North Market street, between seven and eight o'clock last evening, at the age of 78 years. Mr. Sanderson was born in Canada, and was a stone cutter by occupation, but since his residence in this city, which dates from about the time of the closing of the war, he led a retired life, forming but few acquaintances. He was an enthusiastic member of McMartin Post of the G.A.R., in this city, and until his health failed and he became too feeble, was a regular attendant at its meetings. He enlisted in Company G, of the 147th N.Y. Volunteers, in 1862, and we believe served until the close of the rebellion. He leaves one sister to mourn his decease. His funeral will be held from his late residence . . . at 2 o'clock, and from the M.E. church at 2:30 o'clock on Sunday afternoon next. Rev. T. G. Thompson will officiate." William was buried in Johnstown Cemetery. Mary's grave has not been located.

Ernest Schalkenback – Co. A

b. December 9, 1847 Prussia

d. November 20, 1898 Leavenworth, KS

m1. ?

m2. Elizabeth Dobler (September 7, 1857-March 14, 1955) 1886

NOTE: Ernest, the son of Joseph (1823-*post* 1870) and Minna Schalkenback (1821-*ante* 1870), came to the United States when he was three years old. His surname was also spelled Shalkenback and Shalkenbach, among others. He served as a drummer in Co I, 24ᵗʰ Regiment from May 10 until May 16, 1861. He next joined the 81ˢᵗ Regiment and served from September 5, 1861 to February 20, 1862 when he was discharged for "disability." He then enlisted in the 147ᵗʰ and served until mustered out on June 7, 1865. From that point on, he became a professional soldier, serving in the US Army almost continuously until he retired on April 6, 1894. His obituary, published in *The Leavenworth Times* November 22, 1898, 4, summarized a long military career: "Ernest Schalkenback aged 51 years, died at his home on Central and Randolph streets Sunday night at 7:10 o'clock after an illness of several weeks with a complication of diseases. The funeral will be held at the post this afternoon at 2 o'clock and will be a military one. The Rev. Robinson of the Post will officiate. Ernest Schalkenback was very well known in this city and was well liked for his genial disposition. He was a retired soldier, having served thirty years in the service. During this time he was a member of the fifth Infantry band and was noted for his musical ability. Besides being a musician Schalkenback was also the messenger of his regiment and in this capacity he acted for twenty-two years. While filling this position he was always regular and never missed his duties unless on account of sickness. When the men who were formerly stationed at the post delighted the residents there with their minstrels shows Schalkenback was always considered their star player. These accomplishments he retained after his time in the army was up and it was with these that he entertained his friend [*sic*] and gained the good will of all who knew him. Nearly fourteen years ago Ernest Schalkenback married a Miss Doebbler of this city by whom he had one child, a daughter, who survives him. Besides this child he has two sons, by a former wife. Their names are John, who resides in Brooklyn, and Ernest, who lives in St. Louis. The latter arrived in the city yesterday to attend the funeral." Josephine (November 1887-*post* 1955) was the daughter's name. The sons are a mystery. In 1870 Schalkenback was unmarried but by 1880 he was enumerated as a married man. All efforts to find a prior wife and the children have failed. On his pension card, however, extensive reference is made to a man named Edward A. Baldwin (1843-1927) who served in the 125ᵗʰ Regiment. Was this man the second husband of Schalkenback's unknown wife? Elizabeth, Ernest's second wife, successfully filed for a widow's pension in Missouri in 1901. She died in Kansas City, Jackson, MO of congestive heart failure and was cremated. She and Ernest are buried in Fort

Leavenworth National Cemetery. Ernest's father, Joseph, served as a captain in the 24th NY Cavalry from January-August 1864 when he was discharged for "disability."

Charles Scheible – Co. H
b. 1832 Germany
d. December 12, 1903 Kenwood, Madison, NY
m. Mary E. Fairchild Crim (August 1836-November 7, 1925) January 5, 1860

NOTE: Charles' DOB varies from one document to another, as does his surname. His family gravestone assigns him a DOB of 1817 but his government stone shows 1821. In 1900 he said he had been born in May 1820. He came to the United States in 1850 and was naturalized. His parents are unidentified. He was transferred to the VRC on July 1, 1863 and must have been discharged late in the year or early 1864 since he applied for a pension on March 13, 1864. Mary, who died in the Utica State Hospital, was first married to Andrew L. Crim (1834-*ante* 1860). In 1855 she was living in his family's home and had been there five months. She and Charles are buried in Stockbridge Cemetery, Munnsville, Madison, NY.

Edward Schenck – Co. D
b. June 28, 1842 Granby, NY
d. July 15, 1920 Brooklyn, NY
m. Barbara Ross (October 1839-March 28, 1921) 1871

NOTE: Schenck's parents were Peter (1796-1868) and Eliza Maria Daggett Schenck (1804-1848). He transferred to the VRC on December 20, 1864 and was discharged on July 13, 1865. After his death Charles L. Rice wrote an *In Memoriam* which appeared in *The Fulton Patriot* July 28, 1920, 7: "Edward Schenck, a native Fultonian, passed to his reward Thursday, July 15th, in a Brooklyn hospital, aged 78 years. He was a descendant of a Hollander who settled in Flatland (Brooklyn) during New Amsterdam years. In those days Brooklyn was a settlement of Hollanders. Descendants of the Schenck ancestor are numerous in Greater New York, and hold honorable positions in banks, trust companies and public office. Edward's father, Peter Schenck, and his brother, William Schenck, migrated up the Hudson and to Oswego Falls, now Fulton, in the early part of the 19th century . . . The sons of Peter Schenck, Edward and Herman, volunteered early in the civil war. Herman was killed at a spring while taking a drink of water, by a cowardly rebel. Edward fought to the close of the war and remained for three or four years in Washington. While a member of a Presbyterian church, of which Dr. Sunderland was pastor, he was introduced to a preceptress of a young ladies' seminary, who became his wife. They have in recent years resided on Brooklyn Heights and have been members of the 'Church of the Pilgrims,' of which he was an honored deacon. Last February as Mrs. Schenck was entering the Brooklyn post office through the revolving door, a boisterous man or boy rushed the door and threw her to the floor, breaking her hip. She has been a patient sufferer at the Brooklyn hospital for five months. The constant anxiety and faithful visits of her devoted husband finally prostrated him and he also became for several weeks an inmate of the same institution, where he died. Edward has been a member of the U. S. Grant post and the funeral service was held under their roof July 17th and mortal remains taken to Fulton by his cousin, William Schenck, for burial in the family plot at the cemetery . . . The writer feels that in the death of Edward Schenck he has suffered the loss of a life-long friend . . . We have traveled along similar paths to old age. Edward Schenck was one of nature's noble men, a consistent Christian and a Grand Army veteran who has won the affection of all who were associated with him. Fulton may well be proud of those boys who served and died in the Civil war . . . ." Herman Schenck (1839-1863) was a member of Co. I, 3rd NY Cavalry. He was mortally wounded on May 24, 1863 and died on May 29th. He is buried in New Bern National Cemetery, Craven County, NC. Barbara's death was reported in *The Brooklyn Daily Eagle* March 30, 1921, 20: "Mrs. Barbara Ross Schenck, of 59 Pineapple st., widow of Edward Schenck, died on Monday at her home, in her 82d year. Mrs. Schenck was an old member of the Church of the Pilgrims, Henry and Remsen sts., and her funeral services will be held in the church on Thursday afternoon at 2 o'clock. Mrs. Schenck's husband, who died last July, was a veteran of the Civil War and was for many years in the U. S. Customs Service in the office of the Board of General Appraisers in Manhattan. He was a member of U. S. Grant Post, No. 327, G. A. R. and Mrs. Schenck was a member of the Ladies Auxiliary of Grant Post." Edward and Barbara are buried in Mt. Adnah Cemetery, Fulton.

Martin Bryant Schenck – Co. D
b. April 29, 1838 Fulton, NY
d. November 5, 1911 Meriden, New Haven, CT
m1. Margaret Wallace Anthony (1830-April 23, 1907) June 13, 1866
m2. Jennie E. Hammell Powers (1840-1923) September 6, 1910

NOTE: Martin was the son of John (1794-1869) and Hannah Perkins Schenck (1804-1887). He had, among other siblings, a twin brother, Marcus P. (1838-1912). His death was widely reported, beginning with *The Norwich Bulletin* November 6, 1911, 1: "Martin B. Schenck, for the past twenty years the manufacturer of the famous Yale castors, died [yesterday] afternoon at his residence on Broad street, after a four weeks' illness of sickness and kidney trouble. Mr. Schenck was born in Fulton, N.Y., in 1838. During the civil war he was clerk in the central guard house in Washington, and knew President Lincoln intimately. In 1882 he started manufacturing castors in New Haven, but after five years' struggle against great odds his plant was destroyed by fire. He came to Meriden and in 1891 founded the M. B. Schenck company, and purchased a plant and began the manufacture of the castors which he invented. His business has been very successful and the product has sold all over the world. Mr. Schenck was a public spirited man and served the town and city in various capacities. He was a member of the town school committee, a councilman and a present member of the tax board. He was a trustee of Merriam post, G.A.R. Mr. Schenck was at one time president of the Y.M.C.A. and was a member of the official board of the First M. E. church. He was trustee of the Meriden Savings bank . . . ." Sands Gardner, a member of the 110th Regiment and local memoirist, wrote the following which appeared in *The Fulton Times* November 22, 1911, 6: "Martin B. Schenck and I attended school together at Falley Seminary in 1865, and were good comrades and have been since. He lived at Jacksonville and I lived at South Hannibal. I was one of his patrons while he was in the hardware business in Fulton . . . The following sketch I copied from the Meriden Morning Record that I received. Martin Bryant Schenck was born April 29, 1838, in Fulton, N.Y. His youth was spent on his father's farm and he acquired his education in the 'little red schoolhouse' and in Falley Seminary in Fulton. He taught school for a while and learned the builder trade just before the war. He laid down his building tools to join the Union army and served from 1862 to 1865 in the 147th Regiment, N.Y. Volunteers. During his term of enlistment he performed clerical duties in the war department at Washington and saw a great deal of President Lincoln, in fact, had often talked to him in the trying days of the war . . . Mr. Schenck was at the front only six months and the remainder of his enlistment was spent in Washington where he held the important post of clerk in the central guard house – the Washington military prison. Mr. Schenck was a fever patient in the army hospital when Lincoln was shot. While at the front, Mr. Schenck's military company was in the battle of Fredericksburg. In camp his feet were frozen so he had special duty assigned him in Washington afterward." Martin was transferred to the VRC on June 9, 1864 and discharged on August 11, 1865 at Washington, DC. He and Margaret were the parents of William Anthony (1867-1930) and Jessie May (1872-1959). His second wife, the mother of five children, was first married to Judge Joseph Powers (1827-1907). They are both buried in Fairview Cemetery, Cedar Falls, Black Hawk, IA. Although Martin and Margaret died in Connecticut, their bodies were shipped to Fulton and buried in Mt. Adnah Cemetery.

William Penn Schenck – Co. D
b. March 10, 1840 Oswego County, NY
d. July 27, 1863 Gettysburg, Adams, PA
m. ------

NOTE: William was the son of William (1800-1878) and Mary Falley Schenck (1805-1891). He was wounded in action on July 1st when a ball passed through his shoulder, breaking two ribs and his collar bone. It also cut an artery and affected his lungs. At first it was thought he would survive and his father went to Gettysburg to visit him. The wounds, however, proved fatal. His father had the body sent home to Fulton and buried in the family plot in Mt. Adnah Cemetery. His brother, Daniel Falley Schenck (1836-1875), served as a captain in the 50th NY Engineers. Post Schenck No. 271 GAR in Fulton was named in his honor. He too is buried in Mt. Adnah.

Although wounded on July 1, 1863 William Schenck clung to life until July 27th. His father who was present when he died had the body shipped home for burial.
Author's Collection

Richard Abijah Schoonmaker – Co. G

b. May 17, 1834 Hannibal, NY
d. June 9, 1913 Fairdale, NY
m. Charlotte Shutts (1836-April 7, 1920) 1857

NOTE: The son of Michael (1800-1882) and Catherine Van Alstine Schoonmaker (1808-1839), Abijah, as he was generally called, was a carpenter. He mustered out on June 7, 1865. In 1890 he claimed heart disease and rheumatism as his disabilities. The enumerator noted that he had served in the light artillery for eight months and his pension card notes his membership in Co. L. 1st NY LA but he does not appear on *The Adjutant-General's Report*. Charlotte's death was reported in *The Oswego Daily Palladium* April 9, 1920, 5: "The news of the death of Mrs. Charlotte Schoonmaker, aged 85 years, was received in Hannibal Wednesday. Mrs. Schoonmaker was the widow of the late Abijah Schoonmaker, who for many years lived near Fairdale, and was well known and highly respected. She died at the home of her son, John, in Syracuse. The body arrived here today for burial." Abijah and Charlotte are buried in Fairdale Cemetery near Hannibal. His gravestone alludes only to his service in the 147th.

James A. Scribner – Co. G
b. 1836 Columbia County, NY
d. January 3, 1863 Regimental Hospital, Falmouth, VA
m. Helen "Nellie" Maria Parkhurst (1840-January 16, 1864) August 19, 1860

NOTE: James, son of John (1806-*post* 1865) and Catherine Scribner (1810-*post* 1865), died of typhoid pneumonia. He and Nellie were the parents of Erwin E. (1861-1915) and Nellie E. (1863-1900). Their mother applied for a pension but died before the process could be completed. Her father, Isaac Robinson Parkhurst (1809-1882), was named the children's guardian. James and Helen are buried in Hillside Cemetery, Scriba.

John S. Seaman – Co. H
b. June 8, 1836 Eaton, Madison, NY
d. September 21, 1925 Parish, NY
m. Florence "Florine" Allen Prior (May 1851-August 18, 1932) 1880

NOTE: John was the son of George Irving (1814-1900) and Amanda M. Spencer Seaman (1819-1848). *The Pulaski Democrat* June 5, 1912, 1 reported that a part of the Memorial Day celebration in Parish, NY consisted of unveiling a statue erected by John in Pleasant Lawn Cemetery. The article spoke in part about his military service: ". . . He enlisted from Parish and was mustered into United States service, Sept. 23, 1862, as a private of Capt. Slayton's Co. H, 147th Regiment under Col. A. S. Warner which left the state Sept. 25 . . . He was sick in the hospital at Washington in the winter of '62 with typhoid fever, sick in all about three months, captured at Gettysburg and imprisoned in Libby and Bell Isle prisons fifty-two days. [He was] paroled Aug. 23 '63 and sent to Annapolis, Md., and then to the hospital, after [illegible] joined regiment and served until honorably discharged as corporal . . . ." His death was announced in *The Pulaski Democrat* September 30, 1925: "In the death of John S. Seamans [*sic*], a veteran of the Civil War, which occurred September 21st, the village and town of Parish lost its oldest inhabitant and one of its most esteemed citizens. John S. Seamans was born in Eaton, Madison Co., June 8, 1936. When eight years of age he came to Parish to reside and had made this his home about eighty years. Mr. Seamans enlisted in the 147th N. Y. Vols., Co. H, and served during the war coming back to Parish where he was engaged in farming and mechanical work during the active days of his life. He was united in marriage with Mrs. Florence Prior Allen . . . Mr. Seamans was a member of the Parish Methodist church. He had been in poor health the past few years. Funeral services were largely attended at the home, Wednesday afternoon, at 2 o'clock, conducted by his personal friend, Byron C. Seamans, of Pulaski, assisted by Rev.

R. A. Tennies, pastor of the Parish Methodist church. Mrs. Earle Golden sang two selections. Floral tributes and the stars and stripes were draped over the casket. But a small delegation of Mr. Seaman's comrades were able to attend the funeral . . . Burial was made in Parish cemetery, near the beautiful monument Mr. Seamans erected several years ago." Florine was born in West Monroe, NY to Orson F. (1828-1918) and Almeda L. Oyer Allen (1830-1899). She was the mother of a son and a daughter by Alonzo Prior, and of a son and a daughter by Seaman. According to her obituary, published in *The Oswego Palladium-Times* August 19, 1932, 5, she succumbed at the age of 81 following a long illness. She was a member of Puritan Chapter #165, Order of the Eastern Star, which met in Parish. She and John were buried in Pleasant Lawn Cemetery.

John Seaman's statue of a Civil War soldier was unveiled on Memorial Day, 1912.
Author's Collection

James F. Sears – Co. B

b. 1837 Madison County, NY
d. July 1, 1863 Gettysburg, Adams, PA
m. Elizabeth LaPlant (1840-*post* 1865) September 10, 1860

NOTE: James' parents were David (1814-1898) and Maria Sears (1811-1885). His muster roll card says he was born in Madison County, but the 1855 New York census gives a POB of Oneida County. He and Elizabeth were the parents of Maria Louisa (1861-*post* 1882). Elizabeth married Charles W. Raymond (1830-?) on March 25, 1865. The 1865 New York census showed his POB was Onondaga County, his occupation was "boatman" and he was in the Army at the time. The only Charles W. Raymond fitting that description joined the 16th US Infantry at Oneida, NY on March 10, 1864 but his DOB was 1820, not 1830. He was discharged in March 1869 in Savannah, GA. If this is the correct man, he applied for a pension on November 14, 1878. His pension card, however, does not include a widow's name or application date. In 1874 her grandfather, David, claimed to be Louisa's guardian. She last appears in the 1882 Oswego City Directory as a milliner living with him. She probably was married a short time later. David Sears served in the original 81st Regiment and in the re-formed 81st Veteran Regiment.

Elhanan Curtis Seeley – Co. E

b. April 24, 1836 Oswego County, NY
d. April 24, 1898 Sandy Creek, NY
m1. Marion Mason (April 12, 1842-March 30, 1881) June 1863
m2. Amelia L. Mason (1834-December 17, 1911) *post* 1881

NOTE: Elhanan, the son of Calvin (1806-1890) and Sarah Lovejoy Seeley (1811-1885), was a captain in the 147th Regiment. He was discharged on February 4, 1863, having resigned his commission. His death was noted in *The Syracuse Standard* April 26, 1893, 3: "Elhanan C. Seeley died at midnight Sunday after two weeks of severe illness. The funeral will occur at the late residence on Lake street today at 2 o'clock, Rev. Mr. Paul of Pulaski, officiating. Mr. Seeley went into the army as captain of Company E, 147th volunteers." Marion and Amelia were sisters. Marion's death was announced in *The Oswego Daily Palladium* March 31, 1881: "Mr. E. C. Seeley has the sympathy of the people in his bereavement by the loss of his wife, whose death occurred [yesterday] morning after a brief illness. Mrs. Seeley was the daughter of Mr. Stephen Mason of Pulaski. She was a faithful wife and a devoted mother. The funeral will be held Friday afternoon." Amelia's obituary appeared in *The Watertown Herald* December 23, 1911: "Amelia L. Seeley, widow of E. C. Seeley, died Sunday morning at the residence of her niece, Mrs. William M. Pruyn, 337 Keyes avenue, aged 79 years. Mrs. Seeley was born near Pierrepont Manor and lived in that section the early part of her life but came to this city years ago and had since lived here. She was well known in this city and had many friends here. She is survived only by her niece Mrs. Pruyn and a nephew, Calvin Seeley of Los Angeles, Cal. The funeral was held Tuesday morning from Mrs. Pruyn's residence . . . Rev. D. C. Huntington, pastor of St. Paul's Episcopal church, officiating. The body was taken to Sandy Creek where the interment was made." Elhanan died on his birthday. He, Marion, and Amelia are buried in Woodlawn Cemetery, Sandy Creek.

Almon Wright Seely – Co. B

b. February 20, 1844 Kemptville, Leeds, Ontario, Canada
d. ? Canada
m. Anna Maria Fell (December 20, 1849-August 1917) *ca.* 1873

NOTE: Almon's parents were Almon (1796-1853) and Sybil Wright Seely (1814-1890). The family was Jewish or "Israelites" as the Canadian census records termed their religion. Although the entry for Almon in *The Town Clerks' Registers* says he was killed at Gettysburg, such was not the case. In fact, he enlisted in Co. B, 12th US Infantry at Ogdensburg, St. Lawrence, NY on June 7, 1865, from which I infer he had been discharged before the rest of the regiment. He served until June 7, 1868 and was discharged at Georgetown, SC. Almon applied for an invalid's pension on February 10,

1905, leading some researchers to conclude he died that day. He probably did die before the process was completed because he did not obtain a certificate. By 1909 Anna and her son Almon were living in Detroit, MI. In the city directory she styled herself Almon's widow. Two daughters moved to Florida. Rosamond (1876-1973) lived in Pensacola, Escambia, FL where Anna died and was buried in St. John's Cemetery.

Frederick Service – Co. C
b. December 1830 Ohio, Herkimer, NY
d. May 26, 1908 Albion, NY
m. Charlotte French (May 1845-February 14, 1911) 1870

NOTE: Frederick, a farmer by occupation, was the son of Samuel W. (1802-*post* 1870) and Olive Vincent Service (1805-1880). He was discharged at Albany, NY on May 22, 1865. In 1890 he claimed no disability but said he had been discharged on April 23, 1865. He and Charlotte, who had been ill for "some time," are buried in Riverside Cemetery, Pulaski.

Albert Gallatin Severance – Co. A
b. March 16, 1843 Oswego City, NY
d. ? probably Chicago, Cook, IL
m. ?

NOTE: Albert was the son of Curtis (1804-1870) and Marcia Tuttle Severance (1815-1846). He was discharged from the service on December 31, 1864 when the 147th and the 76th Regiments were consolidated. In 1869 the city directory said he was living in Oswego but he can also be found, with his father and his brother, Henry, living in Chicago that year. According to *The Town Clerks' Registers* he was married when he enlisted but that is contradicted by *Registers of Officers and Enlisted Men*. In 1890 A. G. Severance registered to vote in Chicago and said he had lived there for 23 years. Whether or not this is the same man is open to question. If so, no other document for him in that city can be located after that date. His brother Henry (1841-March 29, 1904) served in Co. F, 184th Regiment. Henry entered the National Home in Milwaukee in 1887 and gave the name of J. H. Buckley, a cousin residing in Chicago, as his next of kin. He died at the Home and was buried in Woods National Cemetery.

Elam A. Seymour – Co. H
b. 1826 Western, Oneida, NY
d. January 30, 1864 Campbell General Hospital, Washington, DC
m. Harriet Clock (1832-March 27, 1903) *ca.* 1850

NOTE: Elam's parents are unknown. He succumbed to chronic diarrhea and was buried in the Soldiers' and Airmen's National Home Cemetery, Washington, DC. The name on the grave is Elem. Harriet married Lewis A. Cook (1815-December 6, 1892) *ca.* 1870 as his second wife. Her COD was apoplexy. She and Lewis are buried in Gilmore Cemetery, Gilmore, Isabella, MI.

Samuel S. Shear – Co. E
b. 1828 Montgomery County, NY
d. November 26, 1888 Henderson, Jefferson, NY
m. Mary Jane Kelley (October 1837-January 24, 1917) *ca.* 1854

NOTE: Samuel's parents are unknown. He was discharged from the service on January 13, 1863 for "disability" which according to *The Town Clerks' Registers* was "sickness." Since he applied for a pension on January 22, 1863 the disability apparently was severe. When Samuel died his widow applied for and received a pension. For some reason, the widow's name on the pension card is Sarah J. Later in life Mary Jane lied about her DOB, leading some researchers to conclude she was born in 1841. Unless she was only 14 years old when she was married, the date she provided in 1855 must be more accurate. In 1900 Mary Jane said she was the mother of 11 children, of whom four were living. Samuel's death occasioned the following which was published in *The Watertown Re-Union* December 12, 1888: "At his home in Henderson, Nov. 26, 1888, Samuel S. Shear, aged 59 years, 8 months and 3 days. He leaves a wife, five children and one sister to mourn his loss. *I see on the hillside a grave that is new,/It reminds me today of a brother so true,/Of a chair that is vacant, of a dear one at rest,/ With hands meekly folded on his cold, silent breast./'Tis but a few weeks since his form was laid low,/The sorrows of earth never more will he know,/The vision has vanished and all is now past,/And our brother is safe with the Saviour at last."* Samuel and Mary Jane are buried in North Cemetery, Hungerford's Corners, Henderson, Jefferson, NY.

Phineas G. Shorey – Co. E
b. September 20, 1840 Osceola, Lewis, NY
d. January 31, 1917 Herndon, Guthrie, IA
m. Almira J. Goodrich (June 27, 1841-April 30, 1920) February 16, 1861

NOTE: Phineas mustered out with the regiment on June 7, 1865. After the war the couple moved to Iowa, taking along Phineas' parents, Washington (1818-1880) and Rachel Maria Vandewalker Shorey (1821-1906). Almira's brother, Francis E. Goodrich, also served in the 147th Regiment. Phineas, Almira, Washington, and Rachel are all buried in Richland Cemetery, Herndon.

Peter Shutts – Co. G

b. 1831 Montgomery County, NY

d. July 1, 1863 Gettysburg, Adams, PA

m1. Hannah M. Gibbs (1832-March 6, 1859) August 9, 1854

m2. Mary A. DeMott (1841-September 1, 1867) October 23, 1861

NOTE: Peter's parents were Johannes "John" (1790-1863) and Maria Miller Shutts (1795-1879). By his first wife Peter was the father of Byron Pierce Shutts (1855-April 15, 1925). On December 10, 1862 Peter wrote a letter to his sister Harriet Shutts Myers and her husband Edward, describing his experiences as a soldier, part of which is excerpted here: ". . . We are now down in Dixie. Now we are at Aquia Creek in Virginia. We are camped by the side of the railroad. We have soldiers' life here in good earnest. We are within 11 miles of the rebels but we don't fear them. We want to get a crack at them. I think if we do we shall stop some of their wind. But I don't know as we have a chance yet for a while. We came down here on foot all the way till we got to the river then we crossed over in the boat . . . There was 25,000 men on the way at the same time so you may think we had plenty of company. We expect a big fight down this way before long. I am in the hospital now here in camp. I haven't been very well for a few days and this is more comfortable than our tents but I am well again now and shall go out again tomorrow. You want to know how I like Soldiering. Well I can't say that I like it first rate. I never expected to like it. I didn't come because I thought I should like it. Some had to come you know. I think we can stand it. I don't think it will last long. We have some good times and some hard times. I knew this before I came so I fare as well as I expected to . . . Ed you need not wish you were here for you are better off at home for you could not stand it here. It wants a tough man for a soldier, one that can stand anything. I have been tough the most of the time since I came here and I hope I shall be for the time to come . . . ." Shutts is buried in Gettysburg National Cemetery. Hannah and Byron are buried in Rural Cemetery, Oswego Town. Mary is buried with her parents, George (1805-1895) and Ann Eliza DeMott (1812-1897), in Riverside Cemetery, Scriba.

John Sigourney – Co. G

b. June 10, 1821 East Winfield, Herkimer, NY

d. May 27, 1895 Crystal, Montcalm, MI

m. Charlotte Sparks (October 28, 1826-November 21, 1908) November 30, 1845

NOTE: John, whose parents were Samuel (1800-?) and Hannah Sigourney (?-?), transferred to the VRC on May 1, 1865 and was discharged on June 28, 1865. According to his FAG entry, he moved to Michigan in 1867 and became a minister in 1870. He served as commander of William B. Stewart Post No. 324 GAR. He and Charlotte are buried in Burke Cemetery, Carson City, Montcalm, MI.

George Andrew Sisson – Co. D
b. 1836 Fulton, NY
d. May 13, 1863 Falmouth, VA
m. ------

NOTE: George, son of William (1808-1878) and Samantha Sisson (1811-*ca.* 1879), originally enlisted in the 110th Regiment but was sent to the 147th. According to *Deaths of Volunteers*, he died of acute dysentery. An obituary appearing in *The Oswego Commercial Times* May 21, 1863 added details: "Capt. George A. Sisson, son of Wm. Sisson, Esq., of Fulton, died in hospital, near Falmouth, on the 13th instant. He was Captain of Company D, 147th Regiment. He was in the late battles before Fredericksburg and passed through them unscathed. He was taken sick the day succeeding the late retreat, on the march to camp. He succeeded in reaching the camp by riding Dr. Place's horse. His disease, typhoid fever, accompanied by diarrhea, was brought on by exposure and hard marching. Capt. Sisson was 27 years of age. The body had been embalmed, and was expected to arrive in Fulton yesterday. He entered the service as a private and rapidly rose to the first position in his company." His body was buried in Mt. Adnah Cemetery, Fulton. His brother, William H. (1846-1886), served in Co. F, 81st Regiment. His COD was consumption. He too is buried in Mt. Adnah.

Charles B. Skinner – Co. F
b. 1837 Mexico, NY
d. July 6, 1896 Oswego City, NY
m. Sarah L. Mayber (1844-August 22, 1923) *ca.* 1865

NOTE: Charles, son of Hiram (1798-1865) and Noralla Brusie Skinner (1801-1881), originally enlisted in the 110th Regiment but was sent to the 147th. He was discharged for "disability" on May 6, 1864. His obituary, published in *The Oswego Daily Times* July 7, 1896, 4, summarizes his career after the war: "Charles B. Skinner, who for a number of years has kept a candy and notions store at the corner of East Bridge and Fifth streets, died yesterday afternoon at three o'clock, after a short sickness of a little over twenty-four hours. The deceased was born at Union Square fifty-eight years ago. When the war broke out he enlisted in the 147th regiment as a private and went to the front. When the war closed he came back as a lieutenant, having gained the rank by meritorious conduct. In 1871 he came to this city and was employed as armorer at the state armory. At the conclusion of which service he established himself in the store at the corner of East Bridge and Fifth streets, which is connected with his home where he died. He leaves a wife but no children. The remains will be taken to Union Square at 1:30 o'clock Wednesday afternoon for burial." Sarah's death was reported in *The Oswego Daily Palladium* August 23, 1923, 5: "Mrs. Sarah L. Skinner, wife of the late Charles B. Skinner, a former well known resident of this city, died yesterday morning at the home of her sister, Mrs. Charles Miles, 338 Emma street, Syracuse, at the age of 79 years. Mrs. Skinner had lived in this city on the East side for many years before going to Syracuse. She was a member of the Women's Relief Corps of this city and frequently visited the regular meetings of the organization. She was highly regarded by a large circle of friends. Funeral will be held from her late home . . . Friday at 1:30 o'clock . . . Mrs. Skinner was a member of the First Universalist church, Syracuse." Charles and Sarah are buried in Maple View Cemetery, Mexico.

William Henry Avery Skinner – Co. F
b. September 23, 1839 Mexico, NY
d. December 22, 1910 National Soldiers' Home, Milwaukee, Milwaukee, WI
m. Amelia Sampson (1841-August 8, 1875) 1862

NOTE: Like his brother Charles, William attempted to enlist in the 110th Regiment but was sent to the 147th. He was discharged from the service for "disability" on June 27, 1863 at a hospital in Philadelphia, PA. Although his admission forms to national homes show he was born in Maine, the 1855 New York census clearly indicates all the Skinner children were born in Oswego County. In 1855 William and Amelia's families were near neighbors in Mexico. Her grave has not been located but he was buried in Wood National Cemetery in Milwaukee. His COD was heart disease.

John Skippen – Co. B
b. February 27, 1843 Guelph, Ontario, Canada
d. February 6, 1865 Hatcher's Run, VA
m. ------

NOTE: John was the son of William Thomas (1817-1890) and Maria Skippen (1816-post 1899). An article appearing in *The Herkimer Democrat* December 1, 1863 spoke about John's current status: "Most of our citizens will remember a young man who worked in this office about a year since, named John Skippen. He went to Oswego from this place, where he enlisted in the 147th Regiment, and thence to Virginia. His regiment has been in all the engagements since that of Chancellorsville, and John has been with it, until the 4th of October, when he was taken prisoner near Haymarket, and sent to Richmond, where he was confined on Belle Island, and where our soldiers are said to be suffering terribly. We have a letter from him dated the 19th of October, in which he said he expected to be paroled very soon – an expectation that has been disappointed. Where our young friend is now it is impossible to say." The date of John's exchange is unknown but since he died early in 1865 it is evident he had been freed. In 1899 his brother, Daniel Linderman Skippen (1856-1925), acting as guardian, filed for a pension for their mother in New York State. She did not obtain a certificate and probably died before the application could be completed.

Patrick W. Slattery – Co. B
b. 1836 Ireland
d. October 11, 1887 Oswego City, NY
m. Elizabeth Reid (1834-December 26, 1917) *ca.* 1858

NOTE: Patrick, son of Patrick (?-?) and Mary Fitzgerald Slattery (?-?), had an interesting enlistment. He enrolled at Oswego City on August 30, 1862 and mustered in as a first lieutenant. He was discharged for "disability" on February 23, 1863, then re-mustered in as first lieutenant of Company B and promoted to captain on April 7, 1863. He was wounded in the right thigh on July 1, 1863 and, as part of the Harney "shake-up", was discharged on November 5, 1863. By Special Order he was restored to his command on March 9, 1864. On the 1865 New York census he was listed in the "formerly in Army" column but in 1890 Elizabeth stated he had served until June 27, 1865. She also said that his wounded thigh prevented him from working at his occupation. By 1870 he was a police officer in Oswego. His obituary, published in *The Oswego Daily Palladium* October 11, 1887, described his post-war career: "While at work near his home on West Sixth street this afternoon, Mr. Patrick W. Slattery, father of Mr. James P. Slattery, of the *Palladium*, suffered a stroke of paralysis. He was carried into the house and breathed but a few minutes. Mr. Slattery was one of our best known citizens. For years he was connected with the Oswego Police force in the capacity of a detective and patrolman, and established an enviable reputation in the unraveling of difficult cases. He was Captain of Co. 'B' in the 147th regiment, N.Y.V., and served with that gallant regiment with great credit to himself and his Company. He was wounded at Gettysburg . . . ." Elizabeth outlived her husband by many years. When she died, *The Oswego Daily Times* December 26, 1917, 4 published the following: "Elizabeth R., widow of Patrick W. Slattery, died this morning at 8:30 o'clock at her home, 172 West Sixth street. She was stricken on Saturday afternoon at 5:30 with cerebral hemorrhage. Mrs. Slattery was born a few miles from the city of Limerick, Ireland, 84 years ago and came here with her parents when fourteen years old and had made her home here for 69 years. She was a member of St. Mary's church, of the Altar and Rosary Societies and the League of the Sacred Heart of that parish. For the past fifteen years Mrs. Slattery had suffered severely from rheumatism and had seldom left her home in these years . . . ." Patrick and Elizabeth are buried in St. Peter's Cemetery, Oswego City.

Reuben W. Slayton – Co. H

b. September 12, 1826 Prattsburgh, Steuben, NY

d. November 24, 1893 Tully, Onondaga, NY

m. Eliza F. Fyler (November 12, 1828-July 2, 1904) June 26, 1850

NOTE: Reuben's parents were James (1790-1832) and Phoebe Wood Slayton (1791-1839). His father died of cholera and his mother succumbed to consumption. Why he went to Parish depends upon the source, one of which says he was sent there to live with relatives, another which says he was "bound out" to a local farmer. He and Eliza were the parents of three children, including a set of twins, Frances Ruth (1859-1860), and Frank Reuben (1859-1894). In 1862 Slayton raised a company of soldiers in the Parish area and on September 12th a group of women, headed by Eliza, presented a company flag to the men. According to an article appearing in *The Mexico Independent* September 18, 1862, Slayton responded for the group: ". . . Representing as I do this noble body of soldiers, before you assembled, I most heartily and sincerely thank you for this generous token of confidence you express in our ability to protect by force of arms this flag, which has been insultingly taken down and another placed by traitors over our common inheritance. We have voluntarily enlisted to aid in suppressing this rebellion; your words of confidence in our patriotism shall ever nerve us on to duty. This flag shall never trail in dishonor, but shall continue to wave until the last man in the ranks of this company is fallen. We go forth freely to avenge its insults, to effectually suppress treason, and restore law, order, and prosperity where rebellion and confusion now reign. As soldiers, we go forth to battle with the faithful assurance of the justness of our cause, and the ultimate triumph of universal liberty . . . ." Asa Slayton's *History of the Slayton Family*, 105 contains the following: "July 1st, 1863, having marched 27 miles the previous afternoon and five that morning they [Slayton's company] were sent into the fight at Gettysburg against heavy odds, were badly cut up and he and most of his Co. taken prisoners, he being wounded in one foot. Being disabled he was discharged at Rappahannock Station, Sept. 8, 1863." Slayton was wounded in the foot at Gettysburg, although "not seriously," and his military records do contain a Memorandum of Prisoner of War Record which states he was captured on July 2, 1863 and paroled. None of this, however, is found in *The Adjutant-General's Report* of 1904. It is impossible to state with any certainty the source of Asa Slayton's information but it is patently untrue. Captain Slayton was summarily and dishonorably dismissed from the service by order of President Lincoln and the War Department on September 1, 1863 for cowardice according to the terms of Special Order No. 392, which is detailed in Dennis W. Brandt's *From Home Guards to Heroes: The 87th Pennsylvania and Its Civil War Community*, 72: "George 'Old Snapping Turtle' Meade took a dim view of officers who refused to advance in battle. On September 1, 1863 the Office of the Adjutant General issued a long series of diverse commands entitled Special Order No. 392. One of those orders dishonorably expelled Capt. Vincent C. S. Eckert from the Army of the United States." *The Town Clerks' Registers* are strangely silent about Slayton and I have found neither newspaper articles nor letters from soldiers concerning the matter which suggests that those who knew him held a different opinion from Meade's. Life, however, went on, and when Slayton died his obituary in *The Tully Times* December 2, 1893 revealed with what esteem he had been held in the community: "Reuben W. Slayton died at his home in this place on Friday evening of last week. Mr. Slayton was born in Prattsburg, Steuben County . . . When very young he moved with his parents to Springfield Centre, Otsego county, N.Y., where his parents died. Soon after the death of his parents he was, though a young lad, bound out to a farmer, Joseph Osborn, of Parish, N.Y., with whom he remained until his 21st birthday. On leaving the employ of Mr. Osborn, he engaged in the mercantile and lumber business. On June 26, 1850, he was united in marriage to Miss Eliza F. Fyler, of Parish, N.Y., who survives him. He served his country with distinction, in the civil war, being captain of company H, N.Y.S. Vols. In 1877 he moved with his family to Philadelphia, Pa., where until 1880 he was engaged in the wholesale produce business. On leaving Philadelphia he moved to Tully, taking possession of the Empire House, which property he previously acquired. In 1885 he disposed of the Empire House and built Hotel Slayton, which he was proprietor of for a period of two years, when he leased the same and went to Philadelphia, where he remained for some three years. Feeling compelled, on account of failing health, he gave up his business there and returned to Tully, where he spent the remainder of his days with his family. Although his sickness – a valvular trouble of the heart – extended over a period of more than ten years, the symptoms were not alarming until the spring of 1890, when he was so severely attacked that Dr. F. L. Harter, of Syracuse, was summoned . . . He again partially recovered, and though suffering a number of severe attacks, his robust constitution stood the strain, and aided by the untiring efforts of his physicians, the grim monster was kept at bay until nature's resources were exhausted and tender nursing and skill could do no more. For the past three years he has at times been a great sufferer. Unable to lay down day or night, he got little, if any, natural rest. When able to sit up he sat in a chair during the day and at night, supported by pillows, sat up in bed and, in order to sleep, was forced to lean forward and rest his forehead upon a support. While engaged in business in Tully he made many friends. Strictly honorable in business transactions he won the confidence and respect of all with whom he came in contact in business matters. He was one of the first to buy and ship produce from here and though he expended many hundred dollars each year among the farmers, he never in any way took advantage of them. His honesty and integrity were never questioned . . . The funeral services, which were conducted on Monday by the Rev.

F. W. Betts, of the First Universalist church, Syracuse, assisted by Rev. E. Pittman, of the M. E. church, Tully, was largely attended by the citizens of this place. A number from Syracuse and Parish were present and accompanied the remains to Parish, where they were taken for interment. The masonic order of that place, of which the deceased was an honored member, took charge of the services at the cemetery and in a solemn and impressive manner tenderly laid their brother in the tomb. Much might truthfully be said of the deceased without exaggeration; but suffice it to say, he was an honest, honorable man, truly loyal to his country, a good citizen and a kind and indulgent husband and father. Possessed of a broad mind and tender heart, he scorned deception, hypocrisy and falsehood and truly loved all that was noble and good." Eliza died at the home of her son, James (1853-1928), and was buried with Reuben in Pleasant Lawn Cemetery, Parish.

Reuben Slayton's dishonorable discharge from the military was a well-guarded secret. *Author's Collection*

Alonzo Smith – Co. F

b. April 15, 1809 Leicester, Addison, VT
d. December 20, 1893 New Haven, NY
m. Deborah Looker (1796-September 11, 1886) November 16, 1834

NOTE: Alonzo was the son of Thaddeus (1786-1870) and Abigail Aldrich Smith (1787-1859). His DOB is variously given. I use that found in the family Bible. Alonzo attempted to enlist in Co. K, 81st Regiment but was discharged at Fort Ontario, Oswego City for being over age on December 20, 1861, the day the regiment was mustered in. He claimed a DOB of 1818 when he enlisted in the 147th. He was discharged from Armory Square Hospital, Philadelphia, PA at an unknown date. In 1890 he listed no disability. Deborah, born in New Jersey, and Alonzo were the parents of one child but they also had two adopted children. In 1880 Deborah was suffering from amaurosis or total blindness. The couple is buried in New Haven Rural Cemetery. Deborah's gravestone erroneously shows a DOD of 1887.

George DePew Smith – Co. E

b. September 7, 1841 West Troy, Rensselaer, NY

d. February 18, 1895 LaBette, LaBette, KS

m1. Martha Jane Babcock (August 11, 1845-April 23, 1887) 1867

m2. Eliza Jane "Dicy" Ragle (January 1, 1855-February 10, 1942) February 12, 1888

NOTE: George was the son of Samuel (1813-*post* 1865) and Angeline M. Brothers Smith (1817-*post* 1865). His DOB is taken from a family Bible. He was wounded at Five Forks, VA on April 1, 1865 and apparently was in hospital when the regiment mustered out. He applied for a pension on August 28, 1865. Martha Jane died in Siloam Springs, Benton, AR. George died of "lung fever" and Dicy was appointed administrator of his estate although Martha's adult children were appointed guardians of their minor siblings. Dicy lost no time disposing of the property. In 1940 she was living in the Methodist Home for the Aged in Topeka, Shawnee, KS. She is buried in Mt. Hope Cemetery, Topeka. George is buried in LaBette Cemetery. Martha's grave has not been located.

Gordon Lucian Smith – Co. H

b. 1841 Oswego County, NY

d. June 4, 1863 1st Division Hospital, Aquia Creek, VA

m. ------

NOTE: Gordon, also called Lucian, was the son of Ephraim (1802-1860) and Abigail Hall Smith (1814-1895). He was the second son in the family to serve in the military. His brother Riley Ephraim (1838-October 7, 1862) was a member of the 2nd NY HA. Although his gravestone in Amboy Center Cemetery says he died in 1863, military records conclusively prove he died a year earlier. Another brother, Don Alonzo (1845-*post* 1880), served in the 1st NY ART. After his father died Gordon became his mother's principal support, working to supply groceries and other necessities for her and several younger children. He gave her $110 of his bounty money to help with family expenses. Captain Reuben Slayton asked the editors of the *Mexico Independent* June 18, 1863 to publish a letter announcing the young man's death: "*To the friends of Gordon S.* [sic] *Smith and James E. Dodd:* It becomes my painful duty to inform you that these two brave and noble young men are no more. They both died in 1st Division Hospital near Acquia Creek, Va. of typhoid fever; Smith on the 4th and Dodd on the 7th inst. – They were both taken from the Regimental Hospital on the 29th of May and at that time were not considered dangerous; but being jolted in an ambulance some ten miles through the hot sun, was more than they could bear. Had necessity not compelled them to be moved, it is my opinion they both would have recovered. There seems to be no manner of suffering that this unjust and uncalled-for war does not inflict. Fathers and mothers are made to feel the loss of their beloved sons. The wife is made a widow and for many years keenly feels and mourns the loss of her beloved husband. The kind and loving sister has bade farewell to her brother, never again to meet on earth. All these and many other sufferings are freely borne when we consider the good of the country demands it. Let us pray that the many sufferings we are so nobly bearing, and the many sacrifices that are so freely made will not be in vain: but that our country will soon be restored to peace, and the old flag be allowed to float unmolested. Then shall we be paid." Slayton's re-mark about the sufferings of mothers certainly applied to Abigail. When she applied for a pension in October 1863 she said she had a thirteen-year-old daughter, Emma "Emily" Trifene, who "works out" and a ten-year-old son, Irwin, who was crippled for life. Abigail was subject to all the bureaucratic red tape that pension applicants had to endure and eventually her lawyer, N. W. Nutting, was frustrated to the point he wrote the following, concerning a statement of "disinterest" Jacob Fulmer, a witness, was compelled to sign: "Is this sufficient? If so for God's sake and the woman's sake send her certificate immediately for if any woman ever needed it she now does. No one to help her and a poor crippled child to care for besides others in the family . . . ." The pension was finally admitted for approval on November 18, 1865, retroactive to June 11, 1863. Ephraim and Abigail, together with several children, are buried in Amboy Center Cemetery. Gordon's gravesite is unknown.

John C. Smith – Co. D
b. 1839 Granby, NY
d. December 7, 1863 Armory Square Hospital, Washington, DC
m. ------

NOTE: John's parents were John L. (1804-*post* 1879) and Maria Smith (1807-*post* 1860). According to *Deaths of Volunteers*, he died of chronic diarrhea although his muster card states COD was "fever." He is buried in the Soldiers' and Airmen's Home National Cemetery, Washington, DC. His father, whose name is also given as David, applied for a pension in April 1879 but did not receive a certificate.

Willard S. Smith – Co. B
b. 1843 Oswego City, NY
d. June 1, 1924 Johnson City, Broome, NY
m. Harriet "Hattie" Wadleigh (1843-March 26, 1914) 1871

NOTE: Willard was the son of John W. (1805-1868) and Amelia L. Shaw Smith (1820-1895). His father was born in Stockholm, Sweden. According to *The Town Clerks' Registers,* Willard was taken prisoner at the battle of the Wilderness and imprisoned ten months. In 1890 he stated he had endured Andersonville for nine months and 18 days. The enumerator put him in the 184th Regiment which cannot be correct since Willard mustered out with the 147th on June 7, 1865. After the war he worked as a carpenter. When Harriet died, *The Oswego Daily Palladium* March 27, 1914 published the following: "The Binghamton Press today says: Mrs. Harriet A. Smith, wife of ex-commander Willard S. Smith, of Bartlett Post, G.A.R., died at her home, No. 27, St. Charles street, Lestershire, last evening, in her seventy-first year. She was born in Jefferson county, and after her marriage to Mr. Smith in Oswego, she removed to this city in 1875, where the family has since made its home. Mrs. Smith was for years a well known and highly esteemed resident of the North Side. She was a member of the Calvary Baptist Church, of the Minnehaha Council, No. 4, Degree of Pocahontas, and of Bartlett Women's Relief Corps . . . ." In April of that year Willard was a member of the official delegation which traveled to Andersonville for the formal dedication of the New York Monument. He and Harriet are buried in Floral Park Cemetery, Johnson City.

Albert Snell – Co. G

b. May 1830 Granby, NY
d. August 24, 1911 Oswego City, NY
m. Hannah _____ (June 1830-July 23, 1900) *ca.* 1856

NOTE: Albert, son of Hiram (1804-1884) and Lydia Scouton Snell (1808-1835), was transferred to the VRC on March 28, 1864 and discharged at Washington, DC on July 10, 1865. In 1890 he said his disability was "kidney trouble & rheumatism." The enumerator added, "Been able to work but 3 ms. this year." His obituary appeared in *The Oswego Daily Palladium* August 25, 1911: "Albert Snell, an old and respected resident of this city, died at his home, No. 119 West Seneca street, last night after a short illness. Mr. Snell was born in Oswego Town eighty-one years ago. He was a carpenter by trade, but had lived a retired life for the past seventeen years. He was a veteran of the Civil War, being a member of the 147th Regiment, New York Volunteers. He was also for many years a prominent member of Post O'Brian, G.A.R. Mr. Snell had planned to attend the National Encampment in Rochester this week, but was taken ill on Saturday morning and continued to get worse until death came last night. A cancer was the cause of death . . . The funeral will take place from his late home on Sunday afternoon at 2:30 o'clock, the Rev. C. H. Young, pastor of the First Baptist church, officiating. Members of the G.A.R. will conduct the services at the grave in Riverside cemetery." Snell's muster roll card says he was born in Granby and despite what the obituary says, Albert was buried in Rural Cemetery, Oswego Town, with Hannah and his parents.

Chauncey C. Snell – Co. F

b. 1844 New Haven, NY

d. July 5, 1863 Gettysburg, Adams, PA

m. ------

NOTE: Chauncey was the son of Steven Burrell (1798-1878) and Emily Hinman Snell (1804-1873). He originally enlisted in the 110th but was sent to the 147th. His DOD is disputed. His Interment Control Form dates his death to July 1st but that is probably not correct since his muster roll card states he died in hospital, although no date is given. His entry in Veterans' Gravesites also provides a DOD of July 1st. His FAG entry shows a DOD of July 5th and a note in *Registers of Officers and Enlisted Men* assigns a death date of July 7th. The list of casualties published in *The Mexico Independent* July 23, 1863 does not show a date at all. Snell was first buried in the Presbyterian Graveyard at Gettysburg. His body was later moved to the Gettysburg National Cemetery.

George W. Snell – Co. G

b. May 25, 1841 Oswego Town, NY

d. May 10, 1864 Laurel Hill, VA

m. ------

NOTE: George, son of Hiram (1804-1884) and Louisa Coon Snell (1818-1893), was Albert's half brother. He was killed in action and his gravesite is unknown. A full brother, Charles A. (1839-1883), served in the 24th NY Cavalry and was severely wounded at the battle of Cold Harbor in June 1864. He is buried in Rural Cemetery, Oswego Town.

Phineas B. Snyder – Co. I

b. 1841 Oswego, NY

d. ? ?

m. ?

NOTE: Phineas, a lake sailor, was the son of Nicholas (1806-*ante* 1865) and Diana Snyder (1810-1892). He was discharged from the army on April 22, 1864 in order to join the US Navy. On May 4, 1864 he was enrolled at the Brooklyn dockyards for a term of a year and a half. Records indicate he served aboard the Ticonderoga and the Fort Jackson. The last known reference to him in Oswego is found in *The Oswego Daily Palladium* February 14, 1866, when the city council voted to pay him $3.00 for watching Engine House #2 on February 12th. He applied for a pension on October 16, 1879 in Minnesota but no certificate was issued. Since he is not found on the 1880 census it is altogether possible he died in late 1879 or early 1880, although I have not found him on any Mortality Schedules. His mother Diana applied for a pension on September 23, 1890 but no certificate was granted, probably because she died before the process could be completed. It also appears she applied for a Navy pension which was disapproved. Diana was buried in New Haven Rural Cemetery.

William H. Snyder – Co. I
b. August 1821 Oneida County, NY
d. November 24, 1914 Cato, Cayuga, NY
m. Mary E. Adle (1828-March 2, 1909) *ca.* 1848

NOTE: William, son of Paul C. (1799-1874) and Hannah Snyder (1803-1879), deserted on September 22, 1862 and was not apprehended until February 1865. His muster roll card says he was sentenced to forfeit all his pay and allowances and to pay all the expenses pertaining to his arrest. On June 5, 1865 he was transferred to Co. C, 91st Regiment and discharged on June 9th. Despite his extended absenteeism, he successfully applied for a pension in 1891. In 1865 Mary said she was the mother of eight children. She and William apparently parted company because her obituary in *The* [Williamsport, PA] *Daily Gazette and Bulletin* March 3, 1909 makes no mention of a husband: "Mrs. Mary E. Snyder, who died on Tuesday morning at the residence of her daughter, Mrs. Anna M. Drinkwater, 829 Third avenue, was aged eighty three years. She had been an invalid for a long time and was a great sufferer. Mrs. Snyder had been a resident of this city since 1877, having been born in Oswego, N.Y. . . . The funeral will be held on Thursday at 2 p.m. at the house . . . the services to be in charge of the Rev. Robert F. Gibson, rector of Trinity Episcopal church." Mary's COD was senility with apoplexy a contributing factor. Her death certificate stated she was widowed. She is buried in Wildwood Cemetery, Williamsport. William's death was reported in *The Cato Citizen* November 27, 1914, 1: ". . . The death of William Snyder occurred at the home of John Goodrich Wednesday morning. He was 95 years old and had resided in this section for about 35 years. He was a veteran of the civil war. The funeral will be arranged by friends from Oswego . . . ." To date his grave has not been located.

Cazimire Sorel – Co. A
b. January 1826 Quebec, Canada
d. March 30, 1907 Oswego City, NY
m. Julia Simons dit Arpentigny (December 1832-October 21, 1909) *ca.* 1850

NOTE: This man's name was variously spelled but by the end of his life he was calling himself Cassimere Syrell. His parents were Michel (?-1855) and Marguerite Tetreault-Ducharme Sorel (?-1830), both of whom died in Canada. According to the 1900 census Cassimere immigrated to the United States in 1847 and became a naturalized citizen in 1875. He was wounded at Gettysburg on July 1, 1863 and transferred to the VRC on November 28, 1863. He was discharged at Rochester, NY on July 24, 1865. He and Julia, the mother of nine children, are buried in St. Peter's Cemetery, Oswego.

Nathaniel Dawes Spaid – Co. K

b. May 1844 Oswego County, NY

d. March 12, 1902 Granby, NY

m. Anna Dell Spickerman (1849-January 30, 1923) July 4, 1868

NOTE: Nathaniel's surname was generally spelled Spade. His parents were Jacob Dawes (1812-*post* 1860) and Martha Spade (1816-*post* 1865). His military career was fraught with disease and wounds. He apparently contracted typhoid fever at some point; he was bothered with chronic diarrhea and rheumatism; and he was lame for the rest of his life because of a gunshot wound to his coccyx at the Battle of Laurel Hill, VA on May 10, 1864. His 100+ page pension file bears witness to his suf-ferings in later life and his continual struggle to obtain more pension money. He and Anna were the parents of one son, Charles Eugene (*ca.* 1869-*post* 1913). According to Anna, Nathaniel deserted her, saying he was "going west." Several months later he returned, alleging he wanted to get back together. A trip to see his parents in Granby, however, resulted in a complete separation. Anna said he packed his things and left. With a small child to support Anna became the housekeeper for George Lamphere (?-February 1898). As she said, she "had to do something." By Lamphere she was the mother of Florence (1878-1967) and Burton A. (1880-1965). In the meantime Harriet Emma Dolbear (1860-1939) went to work for Nathaniel who was sick much of the time. She bore a child, Walter H. Spade (1882-1926). Spade's COD was dia-betes. He is buried in Merritt Cemetery, Bowens Corners, NY. After he died, Charles encouraged his mother to apply for a widow's pension since she had never been divorced from his father. The details of this application revealed the tangled relation-ships among the members of the family. Anna lived with her son, Burton, until her death. On April 5, 1920 he wrote a letter to the Pension Bureau complaining that her $25 per month pension was insufficient to care for her: "Anna D. Spade . . . is living at my house she is getting 75.00 evry 3 months and she is 72 years old and in the last 2 years she has had 3 stroaks and about 2 months ago she fell and broke her knee cap she is feeble minded and absolutely helpless and here pencion is not half enough to pay for her care say nothing about Dr. bill she is so helpless we half to waight on her day and nite and I am not able to pay her Dr. bills and nurse day and nite and I think the pencion department ought to do sompthg about it at once . . . ." On July 25, 1921 an anonymous person living in Auburn wrote to the Pension Bureau complaining about the ill treatment Anna was receiving: ". . . do you think it right for her son to sign her papers and keep her locked up in a close filthy room and such care as she has is terrible . . . ." The Pension Bureau contacted local authorities who sent H. Fuller Knight, Health Officer for the Village of Meridian, to investigate. He reported on November 28, 1921: "I have this day inspected the premises of Mr. Bert [*sic*] Lamphere, whereon and wherein, is the home of his mother, and concerning which complaints of unsanitary conditions have been reported. Previous inspections to the Board revealed quarters reeking in filth with insufficient screen protection and no adequate provisions for toilet appoint- ments nor other acceptable means for the disposal of excreta. Today, however, I find the place renovated; the filth removed; the person of the occupant kept cleanly as possible; the floor covered; one window properly screened and a stove and sanitary toilet installed. This embraces a revolution- ary change . . . ." Anna died in Meridian but her grave has not been located. Harriet,

Nathaniel Spaid's gravestone lies par- tially buried in Merritt Cemetery, Bowen's Corners, NY.
Author's Collection

also known as Emma, married Frank A. Fancher (1861-*post* 1935) *ante* 1905. Her di- vorce from him became final on August 8, 1920 and on August 11, 1920 she married Adelbert Sixberry (1875-1945). She and Sixberry are buried in Sandridge Cemetery, Pennellville.

William C. C. Spaid – Co. K
b. 1842 Oswego County, NY
d. March 19, 1863 Belle Plain, VA
m. ------

NOTE: William was Nathaniel's brother. He transferred to Co. B on December 1, 1862. His COD was typhoid fever. Originally buried at Wallace's Farm, VA today he lies in Fredericksburg National Cemetery.

William Elijah Sparks – Co. E

b. April 13, 1834 Sandy Creek, NY
d. May 15, 1911 Orwell, NY
m. Orilla Myers (1837-April 14, 1917) 1855

NOTE: William was the son of Major Andre (1810-1891) and Caroline Stowell Sparks (1816-1890). At some unspecified date he transferred to Company K. He and Orilla were the parents of four children. Upon his death, *The Sandy Creek News* June 8, 1911 published a lengthy, informative obituary: "Died at his home in Orwell, May 15, William E. Sparks, aged 78 years. Thus another veteran has answered to the last bugle call and has passed on to his rest. Mr. Sparks was born in Orwell where he has lived practically all his life. He enlisted in the Civil War in sixty-two and served Company K 147, till end of war, and was mustered out with company on June 7, 1865, near Washington, D.C. Mr. Sparks had been blind many years brought on by the hardships of the army, and for the past year had been a great, but patient sufferer with cancer. Mr. Sparks was loved and respected by all who knew him for his upright, quiet and kind disposition. He was a member of Post Olmstead, Orwell, N.Y., where he will be greatly missed as well as in his home, where he was always a tender and loving husband and father . . . ." Orilla was remembered in *The Sandy Creek News* April 19, 1917: "Mrs. Orilla Sparks, widow of the late William Sparks, Sr., passed away Saturday morning, April 14, after a short illness from pneumonia, aged 80 years . . . Mrs. Sparks has been a member of the W.R.C. ever since its organization and was always interested in the welfare of the order. The funeral services were conducted in the late home Monday afternoon by Rev. T. T. Davies . . . .: William and Orilla are buried in Evergreen Cemetery, Orwell.

Jabez Eugene Spaulding – Co. F

b. 1846 New Haven, NY
d. February 29, 1864 General Hospital No. 21, Richmond, VA
m. ------

NOTE: This soldier's father is unknown. By 1850 his mother, Martha (1818-*post* 1879), was married to John Mason (1806-*post* 1865) as his second wife. Although Jabez claimed to be 18 when he enlisted, the 1850 census proves he was born in 1846. He was wounded at Gettysburg on July 1, 1863. His muster roll card shows he was in hospital at least until September 1863 at which point he must have rejoined the regiment. His muster card also contains a notation that exchanged prisoners reported he had died while a POW. A J. E. Spaulding from Co. F, 147th PA who died of erysipelas in Richmond, VA on February 29, 1864, is listed in *Deaths of Volunteers*. No such man can be found on that regiment's roster in Company F. The 147th NY and the 147th PA were organized in the same time frame and it is altogether possible that this man was mistakenly assigned to the wrong state in the hospital records. His mother successfully applied for a pension in 1879.

David William Spencer – Co. F

b. ? Paris, Oneida, NY
d. December 13, 1898 Albion, NY
m1. Ruhanna Murall (1809-December 16, 1886) *ca.* 1830
m2. Lucina _____ (?-post 1899) *ca.* 1893

NOTE: This man's entry in *The Town Clerks' Registers* says his parents were David (?-?) and Jane Walden Spencer (?-?) and his DOB was February 16, 1810, but he was probably born closer to 1805 even though on his muster roll card he claimed to have been born in 1822. He was discharged from the army for "disability" at Belle Plain, VA on February 3, 1863 and in 1890 said he suffered from lameness in the leg. He and Ruhanna were the parents of numerous children, one of whom, Orrin Franklin (1847-*post* 1870), served in the 24th Regiment from 1861-1863. Lucina has been difficult to track. In 1892 David was unmarried and styled himself a "gentleman." On September 4, 1893 he made his will, leaving everything to Lucina for her lifetime. From this I infer the couple had married recently. *The Pulaski Democrat* January 4, 1899 reported Lucina had moved to Syracuse to live with a daughter. On January 9th she applied for a pension but no certificate was issued. After that the trail ends. She does not appear on the 1900 census. David and Ruhanna are buried in Dugway Cemetery, Albion. David's brother, Lyman (1825-September 26, 1878), served in Co. E, 59th Regiment from September 1861-April 1862.

Jerome John Spencer – Co. H

b. 1832 Madison County, NY
d. May 11, 1867 Parish, NY
m. Sophronia A. Gordinier (1835-April 4, 1900) December 22, 1852

NOTE: Jerome, son of John D. (1795-1840) and Polly Spencer (1793-1867), was often called by his middle name. He was a wagoner in the regiment and on December 1, 1862 his team panicked and threw him out of the wagon down a ten-foot embankment. He was knocked unconscious and when he awoke he found he had no feeling in his right leg and right arm. After spending months in various hospitals he was finally discharged for "paraplegia" at Christian Street Hospital, Philadelphia, PA on January 1, 1864. In his application for a pension he avowed he was totally unable to earn a living, a statement confirmed by Dr. Tobias Greene, the family physician. His death left Sophronia with two minor children, Addie (1857-1913) and Nellie Violet (1859-1917). She applied for and obtained a widow's pension. Sometime after

1875 she and the girls moved to Syracuse where she worked in a restaurant and ran a boarding house, among others, to make ends meet. In 1883 malicious gossip that she was co-habiting with a man named Frank Bryant resulted in a special examination by the Pension Bureau. Witnesses were unanimous in their assessment that such was not the case and the examiner ruled in her favor. She collected the pension until her death in 1900. Jerome is buried in Bidwell Cemetery, Parish. Sophronia's grave has not been located.

Robert Hamilton Spencer – Co. G

b. 1818 Albany, Albany, NY
d. November 24, 1873 Great Bend, Barton, KS
m. Elmina Pleiades Keeler (September 15, 1819-December 29, 1912) November 14, 1840

NOTE: Robert was the son of Abner (1786-1848) and Apollonia Isabella Ingersoll Spencer (1794-1872). His was a varied career, sometime teacher, sometime lake captain. In 1862 he enlisted even though he was beyond draft age and performed duty in various field hospitals. In 1864 he was discharged in order to enlist in the US Army as a hospital steward. He was a frequent correspondent to the local newspapers, sending home casualty lists and reporting events occurring within the regiment, an example of which appeared in *The Oswego Daily Palladium* March 4, 1864, which is excerpted here. The letter was sent from Brandy Station, VA and dated February 24, 1864: "About a week ago a wholesale dealer in New York sent over two hundred dollars' worth of the best tobacco for distribution. You may guess how this pleased the boys who have had no pay for nearly four months, and have exhausted their pay at the Sutlers. The 42 dozen papers were distributed among the boys of the New York and Connecticut regiments, who were wounded at Morton's ford quite lately. – Could the good people of the North stand by and witness the glad expression of the wounded soldier, as the agent enters and asks, 'Who is here from New York?' – 'I am,' says a young lad, 'and I!' 'And I!' is the response from a dozen cots. 'Here is some tobacco, good fine cut, from New York, which Thomas Hoyt & Co., 404 Pearl street, has sent for you.' Oh that proud gratified look! That expression of gratitude. It pays for all the toil and privation a hundred fold. And then again here is a wounded patriot who has made no response, but who is eagerly watching the proceedings; the agent catches his eye, and asks, 'Will you have a paper?' perhaps in a feeble voice he answers, 'I am not from New York, I am of the Connecticut 14th.' 'You are a Union soldier, and we make no distinction in Hospitals, our instructions from the Governor are to help all we can, and especially New Yorkers.' He receives his paper, a tear dims his eye and unexpected pleasure chokes his voice. What a picture some of these scenes would make. – I wish I could describe it, so that those who give might realize how 'much better it is to give than to receive.' Let me describe another scene . . . Of late the Government furnishes neither mittens nor gloves, and the sutlers charge from one to three dollars a pair, which is more than a soldier can pay, who has some 'dear one at home' to whom he remits a portion of his thirteen dollars per month. Those detailed for picket have to remain out on the extreme front three days, during which time they have to be on the alert, and those in the front line have to stand sentry by turns night and day, so near the rebel lines as to forego the comfort of a fire. Now imagine 70 men detailed from the 147th, about to march with their three days' rations, armed and equipped and well clothed in every respect, except that many of them are bare handed. They cannot go whistling along with their hands in their pockets like civilians, neither can they stop to whip them over the shoulder or otherwise warm them. They are soldiers and must submit to military discipline, mittens or no mittens, cold or rain, or sleet, or snow, the gun must be carried in the bare hands and in a proper manner. As the detail is about to march, the officer commands attention, and an agent appears in front of the line with large bundles of woolen mittens, which the Christian Commission had furnished the New York Agent for distribution. The eager, joyous shout, despite the stern rebuke of the officer in command! The restless uneasiness of those on the extreme left of the line for fear the supply would be exhausted before they were furnished with a pair! And when they were found to be soldiers' mits, knit with a fore finger, to enable them the better to handle the gun, you should have seen the boys as they fitted them to their hands and grasped the gun. Talking was not then in order – action was then the word – and as they received the command, 'forward, march,' the firm erect position, the elastic tread, and haughty defiant toss of the head, indicated how well they were pleased with the gift, and how cheerfully they moved to watch the wily foe, to guard the front, and if need be to repel the stealthy assault . . . ." Spencer was discharged on June 15, 1865. After the war he applied for a land bounty and, with Elmina's father, went to Kansas. She went later with the two mothers. He is buried in an unmarked grave in Great Bend Cemetery. Elmina returned to Oswego where she resided until her death. (For her story, see "Et Cetera Nomina.")

Edwin Menzo Sperry – Co. C
b. July 8, 1835 Boonville, Oneida, NY
d. February 25, 1905 Boonville, Oneida, NY
m. Harriet Eliza Rich (October 1843-July 21, 1931) 1861

NOTE: Edwin was the son of Eneas (1793-1853) and Thankful Ames Sperry (1799-1867). He rose through the ranks to become a first lieutenant in the 147th Regiment and mustered out on June 7, 1865. His death was announced in *The Utica Sunday Tribune* February 26, 1905, 1: ". . . Edwin M. Sperry was born in Boonville in 1835 and except for a few years, when he lived in Oswego County, this place had been his home. Always an active, stirring citizen, he took an active interest in public affairs and was looking after the interests of his town and community, but was not a seeker for public office. For several years he served as Excise Commissioner for the town. He enlisted in 1862 from Oswego County in the One Hundred and Forty-seventh New York State Volunteers, as lieutenant in Company C, and served until the close of the war. H was married in 1861 to Miss Harriet E. Rich . . . ." Edwin was a member of Wheelock Post No. 97 GAR which officiated at his funeral. Harriet's death was reported in *The Rome Daily Sentinel* July 21, 1931, 2: "Word was received [in Boonville] this afternoon of the death of Mrs. Harriet E. Sperry, 83, widow of Menzo Sperry, which occurred this morning at the home of her daughter, Mrs. Lula Yauger, at Yolanda Beach, California. Mrs. Sperry formerly resided here and is the mother of Supervisor Clarence Sperry of this village . . . Mrs. Sperry removed to California about 20 years ago, where she had resided, making her home with her daughter." Edwin and Harriet are buried in Boonville Cemetery. His brother, John Dickerson Sperry (1816-1886), served in Co. G, 52nd IL Infantry. Another brother, Cyrus Sanford Sperry (1838-1872), was a member of Co I, 117th NY Infantry. Clarence, Edwin and Harriet's son, died June 18, 1936 at the age of 47 after suffering a heart attack.

Ira A. Sperry – Co. D
b. 1840 Volney, NY
d. June 22, 1863 Lincoln Hospital, Washington, DC
m. Lovina H. Osborn (1839-June 20, 1915) November 7, 1860

NOTE: Ira was the son of Peter Worden (1804-1870) and Eleanor Burns Sperry (1805-*post* 1855). He and Lovina were the parents of Harriet Eleanor (1861-1938) who married William T. Brown, an attorney. Ira's COD was typhoid fever. He is buried in the Soldiers' and Airmen's National Home Cemetery, Washington, DC. A cenotaph for him is located in Mt. Adnah Cemetery, Fulton. Lovina never remarried and lived in many places across the United States with her daughter and son-in-law. Her COD was chronic Bright's disease and arteriosclerosis. She is buried in Mt. Adnah Cemetery, as are Harriet and William.

Wheaton Spink – Co. C
b. 1819 Floyd, Oneida, NY
d. January 1, 1863 Windmill Point Hospital, VA
m. Laura Farmer (1819-?) October 2, 1861

NOTE: Wheaton, son of Seneca (1765-1849) and Charlana Wheaton Spink (1773-1864), died from chronic diarrhea and was buried in Virginia. Laura's later life is a mystery. In 1875 she lived with her brother-in-law, Ishmael Spink (1810-1880), and was the executor of his will which went to probate in March 1880. The pension file reveals she was last paid on September 4, 1880, but her death was not reported until January 4, 1884. It is possible she died before the end of the year. Wheaton's parents are buried in Fairview Cemetery, Williamstown and she may be buried there too.

James Spoon – Co. H
b. March 3, 1842 Amboy, NY
d. July 1864 Andersonville, Sumter, GA
m. ------

NOTE: James was the son of Peter (1794-1884) and Sally Hall Spoon (1802-1881). According to *The Town Clerks' Registers,* he was taken prisoner on May 14, 1864 and died at Andersonville on July 17th. COD was chronic diarrhea. *The Adjutant-General's Report* places his death on July 18th. He is buried in Andersonville National Cemetery.

Justus Sprague – Co. E
b. June 25, 1837 Sandy Creek, NY
d. October 11, 1919 Minneapolis, Hennepin, MN
m. Mary E. Hinman (August 13, 1840-July 22, 1927) July 4, 1857

NOTE: Justus, whose name was also spelled Justice, was the son of Smith (1802-1857) and Talitha Heath Sprague (1805-*post* 1860). He was a member of James Bryant Post No. 119 GAR and upon his death B. M. Hicks, historian of James Bryant Post No. 119 GAR, wrote a moving *In Memoriam* which is here excerpted: "Death always comes to us with a shock, and in this case doubly so, as this comrade was out to the last Post meeting in September, and in apparent good health. We missed him at our last Post meeting, but as he was not reported sick his death came to us unexpectedly, and it again becomes our duty as comrades to tenderly lay away this beloved comrade in his last bivouac. Justice Sprague was born June 25th, 1837, in Oswego Co., New York, and died at his home in this city . . . at the advanced age of eighty two years and three months, surely a ripe old age . . . Comrade Sprague at the age of twenty-five years with a young wife and two small children to support after curbing his patriotic desire to go to his country's defense for over a year, then with the consent of his loyal wife enlisted . . . and was mustered into the service . . . as a private in Co. E, 147th N.Y. Vol. Infty . . . . Comrade Sprague was discharged with his regiment . . . June 7, 1865, having served his country for two years and ten months, always faithful in performance of his duties. Comrade Sprague was married on the fourth day of July, 1857, at the age of twenty years to Miss Mary E. Henman [*sic*], at Sandy Creek, N.Y. . . . Our comrade joined the Grand Army by becoming a member of James Bryant Post in 1893, twenty-six years ago, for nearly one half of that time he faithfully served the Post as Quartermaster Sergeant diligently attending to its duties and being of much assistance to the Quartermaster. After being discharged from the army he resided at Sandy Creek and then moved to Northfield, Minn., where he engaged in farming, and then to this city of which he has been a resident for over 48 years. He drove the first electric car in our street car service. For two years he has been too feeble to engage in any active work and has gradually failed in strength until the painless end came to him. A faithful patriotic and brave defender of the Union has answered his last roll call and joined the ever increasing army of the Blue on the other shore. A tried and true comrade has been taken from our ranks, we shall miss this faithful comrade but will hold his quiet and unassuming manner in grateful memory. A law abiding conscientious citizen of our city has been removed from us, may his example be emulated by future generations . . . ." Mary was active in the Women's Relief Corps and the Park Avenue Congregational Church. She and Justus are buried in Lakewood Cemetery, Minneapolis.

Orrin Nelson Sprague – Co. E

b. June 28, 1847 Sandy Creek, NY
d. May 5, 1924 Fernwood, NY
m. Mary Cordelia Bumpus (1849-January 23, 1918) 1868

NOTE: Orrin, whose parents were Alonzo, Sr. (1823-1898) and Matilda Cristman Sprague (1818-1899), lied about his age when enlisting, claiming to be 18. He was captured at Gettysburg and paroled at an unknown date, mustering out with the regiment on June 7, 1865. Upon his death *The Pulaski Democrat* May 14, 1924, 1 published the following: "Mr. O. N. Sprague, a life long resident of Fernwood, passed away, May 5, aged 77 years at the home of his son, Herbert Sprague. Mr. Sprague was born in the town of Sandy Creek but for many years had lived in Fernwood and engaged in farming until the past few years his health failed. He made his home with his son and family. He enlisted in the 147th regiment, N.Y. Volunteers. He was a member of the J. B. Butler Post, G. A. R. and of South Richland Grange. In his quiet way he was a man of worth and will be missed. He was a most kind, loving father also an obliging neighbor. As the days passed and his suffering was great convincing him his stay was but short here, he tried to forget all worldly things, turning to those things which perish not, putting his trust in Him who saves to the uttermost. Clinging to the old rugged cross and at last exchanging it for a crown . . . Beautiful flowers rested on his casket and friends and neighbors gathered to pay their last tribute of respect to him who had so long been friend and neighbor. For many years Mr. I. J. Rich and Mr. O. N. Sprague were delegated to place flags by the soldiers' graves in the Willis cemetery . . . Services were concluded by the members of the Grand Army." Orrin and Mary were the parents of four children. Her death was announced in *The Pulaski Democrat* January 30, 1918, 1: ". . . Died at her home, January 23, Mrs. Mary Cordelia

Sprague, wife of Mr. O. N. Sprague, aged 68 years. Mrs. Sprague has been in failing health for the past four years, suffering often intensely, but without complaint. It seemed to have been given her to know the summons of the Master was near at hand, by the little things she said and did just a few days before her death. Last fall, when Mr. Sprague's wheat field was golden and ready for the harvester, she gathered a fine bunch and carefully laid it away. One day she said to one daughter, 'get a ribbon,' told her the length and width and said 'use it.' Rarely was she from home for home and her family were all the world to her. No place like the home where she was born and grew to womanhood and with her family and loved ones she was content when the call [came] for her to leave all. Her husband and all her children but one were at her bedside . . . ." Orrin and Mary are buried in Willis Cemetery, Fernwood. Two of Orrin's brothers also served the Union. Alonzo, Jr. (1845-1918) was a member of Co. G, 24th Regiment and Milo (1846-1918) was a soldier in Co. G, 184th Regiment.

David Stay – Co. D
b. 1826 Canada
d. June 11, 1863 Regimental Hospital near Falmouth, VA
m. Saloma LaBonte (1826-December 25, 1883) February 10, 1848

NOTE: David's parents are unidentified. His COD was typhoid fever. He and Saloma were married in Sandy Hill, Washington, NY and became the parents of eight children, one of whom, Jay David (1856-1946), graduated from Syracuse University and was, among others, vice president of Leland University in New Orleans, LA. Another, Anson (1851-1924), served in the US Army. Saloma is buried in Mt. Adnah Cemetery, Fulton.

John B. Steenbergh – Co. D
b. January 1, 1817 Schenectady, Schenectady, NY
d. January 25, 1899 Yale, St. Clair, MI
m. Sophronia Cooper (June 1828-August 31, 1904) 1849

NOTE: John, a wheelwright, was the son of John Steinburg (?-?) and an unidentified mother. He was discharged from the service on December 8, 1862 for "disability." In 1890 he claimed "rupture" as his disability. His COD was heart failure and upon his death, *The Yale Expositor* January 27, 1899, 1 published the following: "Died, at his home in Yale, Wednesday, January 25, 1899, John Steinberg, at the advanced age of 84 years. For the past thirty years Mr. Steinberg has been a familiar figure of the place and his absence will be missed not only by his family, but by hosts of friends. Honest, conscientious, full of Christian purpose and good will toward men he was an example for all men to follow. Deceased was born in Schenectady, N.Y., and in 1849 he was married to Sophrona [sic] Cooper at Fulton, N.Y. In the year 1863 they moved to Michigan. Six children were born to them, three only now living and the wife to mourn the loss of husband and father. Mr. Steinberg was a veteran of the late war and fought bravely for his country . . . ." Sophronia, whose COD was a combination of old age and nephritis, died in Brockway, St. Clair, MI. She and John are buried in Elmwood Cemetery, Yale.

Charles Wesley Stewart – Co. F

b. December 11, 1832 Western, Oneida, NY
d. February 26, 1924 Brook Park, Pine, MN
m. Ann Martin (June 11, 1832-December 24, 1919) 1852

NOTE: Charles, a farmer, was the son of Jonathan (1786-1872) and Emily Theresa Edgerton Stewart (1790-1850). He mustered out with the regiment on June 7, 1865. He and Ann were the parents of four children. They are buried in Brook Park Cemetery.

Orin Stewart – Co. C

b. 1835 Richland, NY
d. March 11, 1870 Pulaski, NY
m. ------

NOTE: Orin, son of Joel (1804-1894) and Betsey Jane White Stewart (1811-1898), was transferred to the VRC on August 10, 1864 and discharged from the service on June 28, 1865 at Washington, DC. His COD was "consumption of lungs." He is buried in Pulaski Village Cemetery.

John Titus Stillman – assistant surgeon

b. February 12, 1827 Brookfield, Madison, NY
d. February 15, 1909 Brookfield, Madison, NY
m. Ann Janette Denison (1828-November 14, 1898) September 9, 1850

NOTE: John was the son of Ethan (1801-1879) and Clarissa Bailey Stillman (1806-1900). His obituary, published in *The Brookfield Courier* February 17, 1909, detailed a long career: "John T. Stillman, who had been very feeble for a long time past died at the home of his daughter, Mrs. Lenthel Bacon, at an early hour Monday morning. His death can be ascribed only to the infirmities of age. He was a son of Ethan and Clarissa Bailey Stillman and was born in this town Feb. 12, 1827. After obtaining a good education he studied medicine and graduated from the Albany medical college. In 1850 he married Janette Denison of this village and they moved to West Edmeston where for a time he practiced medicine, going from there to Orwell, Oswego county, where he continued his profession until his enlistment in the 147th Regiment N.Y.S. volunteers Sept. 23, 1862. He served as assistant surgeon until Dec. 27, [1864] when he re-enlisted as surgeon in the 88th Regt. He was mustered out June 30, 1865, leaving a record unexcelled for patriotic and faithful performance of service in the cause of the Union. In after years he never tired of relating the stirring incidents of the several campaigns in which he took part and his recitals were always listened to with the greatest interest. At the close of the war he and his wife located in this their native village and he for reasons best known to himself discontinued the practice of medicine and engaged in the hardware business which he followed until growing feebleness caused him to turn over the business to his son, John L. Stillman. Since war times Mr. Stillman had been a Democrat although he could more properly be classed as independent, being one who would not condone the evil in any party. His veracity and honor were unswerving and he was held in the highest respect by all our people. Though possessed of unusual ability he had no ambition for place or notoriety but was nevertheless several times honored at the hands of his party. He had been for many years a member of Searle Post being the fourth member of the organization to answer to the final roll call during the present winter . . . The funeral was held at the Bacon home today, Wednesday at 11 a.m., conducted by Rev. Walter L. Greene." The following was published in *The Brookfield Courier* November 16, 1898 announcing Ann's death: "It had not been generally known, outside the family, that Mrs. John T. Stillman was seriously ill, and so her death which occurred Monday evening was a great surprise and shock to the entire community. Last Thursday she was preparing to go on a visit to her daughter in Utica, but was prevented from starting by the violent storm. That night she was taken with peritonitis and became violently ill. Dr. Brown was called and soon had the disease well under control, but a weakness of the heart developed, which caused her death after four days of suffering. Mrs. Stillman was the daughter of the late James Denison . . . She was born and married in this village and the greater part of her life has been spent here. She was a bright, attractive, handsome woman, devoted to her home, her husband and her children, who have the sympathy of their friends in this bereavement. After more than forty years of married life, solitary and comfortless, indeed is the lot of the one left to finish out the journey alone . . . Her funeral will be held this afternoon at 2 o'clock from her late home, conducted by Rev. C. A. Burdick." The Stillmans are buried in Brookfield Rural Cemetery.

Frederick Stinger – Co. H
b. 1829 Oneida County, NY
d. June 9, 1884 Cleveland, NY
m. Ann Jewell Cadman (1829-1894) *ca.* 1858

NOTE: Frederick, the son of Louis (1792-?) and Huldah Stinger (1793-?), was discharged from the service on August 12, 1863 although no reason was provided on his muster roll card. When he married Ann, born in England, she had already been married and was the mother of six children. To date identifying her first husband has been unsuccessful. She and Frederick were the parents of one child, Frederick, Jr., (1859-1885). By 1880 Ann was living with her son and claiming to be a widow. The elder Stinger cannot be found on the 1880 census. After his death, Ann applied for a pension but no certificate was issued. Frederick Sr., Ann, and Frederick, Jr. are all buried in Cleveland Village Cemetery.

Robert Stinson – Co. E
b. 1834 Sheffield, Canada West
d. April 28, 1891 Boylston, NY
m. Alvira Matilda Rowe (January 16, 1837-October 11, 1915) November 28, 1856

NOTE: Stinson, whose parents are unknown, was discharged from the service on February 5, 1865 after the 147th and the 76th Regiments were consolidated. His pension card says he also served in Co. E, 76th Regiment, but *The Adjutant-General's Report* for that organization does not include his name. In 1890 he was living in Mannsville, Jefferson, NY and said his disability was a "shell wound in head." He is buried in Phelps Cemetery, Boylston Center. Alvira died at the home of her daughter in Lorraine, Jefferson, NY and is buried in the Lorraine Village Cemetery.

Joseph Stoughtenger – Co. G
b. 1844 Oswego County, NY
d. July 16, 1863 Gettysburg, Adams, PA
m. ------

NOTE: Joseph, whose surname is variously spelled, was the son of George Washington (1818-1892) and Betsey Loop Stoughtenger (1823-1911). He was wounded in action on July 1, 1863 and his leg was amputated, resulting in his death. In her poem *Before He Was Twenty: A Tribute to Joseph Stoughtenger*, Michele Davis alludes to his death: "*. . . Bullets rang out from the side of the gray./He was struck, and then in his blood he lay./Alone he was in long hours of woe./Alone when told the leg would go.—Before he was twenty./Alone he bore the tremendous pain,/And two weeks later, his life was claimed./In Gettysburg then he was laid to rest./Through death, our country was free and blessed./--Before he was twenty.*" Joseph is buried in Gettysburg National Cemetery.

Hiram Stowell – Co. G
b. May 25, 1829 Orwell, NY
d. July 1, 1863 Gettysburg, Adams, PA
m. Charlotte Lester (1835-June 4, 1878) ca. 1855

NOTE: Hiram, son of Oren Crocker (1785-1847) and Lovisa Kilburn Stowell (1788-1853), was killed in action with Fred Rife. He and Charlotte were the parents of Rozell Hiram (1858-1911) and Ernest Lawrence (1861-1922). Charlotte's grave has not been located. Two brothers served in the 110th Regiment. Albert Stowell died of typhoid fever on January 16, 1863 in New Orleans. Linus Stowell died on October 2, 1863 of chronic diarrhea. He had been discharged from the service but died without ever leaving St. James' Hospital, New Orleans.

Joseph Stuyvesant – Co. C
b. 1834 Oswego County, NY
d. July 2, 1863 Gettysburg, Adams, PA
m. Frances J. Rice (July 18, 1834-November 29, 1916) June 3, 1861

NOTE: His entry in *The Town Clerks' Registers* says that Joseph's father was Christian Stuyvesant (?-?) but he and his unknown wife must have died quite young since in 1850 Joseph was living with Charles and Zipporah Rice, his future wife's paternal grandparents. He and Frances were the parents of one daughter, Zipporah E. (1862-1942). Joseph was WIA on July 1, 1863 and, according to *The Town Clerks' Registers*, "died in a few hours." He was buried on the battlefield. Frances never remarried. Her death was announced in *The Pulaski Democrat* December 6, 1916, 1: ". . . The many friends of Mrs. Frances J. Stuyvesant were saddened last Wednesday when they heard of her death from pneumonia. She lived nearly all her life of 82 years in this place [Pineville] and was loved and respected by old and young. The funeral was held from the Rice home, Sunday at 2 p.m., Rev. C. E. Perry of the M.E. church officiating . . . She leaves one daughter, Mrs. Orrin Catlin with whom she lived . . . She will be greatly missed in her home and by her friends and neighbors." Frances, Zipporah, and Orrin are all buried in Pineville Cemetery, as are many of her Rice family members.

William J. Sullivan – Co. I
b. August 27, 1835 Oswego, NY
d. June 13, 1915 Buffalo, Erie, NY
m. Mary E. Garahan (1840-December 15, 1902) December 8, 1864

NOTE: William's parents were Thomas (1810-?) and Margaret McKay Sullivan (1814-1900). He was a ship carpenter by occupation. Sullivan was captured on July 1, 1863 and paroled at an unknown date. He was promoted to second lieutenant on July 2, 1864 and discharged on July 14, 1865 at Washington, DC. A pension payment card listed rheumatism and heart disease as his disabilities. William was a member of Daniel D. Bidwell Post No. 9 GAR in Buffalo. He and Mary are buried in Holy Cross Cemetery, Lackawanna, Erie, NY.

Benjamin Taber – Co. F

b. 1820 Otsego County, NY

d. November 14, 1864 Salisbury, Rowan, NC

m. Susan Marie _____ (1823-October 25, 1893) *ca.* 1840

NOTE: Benjamin was the son of Joseph (1791-*post* 1874) and Elizabeth Sherman Taber (1789-*post* 1874). He served in Co. B, 7th New York Cavalry from October 1861-March 1862. He attempted to enlist in the 110th but was sent to the 147th. In August 1863 he was in an invalid detachment and was discharged for "disability" on August 31, 1864 from a hospital in Philadelphia. Although that discharge was dated August 31st, he enlisted in Co. K, 111th Regiment at Syracuse, NY on August 30, 1864 as a substitute for Torris F. Deyo. He was captured while on picket duty near Petersburg, VA on October 30, 1864 and died at Salisbury, NC on November 14, 1864, allegedly from disease. Susan died in Brewerton, Onondaga, NY but was buried in Union Settlement Cemetery, West Monroe, NY. Her gravestone also serves as a cenotaph for Benjamin although the DOD of December 14, 1865 is inaccurate. He is buried in Salisbury National Cemetery.

John Tanner – Co. E

b. 1844 Herkimer County, NY

d. December 12, 1864 Salisbury, Rowan, NC

m. ------

NOTE: John was the son of Charles (1821-1899) and Mary Hamer Jones Tanner (1815-1902). When and where he was captured is unknown but his official COD was "disease." He is buried in Salisbury National Cemetery.

Charles H. Taylor – Co. A

b. April 25, 1838 Theresa, Jefferson County, NY

d. February 14, 1919 Syracuse, Onondaga, NY

m. Mary Jane Sullivan (1849-October 3, 1942) August 6, 1869

NOTE: Charles' parents are unknown. Dates for him and Mary Jane vary widely. It appears that he originally attempted to enlist in the 110th but was sent to the 147th. According to *Registers of Officers and Enlisted Men* he was held captive by the Confederates for eight months although this is questionable since his muster roll card says he was captured on December 23, 1864 and discharged from the service on May 30, 1865. In 1890 he said he was troubled by deafness and rheumatism and was entirely deaf in his left ear. Charles and Mary Jane were living together in 1905 but by 1910 they were living apart. His obituary, published in *The Oswego Daily Palladium* February 14, 1919, 7, makes no mention of a wife. That they were still married, however, is corroborated by the fact that Mary Jane applied for and obtained a widow's pension. Mary Jane claimed in 1900 to be the mother of ten children, eight of whom were living. She and Charles, along with several of them, are buried in Rural Cemetery, Oswego Town. His gravestone erroneously says he died November 19, 1921.

James Taylor, Jr. – Co. A
b. April 16, 1845 Canada East
d. June 6, 1908 Chicago, Cook, IL
m. ?

NOTE: James was the son of James (1818-*ante* 1900) and Sophia Roberts Taylor (1821-1902). He was wounded in action during the battle of the Wilderness on May 5, 1864 and transferred to the VRC on March 20, 1865. According to *The Town Clerks' Registers*, he was wounded in the left foot. He was discharged on June 24, 1865 at Washington, DC and applied for a pension on September 16, 1865. His death certificate indicates he was a widower but I have located no wife. By 1870 the family was living in Chicago where James, a single man, worked as a bartender. He was still single in 1880. He is buried in Elmwood Cemetery and Mausoleum, River Grove, Cook, IL.

James Martin Taylor – Co. H
b. September 1844 West Monroe, NY
d. March 14, 1913 National Soldiers' Home, Bath, Steuben, NY
m. Ann Eliza Banning (February 1850-April 1, 1904) 1877

NOTE: James, son of Archibald (1801-1878) and Matilda Riker Taylor (1805-1880), mustered out with the regiment on June 7, 1865. By 1890 he and Ann Eliza were living in Oneida, Madison, NY. They had no children. His page in the Bath National Home register erroneously states he died in 1917. James and Ann Eliza are buried in Gilbert Mills Cemetery, Pennellville.

Samuel Taylor – Co. G
b. November 6, 1839 Oswego Town, NY
d. March 15, 1917 Oswego City, NY
m1. Martha J. Stone (1850-March 3, 1888) *ca.* 1866
m2. Phoebe Jane Parmelye (1859-June 29, 1929) 1888

NOTE: Taylor's parents were Samuel (1803-*ante* 1880) and Matilda (1806-*ante* 1880). According to *The Town Clerks' Registers*, an "endorsement on his discharge signed by his captain states that he took part in 15 battles and was not absent from his Reg't a day." He mustered out with the regiment on June 7, 1865. Upon his death *The Oswego Daily Times* March 16, 1917, 4 published the following: "Samuel Taylor, aged 77 years, one of the oldest and best known residents of the Seventh ward, died in his home, No. 22 Murray street, last evening following a short illness. Mr. Taylor was born in Oswego Town but has lived most of his life in this city. He was a Civil War veteran, having been a member of Co. D [*sic*], 147th Regiment, New York Volunteers. He was employed for 40 years as a starch maker in the Kingsford's Starch factory. He retired from that company's employ about five years ago . . . ." Samuel was a member of May Stacy Post No. 586 GAR, Oswego. He and his two wives are buried in Rural Cemetery, Oswego Town. A brother, Myron (1841-1864), served in the 12th NY Cavalry. He died of scurvy at Andersonville. His cenotaph can be seen in Rural Cemetery.

Sylvester J. Taylor – Co. E
b. April 2, 1834 Ellisburg, Jefferson, NY
d. July 3, 1863 Gettysburg, Adams, PA
m. Eliza A. Moore (1841-November 26, 1899) August 15, 1857

NOTE: Sylvester, son of Jeremiah (1811-1890) and Amanda Isabel Presley Taylor (1813-1889), saw prior service in Co. B, 7th New York Cavalry from September 1861-March 1862. He was killed in action. He and Eliza were the parents of three children for whom their mother obtained pensions. She never remarried and died in Salmon River, NY. An obituary appeared in *The Sandy Creek News* December 14, 1899: "Died November 26, 1899, Mrs. Eliza A. Taylor. She suffered a shock last August from which she never recovered. Her daughter Mrs. Ida Shinners had the constant care of her mother through her sickness. Her children all did what they could to make her last days happy ones . . . Mrs. Taylor had a host of friends who will sadly miss her. Her funeral was held from her home Wednesday at 11 o'clock. She was buried at Sandy Creek . . . ." Eliza is buried in Woodlawn Cemetery, Sandy Creek.

John Tester – Co. K
b. 1839 Kent, England
d. September 10, 1921 National Soldiers' Home, Bath, Steuben, NY
m. Julia Holman (August 1859-October 4, 1939) 1875

NOTE: John Tester was an alias used by Joseph Todman. An informative obituary appeared in *The* [Tonawanda] *Evening News* September 12, 1921, 1: "Joseph Todman, 73 years old, who served with the Union Army in the Civil War, died Saturday at the Soldiers' and Sailors' Home, Bath, N.Y. The body was brought to his home . . . this morning. The funeral will be held there Tomorrow afternoon at 2:30 o'clock. Rev.

Benjamin S. Sanderson of St. Mark's Episcopal church will officiate and burial will be in City Cemetery. For the past few years, Mr. Todman divided his time between the Bath institution and his Twin City home. He left his residence two months ago for Bath, intending to return to his home this fall. He had long been in feeble health but it was not until a short time before his death that his condition became serious. Mr. Todman was born in England. He came to America when a boy and, while still a young man, joined the 147th New York Volunteer Infantry at Oswego . . . With the exception of a few months in 1863, when he was laid up with a shell wound in his right leg, received during the Battle of Gettysburg, he served with his command until the end of the war . . . At the close of the war, Mr. Todman took up his residence in Buffalo. Thirty years ago, he came to North Tonawanda with his family and continued his residence here during the remainder of his life. He was a charter member of L. S. Payne Post, G.A.R. . . . ." An interesting editorial appeared in *The Evening News* September 13, 2: "The tall figure of Joseph Todman was a familiar figure in the Tonawandas for years. His civil war record included a serious wound in the battle of Gettysburgh. Grand Army veterans will miss a faithful comrade and numerous acquaintances lose a friend whose smile and cordial greeting will not soon be forgotten." Julia, also born in England, was a member of St. Mark's Episcopal Church and the Women's Relief Corps. She was buried beside her husband in the City Cemetery, Tonawanda.

William H. Thompson – Co. C
b. 1841 Richland, NY
d. August 15, 1871 Ferris, Montcalm, MI
m. Melissa Johnson (1842-October 6, 1909) September 8, 1862

NOTE: William was the son of James (1815-1888) and Martha Kelley Thompson (1813-1893). He contracted typhoid fever in the army, was transferred to the VRC on December 6, 1864, and discharged at Washington, DC on July 26, 1865. He and Melissa were the parents of John J. (1867-1954) and Mary J. (1869-1940). According to Melissa's pension application, William went to Michigan to establish a home and she traveled there with John and Mary, then two months old. At first they lived in Ionia City but soon moved to Ferris Township, where he died of scrofula, a form of tuberculosis which manifests itself in swellings on the patient's neck. On January 22, 1872 she applied for a pension, alleging William had contracted the disease in the army. Melissa and her children returned to New York State to be near her parents who lived in Ellisburg, Jefferson County. She married Frank Hurley, a barber, on September 2, 1875. A month later he was killed when a train ran over him near Sandy Creek. Melissa, who supported herself by working as a cook in various local hotels, married Edward Tompkins (1823-February 15, 1891), a tailor, as his second wife on April 8, 1876. He had served in Co. L, 10th NY HA from August 1864-June 1865. Apparently unknown to Melissa, Tompkins was never divorced from his first wife, Phoebe Aurelia Cardinelli (1825-December 27, 1913). In 1869 Phoebe had traveled to California to visit her family and Tompkins was supposed to follow her. Instead he remained in Sandy Creek. He died of an overdose of opium, and Melissa, who had lost her pension when she married Hurley, applied for a widow's pension as Tompkins' wife. After Phoebe's existence was discovered the application was rejected. On April 9, 1904 Melissa applied for and ultimately obtained William's pension as a remarried widow. She died in Syracuse at the home of her daughter. Melissa and Edwin Tompkins are buried in Woodlawn Cemetery, Sandy Creek. William's grave has not been located.

Walter B. Thorp – Co. A
b. 1839 Hannibal, NY
d. July 1, 1863 Gettysburg, Adams, PA
m. Edith Eliza Thorp (January 1843-March 29, 1915) ca. 1862

NOTE: Walter, son of Walter (1794-1867) and Eunice Thorp (1804-1877), was a harness maker. He served previously in the 8th US Army and in Co. I, 81st Regiment. He was KIA and his remains buried on the battlefield. He was a brother of Loren LaMonte Thorp (1837-1863), a member of the 110th Regiment who died of typho-malarial fever and diarrhea at Baton Rouge, LA. A cenotaph for them can be seen in Lewis Cemetery, Granby, NY. Edith, whose parents were Monson (1801-1888) and Lany Cooper Thorp (1815-1886), married George Beech Surdam (1834-1898) ca. 1869. He served in the 29th IN Infantry from 1861-1865. They are buried in Lake View Cemetery, Skaneateles, Onondaga, NY.

Warren Delos Tidd – Co. B
b. 1844 Fleming, Cayuga, NY
d. July 1, 1863 Gettysburg, Adams, PA
m. ------

NOTE: Warren was the son of Isaac Chauncey (?-1846) and Permilia Ryerson Tidd (1812-July 7, 1903). Also called Delos, he was a bookbinder for Oliphant and Co., in Oswego. His mother applied for his pension, claiming he was her primary support. Warren gave her $80.00 of his bounty money and sent home $10.00 per month from his army pay. Several surviving letters attest to his generosity and concern for not only his mother but also for two unmarried sisters. Although there were other sons in the family, it appears only Warren supported her. His brother Maurice (1839-1898) served in Co. D, 81st Regiment. John (1835-1904) was a member of Co. E, 9th NY HA.

Edward Toppings – Co. D

b. 1835 Upper Canada

d. May 11, 1865 Islington Lane General Hospital, Philadelphia, PA

m. Mary M. _____ (1835-January 11, 1915) *ca.* 1853

NOTE: Edward, whose parents are unknown, was a furnace man by occupation, according to the 1860 census. He was first wounded at Gettysburg on July 1, 1863. On June 18, 1864 he lost a leg during the ill-fated charge on Petersburg, but he died of smallpox. Originally buried in Mt. Moriah Cemetery, today he lies in Philadelphia National Cemetery. He and Mary, born in Ireland, were the parents of six children. Most of them died young and were buried in Mt. Adnah Cemetery, Fulton, NY. Only Mary (1855-November 14, 1920), William J. (1858-*post* 1915), and Kate (1861-*post* 1880) were still living in 1880. In 1871 their mother was still a widow but by 1875 she was married to Jeremiah "Jerry" Wilcox (1845-March 30, 1921). Jerry and Mary are buried in Mt. Adnah Cemetery.

Francis Monroe Towsley – Co. H

b. 1842 Williamstown, NY

d. June 7, 1923 Parish, NY

m1. Ann Jane McCullock (1848-*post* 1870) June 1, 1868

m2. Ida Frances Champine (December 1859-1929) 1881

m3. Carrie Martell Keeler (1865-February 16, 1939) August 11, 1908

NOTE: Francis, also known as Franklin and Frank, was the son of Thomas (1819-1907) and Catherine Shell Towsley (1819-1905). He mustered out with the regiment on June 7, 1865. In 1890, while living in Bath on Hudson, Rensselaer, NY, he claimed that he had been "injured in side by horse falling on him." He had a varied civilian career. He was living in New York City in 1868 where he married Ann Jane. He gave his occupation as undertaker. He and Ann lived in Orwell in 1870 where he was a farm laborer. In February 1875 he was appointed postmaster of Amboy Center, NY but he cannot be found on the 1875 New York census. He was a grocer in Bath on Hudson in 1900. The 1905 Albany city directory announced that he had moved to North Constantia. Ida, however, was living in Albany and working as a milliner. It is apparent that Ida and Francis parted company in 1905. She married Thomas E. Evans (1854-*post* 1910) on November 20, 1906. Ida is buried with her parents, Charles L. (1832-1902) and Esther Harrison Champine (1842-1929), in Beverwyck Cemetery, Rensselaer, NY. When Francis married Carrie he falsely stated he had two dead wives. Carrie was first married to James S. Keeler (1860-October 19, 1907). She died in the Philadelphia State Hospital. COD was arteriosclerosis and senile psychosis. Her body was shipped to Parish and she was buried beside Francis in Pleasant Lawn Cemetery. Francis' brother, Lorenzo (1846-1863), served in Co. D, 24th

NYV from November 1862-May 13, 1863 when he was transferred to the 76th Regiment. He was killed on July 1, 1863 at Gettysburg, PA. The 1865 New York census erroneously assigned him to the 147th Regiment.

Herman F. Trapp – Co. G

b. August 21, 1836 Prussia

d. January 15, 1886 Oswego Town, NY

m. Elvina Wacholz (1847-December 25, 1926) *ca.* 1867

NOTE: Herman, son of Martin (?-?) and Louisa Knapp Trapp (?-?), was wounded in the hand and leg at Gettysburg on July 1, 1863 and was discharged for "disability" in September. Although his entry in *The Town Clerks' Registers*, under the name "Hammond Tropp," says he left the service on November 15, 1863, the earlier date of September is more correct since he applied for a pension on September 11th. He and Elvina are buried in Riverside Cemetery, Scriba.

Henry A. Trask – Co. D

b. 1838 Herkimer County, NY

d. May 3, 1909 Volney, NY

m. Mary Ann Conroy (September 1838-October 3, 1920) 1858

NOTE: Henry, a farmer, was the son of James (1806-1892) and Sally M. Knight Trask (1811-1884). He mustered out of the regiment on June 7, 1865. He and Mary Ann were the parents of at least seven children. She died in Bridgeport, CT at the home of her daughter, Mrs. R. J. Hoff. Her body was shipped home and buried beside her husband in Mt. Pleasant Western Cemetery, Volney.

George W. Tryon – Co. E

b. 1841 Madison, County, NY

d. July 1, 1863 Gettysburg, Adams, PA

m. ------

NOTE: The son of Peter (1813-1880) and Mary Hungerford Tryon (1808-1864), George was first considered MIA but was ultimately declared KIA. He was erroneously listed as "deserted" in *The Town Clerks' Registers* and also in Johnson's *History of Oswego County*, 386. He was buried in Gettysburg National Cemetery and in July 1866 his father successfully applied for a pension. George's sister was Adelia Tryon (1834-June 4, 1898), wife of Charles B. Philbrick (1825-September 7, 1890), who enlisted in the 147th Regiment and deserted at Tenallytown, DC on November 22, 1862.

Ira J. Turner – Co. E

b. May 1, 1817 Williamstown, Berkshire, MA
d. January 30, 1890 Elk, Nobles, MN
m. Sally M. Meyers (1821-*ca.* 1878) April 13, 1843

NOTE: According to *The Town Clerks' Registers*, Ira was the son of William (?-?) and Betsey E. Marks Turner (?-?). He transferred to the VRC on September 26, 1863 and was probably discharged shortly thereafter since he applied for a pension on March 14, 1864. In 1865 Sally said she was the mother of nine children. Arthur P. Rose's *An Illustrated History of Nobles County, Minnesota*, 378-9 features a biography of Ira's time in Minnesota: "Ira Turner (1817-1890) was one of the pioneer settlers of Elk township, in which he resided from 1872 until his death eighteen years later. Mr. Turner was born in Massachusetts May 1, 1817. Early in life he moved to Oswego county, N.Y., where he resided until his removal to Nobles county in 1872, being engaged in farming and other occupations. There he was married April 13, 1843, to Miss Sallie M. Myers, who died about 1878. Mr. Turner was a veteran of the civil war, having enlisted at Oswego, N.Y., in the 47th [*sic*] New York volunteers in 1862. He served fifteen months, taking part in the battle of Gettysburg and other noted engagements. He came west in May, 1872, and took as a homestead claim the northwest quarter of section 18, Elk township. There he lived and engaged in agricultural pursuits until his death on Jan. 30, 1890. He united with the Methodist church in 1850 and continued a member until his death." Sally's exact DOD cannot be established and gravesites for her and Ira have not been located. Their son Franklin C. (1858-1929) and wife Emma (1860-1958) are buried in Worthington Cemetery, Worthington, Nobles, MN but there is no evidence the parents are also there.

William Upcraft – Co. A

b. 1833 England
d. June 1, 1864 Cold Harbor, Hanover, VA
m. Charlotte Blythe (1844-September 1880) September 10, 1858

NOTE: William, son of James (1799-1874) and Ann Manchett Upcraft (1807-?), immigrated with his family to the United States in December 1854. The family settled in Sterling, Cayuga, NY. The date and site of his death were, according to Records and Profiles, Gettysburg, PA on July 1, 1863. A notation in *The Town Clerks' Registers* claims he died at Spotsylvania on May 27, 1864. Charlotte's deposition of October 13, 1865 placed his death at the battle of the Wilderness on May 5, 1864. That he died at Cold Harbor is proven by *The Adjutant-General's Report* and corroborated by information located in his pension file. He and Charlotte were the parents of Sarah Ann (1860-1949) and Mary Jane (1863-December 9, 1961). Charlotte married Jonathan Neal (1845-February 1911) November 27, 1864. He served in the 9th NY HA. Following her mother's death, Mary Jane married Jonathan in 1881. William's gravesite has not been identified. Charlotte and Jonathan are buried in North Wolcott Cemetery, Wayne, NY. Mary Jane, who died in Clearwater, FL at the age of 98, is also buried there.

Joseph A. Upton – Co. E
b. 1838 Sandy Creek, NY
d. January 20, 1863 Armory Square Hospital, Washington, DC
m. ------

NOTE: Joseph was the son of Elijah (1794-1863) and Nancy Vincent Upton (1802-1872). According to *Deaths of Volunteers*, his COD was rubella. He was originally buried in the Soldiers' and Airmen's Home Cemetery in Washington, DC but on January 27, 1863 his body was exhumed and sent to Sandy Creek. Today he lies in Scripture Cemetery, Sandy Creek, with his parents.

Willard Ure – Co. F
b. 1838 Palermo, NY
d. January 3, 1886 Mexico, NY
m1. Mary Jane Burt (1844-ca. 1879) 1860
m2. Anna "Annie" Albee (December 1858-April 21, 1924) 1880

NOTE: Willard, son of James (1790-1850) and Polly Seeley Ure (1805-1865), was the brother of Albert Ure (1829-1893) who served in the 110th Regiment. According to *The Town Clerks' Registers*, Willard was wounded in the hip at Gettysburg on July 1, 1863. He was transferred to the VRC at an unspecified date and discharged at Washington, DC on June 12, 1865. *The Mexico Independent* January 6, 1886 reported his death: "Willard Ure, who has been ailing for two years, died of consumption Sunday last." He is buried in Clifford Cemetery. To date Mary Jane's grave has not been located. Annie married Lorenzo H. All (1841-November 4, 1920) in 1891 as his second wife. He had served in the 21st Independent Batt. NY LA. They are buried in Mexico Village Cemetery.

John Valliere – Co. B
b. 1838 ?
d. ? ?
m. ?

NOTE: Very little can be learned about this soldier. His muster roll card says nothing about birthplace or occupation. His entry in *The Town Clerks' Registers* spells his name Vallier but gives no information. His muster roll card states he was absent, sick, at the time the regiment mustered out. According to *Records and Profiles*, he survived the war but such may not be the case.

Walter Evander Van Alstyne – Co. B
b. 1844 Scriba, NY
d. April 14, 1924 Oswego City, NY
m1. Lydia "Liddie" Jane Cole (1843-January 7, 1907) *ca.* 1875
m2. Ada Hinman (1842-July 31, 1914) May 27, 1911
m3. Virginia Sarah Proud Blair (1850-May 3, 1933) July 5, 1915

NOTE: Walter, son of John (1819-*post* 1865) and Marinda Read Van Alstyne (1822-*post* 1865), saw service in the 81st Regiment from September 1861-April 1862. He served with the 147th until discharged on June 9, 1865. His obituary which appeared in *The Oswego Daily Palladium* April 15, 1924 makes no mention of his time with the latter organization: "Walter E. VanAlstyne, 80, Civil War veteran and former Oswego city letter carrier, died late Monday afternoon at his home, 213 West Fourth street, after an illness of several months. However, he had been confined to his bed only two weeks prior to his death. Mr. VanAlstyne was a native of Scriba and when the call for volunteers came at the outbreak of the Civil War in 1861 he responded and enlisted in the 81st New York Volunteers, this being the second Oswego county regiment in the field, the 24th alone preceding it. Serving all through the war and being engaged in many battles of that memorable struggle, Mr. VanAlstyne returned at its close to Oswego. He was appointed a letter carrier many years ago and served until he had reached the age of retirement. His health was never particularly robust and he had not been actively employed since retiring from the Government service. Mr. VanAlstyne was an organizer of Post J. D. O'Brian, No. 65, G.A.R. . . . and he was also a member of the First Baptist church. The deceased is survived by his wife and a sister, Mrs. George W. Allen of Oswego. By the death of Mr. VanAlstyne but one member of the 81st Regiment remains in this city, Dr. H. B. Ensworth, the veterinary." Lydia died after a "long illness." Ada succumbed after being sick for three months. Virginia's first husband was Elbridge G. Blair (1843-1905), a veteran of the 21st Independent Batt. NY LA and Co. F, 24th Regiment. He is buried in Riverside Cemetery, Scriba, as are Walter, Lydia, Ada, and Virginia.

Elijah Van Auken – Co. E
b. 1840 Boylston, NY
d. 1884 Boylston, NY
m. ------

NOTE: Elijah was the son of Peter P. (1819-1907) and Mary Ann Orlup Van Auken (1818-1898). He was wounded on May 5, 1864 at the battle of the Wilderness, transferred to the VRC on January 10, 1865, and finally discharged on June 29, 1865. An exact DOD and COD have not been discovered. According to his father's FAG entry, Peter and Mary Ann were divorced. Peter died October 12, 1907 after a botched attempt to commit suicide. The elderly man tried to hang himself and when that did not work he cut his throat with a jack knife. Elijah, his parents, and several other family members are buried in Boylston-Sandy Creek Wesleyan Cemetery, Lacona, NY.

George Washington Van Delinder – Co. D
b. 1820 Washington County, NY
d. February 19, 1891 Hitchcock, Beadle, SD
m. Laura Jane Dumas (January 11, 1832-April 10, 1912) May 14, 1854

NOTE: George was the son of Abram (1793-1863) and Elizabeth Chapman Van Delinder (1792-1889). He mustered out with the regiment on June 7, 1865. After the war, the family moved west, settling in South Dakota. He and Laura, the parents of numerous children, are buried in Altoona Cemetery, Hitchcock, SD. George was a brother of Jacob Van Delinder (1829-1881) who was a member of the 110th Regiment.

Daniel Vandewarker – Co. K
b. 1833 Onondaga County, NY
d. May 5, 1864 Wilderness, VA
m. Minerva _____ (1829-post 1860) ca. 1856

NOTE: Daniel's father is unknown but his mother was Maria C. Reede Vandewarker Eastland (1812-1886). He and Minerva were the parents of Josephine (1857-post 1860). Because Maria applied for her son's pension in 1882 I infer that Minerva and Josephine were deceased. I have located no pension applications for them. Other documents such as entries in *Town Clerks' Registers* or *Records of Officers and Enlisted Men* are also lacking. Under the surname Vanderwalker, Daniel is listed as "killed in battle" in *Deaths of Volunteers*. His gravesite is unknown.

Abraham Vandish – Co. B
b. 1815 Plattsburgh, Clinton, NY
d. October 28, 1894 Oswego City, NY
m. Eveline _____ (1817-April 2, 1900) ca. 1839

NOTE: Abraham was the son of Abraham (?-?) and Mary C. Carlton Vandish (?-?). Although he claimed to have been born in 1818 in 1862, subsequent documents prove conclusively that his DOB was 1815. He was discharged for "disability" at

Belle Plain, VA on February 3, 1863 and applied for a pension on March 9ᵗʰ although in 1890 he claimed no disability. According to *The Town Clerks' Registers*, he was "disabled by accident." His death elicited the following obituary in *The Oswego Daily Palladium* October 29, 1894: "Abraham Vandish, for fifty-five years a resident of this city, died at his home, No. 40 East Mercer street, yesterday, aged seventy-six years and eight months. No man in the Second ward had more friends or was more respected and honored by friends and acquaintances than Mr. Vandish. In the days when the war clouds were blackest he shouldered a musket and went to the front as a member of the gallant 147ᵗʰ New York Volunteers. When the war had been concluded Mr. Vandish returned to Oswego and resided here up to his death . . . ." Abraham and Eveline are buried in Riverside Cemetery, Scriba.

David G. Van Dusen – Co. D
b. 1830 Onondaga County, NY
d. July 1, 1863 Gettysburg, Adams, PA
m. Rosena Arnold (September 4, 1834-December 27, 1905) January 1, 1857

NOTE: David was the son of Mark (1788-1869) and Mary Cline Van Dusen (1793-1853). He and Rosena, married in Hannibal, NY, had no children. His pension file notes he was KIA. Rosena married George Henry Salmon (1830-1906) on September 15, 1868. Her death was marked by a lengthy obituary in *The Fulton Times* January 3, 1906: "'Sleep sweetly, tender heart, in peace,/Sleep, holy spirit, blessed soul,/While the stars burn, the moons increase/And the great ages onward roll.' The death of Mrs. Rosene A. Salmon, Dec. 27, was a sad reality to her many friends in Fulton and elsewhere. She was stricken on Christmas day with fatal illness and lived only two days. The deceased had prepared with loving hands the Christmas cheer; packages were all arranged and labeled for her loved ones, and a stocking filled for the dear little grandson whom she so tenderly loved and was never to see again on this earth . . . Mrs. Salmon had been in delicate health for many years, but she was never content except her hands were active in service for someone. In her church, in her home, where she was always a sweet, patient, ministering spirit, and in her association with others in literary pursuits, 'None knew her but to love her;/None named her out but to praise.' With all her delicacy of health her life was a most useful one and filled with good cheer. She always saw the silver lining to the cloud; was never discouraged, but hopeful and young in her feelings. No reader of human character ever looked upon the sweet, modest face of Mrs. Salmon without believing that purity of soul reigned supreme within. Truly she was one of the best of earth and one of those rare women – loyal, consistent, Christian, charitable, conscientious and good. She had a most unassuming and retiring nature, and the hallowed atmosphere of a perfectly pure life, unspotted by the world, shone in every lineament of her face. There was no room in her life but for thoughts born of God; she was blessed among women, for no one doubted her integrity. She was always interested in literary work and very capable with the pen. Many choice poems and rich, pure thoughts in prose found their way to her friends. Her life was quiet and uneventful, but she filled her allotted sphere in a manner which must have been acceptable to the 'Master.' She was the bright star of her home and was constantly dispensing the 'little, nameless, unremembered acts of kindness and of love' all about her. We believe she was fitted for the great temple above, and that our Heavenly Father had need of her, and so He called her from us all. Mrs. Rosene A. Salmon was born Sept. 4, 1834, in Fulton, and was married Jan. 1, 1856 [sic], to Lieutenant D. G. Vandusen, who was killed in the battle of Gettysburg . . . Mrs. Salmon was a member of the First M. E. Church, and while her health permitted was active in every good work. She was a member of the Woman's Foreign Missionary Society and recording secretary of the same for many years. She was the president of the Chautauqua Circle when it was first organized in Fulton, and filled the position with great honor. Mrs. Salmon was also a charter member of the Fortnightly Shakespeare Club, the members of which have been in close association with her for eighteen years and well know she possessed an intellect of unusual order. She was always an inspiration at the meetings and we shall never cease to miss her. No one can fill her place. She had a little niche in each heart (all her own) which time can never take from us. We deplore her loss and shall always cherish a blessed memory of her . . . Funeral services were held on Friday afternoon at the late home, and were conducted by the Rev. John Richards . . . ." George died nine months later after suffering a stroke. He and Rosena are buried in Mt. Adnah Cemetery, Fulton.

William Henry Vannetten – Co. G

b. September 16, 1846 Oswego Town, NY
d. December 3, 1915 Boardman, Kalkaska, MI
m. Mary Elizabeth Vader (July 21, 1855-October 20, 1937) 1875

NOTE: William was the son of Peter (1822-*post* 1858) and Magdalena "Lany" Marie Shutts Vannetten (1822-1894). His surname was variously spelled. I use that found on his gravestone. Although he claimed to be 18 when he enlisted, *The Town Clerks' Registers*, other documents, and his gravestone confirm he was born in 1846. He was wounded at the battle of Gravelly Run on March 31, 1865 and discharged on June 14, 1865. He applied for a pension on June 30th and in 1890 he claimed he had suffered a "gunshot wound in left leg" and was discharged on a surgeon's certificate. In 1866 he enlisted in Co. K, 4th US Infantry but deserted. After being apprehended he was dishonorably discharged on December 22, 1872 at Louisville, KY. William died of heart disease. Mary married John Thomson (1842-1930) on November 11, 1917 as his third wife. She died in Grand Rapids, Kent, MI of a cerebral hemorrhage. She and her two husbands are buried in Boardman Township Cemetery. William's brother, Edward (1848-1922), served in the 2nd NY HA from 1864-1865.

Charles F. Vauvilliez – Co. A

b. 1838 Sharon, Schoharie, NY
d. February 17, 1908 Ilion, Herkimer, NY
m. Mary Brown (1851-June 12, 1883) *ca.* 1875

NOTE: Charles was the son of Francois "Francis" (1815-1904) and Mary Vauvilliez (1813-1871). His surname was variously spelled. His muster roll card contains the notation that he was "reported killed, since returned to Annapolis, Md. as a prisoner of war – no discharge furnished." *The Adjutant-General's Report* stated that no information concerning his capture and parole was available, but letters published in local newspapers in 1865 amply reveal the story. A letter to his parents from Captain John McKinlock, dated February 9, 1865 and published in *The Oswego Commercial Times* February 15, 1865, announced sad news: "It is with most painful feelings that I am under the necessity of transmitting to you the heart-rending tidings of the death of your son, who was killed on the 6th instant, while gallantly urging his men to follow him in a charge made by our forces upon the works of the enemy at Hatcher's Run. He was wounded in two places, the first taking effect in the right side, passing through the body and coming out in the region of the heart; the second striking back of the left ear and passing out of the mouth. Every effort was made to secure his body, but in vain. Our forces were so hotly pursued that all attempts to recover it proved futile. We would gladly have forwarded his remains to Oswego that you might have had the consolation of gazing once more upon those features so dear to you even if they were cold in death, but circumstances would not permit. I know not that anything I can say will give any consolation to you who so dearly loved the departed one, but may God in His infinite mercy give you fortitude to bear up under this painful affliction. It is the will of Him who holdeth all our lives in His hand, and to His will we bow . . . ." McKinlock's sympathetic letter of condolence was a bit premature, as another letter, written by John V. Stouffar of Dunbar, Fayette, PA, to Charles' father, dated March 13, 1865 and published in *The Oswego Commercial Times* March 16[?], 1865, demonstrates: "By the request of C. F. Vauvilliez, who was a prisoner with me in Petersburg, I take the liberty to address a few lines to you to let you know that he is living and doing as well as could be expected. He was wounded through the right breast but was getting much better and was able to walk about and expected would be able to be sent to Richmond for parole in a few days. You need not be uneasy about him for he is well taken care of and expected to be home in a few days . . . ." Charles returned to Oswego, married, and became the father of three daughters. In 1890 he said his disability was a "crippled arm and right shoulder." He spent several months in the Bath National Solders' Home in 1906 and 1907 and his admission form contains interesting details, among them the notations that he had no near relatives and was unable to read and write. An obituary appearing in *The Ilion Citizen* February 20, 1908 completes the story: "Monday morning at the home of his daughter Mrs. Howard E. Beach in this village, occurred the death of Charles F. Vauvilliez after an illness of ten days. Paralysis was the cause of death. Deceased was born Mapletown, Schoharie County, October 3, 1838. He afterwards moved to Oswego, where the greater part of his life was spent and where he worked at his trade, being a cooper by occupation, but for the past four years he had made his home with his daughter in this village. He was a member of the 147th Regiment . . . The funeral services were held privately Tuesday evening from the home of his daughter and the remains taken Wednesday to his former home in Oswego for burial." Another obituary, published in *The Oswego Daily Times* February 18, 1908, 8, provided more details: ". . . Mr. Vauvilliez was a cooper by trade and for a great many years he was employed at Kingsford's. He has lived in Ilion for the past

Although reported dead after the battle of Hatcher's Run, Charles Vauvilliez lived a good long life.
Author's Collection

five years. He served throughout the war and was wounded at Hatch's [sic] Run, Va., with Captain David Welsh of this city." Charles and Mary are buried in Rural Cemetery, Oswego Town.

Peter John Vinney – Co. H
b. April 1844 Hastings, NY
d. February 11, 1913 Syracuse, Onondaga, NY
m. Jane "Jenny" Rego (1848-September 10, 1928) 1868

NOTE: Peter's parents were John Peter (1801-1866) and Jana Glode Piguet Vinney (1805-1855). The family surname was variously spelled. I use that on the gravestone. Peter was reported MIA on July 1, 1863 and his muster roll card shows he was still MIA in August 1863. He applied for a pension in April 1882 but did not receive a certificate. There is no widow's claim, either, and it well may be that Peter simply walked away from the war. He was a member of the Knights of the Golden Eagle, a fraternal organization designed to assist members in finding employment and offering aid to the unemployed. He and Jane both belonged to Waseka Tribe No. 106, Degree of Pocahontas, the female arm of the Improved Order of Red Men, whose mission was patriotic and charitable. Peter's COD is unknown but Jane died after suffering a stroke. They are buried in Saint Francis Cemetery, Little France, NY.

Frank Virginier – Co. A
b. 1829 Canada East
d. July 1, 1863 Gettysburg, Adams, PA
m. Catherine LeReaux (1836-January 5, 1908) *ca.* 1850

NOTE: Frank Virginier was an alias for Frank Visinot though by 1860 he was spelling his name Virginia. His remains were buried on the field. He was erroneously assigned to the 184th Regiment in *The Town Clerks' Registers*. Catherine, whose maiden name is also spelled LeRoy, married Louis Bouverain (1830-1869) *ca.* 1867 as his second wife. He was killed in November 1869 when the boiler in his railroad engine exploded. Henceforth, she used Virginia and Bouverain interchangeably but the New York State Death Index uses the latter surname, as does her obituary which appeared in *The Syracuse Post-Standard* January 5, 1908: "Mrs. Catherine Virginia Bouverain of No. 73 East Cayuga street died suddenly this morning of heart failure. She appeared to be in as good health as usual when she retired about 11 o'clock last evening after having busied with domestic duties. When her daughter entered the room this morning to arouse her it was found that she had passed away. Coroner Vowinkel was called and after an examination stated that death had resulted several hours before from heart failure. Mrs. Bouverain was born in Leschaine, Canada, seventy-four years ago, but had been a resident of this city ever since she was 12 years old. She was the widow of Frank Virginia, who was a member of the 147th Regiment, New York Volunteers . . . ." In 1900 Catherine said she was the mother of two, both of whom were living. They were Flora (1852-1924) and Frances Rosa Josephine (1862-*post* 1908). On the 1855 New York census, however, another daughter, Philomen, age 5, appears. This may be Flora, even though the birth dates are different. Catherine and Frances are buried in St. Peter's Cemetery, Oswego, and a cenotaph for Frank may also be seen there.

Frederich Vogelgsang – Co. D
b. 1822 Germany
d. August 3, 1890 Volney, NY
m. Margaretha Barbara Eder (June 6, 1828-October 18, 1910) July 1850

NOTE: Frederich, son of Johann (1795-?) and Christine Burr Vogelgsang (1795-?), immigrated to the United States in June 1844. He was discharged from the army for "disability" on May 25, 1865 although in 1890 he claimed nothing. *The Rome Daily Sentinel* September 15, 1890 alludes to his manner of death. His son Charles (1855-1922) had recently been attacked by a boar as he was attempting to clean out the pen. The writer noted that a month earlier Vogelsgsang's father, unnamed, had been killed by an "infuriated bull." Frederich is buried in Mt. Adnah Cemetery, Fulton. Margaretha moved to California and lived with her daughter, Mary. She is buried in Plainsburg Cemetery, Merced, Merced, CA.

Allen Sanford Vorce – Co. F
b. 1840 Mexico, NY
d. May 5, 1864 Wilderness, VA
m. ------

NOTE: Allen was the son of Joseph (1810-1876) and Clarissa Douglas Vorce (1815-1878). He transferred from Co. F to Co. B on October 17, 1862. One entry in *Deaths of Volunteers* places him in the 147th Regiment PA and says his death was "not stated." Another entry, under Vorse, correctly dates his death to May 5, 1864 at Wilderness, VA, saying he was "killed in battle." An obituary written by W. C. Johnson appeared in *The Mexico Independent* June 23, 1864: "Among those noble men who fell on the 5th of May last, at the Wilderness battle, members of the 147th regiment, N.Y.S., from our intimate acquaintance and high esteem and sympathy with the afflicted family, we notice particularly the name of Allen S. Vorce, aged 24 years. The subject of this brief notice nobly entered the service under Capt. C. Hartshorn, Co. F, Aug. 31, 1862. Fought at Chancellorsville and the bloody field at Gettysburg, and taken prisoner and paroled. I speak what I do know when I say Allen was a young man whose memory may be cherished with satisfaction and example imitated with safely. May the consolation connected with the reflection that a son and brother has concluded a well spent life by and honorable death, soothe their crushed and bleeding hearts. And may they learn from this the uncertainty of all early hopes and attachments, and set their affections on the only object in the universe who is infinitely worthy." His father's application for a pension filed on October 29, 1866 was rejected. His mother was successful in her attempt in 1868. She claimed that her husband had been a diabetic for ten years and was permanently disabled. They had depended on Allen for support for several years prior to his enlistment. Joseph and Clarissa are buried in Mexico Primitive Cemetery.

Joseph Walker – Co. K
b. 1841 Oswego, NY
d. May 5, 1864 Wilderness, VA
m. ------

NOTE: Joseph, a cooper by occupation, was the son of Francis (1818-1887) and Elizabeth Gordon Walker (1815-1872), both Irish immigrants. He was KIA and his remains were buried on the field. In 1878 Francis applied for and obtained a pension. He and Elizabeth are buried in St Paul's Cemetery, Oswego City. Joseph's brother, Thomas (1846-1899), served in the 21st NY Cavalry from 1863-1865.

James Wallace – Co. I
b. 1839 Oswego, NY
d. *post* 1870 ?
m. ?

NOTE: James, a ship carpenter, was the son of John (?-*ante* 1850) and Esther McKenny Wallace (1815-*post* 1864). In 1855 his widowed mother was the head of a household of six children, all of whom had been born in Oswego County. James was captured on July 1, 1863 at Gettysburg and paroled at an unknown date. He was wounded at the battle of the Wilderness and discharged on February 14, 1865 "in the field" for disability. He applied for a pension on March 29, 1866 and last appears on the 1870 census living with his brother Henry (1834-?) in Oswego. There the trail ends. A man named James Wallace is buried in the City Plot of Riverside Cemetery, Scriba, having been removed from the Fifth Ward Cemetery on November 15, 1889, but no dates are available, making corroboration impossible.

Levi M. Wallace – Co. E
b. 1839 Sandy Creek, NY
d. June 27, 1863 Campbell Hospital, Washington, DC
m. ------

NOTE: Levi was the son of Elvin (1808-1881) and Sally Bennett Wallace (1806-1896). His DOD is erroneously given on his muster roll card. He succumbed to typhoid fever. Originally buried in the

Originally buried in Washington, DC, Levi's body today lies with his family in Woodlawn Cemetery, Sandy Creek.
Author's Collection

Soldiers' and Airmen's National Home Cemetery, his body was disinterred and sent to Sandy Creek. He is buried with his mother and father in Woodlawn Cemetery. Two brothers served in Co. G, 24th Regiment. William (1834-1909) was discharged for "disability" on December 19, 1862. Asahel (1832-1879) mustered out with the regiment on May 29, 1863. They too are buried in Woodlawn Cemetery.

Norton Ward – Co. A
b. 1818 Canada West
d. July 25, 1864 Petersburg, VA
m. Hannah Smith (1821-September 13, 1878) July 6, 1846

NOTE: Norton, whose parents are unidentified, was discharged from the 147th on May 7, 1863 for "disability." On January 5, 1864, again claiming he had been born in 1818, he enlisted in the 24th NY Cavalry and on January 19th was mustered into Co. K. He was shot by a Confederate soldier as he sat in his tent on the evening of July 25th and died shortly thereafter. In *Deaths of Volunteers* he is called Martin Ward. He left behind a widow and eight children, only one of whom was over 16 years of age. The family was living in Sterling, Cayuga, NY in 1865. Hannah is buried in Sterling Center Cemetery.

Andrew Sylvester Warner – regimental colonel
b. January 12, 1819 Vernon, Oneida, NY
d. December 26, 1887 Sandy Creek, NY
m1. Mary Elizabeth Greene (1823-June 22, 1859) October 19, 1842
m2. Chloe Monroe (1840-February 14, 1916) October 3, 1861

NOTE: Col. Warner was the son of Andrew (1791-1843) and Elizabeth Clark Young Warner (1794-1866). He was instrumental in forming the 147th Regiment and became its first colonel. He was compelled to resign his commission in February 1863 because he had contracted typhoid fever and was unable to carry out his duties. Upon his death *The Sandy Creek News* December 29, 1887, 1 published a long, laudatory obituary which is excerpted here: "Most of our readers, we suppose, have learned before this of the death of our honored townsman, Col. Andrew S. Warner. This event took place on Monday morning of this week, between two and three o'clock. It was altogether unexpected, though the colonel had been in feeble health for several months . . . On Saturday he went to Pulaski, and returned in fair condition. On Sunday and Sunday night, when he was a little restless, there was no indication that he was so near his end. The probability is that he died simply from the failure of the heart, and that he passed away in unconsciousness. He had often expressed the wish that his death might be so, and his wish was granted him. Col. Warner was so well known to all our people; he had lived here so long; he had been so prominent and active in our local affairs, that it seems almost unnecessary for us to offer any facts concerning him now . . . He came with his parents to Sandy Creek in March 1837, and settled where his home has been ever since. He was married first to Mary E. Greene, daughter of Henry K. Green, of New Haven, N.Y., October 19, 1842. Five children were born of this marriage . . . His wife died June 22d, 1859. He then married, on the 8th of October, 1861, Miss Chloe Monroe, daughter of Barnabas Monroe, of this town. Of this marriage five children were born . . . Col. Warner always took an interest in political affairs, and from the formation of the Republican party he was usually identified with it, although he sympathized in the liberal movement which brought out Mr. Greeley as a candidate for the presidency in 1872. During that time – in 1874 – he ran for congress against the regular Republican candidate, Hon. Wm. H. Baker, but was defeated, although he polled a large vote. He was a member of assembly in 1855 and 1856, and of the state senate in 1860 and 1861. He was also for a short time an officer in the United States service during the war of the Rebellion, being colonel of the one hundred and forty-seventh regiment of New York volunteers when it was organized and was sent to the front. He was compelled to resign this position on account of ill health. Col. Warner, as our readers are well aware, was a man of unusual force and energy of character. He had abundant strength and vitality. Then he was possessed of a powerful will. And so he was well fitted to be a leader of men. And a leader he was. In all his political work he showed this. And more. He was always ready for and always capable of hard and earnest work. But more. Although, no doubt, he made some enemies in the many contests of political life, he made also very many warm and attached friends. He will be missed by the community where he has dwelt so long, and he will be doubly missed in his home . . . We are sure that throughout our town there is a general feeling of sorrow because of the colonel's death." Another obituary, appearing in *The Pulaski Democrat* December 29, 1887, was equally complimentary: ". . . He was a man of great energy, decision, activity and strength of character. He took a prominent part in every public enterprise, and after the breaking out of the war of the Rebellion was active in organizing the 147th N.Y.S. Volunteers, of which he became the Colonel . . . As a neighbor and citizen he was kind, faithful, and true to his convictions. He was every inch a man, with as few foibles as fall to the lot of mortals. We leave to others to declare what he was as a brother, a husband, a father. There in that inner circle where he was best known will he be the most sadly missed." Col. Warner was a member of J. B. Butler Post No. 111 GAR which published Resolutions in *The Pulaski Democrat* January 26, 1888, a portion of which is quoted here: ". . . Resolved, That we tender this expression of sympathy and kindly feeling to his bereaved family in their deep affliction, and while we remember the word 'Rejoice with them that do rejoice,' we need not the injunction

to 'weep with them that weep.' . . . ." *The Sandy Creek News* October 4, 1934 published an extensive sketch of Colonel Warner which fills in details of his life: ". . . In
April, 1837 he came with his father's family from Vernon and settled on the 'Warner
crossroad' four miles southwest of the village on the farm which later he owned, and
which he tilled during the rest of his lifetime . . . In those early days much of the land
was still covered with a dense forest, and with tireless energy he cleared the land,
built many farm buildings, and increased the acreage of the large homestead. He was
a progressive and successful farmer and sustained the reputation of a business man
of superior qualifications. He had the first mowing machine in his section. His large
orchards were noted for the variety of fruit. His live stock and products of the loom
were awarded many prizes at the local fairs. Few men in Oswego County led a more
active life and none were more closely identified with the interests which contributed to the prosperity of a community. Andrew S. Warner early enlisted in the state
militia . . . In politics he was originally a Freesoiler, persistently opposing everything
calculated to further the extension of the institution of slavery, and he was a delegate
to the Buffalo Convention in 1848 which nominated Martin Van Buren for the
Presidency. In this year also he was elected one of the three Superintendents of the
Poor of Oswego County. He early supported with characteristic zeal and determina-
tion the organization and the great cardinal doctrines of the Republican party. In
1855 and again in 1856 he was elected a member of the New York State Assembly,
and he served in the State Senate during the exciting years of 1860 and 1861, just
prior to the Civil War. His conduct in the legislature was characterized by diligence
and promptness in the discharge of the duties of his office. His efforts as a debater
were more distinguished for their plain, practical common sense than for flights of
poetry or flowers of rhetoric. His conduct commanded the approval of his constitu-
ency and he acquired a strong political influence throughout Northern New York . . .
In person he was a large, broad shouldered man with light blue eyes, black hair and
beard and, though somewhat diffident, was kind and sociable toward those with
whom he came in contact. He never used liquor or tobacco in any form. He attended
the Congregational Church as his ancestors did before him. He was a member of the
Sandy Creek Lodge of F. & A. M. and a member of J. B. Butler Post, G. A.R. . . . ."
Chloe's obituary in *The Sandy Creek News* February 17, 1916, 4 described an interesting, intelligent woman: "The news of the sad death of Mrs. Chloe Warner at the
home of her son, Dr. Wilbert C. Warner in Cleveland, Ohio, Feb. 14, 1916, saddened
many a heart throughout eastern Oswego county where she was well known. Her
going severs one more tie which connects the early history of the town with the present. Mrs. Warner was a daughter of Mr. and Mrs. Barnabas Monroe. Their hospitable
home on the ridge a mile north of Lacona is still owned in the family, and has recently been restored. Here on October 3, 1861, she was married to the Hon. A. S.

Warner . . . About half her life Mrs. Warner was a resident of the town of Sandy Creek where she was born, though for the past few years she has made her home in Pulaski, and was spending the present winter with her son in Cleveland where she died of pneumonia, aged 77 years. The remains were brought to Pulaski, where the funeral was held Wednesday at 1 o'clock, at the Congregational church . . . The Monroe family were prominent members of the Sandy Creek Congregational church and till after her late husband's death Mrs. Warner led an active life, being prominently identified with the work of the church and community. The Warner home in the western part of the town was counted one of the most hospitable and attractive . . . ." In addition to being a GAR member, Warner was also a member of Sandy Creek Lodge #564 F & A M. The colonel and his ladies are buried in Woodlawn Cemetery, Sandy Creek.

Conrad Warner – Co. B
b. 1834 Germany
d. July 1, 1863 Gettysburg, Adams, NY
m. Cecelia "Celia" Van Greadwold (1835-*post* 1880) April 27, 1856

NOTE: Conrad was the son of John (?-?) and Catherine Dortnew Warner (?-?) and a butcher by occupation. His entry in *The Town Clerks' Registers* mistakenly says he was born in Granby, NY. His remains were buried on the field. He and Cecelia were the parents of Matilda (1857-*post* 1905) and Catherine (1862-*post* 1905). An interesting letter appeared in *The Oswego Daily Palladium* April 14, 1864, written by Lt. William Gillette, Co. B, 147th Regiment on April 2nd: "It having come to the knowledge of the officers and men of this regiment, that the widow and children of Sergeant Conrad Warner, company B, who was killed at the battle of Gettysburg, were suffering from destitution, they promptly determined to contribute something from their own pockets for the relief of the widow and her family. The sum raised amounts to one hundred and seventy-two ($172.00) dollars, which is herewith enclosed to your address. It is desired by the regiment that you will present the money to Mrs. Warner, now residing in Oswego. The sum, though not large, it is hoped will afford her at least, temporary relief from distress, incident to her sad bereavement. There is nothing more depressing to the spirits of the brave men in the field, battling and suffering hardships in the cause of their country, than the thought of privation and distress among friends and family at home. Upon the knowledge, therefore, of the destitution of one who had lost her all in the battle-field, in the death of our brave comrade, Sergeant Warner, widowing her and orphaning two young children, the sum remitted herewith was freely contributed, mostly by the enlisted men of this regiment, from their meager pay, together with the assistance of commissioned officers . . . ." The letter was addressed to William I. Preston who appended his own letter to the editor: ". . . On the receipt of the money, I hastened to discover the whereabouts of Mrs. Warner, and found her at No. 8, Jefferson Block, sad and lonely indeed, struggling with the conflicts of life. Mrs. Warner has two children, one of whom is sick. She has received no bounty, no back pay, no pension, and indeed nothing from the Government, since the death of her husband; and who will describe her privations and sorrows as she travels life's weary pilgrimage! How her face beamed with joy and gladness when I announced that I held in my hands one hundred and seventy-two dollars for her, the generous offering of noble men who can face the dangers and calamities of war unmoved, but whose hearts melt and eyes moisten, *and pockets* open, when they hear that the loved ones at home are suffering. A ray of sunshine seemed to light up the little pale face that pressed so gently to its mother's bosom, as she looked at the money, and felt the sincerity of that prayer of thanksgiving which went up to the widow's God. May Heaven protect and defend our gallant soldiers! And may we *all* remember, that *he who gives to the poor, lendeth to the Lord.*" Cecilia married Frank Dolt (1825-February 16, 1891) on June 6, 1866 and became the mother of Caroline (1867-1957), Marie (1868-1944), and Franklin (1869-1952). The last reference to Cecilia appears in the 1880 census.

Edward P. Warner – Co. F
b. 1841 Columbia County, NY
d. October 1, 1928 National Soldiers' Home, Sawtelle, Los Angeles, CA
m. ------

NOTE: Edward was the son of Dr. Theron A. Warner (1794-ca. 1858). His mother is unknown although on the 1855 New York census his father was listed as married. One of the administrators of Theron's estate was Mary A. Warner who might have been his wife. Edward was captured at Gettysburg and paroled at an unknown date. He transferred to the Brigade Band on February 27, 1865. After the war he migrated to California. He was admitted to the National Soldiers' Home on March 9, 1927 at the age of 86. When he died of chronic myocarditis and arteriosclerosis, his closest relative was Alice W. Wright, a cousin living in Tacoma, WA. His effects were valued at 80 cents. Edward is buried in Los Angeles National Cemetery.

John Warner – Co. G
b. 1816 Germany
d. April 8, 1863 Regimental Hospital, Belle Plain, VA
m. Christianna "Christina" McCullock (1819-November 15, 1871) April 20, 1854

NOTE: John claimed to have been born in 1820 when he enlisted but other documents prove he was actually born in 1816. Christianna's DOB is also a mystery. In 1860 she claimed to be 41 but in 1865 she alleged she was 35. The couple, who were married in Williamstown, NY, had no children. John's COD was typhoid fever. The DOD given above is correct, according to *Deaths of Volunteers*, but some records assign a death date of April 7th. His gravesite is unknown. Christianna obtained a widow's pension. Her tragic end was reported in *The Oswego Daily Palladium* November 16, 1871: "This morning, at about 6:30, as Mr. F. A. Byrne was proceeding to his ordinary occupation for the day, he found in the gutter on the west side of East Second street, the body of a woman. The body was incrusted with snow, the muscles of the arms were frigidly contracted, and in the mud around there were traces of a slight struggle. He immediately notified the Coroner, and the body, after having been viewed by Dr. Kingston, was removed to Faber's undertaking rooms. A jury was summoned and the Coroner proceeded to take the testimony. By this it was made apparent that there were no discoverable marks of violence on the body; that the deceased had been the habit of drinking; that on at least one occasion previous she had had a fit, lasting nearly fifteen minutes; that her name was Christina Warner, and that she had resided in a small house on East Second street, two doors south of the jail. Dr. Whited also testified that he had occasionally attended the deceased, but never for a serious fit of sickness, merely prescribing to remedy as far as possible, the effects of liquor. Drs. Kingston, Whited, and Dewitt united in the opinion that she died in a fit, and jury accordingly rendered the following verdict: 'The Coroner's jury in the case of Mrs. Christina Warner, found dead on East Second street, in the city of Oswego, N.Y., November 16th, 1871, A.D., find that the said Christina Warner came to her death from causes to the jury unknown; but the most probable cause, as indicated by the testimony, was that she died in a fit superinduced by intoxication.' The deceased, Mrs. Christina Warner, was a woman past the middle age. Her husband was killed in the army, and she was in receipt of a pension from the United States government. She bore the character among her neighbors of a hard working woman, although of late she had become somewhat addicted to drink. The general opinion of the jury was that she died early in the night. On examining her house the door was found locked, but a good fire was found burning within." Christianna's gravesite has not yet been located.

Thomas Warner – Co. F
b. May 10, 1832 England
d. September 19, 1895 Palermo, NY
m1. Eliza M. Nichols (1839-February 6, 1878) *ca.* 1860
m2. Mary Ann Frawley (1852-January 1, 1930) 1880

NOTE: Thomas was the son of James (?-1873) and Elizabeth Warner (?-1860). He mustered out with the regiment on June 7, 1865. In 1890 he claimed "breech" as his disability. I fix his marriage to Mary Ann from the fact that Nellie Frances (1881-July

7, 1968) was born in January 1881. Nellie married Edward Gorman (1870-1948). Her sister, Emma (April 1883-April 1965), married his brother, Richard Gorman (1873-1937). Thomas and Eliza are buried in Palermo Center Cemetery. Mary Ann, her daughters, and their husbands are buried in St. Mary's Cemetery, Fulton.

John D. Wart – Co. E

b. 1843 Jefferson County, NY

d. January 24, 1893 State Hospital, Ogdensburg, St. Lawrence, NY

m. Frances Mathews (1836-April 8, 1898) 1865

NOTE: John's parents were William (1799-1879) and Sarah "Sally" Pruyn Wart (1805-1885). He was discharged from the service at a government insane hospital, location not identified. In 1890 he said his disabilities were rheumatism and heart disease. He was a member of May H. Stacy Post No. 586 GAR in Oswego City and when he died his comrades were requested to attend the funeral on January 27, 1893. John and Frances are buried in Riverside Cemetery, Scriba. Two brothers also served in the Union Army. William (1833-1899) was a member of Co. K, 4th NYSV. George (1836-1904) was a member of Co. G, 24th NY Cavalry and later the 1st Provisional Cavalry.

George Winslow Washburn – Co. D

b. July 11, 1816 Colerain, Franklin, MA

d. April 2, 1895 Scriba, NY

m1. Mary E. _____ (1821-May 15, 1855) *ca.* 1850

m2. Lucetta Harriet _____ (1821-July 22, 1894) *ca.* 1859

NOTE: George was the son of Stoddard (1793-1865) and Martha Patty Armour Washburn (1794-1878). He was overage when he enlisted in 1862 and was discharged for "disability" on January 10, 1863. In 1890 he claimed deafness as a disability. He and his wives are buried in Mt. Pleasant Cemetery, Volney, NY.

Edward F. Watson – Co. B

b. 1842 Kingston, Ontario, Canada

d. December 28, 1925 Syracuse, Onondaga, NY

m. Marion Beardsley Cooper (1843-November 27, 1924) 1870

NOTE: Edward was the son of William (1805-*post* 1858) and Mary Blair Watson (1822-*post* 1850). He mustered out with the regiment on June 7, 1865. In 1890 he claimed chronic diarrhea as his disability and the enumerator added "general health depleted." His death was announced in *The Oswego Palladium-Times* December 29, 1925, 5: "Brief announcement yesterday of the sudden death of Edward F. Watson at the home of his son in Syracuse brought regret to many friends in this city where he had lived for more than half a century in the First Ward. Mr. Watson had been feeling in good health yesterday, and about 10 o'clock in the morning went down cellar to care for the furnace. When he did not return in 15 or 20 minutes, his son investigated and found his father lying unconscious on the floor. Physicians summoned stated he had been stricken by an attack of heart disease, and he died without regaining consciousness. Mr. Watson was born in Canada 83 years ago, and with his parents came to Oswego as a small boy. He was one of the first to enlist in the 147th Regiment, N.Y. Vols, and was a corporal when discharged. Mr. Watson was a member of Post J. D. O'Brian, G.A.R., and in later years had always been interested in the work of that organization. He was a sailmaker and for many years had a loft in West First street, later engaging in the awning business. He retired from active business 15 years ago, and four years ago disposed of his property in Oswego and with his wife went to reside in Syracuse with his son. Mrs. Watson died suddenly a year ago Thanksgiving Day. He was a member of Christ Episcopal church, and is survived by his son Frank T. Watson, and by two grand-children . . . ." Marion's death was reported in *The Oswego Daily Palladium* November 28, 1924: "Many friends in this city today learned with regret of the death in Syracuse yesterday of Mrs. Marion B. Watson, wife of Edward Watson, her demise occurring at the Hospital of the Good Shepherd, where she had been a patient since Monday. Mrs. Watson was born in the town of Sterling 80 years ago and came to this city when a young girl and was married more than 54 years ago to Edward Watson, for many years one of the leading sailmakers of the port of Oswego. She was a lifelong member of Christ church and always took a deep interest in the work of that organization while in this city. She was also a member of the Woman's Relief Corps of Post. J. D. O'Brian, of which her husband, a Civil War veteran, was a leading member. Mr. and Mrs. Watson moved to Syracuse four years ago to make their home with their son, Frank T. Watson. Mrs. Watson had been in poor health for some months, according to information re-ceived by friends here, and her physician advised removal to a hospital . . . ." Edward and Marion are buried on Oakwood Cemetery, Syracuse. Frank (1884-1926) died of a massive heart attack on November 11, 1926 at the age of 41.

William Henry Watson – Co. D
b. February 27, 1828 England
d. July 18, 1909 Fulton, NY
m. Mary J. Hutchins (1836-October 26, 1902) November 19, 1851

NOTE: William, a shoemaker, may have been the son of Thomas (1796-*post* 1841) and Jane Watson (1801-*post* 1841). The family was living in Darlington, Durham, England in 1841 and Thomas was a shoemaker. In 1900 William alleged he migrated to the United States in 1841. He saw service in Co. E, 24th Regiment NYSV from May 4, 1861-May 22, 1862. In 1890 he said he had been wounded in the right shoulder at

Laurel Hill, VA on May 8, 1864. He was mustered out on May 13, 1865. Mary alleged in 1900 that she was the mother of three children, all living, but she actually had borne at least two more, Jacob (1858-?), and Angeline (1859-?). William's obituary appeared in *The Oswego Daily Palladium* July 19, 1909, 6: "William H. Watson died yesterday at the home of his son, F. T. Watson, No. 622 Rochester street. He was 81 years old and had been a resident of Fulton for more than 60 years. He was a member of the One Hundred and [Forty] Seventh Regiment of New York Volunteers and was the last survivor of the old volunteer firemen . . . ." Mary's obituary appeared in *The Fulton Patriot* October 29, 1902: ". . . The deceased had been ill for a long time, yet she bore her affliction with a fortitude that denotes the true woman, never complaining and always trying to look on the bright side. Her last hours were peaceful and she passed away like one going to sleep. Mr. and Mrs. Watson have been married half a century and it has been a season free from any interruptions of happiness in domestic affairs. And her life companion, with three sons . . . mourn together the loss of a faithful, devoted wife and mother in all those endearing words imply, while a large circle of friends and acquaintances will always remember her with kindness for her many traits that denote the true woman and friend . . . ." William and Mary are buried in Mt. Adnah Cemetery, Fulton.

Theodore Horton Weaver – Co. E
b. January 19, 1837 Sandy Creek, NY
d. March 11, 1910 Sandy Creek, NY
m. Mary "Polly" Lillis (August 1844-August 10, 1915) 1863

NOTE: Theodore, frequently called by his middle name, was the son of Reuben (1802-July 4, 1877) and Lorinda Weaver (1800-*ante* 1880). He was WIA at Five Forks, VA on April 1, 1865 and discharged on July 26, 1865 at Elmira, Chemung, NY. In 1890 he said he had been wounded in the left foot. His death occasioned the following obituary in *The Sandy Creek News* March 17, 1910: "Theodore Horton Weaver, a veteran of the civil war, and a life-long resident of the western part of the town of Sandy Creek, died at his late residence on Friday, March 11, 1910. He was the last one of a family of six children born to Reuben and Laurinda Weaver. Mr. Weaver passed the seventy-third mile stone in his journey of life on the 19th of January, 1910. He was united in marriage to Polly Lillis, who survives him, in 1863, at which time he was at his father's home on a furlough. On August 21, 1862, he enlisted and was mustered into the One Hundred and Forty-seventh Infantry to serve three years. He was twice wounded; the first time [*sic*] in the ankle at the battle of Five Forks, Virginia. He came home and staid a few weeks and then returned to his regiment. At the memorable battle of Gettysburg he was wounded in the arm . . . He suffered much from the wound in his ankle, from which several pieces of bone worked out. Mr. Weaver was of a quiet disposition and much devoted to his home. He participated in several hard fought battles. He was a good marksman and a brave soldier. During the last years of his life he did but little more than the chores about the house. His health gradually failed until the end . . . ." I have not located any information pertaining to his wounding at Gettysburg but perhaps that was the reason he obtained a furlough in 1863. Polly's death was announced in *The Sandy Creek News* August 19, 1915: "On Tuesday of last week Mary P. Weaver a lifelong resident of this town died at a hospital in Watertown. She has resided in this locality during the last fifty years. One brother, William Lillis, who resides in this neighborhood, and several nieces and nephews remain to mourn her loss. On Thursday she was buried in Woodlawn cemetery beside her husband the late Theodore H. Weaver." Mary's DOD is not shown on the gravestone.

Fred J. A. Webb – Co. F
b. April 1834 Mexico, NY
d. April 29, 1902 Mexico, NY
m. ------

NOTE: Fred was the son of Nehemiah (1801-1885) and Rhoda Gunn Webb (1805-1888). He was discharged from the service for "disability" on March 24, 1863. In 1890 he said that his disabilities were chronic diarrhea and *phthisis* which had lasted for 27 years. According to an announcement in *The Mexico Independent* April 30, 1902, ". . . Mr. Fred Webb, who has been ill for so long a time, died at his home in this village about 11 o'clock yesterday morning. He was a very quiet, industrious man, a veteran of the Civil War, a kind friend and neighbor. He is survived by two sisters . . . ." Webb's funeral announcement in *The Oswego Daily Palladium* May 5, 1902, provided more details: ". . . The funeral of Mr. Fred Webb was held at the Methodist church on Thursday. Mr. Webb was an esteemed citizen and a member of F. and A. M. No. 136. The Masons attended in a body. The Reverend M. Sill, of the Methodist church, preached the sermon, after which the Masons conducted their very beautiful service." Webb is buried in Mexico Village Cemetery.

Lewis M. Webb – Co. F
b. 1824 Mexico, NY
d. July 30, 1912 National Soldiers' Home, Milwaukee, Milwaukee, WI
m. Emily Zipporah Dudley (March 23, 1830- April 8, 1912) September 18, 1850

NOTE: Lewis, son of Thomas (1799-1885) and Carolyn Ames Webb (1804-1878), was captured on July 1, 1863 at Gettysburg and paroled at an unknown date. He was also captured on June 2, 1864 at Cold Harbor, VA. For a long time people did not know what had happened to him until an article appearing in *The Mexico Independent* April 20, 1865 solved the mystery: "From a letter written at Vicksburg, by a lady, to the

Syracuse Standard, we give the following extract, which shows the whereabouts of Mr. Louis Webb, who enlisted in the 147th regiment and has not been heard from for a long time: 'Yesterday morning, while in Parole Hospital, I saw a man from the town of Mexico, N.Y. His name is Webb. Has just returned from Andersonville prison, where he has been ten months. He belongs to the Army of the Potomac; has not heard from home since he was taken prisoner. His hair is almost white although when he was taken prisoner he had hardly a gray hair'." He was finally discharged on July 8, 1865 at New York City. He never returned to his family. In 1875 he was living with his parents in Mexico. By 1910 he had migrated to Chicago. He entered the National Soldiers' Home on June 28, 1910, suffering from several maladies. His COD was a combination of nephritis and senility. He was buried in Wood National Cemetery. Emily's story is best told in a lengthy obituary appearing *The Fort Collins Weekly Courier* April 17, 1912, which is excerpted here: "Last Saturday afternoon the body of Mrs. Emily Dudley Webb, mother of Mr. George A. Webb, cashier of the Fort Collins National Bank, arrived from Pueblo where she died on Wednesday . . . after a short illness from pneumonia. It was accompanied by Mr. and Mrs. George A. Webb and Mr. George P. Dudley of Denver, a brother of the deceased. The funeral party was met at the train by Rev. M. P. Hunt, pastor of the First Baptist church, undertaker W. T. Hollowell, the bearers and other friends, including the Woman's Relief Corps who proceeded with the body directly from the train to Grandview Cemetery where the casket was tenderly lowered into the grave, following a brief service . . . The burial took place just a month to a day after the only daughter of the departed, Mrs. Louie J. Kunkel, had been laid at rest . . . Mrs. Webb had been a resident of Colorado for nearly 36 years and had a wide acquaintance in Greeley, Denver, Pueblo, and Fort Collins, and other parts of the state. She was an educated, cultured and refined woman with a warm, sympathetic heart, a genial nature and a sweet amiable disposition and had many warm admirers in church and social circles. She had lived a long, devoted and useful life. It can truly be said of her that the world is better for her having living in it. She had unselfishly devoted her time and her strength to the proper raising of her children, to advancing the cause of the Master and to bettering and uplifting the social and moral condition of those about her. She was an earnest, zealous and consistent Christian woman, loyal to her friends, her religion and her church, never missing an opportunity when in health to attend to her religious duties, and never neglecting any duty she owed to her family, her neighbor or her God. Emily Zipporah Dudley was born March 23, 1830 at Cato, Cayuga County, New York. Her father was a Baptist clergyman and she was reared in that faith. On September 18, 1850, she was joined in marriage with Lewis M. Webb at Colosse, N.Y. Her husband enlisted in a New York regiment soon after the breaking out of the Civil War and did not return . . . Mrs. Webb was baptized on March 3, 1843 in Pleasant Lake, Edwardsburg, Cass County, Michigan, her father being pastor of the

Baptist church at that place. She immediately united with the church and remained all through life a loyal and consistent member of that denomination."

Robert Watson Webb – Co. K
b. December 4, 1834 Rangoon, Burma
d. March 28, 1876 Kalamazoo, Kalamazoo, MI
m1. Harriet Sophia Bonner (1842-*post* 1864) July 11, 1861
m2. Sarah J. White (1852-February 23, 1909) October 19, 1872

NOTE: Robert was the son of Abner (1804-1891) and Catherine Watson Webb (1806-1848). His father, a Baptist minister, and his mother sailed for Burma as missionaries in 1832 and did not return to the United States until 1838. Robert and Harriet were the parents of two sons, the latter being born in April 1864. Both children died young. Robert, a teacher and justice of the peace, transferred to Co. B on January 1, 1863. He was discharged on February 29, 1864 to accept a commission as second lieutenant in Co. C, 32nd Regiment USCT which was active chiefly in South Carolina. He mustered out on August 22, 1865. *The History of the Descendants of John Dwight of Dedham, Mass.*, vol. 2, 742-3 states he lived in Summerville, SC for some time growing cotton. He married Sarah in Kalamazoo, MI. They were the parents of a son, Robert Lathrop (1874-1963). *The Kalamazoo Gazette* March 31, 1876, 4 carried the following: "The funeral of Robert W. Webb yesterday was largely attended. Kalamazoo Lodge, No. 22, F. & A. M. were present in regalia and officiated in the last sad rites." His grave has not been located. Sarah married Cenius Henry Engle (1832-1915), a lawyer, as his second wife on September 13, 1882. They are buried in Hartford Cemetery, Hartford, Van Buren, MI.

Adam Webber – Co. B
b. September 1827 Germany
d. September 17, 1909 National Soldiers' Home, Bath, Steuben, NY
m1. Marie _____ (1820-September 19, 1889) *ca.* 1852
m2. Magdalena "Biddie" Faudie (1838-1903) *ca.* 1890

NOTE: Adam, a carpenter by occupation, immigrated to the United States in 1840 and became a naturalized citizen. His parents were Johann Peter (1783-1834) and Anna Elisabetha Kaftenberger Webber (1786-1859). He was transferred to the VRC at any unknown date, re-transferred to Co. B on April 5, 1864, and discharged from the service at Mower Hospital, Philadelphia, PA, on June 17, 1865. In 1890, while living in Phoenix, NY, he claimed no disability although he had applied for a pension in 1883 when living in Martville, Cayuga, NY. He and Marie were the parents of numerous children, one of whom, Adam, Jr., died in November 1869 at the age of

15. According to the Mortality Schedules he was burned to death. He and his mother are buried in Rural Cemetery, Oswego Town. Magdalena is a mystery. She and Adam were living in Sterling, Cayuga, NY in 1892 and she was using the name Biddie. In 1900 Adam claimed to be a widower. A woman by the name of Mrs. M. Webber died in Boulder, Jefferson, MT in January 1903 and was buried in St. John the Evangelist Catholic Cemetery, Boulder. Whether or not this is the correct person is open to question. Adam entered the Bath National Home for the first time on August 3, 1903. He re-entered in 1906. When first admitted, he claimed that he had suffered a bayonet wound in the thigh during the war. His COD was chronic cystitis. He is buried in Bath National Cemetery. His son Henry applied for letters of administration for his father's estate on October 18, 1909. It was valued at $160.00.

Edwin Lyman Weed – Co. E
b. July 30, 1838 Pulaski, NY
d. January 23, 1927 Gouverneur, St. Lawrence, NY
m. Sybil A. Thayer (1828-April 3, 1887) September 13, 1862

NOTE: Edwin was the son of Ezra (1793-1851) and Polly Sampson Weed (1796-1869). He mustered out with the regiment on June 7, 1865. He and Sybil, whose DOB was variously given, were the parents of Rose (1865-*post* 1910), Ida (1866-1926), and Nellie (1875-1911). In 1860 Sybil alleged she was 32. Her gravestone, however, implies she was born in 1826. Upon Edwin's death *The Watertown Daily Times* January 24, 1927, 1 published an interesting obituary: "Edwin L. Weed, 87, Civil war veteran, of three years' service, died early Sunday morning at his home . . . He had been a resident of Gouverneur 27 years. Mr. Weed was born in Oswego county, July 30, 1838 . . . . He enlisted at Sandy Creek, Aug. 21, 1862 in Company E, 147th regiment, New York Volunteer infantry. He was wounded severely in the battle of Spotsylvania Courthouse. His service in the Union armies was largely in the army of Virginia. He was wounded seriously enough to be interned in the army hospitals three times . . . He was a member of Barnes Post 156 G.A.R. of this village. On Sept. 13, 1862 he was married to Miss Sibbel A. Thayer of East DeKalb, who died several years ago. His last near relative, a daughter, Mrs. William H. Burns of East Main street, died last summer. He leaves a granddaughter Miss Myrtle Cobb of Gouverneur, and two nieces, Mrs. Polly Spencer of Maple View and Miss Emma Sampson of Richland . . . ." Edwin and Sybil were buried in Riverside Cemetery, Gouverneur.

Jehial Weed – Co. E
b. 1830 Oswego County, NY
d. December 24, 1864 Salisbury, Rowan, NC
m. Nancy Arvilla Brown (1833-January 13, 1923) October 26, 1854

NOTE: Jehial was Edwin's brother. He was taken prisoner at the battle of Weldon Railroad on October 1, 1864. According to *The Town Clerks' Registers* and Nancy's deposition in her pension application he died of starvation. Jehial and Nancy were the parents of Arthur J. Weed (1850-1936), an inventor and photographer. He was an instrument maker for the US Weather Bureau in Washington, DC and invented the Weed Strong Motion Seismograph, among others. Nancy, the daughter of William (1794-1873) and Celinda Brown (1810-*post* 1870), never remarried. Her death was announced in *The Sandy Creek News* January 18, 1923, 8: "On December 4th, 1922 Mr. and Mrs. Claude Davis removed from William Green's farm , near Belleville, to the farm of Robert Goodenough, near Lacona, having with them to care for, her father's aunt, Mrs. Nancy Weed, in her ninetieth year. Two months ago Mrs. Weed returned from a year's stay in Washington, D.C. with her only child, Arthur J. Weed. A wonderful constitution peacefully yielded to the end the morning of January 13th. Long ago arrangements were carried out and Miss Lester brought the old friend to her home where Tuesday afternoon relatives and neighbors gathered for the service, conducted by Rev. F. Griswold, pastor of the Baptist Church of which no better member is found than Mrs. Weed. She was born in the Brewster Settlement, September 22, 1833. In Oct. 1854, she married Jehiel Weed. He enlisted in the civil war and was one of many to die in Libby Prison. Two sons were their children[;] one died at two years of age, the other, Arthur J. Weed, his son, Harold, and four great grandsons are the descendants . . . ." Nancy is buried in Maplewood Cemetery, Mannsville, Jefferson, NY. It is altogether possible that Jehial was sent originally to Libby because of information contained in a letter sent by Lt. Albert Thomas of the 24th NY Cavalry to his father which was published in *The Oswego Commercial Times* October 25, 1864. Dated October 5, 1864 the letter stated that Thomas was confined at Libby Prison but expected to be sent south very soon. This same letter mentions John Wetherby of the 147th (see below).

David Welch – Co. E
b. 1814 Washington County, NY
d. July 15, 1863 Gettysburg, Adams, PA
m. Rebecca Deremo (April 5, 1832-September 13, 1916) 1851

NOTE: Although David claimed he had been born in 1820 when he enlisted, the 1860 census reveals he was actually born in 1814. His parents have not been identified. In 1860 he and Rebecca were the parents of four children: James, 8; Clarissa, 6; Mary E., 4, and Emma, 1. His DOD is taken from *Civil War Soldier Records and Profiles*. Rebecca applied for and obtained a widow's pension. On April 11, 1892 she married Turner Lillie (1817-October 23, 1897) as his second wife. He had served in Cos. E and G, 94th NYSV from December 1861-December 1864. Lillie was buried in Ellisburg Rural Cemetery with his first wife, Sophronia Ethridge

(1824-January 8, 1890). Rebecca's death was announced in *The Sandy Creek News* September 21, 1916, 5: "On September 13, at the home of her daughter, Mrs. Frank Kiblin, Mrs. Rebecca Welch Lilly [*sic*], died, aged 84 years, 4 months, 29 days. She was the oldest of a family of ten children born to George and Emily Deremo, in this town. In 1851 she was married to David Welch, and to them were born six children . . . David Welch served in the Civil war and was wounded in the battle of Gettysburg in 1863, dying a short time afterward, and was buried in the government cemetery there. Several years later Mrs. Welch was married to Turner Lilly, who passed away several years ago. She has since made her home with her daughter . . . As her body grew weakened with age, her daily prayer was that she might soon be with her Saviour and the many friends that had gone before. Rev. T. T. Davies officiated at the funeral and the interment was in Woodlawn cemetery."

Mark Welch – Co. A

b. 1835 Oswego County, NY

d. *post* 1865 Oswego City, NY

m. ------

NOTE: Mark was the son of Francis (1805-1862) and Mary Welch (1805-1865), both Irish immigrants. He was wounded on July 1, 1863 at Gettysburg and discharged from the service at Satterlee Hospital, Philadelphia, PA on May 19, 1865. He does not appear on the Mortality Schedules for 1870, which narrows the time to June 1865-June 1869. He is buried with his parents in St. Paul's Cemetery, Oswego City. His government gravestone, which contains no dates, misspells his surname and erroneously assigns him to Co. B. His brother, Francis (1839-June 3, 1864), was a member of the 81st Regiment. He was killed at Cold Harbor, VA.

Mark Welch is buried with his parents in St. Paul's Cemetery, Oswego.
Author's Collection

Henry W. Welling – Co. D

b. August 15, 1833 Washington County, NY

d. March 27, 1908 Grand Rapids, Kent, MI

m. Martha J. _____ (1829-October 12, 1890) *ca.* 1856

NOTE: Henry's parents were Isaac (1793-1881) and Betsey Witzell Welling (1797-1887). He mustered out with the regiment on June 7, 1865. In 1860, Henry and Martha were living in Hannibal, NY and were the parents of Ida (1857-1932) and Daniel A. (1858-1936). While their parents both died in Grand Rapids, Ida and Daniel died in California. Henry's COD was chronic albuminuria. He and Martha are buried in Oak Hill Cemetery, Grand Rapids.

David L. Wells – Co. C
b. 1844 Richland, NY
d. 1867 Oswego County, NY
m. ------

NOTE: David was the son of Sylvanus (1810-*ante* 1855) and Catherine Wells (1822-*post* 1875). Although he alleged he was 24 when he enlisted census records point to a DOB of 1844. He was discharged for "disability" on June 5, 1863. His exact DOD is unknown but his mother was granted letters of administration for his estate on December 14, 1867. His grave has not been located.

William Wells – Co. A
b. September 12, 1813 Frederick County, MD
d. January 9, 1880 Sharon Township. Franklin, OH
m. Catherine "Kate" Dubbs (1828-April 1876) *ca.* 1852

NOTE: William's parents were James (?-?) and Mary McPike Wells (?-?). Although he claimed to have been born in 1818 when he enlisted, other documents prove he was born in 1813. He was discharged from the army on January 27, 1863 for "disability." He and Kate, who was born in Pennsylvania, were the parents of numerous children. By 1870 the family was living in Harrisburg, Dauphin, PA. In 1875 Catherine petitioned the Court of Common Pleas that she be declared a *femme sole*, the implication being that he had abandoned her. She made a will which was admitted to probate in April 1876. George C. Smith was appointed executor and the guardian of the youngest child, Catherine (1862-1941). Catherine, as well as several of her children and their spouses, is buried in Harrisburg Cemetery. William's COD was pneumonia, according to the Mortality Schedules for 1880. His gravesite has not yet been located.

David Welsh – Co. K
b. 1846 Montreal, Quebec, Canada
d. April 28, 1919 Oswego City, NY
m. Mary McQueen McNamara (November 23, 1832-January 8, 1923) 1885

NOTE: David, whose parents are unidentified, immigrated to the United States in 1858 and became a naturalized citizen. Although he alleged he was born in 1844, other documents prove he lied about his age to enlist. His obituary was published in *The Oswego Daily Times* April 29, 1919: "David Welsh, veteran of the Civil war, and hero of the gallant 147th regiment, New York Volunteers, died last night at his home, East Bridge corner of Eleventh street. Mr. Welsh was in his 73rd year and had been in poor health for some time. He was born in Montreal, Quebec and came to this city when a young man. He was here during the days of the Civil war and on September 2, 1862, enlisted in Company K and fought to the end of the war. He was at Gettysburg July 1, 1863, and assisted in removing from the battlefield General J. J. Reynolds. At the Wilderness, May 5, 1864, Mr. Welsh was wounded by a gunshot wound in his left thigh and after hours of helplessness on the battlefield he was captured on the following day, May 6, 1864. He escaped June 4 of the same year and reached his regiment. At Hatcher's Run, Va., February 5, 1865, he was wounded for the second time, a bullet striking him in the face and destroying the sight of both of his eyes, making him totally blind. He was honorably discharged from the service May 31, 1865. Returning to this city after the war Mr. Welsh has made his home here ever since. He was a member of St. Paul's church, of the Holy Name society connected with that parish and Post O'Brien, G.A.R. . . . ." Mary was first married to Francis McNamara/Mack (1818-1869). Her death was reported in *The Oswego Daily Palladium* January 9, 1923, 4: "Word was received here today of the death in Bristol, R.I., at the home of her daughter, Mrs. John C. Donoghue, of Mrs. David Welsh, wife of the late David Welsh, a former well known resident of the East side. Mrs. Welsh was born in Ireland and was 91 years of age. Practically all of her life was spent in this city, the family home being at 200 East Bridge street. She was among the oldest members of St. Paul's church and was held in high regard by all who knew her, being kind and charitable towards all. For a woman of her years she was keen of mind and enjoyed remarkable health until within a short time ago. She left here two years ago to make her home with her daughter. Mrs. Welsh was the daughter of the late Mary and Patrick McQueen of Scriba . . . Funeral will be held tomorrow morning upon the arrival of the 8:10 West side train and from St Paul's church." David and Mary are buried in St. Paul's Cemetery, Oswego City, as is Francis McNamara.

Asa Westcott – Co. F

b. October 12, 1807 Williamstown, NY
d. July 25, 1863 Lovell General Hospital, Portsmouth Grove, RI
m. Mary C. Wing (1811-December 12, 1893) July 28, 1829

NOTE: Asa's parents are unknown. He alleged he was born in 1818 when he enlisted but in 1860 he gave his age as 53. His COD was listed as chronic diarrhea but

The Mexico Independent August 6, 1863 told a much different story: "Asa Wescott [*sic*] fell out from the effect of a sunstroke and died in hospital." He is buried in the Lovell General Hospital Cemetery under the name of Isaiah. In 1890 Mary was living in Altmar, NY. *The Pulaski Democrat* December 20, 1893 announced her death: ". . . Mrs. Wescott, wife of the late Asa Wescott, died at her home Tuesday evening, Dec. 12th of pneumonia. She has lived here alone for many years spending part of her winters with her daughter, Mrs. Canfield, at Kasoag. She seemed in usual health Thanksgiving day and ate her dinner with many others at the Hall. Her funeral was attended at the Baptist church, Thursday, Dec. 14th, Rev. J. Ford officiating . . . ." Her grave has not been located. Their son, Allen (1832-1912), served in Co. G, 184th Regiment from August 1864-June 1865.

John Wetherby – Co. G
b. 1844 Oswego, NY
d. December 1, 1864 Salisbury, Rowan, NC
m. ------

NOTE: John was the son of Luther (1811-1893) and Delight Wetherby (1815- 1849). When and where he was captured is open to debate. His muster roll card says he was captured at Gettysburg on July 1, 1863 and his name was included first on a list of missing or captured soldiers in *The Oswego Commercial Times* July 20, 1863. He next appeared on a list of men found at Camp Parole, West Chester, PA. All these men eventually returned to the regiment. He next was reported missing in *The Oswego Commercial Times* May 25, 1864 but an undated letter from Lt. A. J. Dickinson, published on the same page, stated Dickinson saw Wetherby on the 17th at Fredericksburgh guarding prisoners. At some point between May 17, 1864 and October 5, 1864, when Lt. Albert Thomas of the 24th Cavalry wrote to his father (see Jehial Weed, above), Wetherby was again taken prisoner and confined initially at Libby Prison. According to *Records of Officers and Enlisted Men*, he was taken prisoner at the battle of Weldon Railroad which was fought between August 18-21, 1864. It also states he died on November

John Wetherby's family erected this cenotaph for their lost son.
Author's Collection

28, 1864. His COD is equally elusive. His FAG entry says he died of "disease." Johnson's *History of Oswego County,* 192, however, reports he died of "wounds received in service." Col. Miller's letter to *The Oswego Commercial Times* which was reprinted in *The Mexico Independent* March 23, 1865 told of being informed by exchanged prisoners that Wetherby was among the dead, although place of confinement and cause of death were not stated. John is buried with many other "unknowns" at Salisbury National Cemetery, although a cenotaph can be seen in the family plot in Rural Cemetery, Oswego Town.

Charles Fay Wheeler – Co. F

b. June 14, 1842 Mexico, NY

d. March 5, 1910 Lanham, Prince George's, MD

m. Catherine Trask Holbrook (September 1848-February 3, 1922) March 4, 1869

NOTE: Charles was the son of Charles (1811-1899) and Mary Walker Wheeler (1808-1890). He initially served in Co. B, 7th NY Cavalry from October 1861 to March 1862. He was discharged for "disability" from the 147th at Philadelphia, PA on March 21, 1863 because he had contracted typhoid fever in November 1862. After his discharge he moved to Michigan where he opened a drugstore and studied plants in his leisure time. He became an expert in Michigan *flora*, obtained a bachelor's degree, and taught at the Michigan Agricultural College until 1902. In that year he moved to Washington, DC to work in the Economic Gardens of the Bureau of Plant Industry, a branch of the USDA. A lengthy, informative obituary published in *Science* July 15, 1910, 72-75 is here excerpted: "It was with a sense of deep personal loss that the associates of Professor Wheeler learned of his death, March 5, at George Washington University Hospital. While those intimately associated with him were perhaps aware of his gradually failing strength, he was so cheerful in his greeting each day, so uncomplaining, that no one realized the extent or significance of his failing health . . . Following his discharge from the federal army he was induced to go to friends at Hubbardston, Mich., where in the out-of-door life he led it was hoped he might regain his health. It was during this period of recuperation, spent almost wholly in the open air, that he became interested in the vegetation of the vicinity and began to acquire that intimate knowledge of plants that was later to ripen into an all-absorbing interest. As strength gradually returned a systematic study of the plants in his vicinity was carried on. In the autumn of 1866 Professor Wheeler entered the medical department of the University of Michigan, but after one year he returned to Hubbardston, where for the following twenty-two years he conducted a drug and book store. During this period he was the center of the intellectual life of the village. The element of gain in connection with the business apparently entered very little into his consideration. It was a mere incident. The real purpose, the real interest of his life, was the study of his beloved plants and the lending of inspiration to others. He possessed to a remarkable degree that rare ability to create an interest in better things in all with whom he came in contact, no matter how lowly the conditions of their life might be. He formed many intimate friends among young and old, gave them an interest in science, and when they went away he corresponded with them. He sought out too people outside of his village who studied botany, and helped them. It was during this period that he laid the foundations of that rare and peculiarly intimate knowledge of plants that enabled him in his work in the Department of Agriculture later to name off-hand so much of the fragmentary material that no one else could recognize . . . In 1889 his reputation as a painstaking systematic botanist was such that he was called to the Michigan Agricultural College to be instructor in the botanical department . . . The same qualities that endeared him to the people of his village quickly made a place for him in the new life and larger field he had come to fill . . . Professor Wheeler became a moving spirit in the intellectual life of the college community. There existed among the faculty at that time a literary circle, and whether the study of one of the modern languages, the reading of Moliere or Shakespeare, was the object of their attention, Professor Wheeler was always the life of the gathering. He was extremely modest and shrank from participation in anything of a public nature, but among those whom he knew intimately he was at ease, and at these social gatherings of the college faculty it was indeed a pleasure to hear him read Shakespeare, for which he had a special fondness . . . While at the college Professor Wheeler was occupied a part of the time with regular college studies and was gradu-ated with the class of 1891, receiving the degree of bachelor of science. In 1907 his alma mater on the occasion of the semi-centennial celebration of the college honored him with the degree of doctor of science. This was be-stowed in the presence of the President of the United States . . . Well-known to many in the Department of Agriculture, he was induced in 1902 to come to the department, where he entered upon systematic work in the Bureau of Plant Industry, and continued in this work until about two weeks previous to his death . . . He lies buried in the National Cemetery at Arlington, within sight of the hills on the farther side of the river, where in a soldier's camp he contracted the illness that was perhaps the determining cause of his botani-cal career." He and Catherine were the parents of two daughters, Mary Lillian (1874-February 10, 1913) and Clara Fay (1876-July 6, 1928). Both girls were married on the same day, July 2, 1902, Mary to George Nial Eastman (1876-1910), an electrical engineer, and

Charles Fay Wheeler became a student and later a professor of botany after his time in the 147th Regiment.
Larry E. Crosby

Clara to Professor Dick Jay Crosby (1866-1926). Some researchers say Catherine's POD was San Dimas, Los Angeles, CA in 1928. Since she was living in Portland, Oregon, "widow of C F," in 1918 and since Clara lived and died in that city I think she died in Oregon. Her name is given in the Oregon Death Index for 1922. Her grave site has not been identified and it is possible her body was cremated.

Wait W. Wheeler – Co. E

b. July 1839 Sandy creek, NY

d. March 5, 1908 Sandy Creek, NY

m. Mary Ann Philbrick (November 8, 1842-August 22, 1926) 1861

NOTE: Wait's first military service was done in Co. B, 7th NY Cavalry. He was the son of Warren Wheeler (1815-April 17, 1863), a member of the 110th Regiment who died in New Orleans, LA of chronic diarrhea. His mother was Charlotte Harmon (1815-March 13, 1901). Wait's tenure in the 147th Regiment was short as he was discharged for "disability" on December 8, 1862 at Finley Hospital, Washington, DC. He was a member of Lewis B. Porter Post No. 573 GAR in Scriba, NY where he and Mary Ann were living in 1880. According to newspaper accounts, he "died very suddenly." Mary Ann's death was announced in a lengthy obituary in *The Sandy Creek News* August 26, 1926: "Mrs. Mary A. Wheeler, aged 86, widow of the late Waite Wheeler, died Sunday night at the home of her sister, Mrs. Harriet M. Price, in Pulaski following an illness of several weeks. Mrs. Wheeler was born in Pulaski November 8, 1842 . . . Mrs. Wheeler has been a resident of Sandy Creek for many years but since her health became enfeebled, she had spent the winter months with her sister. She went to Pulaski about eight weeks ago and has been ill during that time. For many years she had been a faithful member and attendant upon the services of the First Methodist Episcopal church in Sandy Creek where she has many relatives and warm friends who will mourn her departure. Prayers were made at the home of her sister, Mrs. Price, Tuesday morning, at nine o'clock after which Undertaker F. S. Pratt brought the body to her home here, where funeral services were held with Editor Byron G. Seamans of Pulaski officiating . . . ." Wait and Mary Ann are buried in Woodlawn Cemetery, Sandy Creek. Mary Ann was sister to George W. Philbrick (1847-1909) who served in Co. C, 147th Regiment.

Daniel Decker Whipple – Co. F

b. September 2, 1829 Salina, Onondaga, NY

d. May 28, 1893 Amboy Center, NY

m1. Deborah Patience Barber (1830-July 20, 1867) November 9, 1851

m2. Mary _____ (1845-*post* 1880) ca. 1869

NOTE: Daniel was the son of Reuben Jencks "Jinks" (1797-1860) and Deborah Mapes Whipple (1794-1852). His military career is somewhat of a mystery. According to *The Adjutant-General's Report* of 1896 he enlisted in Batt. L, 1st NY ART on August 15, 1862 at Mexico, for three years and was mustered in on September 9th, 1862. *The Adjutant-General's Report* of 1904 says he enlisted in the 147th Regiment on August 15, 1862 at Mexico and was mustered in on September 22nd! The 1904 report also states he transferred to the artillery on December 28, 1863. He definitely mustered out with Batt. L on June 17, 1865 at Elmira, Chemung, NY, as shown by his discharge paper. In 1890 he claimed "rheumatism 26 years" as his disability. His gravestone, located in Amboy Center Cemetery, lists his service in the 1st Artillery. He and Deborah were the parents of four children. Her grave has not been located. Less is known about Mary. Since Daniel's pension card does not show that a widow applied for a pension, it is probably safe to conclude she died before 1893, although it is also possible she remarried.

Abraham James White – Co. A

b. April 9, 1844 Oswego, NY

d. May 6, 1864 Locust Grove Confederate Hospital, VA

m. ------

NOTE: Abraham's parents were Hans (1815-1888) and Susan Dougherty White (1827-1888). He was wounded and captured on May 5th at the battle of the Wilderness and died as a POW. His parents are buried in Rural Cemetery, Oswego Town, and he is memorialized with a cenotaph.

Abraham's parents erected this gravestone in his memory.
Author's Collection

Burton White – Co. E

b. 1819 Newport, Orleans, VT

d. May 26, 1863 Columbia Hospital, Washington, DC

m. Melisia "Melissa" Abigail Runnells (1839-October 24, 1922) *ca.* 1853

NOTE: Burton was the son of Ziba White (1790-*post* 1865), a War of 1812 veteran, and his wife Zilpha (1793-*post* 1865). His COD was enteritis. He is buried in the Soldiers' and Airmen's Home National Cemetery, Washington, DC. Melisia, the mother of five, married John Henry Moore (1837-1930) in 1874 as his second wife. He had served in Co. A, 15th IA Regiment. Melisia is buried in Hooten Cemetery, Winterset, Madison, IA. John is buried in Primitive Baptist Cemetery, Winterset.

Charles Thomas White – Co. D
b. 1821 England
d. March 25, 1898 Volney, NY
m. Elizabeth _____ (1823-July 2, 1887) *ca.* 1853

NOTE: Charles' parents are unknown. He was transferred to the VRC on November 2, 1863 and discharged on July 19, 1865 at Washington, DC. In 1890 he claimed no disability. Charles, a printer by occupation, was a member of Adam Keeslar Post No. 55 GAR, Wolcott. In 1880 Elizabeth was suffering from "paralysis." She and Charles were the parents of Ellen "Ella" Maria (October 1854-February 20, 1932) who married Edwin Alonzo Laws (1845-1905) on June 6, 1886 in Wolcott, Wayne, NY as his second wife. The witnesses were "Charles T. White and wife." Elizabeth, also born in England, is buried in Glenside Cemetery, Wolcott. Since Edwin and Ella lived in Volney in 1900 it is possible that her father also lived in the area and died there.

Frederick W. White – Co. E
b. September 14, 1845 Watertown, Jefferson, NY
d. ? ?
m. ?

NOTE: Frederick was the son of Frederick W. (1808-October 14, 1852) and Sarah White (1820-November 17, 1849). His father was married four times and produced at least six children. In 1850 the family was living in Watertown. Frederick, Jr. is next found on the 1860 census living with Jeremiah King and family in Sandy Creek. He enlisted at Orwell, giving his age as 18. He was a musician for the 147th and on January 23, 1865 he transferred to the 3rd Brigade Band. According to *The Town Clerks' Registers* he mustered out on June 16, 1865. Beyond that date, I have located nothing confirmable.

William Clothier Whitford – Co. K
b. October 24, 1836 Scriba, NY
d. December 19, 1914 Sandy Creek, NY
m. Polly Rosetta Goodrich (1840-March 5, 1908) 1860

NOTE: William was the son of Hiram (1792-1872) and Polly Lawton Whitford (1798-1872), pioneer settlers in the Town of Scriba. He was discharged from the service on a surgeon's certificate on March 10, 1863 and in 1890 he claimed heart disease as his disability. His death was announced in *The Sandy Creek News* December 24, 1914, 1: "William C. Whitford, who for a third of a century has been a resident of the towns of Boylston and Sandy Creek, died December 19, 1914, at the home of his son, William V. Whitford, on the Box farm in the town of Sandy Creek, near Pulaski. Mr. Whitford was 77 years of age; was a native of the town of Scriba, and was the last of a large family of children. Mr. Whitford moved to Boylston about thirty-five years ago. He was a veteran of the Civil war, serving in the 187 [*sic*] N.Y. Vol. . . . The funeral was held on Wednesday at the home where he died, Rev. T. T. Davies officiating . . . ." Whitford was a member of J. B. Butler Post No. 111 GAR which published "Resolutions" in his memory in *The Pulaski Democrat* December 30, 1914. Polly's death was reported in *The Sandy Creek News* March 12, 1908: ". . . The funeral of Mrs. William Whitford, who passed away on the 5th inst., was held at her late residence last Sunday at 1 o'clock p.m. . . . Mrs. Whitford was a devoted mother and an estimable lady and was very much respected by all who knew her . . . Mr. Whitford and his family wish to thank their friends and neighbors who so kindly assisted them in caring for their loved one during her sickness and death, also to the choir for their good music rendered. Mr. Whitford has a wide circle of friends who deeply sympathize with him in his present bereavement and his irreparable loss." William and Polly are buried in Boylston-Sandy Creek Wesleyan Cemetery, Lacona. A brother, Benjamin Franklin Whitford (1833-December 1902), served in Co. K, 54th and Co. K, 157th Regiments. Another brother, George W. Whitford (1819-1906), has been erroneously assigned to Co. E, 136th Regiment. That man died in 1862 while George died on the family farm in Scriba where he had lived his entire life.

William Whitham – Co. B
b. May 27, 1810 England
d. August 31, 1884 Oswego City, NY
m1. Charlotte Frances _____ (1822-1847) *ca.* 1840
m2. ?
m3. ?
m4. Amanda Mary _____ (1823-July 26, 1897) ?

NOTE: William, whose parents are unidentified, claimed to be 42 years old in 1862 but he lied to be able to enlist. He was a musician and on December 31, 1863 he transferred to the non-commissioned staff as second chief musician. He next transferred to the 3rd Brigade Band on January 7, 1865. When the 1865 New York census was taken he was still in the army. That census showed he had been married four times, but its accuracy is questionable without more evidence. Charlotte, his first known wife, bore him at least three children: Eleanor Charlotte (December 5, 1841-?); Henry William (October 5, 1842-March 24, 1900); George Alfred (November

30, 1844-March 25, 1891). She is buried in the Parish of Woolwich, Kent, England. Henry's obituary states he and his father had migrated from England to Canada. Amanda Mary was born in Jefferson County, NY and it is possible she met and married William in Canada. In any event, her daughter Jessie Ann (1860-February 23, 1948) was born in Canada. Apparently the marriage did not last because by 1880 Amanda and Jessie were living in the Town of Henderson and William was living with a woman calling herself Luella Whitham. That they were not married is confirmed by the fact that it was Amanda who obtained a widow's pension. William's death was noted in *The Oswego Morning Times and Express* September 1, 1884: "Mr. Wm. Whitham, sr., a well-known painter died this morning suddenly it is said from rheumatism of the heart. Mr. Whitham was an old resident and was well known especially to our older citizens. He was in the army serving in the 147th regiment and was a member of Post O'Brien. Members of the post are requested to meet at G.A.R. hall tonight to make arrangements for attending the funeral." He was buried in Riverside Cemetery, Scriba. Amanda, who died in Belleville, Jefferson, NY, is buried in Evergreen Cemetery, Roberts Corners, under the name Whitman. Henry served in Co. H, 12th NY Cavalry. George served in Co. D, 4th NY HA.

Daniel Whiting – Co. K

b. 1817 Mayfield, Fulton, NY

d. February 1, 1863 Regimental Hospital, Belle Plain, VA

m. Harriet Plumb (May 15, 1829-April 30, 1868) July 5, 1847

NOTE: Daniel was the son of Henry (?-?) and Catherine Lasher Whiting (?-?). His COD was a combination of typhoid fever and pneumonia. Some documents place his death on February 2nd, but the date in *Deaths of Volunteers* is that given above. Dr. Simeon Place wrote a letter to Harriet dated March 1, 1863 concerning her husband's death which is excerpted here. I have taken the liberty of regularizing the punctuation and capitalization: "Respected Madam, I receivd a letter from you this morning making inquiry in regard to your late husband Daniel Whiting. The first time I ever saw your husband to know who he was, was when he was brought into the Hospittle. I examined him at the time as I was the attending Surgeon. I found him very low. He evidently had had typhoid feaver for several days. He also had an inflammation of the lungs. He was very restless and unease. Medicine seemed to have little or no effect on him, his limbs were cold. He said but a few words in my hearing, nothing about his family or friends whatever. His case was so singular that I made inquiry in regard to him about the Regiment. I found he had been gon several days from Co. K as he was transferred to that company from Co. D and no one knew where he was two days before he was brought to the Hospittle. He went into a tent of Co. D and was brought from that to the Hospittle. I am unable to learn that he said anything to any boddy about his home or friends. In fact Madam he was senseless almost. The evening he died I set by him and gave him brandy . . . I gave him a dose of Brandy, he swallowed it and stoped breathing. At once I took hold of his puls and waited some five minutes expecting that he would make some motion but alas he was dead; there was no struggle . . . He fell away like one asleep. He is buried on a beautiful high hill that looks out the Mighty Potomac with six more of his fellow soldiers who have died here. The officers of the Company have erected to his head a nice Board, his name, death, Co. on it like this: Daniel Whiting/ Co K 147th Regiment/Died Feb. lst 1863. There to sleep until the graves are called on to give up their dead. From what I know or have heard of Mr. Whiting he was a quiet peaceable man unoffending in his manner towards any one, done his duty as long as he was able and then was gathered home to his God. He undoubtedly has gone where the clangor of the battle is not heard, where the song of the redeemed is heard instead of the Harsh Nots of the bugle, where all is Peace, the place where we are all hastening and but a few more rolling suns and the last soldier of the Army of the Potomac will be as low as Daniel Whiting . . . I can sympathize with you. I have lost two Dear companions, ones that I loved. They are both gon. I am yet here and notwithstanding I have become so familiar with death I feel my heart sink within me when I see a soldier die for I know it breaks hearts at home . . . who love them and long for their return . . . ." Harriet applied for a widow's pension and later for pensions for her four minor children. Two of them, Harriet (1852-1866) and Byron (1858-1867), preceded her in death. Francina (1850-February 22, 1932) and Sarah (1854-April 10, 1930) survived to adulthood. Both died in Fulton. They are buried in Mt. Adnah but their mother's gravesite has not been located.

Hamilton Marks Wilcox – Co. F

b. 1835 Lebanon, Madison, NY
d. November 3, 1862 Georgetown General Presbyterian Church Hospital, Washington, DC
m. Sophia Lucy Reynolds (October 20, 1836-November 22, 1874) March 27, 1862

NOTE: Hamilton, also known by his middle name, was the son of Joseph (?-*ante* 1850) and Sophia Drake Wilcox (1808-1890). Captain Cyrus Hartshorn wrote about his sickness and death in a letter dated November 5th and published by *The Mexico Independent* November 20, 1862, 1: "On my return from Washington . . I called to visit Hamilton M. Wilcox, one of my men then a patient in the Presbyterian Hospital, at Georgetown, sick with typhoid fever. He had been removed here the Thursday before . . . Willing hands and sympathizing hearts administer to the wants and soothe the fevered brows of these noble men who hastened from dear homes in their country's defense . . . Mr. Wilcox expressed his joy on seeing me by the hearty yet feeble grasp of my hand, and said that he thought he was on the gain; but I feared it would be otherwise, and my fears were but too true – he died the next day. He formerly resided in the town of New Haven and leaves a wife and numerous friends to mourn his loss . . . He was buried at the 'Soldiers' Home' not far from Washington . . . ." Hartshorn's letter described the company's funeral for Wilcox and provided the text of a Resolution for the family. Sophia, also known by her middle name, obtained a pension. Her gravesite has not been located.

William Wilcox – Co. I
b. 1844 England
d. ? ?
m. ?

NOTE: Little has been discovered concerning this soldier. He was wounded in the face at Gettysburg but the exact date is unknown. He transferred to Co. A on September 9, 1863 and to the VRC on March 20, 1865. There the trail ends.

Andrew J. Williams – Co. F
b. 1835 Western, Oneida, NY
d. ? ?
m. ?

NOTE: This soldier's story is also a mystery. He transferred to Batt. L, 1st NY ART on December 28, 1863 and mustered out on June 17, 1865 at Elmira, NY. He applied for a pension on November 19, 1887 in New York State. There is no notation of a widow's claim.

David Williams – Co. E
b. 1841 Sandy Creek, NY
d. November 7, 1913 Pulaski, NY
m. Amelia A. Johnson (1844-July 1, 1910) 1865

NOTE: David was the son of William (1805-1859) and Jane Williams (1812-1875), both immigrants from Wales. He was discharged from the army for "disability" on February 18, 1863 at Armory Square Hospital, Washington, DC. His obituary appeared in *The Pulaski Democrat* November 12, 1913, 1: "David Williams, a veteran of the Civil War, died at the home of his son, Wm. W. Williams, at Maltby's Corners, Friday, after an illness of about a week with pneumonia. Mr. Williams was born in the town of Sandy Creek where he resided for many years. He enlisted in the 147th Regiment, N.Y. Vols. He served but a short time owing to disability and came back to Sandy Creek to reside. A number of years ago he moved to this town where he was engaged in farming. Mr. Williams was a member of the Methodist church of this village and a faithful attendant when in health so he could be out. His funeral was held from the Methodist church Monday, at two o'clock, Rev. A. P. Palmer officiating . . . By request of the family J. B. Butler Post G.A.R. had charge of the funeral." Amelia died unexpectedly as reported in *The Sandy Creek News* July 6, 1910: "Mrs. David Williams died suddenly Friday forenoon at her home on the North road. Mrs. Williams who was about sixty years old had been in in her usual health except a slight indisposition a few days ago, resulting from chronic heart trouble, which caused her death. Mr. Williams came to Pulaski during the forenoon for some medicine and when he returned found his wife dead . . . ." David and Amelia, the mother of four, are buried in Pulaski Village Cemetery.

John Williams – Co. E

b. 1835 Remsen, Oneida, NY
d. July 1, 1863 Gettysburg, Adams, PA
m. Delilah Dryer (October 2, 1841-February 9, 1923) June 7, 1858

NOTE: John was David's brother. He was initially listed as MIA, as revealed by a letter from Captain James Coey dated October 13, 1864: "I James Coey Captain Co E 147 Regt. NY Vols. hereby certify on my honor that I was well acquainted with John Williams who was a private in my said company and who died on the 1st day of July 1863 in the service of the United States from wounds received while in the service and in the line of duty. That at the battle of Gettysburg in the State of Pennsylvania, on the 1st day of July 1863 while engaged with the enemy said John Williams was severely wounded and fell on the field, to all appearances in a dying condition. That we were driven from the field, our dead & wounded falling into the enemy's hands. That on the 25th day of July 1863 I was relieved of command of said Co. E 147 Regt NY Vols., the officer succeeding <u>erroneously</u> reporting the said John Williams as missing in action. That I was the officer in command of said company E at the time and that I make this statement from my own personal knowledge, and from information received of those present at the time." Delilah obtained pensions for herself and for her two children. On May 26, 1866 she married Charles L. Learned (1841-April 7, 1915). After his death she applied for a remarried widow's pension which was issued to date July 28, 1915. At the time she was 73 years old. Upon her death *The Sandy Creek News* February 15, 1923 published the following: "Delilah Dryer, widow of Charles Learned died at the home of her daughter, Mrs. Jay Lindsey, Friday February 9, at the advanced age of 81 years. Mrs. Learned had always resided in the town of Sandy Creek. She was a daughter of Mr. and Mrs. Nathan Dryer. She was twice married, first to John Williams, who fell in the Battle of Gettysburg and by whom she had two children . . . Later she married Charles Learned and to this union were born four children . . . The funeral of Mrs. Learned was held from the home of Jay Lindsey Monday afternoon, Dr. William J. Hart, officiating.

The remains were placed in the vault in Woodlawn cemetery to be interred in the family plot beside her husband in the spring. Mrs. Learned and her husband were among the leading residents of the western part of the town of Sandy Creek and were always staunch supporters of the Center Methodist Episcopal church." Two more Williams brothers also served the Union cause. Rollin (1838-1916) was a member of Co. K, 24th NYSV. Isaac (1844-1907) was a member of Co. E, 24th NY Cavalry.

Reuben Williams – Co. C
b. 1827 Jamaica, Windham, VT
d. February 12, 1879 Dubuque, Dubuque, IA
m. Mary Lucy Moffitt (April 13, 1829-October 13, 1909) September 9, 1847

NOTE: Reuben was the son of Selden (1789-1834) and Rachel Brooks Williams (1788-1832). He enlisted in the 3rd US Artillery at Worcester, MA on February 24, 1851 but deserted on April 15, 1851. He was discharged from the 147th on January 18, 1864 for "disability." He is buried in Linwood Cemetery, Dubuque. Mary obtained a widow's pension "by special act" perhaps because Reuben deserted from the US Army in 1851. She is buried in Oakwood Cemetery, Beloit, Rock, WI with her son Selden (1857-1887) and other members of the family.

Warren P. Williams – Co. I
b. 1835 New York City, NY
d. December 4, 1864 Charleston, SC
m. ------

NOTE: Warren P. Williams was an alias for Warren P. Jenness, son of Warren (1810-1887) and Mary Richardson Jenness (1812-1880). He stated he was a mariner when he enlisted but census records show he was a coppersmith. Warren was captured at the battle of the Wilderness on May 5, 1864 and sent to Andersonville, GA. He was subsequently sent to Charleston, SC where he died of chronic diarrhea. He is buried in Beaufort National Cemetery, SC. His father attempted to obtain a pension in 1879 but was unsuccessful.

William Alonzo Williams – Co. K
b. June 17, 1843 Newfield, Tompkins, NY
d. May 2, 1927 Minneapolis, Hennepin, MN
m1. Maria Lucretia Tripp (August 29, 1845-January 23, 1923) *ca.* 1864
m2. Chloe K. Blackford (1865-April 6, 1889) December 31, 1883

NOTE: William was the son of Luther (1809-*post* 1880) and Marabah Rumsey Williams (1815-*post* 1880). His POB is a matter of conjecture. Although he claimed in 1862 that he had been born in Seneca Falls, Seneca, NY, documents point to Newfield, further evidenced by the fact that his parents were living there when the 1840 census was taken. By 1850 they were residing in Seneca Falls. William, using his middle name, enlisted in Co. C, 19th Infantry (3rd NY ART) in April 1861 and deserted on August 25, 1861 at Hyattstown, Montgomery, MD. He next attempted to enlist in the 110th Regiment but was sent to the 147th. He was discharged on March 25, 1863 for "heart disease," according to *Registers of Officers and Enlisted Men*. An entry in *The Town Clerks' Registers* shows he attempted to enlist in the VRC in 1864 but was refused because his enlistment was "contrary to the regulations." At the time the registers were compiled, he was living in Battle Creek, Calhoun, MI. In both 1870 and 1880 his parents were living in Georgetown, Ottawa, MI. In November 1883 he applied for a pension but did not receive a certificate, possibly because of his desertion in 1861. By Maria, William was the father of Myrtle Bell (1865-1958), James H. (1867-?), Maribah (1870-1955), Lewis Alonzo (1876-1947), and one more unidentified child. By Chloe he was the father of Mabell (1885-*post* 1930). Maria, Myrtle, Maribah, and Lewis are all buried in Greenwood Memory Lawn, Phoenix, Maricopa, AZ. Mabell married E. G. Scott (1890-?) in Lisbon, Columbiana, OH on July 21, 1930 and then disappeared. Chloe is buried in Georgetown Township Cemetery, Hudsonville, Ottawa, MI. William is buried in the veterans' section of Lakewood Cemetery, Minneapolis.

Charles Gurley Willis – Co. G

b. June 8, 1824 Winfield, Herkimer County, NY
d. December 24, 1898 Lisbon, St. Lawrence, NY
m. Emily Clarinda Gurley (January 1, 1828- May 30, 1871) 1853

NOTE: Charles was the son of Joab (1782-November 16, 1871) and Lucinda Gurley Willis (1789-1853). Lucinda was sister to Joshua Gurley (1795-April 19, 1870), the father of Emily Clarinda Gurley, making Charles and Emily first cousins. Charles transferred to the VRC on May 31, 1864 and was discharged on June 27, 1865 at Washington, DC. A brief obituary appeared in *The Oswego Daily Times* December 27, 1898, 8: "Charles G. Willis, a former Oswegonian, died at Ogdensburg on Friday last. His remains arrived here yesterday in charge of his son Merrick Willis and were buried at Rural Cemetery. Mr. Willis was seventy-five years old and was born at Redfield. He moved with his father to Fruit Valley and for many years lived two miles west of the city on the Plank Road. He was a veteran of the Civil war and served in Company G, 147th Regiment." The article contains three glaring errors: Charles was not born in Redfield. Between the years 1820-1830 his family resided in Winfield, Herkimer County. He died on December 24th according to the New York State Death Index, not in Ogdensburg, but in Lisbon. Emily and other family members are also buried in Rural Cemetery, Oswego Town.

Russell Gibbs Willis – Co. H

b. June 15, 1838 Constantia, NY

d. June 24, 1916 Bernhard's Bay, NY

m. Harriet "Hattie" M. Hall (May 1846-January 27, 1923) 1865

NOTE: Russell was the son of Wendell (1794-1876) and Sarah "Sally" Gibbs Willis (1796-1883). He was wounded on July 1, 1863 at Gettysburg. He transferred to the VRC on March 10, 1864 and was discharged on June 27, 1865. In 1890 he claimed hydrocele as a disability. His death was noted in *The Oswego Daily Times* July 3, 1916, 7: "Russell Willis, an aged farmer of [Bernhards Bay], was stricken with death Saturday afternoon, June 24, which was due to heart trouble. His friends and relatives were shocked to hear of his sudden death. Mr. Willis was an old soldier of the Civil War. He joined the army in 1862 and endured many hardships. He belonged to the 147th regiment and Company H. He was wounded and taken prisoner, but returned at the close of the war and lived [*sic*] to tell many tales about the war. He loved the Stars and Stripes in his late years as well as in his younger days. He was greatly interested in the wars that are going on now. He had just taken the paper in his hands to read the war news when he was stricken with death. Mr. Willis was an old resident of this town and has always lived here. He has left many friends and relatives who will miss him. His funeral was the largest in this town in many years . . . ." Another obituary, appearing in *The* [Cleveland, NY] *Lakeside Press* June 30, 1916, added to the story: ". . . Industrious, frugal, honorable in his dealings with friend or stranger, Mr. Willis was a man honored and respected by all with whom he had business or other relations. He was a charter member of the Bernhard's Bay Grange and was greatly interested in advanced methods of agriculture. In politics he was a firm believer in the principles of the Republican Party . . . ." If Russell were captured by the Confederates, his captivity was of short duration. The August 1863 muster roll put him in Fort Schuyler Hospital, New York City. Harriet's passing was noted in *The Oswego Daily Palladium* February 3, 1923, 3: "The many friends of Harriet M. Willis were sincerely grieved to learn of her death after a brief illness last Saturday morning at her home near Panther Lake in [Constantia]. Funeral services conducted by Bernhards Bay Grange, of which she was an earnest and valued member, were held at Constantia Baptist church on Wednesday forenoon, the Rev. Mr. Genoung officiating." Russell and Harriet were the parents of four children, one of whom, Eldrich, was the district attorney in Auburn, Cayuga, NY. Russell and Harriet are buried in Constantia Center Cemetery.

Thomas Wills – Co. E

b. March 1829 Devonshire, England

d. March 1, 1904 Sandy Creek, NY

m. Emma Harrison (March 1833-April 2, 1907) October 8, 1853

NOTE: Thomas was the son of Charles (1791-?) and Jane Wills (1796-?). He became a naturalized United States citizen on February 12, 1867. His time in the 147th Regiment was brief since he was discharged for "disability" on November 27, 1862 at Armory Square Hospital, Washington, DC. He re-enlisted on September 13, 1864 in Co. E, 189th Regiment and mustered out on May 30, 1865 near Washington, DC. In 1890 he claimed "partial amaurosis and injury to left arm, ribs, and leg" as his disabilities. Upon his death *The Sandy Creek News* March 3, 1904 published the following: "Thomas Wills, for over a half a century a resident of this county, died Tuesday. For many years he was a much respected resident of Boylston but has more recently resided on the Ridge. The funeral will be held at the home of Will Wills Friday at 2 p.m., Rev. T. T. Davies officiating . . . Mr. Wills was born in Devonshire, England in 1829. He followed the sea for nine years and visited Australia and was married in London in 1853 to Emma Harrison. They came to this country in 1854 and settled in this county . . . ." Emma's death was reported in *The Sandy Creek News* April 4, 1907: "Emma Wills, widow of the late Thomas Wills died on Tuesday April 2, aged 73 years. Mrs. Wills was born in London and was married to Thomas Wills in that city in October 1853. They came to this country and for a short time resided in Scriba, Mr. Wills following the lakes. Later they moved to the town of Sandy Creek locating in Kilburnville. Subsequently they bought a farm in the town of Boylston south of Smartville where they resided for a great many years and where their family grew to the age of responsibility. This was one of the best farms in that part of the town and was always an attractive home . . . The funeral was held at the home of William Wills at 2 o'clock today, Rev. W. M. Hyden officiating . . . ." Thomas and Emma are buried in Boylston-Sandy Creek Wesleyan Cemetery, Lacona.

John Howard Wilson – Co. H
b. August 14, 1837 Thompsonville, Hartford, CT
d. April 14, 1921 York, York, NE
m. Martha Jane Wright (December 31-1840-February 7, 1925) November 1, 1857

NOTE: John was the son of James Stuart (1807-1884) and Jean Orr Wilson (1807-1897). Dates for him and Martha vary. I use those on their gravestones. John mustered out with the regiment on June 7, 1865. The family moved to Nebraska at some time after 1875. On December 23, 1887 John and Martha took out a marriage license in Holdrege, Phelps, NE, both claiming to reside in Colorado. Since 1887 marked their 30th wedding anniversary perhaps they decided to renew their vows. They are buried in Elwood Cemetery, Elwood, Gosper, NE.

John Mills Wiltse – Co. F
b. June 21,1835 Marcellus, Onondaga, NY
d. June 22, 1917 Syracuse, Onondaga, NY
m1. Nancy Jane Gardner (1840-December 1, 1868) *ca.* 1865
m2. Henrietta Thurston (1851-May 18, 1894) October 1869

NOTE: John was the son of Solomon (1809-1878) and Betsey Mills Wiltse (1807-1869). He mustered out with the regiment on June 7, 1865. In 1890 he said his disability was "chronic diarrhea now changed to costiveness." Nancy was the mother of one child, Cora (1868-1869). Henrietta was the mother of seven more. John, his two wives, some of his children, and his parents are all buried in Roosevelt Cemetery, Pennellville, NY.

Atwell Sylvester Winchester – Co. H
b. 1832 Madison County, NY
d. June 19, 1864 Petersburg, VA
m. Nancy Wilbur (March 27, 1832-August 16, 1924) April 7, 1853

NOTE: Atwell, the son of Benjamin Sylvester (1787-1853) and Elizabeth Sarah Negus Winchester (1787-1857), met an unexpected death which was related to Nancy in a letter written by W. W. Berry, a member of the 147th Regiment's band, and dated June 22, 1864: "There is a duty resting upon some one to pen a few lines to you if it has not been done, & it is to write sad news. Not knowing whether any one has written, I will take the responsibility upon myself to inform you that Mr. Winchester was shot dead on the 19th about noon while making his coffee by a bullet passing over the breastwork & hit him in the head. Mr. W— was a friend of mine. Him & I were both musicians of the same company. I think he had not an enemy in the company to which he belonged & everyone regrets his departure. There is a board put up at his grave with his Co - Reg - & date that he was killed." Today Atwell lies in Poplar Grove National Cemetery, Petersburg, VA. He and Nancy were the parents of three children for whom she obtained pensions. On June 25, 1865 she married Ebenezer Childs Lowell (1828-1901) as his second wife. He died in the Madison County Almshouse of "cardiac dropsy and heart failure." After his death Nancy petitioned to have her pension restored as a remarried widow. She was described as a "cripple" and "unable to work." A short but interesting obituary appeared in *The Oswego Daily Times* August 25, 1924, 2: "Mrs. Nancy Lowell, 92, widow of Charles [*sic*] Lowell, died Friday night at the home of her daughter, Mrs. Francis Ashby, Oneida. She was born in Smyrna, and had lived in Oneida for the last 24 years. She is survived by the daughter with whom she lived and one son, Eugene Winchester Lowell of Syracuse. She was a member of the M. E. church of West Amboy. Funeral services were held

Tuesday at 2 p.m., the Rev. Casselbury officiating and burial was made there." Nancy and Childs were actually buried in Cleveland Village Cemetery where there is also a cenotaph for Atwell.

David Wines – Co. H

b. 1810 Burn, New York, NY
d. May 1, 1863 Regimental Hospital, Fredericksburg, VA
m. Mary Ann Sturge (1815-*post* 1883) October 24, 1833

NOTE: David, son of James L. (1774-1850) and Charity Wines (1780-1850), lied about his age in order to enlist. Like many others, he said he had been born in 1818. His death was reported in a letter from Captain Slayton which was published in *The Mexico Independent* May 28, 1863. Dated May 18, 1863, it was addressed to the newspaper's editors: "Again death has entered my Company and chosen for its victim David Wines, a man 44 years of age and a resident of Constantia. The circumstances connected with the death of this man are rather peculiar. On the 1st last, we were in line of battle all day, occupying a position below Fredericksburg, across the river. Just as the sun was going down the rebels set up a tremendous cheer or yell, and to satisfy the rebels that we were ready for them cheers were fast going the length of our lines, and as this man arose and gave one cheer, he fell, and as I supposed, fainted; but on approaching him, to my great surprise I found him dead. He was immediately carried to the rear on a stretcher. The doctors immediately procured and agreed that he came to his death by a fit of apoplexy. This man was the father of two sons, both of whom were members of my company. One of them died not long since, of small pox, and the other has been discharged for disability. I have now, in all, seventy six enlisted men, fifty-six with me, and twenty absent, sick, in different hospitals. We are at present camped in a beautiful pine grove. Our camp is neatly swept every morning, and the boys are generally feeling well. My health continues good. I have not seen a sick day since I left home." The sons mentioned in the letter were George and James. (See below.) David and Mary Ann were the parents of at least three other sons, John S. (1846-*post* 1910), Charles H. (1847-1918), and David O. (1854-1939). Charles served as a substitute soldier in Co. E, 104th Regiment. Mary Ann was noticed in a pensioners' list published in *The Oswego Times and Express* October 17, 1883. A cenotaph for David is located in Constantia Rural Cemetery and it is possible she is buried there too.

George Washington Wines – Co. H

b. 1840 Sterling, Cayuga, NY
d. April 8, 1908 Constantia, NY
m1. Sylvia P. Smith (1850-March 31, 1899) *ca.* 1863
m2. Minnie E. Beggs (1881-October 28, 1932) 1902

NOTE: George's time in the 147th was brief since he was discharged on February 9, 1863 for "disability." In 1890 he said he had had a "fractured ankle 26 years" and had also been "kicked by mule." George and Sylvia are buried in Union Settlement Cemetery, West Monroe, NY. Minnie married John D. Carr (1882-1942) in 1907. They are buried in Mt. Adnah Cemetery, Fulton.

James Orville Wines – Co. H
b. 1836 Cayuga County, NY
d. April 21, 1863 Calorama Hospital, Washington, DC
m. Eliza Chapman (1841-1913) April 23, 1857

NOTE: James succumbed to smallpox and was buried in the Soldiers' and Airmen's Home National Cemetery, Washington, DC. Eliza married Willard Squires (1843-1922), a veteran of the 110th Regiment, on October 21, 1866 at West Monroe, NY. They are buried in Union Settlement Cemetery, West Monroe, NY.

Franklin "Frank" Wing – Co. C
b. February 1839 Mexico, NY
d. January 23, 1914 Richland, NY
m. Mary E. Rider (1844-April 14, 1932) 1870

NOTE: Franklin was the son of Fuller (1785-ca. 1850) and Sarah "Sally" Bailey Wing (1801-*post* 1850). He mustered out with the regiment on June 7, 1865. In 1880 he and Mary were living in the Oswego County Poorhouse and he was suffering from consumption. His obituary was published in *The Pulaski Democrat* January 28, 1914: "Frank Wing, 74, a Civil War veteran, died Friday morning at his home in the southern part of the town after a long illness. Mr. Wing served in Company C, 147th Regiment, New York Volunteers, and was a member of J. B. Butler Post No. 111 G.A.R. He was the first member of the post to die this year. None died last year. Ten died in 1912 . . . Funeral was held Monday." According to *The Pulaski Democrat* April 20, 1932, Mary, who was born in Canada, died in Cleveland, Cuyahoga, OH where she resided with her daughter Clara. She and Franklin are buried in Daysville Cemetery, Richland.

Henry Wing – Co. F
b. 1837 Mexico, NY
d. February 28, 1863 Belle Plain, VA
m. ------

NOTE: Henry was the son of Joseph (1805-1852) and Susan Rice Wing (1810-*post* 1880). He originally enlisted in the 110th Regiment but was sent to the 147th. His

COD was typhoid fever. His mother applied for his pension, claiming he had been her primary support for several years. She had married Joseph on January 18, 1826 at Edmeston, Otsego, NY. According to her son Clark (1830-1870) and family friend Gad Morton, ". . . said Joseph Wing her husband became a profligate and abandoned his family many years since and neglected & refused to provide for his family and died at the time and place [Pike, Wyoming, NY] aforesaid without property & without friends." Mary, it was claimed, had no property except her clothing "of the plainest and cheapest quality." To maintain her family she had been forced to apply to the Poor Master of the Town of Mexico. Clark's will provided for his wife, Martha, his mother Susan, and a mentally disabled sister, Maria. Susan does not appear on the 1883 list of Oswego County pensioners and a bill for reimbursement dated 1884 leads me to conclude she died *ca.* 1882. To date her grave has not been located.

Henry Witt – Co. H

b. May 27, 1828 Unity, Sullivan, NH
d. June 26, 1908 Constantia, NY
m. Eliza _____ (1829-*ante* 1905) 1848

NOTE: Henry, a cooper, was the son of Elisha (1790-1849) and Deidamia Alexander Witt (1794-1848). His DOB varies. I use that found on his gravestone. He was captured on May 5, 1864 at the battle of the Wilderness and spent ten months as a POW in Andersonville and North Carolina before being paroled in early 1865. He mustered out with the regiment on June 7, 1865. He and Eliza were the parents of three children. Eliza is a mystery. According to the 1855 New York census she was born in Oneida County. She last appears on the 1900 census, living with Henry, but she was not enumerated for the 1905 New York census. She does not appear on the New York State Death Index. While Henry is buried in Union Settlement Cemetery, West Monroe with other members of the family, there is no trace of her. Henry's brother, Mosley (134-1888), served in the 110th Regiment.

William W. Wood – Co. F

b. July 17, 1828 Ellisburg, Jefferson, NY
d. February 1865 Florence, SC
m. Susan Abigail Streeter (August 12, 1836-February 5, 1932) April 16, 1856

NOTE: William's parents are unidentified. In 1855 he was living as a servant in the Joseph Butler household in Volney, NY and was a cooper. *The Adjutant-General's Report* of 1904 says William was captured at an unknown date but he was in all probability taken on May 5, 1864 at the battle of the Wilderness. The report also says he died in February 1865 which is corroborated by military records . He is buried among the "unknowns" at Florence National Cemetery. Susan married John Dempster Leigh (1839-1879) on September 13, 1869. He died in Camden, Oneida, NY and is buried in Fairview Cemetery, Williamstown, NY. On June 27, 1901 Susan, still residing in Camden, applied for a pension as a remarried widow. Her death was announced in *The Sandy Creek News* February 11, 1932, 6: "Mrs. Susan Streeter Leigh, aged 95 years, died February 5, 1932 at the home of her daughter, Mrs. E. M. Adams in North Main street, Adams, following an illness of several months. She was born in Frankfort, August 12, 1836, the second of a family of nine children to Rev. Herman and Mariah Brayman Streeter . . . When Mrs. Leigh was a child the family moved to Sandy Creek, the father being a pastor of the Wesleyan Methodist church. In early life she was married to William Wood . . . The Civil War broke out and William Wood enlisted. He was captured by Confederate soldiers and thrown into a rebel prison where he died of starvation. Mrs. Wood received one letter from him written in prison and telling of his capture. Her second husband was John Dempster Leigh of Westdale who died in 1878 [sic]. Mrs. Leigh left Westdale about twenty years ago to make her home with her daughter Mrs. Adams. She was well known in this section . . . Funeral services were held at the home Sunday afternoon, Rev. W. A. Gardner, pastor of the Methodist Episcopal church, officiating. Burial was in Elmwood cemetery." Her gravestone also serves as a cenotaph for William. It is interesting to note that the stone states he enlisted in the 147th on August 5, 1861. His DOD on the stone is November 10, 1864. POD is erroneously given as Andersonville.

Alonzo George Woodard – Co. G

b. 1841 Parishville, St. Lawrence, NY
d. April 11, 1911 Fannie Paddock Hospital, Tacoma, Pierce, WA
m. Mary Vallard (October 1, 1848-April 1, 1924) *ca.* 1870

NOTE: Alonzo, son of Calvin (1812-1887) and Elvira Mitchell Woodard (1817-1891), enlisted in Co. F, 81st Regiment on October 16, 1861. He was discharged on December 20, 1861 because he did not have his parents' consent to enlist which is odd since all records indicate he was over 18. On August 25, 1862 he enlisted in the 147th Regiment and served until the regiment mustered out on June 7, 1865. He is buried in Oakwood Hill Cemetery, Tacoma. He and Mary apparently separated. In 1910 he was living with his daughter Bertha (1871-September 16, 1922). Mary's obituary appeared in *The Morning Olympian* April 3, 1924, 4: "Mrs. Mary Woodard, aged 75, passed away at her home, 311 Puget street, Tuesday evening. The deceased was born in Geddes, NY, 1848, and has resided here for the past 11 years. Surviving is one son, Henry Woodard, residing in St. Louis, and a daughter Miss [sic] Edna Holmberg, of this city. Mrs. Woodard was a member of the Pentecostal Assembly and funeral services will be conducted by Elder Secrist from the Mills Chapel Friday afternoon at 1 o'clock . . . ." Mary was buried in Masonic Memorial Park, Tumwater, Thurston, WA.

Charles B. Woodard – Co. E

b. November 9, 1837 Boylston, NY

d. February 16, 1915 Oswego, NY

m. Harriet J. Ostrom (1840-January 31, 1903) 1859

NOTE: Charles' parents were John (1796-1858) and Phebe Brown Woodard (1800-1861). He transferred to the VRC in 1863 and was discharged on June 28, 1865. His death was reported in an informative obituary in *The Oswego Daily Times* February 24, 1915, 5: "Prayer services for Charles B. Woodard, who died February 16, 1915, was [*sic*] held at the home of his daughter, Mrs. F. L. Davis, 103 East Sixth street, Wednesday evening at seven o'clock and were conducted by the Rev. William F. Kettle, pastor of the Congregational church. The remains were taken next morning at 8:30 o'clock to Sandy Creek, where the funeral services were held at 11:30, the Rev. Mr. Barrett, pastor of the Sandy Creek Baptist church, officiating. The deceased was born in the town of Boylston November 9, 1837, being one of seven children born to John and Phebe Brown Woodard. In 1859 he was united in marriage to Harriett J. Ostrom of the town of Orwell, who died at the age of sixty-two years. After having served nearly three years in the Civil War, he purchased a tract of land near Boylston Center, where their lives were spent excepting the last seven years, when he gave up active life and came to reside with his daughter . . . ." Harriet's death was announced in *The Oswego Daily Palladium* February 13, 1903: "Harriet J. Woodard, wife of Charles B. Woodard, died at her home in Boylston, January 31st, 1903 at the age of sixty-two years. She was a model wife, a true mother, a good neighbor and devout Christian, for many years a faithful member of the Methodist Protestant church. Although her sufferings were hard to bear she was ever patient. She has left to those who came under her influence a testimony that Jesus saves and that his promises are true . . . ." Charles and Harriet are buried in North Boylston Cemetery. Two of his brothers also served in the Union Army. One was Orson (see below). The other was Ezra Hampton Woodard (1842-1923), a member of the 10th NY HA from August 1862-June 1865.

Orson J. Woodard – Co. E

b. May 16, 1835 Jefferson County, NY

d. June 19, 1921 Mannsville, Jefferson, NY

m1. Jeanette Curtis (December 15, 1835-May 4, 1892) *ca.*1856

m2. Emma Warren (January 12, 1848-March 11, 1939) June 20, 1894

NOTE: Orson, son of John (1795-1858) and Phebe Brown Woodard (1800-1863), was discharged from the army for "disability" on August 29, 1863 after seeing action at Gettysburg. In 1890 he said his disabilities were typhoid fever, blood poisoning, and kidney disease. He and Jeanette were the parents of six children. In 1863 Orson had made the acquaintance of Emma Warren, a fourteen-year-old school teacher who lived with her parents near Gettysburg. In 1894 when Orson, now a widower, returned to Gettysburg for a reunion he again met Miss Emma, unmarried and still teaching school. The two married and returned to Mannsville. His obituary was published in *The Sandy Creek News* June 23, 1921: "Orson J. Woodard's death occurred in his home Sunday morning after many months of general decline. A year apart the families of Woodard and Brown came by ox team from Vermont to settle here. John Woodard and Phoebe Brown married and in their home about half a mile west from this place, Orson J. was born eighty-six years ago last May 16. He always lived near here, following the business of grist mill owner, wood, lumber, feed and coal dealer. In 1862 he enlisted in Company E 147th N. Y. Volunteers, became second, then first lieutenant and belonged to the Sandy Creek Barney Post G. A. R. His first wife was Miss Jeanette Curtis, who died over thirty years ago . . . Exactly twenty-seven years ago, returning to Gettysburg, Mr. Woodard married Miss Emma H. Warren, a teacher, who has always been a devoted wife and to her is extended the sympathy of friends. Rev. B. F. Hurlbut of Memphis, complying with the oft expressed wish of his veteran friend, conducted the funeral service in the home Tuesday afternoon, attended by several veterans, friends and relatives from Camden, Oswego, Boylston, Belleville, Sandy Creek and Clinton. Four nephews acted as bearers for the burial in Maplewood cemetery. Many beautiful flowers were around the casket, roses being the favorite flower." Emma's story of her family's participation in the battle of Gettysburg was told by David Shampine, "Handshake with History," *The Watertown Daily Times* September 14, 2003. She described the fight occurring right outside her family home as she, her mother, and siblings hid in the cellar. When President Lincoln came to Gettysburg on November 9, 1863 for the dedication of the cemetery, she was one of many who lined up to shake his hand. Orson, Jeanette, and Emma are all buried in Maplewood Cemetery, Mannsville.

Edwin Woodbourne – Co. I
b. November 22, 1839 England
d. September 20, 1864 US General Hospital, Alexandria, VA
m. Alice Reed (1839-1876) September 12, 1862

NOTE: Edwin, son of Thomas (?-1848) and Sarah Rogers Woodbourne (1818-*post* 1870), was wounded on July 1, 1863 at Gettysburg and again on August 18, 1864 at the battle of the Weldon Railroad. His death was reported in *The Oswego Commercial Advertiser* September 28, 1864: "The death of Corp. Edwin Woodburne [*sic*], of Co. I, 147th N. Y. Volunteers, was briefly announced under our obituary head yesterday. He was severely wounded at the battle of Weldonville, and from the field was carried to the General Hospital at Alexandria, where he died on the 20th instant. He was yet a young man – scarcely 25 – and had volunteered in his country's service from a sense of duty alone. He was widely known in this community, and beloved by a large circle of friends who will sincerely mourn his early death, and who deeply sympathise with his sorrowing wife and mother." He is buried in Alexandria National Cemetery. Alice, daughter of Josiah (1812-1861) and Alice Wheatley Reed (1808-1881), had no children with Woodbourne but her marriage to George W. Autenrith (1845-1918) *ca.* 1867 produced three: Josiah (1868-1960); George A. (1871-?); Alice M. (1873-1938). According to her FAG entry Alice died in Centreville, St. Joseph, MI. She is buried with her parents in Rural Cemetery, Oswego Town. Edwin's brother Richard (1842-?) served in Co. I, 24th Regiment and later in the 9th NY HA.

George L. Woods – Co. A
b. September 3, 1836 Phoenix, NY
d. May 10, 1921 Volney, NY
m. Samantha Malvina Clark (November 14, 1847-October 14, 1934) 1861

NOTE: George's parents are reputed to be William J. (1805-*post* 1836) and Sally Duncan Woods (?-*post* 1836). He was wounded on July 1, 1863 at Gettysburg and transferred to the VRC on March 20, 1865. In 1890 he said his disabilities were disease of the rectum and diarrhea. He ran a grocery store in Fulton for many years. He and Samantha are buried in Mt. Pleasant Western Cemetery, Volney, under the name Wood.

Joseph Woods – Co. A
b. 1844 Canada East
d. January 11, 1883 Oswego City, NY
m. Louise _____ (1849-January 22, 1921) *ca.* 1867

NOTE: Joseph, whose surname was also spelled Wood, was the son of Joseph (?-*ante* 1860) and Sophia Sears Woods (1821-*post* 1865). He mustered out with regiment on June 7, 1865. He worked in the boatyard in Oswego, and, as reported in *The Oswego Morning Post* January 12, 1883, he died from a construction accident: "A distressing accident occurred at the D. L. & W. trestle, in course of construction in the new harbor, yesterday afternoon, which cost Joseph Woods his life. The circumstances of the accident are as follows: About 1 o'clock Woods, who had been at work on top of the trestle all day, was engaged in carrying a keg of spikes from one bent to the other on a plank, fully thirty feet from the ground. Other workmen were raising a heavy bent, the weight of which pulled out the stay lath of the third bent, letting the plank upon which Woods was standing fall. The poor fellow pitched backward, striking upon his head and crushing in his skull. He was conveyed to a building used as an office at the foot of Third street, and Dr. Milne summoned. He could do but little for the unfortunate man, and he died soon after. Woods was a hardworking man and leaves a wife and five children in straightened [sic] circumstances. He resided at No. 12, Church street. He was a carpenter and 38 years old. He served in the Union army during the rebellion and was a member of Post O'Brian, G. A. R. The coroner will hold an inquest this morning." The coroner's jury returned a verdict of accidental death. He and Louise were the parents of numerous children. She obtained a widow's pension and never remarried. She and Joseph are buried in St. Peter's Cemetery, Oswego City.

Thomas Woods – Co. A

b. August 20, 1846 Ottawa, Ontario, Canada
d. February 23, 1924 Schenectady, Schenectady, NY
m. Julia A. Murray (October 28, 1851-March 18, 1940) June 13, 1866

NOTE: Thomas was Joseph's brother. According to the 1900 census he immigrated to the United States in 1860 and became a naturalized citizen. He mustered out with the regiment on June 7, 1865. He claimed no disability in 1890. He and Julia moved to Schenectady ca. 1901. An informative obituary appeared in *The Schenectady Gazette* February 26, 1924, 8: "Thomas Woods, a Civil War veteran, died at his home . . . Saturday as the result of ill health from which he had suffered a number of years. The funeral service will be held Thursday morning in Oswego. The body will leave the city on the 1 o'clock train this afternoon. There will be a service in Oswego in the St. Louis Church. Father Thomas Lange of the Church of St. John the Baptist, this city, conducts a prayer service at the house today. Mr. Woods was born in Ottawa, Canada. He had lived in the city 23 years coming here from Oswego where he had lived since a boy 12 years of age. Mr. Woods was a member of O'Brien Post, G. A. R., of Oswego which will assist with the service on Thursday. Mr. Woods enlisted in 1862, was a corporal in the war and was given his discharge papers in 1865 . . . ." Thomas in reality was a sergeant in his company. He may have belonged to Post O'Brian but he also was a member of May Stacy Post 586 GAR. Julia's death was announced in *The Oswego Palladium-Times* March 20, 1940, 4: "Mrs. Julia Woods, 89, widow of Thomas Woods, died at the home of her daughter, Mrs. Charles H. Pilon . . . at 2:30 o'clock Monday afternoon. Mrs. Woods had been in impaired health since she fractured her hip two years ago. Born in Oswego, Mrs. Woods had resided in Schenectady for a number of years, later returning to Oswego. She was a communicant of St. Louis' church and had a wide circle of friends, among whom she was held in fond affection . . . ." Thomas and Julia are buried in St. Peter's Cemetery, Oswego. Amelia (1842-1924), wife of Charles Dashner, another member of Co. A, was sister to Thomas and Joseph.

Datus Woodward – Co. C

b. May 29, 1816 Onondaga County, NY

d. July 29, 1891 Amsterdam, Montgomery, NY

m. Sylvia Powell Foote (September 28, 1821-February 20, 1891) April 15, 1841

NOTE: Datus' father is unknown but his mother was Azuba Woodward (1783-*post* 1860). Datus was a captain but spent only a few months in the army, being discharged on February 4, 1863. He was overage when he enlisted. In 1867 he was appointed postmaster in Lorraine, Jefferson, NY. His son Charles was a dentist in Amsterdam where both Datus and Sylvia died. Their bodies were returned to Oswego County and buried in Hillside Memorial Park and Cemetery, Central Square.

Robert Lowell Woolman – Co. C

b. 1826 Pompey, Onondaga, NY

d. August 1, 1890 Constantia, NY

m. Harriet W. Parkhurst (1829-October 20, 1874) *ca.* 1847

NOTE: Robert's parents were David (1781-*post* 1860) and Hannah Ward Woolman (1790-*post* 1840). He was discharged from the service on August 23, 1864 for "disability" and in 1890 claimed to be paralyzed on the right side of his body. He is buried in Lakeside Rural Cemetery, Bernhards Bay, NY. Although Harriet's DOD is known, her gravesite is not. It is possible she is buried in Cleveland Village Cemetery with her parents, John (1799-1876) and Betsey Dodge Clark Parkhurst (1800-1876). Lowell M. Woolman (1845-September 1864), Robert and Harriet's son, served with the 13th NY HA. Records show he entered a hospital on August 24, 1864, location unknown. Since the 13th was active in Virginia, he most likely died there.

Nathaniel Albert Wright – Co. K

b. March 16, 1836 Oswego, NY

d. December 20, 1912 St. Joseph's Hospital, Syracuse, Onondaga, NY

m1. Sylvia E. George (1839-July 27, 1882) August 31, 1863

m2. Pattie D. Wood Oliver (1839-June 4, 1909) October 22, 1884

NOTE: Nathaniel was the son of Peter P. (1809-1881) and Eliza A. Rogers Wright (1809-1873). He saw prior service in Co. C, 24th NYSV from May 1861–September 1862 when he mustered out in order to accept a commission in the 147th. He was wounded at Gettysburg on July 1, 1863 and discharged for "disability" on November 5, 1863. In 1890 he claimed a wounded right forearm as his disability and said he had been discharged on account of his wounds. He and Sylvia were married in Oswego City. They had no children. Nathaniel's second wife, Pattie, had previously been married to Robert Oliver, Jr. (1836-March 17, 1871), a lieutenant in the 24th

Regiment. She and Wright married in Chicago, Cook, IL but apparently the marriage was unsuccessful. They were not living together in 1892 and in 1900 she said she was divorced. She applied for a remarried widow's pension on February 26, 1902. Her obituary, published in *The Oswego Daily Palladium* June 5, 1909 makes no mention of Nathaniel: "Pattie D. Oliver, widow of Lieutenant Robert Oliver, Jr., died at the Ogdensburg State Hospital yesterday afternoon at the age of seventy years. The body arrived here this morning and was taken to the home of her only child, Joseph Oliver, 80 Ellen street, where the funeral will be held Monday afternoon at two o'clock. Mrs. Oliver was for many years a resident of this city and had many friends. She has been an invalid for several years. Before marriage she was Miss Pattie D. Wood." She and Robert are buried in Riverside Cemetery, Scriba. Nathaniel's death three years later occasioned a lengthy obituary in *The Oswego Daily Palladium* December 20, 1912: "Major Nathaniel A. Wright, one of Oswego's old residents, keen businessmen and best known veterans, died at St. Joseph's Hospital, Syracuse, at a quarter of eight o'clock this morning after a long illness from bladder trouble, which necessitated an operation and from the effects of which he did not rally. Admitted to St. Joseph's on November 16th the operation was performed four days later and he had gradually been getting weaker, until on Wednesday night he lapsed into unconsciousness. From that time he sank rapidly until the end came peacefully this morning. Mrs. Claude W. Thorp, a niece, had been at his bedside since yesterday. Major Wright was the son of the late Peter P. and Eliza A. Wright, and was born in Oswego March 16th, 1836. His father was a tugman, and as a young man he was employed as wheelman on his father's boat. He was in his twenty-sixth year when the Civil War broke out, and he was quick to offer his services, leaving the lakes to enlist in the Twenty-fourth New York, Colonel Timothy Sullivan, and being made First Sergeant. He signed the muster roll as a member of Captain Francis C. Miller's C Company at Elmira, on the 17th of May, 1861, and the year later was made Captain of K Company, 147th Regiment, under the command of Colonel A. S. Warner. He led his company, in the front rank, at the battle of Gettysburg, and was shot through the right wrist during a charge. For his bravery in this engagement he was given the title of Brevet Major and granted a medal by Congress. On August 31st, 1863, Major Wright married Sylvia E. Creore [*sic*], who died on July 27th, 1882. Two years later he married Pattie D. Oliver and she also is dead. After the war Major Wright returned to make his home in this city and in 1867-68 served as Chief of Police, retiring to enter the feed business with George H. Hunt, continuing as a member of the firm of Wright & Hunt until 1896 when he retired from active business. Since that time he has devoted himself almost entirely to looking after his investments. Major Wright was, during his life-long residence here, prominent in social and fraternal circles. He was an enthusiastic sportsman, a lover of rod and gun and active in the affairs of the old Leatherstocking Club. For nearly fifty years he had been a member of the Odd Fellows, belonging to Oswegatchie Lodge 156 I. O. O. F., Konoshioni Encampment and the Odd Fellows' Club. He was also a member of the Fortnightly Club, Post O'Brian, G. A. R., and of the Loyal Legion, whose insignia he always wore in the lapel of his coat. Although a member of no church, Major Wright was most upright in life; of spotless reputation and keenest honor; kind-hearted and charitable; liberal minded with all. He had the love and esteem of innumerable friends and acquaintances. His surviving relatives are nephews and nieces . . . ." One of them, Fred P. Wright, reminisced about his uncle in *The Oswego Palladium-Times* March 7, 1950, 4: ". . . My uncle, Nathaniel A. Wright, who served as chief of police, 1867-1868, was a Union soldier during the Civil War . . . [He was] promoted March 13, 1865 'Major by brevet for gallant and meritorious service.' His name was placed on 'The Roll of Honor' by Congress. He used to relate how when captain he saved from surplus funds earmarked for mess supplies, enough cash to buy good supplies of tobacco. These he had distributed to his men of Co. K, much to their delight and to the disgust of the other companies whose captains were not so shrewd, looking out for their men. His experiences with army discipline and dangers made him an efficient Chief of police. He related how down on 'The Flats' a wrong doer set himself at top of a stairs landing, pulled a revolver and said he would kill the first man sent to get him. Chief Wright calmly walked up stairs and arrested him . . . Chief Wright retired from police work to enter the retail flour and feed business where the Savas Tavern is now located. George H. Hunt was employed by him, became his partner, the firm being Wright and Hunt . . . . ." The major and Sylvia are buried in Rural Cemetery, Oswego Town. His brother, Peter Orsamus (1841-1910), also served in Co. C, 24th Regiment.

Peter Wright – Co. G
b. 1805 Germany
d. August 10, 1873 Oswego, NY
m. Susan _____ (September 12, 1813-November 22, 1885) *ca.* 1851

NOTE: Peter's parents were Conrad (?-?) and Margaret Wright (?-?). Although he said he was born in 1818 when he enlisted, other documents prove he lied. He was discharged for "disability" on July 15, 1863 at Fairfax Seminary, VA. He applied for a pension on July 23, 1863 but did not obtain a certificate. His unexpected death was reported in *The Oswego Daily Palladium* August 11, 1873: "About 5 o'clock yesterday, while Thos. Smith and Ora W. Babcock were strolling through the woods back of the Oswego Driving Park, they thought they saw at a distance a man standing under a tree. – They walked in that direction, and when quite near saw that the man was Peter Wright, a German, whose family live on East Twelfth street, and that he was hanging from a limb and was stone dead. His hat was lying on the ground, and one foot was caught in a crotch in the tree and the other touched the ground, though none of the weight of the body seemed to rest upon it. The appearance was as if the dead man had stepped into the crotch, made one end of the rope fast to the limb from which he was hanging, tied the other end about his neck, and swung himself off, and that his foot caught either in swinging off, or in the struggle of death. The rope was a clothes line, one end being tied securely to the limb, and the other fastened to the neck with a slip knot, which had turned around so that the rope drew from under the ear. Coroner Barnes was notified, and with Bens & Dain, undertakers, went over, cut the body down and took it to the residence on East 12th street, where an inquest was held . . . Timothy Tows deposed that while at the house of his son-in-law, Paul Sheldon, yesterday, about half past one or two in the afternoon, he saw the deceased go up the road towards the race course, walking leisurely with his hands behind him. John Wright, son of the deceased, testified that his father left home Saturday morning and the family had not seen him since. Witness did not know where he staid Saturday night. He was in the habit of going away sometimes. Witness did not know the reason of his going away. He and his father had some words about work; Saturday morning he asked his father to get up and go to work and he wouldn't. Afterwards he got up and left the house. He was in the habit of drinking but was sober when he left. Witness did not know whether he was sober yesterday. Witness did not tell him to leave or stay away, only to go to work. He was at Cook's butcher shop about half past one, Saturday. Dr. Kingston examined the body and found no marks of violence, but the neck was broken. The verdict was that the deceased, Peter Wright, came to his death by his own hands by taking his life by hanging by a rope to the limb of a tree. The deceased was about 60 years old and leaves a family, consisting of a wife and several grown up children. He enlisted in Co. G, 147th Reg't., and served a few months, but was discharged on account of disability, being too old to endure service. Lately he has been a laborer on the streets and for private individuals. The family is a very respectable one, and feel very keenly the death of the deceased in this particular manner." He is buried in Rural Cemetery,

Peter Wright's gravestone contains no information about him. He is buried in the rear of Rural Cemetery, Oswego Town.
Author's Collection

Oswego Town. Susan died in Chicago, Cook, IL. Her body was returned to Oswego and buried in Riverside Cemetery, Scriba.

William A. Wybourn – Co. I
b. 1840 Martinsburg, Lewis, NY
d. August 23, 1875 Oswego City, NY
m. ------

NOTE: William was the son of William (1810-1887) and Angeline Hughes Wybourn (1815-1900). He is remembered as the man who took up the regimental colors after John Hinchcliff fell mortally wounded at Gettysburg. A report written by General Cutler July 9, 1863 includes the following: ". . . The Color Sergeant of the 147th N.Y. was killed and the colors were caught by Sergeant William A. Wybourn of Co. I 147th N. Y. and brought off the battlefield by him, not withstanding he was himself seriously wounded . . . ." He was again wounded at the battle of Dabney's Mills on February 6, 1865 and lost a foot, as reported in *The Oswego Commercial Advertiser* April 7, 1865: "Lieut. Wm. A. Wybourn, of the 147th, arrived home last evening. His right foot has been amputated – the effect of a rebel bullet. Otherwise he is in good health, and looking well . . . ". Wybourn's military career was detailed in a resolution by Alderman Phelps and recorded in the minutes of the Oswego City Common Council held on August 24, 1875 and reported in *The Oswego Daily Times* August 28, 1875: "Mr. Mayor: -- After a long and protracted sickness our fellow townsman, William A. Wybourn has passed over the River of Death and as he was one of our Municipal officers and having taken an active part on the Federal side in the recent conflict for the existence of this nation, and having like Zebulon and Naphtali been willing to jeopardize his life under death in the high places of the field for his country, I hope you will fully concur with me that it is proper to have the records of this Council bear witness of our high appreciation and esteem for his distinguished service. Mr. Wybourn enlisted as a private in Co. I, 147th Regiment, N. Y. Vol., Aug. 23, 1862, and left our city in the following September. He was soon appointed Sergeant and was actively engaged at the battles of Fredericksburg and Chancellorsville. For his gallantry and heroism in rescuing the flag of his Regiment from the hands of the enemy at the battle of Gettysburg he was commissioned a First Lieutenant and was subsequently engaged in all the battles with the Army of the Potomac under Gen. Meade, and from the Wilderness until the crossing of the James River in June, 1864. At the battle of North Anna he was on the staff of Gen. Rice commanding the 4th Division, Fifth Corps. At this battle his timely discovery of the enemy's approach saved the corps from surprise and destruction and won for himself a Captaincy in his Regiment with which he participated in the numerous battles and siege of Petersburg until the battle of Dabney's Mills, February 6, 1865, where he lost his leg. During his military career he exhibited those qualities which make the true soldier and officer, winning the admiration and esteem of both his superiors and subordinates. As further evidence of our high regard and esteem I would respectfully offer the following preamble and resolutions: Whereas, The death of Captain William A. Wybourn, Collector of Taxes of the City is an event in the local history of Oswego that admonishes us of our duty to recognize in a proper manner his public services, Therefore be it, Resolved, That in the character of Captain Wybourn were united the spirit of a dutiful son, a genial companion, a true friend, a kind neighbor, a good citizen, a brave soldier and a faithful public officer, Resolved, That the heroism that he displayed on the bloody field of Gettysburg in grasping the colors from the hands of a fallen comrade should place his name beside the heroes of Lodi and Lundy's Lane and should forever shed luster on the [annals] of his Regiment and of the citizen soldiery, Resolved, That as representatives of the municipality we regret the loss of this faithful officer and tender in a sympathetic manner our condolences to his

William Wybourn's gravestone also memorializes many members of his family. The marker is located near that of Peter Wright.
Author's Collection

afflicted family . . . ." In addition to his professional duties as a tax collector, among others, Wybourn was also a member of Frontier City Fire Company No. 2 which published its own resolutions in *The Oswego Daily Times* September 4, 1875, here excerpted: ". . . *Resolved,* That we recognize in the deceased, a brave soldier whose conspicuous courage upon the field of battle and long service in the army made our whole country his debtor, -- whose fidelity to the interests of the firemen made them his debtors, whose kindness and affection as a son and brother serves as a bright example to us all – whose conduct as a man commends itself to the public and especially to the members of this company who knew him so intimately and so well, and who in the discharge of his duties as a civil officer under our city government has earned universal satisfaction . . . ." He is buried in Rural Cemetery, Oswego Town. William's brother, Howard (1845-*post* 1900), served in the US Navy from 1863-1865.

George W. Yerden – Co. E

b. 1842 Morristown, St. Lawrence County, NY
d. November 29, 1864 Salisbury, Rowan, NC
m. ------

NOTE: George was the son of Jacob G. (1817-1885) and Elizabeth "Eliza" Livingston Yerden (1817-1894). According to *The Town Clerks' Registers*, he was captured in action at Pelles House near Petersburg, VA at an unknown date. A short article appearing in *The Mexico Independent* March 2, 1865, stated that he died in the hospital at Salisbury Prison. His entry in *Deaths of Volunteers* does not include COD. George is buried among the "unknowns" at Salisbury National Cemetery.

Charles Henry Zee – Co. H

b. August 1837 Parish, NY
d. January 4, 1907 Oneida, Madison, NY
m. Eliza Carley (October 7, 1839-January 4, 1919) *ca.* 1860

NOTE: Charles' father was Peter (?-?). His mother is unknown. On the 1855 New York census he was enumerated as the adopted son of Jacob (1795-1870) and Catherine Jacobsen Fravor (1797-1861). He was wounded on July 1, 1863 at Gettysburg and discharged for "disability" on December 11, 1863. On March 28, 1864 he enlisted in Co. B, 149th Regiment. He was wounded at Resaca, GA on May 15, 1864 and transferred to the VRC on January 16, 1865. He mustered out on September 13, 1865 at Springfield, IL. His death was reported in *The Syracuse Herald* January 4, 1907: "About 6 o'clock this morning Charles Henry Zee, a veteran, died at the home of his son-in-law, Fred Eggleston of No. 4 Warner Street, after a long illness, death having been caused by dropsical conditions. He was born 69 years ago and had spent considerable of his life in this city. He was a veteran of the Civil War, having first enlisted in 1862 in the 147th New York infantry. While with this regiment he was injured, and upon recovering returned to the front as a member of the 149th New York infantry. His record as a soldier was excellent, he having participated in a large number of battles . . . The funeral will be held from the First Baptist Church at 1 o'clock Sunday afternoon, the Rev. Frank T. Latham, pastor of the First Baptist church officiating. Burial will be made in the Glenwood cemetery." He and Eliza were the parents of six children in 1875 but by 1880 they were not living together and he claimed he was a divorced person. On February 21, 1878 she gave birth to a son named Charles Travania Russell in Detroit, Wayne, MI. In later life Charles (1878-1958) would say his father's name was Charles T. Russell but no corroborating evidence has been found for this man. Whether he and Eliza were married is unknown. Eliza apparently married Charles A. Weed (1829-1896) *ca.* 1884 and produced another son, Grover

Cleveland Weed (1886-1945). Eliza's COD was heart disease and it is interesting to note she died on the same date as her first husband. She is buried in Woodlawn Cemetery, Syracuse.

Peter Zeigler – Co. G

b. 1822 Germany
d. July 1, 1863 Gettysburg, Adams, PA
m. Elizabeth _____ (?-September 5, 1899) ca. 1849

NOTE: Peter's surname was also spelled Ziegler. He and Elizabeth were the parents of Augusta (1850-April 27, 1931). She was born in Germany, but by 1856 the family was living on the Hall Road, Oswego. Peter, a tailor by trade, was KIA. Elizabeth obtained a widow's pension and lived at the same address until she died. In 1890 she said her husband's name was George. Augusta married John Yorker (1850-June 1928) and was the mother of numerous children. They are buried in St. Peter's Cemetery, Oswego City. Elizabeth's grave has not been located.

The Draft, Dodgers, and Deserters

Part I: Drafting

Our Charlie has gone for to live in a tent,
They have grafted him into the army;
He finally puckered up courage and went,
When they grafted him into the army;
I told them the child was too young – alas;
At the Captain's fore-quarters they said he'd pass,
They'd train him up well in the infant-ry class,
So they grafted him into the army.
O, Charlie, farewell, your brothers fell,
Way down in Alabamy,
I hoped they'd spare a lone widder's heir,
But they grafted him into the army.[108]

THE ELECTION OF Abraham Lincoln to the presidency in November 1860 precipitated the secession of seven southern states: South Carolina, Mississippi, Florida, Alabama, Georgia, Louisiana, and Texas. The attack on Fort Sumter on April 12-13, 1861 and the subsequent secession of Virginia, Arkansas, North Carolina, and Tennessee drove the government to declare war on the grounds that secession was illegal. The War of the Rebellion, initiated so righteously on both sides, originally depended on voluntary military service. Believing the conflict would be of short duration, men filled with patriotic zeal in North and South flocked to fill the ranks of hastily formed regiments.

At the time the US Regular Army, always a small entity, consisted of 14, 926 enlisted men and 1,080 officers.[109] They were scattered all over the continent and only 18 infantry companies were stationed east of the Mississippi River. On April 15th Lincoln, realizing the need for immediate armed assistance, called upon the state militias to provide men for a stint of three months in order to bolster the standing army.[110] He had not obtained approval from Congress for this action, leading that body to vote to permit and support a volunteer army of up to 500,000 men.

A conflict lasting no longer than 90 days was predicted, a foolhardy, naïve, and misguided notion held by both sides. The North failed to realize how serious Southerners were about defending their way of life. The South did not foresee that the sheer industrial capability of the northern states could and eventually would lead to almost total destruction of their agrarian culture.

The early successes of the Confederate Army changed the perspective on both sides. The first battle of Bull Run, July 21, 1861, the failure of the Union forces to capture Richmond, and the general inability of the United States to identify a competent general, among others, all pointed to a potential defeat for the North and the establishment of a separate country in the South. On April 3, 1862 Secretary of War Edwin Stanton, for reasons still not fully understood, ordered all recruiting offices throughout the Union to be closed, a decision rescinded on June 6th.[111] Even with that action, however, something more drastic had to be done if the war effort was to be sustained.

On June 30, 1862 Secretary of State William Seward, no doubt sensing the gravity of the situation, drafted a letter which he then sent to northern governors, asking them to forward it to President Lincoln under their own names with a date of June 28th, to petition him to initiate a draft to replenish depleted regiments. Lincoln was aware of the fact that the Confederacy had been forced to implement a draft and realized such action would be as unpopular in the North as it was in the South. Nevertheless, on July 1st, he responded to the governors' plea: "Fully concurring in the wisdom of the views expressed to me in so patriotic a manner by you, in the communication of the twenty-eighth day of June, I have decided to call into the service an additional force of 300,000 men. I suggest and recommend that the troops should be chiefly of infantry. The quota for your State would be _____. I trust that they may be enrolled without delay, so as to bring this unnecessary and injurious civil war to a speedy and satisfactory conclusion. An order fixing the quotas of the respective States will be issued by the War Department tomorrow."[112]

Oswego County, which furnished 11,000-12,000 men over the course of the war, had already raised the 24th and the 81st Regiments and was now required to provide another.[113] During the summer of 1862 threats of a draft drove the local War Committee to feverish activity to persuade men to volunteer (and be eligible for generous local and state bounties) rather than wait to be drafted and receive no such reward. During the month of July, local newspapers were full of articles urging men to enlist: "Hon. Elias Root, chairman of the Citizens' Committee to aid the matter of enlistment is at Albany, but will soon return here to set the ball in motion. Meetings should at once be held and efforts put forth to secure a prompt response to the President's call . . . We believe that volunteers must be found. It must not be said that we of the North have been compelled to resort to a draft to fill the lines of our armies in the field. Let us have no unwilling soldiers in the ranks; *that* has been the crowning shame of the rebel confederacy. Let press and pulpit, all public and social influences be brought to bear before the word 'draft' is used. The blood of the nation is again up, and a little money combined with a good deal of management must be made to give the government all the men it will require . . . Oswego County must bear her share of the burdens of war, and furnish her proportion of the troops needed to make out the quota of the Empire State."[114] Appeals to patriotism formed part of the effort: ". . . Soldiers are wanted to uphold the honor and dignity of our Government and to defend the glorious old banner that has waved in triumph on so many fields! Has that appeal ever been made to our people without a response? We feel certain that the call will not be in vain . . . ."[115] If loyalty and patriotism were insufficient to procure volunteers, other, less noble, incentives were available: "In case a draft is resorted to by the Government, the times and penalties for the non appearance on muster call of the drafted man – the law making him a deserter if he does not appear – hold him to a very rigid account. There is no escape from a draft; as requirements must be complied with, or the penalties which are very severe, must soon be met. To avoid these unpleasant results, and to fill up the army, which needs recruits, very liberal bounties are offered to volunteers. But the men who do not volunteer will lose these bounties if they are drafted."[116]

Originally scheduled to be held on August 15th the draft was delayed until September 15th because enrollment procedures had not yet been completed.[117] No draft was necessary in Oswego county in 1862: vigorous recruiting ultimately resulted in 1,025 men for the 110th and 837 more for the 147th. In early November the citizens of Oswego County could finally breathe easily: "We are authorized by the chairman of the War Committee to state that the quota of volunteers in this county has been made out, and that there will be no more draft, unless there is another call for troops."[118]

Although Oswego County did its part to provide soldiers without having to resort to a draft, which was, admittedly, the reason for threatening such action, by early 1863 Lincoln and his military advisers realized that volunteerism by itself would not be enough to bring the war to a successful conclusion. On March 3, 1863 the Enrollment Act passed Congress, instituting a real draft in all northern states. To say it was unpopular is to understate the situation and the Draft Riots of New York City in July were only one manifestation of the discontent. According to the regulations, every man between the ages of 20-45 was liable to be drafted, including aliens who intended to become citizens. Officers visited each home in the various districts to record the names of eligible males. All the names were to be put into a box or wheel, from which sufficient names were to be drawn to ensure the area's quota was reached. It was illegal to leave the country to avoid the draft. Something as simple as the failure to provide one's name could get a man into trouble: "This morning a man named Patrick Downing was arrested by Deputy U.S. Marshal Reid, for refusing to give his name to the officers taking the enrollment for the draft. He will have a hearing this afternoon before Commissioner Perry. – The penalty, we understand, is a fine of $500 and imprisonment for two years."[119] Others resorted to harsher methods of avoiding conscription: "A man by the name of Reuben Flanigan, who had been drafted in the town of Oswego, N.Y., hung himself because he did not want to go soldiering. The coroner was sent for, and the jury returned a verdict of 'exempt.' He was a Copperhead and physically resisted the draft as advised by Gov. Seymour . . . ."[120]

Loopholes existed, however, which led to the oft-repeated opinion that this was "a rich man's war but a poor man's fight." Various persons were automatically exempt, such as the vice president, telegraphers, judicial and executive officers, members of Congress, mail deliverers, custom house collectors.[121] Other exemptions might also be claimed, such as son of a widow; son of aged and infirm parents; only brother of minor children dependent on him for support; father of motherless children.[122] One enterprising young man in Rhode Island suggested he be exempt because "he was entirely dependent upon his mother for support. But the Board concluded she ought to be freed from the burden and took him . . . ."[123]

Physical exemptions were allowed and many men flocked to physicians to obtain that precious certificate. The War Department issued a list of 51 specific ailments or disabilities which automatically exempted a man from military service. Among these were imbecility or insanity; disease of the brain, spine, heart, lungs; consumption; loss of sight; total deafness; loss of an arm, forearm, hand, thigh, leg, foot; total loss of index finger on the right hand; loss of teeth which would prevent "tearing of cartridges."[124] Learning of the potential for avoiding the draft on account of a loss of teeth, a draftee in Rochester, NY presented himself to the doctor after purposefully having several extracted: ". . . Dr. Backus saw the dodge, and expressed his regret at a disfigurement which deprived Uncle Sam of so fine an infantry soldier, but consoled the fellow with the assurance that he would answer just as well for the artillery service and the Board would save a good place for him . . . ."[125]

A letter to the editor revealed how men were avoiding the draft in Utica: ". . . A great crowd was gathered on the pavement near the entrance to the hall, from which the stairs led to the doctor's rooms above. The stairs were literally blocked up, thereby rendering it wholly impossible for one to get by. – Being well acquainted with the doctor, and also with the building, I knew of a private entrance to the office, and soon found myself in the doctor's front room. I found in a room not over 16 feet wide by 18 feet long, as many as 25 *invalids*, all anxiously waiting to be called into an inner room by the doctor and be examined, and, if possible, obtain a certificate of exemption that would get them 'out of the draft.' I must say I never saw a more hardy and rugged set of invalids in my life . . . I conversed with several of them, and asked them what their claim to an exemption was . . . Another, more sociable, told me a long list of ills, among which were the following: he had a blind sister to support, and a large family, and his wife was deaf. He was also deaf, and his lungs were very much affected. He never could stand it to be a soldier, and he thought it would be very cruel to send him. I thought to myself it would be a very foolish thing to send him . . . ."[126]

Men resorted to legal trickery to avoid the draft, such as the overweight farmer from Pennsylvania who implored his attorney to find a way to get him an exemption. The two men visited the local commissioner's office and legal counsel announced he had found a man who wanted to be a substitute. The commissioner said he "won't do; he can't march." After a bit of wrangling, the commissioner firmly said the man was not physically qualified. At that, the lawyer triumphantly stated: "Well, then, scratch his name off the list; *he is drafted, and wants to be exempted.*" Knowing he had been bested, the commissioner "looked at the lawyer for about a minute; then regarded the fat draft, and without speaking a word, scratched off his name!"[127]

After Lincoln issued the Emancipation Proclamation, black men were also subject to the draft. Sometimes they too were less than eager to serve: ". . . – A colored waiter in Hartford, Conn., who had been 'struck' by the draft, hired a lame darkey to personate him before the examining board, with a view to exemption. The leg was not unsound enough, the surgeon 'passed' the bogus conscript, and he was held as a warrior. He turned pale with fear, and divulged the cheat; the result was, both substitute and principal were locked up."[128]

A reporter noted the perceived poor health of military aged men in Oswego County: "It is painful to contemplate the number and diversity of complaints to which frail mortality is heir, as evidenced by the claims for exemption which are now being preferred in great numbers by our patriotic friends from the country. We grieve to think of the enfeebled and diseased race of men by whom we are surrounded, and we do not see what is to prevent the County of Oswego from becoming one vast hospital. Men who have always been considered able-bodied, who have always done man's work in the shop, hayfield, and the dinner table, have suddenly been overtaken by the most insidious, and alarming diseases, and have become possessed of litanies of complaints, any one of which would unfit a man for military duty, and if he were taken into the service, would immediately become the inmate of a hospital . . . ."[129]

Women also had opinions about the draft and exemptions. Sara Payson Wilson (1811-1872), better known as Fanny Fern, was a well known and vocal 19th century social critic. She offered her assessment of men claiming exemptions: ". . . Of course I know there are cases where men ought not to go, if it can be avoided; but it strikes me that many men, who were never known to make any remarkable exertions for the comfort of their wives and families, have been seized with a very sudden and affecting view of the duties they owe them in this war, and the utter impossibility of their leaving them to suffer! I hope every mother's son of them will be 'drafted;' we want no such sham-manliness perpetrated in the next generation. And as to the bachelors, most of whom never see their way clear to this or any other species of self-denial, they ought each to be provided with a sewing machine, and set to making soldier-clothing for some 'Relief Society'."[130]

In an effort to promote fairness and transparency, James B. Fry, Provost-Marshal General, issued the following statement on July 12th: "Let the draft be entirely public, and give the names of all drafted men for publication if the papers want them. The name of every man who is granted exemption by the Board must be published, with cause of exemption clearly stated, except in cases of particular physical disqualifying causes which it might not be delicate to publish; in these cases the fact of exemption must be published and the cause stated in general and suitable terms. The exact cause must in all cases be reported to this office."[131] Thus, one William Woodell, residing in New Haven, NY, was included on such a list.[132]

A man might also apply for commutation, whereby he paid the government $300 to avoid the draft. It has been said that more than 160,000 of 207,000 draftees either paid the commutation fee or hired a substitute.[133] The ability of a man to pay his way out of military service was objectionable because it smacked of class bias. Rich men such as J. P. Morgan and John Rockefeller bought their way out of the obligation and two future presidents, Chester Arthur and Grover Cleveland, escaped the same way.[134] Cleveland hired a lake sailor, George Beniski, to take his place: "The death of George Brinske [sic], Grover Cleveland's war substitute, has already been announced in our columns. He died in the soldiers' home Bath, N. Y., of consumption. One of the last things he did before going on his death bed was to relate the story of his engagement as Grover Cleveland's representative as follows: 'In 1863 I was employed on the pro-peller Acme, and frequently made the port of Buffalo. Drafts were being made and substitutes were in big demand with good money offered. I heard of men getting as high as $300 for going to war, and when Capt. Rhinehardt of Buffalo came to me and asked me if I wanted to make some money, I told him yes. He said Mr. Cleveland, assistant city attorney, wanted a substitute and would give me $150 after I enlisted if I would go to the front. I wanted some money and accepted the offer. The captain took me to Cleveland's office, and the offer was repeated by him. Rhinehardt took me to the office of Squire Ryan and I was sworn into the service. Mr. Cleveland gave me $150 and told me that was all the money he had, and said he had borrowed it from William Rhinehardt. He said to me that he was sorry he couldn't give me more but he promised me that on his word and honor, if I lived to come back from the war, he would give me money and do anything he could for me. I took the money and rode out to Fort Porter with Cleveland and Rhinehardt. I was left at Fort Porter for some time and was then sent to Elmira and to Riker's Island, in New York harbor, and then to Alexandria, Va., where I was assigned to the 76th New York Volunteers, a regiment raised in Schoharie county, and then stationed at Rappahannock.' Brinske then stated that after getting his discharge he returned to Buffalo, 'sick and penniless.' He was sent from one poor house to another, until he [was] finally brought up at the soldiers' home at Bath, where he remained until death took him away. He had repeatedly appealed to Cleveland to make good his solemn promise to give him aid, but all his appeals were in vain. The drafted man he represented at the front had no further use for him after getting his own neck out of the halter. He got his substitute for half price by promising to make up the balance when the substitute returned from the war. He never made up the balance. Such was Grover Cleveland's patriotism during the late unpleasantness . . . ."[135]

Commutations in Oswego County were more prevalent than might be expected. Including Oswego City and twenty towns, the total was 332.[136] Taking into consideration the fact that $300 represented the average yearly wage of a laborer in 1863, it was generally beyond the reach of most. Yet ways were found to ensure that draftees could avoid service. In certain cases localities agreed to pay the fee to keep men home. David Lindley, from Canandaigua, Ontario, NY and Lawrence McMullen, Akron, Erie, NY were both noted in *The Town Clerks' Registers* as being the only drafted men from their respective towns to go into the army. Private citizens also banded together to provide "draft insurance" to anyone in the group unlucky enough to be drafted.[137]

At first commutation meant the draftee would be exempt for three years but the government, acknowledging the inherent unfairness of the system, changed the policy twice. Anyone who paid the fee prior to February 1864 was covered under that provision. After February 1864 the exemption was good for one year only. The law was again changed in July 1864 to eliminate commutation altogether, meaning a man had to serve or provide a substitute.[138] The only exception was conscientious objectors.[139]

Lastly, a man might find a substitute and pay him whatever the two agreed upon, as was the case of Cleveland and Beniski. Theoretically that figure was no more than $299. The draftee, called the "principal," and his substitute were required to appear at the designated rendezvous point where the substitute signed papers officially stating he was taking the other man's place. The substitute, therefore, was considered drafted and the principal had no further obligations.[140] The monetary advantages for a substitute were considerable, at least according to *The Rochester Express* which calculated that with state and federal bounties, substitution fee, three years' pay clothing, and board, the substitute would receive $1,363: "If the war lasts but a year – and every intelligent, candid person believes it will close before that time – the substitute will receive for his year's work, $773, or $64.41 per month and $2.47 per day! If you do not believe this, figure for yourself."[141]

While the financial incentives looked good on paper, in reality the practice of hiring substitutes was disastrous. In some cases, as can be seen in the 147th Regiment, a brother would take the place of a drafted sibling for personal reasons. Generally, however, the practice was a failure. An examination of the 215 confirmed deserters from the 147th Regiment shows that 63 of them were substitutes.[142] So-called "substitute brokers" set up shop and used any means possible to persuade or coerce young men to become substitute soldiers. Plying them with alcohol, then presenting them at the recruiting station, was a favorite tactic.[143] Reports abounded of brokers meeting poor immigrants from Europe at the pier and promising them substantial financial incentives if they would agree to serve in the Union Army as substitutes. What the "marks" did not understand was that the broker pocketed much of the promised bonus money, "essentially stealing a significant portion of the bounties and substitution prices owed to volunteers and substitutes."[144] In April 1864 Hawley D. Clapp, a bounty broker in New York City, was arrested and charged with defrauding enlistees out of their bounties, but he was only one of many who endeavored to make a profit through unscrupulous methods and lax rules governing conscription and enlistment.[145] Old men, sick men, criminals, were all solicited. General Grant complained to Secretary of State William Seward that "for every eight bounties paid he did not receive one good soldier for service."[146]

One of the oddest cases of substitution occurred in Ohio and involved a man named Captain Thomas S. Bunker who attempted to have his dead son re-enlisted as a substitute: "Capt. Thomas S. Bunker of the 88th O. V. I., last September, through the Rev. J. W. Bushing, who by the way, received pay for the part he took in the transaction, managed to have his son, who had died in the service, credited to the Quota of Darke county, O., as a substitute for a drafted man named Calvin Moore. It appears that the son, Charles Bunker, had entered the service as a substitute early in the war, and by good conduct had been promoted to the rank of Second Lieutenant, which position he held until his death, which took place last July. His father then, only two months later, through the Chaplain of the regiment to which he belonged, re-enlisted his dead son as a substitute, receiving the pay and local bounty, part of which he gave his accomplice. So glaring a piece of rascality, and so extraordinary a transaction would not of course long remain a secret. The facts have somewhat about them so unnatural – if anything that occurs may be called by that name – that so soon as known both parties were placed under military arrest to await the result of an examination by Court Martial . . . ."[147]

Despite vociferous opposition, riots, and constitutional challenges, the draft went forward. The drawing of names in Oswego City occurred on August 8th and it was reported that "no riotous demonstration of any kind has occurred."[148] Another draft was scheduled for March 10, 1864 but did not occur because volunteers exceeded the county's quota by 61 men.[149] Events in the coming months, however, were to tax the human resources of the Union to the point where another infusion of troops became necessary. Ulysses S. Grant assumed control of the Union Army in March and in what was called the Overland Campaign, he dogged Lee, engaging in battle after battle. On May 5-6, 1864 the battle of the Wilderness was fought, with an estimated loss of 17,666 Union troops. That bloody affair was followed by Spotsylvania, May 7-19, with another loss of over 18,000 men. The battle at Cold Harbor, May 31-June 12, cost the Union almost 13,000 more casualties. On June 3rd Grant lost 7,000 men in less than an hour.

On July 4, 1864 Congress passed a bill authorizing that the president might "at his discretion, at any time hereafter, call for any number of men, as volunteers for the respective terms of one, two, and three years for military service." If the quotas were not filled by volunteers, then 50 days after the call, the president was permitted to order a draft for one year to complete the quota.[150] In Oswego the proclamation was received with a flurry of activity within the War Committee. Wardwell G. Robinson recalled: "The progress of the war in the year 1863 and the early part of 1864 had been disastrous and barren of results to the Federal Government and army; the country at large, which was favorable to the Federal government, was filled with consternation; the sympathizers at the North with the secessionists were outspoken in their predictions as to the triumph and success of secession, and were giving all the aid in their power to those engaged in destroying the unity of the United States; Canadian lake ports were filled with those plotting the dismemberment of the country. There was a feeling of deep gloom overspreading the whole loyal North; not a city, and hardly a village, town, or school district in this State but that had maimed and wounded exemplars of the fact that a sanguinary war was waging. The North had already contributed freely in men, money, and material, and the end was not yet. The 'On-to-Richmond!' cry had ceased to delude the most sanguine, and the oft-repeated saying, 'The war won't last ninety days,' no longer found believers; on the contrary, it was everywhere and by every one recognized that the Republic was battling for its very existence . . . It was under these gloomy and terrible circumstances and conditions, thus briefly and inadequately stated, that Oswego County, again responding to the proclamation of the later-on martyred President Lincoln, calling for five hundred thousand additional troops to serve for one year, and which proclamation was dated July 18, 1864 set about the enlistment of another regiment to be added to the other Oswego County regiments that had already gone to war, and from which regiments maimed and wounded men were continually returning home as leaves falling to the earth from trees smitten by the autumn frost."[151] The new regiment was dubbed the

184th.[152] By mid-September 1,400 Oswego County men and 200 more from Madison and Cayuga Counties had volunteered. Thus it was reported gleefully that all the sub-divisions of the county had filled their quotas "and there is therefore no necessity for a draft."[153] Just how desperate was the need for replacement troops may be seen in the fact that four companies were sent ahead of the rest of the regiment to Washington, DC.[154]

Lincoln again called for a draft in a proclamation dated December 20, 1864, requesting another 300,000 men because the quota of July had not been reached. If after fifty days the men had not been recruited voluntarily, a draft would be held.[155] The quota for the 22nd Congressional District, composed of Oswego and Madison Counties, was 1,142, of which Oswego was responsible for 852.[156] Drafting did indeed begin within Oswego County on February 28th. By March 9th fifteen towns had completed their drawings.[157] The process lagged in Oswego City because of arguments over the actual numbers required to complete the quota. When the war ended abruptly on April 9, 1865 the US Government lost little time discharging soldiers. On April 13, 1865 Secretary of War Edwin Stanton wrote to Major-General John A. Dix, directing all drafting and recruiting in loyal states to end.[158]

I have concentrated attention concerning the draft on Oswego County but identical efforts were taking place all over New York State as well as other northern states. The work done by war committees, draft commissioners, marshals, constables, local officers, and examining boards to ensure the draft requirements were carried out was not without a price. Officers responsible for enrolling men within their district might face possible death when visiting households containing persons opposed to the war or to serving: ". . . The Enrolling Officer of Sullivan county, Ind., was shot dead on the 18th while riding along the road. An officer in Broom county was captured and held by men while women pelted him with eggs. In Holmes county, Ohio, a large number of men have banded together and armed themselves and troops were sent to disperse them on Wednesday. The troops were fired upon, and the fire promptly returned, followed by a charge, which scattered the Copperheads . . . ."[159] As late as March 1865 a police officer in Oswego City was assaulted by a "substitute broker" who thought the officer was attempting to prevent him from taking in tow a potential "sale."[160]

Part II: Dodgers

IT ALMOST GOES without saying that if money is to be made from someone else's misery, dishonest persons will figure out how to do it. So it was with the government's decision to use bounties to induce men to enlist in the military. Cities, towns, counties, states, as well as the federal government, initially all contributed to the funds appropriated to assist recruits and their families who would need financial assistance in lieu of the labor the soldier might provide. Prior to 1863 local entities might set their own bounties but the New York State Legislature passed a law that year stating that only the state could offer such inducements. The state bounty was fixed at $150 for a man re-enlisting for a year and $75 for a volunteer enlisting after November 2, 1862 and enrolling for three years.[161] Stories abound of young men who turned over most, if not all, their bounty money to mothers who were dependent on them for the welfare of younger children. Nathan Case, a member of the 147th Regiment, provides an excellent example. His mother's pension application showed Nathan had been the sole provider for her and his father, described as imbecilic, for several years. He gave his bounty to his mother, Amy, and made provision for a part of his pay to be sent directly to her.[162] Nevertheless, less honorable men saw a way to make some money without engaging in much work by enrolling in a regiment, collecting the proffered bounty, and then skipping town, usually right before the regiment was about to be transported to duty. *The Adjutant-General's Report* shows that 24 men deserted at Oswego before the 147th Regiment moved out on September 27th. Several, such as George M. Burridge and John McCoy, were lake sailors and probably retreated to the nearest outgoing vessel. Darius Ballou, whose surname endured many variations, was born on April 17, 1836 in Athol, Warren, NY. A volunteer for the 147th, he deserted on September 27, 1862 after collecting a bounty of $50. His saga occupied the columns of at least three issues of *The Oswego Commercial Times*. On October 6, 1862 Lieut. Woodard and a police officer named Southwick left Oswego with sixteen deserters whom they had rounded up.[163] The very next day it was reported that Ballou had arrived in Oswego after the regiment had departed and "upon ascertaining that the train had left evinced considerable trepidation, and expressed much solicitude for fear that he should be considered a deserter. The statement which he made was that he had received a furlough, but unavoidable circumstances had prevented his return before it expired. So fearful was he of being arrested here as a deserter, that he returned immediately to Parish, and proceeding to the Supervisor of that town gave himself up." Two days later the town official delivered him to Oswego where Lieut. Slatterly was hunting for deserters. He too believed the story and declined to arrest him. Ballou "was allowed to go at large, and rendered considerable assistance to the officer in capturing others who had deserted. As an illustration of the confidence placed in him, he was appointed a guard over his fellows, and he promised to keep a sharp eye upon them. At Syracuse, however, Mr. Bellow [sic] was among the missing, and all efforts to ascertain his whereabouts have as yet proved unavailing."[164] Lieut. Slatterly learned by telegram that Ballou had not arrived in Syracuse with the others and set out to find him: ". . . In this, however, he was unsuccessful, and accordingly returned to the city last evening. His surprise was somewhat huge on learning that the missing man was here and had already reported at the police office. Bellow denies, most emphatically, any intention of deserting. He says that upon the arrival of the train at Syracuse he received a pass for one hour; that he returned to the depot in less

than three quarters of an hour, and was just in time to witness the train vanishing from sight[;] he accordingly took occasion to pay a short visit to his friends in Parish. He is now here, ready to make another attempt to reach his regiment. He will probably be sent on this evening with the cavalry company which departs at 5:40."[165] The conclusion of this tale is predictable: "The volunteer Bellows, mentioned on a previous occasion as a member of the 147th regiment who had been left behind at the time of the departure of that regiment, but who was forthcoming immediately after the cars left the depot – the same Bellows, who accompanied a gang of deserters as far as Syracuse, as a guard, but who, in that city, was among the missing himself – the same Bellows who last week wrote from the town of Parish to officer Slatterly making inquiry when that officer intended to leave this city for the seat of war, and who was most anxious that he should receive notice in time to

A notorious dodger/deserter, Ballou completely disappeared from history in 1864.

Shawn Doyle

be here for the purpose of accompanying him – is again among the missing. He arrived in town on Saturday, and was told by Lieut. Slatterly to be on hand on Monday morning, but at the time of the train leaving, no Bellows was to be found. Lieut. S. delayed his departure till the afternoon, but still the missing man was *non est*, and the officer was obliged to depart without him. In all probability, if found again, he will receive quarters from which his passage on the train will be insured."[166]

Thomas Davis (1843-?) did not lose any time leaving Oswego, traveling north after "jumping" and enlisting in Co. M, 9th New York Cavalry at Champlain, NY on October 21, 1862. When the unit mustered on October 29, 1862 he was nowhere to be found.[167] What happened after that date is unknown. Perhaps he tried his trick again or headed for the Canadian border.

Just how prevalent was this practice is illustrated in a letter written by a member of the 184th Regiment, which is here excerpted: ". . . It appears that on the night of the 19th, at the time of the alarm, one of the would-be deserters was captured, and the next day our scouts captured five more of the party, two of whom were seriously wounded, one in the hip and the other in the leg. The scouts deceived them; they (the scouts) had been up to the lines at Richmond, and were coming back, when they fell in with the deserters, who informed them they were on their way to Richmond, where they knew they could get $2,000 a-piece in gold as substitutes. They also stated they had jumped three or four bounties already. From the fact that our scouts were habited in rebel uniform, the deserters were thoroughly deceived, and placing themselves under the guidance of their newly acquired acquaintances, they did not discover their mistake until they found themselves in Col. Robinson's headquarters. -- On the persons of these fellows was found $15,000 in greenbacks, two revolvers and about $100 in gold, thus confirming the fact that they were bounty-jumpers. The letter from which we quoted yesterday stated that they were members of the 24th N. Y. Cavalry . . . ."[168]

John Larney (1836-*post* 1905), AKA Thomas Dolan and George King, is reputed to have been one of the most notorious bounty jumpers, claiming to have collected money from 93 regiments in Ohio, Pennsylvania, Massachusetts, and New York.[169] Larney, a career criminal, was well-known to law enforcement across the United States.[170]

Bounty jumping might end fatally, as was the case in Baldwinsville, NY in August 1864. Daniel Sullivan, a recent recruit for the 184th Regiment, collected a bounty of $1,300 and apparently decided to "jump" with his wife and all their possessions. Unfortunately for him, Sergeant William H. Whalen of the 16th US Infantry was notified to be on the lookout for him. On Monday, August 19th, Whalen found himself sitting in the same railroad car as Sullivan and another would-be bounty jumper named Foley. He immediately arrested them. When the train arrived in Baldwinsville Sullivan bolted from the car. Whalen attempted to capture and subdue him but

Sullivan, who swore he would not be taken, fought back. Whalen defended himself with a knife and fatally wounded Sullivan. Despite loud cries that Whalen ought to be lynched, the verdict of the coroner's jury was that the man had acted in the discharge of his duty.[171]

While some men acted independently in various acts of bounty jumping, others were assisted in their efforts by "agents" whose motives were purely financial: "— Substitute swindlers are at work in Ohio. They induce newly enlisted volunteers to desert, paying them $100 and upwards, and then bring them to Albany, New York, where they sell them as substitutes for $400 or more. A fellow engaged in this infamous business has just been arrested at Cleveland."[172]

Other potential soldiers merely "skedaddled," to use contemporary vocabulary. These men crossed the border into Canada to avoid serving, which was a dangerous action, as David Nichols (1801-1887) discovered. Nichols, a farmer in Mexico, NY, was the father of two sons of military age, Freborn (1837-1922) and Charles (1840-?). In August 1862 he attempted to help them escape to Canada but was stymied in his efforts and arrested. Brought before a judge in Oswego City, he was required to take the oath of allegiance, pay a bond of $1,000 to "do no disloyal act," and promise to keep his sons available for possible drafting.[173] A list of "skedaddlers" from Port Ontario and Mexico appeared in a local newspaper, probably causing considerable embarrassment to family and friends.[174]

Canadian reception to skedaddlers was mixed. On the one hand these men added significantly to the workforce (while simultaneously driving down wages). On the other, however, they were viewed with disdain since many Canadian-born soldiers were serving honorably in the Union Army: "One of the Canadian papers thus welcomes the pitiful sneaks who are fleeing across the border to escape the fancied draft: -- 'The call for 300,000 men across the line will be the means of driving hundreds from that country into Canada. We are informed that quite a number have already made their appearance in this and adjoining counties. They have ignominiously left their country in the hour of her peril, to escape conscription'."[175]

Part III: Deserters

A MAN TECHNICALLY became a deserter if he failed to appear at rendezvous or for medical examination but generally the term referred to a soldier who fled service with the idea of not returning. Penalties could be harsh: desertion was considered a capital offense and punishable by execution.[176] Ella Lonn points out that many reasons existed: disillusionment with military life; encouragement by relatives and disaffected friends; poor weaponry; financial concerns for one's family.[177] James Brown and Charles Bruen, both substitutes enrolled in the 147th, deserted "on the march," the former on October 14, 1863, and the latter on May 4, 1864. Anthony Troy deserted at the end of his furlough, as was noted in the local newspaper: ". . . It is now some three weeks since his departure from here, but as yet, Mr. Troy, or the parcels of which he had charge, have not made their appearance at the camp of the 147th. It is feared he has made a mistake in his destination, and instead of journeying southward, has taken a northern course. This supposition is founded upon his failing to report at the expiration of his furlough, and remarks made while here of dissatisfaction, &."[178] Charles Brown, who was drafted from Chemung County into the 147th, deserted on February 9, 1865 at the end of his furlough. Another notable deserter was Thomas Kearney. Born in New York City in 1844, the son of Irish immigrants Patrick and Mary Dempsey Kearney, he initially enlisted in Co. B, 55th Regiment on January 24, 1862. He transferred to Co. K, 38th Regiment when the two organizations were consolidated in December 1862. According to available documents, he deserted "from hospital" on January 27, 1863. Somehow he made his way to Richland, NY where he enrolled in Co. K, 147th in March 1864. His time with the 147th was occupied by some of its most brutal service, portions of which he described in three letters to his brother John. He was granted a furlough in January 1865 and never returned to duty. What happened to him is unknown.

Not all deserters, however, did so because of a desire to avoid the rigors of army life or the possibility of being wounded or killed. Jacob House is one example. He deserted from the 147th Regiment near Tennallytown, DC on November 30, 1862 and went home to Amboy. His entry in *The Town Clerks' Registers* says it all: "Deserted and dead." It appears that Jacob was sick and when he could not obtain a furlough he simply walked away.[179]

Romance might also lead a recruit astray. Alphonse Lukin, who enlisted in the 147th in August 1862 attempted to avoid service in a novel way: "A soldier named Adolphus Lukin, belonging to Capt. Harney's company, 147th regiment, was arrested last night on board the steamer *Ontario*, while he was attempting to escape in woman's clothing. The arrest was made by Nathan Munger, of Chautauqua county, a soldier of the 110th regiment, who chanced to be here on his way home on furlough. It appears that Lukin, clad in hoop-skirts and fashionable female apparel, attempted to elope in company with a young woman name DuFraine. He had gone to the ladies' cabin, and had commenced to disrobe himself, when some of the ladies were struck with his appearance. Munger had been watching the fellow with some suspicion, and finally made his way to the ladies' cabin, and suggested to Lukin that there was some doubt as to his sex, and recommended that he should be examined by a couple of ladies. Just then Munger happened to discover that there was quite a beard upon the face of the assumed lady, and all further doubt as to his sex was dissipated. An examination under the skirts revealed a pair of pants. Lukin was delivered over into the hands of United State Deputy Marshal Reid, considerably chop-fallen at the discovery. He had taken his pay and bounty, and ought to be severely punished . . . ."[180]

Jacob's desertion was noted in a letter written by Captain Reuben Slayton in February 1863. Little is known about this man, including the name of the person who erected the gravestone.
Author's Collection

Sometimes apprehending deserters led to internecine warfare between the states and the federal government, as illustrated by this story: "Quite an exciting scene occurred Thursday in Washington, at the recruiting office for regulars, near the War Department. An officer of the 147th New York regiment went there to get three men who had deserted, and enlisted as regulars. The officer in charge of the regulars declined to give them up, and a brief scuffle ensued between the two commanding officers. The volunteer officer, with the aid of additional military force furnished by Col. Doster, finally caused the door of the barrack to be broken open, secured the deserters and bore them away to the camp of the regiment near Tennallytown."[181]

Christopher Bouck's case demonstrates how seriously officials took their obligation to apprehend bounty jumpers and deserters: "Too much care cannot be taken by those desirous of obtaining substitutes from being cheated by deserters and bounty-jumpers, for if they are not detected by the Marshal, they are sure to be recognized by officers on Hart's Island as deserters, who are well posted up and can spot such fellows at first sight. Deserters who have re-enlisted are not counted in making up the present quota, and the persons who buy them are not only not relieved from the draft, but in nine cases out of ten lose their money. It behooves those buying substitutes to be careful whom they get, and to be particular in ascertaining where they come from, and what reliance can be placed upon their statements. A case in point occurred at the Provost Marshal's office yesterday morning, the publication of which, we trust, will result in much good here and elsewhere: -- On Saturday last Christopher Bouck, aged 16 years, became a substitute for Aaron Fuller, of Guilderland, for one year and received $300. Saturday evening one of the guard at the Marshal's office ascertained that he was a deserter, and yesterday morning reported the fact to Capt. Parsons. He was immediately arraigned before that officer, when he acknowledged that he belonged to the Seventy-sixth N. Y. S. V. He enlisted at Cherry Valley, October, 1861, and left that place with the regiment. He remained with it about a year, and deserted it while the regiment was at Annapolis. On the 5th of October, 1862 he again enlisted, while in the city of New York, in the Fourteenth New York Cavalry, and received a $50 bounty. He was then taken to Riker's Island and subsequently left with the regiment for New Orleans. On the 15th of June, 1863, he was taken prisoner, was sent to Richmond and subsequently paroled. He was sent to the Parole Camp at Annapolis and from thence to the General Hospital at Philadelphia, from which he deserted July 16th, 1864, came home and remained in the town of Middleburgh, Schoharie county, until a day or two prior to last Saturday. He will now be sent back as a deserter, and Mr. Fuller will be swindled out of $125, as Bouck had spent that amount of his bounty since he last enlisted. Mr. Fuller will also lose what he paid his broker . . . ."[182]

Lonn, whose work on desertion during the Civil War remains seminal, theorized that foreign-born troops contributed to the problem, explaining that the bounty system provided men with few financial opportunities a chance to make money quickly and easily by enrolling, then deserting and perhaps enrolling again elsewhere.[183] To test this theory I looked at the 131 reputed foreign-born members enrolled in the 147th Regiment either as draftees or substitutes.[184] Of that number 42 deserted, representing roughly 33% of the total. Among them were John Downey from Scotland, John and William Malt, Canada, John Olson, Sweden, William Ramsey, Canada, Joseph Dawson, England, and John Williams, Wales.[185]

The federal government expended considerable amounts of time and money searching for and apprehending deserters. A report published in early 1864 showed that 28,000 deserters had been returned to their regiments in 1863.[186] Lists were periodically sent out and local authorities, military officials, and civilians were encouraged to arrest alleged deserters. [187] The bounty for capturing a deserter at the beginning of the war was $30. The amount was inexplicably lowered to $5, effectively reducing the initiative to bring such men to justice. As the war progressed, however, and desertions rose, that fee was again set at $30. Once more unscrupulous persons saw an opportunity to acquire "easy money." Stories abound of men rounded up and accused of being deserters although they had papers proving they had been discharged from the service. George Henry Sherman of the 147th attempted to return to his regiment during a grace period only to be jailed by a bounty hunter planning to earn a fee for turning him over to military authorities. James Phillips, discharged at Philadelphia, PA on June 18, 1864 for "disability," was arrested in Oswego City as a deserter on August 27th. He died in jail that night of *delirium tremens*. (See his biography in "'63 and Beyond.")

The ultimate punishment for desertion was execution either by hanging or by firing squad and soldiers were all too frequently unwilling witnesses. Allen Vorce of the 147th Regiment was one of many men who wrote letters detailing what they saw: ". . . Towards two o'clock we were ordered to fall in, and were all marched out into a large field for the purpose of seeing a man shot. He was a deserter. He had deserted three or four times over to the rebels, and from them to us; told the news on both sides. Finally he was caught, tried and sentenced to be shot. Friday, the 12th (the day we marched), between the hours of twelve and four, he was taken out of an ambulance, sitting on his coffin. It looked hard. The whole corps was then formed around, so that all could see. It took quite a piece of ground. A man was chosen from each regiment in his division, twelve in all. One from our regiment. While they were loading the guns, &c., the chaplain was very busy talking to him. Six of the guns were loaded with balls and the rest were not; so no one knew who shot him. When all was ready he was seated on his coffin, facing the men that were to shoot him. How I pitied him! He was then blindfolded, his hands and legs tied, and all was ready. They then fired. He jumped partly forward, and then fell backwards on his coffin. Then two that were kept for a reserve went round and discharged their guns, to make sure work of it. He was put into his coffin and buried. He was a young man not over 25 . . . ."[188] President Lincoln disliked to sanction executions,

This photograph is one of many with the same theme.
Library of Congress

preferring instead to order sentences of hard labor or lengthy prison terms.[189] In February 1864 by General Orders No. 76 he commuted the sentences of all soldiers condemned to death to imprisonment for the duration of the war at Dry Tortugas where the 110th Regiment was stationed.[190]

Other deserters, among them men from the 147th, were ordered to make up time lost and forfeit wages. In a final effort to encourage deserters to give themselves up to authorities, Lincoln signed the Act of March 3, 1865 whereby the men had 60 days to return to their units or lose their right of citizenship or to become a citizen. Furthermore, they would forever be barred from holding public office.[191] This law also compelled a man who had hired a substitute to complete that man's term if he deserted.[192]

The fates of most deserters remain a mystery but I have been able to trace three from the 147th and further study in this area may be fruitful. The three selected had distinctive names conducive to uncovering evidence of their later lives.

Julius Shortsleeve (December 1833-November 6, 1916) was a son of Peter and Marie Ann Agnon Shortsleeve. His parents were French-Canadian but Julius' own POB is disputed, although it is likely he was born in northern New York. Julius was a volunteer in 1862 but failed to appear at the muster-in of the regiment. He may have gone to Canada to avoid service but it is a fact that he married Angeline LaGrow (May 1834-July 6, 1914) in 1866. In 1870 the couple resided in Oswego. Angeline, who was married at least twice, was the mother of 11 children. Julius died in Carthage, Jefferson County, and was buried with Angeline in St. James' Cemetery.

Charles B. Philbrick (1826-September 7, 1890), the son of Knight and Sally Philbrick, was born in Richland, NY and lived in the area his entire life. He deserted from the 147th Regiment on November 24, 1862 at Tenallytown, DC, subsequently enlisting in the 2nd District of Columbia Infantry and deserting from that outfit on December 20, 1863. Philbrick was married to Adelia Tryon (1834-June 4, 1898) but some time after the 1865 New York census was taken Adelia left him for another man. Although the couple never divorced on January 11, 1870 Charles married Almira Meachem Weaver, whose husband had died in Dry Tortugas on March 18, 1864 while serving with the 110th Regiment. Philbrick persuaded Almira, who was illiterate, that he had indeed been divorced from Adelia by showing her a piece of paper which he said was the final decree. Despite neighbors' knowledge of Philbrick's former marriage, Almira seems to have been unaware of the deception. In 1890 she applied for a pension as his widow and the truth was revealed.[193]

According to *The Town Clerks' Registers*, Solomon Tillapaugh "deserted as soon as he got his bounty" but the official date was September 10, 1862. His muster roll card revealed he was born in Jefferson County, NY and was 41 years old. In 1860 he and wife Eliza Ann (1831-1891) were living in Scriba, NY. They do not appear on the 1865 New York census and they may have left the state shortly after his desertion.

By 1870 the family was living in Port Washington, Ozaukee, WI. The youngest child, Nellie, had been born in that state in 1869. Solomon and Eliza Ann are buried in Union Cemetery, Port Washington. His gravestone shows a DOB of 1816 although extant documents suggest that 1820 was closer to the mark.

All in all, the Union's experiment with the draft was an utter failure. Although 776,829 men were drafted, 161,244 simply failed to report. Exemptions were granted to 315,509, which left only 206,678 liable for service and 86,724 of those paid the commutation fee while another 73,607 provided substitutes. Therefore, only 46,347, or 6% of the total, actually served. Of those, 4% were draftees and 9% were substitutes.[194] In Oswego County, as elsewhere, the repeated threat of a draft, aided and abetted by the promise of generous bounties, was enough to encourage thousands of men to enlist, which was the unspoken reason for the draft in the first place. Nevertheless, corruption existed at all levels, from bounty jumpers to bounty swindlers to "sharks," lawyers who charged exorbitant fees to assist men to obtain an exemption.[195] A war undertaken with the lofty goal of preserving the Union very quickly was contaminated by thieves, scoundrels, and cheats.

NOTES

108. "Grafted Into the Army," *Oswego Commercial Times* (Sat. Eve.) August 29, 1863, n. p. This anonymous poem undoubtedly reflected the sentiment of many mothers about to send their only remaining sons to war.
109. *American Military History,* Chapter 9: "The Civil War, 1861," https://history.army.mil/book/AMH-09.htm, 185.
110. Jamie Malanowski, "Virginia's Moment," *New York Times Opinionator* (Sun.) April 17, 2011.
111. "Northern Draft of 1862," *Online Etymology Dictionary,* https://www.etymonline.com/columns/post/draft.
112. "Last Night's Report," *Oswego Commercial Times* (Wed. Eve.) July 2, 1862, n. p. The letter to Lincoln was signed by seventeen state leaders.
113. Charles McCool Snyder, *Oswego County, New York in the Civil War* (Oswego, NY: Oswego County Historical Society, 1962), 1.
114. "The Volunteer Movement," *Oswego Commercial Times* (Thurs. Eve.) July 11, 1862, n. p.
115. "More Troops," *Oswego Commercial Times* (Tues. Eve.) July 15, 1862, n. p.
116. "Drafting," *Oswego Commercial Times* (Tues. Eve.) July 31, 1862, n. p.
117. "The Draft Postponed," *Oswego Commercial Times* (Sat. Eve.) August 30, 1862, n. p.
118. "No Draft," *Oswego Commercial Times* (Sat. Eve.) November 8, 1862, n. p.
119. "A Refusal and an Arrest," *Oswego Commercial Times* (Thurs. Eve.) June 11, 1863, n. p.

120. "Exempted," *Marysville (CA) Daily Appeal* (Sun.) October 11, 1863, n. p. Versions of this story appeared in newspapers across the country. Reuben Flanigan (1836-1863) was married to Fanny Marie Carnrite and was the father of four young sons. Fanny subsequently married two more times and died in Michigan. New York's Governor Horatio Seymour, a Democrat, vigorously opposed the war in general and the draft in particular.

121. "The Defence of the Nation," *Albany Evening Journal* (Wed.) March 4, 1863, n. p.

122. "The Drafted Men," *Syracuse Daily Courier and Union* (Wed. Morn.) September 9, 1863, 1.

123. "Condensed News," *Mexico Independent* (Thurs.) August 20, 1863, n. p.

124. "Exemption and Rules of Evidence, by Which They Are To Be Determined," *Oswego Commercial Times* (Fri. Eve.) August 8, 1863, n. p.

126. "The Draft – Unsuccessful Experiments," *Oswego Commercial Times* (Wed. Eve.) August 19, 1863, n. p.

127. "How a Lawyer Headed Off a Draft Commissioner," *Mexico Independent* (Thurs.) December 4, 1862, n. p. See also "News Items," *Oswego Commercial Times* (Wed. Eve.) July 29, 1863, n.p., for an equally creative way by which gullible men were advised to avoid the draft.

128. "New Items," *Oswego Commercial Times* (Wed. Eve.) August 5, 1863, n. p.

129. "The Exempt Brigade," *Oswego Daily Palladium* (Thurs. Eve.) August 25, 1864, n. p. As late as March 2, 1865 the editors of the *Mexico Independent* could complain, "In consequence of an enrollment fearfully swollen with a floodwood of exempts, the draft falls heavily upon this town."

130. "Shirkers," *Oswego Commercial Times* (Fri. Eve.) October 10, 1862, n. p.

131. *The War of the Rebellion*, series III, volume 3, 484. The order was sent to Colonel R. Nugent, acting assistant provost-marshal in New York City, and copied to other military officers.

132. William Woodall (1841-1867) was the elder brother of John Joseph (1842-1914) and Granville Sharp Woodall (1847-1864), both of whom served in the Civil War. I have not ascertained his COD but it could have been tuberculosis. See *Oswego Commercial Times* (Sat. Eve.) October 3, 1863, 1.

133. James McPherson, *Battle Cry of Freedom: The Civil War Era* (New York: Oxford University Press, 1988), 601-2.

134. John Sacher, "Conscription," *Essential Civil War Curriculum*, Virginia Center for Civil War Studies at Virginia Tech: www.essentialcivilwarcurriculum.com/conscription.html. To be fair, Arthur did serve as quartermaster for the NYS Militia during the war years.

135. "George Brinske," *Owosso Times* (Fri.) September 2, 1887, 3; this article was reprinted from the *Reed City Clarion*.

136. *Oswego Commercial Times* October 3, 1863, 1.

137. Sacher, "Conscription."

138. "Commutation," *Oswego Commercial Advertiser* (Thurs. Eve.) July 31, 1864, n. p.

139. Sacher, "Conscription."

140. "Twenty Questions Answered Concerning the Draft," *Mexico Independent* (Thurs.) August 28, 1862, n. p.

141. "What Substitutes Will Receive," *Oswego Commercial Times* (Sat. Eve.) August 22, 1863, n. p. What the article omits is the financial disaster likely to come upon a family should the soldier-substitute be killed in action or die from disease.

142. The source of this information is the regiment's muster roll.

143. Donald M. Fisher, "The Civil War Draft in Rochester, Part Two," *Rochester History* 53, 2 (Spring 1991), 15.

144. Timothy J. Perri, "The Economics of Civil War Conscription," *American Law and Economics Review* (2008), 443-444.

145. "Letter From Gen. Dix," *Atlas and Argus* (Thurs. Morn.) April 14, 1864, 1.

146. Ella Lonn, *Desertion in the Civil War* (New York: Century Co., 1928), 141.

147. "A Father Sells His Dead Son as a Substitute," *Oswego Commercial Times* (Wed. Eve.) December 21, 1864, n. p.

148. "The Conscription," *Oswego Commercial Times* (Wed. Eve.) August 5, 1863, n. p.

149. The federal call was for 600,000 men. See "The Draft," *Oswego Commercial Times* (Mon. Eve.) March 23, 1864, n. p.

150. "Proclamation 116-Calling for 500,000 Volunteers," *The American Presidency Project:* https://www.presidency.ucsb.edu./ws/?pid+69996.

151. Wardwell G. Robinson, *History of the 184th Regiment, New York State Volunteers* (Oswego: R. J. Oliphant, 1895), 4-5.

152. "184th Regiment," *Oswego Commercial Advertiser* (Sat. Eve.) August 20, 1864, n. p.

153. "The Draft," *Oswego Commercial Advertiser* (Mon. Eve.) September 19, 1864, n. p.

154. Robinson, 6.

155. "A Proclamation by the President," *Hudson Daily Star* (Wed.) December 21, 1864, n. p.

156. "The Quota of Oswego and Madison County," *Oswego Commercial Times* (Mon. Eve.) February 27, 1865, n. p.

157. See "The Draft," *Mexico Independent* (Thurs.) March 2, 1865, n. p. and "The Draft," *Mexico Independent* (Thurs.) March 9, 1865, n. p.

158. "No More Draft – Recruiting to be Stopped," *Mexico Independent* (Thurs.) April 20, 1865, n. p.

159. "News Items," *Oswego Commercial Times* (Mon. Eve.) June 22, 1863, n. p.

160. "Assault of a Substitute Broker Upon Officer Kenan," *Oswego Commercial Advertiser* (Thurs. Eve.) March 9, 1865, n. p. For a humorous story about substitute brokers see "A Row About a Substitute," *Utica Daily Observer* (Fri.) August 26, 1864, n. p.

161. Another requirement was that the soldier had to give at least one half of his monthly paycheck to his family "or other relatives dependent on him for support." Local communities were permitted to establish relief funds to aid families of absent soldiers. See "Expressly Prohibited," *Oswego Commercial Times* (Tues. Eve.) August 4, 1863, n. p. The forbidding of local bounties seems to have been repealed or simply overlooked because in early January 1865 the Oswego County Board of Supervisors passed a resolution to appropriate a sum of $300 for each one-year volunteer, $500 for a two-year volunteer, and $700 for a three-year volunteer. See "Work Now to Fill the Quota," *Oswego Commercial Times* (Fri. Eve.) January 20, 1865, n. p. The situation became so desperate that near the end of the war draftees who provided substitutes were also collecting federal bounties.

162. Nathan (1843-1863) died of typhoid fever on June 1, 1863.

163. "Departure of Deserters," *Oswego Commercial Times* (Mon. Eve.) October 6, 1862, n. p.

164. "Skedaddled," *Oswego Commercial Times* (Tues. Eve.) October 7, 1862, n. p.

165. "Still Around," *Oswego Commercial Times* (Wed. Eve.) October 8, 1862, n. p.

166. "Still Around," *Oswego Commercial Times* (Tues. Eve.) October 21, 1862, n. p. It would appear that Darius was delivered to the regiment because Captain Slayton sent a letter to the editor dated January 30, 1863 detailing the names of deserters from his company. Ballou was among them. See "Letter from Capt. Slayton," *Mexico Independent* (Thurs.) (Thurs.) February 12, 1863, n. p. He was never heard from again. He left behind a wife, Hulda Tilton Ballou (1843-May 7, 1909), and a son, Darius Lamar Ballou (1860-1934).

167. *Annual Report of the Adjutant-General of the State of New York for the Year 1894,* Vol. III (Albany: James Lyon, Printer, 1894), 88.

168. "From the 184th," *Oswego Commercial Times* (Wed. Eve.) March 29, 1865, n. p.

169. Melinda Musil, "Money Out of Misery," *America's Civil War Magazine* (March 2018): www.historynet.com/money-out-of-misery.html.

170. "Professional Criminals of America – Revised: #11 John Larney (1836-19??)." Extracted from Thomas Byrnes, *Professional Criminals of America* (New York: Cassell & Co., 1886): https://criminalsrevised.blog/2018/03/17/john-larney-11.

171. "Homicide at Baldwinsville," *Oswego Commercial Advertiser* (Wed. Eve.) August 21, 1864, n. p.; "Verdict of the Coroner's Jury in the Case of the Deserter Sullivan," *Oswego Commercial Times* (Thurs. Eve.) September 1, 1864, n. p.; "The Baldwinsville Homicide," *Oswego Commercial Advertiser* (Sat. Eve.) September 3, 1864, n. p. For another, less flattering, version of the story, see "Murder of a Soldier Under 'Military Necessity'," *Syracuse Daily Courier and Union* (Wed. Morn.) August 31, 1864 in which it was alleged that Sullivan was merely going to Syracuse to visit relatives.

172. "Miscellaneous Items," *Oswego Daily Palladium* (Wed. Eve.) November 11, 1863, n. p.

173. "The Case of Mr. Nichols," *Oswego Commercial Times* (Tues. Eve.) August 26, 1862, n. p. Others found themselves in trouble with the law for assisting would-be "skedaddlers" to leave the country. As reported in "Arrested," *Oswego Commercial Times* (Tues. Eve.) September 9, 1862, n. p., the captain of a Canadian schooner was arrested for aiding in the escape to Canada of two men from Captain McKinlock's company.

174. "Sneaks," *Oswego Commercial Times* (Mon. Eve.) August 18, 1862, n. p. The names included Giles and Edwin Hemens, Welcome Manwaring, and George Tillepaugh, among others.

175. "The Coward's Welcome to Canada," *Oswego Commercial Times* (Wed. Eve.) August 13, 1863, n. p.

176. The threat of execution was brought home forcefully to Oswego County in "A Deserter Shot," *Mexico Independent* (Thurs.) July 9, 1863, n. p.: "We learn that Joseph Christman, late a resident near Central Square, in this county, was shot a few days ago for desertion. He enlisted in Co. D, 101st, now 37th N. Y. Volunteers, and deserted from that regiment three times. He also broke from jail once or twice. The execution took place in the presence of the entire Fifth Corps (Gen. Meade then commanding) to which his regiment belongs."

177. Lonn, 127-38. See also "Deserters and Why They Desert," *Oswego Commercial Times* (Tues. Eve.) October 27, 1864: "A few days since we had a conversation with an officer who has been prominently engaged in capturing and forwarding deserters to their regiments. He informs us that seven-eighths of all the deserters arrested, said unequivocally that they deserted upon the inducements of their friends, and from letters sent to them by relatives and partisan friends . . . ." The article was reprinted from the *Chicago Tribune*.

178. "A Supposed Deserter," *Oswego Commercial Times* (Wed. Eve.) March 11, 1863, n. p.

179. Little can be ascertained about Jacob House. His parents are unknown although he was born in Herkimer County, NY. His gravestone incorrectly shows he was 24 years old. His DOB fluctuated from census to census but

he apparently was born *ca.* 1830. According to *Registers of Officers and Enlisted Men* he was married with two dependent children although I have been unable to corroborate that assertion. In 1860 he was single. It is possible that he married later that year but, if so, one would expect the widow to know her husband's age when ordering a monument.

180. "Arrest of a Deserter in Woman's Apparel," *Oswego Commercial Times* (Thurs. Eve.) September 25, 1862, n. p. Although Lukin was called Adolphus in this article, his correct name was Alphonse. See his biography in "The Originals."

181. "Personal," *New York Evening Express* (Mon. Eve.) November 24, 1862, 1.

182. "A Deserter Enlists as a Substitute And Is Detected," *Albany Morning Express* (Wed.) August 17, 1864, n. p. See Bouck's story in "76ers."

183. Lonn, 138.

184. In many cases the nativity of an enlistee was not given.

185. For a different perspective see Don H. Doyle, "The Civil War Was Won by Immigrant Soldiers," *Zocalo Public Square* (Arizona State University Knowledge Enterprise) June 29, 2015: www.Time.com/3940428/civil-war-immigrant-soldiers/.

186. "Enlistments for 1863," *Oswego Commercial Advertiser* (Thurs. Eve.) March 24, 1864, n. p. Lonn, 152, estimated that between the years 1861-1865 the Union Army suffered about 200,000 desertions. New York State alone was responsible for 44,913 but it must be pointed out that New York also provided 465,000 troops, the greatest number of all the states. See "New York in the American Civil War," www.familysearch.org/wiki/in/New_York_in_the_Civil_War.

187. Lonn, 173-74.

188. "Letter from the 147th Regiment," *Mexico Independent* (Thurs.) July 9, 1863, 1. The letter was dated June 22, 1863 and sent from Fairfax County, VA. It is possible that Vorce was reporting the execution of Joseph Christman. See note 176.

189. Doris Kearns Goodwin, *Team of Rivals: The Political Genius of Abraham Lincoln* (New York: Simon & Schuster Paperbacks, 2005), 539.

190. "Miscellaneous Items," *Sabbath Recorder* (Thurs.) March 17, 1864, 43.

191. "Last Night's Dispatches," *Oswego Commercial Advertiser* (Sat. Eve.) March 11, 1865, n. p.

192. Lonn, 166.

193. For more of this story, see Natalie Joy Woodall, *Men of the 110th Regiment: Oswego's Own* (Denver: Outskirts Press, 2016), 520-21. See also "Deserter Arrested," *Oswego Commercial Times* (Fri. Eve.) June 5, 1864, n. p.

194. Sacher, "Conscription."

195. See, for example, "Sharks," *Oswego Commercial Times* (Sat. Eve.) August 22, 1863, n. p.

'63 and Beyond

Abraham Thomas Andre – Co. E

b. 1841 Delaware County, NY
d. April 24, 1894 State Hospital, Binghamton, Broome, NY
m. Isabel "Bell" Shelp (1843-May 7, 1893) *ca.* 1869

NOTE: Abraham was the son of Jacob (1812-1890) and Deborah Ann Hubbell Andre (1811-1879). He joined the 147th on July 14, 1863 at Barton, Tioga, NY as a draftee. He was later transferred to the VRC and discharged on May 31, 1865. He and Bell were the parents of one child, Freeman (1870-1927). Abraham took an active interest in the politics of Tioga County. He was appointed a notary in 1893. His mental health, however, deteriorated, as an article in *The Waverly Free Press* December 23, 1893 points out: "Abram T. Andre, of Lockwood, has for some time past shown evidence of an unsound mind, and last Saturday morning he was found by Chief Brooks walking about the streets in a barefooted condition. The officer placed him under arrest and made him as comfortable as possible in the lock-up. A commission, consisting of Drs. R. S. Harnden and I. S. Vreeland, was appointed to inquire as to his sanity, and on Monday they pronounced him insane. Monday night Andre made a pile of his bedding and applied a match. In a short time smoke was issuing from the door of the city hall and filled the various rooms. Chief Brooks saw it and hastened to the cell. In spite of the stifling smoke he managed to unlock the door and get hold of Andre, and pulled him out. In a short time more the man must have been burned. He was taken to the state hospital, at Binghamton, on Tuesday, by an attendant of that institution. The history of the case for some years past is a sad lesson in the evil effects of intemperance." He was buried in Factoryville Cemetery, Waverly, Tioga, NY. Isabel's death was briefly noted in *The Owego Record* May 11, 1893: "Mrs. A. T. Andre died at her home in Lockwood Sunday morning after an illness of but a few hours. She was about 50 years of age. Funeral services were held at the church Tuesday at 1 o'clock, Rev. S. B. Keeney officiating." Because of his father's mental illness Freeman petitioned the Surrogate Court to administer his mother's estate. Her grave has not been located.

Amaziah Armstrong – Co. A
b. October 1, 1822 Batavia, Genesee, NY
d. April 9, 1904 Vienna, Oneida, NY
m. Clarissa Llewellyn Miller (August 29, 1826-November 15, 1900) December 4, 1842

NOTE: The son of Ezra (1784-1849) and Nancy Dougherty Armstrong (1790-?), Amaziah was a farmer. On September 24, 1863 he was enrolled in the 147th at Utica, Oneida, NY as a substitute for Henry Eaton. Although originally classified as a deserter who abandoned the regiment on May 4, 1864 "on the march," in reality he was captured on May 5, 1864 at the battle of the Wilderness. Where he was confined has not been learned but he was paroled on December 6, 1864. During the next few months he spent time in various hospitals. He was finally sent to General Hospital in Elmira, NY where he was discharged on July 11, 1865. He and Clarissa were the parents of 10 children. James Llewellyn (1846-1925) served in Co. K, 189th Regiment from September 1864-June 1865. Amaziah and Clarissa, together with several of their children, are buried in Maple Flats Cemetery, Vienna.

John Brightman Audlin – Co. F
b. February 1830 England
d. January 26, 1913 Oswego City, NY
m. Sophia Cliff (November 1833-December 12, 1903) *ca.* 1855

NOTE: John, son of William (1806-1850) and Dinah Brightman Atkin Audlin (1809-1894), was drafted into the 147th on August 12, 1863 in Oswego City. He was transferred to Co. A, 91st Regiment on June 5, 1865 but was in hospital when that regiment mustered out in July. He and Sophia were the parents of 10 children. His death occasioned the following obituary in *The Oswego Daily Times* January 27, 1913, 1: "John B. Audlin, an old and highly respected resident of the Second ward, passed away yesterday afternoon, at the family home, No. 46 Mercer street, after a long illness. Mr. Audlin came to this country from England, his birthplace, many years ago and settled in the Second ward. For the past several years Mr. Audlin had not been active and for some time his health had been poor. He was a veteran of the Civil War. Mr. Audlin attended the Church of the Evangelists. Mrs. Audlin died several years ago . . . ." He and Sophia are buried in Riverside Cemetery, Scriba.

George W. Austin – Co. H
b. October 8, 1818 Carmel, Putnam, NY
d. September 14, 1889 Yorktown, Westchester, NY
m. Elmira Dean (October 2, 1829-June 2, 1914) October 3, 1855

NOTE: The son of Silas (1780-1841) and Elizabeth Tompkins Austin (1783-1857), George was a substitute for Granville D. Walker, Butler, Wayne, NY. He joined the 147th at Auburn, Cayuga, NY on July 25, 1863 and was discharged on March 22, 1865. He and Elmira were the parents of seven children, only two of whom survived to adulthood. The couple is buried in the Methodist Cemetery, Mahopac, Putnam, NY.

Garrett S. Ayers – Co. G
b. 1842 Ontario County, NY
d. March 29, 1865 Andersonville, Sumter, GA
m. ------

NOTE: Garrett was the son of Peter (1803-1880) and Margaret Hiligus Ayers (1819-1891). He enrolled in the 147th on August 2, 1863 at Canandaigua, Ontario, NY as a substitute for Byron Randall, Troy, Rensselaer, NY. Where and when he was captured is unknown but he succumbed to scurvy as a POW in Andersonville and is buried in the Andersonville National Cemetery. In 1880 his mother successfully applied for a pension.

Norman Eddy Bachman – Co. I
b. November 1845 Canoga, Seneca County, NY
d. January 30, 1926 Portland, Multnomah, OR
m. Mercy Ann Burgess (July 1847-November 3, 1913) March 12, 1868

NOTE: Norman, whose parents are known only as J. S. (1818-*post* 1850) and M. J. (1830-*post* 1850), first served in Co. K, 50th NY Engineers from January 1-September 25, 1862. A substitute for William Hoster, Fayette, Seneca, NY, he enrolled at Auburn, Cayuga, NY on July 23, 1863 as a musician. He was wounded at the battle of the Wilderness on May 5, 1864. Transferred to the 91st Regiment on June 5, 1865, he was discharged on June 8th from Jarvis Hospital, Baltimore, MD. He graduated from the Medical College of Fort Wayne in 1877 and became a specialist in podiatry. In 1890 he said his disabilities were chronic rheumatism and a gunshot wound in his hip. Mercy died of cancer of the uterus in Stanton, Montcalm, MI. She and Norman were buried in Forest Hill Cemetery, Stanton.

Barnett W. Baker – Co. I
b. 1836 Ontario County, NY
d. August 18, 1890 National Soldiers' Home, Bath, Steuben, NY
m. ------

NOTE: Barnett was the son of Isaac (1803-*post* 1865) and Phebe Cushman Baker (*ca.* 1800-*ante* 1850). He enlisted in Co. K, 3rd NYSV in 1861 and served until May 21,

1863. He was drafted into the 147th at Canandaigua, Ontario, on August 20, 1863. On June 5, 1865 he was transferred to Co. D, 91st Regiment, finally mustering out on July 3rd near Washington, DC. Little is known of his life until he entered the Bath National Home in 1886. His COD was heart failure and *phthisis pulmonalis*. He is buried in Bath National Cemetery. Barnett and his two sisters were farmed out to neighbors and family after their mother died. Ann E. (1838-February 11, 1912) married William W. St. John (November 15, 1831-February 9, 1872). They are buried in Oakwood Cemetery, Syracuse, NY. Frances H. (1843-July 4, 1917) married first Hiram Finger (1838-1877) and had a son, Frederick (1862-September 16, 1907), who was drowned in the Erie Canal near Camillus, Onondaga, NY. She next married Benjamin Franklin Warner (1833-1909) in 1881. Frances and her two husbands are buried in Lakeview Cemetery, Penn Yan.

Benoni Baker – Co. A

b. May 15, 1831 Brownville, Jefferson, NY
d. May 5, 1864 Wilderness, VA
m. Esther Elder Mosher (1829-March 11, 1912) December 22, 1855

NOTE: Benoni, son of Daniel Burbanks (1793-1855) and Nancy Waite Baker (1801-1883), saw prior service in Co. A, 35th NYSV from July 1861-June 1863. He joined the 147th as a substitute for an unknown draftee at Watertown, Jefferson, NY on September 29, 1863. Although some sources claim he died at the battle of Mine Run, it is impossible since that conflict occurred in November-December 1863. He is buried in Fredericksburg National Cemetery, although a cenotaph can be found in the Brownville Cemetery. Esther was first married Cyrus Mosher (1829-1854) by whom she had two children. She and Benoni were the parents of Lorinda (1857-?) and Lucy (1861-1918). Esther's third husband was William Frederick Goedecke (1832-April 6, 1890), by whom she was the mother of three more children. After he died she successfully applied for a remarried widow's pension in 1901. She and Goedecke are buried in Oakwood Cemetery, Anoka, Anoka, MN. Two of Benoni's brothers also served during the Civil War. Daniel B., Jr. (1823-1864) was a member of Co. I, 10th NY ART. His COD was erysipelas and his body was sent home to Brownville. Rolla (1833-1911) was a soldier in Co. B, 186th Regiment.

Francis "Frank" C. Baker – Co. A

b. November 9, 1846 Canada
d. April 3, 1918 East Tawas, Iosco, MI
m1. Jeanette Thurston Carter (September 9, 1843-May 16, 1913) 1878
m2. Lucy Genevieve Arno Griffith (April 1882-February 25, 1947) August 4, 1916

NOTE: Francis was the son of Daniel (?-?) and Alice Maybee Baker (?-?). A substitute for an unknown man he joined the 147th at Watertown, Jefferson, NY on September 24, 1863. He lied about his age, saying he was 20 years old. He transferred to Co. C, 91st Regiment on June 5, 1865 and mustered out on July 3rd near Ball's Cross Roads, VA. He was a farmer in Michigan. His COD was "acute obstruction of the bowels due to strangulation." He is buried in American Legion Cemetery, East Tawas. His government stone contains no dates. Jeanette was first married to John Carter (1839-1910) by whom she had two children. She and Francis had one child, Francis, Jr., who only lived a few months. Jeanette, whose COD was a gastric ulcer, died in East Tawas, but her grave has not been located. Lucy was first married to Ernest "Emmet" Griffith (1889-1915) and had several children by him. He was killed in an accidental dynamite blast on September 23, 1915 and was buried in Sims-Whitney Cemetery, Au Gres, Arenac, Michigan. Lucy married William Wesley Nichols (1866-January 23, 1931) on November 10, 1924 as his fifth wife. Apparently they separated because his death certificate said he was a widower. His COD may be the reason for the separation since his death certificate states he died of an intestinal obstruction, peritonitis, and septicemia with acute gonorrhea as a contributing factor. He is buried in Mason Cemetery, Arenac County, MI. Lucy died in Newberry, Luce, MI and is buried in Forest Lawn Cemetery, Newberry.

Christopher Bakerie – Co. A
b. 1840 France
d. ? ?
m. ?

NOTE: This man's parents are unknown. He was drafted and enrolled in the 147th on August 10, 1863 at Buffalo, Erie, NY. On June 5, 1865 he transferred to Co. C, 91st Regiment and mustered out on July 3rd at Ball's Cross Roads, VA. Nothing further has been discovered. The spelling of his surname may be the reason.

Thomas Baldwin – Co. A
b. 1842 New York State
d. ? ?
m. ?

NOTE: Thomas, the eldest of eight children in 1860, was the son of John (1820-?) and Sarah Baldwin (1823-?). He was drafted, joining the regiment on July 31, 1863 at Southport, Chemung, NY. The notes contained on his muster roll card are confusing. One stated he was discharged on June 6, 1865 at Washington, DC. Another reported he was absent, sick, and transferred to Co. C, 91st Regiment on June 5th. His name, however, does not appear in *The Adjutant-General's Report* for that organization. I have located no pension record for him. In fact, after the 1860 census the entire family disappears.

Joseph Ballard – Co. K
b. 1840 Erie Co, NY
d. May 5, 1864 Wilderness, VA
m. ------

NOTE: Joseph was the son of Louis Francis (1810-1887) and Maria Anna "Mary" Daul/ Doll Ballard (1814-1886). In 1855 the family was enumerated under their French name Poullain. Joseph joined the regiment as a draftee at Hanover, Chautauqua, NY on August 8, 1863. He was originally buried in Lynchburg, VA but today he lies in Poplar Grove National Cemetery, Petersburg, VA. The 1865 New York census carried his name but with the *caveat* "has not been heard from since May 5, 1864." His brother John (1844-*post* 1870) served in Co. B, 49th Regiment from February 22-June 27, 1865. Another brother, Sebastian, served in Co. D, 187th Regiment from September 6, 1864-February 11, 1865 when he was discharged for wounds suffered on October 27, 1864 at the first battle of Hatcher's Run. His entry in Samuel C. Noyes Post 220 GAR erroneously assigned him to the 147th Regiment.

Samuel R. Barbeau – Co. A
b. August 2, 1844 Ottawa, Ontario, Canada
d. March 22, 1924 Sacramento, Sacramento, CA
m. Allie Delphina Rider (July 6, 1862-January 26, 1960) December 29, 1881

NOTE: Samuel, whose parents are unidentified, entered the military at Lockport, Niagara, NY on July 28, 1863 as a substitute for Hiram Benedict, Lockport. He transferred to Co. C, 91st Regiment on June 5, 1865 and mustered out on July 3rd near Ball's Cross Roads, VA. He and Allie were married in Denver, CO and were the parents of one child, Edith Justina (1885-1982). According to his FAG entry, Samuel and Allie lived for a number of years in Mexico. The couple parted ways and apparently divorced. Allie married Louis F. Stetler (1867-May 26, 1929) as his second wife, date unknown. Since his first wife, Laurine "Laura" Essex Stetler (1870-*post* 1930), was still alive when the 1930 census was taken, it is evident that couple too had separated. After Stetler's death Allie applied for a pension as Samuel's widow but the application was rejected, probably because the couple had divorced. Samuel is buried in the Sacramento City Cemetery. Allie is buried in East Lawn Memorial Park, Sacramento.

Israel Lee Barber – Co. B

b. 1820 Chemung County, NY

d. November 8, 1863 First Division General Hospital, Alexandria, VA

m. Christina Ann Van Tile (1826-*ca*. 1882) July 3, 1845

NOTE: Israel was the son of James B. (1790-1865) and Catherine Beardsley Barber (1792-1877). He was drafted, enrolling in the 147th on July 11, 1863 at Bath, Steuben, NY. He succumbed to typhoid fever and was buried in Alexandria National Cemetery. He and Christina were the parents of eight known children. The family lived in Humphrey, Cattaraugus, NY in both 1865 and 1870. Beyond that point, the family history is shrouded in mystery. Charles, born August 30, 1846, is last enumerated on the 1875 New York census. Henry, born in 1847, last appears on the 1860 census. Mary Ann was born on September 22, 1850. She was enumerated in 1865 with the others but by 1866 she was married. Her husband is unidentified. Martha Jane, born on July 11, 1852, married Orsen Leuman Mix (?-1901) probably *ca*. 1872, since her son, Wallace Perl, was born on February 26, 1873. He survived to adulthood, served in the Spanish-American War, and died December 25, 1945. He was buried in Chestnut Hill Cemetery, Portville, Cattaraugus, NY. His mother allegedly died in 1901 but I have not located any details for her or her husband. Charlotte Louisa, born May 13, 1855, married William Hamilton (1846-May 22, 1923) *ca*. 1873. She died in 1919 and the couple is buried in Chestnut Hill Cemetery. Harriet L. was born in 1859. The only reference to her occurs on the 1860 census. In 1864, when her mother applied for a widow's pension, Harriet was not included in the surviving children. David was born on January 20, 1862 and was still alive in 1870. Abraham Lee was a posthumous child, born November 12, 1863. In 1892 he was living in Olean with Charlotte and William. After that date, I have found nothing. Christina presents a mystery too. A letter to the Pension Bureau dated January 5, 1885 stated she had last been paid in September 1881 and had been dropped on account of "statute of limitations." Apparently she died early in 1882 but where she and her children were when the 1880 census was taken is unknown.

Darwin Barrows – Co. A

b. December 24, 1831 Freedom, Cattaraugus, NY

d. October 4, 1864 Petersburg, VA

m. ------

NOTE: Darwin was the son of David Lawrence (1806-1878) and Irena Parmila/Parmily Barrows (1807-1841). His was an interesting military career. He was a member of Co. D, 64th Regiment from December 1861- June 1862. He was drafted, enrolling in the 147th on July 24, 1863 at Hume, Allegany, NY. His muster card says he was a printer, his occupation in 1850. This card claimed he was "absent sick since Oct. 24, 1863, no further record." Another muster card states he enlisted in the 4th NY HA in August 25, 1864 at Hume. This card listed dentist as his occupation, which is that given on the 1860 census. Information provided on the card for the 4th HA stated that "name appears only on recruit roll" and his company was marked "unassigned." A deposition given by Azariah Stewart and Edward Skiff in March 1867 shed some light on the matter. They testified that they were authorized in August 1864 to locate and obtain recruits to fill the county's quota under President Lincoln's call for 500,000 more soldiers and that Darwin Barrows was one such volunteer. He was awarded a bounty of $400 which went to his father David "for his use and support." It is possible that Darwin may have been persuaded to join this organization while home on sick leave. The generous bounty was definitely tempting. Moreover, his brother Byron (1839-1882) was a member of Co. H, 4th NY HA, having enlisted on December 23, 1863 at Hume. When Darwin was killed in October he was a member of Co. F, 4th NY HA. An entry in *Deaths of Volunteers* confirms this date, as do the US Burial Registers. Nevertheless, his card for the 147th claims he was transferred *in absentia* to Co. C, 91st Regiment because he was "absent sick, no discharge." *The Adjutant-General's Report* for that outfit, however, does not list him. Originally buried at Meade Station, VA today he lies in Poplar Grove National Cemetery, Petersburg, VA as a member of the 4th NY HA. In 1867 David Barrows, a physician and surgeon, applied for Darwin's pension, alleging his son had been his sole support for many years. Two doctors testified that David's heart disease prevented him from gainful employment. None of the pension papers mentions anything about the 64th or the 147th Regiment. Barrows had married Louisa Selfridge (1817-*post* 1865) as his second wife and had become the father of several more children. During the course of the pension application the Adjutant-General's Office in Washington, DC twice reported that Darwin's name was not found on any muster rolls for the 4th NY HA and could only be found as a recruit at Elmira, NY on August 24, 1864. Despite his claims of financial hardship, Dr. Barrows left a will which demonstrated clearly that he had sufficient resources to bequeath money and property to his surviving children.

Charles Battey – Co. K
b. July 23, 1848 Lockport, Niagara, NY
d. February 27,1914 Buffalo, Erie, NY
m. Elizabeth Hemming (1854-August 3, 1932) September 1, 1880

NOTE: Charles was the son of Dr. Benjamin Arnold (1805-*ca.* 1855) and Phoebe Hart Wibert Battey (1812-1901). He was only 15 when he enlisted at Utica, Oneida, NY on September 10, 1863. He was discharged on April 1964. To date I have located no muster card or pension record for him. An interesting obituary appeared in *The*

Buffalo Morning Express March 4, 1914: "In the death of Charles Battey, this city lost a citizen who for nearly 40 years had made Buffalo his home, coming here in 1848 [*sic*] when but five years old. His father was Dr. Benjamin A. Battey, one of the pioneer homeopathic physicians in this part of the state. As a young man he was a member of the Q.Q.Q.s, an association of Buffalo's younger men organized in 1869. Many well-known Buffalo men were members, probably the oldest surviving member being R. Porter Lee. He sang in the old Buffalo Choral Union and the Buffalo Liederefel. He also sang at the dedication of Buffalo's Music hall in 1886. This is now the Teck theater. He was a member of Alden Lodge No. 594 F. & A. M. For many years he was with the Sisee Forge company and for the last twelve years had been with Hersee & Co. His life was quiet and unassuming and was characterized by kindness to all and a deep devotion to his family . . . ." He was buried in Forest Lawn Cemetery, Buffalo. Elizabeth's obituary appeared in *The Buffalo Evening News* August 8, 1932, 23: "Funeral services for Mrs. Elizabeth Hemming Battey, 78, former resident of Buffalo, who died in Pasadena, Calif., Aug. 3, will be held in the Forest Lawn chapel Tuesday at 2:30 P.M. Burial will be in Forest Lawn cemetery. Mrs. Battey was the widow of Charles Battey, Buffalo businessman, who died 18 years ago. He was connected with Hersee & Co. while in business here and served as assistant treasurer of the Pan-American exposition in 1901. Mrs. Battey was born in Clymer, Chautauqua county, and came to Buffalo with her parents when a young girl and lived here until she went to Pasadena for her health eight years ago. Mrs. Battey was a lifelong member of the First Unitarian church, West Ferry street and Elmwood avenue, and took an active interest in its work as long as she lived in Buffalo. Mrs. Battey is survived by two sons, Carl Edward of Pasadena, Calif., and Fay H. Battey of Buffalo."

Jonas Slote Bayne – Co. E

b. September 7, 1837 Medina, Orleans, NY
d. June 18, 1864 near Petersburg, VA
m. Eliza "Lizzie" Kirby (1841-January 24, 1905) July 3, 1859

NOTE: Jonas was the son of Jonas (1812-1890) and Mary Runciman Bayne (1813-1883). He served first as a second lieutenant in Co. F, 3rd NY Cavalry from July 1861-February 1862. A draftee, he enrolled in the 147th at Shelby, Orleans, NY on August 3, 1863. He was wounded in the thigh at Petersburg, VA on June 18, 1864 and the injury was so severe that the leg was amputated, resulting in his death. An unsourced article, attached to his muster roll card, says in part: ". . . In August last he was drafted from the town of Shelby, and at the appointed time reported for duty and was assigned to the 147th Reg. where he served up to the 18th inst. We have before us a letter from the Rev. Thomas Barrett, chaplain 19th Regiment Indiana Vet. Volunteers, to the wife of Mr. Bayne, which states that he was badly wounded in the left leg above the knee by a Minnie [*sic*] ball so that amputation became necessary, but that he never recovered from the shock to his [?] caused by the amputation and died some time during the succeeding night. The writer says: 'He was loved and respected by all who knew him. He was a man who could stand up for the right – a noble man. He was brave to a fault almost and yet not rash. He has bequeathed to you and yours that which is invaluable – a good name' . . . ." Lizzie obtained a widow's pension which she received until she married William H. Hastings (?-October 27, 1876) on February 21, 1865 at Medina, NY. He had served from 1858-1863 in Co. I, 1st US Infantry and had contracted rheumatism while in the army. He died quite suddenly while shopping in a drugstore in Northville, MI. COD was ruled to be apoplexy. On December 9, 1884 Lizzie married Timothy P. Thompson (1823-1897). The marriage was unsuccessful and Lizzie obtained a divorce from him on December 28, 1889. At that point she began a lengthy attempt to obtain a pension based on Hastings' military service. The pension file is more than 300 pages long and demonstrates to what lengths widows were required to go to prove their worthiness. After a 17 year battle, the claim was rejected on the grounds that Hastings' death was not war-related. On September 5, 1901 Lizzie penned a letter to President William McKinley which made its way into her pension file. It is a combination of frustration and desperation: "Hon. President McKinley, Pleas excuse this Boldness of a poor helpless & dependant Widdow for I am compelled to ask a favor of you in Behalf of my Pension. My Husband Mr Hastings who died very suddenly without a moments warning with siatic Rheumatism but what seems to Bar me out of it was the Inquest called apoplexy and the commisioner Seems to think that was not a disability in Army but the Dr that treated him says that his diseas was the cause of death. he contracted it while in Army he served his time & has an Honorable discharge. he was my only support. I am sick & poor with no one to care for my Self have no home depend on charity for my living because I am not able to work & I appeal to you to lend me your influence & sympathy to the commissioner to have compassion on me & grant by Back Pension. he seemed so inclined to Reject every time on account of the Inquest. pleas Mr. McKinly do notice this appeal to you & do help me to have it granted. This is no fals plea. Pleas do not throw this by unheaded. I know you time is taken up with your own affairs but give heed to this if it is the last thing you can do for a poor widdow. have your Private secretary reply. I enclose stamp hoping you may listen to this. excuse whatever may not be right in this. Mrs. Lizzie Hastings." There is no indication that anything was ever done for her except to add the letter to the already burgeoning file. Lizzie died at the Grand Rapids Soldiers' Home and was buried in the Home Cemetery. Her death certificate bears witness to her tragic life. The doctor stated she died from "defective nutrition" and a "morphine habit." Two of Jonas' brothers also served the Union cause. Oscar Fitzelan (1842-1892) was a soldier in Co. D, 28th NYSV. Henry Clay (1844-December 17, 1864) served in the 8th NYSV. He was captured at the battle of the Weldon Railroad and sent to Salisbury Prison, where he died after five months' imprisonment.

John Masury Berry – Co. A
b. October 3, 1842 Salem, Essex, MA
d. February 22, 1911 Salem Hospital, Salem, Essex, MA
m1. Mary Howard Perley (1836-1869) July 21, 1866
m2. Sarah Jane Whitney (September 24, 1835-July 16, 1908) October 28, 1886

NOTE: John, son of George E. (1812-1879) and Lydia Masury Berry (1812-1900), enlisted in Brooklyn, NY on April 18, 1861, enrolling in Co. C, 84th Regiment. He was wounded at Gettysburg on July 1, 1863 and discharged on December 2, 1863 to accept a commission as second lieutenant in the 147th. He was promoted to first lieutenant on January 22, 1864. A document attached to his muster roll card, dated February 28, 1865, shows he was granted a furlough of 30 days as a paroled prisoner. I have located no evidence that he was captured but perhaps he was taken prisoner on February 6, 1865 at Hatcher's Run. He mustered out with the regiment on June 7, 1865. After the war he spent some time as a trader in Duluth, St. Louis, MN. His COD was cirrhosis of the liver. He and Mary are buried in Harmony Grove Cemetery, Salem. Sarah is buried in Riverside Cemetery, West Townsend, Middlesex, MA.

Joseph Berry – Co. A
b. 1836 Canada
d. *post* 1891 ?
m. ?

NOTE: Joseph's surname was variously spelled. I use that on the muster roll card. He joined the 147th at Constantia on March 28, 1864 but it is unknown whether he enlisted or was drafted. He transferred to Co. C, 91st Regiment on June 5, 1865 and mustered out near Ball's Cross Roads, VA on July 3rd. He applied for a pension on August 15, 1891 but did not obtain a certificate, suggesting he died before he could complete the process. Either he was unmarried or his wife predeceased him. Beyond these few facts, I have located nothing.

John Besemer – Co. I
b. 1821 Cayuga County, NY
d. October 19, 1903 Richford, Tioga, NY
m1. Celia Vanderhoof (1824-*ante* 1880) ca. 1841
m2. Catharine _____ (?-*post* 1903) ?

NOTE: John, whose surname has many variations, was the son of Abraham (1786-1862) and Rachel Elsworth Besemer (1790-*post* 1865). He was a substitute for Abram Caywood, Savannah, Wayne, NY and enrolled on July 23, 1863 at Auburn, NY. Besemer was wounded at Cold Harbor, VA on June 3, 1864 and in 1890 he said he had been injured in the left leg. He theoretically was transferred to Co. I, 91st Regiment on June 5, 1865 but since he applied for a pension on June 12, 1865 (and obtained it), I suspect he had been discharged prior to the transfer. He and Celia were the parents of numerous children, only a few of whom I have been able to track: Rev. James A. Besemer (1842-1926); Rachel (1844-?); Lydia (1846-?); Abram (1849-*ca.* 1891);William M. (1852-?); John E. (1854-*post* 1891); Harriet S. (1858-?); Jenney (1859-*post* 1876); Prudence Celia (1860-1922); Melissa (*ca.* 1860-*post* 1875). Another girl, Ellen J. (1877-?), may also be their child. If so, her birth may have been the cause of Celia's death. By 1880 John was a widower. He was not married when the 1900 census was taken but when he died in 1903 his widow, Catharine, unsuccessfully applied for his pension. I have located no information on this woman. Since John died in Tioga County and is buried in Highland Cemetery, Richford, it is possible the couple was living there. His gravestone says he died October 17th but the New York State Death Index provides a DOD of October 19th.

Stephen B. Besley – Co. H

b. May 18, 1835 Luzerne County, PA
d. January 15, 1911 Baldwin, Chemung, NY
m. Hannah Ophelia McIntyre Morey (March 24, 1845-August 5, 1928) September 30, 1866

NOTE: The son of Oliver (1805-1881) and Eleanor Stage Besley (1803-1880), Stephen first enlisted in Co. H, 50th NY Engineers, serving from August 1861-October 1862. He had contracted typhoid fever, causing his shoulder and scapula muscles to atrophy. He was drafted, enrolling in the 147th at Elmira, Chemung, NY on July 21, 1863. He suffered a gunshot wound to the right leg on May 5, 1864 at the battle of the Wilderness, but rejoined the regiment. At some point between June 29th and October 4, 1864 he suffered a gunshot wound to the neck, necessitating hospitalization. On October 30th, because of the severity of the leg wound and onset of gangrene, the doctors amputated the limb near the hip. The government provided a prosthetic leg but the stump was too painful to bear it. One report stated, ". . . the bone of the stump protrudes through the flesh and it is impossible and has ever been since his leg was amputated, impossible for him in any way to use an artificial limb." In later years Besley would report to examiners that he was required to use morphine everyday to deaden the pain. Although nominally transferred to the 91st Regiment on June 5, 1865, he never reported and was ultimately discharged from hospital in New York

City on August 17, 1865. Hannah was first married to Samuel Morey, another member of the 147th who died in June 1864. (See below.) Stephen and Hannah were the parents of two sons and two daughters. He was a member of William K. Logie Post No. 420 GAR. They are buried in North Chemung Cemetery. An interesting article appeared in *The Elmira Star-Gazette* June 15, 1912, 5: "Erected Thursday afternoon, in the local burying ground as a tribute by Mrs. Hannah O. Besley, was a becoming memorial to Stephen B. Besley, Company H, 147th New York Volunteers; placed also at the instance of Mrs. Besley, was a counterpart in memory of her first husband, Samuel L. Morey, same regiment, same company, who was killed at Petersburg, June 18, 1864 and buried in Virginia."

Charles Freeman Biddlecom – Co. A
b. February 5, 1832 Farmington, Ontario, NY
d. April 18, 1912 Rochester General Hospital, Rochester, Monroe, NY
m. Esther Aldrich Lapham (November 1827-March 29, 1904) August 31, 1854

NOTE: Charles was the son of Joab (1803-1897) and Olivia Mathewson Biddlecom (1808-1885). He first enlisted in Co. E, 28th Regiment and served from May 21-August 1861 when he was discharged for "disability." On July 28, 1863 he entered the 147th Regiment as a draftee at Canandaigua, Ontario, NY. His muster roll card says he was transferred to Co. C, 91st Regiment on June 5, 1865, but he is not included in *The Adjutant-General's Report* for that regiment. In 1890 he stated he had served until February 24, 1865. In civilian life Biddlecom ran a flour mill. He was a member of George S. Bradley Post No. 450 GAR. He is today well-known because of Katherine Aldridge's book, *No Freedom Shrieker: The Civil War Letters of Union Soldier Charles Biddlecom, 147th Regiment New York Volunteer Infantry,* 2012. An obituary appeared in *The Fairport Herald* April 24, 1912, 1: "Charles Biddlecom of Macedon died at the Rochester General Hospital Thursday. He . . . was born in Deerfield, Oneida county, Feb. 5 1833. On August 31, 1854, he married Esther A. Lapham, who passed away eight years ago. Mr. Biddlecom is survived by one daughter, Mrs. Emma Sweet of Rochester; and one son, Bayard C. Biddlecom of Macedon; also one sister, Mrs. Laura Pound of Lincoln, Neb. Mr. Biddlecom was among the first to respond to President Lincoln's call for volunteers and was mustered into service May 22, 1861, in Company E, 28th Regiment, New York State Volunteer Infantry. He was seriously ill, however, and discharged for disability, August 22, 1861. Later, he was drafted and served in 147th Regiment through the Wilderness campaign and was with the army in the siege of Vicksburg [sic]. The funeral was held from the Macedon Universalist church Saturday under the auspices of George S. Bradley Post, G. A. R." Charles and Esther, the parents of three, are buried in Macedon Village Cemetery.

Charles Biddlecom's letters reveal a man of reflection and introspection.
Paul Kamalsky (FAG)

Henry M. Billings – Co. I

b. 1842 Niagara County, NY

d. October 5, 1913 Elsinore, Riverside, CA

m1. Melissa Hepsibah Shear (July 1847-October 27, 1925) June 20, 1867

m2. Polly Maria Budd Patten (February 16, 1849-September 27, 1922) June 17, 1897

NOTE: Henry, son of John (1811-1893) and Margaret Hornbeck Billings (1812-1894), enrolled at Auburn, Cayuga, NY on July 28, 1863 as a substitute for Fletcher B. Conklin, Romulus, Seneca, NY. He transferred to the VRC on August 24, 1864 and was discharged on November 1, 1865. He married Melissa at Marshall, Calhoun, MI. She died in Salt Lake City, UT, of chronic myocarditis and was buried in Wasatch Lawn Memorial Park, Salt Lake City. The couple had three daughters. Polly Maria was first married to Henry Patten (1841-1890). He died at Manistique Lake, Isabella, MI of cholera morbus and exposure. His death record says he was a widower. His grave has not been located. Henry and Polly were married at Albion, Calhoun, MI. She sued for divorce on September 1, 1898 on the grounds of "extreme cruelty" and obtained the final decree on March 14, 1901. She married John Scramlin (1852-1940) on January 15, 1902. Her COD was an intestinal obstruction, cause unknown, with an embolism causing gangrene in the left foot. She is buried in Breckinridge Cemetery, Breckinridge, Gratiot, MI. John's COD was bronchial pneumonia. He is buried in Lincoln Township Cemetery, Gratiot, MI. Henry, a member of Custer Post No. 6 GAR, Leavenworth, KS, is buried in Mt. Olive Cemetery, Whittier, Los Angeles, CA.

King Birchard – Co. E

b. May 4,1834 New York State

d. November 26, 1880 Athens, Bradford, PA

m. Delphene Angenora _____ (1848-*post* 1890) *ante* 1870

NOTE: King, a baker by occupation, was the son of Seymour (1806-1883) and Sally Caroline Betts Birchard (1811-1902). His POB is variously listed. His muster roll card shows he was born in Sussex County, NY, a place which does not exist. In 1875 he supposedly had been born in Pennsylvania. He joined the 147th as a draftee on July 15, 1863 at Owego, Tioga, NY. He was discharged on May 4, 1864 at Emory Hospital, Washington, DC but no reason was provided. He and Delphene had no children. King is buried in Tioga Point Cemetery, Athens, Bradford, PA. In 1890 Delphene, under her middle name, was enumerated as an Army widow. At the time she was living in Paris, Oxford, ME. In that same year she applied for a pension but did not obtain a certificate. No further information has been located on her.

David Bird – Co. A

b. 1842 Oneida County, NY

d. May 5, 1864 Wilderness, VA

m. ------

NOTE: David was the son of Charles (1812-1873) and Sarah McCleary Bird (1813-*post* 1880). A draftee, he joined the regiment at Utica, Oneida, NY on August 27, 1863. According to *The Town Clerks' Registers*, where he was erroneously assigned to the 14th Regiment, he "was wounded in battle of Wilderness, has not been heard from since." In actuality, he was killed in action. In 1878 his widowed mother applied for a pension but apparently died before the pension could be granted. The last document in the file is dated 1880.

George Blackwood – Co. C

b. 1845 Chenango County, NY

d. ? ?

m. ?

NOTE: I have located no information about this man's parentage. He was drafted and enrolled in the 147th at Elmira, NY on September 5, 1863. On June 5, 1865 he was transferred to Co. C, 91st Regiment but "absent, sick." His card for the 91st Regiment contains the same information. It is quite probable he was dead.

John Blacquer – Co. I

b. 1829 Germany

d. ?

m. Christina Holzman (1830-?) *ca.* 1857

NOTE: A substitute for Joseph Larean, Buffalo, NY, John enrolled in the 147th at Buffalo on August 5, 1863. His service was short-lived since he was discharged for "disability" on October 26, 1863. His parents are unidentified. In 1860 John, surname spelled Blacker, and Christina were the parents of Conrad, 2, and a female baby, aged three months. The family does not appear on the 1865 New York census and further information is unavailable.

Aaron Jermus Blakeslee – Co. B

b. December 7, 1834 Hunter, Green, NY

d. January 18, 1898 Portville, Cattaraugus, NY

m. Julia M. Newell (February 1, 1841-May 6, 1929) *ca.* 1866

NOTE: Aaron was the son of Ebenezer (*ca.* 1806-*post* 1880) and Cynthia Stevens Blakeslee (1808-1862). He was drafted, enrolling in the 147th at Pottsville, Cattaraugus, on August 22, 1863. He was wounded in the left foot at the battle of the Wilderness on May 6, 1864, transferred to the VRC on February 8, 1865, and discharged at Brattleboro, VT on August 3rd. He and Julia, who died in Olean, NY, are buried in Chestnut Hill Cemetery, Portville. His gravestone erroneously says he was born in 1843.

Wesley Blanchard – Co. E

b. October 8, 1845 Murray, Orleans, NY

d. October 18, 1864 David's Island, New York City Harbor, NY

m. ------

NOTE: Wesley, son of Chandler (1800-1859) and Lucy Linsley Blanchard (1819-1861), was a substitute for George Huff of Carlton, Orleans, NY and enrolled in the 147th Regiment on August 3, 1863. According to *The Town Clerks' Registers* he was taken sick at Petersburg, VA. His COD was chronic diarrhea. He is buried in Cypress Hills National Cemetery, Brooklyn. His brother Orrin (1843-1923) served first in Co. K, 27th Regiment and later in the 2nd New York Mounted Rifles.

Sylvester Blauvelt – Co. A

b. 1833 Chemung County, NY

d. July 27, 1911 Van Etten, Chemung, NY

m1. Armena Hill (March 17, 1837-February 24, 1901) January 25, 1853 m2. Susan Loomis (December 19, 1842-April 1, 1907) May 7, 1901

m3. Lovina Brinks Ketchum (1838-November 14, 1917) 1908

NOTE: Sylvester was the son of Peter A. (1806-1866) and Emeline Norris Blauvelt (1809-1886). He was drafted, enrolling at Erin, Chemung on July 25, 1863. Although the exact location and date are unknown, he probably was wounded at the battle of the Wilderness in May 1864. His right leg was amputated and he was discharged on August 24, 1864 at Elmira, NY. In 1890 he claimed total disability because of the amputation. Sylvester was the father of ten children. He was active in the William M. Gregg Post No. 430 GAR. His death was reported in *The Ithaca Daily News* July 29, 1911: "The funeral of Sylvester Blauvelt, aged 78 years, was held at 11:30 o'clock this morning from the home in this village [Van Etten]. The remains were taken to Scottstown, near Erin, where interment will be made in the family plot. Mr. Blauvelt died at 8:30 o'clock Thursday night after an illness of two weeks. He had been in ill health for six months but was taken critically ill about two weeks ago. Mr. Blauvelt came to Van Etten from Erin, N.Y., thirteen years ago and had since resided here. He returned not long ago from a visit with relatives in Ithaca. As a member of the G.A.R. Mr. Blauvelt was very well known. He served throughout the Civil War with Company A, 147th Regiment. He had taken a prominent part in Grand Army affairs for years . . . ." Sylvester and Armena are buried in Scotchtown Cemetery. Lovina, who alleged in 1910 she had been married four times, is buried in Woodlawn Cemetery, Ithaca. Susan's grave has not been located.

Charles Benjamin Bliss – Co. A

b. June 3, 1832 Hemlock Lake, Livingston, NY

d. August 15, 1909 Coopersville, Ottawa, MI

m. Mary Cary (January 12, 1844-January 17, 1922) 1858

NOTE: Charles was the son of Charles (1815-1878) and Sarah Jenkins Bliss (1816-1875). Dates for him and Mary vary widely. I use those on their death certificates. Charles, a draftee, enrolled in the 147th on August 1, 1863 at Canandaigua, Ontario, NY and was discharged on December 1, 1864. When he applied for a pension in 1887 it was found that a charge of desertion had been laid upon him but it was removed and his pension was approved. His COD was heart disease and Mary's was apoplexy. Both are buried in the Coopersville Cemetery.

James M. Boardman – Co. B

b. January 27, 1840 Napoli, Cattaraugus, NY

d. April 22, 1929 Minneapolis, Hennepin, MN

m. Emma Rhodes (December 1845-December 7, 1935) November 18, 1868

NOTE: James, son of Asher Norton (1811-1887) and Thirza Henry Boardman (1810-post 1880), saw prior duty with Co. B, 64th Regiment from September 1861-December 1862 when he was discharged for "disability" at Convalescent Camp, VA. He joined the 147th at Napoli on August 21, 1863, apparently re-enlisting. He was captured at the battle of the Wilderness on May 5, 1864, sent to Andersonville, and paroled at Florence, SC on February 28, 1865. He received his discharge at Annapolis, MD on June 13, 1865. His notable life was summarized in a lengthy obituary appearing in *The Nashua* [Iowa] *Reporter* May 1, 1929: "James M. Boardman was born on Jan. 27, 1840, at Napoli, New York where he grew to manhood. He responded to the first call for volunteers in the Civil War, enlisting in Company B, 64th Regiment at Randolph, New York and served until he contracted typhoid fever . . . In 1862 he was discharged from service in a convalescent camp in Virginia. In 1863, he again enrolled as a private in Company B, 147th New York volunteers. In 1864 he was taken prisoner and sent to Andersonville prison for 5 months, then was transferred to Florence, South Carolina . . . His prison days numbered 299 . . . He was married to Emma Rhodes at Napoli in 1868. Immediately after they came to Iowa to make their home. He spent two years at farming and twelve years in a general store in Plainfield. In 1882, he moved to Valley City, North Dakota, where he farmed for 12 years. He served three years in the legislature of that state. He then went to Washington, D.C., where he held a position in the agricultural department of the government for about 25 years, retiring at the age of 80 years. He was a member of the Grand Army, the Masonic order and a lifelong member of the Methodist church, being a charter member of the Plainfield church. His last years were spent with his sister, Mrs. Mary Freeburg, at Charles City, and in Minneapolis . . . ." He was buried in Willow Lawn Cemetery, Plainfield, Bremer, IA. He and Emma were featured in *History of Butler and Bremer Counties, Iowa*, 1173-4: ". . . On 17 Oct. 1868, he was joined in wedlock with Miss Emma Rhodes, who was born at St. Louis, Mo 28 Mar. 1845, her parents being temporarily located there. When she was three years old, her parents returned to their native place, Sullivan County, New York and at the age of sixteen, the daughter attended Randolph academy, and before her marriage, had taught several terms of school. She and her husband are members of the Methodist Episcopal church. Mr. Boardman is a republican, and while a resident of Butler County, held several local offices. At the present time he holds the office of school treasurer. He is an upright, honest, industrious business man, and is held in high esteem by his large circle of friends and acquaintances." His marriage to Emma was unsuccessful. In 1915 she was living in East Randolph, Cattaraugus County. She fell and broke her hip on April 25, 1935. Since she lived alone she was not found until the next day by which time she was also suffering from exposure. She never recovered. Her ashes are buried in East Randolph Cemetery.

William Miles Bolton – Co. E

b. April 13, 1836 North Royalton, Cuyahoga, OH
d. May 16, 1894 Perry, Wyoming, NY
m1. Rebecca Mitchell (April 15, 1835-*post* 1883) June 14, 1856
m2. Mary A. Amos Waugh (1834-1897) September 24, 1867

NOTE: This man, generally known by his middle name, was the son of Warren (1809-1893) and Almira Olin Bolton (1815-1893) and was a teacher by occupation. He joined the military at Canandaigua, Ontario, NY on September 8, 1863 as a substitute for Leicester S. Rockwood of Canandaigua. He spent most of his time in the Army attached to the Third Division Hospital of Fifth Army Corps. Although he was transferred to Co. D, 91st Regiment on June 5, 1865, he apparently never reported. *The Adjutant-General's Report* for that organization does not list him. I have located no pension card for him although Mary Ann applied for a widow's pension on September 23, 1895. She was unsuccessful in her attempt but whether it was because the claim was rejected or because she died before the process could be completed is unknown. Interestingly enough, the pension card assigned Miles to Co. E, 143rd Regiment. Another oddity is his enumeration on the 1890 Veterans' Schedules. Although his name was included, nothing about his regiment or disability was noted. He and Rebecca legally separated in 1867 and soon after Miles married Mary Waugh, widow of James Michael Waugh (1825-1862). Miles' funeral was detailed in *The Warsaw County Times* May 24, 1894: "The remains of Miles Bolton who died at his residence on the 15th [*sic*], were buried in Prospect Hill cemetery at Perry Center on Thursday. The funeral was held at 4 p.m. The religious services were conducted by the Rev. J. H. Hollingsworth of the 1st Baptist church. Silver Lake lodge I.O.O.F. attended the funeral and the beautiful ritual of the order was carried out at the residence and the grave. The lodge turned out about 40 strong, headed by Noble Grand J. C. Lillibridge . . . Deceased was 57 years old and he leaves a wife and two sons to mourn his loss. The lodge has given him every care during his long sickness. He was also a soldier for the preservation of the Union and although not a member of the G.A.R. the casket was covered with the flag of his country from his late home to the grave through the thoughtfulness of Major W. B. Tallman. There were also several handsome floral tributes, one being from the sisters of Mystic Union lodge Rebecca." Mary's death was reported in *The Wyoming County Times* July 8, 1897: "Mrs. Mary A. Bolton died at the residence of Mrs. Hanna at Pike on July [*sic*] 29. The cause of her death was abdominal aneurism. An autopsy was held by Drs. Dutton and Skiff which revealed a condition, showing that her disease was absolutely incurable. Her former residence was at Perry Center." She is buried in Prospect Hill Cemetery with Miles. Rebecca reportedly moved to California with a son and died there, though the date has not been discovered.

Paris E. Bolton – Co. E

b. December 26, 1837 North Royalton, Cuyahoga, OH

d. May 24, 1899 Perry, Wyoming, NY

m1. Mary Marinda Phillips (1837-June 10, 1871) December 29, 1861

m2. Elizabeth Naomi Judd (September 29, 1835-November 17, 1910) 1876

NOTE: Paris was Miles' brother. A draftee, he enrolled in the 147th Regiment on September 20, 1863 at Canandaigua. For much of his term, he, together with his brother, was assigned to the Third Division Hospital of Fifth Army Corps. He was transferred to Co. D, 91st Regiment on June 5, 1865 and discharged on June 9th. His death was reported in *The Western New Yorker* June 15, 1899: "Paris E. Bolton died at his home in the town of Perry on the morning of May 24th, 1899. The funeral services were held at his late residence on the afternoon of May 26th. They were attended by a very large number of friends and neighbors and by the John P. Robinson G. A. R. Post of Perry in a body. The services were conducted by the pastor of the family Rev. D. A. Bloss, assisted by a friend of the deceased, Rev. F. Gutelius of Moscow. The deceased had a slight of stroke of paralysis during the winter, but had so far recovered that he was able not only to enjoy the company of friends but to be about, and had very recently greatly enjoyed a visit to Perry, so that his friends and family were quite hopeful that he would entirely regain his usual health. But God's ways are not our ways, and unexpectedly the deceased was again stricken and within a few days quietly and peacefully passed away. The autopsy showed other organic difficulties and the surprise was that he enjoyed the fair health he did and lived so long. Mr. Bolton when a mere boy of four came with his parents, both deceased, to the town of Perry where he has resided ever since. He was accordingly widely known in the town and community. He bore a good name and because of his manly bearing and a life of integrity and industry he was held in honor and respect by all. He was social, kindly disposed and greatly esteemed and beloved by all who knew him. Though not a member of the church yet a Christian we believe, he was always interested in religious matters and a regular attendant, with his family of the Congregational church in Perry Center, where he will always be greatly missed. Mr. Bolton was married in 1861 to Miss Mary M. Phillips of Perry, who died in 1871. He was again married in 1876 to Miss Elizabeth N. Judd, of Perry, who, with his only daughter, Miss Clara M. Bolton, survives him. He was a soldier of the late civil war, having served in Company E, 147th N. Y. Vols. He was in the Army of the Potomac and engaged in the battles of Mine Run, Spotsylvania, North Anna River and others. During the latter part of his army life he was detailed to do service in the hospital department where he also was efficient. He was with the army at Petersburg and witnessed the blowing up of the mine there and those other interesting events proceeding and concluding with the surrender of Gen. Lee at Appomattox. The war being over he was mustered

OF BLOOD AND BATTLES: OSWEGO'S 147TH REGIMENT

out near Washington, D.C. and returned to his home. In the death of Mr. Bolton, the town and community have lost an important and worthy citizen and he will long be remembered and missed by his friends and family." Elizabeth's death was reported in *The Western New Yorker* November 24, 1910: "Mrs. Elizabeth Naomi Bolton passed away at her home on Grove street Thursday, Nov. 17th, at the age of 74 years, 1 month and 18 days. Mrs. Bolton was for 67 years a resident of the town of Perry, where she grew up to womanhood, and became the wife of Paris Bolton. They resided on a farm a short distance north of the village until after the death of her husband, which occurred in 1899. After his death she sold the farm, and moved to the village where the last five years of her life was [sic] spent. Mrs. Bolton is survived by one daughter, Miss Clara Bolton, and by one brother, Mr. James Judd who resides at Burke Hill. Funeral services were held at 1:30 o'clock Sunday afternoon from her late residence, and interment was made at Perry Center." Her COD was the effects of a stroke. She, Paris, and Mary are all buried in Prospect Hill Cemetery, Perry Center.

Ferdinand Barnard Bommel – Co. B
b. 1841 Saxony
d. March 4, 1917 Buffalo, Erie, NY
m. Catherine M. Langmyer (1843-January 23, 1927) 1867

NOTE: Ferdinand, who regularly used his middle name, was the son of Franz Joseph (1808-1887) and Catherine Elizabeth Brincks Bommel. His POB, as well as the spelling of his surname, differed from document to document. It appears he enlisted in the US Light Artillery in Buffalo on July 24, 1860, using the name Barnard H., and deserted on July 25th. He next enlisted in the 21st Regiment NYSV in May 1861, again using the name Barnard H., and again deserted on August 30, 1862. He was a substitute for John Pfleiger, 25, of Buffalo, when he entered the 147th on August 8, 1863. He transferred to Co. G, 91st Regiment on June 5, 1865 and was discharged near Washington, DC on July 3rd. Ferdinand was, like his father, a tailor. He was a member of E. L. Hayward Post No. 542 GAR. He and Catherine were the parents of five children, only two of whom survived to adulthood. Ferdinand and Catherine are buried the United German and French Cemetery, Cheektowaga, Erie, NY.

Don Ferdinand Booth – Co. A
b. July 1829 Livingston County, NY
d. May 24, 1903 Rodman, Palo Alto, IA
m. Mary Lurena Collins (September 21, 1830-April 24, 1916) 1851

NOTE: Don, the son of David Ferdinand (1806-1880) and Julia Reynolds Booth (1810-1854), was drafted, enrolling in the 147th at Dunkirk, Chautauqua, NY on August 24,

1863. According to his pension application he was wounded in the left arm at the battle of Laurel Hill on May 10, 1864. He transferred to Co. C, 91st Regiment on June 5, 1865 as Daniel F. Booth but the soldier identified as Daniel Booth in that regiment was 25 years old and had been enrolled in Co. E, 91st on September 20, 1864 at Albany, NY. Both Don and Mary applied for pensions and neither one was successful, perhaps because he was technically considered a deserter. An unsourced obituary reported his death: "On Sunday, May 24th, occurred the death of D. F. Booth, an old and esteemed resident of Fern Valley township. The cause of his demise was catarrh of the bladder. The deceased was in his 74th year and was one of the early settlers of this county. He was a veteran of the Civil war, and in those dark days of his country's history stood manfully by the principles of right and justice. As a citizen he also did his duty, and was honored and respected by all who knew him. The funeral was held Monday, the 25th, and the interment made in the cemetery west of Rodman . . . ." Mary's death was also remarked in an unsourced obituary: "Mary Collins Booth passed away Monday morning at 5 o'clock at the home of her daughter, Mrs. L. Slaughter, who lives 5 ½ miles southeast of Independence on the Quasqueton road. Mrs. Booth's death was due to heart trouble and complications arising from old age. She had been in failing health for six or seven months but her condition was only critical during the three weeks previous to her demise. The deceased has lived in this county since 1865 except for 7 years spent in Rodman, Ia., and during this time she had many friends who, with her devoted relatives, will keenly miss her. Mary Lurena Collins was born near Lockport, N. Y. Sept. 21, 1830, making her over 85 years of age at the time of her death. When nine years old she moved with her parents, William and Margaret Collins, to Cattaraugus Co. N. Y., where she was united in marriage in 1852 to D. F. Booth of that vicinity. Mr. and Mrs. Booth came to Iowa in 1865 and settled near Quasqueton until about 1895 when they moved to Rodman where Mr. Booth was laid to rest in May 1902 [sic]. Since then Mrs. Booth had made her home with her daughter, Mrs. L. Slaughter . . . Short services were held at the Slaughter home, Monday afternoon, Rev. Belmond, of Quasqueton officiating. The remains were accompanied by many of the relatives and shipped Tuesday morning at 8:39 to Rodman in Palo Alto County, where the funeral proper will be held and where Mrs. Booth will be interred beside her deceased husband." Don and Mary are buried in Riverside Cemetery, Palo Alto, IA.

Oliver Phillip Boudreau – Co. A
b. July 18, 1837 Montreal, Quebec, Canada
d. February 20, 1925 Marshall, Harrison, TX
m1. ?
m2. Sophia Maxwell (1843-January 24, 1891) May 11, 1878
m3. Mary "Mamie" Hadley Hayes (July 26, 1864-August 13, 1941) 1902

NOTE: Oliver, a "railroad man," joined the 147th at West Union, Steuben, NY on November 3, 1864 for a period of one year. There is no indication on his muster card that he was drafted. He transferred to Co. C, 91st Regiment on June 5, 1865 and was discharged on July 3rd at Ball's Cross Roads, VA. From that point until 1880 his movements are unknown. In 1880, however, he was enumerated in Marshall, Harrison, TX. The household consisted of himself, his wife Sophia, and two sons, William Oliver, aged eight, born in Kansas, and John, aged four, born in Texas. Since Oliver and Sophia were not married until 1878 the boys cannot be hers. Furthermore, Sophia said she was born in North Carolina and the census clearly shows the boys' mother was born in Canada. Sophia became the mother of Mary Jane (January 21, 1883-January 19, 1968). This girl married John D. Johnson (1880-June 1, 1960). Sophia is buried in Greenwood Cemetery, Marshall, TX. Oliver's third wife was Mary "Mamie" Hadley Hayes. She was the mother of Nellie Laura Hayes (September 17, 1883-December 20, 1946) who married Edward Lee Berry (December 1876-August 24, 1965). Edwin Berry, Nellie's son, provided the information for his mother's death certificate and stated that Nellie's maiden name was Budreou, which cannot be true. Mamie and Oliver did not marry until 1902, as evidenced by the 1910 census. Oliver's death was reported in *The Marshall Messenger* February 27, 1925, 4: "Oliver Phillip Boudreau, a pioneer citizen and railroad man of this city, died at his home . . . after an illness of some time. Mr. Boudreau was born in Montreal, Canada, July 8, 1837, and moved to Marshall 51 years ago, and has made this city his home since. Mr. Boudreau was an employee of the Texas & Pacific railway in the shops here for 43 years, and was a staunch friend of L. S. Thorne, who for many years was vice-president and general manager of the Texas & Pacific railway, and did much to assist Mr. Thorne when he came to the Texas & Pacific railway and went to work as a brakeman, to help him climb the ladder as he went up to the highest position of the road in Texas and they were bosom friends as long as Mr. Thorne lived. Mr. Boudreau is survived by his wife, and two children, Will Oliver Boudreau, of Chicasha, Okla., and Mrs. Mary Jane Johnson, of this city, and a number of grandchildren. The funeral will be held . . . from the family residence, at 4:30 o'clock. Interment in the St. Joseph's Catholic cemetery." *The Marshall Messenger* August 14, 1941, 3 noted Mamie's passing: "Mrs. Mamie Boudreau . . . passed away Wednesday evening at the Kahn Memorial Hospital. Mrs. Boudreau was born in Mobile, Alabama, July 25 [sic], 1864. She had been living in Marshall for the past thirty-five years. She was a member of the Catholic Church. The funeral service will be at 10 o'clock Friday morning at St. Joseph's Church, the Rev. J. P. Erbrick officiating. Mrs. Boudreau is survived by one daughter, Mrs. E. L. Berry of Waco, Texas, one stepdaughter, Mrs. J. B. Johnson, of Marshall, two grandchildren, Miss Lola Berry, of Waco, and Edwin Berry of California, and five step grandchildren . . . ." Mamie is buried with Oliver in St. Joseph's Cemetery. John died in Shreveport, Caddo, LA and is buried in Greenwood Cemetery, Marshall. William, who was married at least two times, disappears after 1935.

John Bovee – Co. I
b. 1837 Livingston County, NY
d. April 4, 1915 Mt. Morris, Livingston, NY
m1. Margaret Lucina Jackson (1841-April 8, 1864) *ca.* 1857
m2. Amanda Jackson (May 16, 1843-May 30, 1923) 1870

NOTE: John, son of Cornelius (1810-1865) and Margaret Helmer Bovee (1814-1886), enrolled in the 147th Regiment as a draftee at Canandaigua, Ontario, NY on September 8, 1863. He was transferred to Co. D, 91st Regiment on June 5, 1865 and mustered out near Washington, DC on July 3rd. Margaret and Amanda were sisters. In 1865 John, a widower, was enumerated with his wife's parents. His brother George was married to Lovina "Lena" Jackson, another sister. Margaret apparently died in Groveland, Livingston, NY but her grave has not been located. John's death was announced in *The Picket Line Post* April 9, 1915, 1: "The death of John Bovee, one of the older residents of the village, occurred at the family residence in South Main street on Sunday, following a lingering illness caused by the infirmities of age. Deceased was born in the town of Groveland 70 years ago, one of the children of pioneer residents of that township. Until recently Groveland had practically been his home during his entire life. Besides his wife he is survived by six sons, three daughters and some thirty grandchildren; also one brother George Bovee of Hornell, who is 86 years of age, and who was able to attend the funeral. Services were held from his late home Wednesday afternoon and burial was made in the new cemetery." John and Amanda are buried in Mt. Morris City Cemetery.

Samuel Bowen – Co. H
b. 1842 New York State
d. July 20, 1864 Andersonville, Sumter, GA
m. ------

NOTE: Samuel may have been the son of Abijah (1807-?) and Phebe Bowen (1804-?) since he was listed in *Registers of Officers and Enlisted Men* as having lived in Van Etten, Chemung NY. He enrolled in the 147th on July 21, 1863 at Horseheads, Chemung as a substitute for James H. Rodburn. The date of his capture is unknown. His COD was chronic diarrhea. He is buried in Andersonville National Cemetery.

John Lester Boyd, Sr. – Co. B

b. 1827 Orange County, NY

d. October 9, 1867 Rutland, LaSalle, IL

m. Mary Winans (August 5, 1832-January 29, 1916) *ca.* 1855

NOTE: Much controversy surrounds this soldier. His parents are unknown and vital statistics are conflicting. For example, his muster roll card gives an age of 36, meaning he was born in 1827. His gravestone, however, assigns a DOB of 1834. If this is the man who served in the 147th, he was a substitute for Abner H. Gale, Dunkirk, Chautauqua. He was enrolled and mustered in on August 17, 1863 and discharged for "disability" on February 25, 1865. He applied for a pension on March 7, 1865 but did not obtain a certificate. Mary Winans was born in Durham, Greene, NY, the daughter of Alva (1798-1871) and Eva Hover Winans (1803-1874). She and John were the parents of Bruce and Charles whose names are inscribed without dates on the family gravestone. They were also the parents of Alvina (September 1857-April 11, 1937); William (1861-September 12, 1945); John Lester, Jr. (April 14, 1866-July 18, 1951). I estimate their marriage date by the birth of Alvina, provided she was born in 1857, as is confirmed by her death certificate, and provided she was the first child. The 1870 census intimates she was born in 1859. All the children were born in Illinois and John and Mary are buried in Rutland Cemetery, Marshall, LaSalle, IL. I suspect the stone was commissioned by the children since it appears to be quite modern. Perhaps the informants did not know John's correct DOB.

Henry Bracy – Co. A

b. August 1838 New Haven, NY

d. 1908 Edgerton, Rock, WI

m. Jeanette Edwards (May 1847-1932) 1865

NOTE: Henry, son of Lyman (1802-1884) and Mary "Polly" Wing Bracy (1809-1888), saw prior service in Co. A, 81st Regiment from August 1861-May 1862 when he was discharged for "disability." A draftee, he enrolled in the 147th at Buffalo, NY on August 15, 1863. On June 5, 1865 he transferred to Co. C, 91st Regiment and was discharged on July 3rd at Ball's Cross Roads, VA. He and Jeanette, whose parents were Daniel C. (1819-1893) and Electa Cheesbro Edwards (1826-1910), are buried in Fassett Cemetery, Edgerton, Rock, WI. Their surname on the gravestone is Brace. Two of Henry's brothers also served in the military. William W. (1835-1925) was a member of Co. I, 184th Regiment from August 1864-June 1865. Hiram (1839-1927) was a member of Co. A, 81st Regiment from September 1861-January 1862).

Thomas A. Branch – Co. I
b. 1840 Dorking, Surrey, England
d. May 28, 1905 Wayland, Livingston, NY
m. Mary E. Bidlack (May 17, 1839-August 19, 1905) *ca.* 1868

NOTE: Thomas, son of Stephen (1816-1855) and Sarah A. Friday Branch Brown (1821-1893), enrolled in the 147th Regiment on September 18, 1863. In 1890 he said he was a "drafted man." He transferred to Co. I, 91st Regiment on June 5, 1865 although "absent sick." The 1890 Veterans' Schedules revealed he was discharged from the service on July 7, 1864. He and Mary were the parents of at least six children, among them Rufus (1869-February 4, 1883) who died from diphtheria and Montgomery Wells Branch (June 9, 1880-December 3, 1954) who became an ordained minister and missionary. Thomas' death was reported in *The Livonia Gazette* June 16, 1905: "Thomas Branch, whose death was referred to in this correspondence last week, was born near London in 1840, and came with his parents when a child to this country. His father settled at first near Livonia but later moved to Canadice and there raised a family of five children. Mr. Branch lived in Canadice for over thirty years, where he had a large farm, and only last March moved to Wayland . . . The deceased was an earnest church worker and for over twenty-five years was superintendent of the Sunday school and was called by many the 'father of the Sunday school'." He and Mary, who died only months after her husband, are buried in Pleasant Valley East Cemetery, Springwater, Livingston, NY.

Freeman Brasseer – Co. A
b. 1827 Canada
d. ? ?
m. ?

NOTE: This man, whose name was probably spelled much differently, perhaps Fremont Brasseur, was a butcher by trade. His parents are unknown. He enrolled in the 147th at Buffalo, NY as a substitute for Uri H. Moore, Buffalo on August 8, 1863. He was wounded at the battle of the Wilderness on May 5, 1864. Although he transferred to Co. C, 91st Regiment on June 5, 1865, he was "absent, sick." Another notation says he was discharged by General Order 77 dated April 28, 1865. It is possible he returned to Canada. It is also possible that he died from his wounds.

Jacob Brennan – Co. I
b. 1844 New York State
d. ? ?
m. ------

NOTE: Jacob was a substitute for John Davison of Geneseo, Livingston, NY, enrolling at Canandaigua, Ontario, NY on August 8, 1863. His muster card shows he was MIA at the battle of the Wilderness on May 5, 1864. A further notation appears at the bottom: "No later record found. Pay allowed to May 5/64." Although he was presumed to be a POW no evidence exists of his death or burial. His mother Margaret successfully applied for a pension on August 3, 1865. I have located no other information about this man or his family.

John Bressen – Co. I
b. 1837 Ireland
d. ? ?
m. ?

NOTE: John, a draftee, enrolled at Oswego, NY on August 10, 1863 and served until transferred to Co. I, 91st Regiment on June 5, 1865. He was discharged from the military on July 3rd near Washington, DC. Nothing else has been learned. Spelling may be a problem.

Irving Washington Brewster – Co. H
b. March 22, 1834 New York City, NY
d. June 20, 1919 Waverly, Tioga, NY
m1. Amanda _____ (1836-*ante* 1867) *ca.* 1860
m2. Delphine "Della" McGill (February 12, 1846-May 26, 1924) 1867

NOTE: Irving, son of John Tartulus (1808-1874) and Eliza Austin Brewster (1809-1891), was a mason by occupation. A draftee, he enrolled in the 147th at Horseheads, Chemung, NY on July 26, 1863. He transferred to Co. F, 91st Regiment on June 5, 1865 and was discharged on July 3rd, place unspecified. In 1890 he claimed "rheumatism & disease of back" as disabilities. Although his gravestone in Factoryville Cemetery, Waverly says he died in 1920 the New York Death Index confirms he died in 1919. Furthermore, Delphine applied for a widow's pension on June 28, 1919. Little is known about Amanda, including her DOD. In 1860 she and Irving (Ervine) were living with Charles and Rebecca Willour but I have located no evidence that she was their daughter. Delphine, mother of two, died of complications of bowel disease in Robert Packer Hospital, Sayre, Bradford, PA. She is buried with Irving but her gravestone does not give a DOD.

Levi A. Brigden – Co. I
b. January 1, 1831 Spencer, Tioga County, NY
d. March 5, 1913 Ithaca, Tompkins, NY

m1. Elizabeth A. Morey (January 1835-July 5, 1900) 1852
m2. Mariette Ackles Cowell (1833-September 4, 1912) *ca.* 1903

NOTE: Levi, son of William J. (1811-?) and Eliza Brigden (1811-?), was drafted, enrolling in the 147th at Van Etten, Chemung, NY on July 21, 1863. At some unknown date he was tried for desertion but the sentence, to forfeit two months' pay, was disallowed by the commanding officer and he was returned to duty. He transferred to Co. I, 91st Regiment on June 5, 1865 and mustered out on July 3rd, location unknown. In 1890 he claimed no disability but his entry in the log of Post 420 GAR says he was wounded in the right hand. At his death, *The Ithaca Daily News* March 5, 1913, 2 published the following: "Levi Brigden, aged 82 years, died at 10:30 o'clock this morning at the home of his daughter, Mrs. May Ackles, 215 Dryden Road, following a short illness. Mr. Brigden was born in the Town of Spencer where he spent the greater part of his early life, later moving to Van Etten where he lived for over 60 years until a few weeks ago when he came to this city to reside with his daughter. He was a veteran of the Civil War and was a member of the G. A. R. at Van Etten, and also of the Methodist Church . . . The funeral will be held at 3 o'clock Friday afternoon, from the home of Mrs. Ackles. The remains will be taken to Van Etten for burial." Levi and Elizabeth are buried in Mount Hope Cemetery, Van Etten. Mariette was previously married to John Asa Cowell (1832-1882). They are buried in North Spencer Cemetery.

William Brock – Co. F
b. 1831 Chenango County, NY
d. ? ?
m. ?

NOTE: William, a draftee, joined the 147th Regiment on July 17, 1863 in Lindsey, NY. No such place exists in New York State but perhaps was Lindley, Steuben County. Brock was a lumberman by trade. He transferred to Co. A, 91st Regiment on June 5, 1865 and mustered out near Washington, DC on July 3rd. Nothing else has been discovered.

William Bromley – Co. A
b. 1831 Monroe County, NYS
d. January 21, 1903 Evans, Erie, NY
m. Mary Kennedy (1840-*post* 1870) *ca.* 1856

NOTE: William, son of Martin (1811-*post* 1850) and Lovina Bromley (1811-*post* 1875), was drafted, enrolling in the 147th Regiment on October 6, 1863 at Canandaigua, Ontario, NY. He was wounded in action at the battle of the Wilderness on May 5, 1864. In 1890 he said he "lost left leg at Wilderness VA – Amputation at White House Landing." He and Mary were the parents of five children, the youngest of whom, Frank, was born in March 1870. By 1875 Mary was gone and William and most of the children were living with his widowed mother. William is buried in Brant Cemetery, Brant, Erie, NY. The grave marker shows that he belonged to the GAR. Mary's grave has not been located.

James Brophy – Co. K
b. 1825 Kilkenny, Ireland
d. ? ?
m. ?

NOTE: Brophy, whose parents are unknown, enrolled in the 147th on August 8, 1863 at Buffalo, Erie, NY as a substitute for Eli Long, Amherst, Erie, NY. On June 5, 1865 he transferred to Co. K, 91st Regiment and mustered out on July 3rd near Washington, DC. After that nothing has been discovered. A man named James Brophy served in the 27th Regiment NYSV from 1861-1863. He enlisted at Rochester on August 28, 1861 and was discharged at Elmira, Chemung, NY on May 31, 1863. Whether or not this is the same man is unknown.

Arnold Asa Brown – Co. A
b. 1834 Yates County, NY
d. May 8, 1864 Virginia
m. ------

NOTE: Arnold, son of John G. (1812-1896) and Nancy Townsend Brown (1812-1898), was drafted, joining the 147th Regiment on October 2, 1863 at Canandaigua, Ontario, NY. Although his muster roll card says he was KIA at the battle of the Wilderness on May 5, 1864 all other documents, including *Deaths of Volunteers*, report he was killed in battle at Spotsylvania, VA on May 8th and was buried there. His mother applied for and obtained a pension in 1884.

Charles Edward Brown – Co. G
b. May 18, 1847 Columbus, Warren, PA
d. August 30, 1927 Bear Lake, Warren, PA
m. Mary C. White (March 9, 1845-March 22, 1935) February 5, 1871

NOTE: Charles was the son of Lorenzo Daniel (1819-1888) and Susan Adelia Humphrey Brown (1822-1859). Although he claimed to be 19 when he entered the military on August 19, 1863 at Colden, Erie, NY he was actually only 16, enrolling as a substitute for Nelson Chunley. His muster card says he was MIA on October 1, 1864 at Poplar Spring, VA and "supposed to have been killed." There is no evidence that he transferred to the 91st Regiment and on his pension index card "91st" has been crossed out. I have not located him in the 1890 Veterans' Schedules. Perhaps he merely walked away from the war. Nevertheless he applied successfully for a pension in 1890 and Mary applied for and obtained a widow's pension in 1927. They were the parents of five children, all of whom survived to adulthood. Charles' COD was arteriosclerosis and cerebral congestion. Mary succumbed to erysipelas of the face and arteriosclerosis. They are buried in Bear Lake Cemetery.

Charles W. Brown – Co. I

b. January 31, 1838 Chemung County, NY
d. May 10, 1911 Elmira, Chemung, NY
m. Naomi Phylena Starks (March 1838-September 11, 1917) November 16, 1860

NOTE: Charles, son of Nathaniel (1805-1888) and his second wife Eunice Bonny Brown (1808-*post* 1870), was drafted, enrolling in the 147th at Veteran, Chemung on July 21, 1863. He transferred to Co. I, 91st Regiment on June 5, 1865 and mustered out near Washington, DC on July 3rd. His death was announced in *The Elmira Star-Gazette* May 10, 1911, 7: "Charles W. Brown of 256 South Avenue, a foreman of carpenters in the Northern Central railroad shops for 38 years, died this morning at 4 o'clock after a brief illness, aged seventy-three years. Mr. Brown had been a resident of Elmira many years and was a veteran of the civil war, having served as a private in Co. I, 147th New York infantry. He was also a member of Baldwin Post No. 6, G. A. R. The decedent was greatly interested in the extension of the Christian faith and organized the Sunday school on the southside 18 years ago, which resulted in the organization of the Southside Baptist church. Mr. Brown was the senior deacon and clerk of the church many years and was regarded as one of the leaders of the society and its founder. In his every day life Mr. Brown endeavored to exemplify the life of a Christian . . . ." Like her husband, Naomi was a charter member of the Southside Baptist Church. They are buried in the Fulton Street Cemetery, Elmira. Alonzo Brown (1832-1919), Charles' half-brother, served in Co. G, 50th NY Engineers. Henry E. (1841-September 17, 1862), a full brother, was a member of Co. F, 23rd Regiment. He was killed at the battle of Antietam and is buried in Antietam National Cemetery.

Thomas Brown – Co. A

b. 1836 ?
d. ? ?
m. ?

NOTE: Little can be ascertained concerning this soldier. No POB was provided on his muster roll card. He was drafted, enrolling at Perrysburg, Cattaraugus County on August 20, 1863. He transferred to the US Navy in April 1864.

Michael Buckley – Co. A

b. December 25, 1832 New York City, NY

d. September 14, 1909 York County, PA Almshouse

m. ------

NOTE: Michael, a shoemaker, claimed to have been born in 1837 when he was inducted into the army but his death certificate provides the date given above. His parents are unidentified. A draftee, he joined the 147th Regiment at Elmira on July 20, 1863. A notation on his muster roll card suggested Buckley was "supposed to be identical" to John M. Bulkley of Co. A, 76th Regiment, but that is not true. Bulkley, a draftee, enrolled in the 76th Regiment at Thurston, Steuben, NY on July 15, 1863. It hardly seems likely he traveled to Elmira five days later to join the 147th. His muster roll card gives no age but his Draft Registrations listing said he was 28 in 1863 and therefore born in 1835. John allegedly was wounded and considered MIA on June 2, 1864 near Cold Harbor, VA. No further record exists and in all probability he died on June 2nd and his body was buried on the field. According to an entry in an early admission to the Dayton National Soldiers' Home, Michael had lost the ring finger of his left hand on May 5, 1864 at the battle of the Wilderness. That date would later become May 16th, suggesting he was wounded at Spotsylvania. Nevertheless, he could not have been near Cold Harbor on June 2nd. On March 22, 1865 he was transferred to the VRC and finally discharged at Philadelphia on January 19, 1866. Despite the fact that he said he had been born in New York City when he was mustered in, I have located no parents for him. His admission forms for various national homes listed Mrs. Fanny Clark, Norristown, PA as his nearest relative. She was probably the sister mentioned in the articles quoted below. His experiences in the soldiers' homes seem to have been less than satisfactory. He deserted from the home in Dayton, OH. He was last in the National Home in Hampton, VA, which he left at his own request on March 23, 1909. It was the beginning of the end. A short piece in *The Philadelphia Inquirer* September 11, 1909, 3 reported the following: "YORK. – Michael Buckley, 77 years old, claiming Arizona as his home, was found exhausted in a woods near Windsor yesterday. It is believed that he had been lying there for three or four days before being found." Details were furnished in *The York Daily* September 11, 1909, 9: "Red Lion, Sept. 10. – It was learned today that the man found yesterday in the woods near here, was, by the story he told Justice of the Peace D. A. Heindel of Bittersville, who committed him to the almshouse, Michael Buckley, of Arizona. He had come east, he said, to find a sister who was living in York county. When he arrived here, however, he found that the sister had died. He was on his way to Red Lion to attend to the changing of his pension papers from Chicago to the east, when he was taken sick. This story will be looked into by the authorities." The saga was concluded three days later, as reported by an article fraught with historical errors in

The York Daily September 16, 1909, 6: "Michael Buckley, 77 years old, who was found several days ago by two Red Lion boys wandering homeless and starving in a field in Windsor township, and who was removed to the York county almshouse, died at that institution at 6:15 o'clock Tuesday evening. Before his death the old man made known that he was a veteran of the civil war and had served in Company A of the immortal One Hundred and Forty-seventh regiment, New York volunteers, which was almost wiped out in the first day's fight at Gettysburg, and instead of occupying a pauper's grave he will be laid to rest in the soldier's plot in Prospect Hill cemetery with military services by General John Sedgwick post No. 37, Grand Army of the Republic. Buckley gave his home as Troy, Bradford Co., Pa., but he is not known to have any relatives living. He enlisted at the outbreak of the rebellion at Elmira, N.Y. The regiment of which Buckley was a member was in the Second brigade, First division, First Army Corps, under General John F. Reynolds. Exposed to a heavy fire on the first day at Gettysburg, it was ordered to retreat, but its colonel being killed and its lieutenant colonel and major each wounded, there was no one to transmit the command, and it retained its position until literally cut to pieces. After the war Buckley belonged to the United States invalid corps. Services over the body will be held at the Hartman Memorial chapel, Prospect Hill cemetery, Thursday afternoon at 3 o'clock and all war veterans are invited to participate." Buckley's funeral took place on September 16th. His official COD was gastroenteritis and arteriosclerosis.

George Bull – Co. A

b. 1838 Lockport, Niagara, NY
d. May 5, 1864 Wilderness, VA
m. ------

NOTE: George, son of Robert (1808-*post* 1865) and Frances Roberts Bull (1807-1871), saw previous duty as a member of Co. D, 28th Regiment from October 1861-June 2, 1863. He had been wounded at Cedar Mount, VA on August 9, 1862. On July 28, 1863 he joined the 147th Regiment at Lockport as a substitute for his brother Martin (1842-March 1870). An article written by I. Richard Reed and published in *The Niagara Falls Gazette* May 4, 1964, 9 provides a few details about this soldier: ". . . Last man on our list was another man from the Township of Lockport. He was 25-year-old George Bull who was serving his second enlistment. He had originally enlisted at Lockport in October 1861 and served as a private in the 28th Infantry. At the completion of his first term of enlistment he had re-enlisted in the 147th New York Infantry and was serving as a private in Company A when he was killed in action on May 5. Location of grave unknown. Recently, Mrs. Mary Hall of Lewiston produced a picture of George Bull. It seems that Bull was a tent mate or 'buddy' of her father's. Her father, Milton E. Perrigo, was a neighbor of Bull's before the war and they enlisted together. Mrs. Hall tells me that she can still remember her father speaking of George Bull when she was a little girl. He never spoke of his old friend but what a tear came to his eye."

Albert Burch – Co. K

b. May 20, 1846 Cayuga County, NY
d. April 22, 1922 Dryden, Lapeer, MI
m1. Ida Inez Thornton (1849-?) *ca.* 1872
m2. Henrietta Miller (1854-July 5, 1926) June 20, 1880

NOTE: Albert was the son of Hezekiah (1795-1888) and Emily Burch (1810-*ante* 1888). Although his muster roll card states he was born in Wayne County, the 1865 New York census shows he was born in Cayuga County, as were all his siblings living at home at that time. His DOB varies. I use that provided on the 1900 census. Albert enrolled in the 147th on July 23, 1863 at Auburn, Cayuga, NY as a substitute for John Berger of Savannah, NY. He was transferred to Co. K, 91st Regiment on June 5, 1865 and mustered out on July 3rd near Washington, DC. He and Ida were the parents of Etta M. (1873-1884) and Inez (1877-?). A woman by the name of Ida Birch died at Ionia, MI on March 16, 1877 but whether or not this is the correct woman is open to question. Albert and Henrietta were married in Dryden. His COD was heart disease. He and Henrietta, who died in Genesee County, MI, are buried in Thornville Cemetery. Ida's grave has not been located. Albert's half brother, John H. (1829-November 5, 1916), served in the 9th NY HA from December 1863-July 1865. He too is buried in Thornville Cemetery.

John Irish Burch, Jr. – Co. K

b. February 17, 1838 Columbia County, NY
d. March 20, 1866 Canadice, Ontario, NY
m. Mary Eliza Morley (1843-1862) *ca.* 1860

NOTE: John was the son of John (1802-1871) and Fidelia Race Burch (1808-1899). His POB is a mystery. His birth place in 1855 was Columbia County. In 1863 it was Bridgeport, Fairfield, CT. In 1865 it was Ontario County. *The Registers of Officers and Enlisted Men* place his birth in Ontario County but *The Town Clerks' Registers* allege he was born in Claverack, Columbia, NY. His entry in *The Town Clerks' Registers* erroneously assigned him to the 127th Regiment. As a matter of fact, he attempted to join the 1st NY Cavalry on August 4, 1862 but was unassigned. He was drafted in 1863, enrolling in the 147th at Canadice on July 28th. He was transferred to Co. K, 91st Regiment on June 5, 1865 and discharged near Washington, DC on July 3rd. On July 13, 1889 Fidelia applied for a mother's pension but did not obtain a certificate. John,

Mary Eliza, John, Sr., and Fidelia are buried in Canadice Corners Cemetery, Canadice. A brother, Thomas Jefferson Burch (1842-1918), served in Co. G, 13th Regiment.

Lewis Burdick – Co. A
b. September 29, 1829 Madison County, NY
d. October 25, 1877 North Brookfield, Madison, NY
m. Esther Frances Morgan (February 7, 1833-June 21, 1912) March 1852

NOTE: Lewis may have been the son of Jason (1800-?) and Sarah Burdick (1810-?). He was drafted, enrolling in the 147th at Buffalo, Erie, NY on September 4, 1863. He was "absent" when transferred to Co. C, 91st Regiment on June 5, 1865. On June 13th he was discharged at Elmira, Chemung, NY "as of Co. A, 147th Inf." I have located no obituary for Lewis but when Esther died *The Waterville Times* June ?, 1912 published the following: "Mrs. Esther Frances Burdick, after an illness of three weeks during which she received the tender, loving care of her son and his wife, and their children, went to join the great company awaiting her on the heavenly shore, Friday evening, June 21. She was the daughter of Harry and Weltha Morgan, and was born in Brookfield, N. Y., Feb. 7, 1833. Ten brothers and sisters had lived and died, leaving her the last of the early home circle. In March, 1852 she was united in marriage with Lewis Burdick. One son, Mansel E., was born to them, and her husband died in October, 1877. For many years she lived in North Brookfield, and in this township all her life was spent until, with her son and his family, she moved to Clayville seven years ago, and when the death angel came she was separated from her son for the first time, their home having always been one and the same. A devoted, loving mother, kind friend and neighbor, always ready with a helping hand, she will be sadly missed . . . Memorial services were held from her late home Monday afternoon, conducted by Rev. Edgar Brown of the Clayville M. E. Church. The choir sang 'Nearer My God to Thee,' and 'The Beautiful Isle of Somewhere,' and amid a profusion of flowers, which she loved so well and had enjoyed cultivating she was laid to rest in the beautiful Sauquoit Valley Cemetery. After a long life she sleeps well, and we hope to meet her in the bright hereafter . . . ." Lewis is also buried in this cemetery.

Eugene Burlingame – Co. B
b. April 24, 1841 Ischua, Cattaraugus, NY
d. July 2, 1864 Ischua, Cattaraugus, NY
m. ------

NOTE: Eugene, son of Philo (1809-1873) and Sarah "Sally" Dodge Burlingame (1806-1871), was drafted. He joined the 147th at Ischua on August 21, 1863. He was wounded at the battle of the Wilderness on May 5, 1864 and evidently sent home on furlough to recover. His entry in *Registers of Officers and Enlisted Men* states he died at Ischua on July 2, 1864 and was buried there. He and his parents are buried in Union Hill Cemetery, Ischua.

Charles Burroughs – Co. I

b. 1835 Napoleon, Jackson County, MI

d. September 29, 1892 Napoleon, Jackson, MI

m. Susan Jane Redner (January 14, 1845-May 15, 1935) November 30, 1867

NOTE: Charles was the son of John (1793-1862) and Sarah "Sally" H. Lewis Burroughs (1801-1872). His was an extensive military career. From April-July 1861 he was a member of Co. D, 1st Michigan Infantry. He next served in Co. C, 9th Michigan Regiment from September 1861-November 1862. He joined the 147th at Auburn, Cayuga, NY on July 24, 1863 as a substitute for John A. Stoughtenburg, Williamson, Wayne, NY. He was transferred to Co. I, 91st Regiment on June 5, 1865 and discharged on July 3rd near Washington, DC. In 1890 he claimed chronic diarrhea and "piles" as his disabilities. His official COD was chronic diarrhea. Susan married James L. Hawley (1841-1917) as his second wife on September 7, 1893. He had served in Co. G, 3rd Michigan Cavalry. Hawley, whose COD was prostatitis, is buried in Greenwood Cemetery, Fowlerville, Livingston, MI. Susan's death was caused by acute circulatory failure and pneumonia. She had fractured her left hip and left humerus in a fall at her home. She and Charles are buried in Oak Grove Cemetery, Napoleon.

George Howard Bush – Co. E

b. March 24, 1830 Tioga County, PA

d. March 12, 1912 Lake View, Sac, IA

m1. Servilia B. Gould (December 27, 1833-December 18, 1884) December 1853

m2. Catherine Buck Jones (September 1840-April 18, 1917) *ca.* 1875

NOTE: George was the son of Joseph (1796-1845) and Lucretia Putnam Bush (1795-1842). He had an extensive military career. He first served in Co. B, 72nd IL Regiment from August 1862-March 1863 when he was discharged for "disability." He next served with Co. F, 68th NY National Guard from June 25, 1863-July 27, 1863. On August 18, 1863 he enrolled in the 147th at Hanover, Chautauqua as a draftee. He transferred to Co. A, 91st Regiment on June 5, 1865 and was discharged near Washington, DC on July 3rd. It appears that George and Servilia's marriage was unsuccessful. Her gravestone, located in Evergreen Lawn Cemetery, Hanover, NY, gives only her parents' names. George married Catherine in Illinois. Their wedding date varies. She had previously been married to Edward R. Jones (1829-1869). George's somewhat fanciful obituary appeared *The Lake View Resort* March 14, 1912: "George Howard Bush died at his home in Lake View, Iowa, Tuesday, March 12, 1912, at 6:45 o'clock p.m. Mr. Bush had been in ill health all winter long and continued growing weaker until the end. Mr. Bush was born in Tioga county, Pa., March 24, 1830, and when six years old his parents moved to Poppy Hill, N.Y., where he grew to manhood and then he located in Chautauqua county, N.Y., and was married in December, 1853 to Miss Servilia Gould, to which union two sons, Virgil and Orville, were born. Virgil is a resident of Lake View and Orville died in childhood. The family moved to Michigan in the fall of 1861 and from there to Illinois in the spring of 1862. Mr. Bush joined the Union army August 5th, 1862 and had his full share of hardships in the Civil war. He was discharged at Keokuk, Iowa, Feb. 17, 1863, on account of physical disability and went to New York, and with the state militia went the same year to oppose General Lee's northern march. In the fall of 1863 he enlisted in the 147th N. Y. infantry, which was cut to pieces in battle and Mr. Bush was taken prisoner but in a short time was exchanged back, and was then transferred to the 91st N. Y. He was mustered out of the army at Balls Bluff, Virginia, at the close of the war. In the year 1874 the family moved from New York to Illinois and in 1881 they moved to Crawford county, Iowa, and in 1882 they came to Sac county and have lived in this vicinity ever since. The funeral occurred from the M. E. church in Lake View, Rev. C. J. Hunt of Deloit, assisted by Rev. Carroll of Auburn and Rev. Tumbleson of Lake View, conducting the services at 2:00 o'clock p.m., after which the remains were laid at rest in the Ferguson cemetery. Mr. Bush has gone to his just reward and may heaven bless him." Catherine's death occasioned the following obituary in *The Lake View Resort* April 26, 1917: ". . . Miss Catherine Buck was born Sept. 1, 1840, at Bockville [sic], Canada, and went to Illinois with her parents in 1851. In 1858 she was married to E. R. Jones at Morris, Ill., and to this union four daughters were born . . . Miss Viola Blecker has made her home with her grandmother for the past sixteen years and has been in almost constant attendance since Mrs. Bush developed cancer about eight months ago. In 1869 Mr. Jones died and three years later his widow married Geo. H. Bush, this ceremony taking place at Morris, March 30, and in 1883 the family located on a farm southeast of Lake View, where they resided until 1903, when they came to town, where Mr. Bush died in 1912, leaving a son Virgil by a former marriage. Mrs. Bush joined the Latter Day Saints church at Grant City, but since moving here has attended and been an active worker in the Methodist Episcopal church. She was also a member of the Woman's Relief Corps. The deceased will be mourned by a large circle of friends who have learned her estimable qualities through long acquaintance, though she was of a retiring disposition. The survivors will have the sympathy of the entire community." Catherine is buried with George in Ferguson Cemetery.

Alexander Palmer Campbell – Co. B

b. February 13, 1842 Barrington, Yates, NY
d. April 12, 1867 Starkey, Yates, NY
m. ------

NOTE: Alexander was the son of Henry William (1805-1894) and Abigail Morrison Campbell (1805-*post* 1880). He enlisted in the 85th Regiment on October 29, 1861 at Geneva, Ontario, NY and was assigned to Co. G. He was discharged for "disability" at New Berne, NC on December 31, 1862. He was a substitute for Henry A. Peck, Benton, NY and enrolled in the 147th on August 2, 1863 at Canandaigua, Ontario County. His time with the 147th was brief since he was discharged on December 28, 1863 at Culpeper, VA. On March 31, 1864 he enlisted in Co. B, 179th Regiment at Batavia, Genesee, NY and deserted at Elmira, Chemung, on April 28th. He is buried in the Old Baptist Cemetery, Dundee. He has a government gravestone.

Job G. Campbell – Co. A

b. May 10, 1832 Yates County, NY
d. May 5, 1864 Wilderness, VA
m. Catherine Wood (September 1840- March 27, 1927) *ca.* 1856

NOTE: Job was the son of Samuel (1791-1859) and Maria Mulford Campbell (1800-1882). He was drafted, enrolling at Campbell, Steuben, NY on July 17, 1863. His body was probably buried on the field. Catherine married Myron F. Lovell (1837-March 14, 1880) probably in early 1865. They were married when the 1865 New York census was taken. Lovell had served in Co. D, 107th Regiment. His COD was kidney disease. Catherine's death was reported in *The Steuben Courier* April 8, 1927, 4: "The funeral of Mrs. Catherine Lovell was held in her late home on Center street last Wednesday afternoon, Rev. T. Francis Smith officiating. The bearers were her grandsons, Harry, Myron, and Verne Lovell and Raymond Jones. Interment was made in Hope cemetery where she was laid to rest beside a beloved grandson, Somers Lovell, who died a few years ago."

George B. Canfield – Co. B

b. November 1839 Cazenovia, Madison, NY
d. April 21,1913 Scranton, Lackawanna, PA
m. Mary E. _____ (June 25, 1848-June 25, 1934) 1875

NOTE: George was the son of Asa Burr (1810-1854) and Lucy Electa Ives Canfield (1813-1843). A bookkeeper, he was drafted, enrolling in the 147th on August 11, 1863 at Oswego City, NY. He transferred to Co. G, 91st Regiment on June 5, 1865 and mustered out near Washington, DC on July 3rd. His death was announced in *The*

Scranton Truth April 21, 1913, 5: "George B. Canfield, a veteran of the Civil war, died at 4 o'clock this morning, following a protracted illness, at his home, 1017 Webster avenue. Deceased had an enviable war record. He was a native of Cazenovia, N. Y., and was 74 years old. He enlisted first in Company G, 147th New York Volunteers and re-enlisted in Company B, 91st New York Volunteers, rising to the rank of corporal. For many years he had been a resident of Scranton. For some time he was employed as bookkeeper for the old Republican and also for the Hill & Connell company. He is survived by his widow. The funeral will be held Wednesday, the time of which will be announced later. The Ezra H. Griffin post, G .A. R., will attend." George's COD was apoplexy. Mary's death was reported in *The Scranton Republican* June 26, 1934, 4: "Mrs. Mary E. Canfield, widow of George B. Canfield, died yesterday on her eighty-sixth birthday. While she had been in failing health for some time, her death came suddenly. She was a member of St. Luke's Episcopal Church and had been affiliated with the Women's Guild. Mrs. Canfield resided in Scranton most of her life. Her husband had been employed for a number of years as a bookkeeper by The Republican . . . ." Mary's COD was *angina pectoris*. She and George are buried in Hickory Grove Cemetery, Waverly, Lackawanna, PA.

Thomas Carden – Co. D

b. 1844 County Kings, Ireland

d. ? ?

m. ------

NOTE: Carden, a boatman, joined the 147th at Auburn, Cayuga, NY on July 24, 1863 as a substitute for A. E. Hathaway, Summerhill, Cayuga, NY. According to his muster roll card he was "wounded May 5/64 in the Wilderness, Va. No later record found." He transferred to Co. B. 91st Regiment *in absentia* on June 5, 1865. In all probability he was killed during the two-day battle and his body buried on the field. His parents are unknown.

George W. Carey – Co. I

b. November 19, 1835 Romulus, Seneca, NY

d. probably 1879 Cottonwood County, MN

m. Eliza A. _____ (?-?) *post* 1870

NOTE: George, son of Harvey (1807-1861) and Maria Gulick Carey (1810-1887), was drafted, enrolling in the 147th at Auburn, Cayuga, NY on July 25, 1863. He transferred to the VRC on March 26, 1864 and was discharged on July 29, 1865 at Providence, RI as a member of Co. C, 11th VRC. Eliza applied for a pension on April 19, 1879, place unknown, although in all likelihood it was in Cottonwood County where George and several of his brothers were living. I have located no information about Eliza except that her application for a pension was rejected. George's grave has not been found. Three brothers also served the Union cause. Edward Carey (1838-January 26, 1864) was a member of Co. K, 110th Regiment. He died at Baton Rouge, LA from chronic diarrhea and typhoid fever. John Carey (1845-1928) and Ralph Carey (1847-1917) served in the 148th Regiment.

Lewis Carpenter – Co. B
b. 1839 Madison County, NY
d. ? ?
m. ?

NOTE: Lewis was drafted, nrolling in the 147th at Oswego City, NY on August 28, 1863 although he lived in Eaton, Madison, NY. He transferred to Co. G, 91st Regiment on June 5, 1865 and mustered out near Washington, DC on July 3rd. That same year he was enumerated for the New York census, a single man living in the Leach household in Eaton. I have located no other confirmable information.

Silas Case – Co. F
b. November 1, 1837 Delaware County, NY
d. May 5, 1908 Sayre, Bradford, PA
m. Mary Elizabeth Brock (May 15, 1840-June 11, 1932) 1865

NOTE: Silas was the son of Thomas (1800-*post* 1870) and Christine Strader Case (1801-*post* 1870). He enrolled in the regiment as a substitute for Henry Barrett on July 14, 1863 at Barton, Tioga, NY. He transferred to Co. A, 91st Regiment on June 5, 1865 and mustered out on July 3rd near Washington, DC. His death was reported in *The Waverly Free Press and Tioga County Record* May 8, 1908: "Silas Case, a well-known citizen of Sayre and formerly a member of the borough council, died at his home in that place, Tuesday morning, May 5, 1908. Mr. Case was taken ill one week before Christmas, but later his condition improved so that he was able to leave his home. Ten days ago his condition became worse and the past few days the family realized that death was imminent. The deceased was seventy years of age, and thirty of those years had been spent in Sayre and Milltown. Before that time he was for several years a resident of South Waverly. He was a veteran of the Civil War, having enlisted in Company F, 147th New York Volunteers at the beginning of the rebellion and was discharged from service on July 3, 1865 at Ball's Cross Roads, Va. Mr. Case was an active member of Mallory Post G. A. R., of Sayre, and he had served the borough as councilman representing the Second ward and was faithful to his duties . . . The funeral was held yesterday afternoon from the late home on Stevenson street, the Rev. J. F. Warner, pastor of the Methodist church officiating. Interment was made in the Tioga Point Cemetery." Silas' COD was a gastric ulcer. Mary's death was announced in *The* [Sayre] *Evening Times* June 13, 1932, 2: "Mrs. M. Elizabeth Case, 92 and the oldest native born resident of this valley, died at the home of her daughter, Mrs. P. W. Hocklander . . . at 9 o'clock Saturday night, death being caused by infirmities incident to age. Mrs. Case was born in Factoryville, now East Waverly, and has spent her entire life in this vicinity. Before advancing age made it impossible for her to continue she was for many years an active member of the Sayre Methodist church but during recent years she has spent most of her time at home . . . Funeral services will be held at the Hocklander home at 2 o'clock tomorrow afternoon, Rev. Glen B. Walter, rector of the Church of the Redeemer, officiating. Burial will be in Tioga Point cemetery." Mary's death certificate gives "infirmities of old age" as her official COD. Silas' brother, George W. (1840-1907), was a member of Co. E, 1st NY ART.

Joseph Andrew Caywood – Co. I
b. September 18, 1841 Chemung County, NY
d. probably 1864 ?
m. ------

NOTE: Joseph, also known by his middle name, was the son of Abisha (?-*post* 1847) and Rachel A. Fish Caywood (1823-1901). A draftee, he enrolled in the 147th at Baldwin, Chemung, NY on July 21, 1863. He was MIA at the battle of the Wilderness on May 5, 1864. His muster roll card labeled him a POW but I have located no information to that effect.

Stephen Henry Chandler – Co. F
b. May 29, 1841 Deerfield, Franklin, MA
d. January 30, 1878 Shelburne Falls, Franklin, MA
m1. Eunice Bishop (December 1846-December 31, 1931) July 29, 1863
m2. Elizabeth "Lizzie" Caroline Crane (1851-*post* 1878) December 2, 1868

NOTE: Stephen was the son of Joseph Whitney (1815-1895) and Adaline Goodnow Chandler (1817-1902). He was a member of Co. B, 28th Regiment from May 1861-June 1863. On July 28, 1863 he joined the 147th at Royalton, Niagara, NY as a substitute for Martin I. Dole, Royalton. He was transferred to the VRC on May 9, 1865 and discharged on July 14th. His untimely death was reported briefly in *The Boston Daily Advertiser* February 2, 1878, 4: "Stephen H. Chandler, aged 36, was drowned yesterday in the wheel pit of Bardwell, a tannery at Shelburne Falls." He was buried in Arms Cemetery, Shelburne. His marriage to Eunice, who had been born in Lockport, Niagara, NY, was unsuccessful. She next married Perry J. Crull (1847-1893). In 1870 she and Perry, together with their daughter Jennie, aged two, were living in Newstead, Erie, NY. The family moved to Michigan where Krull died. In 1900 Eunice stated she was the mother of 10 children, of whom eight were still living. It is interesting to note that on October 1, 1906 Eunice, using the surname Chandler, filed a claim for Stephen's pension in New York State. It was rejected. Shortly before her death, her children celebrated her birthday, which was reported in *The Port Huron Times Herald* December 12, 1931, 5: "A birthday dinner was given in honor of Mrs. Eunice Crull, 80, in her home Friday by her children and grandchildren. Mrs. Crull has lived the greater part of her life in Armada and vicinity." Eunice died of a coronary occlusion. She and Perry are buried in Willow Grove Cemetery, Armada, Macomb, MI. Little has been learned about Elizabeth. She was the mother of two children, Frank (1873-1885), who died from a head injury, and Annie Nora (1876-?), a teacher who married Thomas Malachi Fallon (1864-?) on September 15, 1902 at Boston. Since Lizzie was a very young woman when Stephen died, it is possible that she remarried. Stephen's father, Joseph, also served in Co. B, 28th Regiment. A brother, Amariah (1839-1938), was a soldier in Co. H, 10th MA Infantry from 1861-1863.

Horace Chapin, Jr. – Co. I
b. 1829 Herkimer County, NY
d. June 25, 1864 Petersburg, Fauquier, VA
m. ------

NOTE: Horace was the son of Horace, Sr. (1797-1851) and Almira Briggs Chapin (1808-1893) who had married in 1823 and by 1850 were the parents of 10 children, ranging in age from 24 to 1. Horace, Jr. saw prior military service in Co. F, 5th Wisconsin Regiment, serving from 1861-January 1, 1863. He joined the 147th as a substitute for his younger brother, William Henry Harrison (1840-1932), on August 7, 1863 at Rochester, Monroe, NY and was KIA. Almira successfully applied for a pension, claiming Horace had been her sole support for several years.

Reuben C. Chapin – Co. D
b. 1832 New York State
d. January 30, 1914 National Soldiers' Home, Bath, Steuben, NY
m. Jane Snooks (September 15, 1832-April 18, 1920) *ca.* 1859

NOTE: Reuben Chapin's DOB has mystified researchers because of the seeming discrepancies in various documents. When he was enrolled in the 147th on July 21, 1863 his age was recorded as 21, meaning he had been born in 1842. He was 29 when he was mustered in, however, and therefore born in 1832. It is difficult to believe he aged eight years in such a short period of time. Every verifiable document points to a birth date of 1832. With that fact in mind who were his parents? I think they were Jason (1807-1887) and Caroline Chapin (1813-?). In 1850 the Chapin family was living in Springfield, Bradford, PA. The six children ranged in age from 19 to five months. The second child was Reuben, 17, born in New York State. In 1859 Jason was convicted of "incestuous adultery and fornication" and sentenced to two years in Pennsylvania's Eastern Penitentiary. He died in the Bradford County Almshouse on June 23, 1887 and was buried in the almshouse cemetery. Caroline and most of the children disappeared. Reuben joined the 147th at Chemung, Chemung, NY on July 21, 1863 as a draftee. He transferred to Co. B, 91st Regiment on June 15, 1865 but his muster card shows he was absent, sick in Augur Hospital, near Alexandria, VA and no discharge was provided. In 1890 while living in Vestal Center, Broome, NY, Reuben told the enumerator that he had been discharged on August 26, 1865. Although he claimed no disability in 1890 he had applied for a pension on May 2, 1866. His marriage to Jane Snooks produced six children but by 1900 the couple had separated. Their wedding date is conjectural, based on the birth date of their first known child. In 1900 Jane was reported to have been married 45 years but since her birth date, 1826, was an obvious error, the marriage date might also be incorrect. In 1910 her birth date had returned to 1832. When Reuben entered the national home he said his daughter, Alice, was his nearest kin. He was suffering from heart trouble at the time. He is buried in the Bath National Cemetery. Jane's COD was acute bronchitis with heart disease as a contributing factor. She is buried in Franklin Hill Cemetery, Halstead, Susquehanna, PA.

Duane Chapman – Co. D
b. 1846 Oswego County, NY
d. March 13, 1919 Saginaw, Saginaw, MI
m1. Ellen _____ (1850-*post* 1880) *ca.* 1865
m2. Alice Frances Umberfeld Williams (1858-April 16, 1918) October 17, 1916

NOTE: Duane, brother of Daniel Chapman, joined the 147th on February 23, 1864 at Granby, NY., apparently enlisting. At the time both his father, John, and his brother were serving in the military. He transferred to Co. B, 91st Regiment on June 5, 1865 and was discharged near Washington, DC on July 3rd. In 1910 Duane said he had been married twice but identifying his first wife has been a challenge. From his pension payment cards I learned that he had a daughter, Harriet "Hattie," married to James O'Connell. Her death certificate lists Duane as her father and shows she was born on November 13, 1866. A record for her first marriage to Frank E. Clapp in 1883 gave her POB as Fulton, Oswego, NY. It is possible that Duane and Ellen were married soon after he returned home but certainly no later than February 1866. In 1870 Duane was living with his parents and unmarried siblings in Flint, Genesee, MI. He was single. In 1880 he was an inmate in the Michigan State Prison, Jackson, Jackson, MI and married. That same year Ellen Chapman, 30, single, was living in Flint, Genesee, MI with her daughter, Harriet, 13, in the same house as Henry Chapman, 33, Duane's brother. Ellen disappears after that census. Hattie married Frank Clapp in 1883 but apparently the marriage did not last. In 1886 she married O'Connell, with whom she lived until he died of a cerebral hemorrhage in Detroit, MI on February 4, 1922. Hattie died on February 3, 1929 of uterine cancer. They are buried in Forest Lawn Cemetery, Saginaw. Alice was first married to DeWitt Clinton Williams (1835-July 4, 1892). Although she and Duane did not get married until 1916 they were living together in 1910 and claimed they had been married for eight years. Alice's COD, according to her obituary, was senility. She is buried in Elm Lawn Cemetery, Bay City, Bay, MI where Williams is also buried. Duane, who died of a cerebral hemorrhage, is buried in Forest Lawn Cemetery, Saginaw.

Henry Chase - Co. B
b. February 6, 1838 Richmond, Ontario, NY
d. April 13, 1908 Avon, Livingston, NY
m. Maria J. Hayes (April 1854-February 16, 1946) December 27, 1871

NOTE: Henry was the son of Jasper (1812-1897) and Harriet Carpenter Chase (1812-1890). A draftee, he enrolled in the 147th at Canandaigua, Ontario, NY on August 2, 1863. He transferred to Co. G, 91st Regiment on June 5, 1865 and mustered out near Washington, DC on July 3rd. His death was announced in a lengthy obituary in *The Avon News* April 15, 1908: "Henry Chase died at his home in this village about 7:30 Monday evening after an illness which began early last winter and which had confined him to his bed for the past twelve weeks. He was born in Richmond, Ontario county on February 6th, 1838, and was the last surviving member of a family of eight children born to Jasper S. and Harriet Carpenter Chase. In 1863 he enlisted in Co. C, 147th N.Y. Volunteer Infantry and later was transferred to Co. G, 91st N.Y. Volunteer Infantry with which he served until the end of the war. He was a member of H. C. Cutler Post No. 235, G.A.R., and had always been active in the work of that organization. On December 27, 1871 he was united in marriage to Miss Maria Hayes of Lima, and in 1876 he came to this village, which he since made his home. Mr. Chase was a contractor and well known throughout this section. He was in partnership with the late Benjamin Long for several years, and since the dissolution of that firm he has been in business for himself, and he has the reputation of generally doing more than the contract called for, and of never having slighted a job in the slightest manner. In the death of Mr. Chase his wife loses a kind and loving husband, his children are bereft of an indulgent father, while Avon suffers the loss of a man who can never be replaced, and who did much while here toward the up building and uplifting of the village. He had the contract for the new $15,000 town hall which is being erected in Lima, and which is nearing completion. The funeral was held from the house this afternoon, the Rev. H. C. Milliman officiating. Interment in the Avon Cemetery . . . The sincerest sympathy is expressed by the whole community for the bereaved family." At the time of his death, Henry was vice commander of the GAR Post. He and Maria were the parents of six children. Her death was announced in *The Lansing State Journal* February 19, 1946, 4: "Ovid, Feb. 19. – Funeral services were to be held Tuesday afternoon for Maria Chase, daughter of John and Catherine Hayes, who was born at Lima, N.Y., April 8, 1854, and died February 16 at the Ovid Nursing home after several months' illness at the age of 91 years 10 months 8 days. Rev. William Blanding was to officiate and interment was to be made in the Maple Grove cemetery. In 1872 she was married to Henry Chase, a Civil war veteran, at Lima, N.Y., and her early life was spent at Lima and Avon, N.Y. Mr. Chase died in 1911 [*sic*] and she moved to Seattle, Wash., where she spent 35 years with her son. After his death she moved to Michigan and lived in Ann Arbor and Flint until moving to Ovid about a year ago. She was a member of the M. E. church and a faithful worker in the church as her health permitted . . . ." Henry's brother Nathan (1822-1886) was a member of Co. B, 110th Regiment.

Charles W. Cheney – Co. B
b. 1840 Oswego County, NY
d. October 10, 1899 St. Alexis Hospital, Cleveland, Cuyahoga, OH
m. Mary A. Walker (1845-*ante* 1899) November 11, 1861

NOTE: Charles was the son of Samuel (1803-1870) and Charlotte Edna Cheney (1808-*post* 1865). A sailor, he was drafted, enrolling in the 147th at Oswego City on September 1, 1863. He transferred to Co. G, 91st Regiment on June 5, 1865 and mustered out at Ball's Cross Roads, VA on July 3rd. He and Mary were married in the Presbyterian Church in Oswego. He was last mentioned in the city directory in 1869 and tracking them from that date until 1890 has been impossible. In 1890 Charles was living in Independence, Cuyahoga, OH. He told the enumerator he had been wounded in the shoulder at Cold Harbor in 1864. His tragic end was reported in *The Cleveland Leader* October 12, 1899, 5: "About 6:45 o'clock Tuesday evening Charles W. Cheney, an old soldier sixty-five years of age, of Macedonia, O., was killed while walking on the suburban railway tracks between Calvary cemetery and Garfield Park. At that point there is a double track. A car passed west and he stepped from one track to the other to avoid it. In so doing, he stepped directly in front of an A, B & C electric car, in charge of Conductor Frank Tracey and Motorman Joe Segar, going east. Before the motorman could stop his car Cheney was struck. He was thrown sideways. He sustained a fracture of the skull, a serious scalp wound over the right eye, and a fracture of the leg. In an unconscious condition he was conveyed to St. Alexis Hospital in Richards' ambulance. At 10:45 o'clock he died. A brother of the dead man, who lives at No. 1416 Lorain street, was notified." When the inquest was held on October 12th, Segar testified that Cheney stepped right in front of the car and was hurled to the side. He was buried in Woodland Cemetery, Cleveland. The brother mentioned in the article was William (1836-?). I have located no information about Mary.

John Kilburn Church – Co. G
b. December 1836 Oswego County, NY
b. January 21, 1926 Fulton, NY
m. Harriet M. Flower (May 1848-November 25, 1912) 1870

NOTE: John was the son of Asa (1800-*ante* 1850) and Florentine Church (1809-*post* 1855). He was drafted, enrolling in the 147th on August 14, 1863. He transferred to Co. F, 91st Regiment on June 5, 1865 and mustered out near Washington, DC on July 3rd. In 1890 he claimed pleurisy as his disability. He and Harriet were the parents of three children, only one of whom, Elam (1871-1949), survived to adulthood. John and Harriet are buried in North Volney Cemetery. His DOD is not inscribed on the stone. It was located on a pension payment card and confirmed by the New York State Death Index.

George Clark – Co. K
b. 1828 England
d. ? ?
m. ?

NOTE: Very little can be determined about this soldier. He enlisted in the 147th as a substitute for an unknown draftee under the name Clack at Watertown, Jefferson, NY on September 3, 1863. He transferred to the 91st Regiment on June 5, 1865 but was "absent, sick." When he was discharged on June 29th, it was from the 147th. He applied for a pension on December 18, 1869 using the name Clark but did not obtain a certificate. Nothing verifiable beyond that date has been found.

John G. Claus – Co. F
b. 1835 Schoharie County, NY
d. September 27, 1899 National Soldiers' Home, Bath, Steuben, NY
m. Eliza J. Richard (1843-April 25, 1875) *ca.* 1860

NOTE: John was the child of George Washington (1813-?) and Electa Claus (1816-*ante* 1855). He was drafted, enrolling in the 147th at Oswego City on August 11,

1863. He transferred to Co. E, 91st Regiment on June 5, 1865 and mustered out on July 3rd near Washington, DC. His death was reported in an interesting article appearing in *The Oswego Daily Palladium* September 27, 1899, 5: "Chester Penfield received a telegram from A. C. Brundage, Adjutant of the Soldiers' Home at Bath, yesterday, addressed to Mrs. Mary J. Heiman, which reads: 'Your father died this morning. Funeral Friday at 2:30 o'clock unless otherwise ordered.' The dispatch, coming to the care of Mr. Penfield, and he not knowing Mrs. Heiman, it was opened by him. Mr. Penfield is not acquainted with the person for whom it was intended and could not find anyone that is. The directory contains no such name and as the name of the dead man is not given there is much speculation among the members of the G.A.R., as to his identity, there being several there from Oswego. A special dispatch to the *Palladium* from Adjutant A. C. Brundage, of the Soldiers' Home, at Bath, says that the dead man is John G. Claus. When last here Mr. Claus was employed as a coachman by Dr. W. J. Bulger. He was a private in Company G, 147th New York Volunteers, and served until his regiment was mustered out. His wife died several years ago. The only other member of his family known here is Mrs. Lewis Hinman, of Lincoln, Nebraska. She was in Oswego last Spring and visited with her father." John and Eliza were the parents of two known children, Mary Jane (1862-1926) and George W. (1863-1947). John is buried in the Bath National Cemetery. Eliza is buried in Rural Cemetery, Oswego Town.

Joseph Clegg – Co. I

b. November 27, 1829 Yorkshire, England
d. September 25, 1868 Dunkirk, Chautauqua, NY
m. Sarah Thompson Rostron (January 20, 1828-November 21, 1896) *ca.* 1867

NOTE: Joseph, whose parents are unidentified, enrolled in the 147th on August 19, 1863 as a substitute for Eli Durfee, a draftee, at Arkwright, Chautauqua. At an unknown date he was discharged from the service at Point Lookout, MD "by order of surgeon in charge." He applied for a pension on March 20, 1865. In 1890 Sarah told the enumerator that Joseph had lost his right arm. Her death was reported in *The Buffalo Courier* November 22, 1896: "Dunkirk, Nov. 21. – Mrs. Sarah Clegg died suddenly this morning of heart disease. She had been ill during the last week but was so much better that she arose and attempted to dress but while doing so fell upon the floor dead. The deceased was the daughter of Joseph Thompson and was born January 20, 1828, in Leeds, England. She was married in Leeds to Richard Rostron and with her husband came to Dunkirk about 40 years ago. They kept a hotel on Washington Avenue, when most of the business of the place was confined to the north end of Washington and central avenues and Front Street. Mr. Rostron enlisted early in the late War and died in the army. His widow after a time was married to

Joseph Clegg, who also enlisted and lost an arm in the service of the country. He died a few years after the War. Mrs. Clegg was the mother of eight children, seven by her first marriage . . . After Mrs. Clegg's second marriage the name of the hotel was changed to Lancashire House in compliment to Mr. Clegg's English home, and after his death she continued proprietor of the same hotel. She banished the bar and made her house a popular home-like boarding house as the Lancashire the remainder of her life. Numbers of her boarders remained with her for many years and to them she was a valued friend. She was an excellent business woman and her reputation for integrity and prompt discharge of business duties was of the highest grade. She was a good wife, mother, and friend. She was a member of the English Church in England and after coming to Dunkirk became a member of St. John's Episcopal Church." Joseph and Sarah are buried in Forest Hill Cemetery, Fredonia, Chautauqua. Richard Rostron (1825-1863), a blacksmith, enlisted in Co. I, 2nd US Infantry on January 23, 1863 and died of *phthisis* near Falmouth, VA on March 12, 1863. He and Sarah, who was his second wife, were married in Leeds, York, on February 15, 1849.

William Cline – Co. D
b. 1841 New York State
d. September 25, 1864 Andersonville, Sumter, GA
m. ------

NOTE: Very little is known about this soldier before he joined the 147th at Buffalo on August 7, 1863 as a substitute for Thomas Perkins, also of Buffalo. At some unknown date Cline was captured by the Confederates and sent to Andersonville where he died on September 25, 1864 of acute diarrhea. He has been confused with William Kline, also born in 1841, who joined Co. F, 76th Regiment, at Buffalo, on August 3, 1863. Kline was transferred to Co. D, 76th, on July 1, 1864. He too was captured, date unknown, and died at Andersonville on September 24, 1864.

Joseph P. Clyens – Co. B
b. 1824 Ireland
d. August 17, 1864 Andersonville, Sumter, GA
m. Mary Elizabeth Murray (1820-1875) November 24, 1842

NOTE: Joseph, parents unknown, was a substitute for Nelson P. Wheeler and enrolled in the 147th at Portville, Cattaraugus, NY on August 26, 1863. He was captured on May 5, 1864 at the Wilderness and died of chronic diarrhea. He is buried in Andersonville National Cemetery. Mary was the mother of eight children, one of whom was Patrick (1843-December 13, 1862), a member of Co. I, 42nd Pennsylvania Vols. who was KIA at Fredericksburg, VA. The youngest child was Francis (1859-December 13, 1879).

He and two sisters, Mary E. (1850-1933) and Evalina (1854-?), drew pensions as minor children. Francis died in Denison, Grayson, TX and is buried in Oakwood Cemetery, Denison. Their mother Mary died in 1875, according to a letter written to the Pension Board by her daughter, Mary. Her gravesite is unknown.

Edgar P. Coats – Co. F
b. May 15, 1843 Cattaraugus County, NY
d. January 18, 1894 Kennedy, Chautauqua, NY
m. Julia M. Price (1848-March 16, 1916) *ante* 1870

NOTE: Edgar, also known as Edward, was the son of Joseph (1810-1893) and Harriet Jane Baldwin Coats (1813-1897). A draftee, he enrolled in the 147th at Busti, Chautauqua, NY on August 20, 1863. He transferred to Co. A, 91st on June 5, 1865, and mustered out near Washington, DC on July 3rd. I have not located an exact wedding date for him and Julia but in 1870 they were living in Colorado Territory where he was a telegrapher. In 1880 they were residing in Harmony, Chautauqua. They had no children. Edgar's fate was chronicled in local papers in 1894, beginning with an article in *The* [Jamestown, NY] *Evening Journal* January 18, 1894, 1: "Kennedy, Jan. 18. – [Special]. – Edgar P. Coats, a telegraph operator formerly of Grant more recently of Elma, near Buffalo, whilst returning to Grant in feeble health escaped from the home of F. L. Darrow, the agent here of the Nypano, early this morning in his night clothes. He was stopping here over night. Up to 11 a.m. no clue of his whereabouts had been found. Anyone seeing or hearing of him will please advise F. L. Darrow, agent, Kennedy. This afternoon the creek is being dragged in the hope of finding Coats's body." Over the next two weeks the local newspapers reported that he was still missing. *The Chautauqua News* January 24, 1894, 1 carried the following: ". . . George Benjamin was at Kennedy last week, assisting in the search for his wife's uncle, Edgar P. Coats . . . The missing man was insane." Coats was located on January 31st, as reported in *The Evening Journal* February 2, 1894, 7: ". . . The body of Edgar Coats who disappeared about two weeks ago, was found Wednesday afternoon by Melvin Jackson in the Conewango [Creek] about a half mile below the village. The remains were taken to Harris & DeGraff's undertaking room where they were viewed by Coroner Bowers on Thursday morning, and then taken by train to Grant Station where the funeral services will be held." He and Julia, who died in Harmony, are buried in Grant Cemetery, Niobe, Chautauqua, NY. Nypano was an abbreviation for New York, Pennsylvania, and Ohio Railroad.

Halsey Cole – Co. B
b. 1840 Nichols, Tioga, NY
d. February 12, 1909 Nichols, Tioga, NY
m. Ann _____ (1837-*post* 1880) *ca.* 1875

NOTE: Halsey, not to be confused with Halsey D. Cole (1842- 1932), was the son of Edward/Edmund (1818-?) and Miranda Cole (1825-?). He was drafted, enrolling in the 147th at Nichols on July 15, 1863. He had seen prior service in Co. E, 86th Regiment from September 1861-November 1862 when he was discharged for "disability." He was discharged from the 147th at Culpeper, VA on January 9, 1864, again for "disability." He subsequently served in Co. I, 187th PA from May 1864-August 1865. In 1890 he claimed he had been "wounded in the right hand." He and Ann were living in Pennsylvania in 1880 and were the parents of Ida (1876-?) and Charles (1879-), both of whom had been born in that state. Ann was listed as "insane." Neither she nor Halsey was literate. What happened to her is unknown but since she does not appear on the New York Death Index she may have died in Pennsylvania. In 1898 when Halsey applied for admission to the National Soldiers' Home at Bath, NY he claimed to be a widower. For his next of kin he gave a cousin's name, implying that his children were deceased as well. For the next few years Halsey was in and out of the home. On January 7, 1909 he suffered a stroke. He died at the home of his cousin, Truman Cole, and was buried in East Nichols Cemetery.

Horace A. Cole – Co. F

b. 1831 Nichols, Tioga, NY
d. January 15, 1900 Hooper's Valley, Tioga, NY
m1. Mary E. Walterman (November 1832-December 23, 1869) *ca.* 1848
m2. Mary Ann Webb (July 1851-June 21, 1903) *ca.* 1877

NOTE: Horace, son of James (1797-1869) and Elizabeth Hoover Cole (1802-*post* 1860), was drafted, enrolling in the 147th at Nichols on July 15, 1863. He transferred to Co. A, 91st Regiment on June 5, 1865 and mustered out near Washington, DC on July 3rd. In 1890 he claimed a gunshot wound to the shoulder and rheumatism as his disabilities. He was a member of William Warwick Post No. 529 GAR, Nichols. Mary E. died in childbirth. She and Horace are buried in Asbury Cemetery, Nichols. Mary Ann died in Nichols but her grave has not been located.

Minor B. Colegrove – Co. I

b. February 3, 1839 Chemung County, NY
d. August 1, 1914 Russell, Lucas, IA
m. Sarah Caroline "Callie" McKinley (1843-December 27, 1904) December 26, 1871

NOTE: Minor was the son of Nelson J. (1812-1882) and Roxie Fulkerson Colegrove (1815-1897). A draftee, he enrolled in the 147th at Catlin, Chemung on July 21, 1863. According to *The Town Clerks' Registers* he was WIA on May 5, 1864 at the battle of the Wilderness. He transferred to Co. I, 91st Regiment on June 5, 1865 and mustered out on

July 3ʳᵈ near Washington, DC. He and Callie, mother of three, were married in Iowa. Callie's COD was cancer. She and Minor are buried in Ragtown Cemetery, Russell.

Robert Collingwood – Co. A
b. 1841 Chemung County, NY
d. May 5, 1864 Wilderness, Virginia
m. ------

NOTE: Little has been learned about Collingwood's early life, except that he was a carpenter. Because he said he was 22 when he joined the Army I assign him a DOB of 1841. His entry in *The Town Clerks' Registers* says he was born in 1843 (with 1841 stricken over). He entered the military on July 14, 1863 as a substitute for John Morris, Bradford, Steuben, NY. A notation on his muster roll card states he was wounded in action on May 5ᵗʰ and adds that no later record was to be had. He transferred to Co. C, 91ˢᵗ Regiment on June 5, 1865 but "absent, sick, no discharge." His name does not appear in *The Adjutant-General's Report* for that regiment. In all likelihood, he died on the battlefield and was buried there.

Seth Colvin – Co. C
b. 1843 Cattaraugus County, NY
d. March 24, 1886 Allegan, Allegan, MI
m. Lydia J. Miller (November 18, 1845-December 16, 1900) July 1, 1865

NOTE: Seth was the son of Noah (1799-1873) and Caroline Beach Colvin (1809-*post* 1870). Although he said he was born in 1835 when he joined the military, early census records show he was born in 1843. He was drafted, enrolling in the 147ᵗʰ at Cold Spring, Cattaraugus on August 22, 1863. He was discharged for "disability" on January 1, 1864. He next was a member of Co. C, 187ᵗʰ Regiment, serving from October 1864-June 1, 1865, mustering out at Arlington Heights, VA. It is noteworthy that he gave his correct age, 21, when he mustered into this outfit. He and Lydia were the parents of four children by 1880. Fanny, the second child, was born in Michigan in 1869. Seth is buried in Oakwood Cemetery, Allegan. Lydia married Tyler A. Stewart (1841-May 29, 1900) as his fourth wife, date unknown. He had served in Co. I, 39ᵗʰ PA and Co. K, 191ˢᵗ PA. Tyler and Lydia are buried in Kingsley Cemetery, Townville, Crawford, PA.

Stephen Colvin, Jr. – Co. A
b. November 19, 1830 Deerfield, Tioga, PA
d. June 26, 1880 Woodhull, Steuben, NY
m1. Mary Wood (January 12, 1841-July 2, 1868) *ca.* 1856
m2. Catherine A. _____ (1840-*post* 1882) *ca.* 1871

NOTE: Stephen, son of Stephen (1799-1873) and Roxanna "Roxie" Mattison Colvin (1802-1872), was drafted, enrolling in the 147th on July 1, 1863 at Woodhull. He transferred to Co. C, 91st on June 5, 1865 and was discharged on June 19th near Ball's Cross Roads, VA. According to Jackson and Jackson's *Death Notices from Steuben County, New York Newspapers, 1797-1884*, 7, Mary, mother of four children by 1865, died in 1868. In 1870 Stephen was unmarried. In 1875 he was married but his wife was not enumerated with the family. Catherine finally appears on the 1880 census. She applied for a pension on September 17, 1880 but did not obtain a certificate. She was still a widow in 1882 when she was named a defendant in a foreclosure sale. Stephen and his parents are buried in Woodhull Cemetery but Mary's gravesite is unknown. Catherine may have remarried.

Edmund Comfort – Co. I
b. May 1836 Chemung County, NY
d. January 18, 1902 Southport, Chemung, NY
m1. Delilah Conklin (1840-January 1, 1883) 1859
m2. Melissa Beckwith Clark (1865-July 15, 1885) October 6, 1884
m3. Caroline Van Scoy (July 14, 1861-May 27, 1935) 1891

NOTE: The son of Jacob (1820-1891) and Zylia Ann McCann Comfort (1820-1867), Edward was drafted, enrolling in the 147th at Southport on July 20, 1863. He was WIA at Five Forks, VA on April 1, 1865. Although nominally transferred to Co. I, 91st Regiment, he was discharged on June 8th at Petersburg, VA as a member of the 147th. In 1890 he said he suffered from chronic rheumatism caused by exposure. He and Delilah are buried in Christian Hollow Cemetery, Chemung County. Melissa's grave has not been located. Caroline is buried in Maple Grove Cemetery, Horseheads, Chemung.

Martin Van Buren Comstock – Co. F
b. September 15, 1840 Cuba, Allegany, NY
d. April 23, 1924 Belfast, Allegany, NY
m. Mary Ann Fritts (September 13,1837-August 9, 1929) July 4, 1860

NOTE: Martin was the son of Morgan Lewis (1800-*post* 1880) and Margaret Homer Comstock (1813-*post* 1880). A draftee, he enrolled in the 147th on July 11, 1863 at Bolivar, Allegany. In 1890 he said he had been wounded twice on May 5, 1864, once in the left forearm and once in the right thigh. Although nominally transferred to Co. A, 91st Regiment on June 5, 1865, he was discharged from the service for "disability" on June 22, 1865 at McClellan Hospital, Philadelphia. He and Mary Ann are buried in Riverside Cemetery, Belfast.

John Connors – Co. A

b. 1845 Limerick, Ireland

d. ?

m. ?

NOTE: John, a laborer, was drafted, enrolling in the 147th at Buffalo, Erie, NY on August 14, 1863, serving until June 5, 1865 when transferred to Co. C, 91st Regiment. He mustered out near Ball's Cross Roads, VA on July 3rd. His parents are unknown and because of the numbers of men with this name his subsequent life cannot be verifiably traced.

John W. Cook – Co. K

b. 1845 Germany

d. ? ?

m. ?

NOTE: John may have been the son of John (1811-*ante* 1870) and Elizabeth Cook (1813-*post* 1875), German immigrants who lived in Jefferson County. John W. enrolled in the 147th at Watertown on September 3, 1863 as a substitute for an unidentified draftee. John deserted on July 25, 1864 from Central Park Hospital, New York City. On March 11, 1865 President Lincoln issued a proclamation which offered a pardon to deserters who surrendered to a provost-marshal or returned to their units within 60 days. John turned himself in at Watertown and arrived at Fort Columbus, NYC Harbor on May 12th. He was discharged on May 15th but "not honorably." Nothing confirmable after that date has been located.

Bruen Cooley – Co. B

b. 1840 Penn Yan, Yates, NY

d. January 30, 1875 Penn Yan, Yates, NY

m. Anna Mary Carley (1846-December 24, 1869) *ca.* 1866

NOTE: The son of James (1801-1872) and Elizabeth Bruen Cooley (1801-1863), Bruen saw prior duty in Co. I, 33rd Regiment from May 1861-February 1863 when he was discharged for "disability" at the New Convalescent Hospital, Alexandria, VA. On August 18, 1863 he joined the 147th at Canandaigua, Ontario, NY as a substitute for George A. Fordon, Seneca, NY. He was captured during the campaign known as Spotsylvania Court House, contested from May 8-21, 1864, although the exact date is unrecorded. He was sent to Andersonville. When and where he was paroled is also unknown. Although nominally transferred to Co. G, 91st Regiment, he was actually discharged from the service as of 147th Regiment on June 19, 1865 at US Hospital #2, Annapolis, MD. His death was announced in *The Corning Journal* February 11, 1875:

"Bruen Cooley died at his residence in Penn Yan, on the 30th of January. He was a soldier during the war for the Union, was wounded, and a prisoner at Andersonville for nine months. He was 35 years old." He and Anna Mary are buried in Lakeview Cemetery, Penn Yan.

Marcus P. Cortright – Co. I
b. 1838 Ontario County, NY
d. January 22, 1898 Elmira, Chemung, NY
m. Mary Elizabeth _____ (1838- October 18, 1909) *ca.* 1860

NOTE: Marcus, who may have been the son of Margaret (1808-*post* 1860), also spelled his name Courtright. He saw prior duty in Co. A, 107th Regiment from August 1862-January 18, 1863 when he was discharged at Alexandria, VA for "disability." He was drafted, enrolling in the 147th at Southport, Chemung on July 20, 1863. He was discharged at Elmira, Chemung, NY on May 12, 1865. His marriage to Elizabeth produced two children, Walter (1861-1904) and Louisa (1867-?) but it was not successful. By 1880 they were living apart. His death was reported in *The Elmira Telegram* January 23, 1898: "Marcus P. Courtright died yesterday afternoon at 4 o'clock in his rooms in the Stancliff block, where he had been employed as janitor for the past fifteen years. Death was due to heart trouble, from which he had been suffering for six weeks, and for the past three weeks had been confined to his bed. Deceased was sixty-three years of age, and is survived by a wife and two children . . . Mr. Courtright enlisted in 1861 in company A, 107th volunteers, Captain Wilkins, but after serving several months was taken ill and honorably discharged. After his recovery he was drafted and spent two years in the service, from which he was again honorably discharged. He was a member of Hoffman post, G.A.R., which will have charge of the funeral, which will be held Tuesday afternoon at the Stephens Memorial chapel, Woodlawn cemetery . . . ." Mary Elizabeth, who, according to her FAG entry, died from a fractured skull, is also buried in Woodlawn. Her gravestone erroneously states she was born in 1857.

Talcott B. Cotton – Co. F
b. 1833 Friendship, Allegany, NY
d. 1867 Friendship, Allegany, NY
m. Zelinda "Linda" Norton (1838-*post* 1867) *ca.* 1855

NOTE: Talcott, son of Chauncey (1791-1869) and Anna Gold Cotton (1797-1869), was substitute for Lambert Wesley and joined the regiment on July 3, 1863 at Friendship. He transferred to Co. F, 91st Regiment on June 5, 1865 and mustered out on July 3rd near Washington, DC. He and Zelinda had no children. On August 21,

1863, shortly before he mustered into the 147th, he made his will leaving everything to her. She petitioned to have the will proved in November 1867. Talcott is buried with his parents in Nile Cemetery, Nile, Allegany. Zelinda does not appear on the 1870 census and probably remarried.

Adolphus Cousino – Co. F
b. February 1836 Montreal, Quebec, Canada
d. May 31, 1902 Watertown, Jefferson, NY
m. Caroline Bondiette (January 1838-*post* 1921) 1865

NOTE: Tracing this man has been a challenge, in part because of the multiple variants for his surname and numerous birthdates. I use the DOB provided on the 1900 census. According to that census he came to the United States in 1845 and became a naturalized citizen. His parents are unknown. His pension cards state he was a member of Company E, 35th Regiment which his government grave marker confirms. The grave marker also says his name was Alphonso Cousins. *The Adjutant-General's Report* for the 35th Regiment does not include anyone named Cousino or any variation thereof. Nowhere have I been able to locate anyone named Alphonso Cousins/Cousino. Adolphus, a shoemaker, enrolled in the 147th at Oswego on August 12, 1863, a substitute for John Cousino, probably his brother. When he was enrolled he was 24, but when mustered in he had suddenly become 26! His muster roll card provides little information except that at one point he was "in arrest." On June 5, 1865 he was transferred to Co. A, 91st Regiment and was discharged near Washington, DC on July 3rd. The family moved frequently. In 1870 Adolphus and Caroline lived in Oswego. They had no children. Their first known child, Josephine, was born in 1871. John (1873-1961) was born in the Town of Adams, Jefferson, NY. By 1880 the family had moved to Pulaski, NY. In 1890 the family lived in Gouverneur, Jefferson, NY. Adolphus made no mention of service in the 35th when the Veterans' Schedules were compiled. He did say he had been shot in the shoulder. In 1900 he and Caroline still resided in Gouverneur. They claimed to have been married in 1865. Caroline said she was the mother of 11 children, all living. Adolphus' death was briefly noted in *The Jefferson County Journal* June 3, 1902, 4: "COUSINO – In Watertown, May 31, Adolphus Cousino, aged 65 years. Formerly of Adams." Adolphus (if it is he) is buried in North Watertown Cemetery. Caroline last appears in the Watertown City Directory in 1921, but I have been unable to determine a DOD. It is interesting to note that by the time their son Frank (1874-*post* 1910) died family members had reverted to spelling their surname in its original French form of Cousineau.

Nathaniel Covert – Co. K

b. 1847 Schuyler County, New York

d. January 17, 1864 Division Hospital, Culpeper, VA

m. ------

NOTE: Nathaniel was the son of Abram (1808-1875) and Miranda Buck Covert (1815-1899). Although he said he was 20 when he enrolled in the 147th, he was only 16. He was a substitute for Mulford Grey when he joined the regiment on July 27, 1863 at Tyrone, Schuyler, NY. His COD was chronic diarrhea. His muster roll card says he died January 18, 1863 but his entries in both *Deaths of Volunteers* and the Burial Registers show he died on the 17th. He is buried in Culpeper National Cemetery. In 1878 his mother applied for and obtained a pension.

Ambrose Cox – Co. A

b. January 1841 England

d. March 6, 1924 National Soldiers' Home, Dayton, Montgomery, OH

m. ------

NOTE: Ambrose's parents are unknown but on his various soldiers' homes admission forms he gave his sister, Mrs. Mary Ann Sims, 182 Lodge Road, Birmingham, England as his nearest kin. On later census records he stated he arrived in the United States in 1863 and became a naturalized citizen. He was a silversmith. On August 4, 1863 he joined the 147th Regiment at Buffalo, Erie, NY as a substitute for Julius Bennett, Marietta, Onondaga, NY. He transferred to Co. C, 91st Regiment on June 5, 1865 and mustered out at Ball's Cross Roads, VA on July 3rd. On November 3, 1865 he enlisted in Co. A, 18th US Infantry, serving until November 3, 1868. He then enlisted in the US Navy at Detroit, MI on December 6, 1871, serving on the USS St. Mary until discharged on June 17, 1873. His next term was begun in Boston, MA in Co. D, 11th US Infantry on December 1, 1873. He served with this unit until December 1, 1878. His last enlistment began at New York City on August 14, 1879 when he joined Co. I, 3rd US Infantry. He was discharged on November 18, 1882. Over the next few years he was in and out of soldiers' homes across the country. His COD was erysipelas. He is buried in Dayton National Cemetery.

Michael Coyle – Co. B

b. 1829 Ireland

d. *post* 1866 ?

m. ?

NOTE: Little has been learned about this man. His muster roll card says he was born in Braceborough, Ireland but probably it was Brookeborough, Northern Ireland.

Braceborough is located in Lincolnshire, England. Coyle said he was a sailor when he joined the 147th on August 14, 1863 at Buffalo, Erie, NY as a substitute for Marvin C. Amidon, a draftee from Marshall, Oneida, NY. Coyle was captured at the battle of the Wilderness on May 5, 1864. Where he was confined is unknown but he was in a parole camp in April 1865. A notation on his card says he left the camp on April 29, 1865. Though nominally transferred to Co. G, 91st Regiment on June 7, 1865 he never reported and was discharged that day at Ball's Cross Roads, VA as a member of the 147th. He applied for a pension on March 3, 1866 and obtained a certificate. No widow is listed. There the trail ends.

Andrew W. Craig – Co. K

b. 1842 Camden, Oneida County, NY

d. December 8, 1863 First Division, First Army Corps Hospital, Mine Run, Orange, VA

m. Isabelle "Belle" J. Lambie (May 15, 1846-March 23, 1916) March 16, 1863

NOTE: Andrew was the son of Robert (1807-1863) and Elizabeth Craig (1805-1860), both of whom were born in Scotland. He was drafted, enrolling in the 147th at Utica, Oneida, NY on August 26, 1863. His COD was measles and typhoid pneumonia. Isabelle gave birth to a son, Andrew, in 1863 but he died soon thereafter. She married William Henry Crennan (1848-1893) in 1876 as his second wife and had several children by him. Craig's burial site is unknown. Isabelle and William are buried in Forest Park Cemetery, Camden.

George Whitefield Cranston – Co. C

b. December 22, 1842 Springville, Erie, NY

d. May 22, 1923 Fredonia, Chautauqua, NY

m. Mary H. Haskin (July 3, 1847-July 23, 1914) December 22, 1870

NOTE: George was the son of John Clemmons (1814-1876) and Melissa Newell Cranston (1814-1864). He first served in Co. C, 112th Regiment from August 1862-April 1864 when he was discharged for "disability." In 1890 he claimed malaria as his disability and stated he had been discharged on a surgeon's certificate. He enlisted in the 147th at Bainbridge, Chenango, NY on January 25, 1865, after having first attempted to join the 76th on the same day. On June 5th he transferred to Co. H, 91st Regiment and mustered out on July 3rd near Washington, DC. His long, eventful life was catalogued in an obituary appearing in *The Fredonia Censor* May 30, 1923, 1: "George Whitefield Cranston, son of John C. and Melissa Newell Cranston, was born Dec. 22, 1842 at Springville, N. Y., and died at his home in Fredonia, May 22, 1923. Mr. Cranston was the last of his family, his brother, A.

B. Cranston having died four months ago. In 1854 the family moved to Newell's Corners in Sheridan. For three terms Mr. Cranston was a student in the Fredonia Academy, walking to school four miles from his home. For thirteen winters he taught Common District Schools. Twelve of these were in Sheridan, seven of them at Dist. No. 7, and the thirteenth at Harmon Hill, Pomfret. Responding to President Lincoln's call for '300,000 men' he enlisted in the 112th Rgt. Infantry in August 1862, serving until discharged in 1864. On Dec. 22, 1870 he was married to Mary Haskin of Sheridan, daughter of F. C. and Sarah Keach Haskin. In July 1883 he took the first examinations held in the United States under the then called Pendleton Civil Service Law for admission to the Railway Mail Service and was certified for appointment which he received in Feb., 1884. He ran for nine years between Buffalo and Pittsburg and after that on the Route between Dunkirk and Titusville until retired August 20, 1920, by the Civil Service Retirement Law. During the 41 years he lived in Sheridan, he held a few minor offices and was twice Supervisor of the town. In 1895 Mr. Cranston and his family moved to Fredonia, where Mrs. Cranston died in 1914. They were both devoted members of the Baptist Church of Fredonia which they joined in 1877. Mr. Cranston was a comrade in Holt Post G. A. R. from its organization in Oct. and Nov., 1883, until his death, holding this comradeship second only to the brotherhood of the church. He was also a member of Forest Lodge F. and A. M. joining in 1867. Mr. Cranston was a man of sterling character, fine literary discernment and a clear thinking student of contemporaneous affairs. In his home, his church and his community he was an outstanding figure . . . The funeral services were held at the late residence, 41 Maple Ave., May 26 . . . Burial was in Forest Hill Cemetery . . . ." Mary, whose life was equally active, was eulogized in *The Fredonia Censor* July 29, 1914, 8: "In this village, Thursday, July 23, at her home . . . Mrs. Cranston entered into rest. She had degeneration of the heart and had been quite ill about seven weeks the last three being a struggle that a resolute nature like hers would make, but unavailingly. Sheridan was her birthplace; born July 3rd, 1847 she was the youngest daughter of the late Fernando Haskin and Sarah Keach Haskin. Sixty-seven years are not so very many yet, they go back to the days when, as a little girl she would be on the varanda [sic] of her grandfather's tavern – 'The Haskin Inn' – and see the stage coach arrive with its load of passengers for the 'great west' – the Western Reserve and Michigan. From her father's doorstep she saw a hundred rods away, the first train from New York City on the Erie, going to Dunkirk; having on board men of affairs, in what now seems a far away past, Governor Hunt of New York, President Fillmore and the greatest of all Daniel Webster. A short life links the past and now! December 22, 1870, she married George Cranston of Sheridan. After 25 years of strenuous life on a farm in Sheridan, they moved to Fredonia. She had a sound, permanent

Christian experience in meetings in Sheridan conducted by Rev. Mr. Hurd, and in 1877, joined the Baptist church of which her mother had been a life long member. She also belonged to the Order of the Eastern Star and was a member of Prescott Chapter of the Daughters of the Revolution. Her forebear the 2nd Enoch Haskin lived near Bennington, Vt. He was not in that battle, but later though only 14 years old, he was in Washington's Army at Yorktown and was knocked over by a spent cannon ball. He was thrown into a ditch for burial, but fortunately became conscious in time to escape. Enjoying associations like these, and the care of her household, her last years were spent . . . The funeral was held at 41 Maple avenue, Monday, July 27 . . . Burial in Forest Hill Cemetery. George was also a descendant of a Revolutionary War soldier, Samuel Cranston (1752-1830), from Rhode Island.

After the war George Cranston had a long career with the railroad.
Wayne Ashley

David H. Crosier – Co. A
b. 1842 Sterling, Cayuga, NY
d. *ante* 1870 Sterling, Cayuga, NY
m. ------

NOTE: David, son of James M. (1805-*post* 1870) and Catherine Helmer Rasmussen Crosier (1819-*post* 1880), was a sailor. He saw prior duty in Co. D, 81st Regiment from September 1861-February 17, 1862 when he was discharged for "disability." He re-enlisted on July 11, 1862 but was discharged at Albany, NY on December 8, 1862, again for "disability." He joined the 147th as a substitute for Frank Hooper, Ontario, NY at Auburn, Cayuga, NY on January 24, 1863. At some time he was arrested for desertion and sentenced to forfeit his pay for the two weeks lost and then returned to duty. Although nominally transferred to Co. C, 91st Regiment, he was discharged on June 29, 1865 at Washington, DC as a member of the 147th. He was enumerated on the 1865 New York census with his family but that is the last record for him. He does not appear on the 1870 census. The government contract for his headstone did not provide a DOD but it did reveal that he was buried in Sterling Center Cemetery.

George E. Cummings – Co. B
b. 1826 Clarence, Erie, NY
d. May 28, 1890 Nelson, Kent, MI
m. Rosanna McMullen (September 18, 1830-February 4, 1923) January 17, 1848

NOTE: George, whose surname was variously spelled, was the son of Stephen (1763-1857) and Hannah Porter Cummings (*ca.* 1795-1880). He was a substitute for Alfred Wood, Sardinia, NY, and joined the regiment at Buffalo, on August 13, 1863. He transferred to Co. G, 91st Regiment on June 5, 1865 and mustered out near Washington, DC on July 3rd. He and Rosanna were married in St. John's Catholic Church, Lockport, Niagara, NY and were the parents of nine children. His COD is unknown. He is buried in Elmwood Cemetery, Cedar Springs, Kent, MI. On September 10, 1892 Rosanna married John F. Misner (1848-February 6, 1914) in Fremont, Newaygo, MI as his fourth wife. Misner died in St. Luke's Hospital, Duluth, St. Louis, MN, after an illness of three weeks. His gravesite is unknown. Rosanna reportedly is buried in Greenwood City Cemetery, Clark, WI.

John Ernest Cummings – Co. I
b. September 12, 1844 New York State
d. December 26, 1901 Fredonia, Chautauqua, NY
m. Emeline "Emma" Timperley (1843-December 20, 1892) *ca.* 1869

NOTE: John was the son of Dominic (1813-1880) and Elizabeth "Betsy" Cummings (1820-1880). Although John's POB on his muster roll card was Canada, early census records consistently show he and his siblings were born in New York. He entered the 147th at Dunkirk, Chautauqua, NY on August 17, 1863 as a substitute for Samuel Hall. Cummings was wounded at the battle of the Wilderness on May 5, 1864. He was transferred to Co. I, 91st Regiment on June 5, 1865 and mustered out near Washington, DC on July 3rd. He and Emeline, who was born in England, were the parents of three daughters. They are buried in Forest Hill Cemetery, Fredonia.

Marchant "Martin" Cummings – Co. I

b. 1807 Massachusetts

d. *ca.* 1886 Watertown, Jefferson, NY

m1. Rebecca Robbins (?-*ante* 1850) 1836

m2. Caroline Packard (1830-March 12, 1889) *ca.* 1852

NOTE: Marchant was the son of Alanson (1780-1867) and (probably) Abigail _____ French Cummings (1781-*ante* 1823) who were married in November 1804 in Massachusetts. He was the eldest of five known sons. The others were Nathaniel (1809-1889); Alanson Bonaparte (1812-*ante* 1875); Leonard (1819-1853); and Enoch (1822-1887?). In 1823 the elder Alanson married Mary Clarke (?-*ante* 1850). She was the mother of Sylvester (1830-?). By 1850 Alanson was married to Rebecca Ralph (1784-1854). Marchant and Rebecca were the parents of John (1839-?) and Alanson (1842-?) In 1850 he and the boys were living in Worth, Jefferson, NY with his brother Nathaniel. By 1855 he was living in Pamelia, Jefferson with Caroline and Charlotte, 2, and Benjamin, nine months. He and Caroline were also the parents of Maitland (1857-*post* 1900); Caroline "Carrie" (1859-*post* 1880), Eva (1860-*ante* 1870); Alice (1864-*post* 1880). There may have been others. Marchant claimed to be 42 when he entered the 147th Regiment but the 1850 census shows that he was actually born in 1807. He saw prior service in the 1st NY LA, enlisting on July 21, 1862. He was discharged on September 21, 1862 at New York City for "disability." On September 7, 1863 he enlisted as a substitute for Harrison Smith of Watertown and discharged, again for "disability," on December 8, 1863. It appears that he and Caroline parted company because in 1880 he was enumerated twice, with Caroline and with another son by his first wife, William (1837-?), and his family. I have not located an exact DOD for him but Caroline applied for a pension on September 30, 1886. Census records indicate she took in laundry and it stands to reason she would apply for a pension as soon as possible after her husband's death. She did not obtain a certificate. The reason is unknown. Her obituary appeared in *The Watertown Times* March 15, 1889: "The funeral of the late Mrs. Caroline Cummings occurred from her late residence this morning at 10:30. The officiating clergyman was Rev. Thomas Richey, of this city. Mrs. Cummings has long been a resident of this place. Her husband died some years since. She leaves four daughters and two sons . . . The family wish to extend their heartfelt thanks for the great sympathy extended to them by their many friends . . . The remains will be interred in the Banister burying ground on the family plot." Caroline's parents were Allen (1796-*post* 1855) and Fanny Fuller Packard (1798-*ca.* 1852). Her sister, Sophronia Jane (1827-1896), married Alanson Bonaparte Cummings, Martin's brother.

Patrick Cunningham – Co. B
b. 1839 Ireland
d. ? ?
m. ?

NOTE: Patrick's occupation on his muster roll card was painter and lithographic printer. He enrolled in the 147th as a corporal on August 21, 1863 at Ellicottville, Chautauqua County as a substitute for John O'Dea. He transferred to Co. G, 91st Regiment on June 5, 1865 as a corporal and mustered out near Washington, DC on July 3rd. I have located no other information.

Leonard Dade – Co. I
b. March 7, 1831 Suffolk, England
d. February 26, 1909 Hartford, Van Buren, MI
m. Sarah Warrilow (March 31, 1830-March 31, 1874) February 10, 1852

NOTE: Leonard, son of John (1796-1851) and Mary Anne Davis Dade (1801-1878), was a substitute for Samuel B. Ehelman, Niagara County, enrolling at Lockport, Niagara on July 28, 1863. On January 15, 1864 he was discharged at an unknown location. He and Sarah were married in Toronto, Ontario, Canada. Leonard's death was noticed in a lengthy obituary in *The Watervliet Record* March 5, 1909: "The subject of this sketch, Leonard Dade, was born in Suffolk, England, March 7, 1831, and departed this life February 26, 1909, at the home of his daughter, Mrs. Chas. Kelley, in Hartford township, Michigan at the ripe age of 77 years, 11 months and 21 days. When seventeen years of age Mr. Dade, accompanied by his sister Hannah, came to Canada, where at the age of 18 years he was united in marriage to Sarah Warallow [sic], from whom he was separated by death in the spring of 1874, her age being 44 years. To this union twelve children were born, six sons and six daughters . . . In the spring of 1858 Mr. Dade removed with his family to the State of New York, settling in the vicinity of Niagara Falls. Here in the spring of 1863 he enlisted in the 8th regiment New York infantry, serving one year. On leaving the army he located with his family in the state of Illinois, where he remained two years. He also spent a portion of his days in Indiana, Michigan and Minnesota, the latter state being his place of residence till about eight months ago, when he returned to Michigan, assigning to his children the reason that prompted him in this act was his desire to be buried at the side of his companion whose departure is noted above. In this connection the statement should not be omitted that in the early spring of 1872 Mr. Dade, together with his wife, experienced, at a revival held in the school house in District. No. 7, north of Coloma, a change of purpose, or in other words took upon themselves the work of Christianity – a faith held by them to the last. In this faith Mr. Dade's departure was peaceful and serene as the fading out of stars in the quietude of summer morning." His COD was senility with chronic bronchitis as a contributing factor. He and Sarah are buried in Coloma Cemetery, Berrien, MI.

John Daly – Co. K
b. 1846 Oswego, NY
d. June 19, 1864 4th Division, 3rd Army Corps Hospital, Petersburg, VA
m. ------

NOTE: John was the son of John (1800-1877) and Mary Daly (1824-January 1, 1885) and the brother of Michael (1839-1868), also a member of Co. K, 147th. He enlisted on January 1, 1864 at Oswego. On June 18th he was shot in the abdomen and removed to the hospital where he died the next day. In 1869 his mother applied for and secured a pension, claiming that John had been her family's primary means of support since his father, who suffered from rheumatism, had broken his leg, becoming permanently disabled. John, Jr. was a cooper and his employers testified that he used his wages to pay for the family's food, clothing, and other necessities for several years before joining the army. In her initial petition Mary pointed out that she had lost three sons to the war. While Michael had survived the conflict he died on June 3, 1868 from health problems incurred while in the service. Daniel (1843-1863) was a member of Co. K, 160th Regiment. His COD at a hospital in Brasher City, LA was chronic diarrhea.

John W. Davidson – Co. I
b. 1842 England
d. *post* 1886 ?
m. ?

NOTE: John, whose parents are unidentified, styled himself a laborer on his muster roll card. He enrolled in the 147th at Watertown, Jefferson, NY on September 8, 1863 as a substitute for an unknown draftee. He had auburn hair, blue eyes, florid complexion, and stood 5' 11" tall. He was captured at the battle of the Wilderness on May 5, 1864 and sent to Andersonville. He was paroled, location unknown, on April 26, 1865 and discharged to date that same day. Somehow he was charged with desertion on March 23, 1865 at Hatcher's Run, VA which in itself is extraordinary since that battle had been fought in February. Another oddity is that he was called James in the War Department letter. Nevertheless, on September 10, 1886 the charge was rescinded. There the trail ends.

Joseph Nelson Decker – Co. F

b. December 1838 Owego, Tioga, NY

d. May 22, 1912 Owego, Tioga, NY

m. Sarah Jane Clark (August 1843-March 24, 1913) June 18, 1865

NOTE: Joseph, son of Reuben (1800-1875) and Rebecca Nelson Decker (1799-1875), was drafted, enrolling in the 147th at Owego on July 15, 1863. His muster roll card erroneously states he entered the military at Oswego. He was discharged at Harewood Hospital, Washington, DC on June 3, 1865, two days before he was nominally transferred to Co. A, 91st Regiment. In 1890 he stated that his disability was a "gunshot wound of right knee." He and Sarah were the parents of two. His death was reported in *The Waverly Free Press and Tioga County Record* May 24, 1912, 8: "Joseph H. [*sic*] Decker died Wednesday afternoon at his home at Park Settlement, about five miles north of this village, aged 73 years . . . The funeral will be held Sunday afternoon from Flemingville church, Rev. Mr. Carey officiating . . . He was a veteran of the civil war, having served in the 147th Regt., N. Y. V., and was prominent in Grand Army circles. He had resided in the vicinity of his home about 35 years, and was highly respected in the community." Sarah died less than a year later at the home of her son, Lewis. She and Joseph are buried in Flemingville Cemetery.

Levi Decker – Co. I

b. 1830 Chenango County, NY

d. November 24, 1863 Armory Square General Hospital, Washington, DC

m. Emeline Sparks (1844-*post* 1880) January 1, 1862

NOTE: Levi was the son of Isaac (1804-?) and Clarissa Decker (1804-?). He was drafted, enrolling in the 147th on July 21, 1863 at Irving, Chautauqua, NY. His COD was chronic diarrhea and hemorrhage of the bowels. He is buried in the Soldiers' and Airmen's National Home Cemetery, Washington, DC. Levi and Emeline were married in Big Flats, Chemung, NY. They had no children. Emeline's application for a pension on January 19, 1864 was successful. In 1866 she moved into William Greaves' (1828-1906) home and they began "living and co-habiting as man and wife." Emeline gave birth to Roseltha "Rosey" (1867-*post* 1880); Samuel (1869-*post* 1880); Franklin (1871-*ante* 1880); and Emma (1876-*post* 1880). In 1873 an anonymous source alerted the Pension Bureau that Emeline was "married" to Greaves and still collecting her widow's pension. Special agent John Parker was sent to investigate. Emeline told him that her relationship with Greaves was "just as pure as the intercourse between husband & wife married by a minister." She did not consider her children illegitimate nor did she consider what she had done immoral or illegal. For his part, Greaves, who appeared to be intoxicated when interviewed, said: "No marriage ceremony was never performed between us, but we have lived together just as we would if married. I never did go back on her & shall not. The fact of our living & cohabiting together is notorious, we never had to conceal it." Parker's conclusion was that, according to the laws of New York State, the couple had to be considered married and he recommended that the pension be stopped. The family last appears on the 1880 census but something must have happened that year to disrupt domestic unity because on May 25th, Emeline, asserting she was still Levi's widow, applied to have her pension restored under the provisions of the Act of March 9, 1878. Unfortunately for her, that law only applied to widows of veterans of the Revolutionary War and the War of 1812. What happened to her and her surviving children is a mystery but it appears that she and Greaves parted company, perhaps because of his drinking problem. Greaves had been born in Tompkins County and may have served in the 15th NY Cavalry. Someone named William Greaves was admitted to the Erie County Poorhouse on September 27, 1887. He claimed to be 59, single, and born in Ithaca, Tompkins Co. His "dependence" was "sickness, abscess, and diet" but the prospect for recovery was "favorable." In 1889 William Greaves, veteran of the 15th NY Cavalry, applied for and obtained a pension in New York State. No widow was named. In 1890 he was living in Ithaca and claimed chronic kidney disease as his disability. By 1900 he was an inmate in the Bath National Soldiers' Home and that is where he died on July 14, 1906. He is buried in the Bath National Cemetery. Whether or not this is Emeline's William is conjectural, but a more important question is, what happened to her and to her children? I have attempted to trace her family. John (1806-1879) and Sybil Calkins Sparks (1810-*post* 1880) were the parents of at least 10 children. In 1865 Emeline Decker was living with them in Corning. Her father died in July 1879 of "paralysis." Her mother last appears on the 1880 census with two sons, Joseph (1853-*post* 1915) and John (1860-?).

Dennis Degan – Co. K

b. May 2, 1844 Oswego, NY
d. August 31, 1927 Davenport, Scott, IA
m. Ella May Seaver (December 1861-July 2, 1932) September 5, 1883

NOTE: Dennis Degan was an alias for Edward "Ned" D. Lee. To date his parents have not been identified. A sailor, he enlisted in Co. G, 1st Regiment NY Marine Artillery in Chicago, IL in May 1862 and was discharged at Newberne, NC on January 25, 1863. He apparently enlisted in the 147th at Oswego City on March 29, 1864. Captured at the battle of the Wilderness on May 5, 1864, he was sent to Andersonville. He was paroled on April 28, 1865. Although nominally transferred to Co. K, 91st Regiment he never served in that outfit. He was discharged on July 22, 1865 at New York City, his discharge to be dated May 12th. He also served in the US Revenue Cutter Service.

In 1890, living in Oswego City, he said his disability was "poor health from confinement in Andersonville." The balance of his life is best described in a lengthy obituary published in The [Davenport, IA] Quad-City Times September 1, 1927, 1 which is excerpted here: "Ned Lee, the friend of the poor and the children, is dead. The genial old settlement worker, who for 33 years worked among the needy and unfortunate of Davenport, and who had a distinguished Civil war record with the northern armies, passed away at his home 515 Kirkwood Boulevard at 2:57 p. m. Wednesday. He was 83 years old. Ned Lee was widely known as the 'ain't gonna rain no mo' man, -- the weather prophet who always picked a day on which it wouldn't rain for his annual children's picnic . . . There was mourning in thousands of Davenport homes today for the kindly, picturesque old gentleman who made friends of all with whom he came in contact. Ned Lee and his broad rimmed hat, and his cane and watch-chain and his big smile were a part of the city. Not only to those whom he had befriended, but to Civil and Spanish War veterans, to members of the Elks' lodge, with which he always worked in close cooperation, and of the T. P. A., of which he was state chaplain, mourned his passing. Before coming to Davenport Mr. Lee was engaged in settlement work in Oswego, N.Y., the city of his birth, and also in the Bowery district of New York City . . . On picnic day, at New Year's and on other occasions Mr. Lee had the assistance of the local Elks. Their lodge hall was always the headquarters for his tag day drive and he aided them in the work of distributing shoes to the poor. Mr. Lee has been in ill health for some time, and it was while on a recent vacation trip to Lake Delevan, Wis., that he suffered the first of a series of heart attacks that were to prove fatal. He was brought home from Lake Delevan, but his strength was waning and for the last few days his condition was regarded as very critical. He maintained his courage to the last. Mr. Lee once expressed in a poem his philosophy of life: 'Think gently of the erring,/O, do not thou forget./However deeply stained by sin,/He is thy brother yet./Heir of the self-same heritage,/Child of the self-same God.' The sentiment, he often quoted, explained why he chose to spend his life working in the 'outer fringe' of society. Edward D. Lee was born in Oswego, N.Y., May 2, 1844, and was related to the southern family of Lees of which Robert E. Lee was a member. He was reared in Chicago, served in the Civil war, became a missionary and worked for many years in New York state. He was married to Ella M. Seaber [sic] at Wolcott, N.Y. on Sept. 5, 1883. He moved to Davenport 33 years ago. Mr. Lee was a member of Davenport Lodge No. 298, B. P. O. E., a member and past commander of the August Wentz Post No. 1 G. A. R. and of Post D. of the Travelers Protective Association of which organization he was the state chaplain . . . The career of Ned Lee was varied and interesting as is always the life of the man who works for the good of others . . . he enlisted for naval service at the outbreak of the Civil war and saw action on the gunboat Pioneer in its adventurous attempt to cut the blockade chains off Cape Hatteras. After his term of enlistment in the navy expired he entered the army and served in most of the important battle of the Potomac campaigns. He was with 'Little Mac,' Burnside, Hooker and the other Union generals in many sanguine struggles. On that sultry May afternoon of May 4 [sic], 1864, when Grant first came to grips with Lee in the Wilderness, Ned Lee was captured by a troop of Confederate cavalry and went to the Andersonville prison. The torture of that infamous military prison was too much, and finally on Sept. 12, after three unsuccessful attempts, he escaped. Early of an evening he slipped thru the stockade and made for the river banks under fire from the guns of the Confederate guards. Then he swam out into the river and clung to the rudder of a small boat, hiding in the water until darkness. He escaped thru the woods, sleeping by day and making his way by night thru the Carolinas and Virginia to the Union army. After the war he acted as assistant to a temperance lecturer, and later he became a minister. He worked in various cities of New York state, and finally established a mission in Oswego. Later he moved to New York City where he did valiant work for years in the Bowery district . . . Finally Mr. Lee's health gave way under the strain of year after year of his unselfish work, and physicians told him that he must leave New York City. He had offers from Washington, D. C., and Denver, and also a letter from a clergyman in Davenport, Iowa, requesting him to turn his attention to the middle western city. Mr. Lee decided to go to Denver, but agreed to stop off at Davenport for a conference on the way. He stopped off at Davenport and spent the rest of his life working for the community . . . But Ned Lee was not one of your 'hell and brimstone' reformers. His method was to make friends with the unfortunate and wayward, -- to lead them back to the path of righteousness rather than to drive them back. His mission became the gathering place of the poor and needy . . . Ned Lee is dead, but his work lives on." The esteem with which Lee was held in the community is demonstrated in an editorial found on page 6 of the same edition: "'What doth the Lord require of thee, but to do justly, and to love mercy, and to walk humbly with thy God?' Theodore Roosevelt was wont to quote these words from the prophet Micah as embodying his conception of the basic requirement of

Edward "Ned" Lee interrupted his missionary work to serve in the Union Army.
The Quad-City Times

true religion. They come to mind now as one looks back across the years that Ned Lee carried on his mission of practical and applied Christianity here in Davenport. Full of years – he was 83 – and with a third of a century back of him here in our midst, Ned Lee passed on to his reward Wednesday afternoon. He will be remembered as a kindly and helpful influence in the days when Davenport needed a man of his type to take the part of the children and the unfortunate, to help the former to a better start in life and the latter to a better chance. For years he was a liaison officer between the large proportion of our population which was glad to share its better fortune with the underprivileged and the thousands of his wards who could accept from him the help that was extended without condescension, and that raised the standards of living of many during the years when Ned was our city missioner. His record as a soldier, as a worker in the vineyard of the Lord, and as a private citizen, is told elsewhere in this issue. There is no call to enlarge on it, but the passing of Ned Lee recalls to our older residents a city quite different from that of today, in which Ned filled a place of conspicuous helpfulness. He will be missed by many." After his death, Ella continued the ministry. Both are buried in Oakdale Memorial Gardens, Davenport.

Charles Deiott – Co. C
b. 1810 France
d. December 19, 1896 Eaton, Madison, NY
m. Caroline _____ Bennett (August 1832-September 28, 1901) *ca.* 1862

NOTE: Charles' surname was variously spelled. I use that on family gravestones. Charles alleged he was born in 1816 but 1810 is found on his gravestone. He initially was recruited for the 86th Regiment at Eaton, but apparently was sent to the 147th into which he was mustered on September 6, 1864 as a substitute for Myron De Groodt. He was captured and paroled at unknown dates but was able to muster out on June 7, 1865 near Washington, DC. Caroline was previously married to _____ Bennett, by whom she had a son, Charles B. (1855-*post* 1920). Charles and Caroline are buried in Pratt's Hollow Cemetery, Madison, NY. Her DOB and DOD are not inscribed on the stone.

George W. M. Delph – Co. H
b. August 1824 Kentucky
d. July 11, 1903 National Soldiers' Home, Milwaukee, Milwaukee, WI
m. ------

NOTE: George was the son of Colonel Jeremiah (1801-1858) and Sarah H. Campbell Delph (?-?) who were married May 21, 1823. He was a member of Co. K, 1st KY Cavalry during the Mexican War in 1846. He was a merchant when he enrolled in the 147th at Buffalo, NY on August 11, 1863 as a substitute for Samuel E. Britton, Boston,

Erie, NY. Delph was discharged for "disability" at Culpeper, VA on March 21, 1864. He was living in Kansas City, MO in 1880 and entered the National Soldiers' Home from there on August 30, 1885. He apparently never left. In 1890 he claimed diarrhea, rheumatism, and hemorrhoids contracted "during service [in] 1863." His COD was senility and arteriosclerosis. An interesting mystery surrounds his pension. The application date was May 9, 1885 with a notation that he used an alias, George W. Williams, although I have discovered nothing to corroborate the note. The pension card shows that no certificate was issued but in 1903 when George died his account at the National Home contained $36.00 in pension money. Furthermore, his certificate number was given on the record. Perhaps he obtained a pension from his service in the Mexican War although I have located no record to that effect. George's body was sent home to Lexington at the request of his brother Jeremiah "Jerry" Delph (1835-1918) and was buried in Lexington Cemetery.

Edward Alexander Denison – Co. G

b. May 2, 1841 Havana, Schuyler, NY
d. February 10, 1921 Geneva, Ontario, NY
m1. Caroline Augusta Prosser (1832-November 11, 1878) November 10, 1859
m2. Areana "Anna" "Ara" Woodyard (February 1862-December 21, 1918) December 13, 1879

NOTE: The son of Oliver (1807-1888) and Laura Boothe Denison (1814-1888), Edward saw three months' service in Co. F, 2nd Michigan Regiment. He next joined Co. I, 103rd Regiment NYSV, serving from March-December 1862 when he was discharged at Washington, DC for "disability." He saw action at New Berne, NC and Antietam, MD while a member of this regiment. On September 22, 1863 he enrolled in the 147th at Canandaigua, Ontario, NY as a substitute for Edward R. Randall, Milo, Yates County. He was wounded in the right hand, left leg, right shoulder, and left hand at the battle of the Wilderness on May 5, 1864 and discharged on September 14, 1864 as "unfit for duty." He and Caroline, who died in Barrington, Yates County, were the parents of five children. Her grave has not been located. Areana's parents were Abraham (?-?) and Mary Ferguson Woodyard (1845-?). Her maiden name was variously spelled. She and Edward were married in Cabell Township, WV, where she had been born. In 1900 Areana claimed that she was the mother of four, two of whom survived. Edward and Areana are buried in Glenwood Cemetery, Geneva. Two brothers served the Union cause. Charles E. (1835-May 24, 1864) was a member of Co. B, 141st Regiment. He was KIA at Dallas, GA and "buried on the field." Benjamin Adam (1843-December 15, 1919) served in Co. I, 103rd Regiment.

DeWitt Clinton Dickinson – Co. C

b. 1833 Chautauqua County, NY

d. February 8, 1900 State Soldiers' Home, Hot Springs, Fall River, SD

m1. Elizabeth Elestine Muckler (1841-September 15, 1868) February 16, 1858

m2. Sarah Elizabeth Mann (1849-*post* 1905) January 5, 1869

NOTE: DeWitt was the son of Hiram (1799-1848) and Sally Pierce Dickinson (1801-1891). A draftee, he enrolled in the 147th at Carroll, Chautauqua, NY on August 20, 1863. Although nominally transferred to Co. H, 91st Regiment on June 5, 1865, he had already been discharged on May 29th at Davenport, Scott, IA. DeWitt had several occupations. In 1860 he was a boot and shoe manufacturer. In 1880 he was a traveling agent for furniture. By 1885 he was running a hotel in Nemaha, NE. DeWitt succumbed to carcinoma on chin and face and was buried in the State Soldiers' Home Cemetery. He and Elizabeth were the parents of several children. She died in Manchester, Delaware, IA but her grave has not been located. Sarah and DeWitt were also married in Manchester and became the parents of Harry James Dickinson (1887-1969). Reportedly DeWitt and Sarah were divorced in Auburn, Nemaha, NE on September 4, 1896. In 1905 Sarah attempted to claim a widow's pension from Wisconsin but was unsuccessful. Beyond that date I have located no information. She may have remarried.

William Dickinson – Co. F

b. 1832 Connecticut

d. July 11, 1921 Hannibal Center, NY

m. Mary A. Gardenier (January 1841-February 19, 1923) 1867

NOTE: William was the son of Samuel (1794-1850) and Elizabeth Dickinson (1807-1887). Although his muster roll card indicated that he had been born in Canada, census records prove he and all the members of his family came from Connecticut. In 1855 he, his widowed mother, a brother, and a sister had lived in Hannibal for 11 years. He was drafted, enrolling in the 147th on August 30, 1863 at Oswego City. He transferred to Co. A, 91st Regiment on June 5, 1865 and mustered out at Washington, DC on June 16th. I have found no obituary for him but when Mary died *The Fulton Patriot* February 28, 1923, 2 noted her passing: "On Monday, Feb. 19th, occurred the death of Mrs. Mary Dickinson, widow of the late William Dickinson, at her home in Hannibal Center. Mrs. Dickinson was one of the oldest residents of Hannibal, being 82 years of age. She was born near Hannibal Center and lived most of her life in that village. She was interested in all things that tended to raise the morals of the community. For many years she was a member of the M. E. church and for a long time was the treasurer of the Ladies' aid society. In this capacity she endeared herself to all its members and will be sadly missed. Mrs. Dickinson was a regular attendant at the church services and a regular visitor at the homes of the sick. While doing that work she received a fall, breaking her hip, which was the cause of her death. She was the daughter of Henry and Emeline Gardenier who lived many years near Hannibal Center and is survived by one sister, Mrs. Harvey Perkins of Hannibal, and two brothers, Leslie Gardenier of Fulton, and Berlin Gardenier of Hannibal." William and Mary are buried in Hannibal Center Cemetery.

Leger Diss, Jr. – Co. C
b. April 21, 1839 France
d. May 14, 1878 Oswego City, NY
m. Catherine "Kate" _____ (1839-*post* 1905) *ca.* 1865

NOTE: Leger, a gunsmith, was the son of Leger (1803-*post* 1860) and Ann Mary Diss (1807-*post* 1860). He and his family came to the United States aboard the Zurich in 1849. He saw prior service in Co. I, 81st Regiment from February-April 1862 when he was discharged for "disability." He was drafted, enrolling in the 147th at Watertown, Jefferson, NY on August 26, 1863. He transferred to Co. H, 91st Regiment on June 5, 1865 and mustered out near Washington, DC on July 3rd. He is buried in St. Peter's Cemetery, Oswego City. In 1892 Catherine and several of the children were living in Oswego but soon thereafter they migrated to New York City. She was last enumerated on the 1905 New York census. A stone marked "Mother" is found in St. Peter's but it is unknown whether or not she is actually buried there. No dates are available.

Frederick "Fred" S. Doane – Co. K
b. March 12, 1844 Richland, NY
d. January 16, 1897 Brooklyn, Kings, NY
m. Mary Elizabeth Mills (1850-*post* 1880) May 1, 1867

NOTE: Frederick's parents were Bernice Levi (1819-1871) and Irene Lyman Doane (1819-1886). Bernice was Oswego county clerk for several years. Irene was a sister of H. H. Lyman. Frederick served as a musician in Co. B, 32nd Regiment from 1861-June 9, 1863, mustering out in New York City. He joined the 147th on March 12, 1864 at Richland, NY, apparently enlisting. At some point he transferred to the 3rd Brigade Band from which he was discharged at Albany, NY in July 1865. He and Mary were the parents of one child, Alice (1868-*post* 1870). In 1875 he entered the National Home in Milwaukee, WI, claiming chronic diarrhea as his disability. He left the home on August 31, 1877 because of "desertion from furlough." In 1880 he and Mary were living in Waukesha, Waukesha, WI. In 1890 Fred resided in Minneapolis, Hennepin, MN but whether or not Mary was still living is unknown. In 1897 he lived in Brooklyn. *The Pulaski Democrat* January 20, 1897 announced his death: ". . . On Sunday Mr. Sidney Doane received a telegram from Brooklyn announcing the death of his only brother, Frederick Doane. The news of his illness was received the day Mr. Lyman Doane died, so the grief-stricken father could not go to the city, and as the information was of such a character that sudden death seemed improbable, he had not gone. He left Monday morning and returned with the remains this morning. The funeral will be held this afternoon at the home of Mr. W. H. Austin . . . Mr. Doane has been in the west for some time past, but will be remembered by a good many here, as he formerly lived in this place . . . He was about fifty years of age and leaves no family." Frederick is buried in Pulaski Village Cemetery. Lyman Doane was his nephew. He had died on January 9th.

Charles Henry Dolan – Co. C
b. November 28, 1838 Boston, Suffolk, MA
d. ? ?
m. Margaret L. Duffy (1843-March 2, 1868) *ca.* 1861

NOTE: Charles was the son of Charles (1798-June 8, 1870) and Ann Dolan (1810-?). In 1855 the family had lived in Ellicottville for six years. Charles H., a draftee, enrolled in the 147th at Allegany, Cattaraugus County on August 22, 1863 as a sergeant. Although nominally transferred to Co. E, 91st Regiment on June 5, 1865 he was discharged at Buffalo, Erie, NY on June 19th as a member of the 147th. He and Margaret were the parents of four children. In 1870 they were living with their grandfather and aunt/step-grandmother, Catherine Duffy Dolan (1835-1911), their mother's sister. Margaret is buried in Saint Bonaventure Cemetery, Allegany, as are Charles and Catherine. What happened to Charles Henry is unknown. Catherine Duffy Dolan brought up the children. I have uncovered no evidence that she attempted to obtain pensions for them, leading me to conclude their father abandoned the family.

Robert Donaldson – Co. K
b. 1823 Maryland
d. August 28, 1896 Baltimore, Baltimore, MD
m. Mary Ann Elizabeth Jeffries Buckley (January 1826-*post* 1910) October 20, 1850

NOTE: Robert was the son of Robert (1780-1844) and Orpah Logan Saga Donaldson (?-?) who were married May 22, 1805. A sailor, he enlisted in the 147th on August 7, 1864 at Oswego City, NY. He transferred to Co. K, 91st Regiment on June 5, 1865 and mustered out near Washington, DC on July 3rd. Most of his life was spent in Maryland. In 1890 he claimed no disability but a notation stated he had re-enlisted in the heavy artillery. No corroboration for that is found on his pension card. He is buried in Cedar Hill Cemetery, Brooklyn Park, Anne Arundel, MD. Mary Elizabeth was formerly married to Thomas Buckley (1814-April 11, 1850) and had two children by him, Mary (1846-?) and

David (1850-?). In 1900 she claimed to be the mother of 10, of whom three survived. By 1910 she had revised those figures to 12 and one. She disappears after the 1910 census.

Peter Douglass – Co. C
b. 1833 Ireland
d. October 5, 1864 Andersonville, Sumter, GA
m. Ann Wheeler (May 2, 1829-March 27, 1911) June 11, 1851

NOTE: Peter Douglass was an alias for Peter Francis Donnelly. Although he lived in Brooklyn he joined the 147th at Canandaigua, Ontario, NY on August 23, 1863 as a substitute for Abel Armstrong from Geneseo, Livingston, NY. The exact date of his capture is unknown. There is some dispute over his actual DOD. His entry in *Deaths of Volunteers* places it on October 5th, but the Andersonville National Cemetery records say he died on October 4th. He and Ann had one surviving child, Sarah (1852-1918). In 1871 Ann applied for and obtained a pension. At one point she was a postmistress but generally she listed milliner as her occupation. She is buried in St. Peter's Cemetery, Staten Island, Richmond, NY.

Duncan Dow – Co. E
b. 1835 Scotland
d. ? ?
m. ?

NOTE: This man's life prior to his military career is unknown. He enrolled in the 147th at Oswego on August 12, 1863 as a substitute for Lester Haskins. He has two entries in *The Town Clerks' Registers*. According to one, he enrolled in the 16th US Infantry. The other states he enrolled in an unnamed organization on August 8, 1863. Both confirm he was paid a bounty of $300. It may well be that he was brought to Oswego by a bounty agent for the purpose of offering himself as a substitute. He transferred to the US Navy on April 22, 1864. Nothing is available after that date.

Neil Dunbar – Co. C
b. 1820 Scotland
d. ? ?
m. ?

NOTE: Very little has been learned about this soldier, a teacher in civilian life. He was a substitute for Allen Bates and enrolled at Otto, Cattaraugus, NY on August 20, 1863. His stint in the army was short-lived since he was discharged for "disability" on December 29, 1863. He applied for a pension on March 14, 1864 but did not obtain a certificate. It is possible he died before the process could be completed.

Henry Dunn – Co. B
b. 1832 Canada
d. 1864 Fort Lawton, Millen, Jenkins, GA
m. ?

NOTE: Little is known about Henry's life prior to his military service. He was a substitute for Daniel Deming, Rochester, Monroe, NY and entered the 147th on August 5, 1863 in that city. His muster roll card initially listed him a deserter on both May 23 and May 28, 1864 at North Anna River but he was actually captured in Caroline County, VA on May 26th and sent to Richmond before being transported to Andersonville. The terrible overcrowding at that place persuaded General John H. Winder, superintendent of Confederate prisons, to build a new stockade at Millen's Junction. The site was favorable because of a good water supply and nearby rail service. The camp encompassed 42 acres and was touted as the largest in the world. Although it was only in operation for three months, it housed more than 10,000 soldiers, of whom 725, including Henry Dunn, died and were buried in nearby cemeteries. Henry's exact DOD, however, is unknown. After the war, the bodies were disinterred and reburied in Beaufort National Cemetery, VA. The fort was evacuated on November 22, 1864 because the Confederates knew that Sherman was coming. When he arrived, he burned the empty fort together with the entire community of Millens Junction.

Fort Lawton was estimated to be the largest POW camp in existence. After its evacuation Sherman's soldiers burned it to the ground.
Library of Congress

Milton C. Dunten – Co. A

b. 1836 Oxbow, Jefferson County, NY
d. April 16, 1913 Watertown, Jefferson, NY
m. Anna E. Brown (1860-April 17, 1913) 1883

NOTE: The son of Thomas (1811-December 2, 1903) and Sally Kingsbury Dunten (1811-1882), Milton enrolled at Watertown on September 19, 1863 as a substitute for an unknown draftee. He was discharged for "disability" on May 27, 1865. He and Anna were the parents of three children. Their tragic deaths were reported in several news articles. That published in *The Syracuse Herald* April 18, 1913, 6 is perhaps the most inclusive: "Less than twenty-four hours after the death of her husband, of whose passing away she had not been informed, Mrs. Anna C. Dunton [*sic*], widow of Milton C. Dunton, died yesterday morning at their home near Sanford's Corners, about six miles north of this city, after a short illness. Mr. Dunton, who was 76 years of age and who was born at Oxbow, Jefferson county, but who had spent most of his life on a truck farm at Sanford's Corners, was taken ill about six weeks ago while on a visit to his son, Roscoe Dunton in Florida. The son brought him home and remained with him until about two weeks ago. A few days ago the sick man was brought to the City hospital [in Watertown], where he died early Wednesday morning. The remains were taken to the home at Sanford but Mrs. Dunton, who was a native of Fulton county and was 54 years of age, had meanwhile been taken ill with symptoms similar to those of the husband and was delirious, so all knowledge of her husband's death was kept from her until the end. While the exact nature of the disease from which the couple suffered has not been given out, it is stated that both died from natural causes. Mr. Dunton was a veteran of the civil war, serving with Company A, 147th New York volunteers, and fought under Grant at the battle of the Wilderness. Mrs. Dunton was an active member of the Union church at Sanford's corners . . . A double funeral will be held at the family home at Sanford's Corners at 5 o'clock tomorrow afternoon, the Rev. J. C. Barber of Black River officiating. The burial will be made at the Sanford's corners cemetery." An earlier article published in *The Watertown Daily Times* April 16, 1913 claimed their deaths were caused by eating poisoned strawberries while in Florida.

Charles Andrew Durkee – Co. I

b. September 14, 1842 Barton, Tioga, NY
d. January 16, 1926 Columbia, Fluvanna, VA
m. Katherine "Kate" Louise McKinney (December 20, 1854-June 24, 1909) 1876

NOTE: Charles was the son of George Walcott (1806-1852) and Malinda Swartwood Durkee (1810-1881). He entered the 147th as a draftee on July 14, 1863 at Barton. He transferred to Co. I, 91st Regiment on June 5, 1865 and mustered out near Washington,

DC on July 3rd. He and Kate were the parents of five, all of whom survived to adulthood. One son, Charles C. (1877-1967), became an Episcopal priest. Charles and Kate are buried in Fork of Willis Baptist Church Cemetery, Columbia.

Virgil Young Duryea – Co. A

b. September 20, 1838 Ulysses, Tompkins County, NY

d. February 18, 1890 Elmira, Chemung, NY

m. Emeline Sarah B. _____ (1840-July 17, 1913) *ca.* 1862

NOTE: Virgil, son of Walter (1812-1892) and Jane Creque Duryea (1809-1882), was drafted, enrolling in the 147th on July 20, 1863 at Southport, Chemung. He was transferred to the VRC on February 27, 1865 and discharged at Washington, DC on July 31st. He was a sadler by occupation. He and Emeline, the parents of two children, are buried in Woodlawn Cemetery, Elmira.

Albert Eastman – Co. C

b. 1830 Cattaraugus County, NY

d. March 3, 1913 Flat Creek, Franklin, KY

m. Mary Jane Beverley (1840-*ante* 1880) *ca.* 1861

NOTE: Albert was the son of Bartlett (1800-*ante* 1880) and Lucy Grover Eastman (1803-*ca.* 1880) who were married in Pompey, Onondaga, NY on August 13, 1823. A draftee, he joined the 147th at Buffalo on August 12, 1863. On an unknown date while on picket duty near Culpeper, VA he was shot in the right hand and lost two fingers. His muster roll card shows he was in Carver Hospital, Washington, DC on September 26, 1864. He was nominally transferred to Co. C, 91st Regiment on June 5, 1865 but did not serve in that unit. I have located no pension card for him and it is possible he simply walked away. He and Mary had one child, William A. (1863-1943). In 1870 Albert, Mary, and William were living in Boulder, Linn, IA. On one side of them were his mother and father, plus a brother, Vesper. On the other side were a sister, Alzina, her husband Lindsey, and their children. By 1880 Albert, a widower, and William were living in Orchard, Mitchell, IA. When the 1910 census was taken, William, wife Nancy (1869-1939), Albert, and 11 children resided in Crutchers Schoolhouse, Franklin, KY. Albert's COD was acute indigestion. He is buried in Bethel Baptist Church Cemetery, Frankfort, Franklin, KY. Mary Jane's grave has not been located. Albert's brother, Byron H. (1839-1862), was a member of Co. G, 59th NYSV. He died at Antietam, MD on February 17, 1862 of *vulnus sclopeticum* (gunshot wound).

Isaac W. Easton – Co. F

b. February 3, 1834 Angelica, Allegany, NY

d. May 30, 1902 Petrolia, Allegany, NY

m. Lavancha Van Husen (May 1835-April 10, 1905) 1866

NOTE: Isaac, son of Stephen (1794-1885) and Lavilla Content Austin Easton (1801-1873), was drafted, enrolling in the regiment on July 13, 1863 at Ward, Allegany County. He was discharged for "disability" at Washington, DC on May 13, 1865. His muster roll card identified the disability as "insanity." He applied for and obtained a pension in 1873 but in 1890 claimed no disability. He and Lavancha were the parents of five children. One of them, John (1868-1931), was a Methodist minister who died of a skull fracture after being struck by a car. According to a death notice in *The Butler Citizen* April 13, 1905, 2, Lavancha died in Butler County, PA of pneumonia. She and Isaac are buried in Bellamy Cemetery, Alma, Allegany, NY.

Thomas Paul Edwards – Co. D

b. December 1834 New York City, NY

d. July 20, 1901 Elmira, Chemung, NY

m. Mary C. _____ (September 1833-April 8, 1908) 1859

NOTE: Thomas, son of Thomas (1803-?) and Mary J. Edwards (1810-?), was drafted, enrolling in the 147th Regiment on July 20, 1863 at Southport, Chemung. He had previously served in Co. I, 11th NYSV from May 1861-June 1862. He was transferred to Co. D, 95th Regiment on January 10, 1864 and was mustered out "at camp in the field, Virginia" on July 16, 1865. In 1890 he claimed "rupture" as a disability. His attitude towards being drafted in 1863 is demonstrated by his remark: "Discharged and drafted 21 July '63." His gravestone commemorates his service in the 11th and the 95th Regiments but makes no reference to his time in the 147th. His obituary was published in *The Elmira Daily Gazette and Free Press* July 22, 1901: "The death occurred Saturday of Thomas P. Edwards of No. 412 West Fourth street. The deceased was sixty-six years of age and was a veteran of the civil war, in which he served with faithfulness and bravery. He is survived by a widow and two sons – Thomas K. Edwards and Ernest C. Edwards, both of this city. Mr. Edwards was a member of the 147th Regiment, New York Volunteers, served three years and received his honorable discharge. He was also a member of Newtown lodge No. 89, I.O.O.F. For nearly ten years he had suffered from ill health and death came as a happy release from long suffering. His business was that of a carpenter. The funeral services will be held this Monday afternoon at 5 o'clock and will be attended by his fellow veterans and fraternity brethren . . . ." Mary was a member of Class No. 24 Sunday School, Methodist Church, Elmira. When she died, the class attended her funeral in a body. She and Thomas are buried in Woodlawn Cemetery, Elmira.

Nathaniel Ellison – Co. E

b. September 5, 1829 New York City, NY
d. May 11, 1909 Wells, Bradford, PA
m. Angeline S. Wing (December 26, 1833-December 22, 1890) *ca.* 1852

NOTE: Nathaniel was the son of Ira (1800-1875) and Sarah "Sally" Ayres Ellison (1805-?). A draftee, he enrolled in the 147th at Amity, Allegany, NY on July 10, 1863. The surname on his muster roll card is Allison. Although nominally transferred to Co. D, 91st Regiment on June 5, 1865 under the name of Nathan Ellison, he was "absent, sick." He is not in *The Adjutant-General's Report* for that regiment. I have located no pension record for him or an entry in the 1890 Veterans' Schedules. Nathaniel and Angeline lived most of their lives in Wells. His COD was pneumonia. They are buried in Pine City Cemetery, Chemung County, NY. Their gravestone does not show his DOD.

Dietrich August Benjamin Erdmann – Co. A

b. 1826 Germany
d. March 21, 1907 Riverside Accident Hospital, Buffalo, Erie, NY
m. Sophie Frederike Henriette Kniephoff (August 1822-May 28, 1902) 1850

NOTE: Dietrich was the son of Friedrich Wilhelm (1798-1839) and Caroline Wilhelmine Eckelt Erdmann (1787-1851). The family name was also spelled Erdman. He and Sophie were married in Germany and immigrated to the United States the same year. They were the parents of numerous children although in 1900 Sophie alleged she was the mother of four, three of whom were living. Dietrich was a blacksmith. On August 8, 1861 he enlisted in Co. I, 1st NY ART at Buffalo with the rank of second lieutenant. He resigned his commission on September 1, 1862. On August 14, 1863 he enlisted as a substitute for John Heil, Hamburg, Erie, NY, serving until January 27, 1864 when he was discharged for "disability." His tragic end was reported in *The Buffalo Courier* March 22, 1907, 8: "The peculiar accident which happened to Diedrich Erdman, the old man who was injured at Clinton and Ellicott streets, on March 11th, when he slipped on a banana peel and fell to the sidewalk, resulted fatally yesterday morning when the old man died in Riverside Hospital, where he was taken after his injury. Erdman, who was 85 years old, sustained a fractured leg and numerous lacerations of the scalp . . . ." Another article noted that the sidewalk was very slippery. The old man broke his hip when he fell. A death notice published in *The Buffalo Evening News* March 23, 1907, 1 revealed he had been a member of Chapin Post No. 2, GAR and the members attended the funeral in a body. Dietrich is buried in Pine Hill Cemetery (United French and German Cemetery), Cheektowaga, Erie. It is probable that Sophie is also there.

Josiah Farrington – Co. F

b. August 23, 1841 Clarksville, Allegany, NY

d. November 12, 1863 Rappanannock Station, VA

m. ------

NOTE: Josiah, son of Jabez, Jr. (1814-1874) and Amanda Melvina Hill Farrington (1821-1890), was drafted, enrolling in the army on July 10, 1863 at Clarksville. His DOD is much disputed. I use that provided in *Death of Volunteers*. COD was typho-malarial fever. He was originally buried at Rappahannock Station but today rests in Arlington National Cemetery. In 1887 his mother successfully applied for a pension.

Christian Feil – Co. B

b. 1842 Germany

d. May 25, 1864 North Anna River, VA

m. ------

NOTE: Christian, son of Charles (?-ca. 1853) and Elizabeth Feil (1811-1878), was a substitute for Jacob Lepp, Eden, Erie, NY, enrolling on August 13, 1863 at Buffalo, NY. He was KIA. A gravestone may be seen in Allegany Cemetery, Allegany, Cattaraugus, but it is probably a cenotaph. His mother successfully applied for a pension in 1872.

Charles Henry Ferris – Co. H

b. April 15, 1846 Spencer, Tioga, NY

d. May 24, 1870 Spencer, Tioga, NY

m. ------

NOTE: The son of Chauncey Marshall (1808-1858) and Nancy Elizabeth Newton Ferris (1820-1868), Charles was a substitute for Frederick S. Barrows, Catharine, Schuyler County, enrolling on July 27, 1863 at Montour, Schuyler County. On June 27, 1864 he suffered a broken arm in a skirmish at Petersburg, VA. He was discharged from the service on June 5, 1865 at Washington, DC, the same day he transferred to Co. A, 91st Regiment. To date his COD and grave have not been found.

Samuel R. Fessenden – Co. D

b. 1830 Pennsylvania

d. April 10, 1865 Campbell Hospital, Washington, DC

m. Sarah C. West (1834-August 10, 1914) *ca.* 1856

NOTE: Samuel, a draftee, was the son of Joel Crosby (1807-1891) and Matilda Judd Fessenden (1813-1902). He joined the regiment on August 21, 1863 at Humphrey, Cattaraugus. He was wounded at Five Forks, VA on April 1, 1865 and died of his wounds. His entry in *Deaths of Volunteers* says he fractured his clavicle. He is buried in Arlington National Cemetery. He and Sarah were the parents of one child, Alonzo Seth (1857-*post* 1880), who was mentally disabled. Sarah married Thomas Ross (1841-*post* 1885) in Cedar County, IA on February 3, 1870. In 1880 and 1885 they were living in Battle Creek, Madison, NE. It is unknown whether Ross died or whether he and Sarah separated, but from 1891-1893 Sarah, using the surname Fessenden, lived in Binghamton, NY. She was listed in the Syracuse, NY city directory from 1904-1908. On August 8, 1914 Sarah Fessenden, aged 80, entered the Onondaga County Poorhouse. She claimed to be married but gave a niece, Miss Frink, as her nearest relative. She was suffering from cancer and died two days later. Her gravesite is unknown but she might have been buried in the poorhouse cemetery.

Jacob Fetterhoff – Co. C
b. 1840 New Amsterdam, Somerset, PA
d. ? ?
m. ?

NOTE: Jacob, whose parents are unidentified, was a sailor. He enrolled as a substitute for George Kreis, Buffalo, in that city on July 21, 1863. He was wounded at the battle of the Wilderness on May 5, 1864 and sent to McClellan Hospital, Philadelphia, PA on May 31st. According to his muster roll card he returned to duty on February 26, 1865 although no further record was available. He transferred to Co. H, 91st Regiment on June 5th but was "absent, sick." He does not appear in *The Adjutant-General's Report* for that regiment. I suspect he died.

Eli Fields – Co. C
b. March 15, 1844 Barton, Tioga, NY
d. February 5, 1905 Chicago, Cook, IL
m1. Eva A. Shaw (1850-January 29, 1925) *ca.* 1875
m2. Ingebor "Emma" L. E. Larson (September 1862-*post* 1949) July 5, 1889

NOTE: Eli was the son of Noah (1811-1889) and Eleanor Stebbins Fields (1810-1860). He was a substitute for Hiram L. Roberts and enrolled at Reading, Schuyler, NY on July 22, 1863. He transferred to Co. H, 91st Regiment on June 5, 1865 and was discharged at Elmira, Chemung, NY on June 20th. Eli and Eva were the parents of two children, Matie (1876-?) and Frank (1878-1939). In 1918 when Frank enrolled for the draft he was living with his mother, now married to William Anderson. Emma also had two children, Grace (1893-1970) and Irene (1895-?). Eva died in Chicago but her grave has not been located. Emma was last listed in the Miami, Dade, FL directory in 1949. Eli, who gave his occupation as druggist in 1880, is buried in Montrose Cemetery, Chicago.

John Fitts – Co. C

b. 1848 Canada
d. June 6, 1906 Buffalo, Erie, NY
m. Elizabeth Lahey (1859-July 6, 1907) 1877

NOTE: John Fitts/Fitz was an alias used by Alexander Conway, son of Patrick (1815-1857) and Mary Conway (1807-*post* 1880), when he joined the military. Although he claimed to be 20 years old when he enlisted, he was only 15. He substituted for John Archibald from Lackawanna, Erie, NY and was enumerated on the 1865 New York census with this alias. Alexander was captured on May 5, 1864 at the battle of the Wilderness and confined at Andersonville. He was finally released at Wilmington, NC on March 1, 1865 and discharged at Annapolis, MD on June 19th. He and Elizabeth were the parents of five children. He was a member of Bidwell Wilkeson Post No. 9, GAR and Branch 7, Catholic Mutual Benevolent Association (CMBA). His tragic death was widely reported. *The Buffalo Commercial* June 6, 1906, 3 carried one article: "Alexander Conway, foreman fireman at the waterworks pumping station, was crushed to death while he was at work in the pumping station at the foot of Massachusetts avenue at 2 o'clock this afternoon. Conway's clothing caught in one of the buckets of the new automatic coal-conveyors, and he was crushed to instant death. One of the firemen found Conway's body squeezed between two of the conveyors. Conway lived at 492 Fargo avenue, and had been employed at the pumping station for the past 15 years. When the new automatic coal-conveyors were installed some months ago, Conway was made foreman fireman in charge of one of the shifts of men. No one witnessed the accident, and Deputy Water Commissioner Lyon is investigating to determine in exactly what manner the accident occurred. Medical Examiner Danser was notified, and took charge of the case." Another article revealed his skull had been fractured and his torso and abdomen had been crushed. Although the coroner ruled no one was at fault for the accident Elizabeth filed a lawsuit against the city for $10,000. Her own death the very next year may have ended the case. She was a member of the Ladies' Catholic Benevolent Association (LCBA). Her daughter Laura (1886-?), now married to Fred Wood, was named guardian of the youngest child, John (1895-?) for whom a pension was secured. Alexander was buried in Holy Cross Cemetery, Lackawanna, Erie, NY. Elizabeth's grave has not been located.

John Fitzgerald – Co. D

b. 1845 Philadelphia, Philadelphia, PA
d. May 30, 1864 Dabney's Ford, VA
m. ------

NOTE: Little can be ascertained about this soldier. His parents are unknown. A substitute for Henry Campbell, he entered the service at Ischua, Cattaraugus, NY on August

21, 1863. The date and location of his death are a matter of some dispute. According to his muster roll card John Fitzgerald, member of Co. D, 147th NYSV, died at Bethesda Church, VA on June 2, 1864 but that battle was fought on the afternoon of May 30th. It was part of the Union offensive known as Totopotomoy and included Bethesda Church, Crumps Creek, Shady Grove, Hanovertown (Dabney's Ferry/Ford) which lasted from May 28-30th and culminated with the bloody battle of Cold Harbor which lasted from May 31-June 12. *Deaths of Volunteers* shows this man "killed in battle" on May 30, 1864 at Dabney's Ford (Dabney's Ferry). This fact is confirmed by Grove Dutton, 130: ". . . Gallagher and Fitzgerald, both young men, were detailed [to cut down trees]. Fitzgerald almost refused to obey but finally went over the works as ordered. In a few minutes Gallagher came back much frightened and said that Fitzgerald was killed. Sergeant Emblem of Company C and another went outside and brought him in. Poor Fitzgerald had a ball through the head, killing him instantly. 'Trask and Dutton, get a spade and bury him,' was the order, and we selected a place under a pine for his grave. We had dug a hole less than two feet in depth when 'fall in; fall in,' was called and we placed him in the grave, hurrying away, but intending to return and complete our sad duty. The rebels made a feint and their charge at this place did not materialize, but we moved immediately to our left and engaged them and never returned, and in this unknown grave with no covering save the fallen leaves and the blue sky he sleeps his last sleep until he awakes at the bugle call . . . ." *Deaths of Volunteers* contains an entry for John Fitzgerald, Co. D, 147th Regiment PA who died on June 2, 1864. The location is merely noted as 5th AC. No COD or attending physician's name is provided. A search of the roll for the 147th PA has not revealed any man named John Fitzgerald in any company. It is altogether possible and probable that his death was doubly and inaccurately reported as a result of the chaotic and confusing nature of the fighting.

William FitzPatrick – Co. K
b. 1845 Canada
d. August 19, 1864 Weldon Railroad, VA
m. ------

NOTE: William's parents have not been identified but his mother successfully applied for a pension in 1874. He was a substitute for Menzo Hayes, Three Mile Bay, Jefferson, NY, and entered the regiment on September 3, 1863 at Watertown, Jefferson, NY. He was KIA.

John Flinn – Co. F
b. 1842 England
d. ? ?
m. ------

NOTE: Very little is known about this man. He was a substitute for Jacob Lisk, Rochester, Monroe, NY, enrolling in the 147th on August 5, 1863 at that place. He was listed as MIA on May 5, 1864 at the battle of the Wilderness and almost certainly died there and was buried on the field.

Orville Flint – Co. D

b. September 14, 1837 Great Valley, Cattaraugus, NY
d. March 15, 1910 Westhampton, Hampshire, MA
m1. Sarah Hermina Kingsley (August 23, 1838-May 23, 1883) July 3, 1861
m2. Louisa Elizabeth Jewett (Dece4mber 3, 1854-June 26, 1943) May 20, 1885

NOTE: Orville, son of Nicholas (1801-1871) and Phebe Burt Willoughby Flint (1814-1900), was drafted, enrolling in the 147th at Great Valley on August 21, 1863. His time in the army was brief since he was discharged for "disability" on November 28, 1863. In 1890 he claimed rheumatism as his disability. He and Sarah were the parents of a daughter, Isadora (1862-1870). The couple lived in Easthampton in 1880 and according to Massachusetts Vital Statistics, Sarah died there of bronchial pneumonia. She apparently is buried in Willoughby Cemetery, Great Valley. Her name on the gravestone is "Herminia." Orville and Louisa were the parents of three children. His obituary appeared in *The Springfield Republican* March 19, 1910, 15: "Orville Flint died at his home in Westhampton Tuesday night after a long illness with asthma and heart trouble. Mr. Flint was born in Great Valley, N. Y., September 14, 1837, the son of Nicolas and Phoebe Flint. He was a carpenter by trade and also operated a small farm. He was a Grand Army man, enlisting from New York. Mr. Flint was twice married, his first wife being Almena [*sic*] Kingsley, sister of N. A. Kingsley of Westhampton, whom he married July 3, 1861. He married Elizabeth Jewett, daughter of A. D. Jewett of Westhampton, May 20, 1885, and had since made his home in Westhampton. Mr. Flint identified himself with the church and the best interests of the town, serving for several years on the school board and for many years as a member of the library committee, which office he held at the time of his death. He was a close student of Nature and a great lover of flowers and for many years furnished the flowers for the church . . . Funeral services were held at the church Thursday afternoon, Rev. H. S. Ives officiating . . . ." Louisa's obituary appeared in *The Springfield Republican* June 29, 1943, 2: "Mrs. Louisa Elizabeth (Jewett) Flint, 88, died at her home early Saturday morning after a long illness. She was born in Westhampton, the daughter of Albert G. and Vileria (Loud) Jewett on December 3, 1854. She was married to Orville Flint of Great Valley, N. Y., on May 20, 1885. Seven years ago she broke her hip and had been in bed ever since. For 25 years she made her home with her daughter, Mabel Flint, in Northampton, who cared for her in her recent illness. Last fall she returned to Westhampton and lived with her son Gilbert, and later she was moved to her old home, where her son, Orville and his wife cared for her in her last months of illness. She was a member of the Westhampton Congregational church . . . The funeral was held at her home on Sunday afternoon at 4, Dr. Paul T. McClurkin of Northampton officiating." Orville and Louisa are buried in Center Cemetery, Westhampton.

Edwin Fogg – Co. K
b. 1840 Maine
d. ? ?
m. ?

NOTE: Little has been learned about this soldier. His muster roll card spells his name Fagg. He was a substitute for John Hamble, Buffalo, Erie, NY and enrolled at that place on August 8, 1863. He transferred to the VRC on January 25, 1865. Edwin, a farmer, had blue eyes, auburn hair, fair complexion, and stood 5' 4 ½" tall. I have located no other confirmable information about him. He supposedly survived the war.

James Foley – Co. I
b. March 15, 1843 Ireland
d. May 14, 1918 National Soldiers' Home Hospital, Bath, Steuben, NY
m. ------

NOTE: The son of Patrick (1803-1890) and Ann Foley (1814-1886), James was a substitute for his married brother Frank (1836-1891). He transferred to Co. I, 91st Regiment on June 5, 1865 and mustered out on July 3rd near Washington, DC. In 1870 he lived in Ontario, Wayne, working in a mine. It is unknown when he entered the home but he was enumerated there for the 1915 New York census. He is buried in the Bath National Cemetery. It is interesting to note that Frank enrolled in Co. A, 111th Regiment on September 6, 1864 at Manchester, Ontario County to serve one year. He mustered out on June 4, 1865 near Alexandria, VA.

Erastus Bailey Foote – Co. F
b. July 4, 1841 Virgil, Cortland, NY
d. March 1880 Oxford, Sumner, KS
m. Ruth A. King (1849-*post* 1919) 1866

NOTE: Erastus, commonly known by his middle name, was the son of Justin (1816-April 21, 1857) and Sarah Ann Edgecomb Foote (1820-October 3, 1851). After his mother died he and his three siblings were "farmed out" to her relatives. He joined the 147th at Barton, Tioga, NY on July 18, 1863 as a substitute for John D. McErving. He transferred to Co. A, 91st on June 5, 1865 and mustered out on July 3rd near Washington, DC. He and Ruth were in Kansas when the 1870 census was taken. They were still together in 1875 but when Erastus died, his entry in the 1880 Mortality Schedules showed he was divorced. His COD was *delirium tremens*, which may explain why the marriage failed. He is buried in Oxford Cemetery, Oxford. Ruth attempted to obtain a pension in 1919 in New York State. Her surname on the card was Foote "also known as Ruth King." She did not obtain a certificate, in all likelihood because she and Erastus had legally divorced. I have located nothing more about her.

Gilbert Edgecomb Foote – Co. F
b. June 8, 1843 Barton, Tioga, NY
d. January 15, 1918 Waverly, Tioga, NY
m. Isadore W. Davis (1850-May 28, 1930) September 28, 1870

NOTE: Gilbert was Erastus' brother. He was drafted, enrolling in the 147th at Barton, Tioga, NY on July 14, 1863. He was discharged for "disability" at Chester Hospital, Chester, Delaware, PA on November 21, 1864. His obituary appeared in *The Binghamton Press* January 17, 1918: "Gilbert E. Foote, aged 74 years, died at 11:30 o'clock Tuesday night at his home in Fulton street due to apoplexy. Mr. Foote is survived by his wife, one daughter, Mrs. G. Edson Blizzard of Waverly, and one brother, Charles Foote of Cortland. Mr. Foote had been a life-long resident of this locality. He served the Union during three years of the Civil War and lost his left arm at the Battle of the Wilderness. After the war he became a clerk in the patent office at Washington, but always retained his residence here. He was bookkeeper at the Citizens' Bank for the last 18 years. Mr. Foote was not politically prominent but had frequently been a village trustee. Not long ago he refused nomination for the village presidency. He was village treasurer for many years. He was also a vestryman in the Grace Episcopal church . . . ." Gilbert and Isadore were the parents of two children. In 1930, shortly before her death, Isadore's pension was increased to $50.00 per month. They are buried in Forest Home Cemetery, Waverly.

Clark Forbush – Co. C
b. 1812 Herkimer County, NY
d. April 25, 1885 Morris, Otsego, NY
m. Mary Thomas (1815-*post* 1863) *ca.* 1854

NOTE: Clark, a blacksmith, was the son of Aaron (1780-*post* 1855) and Selinda Forbush (1873-*post* 1855), both born in Massachusetts. He alleged he was 40 years old when he entered the military as a draftee on August 21, 1863 at Mansfield, Cattaraugus, NY. He also stated he was born in Chenango County, but census records prove he was born in Herkimer County. Although nominally transferred to the 91st Regiment on June 5, 1865, he had already been discharged as of May 30th. Clark and Mary were the parents of three children, the youngest of whom, Charles, was born in 1863. Clark is buried in Hillington Cemetery, Morris. Mary's grave has not been located.

Albert A. Ford – Co. D
b. 1845 Chautauqua County, NY
d. May 6, 1864 Wilderness, VA
m. ------

NOTE: Albert was the son of Milton (1805-1892) and Eliza B. Lovell Ford (1811-1886). He was a substitute for Abner Hazeltine, Jr., enrolling in the 147th on August 19, 1863 at Ellicott, Chautauqua, NY and transferring to 7th Co., 1st NY Battalion, Sharp Shooters on November 4th. He died of wounds suffered in the battle of the Wilderness. His gravesite is unknown.

Charles Milton Ford – Co. D
b. March 7, 1843 Chautauqua County, NY
d. March 30, 1883 Washington, DC
m. Mary Catherine Hopping (April 1849-June 15, 1933) April 25, 1870

NOTE: Charles was Albert's brother. He was a substitute for Coleman E. Bishop, enrolling in the 147th on August 19, 1863 at Ellicott, Chautauqua, NY. He too transferred to 7th Co., 1st NY Battalion, Sharp Shooters on November 4th. In 1880 his occupation was watchman. He and Mary are buried in Glenwood Cemetery, Washington, DC together with his parents.

Henry P. Foster – Co. C
b. 1837 Clarendon, Orleans, NY
d. June 18, 1864 Petersburg, VA
m. ------

NOTE: Henry was the son of Michael (1793-1864) and Mehitable Singletary Jennison Foster (1802-1893) and one of 14 children. He was drafted, enrolling in the 147th at Byron, Genesee, NY on July 25, 1863. He was KIA. His brother Orrin M. (1833-1928) served two stints in Co. F, 3rd NY ART from 1861-1865.

Drisdor Founeer – Co. A
b. 1821 ?
d. August 16, 1864 ?
m. ?

NOTE: This soldier's life and military career are a mystery, undoubtedly on account of the spelling of his names. His muster roll card contains no vital information. He was drafted, enrolling in the 147th at Oswego, NY on September 1, 1863. He died as a result of wounds suffered at the battle of the Wilderness.

Michael Franey – Co. I
b. 1820 Ireland
d. March 8, 1901 Weedsport, Cayuga, NY
m. Frances "Fanny"_____ (1821-February 24, 1901) 1851

NOTE: Michael, a stone cutter, was the son of James (?-?) and Mary Hadden Franey (?-?). He immigrated to the United States in 1850. He enlisted in Co. K, 19th Regiment on November 5, 1861, an outfit which later became the 3rd NY ART. He was discharged in April 1863. He enlisted in the 147th as a substitute for Benijah Smith, Brutus, Cayuga, NY on July 23, 1863 at Auburn, Cayuga, NY and served until May 19, 1865 when discharged from Satterlee Hospital, Philadelphia, PA. His obituary in *The Post-Standard* March 10, 1901, 9 alluded to his wife's recent demise: "Weedsport, March 9. -- Michael Franey, one of Weedsport's oldest residents, died at his home on Hanford street last evening of a complication of diseases. He was upward of 80 years of age and had been confined in his house for over a year. Mr. Franey's wife died February 24, just two weeks to a day before her husband . . . The funeral will take place at St. Joseph's Church Monday at 9:30 o'clock." Gravesites for Michael and Fanny have not been located but they may be buried in St. Joseph's Cemetery, Weedsport.

George Freeman – Co. D
b. 1842 Canada
d. ? ?
m. ?

NOTE: Little has been learned about this soldier who was a sailor. He was a substitute for Robert W. Scott and enrolled at Conewango, Cattaraugus, NY on August 21, 1863. He transferred to the US Navy on April 22, 1864.

Henry Gilbert French – Co. D
b. May 10, 1841 Weathersfield, Wyoming, NY
d. September 7, 1917 in woods near Olean, Cattaraugus, NY
m. Hester Ann Reed (August 1845-October 26, 1917) 1866

NOTE: Henry, sometimes known by his middle name, was the son of Frederick Cleveland (1811-1844) and Julia Waterman French (1813-1885). A draftee, he enrolled at Great Valley, Cattaraugus County on August 21, 1863. He transferred to Co. B, 91st Regiment on June 5, 1865 and mustered out near Washington, DC on July 3rd. In civilian life he was a deputy sheriff and game warden. His unexpected death was reported in *The Whitesville News* September 13, 1917, 1: "Olean, Sept. 9. – Henry French, 76 years old, a veteran of the Civil War, and formerly a deputy sheriff in Cattaraugus County, was found dead in the woods about two miles from his home early this evening. Death is believed to have occurred about noon yesterday and to have been due to natural causes." His pension index card states he died September 7th. An article in *The Cuba Patriot and Free Press* September 14, 1917 added that he had gone berry picking. Hester's death was reported in *The* [Ellicottville] *Post* October 31, 1917, 3: ". . . C. Reed received the sad news of the death of his sister Mrs. Hester Reed French of Olean which occurred Oct. 26th of heart disease. She was 71 years of age. Her husband died seven weeks ago of the same disease." Henry and Hester are buried in Allegany Cemetery, Allegany, Cattaraugus. Although her gravestone gives a DOB of 1848 it is more likely she was born in 1845 or 1846. In 1900 she stated she had been born in August 1845.

Henry M. French – Co. C
b. 1831 Yates County, NY
d. May 5, 1864 Wilderness, VA
m. Permilia A. Maxfield (1833-September 12, 1906) October 6, 1858

NOTE: Henry was the son of Ebenezer (1793-1875) and Phila Lindsley French (1805-1875). A draftee, he enrolled at Canandaigua, Ontario, NY on July 31, 1863. According to *Registers of Officers and Enlisted Men*, he was "wounded and taken prisoner at battle of Wilderness. His friends consider him dead." His entry in *The Town Clerks' Registers* states, "Was in the Battle of the Wilderness and has not been heard from since." His muster roll card contains the most likely scenario: "1st Lieut. Henry H. Lyman, C, 147 NY, testifies that French received a severe gunshot wound in the battle of the Wilderness, Va., which wound affiant believes to have been mortal; that French was unable to leave the field and was left there and affiant has no doubt he died there." Permilia successfully applied for a pension on August 31, 1865. She married Benjamin MacDonald (1814-1883) on March 19, 1874 in Yates County as his second wife. She and Henry were the parents of one child, Phila (1860-1912), and by 1900 Permilia was living with her and her husband Lemuel D. Gillette (1856-1944). In 1901 Permilia applied for the restoration of her pension under the Remarried Widows Act. She died in Johnstown, Fulton, NY but her grave has not been located. Lemuel and Phila both died in Gloversville, Fulton, and he is buried in Prospect Hill Cemetery. It is possible mother and daughter are there too.

Albert Fuller – Co. C
b. 1838 Yates, Orleans, NY
d. September 1, 1864 Lincoln General Hospital, Washington, DC
m. ------

NOTE: Albert, son of Joel (1802-1860) and Jane Field Fuller (1808-1848), was a draftee, enrolling in the 147th at Oakfield, Genesee, NY on July 27, 1863. His name is entered twice in *Deaths of Volunteers*, August 31st and September 1st. His COD was chronic diarrhea. He is buried in Arlington National Cemetery.

James Galliger – Co. D
b. 1844 Chicago, Cook, IL
d. ? ?
m. ?

NOTE: Research on this soldier has been hampered by the vast number of men with the same name. He enrolled at Buffalo, Erie, NY on August 8, 1863 as a substitute for A. H. Coit, Buffalo. Galliger was a boatman. He transferred to Co. B, 91st Regiment on June 5, 1865 and mustered out on July 3rd near Washington, DC. I located a James Galliger, living in Quincy, Adams, IL in 1870. His occupation was "boating wood" and he was born in 1844 in Illinois. He was living with John and Elizabeth Rogers. John was from NYS but Elizabeth was born in Illinois and may have been a sister. Also in the household was William Galliger, 18, who was involved with "boating wood." There the trail ends. Whether or not this is the correct man is open to debate.

Ansel Gannon – Co. F
b. 1831 Bradford, Steuben, NY
d. September 12, 1864 Andersonville, Sumter, GA
m. ?

NOTE: Ansel, son of David (1808-1900) and Sarah Whitehead Gannon (1809-*post* 1865), was a draftee and joined the regiment on July 10, 1863 at Friendship, Allegany, NY. It is unknown when he was captured by the Confederates but it could have been May 5th at the battle of the Wilderness. His muster roll card carries the notation that his death was "reported by exchanged prisoners who saw him." COD was "disease." He is buried in Andersonville National Cemetery.

William Ganonny – Co. B
b. 1832 ?
d. ? ?
m. ?

NOTE: Researching this man has been nearly impossible because of the spelling of his surname. It is possible the correct spelling was Gagner. His muster roll card indicates he enrolled in the regiment on July 21, 1863 at Catlin, Chemung, NY but it is unknown if he was a draftee or a volunteer. His age was given but no POB. He was discharged for "disability" on March 17, 1865, location unknown. I have found no pension application for him or surviving spouse or order for a government headstone.

Martin B. Gardner – Co. A
b. 1840 Oneida, NY
d. ? ?
m. ------

NOTE: Martin was the son of Adam (1799-1864) and Margaret Dillenbach Gardner (1800-?). A draftee, he enrolled in the 147th on August 29, 1863 at Utica, NY. He was reported WIA at the battle of Spotsylvania on May 15, 1864. He was nominally transferred to Co. C, 91st Regiment on June 5, 1865 but "absent, sick." In all likelihood, he was mortally wounded and buried on the battlefield.

John Garvey – Co. A
b. 1842 New York
d. ? ?
m. ------

NOTE: John Garvey was a draftee and enrolled in the 147th on August 20, 1863 at Utica, Oneida, NY. He transferred to Co. C, 91st Regiment on June 5, 1865 and mustered out at Ball's Cross Roads, VA on July 3rd. A man named John Garvey, aged 23, enlisted in the US Army at Buffalo, Ny on May 11, 1867. His physical description was similar to this soldier. He was discharged on May 11, 1870 at the expiration of term of service. It is unknown if these men are identical. No other information has been discovered.

James M. Geer – Co. F
b. 1842 Allegany County, NY
d. January 1864 4th Division, 5th AC Hospital, Culpeper, VA
m. ------

NOTE: James was the son of Marshall (1815-1902) and Almira Ives Geer (1822-1885). Their surname was also spelled Gere. He was drafted, enrolling in the 147th at New Haven, NY on July 11, 1863. His DOD is a matter of dispute. He has two entries in *Deaths of Volunteers*. One says he died on January 20, 1864 and was signed by Dr. A. S. Coe, regimental surgeon. Another says he died on February 20, 1864 and contains the notation, "Regt. Regr. on file." His gravestone in Culpeper National Cemetery gives a DOD of January 22, 1864. The burial register also gives an AKA of James M. Green. COD was remittent fever. A cenotaph for him may be seen in Bellville Cemetery, Bellville, Allegany Co., where his parents are buried.

Thomas Gerstner – Co. B
b. 1839 Baden, Germany
d. October 24, 1921 National Soldiers' Home, Bath, Steuben, NY
m. Frances _____ (1843-September 14, 1892) *ca.* 1870

NOTE: The son of Frank (1807-1899) and Franziska Sabbcher Gerstner (1815-*post* 1865), Thomas was drafted. He enrolled in the 147th at Buffalo, Erie, NY on August 5, 1863, transferred to Co. G, 91st Regiment on June 5, 1865, and mustered out on July 3rd near Washington, DC. In 1890 he claimed no disability but when he entered the home on July 13, 1921, his ailments included arthritis, heart trouble, and arteriosclerosis. He is buried in Bath National Cemetery. Frances died in Ebenezer, Erie, NY but her grave has not been located.

George Getman – Co. B
b. 1845 Paris, Ontario, Canada
d. ? ?
m. ?

NOTE: Little has been learned about this soldier. He enrolled as a substitute for James Ferris, residence not noted, at Utica, NY on August 20, 1863. He transferred to Co. G, 91st Regiment on June 5, 1865 and mustered out on July 3rd near Washington, DC. His muster roll card gives an address of Town of Otto, Cattaraugus, NY but I have not found him there on any census records, nor have I located any pension applications.

Lucian Charles Gibbs – Co. C
b. May 14, 1834 Cooperstown, Otsego, NY
d. February 2, 1864 Lima, Livingston, NY
m. Melinda "Minnie" Pratt (1838-December 7, 1926) *ca.* 1857

NOTE: The son of Evander (1808-1874) and Lydia Scribner Gibbs (1805-1899), Lucian was a draftee, joining the regiment at Canandaigua, Ontario, NY on July 5, 1863. He was sent home on furlough dating from November 1, 1863 and died there of chronic diarrhea. He is buried in Oak Ridge Cemetery, Lima. He and Melinda were the parents of two children, Sarah (1858-?) and George Nelson (1860-1938). In 1865 Melinda was living with her parents Lorenzo (1805-?) and Catherine Jones Pratt (1805-?) in Lima, but by 1870 the family had moved to Buffalo, Buchanan, IA. The children resided with the grandparents and Melinda was a live-in servant in the Price household. In 1880 George was teaching school and his mother lived with him Sioux City, Woodbury, IA. On November 30, 1883 Melinda married Wanton G. Moon (1837-December 21, 1916), a veteran of the 66th Illinois Volunteers. By 1900 they were living in Springfield, Greene, MO where both of them died. Her obituary appeared in *The Springfield News-Leader* December 10, 1926, 9: "Funeral services for Mrs. Malinda Moon, 84 years old, who died Tuesday morning at her home, 2145 North Main avenue, will be held this afternoon at 1:30 o'clock at the Klingner funeral chapel. Rev. Anna Shaw will officiate, and the McCroskey Relief Corps No. 22, of which Mrs. Moon was a member, will hold a brief service. Mrs. Moon was a nurse in the civil war. Interment will be made in the National cemetery. She is survived by one son, Charles, of the home address." Melinda and Wanton are both buried in Springfield National Cemetery. Her gravestone says she was an Army nurse. The burial records for that cemetery add that she was a nurse at Emery Hospital, Washington, DC. About the only time available to her was the period after Lucian's death. Wanton's COD was pneumonia while Melinda's was classified as senility.

Pope Gibbs – Co. K

b. June 13, 1846 Janesville, Rock, WI
d. May 11, 1916 Chelsea, Kennebec, ME
m1. Hattie A. Plummer (1861-August 10, 1889) October 2, 1886
m2. Elizabeth Ayen (May 1865-January 1942) December 31, 1891

NOTE: Pope was the son of Judge Charles Rollins (1813-1907) and Martha Hill Pope Gibbs (1818-1860). He enlisted in the US Navy at New York City on February 25, 1862 at the age of 16 for a term of three years. On April 19, 1862 he was admitted to the hospital for tonsillitis from the USS Sabine. He apparently was discharged from the Navy because he was working as a waiter in Buffalo in 1863. He enrolled as a substitute for Theron V. N. Penfield at Buffalo on August 8th, giving an age of 23! Between that date and August 20th his age decreased to 20. He transferred to Co. K, 91st Regiment on June 5, 1865 and mustered out on July 3rd near Washington, DC. In 1890 he claimed he had suffered a gunshot wound to the right eye and when he was admitted to the Togus National Soldiers' Home, Chelsea, in 1884 his disability was the loss of sight in that eye due to the wound. Hattie is buried in Chase-Riverside Cemetery, Chelsea. Pope's COD was chronic heart disease. He and Elizabeth are buried in Bien Venue Cemetery, Augusta, Kennebec, ME.

John Robert Gifford – Co. C

b. January 26, 1845 Hannibal, NY
d. December 19, 1927 Rantoul, Champaign, IL
m. Caroline Rosaline Gates (December 11, 1850-March 30, 1941) March 4, 1875

NOTE: John, a farmer, was the son of Robert (1820-1894) and Mary E. Dennason Gifford (1825-1845). He enrolled in the 147th at Hannibal, NY on March 14, 1864 for a term of three years. His muster roll card does not indicate that he was a draftee.

On June 5, 1865 he transferred to Co. H, 91ˢᵗ Regiment but was absent at mustering out of company. I have located no pension card for him or his wife. He and Caroline, the parents of two sons, are buried in Maplewood Cemetery, Rantoul. Although his gravestone says he was born in 1846 all early census records and the Illinois Death Index fix his birth at 1845. Furthermore, his mother died in 1845.

Charles Howard Gilbert – Co. E
b. January 14, 1842 Connecticut
d. March 7, 1917 National Soldiers' Home, Sawtelle, Los Angeles, CA
m. Sarah Frances Glass (May 27, 1847-July 6, 1906) 1872

NOTE: Charles, son of Aaron B. (1807-1879) and Caroline Gilbert Gilbert (1820-1854), was drafted and enrolled in the 147ᵗʰ on August 5, 1863 at Buffalo, Erie, NY. He transferred to the VRC on May 15, 1865. He and Sarah, who was born in Kentucky, were the parents of six children. She died in Eugene, Lane, OR. Charles entered the National Soldiers' Home on February 10, 1915. Among his disabilities were defective vision, rheumatism, and heart disease which was his COD. An obituary appeared in *The Eugene Guard* March 12, 1917, 5: "Charles H. Gilbert, a resident of this city for many years, passed away at the soldiers' home at Sawtelle, Cal., last Wednesday at the advanced age of 75. The news of his death was at once received by his son, William A. Gilbert . . . Mr. Gilbert had been a member of the 147ᵗʰ New York infantry regiment during the Civil war and was a member of the local post of the G. A. R. He was born in the state of Connecticut on January 14, 1842, and came to Eugene with his family from Kansas twenty-seven years ago. Mrs. Gilbert's death occurred in the year 1906. Mr. Gilbert spent two years in the soldiers' home at Roseburg before going to the California institution. It is probable that the remains will be brought to Eugene this week, although arrangements have not yet been made . . . ." Charles' body was shipped to Eugene and buried with Sarah in Eugene Pioneer Cemetery.

Ira Gilbert – Co. B
b. August 16, 1829 Buffalo, Erie, NY
d. October 27, 1904 Olney, Lincoln, MO
m. Elizabeth "Jane" Borne Starks (September 18, 1834-November 8, 1911) November 19, 1849

NOTE: Ira, son of Eliphalet (1810-*post* 1865) and Phoebe Howard Gilbert (1810-?), was a draftee, enrolling in the 147ᵗʰ on August 13, 1863 at Buffalo. According to *The Town Clerks' Registers* he "participated in 13 battles." He transferred to Co. G, 91ˢᵗ Regiment on June 5, 1865 and mustered out on July 3ʳᵈ near Washington, DC. In

1900 Elizabeth said she was the mother of eight, five of whom were living. She and Ira are buried in Macedonia Cemetery, Montgomery, MO.

Francis Gill – Co. K
b. 1845 Ireland
d. February 24, 1918 Manhattan, NY
m. ------

NOTE: Francis, son of Michael (1814-1869) and Bridget Gill (1816-*post* 1870), was a boatman. He apparently enlisted in the 147th at Oswego, NY on January 1, 1864, collecting a bounty of $300. According to *The Town Clerks' Registers*, he "had finger shot off." He transferred to Co. K, 91st Regiment on June 5, 1865 and mustered out on July 3rd near Washington, DC. Some time after 1870 he moved to New York City where he became a member of Post Mansfield No. 35 GAR. His body was returned to Oswego where the funeral was held on March 4, 1918. Francis is buried in St. Paul's Cemetery.

Joseph Gonzales – Co. K
b. ? ?
d. ? ?
m. ?

NOTE: Very little is known about this soldier. He was a substitute "for man actually drafted" and enrolled in New York City on July 24, 1863. His muster roll card contains no biographical material. He nominally transferred to Co. K, 91st Regiment on June 5, 1865 but was "absent, sick." When discharged at Elmira, Chemung, NY on August 1, 1865 it was "as of 147." Someone named J. Gonzales, Civil War veteran born in Portugal, is buried in Holy Cross Cemetery, Brooklyn, but the stone contains no dates or other information.

Jacob F. Goodbread – Co. B
b. 1829 Wurtemburg, Germany
d. August 28, 1864 Andersonville, Sumter, GA
m. Mary A. _____ (1831-1884) *ca.* 1854

NOTE: Jacob, son of John (?-?) and Mary Goodbread (?-?), was a shoemaker. He was drafted, enrolling in the 147th at Ashford, Cattaraugus, NY on September 20, 1863. He was captured on May 5, 1864 at the battle of the Wilderness and sent to Andersonville where he died of dysentery. Jacob is buried in Andersonville National Cemetery. He and Mary were the parents of four. She successfully applied for a pension in 1866 and never remarried. She is buried in Maplewood Cemetery, Springville, Erie, NY.

Isaac James Gorssline – Co. H
b. May 22, 1842 Ontario, Canada
d. November 27, 1863 Richmond, VA
m. ------

NOTE: Isaac was the son of Reuben Cronk (1813-1895) and Jane C. DeMille Gorssline (1816-1854). In 1861 he was living with his father and stepmother, Sarah Ann DeMille Gorssline (1825-1904), Jane's sister, in Hastings, Canada West. He enrolled in Watertown, Jefferson, NY as a substitute for an unnamed draftee on September 9, 1863. According to his muster roll card he was captured at an unknown date and died as a POW. It is possible he was captured at Haymarket, VA on October 19, 1863 when several members of the regiment were doing picket duty. A brother, Richard M. (1840-1862) was a member of Co. G, 49th Regiment from August 16, 1861-March 12, 1862 when he died in US General Hospital, Georgetown, DC. He is buried in Soldiers' Home Cemetery, New York City.

Evander Orsamus Gould – Co. C
b. April 1829 German Flats, Herkimer, NY
d. July 11, 1900 Brookfield, Madison, NY
m. Mary Ann Crumb (1835-*post* 1880) *ca.* 1854

NOTE: Evander, son of Orsamus (1799-1882) and Mary Browning Gould (1799-1881), was a peddler when he enlisted. A substitute for Charles W. Mallery, he enrolled at Norwich, Chenango, NY on September 3, 1863. He transferred to Co. H, 91st Regiment on June 5, 1865 and mustered out on July 3rd near Washington, DC. Mary last appears on the 1880 census when the family was living in Grant, Jewell, KS. Evander was still living in Kansas in April 1893 when he and granddaughter Minnie came to NYS to visit relatives. By 1900 he was with son Frank in Brookfield. He is buried in Brookfield Rural Cemetery. Mary's DOD and gravesite have not been located.

Henry Grawbarger – Co. K
b. November 8, 1846 Savannah, Wayne, NY
d. July 16, 1943 Ft. Lauderdale, Broward, FL
m. Electa Jepson (July 8, 1848-December 28, 1927) February 11, 1872

NOTE: Henry was the son of Daniel (1817-1869) and Lucette Sarah Grawbarger (1829-*ante* 1860). Despite the fact that he said he was 18 when he enlisted as a substitute for Silas Van Nostrand at Auburn, Cayuga, NY on July 25, 1863, he was only 15. According to an article appearing in *The Cayuga Chief* August 28, 1936, 1, ". . . Mention was made . . . that Mr. Grawberger [*sic*] is the only living Northern soldier who was a prisoner of the Confederate army in Libby prison. He fell into [the] hands of Confederate soldiers during the battle of Kelly Ford in 1864 . . . ." Although the article provides a date of 1864, it is more likely Henry was captured there on November 7, 1863. It is unknown how long he spent in Libby Prison but he was discharged from the service at an unnamed hospital in April 1864. In 1890 he was living in Fairport, Monroe, NY and said his disability was "catarrhal difficulty." Over the years his fame and legend grew and sometimes information found its way into newspaper accounts which was not exactly accurate, witness the following published in *The Port Byron Chronicle and Cayuga County News* May 28, 1938, 1: ". . . Mr. Grawbarger, who lives at the home of a niece, survived the horrors of the notorious Libby and Belle Isle prisons . . . He was in the first day of battle at Gettysburg. In 1864 he was taken prisoner by the Confederates and for eight months was confined in the Rebel prisons in which many others perished." Since Henry did not enlist until after Gettysburg, it was impossible for him to have been there and since he was discharged in April 1864 he could not have spent eight months in a POW camp. There is no evidence that he spent any time at Belle Isle, although that is possible. An article published in *The Auburn Citizen-Advertiser* June 28, 1938, 1 mentioned that Henry would attend the 75th anniversary of "The Blue and Gray," where survivors of both sides met "in peace and brotherhood on the scene of the history-making battle fought during the crucial period of the Civil War. Comrade Grawbarger, who it is expected will be Cayuga County's only veteran at the reunion, will be attended by Henry W. Owen, commander of Seward Camp, Sons of Union Veterans, of this city. They plan to remain over July 6. The veterans will attend the reunion, probably the last of its sort, as guests of the federal government and the State of Pennsylvania . . . Mr. Grawbarger is 90 years old. He fought in the Civil War with the 147th New York Infantry." For many years Henry and Electa lived in Fairport where he was a carpenter and later a janitor at the Perinton Town Hall. He was a member and past commander of E. A. Slocum Post No. 211 GAR, Fairport. They were the parents of Grace (1880-1881) and Lillie (1886-1899). Electa's death was announced in *The Fairport Herald-Mail* December 22, 1927, 1: "Electa Jepson Grawbarger died at her home in Perrin street at 4:30 Sunday afternoon, aged 79 years. She had been ill with pneumonia for about ten days, and on account of her advanced age and weakened condition she could not rally. She was born in Lakeport on July 8, 1848. On the 11th day of February, 1872, she married Henry Grawbarger, and for 54 years she resided with her husband in this village. She was a member of the W. R. C.; Avalon Rebekah Lodge, No. 282, of East Rochester; the Lomb Circle, of Rochester; the Spear Bible class of the Raymond Baptist church, and was active in all these organizations. She is survived by her husband and two brothers, Porter J. Jepson, of Detroit, and Charles Jepson, of Syracuse. The funeral was held at the home Tuesday afternoon, Revs. C. H. Colegrove and

H. R. Saunders officiating, and the remains were taken to Bridgeport yesterday." Henry's later life was detailed in a somewhat fanciful obituary in *The Rochester Times-Union* July 24, 1943, 1: "Interment services for Henry M. Grawbarger, 96, Cayuga County's last Civil War veteran and commander of Fort Slocum Post, G.A.R., at Fairport for many years, were held this week at Bridgeport, N. Y. He died Friday, July 16, 1943, at Fort Lauderdale, Fla. A veteran of many campaigns and battles of the Union Army, Mr. Grawbarger enlisted July 23, 1862 [*sic*] and was discharged June 20, 1864. He was twice made prisoner of the Confederate Army, and for several months was confined to Libby Prison in the South. Since the death of his wife 16 years ago, Mr. Grawbarger had resided with his niece, Mrs. Marvin Glazier, of Auburn. For seven years

Henry Grawbarger outlived most of his comrades in arms.
John Hart (FAG)

the two spent the winters in Florida and summers in Auburn, but for the past three years they remained at Fort Lauderdale because of Mr. Grawbarger's health. At Fort Lauderdale, the Civil War veteran stayed at the Gilbert Hotel, where his friends called him 'Uncle Henry.' Each November, on his birthday, a party was given for him there. The body was cremated in Florida, and the ashes sent to Bridgeport." The Grawbarger family is buried in New Bridgeport Cemetery, Onondaga, NY.

Alvah Green – Co. I
b. September 1838 Morris County, NJ
d. December 15, 1913 Campbell, Steuben, NY
m. Jane Atwood (1838-November 16, 1896) *ca.* 1870

NOTE: Alvah, son of Elias (1795-1881) and Rachel Davenport Green (1798-1863), was a draftee and enrolled in the 147th at Catlin, Chemung, NY on July 21, 1863. Although *The Adjutant-General's Report* states he was captured at the battle of the Wilderness on May 5, 1864 and paroled at an unknown date, his muster card tells a different story. He was listed as MIA but was on the roll at General Hospital, Annapolis, MD to June 30, 1864. The roll taken on August 31, 1864 shows that he was absent on furlough and that there was no further record. He had been paid on July 19th and apparently never returned to duty. He nominally transferred to Co. I, 91st Regiment on June 5, 1865 but was "absent, sick." I have located no pension record for him nor does he appear in the 1890 Veterans' Schedules. He and Jane were the parents of Edna (1873-?). Alvah's death was announced in *The Elmira Star-Gazette* December 17, 1913, 4: "Campbell, Dec. 17. – Alvah Green aged 75 years, died at his home on the Theodore Barrett farm, just outside this village Monday, after a few days' illness of pneumonia. Mr. Green had been a resident of this town for many years and is well known here. He leaves a daughter, now living in New York, also a sister in Lawrenceville, Pa., and a sister Mrs. Katherine Jennings with whom he re-sided." He and his parents are buried in Hope Cemetery, Campbell. Jane's grave has not been located.

Sheffield Wells Green – assistant surgeon
b. July 15, 1814 Hopkinton, Washington, RI
d. November 27, 1899 Richburg, Allegany, NY
m. Keziah Noble (May 25, 1816-August 2, 1899) April 27, 1837

NOTE: Sheffield was the son of Rev. John (1792-1863) and Elizabeth Wells Green (1797-1862). His grandfather, Capt. John Greene (1744-1830), was a Revolutionary War soldier with the Rhode Island militia. Sheffield saw prior military duty in Co. D, 15th NY Cavalry from December 1863-February 15, 1865 when he was discharged at Winchester, VA to join the 147th. He mustered out on June 7, 1865 near Washington, DC. His obituary, published in *The Buffalo Evening News* November 28, 1899, chron-icled his medical career: "Dr. Sheffield Green died at his home in Richburg yesterday of paralysis, aged 85 years. He was born in Rhode Island and studied medicine with Dr. J. C. Sibley at Friendship, graduating in 1846. He practiced first at Olean, later in Franklinville, Corry, Richburg and Wellsville. Dr. Green served as surgeon in the Civil War, and during the Appomattox campaign was acting surgeon of the 147th New York Infantry. His son was killed in the Civil War. He came to Richburg in 1893, after receiving a pension and retiring from active practice. He was a member of the Allegany County Medical Society, a gentleman of the old school and one of the most courteous men who ever lived in Allegany County. Mrs. Green died in August last. He leaves three daughters . . . The funeral will be held at the house Wednesday morning." Dr. and Mrs. Green are buried in Richburg Cemetery. The son mentioned in the obituary was William Herbert (1844-September 5, 1862). He died at Bradford, McKean, PA, the area where the family was living at the time. I have been unable to locate any evidence that he died as a casualty of war.

Elijah Greenfield – Co. K
b. December 16, 1836 Hampton, Washington, NY
d. November 21, 1906 Lake View, Montcalm, MI
m. Phoebe A. Brewer (July 1837-Februry 27, 1907) 1861

NOTE: Elijah, son of Benjamin (1809-1897) and Lucinda Greenfield (1808-*post* 1870), apparently enlisted in the 147th, enrolling at Auburn, Cayuga, NY on July 24, 1863. He transferred to Co. K, 91st Regiment and mustered out on July 3rd near Washington, DC. He and Phoebe were the parents of two. His COD was "paralysis – hemorrhage of brain." Phoebe's COD was "la grippe," with heart disease a contributing factor. They are buried in Lake View Cemetery.

George Gregory – Co. B
b. 1831 Wicklow, Ireland
d. ? ?
m. ?

NOTE: George, whose parents are unidentified, was a substitute for Levi Farwell and joined the 147th at Ischua, Cattaraugus, NY on August 21, 1863. He transferred to Co. G, 91st Regiment on June 5, 1865 but was "absent, sick." Beyond that, I have located nothing confirmable. A man by the name of George Gregory or Lawler died in the New York City poorhouse in March 1880 of *phthisis*. He was 47 years old, married, and born in Ireland. Whether or not this is the same man is unknown.

John Grove – Co. F
b. 1839 Beverly, Edmonton, Alberta, Canada
d. ? ?
m. ?

NOTE: John, a farmer, was a substitute for Elnathan K. Terry, Norwich, Chenango, NY and joined the 147th at Hancock, Delaware, NY on September 4, 1863. He transferred to Co. A, 91st Regiment on June 5, 1865 and mustered out near Washington, DC on July 3rd. Nothing else has been learned about him, including his parents' names.

George Grover – Co. D
b. 1838 France
d. ? ?
m. ?

NOTE: George, a baker, was a substitute for Michael Trautman, a draftee from Buffalo. He enrolled in the 147th at Buffalo on August 8, 1863, transferred to Co. B, 91st on June 5, 1865 and mustered out near Washington, DC on July 3rd. No other information has been located.

Ransom Guinness – Co. C

b. 1828 Pennsylvania
d. May 5, 1864 Wilderness, VA
m. Marinda _____ (?-*post* 1867) ?

NOTE: Ransom, whose parents are unknown, was a substitute for Frank W. Fiske, Buffalo, NY. He enrolled in the 147th there on August 10, 1863. He was mistakenly assigned to the 147th PA in *Deaths of Volunteers*. Marinda, whose surname was spelled Guinniss, successfully applied for a pension on February 4, 1867. The state where she made application was not noted. No other information is available.

Perry Gumaer – Co. K

b. 1843 Cayuga County, NY
d. April 12, 1875 Lewanee, MI
m. Rosamond Bennett (December 27, 1842-May 30, 1935) February 24, 1868

NOTE: Perry, son of Harvey (1817-1875) and Marilla Gumaer (1817-*post* 1865), was drafted, enrolling in the 147th at Auburn, Cayuga, NY on July 24, 1863. He transferred to Co. K, 91st Regiment on June 5, 1865 and was discharged near Washington, DC on June 19th. His muster roll card shows he was in the hospital from February 2nd until May 18th. He and Rosamond were married in Medina, Lewanee, MI. They were the parents of one child, Sarah (1869-1949). A brief death notice published in an unnamed newspaper stated he died "this p.m. after suffering from an axe wound a short while back." Perry was buried with "Masonic honors" in Oak Grove Cemetery, Morenci, Lewanee, MI. In 1880 Rosamond married Henry Kirk Goddard (1841-1915). He died in San Francisco, CA. In 1922 Rosamond applied for a pension as a remarried widow. Her COD was chronic bronchitis. She is buried in Cypress Lawn Memorial Park, Colma, San Mateo, CA.

Robert Hager – Co. F

b. 1843 England
d. ? ?
m. ?

NOTE: Robert's parents are unknown. He was a draftee, enrolling in the 147th on August 28, 1863 at Lockport, Niagara, NY. He was captured and paroled at unknown dates. When he transferred to Co. A, 91st Regiment on June 5, 1865 his muster roll card showed he was a paroled prisoner "in hospital." I have located no other information about him. It is possible he did not survive.

William Hagerty – Co. E

b. 1805 Albany, Albany, NY

d. August 26, 1864 Andersonville, Sumter, GA

m1. Ruth _____ (1796-*ante* 1845) *ca.* 1834

m2. Harriet Watson (1828-July 12, 1887) September 21, 1845

NOTE: William's parents are unknown. The family surname was also spelled Haggerty. Although he claimed to be 25 when he entered the army, he actually was 58. In 1860 he had given his age as 55. He was captured on May 5, 1864 at the battle of the Wilderness. His COD was variously described. Scurvy and diarrhea are suggested. His muster roll card states he died of diabetes. His entry in *Deaths of Volunteers* says he died of debility, corroborated by Andersonville records, in which his death was listed as caused by *debilitas*. He is buried in Andersonville National Cemetery. By his first wife he had at least one son, William (1835-?). He and Harriet were the parents of three more. His son Judson (1848-1885) served in the 141st Regiment from September 1864-June 28, 1865. Little is known about Ruth, but Harriet is buried in Hector Union Cemetery.

Irving Hall – Co. H

b. 1843 Remsen, Oneida, NY

d. August 23, 1912 State Hospital, Utica, Oneida, NY

m. Maryett_____ (1846-*post* 1913) *ante* 1870

NOTE: Irving was the son of Raymond (1806-*post* 1880) and Nancy Maria Hall (1813-*post* 1880). A substitute for Delos M. Dudley, Augusta, Oneida, NY, he joined the 147th at Utica, NY on September 7, 1863. He was discharged from an unnamed hospital in Washington, DC on April 11, 1865 for "disability." Nominally he transferred to Co. B, 91st Regiment but never served in that organization. He and Maryett had no children and by 1900 they were living apart. His brother Albert (1846-1927) seems to have become his guardian by 1908 because of a notation on a pension payment card indicating he was required to furnish a bond for $500. In 1910 Irving was an inmate in the insane asylum in Utica. He said he was divorced but such was not the case. On November 26, 1912 Maryett applied for a pension but appears not to have obtained it although, according to the abovementioned pension card, she received an "accrued payment" in July 1913. No further information about her has been located. Irving is buried in Beechwood Cemetery, Forestport, Oneida.

Jonas G. Hamsher – Co. D

b. October 1, 1831 New York City, NY

d. October 30, 1924 Dansville, Livingston, NY

m. Cornelia Rebecca Woodruff (1848-June 21, 1896) April 2, 1867

NOTE: Jonas, son of Bernard (1794-1872) and Rebecca Flick Hamsher (1803-1893), was a draftee, enrolling in the 147th on July 29, 1863 at Canandaigua, Ontario, NY. On June 5, 1865 he transferred to Co. B, 91st Regiment and mustered out on July 3rd near Washington, DC. Sometimes his middle initial was S. His death was reported in *The Tonawanda Evening News* October 31, 1924, 5: ". . . Jonas Hamsher, 94 years old, said to [be] the oldest Grand Army man in the state, died yesterday morning in the Dansville general hospital. He was a member of Seth N. Hodges Post, G. A. R. One of his sons, who served in the World War, died on his father's birthday and the father died on the son's birthday." Jonas and Cornelia were the parents of six children. The son mentioned in the obituary was Dwight Gates Hamsher, who died October 1, 1920. He was a member of the US Marine Corps. Together with his parents, he is buried in Sparta Center Cemetery, Sparta, Livingston.

William Hammersmith – Co. D
b. November 23, 1839 Hesse-Darmstadt, Germany
d. May 9, 1911 Buffalo, Erie, NY
m. Anna _____ (July 26, 1842-February 2, 1904) 1862

NOTE: William immigrated to the United States in 1846 with his parents, Peter (1795-*post* 1860) and Mary May Hammersmith (1800-*post* 1860), and became a naturalized citizen. He seems to have enlisted, enrolling in the 147th in Rochester on August 28, 1863. He was discharged for "disability" by order of General Christopher Augur on October 4, 1864. Hammersmith held a variety of jobs over the years. In 1860 he was a vinegar manufacturer. In 1870 he was a gardener and in 1900 he was a policeman. He and Anna were the parents of eight, six of whom reached adulthood. Their son Oscar (1879-*post* 1940) became a dentist. William and Anna are buried in Mount Hope Cemetery, Seneca, Erie, NY.

Daniel Hammit – Co. I
b. 1830 England
d. April 20, 1880 Walton, Fife Township, Grand Traverse, MI
m. Mary A. _____ (1830-*post* 1890) *ante* 1855

NOTE: Tracing this soldier has been challenging because of the many different spellings of his surname. I use that in his probate papers. His parents are unknown. He and Mary were married in England and George (1855-?) and Maria (1856-?) and probably others were born there. Daniel, Jr. (1864-*post* 1881) and Willie (1866-*post* 1881) were born in New York State. Other children were Charles and Elizabeth for whom birthdates and places have not been established. Daniel was a substitute for Jesse Cook, Lockport, Niagara, NY and enrolled there on July 28, 1863. He transferred to

Co. I, 91st Regiment on June 5, 1865 and mustered out near Washington, DC on July 3rd. It is fairly certain that the family was living in Niagara County in 1870 because Franklin Odell (1845-?), who married Maria, was living in Lockport at the time. Their first two children, C. Franklin (1873-?) and George (1874-1880), were born in NYS. Daniel's gravesite has not been located. In 1890 Mary was living in Mayfield, Grand Traverse, MI. A widow named Mary Hammet died in Kingsley, Grand Traverse, MI on February 2, 1911. It is unknown if this is the correct person.

John Hammond – Co. D
b. 1838 Erie County, NY
d. ? ?
m. ?

NOTE: John Hammond was a substitute for Ira Clinton Bristol, Westfield, Chautauqua, NY, and he enrolled in the 147th on August 18, 1863 in that place. He was captured by the Confederates at an unknown date and location. His muster roll card says he was erroneously listed as a deserter on the June 1864 roll. Another note says he left parole camp, place unidentified, on May 12, 1865. Although nominally transferred to Co. B, 91st Regiment on June 5, 1865 he was discharged on June 9, 1865 near Washington, DC to date April 24, 1865, which was probably the date he was exchanged and paroled. He does not appear in *The Adjutant-General's Report* for the 91st Regiment. I have located no other information for him and it is altogether possible he died shortly after leaving the military.

James D. Hanchett – Co. D
b. 1842 Monroe County, NY
d. January 26, 1929 Appleton, Outagamie, WI
m. Barbara Fallis Gray (1844-1935) 1875

NOTE: James, son of Charles (1812-?) and Zeetna Cook Hanchett (1817-1894), was drafted, enrolling in the 147th at Canandaigua, Ontario, NY on July 25, 1863. He transferred to Co. I, 91st Regiment on June 5, 1865 and mustered out near Washington, DC on July 3rd. He was living in Wisconsin by 1870 where he married Barbara, who had previously been married to _____ Gray, by whom she had a daughter, Amina (1866-?). She and James were the parents of Roy D. (1880-1912) who died in Tacoma, Pierce, WA. James suffered a stroke a few days prior to his death which was reported in *The Appleton Post-Crescent* January 28, 1929, 17: "James D. Hanchett, 87, one of the last of Appleton's Civil War veterans and a former rural mail carrier, died at 4:30 Saturday afternoon at his home . . . Mr. Hanchett, who has been a resident of Appleton since 1863, was a corporal in Company I, Ninety-first regiment, New York, in the Civil war and served from July 30, 1863 to July 3, 1865. For many years he was commander of the George E. Eggleston and Neenah post, Grand Army of the Republic. Survivors are his widow; one brother, George Hanchett, Indianapolis, Ind., and two grandsons. The Spanish American war veterans and the Grand Army post will have charge of the funeral services which will be at 2 o'clock Tuesday afternoon at the Brettschneider funeral parlors. Dr. J. H. Holmes will conduct the services. The body will rest in state at the funeral parlors until the time of the funeral, and burial will be in Riverside cemetery." James had been installed as post commander earlier in the month. Barbara, whose DOB varied with the document, also is buried in Riverside.

John Henry Handy – Co. D
b. October 26, 1844 Carlton, Orleans, NY
d. February 19, 1912 Howard, Ontario, Canada
m. Margaret E. Bury (October 21, 1851-December 5, 1917) June 22, 1872

NOTE: John, son of Sedgwick (1814-1891) and Eleanor Jane Clement Handy (1814-1871), entered the 147th Regiment at Rochester, Monroe, NY on August 8, 1863 as a substitute for Palmer D. Anderson, Carlton, Orleans County. His time in the 147th was short since he transferred to 6th Co., 1st Battalion of Sharpshooters on November 18, 1863. He was discharged at Washington, DC on July 11, 1865. According to *The Town Clerks' Registers*, he "took part in 15 battles, Wilderness, Cold Harbor, Petersburg, capture of Lee, etc." He and Margaret, a native of Canada, were married in Kent, Ontario, Canada. They were the parents of seven children. John's COD was heart disease. Margaret died in Chicago, IL. They are buried in Morpeth Cemetery, Chatham-Kent Municipality, Ontario, Canada.

Andrew J. Harrington – Co. K
b. April 6, 1837 Savannah, Wayne, NY
d. January 19, 1921 Wayne Center, Wayne, NY
m. Mary E. Tolhurst (December 1855-1942) 1880

NOTE: Andrew first saw military service in Co. I, 1st MI Infantry, a three-month unit organized in May 1861. On July 23, 1863 he enrolled in the 147th Regiment at Auburn, Cayuga, NY, apparently an enlistee. He transferred to Co. K, 91st Regiment on June 5, 1865 and mustered out on July 3rd near Washington, DC. Andrew's parentage is of no little interest. According to an unsourced obituary, he was the son of Nehemiah (1800-*ante* 1880) and Jane Patterson/Pettit/Pottit Harrington (*ca.* 1800-1837). I have been able to identify five children from this union: Daniel (1823-1883); James W. (1833-1919); Ellen Jane [m. William Houghtaling, 1830-1916] (1834-1928); Myron

G. (1836-1922); Andrew J. If the available information is correct Andrew was Jane's last child. Because of the gap between Daniel and James there were probably more children. Their father only appears on the 1870 census, aged 70, living with son Daniel. Andrew and Mary were the parents of two. His COD was a cerebral hemorrhage. An exact DOD of August 30, 1942 has been suggested for Mary but I have been unable to confirm it. Andrew and Mary are buried in South Sodus Cemetery, Wayne. Andrew's brother James served in Co. M, 2nd MI Cavalry. Myron served in Co. E, 19th NY Inf. (which became 3rd NY LA).

William Harrison – Co. G

b. 1844 MI
d. May 5, 1865 Wilderness, VA
m. ------

NOTE: William, son of George (?-January 1855) and Jane Harrison (1819-June 5, 1890), worked in a farm implement manufacturing plant from the age of 12, beginning as an apprentice carpenter soon after his father died. In 1861 his mother married Michael Fallon (1801-1866), described as a "small man of delicate health" by Dr. William Ring. Others described him as "very intemperate." All agreed he was a burden to Jane and to William who assumed responsibility for the family's support. In 1860 there were four minor children in the household. William enrolled in the 147th as a substitute for Jeremiah Fogelsonger, Amherst, on August 11, 1863 at Buffalo. Jane and Michael moved to Chicago where he died on October 20, 1866. Jane, described by deponents as "very poor," owned nothing but her clothing and a few pieces of furniture. She successfully applied for a pension on May 13, 1869. At the time of her death in Chicago, she was receiving $12.00 per month.

Ezra Harrison Harwood – Co. K

b. April 24, 1837 Newfane, Niagara, NY
d. December 1869 Chester, Eaton, MI
m1. Lucy Lenaway (?-1862) *ca.* 1861
m2. Elizabeth Wall (December 1837-August 10, 1911) *ca.* 1863

NOTE: The son of Southworth Erasmus (1796-1859) and Almira Mudge Harwood (1799-1852), Ezra saw prior duty in Co. A, 28th NYSV from November 1861-May 8, 1862 when he was discharged for "disability." He was drafted, enrolling in the 147th on July 28, 1863 at Newfane and discharged on January 7, 1864 at Washington, DC. He and Elizabeth were the parents of two daughters, Mary E. (1865-1919) and Almira A. (1867-1944). Ezra was killed by a falling tree. His grave has not been located. In 1870 Elizabeth and her daughters were living in Chicago. Elizabeth and Mary were enumerated in Pasadena, Los

Angeles, CA in 1900. They are both buried in Mountain View Cemetery and Mausoleum, Altadena, Los Angeles, CA. Almira married John Eugene Hanlon (1864-1959). She died in Salt Lake City, Utah but is buried in Calvary Cemetery, Los Angeles, CA.

Shadrach Heaton – Co. K
b. 1828 England
d. 1908 ?
m. ?

NOTE: Shadrach's parents are unknown. His names were variously spelled. I use those found on pension records. He was a substitute for Peter Van Doren, Chaumont, Jefferson, NY and enrolled in the147th on September 19, 1863 at Watertown, Jefferson. He was WIA at Spotsylvania Court House, VA on May 8, 1864, transferred to the VRC on February 3, 1865, and finally discharged at Washington, DC on November 21st. His pension index card shows a DOD of 1908 but nothing else. A man by the name of Shadrach Heaton died in Oldham, England on February 16, 1908 but it is unknown if he is the correct person.

Frederick Jacob Heinold – Co. G
b. 1841 Boston, Suffolk, MA
d. March 14, 1889 Rochester, Monroe, NY
m. Martha Jane _____ (1849-November 16, 1933) *post* 1865

NOTE: Frederick, son of Andrew (1807-1871) and Margaret Heinold (1819-1892), was drafted, enrolling in the 147th on August 5, 1863 at Rochester. A charge of desertion was made against him, alleging he had deserted on August 6, 1864 and again on September 5, 1864. In 1915 when Martha applied for a pension the War Department removed the charges and granted Frederick a discharge to date September 5, 1864. Heinold claimed to be a miller when he entered the service. In later life he was a chair maker and a nursery man. Among others he was a member of Security Lodge No. 9 Empire Order of Mutual Aid (EOMA) and St. Andrew's Brotherhood in Rochester. He and Martha were the parents of three. His grave is located in Mt. Hope Cemetery, Rochester. Martha's grave has not been located.

Andrew Heneka – Co. D
b. 1821 Germany
d. ? ?
m. Elisa _____ (1822-?) *ca.* 1842

NOTE: The spelling of Andrew's surname has hampered research. He was a substitute for George Wochter and enrolled in the 147th at Buffalo, Erie, NY on August 7, 1863.

He was discharged for "disability" on March 24, 1864. The family appears on the 1865 New York census under the name Hennecka. Elisa said she was the mother of 11 children. The trail ends there.

Peter Herden – Co. D
b. 1843 Ireland
d. ? ?
m. ?

NOTE: Spelling may be a hindrance in researching this man. His surname was variously spelled, such as Herdan, Heridan, and Harden. His parents are unidentified. Peter was a substitute for Edward H. Horton, Cato, Cayuga County and enrolled at Auburn on July 23, 1863. He was wounded in action on May 5, 1864 at the battle of the Wilderness. Since no further record for him exists, he most likely died there. He was nominally transferred to Co. B, 91st Regiment on June 5, 1865 but he does not appear in *The Adjutant-General's Report* for that regiment.

William S. Herrick – Co. G
b. 1842 Norwich, Chenango, NY
d. May 22, 1864 Fredericksburg, Virginia
m. ------

NOTE: William, a draftee, was the son of Charles (1815-?) and Almira Herrick (1817-post 1890). He enrolled in the 147th at Oswego City on August 24, 1863 and was wounded at the battle of the Wilderness on May 5, 1864. His death was announced in *The Oswego Daily Palladium* June 3, 1864: "W. S. Herrick, of Co. C [*sic*], 147th regiment, died in hospital at Fredericksburg on the 21st ult." Almira successfully applied for a pension in 1890 but the place of application was not noted on her card.

Florian Hess – Co. K
b. 1835 Germany
d. August 21, 1864 Weldon Railroad, VA
m. ------

NOTE: Florian's parents are unidentified. A resident of Wilson, Niagara, NY, he was a substitute for Luther Brewer of that place, enrolling in the 147th there on July 29, 1863. He made a will dated June 9, 1864, leaving all his property to the Evangelical Association of America and appointing a friend, John Markle, his executor. After he was killed in action at the battle of Weldon Railroad, he was buried on Brick's farm. Later he was reinterred in Poplar Grove Cemetery, Petersburg, VA.

George W. Hicks – Co. G
b. 1839 Groton, Tompkins, NY
d. September 20, 1909 Virgil, Cortland, NY
m. Permilia "Amelia" Kenyon (1844-April 9, 1921) 1871

NOTE: George was the son of Joseph (1803-1874) and Mary "Polly" Sikes Hicks (1808-1886). He was a draftee and enrolled in the 147th at Groton on July 25, 1863. Transferred to Co. F, 91st on June 5, 1865, he mustered out near Washington, DC on July 3rd. A lengthy, informative obituary appeared in *The Homer Republican* September 30, 1909, 8: "The funeral service for George W. Hicks was held from the Methodist church at Virgil Thursday morning, September 23d. Mr. Hicks was born in Groton in 1839 and was one of a family of eleven children. Early in life he learned the blacksmith trade and was considered an expert workman. In 1871 he married Miss Permilia Kenyon of North Pitcher. After two years' residence in Cortland, Mr. and Mrs. Hicks settled in Virgil where for thirty-eight years they have lived and prospered. In 1862-1863 Mr. Hicks served as a private in Company G, 147th Regiment and Company I, 91st Regiment New York Volunteer infantry. About thirty years ago he became a soldier of the cross and a faithful member of the Methodist church. For fifteen years he was a devoted class leader and also acted as steward for some time. He will be remembered as a faithful Christian man and a kind husband and father and a valued friend. He is survived by his widow whose untiring devotion during his long and painful illness commands high esteem; one son, Frank, who resides in Freeville, an only child greatly beloved of his father . . . He was laid to rest on the hillside in the beautiful cemetery at Groton. The funeral was conducted by the pastor who spoke comforting words to the many relatives and friends. The singing was of choir selections and the flowers were from many of their friends. The ladies of the W. C. T. U. and the G. A. R. were seated in a body. Six of his comrades acted as bearers . . . ." George's COD was heart failure. Permilia was eulogized in *The Cortland Democrat* April 15, 1921, 4: "Virgil – Mrs. Permilia Hicks, widow of the late George W. Hicks, passed away Saturday night at her home here at the age of 76 years. She had been ill several months and was a patient sufferer. She is survived by one son, Frank . . . Mrs. Hicks was a woman who endeared herself to all by her kindly words and deeds. Three of her grandchildren have resided with her more or less for years and her eldest granddaughter has tenderly cared for her during her long illness. Before coming to Virgil Mrs. Hicks, whose maiden name was Kenyon, resided in South Otselic, where she has many friends who will remember her dear face and winning personality. Nothing but good can be said of her and by her life others should pattern. The funeral was held Tuesday at 1 p.m. Burial in Groton." George and Permilia are buried, as are his parents, in Groton Rural Cemetery.

Charles Thomas Hilbert – Co. E

b. November 23, 1836 Germany

d. October 20, 1898 Rochester, Monroe, NY

m. Johanna Nelligan (January 14, 1842-January 27, 1918) October 31, 1859

NOTE: Charles' parents were Jacob (?-?) and Margareta Nie Herbst Hilbert (?-?). A draftee, he enrolled in the 147th in Monroe County, NY on August 8, 1863. He was wounded at the battle of Five Forks on April 1, 1865 and discharged from the service on June 29th at Satterlee Hospital, Philadelphia, PA. Although nominally transferred to Co. D, 91st he was officially discharged from the 147th. In 1890 he claimed rheumatism in his shoulder and legs as well as an injury the description of which is illegible on the form. He claimed he had been injured at Culpeper, Va. He and Johanna, an immigrant from Ireland, were the parents of eight children, six of whom were alive in 1900. His tragic death was reported in *The Rochester Democrat and Chronicle* October 21, 1898, 10: "Charles Hilbert, who was employed on the state scow, was drowned at the western widewaters about 4 o'clock yesterday morning. The scow reached the southern extremity of what is known as the widewaters, and it became necessary for the team drawing the boat to cross over on the other side of the canal, thus necessitating the changing of the tow lines from one side of the boat to the other. Hilbert was steering the boat, and it so happened that he was the only member of the crew on deck, the others being asleep. The driver of the team called to him to shift the lines, and leaving the steering rudder Hilbert proceeded to do so. He caught hold of the line, when it suddenly tightened and he was thrown forward. He could not save himself and plunged headlong into the canal. The driver saw the accident, and leaving his horses ran down to the shore and when opposite the boat hailed the crew. C. H. Fleetwood, a member of the crew, was the first one to appear on deck and the driver told him what had happened. The others of the crew were called, and an effort was made to rescue the unfortunate Hilbert. His body, however, did not come to the surface, and after working about an hour with poles the search was given up, and a man sent to the city to notify Coroner Kleindienst. At the instance of the coroner Morgue Assistant Frank Deaude and a number of assistants dragged for the body from 8 o'clock yesterday morning until 5:30

Charles Hilbert came to a tragic end in a canal boat accident.

Erin Cassidy

last evening without success, and dragging will be renewed today. It is supposed that when Hilbert pitched overboard he sank and then rose under the scow. If his head struck the scow he was probably rendered unconscious. Hilbert was 62 years old and lived at Brockport . . . ." According to an article published in *The Rochester Democrat and Chronicle* October 25, 1898, 8, Hilbert's body was recovered Sunday morning, October 23rd, when James Rowland, a passerby, saw it floating in the canal about 500 feet from where he had gone into the water. Charles and Johanna are buried in Mt. Olivet Cemetery, Brockport. Her DOD is not given on the gravestone.

German Hill – Co. C

b. April 1838 Saratoga County, NY
d. April 2, 1919 Syracuse, Onondaga, NY
m. Mary Eleanor Parks (April 1838-October 22, 1923) 1861

NOTE: German was the son of Eppenetus (1806-1882) and Betsey Bennett Hill (1804-1853). He was drafted, enrolling in the 147th at Oswego City on August 14, 1863. He transferred to Co. F, 91st Regiment on June 5, 1865 and mustered out near Washington, DC on July 3rd. He and Mary lived 40 years in Hannibal, NY but moved to Syracuse to be with their son, Ferris. An interesting but fanciful obituary appeared in *The Post-Standard* April 3, 19191: "German Hill, 81 years, one of the original volunteers of the 147th Regiment of Oswego, died yesterday afternoon at the home of his son, Ferris G. Hill . . . Death followed an illness of about a year. Mr. Hill fought in fourteen battles of the Civil War. Among engagements in which he participated were Bull Run and Fredericksburg and during the latter campaign he was wounded. As a member of Shank Post of the Grand Army of the republic at Fulton, Mr. Hill had always taken a leading interest in veterans' affairs. His home was at Dexterville, near Fulton. He resided there forty years previous to coming to this city . . . The funeral will be held at 11 o'clock Saturday morning . . . and . . . in the afternoon at Dexterville, where the body will be taken . . . ." German was a member of Post Schenck No. 271 GAR, Fulton. In 1890 he claimed a lung had been affected by the war. He and Mary were the parents of six children. They are buried in Fairdale Cemetery, Hannibal.

Robert G. Hill – Co. G

b. 1830 Delaware County, NY
d. 1866 Prattsburgh, Steuben, NY
m. Phoebe G. Brooks (1838-August 14, 1933) *ca.* 1856

NOTE: Robert's parents are unidentified. He was drafted, enrolling in the 147th at Springwater, Livingston, NY on July 25, 1863. He transferred to Co. F, 91st Regiment on June 5, 1865 and mustered out July 13th at Washington, DC. He applied for a pension on May 7, 1866 but died before the process could be completed. Phoebe, who never remarried, obtained a widow's pension. In 1890 she said that her husband had been plagued by chronic diarrhea. Phoebe fell at her son's home on August 13th, fracturing her hip. Her death was reported in *The Steuben Farmers' Advocate* August 17, 1933, 8: "The death of Mrs. Phoebe Hill who was born in Rush, N. Y., 95 years ago occurred at her home in Ingleside, Monday, August 14. She has lived in the town of Prattsburg for the past 53 years. She was the daughter of Joseph and Sally Brooks. She leaves one daughter, Mrs. Albert Graves and a son Delbert Hall, both of Ingleside, besides several grandchildren. The funeral was held this (Thursday) afternoon from the Christian Church at Ingleside. Mrs. Hill was the oldest life long resident of Ingleside and Prattsburg." She and Robert are buried in Ingleside Old Cemetery, Prattsburgh.

Robert Hoag – Co. E

b. 1844 Londonderry, Northern Ireland
d. February 5, 1933 Buffalo, Erie, NY
m. Caroline Houghton (October 2, 1846-December 25, 1927) 1866

NOTE: Robert was the son of Alexander (1816-1911) and Margaret "Peggy" Brown Hoag (1807-1904). In October 1861 he enlisted in Co. I, 37th New York Volunteers at Ellicottville, Cattaraugus, NY and was discharged for "disability" at Philadelphia, PA on September 24, 1862. He was drafted, enrolling in the 147th at Farmersville, Cattaraugus on August 20, 1863, and serving until discharged for "disability" on February 15, 1864. In 1890 he said he had acquired rheumatism and heart disease in 1864. His informative obituary appeared in *The Buffalo Courier-Express* February 8, 1933, 14: "Salamanca, Feb. 7. -- Robert Hoag, who died at his home, 892 West Avenue, Buffalo, Sunday night at the age of 91, was buried in the family plot in Wildwood Cemetery here this afternoon. The Rev. A. C. Elliott of the Congregational Church officiating. Mr. Hoag was an early builder in Salamanca, a carpenter and contractor who erected a number of buildings, among them the three-story business building at the northeast corner of Main Street and Wildwood Avenue, long owned by him. He was a son of the late Alexander Hoag, who came here from Ellicottville when the Erie Railroad was being built. Robert Hoag's brother, the late John Hoag, was at one time mayor of Salamanca. Mr. Hoag was the last survivor of a family which numbered nine children. He leaves two daughters, Dr. Myrtle Hoag and Miss Nellie Hoag of Buffalo." Caroline's death was reported in *The Salamanca Inquirer* December 30, 1927, 1: "The death of Mrs. Caroline Houghton Hoag, wife of Robert H. Hoag, and for many years a well known resident of Salamanca occurred at her home, 892 West avenue, Buffalo, Sunday following an illness of about a month. Mrs. Hoag was born in Bradford, Pa., October 2, 1846, and married Robert Hoag, who is a son of Alexander Hoag, pioneer resident of Salamanca, 61 years ago. She lived here many years, until the family moved to Buffalo 16 years ago. The family was one of the most prominent in Salamanca . . . While residing here Mrs. Hoag was a member of the Congregational church . . . The funeral service was held at the home Monday evening with Rev. Lewis G. Rogers, pastor of the Plymouth Congregational church officiating. The funeral party came to Salamanca Tuesday where burial was made in the Wildwood cemetery Tuesday afternoon . . . ." Their daughter, Myrtle (1868-1955), was director and chief of medical staff at the Protestant Home for Unprotected Children in Buffalo.

Charles Hoaglin – Co. E
b. October 22, 1849 Pennsylvania
d. January 20, 1946 Grapevine, Tarrant, TX
m1. Cordelia A. _____ (1858-ca. 1910) 1876
m2. Mary Frances "Fanny" Daniel McFarland (1868-1952) September 24, 1911

NOTE: Charles, a carpenter, may have been the son of John (1819-*post* 1850) and Fanny Hoaglin (1819-*post* 1850). On November 23, 1863 he enlisted in the 147th claiming to be 18 years and four months of age. His guardian, Thaddeus Cowan, gave consent, affirming the young man was 18, but with the stipulation that "his bounty money is paid to me." Charles transferred to Co. I, 91st Regiment on June 5, 1865 as Hoglan and mustered out near Washington, DC on July 3rd. From August 1873-August 1878 he was a soldier in Co. K, 11th US Infantry. In 1880 he and Cordelia were living in Tuscarora, Steuben, NY but by 1900 they had moved to Arkansas. I have been unable to find an exact DOD or gravesite for Cordelia. Mary Frances had previously been married to Felix McFarland (1867-*ante* 1911). She and Charles were married in Gentry, Benton, AR. His COD was apoplexy. Both are buried in Grapevine Cemetery.

Benton S. Holbrook – Co. G
b. December 1842 Volney, NY
d. October 19, 1920 Volney, NY
m. Harriet R. Coville (1844-November 29, 1924) 1867

NOTE: The son of Jesse (1812-1859) and Mary Lincoln Holbrook (1812-1856), Benton was a farmer. It was said he died in the house where he had lived his entire life. A draftee, he enrolled in the 147th at Oswego City on August 14, 1863. He was wounded at the battle of Hatcher's Run on February 6, 1865 and discharged on June 3, 1865 at Washington, DC. In 1890 he said he had been shot in the left thigh and had a "disease of the throat." He was a member of the Vermillion Grange and Hiram Sherman Post No. 434 GAR, Vermillion. He and Harriet were the parents of three children, two of whom were living in 1900. On the 1910 census the enumerator wrote that Benton had been married twice. I have located no evidence of a previous marriage. He was single in 1865. Benton and Harriet are buried in North Volney Cemetery.

Hamilton T. Holden – Co. K
b. 1842 Lockport, Niagara, NY
d. December 19, 1895 Lockport, Niagara, NY
m. Mary J. Bowen (1845-January 7, 1911) *ante* 1870

NOTE: Hamilton's mother was Nancy M. Holden (1818-*post* 1880), a widow with two children in 1855. His father is so far unidentified. Hamilton's sister Caroline had been born in Seneca County in 1836 and the family had lived in Lockport for 11 years. Hamilton, a shoemaker, served in the 28th NYSV from November 1861-June 1863. He was a substitute for John Manning, Wheatfield, Niagara, NY and enrolled in the 147th on July 2, 1863 at Wheatfield. He transferred to Co. K, 91st Regiment on June 5, 1865 and mustered out near Washington, DC on July 3rd. Hamilton and Mary had no children. He is buried in Cold Springs Cemetery, Lockport. Mary is buried in Schaeffer Cemetery, Lockport.

Christian Holte – Co. C
b. 1830 Bremen, Germany
d. ? ?
m. ?

NOTE: Little is known about this soldier's life prior to entering the military except that he was a cigar maker. He attempted to enlist in the 76th Regiment on March 10, 1865 from the 5th New York Congressional District, which in 1865 was composed of part of Manhattan. He was unassigned and sent the same day to the 147th. On June 5th he transferred to Co. H, 91st Regiment and mustered out near Washington, DC on July 3rd. Nothing confirmable has been located beyond that date.

William W. Hosford – Co. D
b. 1830 St. Lawrence County, NY
d. May 10, 1864 Laurel Hill, Augusta, VA
m. Julia A. Maxwell (August 1834-July 14, 1920) January 1, 1851

NOTE: William's parentage is a mystery. When he applied for a marriage license on December 24, 1850 in Erie County, OH he claimed his father was dead and his mother, name not provided, had given written consent to the union since he was not yet 21 years old. Julia's guardian, H. Burton, gave his consent since she too was a legal minor. Their first son, Joel (1852-?), was born in Ohio but the next five boys were all born in Chautauqua County. William enrolled as a substitute for DeGrant Lapham at Westfield, Chautauqua County on August 18, 1863. His COD was "gsw through the heart." His burial site is unknown. Julia married Charles W. Wright (1840-June 1, 1918) on December 25, 1865 as his second wife. He died in Gowanda State Hospital. Julia died in Albion, Erie, PA at the home of her son, Albert Wright. She and Charles are buried in Mayville Cemetery, Chautauqua County.

Thomas Howard – Co. D

b. 1842 Ireland

d. ? ?

m. ?

NOTE: Thomas was a draftee, enrolling in the 147th at Utica, Oneida, NY on August 21, 1863. According to his muster roll card he was "absent, sick" when transferred to Co. B, 91st Regiment on June 5, 1865. *The Adjutant-General's Report* for that regiment does not list him. I have located no other documents pertaining to him and it is altogether possible that he did not survive.

Ossian Howe – Co. F

b. 1829 Cortland County, NY

d. December 15, 1863 1st Division, 1st Army Corps Hospital, Kelly's Ford, VA

m. ------

NOTE: Ossian, son of Nathan (1797-1851) and Nancy C. Mudgett Howe (1804-1888), was a draftee, enrolling in the 147th at Westfield, Chautauqua, NY on August 18, 1863. According to *Deaths of Volunteers*, his COD was "inflammation of lungs or measles." In 1884 Nancy successfully applied for a pension. Ossian's twin brother Oscar enrolled in Co. I, 187th Regiment at Dunkirk, Chautauqua, NY on September 24, 1864 and was killed in action at Hatcher's Run, VA on October 27th. Nathan and Nancy are buried in Green Cemetery, Great Valley, Chautauqua.

Philander Hudson – Co. D

b. October 22, 1847 Cayuga County, NY

d. February 17, 1910 National Soldiers' Home, Grand Rapids, Kent, MI

m1. Melvina "Mary" Van Buren (1843-1878) *ante* 1870

m2. Elizabeth "Bessie" J. Engle (1837-June 29, 1920) June 20, 1897

NOTE: Philander was the son of Abram (1804-1877) and Elizabeth Calkins Hudson (1806-1860). Their surname was also spelled Hodgson. He was a substitute, as an entry in *The Town Clerks' Registers* noted: "Wells Allen paid Philander Hudson $300 to go for substitute – was discharged a little less than a year on account of disability." Philander lied about his age, claiming to be 18 when enrolling in the 147th at Auburn, Cayuga, NY on July 28, 1863. He was severely wounded at Haymarket, VA on October 19, 1863 and was discharged from Emory Hospital, Washington, DC on September 13, 1864. On admission forms for the various national homes his disabilities were, among others, loss of fingers and paralysis due to wounds suffered at Haymarket. It appears that he lost the mobility of his legs. I have not located a marriage date for Philander and Melvina but in 1870 they were living in Midland Co., MI. They had no children. Beginning in 1893 Philander was in and out of many national homes across the country. He and Bessie were married in Grand Rapids. He said he had been married once and she, twice. He used the surname Hodgson and she, her maiden name but under occupation she listed "matron." Philander, according to his death certificate, was mentally deranged, committing suicide by cutting his throat. He was buried in the Home Cemetery. Melvina's grave has not been located. Bessie's COD was apoplexy. She is buried in Oak Hill Cemetery, Grand Rapids. Philander's brother Orville (1844-1908) was a soldier in Co. F, 94th Regiment.

Alvin A. Hughes – Co. F
b. March 14, 1842 Fulton County, NY
d. *ca.* 1890 ?
m. Sarah E. Burbank (?-?) ?

NOTE: Alvin may have been the son of Samuel (1813-*post* 1865) and Catherine Hughes (1819-*ante* 1865) despite the fact that his muster roll card provides a name of James for his father. It also seems he was born in Fulton County, not Schoharie, although in 1865 his father stated he himself had been born there. Alvin, under the name Alain A. Hughs, enlisted in Co. H, 9th NY Cavalry on October 5, 1861 at Hermitage, Wyoming, NY. He was discharged in Washington, DC on May 13, 1862 for "disability." In 1863 he was drafted, enrolling in the 147th on July 15th at Bolivar, Allegany, NY. He was again discharged for "disability" on Washington, DC on August 31, 1864. Someone named Sarah E. Burbank, claiming to be his widow, successfully applied for a pension in New York State on March 23, 1891. No other information is available.

Enderson Hunt – Co. K
b. September 1843 Nichols, Tioga, NY
d. November 22, 1910 Nichols, Tioga, NY
m. Eliza A. Loveland (March 7, 1846-May 29, 1922) 1885

NOTE: Enderson, whose name was also spelled Anderson, was the son of Seth (1799-1882) and Mary Hunt (1810-1886). He was a draftee, enrolling in the 147th at Nichols on July 15, 1863. Though nominally transferred to Co. K, 91st Regiment on June 5, 1865 under the name Andrew, he actually was discharged on May 27th. In 1890 he said he had been shot through the thigh. The date of his wounding is unknown but since he applied for a pension on June 10, 1865 the injury was serious. Enderson was a member of William Warwick Post No. 529 GAR, Nichols. He and Eliza, a native of Pennsylvania, had one child. They are buried in Osborne Hill Cemetery, Windham, Bradford, PA. Eliza's COD was "aortic insufficiency" combined with chronic nephritis. She died in South Creek, Bradford, PA. Her DOD is not inscribed on the gravestone but is found on her death certificate.

Edward Hunter – Co. I
b. 1845 Canada
d. ? ?
m. ?

NOTE: Edward, a farmer, was a substitute for Robert Barren, Jr., Rochester, Monroe, NY. He enrolled in the 147th on August 4, 1863 at Rochester and was discharged on September 3, 1864. Nothing else has been learned, including parents' names.

John Hurley – Co. K
b. May 1846 New Brunswick, Canada
d. December 10, 1900 Oswego City, NY
m. Bridget Griffin (May 1851-July 10, 1936) 1868

NOTE: John, a ship master, enlisted in the 147th at Oswego on March 27, 1864 for a term of one year. He transferred to Co. K, 91st Regiment on June 5th, 1865 and was discharged at an undisclosed date at Washington, DC. An obituary, appearing in *The Oswego Daily Times* December 10, 1900, 8, paid homage to an esteemed member of the community: "Capt. John Hurley, one of Oswego's best known citizens and pioneer vessel captains died this morning at his home in West Van Buren Street, after a brief but fatal illness. Captain Hurley was fifty-four years old and since a boy had followed the lakes and while yet a young man was in command of vessels plying between Oswego and Chicago. Among those he sailed were the Guiding Star, Blazing Star, Mystic Star, White Star, Iron City. He also served as mate of the Iron Duke and the past season he was mate of the steamer Bulgaria which burned at the wharf at Buffalo about a month ago. Captain Hurley was aboard when the fire was discovered and with the firemen worked hard to save the steamer from the flames. He contracted a severe cold which resulted fatally. Captain Hurley was one of the best known masters along the chain of lakes and justly so for he was a thorough seaman, just in all his dealings with his men, of cheerful disposition and a devoted husband and father. He was a member of the Ship Masters' Association, B. P. O. Elks and Branch 140, C. M. B. A. He is survived by a widow and seven children . . . ." An editorial published in *The Oswego*

Palladium-Times on December 11, 1900 contained further praise for the captain: "There may have been better fresh water sailors than Captain 'Johnny' Hurley, who died in this city yesterday, but this generation has never met them . . . ." Bridget's death was reported in *The Oswego Palladium-Times* July 11, 1936, 2: "Oswego friends of Mrs. Bridget Griffin Hurley, widow of Captain John Hurley, former highly esteemed resident of Oswego, will regret to learn of her death which occurred shortly after 8 o'clock Friday evening at the home of her daughter, Mrs. Nelson M. Owen . . . Rochester with whom she had made her home for upwards of fifteen years. Mrs. Hurley was born in Oswego and passed her entire life in the First Ward with the exception of the years she lived in Rochester. In her long and useful life, Mrs. Hurley gained many friends and was known as a kindly neighbor and earnest Christian woman. Her husband was one of the best known vessel masters plying the Great Lakes. The family home for many years was located in West Van Buren street and was always one of hospitality to friends and acquaintances. Mrs. Hurley was gracious and helpful in her personal contacts

Captain John Hurley was a well-known and much respected lake sailor who put his career on hold to serve in the Union Army.
Author's Collection

and was happiest in her home surrounded by her family. Mrs. Hurley always retained her membership and interest in St. Mary's church where her marriage to Captain Hurley took place. She was affiliated with the Rosary and Altar societies and was a member of the L. C. B. A. . . . ." The captain and his lady are buried in St. Paul's Cemetery, Oswego. His parents' names are unknown.

Calvin C. Hyde – Co. F
b. 1842 Allegany County, NY
d. September 16, 1864 Andersonville, Sumter, GA
m. ------

NOTE: Calvin C. was an alias used by Clark C. Hyde, son of Clark Kendrick (1813-1899) and Caroline Hyde (1818-1900). A draftee, he enrolled in the 147th at

Friendship, Allegany, NY on July 16, 1863. Although originally listed as MIA after the battle of the Wilderness, May 5, 1864 he was captured by the Confederates and sent to Andersonville where he died of *scorbutus* (scurvy). He is buried in Andersonville National Cemetery. He was erroneously listed as a member of the 14th Regiment in *Deaths of Volunteers*.

Henry Hyde – Co. B
b. January 17, 1820 Germany
d. March 10, 1899 Allegany, Cattaraugus, NY
m. Susanna Elizabeth Holl (1817-February 23, 1899) January 1, 1846

NOTE: Henry, a shoemaker, was born Georg Heinrich Heid, son of Johann Valentin (1794-1837) and Elizabeth Kolb Heid (1798-1880). He was a substitute for Theodore Ballen, Allegany, and enrolled in the 147th at that place on August 20, 1863. He transferred to Co. G, 91st Regiment on June 5, 1865 and mustered out at Ball's Cross Roads, VA on July 3rd. In 1890 he said he had suffered a gunshot wound. When he was admitted to the Bath National Home on April 20, 1897 he elaborated, saying he had been wounded in the head and in the right thigh. He was a member of Ira Thurber Post No. 584 GAR. He and Susanna were the parents of seven children. Phoebe (1846-1929), the eldest, was born on board the ship conveying the family to America. The youngest, Henry (1859-1859), died after a 38-day illness deemed the "summer complaint." Henry and Susanna are buried in Allegany Cemetery.

George Jakes – Co. B
b. 1836 Toronto, Ontario, Canada
d. March 2, 1913 National Soldiers' Home, Hampton, VA
m. ------

NOTE: George, whose parents are unknown, was a railroad engineer. A substitute for Philip J. Bottleberger, Lancaster, Erie, NY, he enrolled at Buffalo on August 14, 1863. He claimed to be 21 but on his admission form to the National Home in Hampton, VA in 1909 he was 73, suggesting he was born in 1836. He transferred to Co. G, 91st Regiment on June 5, 1865 and mustered out near Washington, DC on July 3rd. His COD was "aortic and mitral regurgitation." He is buried in the Hampton National Cemetery.

Henry B. James – Co. G
b. 1840 Greenwich, Washington County, NY
d. August 30, 1905 Pittsburg, Crawford, KS
m. Sarepta C. Rice (February 29, 1844-October 10, 1914) April 29, 1860

NOTE: The son of Gardner LeRoy (1816-1894) and Catharine Caulkins James (1821-1864), Henry was drafted, enrolling at Oswego City on August 13, 1863. He was wounded at the battle of Cold Harbor, VA on June 1, 1864. His injury was described as a gunshot wound of the right ilium, fracturing the bone. Although nominally transferred to Co. F, 91st Regiment on June 5, 1865, he was discharged for "disability" from Ira Harris Hospital, Albany, NY on October 13, 1865 "as of 147th." He had a variety of occupations. When he entered the military, he was a shoemaker. In 1900 he was a teamster. He joined the Baxter Springs Post No. 123 GAR shortly before he died. His death was announced in *The Pittsburg Daily Headlight* August 30, 1905: "Henry James, an old resident of Pittsburg, died this morning about 6:20 o'clock, at the family home, 115 East 13th street, from the effects of a stroke of paralysis which he received Saturday evening. Mr. James had, about a week ago, purchased a restaurant on West Fourth street, near the fire department, and he was in the restaurant when he was stricken with what at first was thought to be sun stroke, but later proved to be paralysis. His entire side was paralyzed. From Saturday evening until death came the old gentleman was in a helpless condition, and all hope for his recovery was given up. He was an old resident of Pittsburg and had for years been engaged in the restaurant business in this city. During the past year he was located at Baxter, but he recently returned to Pittsburg. The deceased was an old soldier. He was 65 years old . . . The remains will be shipped to Baxter Springs on the Frisco tomorrow morning, and the funeral will occur at Baxter tomorrow." He and Sarepta, who died in Baxter Springs, Cherokee, KS, were the parents of three children. The couple is buried in Baxter Springs Cemetery.

Lyman James – Co. C
b. 1833 Greenwich, Washington, NY
d. ? ?
m. Mary Gillis (1831-1897) *ante* 1860

NOTE: Lyman was the son of James (1799-1882) and Elizabeth E. Ragnatz James (1803-1853). He apparently enlisted in the 147th at Hannibal, NY on March 14, 1864 for a term of one year. He was captured at the battle of the Wilderness on May 5th and sent first to Andersonville and then to Florence, SC. He was paroled on December 9, 1864 and discharged at Elmira, Chemung, NY on January 2, 1866. His muster roll card states he "never joined Regt after capture." He applied for and obtained a pension in 1880. He was enumerated with Mary in Hannibal in 1865, 1870, and 1875. In 1880 he and Mary may have been living in Victory, Cayuga, NY where he was a hotel keeper. In 1882 a man named Lyman James was working as a clerk and boarding in the Cleveland Hotel in Oswego. Some researchers have claimed he died in November 1887 but I have found no evidence for that. Mary was enumerated in

1892 in Hannibal and it is altogether possible Lyman was dead, but, since she did not apply for a widow's pension although she lived until 1897, it is possible that he moved away and outlived her. Mary is buried with her parents, Hector (1796-1864) and Mary Hawley Gillis (1805-1871), in Hannibal Village Cemetery. A man named Lyman James (1806-1888) is buried in the James lot in that cemetery but he was a son of Brinton (1779-1863) and Abigail Phillips James (1773-1840). Mary's brother Charles (1837-1865) was a member of the 110th Regiment.

Thomas James – Co. E
b. 1828 Rutland County, VT
d. January 21, 1886 East Sharon, Potter, PA
m. Ruth Lunn (1836-1904) *ca.* 1856

NOTE: Thomas was the son of Thomas, Sr. (1790-1867) and Mary Ann White James (1796-1860). His DOB and POB are matters of conjecture. Early census records show him born in England but later ones place him in Vermont, where his parents are buried. Although he claimed to have been born in 1828 when he entered the service, his gravestone puts his birth date at 1831. He was a draftee and enrolled in the 147th at Nichols, Tioga, NY on July 15, 1863. He was wounded and captured at the battle of Hatcher's Run on February 6, 1865. According to his muster roll card, he was admitted to a Confederate hospital at Petersburg, VA on February 18, 1865. After being paroled on April 1, 1865 he was sent to Stanton Hospital, Washington, DC where his left thigh was amputated. He was discharged from that place for "disability" on September 6th. He and Ruth were the parents of five children, only two of whom lived to adulthood. Thomas and Ruth are buried in East Sharon Cemetery, Honeoye, Potter, PA.

Robert Tubbs Jenkins – Co. E
b. May 28, 1845 Chemung County, NY
d. April 28, 1935 Yuba City, Sutter, CA
m. Hannah Brewster Pedrick (September 1844-October 2, 1920) 1867

NOTE: Robert, son of Samuel Tubbs (1814-1849) and Catherine Mosher Jenkins (1823-1907), was a substitute for George O. Reynolds and enrolled in the 147th at Elmira, Chemung on July 20, 1863. He was transferred to the VRC on October 20, 1864 and finally discharged on November 28, 1865 at David's Island, New York City Harbor. By 1880 the family, including four children, had moved to Garfield, Pawnee, KS. The youngest, Robert Wheeler, was born in Kansas in 1886. In 1920, the year Hannah died, the couple was living in Yuba. An obituary appearing in *The Yuma City Appeal Democrat* April 29, 19355 outlined his long, interesting life: "Robert Tubbs Jenkins, 89, believed to be the last Civil War veteran in Sutter county and famed as probably the last survivor of the military guard of honor at the bier of Abraham Lincoln following his assassination, died early Sunday morning at the home of his son, H. B. Jenkins, on Wilbur avenue, Yubba City. Jenkins, a resident of Sutter county for the past 23 years, had been in failing health for several years. He was a native of Elmira, N. Y., and would have observed his 90th birthday next May 28. The veteran soldier, although not a member of any local G. A. R. post, since he enlisted in New York, became known as probably the last local Civil War survivor at the time of the death of Judge W. E. Tucker of Yuba City several years ago. Jenkins treasured among his possessions his army service record and the mourning insignia he wore when assigned to his solemn post in the guard of honor of Lincoln's bier in New York. All local military organizations today were to plan for joint participation in full military rites at Jenkins' funeral . . . ." Both Robert and Hannah are buried in Yuba City Cemetery.

Benjamin Jennings – Co. E

b. 1827 Massachusetts

d. ? ?

m. ?

NOTE: Little is known about Benjamin, a bartender, who was a substitute for Conrad Tealhoner, Buffalo. He enrolled in the 147th on August 7, 1863 at Buffalo, allegedly 36 years of age. On September 20th, his age was 20. On January 1, 1865 he was transferred to Co. C, 23rd Regiment, VRC. That outfit mustered out on December 5, 1865. No other information is available.

Charles H. Jennings – Co. K

b. January 24, 1842 Walworth, Wayne, NY

d. October 12, 1864 Andersonville, Sumter, GA

m. ------

NOTE: Charles was the son of David (1817-1900) and Hester Weaver Jennings (1819-1894). He was a draftee and enrolled in the 147th at Auburn, Cayuga, NY on July 24, 1863. His muster roll card shows he was captured and died from wounds. Although the date of his capture was not noted on the muster card, *The Town Clerks' Registers* claimed he was "killed or taken prisoner at the Battle of the Wilderness May 4 [sic], 1864." *Deaths of Volunteers* and Andersonville Interment Records concur that he died on October 12, 1864. His entry in *Deaths of Volunteers* recorded his COD as *vulnus sclopeticum* (gunshot wound) although erroneously placing him in the 149th Regiment. In 1866 his parents both successfully applied for pensions. They died in Bushnell, Montcalm, MI and are buried in Sunny Hill Cemetery.

Amos Johnson – Co. C

b. 1839 Tompkins County, NY

d. February 27, 1893 Mountain Grove, Wright, MO

m1. Emily _____ (1840-May 3, 1863) *ca.* 1860

m2. Mary Jane _____ (1846-*post* 1893) *ca.* 1864

NOTE: Amos, son of James A. (1805-1875) and Mary Esther Johnson (1801-1864), was drafted, enrolling in the 147th at Catlin, Chemung, NY on July 21, 1863. His time in the military was short since he was discharged for "disability" on October 9, 1863, his disability described in *The Town Clerks' Registers* as "constitutional weakness." In 1890 he reported no disabilities. Amos and Mary Jane were the parents of Emma (1871-?). In 1880 the family was living in Tuscarora, Steuben, NY but by 1890 was in Missouri. Amos is buried in Mountain Valley Cemetery, Mountain Grove, Wright, MO. Mary Jane applied for and obtained a pension but what happened to her after Amos' death is unknown. She may have remarried. Emily is buried with James and Mary Esther in Moreland Cemetery, Dix, Schuyler, NY.

William Johnson – Co. G

b. 1834 New York State

d. ? ?

m. ?

NOTE: William, a sailor, was a substitute for James H. Kamerling, Buffalo. He enrolled in the 147th at Buffalo on August 7, 1863 and transferred to the VRC on March 25, 1864. Nothing else has been learned.

William Johnson – Co. B

b. 1846 Cayuga County, NY

d. ? ?

m. ?

NOTE: William was a draftee although he was still underage if the age, 17, given on the muster card is correct. He enrolled at Dunkirk, Chautauqua, NY on August 8, 1863. He was discharged on June 3, 1865 at Elmira, Chemung, NY, suggesting he had been wounded or was so seriously ill that he was sent to a hospital. His muster card shows he transferred to Co. G, 91st Regiment on June 5, 1865 but his name does not appear in *The Adjutant-General's Report* for that regiment. Nothing else confirmable has been learned about him. Someone named William H. Johnson, born in Cayuga County in 1846, married Elizabeth Devone in Oshtemo, Kalamazoo, MI on March 28, 1868 but whether or not this is the correct person is unknown.

Edwin Peters Jones – Co. E

b. 1845 England
d. March 17, 1888 Chicago, Cook, IL
m1. Emily Randall Hartgrove (November 1846-September 22, 1910) June 10, 1864
m2. Mary C. _____ (?-?) *ca.* 1881

NOTE: Edwin, a house painter, was a substitute for Robert Neale, Jr. He enrolled at Big Flats, Chemung, NY on July 27, 1863, transferred to Co. K, 91st on June 5, 1865 and mustered out near Washington, DC on July 3rd. Emily had previously been married to John Hartgrove (1841-1868). She and Edwin were divorced before 1880. Little is known about Mary except that she applied for and obtained a widow's pension. Many women named Mary Jones lived in Chicago and it has been impossible to determine the correct one. Edwin was buried in Rosehill Cemetery, Chicago and a Mary Budlong Jones (1857-1926) is also buried there. Whether or not she is the correct person is unknown. Edwin's death was reported in *The Inter Ocean* March 24, 1888, 16: "Edwin Jones, a member of Godfrey Weitzel Post, No. 425, G. A. R., and Wicker Park Lodge, No. 1,967, Knights of Honor, died Saturday morning at his residence, No. 330 Milwaukee avenue . . . While about to be seated at the breakfast table, he was attacked with a stroke of paralysis, which affected his right side from head to foot, and was unconscious to the time of his death. The funeral takes place at his residence, Monday at 1 p.m., the services to be held by Wicker Park Lodge, No. 1,967, thence to Rose Hill by carriages. The funeral services will be held at the grave by the Godfrey Weitzel Post. Comrades and brothers of the deceased are invited to attend." His parents are unidentified.

Ezra Curtis Jones – Co. E

b. October 31, 1836 Greenfield, Hillsborough, NH
d. October 12, 1864 Andersonville, Sumter, GA
m. ------

NOTE: Ezra, also known by his middle name, was the son of Rev. Ezra (1804-1888) and Cyrintha B. Richards Jones (1807-1860). Like his father, he was a clergyman. He first saw duty in Co. G, 18th Regiment NYSV from May-September 1861 when he was discharged for "disability." He was then drafted, enrolling in the 147th at Auburn, Cayuga, NY on July 25, 1863. He was wounded and taken captive on May 5, 1864 at the battle of the Wilderness. Sent to Andersonville, he died of chronic diarrhea, according to *Deaths of Volunteers*. His entry in *The Town Clerks' Registers* says he died of starvation. Although he is buried in Andersonville National Cemetery, a cenotaph for him can be seen in Resthaven Cemetery, Phelps, Ontario, NY. His brother, Edward Richard (1841-1905), was a member of Co. B, 85th Regiment, serving from September 1861-August 1862 when discharged for "disability."

George Jones – Co. B

b. 1842 Canada

d. ? ?

m. ?

NOTE: George, a boatman, was a substitute for William A. Farnsworth and enrolled in the 147th at Pomfret, Chautauqua, NY on August 17, 1863. Little can be deduced about him or his military career. He was accused of desertion because he left a hospital in Elmira, Chemung, NY on August 29, 1864. On November 25, 1887 the War Department notified the New York Adjutant-General's Office that the charge had been removed and George was considered discharged as of August 29, 1864. It appears, therefore, that someone was attempting to obtain a pension but the identity of the applicant is unknown. I have located no pension record for him.

Thomas Jones – Co. C

b. 1832 Monroe County, NY

d. *post* 1895 ?

m. ?

NOTE: Jones, a farmer, was a substitute for Willard H. Presley. He enrolled in the 147th at Olean, Cattaraugus, NY on August 22, 1863. At some point he was on "detached duty in division train." He transferred to Co. H, 91st Regiment on June 5, 1865 and mustered out on July 3rd near Washington, DC. He applied for a pension on October 28, 1895, place not specified, but did not obtain a certificate. He may have died before the process could be completed.

William D. Jones – Co. D

b. 1842 Cayuga County, NY

d. November 23, 1907 Altoona, Blair, PA

m. Catherine "Kate" Stout (September 2, 1862-October 7, 1933) 1884

NOTE: William's parents are reputed to be Horatio (1809-?) and Almira Jones (1817-?). A draftee, he enrolled in the 147th at Canandaigua, Ontario, NY on July 25, 1863. He was wounded in action at Bethesda Church, VA on June 2, 1864 and listed as a patient in Haddington General Hospital, Philadelphia, PA on August 31, 1864. His muster card contains no further information but his Pennsylvania Veteran's Burial Card shows he left the service on December 13, 1864. Both he and Catherine applied for pensions but neither was successful. It may be that William left the military without being formally discharged. Hs death was reported in *The Altoona Morning Tribune* November 25, 1907: "At 11:30 Saturday morning William D. Jones, a well known resident of the Eighth ward, and a veteran shopman, died at his home, 607

Sixth street, of a complication of diseases. He had been ailing for the past several weeks but his condition was not considered serious, he being able to attend to his work daily. Saturday morning he was unable to go to work and later went to bed, grew rapidly worse until he passed away. Deceased was born in New York state and was aged 62 years. He had resided in this city for many years and was employed in the Pennsylvania Railroad company's car shops. He is survived by his wife and five children, all at home . . . The funeral will take place at 2 o'clock Tuesday afternoon . . . ." COD was apoplexy and arteriosclerosis. Catherine's passing was noted in *The Altoona Tribune* October 9, 1933, 12: "Mrs. Catherine Jones, widow of William D. Jones . . . died at her home at 9:45 a. m. Saturday, after an extended illness. She was born September 2, 1862, in Altoona, a daughter of John and Fanny (Whitman) Stout. Her husband died 25 years ago . . . She was a member of First Baptist church. The body may be viewed at the Tobias and Laughlin funeral home where services will be held at 2:30 p. m. Tuesday, in charge of Rev. Carey S. Thomas . . . ." Catherine's COD was tuberculosis. She and William are buried in Rosehill Cemetery, Altoona.

William Jones – Co. C

b. 1826 Cumberland County, ME
d. ? ?
m. ?

NOTE: William, a sailor, was a substitute for Moses McMillan and enrolled in the 147th at Laona, Chautauqua, NY on August 21, 1863. He transferred to the US Navy at an unknown date. A man named William Jones, born 1826 in Maine, was inducted into the US Navy at Brooklyn, NY on May 4, 1864. His description is roughly the same as that on the muster roll card but identity cannot be established with certainty. No other information is available.

William Thompson Judson – Co. G

b. 1829 Orange County, NY
d. November 28, 1892 Webb Mills, Chemung, NY
m. Isadora "Dora" Marshall (March 1849-March 31, 1929) October 9, 1871

NOTE: William, son of Elijah (1800-1892) and Mary Elizabeth Thompson Judson (1809-1886), was a substitute for Henry W. Beadle, enrolling in the 147th at Elmira on July 20, 1863. He transferred to Co. F, 91st Regiment on June 5, 1865 and mustered out near Washington, DC on July 3rd. He and Isadora, the mother of at least four children, are buried in Woodlawn Cemetery, Elmira.

William Kaswurm – Co. F

b. 1835 Germany

d. ? ?

m. ?

NOTE: William's parents are unidentified. A furmaker by occupation, he enrolled in the 147th as a substitute for George Weaver at Oswego City on September 2, 1863. The records are sketchy but apparently he transferred to Co. G, 95th Regiment in February, 1864 and was captured at the battle of the Wilderness on May 5th. The muster rolls from June 30, 1864 through February 28, 1865 show he was absent. He was paroled, place unknown, on December 15, 1864 and while he was in the hospital he was transferred to Co. D. He rejoined the regiment on May 16, 1865 and mustered out July 16th at Washington, DC. The interesting part of this story is that he does not appear on the muster roll of the 95th Regiment. On August 30, 1869 a man named William Kaswurm enlisted in the US Marine Corps and was honorably discharged on August 31, 1873. He may or may not be the same person.

Frederick Kelkenberg – Co. F

b. January 24, 1839 Hanover, Germany

d. May 9, 1909 Akron, Erie, NY

m. Sybil E. Bratt (1830-June 2, 1914) 1867

NOTE: Frederick's surname was variously spelled. I use that on the gravestone. According to the 1900 census he immigrated to the United States in 1861 and became a naturalized citizen. He was a substitute for J. C. S. Choat, Lancaster, Erie, NY. He enrolled in the 147th at Buffalo on August 14, 1863, transferred to Co. A, 91st Regiment on June 5, 1865, and mustered out on July 3rd near Washington, DC. Kelkenberg was a farmer and lived in Erie County for the remainder of his life. He and Sybil had one child, Franklin (1868-1875). All three are buried in Evergreen Cemetery, Akron. Sybil's DOD is not on the stone. It was located on a pension payment card.

James McFee "Mac" Keller – Co. F

b. December 15, 1837 Hume, Allegany, NY

d. June 25, 1919 Portville, Cattaraugus, NY

m. Elvira G. Burdick Tanner (1840-June 8, 1924) *ca.* 1862

NOTE: Mac, son of John Henry (1795-1875) and Elmina Margaret Reury Keller (1793-1860), was drafted, enrolling in the 147th at Genesee, Allegany, NY on July 10, 1863. He received a gunshot wound to the left side of his chest at Petersburg, VA on June 12, 1864 and was discharged for "disability" from DeCamp Hospital, David's Island,

New York Harbor. He and Elvira, who had previously been married to Albert H. Tanner (1831-1859), were the parents of six, five of whom survived to adulthood. Keller's death was reported in *The Portville Review* June 26, 1919, 1: "M. J. Keller, a well known and highly respected citizen of Portville, died at his home on Brooklyn street yesterday morning at 2:30 after an illness of two days from paralysis. He was stricken Monday morning about 5 o'clock and never regained consciousness. He had suffered severely from pains in his head but aside from that was as well as usual. Deceased was born at Hume, Allegany county, December 15, 1837 and at the time of his death was 81 years old. He came to this vicinity when ten years of age, and has been a resident in and near Portville for 71 years. He followed farming

James McFee Keller was wounded in the chest at Petersburg, VA and discharged for disability.
Mary Lou Thomas

all his life until seven years ago, when he retired and moved to Portville, where he has lived since. He served in the Civil War a member of Company A, 147th New York Regiment. He was a member of H. W. Wessel Post G. A. R., and Portville lodge of Masons . . . Funeral services will be held at his late home Saturday afternoon at 2 o'clock, interment in West Genesee cemetery." More information is found in John S. Minard's *Allegany County and Its People. A Centennial Memorial History of Allegany County, New York,* 1896, 896: ". . . Mr. Keller has been assessor for three years, and in 1875 was census enumerator. He has always affiliated with the Democratic party . . . ." Elvira, whose death was reported in *The Bolivar Breeze* June 12, 1924, died at her daughter's home in Obi, Allegany, NY. She is buried with her husband in West Genesee Cemetery, Obi.

Lutheran Theron Kelley – Co. G
b. 1831 Barton, Tioga, NY
d. December 30, 1909 Lockwood, Tioga, NY
m. Mary E. Lyons (1834-December 11, 1917) 1855

NOTE: The son of John (1808-1874) and Rebecca Elston Kelley (1810-?), Lutheran was drafted, enrolling in the 147th at Barton on July 14, 1863. He was discharged from the service at Elmira, NY on July 17, 1865 as a paroled prisoner. His muster roll card says he was MIA at an unknown date. No other information is available. In

1890 he did not report any disability. He and Mary were the parents of five, three of whom were living in 1900. His death was reported in *The Waverly Free Press and Tioga County Record* January 7, 1910, 3: ". . . The funeral of Lutheran Kelley, the well known Reniff farmer, was held at his home Sunday, a large number of friends being present. The pastor of the Spencer M. E. church conducted the service. The burial, which was at the Forest Home [Cemetery] in this village, was in charge of Waverly Lodge, F. &. A. M. . . . ." Mary is also buried in Forest Home Cemetery, Waverly.

John Key – Co. C
b. 1843 Wabasha County, MN
d. ? ?
m. ?

NOTE: John apparently enlisted in the 147th at New York City on March 14, 1865. Although his muster roll card says he was born in Wabash County, Minnesota, it was more likely Wabasha. He transferred to Co. H, 91st on June 5, 1865 and mustered out near Washington, DC on July 3rd. Nothing else is known.

Morrill Woodworth Kidder – Co. F
b. March 20, 1832 Enosburgh, Franklin, VT
d. October 22, 1920 Kendall, Orleans, NY
m. Emma A. Wilson (May 1839-February 18, 1936) October 27, 1857

NOTE: Morrill, son of John (1804-1850) and Charlotte Eliza Woodworth Kidder (1807-1833), was a draftee, enrolling in the 147th at Kendall on August 8, 1863. An informative biography of him appeared in *Landmarks of Orleans County, New York*, 1894, Part III, 191: ". . . Morrill W. Kidder was enrolled in Co. F, 147th N. Y. Infy., August 14, 1863, and soon after was promoted Scout of 2d Brigade 1s Division 1st Army Corps. In the spring of 1864 the corps was attached to the 5th Corps, forming the 4th Division, and on May 6th Mr. Kidder was made chief of the scouts of this division, being brevetted second lieutenant by General James S. Wadsworth. He served in this capacity until June 18, when, in front of Petersburg, he was severely wounded in the shoulder joint of the right arm, which he was obliged to have amputated, and was honorably discharged November 30, 1864. Mr. Kidder is the only survivor of a party of six soldiers who attempted to break through the Confederate ranks on May 6th, at the battle of the Wilderness, when General Wadsworth was killed, to secure the body of that brave officer. In local affairs Mr. Kidder has been very active serving as justice of the peace twelve years, collector nine years, and deputy sheriff one term, and was a charter member and organizer of David Jones Post, No. 298, G.A.R., in 1882, which he has continually served as commander or as senior vice commander. At the formation of the Orleans County Veteran Regiment he was elected its major, serving one term, and since then until 1893 was its lieutenant colonel. In June, 1893, that organization became the Orleans County Veteran Association and Mr. Kidder was elected its president. October 27, 1857 he married Emma A., daughter of Edson Wilson, and granddaughter of Captain Daniel Wilson, who commanded a body of troops which prevented the British from landing at Charlotte in 1812. Their children are Mary E. (Mrs. H. J. Merrill) and Etta A. (Mrs. W. P. Whitney)." Emma's death was announced in *The Clyde Herald* February 26, 1936, 4: "North Rose. – Mrs. Emma A Kidder, widow of the late Morrill W. Kidder of Kendall, New York died at her home in North Rose on Tuesday, February 18th. Mrs. Kidder was probably the oldest person in the town of Rose. She was born in Penfield, N.Y., May 7, 1839, the fifth of eight children of Edson and Polly T. (Nichols) Wilson. At an early age she removed with her parents to Kendall where on October 27, 1857 she was married to Morrill W. Kidder . . . Until about two years ago Mrs. Kidder was in splendid health and enjoyed life but since that time she has been an invalid. Funeral services were held from the home of Mrs. Estella Roney on Sunday p.m. and the remains were taken to Clyde and placed in the vault in Maple Grove Cemetery. In the spring burial will take place at Kendall, N. Y." Morrill and Emma are buried in Beechwood Cemetery, Kendall.

Victor Putnam Kinnan – Co. H

b. August 20, 1842 Southport, Chemung, NY
d. February 4, 1931 Canandaigua, Ontario, NY
m1. Susan M. Barber (1844-October 17, 1881) *ca.* 1866
m2. Mary J. Inick Roberts (March 11, 1843-August 8, 1933) November 8, 1882

NOTE: Victor was the son of Joseph Smith (1807-1875) and Mary Rhodes Kinnan (1810-1895). A draftee, he enrolled in the 147th at Caton, Steuben County on July 17, 1863. He was wounded at Petersburg, VA on June 18, 1864 and his right leg was amputated. He transferred to Co. B, 91st on June 5, 1865 and was discharged at Ira Harris Hospital, Albany, NY on October 30, 1865. Mary was previously married to Hiram Roberts (1828-1882). All three are buried in Elmwood Cemetery, Caton, Steuben, NY. Three brothers also served the Union cause. Isaac (1838-July 21, 1861) was a member of Co. I, 38th Regiment. He was MIA after the battle of Bull Run and, according to *The Town Clerks' Registers*, "has never been heard from." David (1843-May 15, 1864) was a member of the 24th NY Cavalry. He died of typhoid fever at Alexandria, VA. Harvey (1845-1923) served in Co. F, 1st NY LA.

William Kirk – Co. F
b. 1827 Grant County, KY
d. March 3, 1886 National Soldiers' Home, Dayton, Montgomery, OH
m. ?

NOTE: William, a tobacconist, was a substitute for William A. Comstock. His muster roll card shows he enrolled in the 147th at Auburn, Cayuga, NY on August 23, 1863 although his admission form to the national home placed his enrollment at Olean, Cattaraugus. He apparently never applied for a pension but his admission form stated he suffered from "rheumatism – winter '64-'65 Petersburg." William's wife is unidentified. He claimed his daughter Estella Kirk Jordan (1852-*post* 1890) as his next of kin. A notice in *The Dayton Daily Journal* March 15, 1886, 1 announced his death: "KIRK – At the Hospital, Central Branch, National Home for D. V. S., at 1:30 o'clock a. m., March 3, 1886, William Kirk, late of Company A, 91st Regiment New York, aged 58 years. Cause of death, general debility, mental & physical." He is buried in Dayton National Cemetery. The names of his parents are unknown.

William Knight – Co. G
b. 1847 Prince Edward County, Ontario, Canada
d. August 21, 1864 4th Division, 5th Army Corps Regimental Hospital, VA
m. ------

NOTE: Much of what is written on this man's muster roll card is false, starting with his alleged birth in Oswego County in 1844. William Knight was an alias for Royal A. Ketchum who was born in Prince Edward County, Ontario, Canada in 1847, a son of Thomas (1802-1855) and Caroline Jackson Ketchum (1811-September 23, 1890). According to his muster roll card he was a substitute for W. W. Weston, residence unknown, and enrolled at Coltsville, NY on August 20, 1863. Coltsville does not exist. He was wounded at the battle of Weldon Railroad and died after his leg, which was fractured by gunshot, was amputated. Dr. A. S. Coe signed the register. His grave has not been located. His mother was married to Bernard Dainard in 1871 but by 1890 she was a widow. She applied for Royal's pension, using the name Caroline Deynard, on August 28, 1890 and died September 23rd.

Lorenz Kranz – Co. F
b. 1818 Prussia
d. August 9, 1889 National Soldiers' Home, Hampton, VA
m. Franziska DeLorneaux (1818-*ante* 1887) *ca.* 1843

NOTE: This man's name was variously spelled. I use that on his pension index card. His parents are unidentified. Lorenz saw prior duty in Co. A, 3rd Batt. ART, enlisting on September 18, 1861 at New York City. This outfit became Co. A, 15th Artillery. He transferred to the 2nd Ind. Batt., date unknown, and was discharged for disability at Brooks Station, VA on March 24, 1863. On August 10, 1863 he enrolled in the 147th at Buffalo as a substitute for Andrew Stelinger, Buffalo. He probably was wounded at the battle of the Wilderness on May 5, 1864 because his muster card states he had been in hospital since that date. He nominally transferred to the 91st Regiment on June 5, 1865 but he is not in *The Adjutant-General's Report* for that regiment. His admission form for the national home shows he served from 1861-1864. He was admitted to the home on November 19, 1887 and gave his daughter, Ottilie, as his next of kin. His disability was deafness. He died in the home hospital of senile dementia and was buried in Hampton National Cemetery. .

Cornelius E. Krom – Co. G
b. 1841 Tioga County, NY
d. July 25, 1864 Andersonville, Sumter, GA
m. ------

NOTE: Cornelius' parents were Peter I. (1810-1886) and Eleanor M. Hermance Krom (1806-1892). A draftee, he enrolled in the 147th at Candor, Tioga, NY on July 14, 1863. The date of his capture by the Confederates is unknown. He was buried at Andersonville but a cenotaph for him is located in Maple Grove Cemetery, Candor. His brother, Abraham (1837-1910), was a major in the 5th NY Cavalry.

John Kurc – Co. F
b. 1838 Germany
d. ? ?
m. ?

NOTE: John, whose surname was given as Kunck on his muster roll card, was a shoe-maker. His parents are unknown. He enrolled in the 147th at Buffalo on August 5, 1863 as a substitute for John Jones, of that city. He was listed as MIA on May 5, 1864 and probably died during the battle of the Wilderness.

Stephen S. Lacey – Co. E
b. May 29, 1841 Cohocton, Steuben, NY
d. March 10, 1864 Emory Hospital, Washington, DC
m. Lucy A. McCray (1841-*post* 1865) *ca.* 1862

NOTE: Stephen, son of James (1813-1883) and Polly Barney Lacey (1815-1897), was a draftee and enrolled in the 147th at Canandaigua, Ontario, NY on October 1, 1863. According to *Deaths of Volunteers*, he died on March 9, 1864 of pneumonia. He is buried in Soldiers' and Airmen's Home National Cemetery, Washington, DC. Stephen and Lucy were the parents of Charles (October 26, 1863-September 13, 1938). In 1865 Lucy and Charles were living with her mother, Mary McCray, in Burns, Allegany, NY. Charles was living with Mary in 1870 and 1880 but Lucy was gone, presumably because she died. It is also possible she remarried.

Marcus A. Lafler – Co. A
b. August 1839 Hartland, Niagara, NY
d. December 4, 1907 Hersey, Osceola, MI
m. Medora E. Tuttle (July 1850-December 11, 1926) February 17, 1870

NOTE: Marcus, son of Jacob (1798-1885) and Emily Bryan Lafler (1809-1884), was drafted, enrolling in the 147th at Newfane, Niagara, NY on July 28, 1863. His muster card says he was detailed to the Commissary Department. He transferred to Co. C, 91st Regiment on June 5, 1865 and mustered out on July 3rd at Ball's Cross Roads, VA. Lafler and Medora were married in Portland, MI and became the parents of two children, both of whom died young. Marcus was an attorney in Michigan. His COD was apoplexy. Although he died in Hersey, he was buried in North Ridge Cemetery, North Ridge, Niagara, NY. Medora died at the home of a nephew, Roy Tuttle, Wrights Corners, Niagara and was also buried in North Ridge Cemetery.

Joseph Lane – Co. F
b. May 17, 1832 Brookfield, Tioga, PA
d. November 20, 1915 Potterbrook, Tioga, PA
m1. Orpha R. Lewis (1839-1892) ca. 1854
m2. Mary H. _____ (May 9, 1844-December 24, 1921) 1893

NOTE: According to his death certificate, Joseph was the son of Elihu (?-?) and Eunice Bently Lane (?-?). He was a substitute for John Wilson, Troupsburg, Steuben County, enrolling in the 147th on July 18, 1863, 29th Congressional District, and mustering in at Troupsburg on September 17th. At some unknown place and time he was taken prisoner. His parole date is also unknown but he was discharged from the service at Elmira, NY on May 25, 1865. Joseph and Orpha were the parents of two daughters, Eulalia (1856-?) and Genette (1866-?). In 1910 he and Mary both claimed to have been married twice. Mary had no children. Joseph and Orpha are buried in Potterbrook Cemetery. Mary is buried in Sabinsville Cemetery, Tioga, PA.

Burr Bartram Lathrop – Co. F

b. June 2, 1843 Genesee County, NY

d. 1864 probably Florence, SC

m. ------

NOTE: Burr was the son of Anson (1803-1891) and Elizabeth Bartram Lathrop (1807-1880). He was drafted, enrolling in the 147th at Darien, Genesee, NY on July 29, 1863. He was captured on May 5, 1864 at the battle of the Wilderness. Although his cenotaph in Darien Cemetery, Genesee, NY says he died on May 15, 1864 both *The Town Clerks' Registers* and *Registers of Officers and Enlisted Men* indicate he was living in July, a prisoner in Danville, VA. His muster roll card notes he was "reported died of disease at Florence, SC." His brother Samuel (1835-1865) served in the 22nd and 9th NY HA. He reportedly was captured on July 7, 1864 and died in hospital at Danville Prison on February 1865. Another brother, Henry B. (1837-1864), served in the 150th PA Infantry and died in Fredericksburg, VA in May 1864.

Augustus Laue – Co. F

b. 1838 Germany

d. October 14, 1893 Enfield, Tompkins, NY

m. Helene Viemann (1839-September 18, 1907) *ca.* 1867

NOTE: This soldier's parents are unknown and their surname was variously spelled. I use that on the gravestone. Augustus was a substitute for John E. Jones and enrolled in the 147th at Montour, Schuyler, NY on July 27, 1863. He transferred to Co. A, 91st on June 5, 1865 and mustered out on July 3rd near Washington, DC. In 1890 Laue claimed he had been wounded in the right leg. He and Helene were the parents of George W. (1869-1943) and Carrie E. (1876-1959). August is buried in Grove Cemetery, Trumansburg, Tompkins, NY and presumably Helene is there too.

George Lawrence – Co. E

b. May 1837 Columbia County, NY

d. July 12, 1912 National Soldiers' Home, Bath, Steuben, NY

m. Rachel Keller (April 9, 1844-September 10, 1912) *ca.*1866

NOTE: George was the son of Orrin (1810-?) and Phoebe Finch Lawrence (1810-?). A draftee, he enrolled in the 147th at Leon, Cattaraugus, NY on August 22, 1863. For some unknown reason his age was given as 37 on his muster roll card although every record confirms that he was born in 1837! He was captured at Weldon Railroad on October 1, 1864. Where he was imprisoned is unknown but he was paroled at North East Ferry, NC on March 1, 1865. He was furloughed from Camp Parole, MD on March 19, 1865. On May 19, 1865 he was charged with desertion, a charge later dropped.

He was discharged from the service as of May 19, 1865. In 1890 he was living in Olean, Cattaraugus, NY and said he had been shot through the leg. He is buried in Bath National Cemetery. George and Rachel were the parents of Ada Edith (1867-?). The couple was living together in 1880 but apparently separated. In 1900 George claimed to be single. In 1910 Rachel, using the surname Akeley, said she was a widow. I have found no evidence of a Mr. Akeley. In 1910 she was living on Akeley Road, Pine Grove, Warren, PA. According to her death certificate which also states her last name was Akeley, she succumbed to an exophthalmic goiter and chronic nephritis. She is buried in Pine Grove Cemetery.

George Washington LeFever – Co. H

b. September 26, 1836 Hinsdale, Cattaraugus, NY
d. May 10, 1914 Olean, Cattaraugus, NY
m1. Fannie Maria Carrier (August 30, 1841-February 9, 1908) January 17, 1862
m2. Jane "Jennie" Giering _____ Capron (April 1863-July 4, 1921) October 21, 1908

NOTE: George, a farmer, was the son of John (1804-1871) and Maria Louisa Cowdry LeFever (1809-1881). A draftee, he enrolled in the 147th at Clarksville, Cattaraugus, NY on July 13, 1863. He was taken prisoner on May 5, 1864 at the battle of the Wilderness and spent ten months in captivity. Although no date is provided he probably was paroled in February or March 1865. He was nominally transferred to Co. B, 91st Regiment but is not listed in *The Adjutant-General's Report* for that outfit. He was discharged at Elmira, NY on October 2, 1865. In 1890 he stated his disability was "chronic bronchitis contracted in prison." George's death was reported in *The Olean Evening Herald* May 11, 1914 which stated he died from "a complication of diseases." He was a member of Bayard Post No. 222 GAR. He and Fannie are buried in Chestnut Hill Cemetery, Portville, Cattaraugus. Jennie had two husbands before she married George. The first is unidentified but the second was George Capron (1843-January 9, 1907) whom she married in 1898 as his second wife. According to her obituary, published in *The Olean Times Herald* July 5, 1921, 9, Jennie was to be buried in Maplehurst Cemetery in Hinsdale, Cattaraugus.

Michael Lehmeier – Co. F

b. 1826 Germany
d. ? ?
m. ?

NOTE: Michael's surname was variously spelled. I use that on his Union Index Card. He was a substitute for Jacob Blessing, Buffalo, enrolling in the 147th at that place on August 5, 1863. He was discharged for "disability" on December 22, 1864 at Washington, DC.

Nothing else confirmable has been located, including his parents' names.

Edwin Greer Lepar – Co. H
b. July 8, 1833 Erie County, PA
d. January 21, 1895 Jamestown, Chautauqua, NY
m. Lucy Loraine Root (1846-April 4, 1921) 1866

NOTE: Edwin was the son of James (1793-*post* 1860) and Hester Lotta Lapar (1793-*post* 1860). He was drafted, enrolling in the 147th at Ellicott, Chautauqua, NY on August 29, 1863. He transferred to Co. F, 91st on June 5, 1865 and mustered out near Washington, DC on July 3rd. He and Lucy, generally known as Loraine, were the parents of three daughters. His obituary appeared in *The Jamestown Evening Journal* January 21, 1895, 4: "The death of Edwin G. Lepar occurred today at his home, 16 Fillmore street, at the age of 61 years, 5 months, 19 days . . . Mr. Lepar has resided in Jamestown over 40 years. He was a contractor and builder who has done much good work in this region, especially in this city and Chautauqua, and was known as a capable and honorable business man. At Chautauqua many of the largest and finest buildings were erected by him. Among other buildings in Jamestown he filled the contract for the brickwork on the state armory. Mr. Lepar was a veteran of the late war, serving as a member of Co. H, 147th regiment, N. Y. S. Vols. He was highly regarded by his comrades and all who had business or neighborly dealings with him . . . ." Edwin was a member of James M. Brown Post No. 285 GAR. Gravesites for him and Lucy Loraine have not been located.

Thomas R. Leslie – Co. H
b. 1837 Scotland
d. ? ?
m. ?

NOTE: Thomas, an artist, was a substitute for Franklin S. Hoover, Amherst, Erie, NY, enrolling in the 147th at Buffalo on August 11, 1863. He was captured at the battle of the Wilderness on May 5, 1864 and sent to Andersonville. His release date is unknown but he was on furlough on February 28, 1865. He nominally transferred to Co. B, 91st Regiment on June 5, 1865 but is not listed in *The Adjutant-General's Report* for that organization. His muster roll card says he was not discharged and it is possible he died shortly after going on furlough. His parents' names are unknown.

Gideon Lester – Co. K
b. ? ?
d. ? ?
m. ?

NOTE: Very little is known about this man. He allegedly was drafted, joining the 147th at Westhampton, Suffolk, NY, date unknown. He was not borne on any roll for the 147th until April 3, 1865 when he was reported absent. Supposedly he was a paroled prisoner but no record of his captivity exists. The name might have been an alias. He transferred to Co. K, 91st Regiment on June 5, 1865 but does not appear in *The Adjutant-General's Report* for that outfit. A man named Giddings H. Lester (October 9, 1824-June 19, 1881) worked for the railroad on 1880. He is buried in Yantic Cemetery, Norwich, New London, CT. Whether or not this is the correct person is unknown.

John Jay Lester – Co. F
b. December 1836 Washington County, NY
d. April 7, 1911 Glens Falls, Warren, NY
m1. Eliza M. _____ (1838-*post* 1875) *ca.* 1859
m2. Frances "Fannie" Wilson (August 1855-January 31, 1932) 1877

NOTE: John, a blacksmith, was the son of John L. (1809-1879) and Lydia Moore Lester (1810-1895). He was drafted, enrolling in the 147th at Oswego City, NY on August 11, 1863. He transferred to Co. A, 91st Regiment on June 5, 1865 and mustered out near Washington, DC on July 3rd. He and Eliza were the parents of Ida (1860-?) and Robert J. (1864-?). He and Fannie were the parents of three more. The family was living in Fort Edward, Washington, NY in 1875 and that is probably where Eliza is buried. John and Fannie are buried in Glens Falls Cemetery.

Henry Lewis – Co. E
b. 1842 Paris, France
d. ? ?
m. ?

NOTE: Henry, whose parents are unknown, claimed to be a student when he enrolled as a draftee in the 147th on August 10, 1863 at Buffalo, NY. Although transferred to Co. D, 91st Regiment on June 5, 1865 he mustered out on June 7th at Washington, DC. His muster roll card states he was a paroled prisoner but I have not located any documents to that effect.

Joseph Lewis – Co. I
b. 1845 Chemung County, NY
d. April 18, 1865 Catlin, Chemung, NY
m. ------

NOTE: Joseph was a substitute for Joseph Joslyn, Chemung, Chemung, NY and enrolled in that place on July 21, 1863. He was wounded at Cold Harbor, VA on June 3, 1864 and, according to his muster roll card, died while on furlough. An entry in *Deaths of Volunteers* places him in the 91st Regiment, gives the date cited above, but provides no COD or POD. He nominally transferred to Co. I, 91st Regiment on June 5, 1865 but he was already dead. I have located no familial records for him.

James Like – Co. C
b. 1836 Cattaraugus County, NY
d. probably May 5, 1864 Wilderness, VA
m. Sophia E. Wells (July 1845-February 5, 1917) December 26, 1861

NOTE: James, son of David (1793-1873) and Mary Abrams Like (1797-*post* 1870), was drafted, enrolling in the 147th at Persia, Cattaraugus, NY on August 20, 1863. He was MIA after the battle of the Wilderness and presumed dead. He and Sophia had one child, James (1863-1920). When the 1865 New York census was taken, Sophia and her son were living with her brother. She was still classified as a married woman. She married Lafayette Matteson (1846-May 2, 1904) on January 1, 1866 in Bowens Prairie, Jones, IA where several members of the Like family had moved. Lafayette had served in Co. D, 5th IA Cavalry. She is buried in Bear Butte Cemetery, Sturgis, Meade, SD. Lafayette is buried in Pleasant Valley Cemetery, Tilford, Meade, SD.

Orlando Lillie – Co. D
b. November 1841 Montville, Cayuga, NY
d. December 1, 1904 Moravia, Cayuga, NY
m. Maryette White (October 1849-March 28, 1929) 1870

NOTE: The son of Daniel G. (1808-1873) and Hannah Laura Corey Lillie (1815-1856), Orlando was a substitute for John Lick, Varick, Cayuga, NY, enrolling in the 147th at Auburn, Cayuga, NY on July 25, 1863. He had previously served in Companies A, F, 19th NY Regiment (later 3rd NY ART). He transferred to Co. B, 91st Regiment on June 5, 1865 and mustered out near Washington, DC on July 3rd. Orlando and Maryette had one child, Fay Seward (1876-October 25, 1928). Maryette married James G. Loyster (1843-April 30, 1921) as his second wife on April 12, 1909. She was struck by an automobile in Moravia on March 22, 1929 and suffered severe head and shoulder injuries. Her death was announced in *The Auburn Citizen* March 29, 1929, 7: "Moravia, March 29. -- Mrs. Maryette Loyster, 79, of Main Street, died early Thursday morning in Cortland Hospital as the result of injuries received Friday evening when she was struck by an automobile in West Cayuga Street driven by Wallace Roden, also of Main Street. Mrs. Loyster passed her entire life in Moravia and vicinity . . . Funeral services will be conducted from the home at 2:30 o'clock on Saturday afternoon. The

Rev. F. H. Butman, pastor of the Methodist Church, will officiate . . . ." Orlando and Maryette are buried in Indian Mound Cemetery, Moravia. James Loyster is buried in Owasco Rural Cemetery, Skaneateles, Onondaga. Orlando's brother Alonzo (1837-1905) served in Co. I, 111th Regiment.

Russell Austin Lincoln – Co. D

b. July 8, 1835 Dundee, Yates, NY
d. *post* 1865 probably Starkey, Yates, NY
m. Anna Timms (July 10, 1842-August 15, 1913) *ca.* 1862

NOTE: Russell was the son of Royal (1804-1887) and Jane Young Kingin Lincoln (1807-1888). He saw prior service in Co. A, 126th Regiment from August 1861-December 31, 1862. He was taken captive at Harper's Ferry on September 15, 1862 and paroled the next day. He was discharged at Judiciary Square Hospital, Washington, DC on December 13, 1862 for "disability." Russell was then drafted, enrolling in the 147th at Canandaigua, Ontario, NY on September 30, 1863. He was discharged for "disability" at St. Joseph Hospital, New York City on April 16, 1864. He and Anna were the parents of Royal (1862-1879) and Caroline "Carrie" (1867-*post* 1880). Russell's DOD has not been discovered but Anna married Charles Augustus Van Horn (July 1842-August 27, 1909) on September 17, 1869. Sometime after the 1875 New York census the family moved to Kansas. Charles had served in Co. A, 38th NJ Regiment. He was a member of Franklin Post No. 68 GAR, Olathe, Johnson, KS. Anna's death was reported in *The Irving Leader* August 22, 1913, 1: "Mrs. Anna J. Van Horn was born in the city of Honeoye, N. Y., July 10, 1842, departed this life at the home of her daughter, Mrs. George Briner, of Irving, Aug. 15, 1913, at the age of seventy-five years, one month and five days. Mrs. Van Horn came to Kansas in 1875 and has resided here ever since. She having spent nearly forty years in Kansas she was truly a pioneer; was one of few brave characters that was willing to face hardships and deprivations for the purpose of bettering the interests of her family, and Kansas is largely indebted to these brave women for what it is today. Mrs. Van Horn took a stand for Christ at the age of fifteen and at that time united with the Presbyterian church. Three sons and two daughters are left to mourn the loss of a loving mother, and a faithful friend, the husband and father having entered into rest five years ago. The funeral was conducted at Methodist church by the pastor and interment took place in the Greenwood cemetery."

David Lindley – Co. E

b. 1840 Watertown, Jefferson, NY
d. October 9, 1864 Andersonville, Sumter, GA
m. Anna "Annie" Hibbard (1843-November 5, 1907) December 30, 1862

NOTE: David's parents are unknown. In 1850 he was living with Asa Parkinson and family in Rutland, Jefferson, NY. He enrolled in the 147th at Canandaigua, Ontario, NY on September 29, 1863. An entry in *The Town Clerks' Registers* makes for interesting reading: "This is the only draftee that went from this [place] personally into the Army . . . ." He was captured May 5, 1864 and sent to Andersonville. He was admitted to the prison hospital on September 12, 1864 and died there from chronic diarrhea. He is buried in the Andersonville National Cemetery. Annie married Elijah L. Baker (1834-April 27, 1900) on October 16, 1867 at Ionia, Ontario, NY. They were the parents of one child, Orletta (1869-1939). Annie and Elijah both died of heart disease. Their graves have not been located but since his parents and Orletta are buried in Millers Corners Cemetery, Ionia, Ontario, NY they may be there too.

Newton Adams Lindley – Co. H

b. July 26, 1841 Natal, South Africa
d. September 28, 1878 Manhattan, New York
m. Katharine Caroline Parker (1841-July 23, 1879) *ca.* 1869

NOTE: Dr. Newton Lindley was the son of Rev. Daniel (1801-1880) and Lucy Virginia Allen Lindley (1810-1877). Rev. Lindley was an ordained minister in the Presbyterian Church who served two tours of missionary work in Natal, South Africa where several of the children, including Newton, were born. Newton was a member of Co. G, 1st New York Mounted Rifles, enlisting in New York City in August 1862. He was discharged on January 27, 1864 to accept a commission as second lieutenant in the 147th Regiment from which he was discharged on July 1, 1864. His story is best told in an article in *The New York Herald* September 29, 1879, 8 published upon his death from yellow fever: "The case of Dr. N. A. Lindley, which has been reported daily in the *Herald* since his first attack on Monday last, terminated fatally at Quarantine yesterday forenoon at half-past eleven o'clock. He had passed through the usual stages of the disease, and on Friday afternoon rallied. His pulse and skin became natural and his eyes cleared of the yellowness common to the malady. Dr. Vandepoel [the health officer] had hopes of his ultimate recovery, and left him with that impression late on Friday afternoon. The patient continued in this improved condition until ten o'clock Friday night, when the cold snap occurred, and although the ward had been warmed by the steam pipes of the establishment he was suddenly seized with a fit of blood vomiting, and at once became unconscious, in which state he lingered until his death. The deceased reached Quarantine boarding station on Monday last, having left the city by the Staten Island boat and taken the cars to Dr. Vanderpoel's place. Here he was first seen by a *Herald* reporter in the boat house of the boarding station lying on a rude settee. He said he perfectly knew what was the matter with him, and asked for a drink of hot lemonade. This was furnished; but his stomach refused to retain it. He then said that he desired to be well taken care of, would pay all expenses, and counted out $390, which amount is in the hands of his friends. Dr. Vanderpoel administered the remedies usual in such cases, and the patient was removed, at his own urgent request, to the Quarantine Hospital at West Bank. Previous to his removal the deceased said if it was God's will he should die he was prepared to go. That he had done nothing more than his duty in giving relief to his sick brethren in Memphis and Grand Junction, Tenn., and remarked that he had seen by the papers that two or three of the persons he attended had died since he left. At the hospital Dr. Lindley received every at-

Dr. Lindley's medical career was cut short when he contracted yellow fever in Tennessee and died in quarantine in New York City.
Diane Gravlee (FAG)

tention from the moment of his reception until his death . . . Dr. Lindley . . . was born in the colony of Natal, South Africa, in the year 1841. His father was Daniel Lindley, D.D., a missionary from the American Board of Foreign Mission and a native of Pennsylvania. The deceased came here in 1859 from Africa, having been with his father up to that period for the purpose of being educated. He entered the College of Physicians and Surgeons in this city, but, before graduating, enlisted in the New York Mounted Rifles at the commencement of the civil war and was stationed on the Nansemond River, at Dismal Swamp. He was there constantly employed as a scout in consequence of familiarity with forest trails and nomadic habits acquired in Africa. He was subsequently promoted to a lieutenancy in the 157th [*sic*] New York Volunteers. Owing to malarial disease, contracted in the Swamp, he was compelled to resign his commission, and for several years suffered considerably from these complaints. He then resumed his studies in medicine in the office of Dr. Willard Parker, in this city, whose daughter became his wife. He returned to Africa after completing his studies, and practiced under a commission from the British government. He came again to America upon a visit, but went to Florida, where he was induced by the character of the climate to settle. He remained there, on the St. John's River, in Putnam county, and was conspicuous among the inhabitants for his kindness and attention to the sick. This was especially the case during the occurrence of yellow fever in various parts of Florida, particularly last year in Jacksonville. Being in the Blue Mountains of Georgia this season spending the summer with his family, he met a physician who was on his way to the yellow fever district in Tennessee, and he immediately made up his mind that it was his duty to offer his services. Sending his family on North, he repaired to the infected region and labored assiduously until he was so run down that the doctors told him he had better leave, for if he remained he would only be one more to nurse. The sequel of this melancholy, but noble career, has been already related. The deceased was noted for his cool courage and his kindness to the sick and to little children. He was a famous marksman, and in the jungles of Africa astonished the English officers while a youth by the accuracy of his aim and by his fearlessness and endurance under severe trials . . . The remains will be placed in an hermetically sealed casket and interred in the family vault at Tarrytown." He was buried in Sleepy Hollow Cemetery, Westchester. Katharine, who is buried in Lakeview Cemetery, New Canaan, Fairfield, CT, died in New York City from "bilious remittent fever."

John Lord – Co. H

b. February 13, 1833 Middleburg, Schoharie, NY
d. September 16, 1901 Newark Valley, Tioga, NY
m. Arrenia Wainwright (May 20, 1831-December 11, 1894) *ca.* 1853

NOTE: John, son of Palmer (1797-*post* 1870) and Eleanor Lord (1798-*ca.* 1862), was a draftee, enrolling in the 147th at Newark Valley on July 14, 1863. Although nominally transferred to Co. B, 91st Regiment on June 5, 1865 he was discharged from Mower General Hospital, Philadelphia, PA as a member of the 147th. In 1890 he claimed no disability. John was a member of Charles H. Williams Post No. 245 GAR, Newark Valley. He and Arrenia, the parents of six children by 1875, are buried in Hope Cemetery, Newark Valley.

George B. Lyons – Co. H

b. 1842 Barton, Tioga, NY
d. August 27, 1868 Barton, Tioga, NY
m. ------

NOTE: The son of Jonathan Corey (1805-1895) and Susan Ilett Lyons (1809-1891), George was a draftee., enrolling in the 147th Regiment on July 14, 1863 at Barton. He was wounded in action at an unknown date and although nominally transferred to Co. B, 91st Regiment on June 5, 1865 was discharged for "disability" from his wounds at Elmira General Hospital on July 21, 1865 as a member of the 147th. He is buried with his parents in King Cemetery, Barton.

Enos Cook Mack – Co. C
b. March 17, 1834 Gainesville, Wyoming, NY
d. November 27, 1891 Maryville, Nodaway, MO
m. Crescentia "Cynthia" Romesser (1840-September 24, 1929) *ca.* 1860

NOTE: A draftee, Enos was the son of Moses B. (1793-?) and Mary "Polly" Suel/Sewel Mack (1792-?). He enrolled in the 147th at Hume, Allegany, NY on July 16, 1863 and was discharged for "disability" on February 20, 1864. Although his pension index card says he died in 1891 the order form for a government headstone carries a DOD of March 10, 1892. Since Crescentia applied for a widow's pension on December 7, 1891, the earlier date is correct. They are buried in St. Mary's Cemetery, Maryville.

Martin Mack – Co. C
b. 1836 Herrick, Nassau, NY
d. ? ?
m. ?

NOTE: Martin was a draftee and enrolled in the 147th at Hume, Allegany, NY on August 22, 1863. His muster card says he was born in Herrick, NY and the only place with that name is in Nassau County. He transferred to Co. H, 91st Regiment on June 5, 1865 and mustered out on July 3rd. I have found no other information about him.

LaFayette Magee – Co. G
b. 1842 Erie County, NY
d. March 25, 1921 Wichita, Sedgwick, KS
m1. Dorothy _____ (1850-*ca.* 1887) *ca.* 1871
m2. Mary Catherine Whitmer (February 4, 1850-October 27, 1914) 1894

NOTE: LaFayette, a carpenter, was the son of Joseph (1817-1901) and Sally A. Magee (1816-1890). A draftee, he enrolled in the 147th at Olean, Cattaraugus, NY on August 22, 1863. He was discharged for "disability" on May 15, 1865 although he nominally transferred to Co. F, 91st Regiment under the name of McGee on June 5, 1865. He and Dorothy were the parents of six children. The 1880 census noted that Dorothy was in an insane asylum and Dwight, 9, was "dead." I date Dorothy's death to approximately 1887 because the 1900 census included Ida M., 18, and Anna B., 16, and because LaFayette's obituary stated he moved to Kansas in 1887. LaFayette was struck by a streetcar on March 18, 1921. An account, published in *The Wichita Daily Eagle* March 19, 1921, stated the elderly man had very poor eyesight and probably did not see the car coming towards him. His injuries were fatal, as reported in *The Wichita Beacon* March 25, 1921, 5: "LaFayette Magee, age 79, died at a local hospital at 1:35 o'clock, Friday morning from injuries received last Friday when he was struck by a street car as he was crossing the street in the third block on East Douglas Avenue. He did not regain consciousness. Mr. Magee was born in Erie County, New York, and came to Wichita from there in 1887. For a number of years he was engaged in the furniture business here but has been retired for some time. He was a veteran of the Civil War, having served in Company G, 147 New York Volunteers. He was a member of the Eggleson Post of Wichita and a charter member of the Fraternal Aid Union . . . The time of the funeral has not been set but the Eggleson Post will have charge of the services. City Undertaking Company has charge." LaFayette and Mary are buried in Highland Cemetery, Wichita. LaFayette's parents and son Dwight are buried in Mount View Cemetery, Olean, and it is possible that Dorothy is also there.

James Maloney – Co. G
b. 1843 Buffalo, Erie, NY
d. ? ?
m. ?

NOTE: James may have been the son of James (1803-?) and Elizabeth Maloney (1803-?). In 1855 this family was living in Buffalo and James' POB was Erie County. The family again appears on the 1865 New York census, although James was now reputed to have been born in Ireland. He was a bartender by occupation but was in the army. Mahoney was a substitute for Martin E. Welbeck and enrolled in the 147th at Salamanca, Cattaraugus, NY on August 22, 1863. A note attached to his muster roll card reveals he had been court martialed for an unspecified offense and sent to Fort Jefferson, Florida to serve his sentence. By a special order from the War Department dated May 10, 1865 his sentence was remitted and he was ordered to return to duty. He transferred to Co. F, 91st Regiment on June 5, 1865 and mustered out on July 3rd near Washington, DC. I have located no other information.

John W. Manning – Co. A
b. August 1840 Niagara County, NY
d. November 30, 1914 Rochester, Monroe, NY
m. Anna M. Gaing (December 1855-January 30, 1928) 1879

NOTE: The son of Benjamin (1799-1885) and Mary "Polly" Simmons Manning (1812-1899), John was drafted, enrolling in the 147th at Bergen, Genesee, NY on July 29, 1863. He transferred to Co. C, 91st regiment on June 6, 1865 and mustered out at Ball's Cross Roads, VA on July 3rd. In 1890 he claimed "defective hearing" as a disability. In 1900 he ran a laundry. He and Anna, who was born in Germany, were the parents of two. The couple is buried in Riverside Cemetery, Rochester.

Joel E. Mapes – Co. D
b. 1844 Cayuga County, NY
d. October 29, 1911 Fulton, NY
m. Emily "Emma" Ladd (1855-February 5, 1940) 1877

NOTE: Joel, the son of James S. (1800-*post* 1865) and Jenette Mapes (1820-*ante* 1865), apparently enlisted in the 147th, enrolling at Granby, NY on February 27, 1864. He transferred to Co. B, 91st Regiment on June 5, 1865 and was discharged at Elmira, NY on August 4, 1865. In 1890 he was living in Lapeer, Lapeer, MI where he applied for a pension. He claimed no disability when enumerated for the Veterans' Schedules. His unexpected death was reported in *The Syracuse Daily Journal* October 30, 1911, 2: "Fulton, Oct. 30. – Joel Mapes, aged 65, was suddenly stricken with a severe attack of heart trouble last night while walking home and died within an hour. Mr. Mapes, who is well known in Fulton, residing at the corner of Fifth and Ontario sts., was returning with his wife about 10 from a call on her sister, Mrs. George Ralph of the West Side when without warning, in Erie st., Mr. Mapes fell to the sidewalk and became unconscious. Mrs. Mapes called for assistance, but it was some time before any one was aroused. The stricken man was removed, finally, to the Pooler home nearby. A physician was called and was able to revive him slightly so that an attempt was made to remove him to his home. They had just taken Mr. Mapes into his home when he passed away. Death was attributed to acute heart trouble. Besides his widow, the deceased has several relatives in this city." For Emily, Joel's passing was a double shock since a sister, Mrs. N. W. Althouse, had died in Brooklyn, NY on October 25th. Emily's death was reported in *The Oswego Palladium-Times* February 6, 1940, 6: "Fulton, Feb. 6. – Mrs. Emily Mapes, 89, widow of Joel Mapes, 211 Oneida street, died at the family home Monday after an illness of several weeks. Mrs. Mapes was stricken last fall when she suffered a fracture of a hip in a fall. Mrs. Mapes has been a resident of Fulton for many years and was a member of the First Methodist church and of the Ladies of the G. A. R. Survivors include several nieces and nephews. Funeral services will be held at the Springer memorial home . . . at 2:30 p.m. Thursday. The Rev. Charles Bollinger will officiate . . . ." Joel and Emily are buried in Mt. Adnah Cemetery, Fulton.

Ambrose Marcely – Co. K
b. December 7, 1830 Quebec, Canada
d. July 4, 1878 Oswego City, NY
m. ------

NOTE: Ambrose, a cooper, was the son of Paschal Lemire de Marcelet (1793-*post* 1875) and Victoria Turgeon (1796-*ante* 1870). His name was variously spelled, for example, Marcello, Marcellus, Marsaline. In 1855 the family had lived in Oswego for six years. The 1865 New York census and Johnson, *History of Oswego County,* 199 both allege he enlisted in the 81st Regiment in 1861 and was assigned to Co. K. Nevertheless, he does not appear in *The Adjutant-General's Report* for that outfit under any spelling of his surname. He was a substitute

Ambrose Marcely was one of many unfortunates to drown in the Oswego River.
Sue Sullivan (FAG)

for Charles E. Cameron and enrolled in the 147th on August 31, 1863. He was discharged for "disability" at an unknown date but on July 21, 1864 he re-enlisted at Utica and was placed in Co. H, 86th Regiment. His muster roll card for that organization shows he was a paroled prisoner on February 28, 1865. He mustered out on June 27, 1865 near Washington, DC. According to an article appearing in *The Oswego Commercial Times* November 26, 1862, Ambrose was well known in city court: "Ambrose Marceline who has appeared dozens of times at the bar of the police court, was again brought up on the old charge – drunkenness. He was conveyed to the station on a wheelbarrow, regarding which mode of conveyance he was perfectly oblivious to until informed . . . ." His postwar life was equally unhappy. In 1875 he and his father were both living in the Oswego City Poorhouse. His tragic end was reported in *The Oswego Daily Times* July 8, 1878: "About eleven o'clock this morning, Frank Champion discovered the body of a drowned man in the river near the foot of East Schuyler street. Benjamin Denne helped Champion to remove the body from the water. Coroner Barnes was notified and held an inquest, when it was ascertained that the deceased was Ambrose Marcely, a man about 45 years of age. His cousin, Nelson Marcely, testified that he last saw the deceased about 10 o'clock on the morning of the Fourth. He was of intemperate habits and when drunk was subject to fits. It is surmised that he got drunk on the Fourth and fell into the river while in a fit. The deceased was a pauper and vagrant and had frequently been sent to the poorhouse. The coroner's jury rendered a verdict of accidental drowning. The body was much decomposed when found and was buried this morning." Ambrose is buried in Riverside Cemetery, Scriba. His gravestone says he died on July 5th.

Augustus Marks – Co. F

b. 1836 Wurtemberg, Germany

d. ? ?

m. ?

NOTE: Augustus, a sailor, was a substitute for Edward Ellingworth, Cheektowaga, Erie, NY, enrolling in the 147th at Buffalo on August 12, 1863. He transferred to Co. A, 91st Regiment on June 5, 1865 and mustered out near Washington, DC on July 3rd. No other confirmable information has been located.

John Marsh – Co. C

b. 1833 Chenango County, NY

d. *post* 1880 ?

m. Mary _____ (1838-?) *ca.* 1865

NOTE: John, whose parents are unidentified, was a substitute for Edwin R. Shattuck and enrolled in the 147th on August 22, 1863 at Portville, Cattaraugus, NY. His age when enrolled on August 22nd was 30, but when he was mustered the same day his age was 39. He was wounded at the battle of the Wilderness and was listed as "absent, sick" on August 31, 1864. His muster roll card says he was not borne on subsequent rolls. He was nominally transferred to Co. H, 91st Regiment on June 5, 1865 but was "absent, sick." He applied for a pension on January 13, 1880 but received no certificate. The index card does not provide a discharge date and it is possible John simply walked away from the war and was therefore ineligible for a pension. The last record for the family was the 1880 census for Portville, Cattaraugus. He was working in a saw mill. He and Mary had two children, Elizabeth, 14, and John, 11.

Edwin Marshall – Co. G

b. 1842 Boonville, Oneida, NY

d. June 18, 1864 Stanton General Hospital, Washington, DC

m. ------

NOTE: Edwin's parents are unknown but a newspaper article in *The Oswego Commercial Advertiser* June 11, 1864 reported he was in hospital in Washington, DC and gave his home address as Elizabethtown, Essex County. A fifteen-year-old by that name was living with Jacob and Mary J. Deyoe in North Hudson, Essex, in 1860. Mary may have been his mother. He was a substitute for Peter Phillips, Boonville, and enrolled in the 147th at Utica, Oneida, NY on August 25, 1863. The article cited above, which was a letter to the editor from J. L. Lake, stated that Marshall had been wounded on May 28th "by way of the White House," and he was probably injured at Totopotomoy, a battle fought between May 28-30. Lake considered his recovery "doubtful." His right leg had been so severely wounded that it had to be amputated at the knee. *The Oswego Commercial Advertiser* June 23, 1864 published another letter from Lake, which stated the young man had died of septicemia. Edwin is buried in Arlington National Cemetery.

Edward Adolphus Martin – Co. H
b. April 1839 New York City, NY
d. June 12, 1914 Lockport, Niagara, NY
m. Abbie E. McKinley (August 1842-May 12, 1922) 1878

NOTE: Edward was the son of Jared W. (1796-1870) and Elizabeth Albertson Martin (1803-1874). A draftee, he enrolled in the 147th at Gaines, Orleans, NY on August 8, 1863. On June 28, 1864 he was discharged in order to accept a commission as first lieutenant in Co. D of the newly formed 108th Regiment USCT. He mustered out as a captain on March 21, 1866. In later life he was a letter carrier. He and Abbie, who was born in Canada and immigrated to the United States in 1866, were the parents of 10 children, none of whom survived to 1900. Edward and Abbie are buried in Cold Springs Cemetery, Lockport. His parents are buried in Glenwood Cemetery, Lockport.

John T. Martin – Co. C
b. 1835 Canada
d. *post* 1880 ?
m. ?

NOTE: John's record is scant. A substitute for an unnamed man he enrolled at Watertown, Jefferson, NY on September 1, 1863. He transferred to Co. H, 91st Regiment on June 5, 1865 but was "absent, sick" at muster out. He applied for a pension on June 23, 1880 and obtained a certificate. No widow is listed. His muster roll card shows he was a farmer. In 1860 a man named John Martin, 26, was living in Orleans, Jefferson, NY with Maryette, 30, who may or may not have been his wife. Beyond these few facts, nothing has been discovered.

Joseph Mason – Co. E
b. 1840 England
d. ? ?
m. ?

NOTE: A butcher by occupation, John enrolled at Porter, Niagara, NY on July 23, 1863 as a substitute for Judson Eaton, Porter, NY. He nominally transferred to Co. D, 91st Regiment on June 5, 1865 but apparently never joined that outfit since his name does not appear in *The Adjutant-General's Report* for that organization. He was discharged on June 29, 1865 at Buffalo, NY. No other information is available, including parents' names.

James McClellen – Co. F
b. April 27, 1829 Ireland
d. ? ?
m. ?

NOTE: James' surname was variously spelled. When he entered the 147th, it was spelled McClellen. The surname for his parents, Shae (?-?) and Jane (?-?), was McClelland. When he transferred to Co. A, 91st Regiment on June 5, 1865 it was McClellan. He lived in Clayton, Jefferson, NY and was a substitute for an unnamed draftee. According to *The Town Clerks' Registers* he enrolled in the 147th Artillery. He was supposed to be married. He mustered out of the 91st Regiment on July 3, 1865 near Washington, DC. A man named James McClellan, who lived in Clayton in 1880, died in 1883, leaving a minor child Maggie as his sole heir. Whether or not this is the correct man is a matter of conjecture.

Henry McConnell – Co. H
b. 1830 Chemung County, NY
d. September 30, 1903 Elmira, Chemung, NY
m. Mary _____ (1843-*ante* 1900) *ante* 1870

NOTE: Henry, son of David (1801-1870) and Sarah "Sally" Ervay McConnell (1806-*post* 1880), was a substitute for Edward Ford, enrolling at Elmira on July 20, 1863. He was captured and paroled at unknown dates. Although nominally transferred to Co. B, 91st Regiment on June 5, 1865 he was discharged as of the 147th on May 24, 1865 at Elmira. Little is known about Mary. The couple was married when the 1870 census was taken. In 1900 Henry was a widower. They had no children. Henry worked in an iron foundry. He is buried in Woodlawn National Cemetery, Elmira. At least four of Henry's brothers served the Union cause. Matthew (1833-?) was a member of Co. I, 5th Ind. Artillery from January 1864-September 1865. Andrew (1834-1907) served in Co. F, 179th from May 1864-June 1865. Charles (1837-?) was a member of Co. I, 33rd from July 1861-June 1863. Andrew (1841-?) served in the 5th NY HA from September 1862-June 1865.

John B. McCord – Co. H
b. 1834 Orange County, NY
d. February 16, 1864 Judiciary Square Hospital, Washington, DC
m. Olive A. Roblyer (1840-July 22, 1901) May 11, 1856

NOTE: John was the son of Samuel G. (1803-*post* 1875) and Frances "Fannie" Budd McCord (1815-*post* 1875). A draftee, he entered the 147th at Corning, Steuben, NY on July 16, 1863. His COD was variously described, ranging from diphtheria to laryngitis. A letter written by Captain Alexander Penfield, dated May 24, 1865, clarifies the matter: ". . . Said John B. McCord contracted [typhoid fever] by fatigues and hardships consequent upon the campaign to Mine Run, Va. between the 26th of Nov. and 9th of Dec. 1863. My knowledge of the above facts is obtained from the following source: I was present with my company during the entire campaign." John is buried in the Soldiers' and Airmen's Home Cemetery, Washington, DC. He and Olive were the parents of three children. Olive married John H. Webber (1839-November 23, 1901) on March 4, 1866. He had served in Co. C, 50th NY Engineers. They are buried in Rural Home Cemetery, Big Flats, Chemung, NY.

William McCoy – Co. F
b. 1838 Massachusetts
d. ? ?
m. ?

NOTE: McCoy, a clerk, was a substitute for William Lickley, Rochester, Monroe, NY. He enrolled in the 147th at Rochester on August 5, 1863. The last reference to him is found on his muster roll card which states he was "absent, sick" at Carver Hospital, Washington, DC on October 31, 1863. The card also notes he was never paid and no further record was available. It is probable that he died in November 1863. His parents are unknown.

James McGuire – Co. E
b. 1827 Ireland
d. ? ?
m. ?

NOTE: James was a substitute for Robert Ransbury, a draftee, enrolling in the 147th on August 21, 1863 at Franklinville, Cattaraugus, NY. Although his muster roll card says he transferred to Co. D, 91st Regiment on June 5, 1865 and mustered out on July 3rd near Washington, DC, he does not appear in *The Adjutant-General's Report* for that regiment. A notation says he was "absent, sick" but gives no dates. No other information has been discovered, including names of parents.

George McIntosh – Co. G
b. 1836 Scotland
d. ? ?
m. ?

NOTE: George, a painter, was a substitute for Rinaldo E. Jones and enrolled in the 147th on August 13, 1863 at Ellicott, Chautauqua, NY. At an unspecified date he transferred to the 3rd Brigade Band. Nothing else has been learned about him. His parents are unknown.

John McMahon – Co. G

b. 1828 Ireland
d. *ante* 1870 Dunkirk, Chautauqua, NY
m. Mary _____ (1838-*post* 1870) *ca.* 1853

NOTE: John's parents are unknown. A blacksmith, he saw prior service in Co. H, 72nd Regiment from October 1861-March 1863 when he was discharged from Mt. Pleasant Hospital, Washington, DC for "disability." He enrolled in the 147th as a substitute for Frederick Koch at Dunkirk on August 17, 1863. He was captured on December 10, 1864, place unspecified, returned to his company on June 7, 1865 and was discharged on June 9th. In 1865 Mary said she was the mother of six, four of whom were living. By 1870 she was living with two of them in Dunkirk, apparently a widow.

Lawrence James McMullen – Co. F

b. August 31,1828 Lockport, Niagara, NY
d. March 24, 1918 Akron, Erie, NY
m. Olive Bishop (1838-June 1888) 1860

NOTE: Lawrence was the son of James (1803-1865) and Jane McMullen (1808-1882). His DOB varies, depending on the document. I use that inferred from his muster roll card. He was drafted and his entry in *The Town Clerks' Registers* states he was "the only drafted man in service from this town." He enrolled in the 147th at Buffalo, NY on August 12, 1863. On June 5, 1865 he transferred to Co. A, 91st Regiment and mustered out near Washington, DC on July 3rd. His pension index card also shows service in Co. F, 9th NY HA but he does not appear in *The Adjutant-General's Report* for that outfit. He and Olive were the parents of a son and a daughter. Olive is buried in Pioneer Cemetery, Akron, Erie, NY. Lawrence is buried in St. Teresa Cemetery, Akron. His COD was "cancer of the stomach and chronic interstitial nephritis."

John McMurray – Co. G

b. 1846 Ireland
d. June 20, 1864 4th Division 5th Army Corps Hospital, Petersburg, VA
m. ------

NOTE: John McMurray/McMurry/Murry was an alias for Lawrence John Dorsey, son of Michael (1820-?) and Ann Dorsey/Darcy (1823-?). Although he claimed to be 19 when he entered the military, the 1850 census proves he was only 17. His muster roll card states he was born in New York State but the same census indicates he and all the members of his family had been born in Ireland. Perhaps he used the alias because he was underage. He was a substitute for Andrew Chamberlin and enrolled in the 147th at Ischua, Cattaraugus, NY on August 21, 1863. John was wounded in the side at Petersburg, VA on June 19, 1864 and died the next day. Captain William Gillett, Co. G, deposed that Michael Dorsey had had his son's body exhumed and sent to Lansingburgh, Rensselaer County, where the family resided, an assertion confirmed by a short article located in *The Lansingburgh Semi-Weekly Chronicle* October 19, 1864: "John B. Lavender has returned from a successful trip to Washington in search of the bodies of several deceased soldiers. He brought home four bodies, Cornelius Murphy, Andrew Kirkpatrick, L. Dorsey, and a Mr. Kiefe." On May 16, 1866 Ann Dorsey applied for a pension, claiming that for four years her son had been the sole support for her and Michael who was described in 1866 by Dr. A. D. Hull, the family physician, as a man "of advanced age" incapable of earning a living "by reason of natural decrepitude." The doctor estimated Michael's age to be 70 but for the 1850 census Dorsey had stated he was 30. Lawrence had given his mother almost all his earnings for the several years he worked prior to entering the military, a practice he continued after enlisting, as witnessed by a letter he sent home from Alexandria, VA and dated October 13, 1863: "My daer father I Sent you $50 dollars to you By Adams Express Comp you go to the Express office and you will git it from your Son, John Dorsey. To his father Mich Dorsey I go her By the name of John Murry." Friends and neighbors testified that Ann and Michael were "in indigent circumstances," owning no property except a few pieces of furniture and some clothing. Ann was granted the pension which began at $8.00 per month. By the time she died that amount had increased to $12.00. She was dropped from the rolls on March 27, 1900 for "failure to claim M.O." but it is likely she died in late 1896 or early 1897 because she was last paid to November 4, 1896. Graves for these people have not been located.

Duncan McNiel – Co. G
b. 1839 Canada
d. ? ?
m. ?

NOTE: Little can be ascertained about Duncan's life before or after his military service. He was a substitute for Henry Lawrence, Tonawanda, Erie, NY and enrolled in the 147th at Buffalo, NY on August 15, 1863. A sailor by occupation, he reportedly was discharged from the army on April 15, 1864 in order to enlist in the US Navy. His description for the 147th was as follows: hazel eyes, brown hair, dark complexion, 5' 7" tall. A man named Duncan McNiel, born Canada, a transferred soldier, was enrolled at the Brooklyn Navy Yard on May 4, 1864. He had blue eyes, black hair, florid complexion, and stood 5' 7 ½" tall. This may or may not be the identical man.

William D. Melville – Co. I
b. 1837 Canada
d. ? ?
m. ?

NOTE: A farmer, William was a substitute for George H. Horner, a draftee from Buffalo, Erie, NY. He enrolled in the 147th at Buffalo on August 8, 1863 and was discharged from the service on a surgeon's certificate of disability on March 17, 1864. No other information is available including the names of his parents.

Lavinous William Merrick – Co. E
b. 1844 New York City, NY
d. February 2, 1920 Lorain, Lorain, OH
m. Jane Brown (1833-*ante* 1900) *ca.* 1869

NOTE: Lavinous was the son of Levi (1800-1860) and Ann E. Merrick (1807-1860). His name was variously spelled. I use that on his death certificate. Although he stated for his muster roll card that he had been born in New York City, the 1855 New York census showed that he and a younger sister, Mary, were both born in Erie County. His DOB is also a mystery. His death certificate provides a date of November 8, 1840. In 1855 he was 13. In 1880 he was 37. Lavinous was drafted, enrolling in the 147th on August 18, 1863. He transferred to Co. I, 91st Regiment on June 5, 1865 and mustered out near Washington, DC on July 3rd. He and Jane lived in Scriba and he joined Lewis B. Porter Post No. 573 GAR on January 1, 1887. The entire family, composed of Lavinous, Jane, and two sons, Lavinous (1870-March 27, 1944) and William (1873-December 26, 1925), was living in Scriba in 1892. It is unknown if Jane died in New York State or Ohio. Lavinous died from uremia and chronic nephritis and was buried in Elmwood Cemetery, Lorain. His two sons and their wives are also buried there.

Fayette T. Mersereau – Co. F
b. 1847 Union, Broome, NY
d. July 9, 1899 Binghamton, Broome, NY
m. Sarah Jennett Brundage (1852-December 8, 1928) *ca.* 1876

NOTE: Fayette's DOB varies. I use that on his gravestone. He was the son of John Putnam (1822-1883) and Phebe Ann Dutcher Mersereau (1826-1910). A draftee, he enrolled in the 147th on August 9, 1863 at Rochester, Monroe, NY. He was discharged at Washington, DC on February 28, 1864 for "disability." On January 17, 1865 he enlisted in the 15th New York Engineers, serving until June 13, 1865. His brother Jerome (1845-*post* 1880) enlisted in the same outfit on January 30, 1865. Their entries in *The Town Clerks' Registers* say they were at Petersburg [*sic*] when Lee surrendered. In 1890 Fayette claimed heart trouble and rheumatism as disabilities. His death was announced in *The Susquehanna Weekly* July 18, 1899: ". . . Fayette F. [*sic*] Mersereau, formerly an Erie engineer, but of late years engaged in the ice business in Binghamton, died suddenly at his home, Saturday last, of apoplexy. The funeral was attended Tuesday. Interment at Union, his former home. . . ." He and Sarah are buried in Riverside Cemetery, Endicott, Broome, NY.

Charles Meyers – Co. G
b. 1842 Germany
d. ? ?
m. ?

NOTE: Charles was a substitute for Henry H. Graves, enrolling in the 147th on August 19, 1863 at Harmony, Chautauqua, NY. On June 5, 1865 he transferred to Co. F, 91st Regiment under the name Myers and mustered out on July 3rd. No other confirmable information is available.

Martin Miller – Co. G
b. 1824 Prussia
d. April 10, 1913 ?
m. Catherine _____ (1829-*ante* 1913) *ca.* 1850

NOTE: Martin, whose parents are unknown, was a farmer. His DOB is variously given. He enlisted in Co. H, 21st Regiment and served from May 1861-May 1863. In 1863 he was a substitute for Norman Beebe, Concord, Erie, NY and enrolled in the 147th on August 12th at Buffalo. He suffered a gunshot wound to the right leg on May 5, 1864 at the battle of the Wilderness. Although nominally transferred to Co. F, 91st Regiment on June 5, 1865, he was discharged on June 6th. He and Catherine were the parents of at least eight children. On September 17, 1899 Martin entered the National Soldiers' Home in Wauwatosa, Milwaukee, WI. He gave Catherine as his next of kin and said their address was Wilmette, Cook, IL. He left the home on "own request" on April 3, 1903. He was still alive on March 7, 1907 because he reapplied for his pension. No widow is listed on the pension index card but I have been unable to find Catherine's DOD. Martin's DOD is found on his pension index card. I have been unable to discover where he died.

John Edward Milner – Co. H
b. 1842 London, England
d. March 28, 1888 Baldwinsville, Onondaga, NY
m1. Rosalinda "Rosa" Hilliard (October 1849-January 20, 1924) *ca.* 1865
m2. Jane "Jennie" _____ (1848-*post* 1890) *ca.* 1870

NOTE: Milner, a teacher by occupation, saw prior duty in Co. H, 24th Regiment from May 1861-May 1863. He apparently re-enlisted, enrolling in the 147th at Elmira, Chemung, NY on November 17, 1863. According to *Registers of Officers and Enlisted Men*, he was "shot in back at battle of Wilderness." He was discharged for "disability" on August 29, 1865. Notations on his muster card suggest he was in hospital in Elmira when discharged. Rosalinda was the daughter of Isaiah (1827-?) and Jerusha C. Bovier Hilliard (1828-?). In 1865 she and John Edward, AKA Edward J., were living with her mother in Elmira. It seems, however, that the marriage did not last. By 1870 Rosa was married to Charles David "Dodge" Canfield (1846-1920). In 1900 Rosa claimed she had been married 36 years while David said he had been married 32 years. In 1910, however, Rosa averred she had only been married once. Both Rosa and Charles, who had served in the 12th New Jersey Infantry, died at the Minnesota Soldiers' Home. They are buried in Lakewood Cemetery, Minneapolis. Little is known about Jane. She was born in Onondaga County, NY. In 1875 she and John had a son, Edmund (1872-?), also born in Onondaga County. The family was living in Van Buren, Onondaga, NY in 1880 where John was teaching school. He applied for a pension in 1884. Upon his death Jane obtained a widow's pension. In 1890 Jane, still living in Baldwinsville, was enumerated as a widow on the Veterans' Schedules. After that date, she disappeared. What happened to Edmund is unknown. John is buried in Warners Village Cemetery.

William Miner – Co. C
b. 1833 New Haven, New Haven, CT
d. August 10, 1864 Armory Square Hospital, Washington, DC
m1. Sarah _____ (1836-*ca.* 1862) *ca.* 1860
m2. Helen "Nellie" Wallace (1848-*post* 1905) March 15, 1863

NOTE: Little is known about William's life prior to his military career. He appears on the 1860 census, living in Elmira, Chemung, NY with Sarah, whom he had married "within the year." Evidently she died because on March 15, 1863 he married Nellie, proven by a notarized letter from Rev. E. J. Hermans, the Methodist minister who performed the ceremony. William was drafted, enrolling in the 147th on July 2, 1863. His surname was spelled Minor on his muster roll card. He was wounded at Petersburg, VA in June 1864 and died of his injury. His card says a gunshot wound fractured a femur. He is buried in Arlington National Cemetery. Nellie is an interesting case. She applied for a widow's pension on July 31, 1865 and obtained it. In 1867, however, a complaint was made and her pension was suspended pending the outcome. It appears that in August 1861, when she was only 13 years old, she married James Odell, 14, at Elmira. Her mother, Mary Barden (1825-?), testified that she forced Nellie to return home after living with Odell for approximately ten days. In the eyes of the Pension Bureau, however, it looked as if she had a prior husband living. What is not made clear in the proceedings is that by 1865 Nellie was married to Jacob Fountain (1833-*post* 1905) and was the mother of a baby, Elizabeth! Nellie's second child, John (January 5, 1876-April 9, 1930), was born in New York City. The last known reference to this couple is found in the 1905 New York census. Elizabeth's name was now Smith and she had an 11-year-old son, William. John was not enumerated with the family. He married Kathryn Holfield Floyd in Cleveland, Cuyahoga, OH on May 18, 1920. He died in Michigan City, LaPorte, IN, of tuberculosis, an inmate in the Indiana State Prison.

John Mitchell – Co. I
b. 1846 Ireland
d. June 20, 1864 4th Division 5th Army Corps Hospital, Petersburg, VA
m. ------

NOTE: John was the son of John (?-?) and Ann Mitchell (?-*post* 1867). His mother was a widow when John, her only surviving child, came to the United States from Galway and settled in Oswego. He befriended other Irish immigrants and found work. He regularly sent money to Ann and in early 1864 he mailed her passage money. In the meantime he apparently enlisted in the 147th, enrolling on February 23, 1864 at Oswego City. He left $200 with friends for his mother's use. She arrived in March and settled into a small house he owned on some leased land in the city. On June 19th John was fatally shot. Ann received the following letter from Sergeant Anthony Griffin, dated June 20th: "Mrs. Mitchell, It is with regret that I have to inform you of the death of your son, John Mitchell. While in the act of coming into the breastworks yesterday after cooking breakfast he got hit in the belly by a Minnie ball, passing through him and coming out in his side. He lived 20 hours after getting hit. The officers and men of the company sympathize with you deeply in losing your only Son and support. I gave him three letters before he got hit which he read and I got two More by Mail last night for him which I will return. One is from Mr. Shatzel. His ring also which he sent me from hospital I will send you in this letter. I have no time to write any more at present. I feel sorry for you and also for poor Johnny for he was a good soldier." Mr. Shatzel was a friend who assisted John with sending money to his mother. What happened to Ann is unknown. She obtained a pension and in 1867 moved to New York City.

Joseph F. Moore – Co. F
b. 1841 Glasgow, Scotland
d. ? ?
m. ?

NOTE: Joseph was a substitute for Charles D. Watson, a draftee. He joined the 147th on August 22, 1863 but where he enrolled is a mystery because Perlville, NY seems not to have existed. On June 5, 1865 under the name Joseph G. Moore he transferred to Co. A, 91st Regiment, mustering out on July 3rd near Washington, DC. Nothing else has been located.

John Moran – Co. K
b. 1836 Ireland
d. November 19, 1916 Oswego City, NY
m. ------

NOTE: John was the son of Michael (?-*ante* 1860) and Mary Hare Moran (1799-1879). He seems to have enlisted in the 147th, enrolling on March 29, 1864. It is interesting to note that he has no muster roll card and that *The Town Clerks' Registers* show he was enrolled in Co. K in July 1863. He transferred to Co. K, 91st Regiment on June 5, 1865 and mustered out near Washington, DC on July 3rd. His death was reported in *The Oswego Daily Palladium* November 20, 1916, 5: "John Moran, aged eighty-seven years, died at the home of his niece Mrs. Marcus McCormick, 149 West Mohawk street, at 10:38 yesterday morning. Mr. Moran was born in Ireland and came to this city when a youth. His parents built a home in West Eighth between Oneida and Mohawk streets and lived there for many years, the garden and grape vines being the envy of the boys in the neighborhood. With the death of the older people Mr. Moran and his brother, Patrick, lived there for many years. The latter died several years ago. Recently the deceased had made his home with his niece. During the Civil War he enlisted under Captain N. A. Wright in K Company, 147th New York Volunteers, and served through the campaigns with his regiment. Returning from the war he took up his occupation as gardener and worked about many of the homes in the city. He was a member of St. Mary's Church. Nieces and nephews are the only surviving relatives." Patrick, described as a "recluse," died on November 1, 1910. John and Patrick, together with their parents, are buried in St. Paul's Cemetery, Oswego City.

Samuel L. Morey – Co. K
b. August 18, 1836 Tompkins County, NY
d. June 18, 1864 Petersburg, VA
m. Hannah Ophelia McIntire (March 24, 1845-August 5, 1928) July 4, 1861

NOTE: Samuel was drafted, enrolling in the 147th on July 21, 1863 at Van Etten, Chemung, NY. He was shot in the head. The letter sent to Hannah quoted below says he died on June 18th although the entry in *Deaths of Volunteers* signed by Dr. A. S. Coe says "killed in battle" on June 20th. Captain Joseph Dempsey's touching letter of condolence was dated July 3, 1864: "It is with feelings of the deepest regret that I sit down to write and inform you of the death of your Husband Samuel L. Morey of my Co. K. He was killed on the 18th day of June while we were charging the Enemy's works In front of Petersburgh, Va. – he was behind me when he was struck by a rifle ball which went through his head and wounded another man. I regret his loss very much for he was one of the very best men in my company. We remained under fire of the Enemies' Batteries all the afternoon of the 18th – we could not get away until it was dark. I dug a grave for him with a Bayonet and covered him up as there was no hope at that time of carrying off our dead – as soon as night came I sent out a party and had him taken in where we had him decently interred placing a board at his head with his name age Co. Regt etc printed on it. I made the men search his Body also and whatever Little things or Relics he had from home I sent them to his Brother in law Ira Perrin. The men of my command are very Sorry for Samuel for he was a brave courageous Soldier and he fell fighting in a good cause. I have nothing more to add at present but my sincere sympathy for your sudden Bereavement. I hope god will protect you and your children." Samuel and Hannah were the parents of William (1862-?) and Anna E. (1864-?). Hannah married Stephen Besley, also a member of the 147th, on September 30, 1866. They are buried in North Chemung Cemetery. The gravestone is also a cenotaph for Samuel. Ira Perrin, mentioned in Dempsey's letter, was a member of the 147th. See his story below.

Andrew Morrison, Jr. – Co. G
b. 1831 Humphrey, Cattaraugus, NY
d. March 31, 1865 3rd Division, 5th Army Corps Hospital, Petersburg, VA
m. ------

NOTE: Andrew, son of Andrew (1798-August 18, 1869) and Jeanette Morrison (1795-October 1872), was drafted, enrolling in the 147th at Humphrey on August 21, 1863. According to *Deaths of Volunteers*, he died of a gunshot wound to the abdomen received in battle at Gravelly Run, VA. He is buried in Poplar Grove National Cemetery, Petersburg, VA. After his father died, his mother successfully applied for a pension. They are buried in Sugartown Cemetery, Cattaraugus County.

Charles E. Morse – Co. H
b. May 1843 Java, Wyoming, NY
d. July 25, 1919 Cuyahoga Falls, Summit, OH
m. Amanda E. _____ (September 1847-June 20, 1902) 1863

NOTE: Charles was the son of Benjamin (1803-1883) and Frances Nicholas Morse (1809-1908). A draftee, he enrolled in the 147th at Java, Wyoming County, NY on July 30, 1863, after having seen prior service in Co. I, 44th Regiment from October 1861-May 1862 when he was discharged for "disability." He transferred to Co. B, 91st Regiment on June 5, 1865 and was discharged on July 21st, probably at Augur Hospital, Washington, DC where he was when the regiment mustered out on July 3rd. In 1890 he claimed he had lost a finger and suffered from chronic diarrhea. He and Amanda were the parents of two children. Charles' parents and Amanda are buried in Curriers Rural Cemetery, Wyoming County. His name is on the gravestone without a DOD and it is unknown if he is also there.

William H. Morse – Co. H

b. 1829 Otsego County, NY

d. August 30, 1864 Douglas Hospital, Washington, DC

m. Sarah Evaline "Eva" Hubbard (1840-March 25, 1905) March 14, 1863

NOTE: William's parents are unidentified. He married Sarah in Campbell, Steuben, NY and she later testified it was a first marriage for both. William, a blacksmith, was drafted, enrolling in the 147th at Holmsville, Chenango, NY on July 17, 1863. He contracted dysentery during the siege of Petersburg and was sent to hospital where he died. He is buried in Arlington National Cemetery. On March 12, 1874 Sarah married James D. Greek (1818-August 29, 1895) as his second wife. He died of "exhaustion" with asthma as a contributing factor. An obituary, published in *The Steuben Advocate* September 4, 1895, reported he had been poor master for several years. Sarah's death was announced in *The Bath Farmers' Advocate* March 29, 1905: "Mrs. Sarah Eva Greek, widow of the late James Greek, died at her home here last Friday morning, after a long illness covering a period of some years. Her funeral was held from her late residence Saturday afternoon, burial in Hope Cemetery. Mrs. Greek left no family. She left her property to the trustees of the First Presbyterian church, of which she had been a member for some years." James is also in Hope Cemetery.

Alexander F. Mudgett – Co. K

b. 1840 Cattaraugus County, NY

d. ? ?

m. Annette "Nettie" Howland (1852-October 29, 1890) May 13, 1869

NOTE: The son of Abram (1814-1874) and Marian Roy Mudgett (1812-1911), Alexander was a draftee, enrolling in the 147th on August 21, 1863 at Great Valley, Cattaraugus County. He transferred to Co. K, 91st Regiment on June 5, 1865 and mustered out on July 3rd near Washington, DC. He and Annette were the parents of

William (1871-1880) and Harry (1874-*post* 1900). In 1875 the family was living in Salamanca, Cattaraugus County. By 1880 Nettie and the boys were living with her mother, Phoebe Osborn, in Great Valley. According to a summons and notice appearing in *The Randolph Weekly Courant* July 22, 1882, Nettie sought an absolute decree of divorce from Alexander. She claimed in court papers that her husband left her on March 10, 1878 and never returned. She thought he had moved out of state. Witnesses were produced who corroborated Nettie's claim that Alexander had committed adultery with several area women. One witness even claimed Alexander and a woman named Mary Roland, a reputed prostitute, attempted to lure him into what today would be termed a "threesome" in the Rock City Hotel in Little Valley, NY. It was rumored that Alexander had gone with Mary Roland to West Virginia and Kentucky. Nettie obtained her divorce when Alexander failed to appear at the hearing. The decree was dated November 29, 1882. She subsequently married Frank H. Maher (1858-1919) and had at least four children by him: Winifred (1883-*post* 1930); Elizabeth B. (1885-?); William S. (1888-?); Helen A. (1890-?). Nettie's death was reported in *The Ellicott Post* November 1890: ". . . On Wednesday afternoon Mrs. Annette Maher wife of our depot agent F. H. Maher departed this life. Deceased had been sick but a short time and her untimely death has brought sorrow to many hearts. She leaves a husband and two children, besides sisters and brothers to mourn their loss. Funeral was held on Friday and the remains laid at rest in the cemetery at Green's. The afflicted family have the sympathy of the entire community . . . ." Green Cemetery is located in Great Valley. Alexander's brother Abram (1841-*post* 1908) served in the 10th Iowa Infantry from 1864-1865. On September 16, 1908, *The Ellicottville Post* reprinted an article from an Enid, OK newspaper touting the success of Dr. Abraham G. Mudgett in curing cancer patients. According to the article, Mudgett had been a physician for 30 years and was well-regarded in Oklahoma. What happened to Alexander is a great mystery. His mother died on April 30, 1911. Her obituary stated she was the mother of nine children and listed survivors. Alexander was not among them. Whether he was dead or purposefully omitted is a question which cannot at this time be answered.

Patrick Murphy – Co. H
b. 1842 Ireland
d. August 1, 1893 ?
m. ?

NOTE: Little has been learned about this man, including parents' names. He was a draftee and enrolled in the 147th at Utica, Oneida, NY on September 8, 1863. He was captured, exact date unknown, during the battle of Weldon Railroad, which occurred from August 18-21, 1864 and released on February 28, 1865, location unknown. On

June 5, 1865 he transferred to Co. D, 91st Regiment and was discharged on July 7th at McDougal Hospital, New York Harbor. He applied for a pension on October 9, 1865. His pension index card provides a DOD but does not say where he died. No widow is listed on the card.

Noah Larkin Myers – Co. H
b. 1837 Machias, Cattaraugus, NY
d. August 7, 1864 Andersonville, Sumter, GA
m. ------

NOTE: Noah was the son of Eliphalet (1806-1891) and Nancy Robinson Myers (1807-1893). He was a draftee and enrolled in the 147th on July 14, 1863 at Hume, Allegany, NY. The date of his capture is unknown. His COD was dysentery. He is buried in Andersonville National Cemetery. Three brothers also served the Union cause. John (1839-October 23, 1862) was a member of Co. D, 154th Regiment. He died at Fairfax, VA of "disease." Eli (1828-1897) also was a member of Co. D, 154th. Delos (1837-1874) served in Co. F, 19th NY Cavalry.

John Neal – Co. H
b. October 20, 1841 Lowell, Middlesex, MA
d. February 7, 1876 Cincinnati, Hamilton, OH
m. Carrie Ganter (?-post 1892) December 21, 1869

NOTE: John, whose parents are unidentified, was a shoemaker. He saw prior service in Co. A, 24th Regiment from May 1861-May 1863. It appears he deserted and returned to his regiment under President Lincoln's Proclamation of April 10, 1863. On July 25, 1863 he enrolled in the 147th at Wellsville, Allegany, NY as a substitute for Samuel Carpenter. He was taken prisoner on November 25, 1863, place not specified, and paroled. He was sent to parole camp which he left on May 3, 1865. He transferred to Co. B, 91st Regiment on June 5, 1865 and was discharged on June 9th near Arlington, VA. He and Carrie were married in Cincinnati, Hamilton, OH at Holy Angels Church. He is buried in Mount Washington Cemetery, Mount Washington, OH. Carrie successfully applied for a pension in 1888. She appeared in the Cincinnati City Directory until 1892.

John Newman – Co. G
b. February 13, 1833 Germany
d. September 30, 1909 Buffalo, Erie, NY
m. Amy Margaret Shaw (January 17, 1838-June 14, 1912) 1871

NOTE: John, a machinist, was drafted, enrolling in the 147th at Buffalo on August 8, 1863. In April 1864 he was discharged in order to enter the US Navy. An informative obituary in *The Buffalo Evening News* September 30, 1909, 49 detailed his long, active life: "John Newman, a widely-known resident of the South Park district, died this morning at his home . . . after a long illness. Mr. Newman was born in Germany 77 years ago, and came to this country with his parents when four years of age. He spent his early life in Eastern New York, coming to Buffalo to live about 40 years ago. Mr. Newman was one of the oldest members of St. Mark's Church. He was also a member of Bidwell-Wilkinson Post; having served throughout the Civil War, seeing a term of service in the Navy, and in the ranks of the 147th New York Infantry, participating in many important engagements. Surviving Mr. Newman are his wife Amy Louise [*sic*] Newman, and three children, Angie M., John B. and George S Newman. The funeral will be held from the family home Saturday afternoon, and the remains will be taken to Gansevoort, Saratoga county, for interment." John and Amy are buried in Gansevoort Cemetery. His parents are unidentified.

Alford S. Nicholas – Co. E
b. 1845 Otsego County, NY
d. April 1, 1865 3rd Division 5th Army Corps Hospital, Petersburg, VA
m. ------

NOTE: Alford, whose name was also spelled Alfred, was the son of Samuel (1817-?) and Eliza Nicholas (1817-?). The family lived in Ellisburg, Jefferson, NY in 1863 when Alford volunteered as a substitute for James J. Cook, a resident of Salisbury, Herkimer County. He enrolled in the 147th on September 9, 1863 at Watertown, Jefferson, NY. He was fatally wounded in the abdomen at Boydton Road, VA and died in hospital. According to *Registers of Officers and Enlisted Men* he was KIA and buried at Petersburg, but his entry in *Deaths of Volunteers* makes it clear he did not die on the battlefield.

David Nichols – Co. I
b. 1840 Pennsylvania
d. *post* 1870 ?
m. Catherine Madden (1841-*post* 1870) *ca.* 1861

NOTE: David, son of Jacob (?-?) and Catherine Davis Nichols (?-?), was a blacksmith. His surname was sometimes spelled Nickols. A draftee, he enrolled in the 147th at Oswego on August 14, 1863. He was wounded during the battle of the Wilderness on May 5, 1864 and, according to *Registers of Officers and Enlisted Men*, lost his right foot. Although nominally transferred to Co. I, 91st Regiment on June 5, 1865, he was discharged at Washington, DC on June 6th. He and Catherine were the parents of the following in 1870: Mary (1862-?); Ellen (1866-?); Alice (1868-1934); William F.

(1870-?). The last known reference to the family is the 1870 census when they were living in Oswego City. Alice married James McPherson (1848-1926) as his second wife in 1887. They lived in South Gibson, Susquehanna, PA and it is possible the whole family moved to that state.

Harrison Nichols – Co. H

b. November 15,1831 Amherst, Hillsborough, NH
d. July 18, 1896 Java, Wyoming, NY
m1. Sophia Morse (1837-1884) September 25, 1853
m2. Hannah Nash (1848-February 26, 1929) May 1, 1886

NOTE: Harrison, a farmer, was the son of George (1806-1888) and Mary Robertson Nichols (?-1850). He was drafted, enrolling in the 147th on July 3, 1863 at Java. He was discharged for "disability" on March 22, 1865 and in 1890 said he had cut his foot in Virginia while in the army. Harrison and Sophia were the parents of at least three children. He and Hannah were the parents of Laverne (1894-*post* 1929) who was disabled and in later life resided at the Newark State School. Harrison and Sophia are buried in Curriers Rural Cemetery, Curriers, Wyoming, NY. Hannah's obituary appeared in *The Perry Record* February 28, 1929, 1: "Mrs. Hannah Nichols, a resident of Perry for many years, died last Tuesday at the Woman's Relief Corps Home at Oxford, N.Y. Her age was 82 years. She had been in failing health during the past four years. The deceased was born in the town of Covington, from whence she removed to Perry, where most of her life was spent. Her husband, a veteran of the Civil War, died about 25 years ago. She is survived by one daughter and three sisters, viz.: Miss Laverna [*sic*] Nichols of Newark, N.Y.; Mrs. Leo Bennett, Mrs. Mary Wicking and Mrs. Philinda Fisk, all of Batavia. Her remains will be brought to Perry, where private funeral services will be held in the M. E. Church at 2 p.m. tomorrow, Rev. J. W. Searles officiating." She was buried in Glenwood Cemetery, Perry. Harrison's brother George H. (1827-1912) served in the 187th Regiment. Another brother, Gardiner (1835-1888), served in the 44th Regiment.

John Nichols – Co. H

b. 1841 New York State
d. July 10, 1924 Jackson County, MI
m. ?

NOTE: Little has been learned about this soldier. A draftee, he enrolled in the 147th at Buffalo, Erie, NY on August 13, 1863. He transferred to Co. F, 91st Regiment on June 5, 1865 and mustered out near Washington, DC on July 3rd. He applied for a pension on June 24, 1880, place unknown. His DOD is given only on his pension index card for the 91st Regiment.

John Nolon – Co. C

b. 1844 New York State

d. ? ?

m. ?

NOTE: This man was a substitute for Henry B. Jenkins and enrolled as a sergeant at Elmira, Chemung, NY on July 20, 1863. He was discharged for "disability" on May 10, 1865. No other information has been located.

John Byron Nolton – Co. H

b. September 2, 1842 Newark Valley, Tioga, NY

d. December 4, 1911 Newark Valley, Tioga, NY

m. Roxanna Andrews (September 2, 1842-January 25, 1911) 1875

NOTE: John's parents are unknown. A farmer, he was drafted, enrolling in the 147th at Newark Valley on July 14, 1863. He was discharged at Satterlee Hospital, Philadelphia, PA on June 29, 1865. John was a member of Charles H. Williams Post No. 245 GAR at Newark Valley. He and Roxanna were the parents of one child, Deborah (1885-?). They are buried in Hope Cemetery, Newark Valley. According to the gravestones they were born on the same date.

George Merwin Norwood – Co. F

b. November 14, 1846 Allegany, Cattaraugus, NY

d. 1869 Wyoming Territory

m. Emeline "Emma" Prescott Dudley (October 4, 1841-December 27, 1918) April 26, 1868

NOTE: George was the son of Francis Micah (1808-1904) and Mary Sperry Bush Norwood (1819-1911). He saw prior duty in Co. D, 85th Regiment from August 1862-June 1863. He was a substitute for John Stowell, Allegany, NY, enrolling at Allegany on August 22, 1863. He was wounded in the knee at the battle of Weldon Railroad in August 1864 and discharged from the service on June 7, 1865 at McClellan Hospital, Philadelphia, PA. After the war the family moved to Monona County, IA where George and Emeline, a native of Maine, were married. They became the parents of a daughter, Myrtle Adele (December 2, 1869-1958). Her birth date is important because George, according to his muster roll card for the 85th Regiment, was reported killed by Indians in 1868. A letter written by his father in 1897 revealed he had reportedly been killed while serving as a captain in the US Cavalry. It is evident that the date is incorrect. Emeline married Joseph Hite (1832-July 1, 1900), a veteran of Co. H, 108th IL, on September 10, 1870 in Monona, IA as his second wife. While Gertrude, the first of their five children, was born in Iowa in 1875, Ernest, the second, was born in

Oregon in 1878. Joseph and Emeline are buried in Crescent Grove Cemetery, Tigard, Washington, OR. Eugene Francis Norwood (1839-August 1, 1864), George's brother, served in Co. D, 85th Regiment. He was captured and sent to Andersonville, GA where he died. Another sibling, Delos Mortimer Norwood (1844-1921), served in the 64th Regiment, attaining the rank of lieutenant.

John Nunberg – Co. H
b. 1836 Sax-Gotha, Germany
d. ? ?
m. ?

NOTE: Little is known about this soldier, whose real name was Johan Noanberg. A substitute for Samuel Marsh, he enrolled in the 147th at Allegany, Cattaraugus, NY on August 22, 1863. He was captured on December 2, 1863 at Mine Run, VA. From the available records it appears he was paroled on April 28, 1864 and sent to hospital. The muster roll card shows he "joined from missing in action April 30, 1864." On all subsequent rolls he was reported "absent sick since April 28, 1864." He was nominally transferred to Co. B, 91st Regiment but was "absent, sick" and no discharge was given. There are no records for him after April 1864.

Sylvester Oakley – Co. I
b. June 15, 1838 Pleasant Valley, Dutchess, NY
d. November 6, 1864 Florence, SC
m. Mary Delphina Goodwin (May 27, 1844-June 2, 1906) July 23, 1863

NOTE: Sylvester was the son of Tobias G. (1805-1890) and Helen Medgadth Oakley (1807-1853). He was a substitute for Robert D. Taylor and enrolled in the 147th in Binghamton, Broome, NY on July 17, 1863. A week later he and Mary were married in Candor, Tioga, NY. Sylvester was captured on May 5, 1864 at the battle of the Wilderness. On August 29, 1865 William C. Rose, Hannibal, NY, and William Collins, Oswego City, NY gave the following deposition: ". . . they were Privates in Co. I of the 147th Regt. N.Y. Vols. That deponents were taken prisoners of war at the Battle of the Wilderness, Va. on the 5th day of May, 1864; that they were taken as such prisoners to Andersonville, Georgia, where they remained from the 19th day of May, 1864, until the 12th day of September, 1864. Then they were taken to Florence SC. That deponents were well acquainted with Sylvester Oakley who was a Private in said Co. I and was taken prisoner of war at the same time deponents were taken prisoners. That said Oakley was taken with us to Florence aforesaid. That said Sylvester Oakley died about the 6th day of November, 1864, in the Hospital at Florence, That he was sick with the pluracy [sic], as it was then called about four days before his

death. On being taken sick he was removed to the Hospital Department and deponents visited him every day and some days twice a day while he was in the Hospital.
That his health was good until attacked with the disease of which he died as above
stated." Sylvester was nominally transferred to Co. D, 91st Regiment on June 5, 1865
but he was already dead. Mary married Solomon Vergason (1827-1894) as his second wife in 1875. They are buried in Chapel Hill Cemetery, Candor. Sylvester's grave
has not been located.

Patrick O'Brien – Co. H
b. 1836 County Clare, Ireland
d. ? ?
m. ?

NOTE: Little is known about this soldier. He was a substitute for Rush Craig, Hamburg,
Erie, NY and enrolled in the 147th at Buffalo on August 14, 1863. He was captured by
the Confederates at an unknown date and reportedly paroled at Annapolis, MD on
December 31, 1864. He next was reported "absent at Annapolis" on March 2, 1865.
The record is silent beyond that point. It is possible he died.

John Sanford Odell – Co. E
b. February 1834 Paris, Oneida, NY
d. January 26, 1904 Auburn, Cayuga, NY
m. Laura Earles (December 11, 1843-January 10, 1919) 1862

NOTE: John, a farmer, was the son of Daniel (1799-1872) and Abigail Odell (1803-
1872). He was drafted, enrolling in the 147th at Utica, Oneida, NY on August 25,
1863. He was discharged for "disability" at Camp Distribution, VA on February 11,
1864. He and Laura were the parents of 11 children, ten of whom were living in
1900. The Odells are buried in Evergreen Cemetery, Lee, Oneida, NY.

John O'Hanley – Co. D
b. 1845 Canada
d. May 12, 1864 Laurel Hill, VA
m. ------

NOTE: John, a farmer, was a substitute for Adam Blust, Buffalo, Erie, NY, enrolling
in the 147th at Buffalo on August 10, 1863. His muster roll card states he "died of
wounds received in action." Nothing else is known.

Ansel Orr – Co. C

b. 1819 Yates County, NY

d. July 22, 1864 DeCamp Hospital, David's Island, New York Harbor

m. Polly Van Horn (1820-October 25, 1892) *ca.* 1844

NOTE: Ansel, whose DOB varies from document to document, was a substitute for Edward V. Cole. His muster roll card indicates he was born in Steuben County, but the 1855 New York census shows his POB was Yates County. Furthermore, his younger brother William was born in Yates County. Ansel enrolled in the 147th at Fremont, Steuben, NY on July 18, 1863. His COD was chronic diarrhea. He is buried in Cypress Hills National Cemetery, Brooklyn. Some time before 1870 Polly married Ansel's brother William (1825-September 9, 1892). His death was reported in *The Canisteo Times* September 15, 1892: ". . . William Orr, an old and respected resident of Canisteo, died of pneumonia at his home on Glen avenue last Friday, aged 66 years. The funeral services were held at the house, Rev. W. E. Searles officiating, and interment was in Hillside cemetery. His widow survives but is very low from cancer . . . ." Polly, who died a little more than a month later, is also buried in Hillside. The parents of Ansel and William are uknknown.

Oscar Overton – Co. E

b. 1841 Monroe County, MI

d. April 16, 1900 National Soldiers' Home, Dayton, Montgomery, OH

m1. Martha Skellan (1845-December 18, 1913) *ca.* 1862

m2. Elizabeth Good Wirshing (1844-*post* 1890) December 1, 1887

NOTE: Oscar was the son of Oscar (1806-?) and Jane Overton (1816-?). A farmer, he saw prior duty in Co. K, 13th Regiment from October 1861-May 1862 when he was discharged from Carver Hospital, Washington, DC for "disability." He was a substitute for Clinton Perry, Kendall, Erie, NY and enrolled in the 147th at Rochester, Monroe, NY on August 8, 1863. He was wounded at Five Forks, VA on April 1, 1865 and discharged from Satterlee Hospital, West Philadelphia, PA on July 24, 1865. He lost his little finger in the battle. He and Martha were the parents of Isabella (March 12, 1864-March 24, 1948). By 1875 the couple was living apart. In 1880 Martha was living in Brockport, Monroe, NY with Isabella and husband Albert Mufford (1859-1925). Oscar was living in Rochester with "wife" Libby, 25, and son John, 1. Oscar was admitted to the Monroe County Almshouse on June 16, 1883 for "injury." He gave his son, John, residing in Chicago, IL, and a sister, Lucinda Birch, Brockport, as his next of kin. By September 1883 he was an inmate at the Bath Soldiers' Home. He left there at his own request on November 4, 1884. He seems to have spent time in Milwaukee, but his last admission was to the Dayton Home on June 25, 1885. On

December 1, 1887 Oscar married Elizabeth Wirshing, whose husband was Lucien Wirshing (1843-April 28, 1890), whom she had married in 1865 and by whom she was the mother of four sons and a daughter. The information on the 1890 Veterans' Schedules for Dayton, OH is intriguing. Elizabeth Overton called herself the widow of Lucien Wirshing, who had served in the 11th OH. Two lines below Oscar Overton claimed to have been a member of Co. K, 37th Regiment but could not remember the dates. His death was reported in *The Marietta Daily Leader* April 20, 1900, 2: "Dayton, O., April 20. – Oscar Overton, aged 75, an inmate of the soldiers' home, while in Yoder's saloon, on Washington street, was taken with a fit of coughing. He fell to the floor and died before medical attention could be summoned. Death resulted from the bursting of a blood vessel." Oscar, a member of William F. Barry Post No. 248 GAR, was buried in Dayton National Cemetery. Since no widow claimed his pension, it is possible that Elizabeth predeceased him. It is also possible she did not apply because the Pension Bureau would deny the claim, based on the fact that she had a living husband when she married Oscar. I have found no records for her beyond 1890. Martha, however, found a measure of happiness after being abandoned. She married John Cowlin (1826-July 20, 1914), date unknown, as his second wife. Their only daughter, Emma J. (June 2, 1886-July 16, 1976), was born in Albion, Calhoun, MI and it is evident that John and Martha accompanied Isabella and Albert to Michigan, where their only child, an infant daughter, died on August 31, 1886. John had served in Co. H, 21st NY Cavalry. Martha, John, Isabella, Albert, and the unnamed baby are all buried in Riverside Cemetery, Albion. John Overton's fate is unknown. Emma was twice married, first to Edward J. Eckstein (1884-*ante* 1938) and second to Alfred Brooker (1887-1973).

DeWitt Clinton Owen – Co. E

b. 1841 Dix, Schuyler, NY
d. June 22, 1884 Dix, Schuyler, NY
m. Josephine Willey (1855-February 10, 1927) *ca.* 1880

NOTE: DeWitt was the son of Jonathan (1819-1865) and Betsy Owen (1821-1905). A draftee, he enrolled in the 147th on July 29, 1863 at Dix. He was discharged at Elmira, Chemung, NY on May 24, 1865. His death was announced in *The Havana Journal* June 28, 1884: "DeWitt Owens is suffering very much at present from the effects of a bad breach. He is in a dangerous condition. Later, the 22d. He died today about 11:15 a.m. . . . The funeral of DeWitt Owens was very largely attended at his house on Monday last." He is buried in Moreland Cemetery, Moreland, Schuyler, NY. Josephine was the daughter of Richard (1820-1855) and Rachael Perry Willey (1824-*post* 1860). After their father's death the Willey children were "farmed out" to paternal and maternal grandparents. In 1870 Josephine was living with her uncle

Ebenezer Perry but by 1875 she was living alone in Caroline, Tompkins, NY with two sons, Grant Willie [sic], 2, and Charles Willie, 1. Charles' fate is unknown but in later life Grant took the surname of his stepfather, Joseph W. Miller (1850-November 12, 1916), whom his mother married ca. 1885. In 1900 and 1905 Maude B. Miller (January 1894-December 8, 1940) was living with Joseph and Josephine and was listed as their granddaughter. By 1910 she had become their daughter and when she married John DeMun in 1911 they were listed as her parents. In actuality Grant Willey Miller and Eva Wagar (1874-1949) were the parents of Maude and another daughter, Blanche (1895-1967). Grant died at Josephine's home on February 6, 1927, only four days before his mother. Graves for Joseph and Josephine have not been located but Grant, Maude, and Blanche are all in Lakeview Cemetery, Ithaca.

James B. Owen – Co. E

b. 1828 Schuyler County, NY
d. September 22, 1876 Schuyler County, NY
m. ------

NOTE: James, son of John (1800-post 1855) and Harriet Owen (1795-post 1855), was a mason by occupation. He enrolled in the 147th at Catharine, Schuyler, NY on July 25, 1863 as a substitute for his brother Jesse B. (1831-post 1900). Although nominally transferred to Co. D, 91st Regiment on June 5, 1865 he was discharged on June 6th as a member of the 147th. He applied for a pension on October 30, 1871 and because no widow applied I have inferred he was unmarried. He is buried in Eldred Cemetery, Reynoldsville, Schuyler.

Henry Newman Palmer – Co. E

b. August 22, 1839 Washington, Orange, VT
d. January 21, 1923 Elberton, Elbert, GA
m. Mary Ann Bennett (November 7, 1842-March 29, 1923) February 20, 1866

NOTE: Henry, a farmer, was the son of Elijah (1808-1890) and Adeline Bennett Palmer (1809-1882). He was a substitute for Henry Gleason and enrolled at Oswego City, NY on August 11, 1863. On October 31, 1863 he was reported "absent, sick" at Carver Hospital, Washington, DC. He nominally transferred to Co. D, 91st Regiment on June 5, 1865 but was "absent, sick." In fact, no military records for him can be located. He did not apply for a pension nor did he appear on the 1890 Veterans' Schedules. In 1910 he did not claim to be a Civil War veteran and his grave is marked with a private headstone. In all likelihood, he simply walked away from the war. He and Mary Ann were married in Royalton, Windsor, VT. They were the parents of seven children, four of whom were living in 1900. Their eldest, Eugene Henry

(September 19, 1866-January 9, 1923), died only a few days before his father. Mary Ann died three months later. They are all buried in Elmhurst Cemetery, Elbert County.

John Baum Parslow – Co. C
b. September 24, 1839 Cazenovia, Madison, NY
d. December 1, 1910 Danbury, Fairfield, CT
m. Sarah A. Chambers (April 25, 1849-March 12, 1929) 1871

NOTE: John was the son of John Snyder (1806-1857) and Elizabeth Woodcock Parslow (1804-1848). He saw prior service in Co. B, 76th Regiment from November 25, 1861-January 27, 1863 when he was discharged for "disability" at Alexandria, VA. He enlisted in the 147th at Bainbridge, Chenango County on January 25, 1865 for a term of three years. On June 5, 1865 he transferred to Co. H, 91st Regiment, mustering out on July 3rd near Washington, DC. In later life he was a grocer. John and Sarah, who had been born in Ireland, were the parents of two children, both of whom were alive in 1910. John and Sarah are buried in Wooster Cemetery, Danbury.

John Paulson – Co. H
b. 1843 New Jersey
d. February 24, 1923 National Soldiers' Home, Hampton, VA
m. ------

NOTE: John's parents are unknown but he gave a sister, Cornelia Ligett, Plymouth, IN as next of kin when he entered one of the soldiers' homes. A draftee, he enrolled in the 147th at Hinsdale, Cattaraugus County on August 21, 1863. He was discharged from the service on June 17, 1865 at Mowers Hospital, Philadelphia, PA. He lived with his sister for some time after the war. He also resided in San Antonio, TX because he was shot in the head there in 1881. It appears he was sent to one national home after another. His last transfer occurred on January 2, 1922 when he entered the home in Hampton. At the time he was collecting a pension of $50 per month. His COD was a heart attack. He is buried in Hampton National Cemetery. The name on his gravestone is Poulson.

Alonzo Payne – Co. A
b. Apri 30, 1837 Steuben County, NY
d. June 28, 1927 Liberty, McKean, PA
m1. Rosetta Glover (1843-January 4, 1900) ca. 1862
m2. Phoebe Ann "Eva" Algor _____ (January 11, 1850-January 22, 1922) 1884
m3. Lydia Jane Strang Grimes (1855-1944) ca. 1923

NOTE: Alonzo, son of Isaac (1810-post 1850) and Charity Hess Payne (1816-post 1850), was drafted, enrolling in the 147th on July 18, 1863 at Wayland, Steuben, NY.

He transferred to Co. C, 91ˢᵗ Regiment of June 6, 1865 and mustered out on July 3ʳᵈ at Ball's Cross Roads, VA. Alonzo applied for a pension in 1879 and in 1890 said his disabilities were heart and lung problems. A pension payment card elaborated, saying his disability was disease of the heart and lungs resulting from measles. It appears that he and Rosetta parted company. In 1910 both he and Phoebe said they had been married twice. Alonzo's COD was a cerebral hemorrhage. Phoebe succumbed to heart disease. Rosetta's COD is unknown but she, Alonzo, and Phoebe are all buried in Oak Hill Cemetery, Eldred, McKean, PA. Lydia, usually called by her middle name, was previously married to Samuel Grimes (1843-1921). They are buried in Grimes District Cemetery, Port Allegheny, PA.

James J. Peachey – Co. I
b. September 5, 1840 Cambridge, Gloucestershire, England
d. April 30, 1921 Albion, Calhoun, MI
m. Marian Skellen (April 16, 1842-November 30, 1924) February 27, 1861

NOTE: James, son of James (1815-1876) and Eliza Campbell Peachey (1815-1870), immigrated to the United States in 1846 and became a naturalized citizen. A farmer, he was drafted, enrolling in the 147ᵗʰ on August 7, 1863 at Rochester, Monroe, NY. He transferred to Co. I, 91ˢᵗ Regiment on June 5, 1865 and mustered out near Washington, DC on July 3ʳᵈ. He and Marian were the parents of two children, Clara Belle (1862-1941) and Elmer James (1866-1933) but in 1900 Marian claimed to have had no children at all. James' COD was arteriosclerosis and heart failure. His death was announced in *The Battle Creek Enquirer* May 4, 1920, 12: "James J. Peachey, 80, civil war veteran and resident of Albion for the past forty-five years, is dead at his home on East Pine street after a sickness of only one day. He had not been in good health since a fall on an icy sidewalk last winter. He was a native of England. The funeral will occur at the home Wednesday afternoon, with burial here." He and Marian are buried in Riverside Cemetery, Albion.

George A. Peckham – Co. F
b. 1833 Oneida County, NY
d. ? ?
m. ------

NOTE: George's father is unknown. In 1850 his mother, Maria (1800-*post* 1865), was married to Amasa Chase (1794-*post* 1865). George, a blacksmith, was drafted, enrolling in the 147ᵗʰ on August 2, 1863. At an unknown date he transferred to Co. K, 22ⁿᵈ VRC and was discharged at Camp Dennison, OH on July 28, 1865. At some time after 1875 he moved to Orleans, Ionia, MI where he was enumerated in 1880. He does not appear in the General Index to Civil War Pensions or the 1890 Veterans' Schedules.

Alexander R. Penfield – Co. H

b. September 1940 Wayne County, NY
d. September 7, 1905 Oswego City, NY
m. Rose Althea Parmiter (December 1842-January 13, 1917) 1865

NOTE: Alexander was the son of Alexander (1790-1860) and Betsey Goodenough Penfield (1796-*post* 1850). He was a prominent citizen in Oswego City. In 1885, for example, he sought the position of post master in Oswego and traveled to Washington, DC to consult with President Cleveland. *The Oswego Daily Times-Express* November 16, 1885 reported on the event with an extensive article which included information about his military career: "A day or two since we noticed that Maj. A. R. Penfield was in Washington looking after his own interest in connection with the postoffice in this city. The major has returned, but not with the commission in his pocket as his personal and political friends and probably a large share of the democratic party would have been glad if he had been able to do. Major Penfield is reticent in relation to what was said to him by the president, with whom he was fortunate enough to secure a pleasant interview. He says the president is unquestionably anxious to please the democracy in this appointment, and will not, he thinks, knowingly make an appointment which will displease or make a disturbance in his own party. Our own opinion is that under the circumstances of the case the president finds it quite a difficult matter to set Major Penfield's claims aside. The major is backed by the Veteran's Union, of the United States, and the president has said, that all other things being equal he shall select honorably discharged soldiers in his appointments, a rule, we think, which, if he follows it in good faith, will meet with the approbation of the entire country. With reference to the war and civil record of Maj. Penfield it is so entirely creditable that, if the president is sincere in the expression alluded to, it is difficult to see how he can disregard it. Major Penfield, when a mere boy, so to speak, of 19 years of age, enlisted in the second company raised in this city, Capt. F. C. Miller's, of the 24th N. Y. V., which was a 2 years' regiment, on the 27th of April, 1861. By his sober and soldierly conduct he was early made a sergeant, and for brave and meritorious conduct he was promoted to second lieutenant immediately after the battle of Antietam. While in the 24th, he was in the battles of Fredericksburgh, Rappahannock station, 2d Bull Run, South Mountain, Antietam, Fredericksburgh, (under Burnside) and Chancellorsville. On his return to Oswego, on the mustering out of the 24th, in 1863, 2d lieutenant Penfield found a first lieutenant's commission awaiting him in the 147th N. Y. volunteers, which regiment he joined while it was at Rappahannock Station, and was immediately assigned to the command of a company, and was very soon afterwards commissioned as captain. In the 147th he was in the battles of Hatches' [sic] run, Weldon Rail Road, Yellow Tavern, near the Wilderness. In the battle of the Wilderness, on the 6th of May, the day upon which Gen. Wadsworth was killed, Captain Penfield, while leading his company, was severely wounded in the ankle from a shot from a masked battery, and was taken from the field. He rejoined his regiment before Petersburg, was present at the famous mine explosion and during the siege of Petersburg, was also present with his regiment at Five Forks and at the surrender at Appomattox. His whole time of service was four years and three months, and he was only absent during that time two months from the effects of his wound in the battle of the Wilderness. While still in the service Capt. Penfield was commissioned as major for meritorious conduct in the field. To show the estimation in which Maj. Penfield was held by his superiors, we will state that while still a captain he was assigned a separate command of two companies to garrison Fort McMahon. He was named in the order and the general told him the position was one of peril and he had selected him, young as he was, for the reason that he was sober, discreet and reliable and he knew that he could be relied upon to hold the position, which was a matter of great importance to the Union forces. We think but few young men of this section of the country returned from the war with a more creditable record than Maj. Alexander R. Penfield. What he has been since all our people know, -- a respected, reliable, honorable business man, and as a citizen without a flaw in his character. His qualifications for the postoffice are unquestioned. It remains to be seen whether such a record is of any value in the selection of civil officers under Mr. Cleveland's administration." He did not obtain the appointment. Penfield was a member and past commander of Post O'Brian No. 65 GAR and also served as assistant adjutant-general and assistant quartermaster-general at the state level. If he had lived it was predicted he would have been elected senior vice commander of the state department. In one of several obituaries appearing after his death, *The Oswego Daily Palladium* September 9, 1905, 4 eulogized him thus: ". . . A genial, warm-hearted man, progressive and deeply interested in the welfare of the community in which he lived, he was a representative citizen whose loss will be deeply felt in Oswego and wherever he was known." Rosa moved to Syracuse after her husband's death where she resided with their only child, Cora (1867-1954). She died there "suddenly" and her body was shipped to Oswego for burial. Her COD was myocarditis. The major and his lady are buried in Riverside Cemetery, Scriba.

Benjamin F. Peppard – Co. K
b. May 14, 1838 Chemung, Chemung, NY
d. December 13, 1865 Chemung, Chemung, NY
m. ------

NOTE: Benjamin, son of Francis (1790-December 1849) and Jane Peppard (1790-*post* 1850), was a draftee, enrolling in the 147th at Chemung On July 27, 1863. He transferred to Co. K, 91st Regiment on June 5, 1865 and mustered out July 3rd near

Washington, DC. He made his will on June 24, 1863 in anticipation of entering the military, leaving everything to his brother Charles (1828-1872) who was also named sole executor. COD is unknown. Benjamin is buried in Chemung Village Cemetery.

Daniel Perigo – Co. E
b. 1841 Yates County, NY
d. January 22, 1917 Newfield, Tompkins, NY
m. ------

NOTE: Daniel, son of John (1800-*ca.* 1875) and Betsy Savercool Perigo (1805-*post* 1860), enlisted in Co. G, 3rd Regiment on April 23, 1861 at Albany, NY. He deserted from that outfit at an unknown date and when apprehended was sentenced to join the 147th to carry out the remainder of his term. He joined the regiment on September 16, 1863 and mustered out on June 7, 1865 near Washington, DC. In 1890, while living in Catharine, Schuyler, NY he claimed no disability but when he entered the Bath National Home on April 26, 1909 he was suffering from high blood pressure. He left the home abruptly on July 6th. In 1915 he was living in Newfield. He is buried in Trumbulls Corners Cemetery, Newfield. His government stone does not contain his DOD. That was located on a pension card.

Orlando Amos Perkins – Co. G
b. 1837 Erie County, NY
d. May 14, 1884 Mondovi, Buffalo, WI
m. Hannah Holmes (1837-December 7, 1909) *ca.* 1861

NOTE: Orlando, son of Orley (1812-1858) and Mary Ann Stanbro Perkins (1818-1858), was drafted. He enrolled in the 147th on August 20, 1863 at Yorkshire, Cattaraugus, NY but was discharged for "disability" on December 12th at Convalescent Camp, VA. He and Hannah, the parents of eleven children, were homesteaders in Wisconsin. Orlando's COD is unknown. Hannah's COD was revealed in an article published in *The Eau Claire Leader* December 18, 1909, 4 which reported she had slipped on the porch of her home and had been fatally injured. At her death eight of her children were still living. Orlando and Hannah are buried in Oak Park Cemetery, Mondovi.

Robert Perkins – Co. E
b. 1836 Quebec, Canada
d. ? ?
m. ?

NOTE: Robert's parents are unidentified although it is known he had a sister, Mary, and a brother, Thomas. He was a substitute for Emerson White, Aurelius, Cayuga, NY and enrolled on July 23, 1863 at Auburn, NY. The information on his muster roll card is confusing but it appears he deserted on September 24, 1863 at Culpeper, VA and returned in April 1864. He was listed as MIA on May 5, 1864. He nominally transferred to Co. D, 91st Regiment on June 5, 1865 but does not appear in *The Adjutant's General's Report* for that organization. It is altogether possible he died on May 5th or was taken prisoner and died as a POW.

Milton Ebenezer Perrigo – Co. A

b. December 29, 1840 Newfane, Niagara, NY
d. January 11, 1924 Lewiston, Niagara, NY
m1. Margaret "Maggie" L. Mix (1849-February 16, 1872) April 2, 1867
m2. Sarah C. Mix (1846-August 22, 1900) 1873

NOTE: The son of Albert Ebenezer (1812-1901) and Elizabeth C. Woodward Perrigo (1818-1897), Milton was a substitute for his brother, Franklin H. (1839-February 16, 1906). He enrolled in the 147th on July 28, 1863 at Newfane. He was transferred to Co. C, 91st Regiment on June 5, 1865 and mustered out at Ball's Cross Roads, VA. Margaret and Sarah were the daughters of Benjamin (1809-?) and Jane Mix (1810-?). They were born in St. Lawrence County, NY. Milton and Margaret are buried in Wrights Corner Cemetery, Newfane. It is probable that Sarah is buried there too.

Ira Perrin – Co. K

b. 1840 Chemung County, NY
d. March 18, 1905 Elmira, Chemung, NY
m1. Mary Morey (1846-*post* 1865) *ca.* 1863
m2. Eliza _____ (1850-*ca.* 1875) *ca.* 1867
m3. Helen Imogene "Emma" Larmond (August 1853-March 20, 1951) 1880

NOTE: Son of Hezekiah (1810-1874) and Rhoda Cowell Perrin (1813-1887), Ira was a draftee. He enrolled in the 147th on July 21, 1863 at Van Etten, Chemung, NY where he and his family were living. On June 5, 1865 he transferred to Co. K, 91st Regiment, mustering out on July 3rd near Washington, DC. It appears he was married three times. Mary may have been the sister of Samuel Morey. (See his entry above.) Ira and Eliza were the parents of F. M., who may be the Freddie Perrin who died in 1869 of brain fever, and Juliette (1869-?), who also seems to have died young. They were also the parents of Marguerite (1874-1968). Ira was a member of Louis A. Hazard Post No. 650 GAR, located in Elmira. He is buried in Woodlawn Cemetery, Elmira. Helen was active in the Women's Relief Corps, serving as senior vice-commander in 1902 and commander in 1904. On October 31, 1908 she married Chauncey L. Call (1848-1926) as his second wife. She too is buried in Woodlawn Cemetery.

Levi Perry – Co. C

b. 1842 Schroeppel, NY

d. ? ?

m. ------

NOTE: Levi, a boatman, may have been the son of Eli (1818-*post* 1860) and S. Catharine Perry (1825-*post* 1860). He enlisted in the 147th at Hannibal, NY on March 15, 1864. He was wounded on May 5, 1864 at the battle of the Wilderness and sent to Douglas Hospital, Washington, DC. A letter from J. L. Lake, dated May 23, 1864 and published in *The Oswego Commercial-Advertiser* May 26, 1864, said Perry had been transferred to a hospital in Philadelphia, PA, although another list sent by D. C. Littlejohn dated May 25th and published in the *Advertiser* on May 30th still placed Perry at Douglas Hospital. These seem to be the last references to the man. He is not mentioned in *Deaths of Volunteers* or in *Registers of Officers and Enlisted Men*. No one attempted to obtain a pension.

James Phillips – Co. E

b. 1816 Canada

d. August 27, 1864 Oswego City, NY

m. Jane _____ (1828-?) ?

NOTE: James, according to *The Town Clerks' Registers*, was the son of Elias (?-?) and Susan Roadbud Phillips (?-?). He is not listed in *Registers of Officers and Enlisted Men*. His muster card shows he enrolled in the 147th at Watertown, Jefferson, NY on September 2, 1863 as a substitute for Henry Phillips, who may have been his son (1833-1917), since a man by that name lived in Adams for his entire life. One has to wonder how James managed to enlist since he was too old for military service. Although he was discharged for "disability" at McClellan Hospital, Philadelphia, PA on June 18, 1864, he came to a tragic end and was regarded a deserter, as reported in *The Oswego Commercial Times* August 30, 1864: "On Saturday last a man named Phillips, a deserter from the 147th regiment, was sent to the jail in this city by Provost Marshal Scott for safe keeping. During the night he died from delirium tremens. He had been drinking heavily sometime previous to his arrest."

Stephen Bradley Pierce – Co. E

b. August 14, 1841 Tioga County, NY

d. January 25, 1920 Los Angeles, Los Angeles, CA

m. Sarah Ett Clark (May 1844-September 27, 1901) December 30, 1867

NOTE: Stephen was the son of Addison (1807-*post* 1860) and Sarah Stillwell Pierce (1811-*post* 1860). Although his muster roll card indicates that he was born in Tompkins

County, his birthplace was actually Tioga County, as evidenced by the 1860 census, for which the enumerator entered the county where each person was born. Stephen was drafted, enrolling in the 147th at Auburn, Cayuga, NY on July 23, 1863. He transferred to Co. K, 91st Regiment on June 5, 1865 and mustered out near Washington, DC on June 19th. In 1890 he claimed as his disabilities a hernia and something which might say "throat often disgorges." The enumerator's penmanship and spelling make accurate transcription impossible. Sarah's death was reported in *The Farmer Review* October 5, 1901, 1: ". . . Mrs. Stephen Pierce died very suddenly last Friday evening. She had been in feeble health for some time, and of late has failed very rapidly, but was about the house as usual on Friday. About 8 in the evening, while sitting in her chair, she passed away without a struggle. She leaves, beside her husband, two sons and two daughters, who will have the sympathy of all in their bereavement. The funeral was held at her late home Sunday afternoon, conducted by Rev. W. E. Wells, and burial at Sheldrake. Her age was 58 years. The coroner decided that paralysis of the heart was the cause of death." Sarah was buried in Sheldrake Cemetery, Ovid, Seneca, NY. Stephen moved to California to live with a daughter. His grave has not been located.

Clayton Pierson – Co. E
1842 Canada
d. ? ?
m. ------

NOTE: Little can be ascertained about this soldier, partly because of the wide variations of spelling of his name. He was a substitute for William A. Tanner, Town of Ridgeway, Orleans County, NY, enrolling in the 147th on August 8, 1863 at Rochester, Monroe, NY. He was wounded at the battle of the Wilderness on May 5, 1864 and listed as "absent, wounded" on the roll dated August 31, 1864. He nominally transferred to Co. D, 91st Regiment on June 5, 1865 but was "absent, sick." I suspect he did not survive.

Moses D. Pike – Co. H
b. 1837 Hudson, Columbia, NY
d. March 31, 1865 Cape Hatteras, NC
m. Phila Sophia Leavitt (January 16, 1847-October 15, 1900) 1862

NOTE: Moses was the son of Daniel (1804-1884) and Sarah Akins Pike (1809-1883). So far as can be ascertained, the following is his military career. Moses, a seaman, was a substitute for Oliver Bullard, and joined the 147th at Little Valley, Cattaraugus, NY on August 21, 1863. He transferred to the US Navy at Philadelphia, PA on May 4, 1864. It appears that some time between that date and August 19, 1864 he left the

Navy and made his way to Meadville, Crawford, PA where he joined the 3rd PA HA. At another unknown date he was captured by the Confederates and spent time in Andersonville Prison, from which he was paroled in early spring 1865. He was a passenger on the steamer Gen. Lyon which set out from Wilmington, NC on March 29th with more than 500 passengers and crew heading for Fortress Monroe, VA. The passengers included paroled prisoners, civilians, and refugees. As the steamer rounded Cape Hatteras, NC it was swept up in a hurricane and caught fire. Only 29 persons survived. Phila applied for a pension on

Photo # NH 53866 12-Pounder howitzer on upper deck of USS General Lyon

Moses Pike was one of almost 500 passengers who perished in a hurricane aboard the USS General Lyon.
US Naval History Center

June 19, 1865 and the pension index card states specifically that Moses had been a member of the 3rd PA HA. Another card states he died in the burning of the Gen. Lyon. What is odd about all this is that pension cards ordinarily listed all military service. Pike's only mentioned his time in the 3rd PA HA. It is hard to believe that Phila was unaware of the organization her husband entered in 1863. She obtained the pension although when she obtained it is unknown. She reportedly married Lucius G. Adams (1844-1914) in 1865, if the dates on the 1900 census are to be believed. Her first son, Adelbert, was born in 1867. That same census reveals that Phila and Lucius had parted company. Phila made a will on October 1, 1900, leaving everything to her children and totally excluding Lucius. She obviously wanted to ensure he was unable to claim any part of the property which she stated in her will she herself had purchased. Phila is buried in Spring Cemetery, Springboro, Crawford, PA.

James H. Poulson – Co. H
b. March 1845 in Salem County, NJ
d. February 24, 1923 Roseburg National soldiers' Home, Hampton, VA
m. ------

NOTE: This soldier's parents were Jeremiah (1807-post 1880) and Pachanci [Paceton] Poulson (1811-ante June 7, 1860). The family was living in Philadelphia, PA in June 1850. Poulson had an extensive military career and employed numerous aliases. To simplify comprehension, I have listed the many outfits to which he belonged.

JAMES R. POULSON – 1860 living with father and new stepmother Abigail Babcock in Center, Marshall, IN.

JAMES POULSON – Co. C, 48ᵗʰ Indiana Infantry: enlisted December 24, 1861. **"Transferred to Marine Brigade."**

JAMES POULSON – Co. D, 1ˢᵗ Mississippi Marine Brigade: enlistment date unknown but unit raised in early 1863. By May 29, 1863 was at Vicksburg, MS. In June were on Louisiana side of Mississippi River.

JAMES PARKER – Co. H, 147: August 21, 1863-June 17, 1865. Enlisted Utica, NY. Discharged Washington, DC.

JAMES K. POULSON – Co. L, 4ᵗʰ US Cavalry: September 19, 1866-September 19, 1871. Enlisted Indianapolis, IN. discharged Fort Richardson, TX.

JAMES K. POULSON – US Marine Corps: enlisted October 26, 1871. On board the USRS Vermont from October 26, 1871-February 29, 1872.

JAMES K. POULSON – Co. L, 3ʳᵈ Cavalry [2 L]: March 28, 1872-?. Enlisted New York City. Deserted July 13, 1872, then surrendered December 5, 1873; transferred to **Co. E, 2ⁿᵈ Cavalry** (revoked). Deserted May 15, 1874, as of **3ʳᵈ Cavalry**.

ROBERT GAFFIN – Co. E, 2ⁿᵈ US Cavalry "Enlistment cancelled": November 8, 1873-December 3, 1873. Enlisted Fort Laramie, KS. Surrendered on December 5, 1873 as James K. Poulson, a deserter from **Co. L, 3ʳᵈ Cavalry.**

JOHN POULSON – Co. H, 1ˢᵗ US Infantry: September 3, 1878-September 2, 1883. Enlisted Columbus, OH. Discharged Fort Leavenworth, KS.

JOHN POULSON – Co. A, 20ᵗʰ US Infantry: October 1, 1883-February 16, 1887. [Deserted May 1, 1884 and apprehended November 15, 1886.] Enlisted Fort Laramie, KS. Discharged San Antonio, TX.

JOHN POULSON – Co. F, 3ʳᵈ US Artillery: July 6, 1886-October 28, 1886 ["Dropped"].

JOHN POULSON – First entered a National Home in 1899.

JOHN POULSON – 1900 living in Tippecanoe, Marshall, IN with nephew James M. Poulson.

JOHN POULSON – Died at Roseburg National Home, Hampton, VA on February 24, 1923. Buried in Hampton National Cemetery as John Poulson, Co. H, 147th.

John Powell – Co. H
b. 1838 Dublin, Ireland
d. ? ?
m.?

NOTE: John, who described himself as a laborer on his muster roll card, was a substitute for Frederick Wegner, Tonawanda, Erie, NY, enrolling in the 147th on August 16, 1863 at Buffalo, NY. He transferred to Co. F, 91st Regiment on June 5, 1865 and mustered out on July 3rd near Washington, DC. Nothing else confirmable has been located.

Aaron Preston – Co. F
b. June 30, 1840 Vermont
d. April 24, 1917 Wallingford, Rutland, VT
m1. Sophia Mills (1843-*post* 1865) 1858
m2. Sarah Ella Taylor (November 22, 1847-January 10, 1938) December 15, 1868

NOTE: Aaron, son of Royal (1807-1850) and Caroline Cooper Preston (1812-1845), was drafted, enrolling in the 147th at Canandaigua, Ontario, NY on October 1, 1863. He was WIA at an unknown date and discharged from Columbia Hospital, Washington, DC on May 29, 1865 in consequence of that wound. He and Sophia were the parents of Charles (1859-?) and an unnamed infant (1864-?). Sophia probably died in New York State. Aaron and Sarah were married in Wallingford where his parents had lived. He held a variety of jobs, such as farmer, teamster, and finally grocer. He and Sarah are buried in Green Hill Cemetery, Wallingford.

Peter E. Prior – Co. D
b. April 14, 1830 Bexhill, Sussex, England
d. January 1, 1903 Springville, Erie, NY
m. Mary Ann Meacham (August 11, 1836-May 1, 1910) 1854

NOTE: Peter, a painter, was the son of James E. (1791-April 16, 1834) and Judith Badcock Prior (1784-August 2, 1869). The family set sail for America in 1834 aboard the Emma and James fell overboard, drowning. Judith and the children arrived in America and settled in Erie County, where she died. Peter was a substitute for Burr

S. Bentley and enrolled in the 147th at Ellicottville, Cattaraugus, NY on August 21, 1863. He transferred to Co. B, 91st Regiment on June 5, 1865 and mustered out on July 3rd near Washington, DC. He and Mary Ann were the parents of five children. The couple is buried in Maplewood Cemetery, Springville.

Patrick Quinn – Co. H
b. 1819 Ireland
d. ? ?
m. ?

NOTE: Quinn was drafted, enrolling in the 147th on August 26, 1863. He was captured on October 1, 1864 during the battle commonly called Poplar Spring Church, but also known as Peebles Farm, which was fought September 30th- October 1st as part of Grant's Richmond and Petersburg Campaign. Where he was imprisoned is unknown. He left parole camp on May 5, 1865, transferred to Co. C, 91st Regiment on June 5, 1865, and was discharged on June 9th at Arlington, VA. His application for a pension, dated June 25, 1879, was successful. Nothing more has been learned, partially because of the number of men with this name.

William Quinn – Co. D
b. 1833 Ireland
d. ? ?
m. ?

NOTE: William was a blacksmith. On September 10, 1863 he enrolled in the 147th at Watertown, Jefferson, NY as a substitute for Albert B. Maher, Point Peninsula, Jefferson, NY. He transferred to Co. B, 91st Regiment on June 5, 1865 and was discharged "to date on July 3, 1865" near Washington, DC. I have located no other information for him.

Abraham "Abram" Ralyea – Co. G
b. February 1840 Erie County, NY
d. April 7, 1905 East Aurora, Erie, NY
m1. Maryette Paxton (1846-January 14, 1893) ca. 1862
m2. Sarah J. _____ (June 1842-?) 1894

NOTE: Abraham, son of Abram Ralyea (1786-1861), a widower in1850, was a substitute for Albert L. Jenks, enrolling in the 147th on August 19, 1863 at Harmony, Chautauqua, NY. He was wounded on February 6, 1865 at Hatcher's Run. On June 5, 1865 he transferred to Co. F, 91st Regiment, mustering out on July 3rd near Washington, DC. Abraham and Maryette are buried in Oakwood Cemetery, East Aurora. Sarah, who was Canadian and immigrated to the United States in 1851, probated her husband's will in 1906 and then disappeared.

Barnabas Raymond – Co. G

b. 1822 Vermont

d. September 19, 1866 Durhamville, Oneida, NY

m. Louisa _____ (December 1824-*post* 1900) *ca.* 1845

NOTE: Barnabas, son of Barnabas (1773-1862) and Mary Mayo Raymond (1781-1865), was a substitute for James R. Porter. He enrolled in the 147th at Oswego City, NY on April 4, 1863. He transferred to Co. F, 91st Regiment on June 5, 1865 and was discharged the same day. Barnabas is buried in the Protestant Cemetery, Durhamville. Louisa, also born in Vermont, never remarried. In 1900 she lived with her two surviving children, Polly (1846-1916) and William (1862-1929), in Verona, Oneida, NY.

Asa Reddick – Co. D

b. 1838 Canada

d. February 6, 1865 Hatcher's Run, VA

m. Nancy A. Chambers (1837-*post* 1905) *ca.* 1856

NOTE: Asa's surname had several variants. He was drafted, enrolling at a place identified as May Pole on August 21, 1863. No such place exists but may have been Maple Springs, Chautauqua, NY. He was KIA at the battle of Hatcher's Run. Nancy never remarried. She and her two children, Mary Samantha (1857-1904) and David James (1860-1915), both of whom were born in Canada, moved to Wisconsin. The last reference to her is contained in the 1905 Wisconsin census. Mary died in Wisconsin and David in Iowa.

Herman L. Redner – Co. E

b. October 19, 1828 Tompkins County, NY

d. March 21, 1914 Cayutaville, Schuyler, NY

m. Lorena "Loraney" Bement (May 1841-May 17, 1909) 1865

NOTE: Herman was the son of Alexander (1798-1895) and Catherine Miller Redner (1800-1860). Although he stated for his muster roll card that he had been born in Berkshire, PA all other documents point to a POB of New York State and the 1865 New York census revealed he had been born in Tompkins County. In 1900 he and Lorena said they had been married in 1855 but on the 1865 New York census, his marital status was single. His entry in *A Biographical Record of Schuyler County,* 509-10 provides a good review of his life: "Herman L. Redner is a native of Schuyler county, his birth having here occurred October 19, 1828. He has passed the Psalmist's allotted span of three score years and ten, and is now one of the honored and venerable citizens of the town of Catharine, where for many years he has devoted his attention to agricultural pursuits. In the common school he obtained his education, but put aside his text books at the age of sixteen in order to devote his time and attention to agricultural pursuits, which he followed continuously until the 8th of July 1863. On that day he offered his services to the government, enlisting as a member of Company E, One Hundred and Forty-seventh Regiment of New York Volunteers, the command being raised in Brooklyn, New York. He served for two years, during which time he participated in the battle of the Wilderness and of Culpeper. In the former he was taken prisoner and sent to Andersonville, where he remained for five months. He was then transferred to South Carolina, where he continued for four months, after which he was ordered to Wilmington. He was also for three weeks in the Rebel prison at Goldsboro, North Carolina, after which he was returned to Wilmington, where he was paroled. Later he was sent to Washington and from there he was ordered to the hospital in Baltimore because his health had been largely undermined by the hardships of prison life. He spent eight weeks in the hospital, after which he returned home by way of New York city, on a thirty-days' furlough. When his leave of absence had expired he was still unable to rejoin his regiment and his time was extended for thirty days longer. Before that period had elapsed he was directed to go to Elmira and obtain his discharge, which he did on the 2d of August, 1866. After the war Mr. Redner went to Cayuta, and was united in marriage to Miss Loraine Bement, who was born in the town of Hector, May 19, 1841 . . . At the time of his marriage Mr. Redner purchased a farm in Cayuta township, comprising sixty acres, and has since devoted his efforts continuously to agricultural pursuits with the result that his well tilled fields have brought to him a profitable return and a comfortable living as a reward for his labors. In his political views he is a Republican and in religious faith is a Methodist." The biography is accurate in the main, but Herman was enrolled and mustered into the 147th at Catharine on July 27, 1863. He was indeed discharged at Elmira but the date was August 2, 1865. He and Lorena had no children. They are buried in Laurel Hill Cemetery, Odessa, Schuyler.

William Reid – Co. D
b. 1838 Scotland
d. ? ?
m. ?

NOTE: William, a carpenter, was a substitute for George Wippert, Buffalo, Erie, NY, enrolling in the 147th in that city on August 7, 1863. He transferred to Co. B, 91st Regiment on June 5, 1865 and mustered out near Washington, DC on July 3rd. His surname was also spelled Reed but I have located no other information for him under either one.

Stephen Rhinesmith – Co. A

b. July 10, 1830 Passaic County, NJ

d. October 14, 1902 Web Mills, Chemung, NY

m. Julia Staples (September 22, 1834-March 4, 1918) 1858

NOTE: The son of Godfrey E. (1804-1890) and Hannah Bailey Rhinesmith (1811-1883), Stephen was a draftee. He enrolled in the 147th at Southport, Chemung, NY on July 31, 1863 and was discharged on May 15, 1865, place unknown. In 1890 he claimed "deafness of left ear & bronchitis" as his disabilities. He and Julia were the parents of two children. Stephen's death was remarked by only a brief funeral announcement but when Julia died, an obituary appeared in *The Elmira Star-Gazette* March 5, 1918: "Mrs. Julia Rhinesmith, widow of Stephen Rhinesmith, died last night at 9:15 o'clock at the home of her daughter, Mrs. Walter A. Graves, 461 South avenue. She was eighty-three years old and had been a resident of Webb Mills and had been spending the last few months with her daughter. She was a member of the Webb Mills Methodist Church and was a member of sterling character, much beloved by her friends and family . . . The funeral will be held at the home of her daughter Thursday at 1 o'clock. The Rev. Mr. Whiting will officiate. Burial in the Webb Mills cemetery." Stephen is also buried there.

Syrenus A. Rice – Co. G

b. March 16, 1841 Georgetown, Madison, NY

d. January 19, 1896 Kalkaska, Kalkaska, MI

m. Henrietta Dorman Morton (February 14, 1846-November 29, 1915) August 30, 1871

NOTE: Syrenus, son of Horace (1807-1868) and Betsy Coburn Rice (1812-?), was a draftee, enrolling in the 147th at Oswego City on August 2, 1863. He transferred to Co. F, 91st Regiment on June 5, 1865 and mustered out near Washington, DC on July 3rd. Henrietta's first husband was Charles Morton (1842-1867) whom she married on February 13, 1867. He died on October 5th. She and Syrenus were married in Cazenovia, Madison, NY. According to Dawn Triplett's *Brave Boys Were They,* 226, Syrenus and Henrietta settled in Rapid River Township, Kalkaska in the 1870s. Syrenus' COD was a hernia. Henrietta succumbed to pneumonia. Both are buried in Evergreen Cemetery, Kalkaska. Syrenus' brother, Loren (1831-1916), was a member of Co. L, 2nd MI Cavalry from 1861-1865.

Murray J. Richmond – Co. I

b. February 10, 1836 Allegany County, NY

d. July 16, 1864 Petersburg, VA

m. Julia A. Richmond (March 20, 1843-February 16, 1920) June 13, 1859

NOTE: Murray, also known as John Murray, was the son of Ebenezer (1793-1869) and Lois Ann Gott Richmond (1797-1890). He was a first cousin of Anson Richmond (1819-1874), Julia's father. A draftee, Murray enrolled in the 147th at Independence, Allegany, NY on July 10, 1863. He was KIA at Petersburg and his remains were buried on the field. He and Julia were the parents of Ida (1861-?). On December 12, 1865 Julia married Leonard Briggs (1830-1910), who had been a lieutenant in the 189th Regiment. By 1871 the family was living in Pomona, Franklin, KS. In 1904 Julia, now residing in Lewiston, Nez Pierce, ID, sued Leonard for divorce, citing abandonment. She alleged he had failed to support her for more than a year, forcing her to depend on friends and her three children by him. She claimed he was worth at least $4,000. He also drew a pension because he had been wounded in the battle of Lewis Farm, VA on March 29, 1865. Briggs, for his part, responded that the "complaint does not state facts sufficient to constitute a cause of action." The judge granted the divorce after he failed to appear at the hearing. Julia successfully applied to have her pension based on Murray's service restored retroactive to March 24, 1904, the date of her final divorce decree. She died in Moscow, Latah, ID but by her own request she was buried in Crystal Lake Cemetery, Corvallis, Benton, OR. Her COD was a cerebral hemorrhage.

John W. Rigby – Co. G
b. 1833 Rathbone, Steuben, NY
d. December 10, 1864 Salisbury, NC
m. Adelaide A. Jones (1838-January 2, 1906) July 20, 1859

NOTE: The son of Loren (1810-?) and Jane Rigby (1815-?), John was drafted, enrolling in the 147th at Elmira, Chemung, NY on July 13, 1863. According to Adelaide's deposition for a widow's pension, he was "taken prisoner at or near Petersburg, Va. about the 1st of October 1864 and died at Salisbury prison NC about the 10th day of December 1864." His entry in *The Town Clerks' Registers* states he died of starvation. He is buried among the "unknowns" at Salisbury National Cemetery. Adelaide married Walter F. Bullard, Jr. (1831-January 5, 1899) on December 12, 1870 as his second wife. On June 4, 1901 she applied for a remarried widow's pension. She and Walter lived in Wellsboro, Tioga, PA and are buried in Wellsboro Cemetery.

Patrick Riley – Co. I
b. 1843 Ireland
d. ? ?
m. ?

NOTE: Little is known about this soldier who claimed to be a "horse shoer" when he joined the 147th. He saw prior service in the 69th NY Militia in 1861 soon after Fort

Sumter was fired upon and war was declared. He applied for a pension on November 29, 1861 and obtained a certificate. He was a substitute for William H. Collins, Buffalo, and enrolled in the 147th in that city on August 1, 1863. He suffered a slight wound to his right hand at the battle of Mine Run, VA on November 27, 1863 and transferred to the VRC on July 1, 1864. No other confirmable information has been locatedd, partially due to the large number of men with this name.

John F. Rilley – Co. G
b. 1843 Ireland
d. ? ?
m. ?

NOTE: Rilley, a driver, is another soldier for whom records are scant. He was a substitute for Moses Dart, Jr., Hamburg, Erie, NY, and enrolled in the 147th at Buffalo on August 14, 1863. He was captured at the battle of Poplar Springs Church, VA, also known as Peebles Farm, fought on September 30th and October 1, 1864. Where he was held is unknown but he was paroled on May 22, 1865 and discharged from the service at New York City as "Killy" on July 11, 1865. I have located no other information.

John F. Roberts – Co. K
b. 1842 Butterfield, PA
d. August 1864 3rd Division USA General Hospital, Alexandria, VA
m. Julia Loretta Cooper (1840-post 1902) December 31, 1857

NOTE: John's parents are unknown. His muster roll card states he was born in Butterfield, PA but no such place exists. He was drafted, enrolling in the 147th at Chemung Village, Chemung, NY on July 21, 1863. He was WIA at the battle of the Wilderness on May 5, 1864 and died after his left leg was amputated. The exact DOD is disputed, but Captain Joseph Dempsey testified he died on August 2nd. Although he is buried in Alexandria National Cemetery a cenotaph for him stands in Chemung Village Cemetery. He and Julia were the parents of William H. (1858-post 1919). On September 14, 1865 Julia married Edward Nickerson (1841-post 1919). They appear on the 1870 census with three children, Martha, 3; Rhoda, 2, Harrison, 1. William's whereabouts at that time is unknown. Several more children were born later. The entire family disappears after this census only to reappear in Elmira in the early 1900s. It seems that Julia's second marriage disintegrated. In 1900, while living in the Chemung Almshouse, she claimed to be a widow but her husband was alive until at least 1919. An exact DOD for either one has been impossible to find.

Chauncey N. Robinson – Co. D

b. September 5, 1836 Chemung County, NY

d. March 22, 1916 South Bethlehem, Northampton, PA

m. Clarissa C. Sprague (August 1838-March 13, 1904) 1857

NOTE: Chauncey was the son of Freeman (1812-1877) and Polly Pearce Robinson (1812-1884). A draftee, he enrolled in the 147th on July 21, 1863 at Catlin, Chemung, NY. He was discharged on June 9, 1865 at Whitehall Hospital, Philadelphia, PA for "diarrhea and general disability." His death was reported in *The Elmira Telegram* March 26, 1916: "Chauncey N. Robinson, a former resident of Elmira, died Wednesday evening at the home of his son, William A. Robinson, in South Bethlehem, Pa., after an extended illness. Mr. Robinson resided in this city many years but moved to South Bethlehem about two years ago. He was a veteran of the civil war and a member of C. Edgar Fitch post No. 165, G.A.R. . . . The funeral was held at the undertaking rooms of F. E. Smith at 3:30 o'clock yesterday." Clarissa, mother of four children, died in Elmira. She and Chauncey are buried in Woodlawn Cemetery, Elmira.

George Nelson Robinson – Co. F

b. March 16, 1835 Steuben County, NY

d. March 9, 1904 Dundee, Yates, NY

m. Lydia _____ (December 11, 1841-December 3, 1897) *ca.* 1859

NOTE: George, frequently known by his middle name, was the son of Beverly (1795-1870) and Elizabeth "Betsy" Brown Robinson (1793-1880). A draftee, he enrolled in the 147th on July 2, 1863. According to *The Town Clerks' Registers* he had an "arm shot off at Hatcher's Run Apr. 1st, 1865." He did indeed lose his left arm, as confirmed by the 1890 Veterans' Schedules, but on April 1, 1865 the 147th was engaged in the battle of Five Forks. He and Lydia, the parents of three children, are buried in Hillside Cemetery, Dundee.

James Rodgers – Co. D

b. 1833 Canada

d. September 22, 1909 Mercy Hospital, Bay City, Bay, MI

m. ------

NOTE: James, a boatman, was a substitute for Christian Stadel. He enrolled in the 147th on August 22, 1863 at Olean, Cattaraugus, NY. On June 5, 1865 he transferred to Co. B, 91st Regiment, mustering out July 3rd near Washington, DC. COD was stomach cancer. He is buried in Pine Ridge cemetery, Bay City.

Rollin T. Rogers – Co. E

b. 1836 ?

d. May 10, 1864 Laurel Hill, VA

m. ?

NOTE: The only possible reference to this man before 1863 is Rollin G. Rogers, born in Ohio, residing in Sodus, Wayne, NY in 1860 and working as a farm laborer. He was a substitute for Martin Gibbs, Brutus, Cayuga, NY and enrolled in the 147th at Auburn, NY on July 23, 1863. His muster roll card does not provide a POB. An entry in *Deaths of Volunteers*, under the name "Rullan T. Rogers," states he was killed in action at Spotsylvania. Since Laurel Hill and Spotsylvania were part of the same campaign, either seems acceptable as the POD. A cenotaph, ordered by the American Legion, stands in Pleasant View Cemetery, Port Gibson, Wayne, NY.

William Caleb Rose – Co. I

b. June 16, 1843 Elbridge, Onondaga, NY

d. November 15, 1907 North Rose, Wayne, NY

m. Elizabeth "Eliza" Shattuck (1844-April 11, 1909) July 29, 1865

NOTE: William, a shoemaker, was the son of William J. (1812-1887) and Jane Ann Laird Rose (1812-1873). He saw prior duty in Co. C, 24th Regiment from October 1861-May 1863. A substitute for Nelson D. Putney, he enrolled in the 147th at Oswego City on September 4th, 1863. Though evidence is scant, he seems to have been captured at the battle of the Wilderness and sent to Andersonville. An obituary published in *The Sodus Record* November 22, 1907 mentioned that he celebrated his 21st birthday as a POW in that prison. In 1890 he claimed "asthma, diarrhea, piles" as disabilities and the enumerator noted he had been a "prisoner 8 months." *The Oswego Daily Times* June 4, 1908, 6 published an interesting article detailing his life and career: "Memorial Day was observed at the M. E. Church Sunday by the pastor, Rev. L. B. Chaloux reading the following memoir of the life of Veteran W. C. Rose, who died during the past year: 'William Caleb Rose was born in the town of Elbridge, N. Y., 1843, and died in peace at his home in North Rose, Nov. 15, 1907, at the age of sixty-four years. He received his early education at Oswego, where he enlisted in the army at eighteen years of age. He was a member of the 124th [*sic*] New York Regiment from October 28, 1861, to May 1862, and the 147th New York Regiment from September 4, 1863, to July 6, 1865. Thus he was a soldier in practically the whole course of the Civil War. He was in the famous battle of Antietam and was taken prisoner in the Battle of the Wilderness. For eight long months he was in Andersonville Prison enduring those horrors of war which pen cannot describe. He would much rather [have] been in jeopardy from shot and shell than have been compelled to endure the filth and famine of Andersonville. His best years were given to his country and he was one of the many who suffered that we might have a great and united country founded on freedom. He was married July 20, 1865, and during the last nineteen years of his married life his family has been well known to the members of this church. For some time after his marriage he lived in Michigan and then he settled in Westbury, N. Y., where he was converted and joined the Christian church. He lived to serve for he was full of the Lord's work in this place. He was a trustee of the church, Sunday School Superintendent and teacher. Moving to North Rose in 1880 he joined this church by letter August, 1897[;] elected a trustee of this church he remained faithful in that capacity until February, 1905. Troubled with asthma for many years he was only deprived of active life during his last three years. It was during this time that he had premonitions of his end and communed much with God and went to his last rest in great peace. Concerning his Christian character there was none finer. I was his last pastor and can testify to the gladness and joyfulness with which he received my calls, and to the deep appreciation he showed for all the sermons he was permitted to hear. I observed that he caught the kernel of things. The funeral service was held at his home on the 18th of November, 1907. Rev. J. J. Edwards, a former pastor assisted by the present pastor officiated. Loyal to his home, loyal to his country, loyal to his church and loyal to his God he has been transferred to the Church Triumphant.'" In addition to his church work, Rose was active in the GAR. He joined Godfrey Weitzel Post No. 467 GAR in Westbury, Nassau, NY. He was also a member of John E. Sherman Post No. 401 GAR in Rose, Wayne, NY. Eliza died two years later at her home in North Rose. She and William are buried in Mt. Adnah Cemetery, Fulton.

John Russell – Co. E
b. 1835 Canada
d. probably May 19, 1864 Harris Farm, VA
m. ?

NOTE: John, a farmer, enrolled in the 147th on July 27, 1863 at Wilson, Niagara, NY as a substitute for James Hosmer of that place. He was reported MIA on May 19, 1864. From May 8-May 21, 1864 Grant pursued Lee in what was known as the Overland Campaign, permitting the Confederates little time to escape or regroup after the battle of the Wilderness. On May 19th the Confederates, 6,000 strong, attacked the Federal forces at a place known as Harris Farm. It was a costly error because the Rebels lost 1,000 of their attacking force. They only managed to escape a worse fate because of a rainstorm and the arrival of darkness. In the process, however, the Union forces also lost men, one of whom, it seems, was John Russell. He was never heard from again and his body was probably buried on the field.

James Ryan – Co. I

b. 1834 Waterford, Ireland

d. ? ?

m. ?

NOTE: Ryan, a ship carpenter, enrolled in the 147th at Buffalo, NY on August 14, 1863 as a substitute for Henry Helwig, Lancaster, Erie, NY. He was discharged on May 18, 1865 at Whitehall Hospital, Philadelphia, PA. On February 4, 1867 he applied for a pension but obtained no certificate. It is possible he died before the process could be completed. No other information has been located.

Michael Ryan – Co. D

b. 1843 Bradford County, PA

d. January 25, 1897 National Soldiers' Home, Bath, Steuben, NY

m. ------

NOTE: Michael, whose parents are unknown, served in Co. G, 64th Regiment from November 1861-November 1862 when he was discharged at Convalescent Camp, Alexandria, VA for "disability." He had received a gunshot wound to his elbow at the battle of Fair Oaks, VA on June 1, 1862. He was a substitute for John Lovell and enrolled in the 147th on July 20, 1863. He appears to have been charged with desertion on November 13, 1863 at Culpeper, VA. Since no action was mentioned perhaps the charge was dropped. On April 1, 1865 he transferred to Co. C, 12th Regiment VRC and was discharged from the service on July 22nd at Washington, DC. The discharge was to date from June 7th. It is interesting to note that he had applied for a pension on February 19, 1863. Ryan is buried in the Bath National Cemetery. His gravestone notes only his service in the 64th Regiment.

Thomas Ryon – Co. D

b. 1842 Cayuga, OH

d. ? ?

m. ?

NOTE: Thomas was either born in Cayuga County, NY or Cuyahoga County, OH. His parents are unknown. He was a substitute for David T. Raub and enrolled in the 147th at Pompey, Onondaga, NY on August 21, 1863. Ryon was captured at the battle of the Wilderness on May 5, 1864 and sent to Andersonville. He was paroled on December 11, 1865 and arrived at parole camp on December 18th. Although nominally transferred to Co. B, 91st Regiment on June 5, 1865 he was discharged from the service at Buffalo, NY on June 19th as a member of the 147th. Nothing confirmable has been located beyond that date. It is possible he died shortly after returning home since I have not found a pension card.

Daniel Sanders – Co. K
b. 1844 Cortland County, NY
d. May 25, 1864 Judiciary Square Hospital, Washington, DC
m. ------

NOTE: Daniel, son of Simeon (1795-*post* 1875) and Electa Sanders (1817-*post* 1875), was a substitute for his brother George W. (1842-1914), who became an ordained Presbyterian minister. Daniel's COD was *phthisis pulmonalis* (tuberculosis). He is buried in Arlington National Cemetery. In 1868 Electa successfully applied for a mother's pension.

Wilson Saunders – Co. B
b. 1824 England
d. July 8, 1864 Cape Vincent, Jefferson, NY
m. Ann Jury (1827-June 30, 1909) November 10, 1844

NOTE: Wilson, a substitute for an unnamed draftee, lied about his age in order to enlist, enrolling in the 147th at Watertown, Jefferson, NY on September 8, 1863. Ann stated in her application for a widow's pension that Wilson "died of injuries received at Culpeper, Va." There may be some truth to that statement since the medical form providing information about his service said he died at Cape Vincent while on a furlough from hospital. The official COD was typhoid pneumonia. Ann was left with seven children, six of them under 16. Between that time and 1881 she remained a widow. In 1875 she was enumerated on the New York census as the live-in housekeeper for William Christopher Monroe (1815-1885). Rumors about their "relationship" began to circulate and Ann's pension was suspended. On January 7, 1881 the couple was married in the St. Vincent de Paul Roman Catholic Church, Cape Vincent. When Monroe died he left his wife a house in Cape Vincent for her life use as well as the interest on a $3,000 investment established once the farm was sold, providing she remained a widow. For the next 13 years Ann lived in relative comfort. In 1898, however, all changed, as an article appearing in *The Ogdensburg Daily Journal* March 26, 1898 revealed: ". . . A romantic marriage occurred a few days ago between William Whitworth, of Cleveland, O., and Mrs. Ann Munroe, of Cape Vincent. The parties are aged respectively 75 and 72, and this is the third marriage for each of them. The romantic feature of the case is that they were lovers many years ago but drifted apart, only to renew their former vows in old age. That there is genuine affection at the bottom of it all is shown by the fact that the bride deprives herself of a stated income accruing to the fact of remaining a widow, to enjoying the home and society of one who inspired her earliest affection. That true love is immortal may be a fact after all." Whitworth and Ann were married at Cape Vincent on February 26, 1898. Like her, he had been born in England. Over the next few years they divided their time between northern New York and Cleveland. In 1907 they returned to Cleveland permanently where Ann died. Her lengthy obituary appeared in *The Cape Vincent Eagle* July 8, 1909: "On Wednesday of last week, June 30, at Cleveland, Ohio, occurred the death of Mrs. William Whitworth, aged 86 years. Her death was caused principally from the infirmities of advanced age. Mrs. Whitworth was thrice married, and was best known in Cape Vincent as Mrs. William Monroe, the name of her second husband. Subsequently to her marriage to Mr. Monroe she was married to Wilson Saunders, and became the mother of two sons, Joseph Saunders, of Wolfe Island, and Fred Saunders, of this village. Several years after her second husband's demise she became the wife of William Whitworth of Cleveland, Ohio, the wedding taking place at her home in this village . . . Mrs. Whitworth was a woman of very many commendable traits of character and during her residence in Cape Vincent made very many friends. She was an excellent wife and mother and as such will be mourned and missed. The remains arrived at Cape Vincent Friday evening in charge of her son, Fred Saunders and on Saturday morning at ten o'clock the funeral was held from St. John's church, the remains being interred in the cemetery connected therewith. Mr. Whitworth, on account of his advanced years, was unable to come to the Cape to attend the funeral." Wilson and Ann are buried in St. John's Episcopal Church Cemetery, Cape Vincent. William Monroe is buried in Saint Vincent de Paul's Roman Catholic Cemetery, Cape Vincent. William Whitworth (1822-October 17, 1912) is buried in Woodland Cemetery, Cleveland.

Daniel Scanlin – Co. D
b. 1829 Ireland
d. ? ?
m. ?

NOTE: Daniel, a painter, was a substitute for an unnamed draftee, enrolling in the 147th at Watertown, Jefferson, NY on September 20, 1863. At an unspecified date he was transferred to Co. 4, 2nd Battalion VRC. He was discharged for "disability" on September 14, 1864 at an unspecified place. No other confirmable information has been located.

John Jacob Schwingle – Co. A
b. 1840 Germany
d. June 25, 1911 Wayland, Steuben, NY
m. ------

NOTE: John, commonly known by his middle name, was the son of Jacob (1807-1878) and Anna Mary Gebhardt Schwingle (1805-1875). The family came to the United States in 1850. A draftee, John enrolled in the 147th at Wayland on July 18, 1863. He transferred to Co. C, 91st Regiment on June 5, 1865 and mustered out near Ball's Cross Roads, VA on July 3rd. He is buried in St. Peter's Cemetery, Perkinsville, Steuben, NY.

William Scott – Co. E
b. 1834 Brandt County, Canada
d. probably 1864 ?
m. ?

NOTE: William, a substitute for Robert Disney, was a laborer. He enrolled in the 147th at Allegany, Cattaraugus, NY on August 22, 1863. According to his muster roll card he was wounded on May 5, 1864 at the battle of the Wilderness. Another note shows he was wounded on May 25, 1864 at North Anna River. The accuracy of these two reports cannot be confirmed. He was absent from the regiment through August 31, when he was supposedly in McDougall Hospital, New York City. Since this is the last known piece of information about him it is possible he died shortly afterwards.

William Scully – Co. K
b. 1845 Ireland
d. ? Oswego City, NY
m. ------

NOTE: William, son of Thomas (1808-1888) and Bridget Burns Scully (1822-1889), was a boatman. He enlisted in the 147th on January 4, 1864, receiving a bounty of $600. His entry in *The Town Clerks' Registers* contains some interesting information, namely, he was wounded in the left hip and taken prisoner at the battle of the Wilderness on May 5, 1864 and sent to a hospital in Lansingburg, VA; he was exchanged on August 4, 1864; and discharged June 31 (?), 1861 (?). Lastly, the ball remained in his hip. William applied for a pension on June 15, 1865 and it is evident something is wrong with the dates. In 1865 he was living with his parents in Oswego City. He claimed to have no occupation but had formerly been in the army. He is buried with his parents in St. Paul's Cemetery, Oswego City but his gravestone contains no dates.

Thomas Segrave – Co. G
b. 1838 ?
d. June 19, 1864 4th Division 5th Army Corps Hospital, VA
m. ?

NOTE: Thomas, whose name was recorded as Seriff on a General Index Card, was drafted, enrolling in the 147th at Utica, Oneida, NY on September 5, 1863. He was wounded at Petersburg, VA on June 17, 1864 and died two days later of a "fracture of cranial bones." His grave has not been located.

William G. Seibert – Co. G
b. 1828 Germany
d. December 4, 1895 Minneapolis, Hennepin, MN
m. Marion _____ (1847-*post* 1895) ?

NOTE: Seibert, whose parents are unidentified, was a tailor. He lied about his age to enter the military, alleging he was born in 1832. He was a substitute for Peter Ennis, Pittsford, Monroe, NY and enrolled in the 147th at Rochester on August 7, 1863. He transferred to Co. F, 91st Regiment on June 5, 1865 and mustered out near Washington, DC on July 3rd. William and his wife were living in St. Paul, Ramsey, MN in 1890 when the Veterans' Enumeration was taken. He claimed he had been "injured" but added no details. His sad end was reported by *The Minneapolis Star-Tribune* December 5, 1895, 7: "William Seibert, 67, committed suicide yesterday by hanging in the kitchen of his residence at 2412 Thirteenth avenue south. He was a tailor by trade, but had recently been without employment. For a time he secured work on the court house, and there, too, he was deprived of a means of subsistence. Since then he had been drinking heavily, and the influence of the liquor, combined with despondency, nerved him to the fatal act. His wife, who with himself comprised the family, left him at home early in the morning to assist in caring for a sick neighbor. Noting her departure, the aged man drove a nail in the casement of the kitchen door and tying a rope round his neck and fastening it to the nail, strangled himself to death. A young man named O'Brien discovered the inanimate body and cut it down. Although warm, life was quite extinct. Coroner Kistler viewed the remains and decided that an inquest was unnecessary." Seibert is buried in Lakewood Cemetery, Minneapolis. Marion, born in NYS, was enumerated with William for the 1895 Minnesota census. It is unknown whether she was a first or a second wife.

James Seymour – Co. E
b. 1837 Chemung County, NY
d. ? ?
m. Helen _____ (1851-?) *ca.* 1867

NOTE: James, son of William (1812-1883) and Christiana Dates Seymour (1814-*post* 1892), enlisted in Co. I, 38th Regiment in June 1861 and deserted on July 28th at Camp Scott, Alexandria, VA. After he was apprehended he was sentenced to make up the lost time by joining the 147th and records indicate he joined his company on April 19, 1864. On June 5, 1865 he transferred to Co. K, 91st Regiment, mustering out near

Washington, DC on July 3rd. He and Helen were the parents of Horatio (1868-?). In 1880 the family was living in Osceola, Tioga, PA, as were several of James' siblings. On June 30, 1880 James applied for a pension but no certificate was issued. The entire family disappears at that time. On December 1, 1891 Christiana applied for a mother's pension, implying both James and Helen were dead. She too was unsuccessful in her attempt but it well may be that she died before the application process could be completed. In 1892 she was living in Big Flats, Chemung, NY with her son, William Jr. (1835-1912), who had served in Co. I, 141st Regiment.

Daniel H. Sharpe – Co. K

b. 1835 Ireland

d. January 2, 1864 Division Hospital, Culpeper, VA

m. Mary E. Bennet (1841-May 25, 1903) October 8, 1862

NOTE: In 1860, the first year Daniel appeared on the census, he was journeyman tailor living in Tioga County, NY. He enlisted in Co. E, 23rd Regiment in April 1861, serving until April 1862 when he was discharged for "disability." According to his surgeon's certificate, his disability consisted of "a violent rush of blood to the head occasioning vertigo & congestion of brain on any march. Difficulty was induced by a severe sunstroke in last July 1861, marching on Arlington." Nevertheless in 1863 he was drafted, enrolling in the 147th on January 24, 1863 at Owego, Tioga County. He succumbed to typhoid fever and, based on the testimony of George Wilkinson, was buried near the hospital. Today he lies in Culpeper National Cemetery. His surname is spelled Sharp on the gravestone. When Daniel died he left Mary with an eight-month-old baby, George D. She obtained a pension for herself, and later, one for the boy. She married Lemuel Wheat (1832-April 1, 1890), a carpenter, on November 1, 1865 as his second wife. By him she had three daughters, Rose (1868-1951); Frances (1872-*post* 1903); and Mary (1883-*post* 1940). As reported by *The Hornellsville Weekly Tribune* April 2, 1890, Lemuel was killed by a train near Alfred Station on April 1, 1890. In August 1901 Mary successfully petitioned to have her pension restored as a remarried widow. Graves for her and Lemuel have not been located.

John Shay – Co. F

b. 1847 Canada

d. July 11, 1915 Buffalo, Erie, NY

m. Emma Adaline Dean (1855-April 29, 1946) 1870

NOTE: John, whose parents are unidentified, was a substitute for an unnamed draftee. When enrolled on September 9, 1863, he claimed to have been born in Canada, but all subsequent records for the United States show him born in NYS.

On June 5, 1865 he was transferred to Co. A, 91st Regiment and mustered out near Washington, DC on July 3rd. In 1891 he and Emma, also a native of Canada, were living in Brant, Ontario, Canada, where all six of their children were born, and he said he was a native of Ontario Province. John and Emma immigrated to the United States in 1903 and in 1910 were living with their daughter Carrie (1872-?). John was a member of St. John's Lodge No. 82 AF & AM, Brant Chapter No. 116 RAM, Royal Templars, Court Harmony, A. O. F., and Chapin Post No. 2, GAR. Emma belonged to the Woman's Missionary Society and the Ladies' Aid Society of St. James' Evangelical Church, and the Westside WCTU. They are buried in Paris Cemetery, Paris, Brant, Ontario, Canada.

John Shay, a Canadian, served in the Union Army as a substitute for an unknown American.
St. John's Lodge #82 AF & AM

Chauncey Sheldon – Co. F

b. 1845 Wyoming County, NY
d. August 4, 1909 National Soldiers' Home, Milwaukee, Milwaukee, WI
m. Sophie _____ (1848-*post* 1920) *ante* 1870

NOTE: Chauncey, son of James (1818-1873) and Sarah A. Babcock Sheldon (1824-1887), lied about his age to join the military, claiming to be 22 and using the alias of Albert Babcock. He was a substitute for Wallace V. Smith, enrolling at Hanover, Chautauqua, NY on August 18, 1863. He transferred to Co. C, 9th VRC at an unspecified date, and was discharged July 18, 1865 at Washington, DC. He and Sophie had no children, making an estimated wedding date impossible. In 1870 they were living in Portage, Columbia, WI. Chauncey was admitted to the home on June 5, 1909, suffering from a malignant tumor in his abdomen and high blood pressure. His official COD, however, was cirrhosis of the liver. He is buried in Wood National Cemetery, Milwaukee. Sophie's exact DOD and gravesite have not been located.

Stephen Sherman – Co. A
b. December 20, 1835 Waterloo, Wayne, NY
d. February 7, 1885 Tompkins County Poor House, NY
m. Eleanor _____ (1835-*post* 1880) *ca.* 1862

NOTE: According to *The Town Clerks' Registers*, Stephen's parents were John (?-?) and Lovina Foster Sherman (?-?). His DOB varies from document to document. I use that in the *Registers*. He enlisted in Co. I, 103rd Regiment, serving from January-October 1862 when he was discharged because he had contracted typhoid fever. He was drafted, enrolling in the 147th at Hector, Schuyler, NY on July 27, 1863. He transferred to Co. C, 91st Regiment on June 5, 1865 and mustered out at Ball's Cross Roads, VA on July 3rd. He and Eleanor were the parents of at least five children. She disappears after the 1880 census and perhaps died. *The Ithaca Daily Journal* February 19, 1885 carried the following: "---The commander of Sydney Post G.A.R., was informed yesterday of the death of an old soldier named Sherman at the county poor house. A special meeting of the post was held last evening at which it was ordered that a delegation be sent after the remains and inter them in the soldiers' plot in the Ithaca cemetery." It may be presumed that the "old soldier" was Stephen. He is buried in Ithaca City Cemetery. His gravestone only shows service in the 103rd Regiment.

George Henry Sherwood – Co. E
b. November 25, 1840 Chemung County, NY
d. April 11, 1869 Geneva, Ontario, NY
m. Caroline Rinehart (1845-*post* 1917) July 25, 1863

NOTE: George, a sash and blind maker, was the son of Lambert (?-?) and Irena Maria Sampson Sherwood (1826-1903). His mother married James Butterfield (1826-1898) sometime between 1850 and 1855. In May 1861 George enlisted in Co. H, 33rd Regiment. He deserted at Harrison's Landing, VA on August 5, 1862 and made his way home. According to a letter written by his stepfather, after President Lincoln's proclamation declaring deserters might return to their outfits without fear of punishment provided they surrendered before August 18, 1863, George reported to the local provost marshal and was told to wait until transportation could be arranged. When no transportation presented itself and time was running short, George started back on his own. He was detained again on the promise of transportation and held until the Proclamation expired, then was taken to Albany and turned over to the state adjutant-general, for which the agent received a bounty of $5.00. That night he escaped from the guardhouse and made his way to Washington, DC where he was put to work in the Engineers Department until the 33rd mustered out and he with it. He was re-arrested on September 1, 1863 and sent to Camp Distribution, Alexandria,

VA and subsequently assigned to the 147th although he was detached part of the time to the Quartermaster of 1st Division 1st Army Corps until the spring campaign began and he was returned to Co. E, 147th. On May 16, 1864 Sgt. J. N. Beadle wrote to Butterfield: "Sir—It involves upon me to communicate to you the painful intelligence of the death of your beloved son, Geo. H. Sherwood, who was killed on the 5th day of May while manfully battling for the rights of his county. I was formerly a sergeant in the Co. (E) he belonged to, and I ever found him prompt and efficient in the discharge of the several duties assigned to him. The Company deeply feel the loss of him, as he was honored and loved by all his comrades. His wife and family have the sympathy of the Company in this great bereavement." This letter was published in *The Geneva Daily Gazette* May 27, 1864. Without further information one might assume that this was the end of the story. Years later George's mother applied for a pension, claiming she was entitled since Caroline had remarried and her daughter, Georgeanna, was also grown and married. She claimed that George had not died on the battlefield but had instead been captured by the Confederates and sent to Andersonville, GA where he contracted tuberculosis which ultimately caused his death. Records indicate he was sent to Florence, SC on September 16, 1864 and paroled at Charleston, SC on December 10th. He reported to College Green, Baltimore on December 12th and then was ordered to College Park on April 16th, arriving that same day. He was granted a furlough for 30 days, after which he returned to duty and was discharged on March 6, 1865. He and Caroline were married while he was a deserter and their only child, Georgeanna, was born in May 1864. Caroline applied for and obtained a widow's pension, based on the report of his death. Nevertheless, he was enumerated with her in Geneva in 1865. It is unknown whether she stopped the pension or not. George was originally buried in Washington Street Cemetery but in 1909 his remains were moved to Glenwood Cemetery, Geneva. Caroline married Theodore F. King (1844-March 31, 1904) on November 24, 1870. He died of cancer and was also buried in Glenwood Cemetery. Caroline attempted to obtain a remarried widow's pension but because of the confused nature of George's service record, she was denied on the grounds he was a deserter. The last record concerning her is dated June 5, 1917. She was living in Buffalo and at age 74 was taking in laundry to support herself. She begged for an "increase" in her pension but since she was not getting a pension she was ineligible. The Pension Bureau sent her a form, however, because the law had changed again and she might be able to make a claim. The letter went to the wrong Caroline King. Nothing more has been learned. Why she was in Buffalo is a mystery but perhaps it was because her daughter lived there. I have been unable to find Georgeanna's married name and cannot confirm this theory.

Henry Short – Co. E

b. 1839 ?

d. ? ?

m. ?

NOTE: Little has been learned about this soldier. He enlisted in Co. D, 35th "Jefferson County" Regiment on June 11, 1861 at Elmira, Chemung, NY and deserted at Oak Hill, VA on November 10th. When he was captured he was ordered to make up 18 months and 28 days and assigned to the 147th on August 28, 1863. He was wounded at Petersburg, VA on June 19, 1864. According to his muster roll card he was absent "from wounds" when the regiment mustered out. Since no other documentation seems to exist it is possible he died from those wounds.

Christopher Shults – Co. I

b. 1835 Germany

d. January 17, 1913 Toledo, Lucas, OH

m. Caroline "Carrie" _____ (1835-1915) 1859

NOTE: Christopher, a farmer, enrolled in the 147th at Barton, Tioga, NY on July 24, 1863. There is no indication that he was drafted or was a substitute. He transferred to Co. I, 91st Regiment on June 5, 1865 and mustered out near Washington, DC on July 3rd. He and Caroline are buried in Woodlawn Cemetery, Toledo.

James J. Shultz – Co. G

b. December 5, 1830 Benton, Yates County, NY

d. December 15, 1922 Benton, Yates, NY

m1. Mary E. Bell (September 1835-March 5, 1926) *ca.* 1855

m2. Mary Miller (November 1850-April 10, 1920) 1868

NOTE: James' parents are unknown but a brother, Sydney, survived him. James was a substitute for William W. Sutton, Sparta, Livingston, NY and enrolled in the 147th at Canandaigua, Ontario, NY on October 2, 1863. He transferred to Co. F, 91st Regiment on June 5, 1865 and mustered out on July 3rd near Washington, DC. In 1890 he claimed deafness as a disability. His marriage to Mary Bell was unsuccessful. She married James A. Henderson (1822-October 28, 1898) on April 5, 1888. He is buried in Lake View Cemetery, Milo, Yates County. She is buried in Bennettsburg, Schuyler County. James and Mary Miller Shultz are buried in Seamans Cemetery, Savona, Steuben, NY. Their gravestone does not provide death dates.

Henry Smith – Co. C

b. 1820 Germany
d. May 25, 1864 3rd Division 5th Army Corps Hospital, VA
m. Caroline Kessel (1830-*post* 1880) July 16, 1851

NOTE: The marriage date for Henry and Caroline varies, depending on the document. Their eldest daughter, Matilda, was born July 14, 1851. The family came to the United States in August 1852 and settled in Allegany, Cattaraugus County. Henry was drafted, enrolling in the 147th at Dunkirk, Chautauqua, NY on August 11, 1863. His COD was typho-malarial fever, although Caroline consistently deposed that he died at the battle of the Wilderness. His gravesite is unknown. He and Caroline were the parents of six children, and Caroline obtained pensions for the youngest ones. On March 10, 1866 she married George Walter (1807-*post* 1880), also born in Germany. By 1870 the family was living in Ellsworth, Pierce, WI. George and Caroline disappear after the 1880 census.

James R. Smith – Co. E

b. 1837 Ireland
d. ? ?
m. ?

NOTE: Little has been learned about this soldier. He was drafted, enrolling in the 147th at Utica, Oneida, NY on September 7, 1863. He transferred to Co. K, 91st Regiment on June 5, 1865 and mustered out near Washington, DC on July 3rd. No other confirmable information has been located.

Josiah Smith – Co. G

b. December 22, 1820 Pennsylvania
d. July 30, 1868 Sparta, Livingston, NY
m. ------

NOTE: Josiah, a carpenter, was the son of Adam (1796-*post* 1865) and Elizabeth Kline Smith (1795-*ante* 1860). A draftee, he enrolled in the 147th at Canandaigua, Ontario, NY on July 25, 1863. According to his muster roll card he deserted April 3, 1865 but returned to duty. His entry in *The Town Clerks' Registers* says he took part in the battle of the Wilderness, the siege of Petersburg, and Lee's surrender. He was discharged at Washington, DC on June 3, 1865. His COD is unknown but he is buried in Rau Cemetery, Sparta.

Lewis Smith – Co. I

b. 1831 Newfane, Niagara, NY

d. July 23, 1865 Ira Harris Hospital, Albany, Albany, NY

m. Maria Maham Smith (March 10, 1836-December 17, 1918) January 31, 1859

NOTE: Lewis' parents have not been identified. He was drafted, enrolling in the 147th at Wilson, Niagara, NY on July 29, 1863. Transferred to Co. I, 91st Regiment on June 5, 1865, he mustered out on July 3rd near Washington, DC. According to Captain James McKinley, he had contracted chronic diarrhea near Wilson's Station, VA in May 1865. He accompanied the 91st to New York State. When he arrived in Albany, he was taken to the hospital where he died. Maria had previously been married to Marcus Smith (?-ante 1859), but I have been unable to link him to Lewis. By him she was the mother of Andrew Jackson (April 19, 1854-1938). Maria and Lewis, who were married in Lewiston, Niagara, NY, were the parents of Frances Eliza (November 23, 1859-1935) who was born in Cold Water, Branch, MI. Maria's third husband was Charles Watson Gale (1852-April 2, 1926) whom she married in 1876. Lewis, Maria, Charles, and Andrew are buried in North Ridge Cemetery, North Ridge, Niagara County. Frances is buried in Oakland Rural Cemetery, Ransomville, Niagara County. Marcus' grave has not been located.

Nelson Smith – Co. D

b. 1835 Ithaca, Tompkins, NY

d. November 22, 1893 Van Etten, Chemung, NY

m. Ellenor "Ellen" Cowell Westbrook (1851-1926) ca. 1880

NOTE: Nelson, son of Joseph (1800-post 1870) and Camza Smith (1806-post 1870), was a draftee. He enrolled in the 147th at Elmira, Chemung, NY on July 21, 1863. In 1890 he said he had been wounded in the head and had lost half of his left ear. Exactly when he suffered the wound is open to conjecture. His entry in William M. Gregg Post No. 430 GAR alleges he was wounded at the battle of the Wilderness on May 5, 1864. According to *The Adjutant-General's Report* he was wounded at Laurel Hill on May 12th. If *The Town Clerks' Registers* are to be believed, he was injured during the retreat from White House, VA which began on June 12th. On December 9, 1864 he was captured near Petersburg, VA and confined in Richmond. He spent time in a prison hospital before being paroled at Aiken's landing, VA on February 17, 1865. He obtained his discharge at a hospital in Elmira for "disability" on August 22, 1865. Nelson was a farmer in civilian life. He transferred his GAR membership to Edward Maxwell Post No. 454, Van Etten, at an unknown date. Ellenor, whose name was variously spelled, was previously married to Benjamin Westbrook (1850-post 1875), by whom she bore four children. She and Nelson were childless. He is buried in Old Scotchtown Cemetery, Erin, Chemung. Ellenor married Henry D. Casterline (1861-1931) *ca.* 1902. They are buried in Chemung Village Cemetery.

Robert Smith – Co. H
b. 1833 New York City, NY
d. ? ?
m. ?

NOTE: Little can be said about this soldier. He joined the 147th at Tarrytown, Westchester, NY on August 17, 1864 for a term of one year after attempting to en-roll in the 76th Regiment on the same day. He mustered out on June 7, 1865 near Washington, DC and disappeared.

Theodore Smith – Co. E
b. 1835 Scipio, Cayuga, NY
d. August 24, 1864 Andersonville, Sumter, GA
m. ------

NOTE: Theodore, son of Valson (1803-1889) and Rachel Smith (1804-1897), was drafted, enrolling in the 147th at Auburn, Cayuga, NY on July 24, 1863. It is un-known when he was captured. His COD was *scorbutus* (scurvy). He is buried in Andersonville National Cemetery although a cenotaph can be seen in Scipio Rural Cemetery, where his parents are buried.

Urias Smith – Co. I
b. 1835 London, Ontario, Canada
d. ? ?
m. ?

NOTE: Urias, a tinsmith, was a substitute for Frederick Krauss, Tonawanda, Erie, NY. He enrolled in the 147th at Buffalo on August 15, 1863. He transferred to Co. I, 91st Regiment on June 5, 1865 and mustered out near Washington, DC on July 3rd. Nothing more has been located.

William C. B. Smith – Co. G
b. November 20, 1842 Ontario County, NY
d. July 23, 1930 Jasper, Lewanee, MI
m. Helen L. Potter (November 25, 1840-July 30, 1922) January 21, 1868

NOTE: William, son of Hiram (?-*ante* 1860) and Mahala Stafford Smith (1820-*post* 1860), was drafted, enrolling in the 147th on October 2, 1863 at Canandaigua, Ontario, NY. He was discharged on February 13, 1864 for "disability." In 1890 he said his disability was rheumatism and he had been discharged on a surgeon's certificate. He and Helen were the parents of four children, all living in 1900. Helen's COD was arteriosclerosis with a fractured humerus as a contributing factor. William died of "heat prostration" and "senility." They are buried in Fairfield Cemetery, Fairfield, Lewanee, MI.

Jeremiah Snyder – Co. D
b. 1844 Tompkins County, NY
d. January 30, 1931 Renfrew, Butler, PA
m. ------

NOTE: Jeremiah may have been the son of Samuel (1783-*post* 1860) and Tinty Snyder (1816-*post* 1860). A shoemaker, he saw prior duty in Co. H, 107th Regiment from July 1862-March 1863 when he was discharged at Harper's Ferry, VA for "disability." He was a substitute for John Murray, enrolling in the 147th at Elmira, Chemung, NY on July 20, 1863. He was again discharged for "disability" on August 14, 1864. His grave has not been located.

James R. Spencer – Co. C
b. 1831 Massachusetts
d. ? ?
m. ?

NOTE: James was a substitute for an unnamed draftee, enrolling in the 147th at Watertown, Jefferson, NY on September 11, 1863. He, together with Phineas Snyder, transferred to the US Navy on May 4, 1864. If he completed the entire stint of two and a half years, he was not discharged until 1867. No other information has been located about him.

Charles Vincent Springer – Co. I
b. 1836 South Bainbridge, Chenango, NY
d. October 23, 1864 Florence, SC
m. Ruth Elizabeth Stever (1842-*ante* 1900) November 9, 1859

NOTE: Charles' parents are unknown. A draftee, he enrolled in the 147th at Barton, Tioga, NY on July 13, 1863. He was captured at the battle of the Wilderness on May 5, 1864 and sent to Andersonville. He may also have spent some time in Danville. William C. Rose wrote a letter to Ruth from Hannibal, NY on January 7, 1865 to tell her about Charles' last days. I have added necessary punctuation but retained the writer's spelling: "It becomes my painful duty to be the barer of sad tidings to you. it is of the death of your husband. he died while in prison at Florance South Carolina

& it was at his request that I write this to you. he was with me from the Time of his capture Till he died. he was sick A long time & I took care of him as well as I could Till death took him away from me. he was one of my best friends as we tented together all last winter. he had his right mind Till within half an hour of his death & he knew he had to die so he told me to take the likenesses he had & give one to Mr. Kelly that lives near you & the other he told me to keep & if I ever got out to send it to you. he also sent his dying love to you and his littel boy. he kept up good spirits all through his sickness but his disease was incurable. it was the chronic diarrhea. he died about the last of october if I mistake not. Mr. Kelly has got the date put down in his memorandum book. this is all he requested me to do but if I can be of eney help to you in getting his bounty pay & pension I will do it with pleasure. if you should wish to write to me direct your letter to Wm. C. Rose . . . ." The little boy mentioned in the letter was Clark Vincent (1861-1949). Ruth obtained a pension for herself, was named Clark's guardian, and obtained one for him. On September 15, 1869 she married George M. Springer (1842-February 1, 1926) who had served in the 109th Regiment from August 1862-June 1865. I have been unable to determine if Charles and George were related. By George she had two daughters, Rosa (1872-1937) and Nellie (1876-*post* 1940). Ruth last appears on the 1880 census. In 1900 George claimed to be a widower. He died at the State Hospital in Binghamton, Broome, NY. George and Ruth's graves have not been located. Charles is buried in Florence National Cemetery among the "unknowns."

William D. Squires – Co. B

b. March 11, 1816 Oswego County, NY
d. August 19, 1876 Oswego, NY
m1. Diana Waid/Waite (1823-*ca.* 1865) *ca.* 1851
m2. Lucinda _____ (1830-*post* 1875) *ca.* 1866

NOTE: William, son of William (1796-1878) and Sarah Squires (?-1870), was a carpenter. He enrolled in the 147th at Oswego City on August 28, 1863 as a substitute for Henry L. Goodrich. At an unknown date he transferred to 39th Company, 2nd Battalion, VRC. He was back in Oswego for the 1865 census. His first wife, Diana, claimed in 1865 to have been married twice but no evidence exists for her first husband's name. By 1870 William was married to Lucinda. She and William were the parents of William James (1866-1871). William is buried in Carter Squires Cemetery, Oswego, with his parents and other members of the family. His government stone erroneously provides a DOD of 1871. Diana may be buried there too. A brother, Charles I. (1839-?), served in Hancock's Veteran Corps in 1865. It is unknown what happened to Lucinda. In 1875 she and William were living apart.

Nathan Steinberg – Co. G

b. 1838 Chittenango, Madison, NY
d. ? ?
m. ?

NOTE: Nathan, a boatman, enrolled at Mansfield, Cattaraugus, NY on August 23, 1863 as a substitute for Alson Hollister. He transferred to Co. F, 91st Regiment on June 5, 1865 under the name Steambury and mustered out near Washington, DC on July 3rd. I have located no other documents for him.

George Henry Stevens – Co. I

b. April 15, 1832 Cayuga County, NY
d. December 6, 1914 National Soldiers' Home, Grand Rapids, Kent, MI
m. Cerephna Jane Wheeler (1838-February 24, 1901) 1856

NOTE: George, son of Ira (1803-1884) and Almira Manning Stevens (1805-1885), was a boatman. He was drafted, enrolling in the 147th at Canadea, Allegany, NY on July 14, 1863. He transferred to Co. I, 91st Regiment on June 5, 1865 and mustered out near Washington, DC on July 3rd. He and Cerephna were married at Oramel, Allegany County. Her name was variously spelled. I use that on her death certificate and gravestone. George and Cerephna, the parents of four, are buried in Springport Cemetery, Harrisville, Alcona, MI. His COD was apoplexy. She succumbed to pneumonia.

Philip Jarvis Stevens – Co. C

b. June 20, 1829 Lima, Livingston, NY
d. June 20, 1864 4th Division 5 Army Corps Hospital, Petersburg, VA
m. Zelia Sarah Dunn (April 1827-April 9, 1910) April 8, 1849

NOTE: Philip was the son of Francis (?-ante 1850) and Elizabeth "Betsey" Briggs Stevens (1788-post 1850). A draftee, he enrolled in the 147th at Canandaigua, Ontario, NY on July 30, 1863. He was fatally wounded in front of Petersburg when a bullet severed his femoral artery. It appears he died on his birthday. He and Zelia were married in Livonia, Livingston, NY. They were the parents of Clara J. (1850-?) and William F. (1857-?). Zelia married Van Rensselaer Pratt (March 1843-February 25, 1921) on November 15, 1866. He had served in Co. G, 27th Infantry from 1861-1862 and Co. E, 1st Veteran Cavalry from October 1863-July 1865. He mustered out with the rank of second lieutenant. Pratt entered the Home at Bath, NY on April 20, 1920, suffering from senile dementia and died there. He and Zelia are buried in the Old Baptist Cemetery, Lima.

John E. Stever – Co. I

b. 1833 Schoharie County, NY

d. July 20, 1897 Potter County, PA

m. Eunice Harford (1837-September 4, 1906) *ca.* 1860

NOTE: John's father is unknown but his mother was Mary Chichester Stever (1805-*post* 1870). His sister was Ruth Elizabeth Stever Springer. John was drafted, enrolling in the 147th at Barton, Tioga, NY on July 14, 1863. He transferred to Co. I, 91st Regiment on June 5, 1865 and mustered out near Washington, DC on July 3rd. John, a wagon maker, is buried in John Lyman Cemetery, Roulette, Potter, PA. Eunice's death was announced in *The Waverly Free Press* September 7, 1906: "—Our community is again saddened by death, that of Mrs. Eunice Stever who passed peacefully away Tuesday afternoon, at the home of her daughter, Mrs. Charles Monroe. She was born in this village [Barton] and spent the greater part of her life here and at Smithboro and in Potter county, Pa. She leaves two daughters, Mrs. Charles S. Monroe of this village, Mrs. Lillie Taylor of Elmira, two brothers, John Harford of Windham and Tunis Harford of Waverly, one sister, Mrs. Tuthill of Colorado. The funeral was held at the home Thursday at 11 o'clock. Rev. J. T. Bradburn of the Methodist church spoke brief words of comfort to the sorrowing friends. The burial was in the cemetery at this place." Eunice's grave has not been located but she may be in the Methodist Church Cemetery, Barton.

Benjamin Franklin Stone – Co. I

b. January 8, 1840 Mansfield, Cattaraugus, NY

d. December 20, 1863 1st Division 5th Army Corps Hospital, Kelly's Ford, VA

m. ------

NOTE: Benjamin, frequently known by his middle name, was the son of Russell A. (1818-1902) and Harriet Coe Stone (1824-1877). He was drafted, enrolling at Humphrey, Cattaraugus, NY on August 21, 1863. His COD was chronic diarrhea. His gravesite has not been located but his parents are buried in Five-Mile Cemetery, Allegany, Cattaraugus.

Walter Stone – Co. D

b. June 12, 1812 Newcastle, England

d. February 14, 1895 Port Huron, St. Clair, MI

m1. Elizabeth _____ (1815-*post* 1865) *ca.* 1841

m2. Bridget O'Brien (1827-*ante* 1883) September 8, 1873

NOTE: Walter's parents were Walter (?-?) and Catherine Radcliff Stone (?-?). His muster roll card stated he was born in Scotland but his obituary and other documents confirm he was born in England. When he entered the 147th he claimed to have been born in 1820. In 1855 the family was living in Brighton, Monroe County, and several of the children were born there. The family lived in Buffalo, NY in 1865. A tailor, Walter was a substitute for Jacob Bishler, Hamburg, Erie, NY, enrolling at Buffalo on August 14, 1863. He was discharged for "disability" at Culpeper, VA on March 24, 1864. He enlisted in Co. C, 2nd MA HA at Worcester, MA on June 28, 1864 and served until mustered out at Smithville, NC on September 3, 1865. Elizabeth's DOD is unknown. Bridget and Walter were married in Hamilton, Ontario, Canada. When Walter entered the National Soldiers' Home in Milwaukee, WI on September 23, 1883 he listed his daughter Sarah as his next of kin. When transferred to the Home in Dayton, OH on November 22, 1883 he said he was a widower. He left Dayton at "own request" on September 17, 1885. His obituary appeared in *The* [Port Huron] *Times Herald* February 15, 1895, 5: "Walter Stone died on Thursday afternoon at the home of his daughter Mrs. J. A. [Sarah] Bassett, at 1819 Tenth Avenue. He was born in Newcastle, England, June 12th, 1812, and was nearly 83 years old. He served more than ten years in the British army, and two years in the civil war. He enlisted in Co. D 147th New York Infantry, and afterwards joined the Second Massachusetts heavy artillery. He leaves seven children, two sons and five daughters, of whom Mrs. Bassett is the only one living near Port Huron. Mr. Stone was well connected in England. His mother's maiden name was Radcliff and she was a first cousin of Mr. Gladstone. The funeral will be held from the house of his son-in-law at 2:30 p.m. Saturday. Veterans will act as pall bearers." Walter's COD was neuralgia. Graves for Walter, Elizabeth, and Bridget have not been located. A son, James G. (1847-December 3, 1903), served in Co. D, 61st Regiment from July 1864-July 1865. He lied about his age to enlist. He was an inmate in the National Home in Milwaukee when he died of hydrophobia and was buried in Wood National Cemetery.

Joseph Stoutenger – Co. F
b. 1831 ?
d. ? ?
m. ?

NOTE: Although Stoutenger is the name provided on the muster roll card, it is more likely that the soldier's surname was Staudinger and that he was born in Germany. Drafted at New York City he enrolled on August 24, 1863, apparently as a musician. Later he was promoted to head musician and transferred to Co. D. On February 27, 1865 he was transferred to the Brigade Band. It appears that he survived the war but no other confirmable information has been located.

Alfred A. Stratton – Co. G

b. 1845 Poland, Chautauqua County, NY
d. June 10, 1874 Washington, DC
m. Julia Elizabeth Johnson (1844-?) 1865

NOTE: Although Alfred, whose parents are unidentified, claimed to have been born in Poland, NY, I have found him on no census records before 1870, nor have I been able to identify August Lass, for whom he was a substitute. Alfred claimed to be a blacksmith when he enrolled at Ellicott, Chautauqua, NY on August 19, 1863. On June 18, 1864 in front of Petersburg, VA both his arms were blown off by an exploding cannon ball. Somehow he survived and was discharged at Alexandria, VA on September 27, 1864. It is alleged that he married Julia in Brooklyn. They were the parents of three children: Alfred M. (1866-1867); Alice (1867-*post* 1880); Henry "Harry" Draper (1871-1915). It has been suggested Alfred was a minister in Brooklyn and later in Washington, DC but I have found no evidence for it. When he was enumerated in 1870 he was a clerk in the Treasury Department. Despite the fact that he received an invalid pension, he sat for numerous pictures to increase medical knowledge about amputees and to make extra money. He was an inmate in the National Home in Milwaukee, WI from September-November 1872 when he left at his own request. His disabilities were loss of arms and tuberculosis, the latter of which caused his death. Alfred is buried in Mt. Olivet Cemetery, Washington, DC. It has been suggested that Julia married John J. Sweeney on June 15, 1877 but in 1880 Julia was still a widow, living with Alice and Harry in Washington, although she may have remarried after that time. In 1899 Harry enlisted in the US Army and was enumerated in the Philippines in 1900. In 1910 he resided with his aunt Olivia Johnston and when he entered the National Home in Hampton, VA in 1912 he gave her as his next of kin. He died on August 26, 1915 and was buried in the Soldiers' and Airmen's Home Cemetery, Washington, DC.

Willard Stratton – Co. G

b. 1834 Massachusetts
d. July 26, 1906 Brutus, Cayuga, NY
m. -------

NOTE: Willard's parents are unknown. He was drafted, enrolling in Canandaigua, Ontario, NY on July 27, 1863. He was captured on May 14, 1864 at Spotsylvania, VA and sent to Andersonville. His parole date is unknown but he was discharged from the service on June 6, 1865. Where he spent the next few years is unknown. On January 15, 1890 he entered the National Home at Bath, Steuben, NY, leaving a year later. He said that Weedsport, Cayuga, NY had been his residence immediately prior to applying for admission to the Home. He claimed scurvy as his disability. He is buried in Weedsport Rural Cemetery.

Gabriel Suffriel – Co. I
b. 1845 Baden, Germany
d. *ca.* 1868 Buffalo, Erie, NY
m. ?

NOTE: Gabriel Suffriel was an alias used by Gabriel Leibfried when he enrolled in the 147th. Little is known about him except his military career. He enlisted in Co. F, 65th NY Militia for a tour of 30 days. The outfit left the state on June 19, 1863 and was involved in the Gettysburg campaign. He mustered out at Buffalo on July 30, 1863. It appears he then became a substitute for John Irlbrocker, Buffalo, enrolling in the 147th on August 9, 1863 in that city. According to his muster roll card his "name [was] not borne on any roll of 147th until Apr. 30/65 then 'missing in action May 5/64 and on M.D.R. as above. No further record'." He seems to have been captured and sent to Andersonville. When released he was sent to a parole camp even though no dates were furnished. He nominally transferred to Co. C, 91st on June 5, 1865 but he does not appear in *The Adjutant-General's Report* under either name. He was enumerated for the 1865 New York census in Buffalo as Gabriel Leibfried, 20, born in Germany, single, a soldier, formerly in the army, a naturalized citizen. Finally, someone named Theresa Leibfried was granted permission as his executrix on July 22, 1868 to administer his estate. It is interesting to note that an entry in *Registers of Officers and Enlisted Men* for Buffalo states that Gabriel Libfried [*sic*] joined the 176th Regiment in 1862 and was KIA at Petersburg, VA in 1864. I have found no evidence that he was ever a member of that regiment. His grave has not been located.

George W. Sutton – Co. G
b. 1843 Sparta, Livingston, NY
d. January 11, 1878 Sparta, Livingston, NY
m. Catherine "Kittie" Sawdey (May 24, 1847-December 11, 1919) *ca.* 1865

NOTE: George, son of David (1810-1861) and Polly Dieter Sutton (1812-1890), saw prior duty in Co. I, 136th Regiment from September-November 1862 when he was discharged at Washington, DC for "disability." He was subsequently drafted, enrolling at Canandaigua, Ontario, NY on October 1, 1863. He was again discharged for "disability" on April 10, 1864. By 1870 he and Kittie were the parents of three children. In 1875, however, the couple was living apart. George died at his mother's house, according to a death notice published in *The Dansville Advertiser* January 17, 1878. COD was not given. He is buried in Kiehle Cemetery, Sparta. Catherine married

Henry James Gilman (November 1856-February 11, 1912) soon after George died because in 1880 she had a son, Scott, 2. Henry's COD was "dropsy." Catherine died in the State Hospital, Willard, Seneca, NY. She and Henry are buried in Wayland Village Cemetery.

William Swan – Co. E

b. 1842 England
d. July 1, 1909 National Soldiers' Home Hospital, Grand Rapids, Kent, MI
m. ------

NOTE: William, son of John Swan (?-?) and an unknown mother, was a carpenter. He enrolled in the 147th as a substitute for William Mobbs, Fleming, Cayuga, NY on July 23, 1863 at Auburn, Cayuga, NY. He transferred to Co. K, 91st Regiment on June 5, 1865 and mustered out near Washington, DC on July 3rd. His movements for the next few years are unknown but in 1890 he was living in East Saginaw, Saginaw, MI where he filed for a pension on November 15th. In 1907 he was a resident of the Home in Grand Rapids although I have not located his admission date. His COD was a combination of paralysis, alcoholism, and senility. He is buried in the Michigan Soldiers' Home Cemetery, Grand Rapids, under the name David Thompson.

Andrew M. Swartwood – Co. D

b. December 1840 Chemung County, NY
d. August 17, 1915 Van Etten, Chemung, NY
m1. Elizabeth Decker (1849-February 20, 1871) 1866
m2. Emelie "Emma" Jane Green (November 1853-June 20, 1932) October 20, 1874

NOTE: Andrew, a shoemaker, was the son of John (1801-1875) and Rachel Westbrook Swartwood (1802-1899). He enrolled in the 147th as a draftee on July 21, 1863 at Van Etten. On June 5, 1865 he transferred to Co. B, 91st Regiment, mustering out near Washington, DC on July 3rd. In 1890 he claimed "piles, heart and kidney disease" as his disabilities. By Elizabeth he was the father of Charlotte "Lottie" (1867-1950) and Charles Edgar (1869-1942). They were living in Tioga, NY when Elizabeth died, but her grave has not been located. Emelie was the mother of Lil (Lillian?) who appeared on the 1880 census for Tioga, NY, aged two, and then disappeared; Helen "Lena" (1883-1971); Henry Warren (1889-1959). There may have been another child because in 1900 Emelie claimed to be the mother of four, two of whom were living. Her obituary in *The Elmira Star-Gazette* June 21, 1932 confirms these relationships. Emelie is buried in Mount Hope Cemetery, Van Etten. Andrew's grave has not been located.

Daniel Hale Taylor – Co. K

b. May 19, 1839 Starks, Somerset, ME
d. March 18, 1915 Chicago, Cook, IL
m. Ella Izora Gillett (June 24, 1850-January 22, 1950) *ca.* 1870

NOTE: The son of Daniel Hale (1815-1882) and Rosina Fish Taylor (1817-1888), Daniel was drafted, enrolling in the 147th at Clarksville, Allegany, NY on July 13, 1863. He was reported absent in Mt. Pleasant Hospital, Washington, DC on August 31, 1864. His entry in *The Town Clerks' Registers* shows a discharge date of November 12, 1864 even though he was nominally transferred to Co. K, 91st Regiment on June 5, 1865. His FAG biography states his body was donated to science. Ella, who would have been 100 years old had she lived a few more months, was featured in an article appearing in *The News-Palladium,* Benton Harbor, MI, on January 14, 1950: "Blind and almost completely deaf, Mrs. Ella Isora Taylor, who will be 100 years old next June 24, manages to keep sweet and cheerful despite her handicaps. The snowy haired little old lady who resides with a widowed daughter, Mrs. Edwin Newton, and a granddaughter, Miss Bertha Newton at 458 Ohio street is one of the few living 'Erie canal babies.' She was born on a packet boat owned by her father, Prosper Gillette, who operated it on the famous Erie canal when it was an important artery of transportation between Buffalo and Albany. Her father, at different times, owned a packet, or passenger carrying craft. These were drawn by horses, which walked along the canal bank, and were operated the full length of the canal from Buffalo to Albany and return. Boat owners at that time frequently lived with their families on their craft, which accounts for 'Grandma' Taylor as a host of friends know her, being born on her father's boat. She was born 11 years before the outbreak of the Civil war on June 20, 1850. When Ella was 10 years old her father gave up canal boating and moved with his wife, Delia, and children, to Hannibal, Mo., home of Mark Twain, the novelist and humorist. Mr. Gillette ran a hotel and was section boss on a railroad there. When Mrs. Taylor was 11 years old the Civil war broke out and from then on Hannibal was a hotbed of Union and Confederate strife and much lawlessness and crime prevailed. At the age of 20 Ella married her late husband, Daniel H. Taylor, and the pair moved to Chicago. Mr. Taylor died there over a half century ago. Of Mrs. Taylor's family of four children only Mrs. Newton survives. Three sons, Elmer, Frank, and Daniel H., Jr., are dead. After coming here to live with her daughter, Mrs. Taylor has claimed both Benton Harbor and St. Joseph as her home. She has resided in the twin cities for more than 50 years. For seven years she was employed at Cooper Wells & Co., St. Joseph, where she was affectionately called 'Grandma' by her many associates. The name has clung to her. She has been retired for about 25 years. Cataracts have gradually caused 'Grandma' to lose her eyesight. She is also partially deaf. The hearing in one ear is gone completely but she can hear a little in the other ear if one talks loudly directly into it. Unable to see or hear, there isn't much that

Grandma can do to pass the time of day except rest and sleep. Active all of her life she still can't get used to just sitting around. 'I just don't like it one bit!' she confided. She has been blind for 15 years. Outside of her blindness and deafness she appears to enjoy fairly good health. She has a good appetite and is particularly fond of sweets and fresh fruits . . . ." Ella's sojourn on earth ended eight days later when she suffered a cerebral hemorrhage. She was buried in Crystal Springs Cemetery, Benton Harbor.

James M. Taylor – Co. K
b. 1843 Chemung County, NY
d. December 3, 1875 Horseheads, Chemung County, NY
m. Rocelia _____ (1853-*post* 1880) *ca.* 1866

NOTE: James, son of George (1814-1860) and Nancy Breese Taylor (1817-1879), was a substitute for Joseph Alexander, enrolling in the 147th on July 4, 1863 at Horseheads. He transferred to Co, K, 91st Regiment on June 5, 1865 and mustered out near Washington, DC on July 3rd. He and Rocelia, who was born in Prussia, were the parents of four children: Silas (1867-1880); George (1869-1869); Julia (1870-1880); Ira (1873-1880). Silas, Ira, and Julia all died of diphtheria in early 1880. They, with their father, are buried in Hilltop Cemetery, Breesport, Chemung. Rocelia disappeared after 1880 and probably remarried.

Silas B. Taylor – Co. K
b. 1842 Chemung County, NY
d. September 29, 1864 Andersonville, Sumter, GA
m. Sarah J. Riker (December 1847-November 15, 1907) December 24, 1861

NOTE: Silas, a boatman, was James' brother. Unlike his brother, however, he was drafted, enrolling in the 147th at Horseheads on July 21, 1863. He was wounded and captured at the battle of the Wilderness on May 5, 1864 and sent to Andersonville. According to *The Town Clerks' Registers*, he "died from such wounds and want of proper care." His muster roll card says his COD was *scorbutus* (scurvy) and death very probably was brought about by a combination of factors. Silas is buried in Andersonville National Cemetery. He and Sarah were the parents of Nancy Elizabeth (1864-1908). Sarah married Moses Dow Crandall (1836-1909) as his second wife. In 1900 she said she was the mother of eight children, all living. She and Moses are buried in Woodlawn Cemetery, Elmira.

Braton P. Telford – Co. F
b. 1845 ?
d. August 10, 1873 Castile, Wyoming, NY
m. ------

NOTE: Braton was the son of James (1808-1875) and Lucy Telford (1819-1860). His muster roll card says merely that he was born in New York but since the family was living in New York City in 1855, he could well have been born in New York County. Braton, a substitute for Edward F. Lathrop, enrolled in the 147th at Warsaw, Wyoming, NY on July 30, 1863. He was captured on May 5, 1864 at the battle of the Wilderness and sent to Andersonville. He was released on March 2, 1865 at an unknown location. Though nominally transferred to Co. A, 91st Regiment on June 5, 1865 he never served in that outfit. He was discharged at Elmira, NY on August 21, 1865. He and other members of his family are buried in Grace Cemetery, Castile.

Daniel L. Theetge – Co. K
b. March 14, 1838 Chemung County, NY
d. September 11, 1901 Chemung Village, Chemung, NY
m. Emeline Wheat (September 1843-July 24, 1900) 1861

NOTE: Daniel's parents were Oliver, Sr. (1811-1891) and Mary "Polly" Roberts Theetge (1813-1891). The family name was variously spelled. I use that found on gravestones. Daniel was a substitute for James Theetge but I have been unable to establish any relationship. He enrolled at Veteran, Chemung, NY on July 29, 1863, transferred to the VRC on April 6, 1864, and was finally discharged for "disability" at Cliffburne Barracks, District of Columbia on September 9, 1864. His disability consisted of the loss of parts of three fingers on the left hand resulting from a duty-related accident. He and Emeline were the parents of six sons, all of whom lived to adulthood. Daniel's COD is unknown. Emeline's was heart disease. They are buried in Chemung Village Cemetery.

Albert W. Thompson – Co. G
b. March 1845 Waterfield, NH
d. February 1, 1908 Colchester, Delaware County, NY
m. Mary E. _____ (June 1837-?) 1877

NOTE: Albert, son of William (1813-?) and Mary Thompson (1815-?), was a substitute for John P. Colgrove, enrolling in the 147th Regiment on August 22, 1863 at Allegany, Cattaraugus, NY. He was wounded on June 18, 1864 at Petersburg, VA and in 1890 said he had suffered a gunshot wound to the left foot. He was discharged for "disability" on June 28, 1865 at a hospital in Chester, PA. Albert's muster roll card stated he was born in Waterfield, NH but I have been unable to find the county where it was located. His death was announced in *The Randolph Register and Weekly Courant* February 7, 1908: "Word has been received here of the death of Albert Thompson which occurred in Delaware County on Saturday. The funeral and burial took place Monday. Mr. Thompson was a former resident of Randolph, an old soldier and a member of D. T. Wiggins post G.A.R. He was a brother of Mrs. Hattie Benedict of this village and many friends will learn of his death with regret. He was about 68 years old." Mary applied for a pension on February 24, 1908 but did not obtain a certificate. It is possible she died before the process could be completed. Albert belonged to David T. Wiggins Post No. 297 GAR which met in Randolph, Cattaraugus, NY. Graves for Albert and Mary have not been found.

John Thompson – Co. G
b. 1822 ?
d. ? ?
m. ?

NOTE: Information about this man is scarce. According to his muster roll card, he was drafted, enrolling at Oswego City, NY on September 20, 1863. The card also states he was captured, place unknown, and died, date unknown, as a POW. It is possible that a man named John Thompson, Co. G, 104th Regiment may be this soldier. He died at Andersonville, GA on August 15, 1864 of chronic diarrhea. The only problem is that no one in the 104th Regiment fits this man's description. If this is the correct person, he is buried in Andersonville National Cemetery in grave #5784.

John Thompson – Co. H
b. 1844 Canada
d. ? ?
m. ?

NOTE: Little is known about this soldier. He was a farmer who substituted for John F. Wilmer, enrolling in the 147th at Stockton, Chautauqua, NY on August 18, 1863. He transferred to Co. F, 91st Regiment on June 5, 1865 and mustered out near Washington, DC on July 3rd. Nothing more has been learned.

John Austin Thompson – Co. A
b. July 1836 Steuben County, NY
d. March 28, 1908 Kingsville, Kleberg, TX
m1. Julia E. Patilion (1841-1889) *ca.* 1860
m2. Mary C. Wilson (1857-1902) May 13, 1891
m3. Alice "Allie" Elizabeth Denison McCready (March 10, 1858-June 18, 1930) December 6, 1905

NOTE: John was the son of John Hemingway (1810-1872) and Elizabeth Olive Curtis Thompson (1813-1878). He enrolled in the 147th on July 18, 1863 at Wayland, Steuben, NY as a draftee and was discharged on June 29, 1865 at Washington, DC. After the war

John attended Rush Medical School, graduating in 1870. When he and Julia, with five children, were enumerated in 1880 they were living in Wayland but by 1885 they were in Letts, Louisa, IA. John's death was announced in *The* [Davenport, IA] *Daily Times* April 10, 1908, 7: "Letts, Ia., April 4. – The remains of Dr. J. A. Thompson, who died at his Texas home near Kingsville, were interred in the Letts cemetery Thursday afternoon by the Masonic lodge. Dr. Thompson was 71 years of age, a Civil War veteran, and practiced medicine in Letts a number of years. He is survived by three children, and his widow, Allie McCreedy [*sic*] Thompson . . . ." Dr. Thompson's COD is unknown but he, Julia, Mary, and his parents are all buried in Letts Cemetery. Allie was previously married to George McCready (1857-*ante* 1895) by whom she was the mother of several children. Her COD was listed as "senility" and she was buried in Elm Grove Cemetery, Washington, IA. A brother, Thomas Curtis Thompson (1838-May 5, 1871), served in Co. K, 1st NY Dragoons from August 1862-July 1865. He died of an "abscess of the left lung." He too is buried in Letts Cemetery.

Albert Hugh Tibbals – Co. K

b. January 28, 1843 Canadice, Ontario, NY
d. October 28, 1920 Canadice, Ontario, NY
m1. Lucy Estella Slingerland (1848-December 30, 1902) 1866
m2. Mary Emeline Winch (June 2, 1852-December 29, 1936) November 30, 1904

NOTE: Albert, son of Peter (1821-1878) and Jane Bennett Tibbals (1822-1906), was drafted , enrolling in the 147th on July 28, 1863 at Canadice. He transferred to Co. K, 91st Regiment on June 5, 1865 and mustered out near Washington, DC on July 3rd. His biography in *History of Ontario County*, "Family Sketches," 193-4, details his story: ". . . Albert was educated at the district schools and Dansville Seminary, and worked on his father's farm, teaching school winters for three years. He then enlisted in Company K, One Hundred Forty-seventh New York Infantry, under Colonel F. C. Miller, in July, 1863. He was in several engagements, including all the battles of the Wilderness Campaign to the battle and charge of Petersburg, June 18, 1864 . . . Mr. Tibbals was slightly wounded twice in these battles, but not disabled nor excused from duty till the latter part of June, when he went into hospital on account of sickness. Later he returned to his regiment and participated in the battles of Hatcher's Run, Gravelly Run, Five Forks, and at General Lee's surrender at Appomattox C. H. He was adjutant's clerk at headquarters much of the time when not in active movement, and was discharged in July, 1865. Returning home he taught school fourteen winters and engaged in farming . . . Mr. Tibbals is now serving his fifth term as justice of the peace; he was a notary public several years, a member of the Board of Supervisors in 1884-5, and justice of sessions in 1890-1-2." In 1890 Albert claimed "chronic diarrhea" as his disability. His death occasioned a lengthy obituary in *The Naples Record* November 10, 1920, which is excerpted here: "At his home in this place, on October 28, 1920, Albert H. Tibbals died after an illness of a little more than three weeks. In three months to a day he would have celebrated his seventy-eighth birthday . . . The funeral was held from the church on Saturday, October 30, Rev. W. J. Brown, of Avoca, a former pastor, officiating. Burial was made in the Canadice Valley cemetery. Mr. Tibbals held a large place in this and the surrounding community, also in the church here. He was a soldier in the Civil War, belonged to the G. A. R. His grandsons served in the late war across the sea. Mr. Tibbals was also a member of the Masonic order. For about twenty-five years he was a teacher in this and surrounding communities. He had the office of supervisor for two terms, and had been justice of the peace for many years, holding that office at the time of his death. He had been one of the officials of the church here for many years, and took a keen interest in all its affairs, inquiring in his last illness about the change of pastors." Lucy's death was reported in *The Cohocton Times-Index* January ?, 1903: "The friends of Mrs. Lucy Slingerlands Tibbals regret to learn of her death at her home in Canadice on Wednesday of last week . . from a lingering illness of many years from rheumatism and consumption. She was upwards of 60 years of age . . . The deceased had been a great sufferer for years, which was borne with patience and Christian resignation. Though of a cheerful disposition, she was quiet and domestic in her tastes, and loved her home and her family best of all, where she will be greatly missed. The funeral was held last Friday." Mary's death was announced in *The Livonia Gazette* January 7, 1937, 3: "Mrs. Mary Tibbals passed away Tuesday morning after a brief illness at the home of her cousin, Mrs. Leslie Paine, with whom she had planned to spend the winter. She was born June 2, 1852, and was the second daughter of Lorenzo Winch and Jane Doolittle Winch and the last surviving member of a family of five children. In 1904 she was married to Albert Tibbals. After spending a few years on their Canadice Hill farm, they moved to Canadice Corners, where she has lived since. Mr. Tibbals died in 1920. Mrs. Tibbals was a member of the M. E. church and was always in regular attendance until sickness in the home and her health prevented her. She will long be remembered for her reserved and sweet ways. The funeral services were held Thursday at the church . . . ." Albert, Lucy, and Mary are buried in Canadice Corners Cemetery.

William Tibbitts – Co. A
b. 1839 Livingston County, NY
d. August 27, 1896 Bay City, Bay, MI
m1. ?
m2. Adeline _____ (?-?) ?

NOTE: William has been difficult to trace. The first time he was enumerated appears to be 1865 and since he was still in the service the informant may not have been precise in the reporting. His muster roll card shows a POB of Livingston County but in 1865 he was said to have been born in Steuben County. His parents have not been identified. He was drafted, enrolling in the 147th on July 18, 1863 at Hornellsville, Steuben County. He was discharged from the service at Satterlee US General Hospital, Philadelphia, PA on July 19, 1865. In 1890, while living in Columbiaville, Lapeer, MI, William claimed chronic diarrhea as his disability. According to Draft Registrations Records he was married but I have been unable to identify his wife. Most of the scant documents show him as a single man, but again, there are difficulties. In 1865 none of the boxes for "civil condition" in his entry was checked. He was listed in the Bay City Directory as early as 1871 and in 1880 his age was 35. He was a boarder and the informant may not have known his true age. He was single, so far as the informant knew. The only reference available for Adeline is her (successful) application on October 15, 1896 for a widow's pension. William is buried in Pine Ridge Cemetery, Bay City.

Archibald Timmerman – Co. D
b. 1836 Orleans County, NY
d. 1868 Shelby, Orleans, NY
m. Samantha Mead (1837-*ante* 1865) *ca.* 1860

NOTE: Archibald was the son of Rev. John (1807-1877) and Mary "Polly" Snell Timmerman (1808-1879). Although he alleged his POB was Fulton County when he enrolled in the army, all other extant documents point to Orleans County. A blacksmith, he was a substitute for Charles A. King, Romulus, Seneca, NY, enrolling at Auburn, Cayuga, NY on July 25, 1863. He was wounded on May 5, 1864 at the battle of the Wilderness and sent to hospital in Baltimore, MD, from which he was furloughed on June 24th. It appears he never returned since his muster roll card contains the notation, "no further record." He was also absent when transferred to Co. B, 91st Regiment on June 5, 1865. Little is known about Samantha. She and Archibald were living in Moravia, Cayuga, NY in 1860 and had been "married within the year." When the New York census was enumerated in 1865, however, Archibald was single. He is buried in Boxwood Cemetery, Medina, Orleans. I have been unable to fix an exact DOD.

John T. Tomney – Co. I
b. 1835 Ireland
d. *post* 1865 ?
m. Bridget Smith (1838-?) *ca.* 1854

NOTE: John, whose parents are unidentified, was a freight tally man and was living with his wife Bridget, 22, and three children in Dunkirk, Chautauqua, NY in 1860. He served as a substitute for Cyrus P. Bell, Stafford, Genesee, NY, enrolling in the 147th at Pavilion, Genesee, NY on July 28, 1863. He transferred to Co. C, 9th

Regiment VRC in August 1864 and was discharged at Washington, DC on July 21, 1865. No further information has been located.

George W. Toombs – Co. E
b. January 8, 1832 Argyle, Washington, NY
d. January 8, 1897 National Soldiers' Home, Dayton, Montgomery, OH
m. Sarah J. Grummon (1838-April 8, 1905) *ca.* 1860

NOTE: George, son of William (1789-*post* 1870) and Abigail Toombs (1798-*post* 1870), was a substitute for H. P. Bremester, Rochester, Monroe, NY, enrolling in the 147th on August 8, 1863 in that city. He transferred to Co. K, 91st Regiment on June 5, 1865 and mustered out near Washington, DC on July 3rd. He and Sarah were the parents of Myron (1862-1902); Mortimer (1868-1946); Burt (1877-?). By 1880 the couple had separated. On December 19, 1883 George was admitted to the Monroe County Poorhouse. His "cause of dependence" was kidney disease but he was expected to recover. For next of kin, the clerk wrote, "Has no living relatives – has lived in Rochester 10 years." It is evident he was not telling the truth. In the years that followed George went from one soldiers' home to another. In 1890 he was in Bath, NY. He claimed no disability. It is curious to note that in that same year he applied for a pension but was unsuccessful in his attempt. He spent his last days in Dayton and died of tuberculosis on his birthday. According to the logbook his personal effects were valued at ten cents. George is buried in Dayton National Cemetery. In her later years Sarah lived with members of her family. She reportedly died quite suddenly of edema of the lungs. She is buried in Boxwood Cemetery, Medina, Orleans, NY.

William Toepfer – Co. D
b. *ca.* 1804 Germany
d. February 25, 1864 Regimental Hospital, Culpeper, VA
m. Magdalena "Margaret" Glaser (1823-January 25, 1895) December 1, 1857

NOTE: William, a mason, lied about his age in order to enter the military. On the 1860 census his age was 56, yet when he enlisted in Co. I, 36th Regiment on November 1, 1861, he was 44. He served in that regiment until mustered out on July 15, 1863 at New York City. On August 28, 1863 he enlisted in Co. D, 95th Regiment and gave his age as 46. He transferred to the 147th on January 15, 1864. As reported by Dr. A. S. Coe, his COD was "perforation of the bowels." He is buried in Culpeper National Cemetery, VA. He and Magdalena were married in New York City and were the parents of three children: Anna Mary (1858-*post* 1930); John (1860-*post* 1895); Barbara (1861-1864). Magdalena married Philip Daniel (1837-1906) on April 15, 1866. Upon her death Anna Mary and John were named executors of her will. She left them extensive properties in the New York City area but her husband only $5.00 per month. The family was Roman Catholic but I have been unable to find Magdalena's gravesite.

Joseph Tracy – Co. C
b. 1845 Thistletown, Ontario, Canada
d. ? ?
m. ?

NOTE: Joseph, a farmer, was a substitute for Rozelle Lyman, Buffalo, Erie, NY, enrolling in the 147th in that city on August 8, 1863. According to his muster roll card he transferred to Co. H, 91st Regiment on June 5, 1865 but he is not found in *The Adjutant-General's Report* for that organization. Nothing else has been learned.

William J. Trolan – Co. K
b. 1836 Belfast, Ireland
d. December 31, 1897 Boonville, Oneida, NY
m. Melissa Wood (August 8, 1847-1891) *ca.* 1866

NOTE: According to an obituary for John C. Trolan (1841-1912), William's brother, the boys' parents were Hugh (?-?) and Margaret (?-?) who brought their family to the United States when John was seven. Both parents died soon after immigrating. William was drafted, enrolling in the 147th at Buffalo, NY on August 8, 1863. On December 23, 1864 he transferred to 49th Co., 2nd Battalion VRC and was discharged on June 19, 1865 from Armory Square US General Hospital, Washington, DC. In 1890 he said his disability was a gunshot wound. The enumerator added, "Ball now lies near heart." His obituary was published in *The Utica Daily Press* January 2 (?), 1898: "William J. Trolan died here Friday after an illness of several days. He has been in poor health for some time, having carried a bullet in his body ever since the war. Mr. Trolan was about 60 years of age and has been in the boot and shoe business for a number of years and was well thought of. He is survived by a daughter, Mrs. Henry Grosjean and a brother John of Antwerp." He and Melissa are buried in Boonville Cemetery. John served in Co. E, 14th Regiment from May 1861-May 1863 and in Cos. H and K, 14th NY HA from November 1863-August 1865. He was captured on July 20, 1864 and sent to Andersonville. Until his release, his fellow soldiers thought he had been killed. John became a well-known lawyer in northern New York.

Abner Turner – Co. A
b. February 28, 1823 Springfield, Otsego, NY
d. February 17, 1905 Evans Mills, Jefferson, NY
m. Susan Bort (1828-February 12, 1907) 1844

NOTE: Abner, who styled himself a peddler when he entered the 147th, was the son of Jacob (1797-1880) and Miriam Pickard Turner (1798-1884). He saw prior duty in Co. B, 94th Regiment from November 1861-May 1863. According to his muster roll card he was a substitute for an unnamed draftee and joined the 147th on October 30, 1863 in Watertown, Jefferson, NY. He was discharged near Washington, DC June 5, 1865. In 1890 he claimed "piles and variola" as disabilities. It is interesting to note that he said he had been a member of the 10th NY HA but he is not to be found in *The Adjutant-General's Report* for that outfit. The parents of three children, Abner and Susan are buried in New Evans Mills Cemetery. His COD was a stroke.

Lewis W. Tway – Co. K
b. December 1843 Brooklyn, Kings, NY
d. July 13, 1924 Middletown, Orange, NY
m. Emily "Emma" V. Doughty (December 1848-May 17, 1931) May 6, 1866

NOTE: Lewis' parents are unknown. In 1850 he, a sister Mary J., 10, and a brother, John R., 4, were living in Brooklyn with David Ford, 47, perhaps a relative. He was a substitute for Benjamin Durham, enrolling in the 147th on July 15, 1863 at Nichols, Tioga County. During the battle of the Wilderness on May 5, 1864 he was wounded in the left leg, as he mentioned in his private diary. He transferred to Co. K, 91st Regiment on June 5, 1865 and was discharged from Mower Hospital, Philadelphia, PA on July 14th. He was appointed postmaster of Kelly's Corners Post Office in Delaware County, in January 1886. He also was a salesman for a retail hardware store. According to his funeral notice, published in *The Middletown Daily Herald* July 16, 1924, 12, he was a member of Hoffman Lodge No. 412 F & A M and of Captain William A. Jackson Post No. 301 GAR. He was buried with military honors in Hillside Cemetery, Middletown. In 1930 Emma was living in Brooklyn with her daughter, Helen "Nellie" Miller. Her grave has not been located.

Lewis Tway's diary chronicled the every day life of a soldier.
Special Collections and College Archives, Gettysburg College

Asa Tyler – Co. K
b. 1836 Bath, Steuben, NY
d. March 8, 1896 Springwater, Livingston, NY
m1. Phoebe Guile (1837-*ante* 1865) 1860
m2. Emeline "Emma" E. Brown (July 1845-May 14, 1914) *ca.* 1869

NOTE: Asa was the son of Joseph (1800-*post* 1851) and Irena Caroline Scutt/Schutt Tyler (1803-*post* 1851). A draftee, he enrolled in the 147th on July 29, 1863 at Springwater. He transferred to Co. K, 91st Regiment on June 5, 1865 and mustered out on July 3rd near Washington, DC. In 1890 Asa said his disabilities were "kidney and liver complaint, rheumatism and [illegible]." He and Phoebe were the parents of Edwin (1862-?). He and Emeline were the parents of John (1870-?). Emeline died in Corvina, Los Angeles, CA and her body was returned to Springwater. She and Asa are buried in Mount Vernon Evergreen Cemetery, Springwater. Phoebe's grave has not been located.

Edward Upson – Co. H

b. January 23, 1846 Rochester, Monroe, NY

d. November 6, 1920 Hackley Hospital, Muskegon, Muskegon, MI

m. Sarah Myers Covert (June 1846-January 31, 1923) April 9, 1877

NOTE: Edward, son of Isaac (1817-1850) and Clarinda Raynor Upson (1821-1872), was drafted, enrolling in the 147th at Rochester on August 5, 1863. He was captured at the battle of the Wilderness on May 5, 1864. An unnamed newspaper in Rochester published the following: "Heard From. – Among those who went from this city last fall in substitution for drafted men was a lad named Edward Upson. He was assigned to Co. H, 147th N.Y. Volunteers – an Oswego regiment. The mother of young Upson is a widow lady. The last letter she received from him was dated April 30th, and as the campaign in Virginia commenced a few days later and the 147th was known to have suffered severely she has been in a good deal of anxiety respecting him. Yesterday, however, she received a letter from Capt. Alexander R. Penfield, of Co. H, who is at home wounded, stating that Edward was taken prisoner on the 5th of May, and is now in the hands of the rebels. Of course, this intelligence affords a partial relief to her mind. Capt. Penfield states that those prisoners of his company who have been heard from agree in saying that they are well treated." It is known that Captain Penfield was in Oswego in June 1864 and it is almost definite that the letter was composed at that time. When and where Edward was paroled is unknown but he left parole camp May 4, 1865. He was discharged from the service near Arlington Heights, VA on June 9, 1865. After the war Edward moved to Michigan, settling in Van Buren County, marrying Sarah at Gabbsville. She had been born in Vienna, Oneida, NY. Her first husband was Howe Covert (1816-*ante* 1877), whom she married as his second wife. She died of pneumonia, complicated by old age. Edward succumbed to typhoid fever. They are buried in Lakeside Cemetery, Muskegon.

John Carpenter Vail – Co. K

b. May 13, 1846 Orange County, NY

d. October 27, 1916 Warwick, Orange, NY

m. Mary Reed Van Duzer (June 24, 1859-May 12, 1942) 1882

NOTE: John, a tailor, was the son of William Rundell (1807-1865) and Frances Carpenter Vail (1818-1898). He was a substitute for George Reed, enrolling at Bath, Steuben, NY on July 10, 1863. He transferred to Co. K, 91st Regiment on June 5, 1865 and mustered out near Washington, DC on July 3rd. It is interesting to note that I have found no pension records for either him or Mary. They were the parents of Hazel (1885-1942); Sarah Christine (1888-post 1942); Robert Cornell (1890-1971). It appears that he and Mary parted company, as is suggested in his obituary, published in *The Middletown Times- Press* October 30, 1916, 10: "John C. Vail, for the past 40 years a resident of Warwick, died suddenly in that village on Saturday afternoon, from a hemorrhage, in the 72nd year of his age. Mr. Vail was walking along the street in Warwick, when he was stricken. He was taken to the hospital and after a short period he thought himself strong enough to walk to his brother's home, where he had been living. He walked quite a distance to the house, and just as he reached the door, he was taken with another attack, and he soon expired. The deceased was born in this county, and 30 years ago he met and married a daughter of the late W. W. VanDuzer, of this city. He has resided in Warwick for the greater part of his life . . . The funeral services were held from his late residence this afternoon at 2:30, Rev. W. M. Pickslay officiating. Burial took place in the Warwick cemetery." Mary is also buried in that cemetery. The brother mentioned in the article was Benjamin Franklin Vail (1843-1928).

Francis Van Scroback – Co. B
b. 1831 Antwerp, Belgium
d. ? ?
m. ?

NOTE: Francis, whose surname was also spelled Van Scronbeck, was a substitute for William Emmett, Lancaster, Erie, NY, enrolling in the 147th at Buffalo on August 14, 1863. His muster roll card shows he was captured on May 5, 1864 at the battle of the Wilderness but since no subsequent records have been located he almost certainly died there. He nominally transferred to Co. G, 91st Regiment but that muster card also states he was a prisoner of war and provides no other information.

William L. Voss – Co. H
b. June 1, 1829 Germany
d. February 13, 1890 Wellsville, Allegany, NY
m. Caroline E. Grasstorf (July 29, 1838-April 2, 1902) *ca.* 1858

NOTE: William, a shoemaker, was drafted, enrolling at Scio, Allegany, NY on July 11, 1863. His tenure, however, was brief because he was discharged by "order of Gen. Martindale" on December 14th. He and Caroline, also born in Germany, were the parents of at least 10 children, many of whom died young and are buried with their parents in Fairlawn Cemetery, Scio.

Levinus Wait – Co. E
b. January 6, 1843 Ashford, Cattaraugus, NY
d. November 29, 1863 Armory Square Hospital, Washington, DC
m. ------

NOTE: Levinus was the son of Lorenzo D. (1808-1877) and Nancy Maria Leach Wait (1826-1887). A draftee, he enrolled in the 147th at Ashford on August 20, 1863. He succumbed to typhoid fever and was buried in Soldiers' and Airmen's Home Cemetery, Washington.

Michael Walkenblock – Co. K
b. 1836 Erie County, NY
d. May 5, 1864 Wilderness, VA
m. ------

NOTE: Michael's father is unknown but in 1865 his mother, Catherine Walkenblot (1809-?), and two brothers, John (1835-?) and Lewis (1842-?), were living in Eden, Erie, NY. Lewis reportedly was in the army. Michael's entry in *Registers of Officers and Enlisted Men* provides little information. Almost every category is marked "unknown." His name was included in the section for men who lived in Eden when enrolled. He was probably buried on the field. Variations in spelling the surname hamper research.

Elliott Walker – Co. K
b. September 1839 Nichols, Tioga, NY
d. February 23, 1931 Owego, Tioga, NY
m. Esther D. Hammel (May 1848-December 21, 1907) 1872

NOTE: Elliott, son of Roswell (1806-1869) and Delanie "Delia" Walker (1806-*post* 1880), was drafted, enrolling in the 147th at Owego on July 25, 1863. He transferred to Co. K, 91st Regiment on June 5, 1865 and mustered out on July 3rd near Washington, DC. Elliott and Esther had no children. Her death, announced in *The Waverly Free Press and Tioga County Record* December 27, 1907, revealed she had died after a long illness with cancer. Elliott and Esther are buried in Gibson Corners Cemetery. His brother Aaron (1846-1928) served in Co. K, 85th Regiment from April 1864-June 1865. He was captured on April 20, 1864 at Plymouth, NC and spent 11 months in Libby and Andersonville Prisons.

Charles Ward – Co. B

b. 1845 Niagara County, NY

d. ? ?

m. ?

NOTE: Charles' parents are unknown. He was a boatman when he enrolled as a substitute for Alfred P. Rich at New Albion, Cattaraugus, NY on August 21, 1863. According to his muster roll card he deserted on May 5, 1864 and returned in either February or March 1865. After a court-martial he was sentenced to make up the time lost but on June 19, 1865 he was discharged according to the terms of a telegram sent by the AGO on May 3, 1865. It is possible he was sick and was discharged for an unknown disability. No further information is available.

Edward Ward – Co. F

b. 1820 ?

d. ? ?

m. ?

NOTE: Little is known about this soldier who was a substitute for William Cosgrove, Auburn, NY, enrolling in the 147th in that city on July 23, 1863. His muster roll card provides neither POB nor occupation. He was discharged for "disability" at an unknown date by order of General Lew Wallace. It may be that he lied about his age to enter the military and he was deemed unfit for duty. A man named Edward Ward, 56, born in Massachusetts, married for a second time, a millwright, lived in Mentz, Cayuga, NY in 1865. His wife, Margaret, 52, was also on her second marriage. She was the mother of seven. Four children with the surname White were in the house. There is no indication on the census record that this man had served in the military. He may or may not be the correct person.

George Washington – Co. D

b. 1841 Virginia

d. ? ?

m. ?

NOTE: George was black and in all probability a fugitive slave. Little is known about him. His muster roll card shows he was born in Virginia, was a farmer, and was drafted, enrolling in the 147th at Watertown, Jefferson, NY on September 21, 1863. He transferred to Co. B, 91st Regiment on June 5, 1865 and mustered out near Washington, DC on July 3rd. Information for his later activities is almost non-existent. On February 28, 1913 someone named George Washington, 71, black, child of slaves, born in Virginia, was admitted to the Livingston County Poor House. He was single, in poor physical condition, and admitted because of "sickness." His immediately previous residence had been in Caledonia, Livingston, NY. He died on March 10, 1913 and was buried in the poor house cemetery. This man is a good candidate for the soldier because he said he had lived in New York State for 50 years. If true, he had arrived in New York in 1863.

Edwin E. Waters – Co. E
b. 1842 Sherburne, Chenango, NY
d. December 1, 1921 Norwich, Chenango, NY
m. Marie Bugby (1849-August 10, 1921) 1869

NOTE: Edwin, son of Martin H. (1803-1879) and Athlinda Waters (1809-*post* 1880), saw prior service in Co. H, 76th Regiment, enlisting at New Berlin, Chenango, NY on December 19, 1861. He was discharged on January 16, 1865 at Albany, NY. He re-enlisted in the 147th on March 6, 1865 at Albany for a term of one year and was discharged at Elmira, NY on October 2, 1865. His DOB varies. I use that found on his gravestone. Edwin was a member of Elisha B. Smith Post No. 83 GAR, Norwich. He and Marie, the parents of seven children, are buried in Mount Hope Cemetery, Norwich.

Wilbur Henry Wentworth – Co. G
b. December 1, 1841 Berkshire County, MA
d. June 18, 1864 4th Division, 5th Army Corps Hospital, Petersburg, VA
m. ------

NOTE: The son of William (1813-1883) and Emily Asenath Howlett Wentworth (1818-1844), Wilbur, a draftee, enrolled in the 147th at Almond, Allegany, NY on July 13, 1863. He was mortally wounded in the leg in front of Petersburg, VA. A cenotaph for him is located in Canaserega Cemetery, Allegany County. A brother, William Wallace (June 18, 1840-November 27, 1914), served in Co. G, 23rd Regiment from 1861-June 1863.

David A. Wheeler – Co. H
b. 1833 Livingston County, NY
d. August 23, 1864 Andersonville, Sumter, GA
m. ------

NOTE: David's parents are unknown. A draftee, he enrolled in the 147th on August 21, 1863 at Mansfield, Cattaraugus, NY. His capture date is unknown but he died of chronic diarrhea and is buried in Andersonville National Cemetery.

Richard White – Co. K

b. 1823 Ireland

d. June 20, 1864 Petersburg, VA

m. Elizabeth "Eliza" Robertson (1821-*post* 1882) September 16, 1849

NOTE: Richard enlisted in the 147th at Amboy, NY on March 29, 1864 and was KIA. His burial site is unknown. He and Elizabeth were married in St. Mary's Church, Burlington, VT. At the time of his death they had three minor children: George (1855-1934); Delia Bridget (1857-*post* 1882); Margaret Jane (1861-*post* 1882). On September 12, 1865 Elizabeth married Michael Harvey (1820-*post* 1870), a tailor. By the time the 1875 New York census was taken, Elizabeth was using the surname White and claiming to be a widow. Since there are no records for Harvey after 1870 it is altogether possible he did indeed die. She may have reverted to using the name White because all the children were still living with her. The women disappear after 1882. George died in Oswego on March 10, 1934.

William A. Whitehead – Co. K

b. 1837 ?

d. 1864 ?

m. ?

NOTE: Little can be ascertained concerning this soldier. His POB was listed merely as New York. A substitute for George A. Avery, West Seneca, Erie, NY, he enrolled in the 147th at Buffalo on August 15, 1863. According to his muster roll card he was wounded and captured on May 5, 1864, dying of his wounds while a prisoner of war. To date his prison has not been identified. He is not listed among the dead of Andersonville. It is possible he died en route to a prison camp and was buried along the way.

Samuel Whitford – Co. K

b. December 20, 1825 East Valley, Allegany, NY

d. October 20, 1901 Alfred, Allegany, NY

m1. Maria Wells Langworthy (November 19, 1830-July 28, 1861) October 6, 1849

m2. Cyrenia Sophia Saunders (September 2, 1838-February 28, 1916) October 5, 1866

NOTE: Samuel, son of Jesse S. (1796-1847) and Olive Burdick Whitford (1799-1873), was a draftee, enrolling in the 147th at Alfred on July 13, 1863. In 1890 he said that he had been shot in the left arm but did not specify where it occurred. He was discharged on May 19, 1865 at Satterlee Hospital, West Philadelphia, PA. A lengthy obituary, appearing in *The Sabbath Recorder* November 4, 1901, is excerpted here:

". . . He enlisted in July, 1863, and received a wound in the arm from which he never fully recovered. He was a loving and loyal comrade of the Grand Army. He was converted in young manhood during a revival held by Elder James Cochran, was baptized and joined the Second Alfred Church, from which his membership was transferred to the First Alfred Church two years ago, when his son was baptized He was a regular and punctual attendant until failing health interfered. He was not a man of many words, but constantly aimed to follow the Golden Rule and live a Christian life every day. He was a devoted husband and father, a lover of home, a staunch advocate of good things in public and private life. Whatever he did, he did faithfully and well. Always a great lover of church music, he was for a number of years chorister of the church; and often his home was made cheerful with the grand old hymns in the evening or on Sabbath afternoon . . . Services were conducted at the house Oct. 23, by Pastor Randolph, assisted by Dr. Gamble . . . ." Samuel and Maria had no children. She died quite unexpectedly, as her obituary in *The Sabbath Recorder* August 29, 1861 reveals: "In Alfred, July 28th, 1861, of heart disease, Maria Whitford, consort of Samuel Whitford, aged 30 years. When her husband arose that morning, about 5 o'clock, she appeared to be sleeping quietly. Coming in after about an hour, he found that breath had left her body, though a slight fluttering of the heart was still perceptible. All efforts to resuscitate her proved unavailing. It seems that she had made an effort to get up, as her feet were off the bed. She attended church the day before, and appeared as well as for months. At the family altar, that evening, she expressed gratitude to God that she had been permitted to enjoy one more sanctuary privilege – little thinking, probably, that it was her last on earth. Such is human life. She was noted for her frank and generous nature. She leaves a desolate husband and a large circle of friends to mourn her loss." Samuel and Cyrenia were the parents of one son, Frank (1875-1909). Her obituary appeared in *The Alfred Sun* March 8, 1916, 1: "Mrs. Sophia Cyrenia Saunders Whitford, the fourth child and only daughter of Ethan and Cyrenia Saunders, was born in Darien, Genesee county, Sept. 2, 1838, and died Monday night, February 28, 1916. Early in the year she had suffered an attack of the grip, but was supposed to be far on the way to recovery and the community was not prepared for her sudden departure. Darien was the place of her home until 1864, when her father and her brother Anson came to the town of Alfred with their families. She was united in holy wedlock to Samuel Whitford at Alfred, October 15, 1866. To them was born one child, a son, Frank S., who was one of the proprietors and editors of the Alfred Sun, and died in Boulder, Col., March 6, 1909. For many years their home has been in the village of Alfred and her death removes another life linking ours to the sacred past with its noble characters. By a large circle of old students Mrs. Whitford will always be remembered as having served with efficiency for a number of years as head of the Boarding Department of

The Ladies' Hall. When about thirteen years of age she was baptized by Elder Rouse Babcock and united with the Darien and Cowelsville Seventh Day Baptist Church. Upon coming to the town of Alfred she united with the Second Seventh Day Baptist Church of Alfred of which she remained a member until after coming to this village when she, with her husband and son, united with the church of the same faith here. Years of faithful service and unfaltering trust in her Master had given her quiet serenity and poise which manifested themselves in countenance, voice and conduct while her beautiful Christian character bound friends and neighbors as well as relatives to her . . . ." Samuel, Maria, and Cyrenia are buried in Alfred Rural Cemetery.

Theodore Whitlock – Co. K
b. January 24, 1835 Ithaca, Tompkins, NY
d. February 6, 1865 Hatcher's Run, VA
m. Amanda Newell (1839-August 30, 1868) April 24, 1855

NOTE: Theodore, son of Benijah (1809-1893) and Catharine Ann Apgar Whitlock (1812-1882), was drafted, enrolling in the 147th at Humphrey, Cattaraugus, NY on August 21, 1863. His COD was a "gunshot wound through the bowels." According to *Registers of Officers and Enlisted Men*, he was buried on the field. He and Amanda were married at Ellicottville, Cattaraugus, NY and were the parents of Emily (1856-1908); Caty Ann (1858-1930); Almon Eugene (1860-1945). When Amanda died, her father, Sidney Newell (1805-1901), was named the administrator of her estate and guardian of the children. Amanda is buried in Chapellsburg Burying Ground, Humphrey, as are her parents, Sidney and Emily Eddy Newell (1809-1896).

Auburn M. Wiborn – Co. K
b. 1828 Cumberland, Providence, RI
d. May 19, 1864 Carver Hospital, Washington, DC
m. Mary Elizabeth Wolf (1829-August 4, 1903) August 27, 1847

NOTE: Auburn, a boat builder, was the son of John (1798-1882) and Rosina Vorce Wiborn (1811-1900). He was drafted, enrolling in the 147th at Rochester, Monroe, NY on August 5, 1863. His muster roll card says he was wounded on May 12, 1864 at the battle of the Wilderness but a note in his medical records reveals he was wounded in the left foot on May 10th at Laurel Hill. A letter written to Wiborn's father by Chaplain J. H. Parks and dated May 19th describes his tragic death: "Sir, It has become my painful duty to inform you that your son Auburn Wiborn Co. K 147 Reg NY Vols died in this hospital this morning – he came here on the 16th with a slight wound in the foot – was doing well – up and around – but yesterday unmistakable symptoms of lock jaw manifested themselves, and he died this morning. I saw him and tried to point him to the Saviour of sinners – All was done for him that could be done – I deeply sympathize with you and all afflicted friends but recommend you to the great Comforter." Auburn was buried in Arlington National Cemetery. On January 7, 1865 *The Rochester Evening Express* reported the following: "The remains of Auburn M. Wyborn, who died in Hospital at Washington in August [*sic*] will arrive in this city to-day by Valley Railroad, and the funeral will take place tomorrow (Sunday) afternoon, at 2 ½ o'clock, from Alexander M. E. Church. Friends and acquaintances are invited to attend." A funeral announcement found on the same page added, ". . . Young Wiborn was drafted for the service, in 1862 [*sic*], and went into the army, -- one of the very few who responded to the call thus made upon them. He fulfilled a patriot's duty, and deserves a hero's memory." He was reinterred in the family plot in Mt. Hope Cemetery, Rochester. He and Mary, who were married in Rochester, were the parents of one child, Clara (1850-December 10, 1924). On January 15, 1867 Mary married William Smith (?-1885). In 1901 when Mary applied to have her pension reinstated as a remarried widow, she was living with Clara and her husband, Ambrose McDonald (1852-1918) in Port Huron, St. Clair, MI. The pension was reinstated in 1902. Mary, Clara, and Ambrose are buried in Lakeside Cemetery, Port Huron.

George Washington Wigney – Co. K

b. 1842 New York City, NY
d. March 29, 1883 Detroit, Wayne, MI
m1. Caroline R. Parrish (1844-February 28, 1872) January 1870
m2. Helen Agnes Buell Chidsey (June 1, 1844-November 13,1927) June 20, 1877

NOTE: George, son of William (1807-1880) and Lydia Barraclough Wigney (1806-1889), was a bookkeeper. He was drafted, enrolling in the 147th at Rochester, Monroe, NY on August 5, 1863. Transferred to Co. K, 91st Regiment on June 5, 1865, he mustered out near Washington, DC on July 3rd. He is buried in Woodmere Cemetery, Detroit. He and Caroline were married in Detroit and became the parents of Caroline Armilla "Millie" (August 1870-December 1, 1947). Two years later Caroline died in childbirth. She and her baby, Mattie R. (February-August 16, 1872), are buried with her parents, Philo (1814-1846) and Rosetta Parrish (1813-1845), in Falls Cemetery, Greece, Monroe, NY. Helen had previously been married to Augustus Chidsey (1842-1873) and had three children by him. On July 3, 1889 she married John M. Lake (1840-1924). By 1900 the couple was living apart. Helen's COD was heart disease. A broken leg, occasioned by a fall, may have hastened her death. The name on her death certificate is Helen Agnes Chidsey. She is buried in Elmwood Cemetery, Detroit.

George D. Wilkinson – Co. K

b. 1830 Tioga County, NY
d. August 23, 1885 Waverly, Tioga, NY
m. Margaret R. _____ (September 1827-January 30, 1907) *ca.* 1850

NOTE: George's parents are unidentified. His DOB varies. I use that on his muster roll card. He was drafted, enrolling in the 147th at Barton, Tioga, NY on July 12, 1863. He was wounded on June 18, 1864 before Petersburg, VA and lost a leg. He was discharged from the service on September 14, 1864. George was a harness and carriage maker and a member of Walter C. Hull Post No. 461 GAR, Waverly. On the 1870 and 1875 census records he and Margaret were enumerated with a child, Jennie (1861-?), but she is not seen on the 1865 census. In 1900 Margaret said she had borne no children at all. According to a death announcement published in *The Waverly Free Press* February 1, 1907, 1, Margaret succumbed to *la grippe*. She and George are buried in Forest Home Cemetery, Waverly.

Walter Landon Willett – Co. H

b. December 21, 1841 Lima, Livingston, NY
d. January 5, 1913 Buffalo, Erie, NY
m. Kate A. Rose (1850-February 2, 1913) 1874

NOTE: Walter was a son of Thomas J. (1812-1862) and Phebe Brees Willett (1817-1881). Generally known by his middle name, he was a dentist. A draftee, he enrolled in the 147th on October 1, 1863 at Canandaigua, Ontario, NY. In 1890 he stated that he had spent ten months in Andersonville Prison. Where he was captured is unknown. After the war he was twice appointed postmaster of Newark, Wayne, NY. According to his FAG entry, Kate was a clerk at the post office when they met. Willett was also superintendent of Newark Asylum for Feeble Minded Women for several years. The couple later moved to Buffalo where in 1900 he was working in a hardware store and Kate was matron of the Women's Christian Association. Willett was a member of William B. Vosburgh Post No. 99 GAR, Newark. Kate applied for a widow's pension on January 23, 1913, but died two weeks later. Walter and Kate are buried in East Newark Cemetery. Two of Walter's brothers also served in the military. Oscar (1843-1895) was a member of Co. F, 136th Infantry. Alpheus Cyrene (1846-1864) served in the 8th NY HA. He enrolled on January 4, 1864 and was killed at Cold Harbor on June 3rd.

Francis "Frank" R. Williamson – Co. C

b. 1834 Onondaga County, NY
d. probably December 1864 Alexandria, VA
m. Emeline _____ (1835-April 2, 1861) *ca.* 1855

NOTE: Frank, a carpenter, was the son of Abraham (1802-1872) and Permilia Cooley Williamson (1802-1851). He enlisted, enrolling on March 15, 1864 at Hannibal, NY. His muster roll card shows he was sick in Sickel Branch Barracks Hospital, Division 2, in Alexandria, VA on October 31, 1864. He was paid on December 2nd. No further record was available although he nominally transferred to Co. H, 91st Regiment on June 5, 1865. He is not listed in *The Adjutant-General's Report* for that organization. In all probability he died sometime in December 1864, although he was enumerated for the 1865 New York census as living with a brother, Zenous (1840-?), in Hannibal. Emeline was buried in Hannibal Center Cemetery. Her gravestone says her age was 25 years, six months, and 28 days.

Emeline's death may have provided impetus for her husband, Francis, to enlist in the 147th Regiment.
Author's Collection

William Eugene Williamson – Co. C

b. October 1847 Hannibal, NY

d. April 15, 1910 Hannibal, NY

m. Cornelia Ann Guppy (January 25, 1847-November 15, 1908) November 12, 1866

NOTE: William was Frank's brother. He too enlisted in the 147th on March 15, 1864. His muster roll card states he was absent in Finley Hospital, Washington, DC on August 31, 1864. No further information was available although he nominally transferred to Co. H, 91st Regiment on June 5, 1865. He does not appear in *The Adjutant-General's Report* for that organization. In 1865 he was enumerated in the household of a brother, Lewis, and was "in the army now." What occurred between September 1, 1864 and the end of the war is unknown. In 1890 William said he had served in the 147th Regiment but gave no dates nor did he claim any disability. I have located no pension card for him. He and Cornelia were the parents of four, three of whom were living in 1900. The couple is buried in Hannibal Center Cemetery.

Daniel Willson, Jr. – Co. B

b. 1840 Oneida County, NY

d. December 23, 1863 Douglas General Hospital, Washington, DC

m. ------

NOTE: Daniel, whose surname was also spelled Wilson, was the son of Daniel (1803-1872) and Sophia Betsy Spencer Willson (1808-1880). He was drafted, enrolling in the 147th at Utica, Oneida, NY on August 23, 1863. He succumbed to chronic diarrhea and was buried in the Soldiers' and Airmen's Home Cemetery, Washington.

Daniel Wilson – Co. I
b. June 1846 Oswego, NY
d. May 11, 1910 Thompson, Schoolcraft, MI
m1. Mary Elizabeth Hill (1857-April 29, 1888) January 21, 1871
m2. Sarah Johnson Carpenter (?-June 13, 1913) October 31, 1894

NOTE: Daniel, son of Captain John "Jack" Henry and Susan Laury Wilson, enlisted in the 147th Regiment and was enrolled in Oswego City on January 5, 1864 for a term of three years. He transferred to Co. I, 91st Regiment on June 5, 1865 and mustered out near Washington, DC on July 3rd. An interesting article concerning his life after the war appeared in *The Oswego Daily Palladium* January 29, 1898: "Captain Daniel Wilson, a former resident of Oswego and a well known sailor, is visiting friends in this city for the first time in thirty-two years. Captain Wilson lives in Thompson, Schoolcraft county, Michigan. When there was a call for troops to preserve the Union he went to the front in Company I, 147th regiment. When mustered out at the close of the war in 1865 he returned to Oswego and for a year took up his old occupation as a sailor. He then went to Michigan and has lived there ever since, keeping track of affairs in Oswego through the *Weekly Palladium*, which he has taken nearly all of that time. Tomorrow Captain Wilson and his friends will hold a reunion at No. 112 West Cayuga street." His death was announced in *The Manistique Pioneer Tribune* August 13, 1910 (probably a reprint from another newspaper): "Mr. Daniel Wilson, an old and highly respected citizen of Thompson, died at his home in that village last evening after six o'clock of heart trouble. He was in his usual health at noon, but left his store for the house shortly after dinner, and took to his bed. He grew worse, and when his condition became serious, a physician was telephoned for but death occurred before he reached his bedside. Mr. Wilson had been a resident of Thompson Township for many years and lived on a farm in the Lockhart settlement until a few years ago when age made it impossible actively to pursue farming for a livelihood, and he moved to the village where he conducted a small store. He was a veteran of the civil war and is the second veteran to die within a week." Daniel married Mary in Royalton, Berrien, MI. They were the parents of several children. Sarah had previously been married but her first husband is unidentified. In 1900 she claimed to be the mother of six, none of whom was living. Her DOB varies but her death certificate states she was born on March 23, 1823. COD was senility. She and Daniel are buried in Thompson Township Cemetery. Mary's grave has not been located.

William Wilson – Co. I
b. 1844 Oswego, NY
d. ? ?
m. ------

NOTE: William was Daniel's brother and, like him, a lake sailor. He enlisted in the 147th on January 1, 1864 for a term of three years and received a bounty of $600. On February 6, 1865 he was listed as MIA after the battle of Dabney's Mills (Hatcher's Run). His muster roll card states, "no evidence of death on file" but no further information was available. On June 5, 1865 he nominally transferred to Co. D, 91st Regiment but he is not found in *The Adjutant-General's Report* for that organization. In all likelihood he was killed on February 6th and buried on the field.

Nicholas Wise – Co. D
b. 1827 Luxembourg
d. May 17, 1902 Dunkirk, Chautauqua, NY
m. Maria "Mary" A. Walters (September 19, 1835-May 25, 1924) *ca.* 1855

NOTE: Nicholas, whose surname was spelled Weis on his muster roll card, was a substitute for Frank Noahen, enrolling in the 147th at Yorkshire, Cattaraugus, NY on August 20, 1863. According to his FAG biography, he was wounded at the battle of the Wilderness on May 6, 1864 when a bullet passed through his left thumb and damaged his middle finger, disabling that hand. He was sent to Summit House Hospital, Philadelphia, PA and transferred to Co. D, 14th Regiment VRC. The FAG entry also claims he was one of the soldiers chosen to guard President Lincoln's funeral bier as it lay in state in the Capitol. Nicholas was discharged from the service on August 3, 1865. In later years he was a member of William O. Stevens Post No. 124 GAR, Dunkirk. *The Buffalo Courier* May 18, 1902, 25 reported that he had died after an illness of one year. When the 1900 census was taken, Nicholas and Maria were supposed to have been married in 1846 which would be impossible unless she was only 11 years old at the time. They were the parents of 13 children, all living in 1902. Mary's death was announced in *The Buffalo Commercial* May 28, 1924, 8: "Dunkirk, May 23. – One of the most remarkable residents of this city died today in the person of Mrs. Mary Walter Wise, widow of Nicholas Wise. She left 61 grandchildren, 64 great grandchildren and two great great-grandchildren. She was ninety years old, and a native of Germany. She lived sixty years in Springville and Dunkirk. She was the mother of fourteen [*sic*] children, nine of whom survive, all living in this community. Mr. Wise was a civil war veteran. Mrs. Wise was a member of Sacred Heart church forty years . . . ." Nicholas and Maria are buried in St. Mary's Cemetery, Dunkirk.

Jonathan Taylor Wixson – Co. F

b. June 26, 1843 Wayne, Steuben, NY

d. September 2, 1907 Friendship, Allegany, NY

m1. Alice O. Bassett (1852-November 19, 1899) August 24, 1866

m2. Anna "Annie" J. Enos Jones (January 4, 1860-January 9, 1936) ?

NOTE: Jonathan, son of George (1812-*post* 1865) and Emily Wixson (1813-*post* 1865), served first in Co. K, 136th Regiment from August-December 28, 1862. He was discharged at Washington, DC and since his muster roll card states he had been sick since November 2nd, the cause was probably "disability." On July 13, 1863 Jonathan, a draftee, enrolled in the 147th. He was discharged at Washington, DC on June 3, 1865. He belonged to H. C. Gardner Post No. 247 GAR. His obituary appeared in *The Bolivar Breeze* September 12, 1907, 1: "The funeral of Jonathan T. Wixson was held from the M. E. church in Bolivar at 2 o'clock Thursday afternoon, Rev. J. R. Wells officiating . . . The funeral was largely attended, many members of the G.A.R. Post and Woman's Relief Corps being present . . . Jonathan Taylor Wixson was born Wayne, Steuben County, N.Y., June 26, 1843. He was . . . one of a family of eleven children, seven of whom are now living. When 10 years old he removed to Friendship with his parents. Later he came to Bolivar. At the age of 18 he enlisted in Co. K, 136th regiment and later re-enlisted in Co. F, 147th N. Y. Vol. infantry, from which he was honorably discharged. While in the service he was wounded in the right hand at the Battle of the Wilderness. Aug. 24, 1866, Mr. Wixson was united in marriage to Miss Alice Bassett and they had four children, two boys and two girls. A few years after the death of his first wife Mr. Wixson married Mrs. Annie E. Jones, who survives him. Mr. Wixson was converted and joined the M. E. church in Bolivar in 1901." Jonathan and Alice are buried in Maple Lawn Cemetery, Bolivar. Annie was first married to Levi Jones (1846-1886). The marriage date for Jonathan and Annie is unknown. She was a widow in 1900 and married in 1905. Annie died in Pine Grove, Warren, PA from diabetes and was buried in Hale Cemetery, Russell, Warren, PA.

Theodore Foster Wood – Co. H

b. March 18, 1835 probably Wyoming County, NY

d. February 21, 1883 Dunkirk, Chautauqua, NY

m. ------

NOTE: Theodore was the son of Dwight (1805-*post* 1850) and an unknown mother who probably died shortly after his youngest sister, Mary E. R. (1848-?), was born. A carpenter, Theodore first saw duty as a musician in Co. E, 13th Regiment from May-August 1861. He was drafted, enrolling in the 147th at Canandaigua, Ontario, NY on October 1, 1863. He transferred to the VRC on February 28, 1865, was appointed principal musician on July 6th and discharged at Washington, DC on August 4, 1865. Little can be ascertained about his activities until his death which was reported in *The Fredonia Censor* February 28, 1883: "In Dunkirk, Feb. 21, Mr. Theodore F. Wood, aged 51 years. He was an employee in Brooks Locomotive Works. His death was caused by accidentally stepping into a vat of hot water. He lingered in terrible suffering since Saturday, when the accident occurred." He is buried in Forest Hill Cemetery, Fredonia.

Franklin B. Woodruff – Co. K

b. August 16, 1842 Humphrey, Cattaraugus, NY
d. June 2, 1864 Camden Street General Hospital, Baltimore, MD
m. Louisa Wheeler (1841-May 11, 1928) January 26, 1862

NOTE: Franklin, son of Charles C. (1801-August 14, 1879) and Caroline Reynolds Woodruff (1814-November 6, 1879), was a draftee, enrolling in the 147th at Buffalo on August 15, 1863. He was wounded on May 10, 1864 at Laurel Hill. His arm was amputated and the amputation, together with pneumonia, effected his death. He is buried in Loudon National Cemetery, Baltimore. He and Louisa were the parents of Ulysses Grant Woodruff (April 4, 1864-March 9, 1940). Louisa married J. Elias Whitcomb (1842-1914) on December 25, 1870 at Salamanca, Cattaraugus County. He had served in Co. I, 9th Michigan Regiment. By him she had Frank (1873-?) and Kitty (1878-?). Louisa and J. Elias are buried in Chapellsburg Burying Ground, Humphrey, as are Charles and Caroline Woodruff.

Thomas Pane Wright – Co. H

b. October 2, 1838 Livingston County, NY
d. May 28, 1864 Andersonville, Sumter, GA
m. ------

NOTE: Thomas, a teacher, was the son of Elias C. (1807-*post* 1880) and Elizabeth Turner Wright (1815-*post* 1884). He was drafted, enrolling in the 147th at Canandaigua, Ontario, NY on October 1, 1863. He was wounded and captured on May 5, 1864 at the battle of the Wilderness. His entry in *The Town Clerks' Registers* says he died on September 23, 1864 at Florence, SC which is unlikely since construction on that prison did not begin until September 12th. Thomas is probably buried among the "unknowns" at Andersonville, but a cenotaph for him can be found in New Methodist Cemetery, Lima, Livingston, NY. Elizabeth successfully applied for a mother's pension on April 1, 1884. It seems that Elias abandoned her. He was admitted to the Livingston County Poorhouse on December 31, 1880, claiming to be a widower. His prognosis was poor because he had intemperate habits and was in ill health: the staff thought he would be there the rest of his life. It is possible Elizabeth waited until his death to apply for the pension. If he died at the poorhouse he was probably buried there. Elizabeth's fate is unknown.

Richard Wrye – Co. B
b. 1820 England
d. ? ?
m. ?

NOTE: Information about this soldier is scant. He was a substitute for Benjamin F. Lowry and enrolled in the 147th on August 21, 1863. He was discharged for "disability," place unknown, on March 24, 1864. It is possible he was much older than 43 and for that reason was discharged. Nothing further can be determined.

Harvey Young – Co. D
b. 1830 England
d. ? ?
m. ?

NOTE: Although this man's first name was Harvey on his muster roll card, a notation says his actual name was Henry. The 1855 New York census showed him living in Lyme, Jefferson, NY, single, born in England, and a resident of the area for three years. He was a substitute for an unknown draftee and enrolled in the 147th Regiment on September 10, 1863 at Watertown. He nominally transferred to Co. B, 91st Regiment on June 5, 1865 but was "absent, sick; no discharge." He does not appear in *The Adjutant-General's Report* for that outfit and it is altogether possible, since no subsequent records are to be found, that he had already died.

John Otto Zecher – Co. H
b. December 29, 1836 Germany
d. June 13, 1931 Lowville, Lewis, NY
m. Catherine Wisner (1846-May 19, 1914) April 18, 1863

NOTE: John's parents are unidentified. Known as Otto Zesher on his muster roll card, he was drafted, enrolling in the 147th at Watertown, Jefferson, NY on July 20, 1863. He was wounded in the left hand at the battle of the Wilderness on May 5, 1864. In August he was severely wounded in his right hand, losing the middle finger. He was discharged for "disability from wounds" at Mower Hospital, Philadelphia, PA on June 20, 1865. An extensive obituary published in *The Lowville Journal and Republican* June 18, 1931, 7 detailed his life before and after the war: "John Otto Zecher, one of the five last surviving members of Guilford D. Bailey Post, G. A. R., residing in this immediate vicinity, died at 4:35 Saturday afternoon at the home of his daughter, Mrs. Charles F. Sunderhaft, Shady avenue. Mr. Zecher and Charles Bennsit were the only Civil war veterans to appear in the Memorial day [parade?] in Lowville on May 30th last, and the following day Mr. Zecher was taken seriously ill. His decline was gradual from day to day until the final end. He was the last survivor of Company H, 147th Infantry, and his death leaves but four Civil war veterans in this immediate vicinity. Mr. Zecher was for many years a member and office-holder of Post Bailey. He was born in Mourgburg, Germany, July 15, 1836, and on his 17th birthday he left his native land for this country, making the trip in a sailing ship, the common mode of sea travel of the day, the journey requiring two months and four days. Enlisting in the service of the Union forces, Mr. Zecher took part in a number of battles, the more important being the battle of the Wilderness, Rappahannock, and the battle of Weldon's Railroad. In the latter engagement, in which the commander, General Wadsworth was killed, Mr. Zecher was severely wounded. Following the close of the war Mr. Zecher was engaged in farming in the town of New Bremen until 1890, when he removed to Lowville. His wife, Catherine Wisner, New Bremen, whom he married April 8, 1863, died in May, 1914 . . . Funeral services were held at his late home Tuesday at 3, Rev. G. T. Anderson and Rev. A. W. Ebersole officiating . . . ." Although the obituary claims Zecher was born in July, an article appearing in *The Lowville Journal and Republican* December 30, 1926 announced that he had celebrated his 90th birthday the day before. Otto and Catharine were the parents of eight children, six of whom were living in 1900. Catherine suffered a stroke in May 1914 which led to her death. They are buried in Lowville Rural Cemetery.

76ers

Introduction

THE 76TH "CORTLAND" Regiment New York Volunteers was organized by Col. Nelson W. Green and began recruiting volunteers on September 2, 1861. Although nicknamed the "Cortland Regiment" men from Tioga, Tompkins, Madison, Allegany, Yates, and Chenango Counties also enlisted. In February 1862 the total number of soldiers stood at 1, 012.

The regiment left New York State on January 17, 1862 and eventually became part of the Army of the Potomac, the same group to which the 147th belonged. It suffered its first significant losses at Manassas (2nd Bull Run) in August 1862, then fought at South Mountain on September 14, 1862, and Antietam on September 22, 1862. This regiment is forever linked to the 147th because of its early entry and brave resistance against Lee's Confederate Army on July 1, 1863 at the Battle of Gettysburg. Like the 147th the 76th lost a large number of men at Gettysburg, 234 killed, wounded, or missing. In 1864 the organization participated in the battles of the Wilderness, where 282 were listed as killed, missing, or wounded, Spotsylvania, Laurel Hill, North Anna, Totopotomoy, and Cold Harbor, among others. It also played an important role in the siege of Petersburg. Because of the large numbers of casualties, the regiment was reinforced by transfers from the 24th and the 30th Regiments. Muster out was done by companies and began in late 1864. Re-enlisted veterans and soldiers who had not completed their service were transferred to the 147th on January 28 and January 31, 1865. Total casualties of those killed in action or died from wounds or disease were 13 officers and 328 enlisted men. Fifty-six of these died in captivity.

No account of the 147th is complete without some mention of the men who transferred from the 76th because the outfit saw hard fighting in the months leading up to Lee's surrender at Appomattox in April 1865. Their service is part of the regimental history and deserves to be recognized.

Persons interested in further study of the 76th Regiment are directed to the 76th New York State Volunteer Homepage at www.76nysv.us and the New York Military Museum Homepage at https://dmna.ny.gov/historic/reghist/civil/infantry/76inf/65infMain.htm. Also of interest are R. L. Murray, *First on the Field* (Wolcott, NY: Benedum Books),

1998 and A. P. Smith, *History of the Seventy-Sixth Regiment New York Volunteers: What It Endured and Accomplished* (Cortland, NY: Truate, Smith, and Miles, Printers), 1867 as well as many scholarly and newspaper articles covering the history of this unit and the men who served.

It should be noted that soldiers transferred to the 147th who were unassigned or for whom no record exists have not been included in this section.

Edgar A. Adams – Co. I (tr. January 28, 1865)
b. May 21, 1842 Trumansburg, Tompkins, NY
d. February 18, 1892 Olean, Cattaraugus, NY
m. Pauline Victoria Keller (1857-January 11, 1944) June 19, 1881

NOTE: Edgar, son of Ansel (1804-1886) and Ruth Nichols Adams (1818-1891), enlisted in the 76th Regiment, enrolling on July 17, 1863 at Ithaca, Tompkins, NY. He first served in Co. H and later in Cos. A and B. From the 147th he transferred to Co. I, 91st Regiment on June 5, 1865 and mustered out on July 3rd near Washington, DC. He and Pauline, a native of Indiana, were married in Reedwater, Osceola, MI and were the parents of one child, Ansel Lee (1882-1962). Edgar is buried in Mount View Cemetery, Olean. Pauline married William T. Fletcher (1854-January 5, 1929) on November 25, 1916 in Indianapolis, Marion, IN. He succumbed to a cerebral stroke and his body was cremated. By 1940 Pauline was living in Los Angeles, CA. Her gravesite is unknown but since her son was buried in Forest Lawn Cemetery, Glendale, CA, she too might be there.

James D. Adams – Co. G (tr. January 28, 1865)
b. 1842 Schuyler County, NY
d. June 19, 1893 Ansley, Custer, NE
m. Daisy _____ (1848-November 25, 1922) *ca.* 1870

NOTE: The son of John (1795-1875) and Phoebe Mead Adams (1798-1892), James was drafted, enrolling in the 76th at Hornellsville, Steuben, July 18, 1863 and mustering into Co. D. He was captured at the battle of the Wilderness on May 5, 1884. Where and when he was paroled are unknown. From the 147th he transferred to Co. F, 91st Regiment on June 5, 1865 and mustered out on July 3rd near Washington, DC. He was a painter by occupation. He and Daisy were the parents of one child, Jennie (1873-?). At some point after the 1880 census the family moved to Nebraska where James died and was buried in Ansley Cemetery. Daisy's later movements have been difficult to track but it appears she spent several years in Lincoln, Custer, NE and then moved to California, perhaps to be near her daughter. If the woman who died in 1922 is James' wife, then her death occurred in San Francisco. Her grave has not been located.

Peter Ambirk – Co. A (tr. January 28, 1865)
b. 1843 Buffalo, Erie, NY
d. April 23, 1887 Buffalo, Erie, NY
m. Kunigunda "Cuny" Simon (1854-October 25, 1922) *ca.* 1876

NOTE: Peter, whose parents may have been John (1808-?) and Rosina Ambirk (1804-?), originally enlisted in Co. F, 30th Regiment on August 20, 1862 at Albany, NY. He transferred to the 76th Regiment on May 25, 1863 and was wounded at Gettysburg. On June 5, 1865 he transferred to Co. C, 91st Regiment and mustered out near Ball's Cross Roads, VA on July 3rd. On January 11, 1871 he enlisted in the US Army and was honorably discharged at the expiration of his service. Kunigunda seems to have been married previously since she had a son, Henry P. Meyer (1872-1933). For much of his life he used the surname Ambirk but the 1930 census shows conclusively he was a half-brother of the Ambirk children. Cuny, Henry, and other children are buried in the United German and French Cemetery, Cheektowaga and it is possible Peter is buried there too.

Ambrose Ambridge – Co. C (tr. January 28, 1865)
b. November 17, 1843 Palatine, Montgomery, NY
d. May 2, 1919 Canajoharie, Montgomery, NY
m. Caroline Hulsaver (May 13, 1850-November 12, 1910) 1865

NOTE: Ambrose was the son of James (1808-1897) and Catherine Nihoff Ambridge (1818-1896). Their surname was also spelled Embridge. He enlisted in the 76th Regiment on October 22, 1861 at Cherry Valley, Otsego County and mustered into Co. H. He was taken prisoner on July 1, 1863 at Gettysburg and sent to parole camp. His exchange date is unknown but in later years he was accused of desertion on October 9, 1863, a charge which was dropped in 1890. He re-enlisted on January 3, 1864 at Culpeper, VA and transferred to Co. B on January 1, 1865. From the 147th he went to Co. H, 91st Regiment on June 5, 1865 mustering out on July 3rd near Washington, DC. In 1890 he claimed eye disease and a wounded knee as disabilities. He and Caroline were the parents of four, two of whom were living in 1900. The couple is buried in Canajoharie Falls Cemetery.

Constant Amen – Co. G (tr. January 28, 1865)
b. 1835 Germany
d. ? ?
m. ?

NOTE: Constant, a cheesemaker when he enrolled in the military, was a draftee, enrolling in Co. D, 76th Regiment in Utica, NY on September 26, 1863. He was captured at the battle of Cold Harbor on June 3, 1864 and supposedly paroled at an unknown date. His muster card for the 147th shows him "absent sick" and although he was transferred on June 5, 1865 to Co. F, 91st Regiment he was listed as "absent sick" and he does not appear on *The Adjutant-General's Report* for that organization. I have located no other documents pertaining to this man and theorize he died in captivity.

John Anderson – Co. F (tr. January 28, 1865)
b. 1842 Ireland
d. ? ?
m. Mary _____ (1841-*post* 1891) ?

NOTE: John Anderson was an *alias* used by John Fitzgerald who enrolled in the 76th Regiment at Rochester, Monroe, NY on August 5, 1863 as a substitute for Elias Messner. He was wounded at the battle of the Wilderness on May 5, 1864 and transferred to Co. D on July 1st. Although he was listed as "sick" when the 147th mustered out, he applied for a pension on August 10, 1865. His DOD has not been determined because of the numbers of John Fitzgeralds who died in Rochester shortly before Mary applied for a pension on January 15, 1891. Further information on this couple is not available.

Michael Anstett – Co. I (tr. January 31, 1865)
b. November 1838 Alsace-Lorraine
d. December 6, 1920 Buffalo, Erie, NY
m. Magdalena Stephan (1842-December 25, 1912) November 9, 1865

NOTE: The son of Michael (1810-1890) and Rosina Regina Schmilli Anstett (1803-1886), Michael came to the United States in 1845 and was naturalized. A carpenter, he enlisted in the 76th Regiment on August 12, 1863 and mustered into Co. K. He was captured on May 5, 1864 at the battle of the Wilderness. He was sent to Andersonville and finally released February 25/26, 1865 at North East Ferry, NC. He had been transferred *in absentia* to the 147th Regiment and while it appears he did not spend any time with that organization when he was discharged on June 3, 1865 it was from that regiment. He and Magdalena, also born in Alsace-Lorraine, were the parents of ten children. His obituary appeared in *The Buffalo Evening News* December 8, 1920, 20: "The funeral of Michael Anstett, Civil war veteran and father of the Rev. Michael A. Anstett, rector of Saint Bernard's church who died in the home of his son, 363 Willett street, after a long illness, will be held in the rectory of Saint Bernard's church Thursday morning at 9:45 o'clock. Solemn requiem mass will be celebrated by the Rev. M. A. Anstett assisted by the Rev. Joseph Stephen and the Rev. Roman Nuwer of

Springbrook. Mr. Anstett came to this country from Alsace in 1845 and settled in Lancaster where he lived for many years. He served in the Union army in the Civil war and was taken prisoner at the Battle of the Wilderness. He remained a prisoner until the end of the war. His wife, Magdalena S. Anstett, died eight years ago and since then Mr. Anstett has been living with his son . . . ." Michael and Magdalena are buried in Saint Mary's Cemetery, Lancaster, Erie, NY.

William J. Aumock – Co. G (tr. January 31, 1865)
b. August 20, 1838 Conquest, Cayuga, NY
d. March 7, 1919 Syracuse, Onondaga, NY
m. Katherine "Kate" M. Burke (1844-September 28, 1885) November 20, 1867

NOTE: William, whose surname was mistakenly spelled Americk on the 76th Regiment muster roll, was the son of William (1805-*ante* 1865) and Elizabeth "Betsey" Cowell Aumock (1803-*post* 1865). William enlisted in the 76th Regiment, enrolling in Auburn, Cayuga, NY on July 25, 1863 and mustering into Co. K. He was captured at the battle of the Wilderness on May 5, 1864. After his return on an unspecified date he spent time in Patterson Hospital in Baltimore, MD. Apparently he was discharged as a member of the 147th since his pension cards list both outfits. His interesting obituary appeared in *The Syracuse Post-Standard* March 9, 1919, 2: "William Aumock, 81, veteran of the Civil War, died at 4:45 o'clock Friday night at his home, No. 140 Greenwood place. Mr. Aumock was born in the town of Conquest, Cayuga county, August 20, 1838. He fought in the Civil War, enlisting in Cortland county on July 20, 1863. In one

Michael Anstett.

The funeral of Michael Anstett, Civil war veteran and father of the Rev. Michael A. Anstett, rector of Saint Bernard's church, who died in the home of his son, 563 Willett street, after a long illness, will be held in the rectory of Saint Bernard's church Thursday morning at 9:45 o'clock. Solemn requiem mass will be celebrated by the Rev. M. A. Anstett assisted by the Rev. Joseph Stephen and the Rev. Roman Nuwer of Springbrook.

Mr. Anstett came to this country from Alsace in 1845 and settled in Lancaster, where he lived for many years. He served in the Union army in the Civil war and was taken prisoner at the battle of the wilderness. He remained a prisoner until the end of the war. His wife, Magdalena S. Anstett, died eight years ago and since then Mr. Anstett had been living with his son.

He is survived by four sons, Bernard M., Henry A., Frank and Rev. M. A. Anstett and three daughters, Mrs. L. Schilling, Mrs. _____ and Celia.

A native of Alsace-Lorraine, Anstett enlisted in the 76th regiment and spent time in Andersonville Prison.
Buffalo Evening News

of the hardest campaigns of the war he was taken prisoner and held for seven months in Andersonville Prison. Of four other men and himself who were taken at this time, he was the only one to survive. For some time afterwards he had to remain in the Paterson Park Hospital, Baltimore, Md. By reason of disability he was given his honorable discharge May 20, 1865. Mr. Aumock married Katherine M. Burke of Cato, November 20, 1867. She died September 22, 1885. Mr. Aumock was a member of

Root Post No. 151 G. A. R. While a young man he joined the Methodist Church and when the [illegible] Methodist Church was organized he united with it and had been active in church life. Surviving Mr. Aumock are four children . . . Funeral services will be held at the home of his son, William F. Aumock . . . at 10 o'clock tomorrow morning. Burial will be at Weedsport." William and Kate are buried in Weedsport Rural Cemetery.

Stephen Axtell – Co. D (tr. January 31, 1865)
b. February 14, 1832 Alton, Wayne County, NY
d. March 7, 1900 Sodus, Wayne, NY
m. Cornelia McIntyre (1836-August 22, 1923) June 24, 1855

NOTE: Stephen, son of John (1797-1849) and Sarah Bennett Axtell (1798-*ca.* 1865), was drafted, enrolling in the 76th Regiment at Auburn, NY on July 24, 1863 and mustering into Co. F. He was captured at the battle of the Wilderness on May 5, 1864 and sent to Andersonville. He was transferred to the 147th while still in captivity. He was transferred to the 91st Regiment on June 5, 1865 but discharged on June 9th as a member of the 147th. In 1890 he claimed no disability. He and Cornelia were the parents of one child, Freeman (1857-1946). Stephen's death occasioned the following obituary in *The Rochester Democrat and Chronicle* March 9, 1900: "Sodus mourns the death of Stephen Axtell, one of the most popular men who ever lived in that town. He died suddenly Wednesday night. Mr. Axtell had been feeling unwell for a week, having had neuralgia pains. That night he retired shortly after 9 o'clock, soon complaining of the increase in the pain. He told his wife that he believed that if he changed his position he would be relieved. A moment later he uttered a cry of pain, gasped two or three times and expired instantly, his wife being by the bedside. The deceased was born in Alton sixty-eight years ago. Fifty-one years of that time were passed in the town of Sodus. He was drafted in July, 1863, to Company F, Seventy-sixth Infantry, and later was transferred to the One Hundred and Forty-seventh Regiment, where he was made a sergeant. He was honorably discharged in 1865. During the battle of the Wilderness he was made captive, and passed several months of torture in Andersonville and Florence prisons. His tales of the suffering have been listened to by thousands. He went to New York when a young man and entered politics at the time Tweed was in control. He entered the service of the police department and was one of the shrewdest men on the force. Later he purchased business interests, which for a time were remunerative, but grew to be a poor investment and he sold the property, returning to Sodus, where he resided continually for the past seventeen years. He was one of the best natured men in town, and was always playing jokes on his friends. A widow, one son, Freeman, and a sister, Mrs. James Lewis, survive. His father was John Axtell, and his grandfather, Timothy Axtell, was one of the founders of the Sodus Presbyterian Church in 1812." Stephen and Cornelia are buried in Sodus Rural Cemetery.

Gilbert George Bacon – Co. H (tr. January 28, 1865)
b. February 10, 1841 DeRuyter, Madison, NY
d. December 17, 1912 DeRuyter, Madison, NY
m. Elnora Madison (February 11, 1841-January 28, 1912) 1873

NOTE: Gilbert was the son of Levi, Jr. (1794-1861) and Esther Curtis Bacon (1798-1875). The circumstances surrounding his time in the 76th are murky. He enlisted at Deruyter and mustered into Co. C on October 11, 1861. It appears he did not leave the state with the regiment and was arrested as a deserter in July 1863. A general court-martial sentenced him to make good the time lost. He transferred to Co. B on November 8, 1864. On June 5, 1865 he transferred from the 147th Regiment to Co. F, 91st Regiment, mustering out on July 3rd near Washington, DC. It is interesting to note that in 1890 Gilbert acknowledged he had served in the 76th but he furnished no dates. Gilbert and Elnora are buried in Hillcrest Cemetery, DeRuyter. Levi Bacon was a veteran of the War of 1812. Truman (1839-1917), Gilbert's brother, was a member of the 185th Regiment. Another brother, James Madison Bacon (1835-1909), served in the 10th NY Cavalry from 1862-1865.

John Baer – Co. E (tr. January 28, 1865)
b. 1818 Germany
d. ? ?
m. ?

NOTE: John's surname was variously spelled and his parents unknown. A tailor, he was drafted, enrolling in the 76th Regiment at Niagara, Niagara, NY on July 29, 1863, mustering into Co. E. He was wounded at the battle of Spotsylvania on May 12, 1864. On November 18, 1864 he transferred to Co. C, 76th but it is unknown if he was present. When transferred to the 147th his name was recorded as Beaver. He was "absent, sick; no further record." On June 5, 1865 he was nominally transferred to Co. D, 91st Regiment but he does not appear on the muster roll or in *The Adjutant-General's Report* under any version of his name. It is possible he did not survive.

Aaron Russell Bailey – Co. G (tr. January 28, 1865)
b. 1842 Tyrone, Schuyler, NY
d. August 12, 1917 State Prison, Auburn, Cayuga, NY
m1. Alice C. _____ (1843-November 9, 1876) *ca.* 1870
m2. Georgia A. Simmons (March 1857-January 14, 1919) *ca.* 1880

NOTE: Aaron was the son of Stephen (1819-1885) and Betsy A. Bailey (1826-1895). He enlisted under the name Russell Bailey at Dix, Schuyler, NY on December 30, 1863 and mustered into Co.D. He was transferred to the 147th *in absentia* and listed as "absent, sick." He was discharged from Satterlee Hospital, Philadelphia, PA on June 29, 1865. In June 1913 he briefly entered the Bath National Soldiers' Home, giving heart disease as a disability. His life took a turn for the worse on August 3, 1913 when he shot and fatally wounded Jack Stapleton at his house in Altay. As reported by *The Elmira Star-Gazette* August 5, 1913, 3: ". . . Bailey talks little, only reiterating his first story that they had been drinking somewhat; that Stapleton and he quarreled in the Bailey home that night; that Stapleton made for him with a chair and he (Bailey) fired, fearing that he would be killed or badly harmed by the angered young man . . . In fact, no one knew that Stapleton had been shot until he was found early Monday morning in the Bailey dooryard where he had lain during the night. He was breathing but unconscious and did not live until a physician could be brought . . . ." Details surrounding the killing were brought to light when a coroner's inquest was held, as reported in *The Elmira Star-Gazette* August 6, 1913, 3: ". . . Thomas Maddock of Valois, who is employed on the state road, testified that when going to work Monday morning he saw Russell Bailey coming down the road with a dog cart. Bailey told Maddock he shot Stapleton the night before and was going to Justice of the Peace Littell to give himself up. Bailey went on and Maddock told the Rappleye boys and went with them to Bailey's house, where they found Stapleton lying in the yard about 30 feet from the door. He was unconscious. They arrived at 6:30 o'clock and Stapleton died at 7:10 . . . Bailey told the coroner that he fired the fatal shot but did it in self defense. He said that Stapleton came to his house Saturday night. Sunday morning Bailey's son, who lives nearby, took the two men to Lake Lamoka. They returned Sunday evening to Bailey's house. All had been drinking. Bailey says he went to his bedroom and Stapleton lay on a cot in the sitting room. Some time between 9 and 10 o'clock Saturday [sic] evening Stapleton, he says, came into his room and attacked him. Bailey told him to leave him alone, but Stapleton continued the attack. Then, says Bailey, he got his shotgun and again told Stapleton to keep away. Stapleton raised his arm as if to strike and he fired. He says Stapleton went out of the door and that was the last he saw of him. Bailey went down cellar and out the cellar door, across a berry patch to his son's home. He told no one of the shooting until the next morning. Later Bailey said he might have fired more than one shot but he did not remember. The fact that Stapleton was shot from the rear and that Bailey confided to no one until the next morning that he had shot the man do not coincide, in the opinion of the authorities, with the plea of self defense . . . ." The trial began in early 1914 and Bailey was convicted of first degree murder, a decision overturned on a technicality. His appeal was rejected by the Court of Appeals in November 1914 and he was finally sentenced to not less than five nor more than fifteen years at hard labor. He died from pneumonia. His body was taken to Dundee, Yates County, and buried in Hillside Cemetery. Alice had no children, but Georgia was the mother of five. From accounts given in the newspapers it is evident she and Aaron were not living together. She died in Wayne, Schuyler County from pneumonia after contracting influenza. Graves for the women have not been located.

Charles A. Bailey – Co. F (tr. January 28, 1865)
b. March 1846 Tyrone, Schuyler, NY
d. May 11, 1921 Altay, Schuyler, NY
m. Martha J. "Jennie" Sherwood (October 1846-February 12, 1926) 1874

NOTE: Charles, a farmer, was Aaron Russell's brother. He enrolled the 76th Regiment at Tyrone on December 28, 1863, evidently a volunteer, and mustered into Co. G. On June 5, 1865 he transferred to Co. A, 91st Regiment, mustering out near Washington, DC on July 3rd. In 1890 he claimed no disability. He and Jennie, the parents of two sons, are buried in Tyrone Union Cemetery. His stone gives dates of 1847-1922.

Charles Bailey, Jr. – Co. A (tr. January 28, 1865)
b. January 29, 1829 Morris, Otsego, NY
d. February 17, 1912 Gilbertsville, Otsego, NY
m1. Susannah Collar (1829-October 7, 1854) January 1, 1849
m2. Emily Phelps (1839-February 15, 1921) November 8, 1855

NOTE: The son of Charles, Sr. (1801-1871) and Adria Adams Bailey (1799-1876), Charles was a substitute for an unidentified draftee, enrolling in the 76th Regiment on September 17, 1863 at Norwich, Chenango County and mustering into Co. E. He transferred to Co. A on November 18, 1864. He transferred from the 147th to Co. C, 91st Regiment on June 5, 1865 and mustered out on July 3rd near Washington, DC. In 1890 he claimed he had been shot in the neck. Charles belonged to William W. Jackson Post No. 489 GAR, South New Berlin. According to his death certificate he died of heart disease and pulmonary edema. Charles and Susannah were the parents of Dillwill (1850-1907). He and Emily were the parents of a daughter, Bernice (1877-1959). Although no obituary has been located for Charles, Emily's appeared in *New South Berlin News* February 26, 1921: "At an early hour Tuesday morning, February 15th, the death angel entered the home of Mr. and Mrs. Warren Tillapaugh at Hamden, N. Y., and removed the spirit of the loved mother, Mrs. Emily Bailey. Mrs. Bailey was the oldest daughter of three children of James and Mary A. Coller Phelps . . . She was born near South New Berlin, eighty-one years ago and her entire life was spent here, except the fourteen years which was [sic] very pleasantly spent with her daughter. November 8, 1855, she became the wife of Charles Bailey . . . She was converted early in life and united with the Baptist church of this village and was one of its oldest members at the time of her death. She was a woman of strong Christian character and high ideals of life and found her way into the hearts of many friends . . . . A brief prayer service was held at her late home Wednesday evening and her body was brought the following morning to her old home where funeral services were held at the Baptist church at 1:30 p.m., the Rev. Mr. Silcox, of Gilbertsville, officiating. Beautiful flowers covered her casket and her frail form was tenderly bourn [sic] to its last resting place . . . ." Charles, Susannah, and Emily are buried in Riverside Cemetery, South New Berlin. The gravestone erroneously says he served in the 70th Regiment.

Newton T. Baldwin – Co. F (tr. January 28, 1865)
b. August 5, 1842 Peruville, Tompkins, NY
d. February 18, 1912 McLean, Tompkins, NY
m. Mary E. Hanchett (1846-January 5, 1924) 1866

NOTE: The son of Heman (1809-1865) and Lucinda Brown Baldwin (1815-1908), Newton enlisted in the 76th Regiment on September 16, 1861 at Peruville and enrolled in Co. C. He was captured at the battle of the Wilderness on May 5, 1864 and was sent first to Andersonville and later to Florence, SC. He was still a prisoner when transferred to the 147th but was considered a member of that organization when discharged on June 9, 1865 at Washington, DC. In 1890 he said he had been a prisoner at Andersonville for nine months, had lost an eye, and suffered from rheumatism. His post-war life was eventful and fulfilling, as evidenced by an obituary which appeared in *The Groton and Lansing Journal* February 21, 1912, 1: "Newton Baldwin, of McLean, aged almost 70 years, practically all his life a resident of the Town of Groton and prominent in its affairs, passed away at his home about 8 o'clock Sunday evening from acute indigestion. He was taken ill on Feb. 6. Mr. Baldwin was one of the oldest members of the Groton Masonic Lodge and the funeral, to be held from the home at 11 a.m. tomorrow, will be with full Masonic rites. The Rev. J. J. Farmer, Universalist minister of Cortland, will also participate in the service . . . Mr. Baldwin was born on the Baldwin homestead a mile west of Peruville and except for the years he spent in the famous 76th New York Volunteers during the Civil War he spent his life in this township. He not only fought for his country from 1861 to 1865, but during that time suffered the horrors of the Andersonville Prison for a period of eleven months. Returned from the war, in 1866 he married Miss Mary Hanchett. Mr. Baldwin was active in the Republican party. He was postmaster at McLean for about 27 years and for an even longer time was a justice of the peace. His first term as postmaster was for twelve years and his second term had continued fifteen years when he died . . . ." Newton and Mary were the parents of two daughters. In December 1923 Mary traveled to Ohio for a visit with one of them and died unexpectedly of pneumonia. Her body was returned to McLean and buried next to her husband's in McLean Cemetery. Newton's brother, Carlos (1840-1892), served in the 76th Regiment from May 1863-October 1864.

William H. Baldwin – Co. D (tr. January 28, 1865)
b. April 1838 Otsego County, NY
d. September 13, 1906 Otego, Otsego, NY
m. Mollie Wells (June 26, 1849-December 13, 1919) 1871

NOTE: William, son of Squire (1809-1863) and Millicent Strong Baldwin (1811-1887), enlisted in the 76th Regiment on November 1, 1861 and enrolled in Co. K. He was captured at the battle of the Wilderness on May 5, 1864 but where he spent his captivity is unknown. He was discharged on May 26, 1865 for "expiration of term of service." In1890 he claimed that diarrhea and scurvy were his disabilities and were contracted while a prisoner of war. Like his father, William was a blacksmith. He was a member of C. A. Shepherd Post No. 189 GAR, Otego. He and Mollie were the parents of four children, all living in 1900. I have not located an obituary for him but when Mollie died, the following appeared in *The Otsego Farmer* December 19, 1919, 7: "Mrs. William H. Baldwin, long a well known resident of Otego, died at 2:30 o'clock Saturday morning at the home of her daughter, Mrs. Fred Gilbert, at 107 ½ East street, in Oneonta. The body was taken to Otego, where the more extended service was held from the Baptist church at 2 o'clock, the Rev. R. O. Williamson of Wells Bridge, the pastor of the church, officiating and interment was made in the Evergreen cemetery in Otego. Her maiden name was Mollie Wells and she was the daughter of John and Rachael Wells and was born June 26, 1849, in Milford. When a young woman she removed to Otego and there was united in marriage with the late William H. Baldwin in 1870 [sic]. She had since resided there and enjoyed the respect and esteem of all who knew her. Her husband passed away in 1906 . . . ." William is also buried in Evergreen Cemetery. His brother Hiram (1834-1905) served in the 1st NY Engineers from August 1864-July 1865.

John Frederick Balis – Co. E (tr. January 28, 1865)
b. April 21, 1846 Whitestown, Oneida, NY
d. July 7, 1914 Douglasville, Douglas, GA
m. Sarah F. Stringfellow (January 23, 1852-January 29, 1931) 1872

NOTE: The son of George (1804-*post* 1870) and Alice Coan Balis (1808-1851), John enlisted in the 76th in November 1861 at New York Mills, Oneida County and mustered into

Company D as a drummer. He transferred to Co. H on January 1, 1862. He re-enlisted at Culpeper, VA on January 25, 1864 and transferred to Co. B on January 1, 1865. On June 5, 1865 he transferred from the 147th to Co. I, 91st Regiment, mustering out near Washington, DC on July 3rd. On December 28, 1865 he enlisted in Co. G, 15th USA, serving until December 28, 1868 when he was discharged at Jefferson, TX. During this enlistment he and his father sought unsuccessfully to obtain a commission for him. On November 18, 1869 he enlisted in Ordnance in Alabama. This term ended when he deserted on February 8, 1871. Nevertheless he applied for and obtained a pension. His card makes no mention of his final enlistment. In later life John became a Methodist minister. He and Sarah, who was born in Alabama, had no children but adopted a daughter, Olive Alice (1892-1973). John is buried in Douglasville City Cemetery. Sarah's COD was a lung abscess. Her death certificate says she was buried in Douglasville but I have not located her grave. John's brother, William Henry Harrison (1840-1864), served in the 117th Regiment and was killed at Petersburg, VA on June 15, 1864.

Jerome Ball – Co. E (tr. January 28, 1865)
b. October 20, 1843 Berne, Albany, NY
d. November 22, 1935 Waterford, Saratoga, NY
m1. Isadora Adelaide Settle (March 1848-March 18, 1924) 1870
m2. Mae Temmey LaBlonde (1873-*post* 1940) October 28, 1935

NOTE: Jerome was the son of Peter Mann (1798-1883) and Elizabeth Eve Knieskern Ball (1800-1866). Although in later years he claimed to have been born in 1841, all available records, including his gravestone, point conclusively to a DOB of 1843. He enlisted in the 30th Regiment on September 4, 1862 at Watervliet, Albany County, and enrolled in Co. D. On May 28, 1863 he transferred to Co. I, 76th Regiment and on December 1, 1864 to Co. C. On June 5, 1865 he transferred to Co I, 91st Regiment, mustering out near Washington, DC on July 3rd. In 1890 he claimed chronic diarrhea and rheumatism as his disabilities. He and Isadora were the parents of one child, Delphine (1872-1903). In October 1935 Jerome's birthday was noted in several local papers. The following week he married his nurse, Mae Temmey LaBlonde. His death three weeks later was reported widely. One of the most complete obituaries appeared in *The Troy Times Record* November 23, 1935: "Jerome N. Ball, 94, last surviving member of Post Sheridan, G. A. R., Waterford, died last night at his home, 104 Saratoga Avenue, Northside, after a short illness. Mr. Ball was born at Berne October 20, 1841, and had resided in Northside more than sixty years. He attended the Reformed Church in Cohoes. Mr. Ball was, for a number of years, janitor at School 2, Waterford, and also was employed at the State Barge Canal terminal in that village. At the outbreak of the Civil War, Mr. Ball enlisted in company D, 30th Regulars, of the Union Army at Cohoes. He served three and one-half years in the war and participated in 14 battles. He was severely wounded, never fully recovering from the effects. Survivors include his widow, formerly Mrs. Mae LeBlond, whom he married last month, and several nieces and nephews . . . ." Jerome, Isadora, and Delphine are buried in Waterford Rural Cemetery. His gravestone does not note DOD. Tracing Mae has been difficult. In 1915 someone named Mae Temmey, nursing supervisor, was living in Raleigh, NC. I have located no documents naming her first husband, perhaps because of the variations in spelling the surname. Apparently she was Jerome's nurse for four years. The last reference to her appears in the 1940 census. She was still living in Waterford, was 67 years old, and claimed to have been born in New York State. After that she disappears. Since she is not listed on the New York State Death Index, I theorize she either moved out of state or remarried. It is interesting to note that she apparently did not apply for Jerome's pension.

John Bates – Co. D (tr. January 28, 1865)
b. March 19, 1840 Albany County, NY
d. November 16, 1912 Gaines, Orleans, NY
m. Julia Parker (October 1490-December 3, 1924) 1865

NOTE: John was the son of Thomas (1810-1885) and Sarah "Sally" Whittington Bates (1814-1902). Although his obituary states he was born in Schoharie County, all New York census records show his POB as Albany County. A draftee, he enrolled in the 76th Regiment at Lockport, Niagara, NY on July 28, 1863, mustering into Co. G. His muster card recorded his age as 25. On October 20, 1864 he transferred to Co. C. On June 5, 1865 he transferred from the 147th to Co. B, 91st Regiment and mustered out near Washington, DC on July 3rd. He and Julia were the parents of one daughter, Hattie (1876-1947). His untimely death was announced in *The Medina Daily Journal* November 18, 1912: "John Bates, a well known Gaines farmer, died suddenly of heart failure Saturday afternoon, while riding to Albion from his home near Five Corners, with Samuel Frosdick, of Waterport. He was taken into the home of Ernest Colemyer, just north of the village corporation limits in Main street, and Dr. John Dugan, of Albion, summoned. Coroner Arthur L. Eccleston, of Waterport, was notified and pronounced death due to heart failure. Mr. Bates was born in Schoharie county, 72 years ago, and had resided two miles north of Albion for over forty-one years. He was a veteran of the civil war, having served in Company G, Seventy-six New York Artillery [*sic*]. He was a member of Curtis-Bates Post, G. A. R. . . . The funeral was held from the family home this afternoon at 2 o'clock, Rev. C. H. Burroughs, of Gaines, officiating. Interment was in Mount Albion cemetery." According to a death notice published in *The Orleans Republican* December 10, 1924, Julia died at her daughter's house in Knowlesville where she had lived for many years. She too was buried in Mount Albion Cemetery.

George Baumann – Co. B (tr. January 28, 1865)
b. September 1827 Bavaria, Germany
d. April 7, 1882 Buffalo, Erie, NY
m. Appolonia Lunz (1830-December 4, 1887) December 21, 1855

NOTE: George, a substitute, enrolled in the 76th Regiment on September 15, 1863, mustering into Co. H and subsequently serving in Cos. A and B. He was discharged near Washington, DC on June 22, 1865. He and Appolonia, whose name was variously spelled, were the parents of at least nine children. Graves for these people have not been located.

Silvere Hudon dit Beaulieu – Co. C (tr. January 28, 1865)
b. May 7, 1830 L'Acadie Monteregie, Quebec, Canada
d. November 12, 1905 Elba, Lapeer, MI
m. Henriette "Henrietta" Cordelia Bertrand (March 24, 1824-March 4, 1908) *ca.* 1850

NOTE: This man's surname endured many variations, ranging from Booley to Bolia to Boulier. His parents were Pierre Beaulieu (1792-1867) and Marguerite Henn (1799-1871), both of whom are buried in St. Anne's Cemetery, Colosse, NY. Silvere, also called Sylva and Silver, was a substitute for George H. Patten and enrolled in the 76th Regiment at Oswego, NY on August 14, 1863, mustering into Co. I. He transferred to Co. B on December 1, 1864. Transferred to Co. D, 91st Regiment from the 147th on June 5, 1865, he was discharged near Washington, DC on July 3rd. According to material located in his pension file, he was wounded in the left hand at the battle of the Wilderness, May 5, 1864. He also complained of rheumatism, chronic diarrhea, and severe deafness in both ears. He and Henrietta separated but it is unknown if they divorced. On his death certificate he was "divorced," but on hers she was a widow. In 1884 Henrietta, living in Indiana, unsuccessfully attempted to obtain a pension, implying she did not think he was alive. Silvere was, like his father, a shoemaker. His death certificate, containing the name Sylver Boulier, says he was buried in Lapeer but I have not located his grave. His COD was blood poisoning from an abscess plus senility, with kidney trouble a contributing factor. Henrietta died in Earl Park, Benton, IN from pneumonia. She is buried in St. John the Baptist Cemetery, Earl Park.

George Beckwith, Jr. – Co. E (tr. January 31, 1865)
b. February 1844 Chemung County, NY
d. January 25, 1902 Caywood, Seneca, NY
m. Ella Catlin (January 1858-January 20, 1901) 1877

NOTE: George's parents were George, Sr. (?-*post* 1855) and Elizabeth Beckwith (1823-*post* 1865). He was a substitute for Wayland M. Saunders, enrolling in the

76th Regiment on September 1, 1863 and mustering into Co. B. On June 5, 1865 he transferred from the 147th to Co. K, 91st Regiment and mustered out on July 3rd near Washington, DC. He enlisted in Co. M, 2nd US Artillery on December 10, 1866 and was discharged on May 22, 1867. He and Ella were the parents of two children. I have located no obituaries for either one but a short piece in *The Farmer Review* January 18, 1902, 1 is informative: "George Beckwith is gradually failing and the end does not seem distant." George and Ella are buried in Seneca Union Cemetery, Valois, Schuyler, NY.

Lewis Hamilton Belknap – Co. C (tr. January 28, 1865)
b. May 31, 1838 Little Falls, Herkimer, NY
d. April 27, 1907 Bradford, Penobscot, ME
m. Caroline "Carrie" Mansell (March 8, 1844-*post* 1907) September 10, 1865

NOTE: Lewis, whose name was also spelled Louis, was the son of Philander (?-*post* 1850) and Nancy Ricards Belknap (1818-*post* 1865). He enlisted in the 76th Regiment on November 30, 1861 at Cherry Valley, Otsego County, and mustering into Co. H. He re-enlisted at Culpeper, VA on January 2, 1864. He transferred from the 147th to Co. H, 91st Regiment on June 5, 1865 and mustered out near Washington, DC on July 3rd. By 1870 he and Carrie were living in Wisconsin. In 1890 they were living in Winewoc, Juneau, WI. He claimed chronic diarrhea as a disability. Sometime after 1900 the couple, who had no children, returned to Maine where Carrie had been born. His COD was an ulceration of the bowels and a rupture. He is buried in Hillside Cemetery, Bradford. Carrie, a native of Maine, applied for his pension there on June 24, 1907 and disappeared after that date. Her name is on the gravestone but no DOD is provided. She does not appear on the 1910 census.

William D. Benn – Co. F (tr. January 28, 1865)
b. April 28, 1832 Windsor, Broome, NY
d. April 15, 1915 National Soldiers' Home, Bath, Steuben, NY
m. Caroline Jones (1836-May 18, 1920) October 17, 1852

NOTE: William, son of Hugh I. (1802-1873) and Sophia Grant Benn (1800-1860), was a farmer, enlisting in the 76th Regiment on August 17, 1863 at Kirkwood, Broome, NY and mustering into Co. D. On June 5, 1865 he transferred from the 147th to Co. A, 91st Regiment, mustering out near Washington, DC on July 3rd. William and Caroline were the parents of eight children. In 1899 he deserted her but because of a change in the pension law that year she was able to claim half of his pension. From 1890 until his death William was in and out of various soldiers' homes. In that year he claimed his disability was a problem with his right knee. The admission form for the Marion National Home noted he was crippled in both legs. He is buried in Bath National Cemetery. Caroline worked as a domestic in the years after she and William separated. She died in Binghamton and was buried in Kirkwood Cemetery. Two of William's brothers served the Union cause. Aaron (1834-1886) was in the 137th Regiment, losing his eyesight during the war. Martin (1839-1906) was a member of the 6th NY Cavalry.

William P. Bennett – Co. E (tr. January 28, 1865)
b. *ca.* 1826 ?
d. ? ?
m. ?

NOTE: Little has been learned about this soldier. He was a substitute for Charles B. Potter, Ogden, Monroe, NY, and enrolled in the 76th Regiment at Rochester, Monroe, NY on August 9, 1863, mustering into Co. K, transferring to Co. E on July 1, 1864 and then to Co. C on November 18, 1864. He was nominally transferred to Co. K, 91st Regiment on June 5, 1865 but does not appear in *The Adjutant-General's Report*. His muster roll card gives no biographical or identifying information. On August 13, 1891 he applied for a pension but did not obtain a certificate. Someone named William Bennett died in Rochester on October 17, 1891. If this is the man his death explains the failure to obtain a pension.

Chauncey Guthrie Bills – Co. D (tr. January 28, 1865)
b. November 6, 1840 Addison, Steuben, NY
d. November 15, 1871 Addison, Steuben, NY
m. ------

NOTE: The son of Hiram Philo (1810-1891) and Ama "Amy" Webster Bills (1814-1889), Chauncey was a farmer. He first saw military service when he enlisted in Co. G, 1st NYV on December 31, 1861 at Addison. He was wounded at the battle of White Oak Swamp on June 30, 1862 and discharged for "disability" on January 25, 1863. He was drafted, enrolling in the 76th Regiment at Canandaigua, Ontario, NY on September 21, 1863 and mustering into Co. B. He was captured at the battle of the Wilderness on May 5, 1864 but where he was sent or paroled is unknown. The record says he was "reported as having left Parole Camp May 2/65." He was transferred to the 147th while a prisoner but when discharged on June 9, 1865 he was considered a member of that outfit although he probably never saw any active duty. His gravestone, which can be seen in Presho Cemetery, Lindley, Steuben, NY assigns him to the 147th.

George S. Blake – Co. G (tr. January 28, 1865)
b. October 30, 1836 ?
d. August 19, 1905 Kingsbury, Washington, NY
m. Mary Ann Burt (September 13, 1834-June 20, 1910) 1860

NOTE: The POB of George, son of Solomon (1812-1881) and Jane Bentley Blake (1811-1864), varied from document to document. In 1855 he was supposed to have been born in Warren County but in 1875 his birthplace was Washington County. According to a muster roll card he was born in Trumansburg, Tompkins County. He first saw military duty when he enrolled in Co. H, 22nd Regiment on February 18, 1862. He transferred to Co. B, 76th Regiment on May 28, 1863, transferring several times within the regiment. His discharge date seems to be a matter of conjecture as well. According to the muster card for the 147th he was discharged at "expiration of term of service" but no dates are provided. In 1890 he claimed he had served until July 15, 1865. His pension card, however, shows he was discharged on February 15, 1865. Since he entered the military in February 1862 this date is probably correct. His disabilities in 1890 were chronic diarrhea and deafness. He and Mary Ann, the parents of eight children, are buried in Union Cemetery, Fort Edward, Washington, NY.

Thomas Bond – Co. H (tr. January 28, 1865)
b. December 16, 1818 Newburgh, Orange, NY
d. February 7, 1892 Canandaigua, Ontario, NY
m. Susan E. Boswell (July 12, 1842-July 27, 1889) September 12, 1882

NOTE: Thomas' parents are unidentified. His first military service began when he enlisted at Farmington, Ontario, NY on May 5, 1861 in Co. D, 33rd Regiment. He transferred to Co. G on October 8, 1862 and was discharged for "disability" at Camp White Oak Church, VA on January 3, 1863. Later that year he was drafted, enrolling in the 76th Regiment at Canandaigua on September 4th and mustering into Co. C. He was wounded at Petersburg, VA on June 18, 1864 and transferred to Co. D on November 8th. His time in the 147th was brief since he was transferred Co. C, 3rd VRC on March 22, 1865 and discharged on August 1, 1865 at Augusta, Kennebec, ME. In 1890 he claimed no disability. Thomas and Susan had no children and his will bequeathed everything to his wife's nieces and nephews, the children of William and Sarah Mason. Thomas' sad end was reported in *The Ontario County Journal* February 12, 1892: "Thomas E. Bond, an old war veteran, died at his home on Beeman street Sunday morning from a dose of laudanum which he had taken some time during Thursday night. Dr. Walmsley was summoned Friday morning when the discovery of his condition was made known, but his efforts at resuscitation were of no avail. In his coat was found a bottle of laudanum from which two or three ounces had been taken. About six months ago he attempted suicide in the same manner, but was brought out all right. The deceased was about 60 [*sic*] years of age and was only a wreck of his former self. He was a member of the 33rd New York Volunteers during the war and was twice wounded." Thomas and Susan are buried in West Avenue Cemetery, Canandaigua.

Wright Boodger – Co. B (tr. January 28, 1865)
b. April 1840 Willingham, Cambridgeshire, England
d. February 10, 1928 National Soldiers' Home, Bath, Steuben, NY
m. Maria Kennedy (November 1844-June 18, 1902) 1870

NOTE: Wright's parents were William (1811-1875) and Ann Clack Boodger (1815-1873). He immigrated to the United States with them and became a naturalized citizen. He enlisted in Co. B, 28th Regiment on April 20, 1861 as a musician and was captured at some unknown place and time. According to the records, he was paroled on August 18, 1862. He mustered out at Albany, NY on June 2, 1863. He enrolled in the 76th in Buffalo on August 3, 1863 as a substitute for Casper Walz of East Hamburg, Erie County, mustering into Co. F. He was captured a second time, place and date unknown, and transferred to Co. A in December 1864 while a POW. When discharged at Ball's Cross Roads, VA on June 8th, however, he was considered a member of the 147th. Wright and Maria had no children. Her tragic end was chronicled in *The Medina Tribune* June 26, 1902: "—Mrs. Wright Boodger, of Lockport, 44 years old, died Thursday from burns which she suffered the evening before. She stumbled while going down cellar with a lighted lamp. Her clothing was all burned away and the entire surface of her body was charred." In 1905 Wright entered the Bath National Home and then spent time in and out of other soldiers' homes, finally returning to Bath where he died. He is buried in Bath National Cemetery. Maria's grave has not been located but since Wright's parents are buried in Glenwood Cemetery, Lockport, she may also be there.

Christopher Bouck – Co. E (tr. January 28, 1865)
b. 1846 Middleburg, Schoharie, NY
d. June 16, 1903 Greeley, Anderson, KS
m. Mary Elizabeth _____ (February 1847-*post* 1930) 1865

NOTE: Christopher was a son of Aaron (*ca.* 1825-1901) and Sophia J. Engle Bouck (1822-*post* 1900). His military career was checkered (see "The Draft, Dodgers, and Deserters."). He enlisted in the 76th Regiment on October 12, 1861 and mustered into Co. I. He deserted and enlisted in 14th NY Cavalry at New York City on October 5, 1862. He was captured at Port Hudson, LA on June 15, 1863 and paroled at City

Point, VA on July 2, 1863. After being arrested for desertion in August 1864 he was sent back to the 76th and was transferred to Co. C on December 1, 1864. On June 5, 1865 he transferred from the 147th to Co. A, 91st Regiment, mustering out near Washington, DC on July 3rd. Despite his several missteps he applied for and obtained a pension in 1890. He and Mary were the parents of at least four children. The family moved to Iowa and then to Kansas. *The History of Anderson County, Kansas,* 252 provides pertinent information: "In the spring of 1874 Chris. Bouck, of Newel, Iowa, a practical miller and mill-wright, who had been engaged in that business in Iowa for several years, being desirous of locating in a better wheat country, came to Greeley, where the leading business men gave him some inducements, which he accepted, and immediately commenced the construction of a first-class merchant mill; but meeting unexpected reverses in financial matters, was delayed in the completion of the same until in the fall of 1875, when he enlisted J. K. Gardner and John Weaver, of Albany, N. Y., men of capital, to assist him in the enterprise, as partners, and Greeley can now boast of a fine merchant mill in full operation." Christopher, a member of J. M. Frank Post No. 315 GAR, Greeley, is buried in Greeley City Cemetery. The date given in his FAG entry is incorrect, corroborated by the fact that Mary applied for a widow's pension on September 17, 1903. In 1930 Mary, 84, was living in Walker, KS with her daughter Grace. I have not located a DOD for her. It is possible she was buried with Christopher.

Thaddeus Warsaw Bradley – Co. A (tr. January 28, 1865)
b. December 13, 1837 Warren County, NY
d. April 30, 1914 San Jose, Santa Clara, CA
m. Edith Ann Jenkins (December 27, 1853-July 9, 1924) July 19, 1868

NOTE: Thaddeus was the son of Thaddeus (1812-1889) and Mercy Bennett Bradley (1816-1894). His military career began on April 1, 1862 when he enlisted in Co. B, 22nd Regiment. He transferred to Co. B, 76th Regiment on May 28, 1863 and transferred within the regiment several times. Although nominally transferred to Co. I, 91st Regiment on June 5, 1865 he had already been discharged from the service as a member of the 147th on April 30th at an unspecified location. He moved to Minnesota after the war and married Edith in Stearns County. His obituary, highlighting a long and useful life, was published in *The Mercury News* May ?, 1914 and is excerpted here: "Thaddeus W. Bradley, veteran of the civil war and widely-known resident of this city, is dead, leaving to mourn his passing his widow Edith Bradley, and two daughters, Lillian M. Brannan of Canada and Emma B. Younger of this city, and a host of comrades and friends . . . Mr. Bradley, who was 76 years of age at the time of his death, was a native of Warren county, N. Y., and the son of Thaddeus and Mercy Bennett Bradley . . . He had an interesting war record, and was a member of Sheridan-Dix post, No. 7, department of

California and Nevada, Grand Army of the Republic, in which he had held office as senior vice commander. He was also a charter member of Ketchum post, located at Ada, Minn., and at one time he was a supervisor in Norman county, Minn. Mr. Bradley enlisted in the army from Warren county, N. Y. . . . and was mustered into the United States service at Albany, April 1, 1862, and assigned to Company 'B', 22nd regiment . . . At the second battle of Bull Run, Va., August 29, 1862, Mr. Bradley was captured, paroled and sent to Camp Chase, Columbus, O., where he remained until exchanged . . . he received [an] honorable discharge April 26, 1865. The decedent was with the 76th New York in all its engagements, beginning with Gettysburg . . . Mr. Bradley rendered faithful and meritorious service to his country, and to the day of his death carried with him the scars of war. While building breastworks just prior to the battle of Weldon Railroad, Va., he was injured by a timber striking and breaking his left kneecap, and the injury affected him throughout his long and useful life." Thaddeus and Edith are buried in Oak Hill Memorial Park, San Jose.

Thaddeus Bradley became very involved with the Grand Army of the Republic in the postwar years.
Sebastian A. Nelson

Franklin Brazer – Co. D (tr. January 28, 1865)
b. 1843 Stephentown, Rensselaer, NY
d. ? ?
m. ?

NOTE: This soldier's parents are unknown. He enlisted in the 76th Regiment at Cortland, NY on October 9, 1861, mustering into Co. E. He was captured at South Side Railroad on October 1, 1864 in what was a part of Grant's siege of Petersburg. From September 30th to October 2nd, Grant unsuccessfully sought to cut off this vital railway in an engagement call the battle of Peeble's Farm. Where Brazer was confined is unknown but he was still a POW when transferred to the 147th. He was paroled at North East Ferry, NC on March 3, 1865 and sent to parole camp. His muster card says he was granted a 30 days' furlough to go to Cuyler, Cortland, NY. The card for the 147th states he was "absent, at parole camp, at muster out of company." It is altogether possible that he did not make it home but died along the way. No subsequent records for him have been located.

William Milton Bristol – Co. G (tr. January 28, 1865)
b. July 1841 Cuba, Allegany County, NY
d. February 4, 1929 Shepard Hospital, Montour Falls, Schuyler, NY
m1. Ella Miver (?-*ante* 1875) *ca.* 1867
m2. Eliza Jane Simpson (June 1839-July 16, 1910) 1877
m3. Phoebe Slocum Covell (January 1853-January 15, 1937) July 17, 1913

NOTE: William's parents were Amos Stewart (1814-1873) and Julia Ann Loop Bristol (1819-1892). He was drafted, enrolling in 76th Regiment at Canandaigua, Ontario, NY on September 11, 1863 and mustering into Co. D. He was wounded at the battle of the Wilderness on May 5, 1864. When transferred to the 147th he was "absent, wounded." Although nominally transferred to Co. F, 91st on June 5, 1865, he was in actuality discharged at Alexandria, VA on June 9th. He filed his initial pension claim on June 14th. Little is known about Ella, the mother of Mae (1868-1944). She reportedly is buried in Old Number Nine Cemetery, Seneca, Ontario, NY. Eliza and William were the parents of Edwin Livingston (1879-1972). Phoebe had previously been married to John Wallace Covell (1835-1912), his third wife. It seems her marriage to Bristol was unsuccessful because on June 15, 1919 she married Perry French (1855-1933). William and Eliza are buried in New Number Nine Cemetery, Seneca. Phoebe is buried in Risingville Cemetery, Thurston, Steuben. Perry is buried in Nondaga Cemetery, Bath, Steuben, with his first wife Sarah.

Jay Bronson – Co. C (tr. January 28, 1865)
b. July 7, 1833 Kirkland, Oneida, NY
d. January 15, 1903 St. Mary's Hospital, Detroit, Wayne, MI
m. ------

NOTE: Jay's parents were Allen Wallace (1808-1892) and Tryphena Hudson Bronson (1809-1850). He enlisted in the 76th Regiment at Cherry Valley, Otsego, NY on October 11, 1861, mustering into Co. H. On August 29, 1862 he was captured at Bull Run, VA and later paroled. On January 25, 1864 he re-enlisted at Culpeper, VA. He was wounded at the battle of Weldon Railroad on August 19, 1864, according to the official report of the day: "Private Jay Bronson, of Company H, stretcher-bearer, was wounded in the arm, while going to the skirmish line after a wounded man, in the evening." On January 1, 1865 he was transferred to Co. B. When sent to the 147th he was "transferred, wounded." He was "absent, sick" when transferred to Co. H, 91st Regiment and *The Adjutant-General's Report* for that outfit does not list him. Nevertheless, when he applied for a pension on August 22, 1865 he gave the 91st as his regiment. At some point after the war, Jay moved west. His entry in *The Town Clerks' Registers* says: "Served his time out – reenlisted and discharged at the end of the War – whereabouts not known." His father had moved to Grundy County, IL in 1859 and Jay may have followed him. By 1900, however, he was living in Detroit. His COD was *angina pectoris*. A brief death notice in *The Detroit Free Press* January 17, 1903, 5 stated his body was being sent to Utica, NY. To date his grave has not been located. It is possible that he is buried in Kirkland with his mother. Three of Jay's brothers also served during the Civil War. James Gordon (1840-1883) was a member of the 4th IL Cavalry. Isaac (1845-1909) fought in Captain Henshaw's Independent IL LA. Allen Walter (1847-1918) was in the US Navy.

Nelson Brooks - Co. A (tr. January 28, 1865)
b. 1836 Conquest, Cayuga County, NY
d. May 16, 1919 Union, Broome, NY
m. Mary M. Pier (May 1841-January 27, 1922) 1862

NOTE: Nelson, son of Jesse (1809-1881) and Harriet Butts Brooks (1810-*post* 1860), was drafted, enrolling in the 76th Regiment at Maine, Broome, NY on July 19, 1863 and mustering into Co. E. He was wounded on June 18, 1864 at Petersburg, VA. On November 18, 1864 he transferred to Co. A. On March 22, 1865 he transferred from the 147th to the 14th Co., 2nd Battalion VRC. His exact discharge date is unknown but this unit was discharged in detachments from September 4, 1865-February 1, 1866. Since he applied for a pension on September 14, 1865 he was probably among the first men to be mustered out. His obituary appeared in *The Binghamton Press and Sun-Bulletin* May 17, 1919, 11: "Union, May 17. – Nelson Brooks, aged eighty two years and eleven months, died at his home, 107 Badger street, yesterday noon after a seven weeks' illness of arteriosclerosis and dropsy. The funeral will be held at the home tomorrow afternoon at 2 o'clock, the Rev. Ernest S. Dolaway, pastor of the first Baptist Church, officiating. Burial will be in the Maine Cemetery . . . Mr. Brooks was a member of the Baptist Church for forty years. He also was a member of the G. A. R., and in the interests of both church and army post he was always active and faithful. He saw service of two and one-half years in the Civil War and participated in seven battles, including the Battle of the Wilderness. Members of the G. A. R. will attend the funeral tomorrow in a body. Mr. and Mrs. Brooks became residents of Union thirty three years ago. Mr. Brooks, who was a carpenter by trade, built the house on Badger street, in which he thereafter resided." The GAR post to which Nelson belonged is unidentified but Henry Whittlesey Post No. 350, Union, NY was formed in 1883, only three years before Nelson and Mary moved to the area. According to an obituary published in *The Binghamton Press and Sun-Bulletin* January 21, 1922, 37, Mary, mother of five, died after a nine days' bout of pneumonia. She and Nelson are buried in Maine Cemetery.

David Brown – Co. A (tr. January 28, 1865)
b. February 1831 Jefferson, Schoharie, NY
d. February 6, 1865 Hatcher's Run, VA
m. Zelia Ellen Hine (November 13, 1831-March 8, 1894) December 17, 1856

NOTE: David, son of Silas (1792-1883) and Judith Hicks Brown (1796-1868), was a draftee, enrolling in the 76th Regiment on July 17, 1863 and mustering into Co. E. On November 18, 1864 he transferred to Co. A. Martin Edgcomb testified on August 6, 1866 that "David Brown was an excellent soldier and stood deservedly high in his company." Alonzo Wagoner deposed on August 21, 1866 that he saw Brown's body lying face down on the ground and presumed he was dead. He claimed to have identified him because of a tear in the back of Brown's overcoat. The body was not recovered because it fell into enemy hands. In 1865 Zelia and her three children, Frank A. (1857-1930), Emma C. (1859-June 30, 1880), and Edward M. (1861-?), were living with her parents, Elisha (1803-*post* 1865) and Nancy Hine (1802-*post* 1865) but by 1870 she and the children had moved to Belair, Harford, MD. She never remarried. In 1875 she was appointed postmaster of the Village of Hickory, Harford, MD. In 1880 Frank and Emma were schoolteachers and Edward was a clerk in a store. Emma was suffering from consumption. Zelia's obituary in *The Aegis and Intelligencer* March 16, 1894, 4 tells the rest of the story: "Mrs. Zelia A. Brown, aged 63 years, died of cancer, at her home near the Hickory, on Thursday, March 8th. She was the widow of David Brown, a soldier in the Federal Army, who was killed in battle at Hatcher's Run, Va. Her only surviving children are Edward M. Brown, Principal of Aberdeen Public School, and Frank A. Brown, of the Hickory. The funeral took place on Saturday last from her late residence to Mt. Tabor M. P. Church. Rev. S. A. Whitcomb, of Emmanuel Church, Bel Air, officiated . . . ." She and Emma are buried in Mount Tabor United Methodist Church Cemetery.

William Henry Brown – Co. F (tr. January 28, 1865)
b. November 14, 1838 ?
d. July 5, 1911 Loup City, Sherman, NE
m. Harriet "Hattie" N. Thayer (February 18, 1850-August 23, 1902) June 24, 1866

NOTE: This man's early life is a mystery. Although his obituary states that he was born in Paradise, NY his muster card for the 76th Regiment locates his POB as Carlisle, Schoharie County. Some researchers identify Harriet Crumb (?-?) as his mother but I have found no records confirming this assertion. He may also have been called Henry, further muddying the genealogical waters. There seem to be no records for him prior to 1860. He enlisted in the 76th Regiment at Carlisle, Schoharie County on October 29, 1861 and enrolled in Co. H. Although the exact date is unknown, he was wounded during the battle of Gettysburg. In August 1863 he was hospitalized in York, PA. He re-enlisted at Culpeper, VA on January 25, 1864. On January 1, 1865 he transferred to Co. B. A charge of desertion on March 27, 1865 was later dropped and he was officially discharged on that date as a member of the 147th. His death was noted in *The Sherman County Times* July 13, 1911: "William Henry Brown was born at Paradise, New York, November 14, 1838, and passed away at the home of his daughter, Mrs. E. G. Taylor, July 5, 1911, at the age of 73 years. Mr. Brown suffered a stroke of paralysis about ten years ago and never fully recovered, and as years passed by he gradually grew weaker caused by the severe stroke, and the past year was to [sic] feeble to walk any distance alone. His early life was spent in New York from which state he enlisted in the 76th New York Reg. where he served three years [and] after this was transferred to the 147th New York where he served until near the close of the war being between four and five years in the service. He was a member of the A. Lincoln Post No. 10 David City Neb. After the war he came west and settled in Iowa, and on June 24th, 1866, was married to Miss Hattie Thayer at Cresco, Iowa . . . In 1878 Mr. and Mrs. Brown came to this state making their home at Butler County, and in 1885 they moved to Sherman County and resided on a farm about half way between Rockville and Ashton. From there they moved back to Butler County, where a few years later Mrs. Brown died. Mr. Brown was one of Sherman County's best citizens and had a host of friends. He was nominated a number of times for good political offices in this county but the party to which he belonged was in the minority and he failed of election. At the time of his death he was a member of the Congregational church of David City. A short service was held at the home where he died conducted by the Rev. J. C. Tourtellot of the Presbyterian church, after which the remains were taken to David City where the funeral services were held from the residence of his daughter, Mrs. John Zellinger, David City, Friday, July 7th by Rev. R. A. Harrison, pastor of the Congregational church." William and Hattie are buried in David City Cemetery.

George Washington Brumaghim – Co. D (tr. January 31, 1865)
b. June 27, 1843 ?
d. September 7, 1905 Albany, Albany, NY
m. Catherine Veeder (October 1848-November 22, 1933) 1867

NOTE: George's POB is something of a mystery. On his muster roll card he was alleged to have been born in Saratoga, NY, although all New York census records showed his birthplace as Schoharie County, NY. His obituary said he was born in Sloane, Guilderland, NY. He was a son of Solomon (1799-1881) and Tenah/Tina/Tiney Van Natter Brumaghim. His surname caused all sorts of spelling problems. I use the version found on the family gravestone. George, a substitute for Joseph A.

Long, enrolled in 76th Regiment at Buffalo, NY on August 7, 1863, mustering into Co. F. He was captured on May 5, 1864 at the battle of the Wilderness and was still a prisoner when transferred to the 147th. He was nominally transferred to Co. B, 91st Regiment on June 5, 1865 but was "absent at parole camp." The card also noted that there was no discharge date. He does not appear on *The Adjutant-General's Report* for the 91st. In all likelihood, he simply walked away. I have not found a pension card or an entry in the 1890 Veterans' Schedules. He suffered from tuberculosis. His obituary, which did not mention military service, was published in *The Albany Evening Journal* September 7, 1905, 10: "George W. Brumaghim died this morning, having been a patient sufferer from disease for several years. He was the youngest son of the late Solomon and Tina Brumaghim and was born in Sloane, Guilderland, June 27, 1843. When 14 years of age he came to Albany and entered the wholesale grocery house of Brumaghim & Argersinger. He has resided in Albany ever since. Mr. Brumaghim was a man of quiet tastes and strong friendships, and bore his last days' sufferings without a murmur . . . ." George and Catherine were the parents of seven children, one of whom, Henry, was employed by *The Albany Evening News*. They are buried in Albany Rural Cemetery, Menands.

Charles Calkins – Co. G (tr. January 28, 1865)
b. April 27, 1830 Troupsburg, Steuben, NY
d. January 1, 1920 Woodhull, Steuben, NY
m. Jane L. Sample (July 9, 1833-September 2, 1904) January 28, 1855

NOTE: Charles, son of William (1785-1860) and Cynthia Strong Calkins (1802-*post* 1860), was drafted, enrolling in the 76th on July 18, 1863 at Woodhull and mustering into Co. D. At an unknown date he was wounded accidentally while on picket duty. He transferred to 2nd Battalion, VRC on August 1, 1865 and was discharged on September 16th at New York City. In 1890 he claimed chronic diarrhea as his disability. His death was reported in *The Addison Advertiser* January 6, 1920: "Woodhull, Jan. 5. – Charles Calkins, a highly esteemed citizen, died at his home here Thursday [sic] evening, aged over 89 years. Several years ago he suffered a shock from which he did not recover. His wife has been dead several years. He was a veteran of the Civil War . . . ." Jane was the mother of three. Her obituary appeared in *The Addison Advertiser* September 8, 1904: "Mrs. Charles Calkins, aged sixty-nine years, died Friday September 2 at her home at Woodhull after a long illness. The funeral was held from her late home Sunday, September 4. Burial at Woodhull. She was a lady of many rare traits of character, a devoted Christian and was beloved by all. She bore her severe and lingering illness with true fortitude and her death is sincerely mourned . . . ." Charles and Jane are buried in Woodhull Cemetery.

Brayton Allen Campbell – Co. C (tr. January 28, 1865)
b. July 25, 1836 Cherry Valley, Otsego, NY
d. July 6, 1904 Mason City, Cerro Gordo, IA
m. Anna J. Glendon (March 17, 1843-December 26, 1921) 1864

NOTE: The son of Aaron Putnam (1801-1856) and Jane Thompson Campbell (1806-1858), Brayton enlisted in the 76th Regiment at Cherry Valley on December 18, 1861 and mustered into Co. H. He was wounded at Gainesville, VA on August 28, 1862 and discharged for "disability caused by wound" on February 10, 1863 at Philadelphia, PA. He re-enlisted in the 76th in January 5, 1865 at Morristown, PA but was unassigned until transferred to the 147th. Although nominally transferred to Co. H, 91st Regiment on June 5th he was discharged on June 6th at Washington, DC as a member of the 147th. After the war he and Anna moved to Iowa. In 1900 he was a constable and bailiff. Anna was the mother of seven children, of whom five were alive in 1900. They are buried in Elmwood St. Joseph's Cemetery, Mason City. Her DOD is not given on their gravestone.

John Campbell – Co. F (tr. January 28, 1865)
b. ? ?
d. May 21, 1901 National Soldiers' Home, Bath, Steuben, NY
m. ?

NOTE: John, about whom little is known, enrolled in the 76th Regiment on September 23, 1863 at Utica, Oneida, NY apparently as a volunteer, mustering into Co. E the same day. He gave his age as 44. He transferred to Co. D on November 18, 1864. From the 147th he went to Co. A, 91st Regiment on June 5, 1865, mustering out near Washington, DC on July 3rd. His pension application, dated December 30, 1881, was successful. He first entered the home at Bath in 1888 and gave his daughter, Mrs. Laura Hammond, Utica, NY as his contact. He was enumerated at the home in 1890 and claimed a hernia as his disability. When he died a telegram and letter were sent to his brother, Rev. Amos Campbell, Belleville, Ontario, Canada. A clergyman by that name was living there in 1901. When he died in 1916 his death certificate stated his father's name was Archibald and his mother was Barbara Sager. If this is the correct man then Archibald and Barbara were also John's parents. John's age at his death was 88, leading to the conclusion that he was born in 1813. He was a widower when he first entered the home. COD was senile gangrene. He is buried in Bath National Cemetery.

Levi Campbell – Co. G (tr. January 28, 1865)
b. January 5, 1837 Gerry, Chautauqua, NY
d. August 15, 1904 Poland Center, Chautauqua, NY
m. Sophronia Azuba DeJean (May 1842-January 13, 1916) November 11, 1858

NOTE: Levi was the son of Jonas (1811-1894) and Cynthia DeJean Campbell (1813-1901). His wife, Sophronia, and his mother were first cousins. He was drafted and enrolled in the 76th Regiment on August 15, 1863 at Poland, mustering into Co. D. He was wounded on May 5, 1864 during the battle of the Wilderness. He received his discharge on June 21, 1865 as a member of the 147th while in Whitehall Hospital, Philadelphia, PA. An interesting obituary, published in *The Jamestown Evening Journal* August 22, 1904, 5 chronicles his long, useful life: "Levi Campbell was the oldest son of Jonas Campbell, an early settler, who came from Orleans County, N. Y., about 1830, and settled in the town of Gerry, Chautauqua County, where Levi was born Jan. 5, 1837. In 1840 the family moved to the town of Poland. Nov. 11, 1858 Levi Campbell and Sophronia DeJean were united in marriage and have since resided in this town. Aug. 15, 1863, when there was urgent need of men for the Union army in the Civil war, Levi Campbell was enrolled in Co. G, 147th [sic] N. Y. infantry, to serve three years. May 5, 1864, the first day of the battle of the Wilderness, the 147th was serving with the Fifth corps in the front line of battle and Campbell was severely wounded in the left hip. With other thousands of wounded in that battle he was carried to Fredericksburg, about 30 miles, where he lay on a bare floor many hours before receiving the care of the surgeons. General Grant in his memoirs says of the battle of the Wilderness: 'More desperate fighting had not been seen on this continent than that of the 5th and 6th of May.' May 7, 1864, two days after Levi Campbell was wounded, his brother Joseph, who was serving with Co. C, 9th N. Y. cavalry, was wounded at the battle of Todds Tavern during the movement of the army by its left flank from the Wilderness to Spotsylvania Court House. Levi Campbell was discharged from the service June 21, 1865, at White Hall U.S. hospital and was compelled to carry a crutch during the rest of his life. During the past 13 years he has been postmaster at Poland Center. He was serving his third term as assessor of the town of Poland when he suddenly died of neuralgia of the heart, Aug. 16, 1904 . . . The funeral was held from the family home Thursday, Aug. 18. The burial was at Riverside cemetery, Kennedy. The impressive funeral service of the Odd Fellows was conducted by Kennedy lodge, of which Mr. Campbell was a member. Fifteen veterans of the Civil war and members of the G. A. R. post at Kennedy were present and acted as a guard of honor, six acting as bearers . . . Mr. Campbell was a man of strong and generous sympathies, pronounced political views, well known in political and business circles and will be greatly missed. Newel Cheney, Poland Center, N. Y., Aug. 19, 1904." Levi was a member of H. C. Sturdevant Post No. 282 GAR, Kennedy, NY. He and Sophronia, who was a Rebekah, had no children but adopted a daughter, Fern (1882-1967). His brother, Joseph Lucius Campbell (1838-1902), served in Co. C, 9th NY Cavalry from August 1862-January 1865.

Albert F. Carpenter – Co. E (tr. January 28, 1865)
b. 1846 Cohoes, Albany, NY
d. October 6, 1897 Alexian Brothers' Hospital, St. Louis, MO
m. Elizabeth Wood (1850-*post* 1916) *ca.* 1870

NOTE: The son of Asahel (1807-1876) and Mary F. Schryver Carpenter (1812-1890), Albert lied about his age when he enlisted in the 30th Regiment on September 4, 1862 at Watervliet, Albany, NY, mustering into Co. D. He transferred to Co. I, 76th on May 23, 1863. He was wounded at the battle of the Wilderness on May 5, 1864. He next transferred to Co. C, 76th on December 1, 1864. From the 147th he transferred to Co. A, 91st on June 5, 1865, mustering out on July 3rd near Washington, DC. He and Elizabeth moved to Illinois where their three children were born. They were living in Springfield, Sangamon County in 1880. By 1887 the family had moved to St. Louis where Albert was a merchant. His COD was labeled general paralysis. He is buried in Bellefontaine Cemetery, St. Louis. Their son, Walter (1873-1978), moved to Orange, Essex, NJ and his mother moved with him. She was last listed in the Orange city directory in 1916. Walter, a veteran of the Spanish-American War, died in Dallas, TX. He was 104 years old. Albert's brother, Lorenzo (1843-1925), served in the 43rd Regiment from 1861-1865.

William Carroll – Co. A (tr. January 28, 1865)
b. 1826 ?
d. ? ?
m. ?

NOTE: Few facts are known about this soldier. He enlisted in the 76th at age 38 in Philadelphia, PA on September 1, 1864 for one year and mustered into Co. A. His muster cards show the military authorities were also puzzled by him. He mustered out on June 7, 1865 near Washington, DC. The question remains, who was this man? Although what follows is conjectural until more information is available, a good candidate is Rev. William R. Carroll (February 24, 1826-September 27, 1894), an Episcopal priest. He was married to Martha P. Swift (1828-April 8, 1893). In 1860 William and Martha, who had no children, were living in Philadelphia and they lived there until their deaths. They are buried in Saint James' Churchyard, Bristol, Bucks, PA.

Charles Carver – Co. E (tr. January 28, 1865)
b. 1841 Cayuga County, NY
d. ? ?
m. ?

NOTE: I have located no information about this soldier prior to 1863. He was drafted, enrolling in the 76th on July 28, 1863 and mustering into Co. E. He was wounded at the battle of the Wilderness on May 5, 1864 and transferred to Co. C on November 18, 1864. He transferred from the 147th to Co. I, 91st Regiment on June 5, 1865 and mustered out near Washington, DC on July 3rd. After that date there is nothing.

John D. Cates - Co. H (January 31, 1865)
b. 1840 Middleburg, Schoharie, NY
d. ? ?
m. ?

NOTE: Cates enlisted in the 76th Regiment on October 1, 1861 and mustered into Co. I. He was wounded at Gettysburg on July 1, 1863 and spent several months in hospital in Philadelphia, PA. He reenlisted on March 31, 1864 at Culpeper, Va. He was listed as MIA on October 1, 1864 near Pegram House, VA but more probably the location was Pegram's farm, which was part of Grant's Peeble's Farm campaign fought September 30th-October 2nd. When transferred to the 147th Cates was "missing." On June 5, 1865 he transferred to Co. A, 91st Regiment as John D. Carter and mustered out near Washington, DC on July 3rd. No other information about this man can be ascertained either before or after his alleged discharge. It is altogether possible that he died at Pegram's farm and confusion over surnames resulted in inaccurate reporting. For example, his card for the 91st regiment states he was a draftee.

Robert Chambers – Co. A (tr. January 28, 1865)
b. July 25, 1821 Antrim, Northern Ireland
d. January 26, 1881 Philadelphia, Philadelphia, PA
m. Mary Wylie (1813-April 17, 1895) *ca.* 1853

NOTE: Robert, a shoemaker, was the son of Alexander (1771-1850) and Elizabeth Kidd Chambers (1785-1871). He enlisted in the 22nd Regiment on September 11, 1862 at Greenwich, Washington, NY and mustered into Co. D. On June 1, 1863 he transferred to Co. E, 76th Regiment, although is muster card erroneously states he was sent to the 83rd. His next transfer was to Co. A, 76th on November 18, 1864. He mustered out of the 147th on June 7, 1865. He and Mary were the parents of one surviving child, George Washington Chambers (1854-1922). They are all buried in Greenwood Cemetery, Philadelphia.

George H. Chase – Co. C (tr. January 28, 1865)
b. April 15, 1841 Saratoga Springs, Saratoga, NY
d. November 11, 1911 Warsaw, Wyoming, NY
m1. Harriet P. _____ (1840-*post* 1865) ?
m2. Adaline Burst Craw (April 10, 1839-November 17, 1926) 1880

NOTE: George, son of Hiram (1819-1891) and Amy Wheley Scots Chase (1816-*post* 1855), enrolled in the 30th Regiment at Saratoga, NY on August 31, 1862 and mustered in on October 9th. He transferred to Co. C, 76th on May 25, 1863. On June 5, 1865 he transferred from the 147th to Co. H, 91st Regiment and mustered out on July 3rd near Washington, DC. In 1890 he claimed no disability. Very little is known about Harriet. Adaline's first marriage was to Isaac Craw (1818-1890) in 1856, by whom she had a son, Charles (1859-1927). The marriage had collapsed by 1875 when Adaline was listed on the New York census as the wife of George Benson (1839-1888) which may or may not be true. Isaac died at the Champaign County IL Poor Farm and was buried there. All extant records say that he was insane. George and Adaline had no children. According to an obituary published in *The Wyoming County Times* November 16, 1911, 1, George died "suddenly" from heart disease. Adaline, daughter of Jacob and Johanna Hewitt Burst, was born in Middlebury, Wyoming County. Her obituary, published in *The Western New Yorker* November 18, 1926, 1, stated she had lived in Warsaw for 44 years. Other than her son, her nearest surviving relative was a sister, Charlotte Edson (1841-1928). Charles, who had never married, hanged himself on June 20, 1927. All these people are buried in Warsaw Cemetery.

James Bailey Clark – Co. I (tr. January 28, 1865)
b. February 6, 1842 Sennett, Cayuga, NY
d. December 15, 1910 Roseburg, Douglas, OR
m. Viola Adella "Della" Messenger (1842-August 29, 1922) *ca.* 1878

NOTE: James, son of Peleg Sanders (1796-1854) and Lois Crandall Clark (1810-*post* 1875), enlisted in the 76th Regiment at Spafford, Onondaga, NY on September 4, 1861 and mustered into Co. D. He re-enlisted at Culpeper, VA on January 1, 1864. He transferred from the 147th to Co. I, 91st Regiment on June 5, 1865 and mustered out near Washington, DC on July 3rd. His daughter, Harriet "Hattie" Lois, was born on July 18, 1879 but his marriage to Della was unsuccessful. It is unknown when he migrated to Oregon but it may have been *ca.* 1881 since he was still in NYS in 1880. He first applied for a pension in 1881 but the state is not noted. I have not located James' COD but he is buried in Roseburg National Cemetery. Two brothers also served in the Civil War. George P. Clarke (1833-1863) was a member of Co. D, 157th regiment and died at Stafford Court House VA on April 11, 1863. Chauncey B. Clarke (1840-1864) was a member of Co. B, 117th Regiment and was killed at Fort Gilmer, on September 29, 1864. Della had an interesting life. According to her obituary she moved to Oregon to be with her brothers. In 1888 she married Bynon Johns Pengra (1823-1903), a colorful character in his own right, as his second wife. The marriage did not last and the couple divorced in 1896. Della and Hattie moved to Phoenix, Maricopa, AZ in 1879, only two months before Hattie died. She is buried in Ancient

Order of United Workmen Cemetery, Phoenix, under the name Pengra. On August 18, 1898 Della married Edwin Stanton Gill, another interesting person (1861-1943), as his second wife. She and Gill were the parents of Margaret (1905-?). Della's informative obituary was published in *The Olympia Daily Recorder* August 29, 1922, 5: "Mrs. Viola A. Gill, wife of Major E. S. Gill, of Seattle, died last evening about 9 o'clock at Chambers Prairie. She is survived by Major Gill, her husband, and one daughter, Mrs. H. S. Burrows. Funeral services will be conducted at the Mill's chapel tomorrow at 3:30 p.m. Interment will be in the Masonic cemetery. Viola A. Gill (nee Messenger) was a native of New York state. She was left an orphan at an early age. In 1884 she came to Ashland, Ore., to join her older brothers who had preceded her by a year. In 1889 she entered the Oregon Medical school, intending to become a doctor, but after two years' study was compelled to drop out on account of weakened condition of her eyes. She then took up nursing and was a professional nurse until the time of her marriage to Major Gill in 1898. She became a resident of Seattle in 1903 and for a number of years was active in various women's organizations, being an old member of the Women's Country club, of Myrtle chapter No. 48, of the Eastern Star, one of the organizers of the Women's Auxiliary of the American Legion. At the beginning of the World War she was one of the charter members and incorporators of the War Mothers' League of America, continuing actively in the work until compelled to give up on account of failing health. During the war, notwithstanding the fact of Major Gill's service, she maintained open house for soldiers and sailors and never a weekend passed in which she did not entertain from two to as high as ten, and this notwithstanding the fact that she was to a considerable extent a confirmed invalid, having been in failing health since a serious illness in 1913." Viola is buried in Masonic Memorial Park, Tumwater, Thurston, WA. Gill, who died in Los Angeles, is buried in Los Angeles National Cemetery.

Luther Frost Clark – Co. D (tr. January 28, 1865)
b. March 9, 1817 Tompkins County, NY
d. April 13, 1865 City Point, VA
m. Sarah Kirkham (1819-January 18, 1890) August 8, 1839

NOTE: Luther's parents were Amiz (?-?) and Mary Frost Clark (1775-?). He enrolled in the 76th Regiment on July 17, 1863 at Camden, Oneida, NY as a substitute for Pitt M. Smith and mustered into Co. A. He transferred to Co. I on October 11, 1864 and to Co. E on December 1, 1864. He was wounded in the right leg on March 31, 1865 at Gravelly Run, VA and died in hospital. He is buried in City Point National Cemetery, Hopewell. In 1865 he and Sarah had six children under the age of 16. Sarah, who was illiterate, obtained pensions for herself and for the children. She never remarried. She died in Corning, Steuben County and is buried in Buck Settlement Cemetery, Bath.

Martin Van Buren Clark – Co. D (tr. January 28, 1865)
b. August 1840 Pultney, Steuben, NY
d. March 17, 1916 Wheeler, Steuben, NY
m1. Anna Carman (October 2, 1850-September 1, 1877) January 12, 1870
m2. Clara Carman (March 11, 1861-November 9, 1934) 1879

NOTE: Martin, whose middle initial is erroneously given as D on his military records, was the son of Nelson (1812-1887) and Elizabeth "Betsey" Stratton Clark (1816-1861). Both parents succumbed to consumption. He enlisted in the 76th Regiment on July 15, 1863 at Wheeler and enrolled in Co. E. He transferred to Co. C on November 18, 1864. From the 147th he transferred to Co. I, 91st Regiment on June 5, 1865, mustering out near Washington, DC on July 3rd. In 1890 he claimed to have suffered from varicose veins for 26 years. Anna and Clara were the daughters of Thomas and Margaret Sprague Carman. Martin's death was announced in *The Steuben Courier* March 24, 1916, 5: "Wheeler, March 21. – Martin V. Clark died at his home near here Friday morning, after several weeks' sickness, aged 75 years. Mr. Clark had been an extensive lumberman and farmer during the greater part of his life, and only stopped active work a few years ago when his health began to fail. He served as a soldier in the Civil War, being honorably discharged in 1865, and drew a pension . . . His funeral, conducted by Rev. W. T. H. Bayford, was largely attended at the church at Mitchellsville, Sunday afternoon . . . ." Clara's death was announced in *The Steuben Courier* November 16, 1934, 8: "Mrs. Clara Carman Clark, widow of the late Martin B. [*sic*] Clark, died Friday at 2 p.m. She was 73 years old. She had been in poor health for several months, and for a few weeks past had been with her daughter, Mrs. Bert French . . . She was a member of the Ladies' Aid, several of whom attended in a body. Her funeral services were at 2:30 on Sunday at the home of Mr. and Mrs. French . . . ." Martin, Anna, and Clara are buried in Mitchellsville Cemetery, Wheeler.

Thomas Clark – Co. A (tr. January 28, 1865)
b. May 6, 1843 Philadelphia, Philadelphia, PA
d. January 12, 1903 Phoenix, NY
m. Mary Lucy Moss Morse (October 1839-December 10, 1920) September 12, 1866

NOTE: Thomas, whose parents are unknown, was living in Palermo in 1863. Although not noted on his muster roll card, he may have been drafted, as recorded in his entry in *The Town Clerks' Registers*. He enrolled in the 76th Regiment at Oswego on August 8, 1863, the exact day the draft was held in that city, and mustered into Co. A. He transferred within the regiment several times. From the 147th he was sent to Co. C, 91st Regiment on June 5, 1865, although, according to the *Registers,* he was sent to the 91st HA! On July 3rd he was mustered out near Ball's Cross Roads, VA. He was wounded at the battle of the Wilderness on May 5, 1864 and in 1890 he claimed to have suffered a gunshot wound in the arm. Mary was first married to Lucien Morse (1837-1863), a member of Co. A, 110th Regiment, who was wounded and captured during the ill-fated attack on Port Hudson, LA on June 14, 1863. He died in captivity on July 6th. Thomas and Mary are buried in Phoenix Rural Cemetery.

William Henry Clark – Co. C (tr. January 28, 1865)
b. May 4, 1844 England
d. February 17, 1916 St. Cloud, Osceola, FL
m1. Ellen Hill (1852-October 2, 1883) 1868
m2. Carrie M. Curtis (October 30, 1863-October 2, 1955) November 24, 1883

NOTE: William was the son of William Dutton (1819-1853) and Elizabeth Adelia Soule Clark (1818-1902). He enlisted in the 76th Regiment on October 15, 1861 at Cherry Valley and mustered into Co. H. He re-enlisted in Culpeper, VA on January 6, 1864 and transferred within the regiment several times. On June 5, 1865 he transferred from the 147th to Co. H, 91st Regiment, mustering out near Washington, DC on July 3rd. He and Ellen were married in Cherry Valley but by 1880 they were living in Princeton, White, IN. Her grave has not been located but since William and Carrie were married in Iroquois County, IL shortly thereafter it is possible the family had moved. William and Carrie, who died in Bluffton, Wells, IN are buried in the IOOF Riverview Cemetery, Monticello, White, IN. Her COD was a coronary occlusion.

Marcus J. Clackner – Co. C (tr. January 28, 1865)
b. February 14, 1828 Prussia
d. April 20, 1901 Salamanca, Cattaraugus, NY
m. Elizabeth Elecut (April 6, 1836-June 29, 1911) *ca.* 1860

NOTE: Marcus and Elizabeth immigrated to the United States in 1853 and became naturalized citizens. His name was variously spelled, particularly on military records where Clickner is found consistently. His pension cards refer to Clickner as "alias." Marcus, a substitute for William Cromhar, Marion, Wayne, NY, enrolled in the 76th Regiment at Auburn, Cayuga, NY on July 24, 1863, mustering into Co. A. He transferred to Co. H on October 11, 1864 and to Co. B on January 1, 1865. He went to Co. H, 91st Regiment on June 5, 1865, mustering out near Washington, DC on July 3rd. The Clackners moved several times in the years after the war. They were the parents of five children. Marcus' COD is unknown but Elizabeth died "suddenly" from heart disease. She was a member of the Women's Relief Corps and it can be presumed Marcus was a GAR man. They are buried in Wildwood Cemetery, Salamanca.

Lemuel Clinton Cline – Co. E (January 28, 1865)
b. March 1839 Greene County, OH
d. July 23, 1915 National Soldiers' Home, Dayton, Montgomery, OH
m. Mary Anne Flood (1845-1938) 1866

NOTE: The son of David B. (1807-1888) and Frances Sarah Mortimer Cline (1809-1894), Lemuel worked on the railroad. He saw prior service in Co. D, 12th OH Regiment from April-August 1861 and in Co. B, 74th OH Regiment from October 1, 1861-February 1862. He was discharged from the latter at Nashville, TN for "disability." He was a substitute for Thomas Gunlar when enrolling in the 76th Regiment at Harmony, Chautauqua, NY on August 19, 1863, mustering into Co. A. He was wounded in the left leg at the battle of the Wilderness on May 5, 1864. He was subsequently twice transferred within the organization. From the 147th he was sent to Co. A, 91st on June 5, 1865, mustering out near Washington, DC on July 3rd. He and Mary Anne were married in Farmland, Randolph, IN and became the parents of nine children. Although Lemuel stated he worked on the railroad on his muster card and on his application for admission to the Dayton Home he also engaged in other occupations. In 1880 he was a plasterer and in 1900 he was a professional nurse. When he entered the Dayton Home he had extensive disabilities: loss of teeth, gunshot wound to leg, varicose veins in both legs, and chronic rheumatism, to name a few. His COD, however, was chronic diarrhea. His body was sent home for burial. He and Mary Anne are buried in Woodland Cemetery, Xenia, Greene, OH.

Aaron Closs – Co. A (tr. January 28, 1865)
b. July 25, 1830 Galen, Wayne, NY
d. December 18, 1899 Galen, Wayne, NY
m. Catherine Elizabeth Laughlin (February 13, 1843-December 24, 1924) December 10, 1865

NOTE: Aaron was the son of George (1788-1865) and Katherine "Katjatie" Barnes Closs (1800-1875). According to his FAG entry, Aaron's mother, a full-blooded member of the Six Nations Indians, was born on the reservation in Deseronto, Canada. She came to Galen in 1813 and was George's second wife. Aaron was drafted and enrolled in the 76th Regiment at Auburn, Cayuga, NY on July 24, 1863, mustering into Co. E. He transferred to Co. A on November 18, 1864. From the 147th he transferred to Co. C, 91st on June 5, 1865, mustering out near Ball's Cross Roads, VA on July 3rd. In 1890 he claimed he had been wounded in his left arm. He and Catherine were married in Ernestown, Lennox Addington, Ontario, Canada, where she was born. They were the parents of eight children, five of whom were alive in 1910. Aaron and Catherine are buried in Lock Berlin Cemetery, Lock Berlin, Wayne.

Peter Cody – Co. E (tr. January 28, 1865)

b. 1840 Ireland

d. *post* 1895 probably Great Bend, Barton, KS

m. ?

NOTE: Little can be ascertained about this soldier. He enlisted in the 30th Regiment on October 16, 1862 at Watervliet, Albany, NY, mustering into Co. F. He transferred to Co. E, 76th Regiment on May 25, 1863. He was captured at Gettysburg on July 1st but where he was held is unknown. He rejoined his regiment in December 1864. From the 147th he transferred to Co. I, 91st Regiment on June 5, 1865 and was discharged near Washington, DC on June 21st. In 1890 he was living in Springfield, Greene, MO. He claimed no disability. The last reference to him is found in the roster of Pap Thomas Post No. 52 GAR, Great Bend, where it was noted he had been "discharged."

Albert Colcord – Co. E (tr. January 28, 1865)

b. August 21, 1841 Bath, Steuben County, NY

d. October 10, 1918 Coudersport, Potter, PA

m. Elizabeth "Betsy" Sherer (November 1840-December 30, 1905) December 23, 1861

NOTE: A blacksmith, Albert was the son of Joseph (1797-1862) and Sarah "Sallie" Dickinson Colcord (1804-1887). He enlisted in the 76th on July 9, 1863 at Thurston, Steuben County and mustered into Co. E. He transferred to Co. C on November 18, 1864. From the 147th he transferred to Co. I, 91st Regiment on June 5, 1865, mustering out on July 3rd near Washington, DC. In 1890, while living in Eulalia, Potter, PA he claimed no disability. The family had moved to Pennsylvania in 1867, settling in Potter County. Albert and Elizabeth were the parents of five children, four of whom were living in 1900. He was a member of A. F. Jones Post No. 20 GAR. Albert's official COD was senility. He and Elizabeth are buried in Homer Cemetery, Inez, Potter. Two brothers served the Union cause. David D. Colcord (1821-1905) was a member of the 199th PA Regiment. Amos D. Colcord (1835-1885) served in Co. K, 5th US Regular Cavalry.

William Collier – Co. A (tr. January 28, 1865)

b. probably 1845 England

d. ? ?

m. ?

NOTE: William, a weaver, may have been the son of Thomas (1818-*post* 1860) and Mary A. Collier (1824-*post* 1860), both of whom were born in England. In 1860

William's age was 15. According to *The Adjutant-General's Report* for the 30th Regiment, he attempted to join that outfit at Watervliet, Albany, NY on September 30, 1862 but was unassigned. His muster roll card for the 76th indicates he had transferred from the 30th on May 25, 1863, joining Co. A. He may have been wounded at Gettysburg because his muster roll card shows he had been in the hospital at Fort Schuyler, NY since July 1, 1863. He was transferred to Co. E on October 11, 1864 and back to Co. A on November 18th. He was discharged at Albany on June 21, 1865 as a member of the 147th. He applied for a pension on March 9, 1866 and obtained a certificate. There the trail ends.

Charles W. Cook – Co. H (tr. January 28, 1865)
b. 1833 Madison County, NY
d. June 16, 1923 National Soldiers' Home, Milwaukee, WI
m. Betsey M. _____ (1834-1897) *ca.* 1856

NOTE: Charles, son of Alvah Paul (1812-1903) and Fannie Brown Cook (?- ?), enlisted in the 76th on October 14, 1861 at Cortland, NY and mustered into Co. G. He re-enlisted on March 30, 1864 and was wounded at Petersburg, VA on June 23rd. He transferred to Co. E on October 20th, then to Co. C on November 18th. His time with the 147th was brief because he was transferred to 3rd Regiment, VRC on March 25, 1865 and discharged at Burlington, VT on July 26, 1865. Little is known about his life following the war but in 1880 he and Betsey were enumerated in Harmony, Rock, WI. In later life he wrote several letters published in *The National Tribune* concerning the participation of the 76th in the battle of Gettysburg. He entered the home in 1899, claiming a gunshot wound to the left thigh, partial deafness, and general rheumatism as disabilities. His COD was heart attack. He and Betsey were the parents of at least one child, Charles C. (1857-1891). All are buried in Oak Hill Cemetery, Janesville, Rock, WI.

Ezra G. Coon – Co. I (tr. January 28, 1865)
b. October 11, 1839 Lincklaen, Chenango, NY
d. December 26, 1909 Lawrence, Douglas, KS
m1. Julia A. Bogart (May 3, 1853-October 31, 1877) November 29, 1870
m2. Celinda Benson (August 31, 1838-February 8, 1925) May 5, 1904

NOTE: Ezra was the son of Asaph (1803-1857) and Mary Ann Reynolds Coon (1814-*post* 1860). He enlisted in the 76th on September 17, 1861 and mustered into Co. B. He deserted at Camp Chase in November 1862 and did not return until February 1864 at which time he was court martialed and sentenced "to make good time lost by desertion" and to lose pay and benefits. He transferred to Co. C on July 1, 1864 and to

Co. A on November 8th. From the 147th he transferred to Co. I, 91st Regiment on June 5, 1865 and mustered out near Washington, DC on July 3rd. He and Julia were the parents of four children, including a set of twins. She died in Masonville, Delaware, NY and is buried in Masonville Cemetery. Ezra and Celinda were living in Lawrence, KS in 1905. He belonged to Washington Post No. 12 GAR in Lawrence. According to *The Jeffersonian Gazette* December 29, 1909, 7, Ezra died of asthma. The post participated in his funeral and he was buried in Oak Hill Cemetery, Lawrence. Over the next few years Celinda divided her time between New York State and Kansas. In 1920 she was living with her stepdaughter, Clara, in Masonville. She died at Fort Dodge Soldiers' Home, Lawrence and was buried in Maple Grove Cemetery in that place. The gravestone is also a cenotaph for Ezra.

Clark Coons – Co. G (tr. January 28, 1865)
b. November 1818 Albany, Albany, NY
d. February 26, 1901 Middleburgh, Schoharie, NY
m. Maria _____ (1828-*post* 1875) *ca.* 1844

NOTE: Clark was the son of John (1793-1865) and Selina/Salima/Sylvina Coons (1796-1878). He was a teamster and enlisted as a wagoner in the 76th Regiment on October 1, 1861 at Middleburgh, mustering into Co. I. He was discharged at Culpeper, VA on February 24, 1864 and re-enlisted the next day. On December 1st he transferred to Co. B. At some point he served in the ambulance corps. From the 147th he transferred to Co. F, 91st Regiment on June 5, 1865, mustering out on July 5th. In 1870 he and Maria were the parents of seven children. When Clark entered the National Soldiers' Home, Bath in 1887 he complained of rheumatism and a hernia, among others. He gave his brother Jacob W. (1824-*post* 1890) as his closest relative. Jacob had served in the 134th Regiment from September 1862-June 1865. Clark is buried in Middleburgh Cemetery. Maria's grave has not been located.

Edward Copeland – Co. D (tr. January 31, 1865)
b. 1842 Ireland
d. ? ?
m. ?

NOTE: Nothing has been learned about this man prior to his military service except that he was a shoemaker. He enrolled in the 76th Regiment at Rochester, Monroe, NY as a substitute for Daniel T. Hunt, Greene, NY on August 5, 1863 and was assigned to Co. F. He was MIA on May 5, 1865. According to POW records he was captured and sent to Andersonville as a member of Co. C. He appears to have been transferred to the 147th while a prisoner. His muster roll card for that regiment notes he was supposed to have left Parole Camp on May 2, 1865. Officially he was discharged from the military on June 9, 1865 as a member of the 147th. I have located no other references to him.

Joseph Lorenzo Cotton – Co. H (tr. January 28, 1865)
b. January 1840 Taylor, Cortland, NY
d. January 29, 1915 Santa Monica, Los Angeles, CA
m1. Lucy L. Angell (October 21, 1841-November 5, 1884) *ca.* 1871
m2. Elma Utley Barnes (1865-November 23, 1914) April 28, 1892

NOTE: Joseph, son of Lorenzo (1809-1852) and Mary L. Robbins Cotton (1812-1867), was a farmer. He enlisted in the 76th Regiment at Pitcher, Cortland, NY on September 20, 1861, mustering into Co. B. He was wounded at Gainesville on August 28, 1862 and again on July 1, 1863 at Gettysburg. He re-enlisted on July 1, 1864 and was assigned to Co. E. On November 18th he transferred to Co. A. After being transferred to the 147th he was wounded in the right arm at Hatcher's Run on February 6, 1865. He was discharged from hospital at York, PA on June 20, 1865 for "disability from wounds." He served as Taylor town supervisor from 1875-1881. He and Lucy were the parents of one daughter, May L. (1872-1933), who was dean of girls at Cazenovia Seminary when she died. Lucy's COD is unknown. She is buried in Union Valley Cemetery with other members of her family. Elma was previously married to Barney Barnes (1846-1887) as his second wife. Her death was announced in *The Homer Republican* December 17, 1914, 3: "Mrs. Elma Utley Cotton, whose girlhood and youth were spent in Homer and who after her marriage resided for a time in Homer and Cortland, died at Sawtelle, Cal., November 23. The Veteran Enterprise, published in that place on November 28, says: 'The passing away of Mrs. Elma Cotton at her home on South Eleventh street Monday morning, November 23, occasioned sincere regret. Mrs. Cotton had been in ill health about a year and paralysis was the contributing cause of her death. She was a sweet, lovable character, and during her early life had been active in temperance and other lines of work for the betterment of humanity. The funeral of Mrs. E. J. Cotton who was an earnest, faithful worker in the W. C. T. U. for many years, was held on Wednesday, November 25, at 10 a.m. at the chapel in the undertaking rooms. The W. C. T. U. attended her funeral in a body and furnished a beautiful floral tribute.' Many Homer friends who will remember Mrs. Cotton as a quiet loveable woman, will learn of her death with sincere regret." Graves for Joseph and Elma have not been located.

James Cowden – Co. G (tr. January 28, 1865)
b. 1841 Erie County, PA
d. ? ?
m. ?

NOTE: This soldier's parents are unknown. According to *The Town Clerks' Registers* he was drafted, enrolling at Poland, Chautauqua, NY on August 15, 1863 and mustering into Co. D. One muster card says he was transferred to Co. B but no date is provided. He was "absent, sick" when transferred to the 147th and his time with that outfit was brief because he was discharged for "disability" on May 30, 1865. Nothing can be confirmed after that date.

William Coyle – Co. D (tr. January 31, 1865)
b. 1843 Edinburgh, Scotland
d. November 20, 1898 Brighton, Northumberland, Ontario, Canada
m. Mary Summers (1851-April 22, 1904) October 13, 1868

NOTE: William's parents were William (?-?) and Mary (?-?). He enlisted as a substitute for Morris Moynihan at Rochester, Monroe, NY on August 5, 1863, mustering into Co. F. He was captured on May 5, 1864 at the battle of the Wilderness, returning on December 21, 1864. Where he had been imprisoned is unknown. It appears that after he was transferred to the 147th he was transferred to Co. A, 14th VRC, date unavailable, and discharged on July 24, 1865 at Washington, DC. He is not to be confused with William Coyle, 24, born New York State, who also entered the 76th Regiment at Rochester on August 5, 1863 and was assigned to Co. D. He too was captured on May 5th but died at Andersonville, GA on September 25, 1864 and was buried in grave 9721. After the war William, a blacksmith, moved to Canada. He married Mary Summers, daughter of Patrick Summers and Frances Lee, at Brighton and settled down there. In 1891 the couple had six children. William died of paresis and heart disease. Mary's COD was liver cancer. Their graves have not been located.

William Craig – Co. E (tr. January 28, 1865)
b. 1820 Scotland
d. ? ?
m. ?

NOTE: This soldier's parentage and life before enlisting are unknown. He was a spinner and probably worked in the garment industry in and around Albany, NY. He enlisted in the 30th Regiment at Watervliet on September 15, 1862 and enrolled in Co. D. He transferred to Co. A, 76th on May 25, 1863 and was listed as MIA at Gettysburg on July 1st. His return date is unknown but on November 15, 1863 he was transferred to Co. H, 3rd Regiment VRC, returning to the 76th on March 9, 1864. He again was listed MIA on May 5, 1864 at the battle of the Wilderness. When he returned is not stated but he was transferred to Co. E on October 11, 1864 and to Co. C on November 18th. From the 147th he went to Co. I, 91st Regiment on June 5, 1865, mustering out near Washington, DC on July 3rd. The last known reference to him is the 1880 census. He was a machinist, boarding at a house in Albany. He claimed to be a widower. Since I have found no pension card for him nor any subsequent mention I theorize he died shortly thereafter.

Carlton Cromwell – Co. E (tr. January 28, 1865)
b. 1842 New York State
d. ? ?
m. ?

NOTE: Nothing is known about this soldier prior to his military service. He was a substitute for Benjamin Seamans, whose address is illegible on the muster card. He enrolled in the 76th on September 11, 1863 at Canandaigua, Ontario, NY and mustered into Co. K. He transferred twice within the regiment, to Co. E on July 1, 1864 and to Co. C on November 18th. He went from the 147th to Co. C, 91st Regiment on June 5, 1865 and mustered out near Washington, DC on July 3rd. After that date, nothing has been learned. The various spellings of his names may be a hindrance to further research.

Charles Benjamin Crosby – Co. C (tr. January 28, 1865)
b. 1842 New York State
d. 1924 Weatherford, Parker, TX
m. ?

NOTE: Little has been learned about this soldier. He enrolled in the 76th at Utica, Oneida, NY on September 18, 1863, evidently as a volunteer, and mustered into Co. H. Transferred to Co. A on February 2, 1864, he was re-transferred on April 9th. On January 1, 1865 he went to Co. B. He transferred to Co. H, 91st Regiment on June 5, 1865 and mustered out near Washington, DC on July 3rd. After the war he migrated to Visalia, Tulare, CA and registered to vote in 1892, though he may have been there earlier. He spent time in various soldiers' homes, the last known being that at Danville, IL. He left there at his own request on May 8, 1913. His POD is recorded on his pension cards but where he was between 1913 and 1924 is unknown. It appears he never married.

Lewis Clark Crosson – Co. E (tr. January 28, 1865)
b. November 8, 1835 Barrington, Yates, NY
d. July 17, 1914 State Hospital, Willard, Seneca, NY
m. Phoebe A. Cable (August 1832-November 9, 1816) 1857

NOTE: The son of James (1792-1866) and Sarah Clark Crosson (1791-1863), Lewis was a farmer. His POB and DOB varied from document to document. His name also had several variants. A draftee, he enrolled in the 76th Regiment at Canandaigua, Ontario, NY on September 4, 1863 and mustered into Co. I. On December 1, 1864 he transferred to Co. C. On June 5, 1865 he transferred from the 147th to Co. A, 91st Regiment and mustered out near Washington, DC on July 3rd. In 1890, while living in Batavia, Genesee County, he claimed to have suffered a rupture at the battle of Weldon Railroad. He was a member of Charles M. Pierce Post No. 640 GAR, located at North Cohocton, Steuben County. He and Phoebe were the parents of three children, two of whom were alive in 1900. Lewis is buried in the Willard Asylum Cemetery. Phoebe, who died in Bristol, Ontario County, is buried in Canadice Corners Cemetery.

William H. Cummings – Co. H (tr. January 28, 1865)
b. 1840 Palmyra, Wayne, NY
d. November 20, 1902 National Soldiers' Home, Grand Rapids, Kent, MI
m. Mary L. McFall (1845-?) November 27, 1867

NOTE: According to his death certificate William was the son of Lorenzo (?-?) and Mary Slauson Cummings (?-?), both born in Scotland. He enlisted in the 76th at Cortland on September 19, 1861 and mustered into Co. G. He re-enlisted at Culpeper, VA on February 18, 1864, transferred to Co. H on October 20, 1864 and to Co. B on January 1, 1865. From the 147th he transferred to Co. F, 91st Regiment on June 5, 1865 and mustered out near Washington, DC on July 3rd. Very little evidence for his time with Mary exists. His death certificate indicates he had been married, was a widower, had been the father of one child, deceased. A marriage record for the couple exists which shows Mary was born in Petersburg, MI and the couple married in Tecumseh, Lewanee, MI but nothing more. William applied for a pension in Ohio in 1889 and in 1890, while residing in Mantua, Portage, OH, he claimed no disability. His COD was a combination of chronic Bright's disease, exhaustion, and senility. He is buried in the home's cemetery.

Elliot Alonzo Dailey – Co. C (tr. January 28, 1865)
b. March 8, 1844 Coventry, Peel, Ontario, Canada
d. July 3, 1919 National Soldiers' Home, Grand Rapids, Kent, MI
m1. Blanche Etta Hollinger Prudence (September 5, 1856-September 25, 1906) *ca.* 1880
m2. Mary Ann Nunn Stewart (March 24, 1861-May 30, 1943) June 12, 1907

NOTE: A marriage record for Elliot and Mary Ann lists John W. (?-?) and Charlotte Hill Dailey (?-?) as his parents. His POB is a matter of conjecture. One muster roll card says he was born in Coventry, Canada and another says Montreal. Later census records show a POB of New York State. I think Canada is correct since I have located no early records for him in the United States. He enrolled in the 76th Regiment at Busti, Chautauqua, NY on August 20, 1863 as a substitute for Deloss Hallek and mustered into Co. E. He transferred to Co. C on November 18, 1864. His muster roll card says he was a nurse in 3rd Division 5th Army Corps Hospital. From the 147th he transferred to Co. H, 91st on June 5, 1865 and was discharged on June 17th near Washington, DC. In 1890, while living in Shepherd, Isabella, MI, he claimed rheumatism and diarrhea as disabilities. His COD was endocarditis. Blanche was previously married to Samuel A. Prudence (?-?), by whom she had a son, Charles H. (1874-1957). She had three more children by Dailey. Her COD was tuberculosis. Mary Ann's first husband was George J. Stewart (1849-1906). According to the 1900 census, she was the mother of 13 children. Her third husband was Jacob DeWitte (1857-1938). Elliot and Blanche are buried in Oak Grove Cemetery, St. Louis, Gratiot, MI. Mary Ann is buried in Salt River Cemetery, Shepherd, Isabella, MI with her first husband, George.

Robert Gardner Davidson – sergeant major (tr. January 28, 1865)
b. March 1, 1827 Paris, Oneida, NY
d. January 4, 1917 Homer, Cortland, NY
m. Georgeanna Lawrence (August 8, 1828-October 8, 1912) July 2, 1850

NOTE: Robert, son of John (1796-1874) and Elizabeth Van Slyck Davidson (1801-1880), was an iron worker. He enlisted in the 76th Regiment at McLean, Cortland, NY on September 14, 1861 and mustered into Co. C. He re-enlisted at Culpeper, VA on January 2, 1864, transferring to Co. D on November 18th. He was the regimental armorer. From the 147th he transferred to the 91st on June 5, 1865 and mustered out on July 3rd near Washington, DC. In 1890 he said his disabilities were a hernia and "piles." He was a member of James C. Hatch Post No. 540 GAR. His death was reported in *The Cortland Standard* January 5, 1917, 8: "The death of Robert G. Davidson of McLean occurred about 8 o'clock Thursday evening at the home of his daughter and husband, Mr. and Mrs. Harmon Hooker, in North Main st. He came here about a month ago intending to spend the winter with his daughter. He was nearly 90 years of age, and when prostrated on Monday from an attack of pneumonia, his family were very anxious regarding the outcome. Robert Davidson was born in the town of Ferris [sic], Oneida Co., March 1826 [sic]. He came to McLean to make his home in 1843, and has since resided in that quiet hamlet. On July 2, 1850, he was united in marriage with Miss Georgiana Lawrice, and four children, two sons and two daughters made their home most enjoyable. His wife was taken from him on Oct. 8, 1912, but he has since retained his home in McLean. At the outbreak of the Civil war he enlisted in the famous Seventy-sixth regiment, where he served until transferred to the One Hundred Forty-seventh, with the rank of sergeant major. He was in many of the principal battles and skirmishes receiving his first injury in the battle of the Weldon

Railroad and was in the hospital for four months. He continued in service through nearly the four years and was honorably discharged . . . He built the house where he has resided so many years, sixty-five years ago and was well known in the country round about. Mr. Davidson has been wonderfully well preserved and in his long life of fourscore and ten years has had but little sickness. He was highly esteemed by all who knew him and was particularly friendly with all with whom he had to do . . . Funeral services will be held at the Methodist church at McLean Sunday afternoon at 2 o'clock." Robert and Georgeanna are buried in McLean Cemetery.

Henry L. Davis – Co. G (tr. January 28, 1865)
b. 1842 Germany
d. January 20, 1926 Utica, Oneida, NY
m. Hattie _____ (1846-July 7, 1932) 1863

NOTE: Although Henry's muster roll card says he was born in Little Falls, Herkimer, NY all other documents show he was born in Germany. He immigrated to the United States in 1848 and became a naturalized citizen in 1863. He was a tanner. Henry enrolled in the 76th Regiment at Norwich, Chenango, NY on September 1, 1863 as a substitute for John J. Juliard, and mustered into Co. G. He was WIA on May 5, 1864 at the battle of the Wilderness. On October 20, 1864 he transferred to Co. C and on November 8th to Co. D. He was discharged at Philadelphia, PA on May 19, 1865. Although the nature of his wound is unknown it must have been severe because he applied for a pension on June 27, 1865. He and Hattie were the parents of three. Henry is buried in Forest Hill Cemetery, Utica but Hattie's grave has not been located.

James Dawes – Co. E (tr. January 28, 1865)
b. 1822 Christian County, KY
d. October 11, 1898 National Soldiers' Home, Hampton, VA
m. ?

NOTE: Little is known about this soldier's early life, except that he was a stone mason and illiterate. He enrolled in Co. G, 53rd IL Regiment at Pontiac, IL on January 20, 1862 and mustered into Co. G. He was discharged for "disability" at LaGrange, TN on November 14, 1862. In 1890, while residing at Malta, Saratoga, NY he told the enumerator that he joined the 67th (surely an error for 76th) as a substitute, even though his muster roll cards do not mention such a fact. He enrolled in the 76th at Buffalo on August 14, 1863 and mustered into Co. A. He was twice transferred within the regiment, to Co. I on October 11, 1864 and to Co. C on December 1st. He went from the 147th to Co. K, 91st on June 5, 1865 and mustered out on July 3rd near Washington, DC. Somewhere along the way he married but where, when, and whom is unknown. In 1880 he was an inmate in the Albany County Penitentiary, and an article published in *The Albany Morning Express* April 26, 1880, 1 stated he had been sentenced to 180 days for intoxication. When he entered the soldiers' home on June 14, 1897 he was senile. He claimed to have no near relatives. COD is unknown but he is buried in Hampton National Cemetery. His gravestone alludes to his service in Illinois.

Theodore DeBar – Co. K (tr. January 28, 1865)
b. 1842 Niles, Cayuga, NY
d. May 30, 1893 National Soldiers' Home, Bath, Steuben, NY
m. ------

NOTE: Theodore was the son of Francis DeBar (1816-1887) and an unidentified mother. In 1850, Francis, Theodore, 8, Rhoda, 5,and John F., three months, were living in Parish, NY. It would appear his mother had died in childbirth or soon after. By 1855 Francis was married to Lucy Mae Trass (1832-1872). John was not enumerated, suggesting he too had died. Theodore, a miller, enlisted in the 76th at East Homer, Cortland, NY on October 5, 1861 and mustered in to Co. B. He re-enlisted on January 2, 1864 at Culpeper, VA, was wounded at the battle of the Wilderness on May 5, 1864, and transferred to Co. A on November 8, 1864. His time in the 147th was brief since he was transferred to the 23rd Company, 2nd Battalion VRC, date unknown, and discharged on August 12, 1865 at Washington, DC. In 1890, while living at Truxton, Cortland, NY, he claimed no disability. He was a member of Volney Baker Post No. 517 GAR, Truxton. His COD is unknown but he is buried in Bath National Cemetery. His name is spelled DeBarr on the gravestone.

Abram DeWitt Decker – Co. E (tr. January 28, 1865)
b. September 22, 1832 Westtown, Orange, NY
d. March 29, 1911 Newark Valley, Tioga, NY
m. Lydia C. Goble (1834-March 2, 1897) *ca.* 1860

NOTE: Abram, or Abraham, was the son of Moses (1812-1857) and Elizabeth Winfield Decker (1809-1885). A farmer, he was drafted, enrolling in the 76th on July 13, 1863 and mustering into Co. E. He transferred to Co. C on November 18, 1864 and was discharged from the 147th at Washington, DC on June 6, 1865. In 1890 he claimed no disability. Abram was a member of Charles H. Williams Post No. 245 GAR, Newark Valley. He and Lydia, the parents of at least four children, are buried in Hope Cemetery, Newark Valley.

Nicholas Dennis – Co. G (tr. January 28, 1865)
b. 1849 Niskayuna, Schenectady, NY
d. October 5, 1912 Taft, Orange, FL
m. Helen Jane Tymeson (January 1854-August 19, 1942) 1874

NOTE: Nicholas was the son of Nicholas (1823-*post* 1855) and Cornelia Gegier Dennis (1813-*post* 1865). His DOB varies from document to document but in 1850 he was a year old and later documents all point to 1849 as his correct birth date. He enlisted in Co. K, 30th Regiment at Watervliet, Albany, NY on September 8, 1862 as a musician, transferring to Co. G, 76th Regiment on May 25, 1863 and to Co. D on October 20, 1864. From the 147th he was transferred to Co. E, 91st Regiment on June 5, 1865, mustering out near Washington, DC on July 3rd. In 1894 he and Helen were living in Wichita, Sedgwick, KS where he was a member of Eggleston Post No. 244 GAR. He listed his occupation as laundryman. Upon his death, *The Tampa Tribune* October 9, 1912, 5 published the following: "Taft. – Nicholas Dennis, age 65 years, died at his home in Taft, Florida, Saturday morning, October 5. He was born at Niskayuna, Schenectady county, New York, August 23, 1847 . . . Comrade Dennis was a veteran of the Civil War, having enlisted in Company E, 91st N. Y. Vol. Infy., on the ninth day of September 1862, and honorably discharged July 3, 1865. He was commander of Taft Post No. 37 G. A. R. Dept. of Florida, and had been reelected commander each year from the date of its charter. When Taft was incorporated as a town, Mr. Dennis was elected its first mayor, which position he filled with honor and ability to the time of his death. The citizens of Taft extend to the bereaved family their heartfelt sympathy, in this, their hour of affliction and greatly regret the loss of him who has always had the prosperity of Taft uppermost in his thoughts." Nicholas was buried in Greenwood Cemetery, Orlando. Helen died in Kirkland, King, WA and was buried in Sumner Cemetery, Sumner, Pierce, WA. Her gravestone also remembers her husband.

Cyprian Depore – Co. G (tr. January 28, 1865)
b. March 15, 1842 Beaufort, France
d. January 11, 1915 Mt. Pleasant, Isabella, MI
m. Magdalena Fiegel (April 4, 1856-May 25, 1950) 1882

NOTE: This soldier's name was corrupted to Superd and Supere but his death certificate proves that Cyprian was the correct spelling. He was the son of Frank (?-?) and an unidentified mother. A draftee, he enrolled in the 76th Regiment on August 20, 1863 and mustered into Co. D. From the 147th he went to Co. F, 91st Regiment on June 5, 1865 and mustered out July 3rd near Washington, DC. Magdalena was the mother of seven, all of whom were alive in 1910. Cyprian's obituary appeared in *The Mt. Pleasant Times*

January 21, 1915, 1: "Cyprian DePore died at his home January 11, after a brief illness of only three days. The deceased was born in Belfort [sic], France, March 15, 1842 and when four years of age came with his parents to Erie county, New York. In 1882 he was united in marriage to Miss Magdalene Fiegel and twenty-one years ago they came to Isabella county to make their home, settling on a farm north of Mt. Pleasant, where they have since resided. Mr. DePore was a Civil war veteran . . . The funeral was held Friday morning from Sacred Heart church, Frs. McNeil and O'Conner officiating . . . ." His COD was heart disease and rheumatism. Magdalena's passing was noted in *The Isabella County Times-News* May 26. 1950, 2: "Mrs. Magdelena Fiegel Depore, 94, died May 25 at the home of her daughter, Mrs. Mary Houser in Ithaca. She had made her home with her daughter for the last two years. Mrs. DePore was born April 4, 1856 in New York State. She came to Michigan 57 years ago. She was the daughter of George Fiegel and Mary Stoll Fiegel. Sixty-eight years ago she married Cyprian DePore, a veteran of the civil war. He preceded her in death in 1915 . . . Services will be held Monday morning, May 29 at 10 a.m. from the Sacred Heart Catholic church with burial in Calvary cemetery . . . The body will rest at the Rush Funeral home until service time Monday." Cyprian is also buried in Calvary.

George M. DeWitt – Co. H (tr. January 28, 1865)
b. December 1838 Orange, Schuyler, NY
d. March 1, 1910 Monterey, Steuben, NY
m. Margaret E. Gardner (1853-June 8, 1906) *post* 1870

NOTE: George, son of Charles (1812-*post* 1870) and Samantha DeWitt (1817-*post* 1870), was drafted. He enrolled in the 76th at Orange on July 27, 1863, mustering into Co. A, and transferring to Co. C on October 11, 1864. He was WIA at Hatcher's Run on February 6, 1865 and discharged for "disability" from hospital at Point Lookout, MD on June 21, 1865. In 1890, while living in Montour, Schuyler, NY, he told the enumerator his left leg had been shot off above the knee on February 6, 1865. I have been unable to fix an exact marriage date for him and Margaret. He was not married in 1870 but was in 1875. In 1900 the couple did not indicate how long they had been wed. They had no children. George's death was announced in *The Montour Falls Free Press* March 17, 1910, 1: "George M. DeWitt died at his home in Monterey, Tuesday, March 1st, aged seventy-two years. Deceased was born in that town, and lived there until 1863, when he enlisted as a private in the147th N. Y. Vol. Inft., and was afterwards transferred and appointed corporal in Co. A, 76th N. Y. Vols., where he served until he was wounded in the battle of the Wilderness. After returning from the army he opened a grocery store in the Maltby House where he did business for several years, when he moved to Painted Post where he resided until May, 1909, then returning to Monterey. Mr. DeWitt was married to Miss Margaret Gardner many years ago, his wife dying in 1896 [*sic*]. Deceased was the last of the family, and leaves no surviving relatives except nieces and nephews. He was highly esteemed, and by his death the village loses one of its best citizens." Despite its obvious errors, the obituary is interesting. He and Margaret are buried in Central Valley Cemetery, Hornby, Steuben, NY. His dates do not appear on the stone. A brother, Franklin (1842-1883), served in Co. C, 5th NY HA and in Co. L, 5th US ART.

Jesse Dillenbeck – Co. G (tr. January 28, 1865)
b. 1839 Jefferson County, NY
d. August 22, 1917 National Soldiers' Home, Grand Rapids, Kent, MI
m. ?

NOTE: The son of John (1798-*post* 1865) and Betsy Teachout Dillenbeck (1812-*ante* 1865), this soldier was known as Jason when a boy. Although he claimed to have been born in 1843 later documents point to 1839 as a more accurate date. He was drafted, enrolling in the 76th at Utica, Oneida, NY on August 25, 1863 and mustering into Co. D. He was WIA on Laurel Hill, VA on May 8, 1864. From the 147th he transferred to Co. F, 91st Regiment on June 5, 1865 and was discharged on July 12th at Washington, DC. While living in Burleigh, Iosco, MI in 1890 he claimed his disability was "piles 26 years." In later life he claimed to be married but I have found no trace of a wife. His death certificate stated he was single but also stated his DOB and age were unknown. His COD was arteriosclerosis with senility as a contributing factor. He is buried in the Grand Rapids Soldiers' Home Cemetery. His gravestone credits his service in the 91st Regiment.

George Henry Dodge – Co. B (tr. January 28, 1865)
b. January 10, 1845 Saratoga County, NY
d. July 1, 1907 Oswego City, NY
m. Adeline Opelia O'Hara (August 1846-October 20, 1931) January 25, 1870

NOTE: George was the son of Nathaniel Cleves (1810-1899) and, according to FAG, Lucy Ann Way Dodge (?-*ante* 1850). According to the elder Dodge's obituary in *The Oswego Daily Times* January 3, 1899, 8, the family moved to Oswego City from Saratoga County in 1846. George was a substitute for Frank M. Nichols and enrolled in the 76th Regiment on August 10, 1863 at Oswego, mustering into Co. H. He transferred several times within the regiment, the last being to Co. B on January 1, 1865. He transferred from the 147th to Co. G, 91st on June 5, 1865 and mustered out near Washington, DC on July 3rd. In 1890 he claimed no disability. In 1900 Adeline said she was the mother of eight, only two of whom survived. George's death was announced in *The Oswego Daily Times* July 1, 1907, 4: "George H. Dodge, one of Oswego's best known citizens and business men, died about 4 o'clock this afternoon at his home Corner East Oneida and Third Streets. He had been ill for several weeks with Bright's disease. About four days ago his condition grew serious . . . During his service in the army Mr. Dodge acquitted himself with great credit and was regarded as a fine, loyal and courageous soldier. For many years he was employed at Ames Iron Works and he was also an engineer in the Fire Department up to a few years ago. Mr. Dodge held several public positions. In 1896 he was made a Police and Fire Commissioner. The position of Fire Marshal was created in 1897 and Mr. Dodge resigned as Fire and Police Commissioner and was made Fire Marshal. He proved to be one of the most painstaking and efficient officers in the history of the city. He embarked in the gents' furnishings business several years ago and continued in the business with his sons up to his recent illness. Mr. Dodge was for years active in Republican politics in the Sixth Ward and he was County Committeeman for a long time. He was an enthusiastic member of Oswego Lodge B. P. O. Elks and was Esquire for many years. He had a genial manner and was one of the best liked men in town . . . He had just moved into his new home when stricken." Adeline's death was reported in *The Oswego Palladium-Times* October 21, 1931: "Word was received here today of the death Tuesday at Pittsburgh, Pa., of Mrs. Adeline Dodge, widow of George H. Dodge, at the age of 85. Mrs. Dodge was a former prominent resident of the city, the family home being at East Fourth and Albany streets. Her husband was a well known merchant, member of the firm of Tovey & Dodge, haberdashers in East Bridge street. He also served as the first fire marshal of the city and was a Civil war veteran and member of the Elks. Mrs. Dodge was a member of the Congregational church and was a devout Christian woman. During her long life in Oswego she made many friends among whom she was respected and esteemed. Mrs. Dodge visited Oswego during the past summer . . . ." George and Adeline are buried in Riverside Cemetery, Scriba.

Alfred Duncan – Co. D (tr. January 31, 1865)
b. 1844 Pennsylvania
d. ? ?
m. ?

NOTE: Alfred, whose parents are unidentified, enrolled in the 76th Regiment on August 5, 1863 at Rochester, Mnroe, NY as a substitute for Menzo W. Pooley, mustering into Co. F. He was captured on May 5, 1864 at the battle of the Wilderness. When he was paroled is unknown but he left parole camp on May 2, 1865 and was discharged near Washington, DC on June 9, 1865 as a member of the 147th. His life subsequent to his service is unknown. A man named Alfred Gilmore Duncan (1844-December 19, 1912), son of Samuel (1808-1882) and Elizabeth Caldwell Duncan (1811-1892), died of pneumonia at Bellevue, Allegheny, PA and was buried in Plains United Presbyterian Church Cemetery. Whether or not this is the correct person is conjectural.

John Easterly – Co. C (tr. January 28, 1865)
b. May 1845 Erie County, NY
d. December 25, 1913 National Soldiers' Home, Bath, Steuben, NY
m. ------

NOTE: John, a farmer, was the son of Andrew (1810-1904) and Margaret Weiser Easterly (1819-1902). The family name was originally spelled Oesterle. John was a substitute for Kilian Wettig, Cheektowaga, Erie, NY, and enrolled in the 76th at Buffalo on August 12, 1863. Originally assigned to Co. H, he transferred within the regiment several times. From the 147th he was transferred to Co. H, 91st Regiment on June 5, 1865 and mustered out on July 3rd. In 1890, while living in Lancaster, Erie, NY, he claimed rheumatism and "piles" as disabilities. He never married, instead living with various relatives throughout the years. He is buried in Bath National Cemetery.

Henry Eastham – Co. E (tr. January 28, 1865)
b. January 9, 1831 Preston, Lancashire, England
d. July 16, 1904 Baltimore, MD
m. Sarah Maguire (1830-1919) *ca.* 1857

NOTE: Henry, a weaver by occupation, enlisted in the 30th Regiment on September 29, 1862 at Watervliet, Albany, NY, mustering into Co. D, then transferring to Co. A, 76th on May 25, 1863. He was captured at Gettysburg on July 1st and paroled at an unknown date. He transferred to Co. I on October 11, 1864 and to Co. C on December 1st. He was discharged from the 147th at Washington, DC on June 3, 1865. He and Sarah, who was born in Essex County, NY, lived for many years in Minerva. They were the parents of four children. The youngest was Susannah (1867-1874). At some time after the 1870 census Henry abandoned the family. In 1880 Sarah and the surviving children were living in Adams, Berkshire, MA. They began to spell their surname Eastman. Henry found his way to Baltimore and began a relationship with a woman named Ellen _____ (1828-November 21, 1895). That they never married is confirmed by the fact that Sarah applied for and obtained a widow's pension. I have located no obituary for Henry but he left his estate to an eight-year-old girl, as announced in *The Baltimore Sun* July 20, 1904, 7: "The will of Henry Eastham, filed for probate in the Orphans' Court yesterday, bequeaths all his property of every kind to Marie Christina Smith, youngest child of John S. Smith, 1811 Eagle street. He names the child's mother as her guardian and as executrix of his estate. 'In making this will,' Mr. Eastham states in the document, 'I have not in the slightest degree been influenced by any person, and I make the child my sole legatee because of love and affection for said child, as I am practically alone in the world. I believe I have a brother living somewhere (exactly where I do not know), and also some nephews and nieces living in Massachusetts, with whom I have never continued acquaintance. I direct that my body be buried alongside that of my beloved wife in the Whatcoat section of Loudon Park Cemetery, and that a suitable inscription be placed upon the tombstone standing there now.' The will was executed April 13 last." Indeed, he was buried next to Ellen, whose gravestone bears the inscription "beloved wife." The purposeful omission of his own children from the will is indicative of the bitterness involved in the couple's separation. It is interesting to note that Sarah did not apply for her pension until 1914. Was it pride or ignorance of her spouse's death? Sarah and several of her children are buried in Saint Mary's Cemetery, Irishtown, Essex, NY.

According to his will, Henry wished to be buried by his "beloved wife" Ellen.
Ron Baublitz (FAG)

Martin Edgcomb – Co. D (tr. January 2, 1865)
b. June 7, 1836 Groton, Tompkins, NY
d. August 3, 1920 Cortland, Cortland, NY
m. Emily Giles Merritt (1846-September 7, 1938) 1866

NOTE: Martin was the son of Isaac Allyn (1806-1860) and Clarissa Woodruff Edgcomb (1800-1865). He enlisted at Cortland on October 1, 1861 and mustered into Co. A with the rank of sergeant. He was captured at Groveton, VA on August 29, 1862 and in an article appearing in *The Syracuse Herald* April 7, 1918 he recounted how he was taken and how he made his escape. On January 5, 1864 he re-enlisted and transferred several times within the regiment. He mustered out on June 7, 1865 near Washington, DC as a lieutenant. In 1890 he claimed no disability. He and Emily were the parents of six children. His death was announced in a slightly in-accurate obituary in *The Cortland Democrat* August 6, 1920, 5: "The death of Mr. Martin Edgcomb Tuesday afternoon removed from earth the second member of the aged Edgcomb brothers within six weeks, George W. passing away on June 25 last and the only surviving brother being Isaac Edgcomb, aged 86 years, the eldest in the family. Martin Edgcomb was born in Groton on June 7, 1836, being one of the seven children of Isaac and Clarissa Edgcomb. When the Civil war broke out in 1861 he was a partner with his brother Isaac in the harness business, and he enlisted as a sergeant in Co. A of the 76th regiment and was taken prisoner at the second Battle of Bull Run. He was paroled and sent to Camp Chase in Ohio. He re-enlisted in January, 1864, in the 76th but was transferred to other regiments and participated in several of the great battles of the war. He was mustered out on July 2, 1865. He returned to Cortland and resumed the harness business and later conducted a shoe store. Mr. Edgcomb was for years one of the leading members of the First Methodist church, and had long served on the official board. He was also a member of Grover Post, 98, G. A. R., and had been its commander. He invariably took a prominent part in the annual reunions of the 76th regiment . . . The funeral will be held this (Friday) afternoon at 2 o'clock at the family home . . . ." Emily's sudden death was reported in *The Cortland Democrat* September 9, 1938, 1: "Mrs. Emily Maritt [sic] Edgcomb, 92, widow of Martin Edgcomb, a Civil War veteran, died in her sleep Wednesday morning, September 7. She was active in the last day of her life, wrote a long let-ter, and was making plans for another busy day when she retired Tuesday night. She had passed away when Mrs. Mary Lockwood, with whom she resided . . . went into her room to call her Wednesday morning . . . Mrs. Edgcomb was the daughter of Stephen and Betsy Maritt and was born at Brooklyn, Pa., February 25, 1846, and was the last of that family. She came to Cortland when she was 18 years old and married Martin Edgcomb directly after the Civil War. She was the oldest member of the First Methodist church, both in age and in years of membership . . . ." Emily's COD was deemed a heart attack. She and Martin are buried in Cortland Rural Cemetery.

Keeran Egan – Co. B (tr. January 28, 1865)
b. 1834 Ireland
d. December 5, 1868 Cannonsburg, Kent, MI
m. Ann Hunt (March 1828-August 28, 1908) July 1, 1847

NOTE: Keeran, whose parents are unknown, enlisted in the 76th Regiment on September 19, 1862 at Watervliet, Albany, NY and mustered into Co. E. He was wounded in the thigh at Spotsylvania on May 12, 1864 and sent to Judiciary Square Hospital, Washington. Granted a furlough at the end of May he returned to Cohoes, where the family resided. Dr. Joseph Moore extracted the ball from his thigh and later testified that gangrene had set in and that Egan "suffered greatly." His time in the 147th was limited since he was transferred to Co. C, 18th Regiment VRC on March 8, 1865 and discharged at Washington, DC on July 19, 1865. Dr. Moore testified that after Keeran returned home he was found to be suffering from tuberculosis. He attempted to work in an axe factory but was so weak he had to quit. He went to Michigan, probably hoping his health would return, but succumbed to the disease. His grave has not been located. Ann, who said in 1900 that she was the mother of 11 children, obtained pensions for herself and the four under 16. In a deposition dated May 9, 1869 she stated she was poor and had no property except a small house worth about $100 which was situated on company lands in Cohoes. The company was demanding that she move it. She testified that three of her sons were supporting her and the younger children. John, 20, was making $1 per day; Michael, 18, $20 per month; Francis, 13, $10 per month. All were working in the factory in Cohoes. Ann's death was announced in *The Troy Times* August 29, 1908: "--- The death of Mrs. Ann Egan occurred yesterday at her home, 134 Saratoga Street. She was born in Ireland, but had been a resident of Cohoes for the last fifty-five years . . . The funeral will be held Monday morning at 9 o'clock from the residence and from St. Bernard's Church." Ann's grave has not been located.

John J. Evans – Co. I (tr. January 28, 1865)
b. 1842 Tioga County, NY
d. December 27, 1920 Binghamton, Broome, NY
m1. Josephine Cady (February 26, 1848-March 27, 1866) ?
m2. Sophronia "Frona" A. Japhet (June 1850-*post* 1900) *ca.* 1868
m3. Anna J. _____ (1852-*post* 1910) 1905

NOTE: John was the son of Franklin (1810-1888) and Phila Robinson Evans (1807-1847). He enlisted in the 76th Regiment at Freetown, Cortland, NY on September 14, 1861 and mustered into Co. D. He was wounded at Gettysburg on July 1, 1863. He re-enlisted on January 2, 1864 at Culpeper, VA. He was wounded at Hatcher's Run on February 6, 1865, transferred to Co. D, 91st on June 5, 1865, and discharged on July 3rd. In 1890, while living in Newark Valley, Tioga, he said he had been wounded in the right thigh (place not specified) and wounded in the right hand at Hatcher's Run. His three marriages present many mysteries. In 1865 he and Josephine were married and she was living in Freetown with her grandparents, James (1800-1870) and Eliza Letts Lamberson (1803-1884). They are buried in Galatia Cemetery with Josephine. Her stone, according to FAG, shows she was the daughter of Nelson and

M. A. Cady. I have not located these people who may have died very young since Josephine was living with her grandparents in 1850. Among John's many siblings was Irvin W. (1838-1926), said to be John's only relative when he died. Irvin married Ellen Japhet, daughter of Elijah (1815-1899) and Mary Gordon Pendell Japhet (1816-1882). Sophronia was her sister. She and John were the parents of Carrie J. (1869-*post* 1892). John and Sophronia resided in Maine, Broome County in 1900. She claimed to be the mother of five, all living. She evidently died sometime after that census. By 1905 John and Anna were married. On the 1910 census both claimed to have been married twice and Anna said she was the mother of six, all living. I have found no record for Anna after 1910 and when the 1920 census was taken, John and Irvin were both living with Wallace Japhet, son of Levi (1845-1908) and nephew of Ellen and Sophronia. John said he was a widower. His death was announced in *The Binghamton Press and Sun-Bulletin* December 28, 1920, 9: "Johnson City, Dec. 28. – John J. Evans, a Civil War veteran and for several years street commissioner of Johnson City, died at 159 Washington street, Binghamton, last night at the age of 78 years. Irvin Evans of Endicott, a brother, is the only survivor. The funeral will be held at the funeral parlors of Arthur W. Heilby . . . tomorrow afternoon at 2 o'clock. Burial will be in the soldiers' plot at Floral Park cemetery. Mr. Evans was a member of the Walton Dwight Post, G. A. R. of Johnson City. He served three years in Company E, 91st Regiment, New York Infantry. He has lived in Johnson City for many years but had moved to Binghamton a few months ago." John's father died in Lapeer, MI. He served in Co. F, 10th Michigan Infantry from November 1861-January 1863.

Horace Grenville Fabyan – Co. C tr. January 28, 1865
b. October 1836 New Hampshire
d. March 18, 1884 Lewis County, WA
m. Mary Luella DeForest Cargill (1838-June 11, 1874) July 7, 1857

NOTE: Horace was the son of Horace (1807-1881) and Miriam Eaton Fabyan (1810-1858). The family owned the Fabyan House, White Mountains, NH. Horace first saw military service when he enrolled in Co. D, 53rd Regiment at Poughkeepsie, NY on October 15, 1861, using the name Grenville H. He mustered out with the regiment at Washington, DC on March 21, 1862. He next enlisted in the 30th Regiment at Watervliet, Albany, NY on September 24, 1862, mustering into Co. D, then transferring to Co. B, 76th on May 25, 1863. He was wounded at Gettysburg on July 1st, 1863. He transferred within the regiment several times. From the 147th he went to Co. H, 91st on June 5, 1865, mustering out near Washington, DC on July 3rd. After the war, he and Luella, whom he had married in Lancaster, Coos, NH, moved west. They were the parents of several children. Luella's tragic death was reported in *The Mirror and Farmer* [Manchester, NH] July 18, 1874: "Mrs. Horace G. Fabyan, of Sanders [*sic*] county, Nebraska, and formerly of Lancaster, was recently fatally poisoned by eating powdered corrosive sublimate in place of soda." Her grave has not been located. In 1880 Horace was living in Butteville, Marion, OR and working as a carpenter. According to FAG, the children were sent east to live with relatives. Horace is buried in Toledo Cemetery, Lewis County, WA. His brother, Bernard Douglas (1830-1896), served as a captain in Co. B, 6th VT Regiment.

Peter Fallon – Co. A (tr. January 28, 1865)
b. 1824 Ireland
d. *post* 1892 ?
m. ?

NOTE: The parents of Peter, a shoemaker, are unknown. He enlisted in the 30th Regiment at Watervliet, Albany, NY on August 19, 1862, mustering into Co. D. He was discharged for "disability" on May 7, 1863 at Washington, DC and enlisted in the 76th Regiment the same day, mustering into Co. K. He was transferred several times within the regiment. When sent to the 147th he was "absent, sick" in a hospital in Philadelphia, PA. In 1890 he claimed to have been injured on his right side. Although nominally transferred to Co. C, 91st Regiment on June 5, 1865 he did not join that organization but in all likelihood was discharged from the 147th in early June. He applied for a pension on August 16, 1866 and obtained a certificate. On July 17, 1888 he entered the Soldiers' Home in Togus, Kennebec, ME and remained there until October 25, 1892. What happened after that date is unknown.

John Finnegan – Co. K (tr. January 28, 1865)
b. 1843 Montgomery County, NY
d. ? ?
m. ?

NOTE: Little is known about this soldier's life before he entered the military. He enlisted in the 76th at Cherry Valley, Otsego County on October 24, 1861 and mustered in to Co. H. He re-enlisted on January 3, 1864 at Culpeper, VA and was wounded at Laurel Hill on May 10th. He transferred to Co B on January 1, 1865. From the 147th he was transferred to Co. K, 91st Regiment and mustered out near Washington, DC on July 3rd. According to *The Town Clerks' Registers* he resided in Canajoharie, Montgomery County. The last known reference to him is April 2, 1888 in New York State when he applied for a pension. His name has not been located on the 1890 Veterans' Schedules. He either was unmarried or his wife predeceased him.

Eugene Fisher – Co. G (tr. January 28, 1865)
b. December 27, 1838 Willet, Cortland, NY
d. May 28, 1913 National Soldiers' Home, Dayton, Montgomery, OH
m. Julia Ann Lull (November 1836-*post* 1900) 1865

NOTE: Eugene was the son of John (1789-1869) and Clarissa Palmer Fisher (1795-1872). He enrolled in the 76th at Cortland on November 12, 1861 and mustered into Co. D, re-enlisting at Culpeper, VA on January 2, 1864. From the 147th he went to Co. F, 91st on June 5, 1865 and was discharged on July 3rd near Washington, DC. In August 1866 while living in Kossuth County, IA he provided a deposition for the widow of William Duell, Co. D, who had been captured by the Confederates and died at Andersonville. Anna, Eugene and Julia's daughter, was born in Michigan in 1870. The family resided in Marshall, Calhoun, MI for both the 1870 and 1880 censuses. In 1892, however, they were living in Triangle, Broome County. Anna disappeared after the 1892 New York census and in 1900 Julia claimed she had had no children. I have not found Julia's DOD or her gravesite. When Eugene entered the home in Dayton on May 17, 1913 he gave the name of Carrie M. Fisher as his wife and said they both lived in St. Cloud, Osceola, FL. After he died his effects were sent to her. I have located no information on this woman but they probably were not married. She did not claim a widow's pension and his payment card makes no mention of her as the widow. The city directories for that time period contain no references to either of these people. Eugene is buried in Dayton National Cemetery. His brother, John Jr. (1832-1909), also served in the 76th Regiment. He is buried in Third Street Cemetery, Friendship, Allegany. Their parents are buried in Mount Hope Cemetery, Friendship.

Nicholas Fisher – Co. E (tr. January 28, 1865)
b. October 1837 Buffalo, Erie, NY
d. March 6, 1923 Buffalo, Erie, NY
m. Magdalena "Lena" Streicher (July 1847-November 29, 1929) 1868

NOTE: Nicholas, a moulder, was the son of Nicholas (1802-*post* 1865) and Barbara Fisher (1803-*post* 1865). Their surname was also spelled Fischer. Nicholas enlisted in 21st Regiment at Buffalo on May 1, 1861, mustering into Co. A. He deserted at a camp near Sharpsburg, MD on September 19, 1862. He was a substitute for Cornelius Murphy, Niagara, Niagara, NY, enrolling there on July 28, 1863 and mustering into Co. K. He was captured and paroled although no dates are available. When transferred to the 147th he was a paroled prisoner. From the 147th he was transferred to Co. I, 91st on June 5, 1865 and mustered out near Washington, DC on July 3rd. In 1890 he claimed rheumatism as a disability and the enumerator noted he had been shot in the chest. On October 25, 1890 Fisher applied for a pension and despite his desertion he obtained a certificate. Magdalena reported in 1900 that she was the mother of 10, seven of whom were living. She and Nicholas are buried in United French and German Cemetery, Cheektowaga, Erie.

Michael Fitzgerald – Co. I (tr. January 31, 1865)
b. 1842 Pennsylvania
d. ? ?
m. ?

NOTE: Michael, details for whose early life have not been located, enrolled in the 76th as a substitute for Edwin Markham at Busti, Chautauqua, NY on August 20, 1863 and mustered into Co. I. He was captured on October 1, 1864 during the battle of Pegram's farm, part of the Petersburg Campaign. Where he was confined or when he was released has not been identified. It is doubtful that he ever saw active duty with the 147th but he was discharged at Syracuse, NY on July 28, 1865 as a member of that regiment. The only other known date is June 27, 1895 when he applied for a pension. Since he did not obtain a certificate, it is probable he died before the process could be completed. If he had a wife, she predeceased him because no widow attempted to claim a pension.

John Nicolaus Fleischman – Co. H (tr. January 28, 1865)
b. April 1935 Kilberk, Saxony, Germany
d. April 11, 1920 Cohocton, Steuben, NY
m1. Carolina Elizabeth Mastin (October 20, 1835-June 2, 1877) November 9, 1857
m2. Clara Ahrens (1854-July 16, 1939) 1887

NOTE: John, also known by his middle name, was the son of David (1809-1882) and Catharina Rosina Fleischman (1813-1904). Their surname had many variations. The family immigrated to the United States in 1854 aboard the Hermann Theodor. John enrolled in the 76th Regiment at Cohocton on July 14, 1863, mustering into Co. C. There is no indication he was drafted or a substitute. On November 8, 1864 he transferred to Co. A. From the 147th he went to Co. F, 91st on June 5, 1865 and was mustered out near Washington, DC on July 3rd. In 1890 he claimed "five wounds and loss of teeth" as disabilities. Between his two wives, John was the father of 13 children. He and Carolina, born in Livingston County, were married at Lodi, Seneca, NY. Her COD is unknown but she is buried in Old Saint Paul's Cemetery, Cohocton. Clara, born in Germany, immigrated to the United States in 1887. She and John must have been married soon after her arrival since her first son, William, was born in February 1888. John's death was reported in *The Steuben Courier* April ?, 1920: "John Fleischman, who was born in 1835, died Sunday morning at his home on

Erie street, in the village of Cohocton, his death being the result of paralysis, which rendered him helpless several months ago. Mr. Fleischman was a veteran of the civil war, a member of Rodney E. Harris Post, No. 240, G. A. R., of this village for many years, and much of his life had been passed in or near this village, where he was very greatly respected. Funeral services will be held Wednesday morning at St. Paul's Evangelical Lutheran church, of which he had been a valuable member for most of the time since it was organized in 1860. He was married twice . . . ." Clara's obituary appeared in *The Cohocton Valley Times-Index* July 26, 1939, 1: "The passing of Mrs. Clara Ahrens Fleishman [*sic*] occurred at her home south of the village Sunday, July 16, 1939 following a long illness extending over a period of several years. Her age was 85 years four months and 20 days. She was born in Bromberg, Germany and came to America when a young lady. She was united in marriage with John N. Fleishman who died April 11, 1920 . . . Mrs. Fleishman was of a quiet nature, but a good neighbor and friend to every one and a mighty fine woman to know. Funeral services were held last Wednesday afternoon at 1:30 at the home and at 2:00 at St. Paul's Evangelical church, of which she was a member, with Rev. Walter Labrenz officiating. The burial was in St. Paul's cemetery." John is buried with Clara.

Alfred Foland – Co. C (tr. January 28, 1865)
b. August 8, 1844 Cherry Valley, Otsego, NY
d. July 6, 1930 St. Petersburg, Pinellas, FL
m. Jessica M. Storrs (1850-April 5, 1933) 1868

NOTE: Alfred was the son of Christopher (1817-1903) and Catherine L. Preston Foland (1823-1914). He enlisted in the 76th on January 6, 1862 at Cherry Valley and mustered into Co. B. He was captured at the battle of Bull Run on August 29, 1862 and paroled at an unknown date. On January 5, 1864 he re-enlisted at Culpeper, VA. He was discharged on June 26, 1865 as "supernumerary." In 1890 he claimed "piles" as a disability. He and Jessica had one child, Nathaniel (1869-1944). Alfred's death was announced in *The Tampa Bay Times* July 7, 1930, 10: "Alfred A. Foland, 85, a Civil war veteran and a resident of St. Petersburg for 18 years, died early Sunday morning at his home . . . Mr. Foland came here from Bradenton, where he had lived five years before coming from Worcester, N. Y. Mr. Foland was a Civil war veteran and had been in 26 battles. He enlisted at Cherry Valley, N. Y., Jan. 10, 1862, with Company H, 76th New York infantry. He was discharged at the close of the war with the rank of first sergeant . . . ." Alfred and Jessica, whose obituary appeared in *The Tampa Bay Times* April 7, 1933, 7, are buried in Maple Grove Cemetery, Worcester, Otsego.

George L. Folmsbee – Co. G (tr. January 28, 1865)
b. 1838 Rensselaer County, NY
d. August 10, 1897 Norwich, Chenango, NY
m. Adelia "Polly" Thompson Snyder (1846-June 5, 1924) *post* 1865

NOTE: George was the son of William Henry (1813-*post* 1865) and Margaret Ramy Folmsbee (1822-*post* 1865). His surname was variously spelled. I use that on his gravestone. He was drafted, enrolling in the 76th on July 27, 1863 at Conklin, Broome, NY and mustering into Co. C. He transferred to Co. D on November 8, 1864. From the 147th he transferred to Co. F, 91st on June 5, 1865, mustering out on July 3rd. Someone named George Folmsbee, having the same general description as this person, enlisted in Co. I, 22nd US Infantry on February 6, 1867 in Iowa and was discharged for "disability' at Fort Randall, SD in May 1868. Adelia, also called Delia and Polly, was first married to Charles V. Snyder (1842-April 2, 1865). He served in Co. M, 4th NY HA and was captured at Reams Station, VA on August 25, 1864. According to *The Town Clerks' Registers* he was held at Libby Prison. His entry in *Deaths of Volunteers* shows he died at Camp Parole, Annapolis, MD of diphtheria. He and Delia were the parents of Adda J. (1862-*post* 1880). In later years she lived with her grandmother, Catherine Guile. It is unknown when Polly and George were married but their first child, Hattie, was born in 1872. They were also the parents of George Albert (1875-1914) and Frank (1878-1952). In 1910 Polly said she was the mother of four, all living. George L. and Polly are buried in Mount Hope Cemetery, Norwich. Charles Snyder is buried in Annapolis National Cemetery.

Gilbert M. Fonda – Co. K (tr. January 28, 1865)
b. 1846 Cohoes, Albany, NY
d. April 20, 1899 Fort Porter, Buffalo, Erie, NY
m. Armina "Lina" Margaret Boyle (December 12, 1843-January 15, 1933) *ca.* 1875

NOTE: Gilbert, son of Abraham (1810-1890) and Sarah "Sally" Leversee Fonda (1806-1876), enrolled in the 30th Regiment on October 8, 1862 at Watervliet, Albany, NY, mustering into Co. K as a musician, transferring to Co. I, 76th on May 25, 1863 and to Co. B on December 1, 1864. He was discharged from the military as a member of the 147th on February 13, 1865 at Petersburg, VA. He was a career soldier, serving under the alias of Henry Fuller for his later enlistments. His last posting was with the 13th Regiment, USA stationed at Fort Porter, Buffalo. His death was reported in *The Buffalo Evening News* April 20, 1899, 1: ". . . Henry Fuller, a member of Co. C, died in the post's hospital shortly after noon today. Fuller was one of the most popular men in the regiment. He joined it about a year ago and went all through the Cuban campaign. He had an attack of malarial fever shortly after the return of the regiment.

Ten days ago he was stricken with erysipelas and grew slowly worse. He died this afternoon from a complication of diseases." Gilbert is buried in Forest Lawn Cemetery, Buffalo. He and his wife, generally known as Margaret, were the parents of a son, Leland Gilbert (1876-December 14, 1952). According to his death certificate he died in Philadelphia, PA after falling on the highway and fracturing his skull. He is buried in Harleigh Cemetery, Camden, Oneida, NY. Margaret also died in Philadelphia and, according to her death announcement in *The Philadelphia Inquirer* January 17, 1933, 27, she died "suddenly" at the age of 89. She is buried in Mt. Vernon Cemetery, Philadelphia.

Benjamin Alanson Foote – Co. F (tr. January 28, 1865)
b. September 21, 1843 Unadilla, Otsego, NY
d. January 5, 1910 Kissimmee, Osceola, FL
m. Lydia Melissa Burrows (June 8, 1853-June 20, 1925) 1870

NOTE: Benjamin, son of Elias W. (1801-1851) and Harriet W. Bailey Foote (1810-1867), enlisted in the 76th on November 30, 1861 at Unadilla as a musician and mustered into Co. K. He later was promoted to commissary sergeant. He re-enlisted at Culpeper, VA on January 2, 1864. From the 147th he was transferred to the 91st Regiment as commissary sergeant on June 5, 1865 and mustered out July 3rd. In 1870 he was living with his aunt Eliza Foote (1819-1900), widow of Charles (1812-1868), and working on her farm. Also working there as a dairy maid was Lydia Burrows. After the couple wed, they began their migration which would end in South Dakota. In 1880 they were living in Colfax, Jasper, IA. He and Lydia were the parents of four daughters, all living in 1900. The rest of the story is recounted in an obituary published in *The Otsego Farmer* January 28, 1910, 7: "On January 11th Miss Jane Foote of Oaksville, received, by telegram, the sad news of the death of her only brother, Benjamin Foote, which occurred January 5th at 8:40 p.m., at Kissimmee, Florida, where he had gone to spend the winter on account of his health. He left Highmore, Dakota, December 6th. Mr. Foote was an old-time resident of Otsego County . . . Removing with his family to Kansas, Mr. Foote went first to Ohio [sic], and then to South Dakota, where he invested in land, at one time owning 1,000 acres. He was a large land dealer and, for twelve years acted as county Treasurer at Highmore, Hyde county, Dakota. On December 20th Miss Foote received a letter saying that the deceased intended to build a small residence at Kissimmee." Lydia, whose address was given as Highmore on the 1925 SD census, died in Riverside, Riverside, CA. She and Benjamin are buried in Highmore Cemetery.

Miles Riggs Foster – Co. A (tr. January 28, 1865)
b. March 7, 1841 Hartford, Cortland, NY
d. July 4, 1916 Dryden, Tompkins, NY

m1. Frances A. _____ (*ca.* 1852-1882) *ca.* 1873
m2. Adeline Orton (1866-March 15, 1955) April 23, 1883

NOTE: Son of Amos (1812-1889) and Pauline Maria Barnes Foster (1821-1869), Miles enlisted in the 76th Regiment at Virgil, Cortland, NY on September 19, 1861 and mustered into Co. A. He re-enlisted on January 2, 1864 at Culpeper, VA and transferred to Co. D on October 10, 1864. He was wounded at Hatcher's Run on February 6, 1865 and discharged from hospital, York, PA on June 9, 1865 for disability from his wounds. He and Frances were the parents of a son, Willard (1875-1877) who is buried in Lisle Village Cemetery. Frances' grave has not been located. Miles and Adeline were the parents of 14 children, 13 of whom were living in 1900. The couple is buried in Willow Glen Cemetery, Dryden. Miles' brother, John Lawrence (1842-1906), served in the 138th Regiment from August 1862-July 1865.

Charles Frances – Co. I (tr. January 28, 1865)
b. 1840 Cortland County, NY
d. *post* 1865 ?
m. ?

NOTE: Charles may have been the son of Roswell (1802-1894) and Athelia Frances (1803-1879). The family lived in Virgil, Cortland County where, according to his muster roll card, Charles was born. In 1865 he was enumerated with the family but was "in the army now." Charles, whose surname was also spelled Francis, enlisted in the 76th at Groton, Tompkins County on October 15, 1861, mustering into Co. C. He was wounded at Fredericksburg, VA on December 13, 1862. He re-enlisted at Culpeper, VA on January 2, 1864 and transferred to Co. D on November 8th. From the 147th he was transferred to Co. I, 91st on June 5, 1865, mustering out on July 3rd. The 1865 New York census is the last record for him. No pension card has been located and he does not appear on the 1890 Veterans' Schedules.

James Smith Fritcher – Co. C (tr. January 28, 1865)
b. October 15, 1844 Root, Montgomery, NY
d. 1865 probably Virginia
m. ------

NOTE: James, better known by his middle name, was the son of Peter (1809-1901) and Harriet Mattice Fritcher (1797-1850). His military career began when he enlisted in Co. M, 3rd NY ART at Argusville, Schoharie, NY on October 20, 1861. He transferred to Co. H, 76th on January 17, 1862. He re-enlisted on January 5, 1864 at Culpeper, VA, transferring to Co. B on January 1, 1865. Allegedly he was captured at Hatcher's Run, VA on February 6, 1865 but it is as likely that he died there. According to *The Town*

Clerks' Registers, there was "no knowledge of his whereabouts." Peter applied for a pension on March 7, 1891 but did not obtain a certificate, perhaps because Smith's death could not be established with certainty. The pension card indicates he thought his son had been a member of the 91st Regiment. Peter and Harriet are buried in Shelby Center Cemetery, Orleans County. A brother, Henry Daniel (1831-1910), served in the 8th NY ART and the 10th NY Infantry from January 1864-June 1865.

John Fritton - Co. G (tr. January 28, 1865)
b. June 4, 1843 Germany
d. October 17, 1920 Albion, Broome, NE
m. Mary Herberger (November 1848-July 28, 1927) April 22, 1867

NOTE: John, whose actual name was Johann Friedrich Wilhelm Friton, was the son of George (1808-1894) and Katharina Balluf Friton (1815-1872). His DOB varies from 1841-1843. I use that located on his gravestone. The family immigrated to the United States in 1850 and John became a naturalized citizen. He was drafted, enrolling in the 76th on July 28, 1863 at Hartland, Niagara, NY and mustering into Co. D. According to *The Town Clerks' Registers* he was wounded in the right cheek at Petersburg, VA in 1864 but *The Adjutant-General's Report* states he was injured at Laurel Hill on May 8, 1864. From the 147th he transferred to Co. F, 91st and was discharged near Washington, DC on July 3rd. It is curious to note he does not appear on the muster roll for the 76th Regiment. He and Mary, who was born in New York State, were married in Stark County, IL. The parents of at least 10 children, they are buried in Saint Michael's Cemetery, Albion.

Thomas W. Gardner – Co. C (tr. January 28, 1865)
b. December 31, 1837 New Lisbon, Otsego County, NY
d. June 11, 1911 Hartwick, Otsego, NY
m. Livonia A. Hill (May 17, 1841-May 10, 1924) March 13, 1861

NOTE: Thomas was the son of Mumford D. (1809-1892) and Harriet M. Eldred Gardner (1815-1891). A farmer by occupation, he was drafted, enrolling in the 76th Regiment on August 28, 1863 and mustering into Co. H. He transferred to Co. F on February 2, 1864 and to Co. B on January 1, 1865. From the 147th he transferred to Co. H, 91st on June 5, 1865, mustering out near Washington, DC on July 3rd. In 1890 he said he had been hurt over his right eye with a piece of shell. He was a member of William W. Jackson Post No. 489 GAR, New Berlin. He and Livonia were the parents of four. His death was announced in *The Otsego Farmer* June 16, 1911, 7: "Thomas Gardner of New Berlin, who was visiting his son, Clarence at Hartwick died early Sunday morning. Mr. Gardner had been in feeble health for some time. He was seventy-three years old . . .

His funeral was held Tuesday at 11 o'clock, the Rev. A. J. Cook officiating. Interment at Lena cemetery." He was buried in the same cemetery as his parents, located in New Lisbon, Otsego. On April 26, 1912 at South New Berlin Livonia married John G. Stoddard (*ca.* 1848-?), a native of Alabama. The marriage record shows this was his first marriage. Stoddard was the son of Gridley Blake and Julia Farrell Stoddard. What happened to Stoddard is unknown but on August 24, 1914 Livonia married Walter L. Ritchie (*ca.* 1847-1916) as his fourth wife. Ritchie was a native of Nova Scotia, Canada. He died on December 9, 1916 at Norwich, Chenango, NY. Livonia sought admission to the Women's Relief Corps Home, Oxford, Chenango, NY on June 3, 1919, claiming that she owned no property and that all her husbands were dead. She had poor eyesight and heart trouble. She died at the home and was buried in the New York State Veterans' Home Cemetery, Oxford.

James George – Co. H (tr. January 28, 1865)
b. January 11, 1828 Milton Abbas, Dorset, England
d. March 4, 1871 Cherry Valley, Otsego, NY
m. Thomasine Ann Ridout (1829-November 24, 1894) February 7, 1853

NOTE: James, son of John (1791-1868) and Elizabeth Ballam George (1789-1875), was a stone mason like his father. He and Thomasine, sometimes known by her middle name, were married in Milton Abbas. By 1855 they were living in Cherry Valley. James enlisted in the 76th on October 11, 1861 and mustered into Co. H. He was WIA at Bull Run, VA on August 29, 1862. He re-enlisted on January 3, 1864 at Culpeper, VA. On May 5, 1864 he was captured during the battle of the Wilderness and sent to Andersonville. Debra Harmon relates a family story that while he was a prisoner he carved a set of chess pieces from rat bones. Little is known about his time in the 147th but his wife's pension card confirms his service. He apparently left parole camp on May 4, 1865 and was discharged near Arlington, VA on June 9, 1865. In 1890 Thomasine told the enumerator her husband had been "wounded." He is buried in Cherry Valley Cemetery. Thomasine and the children moved to Amsterdam, Montgomery County. She died in Amsterdam as a result of an "accident," according to her death certificate. She is buried in Green Hill Cemetery, Amsterdam.

Charles Glover – Co. E (tr. January 31, 1865)
b. 1843 Potter County, PA
d. June 30, 1879 Cameron County, PA
m. ------

NOTE: Charles was the son of Jacob L. (1800-*ca.* 1846) and Margaret Glover (?-*post* 1843). His parents must have died young since in 1855 he was living with his uncle,

John Glover, in Cincinnatus, Cortland, NY. A farmer, Charles enlisted in the 76th Regiment on September 26, 1861, mustering into Co. F. He re-enlisted on January 26, 1864 and was taken captive at the battle of the Wilderness on May 5th. His parole date is unknown but he was not discharged until November 21, 1865 at Elmira, Chemung, NY as a member of the 147th. It is interesting to note that his application for a pension was dated July 2, 1879, two days after he died. He is buried in Haine's Farm Burying Ground, also known as Glover Cemetery, near Beechwood, Cameron, PA.

William Glover – Co. A (tr. January 28, 1865)
b. 1843 Glasgow, Lanarkshire, Scotland
d. June 29, 1897 Chicago, Cook, IL
m. Anne "Annie" O'Malley (*ca.* 1852-August 28, 1910) *ca.* 1875

NOTE: William, whose parents have not been identified, was a carpenter. He enrolled in the 76th Regiment on August 5, 1863 at Rochester, Monroe, NY as a substitute for William A. Allen, Rochester, and mustered into Co. E. He was WIA on May 19, 1864 and although his muster roll card says that occurred at the Wilderness, more likely it happened during the Spotsylvania Campaign from May 8-22. He transferred to Co. A on November 18, 1864. As a member of the 147th he was wounded at White Oak Ridge, VA on March 31, 1865. Although nominally transferred to Co. C, 91st Regiment on June 5th he was discharged for "disability from wounds" on July 6th at Washington, DC. He does not appear in *The Adjutant-General's Report* for the 91st Regiment. His wounds must have been serious because he applied for a pension on September 5, 1865. It is unknown where he and Annie were married but Mary (1876-?) and Agnes (1877-?) were born in Pennsylvania, as was their mother. By 1880 the family was living in Lake, Cook, IL. Mary was the mother of five, all living in 1900. William is buried in Calvary Cemetery, Evanston, Cook, IL. Annie is buried in Mt. Carmel Cemetery, Hillside, Cook, IL.

Harrison "Tip" B. Goldsmith – Co. K (tr. January 28, 1865)
b. May 24, 1840 Chemung County, NY
d. October 7, 1920 Erin, Chemung, NY
m. Martha M. McDowell (October 1860-September 4, 1916) 1876

NOTE: Harrison, son of Brewster (1800-1879) and Sarah Shoemaker Goldsmith (1805-1893), was a stone mason. He enlisted in the 14th US Infantry at Elmira, Chemung, NY on December 21, 1861 and was discharged at Perryville MD on February 4, 1862. According to information on his muster roll card for the 147th Regiment, he had "epileptic fits." The note also revealed he had been accepted as a substitute for the 76th. Indeed, he was a substitute for George H. Smith, Elmira, enrolling on July

20, 1863 in that place and mustering into Co. A. He was wounded at the battle of the Wilderness on May 5, 1864, then transferred to Co. I on October 11, 1864 and to Co. C on December 1st. His time in the 147th was brief as he transferred to Co. K, 22nd Regiment VRC on February 3, 1865. At some time he was accused of desertion but the charge was dismissed and he was discharged "to date" July 20, 1865. In 1890, while living in Hicks, Chemung County, he claimed an injury to his arm resulting in the loss of the third finger on his left hand. He also said he had "piles" and possibly a hernia. The penmanship of the enumerator rendered the word almost illegible. Harrison's postwar life has been difficult to trace. In 1870 he was convicted of perjury and sentenced to five years in Auburn State Prison, a crime for which he was pardoned by Governor Grover Cleveland on September 27, 1884. Harrison was a member of William K. Logie Post No. 420 GAR. Martha's parents were John (1821-1880) and Eliza Garson McDowell (1841-*post* 1880). She was the mother of three daughters. Graves for Harrison and Martha have not been located. His brother, Leonard (1835-1903), served in Co. B, Bartlett's Battalion, MN Cavalry and Co. I, 5th IA Cavalry.

Robert Graham – Co. H (tr. January 28, 1865)
b. 1837 Berkshire County, MA
d. ? ?
m. ?

NOTE: Little is known about this soldier, except that he was a boatman. It appears he enlisted in the 76th at Rochester, Monroe, NY on August 8, 1863, mustering into Co. G. He transferred to Co. C on October 20, 1864 and to Co. D, November 8th. His muster cards show he spent time in hospitals but the reason is unknown. He was discharged from the 147th at Washington, DC on June 8, 1865. I have located no pension card. Someone named Robert Graham, who died in August 1885, is buried in Mount Hope Cemetery, Rochester, but whether or not this is the identical person is unknown.

Horace Norman Graves – Co. F (tr. January 28, 1865)
b. January 8, 1831 Locke, Cayuga County, NY
d. September 29, 1899 Carleton, Monroe, MI
m. Samantha King (1840-May 27, 1921) May 27, 1855

NOTE: Horace was the son of Charles (?-?) and Lovina Elwell Graves (?-?), both of whom were born in Vermont. His POB is disputed. In 1855 he was said to have been born in Steuben County, while in 1865 it was Tioga County. Cayuga County is found on his muster roll card. He enrolled in the 76th Regiment on July 18, 1863, perhaps as a volunteer, mustering into Co. A. On May 5, 1864 he was wounded in the left leg at the battle of the Wilderness. He transferred to Co. E on October 11, 1864 and to Co. C on November 18th. He was discharged from the 147th at Mower Hospital, Philadelphia, PA on May 27, 1865. He and Samantha, who was only fifteen when she was married, were the parents of four, two of whom were living in 1900. Horace's death was announced in *The Carleton Messenger* October ?, 1899: "After an illness of eight months our highly respected citizen and business man, Horace N. Graves, passed to his eternal rest at his home in Carleton, Friday morning, Sept. 29. Mr. Graves was born at Locke, Cayuga county N. Y. January 8, 1831. After residing in Pennsylvania for fifteen years [he] returned to New York and was married in 1855 at Howard, N. Y. to Miss Samantha King. He was a veteran of the war of the rebellion enlisting in Co. A 76th New York Volunteers in 1863 and served to the close of the war. He was in many battles, being wounded in the battle of the Wilderness. Not many veterans of the war enjoyed a cleaner record than he. [He] came to Michigan in 1871 and resided on a farm in Raisinville township until 12 years ago when he moved here and purchased a nice home on Harris street, and for the past two years has been in the grocery business. For the past three months Mr. Graves has been confined to his room and suffered that pain and anguish of spirit that always accompanies that terrible disease cancer of the stomach, until a few hours before his death, when the Dark Hand in these last hours seem to wave away the ugliness and bitterness of pain, and with a Christian resignation he bade goodbye to the present and turned to the great beyond. No drowsy child fell asleep more gently, peacefully and tenderly in its mother's arms than did he fall asleep in the rich, cool, somber arms of death . . . ." Samantha's COD was also stomach cancer. They are buried in Carleton Cemetery. His government stone refers to his service in the 147th. Hers mistakenly says she died in 1920.

Jeremiah Gray – Co. B (tr. January 28, 1865)
b. 1838 Middletown, Otsego, NY
d. February 1, 1898 Binghamton, Broome, NY
m. Almira "Myra" _____ (1838-January 23, 1931) November 15, 1877

NOTE: Jeremiah, son of David (1797-*post* 1865) and Rhua Bouton Gray (*ca.* 1800-*ca.* 1844), was a boatman. In later life he seems to have used the name Judson. He was drafted, enrolling in the 76th Regiment at Binghamton on July 17, 1863 and mustering into Co. E. He transferred to Co. A on November 18, 1864. From the 147th he transferred to Co. C, 91st Regiment on June 5, 1865, mustering out at Ball's Cross Roads, VA on July 3rd. He and Almira had no children. On February 9, 1921 Almira applied for admission to the Women's Relief Corps Home, Oxford, Chemung County but it is unknown if she actually resided there. In 1930 she was an inmate in the

State Hospital, Binghamton. It is probable she died there since the New York Death Index states she died in Binghamton. She and Jeremiah are buried in Spring Forest Cemetery, Binghamton. His government gravestone refers to his service in the 91st.

Henry G. Green – Co. A (tr. January 28, 1865)
b. 1827 New York State
d. ? ?
m. ?

NOTE: Little can be ascertained about this soldier. His muster roll card for the 76th Regiment says he was born in Livingston County, but that for the 147th claims he was born in Saratoga County. He enrolled in the 76th on July 14, 1863 at Cohocton, Steuben, apparently as a volunteer, mustering into Co. B. He was wounded at the battle of the Wilderness on May 5, 1864, transferred to Co. C on July 1st and then to Co. A on November 8th. He was discharged from McClelland General Hospital, Philadelphia, PA on July 8, 1865 for "disability from wounds" as a member of the 147th even though he had nominally been transferred to Co. C, 91st Regiment. He does not appear in *The Adjutant-General's Report* for that outfit. One of his muster roll cards states he was married and lived in Hume, Allegany, NY. I have located no records to confirm either of these claims. In fact, nothing has been located which can be employed to examine his postwar life. It is quite possible he died shortly after leaving the military.

John Greenwald – Co. C (tr. January 28, 1865)
b. 1817 Wurttemberg, Germany
d. November 29, 1893 Amsterdam, Montgomery, NY
m1. Christine Louisa H. Shoppe (1828-December 18, 1866) *ca.* 1851
m2. ?
m3. Rosa Rousseau Hoeflinger Sherman (1842-*post* 1893) September 15, 1891

NOTE: John's parents are unidentified. Although he claimed to be 35 when he enlisted, he was much older. According to *Registers of Officers and Enlisted Men* he was born in 1813. He enlisted in the 76th Regiment at Cherry Valley, Otsego, NY on November 7, 1861 and mustered into Co. H. He was captured at Bull Run, VA on August 29, 1862. His parole date is unknown. He re-enlisted at Culpeper, VA on January 3, 1864. From the 147th he transferred to Co. H, 91st Regiment on June 5, 1865, mustering out near Washington, DC on July 3rd. He and Christine were the parents of five children, all born in Montgomery County. She is buried in Canajoharie Falls Cemetery. John moved to Carleton, Madison, Mississippi after the war and was enumerated in Madison County in 1870. He applied for a pension there in 1886. By

1891 he had returned to New York State. He married Rosa in Amsterdam. John's unexpected death was reported in *The Amsterdam Daily Democrat* December 1, 1893: "About 10 o'clock yesterday morning, Henry Hugo, of 44 Grand street, accompanied by his little child, was strolling through Green Hill cemetery when he discovered the body of a man hanging from a tree near the Greene monument. Mr. Hugo at once notified Superintendent Sutton of his discovery and he in turn informed Coroner Johnson of the finding of the body. Dr. Johnson at once had the remains cut down and removed to Undertaker Reid's morgue. A number of those who gathered in the cemetery at once identified the body as that of John Greenwald, an old veteran, who lived at 60 Prospect street. When found Greenwald's body was cold and it is probable that he had committed the rash act some time during the night. The body was suspended by a clothes line which had been doubled. The man's toes were within a few inches of the ground. Lying near by was the suicide's coat, neatly folded, and on top of it was his hat. Mr. Greenwald was about 75 years of age and a member in good standing of Post E. S. Young No. 33, G. A. R. He was somewhat addicted to drink and those who saw him on Wednesday afternoon were of the opinion that he was intoxicated. Superintendent Sutton of Green Hill cemetery said to a *Democrat* reporter today that he saw Mr. Geenwald about the cemetery Wednesday morning and he then appeared to be intoxicated. Mr. Greenwald is survived by his third wife together with two sons, William, of this city, and Herman, who resides near Union Mills. Post E. S. Young, G. A. R., will hold a meeting tonight to arrange for the funeral of Comrade Greenwald, which will be held from his late home on Prospect street tomorrow morning at 9 o'clock. The post will attend the services and will send an escort to Canajoharie, where the remains will be taken on the 10:56 train for interment . . . ." He is buried with Christine. I have located no information about a second wife. Rosa, born in Switzerland, first married John Hoeflinger, later corrupted to Hayflinger (1824-*ca.* 1868), as his second wife. By him she was the mother of several children. Hoeflinger served in Co. A, 7th NY ART from January-April 1864 at which time he was discharged for "disability." Her second husband was Peter Sherman (1823-January 13, 1890) by whom she bore several more children. Rose applied for a widow's pension on December 5, 1893 but did not obtain a certificate. No further information has been located about her.

William H. Grems – Co. B (tr. January 28, 1865)
b. March 6, 1841 Utica, Oneida County, NY
d. April 2, 1918 ?
m. Mary Annette "Nettie" Warren (September 9, 1848-May 8, 1927) September 7, 1869

NOTE: William's father is unknown. He first appears on the 1860 census living with his mother, Nancy (1798-*post* 1870) and stepfather Joseph Gamby (1783-*ante* 1870).

A draftee, he enrolled in the 76th Regiment at Utica on August 26, 1863 and mustered into Co. H. He transferred within the regiment several times. He was wounded near Petersburg, VA on June 5, 1864. From the 147th he transferred to Co. G, 91st Regiment on June 5, 1865, mustering out on July 3rd. He and Nettie were married in Chickasaw County, IA. In both 1860 and 1865 Grems was a teacher but in 1900 he said he was a carpenter. He and Nettie were the parents of six, five of whom were living in 1900. His obituary appeared in *The Manchester Democrat-Radio* April 3, 1918, 1: "On Tuesday of this week death summoned from our midst Mr. Wm. Grems, father of Mr. B. W. Grems, our well-known druggist. About three weeks ago Mr. Grems became afflicted with a severe cold, the effects of which, owing to his advanced age, he was unable to throw off. He died Tuesday morning, April 2, at his home on Union street. William F. [*sic*] Grems was born in Utica, New York, on March 6, 1841, and spent the early years of his life there. In 1863 he entered the army and served until the close of the Civil war. After his discharge from military service he came to Fredericksburg, Ia., where on September 9 [*sic*], 1869, he was married to Miss Nettie M. Warren. After spending three years in Nebraska, the couple returned to Fredericksburg, where they continued to make their home until they took up their residence in Manchester about four years ago. Mr. Grems was a contractor and builder, and was highly respected and beloved in the community where he lived so many years. During the more active period of his life he was an enthusiastic member of the G. A. R. . . . The body will be interred in the cemetery at Fredericksburg, where the funeral services will be held." Both William and Nettie, who also died in Manchester, are buried in Rose Hill Cemetery, Fredericksburg. Her COD was heart disease. William's gravestone refers to his time in the 91st Regiment.

Nathaniel Griffin – Co. G (tr. January 28, 1865)
b. 1841 Clinton County, NY
d. ? ?
m. ?

NOTE: Nathaniel's parents are unknown. He was a substitute for James Barrett, Buffalo, Erie, NY when he enrolled in the 76th Regiment at Rochester, Monroe, NY, mustering into Co. G. He was a shoemaker. A note on his muster roll card says he deserted at Mine Run on November 28, 1863 but if so he returned because he was captured at the battle of the Wilderness on May 5, 1864. Date and place of his release are unknown but he transferred from the 147th to Co. F, 91st on June 5, 1865 and mustered out on July 3rd near Washington, DC. I have located no other confirmable evidence about this soldier.

Henry "Harry" Burdette Griffith – Co. K (tr. January 28, 1865)
b. September 5, 1837 Georgetown, Madison, NY
d. April 7, 1915 New Woodstock, Madison, NY
m1. Maranda Hawks (1843-March 29, 1869) *ca.* 1862
m2. Helen E. White (July 30, 1849-October 25, 1910) July 3, 1869

NOTE: Henry, son of John (1807-1896) and Julia Green Griffith (1813-1871), was drafted, enrolling in the 76th Regiment at Oswego, NY on August 5, 1863 and mustering into Co. F. He was captured at the battle of the Wilderness on May 5, 1864 and sent to Andersonville Prison. According to his obituary he was paroled in December 1864 and on January 8, 1865 he transferred to Co. E. He probably spent little actual time with the 147th because, according to his obituary, he was furloughed after being exchanged, returning to parole camp on May 5, 1865. Nevertheless, he was discharged from that regiment on June 9, 1865 near Washington, DC. According to *The Town Clerks' Registers* his health was impaired by the diet and exposure in prison. In 1890 he claimed rheumatism and chronic diarrhea as disabilities. His lengthy obituary appeared in *The Cazenovia Republican* April 15, 1915: "After a prolonged illness of months of suffering, Mr. Griffith of New Woodstock passed away early April 7. Mr. Griffith was born in Georgetown, September 5, 1837, and was in the 78th year of his age. He was the oldest of four children . . . Mr. Griffith married Miranda Hawks of Georgetown. Four children were born to them . . . Mrs. Griffith died in February [*sic*] 1869. Later Mr. Griffith married Miss Helen E. White of Nelson who died in October 1910 . . . Mr. Griffith was one of the few veterans of the Civil war who remain. He enlisted in August 1863 in the 76th New York Volunteers Co. F; was sent to the 147th Regiment Co. K after the battle of the Wilderness, when his company was almost shot to pieces, only 5 or 6 men surviving that sanguinary struggle. He was taken prisoner May 5, 1864, sent to General Lee's headquarters where he remained over night and then remained in Andersonville prison, where he was held a prisoner for seven months and ten days. He was at Andersonville when the seemingly miraculous opening of Providence Spring in answer to prayer was discovered and he recalled the event quite vividly. He was sent to Florence, S. C., and in December 1864 paroled and exchanged the following March, reaching home in Georgetown April 1865. Later he moved to New Woodstock and had lived in that vicinity for forty years, occupying his present home for the last eleven years of his life, where he has been a well-known figure among us. At the funeral services his comrades of the G. A. R. attended in a body and escorted his remains to the grave . . . ." Helen's death occasioned a lengthy obituary in *The Cazenovia Republican* October 27, 1910, 2: "Tuesday afternoon about 4 o'clock long years of patient suffering ended in glorious victory, when the spirit of Mrs. Griffith returned unto the God who gave it to all who knew and loved her. Helen Eliza Griffith was born in the town of Nelson, July 30, 1849, the daughter of Ebenezer and Eliza Deane White. She was the youngest of eight half brothers and sisters. After completing her education at the Morrisville High school, she taught for several years in the district schools and has always maintained an intelligent interest in public school education. When nineteen years of age she found the Savior and united with the Baptist church in Erieville, and the next year, July 3, 1869, was married to Burdette Griffith of Georgetown. Two children blessed this union . . . Mrs. Griffith lived for several years after her marriage in Georgetown, then in 1875 moving to New Woodstock, where she has found her home until her death. On coming to New Woodstock she united with the First Baptist church of Cazenovia and at once manifested her interest in the work of the Christian people. She was at one time president of the Ladies' Aid society and several years conducted a Sunday school class of fifteen young ladies with great success. She lived to see nearly every one of them brought to Christ and become members of his church. She never wearied of talking of 'her girls' nor of praying for their spiritual welfare. Her devotion to the Master's cause is worthy of emulation. To her Christ and his church meant all that was best in this life and the true preparation for the eternal life. Eleven years ago she was taken ill with the disease which has gradually rendered her more and more helpless and since September 1, 1904, has been unable to walk. Our whole community will miss the cheerful face and the smile of greeting always present in the wheel chair. The arrangement of the funeral service was made several years ago by her own thoughtfulness . . . The service was held at her home on Wednesday, October 26th . . . Of her it may truthfully be said, 'Blessed are the dead who die in the Lord. Yea, saith the Spirit, for they rest from their labors and their works do follow them'." Henry and Helen are buried in New Woodstock Cemetery, Cazenovia. Maranda is buried in Georgetown Baptist Cemetery, as are Henry's parents.

John Rue Griggs – Co. B (January 28, 1865)
b. April 10, 1843 Worcester, Otsego, NY
d. April 29, 1924 San Diego, San Diego, CA
m. Mary A. Atkins (August 24, 1843-March 14, 1936) 1866

NOTE: John's parents were James (1801-*post* 1875) and Chloe Robbins Griggs (February 22, 1805-January 14, 1862). He was a carpenter. He enlisted in the 76th at Cherry Valley, Otsego, on October 24, 1861 and mustered into Co. H. He was taken prisoner at Gainesville, VA on August 28, 1862. His parole date is unknown but he was sent to a camp at Alexandria, VA in November 1862 from which he deserted on December 12th. Although he nominally transferred to the 147th he only returned to duty on April 12, 1865 under President Lincoln's Proclamation of March 3rd. By that time, the war was ended. He transferred to Co. G, 91st Regiment on June 5, 1865 and mustered out on July 3rd near Washington, DC. His application for a pension, dated

April 23, 1892, was successful. After the war John and Mary headed west. In 1910 they were living in Lawrence, Douglas, KS. His obituary, published in *The San Diego Union* April 30, 1924, 1, tells the rest of the story: "Following a general collapse, brought on by a fall in February, Maj. John R. Griggs, past commander of Heintzelman post, G. A. R., and prominent in Masonic circles, died at the Naval hospital last night. His home was at 1744 Granada street. Major Griggs was born in New York in 1843. At the outbreak of the Civil war, Major Griggs was 18 years old, enlisted in the 176th [*sic*] New York regiment. At the expiration of his enlistment he re-enlisted and served in the army until after the grand review at Washington in 1865, following which he received an honorable discharge. He came to San Diego in the spring of 1912, and joined the Heintzelman Post. In 1922 he was elected commander. At the expiration of his term, he declined re-election. Last February he fell while taking a walk and broke his leg. Although he recovered from his injury, the shock is said to have brought about the collapse which resulted in his death. Funeral services will be held at the Benbough chapel at 2:30 o'clock Saturday afternoon, under the auspices of Heintzelman post . . . ." He and Mary, the parents of four, are buried in Mount Hope Cemetery, San Diego. His gravestone notices his service in the 91st Regiment. A brother, William P. (1837-1865), served in Co. I, 121st Regiment. He was killed at Hatcher's Run, VA on February 6, 1865. Although he was buried in Virginia, a cenotaph for him can be seen in Maple View Cemetery, East Worcester, where his mother is buried.

Michael Grimes – Co. E (tr. January 28, 1865)
b. 1840 Ireland
d. ? ?
m. ?

NOTE: Little is known about this soldier. A laborer, he enrolled in the 76th on September 19, 1863 at Utica, Oneida, NY as a substitute for Wallace M. Watt, Utica, mustering into Co. I the same day. On February 21, 1864 he transferred to Co. C. From the 147th he went to Co. I, 91st Regiment on June 5, 1865, mustering out near Washington, DC on July 3rd. There the trail ends.

Adrian M. Griswold – Co. G (tr. January 28, 1865)
b. October 1844 Ridgeway, Orleans, NY
d. November 11, 1919 National Soldiers' Home, Bath, Steuben, NY
m1. Sophia _____ Mail (November 1820-October 7, 1906) ?
m2. Lovina Hawley Brown (1844-October 1, 1926) October 27, 1909

NOTE: Adrian, son of Ebenezer Bishop (1813-1893) and Abigail Corser Griswold (1822-1896), was a blacksmith. A substitute for Byron A. Gilbert, Ridgeway, he enrolled in the 76th at Rochester on August 8, 1863, mustering into Co. F. He was wounded on June 19, 1864 at Petersburg, VA and in 1890 said he had been shot through both shoulders. He transferred to Co. D on July 1, 1864. From the 147th he transferred to Co. I, 91st Regiment on June 5, 1865 and mustered out near Washington, DC on July 3rd. Although in 1900 he and Sophia alleged they had been married 40 years, such was not the case. As late as 1880 Adrian was living with his parents. Sophia Mail, who may be the correct person, was living in Lockport, Niagara County in 1880. She had been born in England in 1820 and was a widow. A young man named George Mail, 18, was living with her but since his POB and that of his parents was Canada, he probably was not her son, as alleged in the census record. Moreover, in 1900 Sophia claimed to have had no children. At this time, the best date for their marriage ranges between 1880 and 1892. Lovina, a native of Canada, had previously been married to Robert Brown (1844-1907), also a Canadian. She was the mother of 13, of whom eight were living in 1910. Sophia's grave has not been located. Adrian and Lovina are buried in Hartland Central Cemetery, Hartland. His gravestone erroneously assigns him to the 176th Regiment.

James Henry Grooms – Co. A (tr. January 28, 1865)
b. November 15, 1838 Clifton Park, Saratoga, NY
d. September 30, 1908 Fork, Mecosta, MI
m. Nancy Phenix (May 29, 1842-April 14, 1926) 1869

NOTE: James, son of William (?-?) and perhaps Catherine Grooms Kelly (1809-?), had an extensive military career. He first enlisted in Co. F, 77th Regiment at Ballston, Saratoga on October 14, 1861. He was discharged for "disability" on January 23, 1862 at Washington, DC. On September 3, 1862 he enlisted in the 30th Regiment at Saratoga, mustering into Co. G. On May 25, 1863 he transferred to Co. C, 76th Regiment, then to Co. A on November 6, 1864. According to the muster roll card for the 147th he transferred while "absent, sick." Nevertheless, he transferred to Co. C, 91st Regiment on June 5, 1865. That muster card also says he was "absent, sick" and notes there was no discharge. He does not appear in *The Adjutant-General's Report* for the 91st. In 1890 he reported no disabilities. The enumerator remarked, "papers lost." He obtained a pension, the card for which cites his service in the 77th and the 147th. He and Nancy, who was born in Ohio, had no children. They are buried in East Fork Cemetery, Barryton, Mecosta, MI.

Albert D. Gross – Co. C (tr. January 28, 1865)
b. June 5, 1840 Cherry Valley, Otsego, NY
d. May 14, 1916 Cherry Valley, Otsego, NY
m. Mary J. Foland (August 31, 1842-December 1, 1926) March 8, 1864

NOTE: The son of Dennison (1809-1888) and Christina Hamilton Gross (1807-1888), Albert enlisted in the 76th at Cherry Valley on October 15, 1861 and mustered into Co. H. He was captured at Bull Run, VA on August 29, 1862 and paroled at an unknown date. On January 1, 1864 he re-enlisted at Culpeper, VA and transferred to Co. B on January 1, 1865. From the 147th he transferred to Co. H, 91st Regiment on June 5, 1865, mustering out on July 3rd near Washington, DC. His death was announced in *The Otsego Farmer and Otsego Republican* May 19, 1916, 4: "Albert Gross, a highly esteemed resident of the village of Cherry Valley, and a veteran of the Civil War, died at his home in that village, Sunday, the 14th inst., death caused by heart's disease. Mr. Gross was born in that village on June 5th, 1840. He enlisted for three years on October 15, 1861, in 76th Regiment, Company H, at the expiration of which time he re-enlisted and served until he was honorably discharged at the close of the war. He held one of the most enviable war records of any enlisted man, fought in twenty-eight battles, was color bearer for more than a year and while honored for daring, courage and activity in engagements he never received the slightest wound. He was a very interesting man to engage in conversation on the war, vividly describing the many battles and all incidents in connection with the conflict as it was impressed on his memory, never boasting of the distinguished part he had taken in it. Mr. Gross was a carpenter by trade and for many years was employed by the late Robert Wales and for the past sixteen or seventeen years had been a valued employee of C. J. Armstrong & Sons. He was a remarkably active and industrious man until within the past year when the development of the disease which caused his death gradually laid waste his health . . . Funeral services were held at his late home, Tuesday, the Rev. J. R. Frets officiating . . . ." He and Mary had no children. She was a sister of Alfred Foland (1844-1930), a member of the 76th. Mary applied for admission to the Women's Relief Corps Home in Oxford, Chenango, NY on September 14, 1920 and died there in 1926. She and Albert are buried in Maple Grove Cemetery, Worcester, Otsego, NY.

Joseph Hagerman – Co. B (tr. January 28, 1865)
b. July 5, 1833 Coburg, Germany
d. February 20, 1893 Niagara Falls, Niagara, NY
m. Mary _____ (1848-January 24, 1902) *ca.* 1862

NOTE: This soldier's name was variously spelled. I use that found on his pension card. His parents were Franz (1803-1881) and Maria Dorothea Ackerman Hagerman (*ca.* 1811-1857). Franz and the children immigrated to the United States in 1857. Joseph first enlisted in Co. I, 28th Regiment on April 22, 1861 at Niagara Falls. He was discharged for "disability" at Berlin, MD on August 7, 1861. He next enrolled, apparently as a volunteer, in the 76th at Niagara on July 28, 1863, mustering into Co. E, and transferring to Co. A on November 8, 1864. He was discharged at Elmira, Chemung, NY on June 8, 1865 as a member of the 147th. In 1890 he claimed no disability. He and Mary were the parents of two sons, Charles (1863-?) and Henry (1871-?). According to an unsourced death notice Joseph died at his home of liver trouble. He was a member of Dudley Donnelly Post No. 67 GAR, Lockport/Niagara. He is buried in Oakwood Cemetery, Niagara Falls. Mary's grave has not been located.

Charles Alexander Hamilton, MD – field and staff (tr. January 28, 1865)

b. February 2, 1832 Butler, Wayne, NY
d. January 14, 1900 Washington, DC
m. Abbie Susan Browning (April 28, 1846-July 4, 1912) May 27, 1867

NOTE: Charles was the son of David Rittenhouse (1806-1898) and Mary Hollister Hamilton (1805-1878), both of whom are buried in Butler-Savannah Cemetery. He enlisted in the 76th Regiment in Washington, DC, according to *The Town Clerks' Registers,* on May 7, 1863 as an assistant surgeon. From the 147th he transferred to the 91st Regiment on June 5, 1865, mustering out near Washington, DC on July 3rd. He and Abbie, a native of Michigan, were married in Eaton, Allegan County. They were the parents of two children of whom only Charles Browning (1881-1934) survived. Dr. Hamilton's death was announced in *The Washington Times* January 16, 1900, 4: "The funeral of Dr. Charles A. Hamilton took place yesterday morning from his late residence, 615 Eighth Street northeast. The Rev. Thomas C. Easton was the officiating clergyman. The services at the grave were under the charge of the G. A. R., of which organization the deceased was a prominent member, having been connected with a post at Syracuse, N. Y. The interment was at Arlington National Cemetery. Dr. Hamilton was born in New York city, and at the outbreak of the war enlisted with the Seventy-first [*sic*] New York Volunteers, and later was promoted to assistant surgeon, which position he filled to the close of the war. He later lived at Syracuse and Savannah, N. Y., and removed to this city less than five years ago . . . ." There is no evidence that he ever served in the 71st Regiment. Abbie died in Lynn, Cambridge, MA of heart disease and arteriosclerosis. She is also buried in Arlington.

Dr. Charles Hamilton enlisted in the 76th Regiment in 1863, serving as an assistant surgeon.

Jeffrey Kowalski

Charles Orley Hardy – Co. A (tr. January 28, 1865)
b. June 3, 1841 Steuben County, NY
d. October 11, 1915 Frankfort, Clinton, IN
m. Lucy Margaret Edwards (August 19, 1843-March 10, 1924) September 1, 1867

NOTE: The son of Adrian (1810-1893) and Lavisa Carroll Hardy (1811-1869), Charles was drafted, enrolling in the 76th at Jasper, Steuben County on July 8, 1863 and mustering into Co. E. He was wounded on May 5, 1864 at the battle of the Wilderness and transferred to Co. A on November 18, 1864. From the 147th he transferred to Co. C, 91st Regiment on June 5, 1865, mustering out on July 3rd near Ball's Cross Roads, VA. He and Lucy, sometimes known by her middle name, were married in Clinton County, IN. They were the parents of three, two of whom were living in 1900. Charles and Lucy are buried in Greenlawn Cemetery, Frankfort. Both died of heart disease. A brother, Simon B. (1846-1902), served in the 9th NY HA from February 1864-September 1865.

Charles Hare – Co. B (tr. January 28, 1865)
b. February 1838 Chenango County, NY
d. July 19, 1919 Harpursville, Broome, NY
m1. Betsey Preston (1847-1875) *ca.* 1863
m2. Emma Gene Olds (April 1848-February 20, 1912) 1879

NOTE: Charles, son of Richard (1808-*post* 1892) and Arvilla Hitt Hare (1809-*post* 1875), was drafted. He enrolled in the 76th at Colesville, Broome on July 17, 1863 and mustered into Co. E. He was wounded on May 5, 1864 at the battle of the Wilderness and according to *The Town Clerks' Registers* and the 1890 Veterans' Schedules he was shot in the head. He transferred to Co. A on November 18, 1864. From the 147th he transferred to Co. G, 91st Regiment on June 5, 1865, mustering out on July 3rd near Washington, DC. He and Betsey were the parents of six children and he and Emma produced one more. Charles and his two wives are buried in Riverview Cemetery, Harpursville. A brother, George R. (1836-1864), joined the 16th NY HA in 1864. He transferred to the 85th Regiment on April 10th and reportedly was captured in North Carolina on April 19th. A notation in *The Town Clerks' Registers* states, "Not heard from since." *The Adjutant-General's Report* for the 85th Regiment says he was captured on April 20th at Plymouth, NC and died in Andersonville, GA on July 4th.

David Harpending – Co. G (tr. January 28, 1865)
b. 1848 Tyrone, Schuyler, NY
d. February 4, 1919 Waterloo, Seneca, NY
m. Frances A. Odell (1849-April 19, 1914) November 27, 1867

NOTE: The son of Minor (1812-1875) and Harriet Adams Harpending (1811-1894), David was underage when he enlisted in the 76th Regiment on December 23, 1863 and mustered into Co. D. He remained in that company until transferred to the 147th. From that outfit he transferred to Co. F, 91st on June 5, 1865, mustering out on July 3rd near Washington, DC. In 1890 David claimed rheumatism and chronic diarrhea as disabilities. He and Frances were married in the Waterloo Presbyterian Church, of which they were members. They were the parents of two, only one of whom lived to adulthood. Frances' COD is unknown. David's death notice in *The Rochester Democrat and Chronicle* February 7, 1919 stated he died "following a lingering illness." He and Frances were buried in Maple Grove Cemetery, Waterloo. Three other Harpending brothers served in the Civil War. Alonzo (1838-1904) was a soldier in the 4th PA Cavalry. Emanuel (1842-1908) was a member of Co I, 103rd NY. For information on Marion Harpending, see "Et Cetera Nomina."

Thompson Truxton Hart – hospital steward (tr. January 28, 1865)
b. March 22, 1838 Cayuga County, NY
d. August 9, 1916 Ira, Cayuga, NY
m. Susan Matilda Townsend (1839-March 5, 1906) March 27, 1867

NOTE: Thompson was the son of Nodiah (1801-1880) and Clarissa Dickinson Hart (1800-1882). He was drafted, enrolling in the 76th Regiment at Auburn, Cayuga, NY on July 23, 1863 and mustering into Co. I. He was promoted to the non-commissioned staff on March 16, 1864 as hospital steward. He was discharged near Washington, DC on June 26, 1865 "by reason of being rendered supernumerary" as a member of the 147th Regiment. He and Susan were the parents of six children, four of whom were living in 1900. His death was reported in *The Cato Citizen* August 11, 1916: "The death of Thompson T. Hart occurred at his home, in the town of Ira, Wednesday evening, after a brief illness due to the infirmities of age. Mr. Hart was born on the Hart farm, near this place March 22, 1838, and the most of his life was spent in this section where [he] enjoyed the confidence and esteem of a host of friends. When a boy he united with the Lysander Presbyterian Church and always maintained an active interest in church work. For 15 years he served as superintendent and teacher in the Sunday school and during this period 99 young men received instruction from him. For a period of three years he was principal of one [of] the public schools at Fulton. In 1863 Mr. Hart responded to the call of his country, enlisted and saw much service in the army. In 1867 he was united in marriage to Miss Susan Townsend, whose death occurred in California in 1906, after a residence there of two years. Since that time Mr. Hart spent his winters in California or Florida and the summers here . . . Three of his children were with Mr. Hart when he passed away. The funeral will be held Saturday afternoon at three o'clock with Rev. T. A. Stubbins officiating." Susan's obituary appeared in *The Baldwinsville*

Gazette and Farmer's Journal April 12, 1906, 5: "April 10 – The body of Mrs. Thompson T. Hart who died in California was brought to this place last Sunday, April 8, 1906. The funeral services were held on Monday at her former residence at two p.m. . . . . Susan M. Townsend, wife of Thompson T. Hart and daughter of the late Justus Townsend, died of heart failure at Long Beach, California, on Monday, March 5, 1906. The subject of our sketch was born in the town of Ira, one mile west of Lysander, on Nov. 11, 1840, where she spent her childhood and youth with the exception of an absence of four years in educational work at Mount Holyoke seminary, Mass., from which she graduated. After a short period spent in teaching she was united in marriage in March, 1863 [*sic*], with Thompson T. Hart, son of Col. Nodiah Hart, of Ira. Establishing a pleasant residence a short distance west of her girlhood home, [she] lived [there] up to the time of her departure with her husband to California, which occurred about two years ago, from whence her return had been fondly anticipated by her large circle of friends; but ere she saw again her native hills the culmination of life's possessions had been reached. It would be useless to dwell long upon the capabilities of the deceased, her active social instincts, her tender relation as wife and mother; we will only say she was a living epistle. Her beautiful Christian character and way of being helpful to others endeared her to all. To the church with which she was identified she was ever loyal and with her influence strove always to promote the interests of its purport and mission. Her refuge and strength lay in Him who has opened the way to her wider and better possibilities . . . [she] has gone to solve the problem of the great mystery which separates time from eternity." Thompson and Susan are buried in Lysander Union Cemetery.

John W. Hay - Co. E (tr. January 28, 1865)
b. 1843 Albany County, NY
d. February 16, 1902 Cohoes, NY
m1. Julia A. Settle (1841-November 28, 1881) *ante* 1870
m2. Jane "Jennie" Saxby (1860-September 26, 1926) *ca.* 1884

NOTE: John was the son of John (1815-1892) and Julia Ann Maple Hay (1815-1883), immigrants from Scotland. He enlisted in the 30th Regiment at Watervliet, Albany, NY on September 16, 1862, mustering into Co. D, and transferring to Co. I, 76th on May 25, 1863. He was WIA at the battle of the Wilderness on May 5, 1864 and transferred to Co. C on December 1, 1864. From the 147th he went to Co. I, 91st Regiment on June 5, 1865, mustering out on July 3rd near Washington, DC. He and Julia had no children, making an estimated marriage date impossible. John and Jennie were the parents of a daughter and two sons. When John entered the military he said he was a clerk. In later life he was a merchant. His obituary appeared in *The Troy Daily Times* February 17, 1902, 4: "—John W. Hay, an old resident of Cohoes, died yesterday morning at his home, 159 Congress Street, after a lingering illness. He was a well known man about town, having conducted an express business in Cohoes for a number of years. The deceased was a veteran of the Civil War and a member of Post Lyon, G. A. R. . . . The funeral will be held tomorrow afternoon at 2 o'clock from the late residence. Rev. Dr. John of the Stillman Memorial Church will officiate . . . ." Jennie's obituary, which appeared in *The Troy Times* September 29, 1926, revealed she had been born in England but had lived in Cohoes for 42 years. She, John, Julia, and John's parents are all buried in Waterford Rural Cemetery, Saratoga County. The GAR post mentioned in John's obituary was Nathaniel G. Lyon No. 43, Cohoes.

Aaron Hayward – Co. E (tr. January 28, 1865)
b. May 12, 1843 Turin, Lewis, NY
d. September 30, 1915 Oneonta, Otsego, NY
m. Emogene Owens (December 1852-*post* 1926) May 22, 1869

NOTE: Aaron, son of Aaron (?-?) and Sarah Hollenbeck Hayward (1823-*post* 1844), enlisted in the 76th Regiment at Middleburg, NY on October 28, 1861, mustering into Co. I. He re-enlisted at Culpeper, VA on January 4, 1864, transferring to Co. C on December 1st. From the 147th he transferred to Co. I, 91st on June 5, 1865, mustering out near Washington, DC on July 3rd. He and Emogene were the parents of five children. A notice in *The Otsego Tidings* September 23, 1915 announced that Aaron had been taken to Fox Memorial Hospital the previous week on account of gangrene in one of his feet: ". . . It was thought that it would be necessary to amputate the offending member, but up to date this has not been done. The bone has been scraped and applications to it have been made in the hope that this will relieve the trouble without further treatment." Such was not to be, as *The Otsego Tidings* October 7, 1915 reported: "The remains of Aaron D. Hayward, who died in the Oneonta hospital of gangrene of the leg last Thursday night, were brought here Friday on the 5 o'clock train and taken in charge by S. H. Sherman & Son, undertakers. The funeral was attended at the Presbyterian Church Sunday at 2:30 PM, Rev. N. S. Becker officiating, and interment was in the Milford cemetery. The deceased was a native of Lewis county and came to Milford several years ago to reside with his son, Tracy Hayward. He was a good citizen and gained many friends. He was a veteran of Company I, 91st Regiment, N. Y. S. V. . . . ." Emogene married Ernest Fowler (1850-?) on July 19, 1926. They promptly disappeared from history, perhaps moving out of state.

Joseph Healey – Co. E (tr. January 31, 1865)
b. September 1835 England
d. November 18, 1905 Cohoes, Albany, NY
m. Martha Jane Fowler (January 21, 1836-January 20, 1902) 1854

NOTE: The son of James (1815-?) and an unidentified mother, Joseph was a weaver. The family surname was variously spelled. Joseph enlisted in the 30th Regiment at Cohoes on September 15, 1862, mustering into Co. C, then transferring to Co. I, 76th Regiment on May 25, 1863. He was taken prisoner at Gettysburg on July 1, 1863 and paroled before October. He was again captured at Pegram House on October 1, 1864. According to the 1890 Veterans' Schedules, he was in Salisbury Prison from October 1864 to February 1865, the period when overcrowding, disease and food shortages led to the deaths of many Union soldiers. In February an exchange of prisoners occurred and in April the Union Army burned the prison. Although Healey was a POW when transferred to the 147th his discharge on June 9, 1865 at Arlington Heights, VA was from that unit. He and Martha were the parents of at least four children. In November 1905 Joseph was living in Cohoes. He disappeared on November 18th and despite a wide-reaching search for the next three weeks, during which time his son George offered a $50 reward for information leading to his father's whereabouts, nothing was learned. Finally on December 1st, two men, Henry Shay and John Conway, walking along the towpath of the Erie Canal near Cohoes, spotted the body in the canal between locks 13 and 14. It was visible only because the canal had been drained. The remains were taken to Valatie, Columbia, for burial. A funeral notice was published in *The Chatham Semi-Weekly Courier* December 6, 1905: ". . . The body of Joseph Healey, which was found in the canal lock at Cohoes, was brought here last Friday and buried from the Methodist church on Sunday morning at the time of the regular service, Rev. J. H. Robinson officiating. Mr. Healey was a member of the G. A. R. Post here and the comrades of the Post attended in a body and the burial service of the G. A. R. was read by Commander Saulsbury and Chaplain Wm. H. Schermerhorn. Interment [was] in the family lot in Prospect Hill cemetery." The GAR post mentioned was Thomas M. Burt Post No. 171. Martha and Emma, their daughter, are also buried in Prospect Hill Cemetery.

Christopher Heffron – Co. A (tr. January 31, 1865)
b. 1844 Rensselaer County, NY
d. August 28, 1893 Cohoes, Albany, NY
m. Ellen Keefe (1853-*post* 1910) *ca.* 1870

NOTE: Christopher was the son of Michael (1809-*post* 1875) and Mary Heffron (1813-*post* 1875). Their surname endured many spelling variations. According to the 1855 New York census, Michael and Mary immigrated to the United States and settled New York State in 1843. All their children were born in Rensselaer County. Christopher, a spinner in the garment industry in Cohoes, enlisted in the 30th Regiment at Watervliet on September 10, 1862, mustering into Co. D and transferring to Co. B, 76th on May 25, 1863. He was wounded at Gettysburg on July 1, 1863 and taken prisoner at the battle of the Wilderness on May 5, 1864. Where he was confined and his parole date are unknown. From the 147th he transferred to Co. C, 91st Regiment on June 5, 1865, mustering out near Ball's Cross Roads, VA on July 3rd. In 1890 he claimed he had been shot in the shoulder and suffered from dysentery. In 1900 Ellen said she was the mother of ten, of whom six survived. Graves for these people have not been located.

Christian Heim – Co. E (tr. January 28, 1865)
b. 1838 Germany
d. April 15, 1907 New Scotland, Albany, NY
m. Catherine _____ (May 1832-*post* 1907) 1867

NOTE: Christian, whose parents are unknown, was a blacksmith. At age 16 he traveled alone to the United States aboard the St. Nicolas. On September 22, 1862 he enlisted in the 30th Regiment at Watervliet, NY and mustered into Co. F, transferring to Co. K, 76th Regiment on May 25, 1863. He was wounded at the battle of the Wilderness on May 6, 1864 and in 1890 said he had been shot in the face. He next transferred to Co. I on July 1, 1864 and to Co. C on December 1st. From the 147th he transferred to Co. I, 91st on June 5, 1865, mustering out on July 3rd near Washington, DC. In 1870 he and Catherine were the parents of George, aged 2. In 1900 Catherine claimed one child, surviving, but I have located no other records for him. Christian's DOD was found on a pension payment card. Catherine applied for the pension on June 10, 1907 in New York State and obtained a certificate but beyond that I have located nothing. Christian's gravesite has not been located.

John Hickey – Co. C (tr. January 28, 1865)
b. 1846 Canajoharie, Montgomery, NY
d. ? ?
m. ?

NOTE: John, son of Michael (1800-?) and Margaret Hickey (1806-?), claimed to be 18 when he enlisted, but the 1850 census clearly shows he was only four years old. What happened to his family is unknown, but in 1860 John was living with Jacob and Joan Eckler in Cherry Valley, Otsego where he enlisted in the 76th Regiment on October 14, 1861, mustering into Co. H. He was wounded at Gettysburg but the exact date is unknown. On January 6, 1864 he re-enlisted at Culpeper, VA. His next transfer was to Co. B on January 1, 1865. From the 147th he went to Co. H, 91st Regiment on June 5, 1865, mustering out on July 3rd near Washington, DC. According to *The Town Clerks' Registers* he participated in the battles of Bull Run, Gainesville, Antietam, as well as Gettysburg. He was present at Lee's surrender. His address in the *Registers* was Canajoharie but I have located nothing to corroborate that statement. He apparently did not apply for a pension and he is not on the 1890 Veterans' Schedules.

Barnabas "Barney" Hill – Co. C (tr. January 28, 1865)
b. April 11, 1840 Saratoga County, NY
d. September 26, 1902 Sturbridge, Worcester, MA
m. Hannah Sheridan (1842-March 24, 1911) *ca.* 1865

NOTE: Barney, a spinner, was the son of Alanson (1810-1885) and Harriet Wright Hill (1807-1860). He enlisted in the 30th Regiment at Watervliet, NY on September 16, 1862, mustering into Co. F. He transferred to Co. E, 76th on May 25, 1863. He was wounded in the knee at Gettysburg on July 1st. He transferred to Co. C on November 18, 1864. From the 147th he transferred to Co. H, 91st Regiment on June 5, 1865, mustering out near Ball's Cross Roads, VA on July 3rd. He and Hannah were the parents of three daughters by 1870. In 1875 Hannah was calling herself a widow. Barney "married" Marie/Mary Savary (1858-*post* 1920) on March 10, 1880 in Massachusetts and had four children with her. In 1890 Barney, living in Fiskdale, MA claimed no disability. Hannah, still in Cohoes, claimed to be his widow. Barney entered the National Soldiers' Home, Togus, ME in 1896 and gave the name of A. H. Edgerton as his nearest relative. His stay was brief. Where he was in 1900 is unknown but his three sons were in the Boston Asylum for Indigent Boys. Barney's COD was a gastric hemorrhage. He is buried in North Cemetery, Sturbridge, Worcester, MA. On May 11, 1904 Mary's guardian, Charles H. Bradley, applied for a widow's pension. Evidently Hannah did not know that her husband had died but on December 7, 1907 she too applied, probably after being informed of the contesting widow's claim. She obtained the pension. When Hannah died in 1911, her three daughters, all unmarried, were living with her. Her funeral was conducted at St. Agnes' Church, Cohoes, and she may be buried in St. Agnes' Cemetery. What happened to Mary is unknown. The last notice of her was the 1920 census at which time she was living with one of her sons. Barney's brother, Joseph Ferris Hill (1832-1890), served in the 91st Regiment in 1864-1865.

Daniel J. Hill – Co. B (tr. January 28, 1865)
b. March 2, 1844 Pitcher, Chenango, NY
d. November 29, 1914 National Soldiers' Home, Center, Grant, IN
m. Maria Katerina "Katherine" Hefner (June 23, 1868-April 19, 1919) April 5, 1885

NOTE: Daniel, son of Lewis (1815-1888) and Laura A. Lincoln Hill (1830-1897), enlisted in the 76th Regiment on September 15, 1862 at Pitcher, Chenango, NY, mustering into Co. B. At Gettysburg on July 1, 1863, according to *The Town Clerks' Registers*, he was "badly wounded in both feet." He transferred to Co. C on July 1, 1864 and to Co. A on November 8th. He mustered out on June 7, 1865 at Washington, DC as a member of the 147th. After the war Daniel became a veterinarian. He and Katherine "Kate" were married in Poughkeepsie, Dutchess County. They were the parents of Carrie (1887-1948); Rudolph (1888-1928); Florence (1889-1972); and Clarence (1890-1959). The marriage apparently failed because when Daniel entered the home in Bath, NY in 1900 he gave Carrie as his next of kin. Katherine and the children were enumerated that year in the home of Charles W. Keller, St. Johnsville, Montgomery, NY and she was using his surname. They were still together in 1915 but since she died in Ilion, Herkimer County the relationship had seemingly ended. Daniel's COD was kidney disease. He is buried in Marion National Cemetery. Katherine's gravesite has not been located but since all her children are buried in West St. Johnsville Cemetery, she may be there too. Charles W. Keller committed suicide by shooting himself in the temple on December 15, 1928.

George Bush Hill – Co. F (tr. January 28, 1865)
b. August 24, 1843 South Valley, Cattaraugus, NY
d. June 13, 1915 Emeryville, Alameda, CA
m. Elizabeth Wheeler (February 1853-June 28, 1925) December 17, 1874

NOTE: George was the son of Charles T. (1805-1864) and Margaretta Bush Hill (1807-1884). He enlisted in the 76th Regiment at South Valley on October 15, 1861 and mustered into Co. A. He was wounded at Gettysburg on July 1, 1863. He re-enlisted at Culpeper, VA on January 2, 1864, was wounded a second time at the battle of the Wilderness on May 5th and transferred to Co. D on December 5th. He attained the rank of second lieutenant. From the 147th he went to Co. K, 91st on June 5, 1865, mustering out on July 3rd near Washington, DC. A biography of him appeared in *An Illustrated History of the State of Idaho* (1899), 322-23 which is excerpted here: "George B. Hill, of the extensive mercantile firm of Hill & Ballentine, of Bellevue, is one of Idaho's prominent business men and statesmen . . . George B. Hill was the youngest but one of the eight children of Charles and Margaret (Busch) Hill. He was being educated in the Cherry Valley Academy for boys, when, in 1861, at the age of eighteen, he enlisted in the Seventy-sixth New York Volunteer Infantry, with which he served in the Army of the Potomac, participating in twenty-two hard-fought battles. In the battle in 'the Wilderness,' the boy soldier received a gunshot wound in his foot . . . he returned to his home at Cherry Valley, and in the spring of 1866 went by steamer by way of Graytown to California. After spending a few months in that state, he went to Virginia City, Nevada, where he was employed as a clerk and became deputy recorder of the city. Later he built the Reno water works, and in 1875 organized what was known as the Carson City Savings Bank, of which for seven years he was cashier and general manager. He subsequently returned to California, where he remained until the spring of 1887, when he came to Bellevue, Idaho, and, in part-nership with Colonel Ballentine, opened the extensive general store of which he has since been the head. Originally a stalwart Republican, he came at last to embrace the principles of the Populist party as being most favorable to his ideas of Abraham Lincoln Republicanism; and since 1892 he has been one of the ablest advocates of them in Idaho. He has six times been elected mayor of Bellevue, and was, in 1898, chosen by his party as its candidate for governor of Idaho; but for business reasons he declined the nomination. He has done much effective campaign work, and when he addresses his fellow citizens on political subjects he speaks from deep conviction and with great energy and power. He has frequently been invited by his comrades of the Grand Army of the Republic to the honored post of orator of the day on Decoration Day. He is a Son of the Revolution and fought through the long civil war and shed his blood in defense of the Union . . . It is doubtful whether in all the country any one can surpass him as a Decoration day orator, for it has been said of him that 'his efforts reach the heights of inspired sublimity.' Mr. Hill was married December 17, 1874, to Miss Elizabeth Wheeler, a daughter of M. W. Wheeler, a Mexican war veteran and a California miner of '49, and she is a native of San Jose, California. Their only child, Miss Grace Hill, was educated at the Michigan State Normal School at Ypsilanti and is an enthusiastic young teacher who is destined to make her mark in her profession. Mr. and Mrs. Hill have a beautiful home at Bellevue, where they dispense a generous and far-reaching hospitality." George did not die in Idaho, however, as his obituary in *The San Francisco Chronicle* June 15, 1915, 6 makes clear: "Oakland, June 14. – George B. Hill, who has lived in the West for the past fifty years, died yesterday at his home, 1080 Forty-third street, aged 72. He had been retired for a number of years; but in early days was a banker at Carson, Nev., and was well-known in that state and Idaho. He was a native of Cherry Valley, New York. He served during the Civil War as an officer in the Seventy-sixth New York Regiment. He was also a Mason. He is survived by his widow and one daughter, Mrs. Grace Hill Hershey of Nebraska, who was at his bedside." George and Elizabeth are buried in Mountain View Cemetery, Oakland.

Silas Wright Holt – Co. D (tr. January 28, 1865)
b. May 6, 1847 Troupsburg, Steuben, NY
d. September 24, 1920 Waterloo, Seneca, NY
m. Alzuma A. Palmer (September 28, 1851-June 19, 1940) July 30, 1871

NOTE: Silas was the son of John (1806-1862) and Charlotte Wright Holt (1808-1870). Although underage, he was a substitute for Dalbert Samuels, enrolling in the

76th on August 20, 1863 at Elmira, Chemung County and mustering into Co. H. He transferred within the regiment several times. From the 147th he transferred to Co. B, 91st Regiment on June 5, 1865, mustering out near Washington, DC on July 3rd. The 1890 Veterans' Schedules show he had served in the 21st NY Veterans (?), but this may have been an enumerator's error. He also claimed his heart was affected by his military service. Silas' death was reported in *The Geneva Daily Times* September 25, 1920, 3: "Waterloo, Sept. 25. – Silas Wright Holt, aged 73 years, died at his home, 303 East Williams street, yesterday morning at about 10:30. Deceased had not been feeling well for several weeks but had been up and about as usual . . . The funeral will be held from the residence, Monday, September 27th, the Rev. J. B. Arthur officiating." Alzuma, whose death was announced in *The Geneva Daily Times* June 21, 1940, 2, succumbed "following a long illness." At 88, she was one of the oldest citizens of Waterloo. She and Silas, the parents of four children, are buried in Maple Grove Cemetery, Waterloo.

Washington Irving Honey – Co. E (tr. April 1865)
b. 1836 Washington County, NY
d. May 5, 1889 Auburn, Cayuga, NY
m1. Clarinda Derby (1840-April 16, 1867) April 30, 1856
m2. Margaret _____ (1840-August 5, 1889) *post* 1867

NOTE: This soldier, also known by his middle name, was the son of Peter (1793-1855) and Lorinda Huntington Honey (1795-1887). A substitute for Charles A. Harris, Savannah, NY, he enrolled in the 76th Regiment on July 23, 1863, mustering into Co. F. He was captured on May 5, 1864 at the battle of the Wilderness and confined at Andersonville. His parole date is unknown. He was added to the roll of the 147th as "taken up from missing in action – at parole camp." When transferred to Co. I, 91st Regiment on June 5th he was still in parole camp. He mustered out on July 3rd near Washington, DC. He and Clarinda were the parents of Nellie Grace (1859-1953) and Horace Derby (1861-1940). Clarinda is buried in Poultney Cemetery, Poultney, Rutland, VT. In 1870 Washington and Margaret were the parents of Kate, aged 2. It appears the child died young. Washington's death was briefly but graphically recorded in *The Union Springs Advertiser* May 1889: "W. Irving Honey, an Auburn carpenter, received $700 back pension money a few weeks ago, which he immediately commenced to spend in buying and drinking liquor, from the effects of which he died Sunday week." Margaret, a native of Ireland, died a few months later. She and Washington are buried in Fort Hill Cemetery, Auburn.

Lyman M. Hopkins – Co. F (tr. January 28, 1865)
b. 1822 Otsego County, NY
d. January 30, 1890 North Lansing, Ingham, MI
m. Elizabeth "Betsey" Grimes (February 18, 1823-March 29, 1900) *ca.* 1848

NOTE: Lyman, son of Owen Hopkins (?-?) and an unidentified mother, enlisted in the 76th Regiment at Flemingville, Broome, NY on December 12, 1861 and mustered into Co. D. His military record indicates he was court martialed for desertion in April 1863 and returned to duty in June. On February 10, 1864 he re-enlisted. From the 147th he transferred to Co. F, 91st Regiment on June 5th and mustered out near Washington, DC on July 3rd. In 1860 he and Betsey were living in Candor, Tioga County and were the parents of six children. The family, now including nine children, was living in Henrietta, Jackson, MI in 1870. At some point after that date, Lyman abandoned his wife, moving to Lansing, Ingham, MI. Here he "married" Clara J. Miller and fathered a son, George (1876-?). His death caused quite a stir in the community, as reported in *The Jackson Citizen Patriot* February 14, 1890: "Lyman W. Hopkins, for a number of years a resident of North Lansing, died three weeks ago leaving, as it was supposed, a widow and one son by a former wife. A short time previous to his death he received $500 back pension, and while on his death-bed suggested to his wife that they may be remarried so that her claim to this money and her contemplated application for a widow's pension might not be imperiled by the loss of all evidence of their marriage at the death of the party who married them. Consequently they were so remarried by Justice Clark a few days before Hopkins died. Mrs. Hopkins was aware of her husband's former marriage and of the fact of his having several grown up children, but at the time of their first marriage she was assured by him that his wife was dead, which assertion was reiterated by him on his death-bed. Wednesday, however, a son-in-law of Hopkins, who says he resides in Mecosta, appeared and claimed the estate on behalf of the first wife, whom [sic] he alleges is still living in that county and from whom Hopkins had never been divorced. The Lansing wife had already made application for a widow's pension." According to the marriage records Hopkins married Clara on December 23, 1889. The son-in-law who claimed the estate was Algernon Sidney Glass (1853-1921), husband of Margaret Hopkins (1856-1932). Betsey got the pension. Lyman is buried in Mt. Hope Cemetery, Lansing. In 1895 Clara married Jesse J. Green but it appears the marriage was unsuccessful because by 1900 they were living apart. She and her son George were living in Bay City, Bay, MI. Someone named Jesse Green died on October 9, 1910 in St. Clair County, MI and this may be the man. By 1907 Clara was again using the surname Hopkins. Someone named Clara Hopkins, 73, died in Meridian, Ingham, MI on February 10, 1910. She had previously resided in Lansing and was to be buried there. Her COD was apoplexy and uremic poisoning. Betsey died in Gilmore, Isabella, MI and was buried in Gilmore Cemetery.

Seth F. Horton – Co. H (tr. January 28, 1865)
b. June 28, 1838 Rensselaer County, NY
d. May 23, 1916 Whittemore, Iosco, MI
m. Elizabeth "Betsey" Hornocker (February 2, 1842-October 3, 1914) July 4, 1859

NOTE: The son of Henry F. (1808-1872) and Julia Moore Horton (1815-1870), Seth was drafted, enrolling in the 76th Regiment at Utica, Oneida, NY on August 25, 1863 and mustering into Co. D. He was wounded at the battle of the Wilderness on May 5, 1864 and in 1890 said he had been shot through the left hip. From the 147th he went to Co. F, 91st Regiment on June 5, 1865, mustering out near Washington, DC on July 3rd. He and Betsey, the parents of five, lived in Boonville , Oneida, NY in 1875 but were in Grant, Iosco, MI by 1880. Seth's COD was cancer of the ear and neck. Betsey's was uremia and nephritis. They are buried in Reno Cemetery, Whittemore.

Thomas Goldsmith Horton – Co. F (tr. January 28, 1865)
b. 1829 Vinton, Athens, OH
d. April 23, 1897 Morton, Mecosta, MI
m. Lucy P. Prentiss (July 31, 1840-January 3, 1914) September 24, 1858

NOTE: Thomas, son of Daniel Moore (1792-1837) and Anna Kimble Horton (1795-1846), was a substitute for William King, enrolling in the 76th on July 16, 1863 and mustering into Co. E. He was wounded at Petersburg, VA on June 22, 1864 and in 1890 said he had been wounded in the breast and left shoulder. He transferred to Co. C on November 18, 1864 and was discharged from the army as of the 147th on June 14, 1865 at Elmira, Chemung, NY. He and Lucy, who was born in Illinois, were married in Tioga, PA. They were the parents of 12 children, nine of whom were living in 1910. The couple's biography appeared in *Portrait and Biographical Album, Mecosta County, Mich.*, 522: ". . . Mr. Horton was married Sept. 24, 1858 to Lucy Prentiss, of Cameron, Steuben Co., N. Y. She was born in Sycamore, De Kalb Co., Ill., and has been the mother of 11 children . . . On his marriage Mr. Horton located in Bath, Steuben Co., N. Y., and removed to Millbrook, Mecosta Co., Mich. where he settled June 7, 1866. He removed to Sheridan in November 1869, and has since been a citizen of that township. He is a Republican in politics, and has been Township Treasurer two terms (1881-2); was Supervisor in 1876, and has served two terms as Justice of the Peace. Mr. Horton served as a soldier in the late war . . . He was wounded June 16, 1864 [*sic*] at the battle in front of Petersburg, while in the act of storming, and was in the hospital one year, receiving his discharge June 14, 1865, at the close of the war." Daniel's COD was rheumatism. Lucy died from *la grippe*. They are buried in Hope Cemetery, Mecosta, MI.

Charles House – Co. B (tr. January 28, 1865)
b. 1840 Burlington, Otsego, NY
d. January 16, 1906 Monticello, Otsego, NY
m1. LaVerne Hungerford (1842-*post* 1880) 1861
m2. Margaret "Maggie" Agnes Hickey (*ca.* 1844-July 12, 1910) April 5, 1864

NOTE: Charles was the son of John (1811-*post* 1880) and Cornelia Vander Walker House (1813-1880). His DOB varies from census to census. He enlisted in the 76th Regiment at Cooperstown, Otsego, NY on November 14, 1861, mustering into Co. K. He re-enlisted on January 5, 1864 and transferred to Co. H on May 3rd. He was WIA on June 18, 1864 at Petersburg, VA and in 1890 said he had a broken right knee. Apparently he fell into a ditch during the night while working on the fortifications. On January 1, 1865 he transferred to Co. B. From the 147th he transferred to Co. G, 91st Regiment, mustering out on July 3rd near Washington, DC. He and Julia were married at Exeter Center, Otsego County. They had no children. Charles applied for a pension in 1886 and upon his death from heart disease a struggle between Maggie and the woman with whom he had lived since 1866, Julia Darby (1844-January 12, 1924), commenced. According to a deposition given by Rev. William M. Brown, dated September 24, 1907, Rev. Lewis Hipple married Charles and Margaret Hickey at Canajoharie, Montgomery, NY on April 5, 1864. During the investigation, however, it was revealed that Charles had married LaVerne shortly before going off to war. They never lived together again. Around 1867 she married William Henry Sickler (1845-*post* 1880) and had several children by him. Nevertheless, in the eyes of the law, she was Charles' legal wife. Maggie alleged she had never heard of Laverne before the inquiry began and Julia readily admitted she and Charles had talked about marriage but he had told her it was impossible because Maggie would "have the law" after him. In the end, neither woman obtained the pension. Charles, who succumbed to heart disease, is buried in Twilight Rest Cemetery, Monticello. LaVerne is buried in Fly Creek Valley Cemetery, Otsego, NY with her parents, William (1814-1877) and Sarah Ann Osterhout Hungerford (1820-1904). Her grave is marked with a stone which merely says "LaVerne." Julia's obituary, published in *The Richfield Springs Mercury* January 17, 1924, stated she was to be buried in Monticello and it is possible she is buried in Twilight Rest with Charles. Maggie's grave has not been located.

Jesse W. Howe – Co. G (tr. January 28, 1865)
b. June 27, 1836 Phoenix Mills, Otsego, NY
d. November 21, 1917 Oneonta, Otsego, NY
m. Elizabeth Slackford (October 1837-November 20, 1920) August 1855

NOTE: Jesse, son of Daniel T. (1813-1864) and Keziah Finch Howe (1815-1880), saw his first military service in the 34th Regiment, enlisting at Herkimer on May 10, 1861 and mustering into Co. I. He was discharged for "disability" at Seneca Mills, MD on August 14th. He next enlisted in the 76th Regiment at Cherry Valley, Otsego, NY on November 17, 1861, mustering into Co. H. He re-enlisted at Culpeper, VA on January 3, 1864. He was wounded at the battle of the Wilderness on May 5th and in 1890 said he had been shot in the right thigh. From the 147th he went to the VRC but was unassigned. He was discharged on September 29, 1865 at Elmira, NY. Jesse's death was reported in *The Amsterdam Evening Recorder* April 23, 1917: "Jesse W. Howe, a veteran of the Civil war who was hit by an automobile driven by C. B. Dibble of Hobart at the corner of Main and Elm streets in Oneonta, November 14, died at his home, 24 Columbia street, in that city, Wednesday afternoon, as a result of his injuries. Mr. Howe, a retired butcher, who had at one time also worked as a carpenter, was 82 years of age. He was born June 29, 1835, at Phoenix, but lived at Cherry Valley until he went to Oneonta 20 years ago. He was married in August, 1855, to Elizabeth Slackford of Cherry Valley and had eleven children, eight of whom survive him. Mrs. Howe, now 81 years of age, also survives him. It was only last August that Mr. and Mrs. Howe celebrated their sixty-second wedding anniversary with their family at the home in Oneonta . . . When the Civil war broke out, Mr. Howe enlisted with his four brothers. He fought all through the struggle as a member of Company H 76th N. Y. regiment, seeing action at the Battle of the Wilderness and at Gettysburg. At the battle of the Wilderness he was shot through the hip. Mr. Howe was a member of the Methodist Episcopal church of Oneonta and of the Grand Army." Jesse's DOB varies. He reportedly is buried in Walton Cemetery, Walton, Delaware, NY. Elizabeth's grave has not been located. The brothers mentioned in the obituary were Henry (1843-1923), who served in Co H, 76th, was wounded at the battle of the Wilderness on May 5, 1864, and discharged on July 22, 1864; Joseph Barrett (1838-1863), a member of the 121st NY Regiment, who was wounded at Salem Heights on May 3, 1863 and died of his wounds and pyemia at Harewood General Hospital, Washington, DC on May 23, 1863; and Solomon, for whom, see below.

Solomon Clark Howe – Co. C (tr. January 28, 1865)
b. September 29, 1842 Cherry Valley, Otsego, NY
d. July 8, 1887 Delevan, Cattaraugus, NY
m. Almantha Achsa Ferrin (November 22, 1842-October 15, 1913) *ca.* 1866

NOTE: Solomon, Jesse's brother, enlisted in the 76th Regiment at Cherry Valley on November 22, 1861 and mustered into Co. H. He was wounded at Fredericksburg, VA on December 13, 1862. He re-enlisted on January 3, 1864 at Culpeper, VA and was transferred to Co. B on January 1, 1865. From the 147th he went to Co. H, 91st Regiment on June 5, 1865, mustering out near Washington, DC on July 3rd. According to *The Town Clerks' Registers* he had participated "in about thirty battles." Solomon was a carpenter. He and Almantha, who had been born in Erie County, NY, were the parents of one child, Chester Dennison (1868-1928), a mail carrier. Almantha moved to Chicago to live with Chester and his family and died there. She and Solomon are buried in Delevan Cemetery. Her DOD is not provided on the gravestone.

Charles Howell – Co. F (tr. January 28, 1865)
b. November 2, 1838 Ancaster, Hamilton, Ontario, Canada
d. October 22, 1921 Charleston, Kanawha, WV
m. Frances "Fanny" Taylor (August 10, 1843-January 6, 1922) July 4, 1863

NOTE: Although this soldier claimed his first name was Charles, in later life he used Clark and that seemingly was correct, as indicated by his baptismal record. He was the son of Moses Hazen (1799-1879) and Deborah Wilson Howell (1801-1870) and was one of 12 siblings. He was a substitute for Frank Rassel of Buffalo and enrolled in the 76th Regiment in that city on August 8, 1863, mustering into Co. E. He transferred to Co. C on November 18, 1864. There is no evidence that he was wounded but when transferred to the 147th he was "absent, sick" and when transferred to Co. A, 91st Regiment on June 5, 1865 he was "in hospital." The muster card for the 91st contains a notation that he was discharged for "impaired health 1865 at Ithaca." The exact date is unknown but he does not appear in *The Adjutant-General's Report* for that regiment. I have not located a pension card for him and he does not appear on the 1890 Veterans' Schedules. Clark was still using the name Charles when the 1870 census was taken in Buffalo. He reported he was a clerk. By 1880 the family had moved to Wolf Creek, Monroe, WV. His occupation now was mechanical engineer and he was called Clark. The 1920 Charleston city directory showed that he and his only surviving son, Ernest (1870-1955), were the officers of the Capital City Supply Co., a firm specializing in groceries. The 1920 census revealed Clark had immigrated to the United States in 1862 and had been naturalized in 1868. Frances, a native of Ireland, arrived in 1855 and had also been naturalized. Clark and Frances are buried in Sunset Memorial Park, S. Charleston.

William LeRoy Hoyt – Co. I (tr. January 28, 1865)
b. February 29, 1840 Springfield, Otsego, NY
d. July 25, 1913 Deposit, Delaware, NY
m. Virginia "Jennie" Sively (January 19, 1850-July 18, 1930) July 4, 1869

NOTE: The son of Reuben (1811-1888) and Asenath Spafford Hoyt (1812-1889), William enlisted in the 76th Regiment on November 5, 1861, mustering into Co. H. He was captured at Bull Run on August 29, 1862 and paroled at an unknown date. He re-enlisted at Culpeper, VA on January 25, 1864. On January 1, 1865 he transferred to Co. B. Although nominally transferred to Co. I, 91st Regiment he was discharged "as of" the 147th on June 9, 1865 at Arlington, VA. His pension cards indicate he had also served in Co. A, 39th Regiment but his name does not appear in *The Adjutant-General's Report* for that organization. He and Jennie were married in Fulton County, IL. They were the parents of eight children, all alive in 1900. William died while visiting his sister. He and Jennie are buried in Ellisville Cemetery, Fulton, IL.

William Harvey "Bill Huggins" Hungerford – Co. H (tr. January 28, 1865)
b. 1842 Granby, NY
d. November 5, 1915 Clyde, Wayne, NY
m1. Sarah Mudge (?-September 19, 1871) ca. 1866
m2. Sarah Lovina Deacons (July 3, 1868-April 18, 1954) December 11, 1886

NOTE: Much of William's early life is shrouded in mystery, partially because of conflicting information he himself provided. His parents were Daniel (?-?) and Anna Bell Deacons Hungerford (?-March 1845). Daniel apparently had several wives and it was rumored in the family that he murdered them. William's aunt Hannah Deacons Carjonelle testified that after administering poison to Anna Bell the old man held the baby to his mother's breast to suck the dead woman's milk, apparently in an attempt to kill him too. William alleged he had two siblings, Jabel (?-?) and Isaac (?-?), but his aunt Hannah said Anna Bell had only two children, George (?-?), who died at age three, and William. Even his DOB is a matter of dispute. Although many records point to a birth date of 1842, William stated the family Bible noted he was born on March 10, 1838. If that is true, however, he could not have been a baby when his father put him to his dead mother's breast in 1845. When completing a questionnaire for the Pension Bureau in 1903, he gave his DOB as March 10, 1845. Should that be true, his mother could not have died, as he alleged, on March 3, 1845. In 1860, while living with George and Mary Deacons in Hannibal, NY, William's age was 15, which leads to the conclusion that he had indeed been born in 1845. Hungerford also alleged that he had become a sailor when he was about 12 years old but his census record for 1860 gives the lie to that statement. On September 22, 1861 he enrolled in the 50th NY Engineers, the same outfit his aunt Hannah's second husband, Norman Carjonelle, had joined a month earlier, at Fulton, NY. He does not, however, appear in *The Adjutant-General's Report* for that organization. He deserted from the 50th on January 6, 1863 because he alleged the officers treated him badly. On August 19, 1863, he enrolled in the 76th Regiment at Oswego City, mustering into Co. I as a substitute for Alonzo Dingman, receiving $300 from him and another $300 bounty. He was wounded on August 21, 1864 at the battle of Weldon Railroad. In September he was sent home on furlough. When he did not return on time he was charged with desertion. He transferred to Co. C on December 1st and from the 147th he transferred to Co. F, 91st Regiment on June 5, 1865. He mustered out near Washington, DC on July 3rd although in later years he alleged he had never served in either the 147th or the 91st. In 1889 the charge of desertion from the 76th Regiment was reduced to AWOL. He applied for and obtained a pension in 1890 and renewed it in 1908. The problems began when the Pension Bureau discovered he had deserted from the 50th Engineers. Even though his tenure in the 76th was finally deemed "faithful," he was still considered a deserter and all subsequent service counted for nothing. Numerous attempts to be reinstated failed. A somewhat imaginative obituary appeared in *The Clyde Herald* November 10, 1915, 7: "William Hungerford, a veteran of the Civil war, died at his home on the South Side of the village last Thursday. He was born in Fulton in 1842, but had spent the greater part of his life in Clyde. He enlisted in Oswego, when 21 years old, in the 76th New York Infantry. In January 1865, he was transferred to the 147th Regiment and was discharged June 5, 1865. He leaves a wife. Funeral services were held at Collier's Undertaking rooms at 2 o'clock Monday afternoon, Rev. F. B. Dovall officiating." William is buried in Maple Grove Cemetery, Clyde. Little is known about Sarah Mudge. Hungerford claimed at one point to have married her in 1857 but more likely the couple married in 1866. In 1898, when responding to a Pension Bureau questionnaire, Hungerford revealed his son, Charles Edward, had been born in 1867, and his daughter, Rosa Lovina, on April 7, 1868. He also claimed that Sarah Mudge died while he was out west prospecting. He first stated she died in 1871 but later alleged she died on July 19, 1875 and had been buried in Williams Cemetery, located near Fulton. This cemetery has not been located. I have been unable to trace Charles or Rosa. Late in life their father admitted he had not heard from them in years. Sarah Deacons' early life is also a mystery, beginning with her parents. Hannah said that she, Anna Bell, and Sarah's father were siblings. Efforts to find corroboration for that statement have proved fruitless but because Sarah herself testified in her widow's pension application that she and Hungerford were first cousins, the relationship must be true. It is possible that George W. (1820-1868) and Lucinda Hall Deacons (1822-1896) were her parents. Sarah testified she had been born in Hannibal, NY and in 1865 these people and their seven children were indeed residing there. By 1870, however, the family had moved to Michigan, as evidenced by the census, marriage, and death records pertaining to members of the family. It is possible that Sarah's earlier claim that she was born in 1866 was correct since George W. died in 1868. When Sarah applied for a widow's pension she said that although she and William were first cousins she did not meet him until he came to visit her aunt, Hannah Carjonelle, with whom Sarah was living at the time. She further testified she only knew him about a week when they got married. Why she married him remains a mystery. William had no particular career. When he enlisted in the 76th he said he was a boatman. On other census forms he claimed to be a laborer. In 1880 he had no occupation. In 1902 both of them were admitted to the Cayuga County Poorhouse. He was described as a "cripple." He had received aid from the GAR. By 1905 they were back in their home in Clyde. Sarah applied for a widow's pension on November 13, 1915. What follows is the rest of the story, as reported in *The Syracuse Herald* April 15, 1916: "Clyde, April 15. – Crossing the canal through water and mud that nearly reached her waist, Mrs. William H. Hungerford, 60, left this village Wednesday and has not been seen or heard from since. She rung [*sic*] her clothes after she reached the opposite side of the canal and disappeared. She carried a satchel. Asked where she was going she answered, 'Illinois.' Knowing

William Hungerford's was one of the most mystifying, intriguing lives of all the men who served in the 76th Regiment.
Robert Byrnes (FAG)

that Mrs. Hungerford did not have money to take her to Illinois, friends here have become greatly concerned over her fate and have informed the neighborhood of her strange action in the hope of finding her nearby. Mrs. Hungerford's strange disappearance is regarded here as the result of mental derangement following the death of her husband on November 5th. Though her husband was a Civil war veteran Mrs. Hungerford could not get a pension because it was discovered that he deserted from the army before the war was over. Friends interceding on her behalf represented her needy condition to the government but without success. It is believed Mrs. Hungerford planned her departure in the belief she could better her condition elsewhere. She has been in poor health and this is believed to have added to her worries. She was last seen on Ford street. She would not stop to talk with friends who asked where she was going. Later she was seen walking along the bank of the canal about a mile east of the village. She started east and that was the last seen of her in this section." What happened to Sarah between 1916 and 1919 is unknown but in 1920 she was an inmate in the Willard State Hospital at Ovid, Seneca County.

She was still there in 1925. She died in Marcy State Hospital, Oneida County, NY of arteriosclerosis and was buried in Mt. Adnah Cemetery, Fulton.

Andrew Jackson – Co. G (tr. January 28, 1865)
b. January 1841 New Berlin, Chenango, NY
d. May 11, 1904 Pharsalia, Chenango, NY
m. Maria Monroe (1849-April 27, 1920) 1867

NOTE: Andrew, son of Malone T. (1794-1866) and Rebecca Jackson (1800-1868), was drafted. He enrolled in the 76th on September 1, 1863 and mustered into Co. G the same day. He transferred to Co. D on October 20, 1864. From the 147th he transferred to Co. F, 91st on June 5, 1865, mustering out near Washington, DC on July 3rd. Andrew was a member of J. E. Parce Post No. 456 GAR. He and Maria were the parents of six, all living in 1900. While Andrew died at home, Maria died at the home of one of her daughters in South Otselic. According to an obituary published in *The DeRuyter Gleaner* May 6, 1920, 2, she "had been in poor health for some time." Maria and Andrew are buried in Pharsalia Center Cemetery.

James Jamieson – Co. G (tr. January 28, 1865)
b. 1821 Scotland
d. ? ?
m. ?

NOTE: Very little can be ascertained about this soldier's life prior to enrolling into the military. According to the 1860 census for Utica, Oneida, NY a man fitting James' description was an inmate in the Utica Insane Asylum. He was a weaver. When Jamieson enrolled in the 76th on September 15, 1863 he was a substitute for Robert J. Ward of Rome, mustering into Co. D. His occupation was gardening. A brief entry in *The Town Clerks' Registers* reveals he collected $1500 in bounties from the town and the county. This note also erroneously states he was born in 1842! He was wounded at the battle of the Wilderness on May 6, 1864 and spent time in hospital. He was discharged at Washington, DC on June 16, 1865 as a member of the 147th. That is the last verifiable reference to him.

William Johnson – Co. A (tr. January 28, 1865)
b. 1825 Ireland
d. *post* 1894 ?
m. ?

NOTE: William's antecedents are unknown. His age on the muster roll card has been misread as 30 instead of 38. He was a substitute for Benjamin S. Tupper of Buffalo,

Erie, NY and he enrolled in the 76th on August 7, 1863 in that city, mustering into Co. A. A notation of the October 1863 muster roll states that he was under arrest and awaiting sentencing for desertion. Another notation states: "Sentenced by Gen'l Court Martial to work on Government fortifications and to forfeit all pay and bounty due, or to become due, except the dues of sutler or laundress during unexpired term of enlistment." That sentence, however, seems to have been overturned because he transferred to the 147th and subsequently to Co. C, 91st Regiment. His transfer date to the 91st was June 5th and he mustered out on July 3rd near Ball's Cross Roads, VA. He does not appear on the 1890 Veterans' Schedules but applied for a pension on October 6, 1894. He did not obtain the pension but an unnamed widow did. It is possible he died before the process was completed. Had he been denied on account of his short-lived desertion, his widow probably would not have been eligible.

John Joyce – Co. F (tr. January 28, 1865)
b. 1813 Ireland
d. January 15, 1891 Ithaca, Tompkins, NY
m. Frances "Fannie" _____ (1813-February 6, 1910) *ca.* 1838

NOTE: John's parents are unknown. A shoemaker, he was a substitute for Garnett Dolan, Batavia, and enrolled in the 76th Regiment on July 28, 1863 at Niagara, NY, mustering into Co. B. Although he alleged he was born in 1819, other records prove that was untrue. He was captured at the battle of the Wilderness on May 5, 1864. His place of imprisonment and date of parole are unknown but he was considered a "paroled prisoner" when transferred to the 147th. At some point he was transferred to Co. B, 76th Regiment but it was probably when he was a prisoner. He was discharged near Washington, DC on June 3, 1865 as a member of the 147th. He and Frances lived for many years in Lockport and were the parents of five children. They were last enumerated together in 1870. By 1875 he was gone and she was working as a domestic in a private home and calling herself a widow. That he abandoned her is made eminently clear by her obituary which is quoted below. In fact, John went to Ithaca, Tompkins County where he established a household and lived with another woman, as yet unidentified. He never applied for a pension and he was not included on the 1890 Veterans' Schedules. He came to a gruesome end, as described in *The Ithaca Daily Journal* January 16, 1891: "The wisdom of the municipal ordinance prohibiting coasting in the corporate limits, and the folly of not enforcing the same, received a sad and forcible illustration in the first ward last night, when an old man was killed by a coaster. The victim of the lamentable accident was John Joyce, an aged laborer, who lived in one of the small houses in Grant row on Cliff street. Joyce came down town yesterday afternoon to obtain some provisions and started to return home about six o'clock last evening. Boys were coasting on the steep hill in front of the school house and their sleds obtained such great momentum that they would cross the street at the foot of the descent and passing over the sidewalk run far out into the vacant lot bordering the highway at that point. As Mr. Joyce, who was very deaf as well as feeble, was making his way along the sidewalk a boy of about fourteen, son of Patrick Hennessy, came down on a small sled called a 'scoop' and struck the old man. He was thrown into the air and fell heavily on his head, striking [illegible]. He lay motionless where he fell, and though still alive it was seen that he had received a dangerous injury. He was taken to his home up the hill where he died shortly before 8 o'clock. He did not recover consciousness after being hurt. The funeral of the victim of this needless accident will take place Saturday afternoon at 2 o'clock. Mr. Joyce leaves a widow who is in very feeble health who with her husband has been supported by the public. She will now have to be removed to the alms house as there is no one left at her squalid home to care for her . . . ." John was given a "simple funeral" but where he was buried is unknown. The "widow" was alive in March 1892 when her attorney sued the town poor master to force him to support her. Frances was named administrator of John's estate and in papers filed in Lockport in November 1891 her son-in-law, George Penfold, was named one of the appraisers. Frances died in Buffalo, as revealed in an obituary appearing in *The Buffalo Express* February 7, 1910: "Mrs. Frances Joyce, 97 years old, died yesterday at her home in the La Salle apartments, Georgia and Chippewa streets. Until a few days ago, when she was slightly injured in a fall in her home, she had enjoyed perfect health. Mrs. Joyce was born in Vermont and moved to Lewiston with her family when a girl. After living there for many years, she went to Lockport to make her home with her son-in-law George Penfold; upon his death seven years ago, she came to Buffalo to make her home with her granddaughter, Mrs. George W. Pound, with whom she was living at the time of her death. During the early years of her life Mrs. Joyce was interested in charitable work and devoted much time to it . . . The funeral will be held from Mrs. Pound's home and burial will be in Lockport." She is buried in Glenwood Cemetery, Lockport.

Horace Kenney – Co. I (tr. January 28, 1865)
b. 1829 Northampton, Fulton, NY
d. March 20, 1890 Mayfield, Fulton, NY
m. Elbertine Hogeboom (1830-September 14, 1894) *ca.* 1861

NOTE: Horace was the son of Theodore (1809-September 8, 1883) and Lovina Houseman Kenney (1802-September 7, 1883). The family name was spelled Kinney at times. He enlisted in the 30th Regiment at Saratoga, NY on August 31, 1862 and mustered into Co. G. On May 25, 1863 he transferred to Co. C, 76th Regiment, transferring to Co. A on November 8, 1864. From the 147th he went to Co. I, 91st Regiment on June 5th, mustering out near Washington, DC on July 3rd. It is interesting to note that Elbertine told the enumerator for the 1890 Veterans' Schedules that her husband had served in Co. D, 93rd Regiment. Horace and Elbertine were the parents of Sarah (1862-April 27, 1920). They also adopted a child, Arthur (1879-1944). Horace and Elbertine are buried in King Cemetery, Northampton, as are his parents.

Charles King – Co. A (tr. January 28, 1865)
b. 1841 Canada
d. June 1, 1922 Oswego City, NY
m. ------

NOTE: Although Charles claimed to have been born in 1838 when he enrolled in the army, all other documents point to a DOB of 1841. He was the son of Charles (1813-1885) and Matilda King (1823-1889). He enrolled in the 76th at Utica on September 21, 1863 and mustered into Co. C, but it is unknown whether he volunteered or was drafted. He was wounded in action at Spotsylvania, VA on May 10, 1864 and apparently spent considerable time in hospital, although in 1890 he claimed no disability. He transferred to Co. A on November 8, 1864 but was "absent, wounded" when transferred to the 147th. His muster card for the 91st Regiment says, "absent, sick; no discharge." Apparently he simply walked away. This theory is borne out by his application for a pension in 1889. It was rejected. As a young man Charles was a boatman but in later life he spent much time in the Oswego City Alms House. He was described as unfit for work. The application form for 1911 stated he had lived in the United States for 58 years and was a naturalized citizen. He was buried in St. Peter's Catholic Cemetery, Oswego City.

Samuel Kipp – Co. H (tr. January 28, 1865)
b. September 25, 1836 Union, Broome, NY
d. November 15, 1892 Endicott, Broome, NY
m. Mary J. Eldridge (1842-*ca.* 1878) *ca.* 1866

NOTE: Samuel, a draftee, was the son of Simeon (1808-1890) and Catherine Baylis Kipp (1811-1899). He enrolled in the 76th at Union on July 17, 1863 and mustered into Co. D. He was wounded in the right arm on June 20, 1864 at Petersburg, VA. His time in the 147th was brief since he transferred to Co. B, 10th Regiment VRC on March 16, 1865 and was discharged at Washington, DC on July 22, 1865. He and Mary were the parents of Carleton (1867-1952); Nelson (1870-1927); and Nellie (June 1878-1953). Mary last appears on the 1875 New York census. In 1880 Samuel was widowed. It is possible that she died during or shortly after giving birth to Nellie. Mary's grave has not been located. Three of Samuel's brothers also participated in the

Civil War. Lewis/Louis (1837-1863) served in Co. D, 76th Regiment and died of ty-phoid fever at Culpeper, VA on November 18, 1863. Edwin (1840-1862) was a member of Co. I, 50th NY Engineers when he died at White House Landing, VA on June 10, 1862 of "disease." Seymour (1845-August 19, 1897) was a member of Co. G, 15th NY Engineers. Edwin and Lewis were buried in Virginia. Samuel, Carleton, Nelson, Simeon, Catherine, and Seymour are all buried in Riverside Cemetery, Endicott. Cenotaphs for Edwin and Lewis may also be seen there.

Michael Kirchner - Co. E (tr. January 28, 1865)
b. June 23, 1843 Darmstadt, Germany
d. November 24, 1865 Buffalo, Erie, NY
m. ------

NOTE: Michael, whose family name was variously spelled, was the son of Adam (1804-*post* 1870) and Maria Kirchner (1810-1861). A substitute for William Volk, he enrolled in the 76th Regiment on August 7, 1863 in Buffalo, mustering into Co. I. He transferred to Co. C on December 1, 1864. From the 147th he went to Co. I, 91st Regiment on June 5, 1865, mustering out on July 3rd near Washington, DC. On September 29, 1865 Kirchner allegedly murdered Henry Henning, a soldier stationed at Fort Porter, Buffalo, with a rock in order to rob him of $100. The case went to trial on October 10th and two days later he was convicted and sentenced to hang on November 24th. Kirchner protested his innocence until the last. A lengthy article in *The Buffalo Evening Courier and Republic* November 24, 1865 contains not only a biography of the young man but excerpts from an interview he gave a reporter the day of his execution, as well as a description of the man's last moments: ". . . Kierchner [*sic*] with his black dress and cap, the rope around his neck, took his seat between his spiritual advisers, and immediately in the rear of the trap which was to launch him into eternity. In the back ground were Sexton Pierce and his assistants. Matters being composed, Kierchner was permitted to address the assemblage and did so at length in a bold, rambling speech, in which, if there was any sympathy in the crowd for him, it must have been crushed out. The speech was as cold blooded and heartless as the murder for which he stood on the gallows . . . He maintained his innocence firmly, talked of dying a game Dutchman, and complained of the unfairness of his trial. He repeatedly asserted his innocence, recited the history of his service in the field, and used language which illy became a dying man . . . While yet Kierchner sat in his chair, the rope was taken from his bosom, and passed through the loop of the cross bar of the gallows. While this was being done Kierchner exclaimed, 'Watch that Dutchman die.' The rope being fastened, and the knot adjusted the convict was assisted to his feet and towards the platform. Here he essayed some remarks, when Sexton Pierce dropped his handkerchief at the feet of the Sheriff, and in an instant the rope was cut the platform dropped, and Kierchner was swung into eternity . . . The body was cut down afterwards and passed over to the friends of deceased, and thus ended the career of Michael Kierchner." The question of Kirchner's guilt or innocence aside, he may have had some justification for his allegation that the trial had been hastily scheduled and he made a scapegoat because he was foreign born. Indeed, the jury deliberated for only two and a half hours before reaching a verdict. A reporter wrote in the article announcing his conviction which was published in *The Buffalo Evening Courier and Republic* October 12, 1865 that he possessed an "evident preponderance of the animal over the mental faculties or the moral sentiments . . . ." Another article published in the same newspaper on October 13th when he was sentenced stated: ". . . He looked at the Judge squarely through his expressionless eyes, and gave no sign of repentance and fear; no evidence of any appreciation of the terrible fate that awaited him; he was as a statue, bloodless and without heart - the an-

Michael Kirchner, a German immigrant and Civil War veteran, was tried and hanged for murder in Buffalo, NY.
Buffalo Evening Courier and Republic

tithesis of all that is good and tender in humanity . . . There is no salvation for the wretch so far as human laws are concerned; and the execution of such a man is demanded now more imperatively than ever before in the history of Buffalo." Kirchner was unmarried but according to articles published about the trial he had been engaged to a young woman named Elizabeth Weaver for six years. She visited him while he awaited execution. Where Michael was buried is unknown. Supposedly five of the Kirchner brothers served in the Civil War, but I have been able to confirm only two in addition to Michael. Jacob (1833-1908) was a member of Co. H, 12th NY Cavalry. Valentin (1848-1916) joined the US Navy and served aboard several ships.

Barnard "Barney" Kishpaugh – Co. B (tr. January 28, 1865)
b. October 20, 1821 New Jersey
d. May 20, 1912 Hector, Tompkins, NY
m. Juliaett Hageton (September 1825-1900) 1843

NOTE: The son of Joseph (1792-1876) and Catherine Snook Kishpaugh (1797-1875), Barney enrolled in the 76th Regiment at Canandaigua, Ontario, NY on September 11, 1863 and mustered into Co. K. Whether he was drafted or enlisted is unknown. He transferred to Co. E on July 1, 1864 and to Co. A on November 18th. He was discharged at Washington, DC on June 3, 1865 as a member of the 147th. In 1890 he claimed "rupture & Rheumatism" as his disabilities. He and Juliaett were the parents of five. Barney died at the home of his daughter Henrietta but he and Juliaett were buried in Hillside Cemetery, Dundee, Yates.

Jacob Knoblauch – Co. E (tr. January 28, 1865)
b. 1840 Germany
d. ? ?
m. ?

NOTE: Little can be ascertained about this soldier. He enrolled in the 76th Regiment at Buffalo, Erie, NY on August 19, 1863 as a substitute for Peter Smith, Eden, Erie, NY and mustered into Co. A. He transferred to Co. I on October 11, 1864 and to Co. C on December 1st. He was discharged at Washington, DC on June 6, 1865 as a member of the 147th. The Buffalo city directories list a man by this name as late as 1873 but many men had the name, making a positive identification impossible.

Christian Korff – Co. F (tr. January 28, 1865)
b. October 26, 1844 Germany
d. February 23, 1906 Newfane, Niagara, NY
m. Fredericka "Ricka" Felton (November 12, 1848-December 2, 1891) *ca.* 1866

NOTE: Christian immigrated with his parents, Joseph Joachim (1804-*post* 1862) and Maria "Mary" Korff (1806-*post* 1880), in the spring of 1862 and became a naturalized citizen in 1868. He enrolled in the 76th Regiment at Newfane on July 28, 1863 as a substitute for Charles W. Lindsay of that place and mustered into Co. I. He was wounded and captured at the battle of the Wilderness on May 5, 1864. According to the 1890 Veterans' Schedules he was shot in the left knee and spent seven months in Andersonville and Florence Prisons. He transferred to Co. C on December 1, 1864 and was paroled at Charleston, SC on December 18th. His next known date is March 6, 1865 when he was sent to Baltimore, MD, perhaps to enter a hospital. He was ultimately discharged on a surgeon's certificate of disability at Summit House,

Philadelphia, PA as a member of the 147th. Christian was active in local politics, standing as candidate for tax collector in 1890, elected Republican elections inspector in 1891, and elected constable for Town of Wilson in 1894. He and Frederika, the parents of six children, are buried in St. Peter's Evangelical Church Cemetery, Cambria, Niagara County. His gravestone does not provide DOD.

Henry Larabee – Co. I (tr. January 28, 1865)
b. August 10, 1837 Denmark, Lewis, NY
d. November 3, 1905 Felts Mills, Jefferson, NY
m1. Adaline Tifft (1841-June 25, 1892) 1868
m2. Anna Booth (October 18, 1857-April 13, 1939) October 9, 1892

NOTE: Henry, son of Pierre LaRivee (1806-1879) and Marie-Desanges Diantha Desautels (1811-*post* 1880), saw prior military service in Co. E, 7th NY Cavalry from September 1861-March 1862. He was drafted in 1863, enrolling in the 76th at Utica, Oneida, NY on August 25th and mustering into Co. D. He was "severely" wounded on June 18, 1864 at Petersburg, VA and according to his GAR roll he was shot in the right hip. (That entry also states he received the wound at Weldon Railroad!) His time in the 147th was short because he transferred to the VRC on March 20, 1865 and was discharged on August 1, 1865 at Augusta ME. The severity of his disability is demonstrated by the fact that he applied for a pension on August 15, 1865. Henry was a member of Charles S. Glass Post No. 409 GAR, Felts Mills. He and Adaline had no children but they adopted Eugene George Geary (1873-1942), son of Henry's sister, Catherine (1851-*post* 1920). Adaline's grave has not been located. Henry and Anna were the parents of Leland Henry (1899-1956). Henry's death was announced in *The Carthage Republican* November 8, 1905, 8: ". . . Henry Larabee died at Felts Mills, Friday night, after a long illness from Bright's disease, aged 67 years. Mr. Larabee was a retired farmer and had lived in that village for many years. He was born in Denmark. Besides his wife he is survived by one son, Leon." Henry is buried in Felts Mills Cemetery. On October 13, 1909 Anna married Richard G. Smith (1839-September 22, 1921) as his second wife. Smith had served in the 86th Regiment from 1861-1865 and his entry in *The Town Clerks' Registers* states he was involved in 28 engagements. He is buried in Black River Cemetery with his first wife, Mary Hall. Anna, who died in Carthage, Jefferson County, reportedly was buried in Felts Mills Cemetery.

George Washington Lason – Co. A (tr. January 31, 1865)
b. July 9, 1840 Harrison, Potter, PA
d. March 18, 1914 Jenksville, Tioga, NY
m. Jane Ann Purdy (October 22, 1840-August 17, 1919) September 2, 1860

NOTE: George, son of Silas Peter (1806-1887) and Nancy Ann Gibson Lason (1824-1858), enlisted in the 76th Regiment at Harford, Cortland, NY on October 9, 1861, mustering into Co. B. According to *The Town Clerks' Registers* he was wounded in the arm at Fredericksburg, VA. He re-enlisted on January 2, 1864 at Culpeper, VA and was taken prisoner at the battle of the Wilderness on May 5th. He was imprisoned at Andersonville and, according to the *Registers*, at Florence, SC. His FAG biography states he was so weak he had to be carried out on a stretcher. His exchange and parole dates are unknown but he left parole camp on May 1, 1865, returning on May 15th. In later life he was in and out of several national homes and his health issues were many, including a loss of teeth, gunshot wounds to arm, sternum, and foot, as well as prostate problems. In 1890 he elaborated on one of his maladies, saying he had "bleeding piles." George was a member of Hiram Clark Post No. 154 GAR, Marathon, Cortland, NY. The parents of eight children, George and Jane are buried in Speedsville Cemetery, Tompkins, NY. Two of George's brothers fought for the Union. Benjamin Franklin "Frank" (1843-1864) was a member of Co. F, 6th NY Cavalry. He was captured near Thoroughfare Gap, VA on October 22, 1863 and died at Andersonville of "remittent fever" on March 6, 1864. George did not know what happened to him until after the war. James (1845-1862) was a member of Co. L, 5th US Cavalry and was killed on May 27, 1862 at the battle of Hanover Courthouse, VA.

Lucas F. Lawrence – Co. C (tr. January 28, 1865)
b. June 6, 1844 Berkshire, Tioga, NY
d. February 7, 1865 5th Army Corps Hospital, City Point, VA
m. Phebe _____ (?-?) ?

NOTE: Lucas was the son of Miles Lewis (1800-1862) and Silvia C. Foote Lawrence (1814-1892). He enlisted in the 76th Regiment on September 22, 1861 at Richford, Tioga, NY and mustered into Co. E. It appears he deserted around February 1863, returning in October. His marriage date is unknown although his entry in *The Town Clerks' Registers* under the name Miles Luke shows he was married upon enlisting. It is possible, however, that he and Phebe were married while he was AWOL. If his DOB is accurate he would be barely 18 in 1861 and it is doubtful Phebe would be any older. When Lucas returned to his regiment he was sentenced to work on government fortifications for the remainder of his enlistment and to make good the time lost after his term of service expired. In other words, he would not be discharged until June 18, 1865. Commanders had the option of redeeming their convicted soldiers and this is perhaps what happened to Lucas since on November 18, 1864 he transferred to Co. A. It is a fact that he was actively involved in the fighting of the 147th since he was fatally wounded during the battle called Hatcher's Run or Dabney's Mills, fought February 5-7. He died from a gunshot wound to the abdomen. The 1865

New York census record for deceased soldiers reveals that his body was sent home. He is buried in Speedsville Cemetery, Tompkins County. Phebe applied for a pension on April 29, 1865 but did not obtain a certificate. She in all likelihood remarried.

John Lee – Co. I (tr. January 28, 1865)
b. 1829 England
d. April 22, 1900 Frankford, Philadelphia, PA
m. Anna "Ann" Highan (1830-March 13, 1916) *ca.* 1850

NOTE: John's parents are unknown but both he and Ann were born in England. In 1855 John was living with his brother Joseph in Watervliet and had resided there for two months which implies that Ann and the children came later. The entire family worked in the textile industry. On October 9, 1862 John enrolled in the 30th Regiment at Watervliet, Albany, NY and mustered into Co. D, transferring to Co. D, 76th on May 25, 1863. He was injured at North Anna River, VA on May 26, 1864 and in 1890 stated that he had suffered a gunshot wound to the left leg. He transferred to Co. I, 91st Regiment on June 6, 1865 and was discharged at Albany, NY on July 14, 1865. By 1880 the family had moved to Philadelphia where several members worked in textile mills. John was a member of Gen. Philip Kearney Post No. 55 GAR in Frankford. He also belonged to Prince of Wales Lodge No. 27 Sons of St. George. His unexpected death was reported in *The Philadelphia Inquirer* April 23, 1900, 5: "Inspired by the martial music, as he saw the funeral cortege of Private Cook pass by, John Lee, a civil war veteran, followed the procession to Cedar hill Cemetery. The excitement was too much for him, and he became ill. A few minutes after reaching home he died. Lee was sixty-five years old, and lived at 4267 Paul Street, Frankford. He was on a visit to his physician, Dr. Pennybaker when he saw the funeral procession, and was led by his patriotism to join it." He and Ann, the parents of at least eight children, are buried in North Cedar Hill Cemetery, Philadelphia.

Frank J. Lewis – Co. B (tr. January 28, 1865)
b. 1836 Montreal, Quebec, Canada
d. August 26, 1914 Buffalo, Erie, NY
m. Julia _____ (1837-November 27, 1924) 1860

NOTE: Frank's parents have not been identified although he stated in 1910 that he had immigrated to the United States in 1842. He enrolled in the 76th Regiment on September 27, 1863 at Hartland, Niagara County as a substitute for William H. Wright, using the alias Joseph and mustering into Co. A. He was wounded on May 7, 1864 at the end of the battle of the Wilderness and a pension payment card reveals he had suffered a gunshot wound to the head. He transferred several times within the 76th. From the 147th he went to Co. G, 91st Regiment on June 5, 1865, mustering out on July 3rd near Washington, DC. A notation that he deserted from a hospital in Buffalo, NY is most likely a clerical error evidenced by the fact that he successfully applied for a pension on September 10, 1865. He and Julia, also born in Canada, were the parents of three children, all living when Julia died. The couple is buried in the United German and French Cemetery, Cheektowaga, Erie, NY.

Leonard H. Littlejohn – Co. A (tr. January 28, 1865)
b. 1822 Colrain, Franklin, MA
d. July 12, 1899 Shoreham, Addison, VT
m. Elvira _____ (1824-*post* 1884) *ca.* 1854

NOTE: Leonard's parents are reported to be David (?-?) and Emeline Littlejohn (?-?). He gave artist as his occupation when he entered the army. He enrolled in the 30th Regiment on October 15, 1862 at Watervliet, Albany, NY and mustered into Co. F, transferring to Co. E, 76th on May 25, 1863. From that company he went to Co. C on November 18, 1864. He was discharged as a member of the 147th on June 26, 1865 at Washington, DC. Leonard's personal life contains many gaps. The only mention of his wife and son, Alexander (1855-?), is found on the 1865 New York census for Albany, NY. In 1875 someone with his name and born in Massachusetts was working as a porter at a hotel in Jamestown, Chautauqua, claiming to be widowed. Beginning in 1884 Leonard was in and out of the Bath National Home on several occasions. He became a member of the William F. Barry Post No. 248 in Bath while a resident at the home. He gave Mrs. E. Littlejohn, Auburn, NY, wife, as his next of kin. It seems that the couple did not live together for many years. Leonard last left the home on May 10, 1899. How and why he traveled to Shoreham where he died is unknown. Leonard is buried in East Shoreham Cemetery. His government stone alludes to his service in the 147th Regiment. His death record contains the names of his parents which implies that someone was familiar enough with him to provide that information. Furthermore, someone had to order the stone. Who that was, however, is unknown. He had applied for a pension in 1890 but no widow claimed the pension upon his death. Elvira presents her own mysteries because on the 1865 census she stated she had been married twice and was the mother of four. She disappeared after 1884. Alexander may have died young.

Morris Loghry – Co. D (tr. January 28, 1865)
b. 1822 Cameron, Steuben, NY
d. *post* 1876 probably Saratoga, Saratoga, NY
m. Almira Bennett (1829-*post* 1910) *ca.* 1847

NOTE: This soldier's story is complicated by numerous errors of spelling and POB. His DOB is even odd, because all records indicate he was born in 1822 except his muster in card for the 30th Regiment which states he was 44 years old, and therefore born in 1818. Various cards place his birth in Candor, Camden, as well as Cameron which is proved by the 1865 New York census. He enrolled in the 30th Regiment at Saratoga Springs, NY on September 3, 1862 as Maurice Laghy and mustered into Co. G, transferring to Co. K, 76th on May 25, 1863 as Maurice Loghey. He transferred to Co. D on October 24, 1864. His muster card for the 147th spelled his name Morris Loughery. On June 5, 1865 he transferred to Co. B, 91st Regiment as Morris Loughery, mustering out on July 3rd. The last reference to him is found in the Saratoga city directory for 1876. He and Almira were the parents of two children, Huldah Elizabeth (1848-*post* 1865), and Joseph Melvin (1857-October 3, 1939). In 1881 Almira, claiming to be a widow, and Joseph were living in Hamilton, Ontario, Canada. In 1890 she was living in Seattle, King, Washington, again claiming to be Morris' widow. For much of his life Joseph, generally known by his middle name, lived with his mother. She is last found on the 1910 census for Seattle. Joseph is buried in Mount Pleasant Cemetery, Seattle. Perhaps his mother is there too.

Edward S. Long – Co. A (tr. January 28, 1865)
b. February 7, 1837 Albany County, NY
d. January 28, 1915 Boggs, Centre, PA
m. Isabelle G. Cryder (July 28, 1842-April 27, 1914) 1876

NOTE: Edward's parents are unknown, although his death certificate indicates that Abraham Long was his father. I have located no information on him. By 1860 Edward was working for a gardener, the occupation he would follow his entire adult life. In 1865 he was enumerated in his brother David's (1829-1904) household. Edward enrolled in the 30th Regiment at Watervliet, Albany, NY on October 16, 1862, mustering into Co. F. He transferred to Co. E, 76th Regiment on May 25, 1863, and to Co. A on November 18, 1864. From the 147th he went to Co. C, 91st on June 5, 1865, mustering out near Ball's Cross Roads, VA on July 3rd. It is interesting to note that in 1890 he claimed not to remember either company or regiment! He did, however, have presence of mind to apply for a pension that same year. He and Isabelle were the parents of five, three of whom were living in 1900. The couple is buried in New Union Cemetery, Wingate, Centre, PA. His COD was chronic nephritis and hers was gall stones.

Levi F. Lowell – Co. I (tr. January 28, 1865)
b. May 10, 1837 Willet, Cortland, NY
d. July 22, 1906 Cortland, Cortland, NY
m. Lydia Maria McClary (1842-July 23, 1914) February 26, 1860

NOTE: Levi, son of Martin (1807-1880) and Phoebe Bradley Lowell (1817-1901), enlisted in the 76th Regiment at Willet on November 11, 1861, mustering into Co. B. He re-enlisted on February 18, 1864 and transferred to Co. C on July 1st. From the 147th he went to Co. I, 91st Regiment on June 5, 1865, mustering out on July 3rd near Washington, DC. He claimed no disability in 1890. Lowell was a member of Hiram Clark Post No. 154 GAR, Marathon. He and Lydia were the parents of four, all living in 1900. The couple is buried in Cortland Rural Cemetery.

Samuel Luth – Co. G (tr. January 28, 1865)
b. 1830 Berne, Switzerland
d. ? ?
m. ?

NOTE: Little is known about this man. His name suffered many spellings and I use that found on his pension card. He was drafted, enrolling in the 76th on August 8,

Photographic Artist
Marathon, N. Y.

Levi Lowell enlisted in the 76th Regiment and served the entire war.
Peter Lowell

1863 and mustering into Co. G, then transferring to Co. D on October 20, 1864. He was wounded on February 7, 1865 at Hatcher's Run. He transferred to Co. F, 91st Regiment on June 5, 1865 and was discharged for "disability" at West Philadelphia, PA on July 18th. He applied for a pension on September 4, 1865. He did not obtain a certificate and since no confirmable further records can be found for him, he may have died before the process could be completed.

Walter Mahaney – Co. B (tr. January 28, 1865)
b. 1828 Springfield, Hampton, MA
d. ? ?
m. ?

NOTE: Mahaney, whose surname was spelled variously, enlisted in the 76th Regiment at Cherry Valley, Otsego, NY on December 15, 1861, mustering into Co. H. He was captured at Bull Run on August 29, 1862 and paroled at an unknown place and time. He was wounded on July 1, 1863 at Gettysburg. He re-enlisted on January 3, 1864 at

Culpeper, VA, was again wounded at Laurel Hill, VA on May 11th and transferred to Co. B on January 1, 1865. From the 147th he went to Co. G, 91st Regiment on June 5, 1865, mustering out near Washington, DC on July 3rd. His pension card indicates his application of October 7, 1865 for a pension was successful. The card also shows he served in Cos. E and I, 17th US Infantry. He enlisted on November 9, 1866 and was discharged at the expiration of his term on November 20, 1869 at Farmville, VA. No further information has been located.

James Frederick Manning – Co. I (January 28, 1865)
b. April 5, 1847 Cohoes, Albany, NY
d. February 2, 1923 Los Angeles, Los Angeles, CA
m. Alice Jane Ostrander (March 1851-February 25, 1925) July 3, 1869

NOTE: James was the son of William (1818-1891) and Agnes Magdalen Whitbeck/ Witbeck Manning (1820-1896). Although he claimed to be 18 when he enlisted, other documents prove he lied about his age. He enlisted in the 30th Regiment at Watervliet, Albany, NY on October 9, 1862, mustering into Co. D, then transferring to Co. D, 76th Regiment on May 25, 1863. He was wounded twice, once at Gettysburg on July 1, 1863 and a second time at the battle of the Wilderness on May 5, 1864. From the 147th he transferred to Co. I, 91st Regiment from which he mustered out on July 3rd. In 1870 he was living with Alice's father in Penn, Osborne, KS and by 1875 the entire family had moved there. In 1900 they lived in Denver, Arapahoe, CO but because his father died there in 1891 the family had probably re-sided in the area for some time prior to his death. In 1909 James was admitted to the National Soldiers' Home in Sawtelle, Los Angeles, CA. Among his disabilities were rheumatism, prostate problems, heart disease, lumbago, and a gunshot wound to the right hand. He died at his home in Los Angeles of myocarditis. He and Alice were the parents of 10 children, six of whom were living in 1900. The couple is buried in Los Angeles National Cemetery. James' brother, Daniel Francis (1839-*post* 1894), served in Co. K, 91st Regiment from August 1864-June 1865.

William Jameson Mantanye – Co. G (tr. January 28, 1865)
b. October 17, 1843 Freetown, Cortland, NY
d. July 9, 1912 Cortland, Cortland, NY
m. Emma Susan Cloyes (1846-July 5, 1922) September 18, 1872

NOTE: William was the son of William C. (1808-1880) and Betsey Fuller Mantanye (1813-1872). He enlisted in the 76th Regiment at Freetown on September 14, 1861 and mustered into Co. D. He was captured on July 1, 1863 at Gettysburg and paroled on the field on July 3rd. He re-enlisted on February 10, 1864. From the 147th he transferred to Co. D, 91st Regiment and mustered out near Washington, DC on July 3rd. His life is best summarized in an obituary published in *The Cortland Standard* July 10, 1912: "W. J. Mantanye, one of the most widely known lawyers of the county, died at his home . . . . yesterday afternoon, shortly before 4 o'clock at the age of 68 years. Death came very suddenly and with no warning illness to precede it. Mr. Mantanye appeared to be in his usual health at noon and was working around the yard, as was his custom, until about 3 o'clock, when he lay down beneath a tree to rest and recover from the heat. When a member of the family went out to him at about 4 o'clock, it was found that he had passed quietly away. Mr. Mantanye was born in Freetown Oct. 17, 1843. He attended a district school in Freetown during his early boyhood and later went to Homer to attend the Homer academy. In the winter of 1860-61 he taught school near Westfield, Pa., in one of the lumbering districts. When the first call for . . . troops in the Civil war was issued, he enlisted in Co. D of the 76th Vol. Inf., and served with distinction during the entire war. At the close of the war he entered the law office of Hon. Arthur Holmes in Cortland, and was admitted to the bar in May, 1867. He opened an office in Marathon shortly afterward, and practiced law there until his removal to Cortland in 1888, where he has since lived. He played a prominent part in the Republican politics of the county until his retirement from the active field several years ago . . . ." Another obituary, published in *The Homer Republican* July 11, 1912, 1, revealed that Mantanye had been a member of the constitutional convention in 1894 and a member of the state's prison commission from June 1895 to 1903. He annually visited many county jails to inspect conditions. He was also a member of Andrew J. Grover Post No. 98 GAR, Cortland, and served as secretary for many years. According to an obituary published in *The Cortland Standard* July 5, 1922, Emma had moved to North Tonawanda to live with her daughter eight years previously. She died in Buffalo General Hospital and her body was returned to Cortland for burial. William and Emma are buried in Cortland Rural Cemetery.

Seth Taylor Marcy – Co. B (tr. January 28, 1865)
b. August 5, 1829 Ames, Montgomery, NY
d. February 20, 1901 White Pigeon, St. Joseph, MI
m1. Delia Jane _____ (1832-*ante* 1880) *ca.* 185
m2. Malona Glover (1857-October 5, 1927) October 29, 1885

NOTE: The son of George Knowlton (1801-1870) and Harriet Coffin Marcy (1809-*post* 1855), Seth apparently was a volunteer when he enrolled in the 76th Regiment on July 17, 1863 at Bristol, Ontario, NY, mustering into Co. E. On November 18, 1864 he transferred to Co. A. From the 147th he went to Co. G, 91st Regiment, mustering out near Washington, DC on July 3rd. Seth was a jeweler by occupation. In 1850 he lived with Asa Talcott, a goldsmith, in Oswego City and it was there he met and married

Delia, generally known by her middle name. The couple lived in Greene, Chenango in 1860. Delia Jane's fate is unknown. By 1880 Seth was living in White Pigeon and was a widower. Malona Glover was born in Davis County, IL and the couple married in White Pigeon. Seth's COD was paralysis of heart and lungs. The doctor noted that contributing factors were "army life and double hernia." Malona died in Grand Rapids, Kent, MI and her COD was chronic alveolitis with senility and arteriosclerosis as contributing factors. Her death certificate states she may actually have died during the night on October 4th. She and Seth are buried in White Pigeon Township Cemetery. Seth's brother Charles (1845-1864) served first in Co. E, 43rd Regiment and subsequently in Co. K, 11th MA. He was fatally wounded on May 5, 1864 at the battle of the Wilderness, dying on May 7th. He was buried on the battlefield.

Anthony Marshall – Co. D (tr. January 28, 1865)
b. 1840 Schoharie County, NY
d. February 4, 1914 Gaines, Genesee, MI
m. Rosalia _____ (August 1842-June 7, 1917) 1876

NOTE: Although Anthony's death certificate says his father was Philip, census records prove his name was Anthony (1805-*post* 1860). His mother was Eliza (1807-*post* 1860). The younger Anthony enlisted in the 76th Regiment at Cherry Valley, Otsego County on October 15, 1861, mustering into Co. H. He re-enlisted on January 25, 1864 and transferred to Co. B on January 1, 1865. From the 147th he went to Co. B, 91st Regiment on June 5, 1865, mustering out near Washington, DC on July 3rd. In 1890 his disabilities were eyesight injured from disease and rheumatism. Anthony's COD was senility and heart disease. Rosalia died after suffering a stroke. They are buried in Greenwood Cemetery, Vernon, Shiawassee, MI.

James McChesney – Co. B (tr. January 28, 1865)
b. November 1844 Scotland
d. May 28, 1865 Campbell Hospital, Washington, DC
m. ------

NOTE: James was the son of William (1821-*post* 1899) and Elizabeth McChesney (1823-*post* 1891) who were immigrants to Canada. He enrolled in the 76th Regiment on August 7, 1863 at Buffalo, Erie, NY as a substitute for Jacob Ekel and mustered into Co. A. He transferred to Co. I on October 11, 1864 and returned to Co. A on December 1st. According to a letter he wrote to his father dated April 2, 1865 he had been wounded on March 31st. Although the letter does not specify, on that date the 147th was at White Oak Ridge. He told his father he was hit "in the shoulder near the shoulder blade and the ball came out on the other side lower down. Do not think it hit the backbone, nor do I think it went inside, but I cannot tell." A letter dated May 21ˢᵗ written by Oliver C. Clark and sent to James' father contained grave news: "I have seated this morning to write you in answer to your letter to your son. he received your letter and was glad to hear from home once more. his health is not as good as he wrote before, he has been confined entirely to his bed and has bed sores more painful then his wound which I believe is getting a long as well as could be expected. his wound effects Spine therefoe has no power over his lower limbs. he is in deplorable condition. to live he never would be any comfort to himself nor to his friends and the Doctor says that he cannot live many days. he is failing fast. he has to be turned every 5 minutes. they have a comfortable bed as can be fixed. he is now on a Water bed which is very comfortable. they take as good care of him as you could if you had him at home so you need not wery about him for they are doing every thing that can be done for any boddy. You need not build yourself up with the hope of evr seeing him a live because he may not live therefore we will have to submit to the divine ruler who ruleth for the best and think that our loss of him on Earth is his gain in Heaven. he I believe is resigned to God's will I think he has a hope of going to a better world where there is no separating of friends. I will now close he sends his undying love to you all and Still hopes to see you all on earth . . . ." Today James lies in Arlington National Cemetery.

Martin McCoy – Co. I (tr. January 28, 1865)
b. November 1834 Otsego County, NY
d. February 13, 1904 Ames, Montgomery, NY
m. Delina _____ (1841-*post* 1900) 1870

NOTE: Martin's parents may have been John (1803-1874) and Ellen S. Beach McCoy (1805-1890), both of whom died in Michigan. He enlisted in the 76ᵗʰ Regiment at Cherry Valley, Otsego on October 21, 1861 and mustered into Co. H. The records are a bit obscure but it appears he deserted on December 26ᵗʰ and was not apprehended until September 28, 1864. As the result of a general court-martial he was sentenced to make up the time and to lose all pay and allowances, in addition to forfeiting $10 per month for 18 months. He transferred to Co. B on January 1, 1865 and then was sent to the 147ᵗʰ as part of his sentence. On June 5, 1865 he transferred to Co. B, 91ˢᵗ Regiment, mustering out on July 3ʳᵈ near Washington, DC. It appears he never applied for a pension. In 1890, while living in Springfield, Otsego, he said he had been a member of the 91ˢᵗ Regiment but claimed no disability. In 1900 he and Delina were living in Ames together with Martin Elmer McCoy (1864-1930) who could not be the elder Martin's son since he and Delina did not marry until 1870. Martin is buried in Ames Cemetery. His stone does not contain any dates. What happened to Delina is unknown but someone with the name of Delina C. McCoy died in Las Vegas, Clark, NV and was buried in Palm Desert Memorial Park. Her stone contains no dates.

John C. McGarry - Co. G (tr. January 28, 1865)
b. 1833 ?
d. ? ?
m. ?

NOTE: This man's POB and parents are unknown. He enrolled in the 76th Regiment at Buffalo, Erie, NY on November 11, 1864, mustering into Co. D. He seems to have been a volunteer. From the 147th he transferred to Co. F, 91st Regiment on June 5, 1865, mustering out on July 3rd near Washington, DC. No other information is available.

Thomas McGill – Co. H (tr. January 28, 1865)
b. 1845 Reading, Berks, PA
d. December 28, 1914 Orting, Pierce, WA
m. ------

NOTE: According to his death certificate Thomas was the son of Thomas (?-?) and Mary McGill (?-?). He enrolled in the 76th Regiment at New York City on March 10, 1864 and mustered into Co. C, apparently a volunteer. He transferred to Co. A on November 8, 1864. From the 147th he went to Co. F, 91st Regiment on June 5, 1865, mustering out on July 3rd near Washington, DC. He was an upholsterer by trade and a member of James Bryant Post No. 119 GAR in Minneapolis, Hennepin, MN. Although he is buried in Washington Soldiers' Home Cemetery, it is unclear whether he actually died at the home.

Miles McGuigan – Co. E (tr. January 28, 1865)
b. October 16, 1830 Ontario, Canada
d. July 30, 1902 Fostoria, Tuscola, MI
m. Urana Theresa Church (August 12, 1837-April 29, 1915) February 2, 1858

NOTE: Miles was the son of Miles (1787-?) and Phoebe Nicholson McGuigan (1788-1878). A draftee, he enrolled in the 76th Regiment at Bath, Steuben, NY on July 16, 1863, mustering into Co. A. He transferred to Co. I on October 11, 1864 and to Co. C on December 1st. Although nominally transferred to Co. D, 91st Regiment on June 5, 1865 he was discharged on June 24th at Washington, DC as a member of the 147th. He and Urana were married in Easton Corners, Leeds and Grenville, Ontario, Canada. They became the parents of 13 children, ten of whom were living in 1902. A brief death notice appeared in *The Saginaw Evening News* August 2, 1902, 12: "Fostoria – Miles McGuigan, a pioneer resident of Watertown township, one mile west of town, is dead, aged 70 years. He had been a great sufferer for years." Miles' COD was cancer of the penis. Urana succumbed to diabetes. They are buried in Watertown Township, Cemetery, Fostoria.

Timothy McKinney – Co. H (tr. January 31, 1865)
b. May 14, 1843 Susquehanna County, PA
d. December 24, 1894 Oakland, Susquehanna, PA
m. Sarah Ellen Hawkins (February 8, 1847-February 22, 1923) *ca.* 1865

NOTE: Timothy, son of James (1811-*post* 1850) and Avis McKinney (1812-*post* 1850), was a substitute for DeValle O. Elsmere and enrolled in the 76th Regiment at Elmira, Chemung, NY on July 20, 1863, mustering into Co. F. He was captured on May 5, 1864 at the battle of the Wilderness and, according to the 1890 Veterans' Schedules, spent eight months in Andersonville. He was discharged on June 9, 1865 at Arlington, VA as a member of the 147th. On September 18, 1879 he was sentenced in Broome County, NY to serve time in the Auburn State Prison for larceny and he was enumerated there in 1880. How long he was a prisoner is unknown but since his daughter Sophia was born on September 7, 1882, he may have been released in December 1881 or January 1882. Timothy and Sarah were the parents of four children. According to *The Montrose Democrat* July 10, 1885, their son Frederick (1870-1885) had attempted to board a freight train the previous Saturday but fell, crushing both feet. The boy died that night. Timothy and Sarah are buried in McKune Cemetery, Oakland. Sarah, whose grave is unmarked, died of chronic Bright's disease.

John O. Merke – Co. E (tr. January 28, 1865)
b. 1835 Switzerland
d. ? ?
m. ?

NOTE: Little is known about this soldier who was a watchmaker. He was drafted, enrolling in the 76th Regiment at Persia, Cattaraugus, NY on August 30, 1863 and mustering into Co. C. He transferred to Co. A on November 11, 1864. From the 147th he went to Co. K, 91st Regiment on June 5, 1865, mustering out on July 3rd near Washington, DC. He was a watchmaker by occupation. I have not located a pension record for him or an entry in the 1890 Veterans' Schedules.

John C. Miller – Co. G (tr. January 28, 1865)
b. December 18, 1832 Remsen, Oneida, NY
d. March 22, 1922 Chadwicks, Oneida, NY
m1. Ann E. _____ (December 26, 1833-May 1, 1858) July 24, 1854
m2. Louisa Mykel (June 18, 1842-June 24, 1917) March 10, 1860

NOTE: John, a mason, was the son of John C. (1801-1866) and Hannah Farley Miller (1811-188). A draftee, he enrolled in the 76th at Ithaca, Tompkins, NY on August 12, 1863, mustering into Co. G and transferring to Co. D on October 20, 1864. From the 147th he went to Co. F, 91st Regiment on June 5, 1865, mustering out on July 3rd near Washington, DC. In 1890, while living in Northwood, Herkimer County, he said his disabilities were rheumatism and diarrhea. He and Ann, whose gravesite is unknown, had no children. Louisa was the mother of eight, all of whom were living in 1900. John and Louisa are buried in Prospect Cemetery, Oneida County.

Lyman H. Miller – Co. C (tr. January 31, 1865)
b. February 13, 1845 Central Bridge, Schoharie, NY
d. May 21, 1916 National Soldiers' Home, Bath, Steuben, NY
m. Mary W. Hamilton (December 4, 1845-October 10, 1945) February 6, 1867

NOTE: Lyman was the son of Isaac Josiah (1805-1870) and Ursula A. Hawes Miller (1825-1885). He lied about his age in order to enlist in the 30th Regiment at Watervliet, Albany, NY on September 29, 1862, mustering into Co. D. On May 25, 1863 he transferred to Co. D, 76th Regiment. The following material is quoted from biographical material submitted to the 76th New York Volunteer Homepage by Bruce Robbins, Lyman's great grandson: ". . . He was wounded in the left thigh the first day's battle at Gettysburg, very near where the monument stands today, which left him with a lifetime limp requiring a cane most of the time for the rest of his life . . . he went on to receive a second wound in the left arm at the battle of The Wilderness in 1864. After recovering from this wound, he was captured at the battle of Poplar Grove Church in October 1864. As a private he and some of his friends were sent to Libby Prison in Richmond. Because this prison was primarily for captured officers, he was soon transferred to Salisbury Prison, NC . . . ." The exact date of his capture was October 1, 1864. Robbins states that Lyman was paroled in March 1865. Miller was in Ford's Theatre on April 14th and witnessed Lincoln's assassination. He was discharged on June 9th as a member of the 147th. He and Mary were married in Cohoes, Albany, NY. According to Robbins, Mary worked in a millinery in Troy, NY and created the bonnets Mrs. Lincoln and Mrs. William Seward wore for the 1861 inauguration. As a youngster Lyman was a spinner in the textile industry but in later life he became a merchant. He entered the Bath Home on May 5, 1916, claiming heart trouble as his disability. Mary died in Hasbrouck Heights, NJ. They are buried in Albany Rural Cemetery, Menands.

John Mooney – Co. H (tr. January 28, 1865)
b. 1840 Ireland
d. April 30, 1895 Cook County, Illinois
m. Fannie Parent (March 11, 1851-January 8, 1920) January 1, 1867

NOTE: John Mooney was an *alias* used by Michael Guiry/Guirie/Guirey whose parentage is unknown. According to his muster roll card, he was a sailor. Under his correct name he enlisted in the 49th Regiment on September 24, 1861 at Buffalo, Erie County, mustering into Co. D. He was discharged for "disability" at Fort Wood, New York City Harbor on December 16, 1862. He enrolled in the 76th Regiment as a substitute for Jacob Reich at Rochester, Monroe, NY on August 5, 1863 using the *alias* of John Mooney, mustering into Co. F. At some point he was captured and paroled. He was discharged on June 9, 1865 at Arlington, VA as a member of the 147th. He and Fannie, who was born in New York State, were married in Sangamon County, IL. It appears that they had only one child, Mary Ellen "Nellie" (1870-February 28, 1929). Michael's grave has not been located. Fannie is buried in Forest Home Cemetery, Chicago.

Joseph Morgan – Co. B (tr. January 28, 1865)
b. 1836 Italy
d. ? ?
m. ?

NOTE: Joseph Morgan was an *alias* used by Giuseppe Pellegrine, whose parents are unknown. He enrolled in the 76th Regiment at Buffalo, Erie, NY on August 7, 1863 as a substitute for Felicien Besancon, mustering into Co. A. He was wounded at Petersburg, VA on June 20, 1864. Subsequent transfers were to Co. G on October 11th, Co. E, October 20th, and Co. A, November 18th. He was discharged on May 29, 1865 as a member of the 147th. The last known date for him is April 12, 1866 when he applied for a pension in New York State.

Hiram Morse – Co. B (tr. January 28, 1865)
b. 1833 Schoharie County, NY
d. ? ?
m. ?

NOTE: Hiram's parents are unidentified. He enrolled in the 76th Regiment at Auburn, Cayuga, NY on July 25, 1863 as a substitute for George W. Nears, Seneca Falls, NY, mustering into Co. C. He was wounded at Petersburg, VA on June 18, 1864 and transferred to Co. H on November 8, 1864. From the 147th he was sent to Co. H, 91st Regiment on June 5, 1865, mustering out on July 3rd at Washington, DC. No further confirmable information has been located.

William A. Mosher – Co. I (tr. January 28, 1865)
b. 1843 ?
d. September 12, 1890 Locke, Cayuga, NY
m. Frances A. Willis (1850-*post* 1940) *ca.* 1867

NOTE: William was the son of Zephaniah (1810-*post* 1860) and Charlotte Mosher (1812-*post* 1860). Although his muster roll card states that he had been born in Dryden, Tompkins County, it is more likely his POB was Cayuga County which was where the family was living in 1850 although by 1860 the family had moved to Tompkins County. He enrolled in the 76th at McLean on October 10, 1861, mustering into Co. C. He deserted at least twice but was present on May 10, 1864 at Spotsylvania where he was wounded. In 1890 he claimed "gunshot wound" as his disability. He was court-martialed at an unknown date and his sentence was referred to General Wadsworth who determined he would serve until April 20, 1865 and lose all pay for the period he was absent. He was discharged at Black and White Station, VA on April 29, 1865. He successfully applied for a pension in 1880 and the cards attest to his tenure in both the 76th and the 147th Regiments. He and Frances were the parents of five sons who were notorious for their behavior in the community. Frances married Alexander Elliott Wood (1850-May 24, 1902) as his second wife probably in early 1894 and bore another son, Charles (November 1894-*post* 1940). Her third husband was Wright Townsend (1867-July 24, 1945) whom she married on January 21, 1905 as a second wife. Townsend's address when he died was Newark, NJ and it is possible Frances died there. The list of his survivors did not include her. She last appears on the 1940 census, aged 90. Graves for these people have not been located.

Francis "Frank" E. Moshier – Co. B (tr. January 28, 1865)
b. April 27, 1845 Point Claire, Quebec, Canada
d. February 26, 1924 Oswego City, NY
m. Melissa Burns Wilfred (January 1, 1844-March 2, 1910) 1865

NOTE: Francis was the son of Luke Bougie/Bushie (1812-1883) and Rosalie LeDuc (1807-1892). The family immigrated to the United States in 1855. Why he chose to enter the military under the name Moshier is unknown but though the family name fluctuated between Bougie and Moshier through the years, the 1890 Veterans' Schedules and pension payment cards all use the latter name. Francis enrolled in the 76th Regiment at Oswego on September 5, 1863 as a substitute for George G. Newton, mustering into Co. C. He was wounded at Petersburg, VA on June 17, 1864. He transferred to Co. A on November 8th. He was discharged at York, PA on May 9, 1865 as a member of the 147th Regiment. Melissa was first married to Paul Wilfred (1839-*ante* 1865) by whom she had two sons. She was the mother of four more children by Frank Bougie. Her death was reported in *The Oswego Daily Times* March 2, 1910: "Mrs. Mellissa Bougie, wife of Frank E. Bougie, died this morning at four o'clock at the home of her son, Frank E. Bougie Jr. Mrs. Bougie had been ill for a number of years past and had been considered seriously ill for the past year. Her death, while not entirely unexpected, came suddenly, for yesterday she was apparently in better health than usual. Mrs. Bougie was born in this city and had always made her home here. For the past thirty years she had been a resident of the Fifth ward where she had a very large number of friends. She had always been a member of St. Louis' church and while her health was good had been very active in church work . . . The funeral will be held at 9:30 o'clock Friday morning at St. Louis' church." Frank's death was reported in *The Oswego Daily Palladium* February 26, 1924, 5: "Frank E. Bougie, 78, one of the best known residents of the this city, died early this afternoon at his home, 38 West Cayuga street, following an illness of five weeks. Mr. Bougie was born in Point Claire, Quebec, coming to this city when very young, where he had since resided. He was a veteran of the Civil War, having enlisted with the 76th Regiment, New York Volunteers, and was afterward transferred to the 147th Regiment. In the battle of Gettysburg [*sic*] Mr. Bougie was seriously wounded and lost half his jaw. In politics Mr. Bougie was a Republican. He served as Commissioner of Fire and Police for six years, being first appointed by Mayor Mitchell and was reappointed by Mayor John D. Higgins. He was a sawyer by trade and a member of St. Louis's church. Mr. Bougie enjoyed the respect and esteem of all who knew him. He was strictly honorable and upright in his dealings with others . . . ." Frank and Melissa are buried in St. Peter's Cemetery, Oswego City.

Thomas Mudge – Co. B (tr. January 28, 1865)
b. 1842 Canada
d. ? ?
m. ?

NOTE: Thomas, whose parentage is unknown, enrolled in the 76th Regiment at Utica, Oneida, NY on September 2, 1863 as a substitute for John Stuber, Herkimer, mustering into Co. H. He transferred several times within the regiment. From the 147th he went to Co. G, 91st Regiment on June 5, 1865, mustering out near Washington, DC on July 3rd. Mudge was a blacksmith and it is possible he returned to Canada because in 1866 someone named Thomas Mudge, blacksmith, lived in Kent County, New Brunswick. No other information is available.

Andrew Murphy – Co. G (tr. January 28, 1865)
b. 1843 Canada
d. ? ?
m. ?

NOTE: Andrew, a painter, enrolled in the 76th Regiment on August 5, 1863 at Rochester, Monroe County as a substitute for Robert Knowles of that city, mustering into Co. K. He was captured at the battle of the Wilderness on May 5, 1864. When transferred to the 147th he was a "paroled prisoner." He transferred to Co. F, 91st Regiment on June 5, 1865 and was discharged at Albany, NY on July 14th. No other information is available.

William H. Myers – Co. I (tr. January 31, 1865)
b. 1841 Cortland County, NY
d. March 14, 1889 Cortlandville, Cortland, NY
m. Nancy Jane "Jennie" Calvert (November 15, 1841-July 3, 1895) January 10, 1867

NOTE: William was the son of John Frederick (1804-1894) and Maria Hunter Myers (1818-1867). He enlisted in the 76th Regiment at Cortland on October 5, 1861 and mustered into Co. A as a corporal, rising to the rank of second lieutenant. He re-enlisted at Culpeper, VA on January 5, 1864 and transferred to Co. F on March 16th. Myers was captured on May 5, 1864 at the battle of the Wilderness but where he was held and when he was paroled are unknown. When transferred to the 147th he was among the missing. He was discharged as of March 12, 1865 through Special Orders No. 121 of that date which provided for the mustering out of paroled officers. In 1890 Jennie said her husband's disability had been "nervous prostration," evidently a reference to the effects of his imprisonment. Upon returning to civilian life, Myers became a grocer. He and Jennie were the parents of four daughters, two of whom grew to adulthood. Jennie's life was celebrated in a lengthy obituary published in *The Cortland Evening Standard* July 8, 1895, 5: "Jennie Calvert, youngest daughter of John and Samantha Calvert, was born Nov. 15, 1841, and died July 3, 1895. She was educated in Cortland academy, and her whole life was spent in Cortland. Early in the spring of 1861 she sent her soldier lover, William H. Myers, with her blessing, to fight for his country. She followed him through the dangers and vicissitudes of those eventful years, and soon after he received his discharge at the close of the war, was united with him in marriage. The home-life of Mr. and Mrs. Wm. H. Myers was a singularly happy one. It was a true Christian home in every sense of the word, father, mother and the two daughters all worshipping in the same church home, the First Methodist Episcopal church of this place. Shadows deep came to the home, and two little ones were laid away in the cemetery, within sight of the door, but no repining or rebellious word was ever spoken. The unselfish mother put aside her grief, and strove to make home still cheerful and bright. The death of her husband, March 15 [*sic*], 1889, seemed to strike her death blow, and although she still tried to banish all outward tokens of grief, and filled her home with light-hearted cheerful young people for her daughters' sake, those who knew and loved her best could see that the light was gone from her eye, and ambition was failing. She saw her daughters through the Normal school course, the eldest, Myrtie Burd married to Fred W. Melvin of this place, and M. Louise thoroughly fitted for her life work, the profession of teaching, when disease took hold of her weakened frame, and after a most pathetic and heroic fight, lasing seven months she gave up the struggle . . . On Sunday afternoon, July 7, she was buried from the home in which she had spent her whole married life, and her body laid to rest beside her husband and children . . . ." Jennie's COD was tuberculosis. She and William are buried in Cortland Rural Cemetery.

William entered the 76th Regiment as a corporal and attained the rank of lieutenant.
Karen Halstead (FAG)

William John Newkirk – Co. D (tr. January 28, 1865)
b. 1846 Milford, Otsego, NY
d. November 9, 1873 Hartwick, Otsego, NY
m. Susan M. Merihew (April 24, 1853-February 5, 1923) November 21, 1871

NOTE: William, son of John C. (1811-1892) and Edith Marjorie Steele Newkirk (1813-1894), lied about his age when he enlisted at Milford on December 1, 1861, mustering into Co. H. He re-enlisted in Culpeper, VA on January 3, 1864 and transferred to Co. B on January 1, 1865. From the 147th he went to Co. B, 91st Regiment on June 5, 1865, mustering out near Washington, DC on July 3rd. Susan married Caleb Clark Aspinwall (1851-September 29, 1929) on October 29, 1879. An interesting obituary for her appeared in *The Otsego Farmer* February 16, 1923, 4: "Mrs. Susan Merihew Aspinwall died at her home on West Main street Monday, February 5th. She had been suffering with heart disease for many years. Services were held from her late home at 11:30 A. M. Wednesday and from the Methodist Episcopal church at 12 o'clock with the Rev. Boyce of that church officiating at both services. Interment will be in Hartwick cemetery. Susan Merihew was born on Bow Hill, April 24, 1853. She was married to William J. Newkirk of Lawrence who died in November 1873. By this marriage there [is] surviving her one daughter, Mrs. William Cronkhite . . . On October 29, 1879 she was married to Clark Aspinwall who survives her. By this marriage she had three children . . . She was a member of the Methodist Episcopal church. Mrs. Aspinwall had been a patient sufferer for many years and the family have the sympathy of a large circle of friends." Susan and her two husbands are buried in Hartwick Village Cemetery. William's father, John, also served briefly in Co. H, 76th Regiment, enrolling the same day as his son. He was discharged at Fort Massachusetts, DC on April 12, 1862 for "old age and disease of the lungs." A brother, Orlando (1844-August 6, 1863), served in Co. A, 43rd Regiment. He died of typhoid fever in Lincoln Hospital, Washington, DC and was buried in the Soldiers' and Airmen's Home Cemetery, Washington.

William Nugent – Co. H (tr. January 28, 1865)
b. 1843 Ireland
d. ? ?
m. ?

NOTE: William, a boatman, enrolled in the 30th Regiment on October 16, 1862 at Albany, NY, mustering into Co. F. He transferred to Co. K, 76th Regiment on May 25, 1863 and transferred several times within the regiment. From the 147th he went to Co. I, 91st Regiment on June 5, 1865, mustering out near Washington, DC on July 3rd. No further information about him has been located.

James E. O'Brien – Co. D (tr. January 28, 1865)
b. 1843 Charlottestown, Prince Edward Island, Canada
d. 1906 ?
m. ?

NOTE: James enlisted in the 30th Regiment on August 26, 1862 at Watervliet, Albany, NY, mustering into Co. F. He transferred to Co. H, 76th Regiment on May 25, 1863 and transferred several times within the regiment. From the 147th he went to Co. B, 91st Regiment on June 5, 1865, mustering out near Washington, DC on July 3rd. He applied for a pension on December 1, 1865. His pension card provides a DOD of 1906 but location is not noted. No other information has been found.

John O'Connell – Co. C (tr. January 28, 1865)
b. 1830 Ireland
d. September 28, 1912 Morris, Otsego, NY
m. Esther Gallup (1832-1882) *ca.* 1860

NOTE: John's parents are unidentified. A farmer, he was drafted, enrolling in the 76th Regiment on August 28, 1863 at Norwich, Chenango, NY and mustering into Co. A. He transferred to Co. I on October 11, 1864 and to Co. C on December 1st. He was discharged from Satterlee Hospital, Philadelphia, PA on June 27, 1865. He and Esther were the parents of six children, the youngest of whom was John A. (1875-1936). He together with his parents is buried in Saint Andrew's Cemetery, New Berlin, Chenango.

John O'Connell – Co. C (tr. January 28, 1865)
b. 1820 Ireland
d. October 19, 1895 ?
m. ?

NOTE: This soldier's parents are unknown. A laborer, John enlisted in the 30th Regiment at Albany, NY on August 26, 1862, mustering into Co. F. He transferred to Co. I, 76th on May 25, 1863 and to Co. C on December 1, 1864. From the 147th he transferred to Co. H, 91st on June 5, 1865, mustering out near Washington, DC on July 3rd. Little is known about his life after the war. He applied for a pension on July 11, 1890 in Maine and it is on his pension cards that his DOD is noted. It is curious that these cards say he was unassigned in both the 76th and the 147th. No widow attempted to claim a pension.

James H. Paine – Co. D (tr. January 31, 1865)
b. June 25, 1836 Caroline, Tompkins, NY
d. May 1, 1918 Hornell, Steuben, NY
m. Polly D. Johnson (December 14, 1838-October 11, 1903) 1860

NOTE: James, a stone mason, was also known as John H. The son of David (1798-1871) and Eveline Doty Paine (1801-1846), he was drafted, enrolling in the 76th Regiment on July 18, 1863 at Woodhull, Steuben, NY and mustering into Co. D. He was captured near Cold Harbor, VA on June 1, 1864 and paroled at Charleston, SC on December 6th. He was discharged at Elmira, Chemung, NY on June 20, 1865 as a member of the 147th. Paine was a member of William C. White Post No. 561, GAR, Greenwood. He and Polly were the parents of five children, four of whom were living in 1900. According to an obituary published in *The Canisteo Times* May 1, 1918, 1, he died at the home of his granddaughter in Hornell. He and Polly are buried in Greenwood Cemetery, Steuben County.

Sylvanus Elisha Parker – Co. G (tr. January 28, 1865)
b. 1831 Russia, Herkimer, NY
d. March 31, 1865 5ᵗʰ AC Divisional Hospital, near Gravelly Run, VA
m. Emily Tisdale (1829-*post* 1866) August 28, 1853

NOTE: According to *The Town Clerks' Registers* Sylvanus' parents were Prentice (?-?) and Annie Mathews Parker (?-?). He enlisted in the 76ᵗʰ Regiment at DeRuyter, Madison, NY on September 21, 1861, mustering into Co. G. He re-enlisted at Culpeper, VA on March 30, 1864 and transferred to Co. H on October 20ᵗʰ. He was wounded at Gravelly Run on March 31, 1865, according to a deposition provided by Captain W. J. Gillett: ". . . Sylvanus E. Parker came to his death while in the line of his duty on the 31ˢᵗ day of March 1865, as follows: while in battle he rec'd a Gun shot wound through the Thigh, for which, on the same day the limb was amputated, he did not survive the operation but about two (2) hours. Said operation took place in Field Hospital near the regiment, and the action at which the wound was rec'd was on the 31ˢᵗ day of March 1865 . . . ." Parker was reportedly buried at Petersburg, VA. Emily applied for and obtained a widow's pension which terminated when she remarried on November 17, 1866. Her second husband's name is unknown.

Robert Parks – Co. I (tr. January 28, 1865)
b. July 1847 Canada
d. May 15, 1908 Troy, Rensselaer, NY
m. Margaret Martin (August 1848-February 6, 1910) *ca.* 1866

NOTE: Robert, son of James (1822-1904) and Matilda Parks (1822-*post* 1865), lied about his age to enlist in the army, enrolling in the 30ᵗʰ Regiment at Watervliet, Albany, NY on August 27, 1862 and mustering into Co. D. He transferred to Co. B, 76ᵗʰ Regiment on May 25, 1863. He was captured at the battle of the Wilderness on May 5, 1864 and paroled at an unknown date and location. From the 147ᵗʰ he transferred to Co. I, 91ˢᵗ Regiment on June 5, 1865, mustering out on July 3ʳᵈ near Washington, DC. Robert and Margaret's marriage date is disputed. January 15, 1866 has been suggested which is probably correct since in 1870 their daughter Jane was three years old, although in 1900 they alleged they had been married 28 years. Margaret died in Buffalo, Erie, NY. Graves for these people have not been located.

Hugh J. Patterson – Co. B (tr. January 28, 1865)
b. *ca.* 1815 Ireland
d. February 4, 1884 National Soldiers' Home, Bath, Steuben, NY

m1. Mary P. _____ (1815-August 28, 1871) *ante* 1850
m2. Maryette _____ (1820-?) *post* 1871

NOTE: Although Hugh claimed to be 44 when he enlisted in the 30th Regiment on August 30, 1862 at Saratoga, NY, other documents point to a DOB of 1815. He mustered into Co. G, transferring to Co. C, 76th Regiment on May 25, 1863. He was captured at Gettysburg on July 1st but paroled before October. He transferred to Co. A on November 8, 1864. His time with the 147th was probably brief since he transferred to Co. K, 14th Regiment VRC, date unknown, and mustered out at Finley Hospital, Washington, DC on July 26, 1865. He and Mary had no children. In 1880 he said he was married but his wife was not living with him. When he entered the home at Bath on November 7, 1883 he gave the name of William Patterson, Albany, NY as his next of kin. Hugh's home immediately prior to entering the home was Saratoga. He and Mary are buried in Greenridge Cemetery, Saratoga Springs. Maryette applied for and obtained a widow's pension. Someone with that name died on February 5, 1894 at Whitehall, Washington County but it is unknown if she is the correct person.

Francois "Frank" Xavier Payment – Co. I (tr. January 28, 1865)
b. April 21, 1835 Quebec, Canada
d. December 13, 1930 Traverse City, Grand Traverse, MI
m1. Louisa Bow (November 7, 1852-October 30, 1915) 1872
m2. Mary Favreau Farrant (May 25, 1855-June 28, 1944) March 31, 1919

NOTE: Frank's parents were Francois Xavier (1809-1900) and Lizzeta Breiner Payment. He was a substitute for an unnamed draftee when he enrolled in the 76th Regiment on August 7, 1863 at Buffalo, Erie, NY, mustering into Co. A. He transferred to Co. I on October 11, 1864 and to Co. C on December 1st. From the 147th he went to Co. I, 91st Regiment on June 5, 1865, mustering out on July 3rd near Washington, DC. In 1890 he claimed "breache" as a disability. Payment, a homesteader in Michigan, was a member of Murray Post No. 168, GAR. He and Louisa were the parents of three, two of whom were living in 1900. Louisa's COD was paralysis. Frank's COD was a diabetic coma, with diabetic gangrene a contributing factor. He and Louisa are buried in Rose Hill Cemetery, Empire, Leelanau, MI. Mary had previously been married to Marshall Farrant (1853-1909), who was killed in a logging accident on Christmas Eve, 1909. She died in Garfield, Grand Traverse but her grave has not been located.

Charles W. Pendell – Co. D (tr. January 28, 1865)
b. 1842 Strikersville, Schoharie, NY
d. August 18, 1930 Aurora, Cayuga, NY
m. Amanda M. _____ (1852-May 26, 1908) *ca.* 1867

NOTE: Charles, a blacksmith, was the son of Rev. David L. (1817-1896) and Adeline A. Stryker Pendell (1823-1887). He enlisted in the 76th Regiment at Unadilla, Otsego, NY, enrolling on January 2, 1862 and mustering into Co. K. According to his muster roll card, he attempted to desert from hospital in 1863 but was arrested and returned to his regiment. He re-enlisted at Culpeper, VA on February 28, 1864 and transferred to Co. G, date unknown, to Co. H on October 20th, and to Co. B on January 1, 1865. From the 147th he went to Co. B, 91st Regiment, mustering out on July 3rd near Washington, DC. In 1890 he said he had been injured by a fall from a horse. He and Amanda were the parents of at least four children. The couple is buried in Oak Glen Cemetery, Aurora. Rev. David Pendell served as chaplain for the 158th Regiment from December 1864-June 30, 1865.

Lyman R. Pender – Co. I (tr. January 28, 1865)
b. 1835 Homer, Cortland, NY
d. May 22, 1865 Campbell General Hospital, Washington, DC
m. ------

NOTE: Lyman's parents are unidentified although his father applied for and obtained a pension. His surname was also spelled Pinder. Lyman saw prior service as a member of Co. D, 12th Infantry from April 1861-September 1861 when he deserted. He enlisted in the 76th on October 9, 1861 at Cortland City, mustering into Co. G. His muster card indicates he again deserted, this time from Fort Slocum, DC. He was returned "under guard" in January 14, 1864. His muster card is contradictory as to the time he rejoined the regiment. It is known, however, that he was wounded in action at Petersburg, VA on June 20, 1864. Subsequent transfers occurred on October 20, 1864 to Co. H and on January 1, 1865 to Co. B. His COD was a gunshot wound to the right thigh but it is unknown if he succumbed to the injury he suffered at Petersburg. He was considered a member of the 147th when he died. Originally buried in Point Lookout Confederate Cemetery, MD, today he lies in Arlington National Cemetery.

Sylvanus S. Pierce – Co. D (tr. January 28, 1865)
b. November 1837 Erie County, NY
d. June 7, 1912 Colden, Erie, NY
m. Roxana "Roxy" Aldrich (June 1848-June 16, 1917) 1872

NOTE: Sylvanus was the son of Serrel (1808-1880) and Philena Gould Pierce (1801-1881). His DOB varies. I use that found on the 1900 census. He enrolled in the 76th Regiment at Buffalo on August 11, 1863, evidently a volunteer, mustering into Co. H. He transferred several times within the regiment. From the 147th he went to Co. B, 91st Regiment and mustered out near Washington, DC on July 3rd. He and Roxy were the parents of two, both living in 1900. The couple is buried in Maple Wood Cemetery, Boston, Erie County.

James L. Pinder – Co. C (tr. January 28, 1865)
b. 1833 Homer, Cortland, NY
d. January 25, 1903 Chicago, Cook, IL
m. Lucina _____ (1837-November 4, 1896) *ca.* 1852

NOTE: James' parents are unidentified and it is possible that he was Lyman's brother. He was a carpenter, enlisting in the 76th Regiment at Cortland on October 10, 1861 and mustering into Co. A. He transferred within the regiment several times. From the 147th he transferred to Co. H, 91st Regiment on June 5, 1865, mustering out July 3rd near Washington, DC. His pension card says he also served in Co. E, 79th Regiment but he does not appear in *The Adjutant-General's Report* for that outfit. He and Lucina, who died in Syracuse, Onondaga, NY, were the parents of three children. James is buried in Woodlawn Cemetery, Syracuse and it is possible that Lucina is there as well. His gravestone acknowledges his time in the 91st Regiment.

Truman Pinder – Co. C (tr. January 28, 1865)
b. 1834 ?
d. December 21, 1909 Syracuse, Onondaga, NY
m1. Ann _____ (1836-*ante* 1860) *ca.* 1855
m2. Ellen Louise Warner (1841-*ante* 1925) *ca.* 1860

NOTE: According to his obituary which appeared in *The Post-Standard* December 22, 1909, 16, Truman was the brother of Alida Pinder Titus (1840-March 4, 1909) whose parents were identified as Benjamin (1801-*post* 1850) and Eliza V. Pinder (1801-*post* 1850) in her FAG entry. His POB is disputed. He reported for his muster roll card that he had been born in Homer, Cortland, NY but in both 1855 and 1875 he reported he had been born in Otsego County. It is unknown if James L. and Lyman R. are related to him. Truman enlisted in the 76th Regiment on December 3, 1861 at Cortland, mustering into Co. A. He transferred several times within the regiment and he also deserted at least once if not twice. He was wounded at the battle of the Wilderness on May 5, 1864 and he claimed when he entered the Bath National Home in 1902 that he had suffered a gunshot wound to the right leg. Although sentenced to make up time lost and forfeit pay, he was discharged on March 13, 1865 at Petersburg, VA. Little is known about Ann who only appears on the 1855 New York census. Truman and Ellen were the parents of Hattie (1862-?) and Fannie Louise (1867-?). Apparently the marriage failed because in 1875 Ellen and the girls were living with Alonzo Murphy (1851-?) in Phelps, Ontario, NY and she was identified as his wife. In 1900 Ellen said she was the mother of six, four of whom were living. By 1925 Alonzo was a widower but Ellen's DOD has not been discovered. Alonzo last appears on the 1930 census but his DOD has not been located. Truman is buried in Woodlawn Cemetery, Syracuse.

Andrew Pinney – Co. B (tr. January 28, 1865)
b. May 22, 1846 Buckland St. Mary, Somerset, England
d. April 23, 1909 Chicago, Cook, IL
m1. Elizabeth "Betsy" Jones (1847-?) ca. 1870
m2. Josephine "Josie" _____ Hansen (1853-May 29, 1933) April 14, 1898

NOTE: Andrew, son of John (1809-1865) and Dinah Bale Pinney (1815-*post* 1855), arrived with his family in the United States in 1851. He enrolled in the 76th Regiment as a substitute for an unnamed draftee at Norwich, Chenango, NY on September 21, 1863, mustering into Co. E. He transferred to Co. A on November 18, 1864. From the 147th he transferred to Co. G, 91st Regiment on June 5, 1865, mustering out on July 3rd near Washington, DC. He and Betsy were the parents of George W. (1870-July 31, 1951) and Ada Dora (1875-?). Andrew apparently abandoned them sometime after the 1875 New York census because in 1880 Betsy and the children were living in Ischua, Cattaraugus County and he was nowhere to be found. When George died his obituary stated he had a half-brother Fred Burnstell but I have located no information about his mother's remarriage or her death. Andrew married Josephine, a native of Austria, in Chicago but the date is disputed. The marriage record apparently shows a date of 1898 but the 1900 census reveals the couple had been married in 1893. Josie's maiden name is unknown. She came to the United States in 1873. In 1900 she stated she had no children but in 1910 she claimed two, both living. Andrew is buried in Mt. Greenwood Cemetery, Chicago. Josephine applied for and obtained a widow's pension, lending credence to the supposition he had divorced Betsy. Josephine is buried in Mt. Olivet Memorial Park, Zion, Lake, IL.

John W. Porter – Co. I (tr. January 31, 1865)
b. 1838 Albany, Albany, NY
d. September 29, 1893 Amsterdam, Montgomery, NY
m. Mary _____ (1848-November 11, 1889) November 8, 1866

NOTE: John's parents are unidentified. When he enlisted in the 76th Regiment at Albany on December 24, 1861, he said he was a farmer but in later life he worked in an oil mill in Amsterdam, NY. He mustered into Co. D, later transferring to Co. I. He was wounded at South Mountain, MD on September 14, 1862 and captured at the battle of the Wilderness on May 5, 1864. He spent time in Andersonville Prison, obtaining parole at Charleston, SC on December 11th, 1864. He mustered out at Albany on March 24, 1865 with a discharge date of January 24th, and was considered a member of the 147th. In 1890 his name appeared on the Veterans' Schedules but his entry contained no information of any kind. He and Mary were the parents of at least five children, the youngest of whom, Ida (1879-1963), obtained a minor's pension. Her sister Elizabeth Porter Borst (1873-1902) apparently was her guardian. John's death was announced in *The Amsterdam Daily Democrat* September 29, 1893, 8: "John W. Porter, a veteran of the late war, died this noon at his home on the canal towpath, of consumption, aged 53 years. He was not a member of the G. A. R. The funeral arrangements are not yet completed." John is buried in Green Hill Cemetery, Amsterdam. His gravestone erroneously assigned him to Co. C, 147th. Mary's grave has not been located but she may also be in Green Hill.

William H. Powers – Co. H (tr. January 28, 1865)
b. June 28, 1842 Lansingburgh, Rensselaer, NY
d. January 26, 1908 Mystic, New London, CT
m. Susan Boutelle (February 11, 1843-November 21, 1907) 1867

NOTE: William was the son of Albert Ebenezer (1816-1910) and Frances Elizabeth Hanford Powers (1816-1850). He enrolled in the 30th Regiment at Albany, NY on August 28, 1862, mustering into Co. A. He transferred to Co. H, 76th Regiment on May 25, 1863 and transferred several times within the regiment. He nominally transferred to Co. A, 91st Regiment on June 5, 1865 but does not appear in *The Adjutant-General's Report* for that outfit. He was actually discharged on June 16, 1865 as a member of the 147th. He and Susan, who was born in Massachusetts, had no children. A funeral notice for William appeared in *The Troy Semi-Weekly Times* January 20, 1908, 5: "—The funeral of William Powers, who died in Mystic, Conn., Sunday, will be held tomorrow morning at 11 o'clock from the residence of his father, Albert E. Powers, on Second Avenue, Lansingburgh, and Rev. Dr. C. M. Nickerson will officiate. Mr. Powers had been in poor health a long time. His wife died several months ago, and Mr. Powers subsequently spent some time with his sister, Mrs. C. H. Dauchy, returning to Mystic shortly after January 1. He was born in Lansingburgh sixty-five years ago, and had resided in Mystic about twenty years. During the Civil War he served in the Union Army for three years, and participated in the battle of Gettysburg. During the war he served in four different regiments. Mr. Powers is also survived by Joseph A. Powers, a half-brother." William and Susan are buried in Oakwood Cemetery, Troy.

Eugene Price – Co. C (tr. January 28, 1865)
b. 1841 Niagara County, NY
d. September 1, 1869 Lockport, Niagara, NY
m. ------

NOTE: Eugene, a tinsmith, was the son of Samuel (1810-1888) and Louisa Bromley Price (1815-1897). He enrolled in the 76th Regiment at Buffalo, Erie County on August 12, 1863, a substitute for George Hellmig, Clarence, Erie, NY and mustered into Co. F. He transferred to Co. I on July 1, 1864 and to Co. C on December 1st. He was discharged for "disability" on May 18, 1865 at Whitehall US General Hospital, Philadelphia, PA. According to the 1870 Mortality Schedules he succumbed to tuberculosis. His exact DOD was found on the order form for his government headstone, which recognizes his service in the 147th but contains no dates. He is buried in West Lake Road Cemetery, Olcott, Niagara. His mother applied for and obtained a pension in 1887.

John H. Putnam – Co. F (tr. January 28, 1865)
b. 1843 Otsego County, NY
d. July 20, 1922 Charleston, Kanawha, WV
m1. Ellen Jane Luther (1852-January 20, 1890) January 30, 1871
m2. Mary _____ (?-?) ?

NOTE: The son of John Lewis (1809-1880) and Catherine Vosburg Putnam (1816-1875), John was drafted, enrolling in the 76th Regiment at Utica, Oneida, NY on August 25, 1863 and mustering into Co. A. He transferred to Co. I on October 11, 1864 and to Co. C on December 1, 1864. He was discharged from Harewood Hospital, Washington, DC on June 19, 1865 as a member of the 147th Regiment. He and Ellen were the parents of four children. His obituary appeared in *The Batavia Daily News* July 20, 1922: "John H. Putnam, for many years a resident of Batavia, died at the home of his son, Louis H. Putnam, at Charleston, W Va. last night. Mr. Putnam who was over seventy years of age and was a Civil War veteran, left Batavia a few years ago. He was employed for several years at the Hotel Richmond. Besides his son in Charleston, Mr. Putnam is survived by a son William Putnam of Schenectady. The body, which will be sent to Batavia, is expected to arrive tomorrow. The funeral will be held at Hartley's undertaking rooms at 2:30 on Friday afternoon." John belonged to Emery Upton Post No. 299 GAR, located in Batavia. The members took charge of the graveside services at his funeral. He and Ellen are buried in Elmwood Cemetery, Batavia. Little is known about Mary, except that her application for a widow's pension filed on September 11, 1922 was successful. I can find no records concerning her marriage to John.

Charles H. Randall – Co. H (tr. January 28, 1865)
b. 1829 Chenango County, NY
d. 1905 Westfield, Chautauqua, NY
m. Mary Covey (1839-December 31, 1882) *ca.* 1857

NOTE: Charles, a shoemaker, was the son of Elijah (1792-1856) and Martha "Patty" York Randall (1798-1875). He was drafted, enrolling in the 76th Regiment at Chautauqua on August 18, 1863 and mustering into Co. A. He transferred to Co. I on October 11, 1864 and to Co. C on December 1st. From the 147th he transferred to Co. F, 91st Regiment on June 5, 1865, mustering out on July 3rd near Washington, DC. He and Mary were the parents of two sons, Willie (1858-?), and Frederick Bennett (1874-1923). The couple lived in Corry, Erie, PA during the 1870s but Mary died in Jamestown, Chautauqua County. Her grave has not been located. Charles is buried in Westfield Cemetery. A brother, William Penn Randall (1832-1919), served in the 112th Regiment from August 1862-June 1865.

Daniel Webster Raymond – Co. I (tr. January 28, 1865)
b. February 18, 1842 Corinth, Saratoga, NY
d. October 15, 1915 Saratoga, Saratoga, NY
m. Anna "Annie" E. Earley (1849-June 2, 1895) *ca.* 1867

NOTE: The son of Henry "Harry" (1808-1851) and Alpha Eddy Raymond (1809-1859), Daniel enlisted in the 30th Regiment at Corinth on October 9, 1862, mustering into Co. G. He transferred to Co. C, 76th Regiment on May 24, 1863 and to Co. A on November 8, 1864. From the 147th he transferred to Co. I, 91st Regiment on June 5, 1865, mustering out on July 3rd near Washington, DC. He claimed no disability in 1890. He and Anna were the parents of two daughters. Daniel's COD is unknown but he died in the Saratoga Hospital. He and Anna are buried in Corinth Rural Cemetery. His gravestone alludes to his time with the 91st Regiment.

James Read – Co. G (tr. January 31, 1865)
b. 1842 Montreal, Quebec, Canada
d. ? ?
m. ?

NOTE: James, whose surname was spelled variously, enrolled in the 76th Regiment at Buffalo, Erie, NY on August 12, 1863 as a substitute for David Barrett, Concord, NY, mustering into Co. K. He was captured on May 4, 1864 and paroled at an unknown date. He was "absent" when transferred to the 147th. According to his muster roll card he was discharged at Arlington Heights, VA on June 9, 1865 as a member of the 147th. No further information has been located.

Melvin Harrison Reed – Co. G (tr. January 28, 1865)
b. August 20, 1844 DeRuyter, Madison, NY
d. October 22, 1916 Morrisville, Madison, NY
m. Jane "Jennie" Wilcox (1852-August 7, 1918) October 6, 1867

NOTE: Melvin, son of Josiah (1814-1861) and Amanda M. Shipman Reed (1815-1890), enlisted in the 76th Regiment at DeRuyter on October 18, 1861 and mustered into Co. G. Although his entry in *The Town Clerks' Registers* states he was captured at the battle of Weldon Railroad, that is incorrect. Weldon Railroad was fought August 18-21, 1864. On October 1, 1864, when he went MIA, the Union Army was fighting the battle of Peeble's Farm. His *Registers* entry further states, "Confined Salisbury Prison five months [and] nearly starved to death." If the time period is correct he was released in February. He was discharged from the service on May 27, 1865 as a member of the 147th. He and Jennie were the parents of eight children, six of whom were living in 1910. The marriage, however, was unsuccessful and by 1892 they were living apart. In 1904 Jennie married James Lunger (1834-1915) as his second wife. He had served in Co. I, 141st PA Infantry and died in Danville, Montour, PA. Melvin's death was announced in *The Madison County Leader and Observer* October 26, 1916, 3: "Oct. 25. – Sunday morning Melvin H. Reed, 72 years old, died at the home of his sister, Mrs. Mary Knickerbocker, after one week's illness of pneumonia. He was a veteran of the Civil war, having been a member of the gallant 76th regiment, New York State Volunteers, and a member of the Morrisville G. A. R. Post . . . Funeral services will be held today at his sister's home at 1 o'clock. Burial will be made in the West Eaton cemetery, Rev. John R. Ellis of Morrisville officiating." The GAR post to which he belonged was Charles H. Tillinghast No. 548. Jennie died in Fayetteville, Onondaga County, at the home of her daughter, Mrs. Claude Isenberg. Her body was taken to Homer and buried in Glenwood Cemetery.

George Reynolds – Co. C (tr. January 31, 1865)
b. ? ?
d. ? ?
m. Ann _____ (?-*post* 1890) ?

NOTE: Much of this soldier's life is shrouded in mystery. He enlisted in the 12th NY Regiment on November 16, 1861 at New York City, mustering into Co. B and using the *alias* Charles A. Fenton, giving an age of 21, and alleging he had been born in New York City. He was wounded at the second battle of Bull Run on August 30, 1862 and deserted from a hospital in Alexandria, VA on December 10th. On August 24, 1863 he enrolled in the 76th as a substitute for James Mall, Rochester, in that city under his real name, again providing an age of 21, alleging he had been born in

England, and mustering into Co. F. He was captured at the battle of the Wilderness on May 5, 1864. His parole date is unknown but he was discharged on June 9, 1865 as a member of the 147th. His DOD is unknown but his wife, Ann, applied for a pension in Pennsylvania on October 11, 1890. She did not obtain a certificate which perhaps indicates she died before the process could be completed.

Charles Richardson – Co. I (tr. January 31, 1865)
b. September 1844 Yorkshire, England
d. May 22, 1911 Milwaukee, Milwaukee, WI
m. Rosaline "Rose" Cleva Lindman (April 3, 1844-November 4, 1912) 1866

NOTE: Charles, a printer, was the son of John (1791-?) and Sarah Nicholson Richardson (1814-1897) and arrived in the United States on October 8, 1851 aboard the Jacob A. Westervelt, eventually becoming a naturalized citizen. His military career began when he entered Co. B, 5th WI Infantry (Hibbard's Zouaves) in which unit he was involved in the bank riots in Milwaukee in 1861. He next persuaded a friend to forge his mother's signature on the consent form so he might enlist in the Navy. He got as far as Buffalo, NY and was aboard the USS Michigan when his mother insisted he be released. Next he joined a regiment known as Rankin's Lancers which took him to Detroit. This effort also came to naught and being unemployed he returned to Buffalo and took a job on the railroad. On August 12, 1863 he enrolled in the 76th Regiment as a substitute for Nathan Beasley of Collins, Erie County. A timeline attached to his muster roll card shows the Army lost track of him: he was declared a deserter but he was also listed as a POW. Many years later Richardson delivered two speeches for his GAR comrades and he revealed to them what actually happened: "Among the very serious losses sustained by the Army of the Potomac during that year of disaster . . . was that which occurred on November 27, 1863 . . . He who is now permitted to burden you with the recital of the events leading up and following that loss was on that day made a prisoner of war. Just as the head of the train we were guarding entered a small piece of woods not more than half a mile from the depot at Brandy Station, going westward, a few shots from a rushing cavalry troop, accompanied by the command 'Surrender you Yanks,' a return volley from the head of the wagon train guard, and the battle was over, and I was a prisoner in the hands of the famous raider, John S. Mosby, within twenty feet of whom I stood, and down, or rather up the muzzle of whose revolver I was looking . . . ." Eventually Richardson and his fellow captives arrived in Richmond where they were held in Libby Prison and Belle Isle: "When I arrived on the island, there were about 100 other prisoners there, and they were sheltered only by poor ragged tents, and about half of those who reached the island with me were sheltered in the same manner. But I had neither tent shelter nor blanket of any kind and I was forced to accept such shelter as the Lee side of the tents afforded. I endured this for more than a week. I suffered terribly from cold and rain. A few days before Christmas I managed to squeeze myself into an already over-crowded tent . . . ." Relief came in the form of the foreman of one of the Richmond newspapers who was looking for someone with printing skills to assist in the office since all his personnel had gone to war. Richardson volunteered, went to work, be-came familiar with the city, and even saw Jefferson Davis and Robert E. Lee one day. The escape of the 109 Union soldiers from Libby Prison spelled an end to his parole and Richardson decided he had to attempt an escape. The attempt failed. He was severely punished and threatened with hanging. When informed that he would live "the reaction was too much for my nerves, and I broke down, and was taken to the hospital the next day, where I spent a month struggling with a fever and erysipelas, from which I recovered in time to be one of the first lot of Richmond prisoners sent to Andersonville, at which place and other stockades I spent altogether 17 months. After leaving Richmond, the real hardships of prison life [were] begun . . . ." First going to Danville, Richardson and his fellow captives then set out for Andersonville which he described in some detail for his audience. He related how it was nearly impossible to find shelter and how he and a friend carefully collected "sufficient ma-terial" to build a shanty. In October 1864 Richardson was sent to Millen, GA where salvation seemed to be at hand: "One day, after we had been at Millen for a couple of weeks, an order came for the sick to appear at the prison gate for exchange, it being stated that a cartel of exchange had been agreed to and that the sick and lame were to receive first benefits . . . But I still remained healthy. I was fat, and correspondingly 'sassy' and I had no means of getting sick. Suddenly it occurred to me to eat my soap ration, and I acted on the idea. I ate a piece – about half an inch thick by two inches square – and vigorously rubbed my tongue with it to make it appear white and furred. When was done . . . I hurried to the sick rendezvous, and found there about five hun-dred men in all stages of decrepitude. I was soon seized with a desire to vomit and I did so. I heaved and belched, and spurted out soapsuds like sewer from a laundry . . . The doctor looked at me and felt my pulse. I stuck my tongue out at him. He asked me how I liked the soap and ordered me back into the stockade . . . ." Shortly thereafter, with rumors flying that Sherman was approaching, Richardson and others were sent to Savannah and then to Charleston, SC. From there he went to Blackshear, FL and thence to Florence, SC. Again, exchanges were arranged but although he now weighed only 75 lbs. he was passed over. Not until February 1865 was he among the fortunates permitted to leave captivity: "I was at last sick enough, and useless enough to be sent home, and with several hundred others was sent to Wilmington, North Carolina; but the authorities were not ready to receive us, and I was hurried off to Goldsboro, where I lay in the woods for three or four days, and then returned to Wilmington, where, late in March, I was sent through the lines, and was once more under Old Glory . . . ." Several days later he was sent to the Naval Academy Hospital at Annapolis, MD: "On getting cleaned up I began to realize the horrors through which I had passed. Every day brought me new arrivals of prisoners from the prisons of the south. Ragged, half clothed, uncleaned, starved to a skeleton appearance, drawn tightly over their fleshless bones, their hollow and lackluster eyes, their ambling unsteady gait, now seemed to me to be real, and I turned from them with feelings of mingled pity and disgust, notwithstanding that I had lived in its midst for a year and a half, and had but a few days before been as bad as the worst of the wretches I now saw. There were here the merest semblances of men, showing by their every act that the treatment through which they had passed had destroyed their minds as well as their bodies; some of them were too dazed even to tell their names, too timid to approach the cleanliness provided for them, they shrank from the comforts to which they had so long been strangers . . . ." A month

Charles Richardson's harrowing tale of imprisonment in Confederate POW camps graphically detailed the awful treatment Union prisoners endured in the last years of the war.
Wes Anderson

later Richardson was sent to Milwaukee where he was discharged on July 26, 1865 as a member of the 147th Regiment. Like all Civil War survivors Richardson began to put his life back together, marrying and beginning a family. He and Rosaline, the mother of nine children, moved to Valley City, ND in 1881 where he became the editor and publisher of *The Valley City Times*, which position he held until retiring and selling the newspaper in 1887. He served on the city council and the elections committee. In 1884 the governor of North Dakota established a state militia and Richardson was appointed *aide-de-camp* with the rank of colonel. He had been a member of E. B. Wolcott Post No. 1, GAR in Wisconsin and in Barnes County, ND helped organize Josiah S. Weiser Post No. 66, serving as its first commander. When he and Rosaline returned to Wisconsin in 1887, he served as adjutant of the Wolcott Post for 14 years. When he died, the GAR took charge of his funeral. He and Rosa, who died in Chicago, Cook, IL, are buried in Forest Home Cemetery, Milwaukee.

Mortimer Richey – Co. I (tr. January 28, 1865)
b. August 19, 1841 Greenwood, Steuben County, NY
d. March 15, 1916 Los Angeles, Los Angeles, CA
m. Ellen "Helen" Ambrosia Malone (May 1848-February 11, 1919) 1869

NOTE: Mortimer, also known as Martin, was the son of Daniel (1818-1891) and Frances Julia Chapman Richey (1821-1877). He enrolled in the 76th Regiment at Elmira, Chemung, NY on July 18, 1863, apparently a volunteer, and mustered into Co. C. He was wounded on May 5, 1864 at the battle of the Wilderness and in 1890 said he had been "shot through right arm." He transferred to Co. H on November 8th. From the 147th he transferred to Co. H, 91st Regiment on June 5, 1865, mustering out near Washington, DC on July 3rd. He was a farmer and miller. In 1898 he was appointed postmaster of Rexville, Steuben, NY Post Office. He was a member of William C. White Post No. 561 GAR, Greenwood. In 1905 Mortimer and Ellen were living in West Union, Steuben County, but by 1910 they had moved to San Bernardino, Los Angeles, CA. Ellen claimed in 1910 to be the mother of nine, six of whom were still living. She too died in Los Angeles but graves for her and Mortimer have not been located.

Charles Rider – Co. D (tr. January 28, 1865)
b. 1844 Oswego County, NY
d. November 11, 1922 Jackson City, Jackson, MI
m. ?

NOTE: Charles' parents may have been Ezra (1785-*post* 1855) and Sarah J. Rider (1823-*post* 1855). His POB and DOB are disputed. One muster roll card says he was born in Oswego while another says Germany. His entry in Draft Registrations claims his native land was Ireland. Since he enrolled, seemingly a volunteer, in Oswego City, I am inclined to believe he was born in Oswego County. Census records for both 1900 and 1920 confirm his POB was New York State. When he enrolled in the 76th Regiment on August 15, 1863, he claimed to be 21 and therefore born in 1842. Later documents all point to a birth date of 1844 except his death certificate which states he was born on December 25, 1859! The death certificate also states that he was a widower but available census records consistently identify him as a single person. He transferred to Co. I on October 11, 1864 and to Co. C on December 1st. From the 147th he transferred to Co. B, 91st Regiment on June 5, 1865, mustering out on July 3rd near Washington, DC. Charles was a farm worker his entire adult life. He is buried in Mount Evergreen Cemetery, Jackson, Jackson, MI.

Charles J. Riggs – Co. C (tr. January 28, 1865)
b. 1845 Ireland
d. March 22, 1897 Fort Mitchell, Kenton, KY
m. Mary O'Hara (1849-December 5, 1913) February 19, 1873

NOTE: Charles J. Riggs was an *alias* used by Charles O'Brien who claimed on his muster roll card for the 76th Regiment to have been born in Germany. He enrolled as a substitute for Franklin Bentley, Summerhill, Cayuga, NY at Auburn on September 24, 1863, mustering into Co. A. He transferred within the regiment several times. From the 147th he transferred to Co. H, 91st Regiment on June 5, 1865, mustering out on July 3rd near Washington, DC. After the war he enlisted in the 19th US Infantry which was consolidated with the 28th US Infantry on March 15, 1869 with the designation of 19th US Infantry Regiment. He and Mary were married in Covington, Kenton, KY. They had no children. Over the years Charles had many jobs but in 1897 he was an hostler. His COD was meningitis. Mary applied for and obtained a widow's pension. Her COD was senility. Both are buried in St. Mary's Cemetery, Fort Mitchell.

Hiram Greenleaf Risley – Co. D (tr. January 28, 1865)
b. April 18, 1833 Oneida County, NY
d. March 9, 1912 Ellisburg, Jefferson, NY
m1. Juliette Van Swall (1840-July 7, 1862) February 2, 1854
m2. Sophia S. Houghton (January 1832-July 25, 1913) 1866

NOTE: Hiram, son of Hiram (1804-1862) and Betsey Greenleaf Risley (1801-December 3, 1871), apparently was a volunteer, enrolling in the 76th Regiment at Columbus, Chenango, NY on August 17, 1864, mustering into Co. H. He transferred to Co. B on January 1, 1865. From the 147th he transferred to Co. B, 91st Regiment, mustering out near Washington, DC on July 3rd. Although his entry in *The Town Clerks' Registers* states, "never wounded or prisoner," he apparently was sick at one time because one of his muster roll cards says he was "absent, in hospital." In 1890, while living at Rural Hill, Jefferson, NY, he claimed "heart & lungs, Diarrhea" as disabilities. He and Juliette were the parents of three: Maryetta (1854-1929); John R. (1856-1929); Lucinda A. (1860-1932). Juliette is buried in Deansboro Cemetery, Oneida County. Hiram and Sophia had no children. A funeral notice appeared in *The Jefferson County Journal* March 20, 1912, 5: ". . . The funeral of Hiram Risley was held on Wednesday, March 13, at his late home in Ellisburg. The service was read by Mr. Robinson, the minister of the Universalist church. Mr. Risley was a soldier in the civil war. He had lived several years in this section and had won the respect of his many friends and neighbors. His death leaves his widow alone in their old home. His sons [*sic*] by a former marriage were present at the funeral." Sophia did not long survive him, as shown by a notice in *The Jefferson County Journal* July 30, 1913, 3: ". . . The community was shocked Friday morning to hear of the death of Mrs. Sophia Houghton Risley, who was a life long resident of this neighborhood." Hiram and Sophia are buried in Stowles Cemetery, Henderson. Hiram's brother, Joshua (1843-1863), was drafted into the 76th Regiment at Shelby, Orleans, NY on August 24, 1863. According to his muster roll card he deserted but in actuality he was taken prisoner at the battle of Mine Run (November 27-December 2, 1863) and sent to Libby Prison, Richmond, VA, where he died. COD is unknown.

Elisha S. Robbins – Co. G (tr. January 28, 1865)
b. June 2, 1841 Bottom Creek, Chittenden, VT
d. July 9, 1908 Shelby, Orleans, NY
m. Ellen _____ (1849-*post* 1913) ?

NOTE: Elisha, son of Nathaniel (1810-1880) and Esther H. Snead Robbins (1816-1880), enrolled in the 76th Regiment on August 8, 1863 at Shelby, apparently a volunteer, mustering into Co. G. He transferred to Co. D on October 20, 1864. From the 147th he went to Co. F, 91st Regiment on June 5, 1865, mustering out near Washington, DC on July 3rd. He was a farm laborer his entire adult life. Little is known about Ellen. In 1900 Elisha said he had married in 1865 but in 1870 he was still living with his parents. In 1875 he, Ellen, and their son, Charles (1872-?), were living in Alabama, Genesee County. I think the couple did not marry until 1871, based on their son's DOB. Beginning with the 1880 census the couple was never again enumerated together. In fact, I have located no census records for her or the child, who may have died young. In 1890 Elisha applied for a pension. When the Veterans' Schedules were enumerated he was living in East Oakfield, Genesee County. He claimed no disability. He renewed his pension in 1907. It is interesting to note that although he died in 1908 Ellen did not apply for a widow's pension until August 11, 1913. She did not obtain a certificate, perhaps because she died before the process could be completed. A DOD has not been located for her. Elisha is buried in East Shelby Cemetery. His stone refers to his affiliation with the 91st Regiment.

Morton L. Roe – Co. E (tr. January 28, 1865)
b. June 6, 1826 Oneida County, NY
d. May 17, 1902 Cherry Valley, Otsego, NY
m. Melissa Rutt (April 5, 1838-December 9, 1913) 1865

NOTE: Morton's parents are unidentified. His name was sometimes given as Martin. He enlisted in the 76th Regiment at Van Harrisville, Herkimer, NY on October 7, 1861, mustering into Co. K. He deserted near Pratts Point, VA on January 20, 1863. His muster roll card states he was tried by court-martial and sentenced to forfeit pay and allowance as well as $10.20 per month, in addition to making up the 18 months he was gone. The date of the trial was not stated but it probably occurred in June 1864. At some point he transferred to Co. I. He transferred to Co. C on December 1, 1864. He was sent to the 147th to make up the lost time. On June 5, 1865 he was sent to Co. K, 91st Regiment, mustering out on July 3rd near Washington, DC. In 1890 he claimed no disability but stated he was a "re-enlisted veteran." In 1900 Melissa said she was the mother of six, three of whom were living. Morton's death was announced in *The Cooperstown Farmer* May 23, 1902: ". . . Morton L. Roe, a veteran of the Civil War, died at his home in this village [Cherry Valley] on Saturday. He was in his 76th year. His funeral, which was held from the Methodist church on Tuesday, was in charge of the G. A. R. and was largely attended." The GAR Post mentioned was Emery Upton No. 224. Melissa's death was announced in *The Otsego Farmer* December 12, 1913, 4: "Mrs. Melissa Roe died at her home in the village of Cherry Valley, Tuesday evening, in the seventy-sixth year of her age, death being caused by dropsy. Mrs. Roe was a highly respected woman of a generous disposition and will be greatly missed especially in her immediate family. She is survived by one son, Louis, and two daughters, Mrs. Patrick Gavin and Mrs. Anna Getman, all of Cherry Valley." Morton and Melissa are buried in Cherry Valley Cemetery.

Peter Rolwine – Co. G (tr. January 28, 1865)
b. 1840 Cohoes, Albany, NY
d. September 7, 1913 Stottsville, Columbia, NY
m. Mary Lee (1848-October 9, 1895) *ca.* 1866

NOTE: Peter's surname was variously spelled. I use that found on gravestone. His father is unidentified but his mother was Margaret "Peggy" (1805-*post* 1850). Peter initially enlisted in the 30th Regiment at Watervliet, Albany, NY on September 17, 1862, mustering into Co. F. He transferred to Co. F, 76th Regiment on May 25, 1863. He was taken captive at Gettysburg on July 1, 1863 and paroled at an unknown date. He next transferred to Co. D on July 1, 1864. From the 147th he went to Co. F, 91st Regiment on June 5, 1865, mustering out near Washington, DC on July 3rd. Peter was a spinner in the textile mills as late as 1900. He and Mary, who was the mother of at least three children, are buried in the Episcopal Cemetery, Stockport, Columbia, NY. Peter's brother, John (1837-1887), served in the 30th Regiment from May 1861-June 1863. He later served in Co. I, 2nd NY Veteran Cavalry from September 1863-November 1865.

Robert Rowland – Co. B (tr. January 28, 1865)
b. January 29, 1843 Oneida County, NY
d. April 25, 1911 St. James City, Watonwan, MN
m. Clarissa Fenno (December 29, 1846-May 1, 1907) June 8, 1867

NOTE: The son of Richard (1810-1875) and Ellen Rowland (1813-1876), Robert was drafted, enrolling in the 76th Regiment on September 25, 1863 and mustering into Co. G. He transferred to Co. H on April 12, 1864 and to Co. B on January 1, 1865. His muster roll card notes he performed extra duty as a brigade guard at headquarters. From the 147th he went to Co. G, 91st Regiment on June 5, 1865, mustering out near Washington, DC on July 3rd. He and Clarissa were married in Blue Earth, Faribault, MN and became the parents of five children, all living in 1900. The couple is buried in Lake Crystal Cemetery, Lake Crystal, Blue Earth, MN.

John Ruloff – Co. F (tr. January 28, 1865)
b. 1833 Cayuga County, NY
d. June 20, 1891 Conquest, Cayuga, NY
m. Ellen Edee (1837-June 8, 1926) *ca.* 1859

NOTE: John was the son of John (1809-1871) and Catherine Coppernoll Ruloff (1811-1873). A draftee, he enrolled in the 76th Regiment at Auburn, Cayuga, NY on July 23, 1863. He was wounded at North Anna River, VA on May 24, 1864 and in 1890 said he had been shot through the leg. He transferred to Co. C on December 1, 1864. He was discharged as a member of the 147th at a hospital in Albany, NY on July 25, 1865. He was a member of E. M. Knapp Post No. 380 GAR in Cato, Cayuga, NY. He and Ellen, who died in Syracuse, Onondaga, NY, were the parents of three children, two of whom were living in 1900. The couple is buried in Union Hill Cemetery, Cato.

Ammi J. Satterly – Co. K (tr. January 28, 1865)
b. August 23, 1844 Broome County, NY
d. September 29, 1906 National Soldiers' Home, Bath, Steuben, NY
m. ------

NOTE: Ammi, son of William Baxter (1820-1896) and Amanda Cole Satterly (1821-1895), enlisted in the 76th Regiment at McLean, Tompkins, NY on September 16, 1861 mustering into Co. C. According to *The Town Clerks' Registers*, he was in such battles as Fredericksburg, Chancellorsville, Wilderness, and Cold Harbor. He was wounded at Second Bull Run, VA on August 28, 1862. On January 2, 1864 Ammi re-enlisted. He transferred to Co. A on November 8, 1864. From the 147th he transferred to Co. K, 91st Regiment on June 5, 1865, mustering out on July 3rd near Washington, DC. He was admitted to the Bath Home on numerous occasions but his last admission occurred on June 4, 1906. Ammi died of septicemia and was buried in Bath National Cemetery. His gravestone erroneously assigns him to the 19th Regiment. Ammi's father served in Co. G, 137th Regiment from August 1862-June 1865.

George Scott – Co. A (tr. January 28, 1865)
b. 1847 England
d. July 7, 1879 Arenac, Arenac, MI
m. Amanda "Mandy" M. Hathaway (1846-May 31, 1927) *ca.* 1869

NOTE: George's parents are unidentified. He lied about his age in order to enter the military, claiming to be 21 in 1863 when he enrolled in the 76th at Watertown, Jefferson, NY as a substitute for an unknown draftee, mustering into Co. F. He was wounded on May 6, 1864 at the battle of the Wilderness and in 1890 Amanda said he had been shot through the left thigh. He transferred to Co. A on December 1, 1864. From the 147th he transferred to Co. C, 91st Regiment on June 5, 1865, mustering out on July 3rd near Ball's Cross Roads, VA. By 1870 he and Amanda were living in Arenac. They were the parents of two daughters, Cora Ann (1870-1871) and Bertha May (1873-1944). George's COD is unknown and his gravesite has not been located. Amanda married William North (1836-1913) on August 11, 1880 as his third wife. Apparently the marriage failed. Amanda's application for a widow's pension on August 6, 1883 was successful. In 1884 North, who had served in Co. B, 15th Michigan, married a fourth time. It would appear, therefore, that their marriage was dissolved in 1883. Amanda resumed using Scott as her surname. Born in Oswego County, NY, the daughter of Daniel Anthony (1785-*post* 1855) and Clara Keiler Hathaway (1810-*post* 1870), she died in Battle Creek, Calhoun, MI after suffering a stroke and was buried in Hicks Cemetery, Penfield, Calhoun, MI.

Samuel Miles Seaman – Co. E (tr. January 28, 1865)
b. April 22, 1833 Yates County, NY
d. August 1, 1886 Watkins, Schuyler, NY
m. ------

NOTE: Samuel, son of Orison (1800-*ante* 1865) and Sarah Kress Seaman (1802-*post* 1865), was a carpenter. He first saw military duty when he enlisted in the 23rd Regiment, serving in Co. I from May 1861-January 1863. He was discharged on a surgeon's certificate. On July 27, 1863 he enrolled in the 76th Regiment as a substitute for his brother, William D. (1834-1905), mustering into Co. A. He transferred to Co. I on October 10, 1864 and to Co. C on December 1st. According to his lengthy entry in *The Town Clerks' Registers,* he participated in the battles of Sulphur Springs, 2nd Bull Run, Antietam, Petersburg, White Oak Swamp, and Hatcher's Run. He was discharged at Elmira, Chemung, NY on June 9, 1865 as a member of the 147th Regiment. In September 1880 he entered the National Soldiers' Home, Bath, Steuben, NY but left in December. A notation of "desertion" indicates the manner of his leave taking. On February 26, 1885 he was admitted to the Chemung County Poorhouse, claiming to be a widower although I have located no evidence of a wife. His habits were described as "intemperate" and his reason for seeking admittance was "sickness and destitution." When he left the poorhouse is unknown as is his COD. He is buried in Glenwood Cemetery, Watkins Glen, Schuyler, NY.

Charles Wesley Sergeant – Co. E (tr. January 28, 1865)
b. August 24, 1837 Buffalo, Erie, NY
d. July 31, 1917 Laingsburg, Shiawassee, MI
m. Harriet O. Bowen (June 9, 1838-April 15, 1926) November 28, 1859

NOTE: Charles, a sailor, was the son of John (1814-1853) and Eleanor "Ellen" A. Burdick Sergeant (1818-1894). He enrolled in the 76th Regiment on August 10, 1863 at Buffalo, apparently a volunteer, and mustered into Co. A. He transferred to Co. I on October 11, 1864 and to Co. C on December 1st. From the 147th he went to Co. I, 91st Regiment on June 5, 1865, mustering out near Washington, DC on July 3rd. He and Harriet were the parents of two children, only one of whom survived to adulthood. An unsourced obituary announced his death: "Charles Wesley Sergeant was born in Erie county, New York, near Buffalo, August 24, 1837. He was married to Miss Harriet Bowen, of Rochester, New York, Nov. 28, 1859. To this union was born one son, Guy L., who resides in Ithaca, Michigan. Mr. Sergeant enlisted in the civil war in 1863, where he served as a soldier until the close of the war, when he returned home to Buffalo, where, with his wife, they lived 3 years longer. In 1872 they moved to Clare county, Michigan, where they remained for 20 years, coming to Laingsburg in 1900, where he made his home until the time of his death. His age was 79 years, 11 months and 6 days. He was a member of the G. A. R. When 45 years of age he felt the desire to become a Christian and sought an entrance into the Kingdom of God by uniting with the Wesleyan Methodist church by immersion. He was a good man, a good neighbor, and though he suffered a long time, he bore it patiently until death allowed his spirit to be free. He leaves a host of friends and relatives to mourn their loss." Charles' COD was heart disease. Harriet, who died in Lansing, Ingham, MI, succumbed to arteriosclerosis. They are buried in Laingsburg Cemetery. His stone erroneously places him in the 79th Regiment.

Arthur Robert Seward – Co. B (tr. January 28, 1865)
b. August 2, 1843 Auburn, Cayuga County, NY
d. June 2, 1918 Indianapolis, Marion, IN
m1. Sophia E. _____ (July 1840-April 4, 1928) ca. 1867
m2. Ary Alice Beswick (April 2, 1868-March 20, 1951) 1889

NOTE: Arthur's parents are unknown. His death certificate states he was born in Maryland, Otsego, NY, but Cayuga County is found consistently in the census records.

He enlisted in the 76th Regiment at Scott, Cortland, NY on September 14, 1861and mustered into Co. D. On January 2, 1864 he re-enlisted at Culpeper, VA. He was taken prisoner on May 5, 1864 at the battle of the Wilderness, sent to Andersonville, and paroled on February 26, 1865 at North East Ferry, NC. After recuperating and taking advantage of a furlough he was discharged at Alexandria, VA on May 27, 1865 at the "expiration of term of service." He and Sophia were the parents of four children. In 1890 she was listed as the "supposed widow of Arthur R. Seward." The enumerator noted she had been "deserted by husband 14 years." Their youngest child, Florence, had been born in 1875. I have been unable to find an entry for him on the Veterans' Schedules. Arthur and Ary had two children. In 1910 he admitted to two marriages but that he never was divorced from Sophia was confirmed in 1918 when she applied for and obtained a widow's pension. His COD was a cerebral hemorrhage with senile dementia as a contributory factor. He is buried in Crown Hill National Cemetery, Indianapolis. Sophia's obituary appeared in *The Cortland Democrat* April 6, 1928. She died at the home of her daughter, Florence, in Homer and was buried in Cortland Rural Cemetery. Ary married Samuel Scott Bethuram (1861-1944) *ca.* 1922 as his second wife. Her death was announced in *The Indianapolis News* March 21, 1951, 11: "Services for Mrs. Ary Alice Bethuram, 82, formerly of 371 Prospect St., who died yesterday in the Evangelistic Center, 3518 Shelby St., will be held at 1:30 p.m. tomorrow in the G. H. Herrmann Funeral Home. Burial will be in Crown Hill Cemetery. Born at Spencer, Mrs. Bethuram had lived in Indianapolis 50 years. She was a member of the Morris Street Methodist Church, its Ladies Aid Society and its Woman's Society of Christian Service . . . ."

Peter Shaffer – Co. K (tr. January 28, 1865)
b. 1828 Germany
d. March 31, 1898 National Soldiers' Home, Bath, Steuben, NY
m. ?

NOTE: Peter's surname was variously spelled. Nothing is known about him before he entered the military. He enrolled in the 76th Regiment at Buffalo, Erie, NY on August 8, 1863 as a substitute for John S. Hopper, Buffalo, mustering into Co. G. He transferred to Co. H on October 20, 1864 and to Co. B on January 1, 1865. From the 147th he transferred to Co. K, 91st Regiment on June 5, 1865, mustering out near Washington, DC on July 3rd. His actions after the war have not been traced but in 1890 he was a resident in the home in Bath. He applied for a pension that year under the name Shoffer. Although most documents show a DOD of March 30, 1898, the NYS Death Index provides that of March 31st. His gravestone in the Bath National Cemetery spells his name Schoffer and refers to his service in the 91st Regiment. I have found no evidence of a wife.

John Shanley – Co. B (tr. January 28, 1865)
b. 1838 Ireland
d. December 9, 1894 National Soldiers' Home, Bath, Steuben, NY
m. ------

NOTE: John's parents are unknown. Although he stated for his muster card that he had been born in Lockport, Niagara, NY in 1840, such was not the case. In fact, he used that lie twice since he enlisted in Co. D, 12th NY Cavalry at Buffalo, Erie, on December 12, 1862. His entry in *The Adjutant-General's Report* for that organization states, "no further record," making it likely he deserted. He enrolled in the 76th Regiment on August 5, 1863 in Buffalo as a substitute for James Finley, mustering into Co. A. He was wounded at North Anna River, VA on May 26, 1864 and in 1890 revealed he had two gunshot wounds in his leg. He transferred several times within the regiment. From the 147th he transferred to Co. G, 91st Regiment, mustering out near Washington, DC on July 3rd. He applied for a pension on May 31, 1867. His subsequent life is a mystery until September 28, 1888 when he was admitted to the Monroe County Poorhouse. His cause of dependence was rheumatism and his habits were described as "intemperate." How long he was there is not noted but in 1890 he was enumerated while incarcerated in the Monroe County Penitentiary, revealing he had an *alias* of John Murphy. He is buried in the Bath National Cemetery.

Charles Shaver – Co. E (tr. January 28, 1865)
b. 1841 ?
d. September 16, 1889 Sisters of Charity Hospital, Buffalo, Erie, NY
m. Jane "Jennie" Virginia Trudel (February 1864-April 2, 1930) *ca.* 1867

NOTE: Charles' POB is disputed. His muster roll card states he was born in New York City but I have located no corroborating evidence for that. His parents are un-identified. Even his DOB is a matter of conjecture. He claimed to be 22 when he enrolled in the 76th Regiment but his gravestone provides a DOB of 1850. In 1870 he was 28 but by 1880 he had advanced to 40. His death notice, published in *The Buffalo Courier* September 18, 1889, placed his age at 40! I think the 1841 date is closer to the mark. He enrolled in the 76th on August 5, 1863 in Rochester, Monroe, NY, mustering into Co. E. Had he been born in 1850 he would only have been 13. I have been unable to determine if he volunteered or was drafted, but he mustered into Co. E. He transferred to Co. C on November 18, 1864. From the 147th he went to Co. D, 91st Regiment on June 5, 1865, mustering out near Washington, DC on July 3rd. He and Jennie, who was born in Canada, were the parents of at least eight chil-dren. Charles was a caulker by occupation. His COD was a stroke. He is buried in United German and French Roman Catholic Cemetery, Cheektowaga, Erie, NY. His stone alludes to his association with the 91st Regiment but places him in the wrong company. Jennie applied for and obtained a widow's pension but strangely enough did not apply for her younger children. Her grave has not been located.

Theodore Shaw – Co. K (tr. January 28, 1865)
b. August 5, 1846 Aurelius, Cayuga, NY
d. August 27, 1919 Blue Lake, Muskegon, MI
m. Mary F. McManus (March 1857-July 1, 1949) December 25, 1873

NOTE: Theodore's parents were Isaac (1810-*ante* 1855) and Lucy Wormer Shaw (1812-*post* 1865). He enrolled in the 76th Regiment at Auburn, Cayuga, NY on July 23, 1863 as a substitute for an unnamed draftee, mustering into Co. K. He was captured at the battle of the Wilderness on May 5, 1864 and sent to Andersonville. According to *The Town Clerks' Registers*, he was exchanged in March 1865, returning from parole camp in early May. He was discharged near Washington, DC on June 9th as a member of the 147th. Shaw was an employee on the railroad when he died of a cerebral hemorrhage. His death certificate states he was buried in Chicago. He and Mary were married in Peoria, Peoria, IL. They became the parents of three children. After her husband died Mary moved to Chicago where she resided with her daughter Rosemary Frances Shaw McCartney (1881-1947). Mary's obituary appeared in *The Chicago Tribune* July 2, 1949, 17: "Mrs. Mary Shaw, 95, of 6519 Ellis av., a Chicagoan for 90 years, died in the Longwood Drive Rest home yesterday. She was the widow of George [*sic*] Shaw, Civil war veteran and a Rock Island railroad conductor who died 25 years ago. She leaves a daughter, Mrs. Mary Ellen Rieg of Los Angeles, and her son-in-law, Frank R. McCartney, with whom she lived . . . Services will be at 10 a.m. Monday in St. Clara's church with burial in Mount Olivet cemetery." It is possible that Theodore is also buried there.

Gideon Silver – Co. K (tr. January 28, 1865)
b. 1830 Bow, Merrimack, NH
d. February 23, 1871 State Prison, Concord, Merrimack, NH
m. ------

NOTE: Gideon was the son of Edmund W. (1796-1836) and Charlotte Isabel Dow Perkins Silver (1789-October 12, 1872). He enlisted in the 16th NH Infantry, a nine months' unit, in October 1862, deserting at Concord on November 7th. On August 21, 1863, he enrolled in the 76th Regiment at Canandaigua, Ontario, NY as a substitute for J. Byron Hayes, mustering into Co. C. He lied about his age, claiming to be 28. He transferred to Co. B on November 8, 1864. From the 147th he went to Co. K, 91st Regiment on June 5, 1865, mustering out near Washington, DC. When the 1870 census was taken for Concord,

NH on June 11, 1870 he was a prisoner in the state prison. His age was given as 40. On January 1, 1873 his half-brother, Artemus Perkins (1813-1894), who had been suggested as the administrator for his sibling's estate, declined the offer. The court document states that Gideon had died "nearly two years since." The reason for his imprisonment may be inferred from an article appearing in *The Manchester Weekly Union* October 5, 1869, 3: "Charles Clifford of Dunbarton recently missed from his pasture a fine two-years old Dutch heifer, and after a while he found her in detail, about the premises of Gideon F. Silver, of that town – hide here, a quarter there, and other parts elsewhere. Silver was arrested – says he knows nothing about it – but is held for trial under $800 bond." Milli Knudsen's *Hard Time in Concord, New Hampshire,* 160-61, tells the rest of the story: "Gideon M. Silver of Dunbarton stole a heifer belonging to Charles Clifford in September 1869 . . . Four witnesses testified about Silver's battle with breathing difficulties before his death on the 23rd of February 1871. Described by Dr. A. H. Crosby as 'one of the most amiable men I ever met,' Silver insisted on working through the day before he died because he felt he could breathe better in the work shop than in his cell. Jeremiah Johnson, a fellow prisoner, helped carry Silver to the prison hospital the night of February 22. Johnson was allowed to rub Silver with hot cloths to relieve his suffering. Stephen B. Eaton, the steward in charge of the prison hospital, gave Silver some whisky that night in an attempt to keep him alive. The next morning Silver's suffering worsened. Dr. Crosby left to get assistance, but didn't return in time. Jeremiah Johnson was there to record Silver's last words, 'I have been murdered in New Hampshire state-prison.' Silver asked that his folks at home be told. Dr. Crosby and a Dr. Conn did a postmortem exam and found air in the heart cavity and his bronchial tubes plugged. An inquiry into this death was presented to the governor and council shortly after Silver died." Gideon's grave has not been located.

John F. Simpson – Co. H (tr. January 28, 1865)
b. March 1821 Yorkshire, England
d. July 7, 1907 Buffalo, Erie, NY
m. Dorothea "Dorothy" _____ (1818-September 10, 1896) *ca.* 1847

NOTE: John's DOB varies. I use that provided on the 1900 census. His parents are unknown but he reportedly came to the United states in 1849 and was naturalized. He enrolled in the 76th Regiment at Buffalo on November 11, 1864, mustering into Co. D. From the 147th he transferred to Co. F, 91st Regiment on June 5, 1865, mustering out near Washington, DC on July 3rd. He was a railroad engineer in Buffalo. He and Dorothy were the parents of at least five children. After Dorothy died, John lived with his daughter Margaret Cummer (1857-July 4, 1907) who died three days before he did. His death notice in *The Buffalo Evening News* July 8, 1904, 1 stated he died "suddenly." John and Dorothy are buried in Forest Lawn Cemetery, Buffalo.

George Sippel – Co. D (tr. January 28, 1865)
b. October 3, 1831 Germany
d. April 15, 1904 Kendall, Orleans, NY
m. Mary Ann Shefler (1829-May 14, 1894) *ca.* 1866

NOTE: George's surname was variously spelled. I use that on the gravestone. His parents are unidentified. He enrolled in the 76th Regiment on August 6, 1863 at Rochester, Monroe, NY as a substitute for Cornelius Fenner, Kendall. He transferred several times within the regiment. From the 147th he transferred to Co. B, 91st Regiment on June 5, 1865, mustering out on July 3rd near Washington, DC. In 1890 he claimed "Rheumatism incurred in the service" as his disability. He and Mary Ann are buried in Beechwood Cemetery, Kendall. His gravestone alludes to his service in the 91st Regiment.

Abram Jacob Sitterly – Co. K (tr. January 28, 1865)
b. September 1844 Schenectady County, NY
d. March 5, 1930 Manhattan, Riley, KS
m1. Helen "Ellen" Van Olinda (1844-*post* 1880) *ca.* 1867
m2. Arminnia Catherine Clover (February 1853-April 26, 1928) November 6, 1878

NOTE: Abram, a carpenter, was the son of Jacob (1823-*post* 1860) and Lois Keefer Sitterly (1814-*post* 1865). The family name was variously spelled. He lied about his age when he enlisted in the 30th Regiment on August 17, 1862, saying he was 27! He mustered into Co. F, transferring to Co. G, 76th Regiment on May 25, 1863. He transferred twice within that regiment. From the 147th he transferred to Co. K, 91st Regiment on June 5, 1865, mustering out on July 3rd near Washington, DC. He and Ellen were the parents of Jacob (1868-?) and Edwin W. (1878-?). It is unknown whether or not he was present for the birth of Edwin. He married Arminnia in Des Moines County, IA. They were the parents of 10 children, according to the 1910 census. Abram declared in 1910 that he had only been married once. In 1880 Ellen was living in Rotterdam, Schenectady, NY with her father, Peter Van Olinda (1817-?). She and the children disappear after that and she may have remarried. Abram and Arminnia lived for many years in Manhattan, KS. He was active in Lew Gove Post No. 100, GAR. The couple is buried in Sunset Cemetery, Manhattan. The surname on the family stone is spelled Sitterley.

George Smith – Co. B (tr. January 28, 1865)
b. 1840 England
d. ? ?
m. ?

NOTE: Nothing is known about this soldier either prior to or after his time in the army except that he was a laborer. He enrolled in the 76th Regiment at Elmira, Chemung, NY on July 20, 1863 as a substitute for an unnamed draftee, mustering into Co. A. He transferred to Co. G on October 10, 1864, to Co. E on October 20th and to Co. A on November 18th. From the 147th he was sent to Co. G, 91st Regiment on June 5, 1865, mustering out near Washington, DC on July 3rd. He does not appear on the 1890 Veterans' Schedules or in *The Town Clerks' Registers*. I have located no pension card for him.

Horace H. Smith – Co. K (tr. January 28, 1865)
b. 1831 Yates County, NY
d. January 12, 1886 Groton, Tompkins, NY
m. Nancy Seaman (1820-*post* 1892) *ca.* 1854

NOTE: The son of Batamson (1806-1866) and Eliza Ann Wooley Smith (1820-*post* 1892), Horace first enlisted in the 76th Regiment on September 16, 1861 and mustered into Co. C. He was wounded at the second battle of Bull Run (August 28-30, 1862) and was discharged for "disability" on November 2nd. He re-enlisted in the 76th Regiment at Groton on July 25, 1863, mustering into Co. C. He was wounded at the battle of the Wilderness on May 5, 1864 and discharged from Harewood Hospital, Washington, DC on May 19, 1865 as a member of the 147th. He and Nancy, who was born in Dutchess County, were the parents of three sons. According to FAG, Horace and Nancy are both buried in Peruville Cemetery, Tompkins, NY. Her DOD is unknown. Their graves are unmarked.

John Smith – Co. F (tr. January 28, 1865)
b. 1819 Germany
d. 1865 probably Hatcher's Run, Virginia
m. Christina Becker (May 21, 1818-February 15, 1902) January 19, 1837

NOTE: John's parents are unidentified. A tanner, he enrolled in the 76th Regiment at Allegany, Cattaraugus, NY on August 22, 1863 as a substitute for Adelbert H. Marsh, mustering into Co. A. He transferred to Co. I on October 11, 1864 and to Co. C on December 1st. He was listed MIA on February 6, 1865 after the battle of Hatcher's Run and probably died there. Christina applied for a pension on June 26, 1865 and obtained a certificate. She never remarried, rearing her seven children alone. She died in Olean, Cattaraugus, NY and was buried in Allegany Cemetery, Cattaraugus, NY.

Melvin O. Smith – Co. D (tr. January 28, 1865)
b. September 12, 1843 Vesper, Onondaga, NY
d. March 19, 1908 National Soldiers' Home, Dayton, Montgomery, OH
m1. Margaret Henderson (1842-*post* 1870) *ca* 1865
m2. Mary E. _____ (?-?) ?

NOTE: Melvin, son of Darius (1813-1869) and Sylvia Hodge Smith (1819-1894), enrolled in the 76th Regiment at Cortland, Cortland, NY on October 19, 1861, mustering into Co. A. He was wounded at White Sulphur Springs, VA on August 25, 1862 and again on Gettysburg on July 1, 1863 when he was also taken prisoner. In 1897 upon entering the soldiers' home he said he had been shot in the chin. On January 2, 1864 he re-enlisted at Culpeper, VA and transferred to Co. I on October 11th and to Co. C on December 1st. He was discharged near Arlington Heights, VA on June 9, 1865. In 1890 Melvin was living in Deer Creek, Bates, MO. Little is known about Margaret. In 1865 she was living with Melvin's parents. She and Melvin were the parents of Nettie M. (1866-January 17, 1940) and Adella "Della" (1868-November 26, 1936). In 1875 Nettie was living with Morris (1833-1900) and Mary Adelaide Merchant (1841-1887) as their daughter. They formally adopted her in 1878. Even less is known about Mary. When Melvin was admitted to the soldiers' home on July 17, 1897 he said he had lived in Lancaster, PA and that Mary, his wife, also lived there. A notation was subsequently made that Mary was dead and that Nettie was now the next of kin. In 1900 Melvin described himself as a widower. His COD was myocarditis. His body was shipped to DeRuyter, Madison, NY where Nettie lived but his grave has not been located.

Nelson William Smith – Co. I (tr. January 28, 1865)
b. September 1841 Coxsackie, Greene, NY
d. August 24, 1922 Blodgett Mills, Cortland, NY
m1. Emma Amelia Jacobs (1844-June 22, 1903) 1867
m2. Alice V. _____ (1855-*post* 1925) 1905

NOTE: Nelson, the son of Jesse (1793-1885) and Mary Ann Green Smith (1796-1848), enlisted in the 76th Regiment at Freetown, Cortland, NY on September 14, 1861, mustering into Co. C. He transferred to Co. D on October 4th. During his time in the army he rose to the rank of sergeant. On January 2, 1864 he re-enlisted at Culpeper, VA. From the 147th he went to Co. G, 91st Regiment on June 5, 1865, mustering out near Washington, DC on July 3rd. He and Emma were the parents of one daughter, Winifred (1872-1956). The marriage to Alice apparently was unsuccessful since in 1910 Nelson was living with Winifred and Alice was in Bridgeport, Fairfield, CT. Alice is last listed in the Bridgeport city directory in 1925. Nelson was a member of William H. Tarbell Post No. 476 GAR and of William B. Shearer Post No. 74 GAR. His obituary appeared in *The Cortland Democrat* September 1, 1922, 4: "Blodgett Mills, Aug. 30 – Nelson W. Smith, 81, died Aug. 24, at the home of his niece, Mrs. J. J. Howard, where he had been cared for during his illness of four months with inflammatory gangrene. The funeral service was held in the Presbyterian church at McGrawville Saturday morning at 10:30 o'clock, Rev. A. M. Brown officiating. Burial in McGrawville rural cemetery. He leaves one daughter, Mrs. Arthur Koenig of Greensboro, N.C., two grandsons . . . two nieces . . . three nephews . . . ." Emma is also buried in McGrawville Rural Cemetery. Nelson's brother, Jesse G. (1848-1895), enrolled in Co. E, 10th NY Cavalry at Norwich, Chenango, NY on January 14, 1865 as a substitute for Thomas E. Porter, lying about his age to do so.

William Henry Snow – Co. K (tr. January 28, 1865)
b. November 30, 1840 Norwich, Chenango, NY
d. July 16, 1901 Yahala, Lake County, FL
m. Sarah Emery (November 2, 1850-July 15, 1932) 1867

NOTE: William, son of John (1812-1892) and Lucinda Kendall Snow (1811-1883), was drafted, enrolling in the 76th Regiment on August 24, 1863 at Norwich and mustering into Co. G. He transferred to Co. D on October 20, 1864. At an unknown date he was captured by the Confederates. According to his muster roll card he was a "paroled prisoner; taken up from missing in action." He was discharged on August 8, 1865 at Elmira, Chemung, NY as a member of the 147th. In fact, his gravestone alludes to his membership in that outfit. William, a sawyer, and Sarah had no children. He is buried in Yahala Cemetery. Sarah and her mother, Martha J. King Emery (1829-1911), moved west. Her mother is buried in Grandview Cemetery, Fayette, Fayette, IA. Sarah died of bronchial pneumonia at the Indiana State Soldiers' Home in Tippecanoe County, IN and was buried in the Soldiers' Home Cemetery.

Jacob Snyder – Co. F (tr. January 28, 1865)
b. 1841 ?
d. April 21, 1865 in hospital, Washington, DC
m. ------

NOTE: Jacob's POB is disputed. Although his muster roll card provides a birthplace of Germany, his parents, Isaac (1811-1882) and Farena Kaser Snyder (?-1852), were married in Switzerland in 1840 and Farena died there. He enrolled in the 76th Regiment in Busti, Chautauqua, NY on August 20, 1863 as a substitute for William Jones, mustering into Co. I. He transferred to Co. C on December 1, 1864. I have been unable to discover where he was wounded but the 147th was heavily involved in the battle of Five Forks on April 1st. His COD was described as "gsw received in action." Jacob is buried in Arlington National Cemetery, VA. In 1867 Isaac applied for and ultimately obtained a pension, claiming he had been unable to earn a living for ten years because of a hernia. Jacob supported him and gave him his bounty of $300 to buy a house. He also sent him money from his army pay. After Isaac died his second wife, Anna Bauman Gottlieb Snyder (1829-*post* 1883), attempted to claim a pension but was rejected on the grounds she was ineligible.

John Stahler, Jr. – Co. H (tr. January 28, 1865)
b. July 1842 ?
d. February 13, 1905 Lockport, Niagara, NY
m. Mary _____ (June 1848-April 18, 1926) 1868

NOTE: John's parents were John, Sr. (1805-1863) and Catharine Wagner Stahler (1810-1860). His POB is somewhat of a mystery. His obituary says he was a life-long resident of Lockport, but other sources suggest he was born in Pennsylvania. In both 1860 and 1870 he claimed to have been born in Michigan! He enrolled in the 76th Regiment at Lockport on July 28, 1863, apparently a volunteer, mustering into Co. D. He was discharged from the service on June 7, 1865 at Satterlee Hospital, W. Philadelphia, PA. He and Mary, who was born in Germany, were the parents of two, both living in 1900. John was a police officer for many years and, according to his FAG entry, his nickname was "Stahler the jailer." His death was announced in *The Lockport Journal* February 14, 1905, 5. Mary's tragic end was chronicled in *The Lockport Union-Sun and Journal* April 19, 1926, 12: "Funeral services for Mrs. Mary Stahler, 77 years old, who was found dead on a couch at her home . . . about 6:30 o'clock Saturday evening, will be held Tuesday afternoon . . . Mrs. Stahler, widow of John Stahler, was found by her granddaughter, Mildred Gunby. Death was due to as-phyxiation. Three gas burners were turned on, but only two were lighted. The woman lived alone . . . ." Mary and John are buried in Glenwood Cemetery, Lockport.

William Steele – Co. D (tr. January 28, 1865)
b. January 10, 1820 Germany
d. July 28, 1901 Adams, Berkshire, MA
m. Sylvina Jennett Purdy Van Olinda (June 27, 1823-June 20, 1905) 1850

NOTE: William's parents are unidentified. He enrolled in the 76th Regiment on September 16, 1863 at Watertown, Jefferson, NY as a substitute for an unknown draftee and mustered into Co. H. He transferred several times within the regiment. On May 10, 1864 he was wounded at Laurel Hill, VA but in 1890 claimed no dis-ability. He transferred to Co. B, 91st Regiment on June 5, 1865 and mustered out near

Washington, DC on July 3rd. Sylvina was first married to William Van Olinda (1820-ante 1850). In 1850 she was living with her father-in-law, John Van Olinda, 76, and her daughter Adeline Van Olinda (1841-1911), in Halfmoon, Saratoga, NY. Also in the household was William Stale, 25, better known as William Steele. Sylvina was the mother of ten children, six of whom were living in 1900. William's COD was "senile debility-exhaustion." Sylvina's was acute gastritis. They are buried in Maple Street Cemetery, Adams.

John "Jack" Stephens – Co. B (tr. January 28, 1865)
b. December 1838 Syracuse, Onondaga, NY
d. October 13, 1928 Noroton Heights, Fairfield, CT
m. Ida "Ireda" Reynolds (March 1850-March 27, 1927) *ca.* 1877

NOTE: The spelling of this man's name presents challenges for the researcher. It would appear that the correct version is Stephen. The surname on the gravestones for his parents, George (1808-1861) and Isabella Mitchell (1814-1856), is Stephen. John enlisted in the 76th Regiment at Cherry Valley, Otsego, where the family lived, on October 15, 1861 and was mustered into Co. H. An interesting but unsourced article attached to his muster roll card tells of his bravery on the battlefield: "We learn from one of the Captains of the 76th Regiment, that at the battle of Gettysburg, as the regiment was falling back [illegible] out the enemy, the color-bearer was shot down and as the flag lay on the ground, one of our village boys, John Stevens, stepped out of the ranks towards the enemy, and amid a shower of bullets, secured the flag and nobly bore it off the field. – For this daring feat 'Jack' was rewarded on the spot by being made color-sergeant, 'which under such circumstances, is as great an honor as could possibly be conferred.' At three different times the color bearer of the 76th has fallen pierced with the enemies' bullets. May that not be the fate of the fourth." John re-enlisted at Culpeper, VA on January 6, 1864. He transferred to Co. B on January 1, 1865. From the 147th he went to Co. G, 91st Regiment on June 5, 1865, mustering out July 3rd near Washington, DC. In 1880 he was living with Ireda and

John Stephens distinguished himself at Gettysburg by rescuing the regimental flag from capture by the Confederates.
Theresa Richardson

their son, Frederick (May 15, 1878-September 11, 1945), in Waterbury, New Haven, CT. The marriage, however, was unsuccessful. In 1900 John and Frederick were living with two of his sisters in Waterbury while Ireda, claiming to be single, was lodging elsewhere in the city. Later in life John lived with his son and family. According to *The Hale Collection of Connecticut Cemetery Inscriptions and Newspaper Notices,* John, a sergeant in Co. G, 91ˢᵗ Regiment and GAR member, died on October 13, 1928, aged 85 years, of "gangrene exhaustion." He was buried, as were his sisters Helen Harper (1835-1914) and Susan G. Stephen (1836-1926), in Riverside Cemetery, Waterbury. Ireda's COD was chronic nephritis. She is buried in the plot next to John's and the cemetery record says she was his wife.

John Charles Stephens – Co. I (tr. January 28, 1865)
b. September 2, 1839 Lewis County, NY
d. August 11, 1916 Port Leyden, Lewis, NY
m. Julia Wise (September 5, 1835-February 10, 1922) October 3, 1861

NOTE: John, called Charles in his father's will, was the son of French immigrants, Charles (1803-1860) and Catharine Smith Stephens (1807-1873). He was drafted, enrolling in the 76ᵗʰ Regiment at Utica, Oneida, NY on August 25, 1863 and mustering into Co. D. He was "severely" wounded at the battle of Bethesda Church, VA on June 2, 1864. He was discharged on June 15, 1865 at Whitehall Hospital, Philadelphia, PA. In 1890 John's disability was "gun shot wound." He and Julia were the parents of four, all living in 1900. John's obituary appeared in *The Lowville Journal and Republican* August 17, 1916: ". . . On Friday afternoon at 4 o'clock occurred the death of John Stephens, an aged and respected resident of this village. Mr. Stephens was born in September 1839, near Constableville, on a farm now owned by William McDermott. October 3, 1861, he was united in marriage with Julia Wise, of the same place. During the Civil war he was a member of Company G, New York Artillery. Having been wounded, he returned home after three years' service. In 1886 he moved his family to the farm of Joseph Wilcox on the East road. For a number of years Mr. and Mrs. Stephens have resided in their present home on North Pearl street. Mr. Stevens [*sic*] was honest in his business relations and a kind husband and father . . . The funeral services were held at his late home Monday afternoon, conducted by Rev. Reuben Klina, assisted by Rev. Miller Scott . . . ." There is no evidence that John served in the artillery. Julia's obituary appeared in *The Watertown Daily Times* February 16, 1922: "Lowville, Feb. 16. – The death of Mrs. Julia Stephens, widow of the late John Stephens, occurred on Friday at the home of her daughter, Mrs. John Scoville of Port Leyden. Mrs. Stephens was born in Alsace-Lorraine Sept. 5, 1835. When 23 years of age she came to the United States and to Constableville, Lewis County where she married Mr. Stephens . . . ." John and Julia are buried in Port Leyden Cemetery.

Robert J. Stephens – Co. G (tr. May 1865)
b. 1840 Montreal, Quebec, Canada
d. ? ?
m. ?

NOTE: Little is known about this soldier. He enrolled in the 76th Regiment at Rochester, Monroe, NY on August 5, 1863 as a substitute for David Waterman of that city, mustering into Co. G. He was captured at the battle of the Wilderness on May 6, 1864. Where he was imprisoned is unknown but he was paroled at Savannah, GA on November 19th. Robert J. Coddington, "Surviving Andersonville," *New York Times* "Opinionator" November 24, 2014 relates the story of one soldier who was exchanged at Savannah in November 1864 and with several hundred other paroled Union prisoners boarded a "flag-of-truce boat" at Savannah on November 21st. It is probable that Stephens was among those soldiers since he reported to Camp Parole, MD on November 25th. On April 4, 1865 he was sent to Camp Distribution, MD. He reported for duty on May 20, 1865. Although nominally transferred to the 91st Regiment on June 5th he was discharged as a member of the 147th at Arlington Heights, VA on June 9th. I have located no pension card. He does not appear in *The Town Clerks' Registers* nor is he included in the 1890 Veterans' Schedules. It is possible he died shortly after leaving the service.

William Stephens – Co. H (tr. January 31, 1865)
b. 1846 Cherry Valley, Otsego, NY
d. May 31, 1930 Brooklyn, Kings, NY
m. Martha E. Osborne (December 1852-October 1, 1925) July 31, 1871

NOTE: William, a sawyer, was John "Jack" Stephen's brother. He enrolled in the 76th Regiment at Albany, NY on April 2, 1864, apparently a volunteer, mustering into Co. H. He was captured at North Anna River, VA on May 26th and paroled at an unknown date. He was discharged at Tilton General Hospital, Wilmington, DE on June 20, 1865. He and Martha were married in Brooklyn. In 1900 she said she had been the mother of one child, now deceased. William and Martha are buried in Green-Wood Cemetery, Brooklyn.

Andrew J. Stephenson – Co. I (tr. January 31, 1865)
b. 1845 Seneca County, NY
d. September 14, 1907 Cleveland, Cuyahoga, OH
m. Mary A. Cooper (1848-April 12, 1921) *ca.* 1867

NOTE: Andrew, son of John (1801-1883) and Susan Wiley Stevenson (1805-1899), enrolled in the 76th Regiment at Auburn, Cayuga, NY on July 25, 1863 as a substitute for William Dahl, Seneca Falls, mustering into Co. K. He was captured on May 5,

1864 at the battle of the Wilderness. Where he was imprisoned and date of parole are unknown but he left parole camp on May 4, 1865 and was discharged near Washington, DC on June 9, 1865 as a member of the 147th. He and Mary were the parents of two children, both living when Mary died. Although Andrew and Mary both died in Cleveland, their bodies were sent to Seneca Falls, Seneca, NY for burial in Restvale Cemetery. His COD was chronic laryngitis and hers was apoplexy.

James Stewart – Co. G (tr. January 28, 1865)
b. 1840 Ireland
d. December 4, 1913 National Soldiers' Home, Bath, Steuben, NY
m. ------

NOTE: James' DOB varied from document to document. I use that found on his muster roll card. His POB also varies. In some cases he was born in Brooklyn, NY while in others he was born in Ireland. He enlisted at Freetown, Cortland, NY on September 14, 1861, mustering into Co. D and re-enlisting at Culpeper, VA on January 2, 1864. From the 147th he transferred to Co. F, 91st Regiment on June 5, 1865, mustering out July 3rd near Washington, DC. After the war he lived in Cortland County. He entered the National Soldiers' Home, Bath, NY in 1895 and was admitted many times up through November 25, 1913. COD was not recorded on his admission form. He is buried in Bath National Cemetery.

Abram Strate – Co. F (tr. January 28, 1865)
b. March 25, 1837 Tioga County, PA
d. November 21, 1915 Olean, Cattaraugus, NY
m. Caroline Augusta Prindle (February 28, 1842-July 30, 1916) 1861

NOTE: Abram, son of James G. (1818-post 1855) and Polly Strate (1812-post 1855), was drafted. He enrolled in the 76th Regiment at Woodhull, Steuben, NY on July 18, 1863, mustering into Co. A. He transferred to Co. I on October 11, 1864 and to Co. C on December 1st. From the 147th he went to Co. A, 91st Regiment on June 5, 1865, mustering out on July 3rd near Washington, DC. In 1890, while living in Alma, Steuben, NY, he claimed no disability. He and Caroline, also known by her middle name, were the parents of seven, six of whom were living in 1900. Both died at the home of their daughter, Una Hanks. They are buried in Maple Grove Cemetery, Shinglehouse, Potter, PA.

Silas Leander Strivens – Co. H (tr. January 28, 1865)
b. 1841 Livingston County, NY
d. 1866 Leicester, Livingston, NY
m. ------

NOTE: Silas, who used his middle name when he entered the military, was the son of James (1806-18790 and Eunice Maria Balcom Strivens (1811-1894). A draftee, he enrolled in the 76th Regiment at Perry, Wyoming, NY on July 30, 1863, mustering into Co. G. He was wounded at Petersburg, VA on June 18, 1864. He transferred to Co. D on October 20, 1864. From the 147th he went to Co. F, 91st Regiment on June 5, 1865, mustering out near Washington, DC on July 3rd. His exact DOD is unknown. His mother's application for a pension on October 6, 1885 in Michigan was rejected. She died in Mt. Morris, Livingston, NY. Graves for these people have not been located.

Nelson P. Swan – Co. B
b. 1835 Massachusetts
d. August 22, 1874 Saratoga County, NY
m. Susan J. Vandenburg (1843-*post* 1870) *ca.* 1860

NOTE: Nelson's POB is disputed. On some census records he reportedly was born in Rensselaer County, NY although both *The Town Clerks' Registers* and *Registers of Officers and Enlisted Men* say he was born in Massachusetts. His parents are unidentified. He first enlisted in the 30th Regiment at Saratoga, NY on August 31, 1862, mustering into Co. G. He transferred to Co. C, 76th Regiment on May 24, 1863 and to Co. A on November 11, 1864. He mustered out on June 7, 1865 near Washington, DC as a member of the 147th. He and Susan were the parents of Estella (1861-?) and Elsie (1863-?). Nelson's estate papers, which provided an exact DOD, stated that the girls were his only living heirs. He is buried in Ballston Spa Village Cemetery and his stone alludes to his time in the 147th. Susan's grave has not been located. The daughters disappear from history after 1874.

John Henry Swartout – Co. G (tr. January 28, 1865)
b. 1831 New York State
d. May 5, 1882 Chicago, Cook, IL
m. Orris "Ora" D. _____ (1835-*post* 1910) *ca.* 1855

NOTE: Nothing has been learned about this soldier's early life. He enrolled in the 76th Regiment at Rochester, Monroe, NY on August 8, 1863 as a substitute for Theodore Slade, Yates County, mustering into Co. G. He was wounded at Poplar Grove Church on October 1, 1864 and in 1890 Orris said he had suffered a shell wound in the right side. John transferred to Co. E on October 20, 1864 and to Co. C on November 18th. From the 147th he went to Co. F, 91st Regiment on June 5, 1865, mustering out on July 3rd near Washington, DC. By 1870 he and Orris were living in Chicago. They were the parents of James L. (1856-1937) and Eleanor "Nellie" (1861-*post* 1910). Orris was living in Syracuse in 1888. She applied for a pension that year. She last appeared on the 1910 census, residing in Fabius, Onondaga, NY. Nothing further has been learned about this couple.

John H. Taylor – Co. G (tr. January 28, 1865)
b. 1831 Rensselaer County, NY
d. November 22, 1902 Troy, Rensselaer, NY
m. Ann Elizabeth Van Auken (1832-May 25, 1881) September 23, 1852

NOTE: John, a blacksmith, was the son of Col. John Taylor (?-?) and an unidentified mother. He enlisted in the 30th Regiment at Watervliet, Albany, NY on September 6, 1862, mustering into Co. D, transferring to Co. D, 76th Regiment on May 25, 1863. From the 147th he transferred to Co. F, 91st Regiment on June 5, 1865, mustering out July 3rd near Washington, DC. John and Ann were the parents of Sarah L. (1855-1886) and Henry J. (1858-?). In 1875 the family was living in Cohoes, but in 1880 Ann and Sarah lived alone. Ann made a will specifically leaving everything she possessed to Sarah. Her COD was heart disease. She and Sarah are buried in Albany Rural Cemetery, Menands, with her father and mother Henry and Ann Van Auken. John applied for a pension in 1892 but nothing else has been learned about him prior to his death. His grave has not been located.

William Kimble Thatcher – Co. F (tr. January 28, 1865)
b. May 1841 Liverpool, Onondaga County, NY
d. June 8, 1917 Canisteo, Steuben, NY
m. Roxy J. Tuller (1847-December 30, 1930) 1866

NOTE: William was the son of Amos (1814-1899) and Mary White Thatcher (1803-1892). He first enlisted in the 12th Regiment in May 1861, mustering into Co. E, but deserted on September 25th. He next enrolled in the 76th Regiment at Hartsville, Steuben County, on July 18, 1863 as a substitute for James A. Alma, mustering into Co. I and receiving a bounty of $300. According to *The Town Clerks' Registers* he was wounded and taken prisoner at the battle of the Wilderness but recaptured, an assertion not noted in any other document. A pension payment card noted he had an injury to his right ankle and suffered from rheumatism, the latter confirmed in the 1890 Veterans' Schedules. Thatcher was transferred to Co. C on December 1, 1864 and discharged "at camp in the field, VA" on May 8, 1865 as a member of the 147th. He and Roxy were the parents of three, all living in 1900. His obituary appeared in *The Canisteo Times* June 13, 1917, 1: "William K. Thatcher died at the home of his daughter, Mrs. Carl Flohr in this village on Friday after a long illness. The final end was caused by cerebral hemorrhage. His death removes one of the most prominent and highly respected residents of Canisteo. He was born at Liverpool, Onondaga county, 76 years ago, and in 1861 he moved to Hartsville where he resided on a farm for a number of years. He then moved to this village and at once took an active part in business and church life. He was justice of the peace in Hartsville for a long time and was a successful and prosperous farmer. He was a member of Morning Star Lodge, No. 65, F. & A. M., of Mountain Lodge, No. 216, I. O. O. F., of Abram Allen Post and of the Baptist church. He served in the civil war in Co. K [sic], 76th N. Y. V. and was in the battle of Gettysburg [sic] . . . The funeral was held at 10 a.m. Monday from the residence and was largely attended. Rev. C. S. Roush officiated and burial was made in Call hill cemetery in Hartsville." The GAR post mentioned in the obituary was Abram Allen Post No. 194 which met in Canisteo. Roxy's obituary stated she would be buried in Hillside Cemetery, Canisteo, but she is actually buried next to her husband in Call Hill.

Frederick Thomas – Co. H (tr. January 28, 1865)
b. October 1841 Dryden, Tompkins, NY
d. August 2, 1912 Lisle, Broome, NY
m. Sarah Ann Brown (November 29, 1846-August 25, 1904) 1866

NOTE: Frederick, son of Michael (1800-*post* 1875) and Sally Goodwin Thomas (1801-*post* 1875), was a farmer. He seems to have been a volunteer, enrolling in the 76th Regiment on July 17, 1863 at Lisle, mustering into Co. D. He was "severely" wounded at the battle of the Wilderness on May 5, 1864 and in 1890 said his finger had been shot off. He was discharged as a member of the 147th at Elmira, Chemung, NY on June 22, 1865. He and Sarah were the parents of six children, all living in 1900. The couple is buried in Killawog Cemetery, Killawog, Broome, NY.

Josiah Thomas – Co. F (tr. January 31, 1865)
b. March 4, 1811 ?
d. July 23, 1910 Savona, Steuben, NY
m. Rebecca Van Lyle (1822-March 20, 1893) *ca.* 1840

NOTE: Although Josiah, whose parents are unidentified, claimed to have been born in 1826 when he entered the military, such was not the case. On his muster roll card he claimed to have been born in Oneida County but no evidence for that assertion exists. In 1855 he said he had been born in Cayuga County; in 1865, Yates County; in 1875, Steuben County. Since his obituary states he was born in Pulteney, he was almost certainly born in Steuben. He enrolled in the 76th Regiment at Thurston, Steuben, NY on July 15, 1863 as a substitute for Albert W. Dimmick and mustered into Co. F. He was wounded and captured at the battle of the Wilderness on May

5, 1864 and in 1890 stated he had been shot in the head and had spent ten months in Andersonville Prison. His actual parole date is unknown but he returned from parole camp in Annapolis, MD in May 1865. He was discharged from the service as a member of the 147th on June 9, 1865. He and Rebecca were the parents of six children. His obituary appeared in *The Bath Plain Dealer* July 30, 1910: ". . . ---Josiah Thomas died at the home of his daughter, Mrs. Wescott, at Savona, last Saturday. Mr. Thomas was born in Pulteney, March 4, 1811, so he was past 99 years old. Mr. Thomas went out as a substitute in 1862 [*sic*], was taken prisoner at the battle of the Wilderness and spent two years in Libby and Andersonville prisons. He had three sons in the army as well as himself . . . ." Those sons were William H. (1841-1893), 126th Regiment; Stephen (1843-1919), 86th Regiment; and Nathaniel (1846-1888), 189th Regiment. There is no evidence Josiah spent any time in Libby Prison. He and Rebecca are buried in Seamans Cemetery, Savona.

John Thornton – Co. C (tr. January 28, 1865)
b. September 1832 Machias, Cattaraugus, NY
d. July 12, 1904 Laurens, Otsego, NY
m. Julia A. Graves (April 1835-February 23, 1914) 1857

NOTE: Although John's POB provided on his muster roll card was Pennsylvania, in reality he was born in Cattaraugus County to Parley (1808-*ante* 1860) and Almira Hadley Thornton (1811-1884). John enrolled in the 76th Regiment at Norwich, Chenango, NY on September 17, 1863, a substitute for an unnamed draftee, muster-ing into Co. K. At an unknown date he was wounded in the left leg above the knee, confirmed by the 1890 Veterans' Schedules. When he was transferred to the 147th he was "absent, sick." He was discharged as a member of the 147th on May 27, 1865 at Elmira, Chemung, NY. John was a sawyer by occupation. He belonged to Charles C. Siver Post No. 124 GAR, Unadilla, Otsego County and later to James and LeRoy Hall Post No. 139, Laurens. He and Julia were the parents of three children. His death was announced in *The Otsego Farmer* July 15, 1904, 4: "John Thornton of Laurens, died Tuesday night at about 11 o'clock. He had been sick for several years with paralysis. Monday he had a shock. He was a soldier in the 76th Regiment, N. Y. volunteers. He leaves a wife, who has patiently cared for him . . . The funeral was held Thursday afternoon, at 2 o'clock, at his late home . . . ." Although Julia's obituary, which appeared in *The Freeman's Journal* February 25, 1914, alleged her maiden name was Green, that was erroneous. She was born in Delaware County and her parents were Thomas (1793-*post* 1855) and Elizabeth Graves (1795-*post* 1855). Julia's obituary spoke highly of her as a person: "Mrs. Julia (Green) Thornton, for many years a resident of Laurens died Sunday, February 22nd [*sic*]. She had been in feeble health for some time and her death was not entirely unexpected. Her death, of cerebral hemorrhage, followed a shock which she suffered on Wednesday of last week. The deceased was born in Delaware county 77 years ago and had been a resident of Laurens for 37 years . . . She was for many years a member of the Presbyterian church and had numerous friends by whom she was highly esteemed and who will deeply regret her death. The funeral was held Tuesday from her late home at 1 p.m. The services were conducted by Rev. A. J. Cook, pastor of the Methodist Episcopal church . . . ." John and Julia are buried in Glenwood Cemetery, Oneonta.

Daniel Barnes Torrey, Jr. – Co. B (tr. January 31, 1865)
b. 1844 Lincklaen, Chenango, NY
d. November 25, 1873 Pitcher, Chenango, NY
m. Harriet "Hattie" Amelia Gorsline (October 31, 1850-November 6, 1937) November 11, 1866

NOTE: Daniel was the son of Daniel, Sr. (1821-November 11, 1896) and Maryette Hyde Torrey (1824-January 26, 1899). He enlisted in the 76th Regiment at Pitcher on September 15, 1862 and mustered into Co. B. He was wounded in the leg at Gettysburg on July 1, 1863. He was captured at the battle of the Wilderness on May 5, 1864 and, according to Pitcher Town records, sent to Andersonville where he was confined until September 10th when he was moved to Florence, SC. He was exchanged on March 15, 1865 and discharged on May 18, 1865 at Baltimore, MD as a member of the 147th Regiment. He is buried in Pitcher Congregational Church Cemetery. Hattie married Sidney Illidge (1839-March 19, 1911) on June 15, 1874. They resided in Portland, Multnomah, OR and Illidge was the steward of the steamboat Mascot. On the night of March 19, 1911 the vessel, which was tied at the wharf, exploded and burned. The only part of Illidge recovered, according to his death certificate, was a hand. Hattie, the mother of seven children, all of them alive in 1900, died in Portland and was cremated.

Uriah Towner – Co. C (tr. January 28, 1865)
b. April 1835 Steuben County, NY
d. March 20, 1912 Howard, Steuben, NY
m. Emeline Finch (July 1838-October 19, 1923) 1859

NOTE: Uriah, a sawyer, was the son of Joseph (1794-1864) and Harriet Harrington Towner (1807-1864). He was drafted, enrolling in the 76th Regiment at Prattsburg, Steuben, NY on July 16, 1863 and mustering into Co. C. He transferred to Co. A on November 8, 1864. From the 147th he went to Co. H, 91st Regiment on June 5, 1865, mustering out near Washington, DC on July 3rd. In 1890 he claimed chronic diarrhea as a disability. He and Emeline were the parents of six, two of whom were living in 1900. His death was announced in *The Steuben Courier* March 29, 1912, 8: "Towlesville, March 27 – In the death of Uriah Towner, this town has lost an upright and respected citizen. Mr. Towner passed away at his home on Campbell Creek, where he had resided for many years, last week Wednesday after an illness of about two months. Death resulted from a stroke. The funeral was held Saturday afternoon at the M. E. church in this village . . . ." He and Emeline are buried in Fairview-Towlesville Cemetery, Howard. Her DOD is not on the gravestone.

Henry Slocum Townsend – Co. K (tr. January 31, 1865)
b. November 14, 1845 Aurelius, Cayuga, NY
d. August 3, 1890 Aurelius, Cayuga, NY
m. Ann "Annie" Swift Warrick (October 2, 1853-December 19, 1918) *ca.* 1873

NOTE: Henry, son of William A. (1824-1892) and Phoebe Jane Slocum Townsend (1824-1863), was drafted, enrolling in the 76th Regiment at Auburn, Cayuga, NY on July 23, 1863 and mustering into Co. F. He was captured and paroled but nothing is known about locations or dates. He was discharged near Washington, DC on June 9, 1865 as a member of the 147th. He and Annie were the parents of four, all living in 1900. Henry's COD is unknown. Annie's obituary appeared in *The Auburn Citizen* December 19, 1918, 5: "After an illness of several months' duration, Mrs. Annie S. Warrick, widow of Henry S. Townsend, died at the home of her daughter, Mrs. S. G. Harmon on the Auburn-Union Springs State Road, near Oakwood Station. Mrs. Townsend was born in Aurora and had lived in Aurelius and vicinity her whole life. She was 65 years, 2 months and 17 days old . . . Funeral services conducted by Rev. E. L. Jones of Meridian, former pastor, will be held at the Presbyterian Church in Cayuga Saturday afternoon next at 2 o'clock. Prayer will be offered at the house at 1 o'clock. Burial will be made in the family plot in Lake View Cemetery in Cayuga." Henry is also buried there.

Stephen Trass – Co. K (tr. January 28, 1865)
b. February 25, 1837 Solon, Cortland, NY
d. January 20, 1930 Oneida, Madison, NY
m. Jane Augusta Bisbee (April 1834-December 20, 1903) 1862

NOTE: Stephen was the son of Joseph (1799-1898) and Catherine Davis Trass (1815-1897). A draftee, he enrolled in the 76th Regiment on September 1, 1863 at Norwich, Chenango, NY, mustering into Co. G. He transferred to Co. H on October 20, 1864 and to Co. B on January 1, 1865. From the 147th he went to Co. K, 91st Regiment on June 5, 1865, mustering out near Washington, DC on July 3rd. In 1928 he was one of only 11 Civil War veterans in Oneida. He and Jane were the parents of three children, all living in 1900. His obituary appeared in *The DeRuyter Gleaner* January 23, 1930, 1: "Stephen Trass, 93, Oneida's oldest Civil war veteran, died Monday forenoon. Funeral services were held on Wednesday at 2 p.m. . . . Mr. Trass was a member of the 76th N. Y. Vol. Infantry, locally known as the Cortland regiment. He was wounded at the battle of the Wilderness, a bullet nipping off a finger on the left hand, but he did not leave the field, bandaging the wound himself and continuing with his company to the end of the fight." Charles Trass (1838-1916), Stephen's brother, served in Co. C, 157th Regiment from 1862-1865. He married Abigail Bisbee (1840-1911), Jane's sister. All are buried in Glenwood Cemetery, Oneida.

Nicholas T. Travis – Co. H (tr. January 28, 1865)
b. 1845 Steuben County, NY
d. April 22, 1915 near Pope, Madison, TN
m1. ?
m2. Mary "Mollie" Almarinda Kirk (March 4, 1866-May 9, 1932) June 17, 1909

NOTE: Nicholas' parents may have been Nicholas (1799-?) and Polly Travis (1820-?). He enrolled in the 76th Regiment at Canandaigua, Ontario, NY on July 19, 1863 as a substitute for Oscar Kenyon, mustering into Co. D. From the 147th he was transferred to Co. K, 91st Regiment on June 5, 1865, mustering out on July 3rd near Washington, DC. His whereabouts for the next 44 years are a mystery. He does not appear on the 1890 Veterans' Schedules. He married Mollie in Perry County, TN and in 1910 they were enumerated with her three children in that same place. He indicated that he had been married twice. Nicholas' DOD is recorded on his pension card but I have not located his grave. Mollie applied for a pension on June 15, 1915 but did not obtain a certificate. Some researchers say she died in 1932 in Arkansas, and indeed, her son, Guy Kirk (1902-1974), lived in that state in 1930. Others claim she died in 1946 in Perry, TN. Her sister Permilia died that year and Mollie was not included among the survivors in the obituary.

Joseph Turner – Co. F (tr. January 28, 1865)
b. 1845 ?
d. March 11, 1913 National Soldiers' Home, Bath, Steuben, NY
m. ------

NOTE: Joseph's parents were John (1808-*post* 1851) and Jane Turner (1810-*post* 1851). In 1851 the family was living in Saltfleet, Wentworth, Ontario, Canada. Joseph's POB was USA. On his muster roll card he indicated he had been born in Hamilton, Ontario. In 1910, however, his POB was New York State. Joseph enrolled in the 76th Regiment on August 7, 1863 at Buffalo, Erie, NY as a substitute for Louis P. Monier, mustering into Co. A. He transferred to Co. I on October 11, 1864 and to

Co. C on December 1ˢᵗ. From the 147ᵗʰ he went to Co. A, 91ˢᵗ Regiment on June 5, 1865, mustering out near Washington, DC on July 3ʳᵈ. His postwar life has been difficult to trace. He first entered the home in Bath on December 12, 1889, not leaving until April 13, 1898. After that time, he was in and out on several occasions. He was a resident at the home in 1910 when the census was taken and apparently never left. COD is not recorded on his admission form. He is buried in Bath National Cemetery.

Karl "Charles" Leopold Valois – Co. F (tr. January 31, 1865)
b. June 18, 1832 Rastatt, Baden, Austria
d. January 16, 1912 Newark, Essex, NJ
m. ------

NOTE: Charles' parents were Francois Joseph Valois (1777-1854) and Maria Anna Francisca Zwiebelhofer (1790-1854). He immigrated to the United States in 1851, arriving in New York City aboard the William Tell on October 4ᵗʰ. By 1860 he was living in Schoharie County. He enrolled in the 76ᵗʰ Regiment on January 23, 1862 at Riker's Island, New York City, mustering into Co. F, and re-enlisting as a veteran at Culpeper, VA on January 26, 1864. At the battle of the Wilderness on May 5ᵗʰ he was wounded in the ankle and thigh and taken prisoner. He was imprisoned at Andersonville and later at Florence, SC. He was exchanged at Charleston, SC in December 1864 and sent to Wilmington on January 22, 1865. He spent several months in various hospitals recovering from his wounds and the effects of being a POW. He suffered from chronic diarrhea, scrofula, rheumatism, gangrene, and blood poisoning the rest of his life. When he returned to duty in April he was a member of the 147ᵗʰ. On June 5ᵗʰ he transferred to Co. A, 91ˢᵗ Regiment, mustering out near Washington, DC on July 3ʳᵈ. In later years he moved to Newark where he lived with his nephew, Louis, and family. His COD was carcinoma of the larynx. Charles is buried in Holy Sepulchre Cemetery, East Orange.

Myron White Van Benthuysen - Co. C (tr. January 28, 1865)
b. October 27, 1841 Gloversville, Fulton, NY
d. September 25, 1891 Cohoes, Albany, NY
m. Jane Warhurst (May 19, 1845-June 16, 1912) *ca.* 1866

NOTE: Myron, son of Jacob (1807-1893) and Mary "Polly" Brooks Van Benthuysen (1802-1867), enlisted in the 30ᵗʰ Regiment at Watervliet on September 13, 1862, mustering into Co. D. He transferred to Co. E, 76ᵗʰ Regiment on May 25, 1863 and to Co. A on November 11, 1864. From the 147ᵗʰ he transferred to Co. H, 91ˢᵗ Regiment on June 5, 1865, mustering out near Washington, DC on July 3ʳᵈ. His COD was "paralysis." His obituary, appearing in *The Troy Daily Times* September 26, 1891, 2, chronicled an active and useful life: "Myron Van Benthuysen, a prominent business man of Cohoes, formerly of the knit-goods manufacturing firm of Horrocks & Van Benthuysen, died about 10:30 o'clock last night at his residence in that city. Mr. Van Benthuysen was born in Pottersville, Warren county, in 1841. At an early age he removed to Cohoes, and had been a resident of that city throughout his life. He enlisted in the war in 1861 [sic], and served with honor during the greater part of the conflict. He married Miss Warhurst, daughter of the late George Warhurst, and they had one child, which died while young. The deceased was a member of Post Griswold of Troy, and several of his comrades of that post will act as bearers. Mr. Van Benthuysen was a printer, having learned that trade in the office of the Cohoes *Cataract.* He had been employed on the Troy *Times.* Mr. Van Benthuysen had been for several years in the knit-goods business in partnership with his brother-in-law, John Horrocks, and together they owned the large manufacturing establishment known as the Atlantic mills. At the close of the war Mr. Van Benthuysen was deputy postmaster of Cohoes, under Postmaster Masten. He is survived by his wife and two brothers. The funeral will take place Monday afternoon at 2:30 o'clock from his late residence on Saratoga street." Although the article says he was born in Warren County, NYS census records consistently show a POB of Fulton County. The GAR post to which he belonged was Griswold-McConichie No. 18, Troy. Myron and Jane are buried in Albany Rural Cemetery, Menands.

Simon Vanderpool – Co. C (tr. January 28, 1865)
b. 1836 Tompkins County, NY
d. ? ?
m. Ellen Booth (?-?) August 1872

NOTE: Simon, a farm laborer, was the son of Jacob (1797-1863) and Delila Larrabee Vanderpool (1804-1865). He enlisted in the 76th Regiment at Dryden, Tompkins, NY on October 9, 1861, mustering into Co. F. According to his muster roll card he deserted in either May or June 1862. His apprehension date is unknown but he was transferred to the 147th to make up the lost time. When transferred to Co. H, 91st Regiment on June 5, 1865 he was "absent, sick." He was also "absent, sick" when the regiment mustered out on July 3rd. It appears he was never officially discharged which may account for the fact that he did not apply for a pension. In 1865 he was working as a farm laborer in Dryden. His parents both died in Berlinville, Erie, OH. Simon was living in Ohio since he and Ellen's marriage license was procured in Erie County, OH in August 1872, as reported in *The Sandusky Weekly Register* September 4, 1872, 3. It is unknown if the couple actually married since no further record for Ellen is available. Although a FAG entry states that Simon was buried in Woodlawn Cemetery, Norwalk, Huron, OH, the cemetery records do not include him. A brother, John (1834-1897), served in Co. E,

76th Regiment from September 1861-October 1864. He was killed by a train on April 1, 1897 after falling asleep on the railroad tracks near Dryden and was buried in Green Hills Cemetery, Dryden. His death announcement stated he was survived by a brother who lived "in the west." That was Isaac (1840-March 18, 1903) who lived at the time of his death in Vermilion, Erie, OH. He had served in Co. G, 72nd Ohio Volunteers from October 1861-1862 when he was discharged on a surgeon's certificate because he was suffering from consumption.

Peter Sarels Van Ryne – Co. K (tr. January 28, 1865)
b. October 5, 1839 Holland
d. June 6, 1917 Williamson, Wayne, NY
m1. Hannah Lourette (March 30, 1844-November 23, 1910) December 13, 1866
m2. Maria "Mary" DeKing Hoste (1843-1926) January 14, 1914

NOTE: Peter was the son of Adriaan Sarels Van Rijn (1796-1845) and Magdalena Deback (1799-*post* 1856). Magdalena and three children arrived in the United States in 1856. Peter was drafted, enrolling in the 76th Regiment at Auburn, Cayuga, NY on July 24, 1863 and mustering into Co. E. He was wounded at Petersburg, VA on June 18, 1864 and transferred to Co. A on November 18th. He was discharged on July 18, 1865 at Syracuse, Onondaga, NY as a member of the 147th. He and Hannah, also born in Holland, were the parents of six, five of whom were living in 1900. Peter was a member of John Hance Post No. 320 GAR, Williamson. For many years the family lived in Rochester, and Peter and Hannah are buried in Mt. Hope Cemetery. His COD was pneumonia and hers was tuberculosis. Maria's first husband was Abraham Hoste (1842-1911). After Peter died she married Marenus Mason (1839-April 15, 1920) on August 12, 1919. His grave has not been located. Maria is buried with Abraham in Sunnyside Cemetery, Williamson. I have been unable to discover her exact DOD. The name on her stone is Mary Hoste.

Alexander Van Valkenburg – Co. F (tr. January 28, 1865)
b. February 1834 Summit, Schoharie, NY
d. April 1, 1915 Burtonville, Schoharie, NY
m. Emeline Hogaboom (July 1, 1849-February 23, 1924) June 1861

NOTE: Alexander's parents are unknown. He enrolled in the 76th Regiment at Albany, NY on September 21, 1861, mustering into Co. I. He re-enlisted at Culpeper, VA on January 4, 1864 and on December 1st he transferred to Co. C. From the 147th he transferred to Co. A, 91st Regiment, mustering out near Washington, DC on July 3rd. According to a statement made by Emeline in 1923 she and Alexander were married one week before her thirteenth birthday at Summit Four Corners, Schoharie. In 1865 she and her first child, Alexander (1864-?), were living with her parents, Jeremiah (1808-?) and Catherine Hogaboom (1808-?). Alexander, Sr. was still in the army. In 1900 Emeline stated she was the mother of 13, eight of whom were still alive. That number climbed to 15 in 1910! Her last child, Purity, was born in 1891 but seems to have died young. Alexander was admitted to the Schoharie County Poorhouse in February 1889 where his habits were described as "very bad" and may have been the reason for marital discord. In 1900 Alexander was living with Etta Clayton and her son, Amos, and Emeline was living with a daughter in Schenectady. Alexander lived with Etta until he died of pneumonia. He is buried in the Clayton Family Burial Ground, Burtonsville. By 1905 Emeline was working as a housekeeper for Frank Cole, 63, in Duanesburg, Schenectady, and calling herself Emma Cole, wife. She lived with Frank until her death but for later censuses she reverted to her legal name. After Alexander died she applied for a widow's pension which was granted but afterward challenged and cancelled because she was living "in open and notorious adulterous cohabitation" at the age of 74! Emeline's death notice appeared in *The Schenectady Gazette* March 1, 1924. She is buried in Grove Cemetery, Delanson, Schenectady County.

Peter Wagner – Co. B (tr. January 28, 1865)
b. 1832 Albany County, NY
d. ? ?
m. ?

NOTE: Peter's parents are unidentified. He enrolled in the 76th Regiment on August 20, 1863 at Canandaigua, Ontario, NY, mustering into Co. C. It is unknown whether he was a draftee, a substitute, or a volunteer. He was wounded at the battle of the Wilderness on May 5, 1864 and transferred to Co. A on November 8th. He was discharged from Campbell Hospital, Washington, DC on June 19, 1865 as a sergeant in the 147th Regiment for "disability from wounds." According to *Registers of Officers and Enlisted Men*, Peter was married when he entered the service. The 1865 New York census showed him living in Farmington, Ontario County, widowed with one child, unidentified. He applied for a pension on June 27th and obtained a certificate. Someone named Peter Wagner, 34, born in Albany, NY, enlisted in the US Regular Army at Rochester, NY on August 22, 1867. He was discharged for "disability" at Fort Porter, Buffalo, NY on June 10, 1869. Whether or not this is the same man is conjectural. No other information is available.

Alonzo B. Wagoner – Co. A (tr. January 28, 1865)
b. November 4, 1842 Dryden, Tompkins, NY
d. October 3, 1898 Syracuse, Hamilton, KS

m. Jane "Jennie" L. Bentley (November 28, 1843-January 3, 1916) November 26, 1872

NOTE: Alonzo, son of William (1812-1893) and Agnes H. Colman Wagoner (1812-1858), enlisted in the 76th Regiment at Dryden on September 26, 1861, mustering into Co. F. He was wounded at Second Bull Run on August 28, 1862. He re-enlisted on January 25, 1864 and was wounded in the leg at the battle of the Wilderness on May 5th. Although captured he managed to escape. Alonzo transferred to Co. E on July 1st and to Co. A on November 18th. From the 147th he went to Co. H, 7th VRC, and was discharged on June 9, 1865 as a member of that outfit. In 1870 he was a student at Cornell University and in 1875 he was living in Cottonwood Falls, Chase, KS practicing law. He was a member of Lodge No. 303 IOOF and of Syracuse Post No. 381 GAR, both in Syracuse, KS. He and Jennie were the parents of one surviving child, Inez (1875-1948), who was born in Kansas. His death was announced in *The Syracuse* [Kansas] *News* October 7, 1898, 4: "A soldier just back from the army stood on the porch of a west side home and with a coronet, softly sounded 'taps.' At the same moment an old soldier, with the weight of nearly three score years upon him, hesitated at his toil and dropped to the earth, never to arise. It was perhaps merely a coincidence that the young musician should sound the soldier's last farewell as the grizzled veteran fell by the wayside. It may have been more. A. B. Wagoner, who had known Syracuse twenty-five years and who was known and liked by everybody in the town and county, had suddenly died. He had gone out from his home in the morning to help work the streets. He was feeling well and volunteered to hold the plow. The work was hard and he was not young and strong as he once was, but he stuck to it. At 11:40, as near as anyone knows, he was seen drop to the ground. Scarcely a minute before he had been laughing and joking with his companions and they at first did not suspect anything serious. But when they went to him they found him unconscious. Rev. Booth, his pastor and physician, who lived but a block away, was hurriedly summoned, and when he came the last spark of life had fled, and so they tenderly carried his remains home. A. B. Wagoner was born at Dryden, N. Y., Sept. 2, 1841. He served in the war of the rebellion four years less one month. He came to Syracuse with the original colony from Syracuse, N. Y., in 1873, and remained here one year, when he removed to Cottonwood Falls where he resided until he returned here with his family about twelve years ago. His wife and daughter survive him and two children died in infancy. Mr. Wagoner was of a gentle, kindly disposition, very social and with a strong vein of humor, all of which made him very popular. He had in him many elements of success. In early life he received a good education having been a student at Cornell University at Ithaca, N. Y. He had good natural talent. He was an adept at many lines of work besides having been admitted to the bar. As a musician he was a success and many of the most happy moments of his life were spent in the pursuit of the divine art. As the world measures success our friend was not successful but when viewed in the sense of making the world happier and a pleasanter place for other to live in, he did not live in vain. His kindly face and voice will be missed more in Syracuse than perhaps any other man would be. He was the children's playfellow and they loved him. He was a Christian and lived up to his professions. He was active in his church, in his Sunday School and in the choir. He was an Odd Fellow and the lodge had charge of his burial. The funeral services were conducted by Rev. H. S. Booth and there were few dry eyes in the audience when the good man concluded." Another obituary, written by an unnamed friend and published in *The Syracuse News* on the same day, contained the following: ". . . November 26, 1872 he was married to Miss Jennie L. Bently [*sic*], a graduate of the N. Y. State Normal at Cortland. In March 1873 they came to this part of Kansas as members of the old colony that named Syracuse, where they remained for something over a year and then moved to Cottonwood Falls, where Mr. Wagoner served several terms as a justice of the peace. Later they lived for a time in Emporia. In 1887 they returned to Syracuse and have since that time resided here continuously. Mr. Wagoner was a man of temperate and industrious habits, and possessed of a lovely home. He has been a justice of the peace for this township . . . His learning, of which he made no display, extended into the most erudite sciences, and his knowledge of current events was something wonderful. He was most genial in his disposition, a friend of all humanity, of children, birds and flowers . . . And dear friend of the long and weary years, we pay this little tribute to your worth, knowing the world is better for your living." Alonzo was buried in Syracuse Cemetery. Inez married William O. Wood (1866-1944) and in 1910 they, together with Jennie, were living in Indianapolis, Marion, IN. Jennie succumbed to influenza and was buried in Crown Hill Cemetery, as were Inez and William.

William Nelson Wait – Co. D (tr. January 28, 1865)
b. 1820 New Brunswick, Medford, MA
d. November 6, 1888 Root, Montgomery, NY
m. Catharine M. _____ (1820-*post* 1892) *ca.* 1845

NOTE: William's parents are unknown. He claimed to be 36 when he enlisted but census records indicate he more likely was 41. He enrolled in the 76th Regiment at Cherry Valley, Otsego, NY on December 20, 1861 and mustered into Co. H. He was wounded at Gettysburg on July 1, 1863 and in 1890 Catharine reported he had been wounded in the thigh. He re-enlisted on January 3, 1864 and transferred to Co. B on January 1, 1865. From the 147th he went to Co. B, 91st Regiment on June 5, 1865, mustering out near Washington, DC on July 3rd. He and Catharine were the parents of at least three children. When he enlisted William was a boatman. In later life he was a miller. He is buried in Canajoharie Falls Cemetery, Montgomery, NY. Catharine was last enumerated on the 1892 New York census. No further information has been located.

Enos W. Walker – Co. D (tr. January 28, 1865)
b. December 25, 1846 Brinkworth, Wiltshire, England
d. August 7, 1912 Dallas, Dallas, TX
m1. Margaret "Maggie" E. Perry (1849-February 11, 1882) October 4, 1871
m2. Emma Catherine Bates Behen (December 20, 1856-February 25, 1940) February 15, 1885

NOTE: Enos' parents were Charles (1820-1886) and Elizabeth Wheeler Walker (1818-1905). The family immigrated to the United States in 1850 and Enos became a naturalized citizen. He enrolled in the 76th Regiment at Wilson, Niagara, NY on July 29, 1863 as a substitute for Samuel P. Case. It appears he lied about his age, claiming to have been born in 1842. He transferred several times within the regiment. From the 147th he went to Co. B, 91st Regiment on June 5, 1865, mustering out near Washington, DC on July 3rd. Maggie, the mother of three, was born in Georgia. In 1880 the family was living in Bossier, LA. Her grave has not been located. Emma, born in Louisiana, had previously been married to William F. Behen (1845-1883) by whom she had three sons. He is buried in Wesley Chapel Cemetery, Ruston, Lincoln Parish, LA. She and Enos had one son, Roy Willington (1887-1972). Enos' COD was reported as two fractured ribs. He is buried in Western Heights Cemetery, Dallas. Emma succumbed to influenza and heart failure and was buried in Oak Grove Cemetery, Irving, Dallas. TX.

Lawrence Walker – Co. K (tr. January 28, 1865)
b. 1846 Yorkshire, England
d. March 11, 1897 Lockport, Niagara, NY
m1. Sarah _____ (1848-?) ca. 1868
m2. Frederika Wahl Dunning (April 1860-March 1, 1923) ca. 1887

NOTE: Lawrence, son of Thomas (1826-1896) and Elizabeth Lambert Walker (1824-1900), was a blacksmith. He enrolled in the 76th Regiment on July 28, 1863 at Niagara, NY as a substitute for Thomas Mullen, mustering into Co. B. He was captured at the battle of the Wilderness on May 5, 1864 and, according to his obituary, spent nine months in Andersonville. His muster roll card shows he was on the roll to December 31, 1864 and to February 28, 1865 as a paroled prisoner at which time he was granted a furlough. It appears he never returned and was not formally discharged. I have located no pension card for him and he does not appear on the 1890 Veterans' Schedules. He and Sarah, who had been born in Canada, were the parents of at least one child, Lily L. (1870-?), who probably died young. Where or when her mother died cannot be determined. Frederika was first married to Frederick Dunning (1834-?) by whom she was the mother of Marie "Mary" (1881-1967), who was born in Germany. By Walker she had a son, Lawrence (January 1888-July 18, 1954). Lawrence, Sr. was originally reported to have died in bed, but that statement was refuted in his obituary which appeared in *The Niagara Falls Gazette* March 15, 1897, 1: "Mr. A. J. Walker of this city contradicts the statement made in press dispatches from Lockport last Friday evening that his brother Lawrence Walker was found dead in his bed on Friday morning. The deceased was unconscious at the time he was discovered and lived about three hours afterward. Mr. Walker had been ill about three months, but was not considered serious. He had been out the day before and his wife had spent the evening at home until 9 o'clock, when she left to attend a patient as a trained nurse. Mr. Walker was 52 years old and was born in this city. He served during the civil war and was nine months a prisoner at the Andersonville prison . . . The funeral was held from his late home . . . The services were conducted by the Knights of St. John and Malta. The interment was in Glenwood Cemetery." On October 16, 1897 Frederika married Joseph Kohl (1861-1927). They too are buried in Glenwood Cemetery.

James B. Walley – Co. D (tr. January 28, 1865)
b. March 21, 1820 Otsego County, NY
d. August 24, 1892 Otsego County, NY
m. Arvilla Abigail Sweetser Thornton (March 22, 1827-August 3, 1914) *ca.* 1860

NOTE: James' parents were Evert (1789-1850) and Sarah Burnside Walley (1789-1854). He and all his siblings were born in Otsego County but baptized in New Scotland, Albany, NY in 1833. James enlisted in the 30th Regiment at Saratoga Springs, NY on September 9, 1862, mustering into Co. G. He transferred to Co. K, 76th Regiment on May 25, 1863. His muster card indicates he was captured and paroled at unknown dates and it is possible that he was taken at Gettysburg. He transferred to Co. H on July 1, 1864 and to Co. B on January 1, 1865. From the 147th he went to Co. B, 91st Regiment on June 5, 1865, mustering out near Washington, DC on July 3rd. Arvilla, whose parents were Stephen, Jr. (1792-1881) and Hannah Willey Sweetser (1792-?), was first married to John Thornton (1819-1855), by whom she was the mother of six children. She, John, and the children were born in Vermont and, according to her gravestone, John died there. In 1860 she was living in Troy, Rensselaer, NY as James Walley's wife. In 1900 she said she had been married 40 years, possibly meaning that she had married Walley in 1860. In 1865 the family was living in Saratoga and James was in the army. At some unknown date between 1865 and 1870, the marriage disintegrated. Arvilla and the children again resided in Troy in 1870 and James was nowhere to be seen. She reverted to using Thornton as her surname by 1875 but in 1880 she was Arvilla Lazell, a widow! Family members who were interviewed, however, had no recollection of a Mr. Lazell. James reappeared in Otsego County for the 1880 census, claiming to be single. In May 1887 he was admitted to the Albany County Poorhouse because he had a broken arm. His habits were described as "intemperate." On October 31, 1887 he was sentenced to $5 or 10 days in the Albany Penitentiary for intoxication. His next incarceration occurred on May 12, 1888, again for intoxication, for 180 days. He was admitted to the National Solders' Home, Bath, Steuben, NY on December 13, 1889 and in 1890 claimed he had "injuries to back caused by fall." Apparently he did not do well in the home since he was "summarily" discharged on July 3, 1891. James' COD is unknown but he is buried in Crumhorn Cemetery, Maryland, Otsego, NY. Arvilla continued to live in Troy with her son Leonard and family until her death. She never claimed a widow's pension, which suggests she and James were legally divorced. She died in Wynantskill, Rensselaer, NY and is buried in Oakwood Cemetery, Troy. The name on her gravestone is Thornton.

John Walton – Co. C (tr. January 28, 1865)
b. July 1839 Eagle, Wyoming, NY
d. March 25, 1920 Castile, Wyoming, NY
m1. Elizabeth Jewell Whitney (September 6, 1832-June 15, 1908) 1868
m2. Laura Morgan Otis (1835-December 13, 1919) 1909

NOTE: John, son of Major W. (1792-1860) and Rachel Gibson Walton (1802-1880), was drafted, enrolling in the 76th Regiment on July 30, 1863 and mustering into Co. C. He transferred to Co. A on November 8, 1864. According to his obituary he was taken prisoner on April 1, 1865 and if so he was captured at Five Forks, VA. He was discharged at Elmira, Chemung, NY on May 22, 1865. In 1890 he claimed no disabilities and "couldn't find dates" of his service. Elizabeth had first been married to Charles Whitney (1832-1864), a member of Co. F, 5th NY Cavalry who was KIA on October 7, 1864 near Fishers Hill, VA. She had two children by him, Ella (1857-?) and Charles (1859-?). Her obituary appeared in *The Wyoming County Times* June 24, 1908: "Elizabeth Walton was born in Orangeville, N. Y., Sept. 6, 1832 and died June 15, 1908. While yet in her teens she was joined in marriage to Chas. Whitney shortly after which he was called to war to which he went and lost his life leaving her with one small son and daughter, for whom she toiled early and late. Sometime after she was married to John Walton of Eagle Center, N. Y., where for over 40 years they have made their home together one child being born to them, John Jr. She was a most devoted wife and mother and respected by all who knew her. If any one in her neighborhood was sick she was tireless in her efforts to alleviate their suffering . . . Funeral [was held] June 17 at the house at 12 m. Interment Lyonsburg, Rev. O. J. Ward officiated." John's death was announced in *The Castilian* April 1, 1920, 1: "The funeral of John Walton was held at the home of Mr. and Mrs. Geo. E. Washburn on Saturday afternoon at three o'clock. The deceased was born in Eagle, July 4, 1838 [*sic*] and died March 25th, 1920, at the age of 84 years. He enlisted in 1863 in Co. C, 76th N. Y. Infantry and participated in many of the big battles, such as the Battle of the Wilderness, South side Railroad, etc. April 1, 1865, he was taken prisoner, being confined only a few days as Lee surrendered April 9, 1865. He was twice married, his second wife being Mrs. Laura Otis of Lamont, who preceded her husband's death by three and one-half months. The body was placed in the vault in Grace cemetery and later will be taken to Bliss for burial beside his first wife . . . ." John and Elizabeth are buried in Lyonsburg Cemetery, Bliss, Wyoming, NY. Laura, who was previously married to Clark Kendrick Otis (1834-April 1, 1872), was buried with him in Lamont Cemetery, Lamont, Wyoming, NY.

William A. Warner – Co. I (tr. January 28, 1865)
b. 1844 Schoharie County, NY
d. November 15, 1907 Bridgeport, Fairfield, CT
m. Frances E. Carnes (1853-May 4, 1931) 1874

NOTE: William's father is unknown. His mother was Hannah (1820-?). In 1850 he and Hannah were living with Peter and Eleanor Houck, who may have been her parents, in Burns, Allegany, NY. In 1855 they were living with her father- and mother-in-law, Marcus and Catherine Warner. Also in this household was her other son, Marcus, 16, who had lived with his grandparents in 1850. William enlisted in the 76th Regiment at Cherry Valley, Otsego, NY on December 5, 1861, mustering into Co. H as a musician. He re-enlisted on January 24, 1864 and transferred to Co. B on January 1, 1865. He was discharged on June 9th near Washington, DC as a member of the 147th. His muster roll card states he was a nurse in City Point Hospital, VA. He and Frances were the parents of Lena May (October 1874-?) and Grace (1880-?), both of whom were born in New York State. William's body was sent to Fulton, NY and buried in Mt. Adnah Cemetery. His gravestone refers to his service in the 147th Regiment. By 1910 Frances and Lena, a music teacher, had moved to Springfield, Hampton, MA. Her obituary appeared in *The Springfield Republican* May 5, 1931, 5: "Mrs. Frances Warner, 77, of 494 Belmont avenue, widow of William A. Warner, died yesterday noon at the Chapin Memorial hospital. Mrs. Warner was born at Fulton, N. Y., and had lived in this city for 23 years. She was a member of the First Christian Science church. She leaves two daughters, Miss L. May Warner and Mrs. Grace W. Peck, both of this city; one brother, George T. Carner [*sic*] of Syracuse, N.Y., and four grandchildren. The funeral will be held at Byron's funeral home Thursday afternoon at 2, with Reader Thomas Powell of the Christian Science church officiating. Burial will be in Hillcrest Park cemetery." William's brother, Marcus (1839-September 7, 1927), served in Co. G,

130th Regiment (1st NY Dragoons) from August 1862-1863 when he transferred to Co. A, 19th VRC. He died in Salmon Hot Springs, Lemhi, ID and is buried in Salmon Cemetery. It is interesting to note that his son, with whom he lived at the time of his death, was named William A.

Velorus Beebe Warriner – Co. K (tr. January 28, 1865)
b. January 15, 1839 Delmar, Tioga, PA
d. April 19, 1907 Harrison, Potter, PA
m. Huldah Maria White (1845-March 1893) September 28, 1862

NOTE: Velorus was the son of James (1803-1862) and Creta Butler Warriner (1809-1873). A draftee, he enrolled in the 76th Regiment at West Union, Steuben, NY on July 18, 1863 and mustering into Co. C. He transferred to Co. A on November 8, 1864. From the 147th he transferred to Co. K, 91st Regiment on June 5, 1865, mustering out near Washington, DC on July 3rd. He and Huldah were the parents of nine children. His obituary appeared in *The Greenwood Times* April 26, 1907. 1: "Velorus B. Warriner died at Harrison Valley Thursday of paralysis and was brought to Greenwood Sunday for burial. Mr. Warriner was for many years a resident of this place and was at his daughter's on a visit at the time of his death . . . Mr. Warriner was a veteran of the Civil war and was known as an upright honest man and kind neighbor and friend. He was buried from the M. E. church in Greenwood Sunday." Velorus and Huldah are buried in Greenwood Cemetery. His father served in Co. E, 42nd PA from May 1861-September 1861.

George Edmund Watrous – Co. K (January 28, 1865)
b. November 21, 1841 Freetown Corners, Cortland, NY
d. November 14, 1925 Corry, Erie, PA
m. Anna "Annie" H. Bathurst (May 15, 1861-April 7, 1908) 1881

NOTE: George, son of George W. (1815-1897) and Jemima Travis Watrous (1820-1843), enlisted in the 76th Regiment on September 14, 1861 at Freetown and mustered into Co. D. He was wounded in the left leg at the second battle of Bull Run on August 28, 1862. George re-enlisted on January 2, 1864 and was wounded a second time at Laurel Hill, May 8, 1864. George Woodward, a descendant, relates that his grandmother, Florence Watrous Woodward (1885-1987), told how her father, wounded in the side, lay on the battlefield for seven days without food or water. When Confederate soldiers began to strip him of boots and clothing, a "high ranking" officer came along and ordered them to stop and to allow the man to die with dignity. The next day, according to Florence, Union soldiers found and rescued him. From the 147th George went to Co. K, 91st Regiment on June 5,

1865, mustering out near Washington, DC on July 3rd. George, a farmer, and Annie were the parents of four children, all alive in 1900. His COD was pneumonia. Annie's was albuminaria with *la grippe* and tonsillitis as contributing factors. They are buried in Pine Grove Cemetery, Corry.

George Washington Webb – Co. G (tr. January 28, 1865)
b. 1836 Broome County, NY
d. November 28, 1915 Endicott, Broome, NY
m. Adelaide A. Hill (1844-July 2, 1924) 1866

Some of George Watrous' equipment may be seen on the 76th Regiment's homepage.
Gary Woodward

NOTE: George, a farmer, was the son of Stephen (1797-1874) and Sylvia Olmstead Webb (1806-*post* 1875). His DOB varies. I use that found on the gravestone. He was drafted, enrolling in the 76th Regiment on July 17, 1863 at Union, Broome, NY and mustering into Co. D. From the 147th he transferred to Co. K, 91st Regiment on June 5, 1865, mustering out near Washington, DC on July 3rd. In 1890 George claimed deafness and kidney disease as disabilities. He and Adelaide were the parents of Frank L. (1867-1926). They are all buried in Riverside Cemetery, Endicott. Two brothers also served the Union cause. Eli (1841-1924) was a member of the 50th NY Engineers. For Levi, see below.

Levi Webb – Co. K (tr. January 28, 1865)
b. October 27, 1842 Broome County, NY
d. September 5, 1912 Maine, Broome County, NY
m. ------

NOTE: Levi, like George, was a farmer and, like his brother, was drafted. He enrolled in the 76th Regiment on July 17, 1863 at Union, Broome, NY, mustering into Co. D. Levi was wounded at Laurel Hill, May 8, 1864 and in 1890 stated he had been shot in the left arm. He is buried in Riverside Cemetery, Endicott. His gravestone alludes to his service in the 91st Regiment.

Henry Webber – Co. H (tr. January 28, 1865)
b. 1844 Germany
d. ? ?
m. ?

NOTE: Henry, a mason, was the son of Henry (1800-?) and Catharine Webber (1817-?) and was living with them in 1860 in Poughkeepsie, Dutchess, NY. He apparently volunteered for the military under the one-year provision on July 13, 1864 at Poughkeepsie, mustering into Co. G. He transferred to Co. D on October 20th. He mustered out on June 7, 1865 as a member of the 147th near Washington, DC. Nothing confirmable has been located after that date.

Orlando Alonzo Wedge – Co. K (tr. January 28, 1865)
b. October 16, 1841 Georgetown, Madison, NY
d. March 19, 1919 Enid, Garfield, OK
m1. Sarah Sharp (1849-July 3, 1912) 1866
m2. Sarah L. _____ Gibson (1841-*post* 1935) January 22, 1917

NOTE: Orlando, son of Alonzo Norris (1820-December 29, 1866) and Harriet Drew Wedge (1821-1893), enlisted in the 76th Regiment at Georgetown on October 22, 1861, mustering into Co. D. He was captured at the second battle of Bull Run on August 29, 1862 and paroled at an unknown date. He re-enlisted on January 21, 1864 and was so seriously injured in the thigh at the battle of the Wilderness on May 5th that he was crippled for the rest of his life. He was discharged as a member of the 147th on January 20, 1866 from DeCamp Hospital, David's Island, New York City Harbor. He and Sarah Sharp were the parents of three children, all born in New York State. The couple is buried in Enid Cemetery. Little is known about Sarah Gibson. She was born in New Jersey and was last listed in the Enid city directory in 1935. Orlando's father, Alonzo, enlisted in the 76th Regiment on October 22, 1861, mustering into Co. D. He was discharged for "disability" at Fort Slocum, DC on April 11, 1862. He is buried in Maple Grove Cemetery, Otselic, Chenango, NY. Brother Oscar (1843-1863) enlisted in the 76th on October 22, 1861, mustering into Co. D. He was discharged for "disability" on October 15, 1862 at Philadelphia, PA and, according to *The Town Clerks' Registers*, was "sick from the time he left the army until his death Feb. 16, 1863." Another brother, Cyrus Austin (1846-1864), enlisted in the 76th Regiment on January 12, 1864, also mustering into Co. D. He was killed at Petersburg, VA on June 18th. Harriet Drew Wedge died in Michigan and is buried in Grant Township Cemetery. Her gravestone carries a poignant inscription: "A mother and a soldier's widow." For another brother, William, see below.

William Riley Wedge – Co. H (tr. January 28, 1865)
b. July 3, 1846 Georgetown, Madison, NY
d. July 30, 1911 Lansing, Ingham, MI
m. Sarah Ann Cash (July 1846-April 9, 1907) 1870

NOTE: William's DOB varies from document to document. I use that found on his death certificate. He enlisted in the 76th Regiment on May 5, 1864 at Delhi, Delaware, NY, mustering into Co. D. From the 147th he transferred to Co. F, 91st Regiment on June 5, 1865, mustering out near Washington, DC on July 3rd. Sarah succumbed to heart disease. William's COD was "gangrene of the lungs" with pneumonia as a contributing factor. His death was reported in *The Lansing State Journal* July 31, 1911, 5: "William R. Wedge died at the residence of his son, Clarence . . . at 4:45 o'clock Sunday afternoon. Funeral services will be held at the home Tuesday afternoon at 2 o'clock, and will be in charge of Charles T. Foster post, G. A. R., Mr. Wedge being a civil war veteran. The deceased was born in New York state, July 3, 1846. He came to Lansing about 30 years ago, and had since made his home in this city. Two daughters and six sons survive him . . . A special meeting of Charles T. Foster post will be held at the G. A. R. hall this evening to make arrangements for the services." William and Sarah are buried in Mt. Hope Cemetery, Lansing.

Jesse L. Weidman – Co. B (tr. January 28, 1865)
b. January 1842 Schoharie County, NY
d. February 7, 1910 Windsor, Broome, NY
m. Elizabeth B. Wagner (November 1841-March 21, 1920) 1866

NOTE: Jesse, son of Garrett (1813-*post* 1865) and Maria Curren Weidman (1819-*post* 1865), was a farmer. He apparently enlisted, enrolling in the 76th Regiment on July 17, 1863 at Windsor and mustering into Co. E. He was wounded at the battle of the Wilderness on May 5, 1864 and transferred to Co. A on November 18th. He was discharged at Washington, DC on July 15, 1865 as a member of the 147th. Jesse and Elizabeth were the parents of two, both living in 1900. The couple is buried in Riverside Cemetery, Windsor.

James Welch – Co. B (January 28, 1865)
b. 1841 Troy, Rensselaer, NY
d. January 11, 1890 National Soldiers' Home, Dayton, Montgomery, OH
m. ?

NOTE: James, a brushmaker, may have been the son of John W. (1813-?) and Sally A. Welch (1817-?). When he entered the Bath National Soldiers' Home in 1887 he gave a brother, John, as his nearest relative. In 1850 this family was living in

Westerlo, Albany, NY. James enlisted in the 30th Regiment at Watervliet, Albany, NY on September 29, 1862, mustering into Co. F. He transferred to Co. H, 76th Regiment on May 25, 1863 and was captured at Gettysburg on July 1st. On his admission form for the Bath National Home he noted he had contracted *phthisis pulmonalis* while held in Libby Prison. His parole date is unknown but he was transferred to Co. I on February 2, 1864 and transferred twice more before joining the 147th. He transferred to Co. G, 91st Regiment on June 5, 1865, mustering out at Ball's Cross Roads, VA on July 3rd. His admission form for the Bath Home indicated he was a widower but when he entered the home at Dayton he claimed to be married. I have found no evidence of a wife. His COD was *phthisis pulmonalis*. He is buried in Dayton National Cemetery and the marker alludes to his time in the 91st.

Thomas Welch – Co. D (tr. January 28, 1865)
b. 1843 Ontario County, NY
d. ? ?
m. ?

NOTE: Thomas was the son of Thomas (1817-*post* 1870) and Mary Welch (1819-*post* 1870). He was drafted, enrolling in the 76th Regiment at Auburn, Cayuga, NY on July 24, 1863 and mustering into Co. H. He transferred to Co. I on February 2, 1864 and, according to a muster roll card, deserted on June 16, 1864 near Prince George General Hospital, not returning until December 26th. On an unknown date he was sent to Co. B. From the 147th he transferred to Co. B, 91st Regiment on June 5, 1865, mustering out on July 3rd near Washington, DC. There the trail ends. He was enumerated with his parents in Brutus, Cayuga, for 1865 but when the 1870 census was taken he was no longer living with them. In 1865 a brother, William, 20, was also in the army but I have been unable to determine the regiment.

John B. White – Co. K (tr. January 28, 1865)
b. 1840 Switzerland
d. October 11, 1901 Rome, Oneida, NY
m. Mary Ann Oatman (?-May 27, 1914) 1866

NOTE: John, whose parents were John (1815-?) and Mary Anna White (1818-?), was a sailor. He enrolled in the 76th Regiment at Buffalo, Erie, NY on August 10, 1863 as a substitute for Theobald Bregas and mustered into Co. G, transferring to Co. H on October 20, 1864 and to Co. B on January 1, 1865. From the 147th he went to Co. K, 91st Regiment on June 5, 1865, mustering out near Washington, DC on July 3rd. Mary Ann's DOB is a matter of conjecture. Her gravestone says she was 63 when she died which translates into a birth date of 1851. In 1860, however, she was 12 years old.

She and John were the parents of seven, five of whom were living in 1900. John is buried in Rome Cemetery. Mary Ann died in a hospital in Utica, NY after an illness of six weeks. She is buried in St. Peter's Lutheran Cemetery, Churchville, Oneida. The inscription on her gravestone reads: "widow of John B. White Civil War Veteran."

Harrison Whitney – Co. H (tr. January 28, 1865)
b. 1842 Worcester, Otsego, NY
d. March 18, 1887 Richfield Springs, Otsego, NY
m. Emma Layton (June 11, 1856-April 17, 1929) *ante* 1875

NOTE: Harrison, son of Orrison (1806-*post* 1884) and Julia Ann Lory Whitney (1819-*post* 1865), was a blacksmith. He enlisted in the 76th Regiment as a musician on November 1, 1861 and mustered into Co. K. He re-enlisted at Culpeper, VA on February 19, 1864 and was transferred to Co. H on July 1st and later to Co. B, date unknown. Although transferred to the 91st Regiment on June 5, 1865 he was unassigned and discharged at Albany, NY on July 17th as a member of the 147th. He and Emma were the parents of a daughter, Katherine (1886-1963). In March 1916 Emma married Fred Garlock (1860-November 11, 1936) as his second wife. It is interesting to note that they were listed as husband and wife on the 1915 New York census. Harrison and Emma are buried in Lakeview Cemetery, Richfield Springs.

Thomas Parker Wilbur – Co. H (tr. January 28, 1865)
b. November 27, 1845 DeRuyter, Madison, NY
d. July 12, 1921 Ancaster, Wentworth, Ontario, Canada
m. Lydia L. Sharp (November 16, 1846-July 5, 1941) April 15, 1865

NOTE: Thomas, son of John A. (1819-1909) and Betsey Ann Roberts Wilbur (1825-1910), lied about his age in order to enlist in the 76th Regiment on November 20, 1861 at Upper Lisle, Broome, NY, mustering into Co. D. He re-enlisted on January 2, 1864. From the 147th he went to Co. F, 91st Regiment on June 5, 1865, mustering out on July 3rd near Washington, DC. He and Lydia were married in Greene, Chenango, NY and were the parents of two sons. The family moved to Canada in the mid-1870s. In 1901 he was the church sexton. His death certificate listed his occupation as painter. His COD was "catarrhal appendicitis and cardiac paralysis." He and Lydia are buried in St. John's Anglican Church Cemetery, Ancaster.

Charles H. Wilde – Co. C (tr. January 28, 1865)
b. December 7, 1831 Saratoga Springs, Saratoga, NY
d. November 21, 1914 Nora Springs, Floyd, IA
m. Alice Stephens (December 1840-April 6, 1921) 1858

NOTE: Charles was the son of Ebenezer Wilde (1812-?) and an unidentified mother. His DOB varies. I use that found on the 1900 census and his gravestone. He enlisted in the 30th Regiment at Saratoga on August 30, 1862, mustering into Co. G. He transferred to Co. C, 76th Regiment on May 25, 1863 and was wounded at Spotsylvania on May 8, 1864. When he transferred to the 147th he was "absent, wounded." His muster card indicates he was transferred to the 91st Regiment but was unassigned. When discharged in Albany, NY on July 3, 1865 he was considered a member of the 147th. He and Alice, a native of Ireland, were the parents of eight, six of whom were living in 1900. His COD is unknown but hers was pneumonia. According to her death certificate she died at the home of her daughter, Catherine, in Charles City, Floyd, IA. She and Charles are buried in Rock Grove Township Cemetery, Nora Springs.

Albert Julius Wildman – Co. F (tr. January 28, 1865)
b. December 5, 1838 Pitcher, Chenango, NY
d. March 15, 1883 South Otselic, Chenango, NY
m1. Alice Jane Nhare (1851-April 29, 1877) September 15, 1867
m2. Juliet Baldwin Dorrance (September 18, 1844-September 5, 1930) December 1877

NOTE: Albert, son of John (1806-1884) and Melissa Baldwin Wildman (1811-1893), enlisted in the 76th Regiment at Pitcher on September 25, 1861, mustering into Co. B. He was injured at 2nd Bull Run on August 28, 1862 and again at Gettysburg on July 1, 1863. He re-enlisted on February 29, 1864 and transferred to Co. E on July 1st and to Co. C on November 18th. From the 147th he transferred to Co. F, 91st Regiment on June 5, 1865 and was discharged at Albany, NY on July 17th. After the war, Albert and his brother, John, Jr., ran a store in Otselic until 1873 when they terminated the partnership and Albert opened a clothing and dry goods store. Albert's obituary was published in *The DeRuyter Weekly Gleaner* March 22, 1883: "Albert J. Wildman was born on the Wildman homestead, where his father and mother now live, in the town of Pitcher, N. Y., in December 1838. There he resided until some sixteen years since, when he and his brother, John Wildman, Jr., came here and started in trade in the store now occupied by John P. Newton. After doing business there a few years, they built a new store over the river, which was burned to the ground soon after. About this time they dissolved the partnership, John taking the grocery trade and Albert the dry goods. Soon after their store burned, Albert, with his characteristic energy and perseverance, rebuilt upon the old site, where, by strict honesty, uprightness, and fair and square dealing with one and all, he had built up one of the most flourishing dry goods trades to be found in this section. Mr. Wildman became a member of the Baptist Church at Pitcher when he was nineteen years old. Soon after moving to South Otselic he identified himself with the Baptist Church here, and has ever since been one of its most valued members. His contributions to the support of the church and religious benevolence were large and regular. His religion was carried into his business, and his every act was marked by the most perfect integrity. He was pleasant and genial in his social intercourse, kind and tender in his family. His aged father and mother are especially afflicted by his loss, as they have been accustomed to lean on him in the midst of many trials and burdens. On September 15, 1867 he married Miss Alice Nhare, daughter of Mr. and Mrs. Jacob Nhare, with whom he lived until her death, which occurred April 29, 1877. In December, 1877, he was married to Miss Juliette Dorrence, of Albion, Orleans Co., N. Y., who survives him. He leaves a son, Willie, by his first wife, aged about twelve years. The funeral services were held from his late residence, at 11 o'clock Sunday, the 18th, Rev. H. C. Leach officiating. The bereaved family have the sympathy of a very large circle of friends and neighbors in this hour of deep affliction." Albert and Alice are buried in Valley View Cemetery, South Otselic. After Albert's death Juliet continued to run the store. She married Giles Chittenden Packard (1824-August 8, 1898), whose COD was cholera, some time before 1892. He is buried with his first wife, Harriet Bingham (1833-1884), in Oakwood Cemetery, Syracuse, Onondaga, NY. In Whiting, IA, where Juliet moved after Giles' death, she was active in the Lonely Ladies Club, composed of widows and unmarried elderly women, which is mentioned in her obituary in *The Sioux City Journal* September 7, 1930, 31: "Whiting, Ia. – Mrs. Juliet Packard, Whiting's oldest resident, died in her home following a four weeks' illness due to a fall. She would have been 86 years old September 18. She had lived in Whiting the last 25 years, coming here from New York state. She was an active member of the Congregational church and the L. L. club and one of the three or four widows of civil war veterans left in this vicinity. She was an aunt of Mrs. W. B. Whiting and Mrs. H. W. Gibson and a sister of Mrs. Mary Rust. Funeral services will be held Sunday, in charge of Rev. Mr. Croker and Rev. Mr. Hoerner." Juliet's death certificate details her injuries: fractured rib, abdominal and extremity injuries. She is buried in Whiting Cemetery.

Henry Rudolf Wilkes – Co. C (tr. January 28, 1865)
b. October 1839 Germany
d. September 15, 1923 North Tonawanda, Niagara, NY
m. Maria "Mary" Butler (1849-July 23, 1899) *ca.* 1865

NOTE: Henry's parents were Martin (1795-*post* 1865) and Wilhelmina Wilkes (1812-*post* 1865.) The family name was also spelled Wilke. Henry enrolled in the 76th Regiment at Wheatfield, Niagara, NY on July 29, 1863, apparently a volunteer, and mustered into Co. E. He was wounded at the battle of the Wilderness on May 5, 1864 and transferred to Co. A on November 18th. From the 147th he transferred to Co. H, 91st Regiment on June 5, 1865, mustering out near Washington, DC on July 3rd. He and

Maria were the parents of at least seven children. Henry died at a daughter's home "after a lingering illness" and was buried in St. Paul's Lutheran German Cemetery, Martinsville, Niagara. His gravestone alludes to his service in the 91st Regiment. Maria's grave has not been located but she is probably buried with her husband.

Hiram Williams – Co. G (tr. January 28, 1865)
b. 1838 Providence, Providence, RI
d. May 26, 1900 Brackenridge, Allegheny, PA
m1. Prudence Rosevelt (1841-October 2, 1877) *ca.* 1860
m2. Mary E. Gilby (April 14, 1852-March 31, 1910) *ca.* 1871

NOTE: Hiram's parents are unidentified. He was drafted, enrolling in the 76th Regiment at Sweden, Monroe, NY on August 7, 1863 and mustering into Co. B. He transferred to Co. I on July 1, 1864 and to Co. C on December 1st. He was discharged at Washington, DC for "disability" on June 3, 1865 as a member of the 147th. He and Prudence were the parents of Carrie A. (1862-*post* 1884) and in 1870 the family was enumerated in Sweden. Hiram must have abandoned them soon after since in 1880 he and Mary, residing in Brackenridge, were the parents of Adda Bell (October 1871-1937). Prudence, daughter of Solomon (1810-1842) and Martha Caroline Rosevelt Rosevelt (1813-February 22, 1884), is buried in High Street Cemetery, Brockport, Monroe, NY. In 1875 she, Martha, and Carrie lived together. Carrie was named in her grandmother's will and was still unmarried. She probably married since she does not appear on the 1892 New York census. Hiram was a pumper in the oil fields of Butler County, PA in 1880. His COD is unknown. Mary next married _____ Bronson, date unknown. She died in Harmony, Butler, PA of *la grippe* and pneumonia. Hiram and Mary are buried in Prospect Cemetery, Brackenridge.

James Dexter Willmarth – Co. C (tr. January 28, 1865)
b. October 25, 1827 Perinton, Monroe, NY
d. August 7, 1894 Cortland, Cortland, NY
m. Amanda H. Stewart (July 1, 1827-March 16, 1900) February 17, 1847

NOTE: James, son of Galon (1801-1867) and Esther Brown Willmarth (1803-1836), enlisted in the 76th Regiment at Pitcher, Chenango, NY on September 15, 1862, mustering into Co. B. He transferred to Co. C on January 1, 1864 and to Co. A on November 18th. He was "absent, sick" when transferred to the 147th and on May 18, 1865, he was sent to Co. H, 7th Regiment VRC. He was discharged on June 29, 1865 at Washington, DC as a member of that organization. His obituary appeared in *The DeRuyter Weekly Gleaner* August 16, 1894: "The funeral services of the late James D. Wilmarth [*sic*] of Cortland, N. Y., occurred from his late residence on the 9th instant, Rev. Mr. Pound officiating. The obsequies were in charge of the Grand Army of the Republic, of which the deceased was an honored member, and the services were largely attended. A quartette from the choir of the Congregational church sang. The deceased had been confined to his bed about six months, and suffered untold and excruciating pain from a cancer which was in his left side. Though he was in the hands of skillful physicians, yet they were powerless to relieve him. Mr. Wilmarth was born near Rochester, N. Y., in 1828 [sic]. When a child his parents removed to Pitcher, Chenango Co., where he resided until about ten years ago when he took up his residence in Cortland. About 50 years ago he was united in marriage to Miss Amanda Stuart, who survives him. The result of this union was four children, two girls and two boys, all of whom are living and married . . . The deceased was in his 66th year. In 1861 [sic] Mr. Wilmarth enlisted and became a member of the 76th Regiment, New York Infantry and served three years. In Grand Army matters he always took a deep interest and was ever ready to lend a helping hand to an old soldier. Mr. Wilmarth was a kind and indulgent father, a good husband and citizen, and was honored and respected by all who knew him." He and Amanda are buried in Cortland Rural Cemetery. The GAR post to which James belonged was probably Andrew J. Grover No. 98, Cortland.

Robert J. Wilson – Co. F (tr. January 28, 1865)
b. May 13, 1837 Cayuga County, NY
d. March 25, 1910 Weedsport, Cayuga, NY
m. ------

NOTE: Robert was the son of William (1812-1895) and Elizabeth Wilson (1811-1882). A draftee, he enrolled in the 76th Regiment at Auburn, Cayuga, NY on July 23, 1863. He was "severely" wounded in the thigh at the battle of the Wilderness on May 5, 1864. He transferred to Co. C on December 1, 1864. From the 147th he went to Co. A, 91st Regiment on June 5, 1865, mustering out near Washington, DC on July 3rd. He is buried in Weedsport Rural Cemetery. His brothers, William John (1835-1900) and Silas (1841-1864), were also drafted and served in the 76th Regiment. Silas was killed at the battle of the Wilderness on May 5th, 1864 and was buried on the battlefield. William John was wounded in the right thigh in the same battle on May 5th and spent nine months in the hospital. He was discharged on August 1, 1865 as a member of Co. I, 14th Regiment VRC.

John Winters – Co. C (tr. January 28, 1865)
b. 1822 Ireland
d. March 4, 1887 National Soldiers' Home, Bath, Steuben, NY
m1. Emma M. _____ (1823-post 1860) ca. 1845
m2. Catherine _____ Teachley (1827-?) ca. 1861

NOTE: John's parents are unidentified. A stone cutter, he enlisted in the 30th Regiment at Watervliet, Albany, NY on August 29, 1862, mustering into Co. D. He transferred to Co. E, 76th Regiment on May 25, 1863 and suffered a gunshot wound to the left leg at Petersburg, VA on June 18, 1864. He transferred to Co. A on November 18, 1864 and was discharged for "disability" on May 20, 1865 as a member of the 147th. Winters entered the Bath Home on July 2, 1879 and left at his "own request" on December 15th. In 1881 he was admitted to the Rensselaer County Almshouse, suffering from paralysis. His habits were intemperate and his chance of recovery "doubtful." When he re-entered the home in Bath is unknown. His COD was chronic bronchitis and senility and he was buried in Bath National Cemetery. His stone refers to his enlistment in the 30th Regiment. Little is known about his wives. It is possible Catherine did not survive him since she did not apply for a widow's pension.

Darius Charles Wolverton – Co. C (tr. January 28, 1865)
b. August 28, 1841 Canandaigua, Ontario, NY
d. December 10, 1918 Painted Post, Steuben, NY
m. Melissa Street (1842-January 31, 1913) 1866

NOTE: Darius, son of Joel (1799-December 1879) and Elizabeth Bucaloo/Buckalieu Wolverton (1799-*post* 1870), was a substitute for Theodore Osborn, Ossian, Livingston, NY, enrolling in the 76th Regiment at Canandaigua, Ontario, NY on August 25, 1863 and mustering into Co. C. He transferred to Co. A on November 8, 1864. From the 147th Regiment he went to Co. H, 91st Regiment on June 5, 1865, mustering out near Washington, DC on July 3rd. In 1890, while living in Watertown, Codington, SD, he claimed his disabilities were rheumatism, chronic diarrhea, eye disease, and heart trouble. His death was briefly noted in *The Bolivar Breeze* December 19, 1918, but Melissa's death occasioned a lengthy, informative obituary in *The Canaseraga Times* January 31, 1913: "Melissa, wife of D. C. Wolverton after nearly a year of suffering is at rest. Her death occurred at the home on Church street north this morning, the cause of death being a nervous disease. She was 70 years of age. Mrs. Wolverton was a quiet every day Christian, showing the fruit of her faith in her home and in all the relations of life. She was a lovable woman, genial, kind, a general favorite and will be greatly missed. She possessed those womanly traits of character, that are cherished in loving memory. In her loss the surviving members of her family have the tender sympathy of all in this community. Mrs. Wolverton was a member of the Presbyterian church and her minister Rev. R. R. Watkins will conduct the funeral services which will be held at the home Sunday afternoon. Mrs. Wolverton is survived by her husband, one son Fred who resides in So. Dakota, three daughters, Mrs. Nineva Mundy, who has tenderly cared for her during all these months of suffering, Mrs. Frank O. Jones of Elmira and Mrs. Walter Breen of Rochester." Darius and Melissa are buried in Canaseraga Cemetery.

Harrison Lysander Woodard – Co. K (tr. January 28, 1865)
b. 1829 Steuben County, NY
d. September 22, 1894 Hammondsport, Steuben, NY
m. ------

NOTE: Harrison, son of Benjamin (1800-1867) and Martha Harrison Woodard (1803-1897), was a cabinet maker. The family name was also spelled Woodward. A draftee, he enrolled in the 76th Regiment at Urbana, Steuben, NY on July 13, 1863 and mustered into Co. E. He transferred to Co. C on November 18, 1864. According to *The Town Clerks' Registers* he was wounded at the battle of Five Forks, VA on April 1, 1865. He transferred to Co. K, 91st Regiment on June 5th and mustered out near Washington, DC on July 3rd. In 1890 he claimed chronic rheumatism as his disability. Harrison is buried in Elmwood Cemetery, Hammondsport. An article in *The Hammondsport Herald* September 23, 1896 reveals that Martha obtained a mother's pension: "Pension Attorney B. J. Wright of this village was notified on Saturday evening that a pension of $12 per month, from June 1, 1894 had been granted to Mrs. Martha Woodard of this place. Mrs. Woodard is the mother of the late Harrison Woodard, upon whose service the pension was granted. She is now ninety-four years of age, and has long been help-less, but kindly cared for by her daughter, Mrs. Cornelia Truesdell."

Frederick A. Wright – Co. B (January 28, 1865)
b. 1833 Schuylerville, Saratoga County, NY
d. September 9, 1903 Brooklyn, Kings, NY
m1. Mary Frances "Fannie" Brisbin (1837-?) October 20, 1858
m2. Kate E. Pettit (April 1865-March 16, 1916) November 4, 1880

NOTE: Frederick may be the son of William M. (1810-*post* 1855) and Charlotte Wright (1810-*post* 1855). He enlisted in the 30th Regiment at Watervliet, Albany, NY on September 10, 1862, mustering into Co. F. He transferred to Co. K, 76th Regiment on May 25, 1863, then to Co. I July 1, 1864 and to Co. B on December 1st. From the 147th he went to Co. G, 91st Regiment on June 5, 1865, mustering out near Washington, DC on July 3rd. In 1865 Wright and Mary Frances were living in Waterford, Saratoga, with her parents, Giles (1808-?) and Matilda Brisbin (1817-?). A DOD of August 7, 1884 has been suggested for Mary Frances but since Frederick and Kate were married in November 1880 she either died before that date or the couple divorced or he was committing bigamy. When the 1880 census was taken Frederick was boarding in Brooklyn and claiming to be single. It is altogether possible the marriage failed and he simply waited until his first wife died to marry the second one. A woman named Mary F. Wright died on March 10, 1880 and was buried in Green-Wood Cemetery,

Brooklyn. If she is indeed the correct person, then Frederick could truthfully say he was single when the census was taken. In 1900 Frederick and Kate alleged they had been married in 1884 but that was untrue, according to marriage records for New York City. Wright's lengthy, somewhat fanciful, obituary appeared in *The Brooklyn Daily Eagle* September 11, 1903, 3: "One of the best known local railroad men passed away in the sudden death on Wednesday at his home, 104 Vernon avenue, of Frederick A. Wright, who at one time was a general superintendent of the Brooklyn City Railroad Co., and later was in charge of the claim agents department of that corporation. He was a familiar figure in the streets of Brooklyn for years by reason of his picturesque habits of dress, and he was known by sight to thousands who did not know of his occupation. During the past six years he had been in the employ of Morris & Whitehouse. Sunday, while fatigued from a trip to Woodlawn, Mr. Wright was seized with apoplexy, and he lay in an unconscious condition until Wednesday. He was born at Schuylerville, this state, April 17, seventy years ago, his parents being Quakers. Fifty years ago he came to Brooklyn, and, beginning as a conductor, he gradually rose through various grades to be probably the best informed railroad man in this borough. When the Civil War broke out he enlisted in the Ninety-first Regiment of New York Volunteers, and was discharged a sergeant of Company G. He was a member of the Dutch Reformed Church, but never made any fraternal or social connections, his whole life being centered in his railroad work. Mrs. Wright, who was Miss Kate E. Pettit of Hempstead, L. I., and a sister and a brother survive Mr. Wright. Funeral services, which are to be held at the late residence this evening at 8 o'clock, will be conducted by the Rev. J. F. Carson, pastor of the Central Presbyterian Church . . . ." Frederick is buried in Cypress Hills National Cemetery. When Kate died she left an estate of almost $15,000 in personal and real property. Her sole heirs were cousins and several of them unsuccessfully contested the will which she had signed only a week before she died, alleging she had not been competent to do so. Her grave has not been located.

Frederick A. Wright.

Frederick Wright, a railroad employee, was known in New York City for his flamboyant mode of dress.
Brooklyn Daily Eagle

William H. Wright – Co. H (tr. January 28, 1865)
b. 1843 Caroline, Tompkins, NY
d. ? Chicago, Cook, IL
m. Rozenia Robinson (February 1848-December 13, 1923) 1868

NOTE: William, whose parents were David (1807-*post* 1880) and Matilda Tuttle Wright (1809-*post* 1880), enrolled in the 76th Regiment as a musician at Speedsville, Tompkins, NY on October 28, 1861, mustering into Co. E. He re-enlisted on January 26, 1864, transferring to Co. A on November 18th. From the 147th he went to Co. K, 91st Regiment on June 15, 1865, mustering out near Washington, DC on July 3rd. He and Rozenia, whose parents were William S. (1816-1900) and Calista Branson Robinson (1820-1906), were the parents of Miriam Helen (1874-1932) who was born in Illinois. In 1880 the family was living in Alden, McHenry, IL where William was a railroad station and express agent. Rozenia's parents lived next door. By 1900 the Wrights were residing in Chicago and he was a depot agent. William's pension card provides a DOD of 1905 and Rozenia applied for a pension on January 30, 1905. It does not appear, however, that anyone with his name died in Cook County that month. Miriam married Willis Blackman (1866-1932) and they are buried in Alden Cemetery as are the Robinsons. It is possible that William and Rozenia are also there. Two of William's siblings served during the Civil War. James (1841-?) was in the 76th Regiment from September 1861-May 1862 when he deserted. On June 1, 1863 he enlisted in the 11th NY HA which became the 4th and served until discharged in September 1865. Aaron (1845-1864) was a member of the 5th NY Cavalry. He was wounded at Milford Station, VA on May 21, 1864 and died on August 17th at Lincoln Hospital, Washington, DC.

Gustave Yager – Co. G (tr. January 31, 1865)
b. 1844 Germany
d. ? ?
m. ?

NOTE: Gustave enlisted in the 76th Regiment in New York City on January 2, 1864, mustering into Co. F. He was captured at the battle of the Wilderness on May 5th. According to the records he transferred from the 147th to Co. A, 91st Regiment on June 5, 1865 and mustered out July 3rd near Washington, DC. I have located no pension record for him and it is possible he died shortly after leaving the military.

James Yarnes – Co. C (tr. January 28, 1865)
b. 1841 Smithville, Chenango, NY
d. 1904 Smithville Flats, Chenango, NY

m. Mary _____ (1836-January 15, 1902) *ca.* 1870

NOTE: James, son of Ward L. (1795-*post* 1860) and Betsey Yarnes (1810-*post* 1860), was a farmer. A draftee, he enrolled in the 76th Regiment at Norwich, Chenango, NY on September 1, 1863, mustering into Co. H. He transferred several times within the regiment. From the 147th he went to Co. H, 91st Regiment on June 5, 1865, mustering out on July 3rd near Washington, DC. He and Mary were the parents of one child, Minnie (1871-1932). I have been unable to determine James' exact DOD but his estate went to probate in April 1904. His brother Thomas (1843-?) was named the administrator. James and Mary are buried in Maple Grove Cemetery, Smithville Flats.

Edward Yarton – Co. K (tr. January 31, 1865)
b. September 15, 1843 Rochester, Monroe, NY
d. March 20, 1908 Soldiers' Home, Grand Island, Hall, NE
m. Olive Boardwell (August 21, 1845-September 5, 1935) August 6, 1865

NOTE: Edward, the son of Isaac (1815-?) and Elizabeth Yarton (1815-*post* 1864), saw prior service in Co. G, 9th NY Cavalry from October 1861-January 1863 when he was discharged for "disability" at Washington, DC. He enrolled in the 76th Regiment at Rochester on August 5, 1863 and mustered into Co. K. He was captured at the battle of the Wilderness on May 5, 1864 and held until February 22, 1865. He was transported first to Washington, DC, and then to Rochester to recuperate. On June 5th he transferred to Co. D, 91st Regiment from which organization he was discharged on October 7, 1865 at Rochester. It is doubtful he ever spent one day on active duty with either the 147th or the 91st but his pension cards credit him with service in both regiments. An interview he gave to a reporter for *The Omaha Sunday Bee* concerning his war experiences appeared May 26, 1904, pt. 3, 1 and is excerpted here: ". . . He was 17 years old when the war broke out and he immediately offered himself as a candidate for the army. He was only a boy and very small for his age. He was refused without hesitation. But he persisted, and in the fall of 1861 he was finally accepted and enrolled in Company G, Ninth New York cavalry . . . In the first five weeks of the campaign in the Army of the Potomac he received five wounds, some of them serious, but never once did he think of going to the hospital and only [on] one occasion did he let the surgeon attend to his wound . . . But at the second battle of Bull Run a bullet went through the cap of the right knee. It was a serious wound, and disabled him entirely. He was taken off the field in an ambulance and sent back to Washington. There he lay in St. Aloysius hospital waiting to have the wound dressed. 'There was groaning and screaming all around me,' he says. 'The doctors were at work cutting and sawing like so many butchers. I saw a pile of arms and legs and feet and hands two feet high. The surgeons were mostly students and they decided pretty quick whether to cut off a limb or not. I was sure if they got hold of me they would cut my leg off. A steward came in and I asked him where a little door which was close to my cot led to. He said it opened onto the road at the back of the hospital. When no one was looking I got up and slipped out the door' . . . He arrived back in time to take part in the bloody battle [of] Antietam, where he sustained two more flesh wounds . . . He took part in the fierce assault . . . at Fredericksburg in December, 1862. There he was again disabled in the very front of the rebel position by a ball which grazed the side of his head and destroyed the hearing of his left ear. He also received a saber cut in the left wrist . . . which nearly severed the hand from the arm. It has been paralyzed ever since. He was sent back to Washington where he again found himself in St. Aloysius hospital. This time he stayed on the assurance he would not be 'butchered up,' and on January 23, 1863, he was discharged from the service as being unfit for further duty. . . He was sent home to Rochester . . . But the war fever had so firm a hold on him that he could not rest . . . He heard from his brother, whose enlistment had run out, and found that he was going to re-enlist in the Seventy-sixth New York infantry. Immediately he also set about getting back into the service. But the recruiting officers declared that he was badly enough scarred up already and refused to take him. But the doughty little fighter persisted. He was successful in the end, though it took considerable tact to get over the matter of the paralyzed left hand . . . One day came orders to march to the north. The rebels had invaded Pennsylvania. Yarton's regiment was hurried to Harper's Ferry and thence north to the field where the greatest battle of the war was to be fought . . . 'It was on the second day of the battle that I got the most painful wound of all. We were assaulting the rebels, who were firmly entrenched. It was a hand-to-hand fight; we on the earthworks and they in the trenches. Suddenly I felt a sharp pain in my cheek and when I put my hand there I felt a bayonet being pulled out and saw a rebel grinning up at me. He had stood on a stone and run his bayonet into my chin. It had gone up through my cheek to my cheek bone . . . The rebel was just about to run me through the body when my brother, who was fighting close to me, knocked his gun away and with the same thrust killed him . . .' May 4, 1864 Yarton's company was at Culpepper Court House when . . . at 3 a.m. orders were given to be ready to march in an hour. All that day they marched and most of the night and early the next morning they were in the thick of the Battle of the Wilderness. There young Yarton received the most serious wound of his life. An officer caught him with his saber on the right side of the neck, cutting a gash deep and long, which bled heavily. In the moment this put him off his guard [and] a soldier hit him over the back of the head with his gun and Yarton knew no more. When he regained his senses he was in the hands of the enemy and a few weeks later he was marched into the great confederate prison. The horrors which he endured there in the nine months he remained a prisoner are almost beyond belief . . . Mr. Yarton was released from the prison February 22, 1865. He tells a pitiful story of his heroic effort to appear well, though he was nearly dead. Had he not done this he would have been kept in prison. Two comrades helped him into the train and then after days of delay they arrived in Washington. He was sent on to Rochester after a short period in the hospital. When he arrived home he weighed just sixty-one pounds. It took months for the recovery, but there was a young woman in Rochester who made a good nurse. She was Miss Olive Boardwell, the girl he had 'left behind him' when he marched away to the war in '61. On August 6, 1865 they were married. They have seven children . . . After the veteran recovered he moved about into various parts of the country working at his trade of carpenter. They finally arrived in Omaha in 1887. Here he worked for a time in the railroad shops and a few years ago he and Mrs. Yarton moved to Benson . . . He still suffers considerably from his wounds. The dent put in his head . . . put there by that rebel at the Battle of the Wilderness gives him more pain than the rest. A silver plate two inches in diameter takes the place of a large piece of skull which the surgeons removed. Five years ago Dr. R. M. Stone and other surgeons performed an operation on Mr. Yarton and took from his abdomen a big and badly battered bullet. That bullet had entered his body at the Battle of Gettysburg and for nearly forty years had lodged in him and given him pain. Mr. Yarton is a Blue Lodge Mason, a member of the Methodist church and, of course, a prominent and honored member of the Grand Army organization, Crook post, No. 262. He still has the Springfield rifle which went with him through his adventures. 'I'll always keep it,' he says, 'and when I die it goes into the box with me. It was my friend in life and in death. I won't be parted from it.'" If one accepts this tale without reservation Mr. Yarton was a model citizen. Other news accounts painted a different picture. Yarton ran a saloon in Omaha and in 1894 his family appeared in court and testified to their husband and father's behavior, as reported in *The Omaha World-Herald* April 13, 1894, 8: ". . . Yarton has been running one of the several saloons near the fort for the last three years, and however suave he may be to the soldiers who drink over his bar he is a terror to his family, beating the children and threatening dire things to his wife. Olive Yarton, his wife, testified that the difficulty between them arose from the fact that he wished her and the children to sell liquor to the soldiers when he was absent and that she did not propose to do so nor to have her children brought up in that way. One boy 12 years old showed the scars on his head where his father had beaten him with a broomstick. Yarton has refused to support his family, although he is drawing a pension of $24 a month, besides what he makes in the saloon. About ten days ago the final row, which led to his arrest, arose when he shut himself into his room, broke furniture and threw things around until his wife came in and remonstrated. Then it was that he threatened to kick her out and knock her brains out . . . He was bound over to the district court." He again was in the news when *The Omaha World-Herald* reported on June 1, 1895, 8 that he had beaten 14-year-old Llewellyn so badly that the boy actually went to the police and swore out a warrant for his father's arrest. The same newspaper reported on July 21, 1896, 3 that a daughter, Olive, applied to the police for shelter, saying he had "turned her out of house and home on Saturday." Edward's body was sent to Omaha where it was buried in Forest Lawn Cemetery. Olive, his long-suffering wife, secured a widow's pension. She later married John W. Vest (1842-April 25, 1938) who had been a soldier in Co. A, 3rd IA Volunteer Cavalry. In 1930 they were enumerated at the same soldiers' home where Edward had died. Olive died at the home of her daughter Stella while visiting her in Omaha. According to an obituary published in *The Omaha World-Herald* September 7, 195, 22, she and Vest had entered the home seventeen years earlier. Olive is also buried in Forest Lawn Cemetery, Omaha. Vest is buried in Burr Oak Cemetery, Burr Oak, Winneshiek, KS. The brother alluded to in Edward's tale of his Civil War adventures was James (1840-June 18, 1864) who was killed at Petersburg, VA.

EDWARD YARTON

Edward Yarton was a controversial figure in Omaha.
Omaha Daily Bee

Et Cetera Nomina

Military record keeping during the Civil War depended on the quality of the clerks given the job of ensuring that all men in their companies were accounted for. Sometimes errors were committed but in general these anonymous soldiers performed masterful service for future generations of researchers. Nevertheless, they did not enjoy the more complete record which has accrued to those who are writing more than 150 years later. The following pages contain biographies, as fully as can be ascertained, of persons associated with the 147th Regiment but who for one reason or another did not actually serve in that outfit.

James Ash – Co. E (tr. January 28, 1865)
b. 1844 Ireland
d. ? ?
m. ?

NOTE: James, a spinner, enlisted in the 30th Regiment at Watervliet, Albany, NY on September 16, 1862, mustering into Co. F. He transferred to Co. E, 76th Regiment on May 25, 1863. He was wounded at Gettysburg on July 1, 1863 and transferred to Co. C on November 18, 1864. When transferred to the 147th he was "absent, sick." He was also "absent, sick" when on June 5, 1865 he was sent to Co. D, 91st Regiment. He does not appear in *The Adjutant-General's Report* for that organization. Although *Civil War Soldier Records and Profiles* claims he survived the war, I have located no other information about him.

Chauncey Barnes – Co. B (tr. January 28, 1865)
b. 1844 Moriah, Essex, NY
d. ? ?
m. ------

NOTE: Little is known about Chauncey prior to his military service. He enlisted in the 30th Regiment at Albany on September 30, 1862, enrolling in Co. G, then transferring to Co. C on December 29, 1862. He was a musician in the service but a tanner by trade. He transferred to Co. C, 76th Regiment at Fitzhugh Farm, VA on May 25, 1863. He was wounded and captured at the battle of the Wilderness on May 5, 1864. According to the muster cards he was a POW when transferred to the 147th and to Co. G, 91st on June 5, 1865, with the notation, "no further record." Although official records claim he survived his time in Andersonville Prison, in all likelihood he died there. The burial records contain a G. Barnes, US soldier, who died on August 5, 1864. The capital letters C and G were written very similarly and this man may be Chauncey. If so, he is in grave # 4782.

Martin Barry – Co. G (tr. January 28, 1865)
b. 1841 New York State
d. ? ?
m. ?

NOTE: Little can be found about this soldier. He enrolled in the 76th Regiment on August 20, 1863 at Friendship, Allegany, NY as a substitute for Alvin Fisher, mustering into Co. A. For the muster roll of October 1863 he was described as being "Left at Culpepper Va. sick when detachment came to Regt." When transferred to Co. D on October 11, 1864 he was "absent, sick." He was also "absent, sick" when transferred to the 147th and to the 91st. Although *Civil War Soldier Records and Profiles* claims he survived the war, that statement is probably erroneous.

Henry Benjamin – Co. I (tr. January 28, 1865)
b. 1833 Wayne County, NY
d. October 8, 1916 Willard State Hospital, Ovid, Seneca, NY
m1. Phoebe Ann Loveless (1831-1868) *ca.* 1856
m2. Sarah Ann Proctor (1857-May 15, 1923) 1872

NOTE: Henry was the son of William (1801-1864) and Nancy Shaver Benjamin (1809-1863). He enrolled in the 76th Regiment on July 25, 1863, apparently a volunteer, mustering into Co. K. He was reported "absent, sick in Hospital, Washington, DC" on October 16, 1863. He transferred to Co. E on July 1, 1864 and to Co. C on November 18th. When transferred to the 147th he was "absent, sick." He nominally transferred to Co. D, 91st Regiment on June 5, 1865 but he does not appear in *The Adjutant-General's Report* for that outfit. Furthermore, his pension cards show service in only Cos. K and C. Henry was the father of two children by Phoebe and three by Sarah. Graves for these people have not been located.

David Benton – Co. A (tr. January 31, 1865)
b. May 17, 1847 Michigan
d. ? ?
m. ------

NOTE: David was the son of David (?-*post* 1847) and Mary A. Thornton Benton (?-*post* 1847). He was a substitute for Martin Bennett and enrolled in Co. B, 76th

Regiment on September 4, 1863 in Oswego, NY. He was captured at the battle of the Wilderness on May 5, 1864 and according to *The Town Clerks' Registers* he was "supposed to have died in Florance [*sic*] Prison." He nominally transferred to the 147th and then to Co. C, 91st Regiment on June 5, 1865 although he does not appear in *The Adjutant-General's Report*. Two brothers served the Union. George (1839-1900) was a member of Co. I, 98th Regiment (1861-1865). Henry (1845-1920) served in Co. C, 160th Regiment (1864-1865).

John Berrigan – Co. I
b. December 1829 Ireland
d. August 26, 1909 Oswego City, NY
m. Elizabeth "Eliza" Kennedy (1835-November 29, 1911) 1856

NOTE: According to Berrigan's gravestone he was a member of the 147th Regiment and Draft Registrations states "9 months in 147 NYV." Nevertheless, he does not appear in *The Adjutant-General's Report* for that organization. His entry in *The Town Clerks' Registers* spells his name Barrigan and reveals he enrolled in the 1st NY LA at Oswego on February 16, 1864, mustering into Co. C. He mustered out of this unit at Elmira, Chemung, NY on June 17, 1865. In 1890 he claimed to have served in the light artillery but provided no dates. He said he had been shot and one hand was totally disabled. He had also suffered an injury to his right kneecap and it was now numb. John and Eliza were the parents of four, all living in 1900. When he died an obituary appeared in *The Oswego Daily Times* August 26, 1909, 1 but other than allude to the fact that he was a Civil War veteran it did not offer any information at all about the outfits in which he served. Berrigan's parents are unknown. He and Eliza are buried in St. Paul's Cemetery, Oswego City.

Clinton DeWitt Bouton – Co. G (tr. January 28, 1865)
b. 1843 Virgil, Cortland, NY
d. February 11, 1927 Ithaca, Tompkins, NY
m. Mary Alice Grant (June 1844-July 21, 1924) 1866

NOTE: Clinton, son of George (1809-1859) and Charlotte Bouton (1816-1856), enlisted in the 76th Regiment at Dryden, Tompkins, NY on October 4, 1861, mustering into Co. F. At some time before July 1, 1864, he transferred to Co. G, 18th Regiment VRC and then to 216th Company, 1st Battalion VRC because on that date he was supposed to go to Co. D, 76th but was described as "absent, sick." He was also "absent, sick" when transferred to the 147th and to Co. D, 91st Regiment on June 5, 1865. He is not listed in *The Adjutant-General's Report* for the 91st. His pension cards refer only to time in the 76th and the VRC. Bouton's life as a civilian was interesting, as shown by his obituary which appeared in *The Cortland Democrat* February 18, 1927, 10: "Funeral services for Clinton DeWitt Bouton, formerly of Dryden, were held at his late home at Ithaca, Sunday afternoon, followed by interment in the family lot in Willow Glen cemetery. His death occurred Feb. 11, after a prolonged illness. Mr. Bouton was born in the town of Virgil, 85 years ago. He was a corporal in Co. F, 76th Regiment, and served three years. For a long time he was a resident and prominent business man in Dryden village, as merchant, postmaster, and member of the Dryden Granite & Marble Works Co. His wife was Miss Alice Grant of this place. After moving to Ithaca over forty years ago, Mr. and Mrs. Bouton kept in touch with their friends here, and on the occasion of a wedding anniversary they chose to hold a reception at Grove Hotel, that they might be surrounded by their old friends and associates. Mr. Bouton manifested his interest in the Dryden Methodist church by generous gifts when the church was being repaired. His wife died about three years ago and he leaves no children. In 1893 Mr. Bouton was elected mayor of the city of Ithaca as an independent ticket. He refused to run for a second term, but served twelve years as a member of the board of education. He joined the J. C. Stowell company in 1901 and was active in the firm until 1920; from 1912 until he retired he was managing director. Mr. Bouton was the son of Rev. and Mrs. George Bouton. His father was a Methodist clergyman, born in 1809, who died Oct. 3, 1859. His mother, Charlotte Bouton, was born Aug. 28, 1816 and died Aug. 28, 1856. The bearers at the funeral were four nephews . . . ." Alice is also buried in Willow Glen.

DeWitt Clinton Bouton is the third man from the right in the second row
in this picture taken at the last reunion of the 76th Regiment in 1922.
Ken Eaton Collection, Homeville, NY Museum

Gilbert Brinner – Co. E (tr. January 28, 1865)
b. January 7, 1836 Steuben Co., NY
d. March 3, 1917 Prophetstown, Whiteside, IL
m. Lucinda Finch (August 1837-July 30, 1908) 1860

NOTE: Gilbert, son of Aaron (1816-1879) and Deidamia Rowley Brinner (1818-1906), was drafted, enrolling in the 76th Regiment at Woodhull, Steuben, NY on July 13, 1863 and mustering into Co. A. He was wounded during the battle of the Wilderness on May 5, 1864 and deserted from a hospital in Rochester, Monroe, NY on July 1st. Even so, he transferred to Co. C on November 10th. He was reported "absent, sick" upon transfer to the 147th. He nominally transferred to Co. D, 91st on June 5th. That he did not serve in that regiment is demonstrated by the fact that he does not appear in *The Adjutant-General's Report* for that unit. He never applied for a pension and he does not appear on the 1890 Veterans' Schedules. His entry in *The Town Clerks' Registers* says merely that he was drafted. By 1870 Gilbert was in Illinois. He and Lucinda were the parents of two children, both living in 1900. The couple is buried in Leon Cemetery, Prophetstown.

Charles S. Brown – Co. B
b. 1838 Oswego, NY
d. June 20, 1882 Oswego City, NY
m. Louisa Wadleigh Haskins (1838-June 7, 1916) *ca.* 1874

NOTE: Charles was the son of Charles S. (1799-1882) and Deluse "Lucy" Wormuth Brown (1804-?). He enlisted in the 147th Regiment at Oswego City on August 23, 1862 and enlisted in Battery L, 1st NY Light Artillery on 24th. He allegedly mustered into Co. B, 147th on September 22nd and into the light artillery on September 23rd. *The Adjutant-General's Report* for the 147th states that he served until February 1, 1863 and then transferred to Batt. L but that for the 1st Artillery specifically states that he was a member of that organization from August 1862 until mustered out on June 17, 1865. Moreover, in 1890 Louisa stated he had served in the light artillery from August 25, 1862-June 17, 1865. Louisa, born in Jefferson County, NY, was first married to Lester Haskins (1836-?), a lake sailor. In 1880 Louisa was Brown's wife. Enumerated with them were Carrie Haskins (1861-December 1, 1949); Jennie Haskins (1863-?); Charles Haskins (1865-?). Two other children, Ward (1875-1905) and Claud (1877-1922), were listed as step-children but when Claud married in 1912 he stated his father was Charles Brown. It seems that the two youngest were indeed Charles' sons. What happened to Haskins is unknown. Charles is buried in Riverside Cemetery, Scriba, as are several of the children. Both Claud and Ward's surname is Brown. Louisa's death notice mentioned no cemetery but she is probably also in Riverside.

James W. Burtch – Co. G (tr. January 28, 1865)
b. 1838 Andes, Delaware, NY
d. April 1, 1900 ?
m. Lydia J. _____ (1836-?) *ca.* 1857

NOTE: James, whose surname was also spelled Burch, was the son of David (1798-*ca.* 1858) and Lydia (1798-*post* 1860). He enlisted in the 76th Regiment at Willet, Cortland, NY on November 11, 1861 and mustered into Co. B. He deserted from the regiment on May 8, 1862, returning on December 7th. He was wounded twice, first at Gettysburg on July 1, 1863 and again at the battle of the Wilderness on May 5, 1864. He transferred to Co. A, 21st Regiment VRC at an unknown date. His discharge date is also unknown. When he applied for a pension on July 16, 1890 he was living in Michigan. The pension card reports only service in the 76th and the VRC. The card also provides a DOD but does not indicate where it occurred. No widow applied for a pension.

Charles Bush – Co. A (tr. January 31, 1865)
b. 1840 Truxton, Cortland, NY
d. 1864 Florence, SC
m. ------

NOTE: Charles, son of John (1792-1872) and Eliza E. Bush (1805-1878), enlisted in the 76th Regiment at Cortland City on October 12, 1861, mustering into Co. B. He was captured near Bull Run on August 29, 1862 and later paroled. He was again captured on May 5, 1864 at the battle of the Wilderness. While *Registers of Officers and Enlisted Men* says his POD and DOD were "unknown," testimony by William J. Crozier on January 12, 1887 revealed that Bush died in the prison pen at Florence, SC, perhaps in October. His testimony was corroborated by a notation in a diary kept by George F. Snell's great great grandfather. Although it is impossible to pinpoint Bush's actual DOD, the Florence POW camp was occupied from September 1864-February 1865. He is probably buried among the "unknowns" in Florence National Cemetery.

John Cahill – Co. B (tr. January 28, 1865)
b. October 7, 1830 New York City, NY
d. January 15, 1865 Salisbury, Rowan, NC
m. ------

NOTE: John, a farmer, was the son of Irish immigrants, Thomas I. (1796-1866) and Johanna Kenneally Cahill (1802-*ante* 1860). He enlisted in the 76th Regiment at Solon, Cortland, NY on February 25, 1864 and enrolled in Co. B. He was taken prisoner at Poplar Grove Church, VA on October 1st and died of "disease" at Salisbury Prison on

January 15, 1865. He is buried among the "unknowns" in Salisbury National Cemetery. His brother, William (1837-1900), was a first lieutenant in the 76th Regiment.

Chester Palmer Card, Jr. – Co. B (tr. January 28, 1865)
b. August 25, 1844 Fayetteville, Onondaga, NY
d. ? ?
m. ------

NOTE: The son of Chester, Sr. (1812-1856) and Julia Goodale Card (1816-1863), Chester enrolled in the 76th Regiment at New Woodstock, Madison, NY on October 20, 1861 and re-enlisted at Culpeper, VA on January 26, 1864. He was captured on May 5th at the battle of the Wilderness and paroled at Charleston, SC on December 10th. The sketchy record indicates he went to parole camp and was furloughed for 30 days on December 25th. It has been suggested he was killed in a railroad accident in Pennsylvania on his way home. This has not been confirmed but since no further record of him exists it is most likely accurate.

Hiram Christopher – Co. K
b. 1839 Germany
d. ? ?
m. ?

NOTE: Hiram's muster card for the 147th indicated he was a blacksmith and was drafted but place and date were unknown. In fact, little information is available for him. He nominally transferred to Co. K, 91st Regiment on June 5, 1865 but he does not appear in *The Adjutant-General's Report* for that organization. No other confirmable information is available.

Charles F. Cline – Co. I
b. June 22, 1844 Oswego, NY
d. September 17, 1927 Cherokee, Alfalfa, OK
m. Ruth Amy Sheldon (January 21, 1844-April 13, 1933) January 1, 1867

NOTE: Charles was the son of George (1823-*post* 1855) and Lovina Felinda Philips Cline (1828-1906). Their surname was variously spelled, even among family members. I use that given on pension cards. Charles enlisted in the 147th Regiment on September 4, 1862 at Oswego City and was assigned to Co. I. On September 23rd he was rejected by the mustering officer. Undeterred, on June 3, 1863 at New York City he enrolled in Co. D, 13th NY Cavalry as a bugler. He transferred to Co. D, 3rd Provisional Cavalry on August 17, 1865, mustering out at Camp Barry, DC on September 21st. According to *The Town Clerks' Registers* Charles was held at Andersonville Prison from July 10, 1863 until August 1864. Since the 13th Cavalry was involved with the Gettysburg Campaign it is possible he was taken prisoner but he probably did not go to Andersonville. That facility did not open until February 1864 and at that time prisoner exchanges were not regularly taking place. Charles was a member of Henry Hopkins Post No. 301, GAR, Strafford, KS. He and Ruth were the parents of six, four of whom were living in 1900. The couple is buried in Cherokee Municipal Cemetery.

Eli Cornwell – Co. I
b. 1848 New Haven, NY
d. January 5, 1865 Military Prison Hospital, Florence, SC
m. ------

NOTE: Eli was the son of John (1815-1885) and Sarah Cornels Cornwell (1826-1899). He enlisted in the 147th at Oswego but was discharged by the mustering officer on September 23, 1862, probably because it was discovered he was underage. He successfully enlisted at Oswego in the 24th Regiment on November 14, 1862, mustering into Co. I. He transferred to Co. I, 76th Regiment on May 13, 1863 and was borne under the name Cornell. He was captured at the battle of the Wilderness on May 5, 1864 and died of chronic diarrhea. His gravesite is unknown.

James M. Curtis – Co. H (tr. January 31, 1865)
b. 1845 Chenango County, NY
d. December 27, 1864 Salisbury, Rowan, NC
m. ------

NOTE: James, son of William (1824-1903) and Jane Curtis (1826-1889), enrolled in the 76th Regiment on July 16, 1863 as a substitute for Charles Rusenbark, mustering into Co. I. His enrollment location, as shown on his muster card, was Cordon, NY, a place which does not exist. Since he mustered in at Corning, Steuben, NY the recording clerk may have made a mistake. James was wounded at the battle of the Wilderness on May 6, 1864 and captured on October 1st near Pegram House, VA. His COD was chronic diarrhea and he is buried in Salisbury National Cemetery.

James W. Davis – Co. K
b. 1833 Kentucky
d. ? ?
m. ?

NOTE: Little is known about this man except that he claimed to be a stone cutter. He enrolled in the 147th Regiment as a substitute for an unnamed draftee at Buffalo, Erie, NY on July 24, 1863, mustering into Co. K the same day. According to his muster roll card he was "not borne on any roll 147th until Feb. 28/65 'absent, sick'; Apr. 30/65 same; same on MOR 147 & 91." In fact, he does not appear in *The Adjutant-General's Report* for the 91st Regiment. It may be that he collected a bounty and then "skedaddled" but was never properly accounted for until February 1865.

Joshua Dolphus Davis – Co. E (tr. January 28, 1865)
b. April 1840 Chenango County, NY
d. August 12, 1917 Horseheads, Chemung, NY
m. Elizabeth Martha McFail (August 1846-July 12, 1916) *ca.* 1870

NOTE: Joshua, son of Eliphalet (1809-1887) and Emiline Lamphier Davis (1812-*post* 1880), was drafted and enrolled in the 76th Regiment on July 27, 1863 at Hector, Schuyler, NY, mustering into Co. C the same day. He was accidentally wounded while on picket duty on October 30, 1863 and discharged because of his wounds at Cliffburne Barracks, Washington, DC on March 7, 1864. In 1890 he stated he had suffered gunshot wounds in both hands. He and Elizabeth, the mother of three, are buried in Maple View Cemetery, Horseheads.

Charles Deneff – Co. K (tr. January 28, 1865)
b. 1829 Germany
d. December 1864 Savannah, Wayne, NY
m. ?

NOTE: Charles' parents are unknown. He enrolled in the 76th Regiment at Auburn, Cayuga, NY on July 24, 1863 as a substitute for an unnamed draftee and mustered into Co. I. He was captured at the battle of the Wilderness on May 5, 1864 and sent to Andersonville. According to the records he was paroled on February 8, 1865 and on February 28th was on furlough. Those dates conflict with probate records filed in Lyons, Wayne, NY on January 6, 1865. On that date Charles Herman petitioned the court to be appointed administrator of Deneff's estate. It would appear, therefore, that Deneff had died late in December 1864. Somewhat surprisingly, Deneff was assigned to Co. K, 147th Regiment in certain documents relating to Andersonville prisoners.

John Desmond – Co. I (tr. January 31, 1865)
b. 1840 Pennsylvania
d. 1864 ?
m. ------

NOTE: John, whose parents are unidentified, was a painter. He enrolled in the 76th Regiment at Rochester, Monroe, NY on August 7, 1863 as a substitute for John H. Williams, Mendon, Monroe, NY, mustering into Co. I. On May 5, 1864 at the battle of the Wilderness he was designated MIA and, since no further information was discovered about him, he probably died and was buried there.

Mathew Devine – Co. B (tr. ?)
b. 1842 Ireland
d. September 8, 1864 Andersonville, Sumter, GA
m. ------

NOTE: Mathew's parents are unidentified. He claimed to be a shipbuilder when he enrolled in the 76th Regiment on August 19, 1863 at Syracuse, Onondaga, NY, mustering into Co. C. He was captured on May 5, 1864 at the battle of the Wilderness and died of scurvy. He is buried in Andersonville National Cemetery. It is curious to note that a muster roll card for the 147th Regiment shows that Mathew Devine, a ship carpenter, enrolled as a substitute for John J. Morse, Manlius, Onondaga, NY on August 19, 1863, mustering into Co. B. He was captured on May 5, 1864 and died at Andersonville on July 12th. Prison records document his membership in the 76th Regiment and his interment card also assigns him to that organization.

George W. Devoe – Co. K (tr. January 31, 1865)
b. 1833 Springfield, Otsego, NY
d. November 15, 1864 Andersonville, Sumter, GA
m. ------

NOTE: George, son of Winard (1805-1842) and Margaret Jewell Devoe (1806-*post* 1880), enlisted in the 76th Regiment on October 14, 1861, mustering into Co. K. He was wounded at 2nd Bull Run on August 28, 1862, then captured at Gettysburg on July 1, 1863 and paroled at an unknown date. He was wounded in both arms at the battle of the Wilderness on May 5, 1864 and taken prisoner. Sent to Andersonville, he died of starvation. Testimony from neighbors and children revealed that George had supported his mother for many years, even buying her a house and sending money home from the army to pay for it. After he died she was forced to sell it since she could not make the payments but her application for a pension in 1869 was successful. The last known reference to her was the 1880 census. Winard is buried in Middle Village Cemetery, Springfield, and she may be there too. George's gravesite is unknown but he probably lies with the "unknowns" in Andersonville National Cemetery.

Horace Dickerson – Co. F
b. 1826 Ellisburg, Jefferson, NY
d. May 17, 1895 Orleans, Ionia, MI

m1. Catherine Cornwell (November 26, 1827-May 6, 1910) October 23, 1852

m2. Pruciann "Prushia" Adams Higley (April 4, 1835-September 2, 1903) June 21, 1877

NOTE: Horace was the son of Elias (1801-1886) and Anna Attridge Dickerson (1806-1849). He enlisted in the 147th Regiment on September 6, 1862 and enrolled in Co. F. His muster roll card shows he was discharged on September 21st without offering any explanation. Crisfield Johnson's *History of Oswego County,* 346 provides the rest of the story. Horace "played crazy, and had fits, and [was] let off before mustered into service." Horace and Catherine were the parents of five children. By 1865 the family had left New Haven, NY. Horace lived in Ellisburg in 1870 but the family was not with him. At some point all of them settled in Michigan, after which Horace and Catherine separated. When he and Pruciann were married she was still the wife of Nelson Joseph Higley (1837-*ante* December 23, 1892), as evidenced by the 1880 census. Catherine allegedly married Henry Allen (1821-March 31, 1911) in 1865 according to the 1900 census but it is unlikely that they were legally married since her death certificate provides a surname of Dickerson. Although Horace never served in the military, nevertheless he applied, unsuccessfully, for a pension in 1889. In 1892 Prushia applied, also unsuccessfully, for Higley's pension! After Horace died, she made a third, unsuccessful, attempt at collecting a pension. Shortly before he died, Horace made a will leaving everything, including his share of his father's estate, to Prushia, disinheriting all his children: "To my children . . . I do not leave anything they being young and able to take care of themselves." Prushia petitioned to have the will probated and was ultimately appointed administrator of the estate. She was not competent to undertake such a position and years passed. Catherine, apparently unaware of Horace's demise, petitioned the court in September 1900 to have the will set aside since Prushia was not his legal wife and had no claim to the property. Prushia responded to the contrary and seems to have won the case. In 1909, however, the surrogate's office sent the now long dead Prushia a letter urging her to complete her duties in order to close the file. Horace's gravesite has not been located. Prushia, whose COD was "dropsy," is buried in Greenop Memorial Cemetery, Orleans. Catherine, who died of senile debility, is buried in Forest Home Cemetery, Greenville, Montcalm, MI. Henry, who in 1910 was living at the Chippewa Township Poor Farm, died in Lincoln, Isabella, MI and was buried in Chippewa Township Cemetery.

Chauncey Bromley Dodge – Co. D (tr. January 28, 1865)
b. August 27, 1845 Coventry, Chenango, NY
d. September 20, 1864 Andersonville, Sumter, GA
m. ------

NOTE: The son of Avery Bromley (1806-1884) and Phoebe Parker Dodge (1807-1891), Chauncey enrolled in the 76th Regiment at Triangle, Broome, NY on July 17, 1863 as a substitute for George Love and mustered into Co. E. His muster roll card for the 147th Regiment contains the following annotation: "1st Sgt. Hiram G. Warner, Co. B, Pvt. Chas. Glover, Co. F, and Eugene Fisher, Co. D, testify that they and Dodge were taken prisoners at the battle of the Wilderness May 5/64 and were confined in the rebel prison at Andersonville, Ga., and according to their best information and belief, he, Dodge, died there on or about Sept. 23/64 of chronic diarrhoea." Chauncey is buried in Andersonville National Cemetery. In 1889 his mother successfully applied for a pension.

Martin Driscoll – Co. I (tr. January 31, 1865)
b. January 15, 1843 Canada
d. ? Andersonville, Sumter, GA
m. ------

NOTE: Martin was the son of John D. (1814-1860) and Mary A. Mahoney Driscoll (1823-1881). He enrolled in the 76th Regiment at on July 23, 1863 at Auburn, Cayuga, NY as a substitute for Martin H. Morley, mustering into Co. K. He was captured at the battle of the Wilderness on May 5, 1864. Nothing more was ever heard from him and all records indicate he died at Andersonville.

William H. Earls – Co. G (tr. January 28, 1865)
b. March 14, 1840 Livingston County, NY
d. May 19, 1909 Traverse City, Grand Traverse, MI
m1. Delia A. Lane Lamson (July 15, 1830-November 11, 1901) *ca.* 1865
m2. Emma Shaw (1859-January 30, 1937) *post* 1901

NOTE: William, son of John (?-?) and Sarah Decker Earls (?-?), was drafted. He enrolled in the 76th Regiment on July 14, 1863 at Cohocton, Steuben, NY and mustered into Co. F. He was seriously injured in an accidental shooting while on picket duty, losing one finger on his right hand and crippling two others. He transferred to Co. K, 20th Regiment VRC on June 1864 and mustered out at Wheeling, WV on July 24, 1865. Delia had first been married to William Wallace Lamson (1824-1865) and was the mother of at least three sons by him. When he died the family was living in Van Buren County, MI. In 1870 William, Delia, Martin Lamson, 20, John Lamson, 10, and Adolphus Earls, 7 resided in Deerfield, Van Buren County. Adolphus may have been another son of William Wallace Lamson. He disappears after the 1870 census. According to Dawn Triplett's *Brave Boys Were They!*, 90, Earls was a barber and at the time of his death was the oldest barber in Traverse City. Delia's COD was neurasthenia. It is unknown when William and Emma married. In 1905 and in 1910 she and her daughter, Mabel Shaw (1886-1966), were living in Grove, Allegany, NY with her father, Harry Griswold Shaw (1827-1912). William's COD was gangrene of the foot caused by Bright's disease. He and Delia are buried in Oakwood Cemetery, Traverse City. Emma died in Olean, Cattaraugus, NY at the home of her daughter and husband, Floyd C. Woods (1875-1961). She is buried in the Shaw plot in Canaseraga Cemetery in an unmarked grave.

John Edwards – Co. E (tr. January 28, 1865)
b. 1842 New York State
d. *post* August 26, 1892 New York State
m. ?

NOTE: This soldier, whose parents are unknown, saw prior service in Co. K, 22nd NY Militia, enrolling under the name of John Robbins on June 6, 1861 at Albany, Albany, NY for a period of two years. He deserted on or about June 9th. On August 21, 1863 he enrolled in the 76th Regiment at Rochester, Monroe, NY as a substitute for Jacob Kroener, mustering into Co. K. He was captured at the battle of the Wilderness on May 5, 1864 and paroled at an unknown date. Although nominally transferred to the 147th on January 28, 1865 he was discharged to date January 25th. On August 26, 1892 he applied for a pension in New York State but did not obtain a certificate. It is possible he died before the process could be completed but it is also possible he was rejected because of his desertion in 1861. He either was unmarried or his wife predeceased him. Nothing else confirmable has been discovered.

Francis "Frank" Eggensperger – Co. E (tr. January 28, 1865)
b. June 19, 1837 Kirchhausen, Baden-Wuerttemberg, Germany
d. August 9, 1889 Poughkeepsie, Dutchess, NY
m. Katharina "Katherine" Jakobina Schippert (1839-January 5, 1937) October 15, 1869

NOTE: Francis was the son of Francis (1803-1862) and Elizabeth Eggensperger (1806-1877). The family name was variously spelled in military records. Frank enlisted in the 30th Regiment at Watervliet, Albany, NY on September 8, 1862, mustering into Co. E. He transferred to Co. K, 76th Regiment on May 25, 1863 and was wounded at Gettysburg on July 1st. He transferred to Co. C on July 1, 1864 and to Co. D on November 8th. At an unknown date he was transferred to the VRC and discharged at Cliffburne, DC on January 28, 1865. On February 22, 1865 he enrolled in the 169th Regiment at Oppenheim, Fulton, NY, mustering into Co. A. He was discharged at Raleigh, NC on July 19th. On October 13, 1865, two days before his wedding, he enlisted in Co. A, 33rd Reserve Infantry and was discharged at the expiration of his term on October 10, 1868 at Mobile, AL. He and Katherine, also a native of Germany, were the parents of six, four of whom were alive in 1900. Frank was a member of Poughkeepsie Council No. 18, Order of United Friends and of Louis Hamilton Post No. 20 GAR. The Eggenspergers were members of the Poughkeepsie German Lutheran Church. Katharine was a member of the church's Ladies' Aid Society. The couple is buried in Poughkeepsie Rural Cemetery.

William H. Ferguson – Co. B (tr. January 28, 1865)
b. 1825 New York City, NY
d. ? ?
m. ?

NOTE: Ferguson, a sailor, enlisted in the 76th Regiment at Groton, Tompkins, NY on September 16, 1861, mustering into Co. C. He was captured at the battle of the Wilderness on May 5, 1864. When transferred to the 147th he was "absent, wounded." Since there is no further record, it is relatively certain that he died in captivity.

Jerome W. Frink – Co. A (tr. January 31, 1865)
b. November 11, 1842 Chenango County, NY
d. *ca.* October 21, 1864 Florence, SC
m. ------

NOTE: Jerome was the son of Prentice (1877-1860) and Amelia E. Frink (1815-1888). He enrolled in the 76th Regiment on October 12, 1861 at Greene, Chenango, NY, mustering into Co. B. He was wounded at Gettysburg on July 1, 1863 and taken prisoner on May 5, 1864 at the battle of the Wilderness. Lewis Fox testified on January 11, 1887 what happened to him and Frink after their capture: "When first captured we remained at Lee Head Quarters all night and was the next morning taken to Orange Court House, Va. We were kept at Orange Court House one night and were then taken to Gordonsville. We stayed there one night and then to Lynchburg we were kept about 3 days, then to Danville for 3 or 4 days, and then to Andersonville where we were kept about 4 months and then sent to Florence, S. C. When we were taken out of the cars at Florence, S.C. there were a large number of the prisoners who were unable to walk to the stockade and they were left near the railroad[:] among those left there was Jerome W. Frink. I was also left there and being in somewhat better condition than the above named members of my company I tried to help them . . . Jerome W. Frink died there about 2 or 3 weeks after we arrived . . . Frink had the Scurvy and the diarrhoea and also had a bad cough. He contracted these diseases at Andersonville and was quite sick when we left there . . . I am positive that the Jerome W. Frink who was a member of Co. B, 76th N. Y. Vol. died and was buried between the railroad and the prison stockade at Florence, S.C. in the month of October 1864 and on or about the 21ˢᵗ of that month . . . ." On January 27, 1880 Amelia Frink had made application for a mother's pension, on the grounds that Jerome had been her primary support after her husband's death. The case apparently stalled because no one knew Jerome's actual fate. On or about December 4, 1884 James Frink (1840-1914), Jerome's brother, bribed Dora Wooldridge Altenberg to sign an affidavit that while on her wedding trip she had seen Jerome in Libby Prison and the following day had seen his dead body. For this false testimony James promised to pay her $100. When he reneged on the agreement, Dora sued him and Amelia for damages. According to an article in *The Syracuse Journal* March 10, 1886, she had in the previous December obtained a judgment in the amount of $100 to "recover that amount, she alleging she had rendered the defendants services with that sum, in helping them obtain a pension . . . ." Sometime later the Pension Bureau became involved, James was arrested, and the case went to trial in July 1886. Many witnesses were called and every effort was made to impugn their integrity and credibility. In the end, however, James was convicted and sentenced on January 22, 1887 to two years in Auburn Prison. After his release he and his family lived in Syracuse where he earned a living as a portrait artist. He and Amelia are buried in Oakwood Cemetery, Syracuse. Another brother, Prentice Stanhope (1835-?), served in the 44ᵗʰ Regiment, the 140ᵗʰ, and the 5ᵗʰ N Y Veteran Infantry, mustering out on September 16, 1865 at New York City. He was never heard from again and the family was told he died there of smallpox.

Everett Fuller – Co. C (tr. January 31, 1865)
b. September 15, 1840 Taylor, Cortland, NY
d. September 25, 1864 Florence, SC
m. ------

NOTE: Everett, son of Sullivan (1801-1892) and Polly Cole Fuller (1802-1885), enrolled in the 76ᵗʰ Regiment at Union Valley, Cortland, NY on September 21, 1861, mustering into Co. B. He was wounded at Bull Run on August 28, 1862 and again at Gettysburg on July 1, 1863. Together with Jerome Frink and Lewis Fox he was captured at the battle of the Wilderness on May 5, 1865 and spent time in Andersonville before being sent to Florence. According to Fox, Fuller was among a group of men too sick to walk into the stockade. A notation on Fuller's muster roll card states that Sgt. Peter G. Brown, Co. B, 76ᵗʰ Regiment "testified he kept a roster of men in 76ᵗʰ in prison; Fuller was prisoner with him at Florence, S.C. where he died September 25, 1864." Fuller is buried among the "unknowns" at Florence National Cemetery. David C. Crankshaw's *Taylor, NY, 217* mistakenly asserts he was buried in Union Valley Cemetery. The stone, which contains an incorrect DOD, is a cenotaph. Everett's parents, however, are buried in that cemetery.

William Kelly Fuller – Co. E (tr. January 28, 1865)
b. October 11, 1839 Taylor, Cortland, NY
d. January 4, 1865 Union Valley, Cortland, NY
m. ------

NOTE: William, son of John (1812-*post* 1870) and Susan Brooks Fuller (1817-February 4, 1899), was a cousin of Everett Fuller. He enrolled in the 76th Regiment at Cortland City on October 25, 1861, mustering into Co. B. He was wounded at South Mountain, MD on September 14, 1862. He re-enlisted on January 26, 1864 and was taken captive on May 5th at the battle of the Wilderness. Where he was held and his parole date are unknown but he was granted a 30-day furlough from Parole Camp at Annapolis, MD on December 16th. After he arrived home he was so sick that a doctor was called who later testified that William "was laboring under disease of lungs of which he died. Causes perhaps were starvation & exposure – together with the effects of a gunshot wound through the right lung." It appears that both John and Susan, who had not lived together since 1858, applied for a pension. John was paralyzed and lived with his sister, Vesta Fuller Ballou (1798-1880). He received his certificate on November 18, 1868 and about this time Susan began her action, claiming William had been her primary support for many years after her husband abandoned the family. She obtained the pension retroactive to January 5, 1865 with a certificate dated April 9, 1870. John appeared on the 1870 census which was taken on June 7th. He does not appear on the 1875 New York census but neither does Vesta, who is known to have died in April 1880. In that year Susan was living with her son, Eugene, claiming to be a widow. She died in Homer, Cortland, NY and is probably buried in Union Valley Cemetery with William.

William Gabsch – Co. E (tr. January 31, 1865)
b. 1840 Germany
d. ? ?
m. ?

NOTE: Gabsch enrolled in the 76th Regiment at New York City on January 2, 1864, mustering into Co. F. He was declared MIA at the battle of the Wilderness on May 5, 1864 and probably died there.

Henry Gremmels – Co. E (tr. January 31, 1865)
b. 1824 Germany
d. ? ?
m. ?

NOTE: Gremmels enrolled in the 76th Regiment on January 2, 1864 in New York City, mustering into Co. F. He was declared MIA at the battle of the Wilderness on May 5, 1864 and probably died on the battlefield.

George O. Guiles – Co. E (tr. January 31, 1865)
b. 1842 Saratoga County, NY
d. ? ?
m. ------

NOTE: George, whose name strangely became Gold on his muster roll card for the 147th Regiment, was the son of Aaron (1806-1892) and Orilla Herrick Guiles (1819-1860). He enlisted in the 30th Regiment at Day, Saratoga, NY on September 29, 1862, mustering into Co. G. He transferred to Co. F, 76th Regiment on May 25, 1863. According to *The Adjutant-General's Report* Guiles was captured at the battle of the Wilderness on May 5, 1864 but his muster roll card says he was listed among the missing. His father applied for a pension in 1889 and the pension card for the 30th Regiment specifically says George died on May 5th. George's brother Daniel (1839-1906) served in Co. C, 2nd NY Cavalry from July 1863-November 1865.

Marion Harpending – Co. C (tr. January 31, 1865)
b. 1846 Steuben County, NY
d. January 28, 1865 Salisbury, Rowan, NC
m. ------

NOTE: Marion was the son of Minor (1812-1875) and Harriet Adams Harpending (1811-1894). Together with his younger brother David he enlisted in the 76th Regiment on December 23, 1863 at Tyrone, Steuben, NY, mustering into Co. D. He was captured near Poplar Grove Church, VA on October 1, 1864. His muster card for the 147th Regiment includes the following: "Sgt. John H. Price, C, 179 NY testifies that while a prisoner of war at Salisbury, N. C., that Harpending died there or about Jan. 28/65 of exposure and starvation." He is buried among the "unknowns" at Salisbury National Cemetery. His mother applied for a pension on May 24, 1880 and someone wrote on the bottom of the card that Marion had died on January 29, 1865.

Stephen Valentine Hart – Co. H (tr. January 28, 1865)
b. August 2, 1845 Tylerville, Jefferson, NY
d. May 1864 Union Army field hospital, VA
m. ------

NOTE: Stephen's parents were Reuben (1817-1862) and Elizabeth "Betsey" Cole Hart (1819-1893). Reuben served in Co. H, 94th Regiment from December 1861-August 30, 1862 when he was killed at the 2nd battle of Bull Run and his body buried on the field. Stephen enrolled in the 76th Regiment at Watertown, Jefferson, NY on September 14, 1863 as a substitute for an unidentified draftee, mustering into Co. F. His exact DOD is disputed. His muster roll card states he was wounded at Laurel Hill, VA on May 8th and died on May 9th. Two friends who were with him when he died, Homer Doney and John W. Sischo, testified that he was wounded at the battle of the Wilderness on May 8th and died the following day. A death notice which appeared in *The New York Reformer* September 7, 1864 stated he had been wounded on May 5th at the battle of the Wilderness and had died on May 7th. If wounded on May 5th it happened at the Wilderness. If wounded on May 8th, the battle took place at Laurel Hill. Stephen's gravesite is unknown. Two brothers also served the Union cause. Americus V. Hart (1838-1898) served in Co. H, 34th Regiment from May 1861- June 1863 and in Co. B, 10th NY HA from September 1863-April 1864. Jairus James William Hart (1842-1920) served in Cos. H and A, 94th Regiment from December 1861-June 30, 1865. Although Reuben was buried on the battlefield, a cenotaph for him stands in Adams State Road Cemetery, Honeyville, Jefferson, NY. Betsey died of pneumonia in Clayton, Jefferson, NY on March 5, 1893. Her obituary in *On St. Lawrence and Clayton Independent* March 10, 1893, 5 said her age was 71 years, 11 months, and 15 days. She is buried in Adams State Road Cemetery.

Hugh H. Harvey – Co. B
b. 1835 Ireland
d. November 5, 1890 Oswego City, NY
m. Margaret _____ (1830-?) *ca.* 1849

NOTE: Harvey was a blacksmith by occupation. He apparently enlisted in two outfits on the same day. His muster card for the 147th Regiment states he enrolled in that organization on August 19, 1862 and transferred to Battery L, 1st Artillery on December 30, 1863. According to *The Adjutant-General's Report* for the 1st Artillery, however, he enrolled in Battery L on August 19, 1862 and was mustered in on August 30th. He mustered out with the battery at Elmira, Chemung, NY on June 17, 1865. He and Margaret were the parents of six by 1865, four of whom were alive and all born in Oswego County. His entry in *The Town Clerks' Registers* includes this odd statement: "Don't know what become of the boy." If that is true, then the man who died on November 5, 1890 cannot be the identical person.

James Hatch – Co. H (tr. January 28, 1865)
b. 1841 England
d. ? ?
m. ?

NOTE: James, a sailor, enrolled in the 76th Regiment on August 7, 1863 at Buffalo, Erie, NY as a substitute for Mathias Gardner, mustering into Co. H. He was captured on November 27, 1863 at the battle of Mine Run. His muster roll card states he was held in both Libby and Andersonville Prisons. He was paroled on April 12, 1865 at an unknown place. His card for the 147th states he "never joined his regt. since captured." He was discharged at Elmira, Chemung, NY on August 5, 1865. No further information has been located.

Gaines Healy – Co. I
b. 1836 Lysander, Onondaga, NY
d. ? ?
m. ?

NOTE: Little can be ascertained about this man who gave "mariner" as his occupation. His muster card for the 147th shows contradictory information. He enlisted on August 26, 1862 but was rejected. The card also says he deserted on September 27th.

Joseph Hemrick – Co. A (tr. January 28, 1865)
b. 1843 New York State
d. ? ?
m. ?

NOTE: Joseph, whose parents are unidentified, enlisted in the 30th Regiment at Watervliet, Albany, NY on September 4, 1862, mustering into Co. D. Although he transferred to Co. K, 76th Regiment on May 25, 1863 he was discharged from the service from Carver Hospital, Washington, DC on a surgeon's certificate of disability on June 2nd and then transferred to Co. K, 76th Regiment. He transferred to Co. G on July 1, 1864, to Co. C on October 20th, and to Co. A on November 8th. By the time he transferred to the 147th he was "absent." From the 147th he was sent to Co. C, 91st Regiment but he does not appear in *The Adjutant-General's Report* for that organization. I suspect something happened to him in late November 1864 which was not reported.

William Herring – Co. F
b. 1834 Cortland County, NY
d. ? ?
m. ?

NOTE: William, who described himself as a laborer, was drafted, enrolling in the 147th Regiment on September 16, 1863 at Watertown, Jefferson, NY and mustering into Co. F the same day. What happened to him after that date is unknown. His muster card called him a paroled prisoner and added, "not borne on any roll 147ᵗʰ until Feb. 28/65 – absent, sick." No other information is available.

Ahial Hibbard – Co. A (tr. January 31, 1865)
b. 1833 Madison County, NY
d. August 30, 1864 Andersonville, Sumter, GA
m. ?

NOTE: Ahial, whose parents are unknown, enrolled in the 76ᵗʰ Regiment on August 8, 1863 at Buffalo, Erie, NY as a substitute for Henry Joslyn of that city, mustering into Co. B. He was captured on May 5, 1864 at the battle of the Wilderness. His COD was *scorbutus* (scurvy). He is buried in Andersonville National Cemetery. The name on his gravestone is Abiel Hibbard.

Charles D. Hilliard – Co. B (tr. January 28, 1865)
b. 1843 Cassville, Oneida, NY
d. November 9, 1864 Florence, SC
m. ------

NOTE: Charles was the son of William A. (1809-April 18, 1863) and Emeline Spicer Hilliard (1814- ?). He saw prior service in Co. B, 14ᵗʰ Regiment from September 1861-June 24, 1863 when transferred to the 44ᵗʰ Regiment where he was unassigned and probably discharged. He enlisted in the 76ᵗʰ Regiment at Utica, Oneida, NY on September 5, 1863 and mustered into Co. C. He was taken prisoner on May 5, 1864 at the battle of the Wilderness. According to Newton Baldwin, also a prisoner at Florence, Charles died of chronic diarrhea. A pension card claims COD was consumption. The official COD, however, was typhoid fever. On May 22, 1865 Emeline applied for a mother's pension, claiming her son had been her primary support since 1859. She was dependent on him since she had no property and no means to earn her own living. One witness said that Charles once remarked that "he could support his mother, Mrs. Emeline Hilliard, easyer [*sic*] when at war than at home at farm labor . . . ." She obtained the pension and allegedly collected it until September 1881. In 1885 the Pension Bureau was informed of her death but no dates were provided. In fact, after the 1870 census Emeline disappeared altogether. Charles is buried among the "unknowns" in Florence National Cemetery.

Charles Robert Hoag – Co. C (tr. January 28, 1865)
b. July 18, 1832 Columbus, Chenango, NY
d. July 23, 1910 Norwich, Chenango, NY
m1. Margaret King (1848-November 5, 1873) 1864
m2. Esther Perkins (August 18, 1843-February 1, 1910) 1875

NOTE: Charles was the only surviving child of Amos (1807-*post* 1875) and Patience Roberts Hoag (1807-1846). He enlisted in the 76th Regiment at Columbus on December 1, 1861, mustering into Co. H. He was captured at 2nd Bull Run, probably on August 28, 1862, and paroled on September 4th. He was sent to Point of Rocks, MD and then to Camp Chase Prison, Columbus, OH. He was exchanged on November 4th. Officially declared a deserter from parole camp he went home but after President Lincoln declared an amnesty on March 10, 1863 he reported at Utica on March 23rd and was sent to Albany the next day. He was sent to Camp Parole, Annapolis, MD and held there until May 15th when he was sent back to his regiment. Hoag had the misfortune to be captured a second time at Gettysburg. He apparently suffered from partial deafness and the cannon fire exacerbated the condition. He was delivered to a makeshift Confederate hospital where he helped with the wounded until released when the Union forces retook the site. He later was treated for "intermittent fever" and chronic diarrhea. On October 10, 1863 he was a patient in the 3rd Division USA General Hospital, Alexandria, MD. Then he developed bronchitis. On March 18, 1864 he was transferred to 99th Co., 2nd Battalion VRC and later transferred to Co. E, 18th Regiment VRC.

He was discharged on January 3, 1865. He and Margaret, a native of Maryland whom he had met and married while in hospital, returned to Columbus. He applied for and obtained a small pension based on his hearing loss. Later, however, that pension was revoked because his deafness was deemed a pre-existing condition. Although poverty-stricken, Hoag was ordered to repay the government $1,108.40 which he had "fraudulently" received. He successfully applied for a pension under the Act of 1890. Margaret's COD is unknown and her gravesite has not been located. Esther died of pneumonia. Upon Charles' death from enteritis an interesting obituary appeared in an unsourced newspaper: "Norwich, July 29. -- Charles R. Hoag died at the home of his daughter, Mrs. R. A. Richardson, on Gold street, last Saturday evening, aged 78. Death was due to a complication of diseases. Funeral services were held on Monday afternoon at 4:30,

Charles Hoag was accepted into the army despite a severe hearing loss which was worsened by his wartime experiences.
Richard Roth

Rev. M. D. Fuller officiating. Smith Post, G. A. R., assisted in the service. The remains were taken to South Edmeston for burial on Tuesday. Mr. Hoag was born in Columbus, N. Y. in 1832, and had lived in the vicinity of his birth the greater share of his life. He had twice married. His first wife, who was Margaret King, of Georgetown, Md., died in 1873. In 1875 he married Esther Perkins, of Sherburne, who passed away in February last since which time he had made his home with his daughter . . . The deceased was a veteran of the civil war with a record of over three years faithful service as a member of Company H, Seventy-sixth New York Volunteer Infantry, and of the Ninety-ninth Company, Second Battalion, V. R. C. He was a member of the G. A. R. and a man of genial disposition . . . ." Charles and Esther are buried in Columbus Corners (Lambs Corners) Cemetery, Columbus. His final medical and funeral bills were paid by the Town of Norwich. The GAR Post to which he belonged was Elisha B. Smith No. 83, Norwich.

Hubert Hurtubis – Co. A
b. 1838 Canada East
d. May 4, 1892 Bay City, Bay, MI
m. Phebe Donahue Archambo (1844-*post* 1892) July 27, 1868

NOTE: Hubert, son of Hubert (1812-?) and Rosa Hurtubis (1819-May 18, 1906), was a ship carpenter. He enlisted in the 147th Regiment on August 9, 1862 and subsequently enlisted in Battery L, 1st NY LA on August 29th, mustering in on August 30th. *The Adjutant-General's Report* for the 147th indicates he was mustered into that organization on September 23rd! He was wounded at Gettysburg on July 1, 1863 and mustered out at Elmira, NY on June 17, 1865. He married Phebe in Wenona, Bay, MI but all their children except Phoebe (1882-?) were born in Oswego County. In 1875 a child named Mary, 12, using the Hurtubis name, appeared on the New York census with the family. She in all likelihood was Phebe's daughter by her first husband. In 1890 Hubert said his disability was "consumption." He is buried in Pine Ridge Cemetery, Bay City. Phebe applied for a widow's pension but apparently did not receive it. She may have remarried or died before the process could be completed.

Ezra G. Jenks – Co. K (tr. January 31, 1865)
b. 1839 Oneonta, Otsego, NY
d. October 14, 1864 Florence, SC
m. ------

NOTE: Ezra was the son of Joseph Griffin (1801-*post* 1865) and Mary "Polly" Strait Jenks (1802-*ca.* 1861). He enlisted in the 76th Regiment at Oneonta on November 1, 1861, mustering into Co. K. He was captured on May 5, 1864 at the battle of the Wilderness. According to Edwin T. Farmer of Co. E, 95th Regiment, he "was a prisoner of war at Florence, S.C., with Jenks and the latter was sick with chronic diarrhoea and scurvy and was taken outside the stockade[;] also was reported to have died Oct. 14/64." Ezra is buried among the "unknowns" in Florence National Cemetery.

John Keith – Co. F (?)
b. 1842 New York State
d. ? ?
m. ?

NOTE: This man's muster card for the 147th Regiment says "date, place of enlistment & m/i not stated." He is most likely John Keif who enrolled in the 76th Regiment at Buffalo, Erie, NY on August 13, 1863, mustering into Co. F. His muster card for that organization states he deserted on October 10, 1863 near Rapidan River, VA and was dishonorably discharged as John Keefe on July 1, 1865. There is also a card for him in Co. A, 91st Regiment which says he transferred to that unit on June 5, 1865 and mustered out on July 3, 1865 near Washington, DC. No other reliable information has been discovered.

Frederick Koster – Co. H (tr. January 28, 1865)
b. 1837 Germany
d. September 4, 1864 Andersonville, Sumter, GA
m. Catherine Schall (1847-December 3, 1917) March 16, 1861

NOTE: Frederick, son of Johannes (1800-1867) and Maria Koster (1800-1890), enrolled in the 76th Regiment at Watertown, Jefferson, NY on September 13, 1863 as a substitute for an unnamed draftee, mustering into Co. H. He was captured at Bethesda Church, VA on June 2, 1864 and sent to Andersonville. He and Catherine were the parents of two sons. In 1870 Catherine married Charles Martin Spencer (1837-1915) by whom she was the mother of two daughters. Martin, as he was known, had been a soldier in the 5th NY HA from 1862-1865. He was a member of Guilford D. Bailey Post No. 200 GAR, Lowville, Lewis, NY. His COD was liver cancer. Catherine's death was reported in *The Black River Democrat* December 6, 1917, 1: "The body of Mrs. Catherine Spencer, a former resident of this village, was brought here Tuesday and funeral services were held Wednesday afternoon at 2 o'clock in the Baptist church. Mrs. Spencer sustained a fall a week ago which resulted in her death at the Watertown City Hospital. She was 70 years old." Catherine and Martin are buried in Lowville Rural Cemetery.

Anthony LaBrock – Co. G
b. 1818 Prussia
d. ? ?
m. ?

NOTE: This man enrolled in the 147th Regiment at Buffalo, Erie, NY on August 11, 1863 as a substitute for Frederick Rodloff. According to his muster roll card he never reported. His surname was variously spelled which hampers identification but it is possible that Anton Leibrecht (August 12, 1816-January 3, 1897), who is buried in Fairport Cemetery, Fairport, Muscatine, IA, is the correct person. His wife was Victoria _____ (1835-1906).

Nelson Lawyer – Co. F (tr. January 28, 1865)
b. June 1842 Schoharie County, NY
d. March 20, 1908 Middleburgh, Schoharie, NY
m. Caroline Rifenberg (1841-April 19, 1896) *ca.* 1866

NOTE: Nelson, the son of David (1814-*post* 1880) and Lana Schramm Lawyer (1818-1898), enrolled in the 76th Regiment at Middleburgh on October 20, 1861 and mustered into Co. I. His military record shows he deserted at some time before May 8, 1863 on which date he returned to duty. He was captured at Gettysburg on July 1, 1863 and later paroled. He was wounded at Laurel Hill, VA on May 12, 1864 and deserted from a hospital in Philadelphia, PA on August 24th. It is interesting to note that in 1890 he gave that date as his leave taking from the military. An article appearing in *The Schoharie Union* December ?, 1865 sheds interesting information on his character: "On the 21st inst. another band of three was hauled up before the same court. These were a notorious fellow named Nelson Lawyer, and William and Lewis Rifenberg. They were likewise convicted and sentenced to imprisonment at hard labor for six months. They too were convicted for stealing chickens from Garret Mattice. As there was no money penalty attached to their sentence they had to 'go up,' and were accordingly taken to Albany on last Saturday by Sheriff Ferris who introduced them to General Pilsbury, by whom they were taken in charge and clothed in the bi-color uniform of the Penitentiary Corps. Lawyer is a desperately bad fellow. Besides being a chicken thief, he is a deserter from the military service. He has many times been pursued by the detectives and marshals, but always escaped arrest. He has often threatened to kill any person who attempted to arrest him as a deserter; and it is believed that he was the ring leader of the party that fired upon Deputy U. S. Marshal Burt and assistants on their visit to 'Polly Hollow' about a year ago, to arrest deserters. As he is now where the Government can get hold of him, he will have a chance to receive his full deserts." Nelson apparently did not mend his ways as he grew older. On June 24, 1886 he was sentenced to 90 days in the Albany Penitentiary after being found guilty of third degree assault. Caroline was the sister of Lewis Rifenberg (1844-?). She and Nelson were the parents of six children. Graves for Nelson and Caroline have not been located.

Henry A. Layman – Co. I (tr. January 31, 1865)
b. 1843 Hamilton, Ontario, Canada
d. ? ?
m. ?

NOTE: Layman's name was spelled Lehman on his muster card for the 147th Regiment. He enrolled in the 76th Regiment at Buffalo, Erie, NY on August 12, 1863 as a substitute for Martin Lewis, Collins, Erie, NY., mustering into Co. I. He was wounded and captured on May 5, 1864 at the battle of the Wilderness. When transferred to the 147th he was "absent, wounded." His muster card for Co. I, 91st Regiment states he was "absent, paroled prisoner." He does not appear in *The Adjutant-General's Report* for that organization. In all likelihood he died after being captured.

Henry W. Lewis – Co. I (tr. January 28, 1865)
b. September 1844 Monroe County, NY
d. April 9, 1915 Rochester, Monroe, NY
m1. Sarah J. _____ (1845-November 23, 1887) *ca.* 1867
m2. Helen "Ellen" _____ (1850-*post* 1905) 1891

NOTE: Henry, a harness maker, was the son of Ebenezer (1805-*post* 1860) and Orpha Lewis (1827-*post* 1855). In 1860 he was working for William Barnhart, Ontario, Wayne, NY and on July 25, 1863 he enrolled in the 76th Regiment at Auburn, Cayuga, NY as a substitute for William's brother, James, mustering into Co. K. In February 1864 he was convicted of larceny at a general court-martial and sentenced to serve the remainder of his term at Fort Jefferson, Dry Tortugas "at hard labor." He was finally mustered out at Albany, NY on March 16, 1866. Henry and Sarah were the parents of two daughters, Sarah A. (1867-1940) and Minnie B. (1885-1964). In 1880 the family lived in Macedon, Wayne, NY. Henry's disability was "loss of limb." When he entered the National Soldiers' Home in Dayton, OH in 1911 it was reported that his right leg had been amputated. Sarah in 1880 suffered from curvature of the spine. Sarah A. and her husband Ara Martindale (1861-1943) are buried in Sand Hill Cemetery, Unadilla, Otsego, NY. Minnie and her husband Ernest Ades (1884-1950) are buried in Grove Place Cemetery, Chili, Monroe, NY. In 1905 Henry and Helen were living in Rochester. She disappears after that date. He gave his daughter Minnie as his next of kin in 1911. Graves for Henry and his two wives have not been located.

Rufus Eugene Lincoln – Co. D
b. May 9, 1835 Groton, Tompkins, NY
d. January 17, 1916 McLean, Tompkins, NY
m1. Maria P. Teed (1837-1868) *post* 1860
m2. Grace A. Crittenden (1852-September 25, 1922) *ca.* 1869

NOTE: Rufus, who used his Christian names interchangeably, was the son of Milton Lewis (1797-*post* 1865) and an unidentified mother. Although he was credited to the 147th Regiment, documents clearly demonstrate that on July 25, 1863 he enrolled in the 157th Regiment as a draftee, mustering into Co. A. On June 22, 1865 he was transferred to Co. B, 54th Regiment, mustering out at Charleston, SC on April 14, 1866. How his name ever became associated with the 147th is a mystery. He was a member of James C. Hatch Post No. 540 GAR. Rufus and Maria had no children but Grace was the mother of five, four of whom were living in 1900. His death was announced in *The Ithaca Daily News* January 20, 1916, 7: "Groton City, Jan. 20. – R. Eugene Lincoln, who has been confined to his bed several months as the result of a stroke of paralysis, died at his home Monday morning, aged 80 years . . . The funeral was held at 1 p.m. yesterday from the home. The Rev. Mr. Ledyard of the Universalist Church of Cortland officiated. Burial was in Cortland Rural Cemetery." Grace's death was reported in *The Journal and Courier* September 28, 1922, 1. She had died on Monday after suffering a stroke the previous Thursday from which she had only partially regained consciousness. She too was buried in Cortland Rural Cemetery along with Rufus and Maria.

George W. Logan – Co. I (January 28, 1865)
b. ? ?
d. ? ?
m. ?

NOTE: Very little can be ascertained about this man. His age, date and place of enlistment, and muster into Co. D were not provided on his muster roll card for the 76th Regiment. When transferred to the 147th he was "absent, sick." He was nominally transferred to Co. I, 91st Regiment on June 5, 1865 but was "absent, sick." He does not appear in *The Adjutant-General's Report* for that organization.

Elijah W. Loomis – Co. C
b. 1845 Albion, NY
d. ? ?
m. ------

NOTE: Elijah was the son of George H. (1812-1873) and Susanna Witherill Loomis (1814-1888). On August 28, 1862 he enlisted in the 147th Regiment at Albion. He was rejected for service because he was underage. At some point after that, the entire family moved to Michigan and Elijah enlisted in the 10th Michigan Cavalry at Grand Rapids, Kent, MI which was mustered in on November 18, 1863 and saw duty in Tennessee. The rest of the story is found in *The Town Clerks' Registers*: "Was initially rejected from the 147th Reg.[;] went to Mich. and re-enlisted in the 10th Mich. Cav. Died in the Hospital. Said to have deserted and was shot in being taken." A DOD of October 31, 1864 has been suggested but I have found no confirmation. His parents died in Muskegon County, MI and were buried in Seaman Cemetery.

James R. Loomis – Co. K (?)
b. July 31, 1836 West Monroe, NY
d. December 6, 1921 National Soldiers' Home, Bath, Steuben, NY
m. Mary J. _____ (1841-January 22, 1917) *ca.* 1860

NOTE: According to the muster roll card, James, son of H_____ (?-?) and Caroline Loomis (?-?), was not borne on any roll for the 147th until February 28, 1865 and then under the name Floomis and was "absent, sick." He was still "absent, sick" when transferred to Co. K, 91st Regiment on June 5, 1865. In reality, this man enrolled in the 149th Regiment at Brewerton, Onondaga, NY on September 3, 1862 and mustered into Co. H, as confirmed by *The Town Clerks' Registers*. His military service was brief. On January 10, 1863 he was discharged on a surgeon's certificate of disability. The confusion over the surname may have arisen because R was misread as F. How his name became associated with the 147th Regiment remains a mystery. He and Mary J. are buried in Mt. Adnah Cemetery, Fulton. His gravestone specifically states "Co. H 149 NY Vol, 1836-1921."

William Madigan – Co. K (tr. January 28, 1865)
b. 1843 Canada
d. ? ?
m. ?

NOTE: William may have been the son of James (?-?) and Mary Ann Powers Madigan (?-?). If so, he was born on April 28, 1842 and was baptized in Kingston, Ontario, Canada the next day. He enrolled in the 76th Regiment at Rochester, Monroe, NY on August 5, 1863 as a substitute for Richard Decker of that city, mustering into Co. I. His military career is sketchy. According to his muster card for the 147th he was listed on the roll of paroled prisoners at Annapolis, MD and was paid from October –December 1864, which seems to indicate he was exchanged in October. The note also says he was present and paid to February 28, 1865 and then was absent on furlough, no further record found. Someone by the name of William Madigan, having similar physical features to the man who joined the 76th Regiment, born in Kingston, Canada, and of the same age, enlisted in the US Army at New York City on November 17, 1865 and was assigned to Co. K, 4th US Cavalry. He died of cholera at Camp Sheridan, TX on September 20, 1866 and presumably was buried there. Whether or not this is the same person is conjectural until more evidence can be discovered.

William Marooney – Co. H

b. 1818 Tipperary, Ireland
d. January 23, 1887 Oswego City, NY
m. Judith "Johanna" Walsh (1820-April 20, 1868) *ca.* 1844

NOTE: William's surname was variously spelled. I use that on his gravestone. Although he alleged at the time of his enlistment in the 147th that he was 44 years old, his DOB also varied. In 1850 he was 31 but in 1875 he was 70. In 1880 he claimed to be 60 and in the article concerning his death he was 52! He enrolled on August 25, 1862 at Oswego City but was absent at the muster in of his company. The circumstances are not explained. He continued to live in Oswego with his family until his tragic and unforeseen death which was reported in *The Oswego Times-Express* January 23, 1887: "Sunday afternoon William Morooney [*sic*], a man 52 years of age, who lived at 272 West Seventh street left his house at about 3:30 o'clock. He did not return and in the evening a search was commenced for him which continued until morning without result. He was heard from in one or two places. The search continued through the morning of Sunday and between 11 and 12 o'clock Hugh Radcliff discovered Marooney lying in the snow upon the bluff overlooking the new harbor near the foot of West Sixth street near the bank. The next person to arrive was Officer Grant, who found that there was some life in the man although he was not able to speak. His heart was still beating. Officer grant took off his coat and put it around the man and waited for a carriage to convey him to the hospital but before reaching that institution Marooney was dead. He had not been able to speak and hence the manner of his death is left open to conjecture. The body was taken to Cullinan's undertaking rooms and Coroner Matteson notified. It is said that previous to this occurrence Marooney has had trouble with his head and has wandered away and got lost. It is thought that he may have had another attack of paralysis of the brain and to have died from this cause combined with exposure . . . In the inquest this afternoon Miss Marooney was sworn, Dr. J. K. Stockton testified that he examined the body and concluded that he had died from exposure although there were some indications that he might have had an attack of vertigo or apoplexy and that the two combined caused his death. Hugh J. Radcliff testified that he was walking up the lake with James McDonald and that his friend saw Marooney first. They then heard him groan and ran and raised him up and asked him his name but he could not speak. After the hack came they started to the hospital but just as they reached the hospital Marooney died. Mrs. Kittie Brown testified that she met deceased on the corner of West Third and Utica street at eight o'clock Saturday night and he appeared to be on his way home. She said he had worked for her husband and she knew him to be a sober, industrious man. After hearing the evidence, the jury returned a verdict of death from exposure." William, Johanna, and several of their children are buried in St. Paul's Cemetery, Oswego.

Thomas Marshall – Co. G (tr. May 1865)
b. August 15, 1843 Jefferson County, NY
d. September 6, 1911 Detroit, Wayne, MI
m. Philomene Jeroy (May 24, 1846-June 25, 1923) February 25, 1867

NOTE: Thomas, son of Canadian natives Isaac (1818-*post* 1901) and Elizabeth Prudhomme Marshall (1818-*ante* 1891), enrolled in the 30th Regiment at Albany, Albany, NY on October 16, 1862, mustering into Co. F. He transferred to Co. G, 76th Regiment on May 25, 1863. He was captured at Squirrel Level Road on October 1, 1864 which was the site of the second day of the battle of Peebles' farm. Where he was held is unknown but he was paroled on February 28, 1865 at Northeast Ferry, NC, reporting to Camp Parole on March 14th. Records indicate he left parole camp on May 5th. His muster card for the 147th says merely that he was transferred to that regiment in May 1865. He was discharged at Arlington Heights, VA on June 6th. Later, when Marshall applied for a pension he claimed to have been a member of the 147th and technically he was, but he saw no action with that unit. Indeed, the war was over when he joined. Thomas and Philomene, who was born on Howe Island, Ontario, Canada, were married in Chatham Township, Ontario, Canada and lived for many years in that country, becoming the parents of at least eight children. It is unknown when they returned to the United States. They do not appear on the 1910 census. Thomas' COD was "paralysis" and heart disease. Philomene succumbed to chronic heart disease. They are buried in Holy Cross Roman Catholic Cemetery, Detroit.

John Martin – Co. I (tr. January 28, 1865)
b. 1820 Germany
d. November 21, 1862 Fort Monroe, Hampton, VA
m. Catherine _____ (1816-*post* 1863) ?

NOTE: John, a farmer, enlisted in the 30th Regiment at Albany, Albany, NY on August 28, 1862, mustering into Co. F on October 16th. According to his muster roll card he was sent to a hospital from Warrenton, VA on November 9th. His burial record does not provide regiment or age but he is buried in Fort Monroe Cemetery. In 1860 he and Catherine lived in Watervliet with their daughter, Caroline, 12. On April 23,

1863 Catherine made a successful application for a pension. On paper John was transferred to Co. G and to Co. D, 76th Regiment before being transferred to the 147th. What happened to Catherine and Caroline is unknown. Like John they were born in Germany. Determining a marriage date is impossible and it is very likely that Caroline was the last child, not the first.

Nicholas W. Martin – Co. K (tr. January 31, 1865)
b. April 23, 1842 Green County, NY
d. July 1864 Andersonville, Sumter, GA
m. ------

NOTE: Nicholas was the son of John (1802-1887) and Abigail Stall Martin (1807-1897). He was drafted and enrolled in the 76th Regiment at Sanford, Broome, NY on July 17, 1863, mustering into Co. B. He was captured on May 5, 1864 at the battle of the Wilderness and sent to Andersonville where he died from dysentery. His DOD is disputed. According to his muster card for the 147th Regiment he "died on or about July 15/64, per testimony of comrades." His cenotaph in Anthony Cemetery, North Sanford, claims he died on July 29th while *Andersonville Prisoners of War*, 131, provides a date of July 30th.

Michael Mason – Co. I (tr. January 28, 1865)
b. 1840 Reach, Cambridgeshire, England
d. May 20, 1915 Phelps, Ontario, NY
m. Alida D. Rogers (October 1848-March 14, 1913) December 25, 1866

NOTE: Michael, son of Michael (1814-1875) and Elizabeth Peachy Mason (1815-1860), immigrated with his family in 1852. He was drafted and enrolled in the 76th Regiment at Auburn, Cayuga, NY on July 25, 1863, mustering into Co. D. He was wounded on May 5, 1864 at the battle of the Wilderness and in 1890 reported he had lost the index finger of his right hand. He transferred to the VRC on January 10, 1865 and discharged on August 2nd. He and Alida were the parents of eight, six of whom were living in 1910. His death was announced in *The Rochester Democrat and Chronicle* May 21, 1915, 16: "Phelps, May 20. – Michael Mason, aged 75 years, a veteran of the Civil war, died this morning in the home of his daughter Mrs. Jesse Dickenson, after an illness of several weeks. Mr. Mason was a native of England, having been born in Cambridgeshire in 1840 and located in Seneca county. Ten years later he enlisted in Auburn with Company G [*sic*] 76th New York Infantry, and served until the close of the rebellion. He was wounded in the battle of the Wilderness but on his recovery again went into active service. Mr. Mason had been in Oaks Corners for the last forty years and since the death of his wife about two years ago had made his home with his daughter, Mrs. Dickenson, in Phelps. He was a member of General J. G. Murray Post No. 597, G. A. R. of this place . . . The funeral will be held Sunday afternoon at 2 o'clock from the home of Hiram Mason in Oaks Corners . . . Rev. Bradley Sayre, pastor of the Oaks Corners Presbyterian Church, will conduct the services." Michael and Alida are buried in Oaklawn Cemetery, Phelps.

David Mattison – Co. F (tr. January 31, 1865)
b. 1843 Virgil, Cortland, NY
d. October 25, 1864 Andersonville, Sumter, GA
m. ------

NOTE: Son of Norman (1810-*post* 1864) and Hannah Mattison (1806-*post* 1860), David enlisted in the 76th Regiment at Dryden, Tompkins, NY on October 23, 1861, mustering into Co. F the same day. He was captured at the battle of the Wilderness on May 5, 1864 and sent to Andersonville. His COD is unknown. His muster card for the 147th shows that his father attempted to obtain a pension. A brother, Lyman Mattison/Matson (1836-1909), served in Co. E, 157th Regiment from 1862-1865.

James McCabe – Co. B (tr. January 28, 1865)
b. 1837 Ireland
d. ? ?
m. ?

NOTE: James, whose parents are unidentified, enrolled in the 76th Regiment at Buffalo, Erie, NY on August 15, 1863 as a substitute for Hilton Wheelock of East Hamburg, Erie, NY, mustering into Co. C. He was accidentally wounded in a skirmish on October 18, 1863 and on May 12, 1864 was transferred to 107th Company, 2nd Battalion VRC. He was discharged for "disability" on September 26, 1864 from Carver Hospital, Washington, DC. His application for a pension dated February 20, 1867 was successful. His father's application at an unknown date was not. Nothing else is available.

Thomas McCormick – Co. B (tr. January 28, 1865)
b. 1832 Ireland
d. ? ?
m. ?

NOTE: Thomas' parents are unknown. He enlisted in the 30th Regiment at Saratoga, Saratoga, NY on August 30, 1862, mustering into Co. G. He transferred to Co. C, 76th Regiment on May 25, 1863 and was wounded at Gettysburg on July 1st. In August he was in a hospital in New York City. Nothing else can be discovered about him after that date. When transferred to the 147th and to the 91st Regiments he was "absent, sick."

William McCormick – Co. B

b. 1841 ?

d. ? ?

m. ?

NOTE: William's parents are unknown. He enlisted in both the 147th Regiment and the 1st NY Artillery at Oswego, NY on August 23, 1862. While his card for the 147th says he transferred to the latter outfit on December 30, 1863, such was not the case. His card for the artillery shows he mustered into Battery L on August 30, 1862 and mustered out with the battery on June 17, 1865 at Elmira, Chemung, NY. No other information has been located.

Harvey Deyo Merritt – Co. G (tr. January 28, 1865)

b. 1841 Dutchess County, NY

d. August 18, 1864 Andersonville, Sumter, GA

m. ------

NOTE: Harvey was the son of Jesse (1810-1870) and Phoebe Deyo Merritt (1813-1896). His POB varies from document to document. He enrolled in the 76th Regiment at Auburn, Cayuga, NY on July 25, 1863, apparently a volunteer, mustering into Co. F. He was taken prisoner at the battle of the Wilderness on May 5, 1864 and sent to Andersonville where he died of dysentery. John Worrell Northrop mentioned the young man in his *Chronicles of a War Prisoner*, 113-15: "I saw by a Rebel sergeant's book that Harvey Deyo Merritt died on the 16th inst. I learn he died laying in the sand outside the hospital having been carried out owing to the crowd. All knew him as Deyo in my company where he was a favorite. He often entertained the boys with songs. He had a melodious voice, was a good singer, a pleasant young man, a faithful soldier." Northrop included a poem "Deyo," which is excerpted here: "Dead he lay upon the sand,/Breathless lips and pulseless hand./Dead he lay, appalling sight;/ In those eyes there is no light;/Dead 'mid living, dying, dead,/And we have no tears to shed!/ . . ./No more his voice in song is heard/That sweetly once his comrades stirred;/Dead within this dreadful place/The peace of God upon his face./Nevermore the ration spare/Of prison pen with him we share./He stood with us in fighting line;/ Alas, together here we pine;/We sat with him in camp at night/Cheered by the Union firelight;/On weary marches night and day,/And with him in embattled fray;/ On picket when the camp did sleep/In wood, and field, and trenches deep/When as skirmishers we creep,/And here where foes their vigils keep!/But now he sleeps in Dixie's soil,/No more, no more with us to toil . . . ." Harvey is buried in Andersonville National Cemetery.

Peter Meyet – Co. I
b. ? Canada
d. ? ?
m. Ann Christinus (1831-?) *ca.* 1851

NOTE: Research for this man has been hampered by the many spellings of his surname, e.g., Meytt, Meiot, Mayette, Meyette. He enlisted in the 147th Regiment at Oswego City on September 1, 1862, claiming to be 40 years old. Census records, however, point to a DOB closer to 1815. He was rejected for military service by the examining surgeon who probably concluded he was too old. Peter and Ann, whose DOB also varied from census to census, were the parents of five known children, all born in New York State: Elizabeth "Betsy" (1852-*post* 1870); Charles (1856-June 12, 1925); Alonzo (1862-July 22, 1890); Joseph (1864-*post* 1870); Martha (1868-*post* 1870). Only by tracing the children has it been possible to track the parents. In 1870 the family lived in Scriba and were still there in 1878 when on February 23rd *The Oswego Daily Palladium* reported that Alonzo Mayette, 13, had been thrown out of his parents' house. The boy stole a package of tobacco in order to get himself arrested and sent to a reformatory. After pleading guilty he was sent to the Western House of Refuge in Rochester, NY where he was enumerated in 1880, still 13. He died in Auburn, Cayuga, NY. Someone by the name of Joseph Mayette was convicted of second degree larceny in Wayne County in May 1893 and sent to the Elmira Reformatory. In August 1893 he was sent to Auburn State Prison "for no apparent reason," according to an article published in *The Buffalo Courier* October 10, 1895, 2. On the recommendation of the district attorney of Wayne County, Governor Morton commuted the sentence. Whether or not this is Ann and Peter's son is conjectural. Charles had his own problems. In 1880 he was enumerated in the Auburn State Prison, having been convicted of third degree burglary on February 28, 1878. His home address was given as Geddes, Onondaga, NY. Charles died in Pontiac State Hospital, Oakland County, MI of arteriosclerotic brain disease complicated by insanity. His death certificate provided his mother's maiden name. He was to be buried in Ann Arbor. After 1878 the rest of the family disappeared, perhaps also migrating to Michigan.

John Mills – Co. F (tr. January 28, 1865)
b. 1837 Halifax, Halifax, Nova Scotia
d. ? ?
m. ?

NOTE: John, whose parents are unknown, was a cabinet maker. He enrolled in the 76th Regiment at Oswego City on August 14, 1863 as a substitute for John H. Statts, mustering into Co. I. He was discharged from the army as a member of Co. I on April

16, 1864 in order to join the US Navy at Baltimore, MD. Nothing more has been learned. His entry in *The Town Clerks' Registers* notes, "not heard from since."

Thomas Mills – Co. G (tr. January 28, 1865)
b. 1844 Canada
d. ? ?
m. ?

NOTE: Thomas, a painter, enrolled in the 76th Regiment at Buffalo, Erie, NY on August 7, 1863 as a substitute for Jacob Wallaber, mustering into Co. C. His military record is sketchy, revealing only that he was captured and paroled. His muster card for the 147th Regiment states he returned on April 9, 1865. He evidently went to parole camp since he left there on May 5, 1865. He was discharged at Arlington Heights, VA, apparently as a member of the 147th. Nevertheless, he saw no duty with that unit. Nothing further has been learned.

Amos Baldwin Miner – Co. A (tr. August 30, 1863)
b. 1839 Pharsalia, Chenango, NY
d. October 1, 1864 Florence, SC
m. Emeline E. Skinner (June 30, 1835-October 2, 1897) December 16, 1860

NOTE: Amos, whose surname was also spelled Minor, was the son of Frederick A. (1795-1876) and Sarah "Sally" Mariah Ashcroft Miner (1807-1883). He enlisted in the 76th Regiment on September 20, 1861 at Pitcher, Chenango, NY, mustering into Co. B and was discharged on a surgeon's certificate of disability at Odd Fellows Hall Hospital on September 12, 1862 for *phthisis pulmonalis*. On August 31, 1863 he re-enlisted in the same regiment and the same company. He was captured at the battle of the Wilderness on May 5, 1864. His wife's pension application, stated that he died from a combination of chronic diarrhea, scurvy, and (perhaps) dropsy. He is buried among the "unknowns" at Florence National Cemetery. According to *The Adjutant-General's Report* for the 147th, however, Amos B. Miron was drafted and enrolled in that outfit on August 30, 1863, mustering into Co. A. Furthermore, he was absent, at parole camp, Annapolis, MD when the regiment mustered out. His muster card for the 147th provides a slightly different story, saying he was "not borne on any muster roll for 147th until m. o. [and] then as above," that is, as Amos Miron. Emeline, daughter of George 1798-1864) and Elizabeth Stebbins Skinner 1796-1877), obtained a widow's pension. She never remarried. Her death was announced in *The Deruyter Gleaner* October 14, 1897, 2: ". . . Mrs. Emeline Miner, who has been an invalid for many years, and who has been staying for some time at Lewis Sergent's, had a shock last week and died Saturday. The funeral was held Tuesday at 1 o'clock at the W. M. church of which she was a member. Rev. F. Pressley officiated. The body was interred in our [Taylor] cemetery by the side of her parents."

George Morgan – Co. D (tr. January 28, 1865)
b. 1842 Toronto, Ontario, Canada
d. ? ?
m. ?

NOTE: George, whose parents are unidentified, enrolled in the 76th Regiment on August 5, 1863 at Rochester, Monroe, NY as a substitute for Martin V. Beemer, mustering into Co. K. His muster roll card shows he was absent in October 1863. He transferred to Co. G on July 1, 1864 and to Co. H on October 20th, at which time he was "absent, in hospital." When transferred to the 147th he was "absent, sick." In all likelihood he did not survive.

Hiram W. Morse – Co. B (January 28, 1865)
b. 1845 Cortland County, NY
d. July 22, 1864 Andersonville, Sumter, GA
m. ------

NOTE: The son of Daniel (1806-1869) and Eliza Morse (1808-1870), Hiram lied about his age in order to enlist in the military. He enrolled in the 76th Regiment at Homer, Cortland, NY on October 22, 1861, mustering into Co. F. His sickness is recorded in John Worrell Northrop's *Diary of a War Prisoner*, 69: "May 30th: Hiram Morse of Co F 76th regiment admitted to the hospital today. He sickened on corn bread, lost appetite, became helpless from diarrhoea and attendant fever; has wasted rapidly to a skeleton, helpless in body, crazed in mind. He has been kept alive by crust coffee and a little black tea we happened to have, since he got here." Hiram is buried among the "unknowns" in Andersonville National Cemetery. The Morse family sent five sons to fight in the war. Besides Hiram, Lewis M. Morse (1833-1913) was a member of Co. E, 76th Regiment from September 25, 1861-May 19, 1863 when he deserted at Fredericksburgh, VA. Daniel B. Morse (1839-1881) served in Co. H, 157th Regiment from 1861-1862. Adolphus (1843-1864) was a member of Co. F, 76th. He deserted and when apprehended was sentenced to death. Efforts on the part of his family and friends convinced President Lincoln to commute the sentence and Adolphus was sent to Fort Jefferson, Dry Tortugas where he died. David Morse (1841-1861) served in the 12th Regiment and died in the service. A Civil War monument in East Homer Cemetery contains the names of David and Hiram.

John Morse – Co. D (tr. January 28, 1865)
b. 1830 New York State
d. ? ?
m. ?

NOTE: Little is known about this soldier. He enrolled in the 76th Regiment at Syracuse, Onondaga, NY on August 19, 1863, apparently a volunteer, mustering into Co. H. He transferred to Co. F on February 2, 1864 and returned to Co. H on April 11th. He then transferred to Co. B on January 1, 1865. When transferred to the 147th he was absent. His muster card for that regiment says: "On Co. roll to Apr. 30/64 present, not paid. June 30/64 Left in camp sick, nothing heard from him since. No later record found." In all likelihood, he died although his death does not appear in *Deaths of Volunteers.*

John Murphy – Co. D (tr. January 28, 1865)
b. 1825 Ireland
d. ? ?
m. ?

NOTE: John, whose parents are unknown, en-rolled in the 76th Regiment at Buffalo, Erie, NY on August 5, 1863 as a substitute for John Dalton, mustering into Co. H. He transferred to Co. F on February 2, 1864 and was sent back to Co. H on April 11th. He next transferred to Co. B on January 1, 1865. His muster card for the 147th states he was present and paid to February 29, 1864 but on later rolls he was "absent, sick." Since no further records have been found he probably died and the death was not recorded. A cenotaph for him is located in St. Paul's Cemetery, Oswego City.

John Murphy's cenotaph in St. Paul's Cemetery, Oswego, contains no dates, implying that his DOD was unknown.
Author's Collection

John Worrell Northrop – Co. E (tr. January 31, 1865)
b. April 15, 1836 Georgetown, Madison, NY
d. September 22, 1923 Los Angeles, Los Angeles, CA
m. Sarah Flavilla Williamson (1844-1931) 1870

NOTE: John, son of Harvey (1796-1884) and Lovina Ellis Northrop (1798-1880), was drafted and enrolled in the 76th Regiment at Oswego

OF BLOOD AND BATTLES: OSWEGO'S 147TH REGIMENT

City on September 8, 1863, mustering into Co. F on the same day. He was captured at the battle of the Wilderness on May 5, 1864 and taken to Andersonville and later Florence, SC. His diary, published as *Chronicles from the Diary of a War Prisoner in Andersonville and Other Military Prisons of the South in 1864,* provides graphic details about the horrible conditions in southern POW camps. Northrop frequently mentions other soldiers with whom he served and whom he met in prison. He was finally paroled on December 4, 1864. He tells in his book how he and others reacted to freedom and the expectation of sufficient food and clothing. He was discharged from the army on June 19, 1865 at Annapolis, MD as a member of the 76th. After the war Northrop, who said he was a clerk in 1863, edited a newspaper in Parish, NY. He and Flavilla were the parents of four children, all living in 1900. Northrop was a

John Northrop's wartime diary is a treasure for the many names it contains and for his details about prison life.

Steve and Linda Malkson (FAG)

member of the GAR, as shown on his gravestone. He and Flavilla are buried in Mountain View Cemetery and Mausoleum, Altadena, Los Angeles, CA. A brother, Martin V. B. Northrop (1844-1915), served in Co. D, 76th Regiment from 1861-1863 and in Co. F, 9th NY HA from 1864-1865.

John Nugent – Co. I (tr. January 31, 1865)
b. 1844 Ireland
d. April 3, 1925 Albany, Albany, NY
m. Cecilia "Celia" T. Madden (1845-December 31, 1926) 1870

NOTE: John, brother of William Nugent (1843-?), enlisted in the 30th Regiment at Albany, Albany, NY on August 20, 1862, mustering into Co. F. He transferred to Co. K, 76th Regiment on May 25, 1863. He was taken prisoner on May 5, 1864 at the battle of the Wilderness, spent time in Andersonville Prison and was finally taken to Salisbury, NC where he managed to escape. He and Cecilia were the parents of six, three of whom were living in 1910. John's informative but somewhat fanciful obituary appeared in *The Albany Times-Union* April 3, 1925: "John J. Nugent, 84, of 78 Lawrence street, commander of Lew Morris Post, G. A. R., of Albany, a civil war veteran and noted railroad engineer, died at 2 o'clock this morning in St. Peter's hospital, where he was brought one hour before suffering from a heart attack. Mr. Nugent in late years had been employed in the State Capitol as a guard. He was a close friend of Governor Alfred E. Smith, and of scores of assemblymen, senators and state officers. He enlisted at the age of sixteen years as a drummer boy in the 91ˢᵗ New York volunteers and served throughout the civil war. He was captured at the Battle of Antietam after being wounded and was held in Andersonville prison for thirteen months before he escaped. Mr. Nugent escaped from prison in a half starved condition. He wandered back in the direction of the Union forces by night [and] slept during the day. For several days he went without food. Finally he stopped at a house and asked for food and he was told that the war had ended two days previous. As a railroad engineer, Mr. Nugent was one of the few New York Central railroad pilots permitted to run on all of the important lines. Advanced age necessitated him giving up railroad work five years ago at which time he was pensioned by the railroad. He was the possessor of five cherished medals as the result of his war service. One represented the Old Iron Brigade; another the Blue and Grey Reunion at Gettysburg; one Mayor Wadsworth First Division of the Army of the Potomac; Late Monument of Gettysburg, Escaped Prisoner of War from Andersonville Prison, which was made of part of a cannon presented to Governor Vance by Queen Victoria . . . The funeral will take place at 9 o'clock, Monday morning from the home and at 9:30 o'clock from St. Joseph's church . . . ." It is interesting to note that although John never spent a day as a member of the 91ˢᵗ Regiment, in 1890 he claimed to have served in that outfit. He and Cecilia are buried in St. Agnes Cemetery, Menands, Albany, NY.

Michael O'Brien – Co. I
b. 1818 Ireland
d. *post* 1880 Oswego City, NY
m. Margaret _____ (1825-*post* 1880) *ca.* 1850

NOTE: Michael, claiming to be 44, enlisted in the 147ᵗʰ Regiment at Oswego on August 29, 1862, mustering in on September 22. On September 23ʳᵈ he was discharged by the US mustering officer, probably for being overage. Birth dates for him and Margaret fluctuated from census to census. In 1880, the last year they were enumerated, he claimed to have been born in 1830. They were the parents of at least five children. Graves for this couple have not been located.

Conrad Ochinger – Co. I (tr. January 28, 1865)
b. 1832 Zurich, Switzerland
d. ? ?
m. Wilhelme Volksdorf (?-?) ?

NOTE: This man immigrated to the United States aboard the Edwiner, arriving in New York City on April 20, 1853. A blacksmith by occupation, he traveled alone. He enrolled in the 76ᵗʰ Regiment on August 7, 1863 as a substitute for Peter Van Orden,

Hamlin, Monroe, NY, mustering into Co. D. He was wounded at Petersburg, VA on June 18, 1864 and when transferred to the 147th he was absent. His muster card for the 91st Regiment states he had obtained a furlough from Augur Hospital, Alexandria, VA for 20 days on January 24, 1865 and deserted at the expiration of his leave. No other information is available. The various spellings of his surname have impeded research.

John Orland – Co. B (tr. January 28, 1865)

b. 1840 England

d. ? ?

m. ?

NOTE: John enlisted in the 24th Regiment at Oswego, NY on November 6, 1862, mustering into Co. D. He transferred to Co. C, 76th Regiment on May 13, 1863 and was wounded at Gettysburg on July 1st. He spent time in a hospital in Philadelphia, PA but returned to his regiment. He was wounded and captured at the battle of the Wilderness on May 5, 1864 and was never heard from again.

Jacob Pfluge – Co. K

b. October 18, 1816 Hanover, Germany

d. September 4, 1864 Andersonville, Sumter, GA

m. Anna Maria "Mary" Facktley (January 14, 1822-January 24, 1892) April 28, 1848

NOTE: Jacob, son of Dars (1790-?) and Ana Pfluge (1790-?), arrived in New York City on November 6, 1849 aboard the Hannah Crookes. He enrolled in the 76th Regiment on January 5, 1864 at Boston, Erie, NY, mustering into Co. K on February 20th. For enlisting he received bounties totaling $600 even though he was clearly too old to serve. He was captured at the battle of the Wilderness on May 5, 1864 and died of *scorbutus* (scurvy). He is buried in Andersonville National Cemetery under the name Fluke. The confusion begins with his entry in *The Town Clerks' Registers* which states he enrolled in Co. K, 76th Regiment on June 5, 1863 and then adds, "After serving four months was taken prisoner and sent to Andersonville Prison and there died September 4th 1864." According to his muster roll card for the 147th Regiment, however, Jacob Fluke enrolled in that organization on January 3, 1864 at Barton, Tioga, NY. On June 30, 1865 Anna applied for a widow's pension. In 1870 she and several minor children were living with Christopher Muller, 57, who had been a witness to a deposition she gave for her pension application. Also living in the household were Christopher, Jr., 5, and William, 2. In 1875 Anna and her children had moved to another house two doors away from the Mullers but by 1880 Christopher, Jr. and William were living with her and their surname was Pfluge. Whether or not Anna and Christopher, Sr. were married and she was the mother of the two boys is debatable. It has been suggested that he died in 1877.

Anna may simply have taken in the boys because they had nowhere else to go. She is buried in St. Aloysius Cemetery, Springville, Erie, NY.

William H. Pierson – Co. K (tr. January 31, 1865)
b. 1843 Canada
d. August 17, 1864 Andersonville, Sumter, GA
m. ------

NOTE: William, son of James Ambrose (1807-1879) and Mary Ann Routledge Pearson/Pierson (1803-1877), enrolled in the 76th Regiment at Niagara, Niagara, NY on July 28, 1863 as a substitute for Horatio N. Griffith, mustering into Co. B. He was taken prisoner at the battle of the Wilderness on May 5, 1864. He succumbed to dysentery and is buried in Andersonville National Cemetery.

Waldo Wesley Pinchin – Co. F (tr. January 31, 1865)
b. 1840 Livingston County, NY
d. March 14, 1865 Division No. 2 Hospital, Annapolis, MD
m. Arvilla L. Tompkins (June 20, 1849-July 10, 1934) ?

NOTE: Waldo, son of Abner (1816-1896) and Julia A. Artrip Pinchin (1822-1902), volunteered, enrolling in the 76th Regiment on July 18, 1863. The place where he enlisted has been interpreted to be Orwell, a hamlet in Oswego County, but more likely was Hornell, Steuben County. He was captured at the battle of the Wilderness on May 5, 1864. Northrop, *Chronicles*, 119, wrote of him at Andersonville: "Pinchen has possession of his papers and the likeness of his wife. He was drafted Steuben county, N. Y." His entry in *Deaths of Volunteers* assigned him to the 76th Regiment. Waldo died of typhoid fever and was buried in Annapolis National Cemetery. Arvilla was only 10 years old in 1860 and married Waldo when she was no older than 14. On October 10, 1868 she married Perry Horace Gardner (1836-February 6, 1897) in Blair, Grand Traverse, MI as his second wife. In 1910 she claimed to have been the mother of four, only one of whom was alive. Perry died in Ohio but was buried in Oakwood Cemetery, Traverse City, MI. Arvilla moved to California to live with her daughter and died there. Her body, too, was shipped to Traverse City and buried next to Perry.

Theodore G. Pindar – Co. K (January 31, 1865)
b. 1837 Unadilla, Otsego, NY
d. September 28, 1864 Florence, SC
m. ------

NOTE: Theodore's surname was variously spelled. I use that on his parents' gravestone. The son of Joseph B. (1811-1880) and Elizabeth E. Pindar (1805-1887), he enlisted in the 76th Regiment at Homer, Cortland, NY on October 21, 1861, mustering into Co. B. He re-enlisted on January 20, 1864 and was taken captive on May 5th at the battle of the Wilderness. According to the testimony of Daniel W. Fox, Co. B, Pindar had been wounded in the foot. He is probably buried among the "unknowns" at Florence National Cemetery. A monument honoring Civil War soldiers in East Homer Cemetery bears his name.

Charles H. Pittsley – Co. B (tr. January 28, 1865)
b. 1831 Greene, Chenango, NY
d. November 26, 1863 Convalescent Camp, Alexandria, VA
m. Sarah J. Wilcox (1833-June 8, 1894) October 18, 1854

NOTE: Charles was the son of Alexander (1792-1864), a War of 1812 veteran, and Fannie Japhet Pittsley (1803-1880). He was drafted, enrolling in the 76th Regiment on July 17, 1863 and mustering into Co. E. He succumbed to chronic diarrhea a mere four months later. He and Sarah were the parents of Permilia Sophronia (*ca.* 1856-*post* 1930) and Jacob Arthur (1861-1937). By 1870 Sarah was living in Wilmington, Will, IL and her household also included Aaron, 5. Although in later life Aaron (1864-1951) claimed Charles was his father, since he was born July 4, 1864 it is relatively certain that was not the case. Graves for Charles and Sarah, who died in Chicago, have not been located.

Vincent Puncience – Co. B (tr. January 28, 1865)
b. 1830 Canada
d. ? ?
m. ?

NOTE: This soldier, whose surname endured many variations, may be the son of Noel Pinsince (1789-?) and Marie-Claire Han-Chausse (1798-1831), born in St. Cuthbert, Quebec, Canada on February 7, 1829. He had a sister, Henriette (1819-1877). Vincent enrolled in the 76th Regiment on August 8, 1863 at Buffalo, Erie, NY as a substitute for David W. Burt, of that city, mustering into Co. A. He was listed as WIA at the battle of the Wilderness on May 5, 1864. His muster card for the 147th Regiment states that his company roll to August 31, 1864 showed him "absent wounded May 5, 1864 at Wilderness, VA. No further record found." It is almost certain that he died on or about that date.

George Rineholdt – Co. I
b. 1842 England
d. ? ?
m. ?

NOTE: Although his muster card for the 147th Regiment says George was a draftee who enrolled in that outfit on August 5, 1863 and mustered into Co. I, it also reveals he was "not found on any roll 147 until April 30/65." Nominally transferred to the Co. I, 91st Regiment he was declared a paroled prisoner. His true identify and his regiment remain a mystery but in all likelihood he did not survive the war.

Christopher Strong Rising – Co. B
b. June 27, 1825 Marlboro, Windham, VT
d. July 18, 1864 Andersonville, Sumter, GA
m. ------

NOTE: Christopher, son of Jonathan (1784-1866) and Lucy Kelsey Rising (1795-1852), enrolled in the 76th Regiment at Watertown, Jefferson, NY on September 17, 1863 as a substitute for an unnamed draftee, mustering into Co. B the same day. On September 19th he apparently enrolled in Co. B, 147th Regiment in the same place as a draftee. He was captured at the battle of the Wilderness on May 5, 1864 as a member of the 76th Regiment and succumbed to diarrhea. He is buried in Andersonville National Cemetery.

James S. Rose – Co. C (tr. January 31, 1865)
b. 1835 Orleans County, NY
d. March 1865 Wilmington, NC
m. Rosanna Fuller (1835-September 2, 1893) January 13, 1859

NOTE: James, whose parents are unidentified, also used Henry as his middle name. According to Sylvester Axtell, he was drafted and enrolled in the 76th Regiment at Ridgeway, Orleans, NY on August 8, 1863, mustering into Co. D. He was captured on June 2, 1864 at Gaines Mills, VA and sent to Andersonville. Sylvester Axtell gave a detailed deposition to assist Rosanna's application for a pension, which is here excerpted: ". . . And deponent further says that said James H. Rose aforesaid was paroled with deponent at Goldsborough, NC on the 24th day of Feb, 1865, & then we were sent back to Wilmington, NC for transportation to Annapolis, Md. Deponent was with W. H. Riley of his deponent's Co & James H. Rose aforesaid about noon on the 2nd day of March 1865 in an old tobacco ware House on the Dock at Wilmington NC when an officer came to the door and said that three hundred men were wanted on board of the vessel for Annapolis, Md, deponent spoke to J. H. Rose aforesaid & William H. Riley aforesaid to go onboard of the boat, they at said time were very sick of Typhoid Fever & Chronic Diarrhea &c, Said Riley & James H. Rose were then to sick to move & he could not prevail on either to make an effort to start. Deponent was hardly able to get on the boat . . . And deponent further states that he never saw the said James H. Rose after he left him on the 2nd day of March 1865 . . . Deponent gives it as his opinion judging from the condition of the said James H. Rose that he must have died soon after he left him . . . ." Rosanna applied for and obtained a pension. She married Benjamin R. Rose (1829-1904), a widower, in Michigan, perhaps in 1874. I have not been able to determine if he and James were related. Benjamin had been a member of Co. K, 6th Michigan Cavalry. He and Rosanna were the parents of one child, Marvin B. (September 18, 1875-July 10, 1876). Rosanna's COD was cancer. Benjamin, who married a third time, died of "acute laryngitis" and senility. He, Rosanna, and Marvin are buried in Fuller Family Cemetery, Carlton, Barry, MI.

Dwight D. Sanderson – Co. K (tr. January 31, 1865)
b. December 1839 Phelps, Ontario, NY
d. February 10, 1865 Florence, SC
m. ------

NOTE: Dwight was the son of William (?-1843) and Margaret Sanderson (*ca.* 1816-*post* 1880). He was a draftee, enrolling in the 76th Regiment at Prattsburgh, Steuben, NY on July 16, 1863 and mustering into Co. K. He was captured at the battle of the Wilderness on May 5, 1864 and sent first to Andersonville and later to Florence where, according to the testimony of William N. Cook and W. L. Bonney, he died. He is probably buried among the "unknowns" in Florence National Cemetery. His was an interesting family. When his mother applied for a pension in 1880 her surname was Lamb. Further investigation revealed that she had married Jabez Lamb (1792-April 18, 1872) at Auburn, Cayuga, NY on October 24, 1845. Her address at the time was Prattsburgh, which may explain why Dwight claimed to have been born in that county when he entered the military. By 1860 Jabez and Margaret, together with their children, Sarah A. (1847-*post* 1880) and Charles Jay (1850-*post* 1900), were living in Coldwater, Branch, MI. Jabez, a native of Montgomery County, NY, died in Coldwater and was buried in Oak Grove Cemetery. In 1880 Margaret was living in Atchison City, Atchison, KS with Sarah and her husband, William H. Williams (1843-?). She applied for a pension that year. Margaret obtained the pension but what happened to her after 1880 is unknown. Sarah and William also disappear. By 1900 Charles, claiming to have been born in 1852, was living in Prattsburgh with his half brother, George Sanderson (1836-1906).

Joseph Schaumberger – Co. K (tr. January 31, 1865)
b. 1841 Byron, Genesee, NY
d. ? ?
m. ?

NOTE: Little is known about this soldier. He enrolled in the 76th Regiment at Buffalo, Erie, NY on August 5, 1863 as a substitute for an unnamed draftee, mustering into Co. K. Although he was allegedly captured on May 5, 1864 at the battle of the Wilderness, it is probable that he died on the battlefield.

John Schroeder – Co. F (tr. January 31, 1865)
b. 1838 Germany
d. ? ?
m. ?

NOTE: Schroeder enrolled in the 76th Regiment on January 4, 1864 in the Ninth Congressional District, which was comprised of Orange and Sullivan Counties, and mustered into Co. F. His card for the 76th Regiment states he was captured at the battle of the Wilderness on May 5, 1864 while his muster card for the 147th shows he was considered MIA. It is quite possible he died on the battlefield.

John Shamphan – Co. E
b. December 25, 1843 Lachine, Quebec, Canada
d. August 12, 1923 Sandy Creek, NY
m. Genette McCarty (1847-May 8, 1930) April 16, 1871

NOTE: This man's surname was variously spelled but I use that on the family monument. He was the son of Joseph Shampang (1811-1903) and Marguerite Hubert (1803-*ca*. 1900). His was a complicated military career. He enlisted in the 59th Regiment at New York City on October 22, 1861, mustering into Co. G. According to *The Town Clerks' Registers* he deserted from that outfit and returned to Oswego County. On August 21, 1862 he enrolled in the 147th at Boylston, mustering into Co. E. The authorities must have found out he was a deserter because on January 5, 1863 he was sent back to Co. A, 59th where he stayed until June 25th when Cos. G and A were consolidated. Around that time he transferred to Co. A, 1st RI LA, mustering out on June 13, 1865. He applied for a pension on August 19, 1865 and obtained a certificate despite the fact that he had deserted his original regiment. His pension cards say nothing about service in the 147th. Although he did not claim a disability in 1890 a pension payment card revealed he had been shot in the left thigh. John's death was reported in *The Sandy Creek News* August 16, 1923, 5: "On Sunday afternoon occurred the death of John Shampan [*sic*], at his residence, the H. C. Shares' dwelling on North Main Street. Mr. Shampan, aged 80 years, was a veteran of the Civil War and a former resident of Sandy Creek, working at one time in the tannery here. Later he lived at Richland where he bought a farm and but recently returned to Sandy Creek. Death was due to a stone cancer in the food pipe. The funeral services were conducted Tuesday, Rev. H. C. Shares officiating. Burial was made at Richland cemetery. Mrs. Shampan is the only surviving relative." Genette, whose name also suffered variations, only had one child and it died young. She died near Watertown, Jefferson, NY. According to an unsourced obituary, she had been born in Redfield, NY on October 4, 1844 although all census records point to a DOB of 1847. Her only surviving relative was Cora Piddock, a niece. John and Genette are buried in Richland Village Cemetery. Their monument does not show DOD for either one. John's brother, Emanuel Joseph Shampang (1842-1913), served in Co. I, 22nd Regiment from May 1861-June 1863.

Franklin W. Shaut – Co. F (tr. January 28, 1865)
b. 1835 Herkimer County, NY
d. ? ?
m. ------

NOTE: Franklin, son of Henry "Harry" (1804-March 1870) and Catherine Shaut (1810-*post* 1870), was drafted. He enrolled in the 76th Regiment at Wheeler, Steuben, NY on July 15, 1863, mustering into Co. I. He was wounded at the battle of the Wilderness on May 6, 1864 and according to his muster card for the 147th he was absent, in hospital, Baltimore, MD on June 30, 1864. No further record is available and he probably succumbed to his wounds.

Martin Shaw – Co. C
b. 1836 Canada
d. September 10, 1864 Andersonville, Sumter, GA
m. Sarah Beckwith (1840-December 26, 1867) July 5, 1858

NOTE: Martin's parents are unknown. He had the distinction of enrolling in two regiments on the same day, September 18, 1863, at Watertown, Jefferson, NY. On the muster roll card for the 147th he was drafted and enrolled in Co. C but on the card for the 76th he was mustered into Co. D as a substitute under the name Martin Shon and his entry in *The Town Clerks' Registers* provides the name of the draftee, Uriel Graves. He was captured on June 3, 1864 near Cold Harbor, VA and sent to Andersonville where he succumbed to various maladies, depending on the document. According to *Death of Volunteers* his COD was *scorbutus* (scurvy) but he might also have been fatally wounded. Diarrhea was also suggested. He is buried in Andersonville National Cemetery. He and Sarah were the parents of three daughters: Ida Elizabeth (1859-*post* 1875); Frances Violetta (1861-1912); Imogene (1863-1943). Sarah came to a tragic end, as reported in a deposition made by Henry Fredenburg and Charlotte Cummings on March 31, 1868: ". . . They were well acquainted with

Sarah Shaw who was the widow of Martin Shaw who was a Private Co. 'D' of the 76th Regt. N. Y. Vols – that said Sarah Shaw died on the 26th day of December A. D. 1867 at Brownville, N.Y. She was frozen & perished in the night – on the night of said 26" day of Dec. 1867 & was subsequently found & recognized & a Post Mortem Examination had upon her body. & we testify from personal knowledge & we have no interest in the claim of the minor children of said Martin Shaw for Pensions." It is unknown whether her death was an accident or a suicide. I have located no newspaper articles about the incident and it well may be the family discouraged reports, particularly if Sarah took her own life. Her grave has not been located. Reuben Day was appointed the girls' guardian and pensions were obtained for them. Ida lived in Watertown in 1875, working in a private home. She may have married after the census. Frances married F. S. Cannon and died in Westfield, MA. Imogene married D. Hugh Anderson and died in Aurora, Erie, NY.

Gilbert Sherwood – Co. B

b. ? Steuben County, NY
d. September 15, 1864 Andersonville, Sumter, GA
m. ?

NOTE: Gilbert may have been the son of Nehemiah (1806-*post* 1870) and Eleanor Jones Sherwood (1805-*post* 1880). His DOB is disputed. In 1855 he was 30 but in 1860 he was 38. His age in the draft registrations records dated June 1863 was 36. When he entered the military in1863 he was 44. According to his muster roll card for the 76th Regiment he was drafted, enrolling in Bath, Steuben County on July 16, 1863 and mustering into Co. B. According to his muster card for the 147th Regiment, however, he was drafted, enrolled in Bath on July 16, 1863 and mustered into Co. B. The card for the 76th Regiment states he was MIA at the battle of the Wilderness on May 5, 1864 and died at Andersonville on September 15th. Information on the card for the 147th is scant, saying only he was captured at an unknown date and died of diarrhea on August 4, 1864. Burial records prove he was a member of the 76th Regiment, died of diarrhea September 15, 1864, and was buried in Andersonville National Cemetery.

John Shotthofer – Co. I

b. 1847 Syracuse, Onondaga, NY
d. ? ?
m. ?

NOTE: John, son of George (1821-*post* 1855) and Elizabeth Shotthofer (1824-*post* 1875), was a barber. He enlisted in the 147th Regiment at Oswego City on August

25, 1862, claiming to be 18, and was assigned to Co. I. On September 25th he was rejected by the US mustering officer. On June 29, 1863, again claiming to be 18, he enlisted in the 15th NY Cavalry, mustering into Co. A. He served with that outfit until mustered out on June 27, 1865 in Virginia. He was last enumerated in Syracuse in 1875.

Richard Elwood Smith – Co. B (January 28, 1865)
b. June 27, 1828 New Lebanon, Columbia, NY
d. April 4, 1891 Lisle, Broome, NY
m. ------

NOTE: Richard, son of John L. (1802-*post* 1875) and Lurena Griggs Smith (1808-*ante* 1875), was a substitute for an unnamed draftee. He enrolled in the 76th Regiment at Nanticoke, Broome, NY on July 17, 1863, mustering into Co. E. A notation in *The Town Clerks' Registers* reveals he "came home sick in November 1863 and is sick yet and has never been discharged." *Registers of Officers and Enlisted Men* offers more information: "Sick with the consumption, home on furlough." In 1890 he stated his disability was Locomotor Ataxia, a condition which attacks the back side of the spinal column and prevents the person from controlling his bodily movements. It is associated with venereal diseases such as syphilis. He applied for a pension on May 4, 1875 and his pension cards indicate he was a member of the 76th and the 91st Regiments, although he does not appear in *The Adjutant-General's Report* for the latter outfit. His muster roll card for the 147th states he was honorably discharged on December 21, 1871 to date July 3, 1865, which is the date the 91st mustered out. His grave has not been located. A brother, Dwight Romano (1844-1907), served in Co. E, 50th NY Engineers from August 1864-June 1865.

Elmina Pleiades Keeler Spencer – nurse
b. September 15, 1819 Mexico, New York
d. December 29, 1912 Oswego City, NY
m. Robert H. Spencer (1818-November 24, 1873) November 14, 1840

NOTE: Elmina was the daughter of Darius Dunham (August 26, 1795-November 4, 1874) and Arethusa Powers Keeler (1797-July 17, 1875). She was a music teacher and in later life a journalist. In 1862 her husband Robert enlisted in the 147th Regiment, intending to become a hospital steward since he was too old for combat duty. Elmina also enlisted. For the next three years she battled alongside the soldiers, nursing them, obtaining supplies for them, providing food, writing letters. Among the families she assisted was that of John and Jane Wray Woodall of New Haven, whose 15 year old son, Granville, enlisted in the 24th NY Cavalry in January 1864 and died of typhoid fever at White House Landing six months later. According to Granville's brother, John Joseph, Mrs. Spencer helped him get Granville's body embalmed and sent home where it was buried in the New Haven Rural Cemetery. Her kindnesses were never forgotten by the men she aided and letters sent home by them were full of gratitude and praise. After the war she, Robert, his mother, and her parents moved to Kansas as homesteaders. Elmina attempted to remain in Kansas after they all died but insects and the resulting destruction of crops drove her to near destitution. Friends in Oswego attempted to help, but she eventually decided to return there. Elmina obtained a pension in the sum of $8.00 per month based on her husband's service. She eventually was granted an increase to $20 but it was scarcely enough. Elmina was an honored member of the community. She accompanied the veterans to Gettysburg in 1888 for the dedication of the monument commissioned by the 147th. She rode in parades and spoke at veterans' reunions. She was a loyal and dedicated member of the Good Templars. As she grew older, however, her physical condition declined and in the last years of her life she lived with several female caregivers. The Women's Relief Corps of Post John D. O'Brien No. 65 GAR provided financial support to supplement her meager pension. In November 1912, suffering from blood poisoning, she had her right leg amputated. Gangrene set in, causing her death.

Her passing was widely reported but the obituary appearing in *The Syracuse Daily Journal* December 30, 1912, 7 is perhaps the most complete: "Mrs. Elmina Spencer, 93 years old, of Oswego, who died yesterday in [Oswego], was born in a log cabin at Mexico . . . Her father was Darius Dunham Keeler, who with a party of French Canadians, settled at Mexico, hewing their log cabins out of the virgin forest. A number of the descendants of these pioneers still live in and around Mexico. Mrs. Spencer's mother was a native of the Green Mountain state . . . Elmina Keeler married Robert H. Spencer and with him went to the War of the Rebellion. She was mustered into the One Hundred and Forty-seventh Regiment, New York Volunteers as hospital nurse and served until the close of the conflict. At City Point while ministering to the wounded she was struck in the side by grape shot and for this the government allowed her a small pension. In the Army of the Potomac there

Elmina Spencer's care for and devotion to the soldiers she assisted was universally praised and generals and politicians gratefully acknowledged the services she performed on behalf of the sick, wounded, and dying.

Author's Collection

was none better known at the close of the war than Mrs. Spencer and few generals elicited more cheers from the men when riding past than she as she rode her favorite horse 'Pete.' Generals, from Grant down, treated her with distinguished consideration and respect. Thousands of 'New York boys' now way beyond their prime as well as veterans of other states remember her with gratitude for her ministrations to them. The state of New York some years ago honored Mrs. Spencer by placing her head and bust in bronze on the main stairway of the Capitol at Albany . . . Bedridden for years, but full of cheerfulness and hope, keen of mind, Mrs. Spencer had been cared for by the Woman's Relief Corps of the G. A. R. With her has passed away the last of the family . . . ." Elmina is buried in Rural Cemetery, Oswego Town. The Women's Relief Corps paid for her funeral expenses.

William A. Stubbs – Co. D (tr. January 28, 1865)
b. 1836 Hector, Schuyler, NY
d. March 4, 1914 Ithaca, Tompkins, NY
m. Antoinette Flint (September 1844-August 11, 1925) 1874

NOTE: William was the son of John W. (1802-1880) and Joanna Ammerman Stubbs (1805-1887). He enlisted in the 76th Regiment at Etna, Tompkins, NY on November 8, 1861, mustering into Co. C. He transferred to Co. H, 10th VRC on June 24, 1863 and mustered out on November 8, 1864. In 1890 he claimed bronchitis, rheumatism, and spinal disease as disabilities. He and Antoinette were the parents of two children, both alive in 1910. The couple is buried in Lake View Cemetery, Ithaca.

Florence Sullivan – Co. B (tr. January 28, 1865)
b. 1846 Canada
d. October 21, 1864 Andersonville, Sumter, GA
m. ------

NOTE: Florence, whose surname was also spelled O'Sullivan, was the son of Timothy (1816-*post* 1891) and Mary (1817-?). In 1851 the family lived on Prince Edward Island. Florence enlisted in the 24th Regiment at Oswego City on November 1, 1862, mustering into Co. D. On May 13, 1863 he transferred to Co. C, 76th Regiment. He was captured at the battle of the Wilderness on May 5, 1864 and died of diarrhea. He is buried in Andersonville National Cemetery.

John Sweet – Co. B (tr. January 28, 1865)
b. 1841 New Brunswick, Canada
d. ? ?
m. ?

NOTE: Sweet, whose parents are unknown, enrolled in the 76th Regiment at Rochester, Monroe, NY on August 5, 1863 as a substitute for Garrett Manning of that city, mustering into Co. C. He said he was a sailor and on April 16, 1864 he was discharged in order to enlist in the US Navy. His rendezvous listing at Baltimore, MD revealed he had been a sailor for 12 years aboard a ship named the Constellation under Captain Fox. No other confirmable information has been located.

Rufus Taggart – Co. D (tr. January 28, 1865)
b. 1835 Genesee County, NY
d. November 7, 1864 Wilson, Niagara, NY
m. ------

NOTE: The son of Rufus (1792-1869) and Eliza Cone Taggart (1805-1872), Rufus was drafted and enrolled in the 76th Regiment at Wilson on July 29, 1863, mustering into Co. H. He transferred several times within the regiment. His muster roll card for the 147th Regiment reveals that while on furlough he died of consumption at Wilson. He is buried in Greenwood Cemetery, Wilson.

Frederick Tompkins – Co. K
b. ? ?
d.? ?
m. ?

NOTE: This soldier's identity is unknown. According to his muster roll card he was not borne on any rolls for the 147th until February 28, 1865. He was transferred to Co. K, 91st Regiment on June 5th "while absent on extra duty." He does not appear in *The Adjutant-General's Report* for that organization.

John H. Tripp – Co. B (tr. January 28, 1865)
b. 1843 New Zealand
d. ? ?
m. ?

NOTE: This man's surname was also spelled Tripps. He enrolled in the 30th Regiment on September 7, 1862 at Albany, NY, mustering into Co. F. He transferred to Co. G, 76th Regiment on May 25, 1863 and was wounded at Gettysburg on July 1st. He was also wounded on May 5, 1864 at the battle of the Wilderness. When transferred to the 147th he was "absent, wounded." He was "absent, sick" when transferred to Co. G, 91st Regiment on June 5, 1865. He does not appear in *The Adjutant-General's Report* for that organization. I have located no other records for him and in all likelihood he did not survive.

Mary Edwards Walker, MD – US army surgeon; Medal of Honor recipient
b. November 26, 1832 Oswego Town, NY
d. February 21, 1919 Oswego Town, NY
m. Albert Miller, MD (1831-April 21, 1913) November 19, 1855

NOTE: Mary was the daughter of Alvah (April 9, 1798-April 9, 1880) and Vesta Whitcomb Walker (April 5, 1801-February 25, 1885). She graduated from Syracuse Medical College in 1855, the only woman in her class. A marriage to a classmate, Dr. Albert Miller, was short-lived but she did not obtain a divorce until 1867. Although never a member of the 147th Regiment, nevertheless she took an active interest in the soldiers she encountered in the various hospitals in and around Washington, DC where she was serving as an assistant surgeon. She wrote many letters to the local newspapers detailing whom she found and what their condition was. At one point during the war she was captured by the Confederates and held for several months until exchanged. She was an advocate for dress reform and was known for her (for the time) eccentric attire. She was the author of two books, *Hit!* (1871) and *Unmasked or, The Science of Immortality* (1878). Dr. Walker was the only woman ever awarded the Medal of Honor and in 1917 when the federal government attempted to take it away from her she stalwartly refused to return it. In 2000, thanks to the efforts of Rosemary Nesbitt, Oswego city historian, Mary Walker was inducted into the Women's Hall of Fame in Seneca Falls, NY. Dr. Walker's death was widely reported in obituaries which may generously be characterized as fanciful. The best one was published in *The Oswego Daily Times* February 22, 1919, 8, which is here excerpted: "Dr. Mary E. Walker died at eight o'clock last night at the home of Mr. and Mrs. Frank Dwyer, Bunker Hill, adjoining her own farm. She had been cared for there during her last illness which covers a period f two or three months. Dr. Mary was born on the farm where she lived practically all of her life . . . At the age of twenty-three, November 19, 1855, she married Dr. Albert E. Miller and for a time they lived in Rome, N. Y., where they practiced their profession, though Doctor Mary never surrendered her maiden name, maintaining it to the end. Dr. Miller died many years ago. Dr. Mary was always reticent about her married life and spoke of it only to her immediate friends and members of the family, and then only infrequently. . . At the age of fifteen she was a teacher and when eighteen was prepared to begin the study of medicine, having saved money enough from her salary to carry her through college . . . Three years later she was graduated a full fledged medical doctor and began the practice of her profession in Columbus, O. About that time the Doctor attracted to herself a lot of attention by her mode of dress. She discarded skirts for bloomers . . . Dr. Walker's career has been a picturesque one. At the outbreak of the Civil War she entered the Union service in her professional capacity. She served as an assistant surgeon in the Patent Office hospital in Washington, D. C., where so many Union soldiers were cared for and in 1862 and 1863 she served at the front, before she was regularly in the service of the government, having been appointed by surgeons in charge of field hospitals because of her efficiency. It was only then that the war department, recognizing her ability, conferred upon her a commission as Assistant Army Surgeon, the first commission of the kind ever conferred upon a woman by any government in the world . . . After the Civil war she resumed the practice of her profession but her time was mostly spent in Washington where, because of her dress and what in those days were considered eccentricities, she became a National character . . . If Dr. Walker had been devoted to any other thing as much as she had been devoted to dress reform it was her project for fighting the inroads of tuberculosis. She has always held that the disease could be fought successfully, and for years her great ambition was to establish a sanitarium for its treatment according to her own theories. Although always an ardent advocate of equal suffrage she has never been in sympathy with the modern method of bringing about the reform. According to her theory the modern suffragists have been inclined to do too much talking and too little acting. Dr.

Walker claimed to have been the [?] woman to attempt to vote at the polls. That was in Oswego town many years ago, and through her persistent advocacy of equal suffrage she was influential in obtaining legislation in several States . . . At one time after the war the Doctor held a clerkship in the pension department. During the latter years of her life she has had only her pension of $20 a month to support her. Two years ago she spent the Winter in Washington and while there had a fall that impaired her health. She returned home and last spring was found at her home badly off and was removed to General Army Hospital No. 5, where she was nursed back to health and strength. Last Fall she returned to her farm and then with the approach of winter went to live with Mr. and Mrs. Dwyer, where she was tenderly cared for and her wants supplied. Her mind was clear and active all during the weeks of illness and dissolution came only after the physical mechanism had worn out . . . The funeral will be held Monday afternoon at two o'clock from the Doctor's own home at Bunker Hill and the services will be conducted by the Rev. Mr. Hand of the M. E. church of Oswego Center. Burial will be

The statue of Dr. Walker which stands outside the Oswego Town Hall shows her touching the Medal of Honor which she proudly wore.
Author's Collection

made in Rural cemetery . . . ." On June 10, 1982 the USPS issued a twenty-cent stamp in Dr. Walker's honor. Walker/Spencer Tent No. 108, Daughters of Union Veterans of the Civil War, New York Department, was installed in Oswego, NY on September 5, 2009, and named in honor of her and Elmina Spencer. A mural portraying her in later life is located near the entrance to the River's End Bookstore on Bridge Street, Oswego. A bronze statue of the young Mary, sculpted by Sharon BuMan, was dedicated at the Oswego Town Hall on May 13, 2012 during a ceremony attended by many dignitaries. On the base of the statue is a statement by Dr. Walker which has been seen as nothing short of prophetic: "I have got to die before people will know who I am and what I have done. It is a shame that people who lead reforms in this world are not appreciated until after they are dead: then the world pays its tribute . . . ."

Hugh Ward – Co. K
b. ? ?
d. ? ?
m. ?

NOTE: Ward enlisted in the 147th on August 14, 1862 at Oswego City, claiming to be 44. He was assigned to Co. K but was rejected for mustering. The most likely candidate for this man is Hugh Ward (*ca.* 1805-1885), born in Ireland. He and his wife Ann (*ca.* 1815-1877) are buried in St. Paul's Cemetery, Oswego.

John Ward – Co. K (tr. January 31, 1865)
b. 1832 Poughkeepsie, Dutchess, NY
d. January 20, 1901 Poughkeepsie, Dutchess, NY
m. Mary Jane Filkins (1832-March 10, 1922) 1855

NOTE: John, son of Elisha (1801-*post* 1865) and Esther Ward (1803-*post* 1865), enlisted in the 30th Regiment at Troy, Rensselaer, NY on April 30, 1861 for two years. He deserted from this outfit on January 17, 1862, was returned under arrest on March 7, 1863, and sentenced by court-martial to serve until July 12, 1864. He transferred to Co. K, 76th Regiment on May 25, 1863, was captured at Gettysburg on July 1, 1863, and subsequently paroled. He again was captured on May 5, 1864 at the battle of the Wilderness. When and where he was paroled is unknown. Although his muster card for the 147th states he was transferred to that unit on January 31, 1865 *Civil War Soldier Records and Profiles* reveals he was actually transferred on January 28th and discharged on January 30th. As proof of that, he does not appear in *The Adjutant-General's Report* for the 147th Regiment. When he applied for a pension in 1890 he claimed service in all three regiments. Despite his desertion he obtained the pension. He and Mary Jane were the parents of eight, five of whom were living in 1900. Graves for these people have not been located.

Daniel Willis Washburn – Co. F (tr. January 28, 1865)
b. 1822 Colerain, Franklin, MA
d. March 1897 Bradford, Kean, PA
m1. Sarah Sophia Barker (1839-January 14, 1859) July 18, 1849
m2. Adelaide Permilia Bentley (1839-December 17, 1927) 1864

NOTE: The son of Stoddard (1794-1864) and Martha Patty Armour Washburn (1795-1878), Daniel enlisted in the 24th Regiment at Oswego City on September 21, 1861, mustering into Co. I. His muster card for the 76th Regiment says he had been absent since July 5, 1862. When he returned he was transferred from the 24th to 75th Company, 2nd Battalion VRC from which, according to the 1890 Veterans' Schedules, he was discharged on September 22, 1864. He and Sarah, who died in Oswego City, were the parents of three children. Her grave has not been located. He and Adelaide were the parents of two children, both living in 1927. Adelaide lived with her daughter in the greater New York City area for many years but she died in Sebring, Florida. Her body was shipped to Oriskany Falls, Oneida, NY where it was buried beside Daniel and his parents in Hillside Cemetery.

Peter L. Webber – Co. F (tr. January 28, 1865)
b. 1833 Switzerland
d. ? ?
m. ?

NOTE: Peter enrolled in the 76th Regiment at Rochester, Monroe, NY on August 5, 1863 as a substitute for William Graebe of that city, mustering into Co. I. He was wounded at the battle of the Wilderness on May 5, 1864 and again at Spotsylvania on May 14th. He was sent to Satterlee Hospital, Philadelphia, PA from which he deserted on June 1, 1864. No other information is available.

William H. Wells – Co. C
b. 1845 Richland, NY
d. ? ?
m. ------

NOTE: William was the brother of David Wells, who served in the 147th Regiment. Although William claimed to be 18 when he enlisted in the 147th on August 29, 1862 at Richland, such was not the case. His muster roll card says he was "absent from muster" probably because his true age was revealed. He was the subject of an interesting article which appeared in *The Sandy Creek News* May 27, 1886, 1: "Mr. William Wells, a man about 40 years of age living with his widowed mother on a little farm one half of a mile east, was taken suddenly ill when repairing a fence last Wednesday afternoon, and started for the station. When at or near the water house he became violently insane, and with a maniac's expression on his face, gave chase to all who were unfortunate enough to come in his path. Mr. Frank Cone saw the danger and thought himself equal for the emergency. He nobly sprang to the rescue, and leaping to the crazy man's back, strove to force him to the ground. The maniac, when well, was a power of strength, and strove to shake him off. Failing in this, he climbed into a locomotive standing near, with the agility of a cat, and seized the fireman. After a hard struggle, with the aid of many strong hands he was conquered and bound hands and feet and tied to a large timber. He remained in this condition, making the air hideous with his noise, until the proper officers with the aid of his conqueror, Frank, took him to Pulaski where he was examined and pronounced hopelessly insane, and removed to Mexico. While there his ravings were so severe they moved him, the following day, to Utica for treatment." No further information has been learned about him and it is possible he died in a hospital for the insane.

Charles M. White – Co. F (tr. January 28, 1865)
b. July 1832 Saratoga County, NY
d. May 23, 1904 Saratoga Springs, Saratoga, NY
m. ------

NOTE: Charles' parents are unidentified although both were born in New Hampshire. In 1850 he was living with several siblings in Saratoga Springs. Charles enrolled in the 30th Regiment at Saratoga on September 29, 1862, evidently deserting before he could be assigned a company. While details are scarce it appears he was arrested and sentenced to make up the lost time in the 76th Regiment which he joined on October 1, 1864. When the 76th and the 147th were consolidated he was listed "absent, sick," and he was still "absent, sick" on June 5, 1865 when he was transferred to the 91st Regiment. It would appear that he again deserted and went home. In the 1865 he was living at home with his siblings. He has no pension card and he does not appear on the 1890 Veterans' Schedules. His grave has not been located.

Edwin Wilcocks – Co. K
b. 1828 England
d. ? ?
m. ?
NOTE: Little can be ascertained about Wilcocks. A sailor, he enlisted in the 147th Regiment at Oswego City on August 23, 1862 but was rejected for service before he mustered in.

Bibliography

Newspapers

Addison Advertiser
Aegis and Intelligencer
Albany Atlas and Argus
Albany Capital
Albany Evening Journal
Albany Morning Express
Alfred Sun
Altoona Morning Tribune
Altoona Tribune
Appleton Post-Crescent
Arizona Daily Star
Arizona Sentinel
Auburn Argus
Auburn Bulletin
Auburn Citizen
Auburn Citizen-Advertiser
Austin Daily Herald
Avon News
Baldwinsville Gazette and Farmers' Journal
Baltimore Sun
Bath Farmers' Advocate
Bath Plain Dealer
Battle Creek Enquirer
Belair Aegis and Intelligencer
Bellingham Herald
Benton Harbor News-Palladium
Binghamton Press and Sun-Bulletin

Bismarck Tribune
Black River Democrat
Bolivar Breeze
Boston Daily Advertiser
Brookfield Courier
Brooklyn Daily Eagle
Buffalo Commercial
Buffalo Courier
Buffalo Courier-Express
Buffalo Enquirer
Buffalo Evening News
Buffalo Morning Express
Butler Citizen
Canaseraga Times
Canisteo Times
Cape Vincent Eagle
Carthage Republican
Castilian
Cato Citizen
Cayuga Chief
Cazenovia Republican
Chatham Semi-Weekly Courier
Chautauqua News
Chicago Inter Ocean
Cleveland Leader
Clyde Herald
Cohocton Valley Times-Index
Cooperstown Farmer
Corning Journal
Cortland Democrat
Cortland Evening Standard
Cortland Standard
Cuba Patriot and Free Press
Dansville Advertiser
Davenport Daily Times
Dayton Daily Journal
DeRuyter Weekly Gleaner
Detroit Free Press
Ellicott Post

Ellicottville Post
Elmira Star-Gazette
Elmira Telegram
Eau Claire Leader
Eugene Guard
Fairport Herald-Mail
Farmer Review
Fayetteville Bulletin
Fayetteville Recorder
Freeman's Journal
Fort Collins Weekly Courier
Fredonia Censor
Fulton Observer
Fulton Patriot
Fulton Times
Geneva Daily Gazette
Geneva Daily Times
Green Bay Press-Gazette
Greenwood Times
Groton and Lansing Journal
Grundy Courier
Havana Journal
Herkimer Democrat
Homer Republican
Hornellsville Weekly Tribune
Hudson Daily Star
Ilion Citizen
Indianapolis News
Indianapolis Star
Irving Leader
Isabella County Times-News
Ithaca Daily News
Jackson Citizen Patriot
Jamestown Evening Journal
Jefferson County Journal
Jeffersonian Gazette
Johnstown Daily Republican
Joplin Globe
Journal and Courier

Kalamazoo Gazette
Lakeside Press
Lake View Resort
Lansingburgh Semi-Weekly Chronicle
Lansing State Journal
Lawrence Gazette
Leavenworth Times
Lewis County Democrat
Livonia Gazette
Lockport Journal
Lockport Union-Sun and Journal
Long Beach Press
Los Angeles Herald
Los Angeles Times
Louisville Courier-Journal
Louisville Times
Lowville Journal and Republican
Lowville Leader
Madison County Leader and Observer
Madison County Times
Madison Courier
Manchester Democrat-Radio
Manchester Mirror and Farmer
Manchester Weekly Union
Manistique Pioneer Tribune
Marietta Daily Leader
Marshall Messenger
Marysville Daily Appeal
Medina Daily Journal
Medina Tribune
Mercury News
Mexico Independent
Miami Daily News-Record
Middletown Daily Herald
Middleton Times-Press
Minneapolis Star-Tribune
Montour Falls Free Press
Montrose Democrat
Morning Olympian

Mt. Pleasant Times
Muskegon Chronicle
Naples Record
Nashua Reporter
National Tribune
New South Berlin News
New York Evening Express
New York Herald
New York Press
New York Reformer
New York Times
Niagara Falls Gazette
Northern Ohio Journal
North Tonawanda Evening News
Norwich Bulletin
Ogdensburg Daily Journal
Olean Evening Herald
Olean Times Herald
Olympia Daily Recorder
Omaha Sunday Bee
Omaha World-Herald
On St. Lawrence and Clayton Independent
Oneida Weekly Herald
Oneida Weekly Herald and Gazette and Courier
Ontario County Journal
Orleans Republican
Oswego Commercial Advertiser
Oswego Daily Palladium
Oswego Daily Press
Oswego Daily Times
Oswego Morning Herald
Oswego Morning Post
Oswego Morning Times and Express
Oswego Palladium
Oswego Palladium-Times
Oswego Semi-Weekly Palladium
Otsego Farmer
Otsego Farmer and Otsego Republican
Otsego Tidings

Ottawa Republican-Gazette
Ottawa Republican-Times
Ottumwa Review
Owasso Times
Owego Record
Perry Record
Philadelphia Inquirer
Picket Line Post
Pittsburg Daily Headlight
Plattsburgh Daily Press
Plattsburgh Sentinel
Port Byron Chronicle and Cayuga County News
Port Huron Times Herald
Portville Review
Potsdam Commercial-Advertiser
Potsdam Courier and Freeman
Pulaski Democrat
Quad-City Times
Randolph Weekly
Randolph Weekly Courant
Rochester Democrat and Chronicle
Rochester Evening Express
Rochester Times-Union
Rome Semi-Weekly Citizen
Sabbath Recorder
Saginaw Daily News
Saginaw Evening News
Saginaw News Courier
St. Cloud Times
St. Lawrence Republican
Salamanca Inquirer
Salem Press
Salina Evening Journal
Salisbury Evening Post
San Diego Union
Schoharie Union Journal and Courier
Sandusky Weekly Register
Sandy Creek News
San Francisco Chronicle

Sayre Evening Time
Schenectady Gazette
Schoharie Union
Scranton Republican
Scranton Truth
Sherman County Times
Sioux City Journal
Sodus Record
Springfield News-Leader
Springfield Republican
Steuben Advocate
Steuben Courier
Steuben Farmers' Advocate
Susquehanna Weekly
Syracuse Daily Courier and Union
Syracuse Daily Journal
Syracuse Daily Standard
Syracuse Evening Herald
Syracuse Herald
Syracuse News
Syracuse Post-Standard
Syracuse Standard
Tampa Bay Times
Tampa Tribune
Tonawanda Evening News
Troy Daily Times
Troy Daily Whig
Troy Semi-Weekly Times
Troy Times
Troy Times Record
Tully Times
Union Springs Advertiser
Utica Daily Observer
Utica Daily Press
Utica Herald-Dispatch
Utica Morning Herald
Utica Sunday Journal
Utica Sunday Tribune
Utica Tribune

Warren Sheaf
Warsaw County Times
Washington Times
Watertown Daily Times
Watertown Herald
Watertown Re-Union
Waterville Times
Watervliet Record
Watkins Democrat
Waverly Free Press
Waverly Free Press and Tioga County Record
Western New Yorker
Whitesville News
Wichita Beacon
Wichita Daily Eagle
Williamsport Daily Gazette and Bulletin
Wyoming County Times
Yale Expositor
York Daily
Yuma City Appeal Democrat

Periodicals

Bastion, Diana Grace Felix. "Omans-Spooner Descendants of William White," Part 2. *The Mayflower Quarterly* 69, 1 March 2003: 134.

Coddington, Robert J. "Surviving Andersonville," *New York Times* Opinionator November 24, 2014.

Fisher, Donald M. "The Civil War Draft in Rochester, Part Two." *Rochester History* 53, 2 Spring 1991: 15.

Malinowski, Jamie. "Virginia's Moment." *New York Times* Opinionator April 17, 2011.

Perri, Timothy J. "The Economics of US Civil War Conscription," *American Law and Economics Review,* 2008: 424-453.

Wight, W. F. "Charles Fay Wheeler," *Science* (New Series) Vol. 32, 811, July 15, 1910: 72-75.

On-Line Sources

American Military History, Chapter 9: "The Civil War, 1861," 185. https://history.army.mil/books/AMH-09.htm.

Doyle, Don H. "The Civil War Was Won by Immigrant Soldiers," Zocalo Public Square, Arizona State University Knowledge Enterprise (June 29, 2015): time.com/3940428/civil-war-immigrant-soldiers/.

Musil, Melinda. "Money Out of Misery," *America's Civil War Magazine* (March 2018). HistoryNet: www.historynet.com/money-out-of-misery.htm.

"New York in the American Civil War." www.familysearch.org/wiki/in/New_York_in_the_Civil_War.

New York Military Museum Homepage. https://dmna.ny.gov/historic/reghist/civil/infantry/76thinf/76thinfmain.htm.

"Northern Draft of 1862," *Online Etymology Dictionary*. https://www.etymoline.com/columns/post/draft.

"Proclamation 116-Calling for 500,000 Volunteers," *The American Presidency Project*. http://www.presidency.ucsb.edu./ws/?pid+69996.

"Professional Criminals of America – Revised: John Larney (1836-19??)." Extracted from Thomas Byrnes, *Professional Criminals of America*. New York: Cassell & Co., 1886: https://criminalsrevised.blog/2018/03/17/john-larney-11.

"Report of Brig. Gen. Lysander Cutler, U.S. Army, Commanding Second Brigade. April 27-May 6, 1863. – The Chancellorsville campaign." http://www.civil-warhome.com/cutlerchancellorsvill.htm.

Sacher, John M. "Conscription." Essential Civil War Curriculum. Virginia Center for Civil War Studies at Virginia Tech. www.essentialcivilwarcurriculum.com/conscription.html.

76th New York State Volunteer Homepage. www.76nysv.us/.

"The 'Mud March' Nor'easter, January 20-23, 1863." http://www.weatherbook.com/Mudmarch.htm.

"$300 and You're Cleared of Duty," The History Engine. https://historyengine.richmond.edu/episodes/view/6244.

Books

A Biographical Record of Schuyler County. New York: S. J. Clarke Publishing Co., 1903.

Aldrich, Lewis Cass and George S. Conover. *History of Ontario County, New York*. Syracuse: D. Mason and Co., 1893.

Aldridge, Katherine M., ed. *No Freedom Shrieker: The Civil War Letters of Union Soldier Charles Biddlecom*. Ithaca, NY: Paramount Market Publishing, Inc., 2012.

Anholt, Betty. *Sanibel's Story: Voices and Images from Calusa to Incorporation*. Marceline, MO: Walsworth Publishing Co., 1998.

_____. *An Illustrated History of the State of Idaho*. Chicago: Lewis Publishing Co., 1899.

Annual Report of the Adjutant-General of the State of New York. Albany, NY: Brandow Printing Co., 1893-1905. 43 vols.

Beath, Robert B. *History of the Grand Army of the Republic*. New York: Bryan, Taylor and Co., Publishers, 1889.

Brandt, Dennis W. *From Home Guards to Heroes: The 87th Pennsylvania and Its Civil War Community*. Columbia: University of Missouri Press, 2006.

Bristol, Lansing. *The Civil War Diary and Letters of Lieutenant Lansing Bristol, 147th New York Volunteers*. Ed. Joyce Hawthorne Cook. Oswego: Mitchell Printing Co., 2004.

Busey, Travis and John Busey. *Union Casualties at Gettysburg: A Comprehensive Record*. Jefferson, NC: McFarland, 2011.

Catton, Bruce. *Reflections on the Civil War*. Ed. John Leekley. New York: Berkeley Books, 1994. Rpt.

Chamberlain, Mildred Mosher and Laura McGaffey Clarenbach, compilers. *Descendants of Hugh Mosher and Rebecca Maxson*. Rev. ed. Madison, WI: Laura M. Clarenbach, Publisher, 1990.

Cobb, Hubbard. *American Battlefields*. New York: Simon and Schuster, 1995.

Cook, Joyce Hawthorne. *Elmina Spencer: Oswego's Civil War Battlefield Nurse*. Syracuse: Avalon Document Services, 2017.

Crankshaw, David C. and Ruby M. Potter. *Taylor, N.Y.* Rev. ed. Taylor Historical Society, 2008.

_____. *Dedication of Monument Erected by the State of New York at Andersonville, Georgia, 1914*. Albany: J. B. Lyon Co., 1916.

Dwight, Benjamin Woodbridge. *The Descendants of John Dwight of Dedham, Mass.* New York: John F. Tron and Son, 1874. 2 vols.

Ebert, Thomas J. *147th New York Volunteer Infantry: September 22, 1862-June 7, 1865, The Oswego Regiment: A Documentary History*. Clovis, CA: T. J. Ebert, 2009. 3 vols.

Goodwin, Doris Kearns. *Team of Rivals: The Political Genius of Abraham Lincoln*. New York: Simon and Schuster, 2005.

Gorski, Glenna and others. *Williamstown Military Veterans*, volume 1. Williamstown [NY] Historical Society, n. d.

Grant, Ulysses S. *Personal Memoirs*. New York: Modern Library, 1999. Rpt. 1885 ed.

Hale Collection of Connecticut Cemetery Inscriptions and Newspaper Notices.

Hendrix, Dorothy Kincheloe. *A Leaf from Army Life: Background and Experiences of a Civil War Soldier*. 2nd ed. Independently published, 1995.

Hugunin, George. *Autobiography of Col. George Hugunin*. Syracuse, NY: January 7, 1889.

Johnson, Crisfield. *History of Oswego County, 1789-1877*. Philadelphia: L. H. Everts and Co., 1877.

Johnson, W. A. *The History of Anderson County, Kansas, From Its First Settlement to the Fourth of July, 1876*. Garnett: Kauffman and Iler, 1877.

Knaer, Kelly, ed. *The Civil War: An Illustrated History*. New York: Time Books, 2011.

Knudsen, Milli. *Hard Times in Concord, New Hampshire*. Berwyn Heights, MD: Heritage Books, 2008.

Ladd, David L. and Audrey J. Ladd, eds. *Bachelder Papers: Gettysburg In Their Own Words*. Dayton, OH: Morningside House Publishers, 1994-1995. 3 vols.

Lee, Edward. *Prison, Camp and Pulpit: The Life of a City Missionary in the Slums*. Ed. Charles Dunning Clark. Oswego: R. J. Oliphant, 1889.

Lonn, Ella. *Desertion in the Civil War*. New York: Century Co., 1928.

Loomis, Mary Louise King. *Loomis Family History*. Unpublished manuscript, n. d.

Lyman, H. H. "Historical Sketch of the 147th Regiment," *Monuments Commission for the Battlefields of Gettysburg and Chattanooga*. Final Report on the Battlefield of Gettysburg. Albany: J. B. Lyon Co., 1900. 997-1010.

McPherson, James. *Battle Cry of Freedom: The Civil War Era*. New York: Oxford University Press, 1988.

Meade, George Gordon, ed. *The Life and Letters of George Gordon Meade*. New York: Charles Scribner's Sons, 1913. 2 vols.

Menard, John S. *Allegany County and Its People. A Centennial Memorial History of Allegany County, New York*. Alfred, NY: W. A. Fergusson and Co., 1896.

Northrop, John Worrell. *Chronicles from the Diary of a War Prisoner in Andersonville and Other Military Prisons of the South in 1864*. Wichita, KS: Wining Printery, 1904.

Norton, Clark H. *Clark H. Norton Papers, 1888-1919*. Albany, NY: New York State Historical Documents.

O'Reilly, Francis Augustin. *The Fredericksburg Campaign: Winter War on the Rappahannock*. Baton Rouge: Louisiana State University Press, 2006.

Pfanz, Harry W. *Gettysburg – The First Day*. Chapel Hill: University of North Carolina Press, 2001.

_____. *Portrait and Biographical Album, Mecosta County, Mich.* Chicago: Chapman Brothers, 1883.

Richardson, Charles. *Story of a Private: Narrative of Experiences in Rebel Prisons and Stockades.* Milwaukee: George Richardson, Printer, 1897.

Robinson, Wardwell G. *History of the 184th Regiment, New York State Volunteers.* Oswego: R. J. Oliphant, 1895.

Rose, Arthur P. *An Illustrated History of Nobles County, Minnesota.* Worthington, MN: Northern History Publishing Company, 1908.

Roth, Lottie Roeder. *History of Whatcom County.* Seattle: Pioneer Historical Publishing Company, 1926. 2 vols.

Scott, Robert N., general editor, and others. *The War of the Rebellion: A Compilation of the Official Records of the Union and Confederate Armies.* Washington, DC: Government Printing Office, 1880-1901. 128 vols.

Shampine, Dave. *New York's North Country and the Civil War.* Charleston, SC: History Press, 2012.

Shue, Richard S. *Morning at Willoughby Run: The Opening Battle at Gettysburg, July 1, 1863.* Gettysburg: Thomas Publications, 1998.

Sickles, Major-General Daniel E. and others. *Final Report on the Battlefield of Gettysburg.* Albany: J. B. Lyon Company, 1902. 3 vols.

Signor, Isaac S. and Others. *Landmarks of Orleans County, New York.* Syracuse: D. Mason and Company, 1894.

Slayton, Asa Walker. *History of the Slayton Family.* Grand Rapids, MI: Dean Printing Company, 1898.

Smith, A. P. *History of the Seventy-Sixth Regiment New York Volunteers; What It Endured and Accomplished.* Cortland, NY: Truate, Smith and Miles, Printers, 1867.

Snyder, Charles McCool. *Oswego County, New York in the Civil War.* Oswego: Oswego County Historical Society, 1962.

The Past and Present of Eaton County, Michigan; Historically Together with Biographical Sketches. Lansing: Michigan Historical Publishing Association, 19--.

Townsend, Luther Tracy, Adjutant. *History of the Sixteenth Regiment, New Hampshire Volunteers.* Washington, DC: Norman T. Elliott, Printer and Publisher, 1897.

Triplett, Dawn. *Brave Boys Were They! Civil War Veterans of Kalkaska, MI.* Independently published, 2012.

Turo, Sharon and Linda Remillard and others. *Brothers of the Past: Selected Biographies of 100 Members of Pulaski Lodge #415 From Two Large Frames.* Richland, NY: Half-Shire Historical Society, 2018.

Union Publishing Company. *History of Butler and Bremer Counties, Iowa.* Springfield, Il: Union Publishing Co., 1883.

Woodall, Natalie Joy. *Men of the 110th Regiment: Oswego's Own.* Denver: Outskirts Press, 2016.

Woodall, Natalie Joy. *Oswego County and the Civil War: They Answered the Call.* Charleston, SC: History Press, 2013.

Index

CPSIA information can be obtained
at www.ICGtesting.com
Printed in the USA
BVHW062132200619
551558BV00004B/26/P